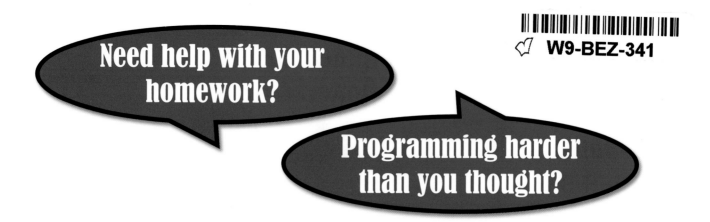

Imagine! Java™
Programming Concepts in Context

Frank M. Carrano
University of Rhode Island

Prentice Hall

Boston Columbus Indianapolis New York San Francisco Upper Saddle River
Amsterdam Cape Town Dubai London Madrid Milan Munich Paris Montréal Toronto
Delhi Mexico City São Paulo Sydney Hong Kong Seoul Singapore Taipei Tokyo

VP/Editorial Director: Marcia J. Horton
Editor in Chief: Michael Hirsch
Executive Editor: Tracy Dunkelberger
Assistant Editor: Melinda Haggerty
Editorial Assistant: Allison Michael
Director of Marketing: Margaret Waples
Marketing Coordinator: Kathryn Ferranti
Vice President, Production: Vince O'Brien
Senior Managing Editor: Scott Disanno
Senior Operations Supervisor: Alan Fischer
Operations Specialist: Lisa McDowell
Senior Art Director: Kenny Beck

Art Director: Kristine Carney
Cover Designer: Rachael Cronin
Photo Researcher: Marta Samsel
Manager, Cover Visual Research & Permissions: Karen Sanatar
Cover Art: Steve Wall
Media Editor: Dan Sandin
Full-Service Project Management: GEX Publishing Services
Composition: GEX Publishing Services

Library of Congress Cataloging-in-Publication Data on File

10 9 8 7 6 5 4 3 2 1

Prentice Hall
is an imprint of

www.pearsonhighered.com

ISBN-10: 0-13-147106-6
ISBN-13: 978-0-13-147106-1

Welcome to *Imagine! Java* a new book for introductory courses in Java programming. This presentation of Java is based upon my experiences during more than three decades of teaching undergraduates their first programming language. I want to share it with you, student and instructor alike.

My instruction is concise, conversational, and full of examples. And questions! *What if...? Suppose...* and, of course, *Imagine...!* Questions are not much help without answers, so answers to the self-test questions appear at the end of each chapter. Some examples are brief; some are lengthy. They all were chosen to clearly demonstrate a concept and often are in the context of varied scenarios.

More extensive examples are presented in the form of "A Problem Solved," in which a problem is posed and its solution is discussed, designed, and implemented. I enjoy the exploration of various design choices and share these as "Design Decisions." As you will see in the next few pages, important ideas, insights, programming tips, and Java syntax are highlighted and appear in context with the presentation. And so do my questions!

You will find that the book's organization, sequencing, and pace of topic coverage are designed to facilitate learning and teaching. Each of its 32 chapters focuses on specific aspects of Java and consists of small, numbered segments that deal with one issue at a time. As we progress, previous ideas that might be applicable are brought back to reinforce and augment the current topic.

Seven debugging interludes occur throughout the text and are positioned after key chapters. They discuss debugging and testing directly related to the Java concepts recently discussed. Debugging is an essential skill to develop. It is my hope that these interludes will encourage both students and faculty to tackle this often elusive topic.

Finally, I have found that my students have enjoyed creating programs that produce pictorial output. A programming construct that results in a picture rather than only textual output is often more appealing and understandable to the reader. To this end, seven chapters devoted to pictorial examples are interspersed throughout the book. Although you could skip these chapters, I urge you to consider them. Interesting ideas about program design arise naturally in a graphical context.

I hope that you enjoy reading this book. Imagine! You can learn, or teach, Java!

Warm Regards,
Frank M. Carrano

Approach ■ Organization ■ Examples ■ Pedagogy

Welcome to *Imagine! Java*. This book teaches critical thinking, problem solving, and sustainable Java-programming skills to students new to programming. Readers of this book should have used a computer and be familiar with basic algebra and some trigonometry. Knowledge of programming is not assumed.

This book is designed to be used for a one- or two-course introduction to programming sequence and is the result of three decades of teaching undergraduates how to program successfully.

- **Approach:** Concise, Conversational, Contextual
- **Organization:** Focused, Methodical, Well-Paced
- **Examples:** Clear, Illustrative, Compelling
- **Pedagogy:** Student Self-Study, Contextually Relevant, Enriching

This is a novel pedagogical approach that will drive the evolution of textbook design strategy, which has been stalled for some time now.
—**Ric Heishman, North Virginia Community College**

Approach and Organization

Using a conversational writing style, Frank Carrano teaches programming concepts in a problem-solving context. Topics are introduced one at a time using simple **everyday analogies and examples** that help students understand and conceptualize abstract programming concepts. For example, *a paper bag helps students understand a container class,* and *a simple grocery or to-do list is the same as how a program can organize data.* Students learn to think critically about the concepts at hand and, therefore, retain the fundamental problem-solving and programming concept being taught. We are very excited about this new approach.

Another hallmark feature of *Imagine! Java* is how each topic is distilled into **small, manageable portions**. This concise and focused content coverage allows for more extensive discussion of a topic and provides an opportunity to explore alternatives and design decisions that support contextual learning. To accomplish this goal, the material is divided into **short, numbered segments** that are organized into 32 relatively short chapters. Each segment presents a single idea and individual chapters focus on specific aspects of Java. As students complete each numbered segment, they achieve a sense of accomplishment. A list of chapter prerequisites appears later in this preface to help you to plan your path through the book.

> I really appreciate this organizational approach. There are two advantages from my point of view: First it is flexible for instructors to pick topics taught in class and homework reading; second, it is much easier for students to focus on main concepts without the distraction of too much material.
> —**Ed Gehringer, North Carolina State**

Frank Carrano is focused and methodical, but also very complete. This is a very good approach to presenting objects.
—Dennis Higgins, SUNY Oneonta

This book was created specifically with **objects and Java** in mind. Objects are introduced in Chapter 1 and mentioned throughout Chapters 2 and 3. Students actually start to use objects of the standard classes that are supplied with Java in demonstrations in Chapters 4 and 5. After readers are comfortable with objects and understand how to use them, they learn how to write their own classes in Chapters 6, 8, and 9.

After the decision and repetition elements of Java are developed, inheritance and polymorphism are introduced as concepts midway through the book. These concepts are then covered in depth later, after the chapters about arrays and recursion.

The following shows the overall composition of the book. A further chapter-by-chapter description appears later.

Another advantage (of the interludes) is that the flow through the text is improved by not interrupting it constantly with what can go wrong.
—Paul Sivilotti, Ohio State University

Appendixes

Brief Table of Contents

I think the clarity of presentation is the book's greatest strength. Ultimately, that is the most important feature because it improves learning by helping students absorb the material better.
—Harish Sethu, Drexel University

Pedagogical Elements

I really like the many short examples that illustrate a single concept. In my experience, the students often look to examples for patterns that they can use in their programs.
—**Doug Twitchell, Illinois State University**

In addition to the concise and methodical presentation of topics, numerous examples illuminate new concepts and often answer the *What If* questions that might come to mind. Often, these examples are presented in the form of **"A Problem Solved,"** in which a problem is posed and its solution is discussed, designed, and implemented.

▓ A Problem Solved: Comparing Classes of Squares

As an exercise, imagine that you are asked to design and implement a class of square objects. Each object should be able to initialize the length of its side, change this length, and report its area.

To give readers insight into the design choices that one could make when formulating a solution, **"Design Decision"** elements lay out such options along with the rationale behind the choice made for a particular example. These discussions are often in the context of *A Problem Solved*.

Details such as the Design Decision on p. 589 are an excellent means for instilling good design technique. This one provides subtle insight into the larger concepts of encapsulation and information hiding.
—**Ric Heishman, North Virginia Community College**

The organization of graphics topics in *Imagine! Java* will raise students' interests and enhance their understanding of other programming constructs.
—**Ed Gehringer, North Carolina State**

Imagine! Java offers optional, yet integrated, **coverage of graphics**. This use of graphical examples adds to the understanding of basic Java topics. Graphical applications appear in their own **optional chapters** and are integrated into the text to illustrate aspects of Java in a more engaging and visual way. Thus, the graphics coverage augments and enhances the learning experience instead of being presented for its own sake.

Notes Important ideas are presented or summarized in highlighted paragraphs and are meant to be read in line with the surrounding text.

Programming Tips Suggestions to improve or facilitate programming are featured as soon as they become relevant.

Java Syntax Concise descriptions of Java constructs are presented as each is introduced.

Debugging Interludes

Another unique feature is the occurrence of seven debugging interludes that discuss debugging and testing of program code. These interludes are positioned after key chapters throughout the text and directly relate to the preceding Java concepts.

The debugging interludes are excellent and definitely are a unique feature of this text. I also like the spacing and periodicity, relative to major sets of topics. There is virtually no comparison for these topics; they are significantly unique relative to other entry-level Java texts.

—Ric Heishman, North Virginia Community College

Debugging
Interlude

1

The Errors Made by Programmers

Contents
Kinds of Errors
Compile-Time Errors
Execution-Time Errors

Prerequisites
Chapter 3   Arithmetic Expressions

Mistakes. We hate to make them, but we all do. Any error that you make in a program is called a **bug**, and the process of finding these errors is called **debugging**. In these *debugging interludes*, we will talk about the common errors that occur in Java programs and try to give you the skills to deal with them. We begin here by describing the kinds of errors that programmers make.

Elements for Student Self-Study

Each chapter begins with a **table of contents**, a list of **prerequisite chapters** that students should have read, and the **learning objectives** for the material to be covered.

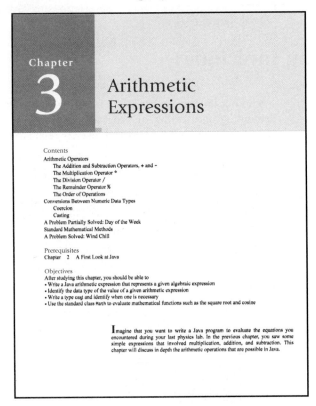

 Self-Test Questions are integrated within the text to reinforce the concept just presented. The reader must pause and reflect on the material to answer the question(s). Solutions to the self-test questions are provided at the end of each chapter. Further practice is available by solving the exercises and programming projects at the end of each chapter.

 Video*Notes* are Pearson's new visual tool designed for teaching key programming concepts and techniques. These short, step-by-step videos demonstrate aspects of Java and how to solve problems from design through coding, and provide students with another way to recap and reinforce key concepts presented throughout the book. Video*Notes* allow for self-paced instruction with easy navigation, including the ability to select, play, rewind, fast-forward, and stop within each video. A unique Video*Notes* icon appears in the margin of this book to let you know when a video is available for a particular concept or problem. A detailed breakdown of the 109 Video*Notes* for this text and their associated location in the book can be found on p. xxv. Video*Notes* are free with the purchase of a new textbook. To purchase access to Video*Notes*, please go to www.pearsonhighered.com/carrano.

Accessing Instructor and Student Resource Materials

■ Instructor Resources

The following protected instructor material is available on the publisher's website at www.pearsonhighered.com/carrano. For username and password information, please contact your Pearson representative.

- PowerPoint lecture slides
- Instructor solutions manual
- Java code as it appears in this book
- Errata
- Link to online premium content
- Video*Notes*
- Web chapters

■ Student Resources

Access to the premium website and access to online content is located at www.pearsonhighered.com/carrano. Students must use the access card located in the front of the book to register and access the online material. If there is no access card in the front of this textbook, students can purchase access by going to www.pearsonhighered.com/carrano, selecting "Premium Content and Web Chapters," and clicking "Get Access." Instructors must register on the site to access the material.

The following content is available through the premium website:

- Instructional Video*Notes*
- Web Chapter 30: Sequential Binary Files
- Web Chapter 31: Random-Access Files
- Web Chapter 32: Generics and Data Structures
- A glossary of terms

Additional content is available to students; this content appears on the initial screen and does not require a password:

- Errata
- Java code as it appears in the book

The Java Class Library is available at

java.sun.com/javase/6/docs/api/

Chapter Overview

The book begins with a brief description of the basic components of a computer that are relevant to learning a programming language. This first chapter introduces Java and sets the stage for a discussion of this language. Chapter 2 provides our first look at a Java program, including how to display text, declare variables, make assignments, read input, and write comments. Chapter 3 develops these points by examining arithmetic expressions, data types, and mathematical functions.

We pause our presentation to turn our attention to debugging. Debugging Interlude 1 describes the kinds of errors programmers make. The main examples here are of syntax errors, but run-time and logical errors are also introduced. Chapter 4 presents several standard classes in the Java Class Library and uses them in sample programs. The goal here is to become familiar with objects and their behaviors. Chapter 5 then introduces the class Graphics and uses it to write simple applications that draw. While setting the stage for future chapters that involve graphics, Chapter 5 reinforces the use of objects. Chapter 6 describes class definitions and methods. Included in this presentation are constructors, public versus private access, passing arguments, and general guidelines for the design of a class.

Debugging Interlude 2 presents examples of some typical run-time and logical errors that novices tend to make at this point in their study of Java. Using these examples, debugging strategies are explored. Chapter 7 discusses decisions within a program and defines the if statement, boolean expressions, and the assert statement. Chapter 8 adds to our discussion of class definitions by introducing boolean-valued methods, private methods, and enumerations. This chapter integrates its coverage of classes with the material about if statements given in the previous chapter. Chapter 9 revises some of the earlier graphical applications by creating and using a class that represents each drawing. These graphical examples provide richer material to demonstrate the design of a class. Chapter 10 continues the discussion of decision statements by examining the multiway if statement and the switch statement. Chapter 11 writes several graphical applications that involve the decision statements given in Chapters 7 and 10. This chapter also provides an opportunity to discuss the interactions among several objects.

Debugging Interlude 3 introduces the topic of testing a program to find logical mistakes. The examples involve typical errors made when using decision statements and the strategies used to find these mistakes. Chapter 12 discusses loops and the while statement. By focusing on one new statement in this chapter, the reader is able to develop the skills necessary to write a loop. The presentation of loops continues in Chapter 13 by examining the for statement and the do statement. Chapter 14 offers several more examples of loops within the context of a graphical application. Again, the graphical approach offers a visual and captivating way to study the effects of repetition within a program. The subsequent Debugging Interlude 4 explores how to find errors that occur in loops.

The discussion of classes continues in Chapters 15 and 16. Elaborating on class design, Chapter 15 introduces some design tools, such as the Unified Modeling Language. We talk about abstraction, specification, and encapsulation; introduce aggregation and inheritance; and cover overloaded methods and the static modifier. Chapter 16 builds on these topics by presenting Java interfaces, polymorphism, inheritance, and the class Object. Inheritance is covered in more detail in a later chapter, as you will see. Chapter 17 examines how interfaces and inheritance are used in the Abstract Windowing Toolkit (AWT) and Swing.

In doing so, the chapter builds on the material of the previous graphical chapters by including listeners for buttons and the mouse to build a basic graphical user interface. This chapter shows interfaces and inheritance in use. Debugging Interlude 5 discusses debugging tools such as those offered by integrated development environments (IDEs).

Chapter 18 introduces one-dimensional arrays and includes many examples of array processiong. Chapter 19 designs and builds a class of bags. Though generally considered to be a topic in data structures, the material is easily understood and shows how to create a non-trivial class. Moreover, the reader exercises what was just learned about arrays and about design in previous chapters. Chapter 20 continues the presentation of arrays by considering multidimensional arrays and how to resize an array. Debugging Interlude 6 explores difficulties when working with arrays.

Chapter 21 introduces the class `ArrayList` as a follow-up to our prior discussion of arrays. Chapter 22 provides more examples of arrays in a graphical context. Chapter 23 sorts and searches arrays using iterative algorithms. We take this opportunity to introduce Big Oh notation at an elementary level. Chapter 24 discusses recursion, and Chapter 25 continues the discussion by presenting recursive methods for searching and sorting an array. Next, Chapter 26 creates drawings recursively. Finally, Debugging Interlude 7—the last one—explores some pitfalls when using recursion.

Chapter 27 considers the details of using inheritance to derive a new class from an existing one. Concepts introduced earlier are reinforced and elaborated. New concepts, such as protected access and package access, are presented. We also define abstract classes and compare them to interfaces. Chapter 28 discusses exceptions. Methods that throw an exception and using methods that might throw an exception are considered. Chapter 29 covers reading and writing text files, including how to handle the exceptions that can occur.

Appendixes A through E provide supplemental coverage of Java. Appendix A shows where one can get Java without charge. Appendix B lists the Java reserved words, and Appendix C gives a table of Unicode characters. Appendix D summarizes programming style and comments. It describes `javadoc` comments and defines the tags used in this book. Appendix E provides an introduction to cloning.

Three more chapters and a glossary of terms are available online at the book's website. Chapter 30 looks at sequential binary files, and Chapter 31 introduces random-access files. Finally, Chapter 32 talks about generics and collections. It includes an overview of basic data structures, such as the list, stack, queue, and binary tree. This chapter also discusses generics in the context of these data structures.

Frank M. Carrano is Professor Emeritus of Computer Science at the University of Rhode Island. His interests include data structures, computer science education, social issues in computing, and numerical computation. He is especially interested in the design and delivery of undergraduate computer sciences courses, and has authored several well-known textbooks. He holds a Ph.D. in computer science from Syracuse University.

Acknowledgments

Thank you to the following reviewers for carefully reading the manuscript and making candid comments and constructive suggestions that greatly improved the work:

Ed Gehringer—*North Carolina State University*
Jainchao Han—*California State University, Dominguez Hills*
Ric Heishman—*North Virginia Community College*
Dennis Higgins—*SUNY College at Oneonta*
Tim Margush—*University of Akron*
Richard Povinelli—*Marquette University*
Nripendra Sarker—*Prairie View A&M University*
Harish Sethu—*Drexel University*
Paul Sivilotti—*Ohio State University*
Doug Twitchell—*Illinois State University*

Several people were my support team during the lengthy process of creating this new book. My editor, Tracy Dunkelberger, gave me her constant enthusiasm, encouragement, wisdom, and guidance. Jake Warde coordinated the review process, and Melinda Haggerty oversaw the development of the supplements. My long-time copy editor, Rebecca Pepper, ensured that my presentation is clear, correct, and grammatical. Scott Disanno directed the production of the book and personally checked every page for accuracy. This team was there for me and made me feel like this was the only important task in their busy lives. Thank you so much!

My gratitude for the previously mentioned people does not diminish my appreciation for the help provided by many others. Tim Henry, my colleague at URI, created 109 Video*Notes* that provide extra instruction for every chapter of the book. Steve Armstrong produced the lecture slides, and Dawn Ellis and Karen Gardner contributed the exercises, programming projects, and their solutions. In addition, I thank Bob Engelhardt, Allison Michael, Louise Capulli, Charles Hoot, and Lianne Dunn for their help and contributions.

Finally, I thank my family and friends—Doug, Ted, Vandee, Nancy, Sue, Tom, Maybeth, and Ed—for giving me a life away from computers.

Thank you, everyone, for your expertise and good cheer.

Frank M. Carrano

Contact Us

Your comments, suggestions, and corrections are always welcome. Please e-mail them to us at

carrano@acm.org

Table of Contents

Table of Contents

Table of Contents

Appendixes

Video*Notes* Directory

This table lists the Video*Notes* that are available online. The page numbers indicate where in the book each Video*Note* has relevance.

VideoNotes

VideoNotes

VideoNotes

Chapter Prerequisites

Each chapter assumes that the reader has studied certain previous chapters or parts of a chapter. This list indicates those prerequisites. You can use this information to plan a path through the book.

	Prerequisites
Chapter 1 Introduction	
Chapter 2 A First Look at Java	1
Chapter 3 Arithmetic Expressions	2
Debugging Interlude 1 The Errors Made by Programmers	3
Chapter 4 Using Classes and Objects	3
Chapter 5 Basic Graphics	4
Chapter 6 Class Definitions: The Fundamentals	4
Debugging Interlude 2 Common Mistakes When Working with Classes	DI-1, 6
Chapter 7 Decisions	4
Chapter 8 Class Definitions: More Details	6, 7
Chapter 9 Classes of Graphical Objects	5, 7, 8
Chapter 10 Multiway Decisions	7, 8
Chapter 11 Decisions and Object Interactions When Drawing	9, 10
Debugging Interlude 3 Introduction to Testing	9, 10, 11, DI-2
Chapter 12 Repetition	7
Chapter 13 Repetition Continued	12
Chapter 14 Repetition When Drawing	5, 9, 10, 11, 13
Debugging Interlude 4 Debugging Loops	12, 13, 14
Chapter 15 Designing Classes	6, 7, 8
Chapter 16 Object-Oriented Concepts	15
Chapter 17 Inheritance and Interfaces in Swing and the AWT	9, 15, 16
Debugging Interlude 5 Debugging Tools	DI-4
Chapter 18 Arrays	10, 13, 16 (16.16–16.21)
Chapter 19 An Array-Based Data Structure	15, 16, 18
Chapter 20 Arrays Continued	8, 13 (13.1–13.10), 18, 19
Debugging Interlude 6 Debugging Arrays	18, 19, 20
Chapter 21 Array Lists	16, 19, 20
Chapter 22 Arrays When Drawing	15, 17, 20, 21 (for Segments 22.32–22.33 only)
Chapter 23 Sorting and Searching	18
Chapter 24 Recursion	10, 12, 15 (15.6–15.10), 23 (23.31–23.34)
Chapter 25 Recursive Array Processing	13, 18, 19 (for Segments 25.8–25.9 only), 23, 24
Chapter 26 Recursive Drawings	12, 18, 24
Debugging Interlude 7 Debugging Recursive Methods	24, 25, DI-5
Chapter 27 Inheritance Continued	16
Chapter 28 Exceptions	7, 16, 18, 24, 27
Chapter 29 Text Files	7, 12, 15, 28
Chapter 30 Sequential Binary Files	Segments 29.1–29.5, 29.17–29.18, 29.21–29.23
Chapter 31 Random-Access Files	30
Chapter 32 Generics and Data Structures	16, 19, Segments 20.2–20.10, 21
Appendix E Cloning	16, 18, 27, 28

Chapter

1

Introduction

Contents

Prerequisites

None

Objectives

After studying this chapter, you should be able to

- Describe the basic operations of a computer
- State the purpose of the four major components of a computer
- Distinguish between the contents of a byte and its address
- Describe the difference between machine language and a high-level language
- Describe the advantages of Java
- Describe the notion of an object and a class
- Describe the purpose of bytecode and the Java Virtual Machine
- Describe the steps one takes to write, compile, and execute a Java application program

Imagine! You are about to learn how to write computer programs in Java. You might be excited by this prospect, fearful, or even bored. In the pages that follow, we hope to keep your interest high and tedium low, and erase any fear by giving you clear explanations that foster a strong understanding of the material.

Our world surrounds us with computerized technology. Computers affect us daily, even without our realization. Every time we use our cell phone, watch television, or even run on a treadmill, a computer is involved somehow. Although this involvement is hidden, you likely have had explicit contact with computers—or computerized game consoles—when playing video games or writing essays. Although the computers involved in these situations might have different electronics, they basically share similar characteristics. Despite their similarities, computers can perform many diverse functions because we can program them by giving them a sequence of **instructions**, called a **program**, to follow. Each task is the result of a particular program. This book will show you how to write such programs in a language called Java.

Before we can really talk about Java, we need to introduce some terminology. Sometimes when people speak of computers, they really mean a **computing system**: the computer itself, or **hardware**, and the programs, or **software**, necessary to perform desired tasks. Discussing each aspect separately is somewhat difficult, as they are so interrelated. A computer can do nothing useful without a program, and a program by itself is like an ignored list of directions. Even so, we begin with a description of the computer as a machine.

■ An Overview of a Computer

videonote
Hardware

The hardware of a computing system includes not only the computer but also peripheral components such as printers, displays, scanners, and so on. We will treat these peripherals as a part of the computer.

What Can a Computer Do?

1.1   Computers can perform astounding tasks, or so it seems. Actually, any major task is the result of many simple, basic operations. Just how rudimentary these operations are may surprise you! For example, a computer can

- Get data from the outside world via a keyboard, a mouse, a disc, a scanner, the Internet, and so on.
- Save data, either temporarily or more permanently.
- Retrieve data that has been saved.
- Add, subtract, multiply, or divide two numbers.
- Compare two values to see whether one is less than, greater than, or equal to another.
- Manipulate data by either breaking it into pieces, joining it to other data, or moving it around.
- Display numbers, words, and other marks on a screen or on paper in various colors.

By performing these simple operations with great speed and accuracy, a computer can achieve impressive results.

The Components of a Typical Computer

A typical computer has these major components, as Figure 1-1 illustrates:

- Primary memory
- Central processing unit

- Secondary memory
- Input and output system

The connections between the various components are collectively called a **bus**.

FIGURE 1-1   The components of a typical computer

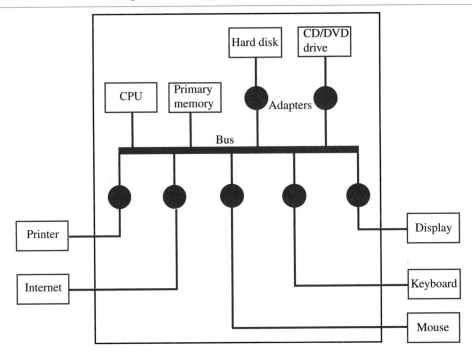

1.2   **Memory.** The **primary memory**—also known as **random access memory (RAM)** or **internal memory**—is where a computer stores both its instructions and the data on which the instructions operate. This memory is **volatile**, and whatever is stored therein is lost when electrical power is turned off. **Secondary memory**, on the other hand, is **nonvolatile**: It does not lose its data without electricity. Hard disks and DVDs are two examples of devices that can be a part of a computer's secondary memory.

A computer can access the data and programs in its primary memory faster than those in secondary memory. However, primary memory is usually more expensive than secondary memory, and so computers have less of it.

1.3   **The input and output system.** A computer can communicate with us—under the control of a program—via its **input and output system**. This system includes various **input devices**—such as a keyboard and mouse—and **output devices**, such as a display and a printer. Various disk drives can be both input devices and output devices, as can network cards and modems, which enable computers to communicate with one another via the Internet. Input and output devices connect to the bus via **adapters**, which make the devices appear similar to the CPU by accommodating their differing characteristics.

1.4   **The central processing unit.** The **central processing unit**, or **CPU**, decodes and **executes** the instructions of a program stored in memory. These instructions direct the CPU to perform arithmetic, make comparisons, and perform other similar tasks. The CPU can move data from one memory location to another. It can direct data from memory to an output device and from an input device to memory. In these ways, the CPU manipulates data in memory according to the instructions in a program. In a sense, the CPU is the heart—or brain—of the machine.

Ordinarily, the CPU executes instructions sequentially in the order in which they appear in memory. Certain instructions, however, can direct the CPU to alter the order of execution by repeating or skipping other instructions. We will learn how to design the logic of a program, and in doing so to determine the conditions that will affect the order in which the CPU will execute instructions.

1.5   Although input and output devices do not communicate directly with the computer's primary memory, they ultimately transfer data either to it or from it, as Figure 1-2 illustrates, as a result of an instruction executed within the CPU. If you type data at a keyboard for a program to **read**, the data is placed into memory. This data is the program's **input**. If a program displays data for us, the data first must be in memory. Anything that a program displays is called its **output**.

FIGURE 1-2   Data is transferred from an input device to a computer's memory, or from a computer's memory to an output device

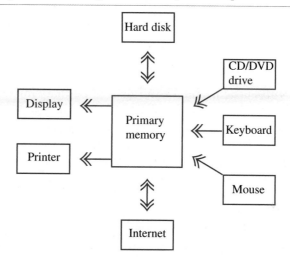

1.6   **More about primary memory.** For our purposes, some knowledge of a computer's primary memory will be helpful. This memory is a collection of locations called bytes. Each **byte** contains a value—known as its **contents**. Also associated with each byte is a fixed numeric name called an **address**. A byte's address is fixed by the designer of the computer. You cannot change the address of a particular byte, but you can change its contents. Thus, your program can refer to a specific byte by its address and then look at or change its contents.

We can make an analogy between bytes and mailboxes in a post office: Each box number (the address) is fixed, but the contents of the box can change. However, unlike a mailbox, a byte can contain only a single piece of data at a time; placing new data into a byte destroys the old data.

Both the contents and address of a byte are represented by a sequence of binary values. Each value is produced by a physical component that can be in one of two states, such as on or off, magnetized or not magnetized, and so on. Such components are usually easier and cheaper to make than those having more than two states each. We typically denote the two states using the binary digits 0 and 1. Binary digits are commonly called **bits**.

A byte contains eight bits. For example, we might represent the contents of a particular byte as the binary numeral 10011100. This sequence of bits represents a **binary number**. The address of a byte is typically 16, 32, or even 64 bits long. Having more bits enables an address to be longer, and thus the computer's memory can be larger because it can have more bytes. Addresses begin at zero and are assigned to the bytes consecutively, as shown in Figure 1-3.

FIGURE 1-3   Bytes in memory

16-bit addresses	Bytes
0000000000000000	
0000000000000001	
0000000000000010	
0000000000000011	
0000000000000100	
0000000000000101	
⋮	⋮
1111111111111101	
1111111111111110	
1111111111111111	

Note: The decimal equivalent of a binary integer
Each bit in a binary numeral has a value that is determined by its position within the numeral. This value is analogous to the value of a digit within a decimal numeral. For example, the decimal numeral 4321 represents four thousand, three hundred, twenty-one: The 4 represents 4000, the 3 represents 300, the 2 represents 20, and the 1 represents 1. The sum of 4000, 300, 20, and 1 is 4321.

Another way to write 4321 is

$$4 \times 1000 + 3 \times 100 + 2 \times 10 + 1$$

but by convention, we reverse the order of the terms and write the sum this way:

$$1 + 2 \times 10 + 3 \times 100 + 4 \times 1000$$

which is

$$1 \times 10^0 + 2 \times 10^1 + 3 \times 10^2 + 4 \times 10^3$$

Analogously, the binary numeral 10111 represents the decimal computation

$$1 \times 2^0 + 1 \times 2^1 + 1 \times 2^2 + 0 \times 2^3 + 1 \times 2^4$$

which is

$$1 \times 1 + 1 \times 2 + 1 \times 4 + 0 \times 8 + 1 \times 16$$

or 23 in decimal. While decimal numerals use a **base** 10 notation, binary numerals use a base 2 notation.

Although the eight bits in a byte permit a rather small range of values, you can group consecutive bytes to represent larger quantities. For numeric values, Java uses groupings of two, four, and eight bytes.

1.7   **Instructions.** A computer's primary memory contains not only data, but also the instructions that enable the computer to perform its task. These instructions reside in consecutive bytes of memory and are in a numeric form called **machine instructions**. In general, each kind of computer has its own unique instruction set, or **machine language**, that is defined by its designers. Whether you write a program in Java or another programming language, the computer ultimately understands only a machine-language version of the program, as you will see.

> ### Aside: Some history of the stored program concept
>
> The IBM Automatic Sequence Controlled Calculator, also called the Harvard Mark I, was the first automatic digital computer. Completed in 1944, it was the result of a collaboration between Howard Aiken of Harvard University and IBM. The Mark I followed instructions that were punched onto a paper tape; a program was not stored internally within the machine. Calculations were carried out electromagnetically by using relays, which are mechanical switches that are activated by electromagnets.
>
> At about the same time that Aiken was building his computer, John Atanasoff of Iowa State University designed and built the first electronic digital computer. Using Atanasoff's ideas, J. Presper Eckert and John Mauchly of the University of Pennsylvania completed the ENIAC in 1946. The ENIAC was the first large general-purpose electronic computer. Although these machines did not depend upon mechanical devices to perform their calculations, they were programmed by plugging wires into special boards and by setting thousands of switches.
>
> While work on the ENIAC progressed, Mauchly and Eckert, along with John von Neumann of Princeton University, proposed the **stored program concept**, whereby a computer's memory would contain both the program and the data to be manipulated. This concept—also known as the **von Neumann architecture**—was a significant advance in the development of computers and remains fundamental to all present-day computers.

■ A Computing System's Software

videonote
Software

1.8   In the late 1940s, programmers actually wrote programs only in machine language. This process was both tedious and error prone, and produced programs that were difficult for humans to read and understand. The mid-1950s saw the development of **high-level languages** that focused on problem solving and not on a particular machine language. Today's programming languages are still called high-level languages, even though they are more powerful than the languages of more than half a century ago. Rather than writing the numeric instructions of a machine language, programmers can write symbolic statements in a high-level language. These statements have more immediate meaning to humans and thus are easier to write, read, and understand. Moreover, one statement in a high-level language generally represents several machine-language instructions.

A program written in a high-level language—called a **source program**—must be translated into the machine language of a specific computer before it can execute, or **run**. Another program performs this translation. A **compiler** is one such program; it translates an entire high-level-language program into machine language. You then run the resulting machine language in a separate step. An **interpreter**, on the other hand, translates a statement written in a high-level-language into machine language and then immediately executes it, alternating between translation and execution. As you will see, Java programs are typically compiled.

 Note: The statements in a program are sometimes called **code**, regardless of the programming language. **Coding**, then, is a synonym for programming.

1.9   Have you ever used a computer to play a video game or write an essay? For each of these endeavors, you actually used an **application program**, or simply an **application**. You are about to use Java to write your own applications. To be able to use any application, your computer needs an operating system. An **operating system** is a set of programs that provides services that enable you to use a computer. For all practical purposes, an operating system is an essential part of a computing system. Current systems—such as Windows, MacOS, UNIX, and Linux—provide an environment in which you can work. For example, they enable you to save files, organize them into folders or directories, use applications, and connect to the Internet. We will assume that you have some basic knowledge of the operating system that is available to you.

The Programming Language Java

1.10   Java was created by James Gosling of Sun Microsystems[1] and presented to the public in 1995. Although that was a while ago, many other current programming languages were introduced much earlier. Originally created for the computers in home appliances, Java has become an important general-purpose language with widespread appeal. Java programs are advantageous because they

- Are object oriented
- Can run on different kinds of computers, making them **platform independent**
- Can run within an Internet browser

Let's talk briefly about each one of these points.

1.11   **Object-oriented programming**. Within an **object-oriented program**, you define basic elements called **objects** by writing Java code. An object stores certain values, or **attributes**, that give it a particular **state**. An object also has **behaviors**, some of which could change its state.

For example, Java objects often represent actual things, such as people, books, or cell phones. You can see that each of these real-life objects has characteristics, or attributes, and some have behaviors. While not all things have behaviors, the Java objects that represent them almost certainly will. For instance, an object representing a rock should be able to give you its weight. The weight is an attribute of the object, and the act of providing the weight is a behavior.

Java objects also can represent abstractions, such as names, songs, numbers, or bank accounts. While these items have attributes in real life, their behaviors likely exist only in the realm of a Java program. For example, a song object should be able to give you its title and composer.

An object has **data fields** to represent its attributes as well as **methods** to perform its behaviors. These data fields and methods are defined within a **class** that describes like objects. A class is like a blueprint or plan for creating objects. You can write your own classes and thereby create objects of your own design, and you can use classes that others have written. Java comes with a collection of useful classes, called the **Java Class Library**. Chapter 4 will show you how to use some of the classes in this library. Chapter 6 will begin to show you how to write your own classes.

Frequently, a new class is based upon an existing class. By using a feature of object-oriented programming called **inheritance**, you can have a class inherit the fields and methods of another class, adding to or revising them as necessary. Inheritance provides a way to create new classes without repeating earlier work. Although we will begin to use inheritance as early as Chapter 5, when we introduce graphics, we will not explore its details until much later in this book.

1.12   **Platform independence**. A **platform** is basically a kind of computer, that is, a computer's architecture and often its operating system. For example, two popular platforms might be described as a Windows machine and a Macintosh running MacOS X. For many programming languages, a compiler must be written for each platform. The compiler for a given platform translates a program written in a particular language into the appropriate machine language for that platform. The disadvantage to this approach is the need for several compilers for the same language.

Java, on the other hand, is platform independent. A Java compiler does not produce machine language instructions for a particular platform directly from a Java program. Instead, it generates an

---

1. Oracle acquired Sun Microsystems on January 27, 2010.

intermediate form of the program called the Java **bytecode**. This bytecode will run on any computer that has the **Java Virtual Machine**, or **JVM**, installed. The JVM is actually another program that converts Java bytecode into the machine language of its host platform. Any platform that has its own version of a Java Virtual Machine, as Figure 1-4 illustrates, will be able to run a Java program.

FIGURE 1-4   The steps a Java program takes to achieve platform independence

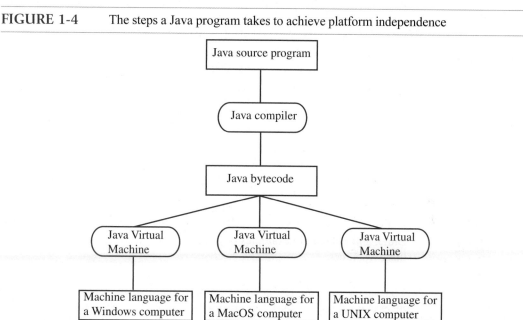

Although this strategy replaces the need for multiple compilers with a need for multiple JVMs, writing the code for a Java Virtual Machine is far easier than writing a compiler. This is because translating bytecode into a particular machine language is easier than translating Java statements directly into machine language. Depending on the way it is written, a particular JVM can act either like an interpreter, alternating between translation of bytecode and execution of machine language, or like a compiler that translates all of the bytecode into machine language before it is executed.

1.13   **Local and remote execution**. One type of Java program is an application designed to reside and execute on your computer. The software that supports the execution of an application, including the JVM and the Java Class Library, is called the **Java runtime system**. Applications whose output is entirely textual are called **console applications**. You also can write applications that have graphical output. We will show you how to write both kinds of applications.

Another form of Java program—called an **applet**—runs inside another program. Typically the other program is a **web browser**. An applet's bytecode can be placed on the Internet, where it can be run at a distant location within a browser to produce its output. Note that the browser uses a JVM to execute an applet. Although our focus is on application programs, once you learn to write Java applications, writing an applet will not be difficult.

Graphics

1.14   Both applets and applications can produce graphical output. You can draw certain shapes as if you were using a pen or paintbrush, display images, or create components of a **user interface**. A program's user interface provides a way for the person who uses the program—the **user**—to interact with it. When the interface involves graphical components such as buttons and menus, it is called a **graphical user interface**, or **GUI**.

Java provides many standard classes that support the use of graphics in a program. The original collection of such classes is called the **Abstract Window Toolkit**, or **AWT**. Subsequent to its development, a more capable collection called **Swing** was written. Rather than replacing the AWT, Swing builds on the classes within the AWT. Thus, both the AWT and Swing are available to us.

We'll cover graphics in separate chapters that support and enhance our presentation of the basic Java concepts. Using graphics as a way to learn Java provides a richer experience and is much more fun.

■ Writing, Compiling, and Running a Java Program

videonote

From idea to
Java program

We will look at our first Java program in the next chapter and begin to describe Java as a programming language. But before we do that, let's look at what you will need and the steps you will take to write and execute a Java program.

Tools and Resources

1.15   You will need a text editor and additional tools to write and run Java application programs. If your platform is Windows or UNIX, you can download Sun Microsystems' free Java 2 Software Development Kit, Standard Edition (J2SE SDK), from the website java.sun.com. If you are a MacOS user, you have Java included with your operating system.

videonote

Using NetBeans

You might prefer to use an **integrated development environment (IDE)**, which provides an editor, compiler, Java Virtual Machine, and other helpful tools for writing Java programs. NetBeans, BlueJ, and Eclipse are examples of IDEs available to you at no charge. Appendix A provides links to these resources.

The Steps

1.16   You can use any simple, plain-text editor, such as Notepad, to write a Java program. You can also use other editors, such as those supplied with an IDE, that use colors to highlight various components of the program. As you type your program, the characters are stored in the computer's primary memory. You risk losing your work if you do not save it in a file on the computer's hard disk. Get in the habit of saving your work often; do not wait until you have finished typing the entire program. Note that Java expects the name of the file to be *name*.java, where *name* is the name of the program.

Once you have your program saved in a file, you will compile it. With an IDE, clicking a button will accomplish this step. With the SDK, however, you would type the command

```
javac name.java
```

More than likely, the compiler will complain about something that you typed in your program! As you will learn, mistakes in your program that the compiler detects are called **syntax errors**. Maybe you made a simple typing mistake, or perhaps you didn't follow Java's rules exactly. The compiler will not try to fix your errors, but it will give you an opinion about what seems to be wrong.

1.17   After fixing your mistakes, you will try to compile the program again. Several repetitions of compiling and fixing mistakes may be necessary before the compiler actually produces bytecode. Once it does so, it will save the bytecode in a file named *name*.class. You now can run the program. In an IDE, clicking a button will execute the bytecode. Frequently, one button can be used to both compile and execute a program, but if compilation is unsuccessful, execution does not occur. Using the SDK, you run a program by typing the command

```
java name
```

Notice that the name of the program is used in this command, not the file name *name*.class.

Did the program do what you expected and planned? Once you are able to run your program, you test to see whether it behaves as it should. You might need to correct errors in the program's logic and repeat the compilation, execution, and testing phases. Figure 1-5 illustrates the steps you will take in writing Java programs.

So let's begin!

FIGURE 1-5   The steps involved in developing a Java program

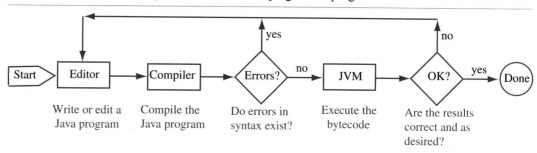

Question 1 Complete the following crossword puzzle by using terms introduced in this chapter.

(crossword grid)

Across

1. A high-level language
3. First word of the concept used by the von Neumann architecture
4. Random access memory
9. One of the three major components of a typical computing system (abbr.)
10. The "G" in GUI
11. A kind of programming error
13. A program that translates Java code into a platform-independent form
15. A person who uses a program
16. A characteristic of an object
18. Elements that interact with one another in an object-oriented program
19. The base of a decimal number system
20. A program that converts Java bytecode into the machine language of its host computer (abbr.)
21. A collection of locations called bytes
22. What you are when you finish this puzzle

Down

2. Primary memory is _____
5. The kind of instructions produced by the JVM
6. Windows, Linux, and MacOS are examples of this kind of system
7. A particular kind of computer and operating system
8. Produced by a Java compiler
10. A kind of user interface (abbr.)
12. To execute a program
13. Like a plan for creating objects
14. Java code to define a behavior of an object
17. Smallest unit of memory

CHAPTER SUMMARY

- A computing system includes both hardware and software components.

- A computer performs its operations at the direction of instructions in a program. The speed and accuracy of a computer allow it to accomplish astounding results, even though its operations are quite basic.

- A typical computer has four major components: primary memory, the central processing unit, secondary memory, and the input and output system.

- A computer's primary memory consists of a collection of locations called bytes. Each byte has contents, or value, and a fixed numeric address. Both the value and address of a byte are thought of as binary numerals. A byte represents eight binary digits.

- Primary memory contains not only data, but also the machine instructions that enable the computer to perform its task. These instructions reside in consecutive bytes of memory.

- Primary memory is volatile, and thus its contents disappear when electrical power is turned off.

- Secondary memory resides on components such as hard disks and DVDs. Access to this memory is slower than access to primary memory. However, secondary memory is less expensive than primary memory. Secondary memory is nonvolatile: The data stored remains even without electricity.

- The central processing unit executes the instructions of a program, performing arithmetic, comparisons, and other similar tasks. It can move data from one memory location to another, and it can direct data to and from the input and output system.

- The stored program concept, or von Neumann architecture, places both the instructions of a program and their data within a computer's primary memory.

- A source program written in a high-level language is translated into the machine language of a specific computer before it can execute. Another program—either a compiler or an interpreter—performs this translation.

- A Java compiler produces bytecode that the Java Virtual Machine can execute. The JVM is actually another program that converts bytecode to the machine language of a particular computer.

- A program can communicate with its user via the computer's input and output system. It can read data from an input device and place it into the computer's memory. It also can transfer data from memory to an output device.

- Java is a programming language that has widespread appeal. Java programs are object oriented, are platform independent, and can run within a web browser.

- An object-oriented program defines objects that interact with one another. An object has attributes, as well as behaviors that could affect the value of its attributes.

- Data fields represent an object's attributes; an object's methods give it behaviors. These data fields and methods are defined within a class that describes groups of like objects.

- The Java Class Library is a collection of standard classes that you can use in your programs.

- A Java application is a program that runs on its own; an applet is a program that runs within an application. Usually an applet travels the Internet and runs within a web browser. Thus, you typically must provide a web page to contain the applet.

- Java provides many classes that support the use of graphics in a program. These classes are organized into the Abstract Window Toolkit, or AWT, and Swing.

- You can use several free tools to develop a Java program. An integrated development environment, or IDE, provides many useful tools not available in Sun's SDK.

EXERCISES

1. What is volatile memory and nonvolatile memory?

2. Name three input devices and three output devices.

3. Data is transferred from a user to which part of a computer? Data is transferred from which part of a computer to its user?

4. Define a memory address.

5. What is a binary numeral?

6. What is the decimal equivalent of each of the following binary numerals? 10110, 11001, 10101

7. Java is a multiplatform programming language. What does this statement mean?

PROJECTS

1. Using a text editor, type the following program. Name your file Welcome.java. From the command prompt, issue the command to compile your Java program,

   ```
   javac Welcome.java
   ```

   If there are any syntax errors, fix them and then recompile the program. When there are no more syntax errors, issue the command to run your program, java Welcome.

   ```
   public class Welcome
   {
      public static void main(String[] args)
      {
        // Display a welcome message
         System.out.println("Welcome to Java!");
      } // end main
   } // end Welcome
   ```

2. Repeat the previous project, but use the following program:

   ```
   public class Welcome2
   {
      public static void main(String[] args)
      {
         String name = "Dawn";
         System.out.println("Welcome to Java, " + name + "!");
      } // end main
   } // end Welcome2
   ```

   The file names and commands must use Welcome2 instead of Welcome. Replace "Dawn" with your name.

ANSWER TO SELF-TEST QUESTION

1. **Across:** 1. Java; 3. Stored; 4. RAM; 9. CPU; 10. Graphical; 11. Syntax; 13. Compiler; 15. User; 16. Attribute; 18. Objects; 19. Ten; 20. JVM; 21. Memory; 22. Done
   Down: 2. Volatile; 5. Machine; 6. Operating; 7. Platform; 8. Bytecode; 10. GUI; 12. Run; 13. Class; 14. Method; 17. Byte

Chapter

2

A First Look at Java

Contents

Prerequisites

Objectives

After studying this chapter, you should be able to

- Create valid Java identifiers
- Write Java statements that display text
- Describe the primitive data types `int`, `double`, `char`, and `boolean`
- Declare variables and assign values to them
- Read numbers and characters from the keyboard
- Write comments in a Java program
- Write a Java program that uses these aspects of Java

At this point, you likely want to see a Java program. In this chapter, we'll look at a few simple programs that use some basic Java components, including statements that get data into the computer from the keyboard, do some arithmetic, and display the results. We begin with a program that displays some text, and we will use it to introduce some terminology central to Java.

A Simple Java Program

2.1   Imagine that you want to write a Java application program to display some text. Listing 2-1 shows one such program. We'll use it to give you a general overview of a Java application as well as specifics of how to use the `println` and `print` statements.

videonote
Basic parts of a program

LISTING 2-1   A sample Java application program

```java
// Sample.java by F. M. Carrano
// Displays strings and provides an example of a Java application.
public class Sample
{
   public static void main(String[] args)
   {
      // demonstrate println
      System.out.println("This string is displayed on one line.");
      System.out.println("This string appears on the second line.");
      System.out.println(); // the third line displayed is blank

      // demonstrate print
      System.out.print("Four ");
      System.out.print("and twenty ");
      System.out.println("blackbirds");
      System.out.println("Baked in a pie.");
   } // end main
} // end Sample
```

Output

```
This string is displayed on one line.
This string appears on the second line.
                                              ◄——————— A blank line
Four and twenty blackbirds
Baked in a pie.
```

This Java program, which is stored in the file `Sample.java`, produces several lines of textual output, as shown below the program. In the Java program itself, each line is a **statement**. The program in the listing begins with some statements that give descriptive information, including its author and purpose. Statements like these, that begin with two slashes, are called **comments** and are ignored by the compiler. That is, comments help the human reader of the program and are not directions to the computer. A comment can appear on its own line or at the end of another statement in the program. Soon you will see other ways to write comment statements. As you will also see, a statement can extend across more than one line.

2.2 Our example program contains the definition of a **class** named `Sample` that begins with the lines

```
public class Sample
{
```

and ends with

```
} // end Sample
```

Statements within this outer pair of braces define a **method** called `main` that begins with the statements

```
public static void main(String[] args)
{
```

and ends with

```
} // end main
```

Statements within this inner pair of braces are the **body** of the method `main`. Generally, a class contains several methods, each defining a specific task and each having a name of the programmer's choosing. Every application program, however, must contain a method that is called `main`.

Identifiers

2.3 Words within the program, such as `public` and `main`, are **identifiers**. An identifier in Java can consist of letters, digits, the underscore (_), and the dollar sign ($), though it cannot begin with a digit. Identifiers are case sensitive, which means that Java considers uppercase letters and lowercase letters to be different letters. Thus, `result`, `Result`, and `RESULT` are three different identifiers. Using these identifiers in the same program would be confusing to others who read your program, so you should avoid doing so, even though it is legal.

Identifiers fall into one of three categories:

- Identifiers that you invent. In Listing 2-1, `Sample` and `args` are examples of identifiers that we chose.
- Identifiers that another programmer has chosen. `System`, `out`, `println`, `print`, `main`, and `String` are examples of identifiers in this category. They were chosen by the designers of Java.
- Identifiers that are a part of the Java language. These identifiers are called **reserved words** or **keywords**. Examples are `public`, `class`, `static`, and `void`. Since reserved words have particular meanings within Java, you should not use them for another purpose. We will say more about reserved words as we discuss the details of Java. You can see a list of Java's reserved words in Appendix B of this book. Note that all reserved words use lowercase letters.

Syntax: Identifiers

An identifier is a word composed of letters, digits, the underscore (_), and/or the dollar sign ($). It cannot begin with a digit. An uppercase letter is distinct from its lowercase counterpart. The following are valid identifiers: `Sphere`, `salesTax`, `draft2`, and `FEET_PER_YARD`.

Note: All reserved words in Java use only lowercase letters.

Question 1 Which of the following are valid Java identifiers?
`2beOrNot2be, room102, salesTax, six%, _inches, FEET, miles-per-hour`

2.4   Conventions. Why do some of our identifiers begin with an uppercase letter, and why are some of the statements in our program indented? The Java language does not define details like this. Rather, programmers follow a **programming style** by convention. Not every programmer follows the same stylistic conventions, however. Often, such conventions are dictated by a programmer's employer or, as in your case, an instructor. The programming style that we use in this book was chosen in the interest of clarity and ease of learning Java.

As shown in Figure 2-1, here are the conventions that the program in Listing 2-1 uses:

- Class names, such as `Sample`, begin with a capital letter.
- Method names, such as `main`, begin with a lowercase letter.
- Each brace is on its own line.
- The braces in a pair of open and close braces align.
- Each close brace is labeled with a comment to identify the portion of the program that it ends.
- Statements within a pair of braces are indented. We use a three-space indent, but two or four spaces are also reasonable as long as you are consistent.
- Blank lines are added to improve readability.

We will mention other conventions as we encounter them.

FIGURE 2-1   The stylistic conventions used in the program in Listing 2-1

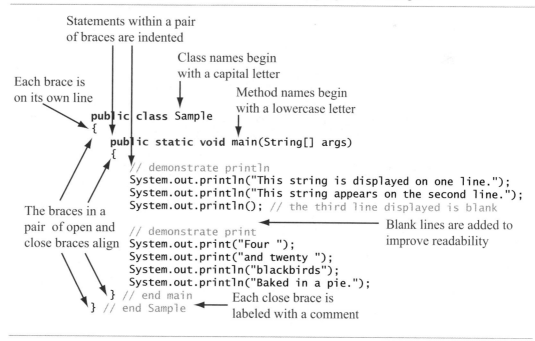

> **Note:** Another common style places the open brace at the end of the line before the code being bracketed. For example, you could begin the class in Listing 2-1 as follows:
>
> ```
> public class Sample {
>     public static void main(String[] args) {
> ```
>
> This style saves vertical space, which is important when viewing a program on a computer screen. We much prefer to align our braces for clarity. You can align your braces *and* save vertical space by writing the open brace at the beginning of the first line to be bracketed. For example, using this style, the class in Listing 2-1 would begin as follows:
>
> ```
> public class Sample
> {   public static void main(String[] args)
> ```

2.5   **White space.** The white areas in Listing 2-1 are caused by blank characters (spaces), tabs, and new-line characters. These characters are known as **white space**. The blanks that separate words are necessary in a program, but other white space that appears as indentations and new lines are there for people, not for the computer.

Displaying Text

2.6   **System.out.println.** The program in Listing 2-1 solves the simple problem of displaying text on the computer's screen. Let's focus on the statements that form the body of the method main.

videonote
Communicating
with a program

The statement that begins with System.out.println displays one line of text. The identifier println means *print line*. Notice that the statement contains text, enclosed in double quotes and placed within a pair of parentheses. The text and quotes are a **string literal**. The text, but not the quotes, is displayed on the next line of the screen output. Thus, the statements

```
System.out.println("This string is displayed on one line.");
System.out.println("This string appears on the second line.");
System.out.println(); // the third line is blank
```

display three lines of output, the last of which is blank.

Notice that each of these statements ends with a semicolon. This punctuation separates one statement from the next within the body of a method. Note the position of the semicolon in the third statement. If you placed it after the comment, it would become part of the comment. Since the compiler ignores comments, the statement would no longer have an ending semicolon, which is a syntax error.

2.7   **System.out.print.** When you use println, text is displayed and then an advance is made to the next line. If you use print instead of println, no advance to the next line occurs. Instead, a subsequent print or println would place text on the same line. For example, the statements

```
System.out.print("Four ");
System.out.print("and twenty ");
System.out.println("blackbirds");
System.out.println("Baked in a pie.");
```

produce two lines of output:

```
Four and twenty blackbirds
Baked in a pie.
```

The second print statement begins where the first print left off, placing and twenty on the same line as Four. The first println statement begins where the second print ends, placing blackbirds on the same line as before, and then advances to the next line. Thus, the text in the last println displays on a new line.

Notice the blank characters at the end of the strings "Four " and "and twenty " in the program listing. You must include these to separate the words that are displayed. Java doesn't insert spaces in output for you.

You'll learn more about using println and print statements later in this chapter.

Question 2 Suppose that you want to display your name on one line, a row of dashes on the next line, and nothing on the third line. What println statements will do this?

Question 3 Repeat Question 2, but this time use both println and print statements.

■ Comments

2.8   Novice programmers tend to omit comments. But comment statements provide an opportunity for you to document your thoughts about what your program does and how it solves the problem at hand. Although comments are important to others who read your program, you should realize that they are useful to you, too. Typical programs are written over a period of time. What might be obvious to you today could be baffling next week.

Listing 2-1 showed one kind of Java comment: a line that begins with two slashes. Use this form of comment within the body of a program to describe the purpose of groups of statements, or to explain anything that is not obvious. Notice how we have divided the method main into two portions separated by a blank line. Each portion begins with a comment that indicates what the statements do.

Another way to use this kind of comment is at the end of another Java statement. For example, the comment in the statement

```
System.out.println(); // the third line is blank
```

clarifies the purpose of that statement. We used this comment in Listing 2-1 because it was the first time you saw this form of the println statement. Generally, you should omit comments that state the obvious. Of course, what is obvious to you might not be obvious to someone else. However, a comment such as the one in the statement

```
System.out.print("Four "); // display "Four"
```

is obvious and should be omitted.

2.9   When a comment spans several lines, you can **delimit** it (begin and end it) by using /* and */. Thus,

```
/* This is another way to write
   a comment */
```

We usually do not use this form of comment for documenting our programs. However, during the development of a program, you might want to disable a group of statements temporarily. An easy way to do this without deleting the statements is to place /* before the group and */ after it.

A variant of this form of comment begins with /** and ends with */. For example, the comment at the beginning of Listing 2-1 could be written as follows:

```
/** Sample.java by F. M. Carrano
    Displays strings and provides an example of a Java application.
*/
```

We will use this form in our programs.

Comments like this one can be processed by a utility program called **javadoc**. This utility produces an HTML document that describes the classes and methods that use this form of comment. Chapter 15 and Appendix D contain more information about javadoc.

■ Data Types

Computers process various kinds of data. For example, an application might use numbers that contain a decimal point, integers, individual characters, and strings. The Java compiler needs to know what kind of data it is working with, and so the programmer needs to specify a **data type**. For example, int, char, and String are examples of data types for integers, characters, and strings, respectively. As you will see, Java's data types are organized into two categories: primitive types and reference types.

Because the program in Listing 2-1 is so simple, we will look at other Java examples as we discuss the topics in this section.

Primitive Types

2.10   Individual numbers, characters, and boolean (true or false) values have **primitive data types**, because they are not objects in Java. The names of these types are reserved words made up of lowercase letters. For example, integers can have the data type int. An integer has no decimal point. Real, or **floating-point**, numbers contain a decimal point and can have the data type double. Individual characters—letters, digits, and punctuation—h ave the data type char. Data of type boolean has only two values, true or false.

Note: Primitive types
The data types of integers, real numbers, characters, and booleans are said to be primitive. Data that has a primitive type has a single value.

The types int, double, char, and boolean are the primitive types that we typically will use in this book. But Java has several other primitive types for integers and real numbers. The choice affects the range of numbers available and the amount of computer memory needed to represent them. Thus, an integer can have one of the types byte, short, int, or long. A byte integer has the smallest range and uses the least memory. A long integer has the largest range and uses the most memory. Similarly, a real number can have one of the types float or double. A double number can contain more digits—and so is more precise—than a float number.

Figure 2-2 lists the available primitive types and shows their sizes as well as the ranges of their values.

FIGURE 2-2   Primitive data types

Data Type	Data	Memory	Minimum Value	Maximum Value
byte	integer	8 bits	−128	127
short	integer	16 bits	−32,768	32,767
int	integer	32 bits	−2,147,483,648	2,147,483,647
long	integer	64 bits	−9,223,372,036,854,775,808	9,223,372,036,854,775,807
float	real	32 bits	-3.402824×10^{38}	3.402824×10^{38}
double	real	64 bits	$-1.79769313486232 \times 10^{308}$	$1.79769313486232 \times 10^{308}$
char	character	16 bits	Unicode 0	Unicode 65,535
boolean	boolean	1 bit	Not applicable	Not applicable

Reference Types

2.11   As you just saw, data with a primitive type has a single value. Other data types, known as **reference types**, are more complex. For example, an object may have one or more pieces of data, as well as methods that work with that data. An object's data type is a **class type**, which is a kind of **reference type**. A string is an example of an object. Its data type is `String`, which is the name of a class in the Java Class Library that is provided with Java. Java has two other reference types that we will encounter later in this book. For the moment, you need not worry about reference types, as we will concentrate on primitive types.

 ## Variables

2.12   You can use a **variable** in a Java program to represent a piece of data. A variable actually represents a memory location that stores the data. The data itself is called the variable's **value**.

You use an identifier to name a variable. By convention, variable names should begin with a lowercase letter. They should also be meaningful. For example, if your variable represents the sales tax for a purchase, name it `salesTax` instead of `st` or `stax`. Multiple-word variable names are common. By convention, the first word begins with a lowercase letter, but subsequent words in the name each begin with an uppercase letter.

> **Programming Tip**
> Java variable names can be long. Favor clarity over brevity. Avoid one-letter names unless the context suggests that they are appropriate. Follow convention by beginning variable names with a lowercase letter.

Declarations

2.13   When you first create a variable, you must choose its data type. That is, you must specify what type of data the variable will represent. For example, if your program involves apples, you might track the number of apples in the variable `numberOfApples`. This count is an integer, so the data type of this variable would be `int`.

You declare the data type of a variable in a **declaration statement**. For example, the following statements declare one `int` variable, two `double` variables, a character variable, and a boolean variable:

```
int numberOfApples;
double pricePerApple, totalCost;
char letter;
boolean done;
```

Each declaration begins with a data type and contains one or more variables of that type. Commas separate variables of the same type, and a semicolon ends each declaration.

> **Note:** You must declare a variable before you can use it. You declare each variable only once, regardless of how often you use it.

Assignments

2.14   When you declare a variable within the body of a method, Java gives it no particular initial value. You can either give an initial value to a variable or change the existing value of a variable by using an **assignment statement**. An assignment statement has the following form:

variable = *expression*;

The **assignment operator** (=) assigns the value of the expression to the variable. An **operator** is a symbol within a programming language that represents a particular operation or action. For example, the operator = assigns a value to a variable, and the operator * multiplies two arithmetic values. An **expression** in a programming language is a combination of operators and other components that represent values. Both operators and expressions have various categories, as you will see.

> ### Syntax: Assignment statement
> An assignment statement has the following form:
>
>   variable = expression;
>
> It assigns the value of *expression* to *variable*.

2.15   **Example.** After declaring the variables numberOfApples, pricePerApple, and totalCost, as we did previously in Segment 2.13, you can assign them values by writing statements such as these:

```
numberOfApples = 15;
pricePerApple = 0.29;
totalCost = numberOfApples * pricePerApple;
```

The 15 and 0.29 are called **literals**. We encountered this term earlier in Segment 2.6 when we defined a string literal. Here we have an integer literal and a real literal. As you can see, a literal is the Java representation of a specific fixed value, rather than a value that results from a calculation.

The expression numberOfApples * pricePerApple is an example of an **arithmetic expression** that we will detail in Chapter 3. The operator * multiplies the current values of the two variables in the expression. The resulting product is assigned to, or given to, the variable totalCost. That is, the value of totalCost becomes 4.35, as Figure 2-3 illustrates. These statements appear in a complete program in the next segment.

> **Note:** Once you declare a variable and assign it a value, you can use it in another assignment statement.

FIGURE 2-3   Depiction of an assignment statement before and after its execution

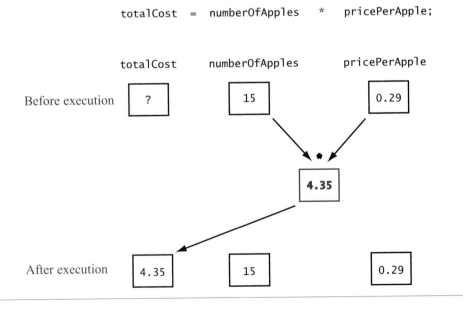

2.16   **Declarations and assignments within a program.** Listing 2-2 shows two of the variable declarations given earlier in Segment 2.13 and the three assignment statements given in the previous segment in the context of a Java program. This program computes the cost of a certain number of apples by multiplying their number by the cost of each one. The total cost then is displayed within a descriptive message.

Note the use of the + **operator** in the `print` statements. This is an aspect of Java that you have not seen previously. When used in this way, the + operator joins, or **concatenates**, one string with another. Although it appears that we are joining a number with a string, in fact Java converts the number to a string of characters before displaying it. So by the time the + operator is considered, we really do have two strings that are joined together and then displayed.

LISTING 2-2   A demonstration of variables in a program

```
/** Apples.java by F. M. Carrano
    Computes the cost of a number of apples.
    Demonstrates the declaration of variables, assignment statements,
    the display of textual data, and the conversion of numeric data
    to a string.
*/
public class Apples
{
    public static void main(String[] args)
    {
        int numberOfApples;
        double pricePerApple, totalCost;

        numberOfApples = 15;
        pricePerApple = 0.29;
        totalCost = numberOfApples * pricePerApple;

        System.out.print(numberOfApples + " apples at $");
        System.out.print(pricePerApple + " apiece cost $");
        System.out.println(totalCost);
    } // end main
} // end Apples
```

Output

```
    15 apples at $0.29 apiece cost $4.35
```

2.17   **Strings spanning two or more lines.** Listing 2-2 uses the following three statements to display one line of output:

```
System.out.print(numberOfApples + " apples at $");
System.out.print(pricePerApple + " apiece cost $");
System.out.println(totalCost);
```

Using several statements in this way is fine, but you could also write one `println` statement, as follows, and get the same output:

```
System.out.println(numberOfApples + " apples at $" +
                   pricePerApple + " apiece cost $" + totalCost);
```

Since this statement is too long to fit on one line, we let it span more than one line. The compiler ignores the intervening white space, as long as it occurs before or after the + operator.

You must be careful when a string literal must span two lines. For example, the following statement would produce a syntax error:

```
System.out.println("The total cost of 15 apples if bought
                    separately is $" + totalCost); // SYNTAX ERROR!
```

The correct way to divide a string literal is to break it into two string literals and then concatenate them, as follows:

```
System.out.println("The total cost of 15 apples if bought " +
                   "separately is $" + totalCost);
```

Note the additional quotes, the space after bought, and the additional + operator.

2.18   **Changing the value of a variable.** Variables are so named because their values can vary. For example, we declared and initialized the variable numberOfApples in the previous examples, but we could change its value by writing

```
numberOfApples = 20;
```

Or you could add 1 to numberOfApples by writing

```
numberOfApples = numberOfApples + 1;
```

If numberOfApples was 20, this statement would assign it the value 21. You should not read the assignment operator as "equals." The statement means

Add the current value of numberOfApples *and 1, and assign the sum to* numberOfApples.

Figure 2-4 traces the effect of executing the following sequence of statements:

```
int numberOfApples;
numberOfApples = 15;
numberOfApples = 20;
numberOfApples = numberOfApples + 1;
```

FIGURE 2-4   The effect of a sequence of assignments

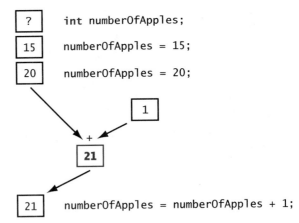

Note: **Tracing the effect of the statements in a program is an essential skill**
To truly understand the effect of an assignment statement, you must imagine the current value of each variable at various points in time. You should be able to trace the effect of any sequence of Java statements, as we have done in Figure 2-4. With this skill, you will be able to locate the mistakes in the logic of your Java code. This ability is key to learning how to program.

Note: When declaring a variable, you can assign it an initial value. For example, you can write

```
int numberOfApples = 15;
```

2.19   **Example.** In Segment 2.13, we declared the variable letter as a char. You can assign a value to letter by using a character literal, as follows:

```
letter = 'a';
```

A character literal is a single character enclosed in single quotes. As noted earlier, you can combine the declaration of a variable and its assignment:

```
char digit = '2';
```

Segment 2.13 also declared the variable done as a boolean. You can assign a value of either true or false to done by using an assignment statement, as in the following example:

```
done = true;
```

The reserved words true and false represent predefined boolean values.

As with variables of other types, you can combine the declaration and assignment of a boolean variable. You will see later that boolean variables and expressions play important roles in Java programs.

Question 4 When the following sequence of statements executes, what is displayed?

```
int count = 0;
System.out.println(count);
count = count + 2;
System.out.println(count);
count = count + count;
System.out.println(count);
```

■ Constants

Unnamed Constants

2.20   As you've seen previously, literals have values that do not change. They are, in fact, **unnamed constants**. Literals that have an integer type have no decimal point or commas, but they can have an optional plus or minus sign.

Like integer literals, floating-point literals have an optional plus or minus sign but no commas. Floating-point literals are written in one of two ways: with an exponent or without. For example, 3.14, 0.07, and -50.0 are all floating-point literals without an exponent. When written in this way, a floating-point literal must contain a decimal point. Sometimes it is more convenient to write real numbers with a power-of-ten multiplier, particularly when they are either very large or very small. For example, in mathematics, you might write 0.00001234 as 12.34×10^{-6}. In Java, you could write this value as 12.34e-6. The letter e—which suggests the word "exponent"—represents both the multiplication operator and the 10. You can omit the decimal point in the number before the e, as long as you adjust the exponent to produce the correct value. The number after the e is an integer; it cannot contain a decimal point. Any plus sign is optional.

The boolean values `true` and `false` are also literals. And a character literal—as you saw earlier in Segment 2.19—is a single character enclosed in single quotes.

Question 5 Which one of the following Java literals does not represent the numeric value 0.00000001?

    `0.1e-7, 10e-8, 0.00000001, 0.00000001e0`

Question 6 Which one of the following Java literals does not represent the numeric value −1,000,000?

    `-0.1e+7, -10e6, -0.00000001e14, -1000000e0, -1000000`

Named Constants

2.21   You can name constants in much the same way that you name variables. Doing so lets you describe the constant and avoid the mistakes that can occur when you repeatedly type their values. To create a **named constant**, you combine its declaration and assignment into one statement. To indicate that the value does not change, you precede the data type with the reserved word `final`.

For example, the following statements define several named constants. Note that by convention, all the letters in their names are capitalized. We use underscores to separate multiple words.

```
final int INCHES_PER_FOOT = 12;
final double MILES_PER_KILOMETER = 0.62137;
final char STAR = '*';
```

> **! Programming Tip**
> When naming a constant, follow convention by capitalizing all the letters in its name. Use underscores to separate multiple words.

2.22   **Apples by the dozen.** The program in Listing 2-3, like the one in Listing 2-2, computes the total cost of a number of apples. This time, however, the number of apples is measured by the dozen. Since the apples are still priced individually, we first multiply the number of dozens by 12 to get the number of apples. Instead of using a literal for 12, however, we define a named constant, `ONE_DOZEN`, to represent this value. Note that this program combines the declaration of a variable with its first assignment of a value.

LISTING 2-3   A program that uses a named constant

```
/** ApplesByTheDozen.java by F. M. Carrano
    Computes the cost of several dozen apples.
    Demonstrates the use of a named constant.
*/
public class ApplesByTheDozen
{
    public static void main(String[] args)
    {
        final int ONE_DOZEN = 12;
```

```
        int dozensOfApples = 3;
        double costPerApple = 0.29;
        double totalCost = dozensOfApples * ONE_DOZEN * costPerApple;

        System.out.println(dozensOfApples + " dozen apples at $" +
                            costPerApple + " apiece cost $" + totalCost);
    } // end main
} // end ApplesByTheDozen
```

Output

```
    3 dozen apples at $0.29 apiece cost $10.44
```

Programming Tip

By using a named constant instead of a literal, you provide yourself, and anyone else who reads your program, with a description of its meaning. Within an expression, the constant ONE_DOZEN has more meaning to a person than the literal 12. For obscure numeric values, especially lengthy ones, a named constant not only gives the value meaning, but also makes a correction to it easier. If you were to accidentally transpose a few digits, you could fix the mistake in one place, rather than check every occurrence of the constant in your program.

■ Simple Input from the Keyboard

2.23   A Java program can read data from either the keyboard or another source, such as a disk, and place it into memory. The Java Class Library provides a class—Scanner—for this purpose. Most of our programs will use the keyboard as their input device. We will use the methods in Scanner to read data typed at the keyboard and place it into variables that we specify. In this section, you will see how to read integers and real numbers.

The Java Class Library is organized into units called **packages**. The class Scanner, for example, is in the package java.util. To use Scanner in your program, you must tell the compiler where to find the class. One way to do so is to write the class's name as java.util.Scanner each time you need to use it. This **fully qualified name** is tedious to write over and over again, so Java provides another way. You can write the following **import statement** before the rest of your program:

```
    import java.util.Scanner;
```

This statement tells the compiler to look in the package java.util for the class Scanner. Then, anytime you write Scanner in your program, the compiler will understand it as java.util.Scanner. As we introduce other classes in the Java Class Library, we will show you the appropriate import statement to use.

Syntax: The import statement

Java

```
    import package-name.class-name
```

To use a class from the Java Class Library, you can write an import statement before the rest of the program. This statement allows you to use just the class name instead of its fully qualified name, *package-name.class-name*, within the program. Although you can avoid import statements by always using fully qualified class names, most programmers do use import statements.

2.24   Before you can use any of the methods in Scanner, you must create a Scanner object by writing a statement such as

```
Scanner keyboard = new Scanner(System.in);
```

This statement assigns the Scanner object associated with the input device that System.in represents to the variable keyboard—which could have any name of your choosing. This input device, by convention, is the keyboard.

Scanner provides several methods that read input data. You can use any of these methods by writing a statement that has the following form, where keyboard is the Scanner object that we defined previously:

variable = keyboard.*method_name*();

The named method reads a value from the keyboard and **returns** it. That is, the expression keyboard.*method_name*() represents the value that was read. The previous statement then assigns this value to the indicated variable.

2.25   Data, like Java statements, can contain white space. Any cluster of symbols other than white space is called a **token**. A Scanner object identifies these tokens and converts them into values of various data types according to the Scanner method you use.

Note: **Using the class Scanner to read numbers typed at the keyboard**
Assuming that a statement such as

```
Scanner keyboard = new Scanner(System.in);
```

has been executed, you can read integers and real numbers as follows:

```
keyboard.nextInt()
```
Interprets and returns the next token encountered in the input data as an integer whose type is int.

```
keyboard.nextDouble()
```
Interprets and returns the next token encountered in the input data as a real number whose type is double.

Each token encountered by these methods must be a number and must have the data type expected by the method. Each of these methods ignores any white space that might precede or follow the number.

The variable keyboard has a class type. We will examine other class types, including strings, in Chapter 4.

Syntax: **The dot operator**
Java uses a period, or dot, to separate identifiers in various contexts. This dot is called the **dot operator**. For example, the dot operator appears in an import statement when referencing a class in the Java Class Library. It is also used when calling an object's method to separate the name of the object from the name of the method.

2.26   **Example.** To read an integer from the keyboard, you can write a statement such as

```
size = keyboard.nextInt();
```

where size has been declared previously as an int variable. The user of your program would type an integer and press the Enter or Return key. The value entered by the user is read by the method nextInt, returned, and assigned to the variable size.

Typically, you should display a message, or **prompt**, for the user that describes the data to be entered. For example, your program might contain the following statements:

```
System.out.println("What is your age?");
int age = keyboard.nextInt();
```

Whatever the user types appears in the same window as the prompt. Here, the prompt would appear on one line and the user would type his or her age on the next.

 2.27   **Example.** To read a real number from the keyboard, you can write statements such as

```
System.out.print("Enter the area of your room in square feet: ");
double area = keyboard.nextDouble();
```

After the user types a real number at the keyboard and presses the Enter key, the value of the number is assigned to the variable area. Since we have used print instead of println, both the prompt and the input data appear on the same line on the display.

 2.28   **Example.** You can read more than one value per line of input. For example,

```
System.out.println("Please enter your height in feet and inches:");
int feet = keyboard.nextInt();
int inches = keyboard.nextInt();
```

The user could type either

    6   2

on one line or

    6
    2

on two lines. In either case, feet is 6 and inches is 2.

 Question 7 Write statements that ask a user to enter the radius of a circle and then read the radius as a real number.

 Note: To simplify our examples in future chapters, we will always use the variable keyboard when we read data from the keyboard. You can always assume that the statement

```
Scanner keyboard = new Scanner(System.in);
```

has been executed sometime prior to our use of keyboard, even if we do not say so.

 Programming Tip: Consult the documentation for the Java Class Library

As mentioned earlier in this chapter, the classes String and Scanner are in the Java Class Library. Standard documentation for the library's classes and their methods is maintained by Sun Microsystems and is readily available online. The link to this documentation appears on the book's website. You should become familiar with this documentation as we introduce various classes in the Java Class Library. Begin now by reading about Scanner's methods nextInt and nextDouble. The more you refer to this documentation, the easier its use will become. Your eventual goal should be to understand and use a class or method not described in this book!

■ A Problem Solved: Apples by the Box

> You're driving your car with your favorite other person and spy a roadside stand. You stop and find a farmer who is selling apples individually and by the box. You buy a box of apples. How much would the apples have cost if you had bought the same number individually? How much did you save, if anything, by buying at the box rate?

2.29   **Discussion.** We really have two problems here, so let's begin by answering the first question: How much would the apples have cost if you had bought them individually? Do we know enough to solve this first problem? No. We need to know

- The number of apples in a box
- The price of one apple
- The price of a box of apples

A Java program that solves this problem can begin by asking the user for this data. It then can make the necessary computations.

So here is a rough outline of what needs to be done to answer the first question:

- Get the data from the user.
- Display the data.
- Multiply the number of apples in a box by the price of one apple.
- Display the result of the multiplication—the product—which is the cost of buying the same quantity of apples individually.

It turns out that we can answer the second question (How much did you save?) by adding the next two steps to our solution:

- Subtract the price of a box of apples from the product.
- Display the difference.

The steps that we have listed in our solution are collectively called an **algorithm**. You can write the steps in English—as we have done here—or in a combination of English and Java, as we will do in the future as you learn more Java. Such a combination of languages is called **pseudocode**.

2.30   **The program.** Listing 2-4 contains a Java program that solves this problem and shows the output for one set of input data. (User input is shown in color.) We have combined the declarations of variables with their first assignments. Although you could declare all of the variables at the beginning of the method `main` and then assign values to them later, you generally should not do so.

LISTING 2-4   A program about the cost of apples

```
/** BoxedApples.java by F. M. Carrano

    Computes the money saved by buying a box of apples
    at the box rate instead of the individual rate.

    Input:  number of apples per box
            cost of one apple
            cost of box of apples
```

```
     Output: the input data
             the cost of apples if bought separately
             the savings if bought by the box
*/
import java.util.Scanner;

public class BoxedApples
{
   public static void main(String[] args)
   {
      Scanner keyboard = new Scanner(System.in);
      System.out.print("How many apples are in a box? ");
      int applesPerBox = keyboard.nextInt();

      System.out.print("How much does one apple cost? $");
      double costPerApple = keyboard.nextDouble();

      System.out.print("How much does a box of apples cost? $");
      double costPerBox = keyboard.nextDouble();

      double costOfApples = applesPerBox * costPerApple;
      double savings = costOfApples - costPerBox;

      System.out.println();
      System.out.println("Apples per box:                        " +
                         applesPerBox);
      System.out.println("Cost per apple:                       $" +
                         costPerApple);
      System.out.println("Cost per box:                         $" +
                         costPerBox);
      System.out.println("Cost of apples if bought separately: $" +
                         costOfApples);
      System.out.println("Savings if bought by the box:         $" +
                         savings);
   } // end main
} // end BoxedApples
```

Sample Output

```
How many apples are in a box? 24
How much does one apple cost? $0.32
How much does a box of apples cost? $7.25

Apples per box:                         24
Cost per apple:                        $0.32
Cost per box:                          $7.25
Cost of apples if bought separately: $7.68
Savings if bought by the box:        $0.4299999999999997
```

Programming Tip

Typically, a program should display, or **echo**, the input data it reads. The user then can check that the data he or she entered matches the data displayed.

2.31   The last line of output shows the amount saved by buying 24 apples by the box instead of individually. The savings should be the difference between $7.68 and $7.25, or $0.43. Instead, it is displayed as $0.4299999999999997.

Typically, computers use binary—that is, base 2—numbers to represent decimal (base 10) numbers. This representation is not always exact. Thus, after the decimal numbers are converted to binary, combined using binary arithmetic, and converted back to decimal, the displayed results are not quite correct. Later, in Chapter 4, you will see how to force output to a certain number of decimal places, so that the answer here will be rounded to $0.43. Chapter 4 will also show you how to perform decimal arithmetic instead of binary arithmetic to avoid this difficulty.

Question 8 Throughout this chapter, we have used `System.out.println` to display output. Using the online documentation for the Java Class Library, answer the following questions:

    a.   Is `System` the name of a class, a method, or an object?
    b.   Is `out` the name of a class, a method, or an object?
    c.   Is `println` the name of a class, a method, or an object?

Question 9 Which identifiers in Listing 2-4 are

    a.   Variables
    b.   Constants
    c.   Literals
    d.   Named constants
    e.   Reserved words
    f.   Data types
    g.   Class names
    h.   Method names
    i.   Package names

videonote
A problem
solved

Question 10 Repeat the previous question, but consider Listing 2-3 instead.

CHAPTER SUMMARY

- An identifier is a word composed of letters, digits, the underscore (_), and/or the dollar sign ($). It cannot begin with a digit. An uppercase letter is distinct from its lowercase counterpart.

- A reserved word is an identifier that has a special meaning in Java.

- You use a Java statement of the form `System.out.println(. . .)` to display text. The text is placed between the parentheses and enclosed in double quotes. Such text is called a string.

- When you use `println`, text is displayed and then an advance is made to the next line. If you use `print` instead of `println`, no advance to the next line occurs. A subsequent `print` or `println` places text on the same line.

- Comments are remarks that you place in a program to describe its purpose and methodology, or to clarify aspects of its logic. You can begin a comment with two slashes or enclose it between /* and */. A third form enables a program called `javadoc` to create HTML documentation. In this form, you enclose the comment between /** and */.

- Java's data types are organized into two categories: primitive types and reference types. For now, we will focus on the primitive types int, double, char, and boolean, although other primitive types exist.

- A variable represents a piece of data stored in memory. An identifier names the variable.

- Before the first use of a variable, you declare its data type, but you do so only once. You then give it a value either by using an assignment statement or by reading data from the keyboard.

- When a variable appears within a println or print statement, its value is converted to a string that is displayed.

- The + operator joins, or concatenates, one string with another.

- An unnamed constant, or literal, has a value that is self-defined and does not change. A named constant, like a variable, has a declared data type and is assigned a value. However, it is tagged with final to ensure that its value does not change.

- You can read a value typed at the keyboard into a variable. The class Scanner provides the methods nextInt and nextDouble to read integers and real numbers.

EXERCISES

1. What are the three categories of Java identifiers? Give an example of each category.

2. Is programming style, such as indentation, a requirement of the Java language?

3. Write statements to display the following phrase exactly as shown:

   ```
   To be or
   not to be
   ```

4. Write statements to display the following phrase on one line of output.

   ```
   To be or not to be
   ```

5. What is the difference between the // comment notation and the /* */ comment notation?

6. What is the purpose of the javadoc utility? Give an example of a javadoc comment.

7. What primitive data type would you use to represent the most precise real number?

8. Write a statement to declare a variable to represent the sales tax percentage. Write a second statement to assign the variable the value of 9.25%. Then write a statement that computes the sales tax on a purchase of $19.95 and stores the result in a properly declared variable called salesTax. What is the value of salesTax?

9. Write a statement that displays the label "Sales tax:" and appends the calculated value from the previous exercise to the end of the label.

10. When the following sequence of statements executes, what is displayed?

    ```
    double length = 5.0;
    double width = 8.5;
    System.out.println("Length: " + length);
    System.out.println("Width: " + width);
    System.out.print("Area: ");
    System.out.println(length * width);
    ```

11. Which of the following are literals?
    count, 'a', 7.5, letter, 10, salesTax

12. Write a statement to declare a named constant for a sales tax rate of 7.5%.

13. Why is it good practice to use named constants, as opposed to using literals?

14. Consult the documentation of the Java Class Library for the Scanner class. What method would you use to read a string from a Scanner object?

15. Write a statement that asks the user to enter the sales tax rate. Write statements to create a Scanner object, and then use it to read and store the rate as a real number.

16. Write an application that displays the following pattern:

```
*
**
***
****
*****
*****
****
***
**
*
```

17. Write an application that prompts for the user's name, address, birthday, and hobby. Display each on a separate line, properly labeled.

PROJECTS

1. Run the following program:

```java
import java.util.Scanner;
/** Project1.java by
*/
public class Project1
{
    public static void main(String[] args)
    {
        final double PI = 3.1428;

        Scanner keyboard = new Scanner(System.in);
        System.out.print("Think of a planet and enter its +
                    "radius in miles: ");
        double radius = keyboard.nextDouble();

        double volume = 4.0 * PI * radius * radius * radius / 3.0;
        double earthVolume = 4.0 * PI * 3963 * 3963 * 3963 / 3.0;
        double proportion = volume / earthVolume;

        System.out.println();
        System.out.println("Your planet has a radius of " + radius +
                    " miles");
        System.out.println("and has a volume of " + volume +
                    " cubic miles.");
        System.out.println("This volume is " + proportion +
                    " times the earth's volume.");
    } // end main
} // end Project1
```

Now make the following changes to the program and run it again:

- Add comments to the program to make it more readable.
- The value of the constant PI is incorrect. Correct this value rounded to four decimal places.
- Replace the unnamed constant 3963 with a named constant. It represents the earth's radius in miles.
- Compute the surface area of the planet and display it. The surface area of a sphere of radius r is $4\,\pi\,r^2$.

2. Write a program that displays your name inside a box on the console screen. Do your best to approximate lines with characters such as |, -, and +. For example, your output might look like this:

```
+-----------+
|   Karen   |
+-----------+
```

3. Write a program that displays a face using text characters. Use comments to indicate the statements that display the face components such as hair, ears, mouth, and so on. For example, your output might look like this:

```
  /////
 | o o |
(|  ^  |)
 | <_> |
  -------
```

4. Write a program that prints a name and address as you would see it written on an envelope. For example, your output might look like this:

```
Romeo Engineering & Technology Center
62300 Jewell Rd.
Washington, MI 48095
```

5. Children like to play with soap bubbles. One recipe for a bubble solution uses dishwashing liquid, sugar, water, and food coloring. The number of cups of water needed and the number of teaspoons of sugar needed are four times the number of cups of dishwashing liquid used. Write a program that, given the amount of dishwashing liquid available, computes the amount of water and sugar needed for the bubble mixture. For example, the program might produce the following output:

```
Enter the cup(s) of dishwashing liquid in decimal format: 0.5

Bubble Recipe
0.5 cup(s) of dishwashing liquid
2 cup(s) of water
2 teaspoon(s) of sugar
Add food coloring for colorful bubbles.
```

ANSWERS TO SELF-TEST QUESTIONS

1. Valid: room102, salesTax, FEET
   Illegal: 2beOrNot2be (does not begin with a letter), six% (% is illegal), _inches (does not begin with a letter), miles-per-hour (- is illegal)

2.
```
System.out.println("Jake Java");
System.out.println("---------");
System.out.println();
```

3. Several answers are possible; here is one:
```
System.out.print("Jake ");
System.out.println("Java");
System.out.println("---------");
System.out.println();
```

4. 0
    2
    4

5. 10e-8

6. -10e6

7.  ```
    Scanner keyboard = new Scanner(System.in);
    System.out.print("Enter the radius of the circle: ");
    double radius = keyboard.nextDouble();
    ```

8. a. System is the name of a class.
    b. out is the name of an object.
    c. println is the name of a method.

9. a. keyboard, applesPerBox, costPerApple, costOfApples, savings
    b. The string literals in the print and println statements.
    c. The string literals in the print and println statements.
    d. None.
    e. import, public, class, static, void, new, int, double
    f. int, double, String
    g. Scanner, Apples, String, System
    h. main, nextInt, print, println
    i. java.util

10. a. dozensOfApples, costPerApple, totalCost
    b. ONE_DOZEN, 12, 3, 0.29, " dozen apples at $", " apiece cost $"
    c. 12, 3, 0.29, " dozen apples at $", " apiece cost $"
    d. ONE_DOZEN
    e. public, class, static, void, final, int, double
    f. String, int, double
    g. ApplesByTheDozen, String, System
    h. main, println
    i. None.
    ```

Chapter 3

Arithmetic Expressions

Contents

Prerequisites

Objectives

After studying this chapter, you should be able to
- Write a Java arithmetic expression that represents a given algebraic expression
- Identify the data type of the value of a given arithmetic expression
- Write a type cast and identify when one is necessary
- Use the standard class Math to evaluate mathematical functions such as the square root and cosine

Imagine that you want to write a Java program to evaluate the equations you encountered during your last physics lab. In the previous chapter, you saw some simple expressions that involved multiplication, addition, and subtraction. This chapter will discuss in depth the arithmetic operations that are possible in Java.

▪ Arithmetic Operators

An arithmetic expression in Java is analogous to an expression in algebra. Both kinds of expressions contain operators, variables, constants, and parentheses.

In Java, you can perform five different operations that involve numeric values: You can add, subtract, multiply, or divide, and you can find the remainder after division. The operators for these operations are, respectively, +, -, *, /, and %. The variables or constants on which the operators act are called **operands**. Each of these operators can have two operands, in which case they are called **binary operators**. However, + and - also can act on a single operand—that is, they can behave as **unary operators**.

The Addition and Subtraction Operators, + and -

videonote
Performing arithmetic

3.1   **As binary operators.** The previous chapter used the operators + and - just as you would use them in ordinary addition and subtraction. For the most part, these operators behave as you would expect them to. For example, the statement

```
int sum = 2 + 3;
```

assigns 5, the result of adding 2 and 3, to the variable sum. Similarly, the statement

```
int difference = 8 - 1;
```

assigns the difference between 8 and 1, or 7, to the variable difference.

When several addition or subtraction operations occur within an expression, the operations occur from left to right in their order of appearance. For example, in the statement

```
int result = 6 - 9 + 2;
```

the subtraction occurs before the addition to produce the value -1. If the addition were to occur first, the sum of 9 and 2, when subtracted from 6, would result in -5. Thus, Java interprets the expression 6 - 9 + 2 as if it were written as (6 - 9) + 2. In fact, Java allows you to use parentheses within an arithmetic expression in much the same way that you use them in an algebraic expression to group operations. For example, note the effect of the following statements:

```
int resultA = 6 - 9 + 2;    // resultA is -1
int resultB = (6 - 9) + 2;  // resultB is -1
int resultC = 6 - (9 + 2);  // resultC is -5
```

3.2   **As unary operators.** When you see values such as +2 and –6, you likely see a plus sign and a minus sign. In Java, however, literals such as +2 and -6, and expressions such as -sum, use the unary operators + and -. The result of each unary operation is equivalent to a corresponding binary operation that has zero as its first operand. For example, you can view -sum as the expression 0 - sum. That is, -sum negates the value of sum, as the following statements indicate:

```
int sum = 5;              // sum is +5
int negativeSum = -sum;   // sum is -5
```

A unary + operator really has no effect on its operand and is usually omitted. The literals +2 and 2 have the same meaning, as do the expressions result and +result. Notice that if result contained a negative value, +result would not be positive:

```
int resultA = -21;        // resultA is -21
int resultB = +resultA;   // resultB is -21
```

The Multiplication Operator *

3.3   The multiplication operator * is a binary operator, so it always has two operands. The values of the operands are multiplied to produce a product that can be either assigned to another variable or used in a subsequent operation. For example, a statement such as

```
double totalCost = numberOfApples * costPerApple;
```

assigns the product of numberOfApples and costPerApple to totalCost. Notice that the values of numberOfApples and costPerApple are not changed.

When consecutive multiplications take place, they occur from left to right in their order of appearance, just as additions and subtractions do. For example, in the statement

```
int product = 2 * 3 * 4;
```

2 is multiplied by 3, and their product, 6, is multiplied by 4 to get 24. In this particular example, we would still get 24 if 3 were multiplied by 4 and that result was multiplied by 2. However, in general, particularly if real numbers are involved, the order of operations can be significant. We will talk more about the order of operations after we introduce the operators / and %.

The Division Operator /

3.4   Like the multiplication operator, the division operator / is a binary operator. The result of a division—that is, the **quotient**—depends on the data type of its two operands. When one or both of the operands are real, the result of the division is real. When both operands are integers, the result is **truncated** to an integer—that is, any fraction in the division is discarded. For example,

- 11.0 / 4.0 returns the real number 2.75, as do 11.0 / 4 and 11 / 4.0.
- 11 / 4 returns the integer 2. Note that this result is not rounded to 3.

Note: Division in Java

Java has two kinds of division, but both kinds are indicated by the same operator, /. When both operands have an integer data type, the quotient is truncated to an integer. Not surprisingly, we call this operation **integer division**. If either or both operands of / have a floating-point data type, such as double, the quotient is a real number that is neither truncated nor rounded.

3.5   **Example: The average of four exam grades.** Imagine that last year you received grades of 80, 85, 95, and 99 on the four exams in your favorite course. The sum of these scores is 359, which, when divided by 4, gives an average of 89.75. You expected to have this average rounded up to 90 and to receive an A in the course. However, your grade was B with a reported average of 89.

Now that you are learning Java, let's examine the program used to find the average of your exam grades. Suppose the key statements are

```
Scanner keyboard = new Scanner(System.in);
System.out.println("On the next line, enter four exam grades: ");
int exam1 = keyboard.nextInt();
int exam2 = keyboard.nextInt();
int exam3 = keyboard.nextInt();
int exam4 = keyboard.nextInt();

int average = (exam1 + exam2 + exam3 + exam4) / 4;
System.out.println("The average of " + exam1 + ", " + exam2 + ", " +
                   exam3 + ", and " + exam4 + " is " + average);
```

The output from these statements is

```
The average of 80, 85, 95, and 99 is 89
```

The problem is the integer division: The value of 359 / 4 is 89 due to truncation.

3.6   **The fix.** How do we get the actual average, 89.75, instead of a truncated result? Clearly, 89.75 is a real number, so the data type of the variable average should be double instead of int. If we replace the computation in the previous segment with

```
double average = (exam1 + exam2 + exam3 + exam4) / 4;
```

we will get the following output:

```
The average of 80, 85, 95, and 99 is 89.0
```

While 89.0 is certainly a floating-point value, we still have lost the fractional portion of the quotient. Changing the data type of average, while correct, does not affect how the division takes place: An integer division still occurs, but then the truncated integer quotient is converted to a floating-point value before its assignment to average.

To avoid the integer division, at least one operand of the division operator needs to have a floating-point data type. The easiest fix here is to replace 4 with 4.0:

```
double average = (exam1 + exam2 + exam3 + exam4) / 4.0;
```

The output is now

```
The average of 80, 85, 95, and 99 is 89.75
```

as desired.

The Remainder Operator %

3.7   The **remainder operator** % returns the remainder after a division. This value is not the decimal part of the result you would get if you used a calculator. For example, the value of the expression 11.0 / 4.0 is 2.75. However, the value of 11.0 % 4.0 is not 0.75. Rather, it is 3.0. Why? The remainder after dividing 11.0 by 4.0 is the difference 11.0 – (2 x 4.0), which is 3.0. In grade-school terminology, 4 goes into 11 twice with 3 left over.

What if the operands have nonintegral values? The remainder is computed in the same way as it is for integral values. For example, 11.5 % 4.5 is 2.5 because the remainder after dividing 11.5 by 4.5 is the difference 11.5 – (2 x 4.5), which is 2.5.

What if we had integer operands? 11 % 4 is the integer 3. The remainder operator is used most often with integers. It provides a way for your program to decide whether an integer is even or odd. A variable n contains an even integer if it is divisible by 2, that is, if n % 2 is zero. In general, you can decide whether the integer n is divisible by an integer m by seeing whether n % m is zero.

 Note: The sign of a remainder
The sign of the result of a remainder operation is the sign of its first operand. For example,

- 11 % 4 is 3
- –11 % 4 is –3
- 11 % –4 is 3
- –11 % –4 is –3

Programming Tip
Generally, the remainder operator is useful only when its operands are positive integers.

Note: Java does not have an exponentiation operator. To square or cube a number, you can use repeated multiplication. You can also raise a number to any power by using a method that is provided with Java. You'll learn how later in this chapter.

Question 1 What is the value of each of the following Java expressions?

    a.   26.0 % 3.0
    b.   15 % 4
    c.   3 % -4
    d.   18 % 4.0
    e.   -14.4 % 4.0

The Order of Operations

3.8   What value does the Java statement

```
int test = (2 + 4) * (3 - 6);
```

assign to the variable `test`? The computations within the parentheses are done first, so `test` is assigned the product of 6 and –3, or –18.
    What would the result be if we omitted the parentheses? In that case,

```
int test = 2 + 4 * 3 - 6;
```

Java performs the operations in a certain order, as listed in the Note that follows.

Note: Order of operations in an arithmetic expression
Operators in an arithmetic expression execute in the following order:

    1.   Operators within parentheses
    2.   The unary operators + and –
    3.   The operators *, /, and %
    4.   The binary operators + and –

Operators at the same level in the previous list execute from left to right within the expression. The level is called the operator's **hierarchy** or **precedence**, and the order of execution is called the **precedence order**.

Thus, the multiplication in 2 + 4 * 3 - 6 is performed first, then the addition, and finally the subtraction, resulting in 8 as the value of the expression. Since the + and - have the same precedence, they are performed in left-to-right order.

3.9   **Example.** In algebra, division is usually indicated with a two-dimensional notation, such as

$$\frac{2 \times a}{b - c}$$

The notation makes it clear that the entire product 2 x *a* is divided by the difference *b* - *c*. No parentheses are necessary in this case. In Java, however, we would indicate this computation by writing a one-dimensional expression, such as

```
2 * a / (b - c)
```

The left-to-right rule applied to * and / indicates that the multiplication occurs before the division. Thus, parentheses around 2 * a are unnecessary—but would be acceptable. However, parentheses are required around b - c so that the subtraction will occur before the division.

3.10   **Example.** What value does the Java statement

```
int test = 9 % -2 * 4 + 6;
```

assign to the variable `test`? The unary operator - has the highest precedence, and so the value is one operand. The operators % and * have the same precedence, which is higher than the precedence of +, so they operate next, in left-to-right order. The result of 9 % -2 is 1, which, when multiplied by 4, is 4. Finally, the sum of 4 and 6 is 10, which is assigned to `test`.

Question 2 What is the value of each of the following Java expressions?

    a. `(2 + 4) * 3 - 6`
    b. `2 + 4 * (3 - 6)`
    c. `2 + 4 * 3 - 6`
    d. `2 - (4 * 3) + 6`
    e. `-8 - 2`
    f. `-(8 - 2)`

Question 3 What is the value of each of the following Java expressions?

    a. `13 / 2 * 2`
    b. `13 / 2.0 * 2`
    c. `9 / 4 + 3 * 5`
    d. `100 / 30 - 4.5`
    e. `3 / 4`
    f. `-3 / 4.0`

Question 4 What is the value of each of the following Java expressions?

    a. `-9 % -2 * 4 + 6`
    b. `-9 % (-2 * 4) + 6`
    c. `9 % (-2 * 4) + 6`

Conversions Between Numeric Data Types

When writing an arithmetic expression or assigning a numeric value to a variable, the data types of the values involved are significant. In certain cases, Java implicitly converts a value from one data type to another, based on the context in which the values appear. At other times, you must explicitly tell Java to make a conversion. Failure to do so in these cases can lead to either incorrect results or an error message. This section examines data-type conversions beginning with the implicit ones.

Coercion

videonote

Data types of
arithmetic expressions

3.11   So far, when we have assigned a value to a variable, we have been careful to match their data types. For example, we assigned a double value to a double variable. Matching data types is not always necessary, however. We can assign a value whose data type is in the following list to a variable whose data type is either the same or appears to the right in the list:

byte → short → int → long → float → double

For example, we can assign an int to a double variable, as in

```
double realNumber = 8;
```

An implicit type conversion, that is, a **coercion**, from int to double occurs.

We cannot, however, assign a double value to an int variable. For example, the following is illegal:

```
int integerPart = realNumber; // ILLEGAL!
```

This statement is illegal even if realNumber contains an integral value such as 25.0. This difficulty does not mean that we cannot extract the integer part of a real number, as you will see shortly.

3.12   If all the values in an arithmetic expression have the same data type, the result has that type. If at least one of the values has a floating-point type, the result will have a floating-point type. For example, if *i* represents an int value, *d* represents a double value, and • represents one of the arithmetic operators +, -, *, /, or %, the result of

- *i* • *i* is an int
- *d* • *d* is a double
- *i* • *d* is a double
- *d* • *i* is a double

Usually you need to know only whether a result's type is integer or floating point. If you must know the exact data type, the following fact will help you:

The value of an arithmetic expression has a data type that matches the data type of one of its operands and appears rightmost in the following list—which is the same list as the one given in the previous segment:

byte → short → int → long → float → double

For example, if x is int, y is float, and z is double, x * z + y is double.

Note: Java can make an implicit type conversion, that is, a coercion, from an integer or real data type to any other primitive data type that appears to its right in the following list:

byte → short → int → long → float → double

SELF-TEST

Question 5 What is the value of each of the following arithmetic expressions? Indicate whether the data type of each result is integer or floating point.

    a.   12.5 + 9 / 2
    b.   4.8 / 4 + 9 % 2
    c.   14.4 % 4 + 14 / 4
    d.   15.0 / 3 - 16 % 3
    e.   15 / 3 - 16 % 3

Question 6 Consider the variables d, f, i, l, and s. If the respective data types of these variables is double, float, int, long, and short, what is the data type of each of the following Java arithmetic expressions?

    a. s * s / i
    b. i + i / d
    c. l * f / i
    d. s / i * f * f - d

Question 7 For each of the following algebraic expressions, write an equivalent Java arithmetic expression. For simplicity, use one-letter variable names and assume that their data types are double. Use the fewest parentheses possible.

    a. $(a + b) \times c - \dfrac{d}{2}$

    b. $\dfrac{a}{-c} + \dfrac{2 \times b}{d - e}$

    c. $\dfrac{a \times b}{c \times d}$

    d. $b^2 - (4 \times a \times c)$

    e. $\dfrac{4}{3} \times \pi \times r^3$

Casting

3.13   Java will not automatically convert a real value to an integer. As you saw in Segment 3.11, the following statement is illegal:

```
int integerPart = realNumber; // ILLEGAL!
```

However, you can force such a conversion explicitly by using a **type cast**. To explicitly convert a value from one data type to another compatible data type, you precede it with the desired data type enclosed in parentheses. For example, to convert the value in the double variable realNumber to an int value, you write

```
(int)realNumber
```

When you type-cast any floating-point type to an integer type, the value is truncated to an integer, not rounded. So if realNumber contains 18.99, integerPart in the following statement will contain 18.

```
int integerPart = (int)realNumber;
```

3.14   **Example.** Type casting is useful within an arithmetic expression when you want the quotient of two integers but do not want truncation to occur. For example, suppose

```
int count = 75;
int maxSize = 100;
double fraction = (double)count / maxSize;
```

The type cast applies to count, not the result of the division, and so count is converted from int to double. Then, since one operand of the division operator is double, the other operand maxSize is implicitly converted to double. The result, 0.75, is double and is assigned to fraction.

    Note that you could write the last Java statement as

```
double fraction = count / (double)maxSize;
```

and get the same result. Also note that the expression

    `(double)(count / maxSize)`

applies the type cast to the result of the integer division *after* truncation occurs.

Note: A type cast is indicated by the **type-cast operator** (*type*), which is a unary operator. Its precedence is just below that of the unary operators + and -.

Programming Tip

While some programmers leave a space between the type-cast operator and its operand, we prefer to omit such space, just as we omit space between the unary operators + and - and their operands. Either style is correct and does not affect the operation of the type-cast operator.

A Problem Partially Solved: Day of the Week

A number of devices in a home record the current date as month, day, and year. When a date is displayed, it often includes the day of the week. Is it possible to ascertain the day of the week from the month, day, and year? The answer is yes, as you will soon see.

3.15   **Discussion.** An algorithm known as Zeller's congruence makes the determination that we need. According to this algorithm, a date such as December 31, 2010, is described as three components, as follows:

- *m* is the month number, but one that is slightly different from what you are used to. March is month 3, April is month 4, and so on to December, which is month 12, but the algorithm considers January and February as months 13 and 14 of the preceding year. Thus, for these months, you subtract 1 from the year before continuing.
- *d* is the day of the month.
- *y* is the year, which was possibly adjusted earlier.

Here are two examples:

    December 31, 2010: *m* is 12, *d* is 31, and *y* is 2010.
    January 2, 1800: *m* is 13, *d* is 2, and *y* is 1799.

Next, you compute

    $f = d + [(26 * (m + 1)) \ / \ 10] + y + [y \ / \ 4] + 6 \ [y \ / \ 100] + [y \ / \ 400]$

where the square brackets indicate that the division is truncated to an integer. You now compute

    $w = f \text{ modulo } 7$

A modulo 7 number system counts from 0 to 6 and then starts over again at 0. Since *f* is not negative, you compute *w* by getting the remainder after dividing *f* by 7. That is, you use the Java operator %. The result *w* represents the day of the week of the given date, as follows: 0 indicates a Saturday, 1 indicates a Sunday, 2 indicates a Monday, and so on.

The computation for December 31, 2010, proceeds as follows. Since m is 12, $26 * (m + 1)$ is 338. Divide this number by 10 and ignore the fraction to get 33. Add 31 for d and 2010 for y to get 2074. Then $[y / 4]$ is 502, 6 $[y / 100]$ is 120, and $[y / 400]$ is 5. Adding 502, 120, and 5 to 2074, we find that f is 2701. Divide f by 7 and get a remainder of 6. This value is w and represents Friday.

Question 8 On what day of the week did February 29, 2000, fall?

3.16 **A pseudocode solution.** You know enough Java to perform the computations necessary to solve our problem, but we have not talked about making decisions within a program. So instead of completing a Java program, we will use pseudocode for a part of our solution. We assume that `month`, `day`, and `year` are `int` variables that represent the date before any adjustments are made. Thus, for December 31, 2010, `month` is 12, `day` is 31, and `year` is 2010.

```
int zellerMonth = month;
int zellerYear = year;

// January and February are months 13 and 14 of the previous year
If month < 3, execute the next two statements:
   zellerMonth = month + 12;
   zellerYear = year - 1;

// Zeller's Congruence
int computation = day + (26 * (zellerMonth + 1)) / 10 + zellerYear +
                  zellerYear / 4 + 6 * (zellerYear / 100) +
                  zellerYear / 400;

int dayOfWeek = computation % 7; // 0 - 6 for Saturday - Friday
```

Observe that the integer divisions in Java perform the truncations that Zeller's congruence requires, and the operator `%` performs the modulo arithmetic.

In Chapter 7 you will see the complete Java version of this solution, and in Chapter 10 you will see how to transform the resulting integer into a string that represents the day of the week.

Note: The results of modulo arithmetic are never negative; however, the result returned by the remainder operator can be negative. Thus, `%` and modulo are not always equivalent. Even so, you can use the remainder operator to perform modulo arithmetic. For example, if x % y is negative, you can add y to the result to obtain the value of x modulo y. Chapter 7 will show you how to test for a negative value.

Standard Mathematical Methods

3.17 Java provides a collection of methods that compute standard mathematical functions such as the square root, the cosine, and so on. The collection also includes two useful constants: `PI`—the value π—and `E`—the base e of the natural logarithms. This collection of methods and constants is organized as the class `Math`, much as the methods that read input data are organized as the class `Scanner`. Figure 3-1 lists some of the available methods in this class. The online documentation for the Java Class Library describes additional methods.

FIGURE 3-1   Some methods in the class `Math`

In each of the following methods, the arguments and the return value are `double`:

`Math.cbrt(x)`	Returns the cube root of x.
`Math.ceil(x)`	Returns the nearest whole number that is $\geq x$.
`Math.cos(x)`	Returns the trigonometric cosine of the angle x in radians.
`Math.exp(x)`	Returns e^x.
`Math.floor(x)`	Returns the nearest whole number that is $\leq x$.
`Math.hypot(x, y)`	Returns the square root of the sum $x^2 + y^2$.
`Math.log(x)`	Returns the natural (base e) logarithm of x.
`Math.log10(x)`	Returns the base 10 logarithm of x.
`Math.pow(x, y)`	Returns x^y.
`Math.random()`	Returns a random number that is ≥ 0 but < 1.
`Math.sin(x)`	Returns the trigonometric sine of the angle x in radians.
`Math.sqrt(x)`	Returns the square root of x, assuming that $x \geq 0$.
`Math.tan(x)`	Returns the trigonometric tangent of the angle x in radians.
`Math.toDegrees(x)`	Returns an angle in degrees equivalent to the angle x in radians.
`Math.toRadians(x)`	Returns an angle in radians equivalent to the angle x in degrees.

In each of the following methods, the arguments and the return value have the same type—either `int`, `long`, `float`, or `double`:

`Math.abs(x)`	Returns the absolute value of x.
`Math.max(x, y)`	Returns the larger of x and y.
`Math.min(x, y)`	Returns the smaller of x and y.

`Math.round(x)`	Returns the nearest whole number to x. If x is `float`, returns an `int`; if x is `double`, returns a `long`.

Each method in the class `Math` can be used by writing a statement in the following form:

variable = `Math`.*method_name*(. . .);

You also can embed `Math`.*method_name*(. . .) within an arithmetic expression. The value or values that occur between the parentheses are called **arguments**. Thus, you pass arguments to a method when you **call**—or **invoke**—it, and it returns a result to you. Note that not all methods require arguments. Even so, the parentheses are always required, though there may be nothing inside them.

3.18   **Example: The square root of a number.** The method `sqrt` computes the square root of a nonnegative `double` number. It returns a `double` value. In the following statements, we read a positive number that a user types at the keyboard, compute its square root, and display the result:

```
Scanner keyboard = new Scanner(System.in);
System.out.print("Type a positive number: ");
double number = keyboard.nextDouble();
double squareRoot = Math.sqrt(number);
System.out.println("The square root of " + number + " is " +
                   squareRoot);
```

Figure 3-2 illustrates the method call `Math.sqrt(number)` when the value of `number` is 90.25.

FIGURE 3-2   A call to the method `Math.sqrt`

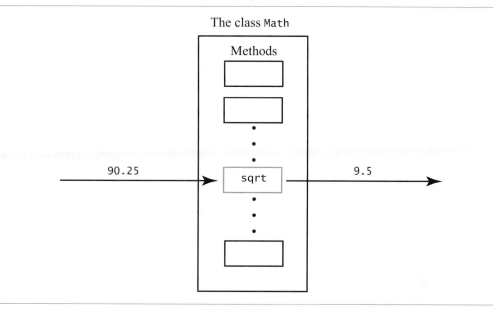
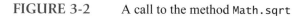

3.19   **Example: The cosine of an angle.** The method `cos` computes the cosine of an angle given in radians as a `double`. It returns a `double` value. The following statements read two angle measurements—one in radians and one in degrees—from the user, compute the cosine of each angle, and display the results:

```
Scanner keyboard = new Scanner(System.in);
System.out.print("Type an angle in radians: ");
double angleInRadians = keyboard.nextDouble();
double cosine = Math.cos(angleInRadians);
System.out.println("The cosine of " + angleInRadians +
                   " radians is " + cosine);

System.out.print("Type an angle in degrees: ");
double angleInDegrees = keyboard.nextDouble();
angleInRadians = Math.toRadians(angleInDegrees);
cosine = Math.cos(angleInRadians);
System.out.println("The cosine of " + angleInDegrees +
                   " degrees is " + cosine);
```

In the second part of this example, notice how we convert an angle given in degrees to one given in radians so that we can use the method `cos`.

3.20 **Example: Raising a number to a power.** Suppose that you want to compute the volume of a sphere. You would use the formula

$$\frac{4}{3} \times \pi \times r^3$$

where *r* is the sphere's radius. You can compute r^3 by using the method pow, as follows:

```
Scanner keyboard = new Scanner(System.in);
System.out.print("Type the radius of the sphere in inches: ");
double radius = keyboard.nextDouble();
double volume = 4 * Math.PI * Math.pow(radius, 3) / 3;
System.out.println("The volume of a sphere of radius " + radius +
                   " inches is " + volume + " cubic inches.");
```

Remember that you precede the name of the constant PI with Math., just as you do when you use a method in this class.

You need to be a bit careful if you compute the fraction 4/3, since in Java 4 / 3 is 1 due to truncation. You might not notice this mistake, as the computed volume likely will be reasonable. Notice how we have avoided the difficulty by changing the order of the operations in an algebraically equivalent way. Instead, we could have begun our Java expression with 4.0 / 3 to ensure a double computation that is not truncated.

Note: You know that the Java Class Library is organized into packages. The class Math is in the package java.lang. The classes in this package are available automatically within any Java program without the need to include an import statement. These classes behave as if they were a part of the language instead of additions to the language. To use other packages, you do need an import statement.

■ A Problem Solved: Wind Chill

> The effect of wind on the human body can make one feel colder than the air temperature might suggest. The combined effect of wind and temperature is called the wind-chill temperature. Suppose that the National Weather Service wants you to write a Java program to compute the wind-chill temperature given the air temperature and wind velocity.

3.21 **Discussion.** According to the U.S. National Weather Service, the wind chill temperature is calculated by the following formula:

$$W = c_1 + c_2 \times T - (c_3 \times V^{0.16}) + c_4 \times T \times V^{0.16}$$

where *T* is the current air temperature in degrees Fahrenheit, *V* is the velocity of the wind in miles per hour, c_1 is 35.74, c_2 is 0.6215, c_3 is 35.75, and c_4 is 0.4275.

When wind speeds are less than 3 miles per hour, the previous formula will give you a wind chill that is higher than the actual temperature. When you are standing still in a light breeze, your body warms the air near you. This warm air insulates your body somewhat from the colder environment. As a result, it may actually feel warmer than the actual temperature.

3.22   **The program.** Listing 3-1 contains a Java program that evaluates the wind-chill formula. The listing also shows the output for one set of input data.

LISTING 3-1   The wind-chill program

```java
/** WindChill.java by F. M. Carrano

    Computes the wind-chill temperature from the actual temperature
    and wind speed.
*/
import java.util.Scanner;
public class WindChill
{
    public static void main(String[] args)
    {
    // describe program
        System.out.println("This program computes the wind-chill ");
        System.out.println("temperature from the actual temperature ");
        System.out.println("and wind speed.\n");

    // get input data
        Scanner keyboard = new Scanner(System.in);
        System.out.print("Enter the temperature in degrees Fahrenheit: ");
        double temperature = keyboard.nextDouble();
        System.out.print("Enter the wind speed in miles per hour: ");
        double windSpeed = keyboard.nextDouble();

    // compute wind chill temperature
        final double CONSTANT1 = 35.74,
                     CONSTANT2 = 0.6215,
                     CONSTANT3 = 35.75,
                     CONSTANT4 = 0.4275,
                     EXPONENT  = 0.16;

        double powerTerm = Math.pow(windSpeed, EXPONENT);

        double windChillTemperature = CONSTANT1 + CONSTANT2 * temperature
                               - CONSTANT3 * powerTerm
                               + CONSTANT4 * temperature * powerTerm;

    // display results
        System.out.println("\nThe actual temperature is " + temperature +
                        " degrees Fahrenheit.");
        System.out.println("The wind speed is " + windSpeed + " m.p.h.");
        System.out.println("The wind-chill temperature is " +
                        Math.round(windChillTemperature) +
                        " degrees Fahrenheit.");
```

```
     } // end main
} // end WindChill
```

Sample Output

```
This program computes the wind-chill
temperature from the actual temperature
and wind speed.

Enter the temperature in degrees Fahrenheit: 35
Enter the wind speed in miles per hour: 5

The actual temperature is 35.0 degrees Fahrenheit.
The wind speed is 5.0 m.p.h.
The wind-chill temperature is 31 degrees Fahrenheit.
```

The program begins by giving a brief description of its purpose to the user. It then prompts for and reads the input data, taking care to indicate the desired units of the input values. Note that we have chosen to declare the data type of the variables `temperature` and `windSpeed` as `double` even though integers often appear in wind-chill tables. This makes the program more flexible, since the user can provide data with or without a decimal point. In addition, `windSpeed` will have the correct data type for the method `Math.pow`, which requires `double` arguments. Note that when we display the resulting wind-chill temperature, we invoke the `Math` method `round` to round the result to the nearest integer.

Although the term $V^{0.16}$ appears twice in the formula, we have computed it only once to save execution time. Also, naming the necessary constants, as we have done, makes it easier to maintain the program in case we need to change their values or precision.

videonote
A problem
solved

Programming Tip

Naming constants makes it easier to maintain your program, especially when you use them more than once. Suppose that you make an error in a particular constant or that you want to provide more digits of precision. With a named constant, you can correct one value. If the constant was unnamed, you would need to hunt throughout the program for every occurrence.

CHAPTER SUMMARY

- Java has five operators for primitive numeric data: +, -, *, /, and %. Each has two operands, but + and - can also have only one operand.

- Operators within an expression have a hierarchy, or precedence. That is, they execute in a certain order, as follows: operators within parentheses; the unary operators + and -; the type-cast operator; the operators *, /, and %; and the binary operators + and -.

- The data type of a binary operation is real if at least one of its operands is real. The data type is integer if both operands are integers.

- The result of dividing two `int` operands is truncated to an integer.

- You can assign a value whose data type appears in the following list to a variable whose data type is either the same or appears to its right in this list:

      byte → short → int → long → float → double

  In all other cases, a type cast is necessary.

- A type cast converts a value from one data type to another compatible data type. You precede the value with the desired data type, enclosed in parentheses.

- The class Math contains methods that perform standard mathematical functions, such as the square root and cosine. You use these methods by writing an expression in this form: Math.*method_name*(. . .).

EXERCISES

1. What is the value of each of the following Java expressions?

    a. 17 + 2 – 5 / 5
    b. 2 + 3 * 5 – 2
    c. 3 * 2 / 3 + 8
    d. 6 / 2 * 3 – 10
    e. 6 % 2 * 10

2. What is the value of each of the following Java expressions?

    a. 12 / 3.0
    b. 12 / 3
    c. 16.0 / 3
    d. 16 / 3

3. Explain how to use Java to determine whether x is an odd integer.

4. Write two different Java statements that each compute the cube of an integer x.

5. Classify each of the following Java statements as either legal or illegal. Let b, s, i, l, f, and d represent variables of type byte, short, int, long, float, and double, respectively.

    a. d = l;
    b. l = f;
    c. i = b;
    d. i = s;
    e. b = s;
    f. i = d;

6. What is the data type of each of the following expressions if i, l, f, and d represent variables of type int, long, float, and double, respectively?

    a. f + d
    b. d * i
    c. l – i
    d. i / f
    e. l % d
    f. l * l

7. Using Zeller's congruence, determine the day of the week for March 17, 2020.

8. For each of the following mathematical expressions, write a Java expression to represent it.

    a. $\sqrt{64}$
    b. $|-17|$
    c. e^{-1}
    d. 2^3
    e. 6^2

9. Write a program that displays the following table. Use the method `Math.min` to compute the smaller of x and y in each case.

```
x       y       Min(x, y)
---------------------------------
10      5       5
13      23      13
100     100     100
-1      -5      -5
0       -8      -8
```

10. Write a program to convert a user-supplied temperature from Fahrenheit to Celsius using the following formula. If C represents a temperature in degrees Celsius, and F represents a temperature in degrees Fahrenheit, then $C = 5 \times (F - 32) / 9$.

11. In a contest, a ticket number wins a prize if it is a multiple of 6. Write a program that reads a ticket number and indicates whether it is a winner. The program's output could appear as follows:

Sample Output 1

```
Is your ticket a winner?
Enter your ticket number: 12
The ticket number 12 is a winner if the following value is zero: 0
```

Sample Output 2

```
Is your ticket a winner?
Enter your ticket number: 37
The ticket number 37 is a winner if the following value is zero: 1
```

12. One integer is a multiple of another integer if the remainder after dividing the first integer by the second is zero. Write a program that tests whether one integer is a multiple of a second integer. The program's output could appear as follows:

Sample Output 1

```
A test of whether one integer is a multiple of a second integer.
Enter the first integer: 25
Enter the second integer: 5
25 is a multiple of 5 if the following value is zero: 0
```

Sample Output 2

```
A test of whether one integer is a multiple of a second integer.
Enter the first integer: 23
Enter the second integer: 7
23 is a multiple of 7 if the following value is zero: 2
```

PROJECTS

1. Write a program to calculate the energy needed to heat a pot roast from an initial temperature to 160 degrees Fahrenheit. Your program should ask the user for both the weight of the pot roast and its initial temperature in degrees Fahrenheit. To compute the required energy, Q, use the following formula:

$$Q = W \times (T_{final} - T_{start}) \times 4184, \text{ where}$$

W is the weight of the roast in kilograms, T_{final} and T_{start} are temperatures measured in Celsius, and Q is measured in joules.

   Since the formula assumes that temperatures are measured in Celsius and the user supplies them in Fahrenheit, your program must make the conversion described in Exercise 10.

2. The body mass index, or BMI, is a measure of weight in relation to height. It is equal to the body weight in kilograms divided by the square of the height in meters. Write a program to compute the body mass index, given a weight in pounds and a height in inches. You can convert pounds to kilograms by dividing the number of pounds by 2.2. You can convert inches to meters by multiplying the number of inches by 0.0254. The program's output could appear as follows:

```
Calculating the body mass index.
Enter weight in pounds: 130
Enter height in inches: 67

The weight is 130.0 pound(s) or 59.090909090909086 kilogram(s).
The height is 67.0 inches(s) or 1.7018 meter(s).
The body mass index is 20.40345116353166.
```

3. Write a program that reads an integer that is greater than or equal to 1,000 but less than 999,999 and displays it with a comma separating the thousands. For example, the result of executing the program could be as follows:

```
Please enter an integer between 1000 and 999999: 34567
The formatted value is 34,567.
```

Your program can assume that the user will enter a valid integer.

4. Write a program that asks the user for the cost of a pizza, the diameter of the pizza in inches, and the number of equally sized slices into which the pizza is cut. It should then report this data, the area of the pizza, the cost of one slice, and the area of one slice.

5. Write a program to convert a measurement given by the user in yards, feet, and inches into an equivalent measurement in meters and centimeters. One yard is 3 feet, one foot is 12 inches, one inch is 2.54 centimeters, and one meter is 100 centimeters.

6. When you exercise aerobically, you should maintain a heart rate within a certain range. To determine this range, first subtract your age in years from 220. Your maximum heart rate should be 85 percent of this value; your minimum heart rate should be 65 percent of this value. For example, if you are 20 years old, your heart rate should be between 130 and 170 beats per minute when you exercise.

Write a program that asks for the user's age and reports the minimum and maximum heart rates desirable during exercise. The program should clearly tell the user what to type, and it should clearly describe all output.

7. Write a program that computes the number of miles per gallon and kilometers per liter of gas used during an automobile trip. Your program should read the following data:

- Your name and vehicle name as strings
- The number of gallons of gasoline used as a real number
- The initial and final odometer readings (in miles) as integers

Display a report of the data read and the results of the computation. Note that one mile is 1.609344 kilometers and one gallon is 3.785412 liters. Use a format as close to the following as possible:

```
Please type your name: Jamie
What vehicle do you drive? Jeep
How many gallons of gas did you use? 5.2
What was the initial odometer reading? 55652
What was the final odometer reading?    55793

Jamie, here are the statistics of your recent trip in your Jeep:
Initial odometer reading: 55652
Final odometer reading:    55793
Miles traveled:            141
Kilometers traveled:       227
```

```
Miles per gallon:        27.115384615384613
Kilometers per liter:    11.532125473751908
```

Bonus: Display the miles per gallon and kilometers per liter rounded to one decimal place.

8. Water droplets in the atmosphere refract light to form a rainbow. If you look at the top of a rainbow, the angle between your line of sight and the horizon is always the same. This angle—call it α—is 42 1/3 (42.333333) degrees.

   Imagine a vertical line from the top of the rainbow to the ground. Also imagine a horizontal line between you and the previous vertical line. The length of this horizontal line is the distance to the rainbow, and the length of the vertical line is the height of the rainbow:

   The height of the rainbow is given by the following formula:

   rainbowHeight = yourHeight + distanceToRainbow x tangent(α)

   Because α is given in degrees, you must convert it from degrees to radians before computing the tangent of α by using the formula

   radians = degrees x π / 180

   Write a program to compute the height of a rainbow given your height and your distance from the rainbow.

9. Imagine throwing, hitting, or kicking a ball, be it a baseball, football, basketball, or soccer ball. Suppose that you know the ball's initial velocity and the initial angle that the ball's trajectory makes with a line parallel to the ground, which we assume is level.

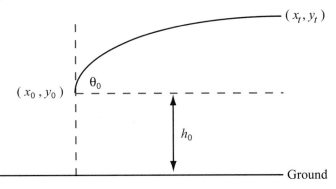

   Some basic equations from physics describe this scenario. Assume that at time $T = 0$, you are given the following values:

   V_0 is the ball's initial velocity in meters per second.

   θ_0 is the initial angle, in degrees, that the ball's trajectory makes with the ground.

   (x_0, y_0) are the ball's initial coordinates. If we place the origin of the coordinate system at the ball's initial position—when it leaves your hand, strikes the bat, or so on—the initial coordinates are (0, 0). This origin is h_0 meters above the ground.

   At time t seconds, the ball has the coordinates (x_t, y_t) and velocity v_t, given as a function of t as follows:

   $x_t = t \times v_0 \times \cos \theta_0$

   $y_t = t \times v_0 \times \sin \theta_0 - g \times t^2 / 2$, where g is the acceleration due to Earth's gravity, or 9.78049 meters per second per second

   $v_t^2 = v_0^2 \times \cos^2 \theta_0 + (v_0 \times \sin v_0 - g \times t)^2$

Write a program that calculates the ball's velocity and position at any given time. Realize that if the ball is at (x_t, y_t), its height above the ground is $y_t + h_0$. The program should read the ball's initial velocity v_0, initial angle θ_0, and initial height h_0. It should also read the time t, in seconds, at which the ball's status is desired. The program should produce clearly labeled output.

ANSWERS TO SELF-TEST QUESTIONS

1.
   a. 2.0
   b. 3
   c. 3
   d. 2.0
   e. -2.4

2.
   a. 12
   b. -10
   c. 8
   d. -4
   e. -10
   f. -6

3.
   a. 12
   b. 13.0
   c. 17
   d. -1.5
   e. 0
   f. -0.75

4.
   a. 2
   b. 5
   c. 7

5.
   a. 16.5; floating point
   b. 2.2; floating point
   c. 5.4; floating point
   d. 4.0; floating point
   e. 4; integer

6.
   a. int
   b. double
   c. float
   d. double

7.
   a. (a + b) * c - d / 2
   b. a / -c + 2 * b / (d - e) or -a / c + 2 * b / (d - e)
   c. a * b / (c * d)
   d. b * b - 4 * a * c
   e. 4.0 / 3.0 * 3.14156 * r * r * r or 4.0 * 3.14156 * r * r * r / 3.0

8. For February 29, 2000, m is 14, and y is 1999. Thus, 26 x $(m + 1)$ is 390. Divide by 10 and ignore the fraction to get 39. Add 29 for d and 1999 for y to get 2067. Then $[y / 4]$ is 499, 6 $[y / 100]$ is 114, and $[y / 400]$ is 4. Adding 499, 114, and 4 to 2067, we find that f is 2684. Divide f by 7 and get a remainder of 3. This value is w and represents Tuesday.

Debugging Interlude

1

The Errors Made by Programmers

Contents

Prerequisites

Mistakes. We hate to make them, but we all do. Any error that you make in a program is called a **bug**, and the process of finding these errors is called **debugging**. In these *debugging interludes*, we will talk about the common errors that occur in Java programs and try to give you the skills to deal with them. We begin here by describing the kinds of errors that programmers make.

Kinds of Errors

D1.1   Just like any natural language, such as English, Java has a set of rules that define it. These rules form the language's **syntax**. They dictate how you form correct phrases and statements. If you do not follow Java's syntax precisely, you will have made a syntax error, and your program will not compile. The compiler will produce a message that attempts to describe what you have done wrong. Most of the time, these error messages will point right to your mistake, but sometimes the messages might seem vague or even misleading. Because the compiler generates a message when it first detects that something is incorrect, it cannot always diagnose the problem specifically. However, you can be sure of one thing: The compiler is right; you made a mistake!

 Note: Compilers detect syntax errors. Any errors detected by a compiler are **compile-time errors**.

D1.2   Even if you follow all of Java's grammatical rules—its syntax—thereby passing the compiler's scrutiny, you might not get the results you desire or expect. It is possible for a statement to be syntactically correct but still be wrong. Perhaps a variable has the wrong data type, or you've omitted a pair of parentheses in an expression. Such an error is a **semantic error**. The semantics of a statement are its meaning. Unlike a natural language, such as English, the semantics of a programming language are unambiguous. A Java statement has one meaning. A statement in English could have several meanings.

Another name for a semantic error is a **logical error**, since it is a mistake in the logic of an algorithm. Although some people differentiate between a logical error and a semantic error, we will consider them to be the same kind of error. These errors are not detected by the compiler, but rather exhibit themselves when the program executes. As such, these errors are known as **execution-time errors**. They could cause your program to **crash**—that is, terminate its execution abnormally—and give you an error message. Such an error is called a **runtime error**. However, logical errors often don't give any obvious indication that something is wrong. This type of error is known as a **silent error**. That is, your program terminates normally, but its results are incorrect.

Silent logical errors are typically the most difficult to find and usually will be our main focus. However, in this first debugging interlude, we will spend more time with examples of syntax errors.

 Note: **The kinds of programming errors**
Programming errors fall into two classifications:

- Compile-time errors—Occur during program compilation due to
  - Syntax errors—Grammatical mistakes in writing Java statements.
- Execution-time errors—Occur during program execution due to mistakes in the program's semantics (logic). These occur as
  - Run-time errors—Cause an abnormal termination of the program and an error message.
  - Silent errors—Cause incorrect results but no error messages; execution ends normally.

Aside: **The First Bug**

Errors, or bugs, have plagued people for decades. Even Thomas Edison complained of a bug in his phonograph. Just like Mr. Edison, most students of programming quickly discover the necessity of debugging. However, one early debugging exercise did not involve a syntax error, but rather a real bug—the six-legged kind.

In the summer of 1945, Grace Murray Hopper and other researchers were working with the Mark II computer as part of the U.S. war effort. It was a hot summer, and often the windows of the aging Navy building were left open to improve the ventilation. One afternoon in early September, the Mark II stopped running. Hopper and her colleagues searched for the problem and found a relay that had failed. When they investigated further, they discovered a moth; it had flown in through an open window and made its way into the computer, where it had been beaten to death by the relay.

In addition to its small revenge of temporarily stopping the Mark II, the insect gained a permanent place in computer history. The amused researchers extracted it with tweezers and taped it in their log book, carefully labeling it with the hour and minute of its discovery. Today, visitors to the Naval Museum in Dalgren, Virginia can view the "first bug," still taped to the log-book page for September 9, 1945. However, you can view it now simply by visiting the web page at
www.history.navy.mil/photos/images/h96000/h96566kc.htm

D1.3   Debugging is an important skill for a programmer to have and, like other problem-solving skills, is one that is developed through practice. The examples provided in these debugging interludes cannot possibly illustrate all of the errors that you might make in your programs, but they describe some common errors made by other novice Java programmers. These descriptions should start you on your way to becoming a successful debugger and programmer.

However, you cannot acquire successful debugging skills simply by memorizing our examples. Although you might not at first recognize the source of your errors, experience and a familiarity with possible causes of an error will give you the intuition that tells you where to begin your search. If your debugging efforts fail, by all means seek another person's help—but play an active role in understanding the steps taken to find the error.

■ Compile-Time Errors

D1.4   We begin our examples by looking at some common errors in syntax and the messages they cause the compiler[1] to generate. The following mistakes are easy to make, particularly for someone just learning Java:

videonote
Programmer errors

- **Missing semicolons**. Each Java statement must end in a semicolon, just as English statements end in a period.
- **Extra semicolons**. An extra semicolon sometimes causes no harm, as the compiler simply ignores it. However, a misplaced semicolon can cause a problem.
- **Spelling mistakes**. Errors while typing Java reserved words or variable names, for example, are typically flagged as unidentified symbols.
- **Capitalization**. Java is case sensitive. That is, your use of uppercase and lowercase letters matters. All Java reserved words are lowercase. Spelling one using one or more capital letters is incorrect. Any identifiers that you use must be consistent in their case.
- **Mismatched parentheses or braces**. Each open parenthesis or brace must match a corresponding close parenthesis or brace, respectively. Usually, an IDE's editor will help you to avoid this error, but if you make it anyway, the compiler will complain.

The examples that follow examine each of these syntax errors.

D1.5   **Missing semicolons.** Let's consider the small program in Listing D1-1 and the messages given during its compilation. The three statements on lines 1, 6, and 7 of the program should end in a semicolon. Each error message explicitly indicates the line number, the offending statement, and, by using a caret (^), the location of the mistake within the statement. Unfortunately, not all compiler messages are this easy to understand. (We began this program with an `import` statement, even though none is required here, simply to illustrate one.)

LISTING D1-1   A program lacking necessary semicolons

```
1 import java.util.Scanner
2 public class Debug1
3 {
4    public static void main(String[] args)
5    {
6       int anInteger = 10
```

```
7        System.out.println("The integer is " + anInteger)
8    } // end main
9 } // end Debug1
```

Error Messages

```
Debug1.java:1: ';' expected
import java.util.Scanner
                        ^
Debug1.java:6: ';' expected
     int anInteger = 10
                      ^
Debug1.java:7: ';' expected
      System.out.println("The integer is " + anInteger)
                                                       ^
3 errors
```

D1.6

Extra semicolons. Let's add semicolons to the previous program where they belong and in some places where they do not. Since we really don't need the import statement, we'll delete it to save some space. Now the compiler produces the output shown in Listing D1-2.

LISTING D1-2   A program containing extra semicolons

```
1 public class Debug2;
2 {
3    public static void main(String[] args);
4    {
5        int anInteger = 10;
6        System.out.println("The integer is " + anInteger);
7    }; // end main
8 }; // end Debug2
```

Error Message

```
Debug2.java:1: '{' expected
public class Debug2;
                   ^
1 error
```

We get only one error message. The compiler expects to see an open brace after Debug2, but instead it finds a semicolon. Since we have written the necessary open brace, the semicolon must be the mistake.

Let's remove the semicolon at the end of the first line of the program and compile it again. Even though we corrected the only recognized error, we now get the following message:

```
Debug2.java:3: missing method body, or declare abstract
   public static void main(String[] args);
                       ^
1 error
```

The mistake is the semicolon at the end of the line, but the message is not as straightforward as the previous messages have been. The semicolon makes the main method appear to have no body—that is, to have no statements that define it. Although you could define a method without a body, as you will learn much later in this book, you would also include the keyword abstract. So the semicolon in line 3 is not wrong in all situations, but it is here.

After we remove the offending semicolon, our program will compile without a problem. But what about the semicolons after the two closing braces at the end of the program? They shouldn't be there, but the compiler sees them as empty statements and so ignores them. No harm is done.

D1.7   **Spelling and capitalization mistakes.** In the program shown in Listing D1-3, the keyword void is spelled incorrectly, Public and Int incorrectly begin with a capital letter, and string and system are lowercase but should begin with a capital letter. Let's see what the compiler does.

LISTING D1-3   A program containing various spelling mistakes

```
1 public class Debug3
2 {
3     Public static viod main(string[] Args)
4     {
5         Int anInteger = 10;
6         system.out.println("The integer is " + anInteger);
7     } // end main
8 } // end Debug3
```

Error Message

```
Debug3.java:3: <identifier> expected
    Public static viod main(string[] Args)
         ^
1 error
```

The compiler expects to see an identifier after Public, but instead it finds the keyword static, so it does not continue. Why would the compiler expect an identifier? Public is not a Java keyword, public is. So Public appears to be the name of a class serving as the data type of the missing identifier. The problem, of course, is that Public should be public.

After correcting that one error and compiling the program again, we get the following messages:

```
Debug3.java:3: cannot find symbol
symbol  : class string
location: class Debug3
    public static viod main(string[] Args)
                              ^

Debug3.java:3: cannot find symbol
symbol  : class viod
location: class Debug3
    public static viod main(string[] Args)
                  ^

Debug3.java:5: cannot find symbol
symbol  : class Int
location: class Debug3
        Int anInteger = 10;
        ^

3 errors
```

The compiler does not know the meaning of the identifiers `string`, `viod`, and `Int`, since they are not reserved words or class names. The compiler does not know what you meant to write, so it reports the unknown symbols. Hopefully, this hint, along with an indication of the identifier's location, will enable you to correct these three mistakes.

After rectifying these errors, the compiler is still not happy, as you can see here:

```
1 public class Debug3
2 {
3    public static void main(String[] Args)
4    {
5       int anInteger = 10;
6       system.out.println("The integer is " + anInteger);
7    } // end main
8 } // end Debug3
```

Error Message

```
Debug3.java:6: package system does not exist
        system.out.println("The integer is " + anInteger);
              ^
1 error
```

Changing `system` to `System` will allow our program to compile correctly.

Programming Tip

We have highlighted Java reserved words in this book, but you might have noticed that `Public`, `viod`, and `Int` are not highlighted in the previous example. Many Java text editors also use highlighting—such as color or boldface—for reserved words, helping you spot these types of errors. The editor you use to compose your program can help you avoid other syntax errors as well. For example, some editors will signal unpaired parentheses or braces. Those sorts of errors are the subject of the examples you'll see next.

Note: Capitalization mistakes: Syntax errors versus failure to follow convention

In the previous example, `Args` begins with a capital letter. As you will see in Chapter 6, `Args` is a special kind of variable called a parameter. By convention, variables should begin with a lowercase letter. However, the compiler did not see `Args` as an error, because it does not enforce naming conventions. Although using `Args` instead of `args` is not a syntax error, you should still follow convention and use `args`.

D1.8 **Missing parenthesis.** Suppose we accidentally omit the closing parenthesis from a `println` statement. For example, consider the program in Listing D1-4 and the result of its compilation. The compiler is precisely correct in identifying the mistake!

LISTING D1-4   A program that contains a missing parenthesis

```
1  public class Debug4
2  {
3     public static void main(String[] args)
4     {
5        System.out.println("Welcome!";
```

```
6    } // end main
7 } // end Debug4
```

Error Message

```
Debug4.java:5: ')' expected
      System.out.println("Welcome!";
                                    ^
1 error
```

What if we had omitted the opening parenthesis instead, so that the statement read as follows:

```
System.out.println"Welcome!");
```

We would get these messages from the compiler:

```
Debug4.java:5: not a statement
     System.out.println"Welcome!");
               ^
Debug4.java:5: ';' expected
     System.out.println"Welcome!");
                                   ^
2 errors
```

Hopefully, the second message would help you to both recognize the missing parenthesis and ignore the first message.

D1.9

Missing brace. Braces, like parentheses, must occur in open-close matching pairs. The program in Listing D1-5 has two open braces but only one close brace.

LISTING D1-5   A program that contains a missing close brace

```
1  public class Debug5
2  {
3     public static void main(String[] args)
4     {
5        int anInteger = 10;
6        System.out.println("The integer is " + anInteger);
7     }
```

Error Message

```
Debug5.java:7: reached end of file while parsing
        }
        ^
1 error
```

The word **parse** means to analyze syntactically. The error message is indicating that the compiler has reached the last statement available while analyzing a program that it knows is incomplete.

Something needs to follow the last brace. It is up to you to figure out that another close brace is necessary to complete the program.

Programming Tip: Pairing braces

You can ensure that braces occur in matching pairs in any or all of the following ways:

- Use an IDE whose editor watches for unpaired braces.
- Align each open brace with its associated close brace.
- Label each close brace with a comment that indicates the construct to which it belongs.

D1.10

Missing double quote. When defining a string literal, you must be careful to write a double quote at its beginning and end. Forgetting to do so is particularly easy when including such a literal within a `print` or `println` statement. Let's examine how the compiler reacts when one or both of these quotes is missing.

In the program in Listing D1-6, we forgot to end the string literal with a double quote. The compiler points to the beginning of the string literal that is in error. After all, it doesn't know where the end is.

LISTING D1-6   A program with a string literal that is missing a closing quote

```
1 public class Debug6
2 {
3     public static void main(String[] args)
4     {
5         int anInteger = 10;
6         System.out.println("The integer is + anInteger);
7     } // end main
8 } // end Debug6
```

Error Message

```
Debug6.java:6: unclosed string literal
        System.out.println("The integer is + anInteger);
                           ^
    1 error
```

If we had omitted the beginning quote instead of the final one, like so:

```
System.out.println(The integer is " + anInteger);
```

the compiler would provide the following messages:

```
Debug6.java:6: ')' expected
        System.out.println(The integer is " + anInteger);
                                           ^
Debug6.java:6: unclosed string literal
        System.out.println(The integer is " + anInteger);
                                           ^
    2 errors
```

The first of these messages is not too helpful, but the second one is.

Finally, what happens when we omit both quotes? If we had written

```
System.out.println(The integer is + anInteger);
```

we would get the following error messages from the compiler:

```
Debug6.java:6: ')' expected
      System.out.println(The integer is + anInteger);
                            ^

Debug6.java:6: ';' expected
      System.out.println(The integer is + anInteger);
                                        ^

Debug6.java:6: not a statement
      System.out.println(The integer is + anInteger);
                                             ^

Debug6.java:6: ';' expected
      System.out.println(The integer is + anInteger);
                                                    ^

4 errors
```

The compiler clearly is aware that this line is wrong, but it really cannot detect the mistakes with certainty. The best message is the third one: "not a statement" implies "not a valid statement." Again, it is up to you to see your mistake.

D1.11 **Missing concatenation operator.** Consider again the program in Listing D1-6, but this time, let's omit the + operator, instead of the double quotes, from the `println` statement as follows:

```
System.out.println("The integer is " anInteger);
```

and name the program Debug7. The compiler would produce the following error messages:

```
Debug7.java:6: ')' expected
      System.out.println("The integer is " anInteger);
                                             ^

Debug7.java:6: not a statement
      System.out.println("The integer is " anInteger);
                                             ^

Debug7.java:6: ';' expected
      System.out.println("The integer is " anInteger);
                                                    ^

3 errors
```

Once again, the compiler is confused by this mistake. We have omitted one character, the +, but we are told we have made three errors. Although the compiler's first message is not quite right, it does indicate the location of our mistake.

 Programming Tip

If the compiler finds an error in the syntax of your program, you made a mistake. The compiler might be unable to tell you exactly what is wrong, but you should assume that something is. Hoping that it is the compiler that has made a mistake, instead of you, will not help you to find the error.

D1.12 **Missing arithmetic operator.** Imagine that we want to evaluate the formula

$$z = \frac{7}{8}x + 2y$$

for some given real values of x and y. Suppose that we express this formula as the following Java assignment statement, where we assume that x and y are `double` variables that contain given values:

```
double z = 7 / 8 * x + 2y;
```

The compiler will flag this statement as follows:

```
Debug8.java:7: ';' expected
      double z = 7 / 8 * x + 2y;
                              ^
1 error
```

The syntax error does occur immediately after the 2, but it is not a semicolon that is missing. Rather the multiply operator * is missing from between 2 and y.

D1.13 **Uninitialized variable.** We conclude this section with a simple example of an uninitialized variable. Let's compile the program in Listing D1-7, which is intended to compute the average of three numbers. The compiler detects that the variable `counter` is not given a value, so this lapse is a syntax error. Sometimes you will get this error when you know that your program is correct. For your program to compile, however, you need to alter your program to the compiler's satisfaction.

LISTING D1-7   A program that contains an uninitialized variable

```
1  import java.util.Scanner;
2  public class Debug9
3  {
4     public static void main(String[] args)
5     {
6        Scanner keyboard = new Scanner(System.in);
7        double counter;
8        System.out.print("Type three numbers; " +
9                         "this program will compute their average:");
10       double first = keyboard.nextDouble();
11       double second = keyboard.nextDouble();
12       double third = keyboard.nextDouble();
13       System.out.println("You typed " + first + ", " +
14                          second + ", and " + third + ".");
15
16       double average = (first + second + third) / counter;
17       System.out.println("Their average is " + average);
18    } // end main
19 } // end Debug9
```

Error Message

```
Debug9.java:16: variable counter might not have been initialized
      double average = (first + second + third) / counter
                                                  ^
1 error
```

Execution-Time Errors

Finding the logical errors in a program is the subject of this section and of subsequent debugging interludes within this book.

D1.14 **Incorrect arithmetic.** Consider the computation we described earlier in Segment D1.12. Let's correct the syntax error in that assignment statement and embed it within a simple program, as follows:

```java
public class Debug10
{
    public static void main(String[] args)
    {
        double x = 50.5;
        double y = 4.8;
        double z = 7 / 8 * x + 2 * y;
        System.out.println("x is " + x + ", y is " + y +
                           ", z is " + z);
    } // end main
} // end Debug10
```

This program compiles without error.

Executing the program produces the following output:

```
x is 50.5, y is 4.8, z is 9.6
```

As tempting as it might be to feel successful, we should check our answer. Substituting 50.5 and 4.8 for the variables x and y, respectively, and using a calculator, we would compute 53.7875 as the value of z. The program computed 9.6. How can we be so far off? Should we trust the computer or our calculator?

We certainly can—and should—repeat the computation using our calculator. We also can **trace** the computation that our program performs by subdividing the expression for z and displaying some intermediate results. For example, z is the sum of the two terms 7 / 8 * x and 2 * y. We could compute and display each of those terms before computing their sum to get z. That is, we could replace the assignment statement for z with the following statements:

```java
double z1 = 7 / 8 * x;
double z2 = 2 * y;
System.out.println("z1 is " + z1 + ", z2 is " + z2); //DEBUG
double z = z1 + z2;
```

When we run the modified program, we get the following output:

```
z1 is 0.0, z2 is 9.6
x is 50.5, y is 4.8, z is 9.6
```

For some reason, the first term, z1, is zero, and so z is equal to the second term, z2. That must be the source of at least a part of our mistake, because z1—that is, 7 / 8 * x—should not be zero when x's value is 50.5. Do you see why it is zero?

Recall from Chapter 3 that the quotient of two integers is an integer. Any fractional part is discarded, or truncated. Thus, the value of 7 / 8 is zero plus some fraction, which is discarded. That is, 7 / 8 is zero. Multiplying zero by x results in zero, which is assigned to z1. How do we fix our program?

Instead of integer division, we need a division of real numbers. Rather than writing 7 / 8 * x, we could write any of the following expressions:

```java
7.0 / 8.0 * x
7.0 / 8 * x
7 / 8.0 * x
```

```
7 * x / 8
7.0 * x / 8
7 * x / 8.0
7.0 * x / 8.0
```

After using one of these expressions in the program, we will get the same value for z that we calculated by hand.

Programming Tip: Display intermediate results

Add temporary `println` statements to your program to display key values and intermediate results of a computation. You can use a comment to identify these statements, as we did in the previous example. After you have finished debugging your program, you can either remove these `println` statements or add two slashes to the beginning of each one. That is, you can **comment out** the statements. In this way, they are available should you need them again at a later time.

Programming Tip: Play computer

A key to becoming a proficient programmer, as well as a successful debugger, is to simulate the logic of your program as if you were the computer. Imagine the state of each variable at each step of the program's computation. In other words, you trace the program's execution by hand. To avoid confusion, write notes as you continue the trace. Practice this process using simple examples so that you will be able to trace the logic of more complex code. Supplement your hand trace by displaying intermediate results, as the previous programming tip describes.

D1.15 **A mistake in capitalization.** Although we treated spelling and capitalization mistakes earlier in Segment D1.7 as examples of syntax errors, not all such errors are detected by the compiler. For example, consider the program in Listing D1-8, which is similar to the one in Listing D1-3. During program execution, a runtime error message tells us that the method main is missing. Every Java program requires a method named main. In this program, the method is named Main, not main. Remember that Java is case sensitive.

LISTING D1-8   An example of a missing method main

```
1 public class Debug11
2 {
3    public static void Main(String[] Args)
4    {
5       int anInteger = 10;
6       System.out.println("The integer is " + anInteger);
7    } // end Main
8 } // end Debug11
```

Error Message

```
Exception in thread "main" java.lang.NoSuchMethodError: main
```

Since the compiler sees Main as a valid identifier, it does not detect the mistake. As we mentioned previously, not following convention is not a syntax error. This mistake, however, is more than a failure to follow convention; we violated an expectation of the JVM by not defining a method named `main`. The compiler is not responsible for finding this kind of mistake.

 Note: The previous error message uses two terms that we have not yet introduced. An **exception** is an unusual event, such as some kind of error, that interrupts program execution. The previous message tells us that an error (exception) called `NoSuchMethodError` occurred because the method `main` is missing. We will say a bit more about exceptions in the next chapter and discuss them in depth later in this book.

A **thread** is a single sequential flow of logic within a program. If a program has one thread, it consists of the sequence of statements that are executed. In the previous error message, these statements are in the method `main`. However, a program can perform several different tasks, some of which can occur simultaneously. Each such task is a thread.

EXERCISES

The source code available online for this book contains the programs referenced by the following exercises.

1. The program `DebuggingInterlude1a.java` compiles and executes correctly, but its form is not useful for human readers. Edit the program so that each statement is clear and properly indented.

2. The program `DebuggingInterlude1b.java` is supposed to find the larger of two numbers entered by the user, but it is in error. Fix the errors so that it compiles and executes correctly.

3. Repeat Exercise 2, but use the program `DebuggingInterlude1c.java` instead.

4. Repeat Exercise 2, but use the program `DebuggingInterlude1d.java` instead.

5. Repeat Exercise 2, but use the program `DebuggingInterlude1e.java` instead.

Chapter 4

Using Classes and Objects

Contents

Prerequisites

Objectives

After studying this chapter, you should be able to

- Describe how a variable of a primitive type differs from a variable of a class type in the way they represent data
- Use the operator new to create an object
- Use methods within the class String to manipulate strings
- Use the class Scanner to extract portions of a string
- Use the class Date to create and compare two Date objects

- Use the class `BigDecimal` to perform decimal arithmetic
- Use a wrapper class such as `Integer` to represent primitive data as an object
- Use the method `parseInt` in the class `Integer` to convert a string containing an integer to an `int`
- Use constants in the class `Integer` to discover the minimum and maximum values of an `int`
- Use the class `Random` to generate random numbers
- Use the class `DecimalFormat` to format numerical output
- Use a dialog box to read input from the user

Chapter 2 introduced the notion of an object, but here we will look at the concept in detail. We will introduce several classes that are standard in Java and show you how to use them.

Introduction

4.1   We begin by reviewing some of the earlier material about objects and classes. An object is a construct in a Java program that represents data and performs certain actions. A Java object can represent a real-world object or an abstraction, such as a name. Objects within a program can act on their own or interact with one another to accomplish a task. Each object has a data type. Objects that have the same type belong to the same class. The data type of an object is the name of a class, so an object's data type is called a **class type**.

videonote
Classes and objects

A class is like a plan for creating objects. That is, the class C describes the data and methods that are associated with each object of type C. Thus, you must have a class—one that either you write yourself or is written for you—before you can create objects of the class. When you create, or **instantiate**, an object, space is typically allocated for the data that the class describes. The process of creating the object is called **instantiation**. Thus, an object is also known as an **instance** of the class type.

4.2   The actions, or behaviors, of an object are the result of executing the methods that the class defines. You **call**, or **invoke**, a method to execute it. You do not need to know how to write a class in Java to be able to use one. If someone else writes a class and describes how to call its methods, you will be able to use the methods in your program. Although you will learn how to write your own classes, it is not unusual to use classes that someone else has written. We have mentioned that Java comes with an extensive collection of such classes called the Java Class Library, sometimes called the **Java Application Programming Interface**, or **API**. The class `Scanner` that you saw in Chapter 2 and the class `Math` that you saw in Chapter 3 belong to this library. The objects that we discuss in this chapter also belong to classes in the Java Class Library.

The Class `String`

Imagine that your program asks for the user's full name. Sometimes, however, you will want to use only the user's first name, other times just the last name, and occasionally the initials. A person's name can be represented by a string. In this section, we explore how to work with strings so that we can solve the problem at hand.

4.3   In Chapter 2, we used string literals and `println` statements to display lines of text. For example,

```
"Java is a programming language."
```

is a string literal. A string literal is an object that belongs to the class `String`. As such, it is a `String` object, or more simply a string, and it has the data type `String`. The class `String` is standard in Java and is a part of the Java Class Library within the package `java.lang`.

You can declare the data type of a variable to be `String` much as you declare variables of other types. You also can assign a string to a `String` variable. For example, you can write

```
String greeting = new String("Hello");
```

The **new operator** creates a new object of the indicated class type—String in this case—and String("Hello") initializes the object's data portion. Here, the String object is initialized to "Hello".

4.4   Although you use the new operator to create an object of any class, you can create a String object more simply. Instead of the previous Java statement, you can write

```
String greeting = "Hello";
```

Thus, you can use a string literal as you would a primitive literal in an assignment statement. Java includes this simplification since strings are so prevalent in Java programs. You will see other classes later in this chapter that allow a similar initialization. For almost all classes, however, you must use the new operator to create a new object.

Note: The new operator
You use the new operator to create a new object of a given class type. For example,

```
String name = new String("Jill");
```

creates an instance of String. For strings, a shortcut exists that does not use the new operator. Thus, you can create a String object by writing a simple assignment, such as

```
String name = "Jill";
```

Note: Constructors
Whenever you create a new object, the instantiation process calls a special method within the class called a **constructor**. A constructor has the same name as the class. Some constructors accept arguments and some do not. You will learn much more about constructors in Chapter 6, but for now, you should be familiar with the term.

Question 1 Define two String variables. Assign your first name to one by using the new operator. Assign your last name to the other without using the new operator.

References

Variables of a class type are a bit different from variables of a primitive type. Let's compare them.

4.5   A variable whose primitive type is int is given enough memory to contain an integer. Figure 4-1a shows two int variables after they are assigned initial values. Each contains its assigned value. Now notice what happens in Part b of the figure when one variable is assigned to another in an assignment statement. Both variables now contain the same value. The old value of size is lost.

FIGURE 4-1   Variables of a primitive type contain their values: (a) two variables are assigned values; (b) one variable is assigned to the other

```
(a)  int size = 12;        12  size

     int newSize = 30;     30  newSize


(b)  size = newSize;       30  size

                           30  newSize
```

4.6 Now consider variables of a class type. Figure 4-2a shows two String variables after they are assigned initial values. These values are objects. A variable of a class type does not contain an object. Rather, it contains a **reference** to the object. A reference is simply the address of the memory that an object uses. The figure uses an arrow to illustrate a reference. Thus, greeting, for example, references the string object that contains "Hello". A variable of a class type is also called a **reference variable**.

FIGURE 4-2   Variables of a class type reference their values: (a) two variables are assigned values; (b) one variable is assigned to the other

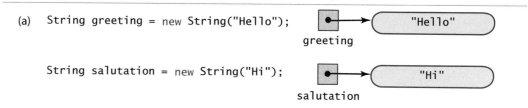

(a)   `String greeting = new String("Hello");`

(b)   `greeting = salutation;`

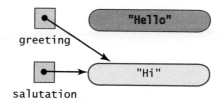

When one variable is assigned to another, one reference replaces the other. In Figure 4-2b, both variables now reference the string object that contains "Hi". Since the object now essentially has two names, these variables are called **aliases**.

The string "Hello" is no longer referenced by any variable. The memory assigned to abandoned objects is collected by the runtime system periodically and used for other purposes. This recycling effort is called **garbage collection**. The process happens automatically for you without any action on your part.

Note: References

- While a variable of a primitive type actually contains a primitive value, such as an integer, a variable of a reference type contains the address of, or a reference to, its value.
- A variable of a reference type can reference one object and then later reference a different object.
- In general, references are much smaller than objects, so copying a reference is easier than copying an object.

Characters Within Strings

4.7 Programming languages typically use integers to represent characters, and so does Java. For example, the digits 0 through 9 are represented by the decimal integers 48 through 57, respectively. The letters *A* through *Z* are represented by 65 through 90, and *a* through *z* are represented by 97 through

122. This notation is called **Unicode**. Although you do not need to know these values, you should notice that their sequence gives an order to the characters they represent.

The Unicode character set includes not only digits and letters, but also punctuation and characters from languages other than English. Most programming languages use a smaller character set called **ASCII** (American Standard Code for Information Interchange). Unicode, the notation used by Java, represents more characters than ASCII, but it also uses more memory to represent each individual character.

Appendix C summarizes the Unicode character set.

4.8 **Escape characters.** Within a single `println` or `print` statement, you can display more than one line by including a **new-line character** within your strings each time you want to start a new line. Two typed characters are necessary to indicate one new-line character. The first of these characters is a blackslash (\) and the second is the letter n. Thus, \n embedded within a string is a signal to go to a new line.

For example, the statement

```
System.out.println("Line one\nLine two");
```

displays the two lines

```
Line one
Line two
```

The notation \n is an example of an **escape character**, as it *escapes* from the usual notation for a character. Figure 4-3 lists other escape characters. For example, the notation \" is necessary to display a quote within a string because quotes are used to delimit the string. So if you wanted to display the lines

```
During the first telephone call, Alexander Graham Bell said
"Watson, come here!"
```

you could write Java statements such as

```
System.out.println("During the first telephone call, " +
                   "Alexander Graham Bell said");
System.out.println("\"Watson, come here!\"");
```

FIGURE 4-3   Escape characters

\n	New line (go to the next line)
\r	Return (return to the start of the current line)
\t	Tab
\\	Backslash
\"	Double quote
\'	Single quote (apostrophe)

Question 2 Replace the previous two `println` statements that display a message about Alexander Graham Bell with one `println` statement.

Joining Strings

4.9   You learned in Segment 2.16 of Chapter 2 that you can use the + operator within a `println` statement to join, or concatenate, two strings. You need not restrict your use of the **concatenation operator** + to `println` statements. For example, you can write the assignment statement

```
String verseStart = "4" + " and " + "20" + " blackbirds ";
```

to assign the string "4 and 20 blackbirds " to the variable `verseStart`.

When one operand of the + operator is a string and the other is a primitive, such as an integer, the primitive value is converted to a string and then joined to the other string. Thus, we could write the previous assignment as

```
String verseStart = 4 + " and " + 20 + " blackbirds ";
```

We have simply written the integer 4 instead of the string "4". You also can substitute integer variables for the integer literals and get the same results.

This conversion to a string works for real numbers and characters as well. For example,

```
String label = "minute";
String pluralLabel = label + 's';
```

sets `pluralLabel` to "minutes".

Note: **The concatenation operator +**

When the operator + has a string as at least one of its operands, it concatenates, or joins, its operands into a new string. If one of the operands has a primitive type, the primitive value is first converted to a string and then concatenated with the other operand. Realize that when the + operator has two primitive numeric values as its operands, addition, not concatenation, occurs. For example, the value of the expression "4" + "4" is "44", while the value of 4 + 4 is 8. You must also consider the precedence and order of operations. The expression "four" + 4 + 4 is equivalent to ("four" + 4) + 4, and so has the value "four44". However, the expression 4 + 4 + "four" is equivalent to (4 + 4) + "four", or 8 + "four", and so has the value "8four".

The following section includes another way to concatenate strings.

Question 3 Using the + operator and your answer to Question 1, give the Java statement that will now assign your full name to a `String` variable `fullName`.

String Methods

In addition to the characters that compose its value, a string has certain behaviors that are defined by the methods in the class `String`.

4.10   **The method `length`.** The method `length` provides the number of characters that are in a string, including any spaces. For example, the statements

videonote
The class **String**

```
String fact = "Java is my dog's name"; // 21 characters
System.out.println(fact.length());
```

display 21. The string object named `fact` calls the method `length` by using a dot notation, `fact.length()`. The pair of parentheses after the method name `length` is required. This method returns an `int` value.

You can use the expression `fact.length()` anywhere that you can use an `int` value. Thus, you can embed the expression within an arithmetic expression.

Question 4 Write a statement that assigns the length of the string in the `String` variable `fullName` to the `int` variable `nameLength`.

> **Syntax: Calling a method**
> You call, or invoke, an object's method by using the notation
>
> *object_name*.*method_name*(...)
>
> The object is the **receiving object**, or **receiver**, as it receives the invocation. For some methods, nothing appears between the parentheses. For other methods, one or more arguments—which can be expressions—occur. Multiple arguments are separated by commas.

4.11   **The method concat.** You can concatenate two strings, either by using the + operator or by using the method concat. For example, if you define the two strings

```
String one = "sail";
String two = "boat";
```

the expressions

```
one + two
```

and

```
one.concat(two)
```

produce the same string, "sailboat". Notice that concat has one argument, the variable two in this example. Also, notice that the strings one and two are unchanged by concat.

Question 5 Repeat Question 3, but use the method concat instead of the + operator.

4.12   The statements

```
String dogName = "Spot";
String fact = dogName + " ";
fact = fact.concat("is my dog's name.");
System.out.println(fact);
System.out.println("The variable dogName references the string " +
                   dogName + ".");
```

display the lines

```
Spot is my dog's name.
The variable dogName references the string Spot.
```

The variable dogName references the string "Spot" and remains unchanged by these statements. The assignment to the variable fact adds a blank space at the end of "Spot", resulting in a new string "Spot ". The invocation of concat returns a new string that is the concatenation of "Spot " and "is my dog's name.". This new string is assigned to fact and then displayed. The string "Spot ", which fact originally referenced, is left for garbage collection.

4.13   **The methods `toUpperCase` and `toLowerCase`.** Two methods are available that change the case of any letters in a given string, returning a new string containing the changes. These methods do not change the original string. The method toUpperCase changes any lowercase letters within a string to uppercase in the new string. It does not change any letters that are already uppercase, nor does it change any characters that are not letters. For example, if phrase is defined by

```
String phrase = "Java, Java, Java!";
```

the statement

```
System.out.println(phrase.toUpperCase());
```

displays

```
JAVA, JAVA, JAVA!
```

The original string referenced by phrase is unchanged, so

```
System.out.println(phrase);
```

displays

```
Java, Java, Java!
```

An analogous method, toLowerCase, changes any uppercase letters within a string to lowercase.

Question 6 If fullName references a String object that contains your name, what is the result of the expression fullName.toLowerCase()?

Note: Methods in the class String do not change any string that is a receiving object or an argument of the method. For example, one.concat(two) does not change the strings one and two, and phrase.toUpperCase() does not change the string phrase. In both examples, the method returns a new string.

4.14   **The method trim.** This method removes any white space, such as spaces, that occur at either the beginning or the end of a string. For example, the statements

```
String line = "   Along came a spider,   ";
String trimmedLine = line.trim();
```

set trimmedLine to the string "Along came a spider,".

Question 7 What string does line reference after the previous two assignment statements have executed and trimmedLine has been assigned a value?

Question 8 Assuming that trimmedLine is as just defined, what is the result of the statement

```
trimmedLine = trimmedLine.trim();
```

4.15   **The method charAt.** The method charAt enables you to access any character within a string, given the character's position. To indicate a position, you number the characters within the string, starting with 0. The last character in a string is numbered $n - 1$, where n is the length of the string. Each of these numbers is called an **index**. Figure 4-4 illustrates a string and its associated indices. Several String methods use this notation to identify characters within a string.

FIGURE 4-4   Indices 0 through 19 for the string "Along came a spider,"

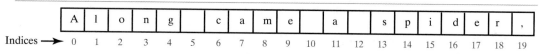

The method `charAt` gets the character that is at a given index within a string. For example, if `trimmedLine`, as defined as in Segment 4.14, represents the string shown in Figure 4-4, the seventh character is the letter *c* at index 6. Thus, `seventhCharacter` in the statement

```
char seventhCharacter = trimmedLine.charAt(6);// character at index 6
```

has the value `'c'`.

Question 9 Write a Java statement that defines a string called `myName` that contains your first and last names. Using this string and the method `charAt`, define `char` variables `firstInitial` and `lastInitial` that contain your first initial and last initial, respectively.

Question 10 What is displayed by the following statements?

```
String line = "    Along came a spider,    ";
String trimmedLine = line.trim();
System.out.println(trimmedLine.charAt(trimmedLine.length() - 1));
```

4.16   **Exceptions.** The index that you pass to the method `charAt` must be valid. That is, it must be either

- Zero, or
- Positive but less than or equal to *n* - 1, where *n* is the length of the string

If you violate this restriction, your program will stop executing and you will see an error message. For example, for the string `trimmedLine` pictured in Figure 4-4, `trimmedLine.charAt(20)` will cause an error message that includes the following:

```
StringIndexOutOfBoundsException: String index out of range: 20
```

Recall from the debugging interlude that preceded this chapter that an exception is an unusual circumstance that interrupts the execution of a program. Here we are trying to access a character at index 20, which does not exist. Exceptions are actually objects of certain classes. In this case, the exception belongs to the class `StringIndexOutOfBoundsException`, which is a part of the Java Class Library. Chapter 28 will discuss exceptions in detail.

4.17   **The method `indexOf`.** The method `indexOf` locates the position of a **substring** within another string. For example, in Figure 4-4, the string `"spider"` is a substring within the string `"Along came a spider,"`. Since this substring begins at index 13, `trimmedLine.indexOf("spider")` returns 13.

Question 11 What is the value of the expression `"Along came a spider,".indexOf("a")`?

Question 12 Given a string `phrase`, what is the index of the first space, if any, in the string? Assign this index to the `int` variable `spaceIndex`.

4.18   **The method `replace`.** The method `replace` returns a new string formed by replacing all occurrences of a given character within the receiving string with another given character. You pass the two characters, `oldChar` and `newChar`, to the method `replace` as arguments. The original receiving string is not changed by this method.

For example, if `phrase` is defined as follows:

```
String phrase = "spamming a homey bum";
```

the expression

```
phrase.replace('m', 'n')
```

returns the string `"spanning a honey bun"`.

4.19   **The method substring.** The method substring has two forms. Each returns a copy of a substring that occurs within the receiving string. For one form of the method, you pass the index of the first character of the desired substring. The substring extends through the end of the original string. For example,

```
String word = "decrease";
System.out.println(word.substring(2));
```

displays the substring "crease". Note that the string word is unchanged by the method substring.

Another form of the method requires two arguments. The first argument is the index of the first character of the substring. The second argument is 1 more than the index of the last character of the substring. Thus,

```
String pluralWord = "decreases";
System.out.println(pluralWord.substring(2, 8));
```

displays the substring "crease".

Notice that the second argument is 8, which indicates the character at index 7. This character is the last *e* in *decreases*.

 Note: When present, the second argument of the method substring must be 1 more than the index of the last character in the desired substring.

 Note: The first index that you pass to the method substring must be greater than or equal to zero but less than or equal to $n - 1$, where n is the length of the string. The second index, if present, must be greater than or equal to the first argument but less than or equal to n. If you violate these restrictions, a StringIndexOutOfBoundsException will occur and program execution will stop.

 Question 13 Assume that phrase references a string that consists of three or more characters. Suppose that the string contains exactly one space that is neither the first nor the last character. The blank character divides the string into two substrings that contain no spaces. Write statements that define two strings, each of which contains one of these substrings.

Comparing Characters and Strings

4.20   When we introduced the Unicode character set in Segment 4.7, we mentioned that characters are ordered by their Unicode values. These values are consistent with ordinary alphabetic order. For example, the letters *A* through *Z* are represented by the integers 65 through 90 in Unicode; *a* through *z* are represented by 97 through 122. When you compare characters, you are actually comparing their Unicode values. Thus, 'A' < 'B', 'Z' < 'a', and 'a' < 'b'. When you compare two strings, you are comparing the Unicode values of the characters within the strings. This ordering of strings is called the **lexicographic order**, or sometimes **dictionary order**. To compare two strings, you use one of the following two methods.

4.21   **The method equals.** The method equals decides whether two strings have equal values. If they do, the method returns the boolean value true. Otherwise, it returns false. For example, given the statement

```
String greeting = "Hello";
```

the expression greeting.equals("Hi") is false. You can display this value or assign it to a boolean variable.

Note: Although this is a natural place to present methods that make comparisons, to have your program react to their results, you will need the Java statements that Chapter 7 describes.

4.22   **The method `equalsIgnoreCase`.** This method behaves like the method `equals`, but ignores the case of the two strings. For example, if `greeting` is defined as in the previous segment, the expression `greeting.equalsIgnoreCase("hElLo")` is true.

4.23   **The method `compareTo`.** The method `compareTo` compares two strings and returns an `int` value that signals the result of the comparison, as follows: If `s1` and `s2` are strings, `s1.compareTo(s2)` is

- Positive if `s1` comes after `s2` in lexicographic order
- Zero if `s1` and `s2` are equal
- Negative if `s1` comes before `s2` in lexicographic order

For example,

```
"able".compareTo("baker") is negative
"bug".compareTo("big") is positive
"Color".compareTo("Color") is zero
"Color".compareTo("color") is negative
"Java".compareTo("A") is positive
"Java".compareTo("a") is negative
```

 Question 14 What is the value of each of the following expressions?

a.   `"Color".equals("color")`
b.   `"bug".compareTo("bugs")`

 Note: The class `String` has other methods that we have not discussed in this chapter. You can see a complete list of these methods online in the documentation for the Java Class Library.

Using Scanner to Read a String

Chapter 2 introduced the class `Scanner` for reading user input from the keyboard. We now look at two of its methods that read strings.

4.24   **The methods `nextLine` and `next`.** The method `nextLine` in the class `Scanner` reads to the end of a line of user input and returns it as a string. For example, if `keyboard` is defined as

```
Scanner keyboard = new Scanner(System.in);
```

then the statement

```
String message = keyboard.nextLine();
```

reads the entire string that the user types before pressing the Enter key and assigns it to the variable `message`. Any spaces in the line are read as characters and are not skipped.

The method `next` in the class `Scanner` reads the next group of contiguous characters that are not white space and returns it as a string. For example, you can use this method to read the next word that appears in the input data, as follows:

```
String word = keyboard.next();
```

A Problem Solved: Processing a String

> Read a person's name, compute its length, and identify the first and last names and the person's initials. If the name is typed on one line, insist that only one space occur between the two names. However, offer some flexibility by allowing spaces to occur before or after the entire name.

4.25   The solution to this problem demonstrates some of the methods we have just discussed. It does so by manipulating strings. Such manipulation is called **string processing**.

Here are the steps that our program will take:

Read the name
Remove any leading or trailing spaces

Locate the position of the space between the first and last names
Get the first name
Get the last name
Get the length of the name

Get the first initial
Get the last initial
Form a string of the initials punctuated by periods

Display the name and its length
Display the first and last names
Display the initials

Listing 4-1 contains the Java program and a sample of its output.

LISTING 4-1   A demonstration of String methods

```java
import java.util.Scanner;
public class StringDemo
{
    public static void main(String[] args)
    {
        Scanner keyboard = new Scanner(System.in);
        System.out.print("Please type your first name, a space, and " +
                        "your last name: ");
        String name = keyboard.nextLine();
        name = name.trim();

        int firstNameIndex = 0;                // start of first name
        int spaceIndex = name.indexOf(" ");
        int lastNameIndex = spaceIndex + 1; // start of last name

        String firstName = name.substring(firstNameIndex, spaceIndex);
        String lastName  = name.substring(lastNameIndex);
        int nameLength = firstName.length() + lastName.length();

        char firstInitial = firstName.charAt(0);
        char lastInitial  = lastName.charAt(0);
        String initials = firstInitial + ". " + lastInitial + ".";
```

```
        System.out.println("Hi, " + name + ".\nYour name contains " +
                            nameLength + " characters.");
        System.out.println("Your first name is " + firstName + ".");
        System.out.println("Your last name is " + lastName + ".");

        System.out.println("Your initials are " + initials);
    } // end main
} // end StringDemo
```

Sample Output

```
Please type your first name, a space, and your last name: Joe Java
Hi, Joe Java.
Your name contains 7 characters.
Your first name is Joe.
Your last name is Java.
Your initials are J. J.
```

Question 15 How can you simplify the previous program by using Scanner's method next instead of nextLine?

Using Scanner to Extract Pieces of a String

4.26 You have seen how to use the class Scanner to read data that a user types at the keyboard. Methods in Scanner process the string of characters that come from the keyboard. For example, methods such as nextInt, nextDouble, and next read a group of characters as, respectively, an integer, a real number, or a string. Such a group of contiguous characters is called a **token**. When more than one token appears in the input data, they are separated by one or more characters known as **delimiters**. By default, Scanner uses white space as delimiters.

In a manner similar to reading data from the keyboard, you can use Scanner to process a string that you define within your program. You simply pass the string to Scanner's constructor instead of passing it System.in.

4.27 **Example.** The statements

```
String phrase = "one potato      two     potato three potato four";
Scanner scan = new Scanner(phrase);
System.out.println(scan.next());
System.out.println(scan.next());
System.out.println(scan.next());
System.out.println(scan.next());
```

display the words

    one
    potato
    two
    potato

We essentially have read tokens from a string instead of from the keyboard. The tokens here are separated by white space, the default delimiter.

4.28   **Specifying delimiters.** Whether you read characters from an input device such as a keyboard or from a string defined in your program, you can specify the delimiters that Scanner will use. The Scanner method useDelimiter sets these delimiters to those indicated in its string argument. For example, to use a comma as a delimiter, you would write

```
scan.useDelimiter(",");
```

where scan is a Scanner object. Thus, the statements

```
String data = "one,potato,two,potato";
Scanner scan = new Scanner(data);
scan.useDelimiter(",");
System.out.println(scan.next());
System.out.println(scan.next());
System.out.println(scan.next());
System.out.println(scan.next());
```

display the words

one
potato
two
potato

Question 16 What Java statements would read the following line from the keyboard and display the two names on separate lines?

```
Joe Java/Colbie Coffee/
```

Immutable Strings

4.29   When you create a string object, you cannot change it. To fully understand this statement, you need to distinguish between a string variable and a string object. The variable can reference one string object, and later reference a different string object. For example, in the program given in Listing 4-1, the variable name is assigned a string read from the keyboard. If Joe Java types spaces before and after his name, the statement

```
name = name.trim();
```

removes those spaces. As a result, the variable name no longer references the original string; it now references another string without leading or trailing spaces. Figure 4-5 illustrates the string objects "   Joe Java   " and "Joe Java". Initially, name references the string object that contains the extra spaces. After the method trim removes those spaces, name references another string object. The two string objects do not change. An object that cannot change is said to be **immutable**, which simply means unchangeable.

FIGURE 4-5   The String variable name references (a) a string that contains extra spaces; (b) another string without the extra spaces

```
(a)  String name;
     name = "    Joe Java    ";
```
name → "   Joe Java   "

```
(b)  name = name.trim();
```
name → "   Joe Java   "
     → "Joe Java"

Note: An object whose methods do not change its data is said to be immutable. The objects of the class `String`—that is, strings—are immutable.

Question 17 In Figure 4-5b, what happens to the string "   Joe Java   " now that no variable references it?

The Class Date

4.30   The Java Class Library contains the package `java.util`, which contains utility classes. Among them is the class `Date`. An object in this class represents the time that it was created, accurate to the nearest millisecond. The time is recorded as a date (year, month, and day) and time of day.

   To create a new `Date` object, you write a statement such as

```
Date dateAndTimeNow = new Date();
```

If you were to display the variable `dateAndTimeNow` by using the statement

```
System.out.println(dateAndTimeNow);
```

you would get a line like

```
Wed Jul 30 16:19:38 EDT 2010
```

Although the object itself is accurate to the millisecond, only the nearest second is displayed.

4.31   **The method `toString`.** The method `toString` of a `Date` object returns a string representation of the object. If `dateAndTimeNow` is defined as in the previous segment, the statement

```
String dateAndTime = dateAndTimeNow.toString();
```

assigns the following string to `dateAndTime`:

```
"Wed Jul 30 16:19:38 EDT 2010"
```

This string is the same one that the `println` statement in the previous segment displays.

4.32   **The method `equals`.** Suppose that we have

```
Date dateAndTimeOne = new Date();
```

and later in the program we have

```
Date dateAndTimeTwo = new Date();
```

Because the first statement executes before the second one, `dateAndTimeOne` is before `dateAndTimeTwo`. Several methods are available to compare two `Date` objects. Each of these methods returns a value that indicates the result of the comparison. As we mentioned earlier in this chapter, you will need the statements that Chapter 7 introduces to fully react to these returned values.

   The method `equals` decides whether two `Date` objects have equal values. If they do, the method returns the boolean value true. Otherwise, it returns false. For example,

```
dateAndTimeOne.equals(dateAndTimeTwo)
```

returns false.

   The following segments describe three other methods that compare two `Date` objects. We will use the objects `dateAndTimeOne` and `dateAndTimeTwo` in our examples.

4.33 **The method compareTo.** The method compareTo compares two Date objects and decides whether they are equal or whether one is before or after the other. The method returns an int value that signals the result of the comparison as follows. If d1 and d2 are Date objects, d1.compareTo(d2) is

- Positive if d1 comes after d2
- Zero if d1 and d2 are equal
- Negative if d1 comes before d2

For example, dateAndTimeOne.compareTo(dateAndTimeTwo) is negative. Note that Date's compareTo behaves like String's compareTo, which you saw in Segment 4.23.

4.34 **The methods before and after.** The method before decides whether one Date object comes before another. For example,

```
dateAndTimeOne.before(dateAndTimeTwo)
```

returns true. The method after decides whether one Date object comes after another. For example,

```
dateAndTimeOne.after(dateAndTimeTwo)
```

returns false.

4.35 **The import statement.** As you saw in Chapter 2, if your program uses a class from a package, you write an import statement that appears before the rest of your program. To import the class Date from the package java.util, you write

```
import java.util.Date;
```

If you use more than one class in a package, you can import the entire package by writing an asterisk instead of a class name, as in

```
import java.util.*;
```

While importing an entire package is common among some programmers, we will import each class separately to help you associate classes with their packages.

Question 18 Write and execute a small program that creates three Date objects. Display the objects and display the results of the four methods discussed previously. Move the definitions of the three Date objects around so that the method equals returns true for one pair of the objects and false for a different pair.

The Class BigDecimal

videonote
Other
interesting classes

4.36 Listing 2-4 in Segment 2.30 of Chapter 2 contains a program that computes the money saved by buying apples by the box instead of individually. For a box of 24 apples, the savings should be the difference between $7.68 and $7.25, or $0.43. Instead of displaying $0.43, the program displayed $0.4299999999999997. This imprecision is the result of using the binary number system to represent decimal values. Although we can force the output to look like $0.43, the internal representation of the result is not quite correct. If we used this value in subsequent computations, the error would propagate and likely get larger. Using binary arithmetic for monetary computations is not a good idea, and is certainly something that banks could not tolerate.

The class BigDecimal enables us to perform accurate decimal arithmetic and to work with arbitrarily large numbers. This class is in the package java.math. Do not confuse this package with the class Math that is in the package java.lang.

Note: An object of BigDecimal has a signed decimal value and a scale, both of which are integers. The value of the scale positions the decimal point within the value. Usually, this representation need not concern you, but the terms *value* and *scale* do appear within the description of some of the class's methods.

4.37   **Creating a BigDecimal object.** To create a new BigDecimal object, you write a statement such as

```
BigDecimal price = new BigDecimal("2.97");
```

You write the desired value of the new object as a string to preserve its accuracy. Writing it as a double is legal, but doing so would involve a conversion to binary and, therefore, an inaccuracy in its representation.

If you want to read the value of the BigDecimal object from the user, you could read it as a string. For example,

```
System.out.print("How much does one apple cost? $");
String input = keyboard.next();
BigDecimal costPerApple = new BigDecimal(input);
```

The user would type a value such as 0.32, and it would be read as a string.

Alternatively, you can use the method nextBigDecimal from the class Scanner to read an input string and create a BigDecimal object from it. For example, the following statements are equivalent to the ones you just saw:

```
System.out.print("How much does one apple cost? $");
BigDecimal costPerApple = keyboard.nextBigDecimal();
```

 Note: Using Scanner to read a BigDecimal value
The following method in the class Scanner creates a BigDecimal object from the next value read:

```
nextBigDecimal()
```
Reads the next input value and returns it as a BigDecimal object.

4.38   **The method add.** The method add adds two BigDecimal objects and returns the result. For example, to add the sales tax to the price of an item, you could write

```
BigDecimal price = new BigDecimal("21.97");
BigDecimal salesTax = new BigDecimal("1.54");
BigDecimal cost = price.add(salesTax);
```

Realize that neither price nor salesTax is changed by the method add. Rather, their sum is returned and assigned to cost.

 Note: The string that you use to create a BigDecimal object must not contain white space or other characters that are not legal in a real number. Even spaces before or after the number would be illegal. If you do not observe this restriction, your program will terminate execution with a NumberFormatException.

4.39   **The method subtract.** The method subtract finds the difference between two BigDecimal objects and returns the result. For example, to subtract the amount of a check from your bank balance, you could write

```
BigDecimal balance = new BigDecimal("204.58");
BigDecimal newCheck = new BigDecimal("15.25");
balance = balance.subtract(newCheck);
```

Neither newCheck nor balance is changed by the method subtract, but since we assign the result of the subtraction to balance, the object that balance referenced originally—its value was 204.58—is lost. This situation is similar to the one for strings that is pictured in Figure 4-5.

4.40 **The methods multiply and divide.** The method multiply forms the product of two BigDecimal objects and returns the result. The two operands are not changed by the operation. Thus, if price and salesTax have been declared as BigDecimal variables, the statements

```
BigDecimal taxRate = new BigDecimal("0.07");
salesTax = price.multiply(taxRate);
```

compute the product of price and taxRate.

The method divide forms the quotient of two BigDecimal objects and is analogous to the method multiply. For example, if price and weight are BigDecimal variables that represent the price and weight of a box of cereal, the cereal's unit price is given by

```
BigDecimal unitPrice = price.divide(weight);
```

Question 19 Write statements that use BigDecimal arithmetic to compute the area of a trapezoid. Recall that a trapezoid has two parallel sides, *b1* and *b2*, that are *h* units apart. The area is (*b1* + *b2*) x *h* / 2.

Note: The objects of the class BigDecimal are immutable.

4.41 **The methods toString, equals, and compareTo.** The method toString returns a string representation of a BigDecimal object. The methods equals and compareTo for this class are analogous to the corresponding methods in Date. However, equals judges two BigDecimal objects as equal only if they have equal values and scales. Thus, 5.0 and 5.00 are not equal according to the method equals. The method compareTo, on the other hand, considers 5.0 and 5.00 as equal.

Programming Tip

Use caution when using the equals and compareTo methods of BigDecimal, as these methods do not judge the equality of two objects in the same way.

Note: If you define the methods equals and compareTo in your own class, write them so that they judge the equality of two objects in the same way.

A Problem Solved: More Apples by the Box

4.42 The program in Listing 2-4 of Chapter 2 computes the difference in cost between a box of apples and the same number of apples if bought individually. We revise that program here in Listing 4-2 so that it performs the computations using BigDecimal objects instead of double primitives. We demonstrate two ways to read the data. One way uses next to read data as a string, and the second way uses nextBigDecimal. In both cases, the input data is ultimately converted to BigDecimal objects for the subsequent computations. Note that the println statements are identical to those in Listing 2-4. Also notice that the final result, $0.43, is correct and not an approximation, as it was in Listing 2-4.

LISTING 4-2   Computing the cost of apples using BigDecimal arithmetic

```java
/** BuyApples.java by F. M. Carrano
    Computes the money saved by buying a box of apples
    at the box rate instead of individually.
*/
import java.math.BigDecimal;
import java.util.Scanner;
public class BuyApples
{
   public static void main(String[] args)
   {
      Scanner keyboard = new Scanner(System.in);
      System.out.print("How many apples are in a box? ");
      String input = keyboard.next();
      BigDecimal applesPerBox = new BigDecimal(input);

      System.out.print("How much does one apple cost? $");
      BigDecimal costPerApple = keyboard.nextBigDecimal();

      System.out.print("How much does a box of apples cost? $");
      BigDecimal costPerBox = keyboard.nextBigDecimal();

      BigDecimal costOfApples = applesPerBox.multiply(costPerApple);
      BigDecimal savings = costOfApples.subtract(costPerBox);

      System.out.println();
      System.out.println("Apples per box:                      " +
                         applesPerBox);
      System.out.println("Cost per apple:                      $" +
                         costPerApple);
      System.out.println("Cost per box:                        $" +
                         costPerBox);
      System.out.println("Cost of apples if bought separately: $" +
                         costOfApples);
      System.out.println("Savings if bought by the box:        $" +
                         savings);
   } // end main
} // end Apples
```

Sample Output

```
How many apples are in a box? 24
How much does one apple cost? $.32
How much does a box of apples cost? $7.25

Apples per box:                      24
Cost per apple:                      $0.32
Cost per box:                        $7.25
Cost of apples if bought separately: $7.68
Savings if bought by the box:        $0.43
```

Wrapper Classes

4.43   For each primitive data type, the Java Class Library contains a corresponding **wrapper class**. These classes enable you to represent primitive data as objects. They also contain constants that indicate the range of such data and provide useful methods for processing input data. It is these latter two features that are most important to us right now.

   For example, the class `Integer` represents integers whose data type is `int`. This class contains two constants that indicate the range of `int` values. The constant `Integer.MAX_VALUE` contains the largest `int` value, $2^{31} - 1$, and `Integer.MIN_VALUE` contains the smallest value, -2^{31}. Note that the data type of these constants is `int`, not `Integer`.

4.44   The method `parseInt` takes an argument that is a string containing an integer literal and returns an `int` representation of that integer. For example,

```
int feetPerMile = Integer.parseInt("5280");
```

returns the `int` value 5280. Note that you use `parseInt` much as you use the methods in the class `Math`. You simply write the name of the class before the method name, instead of the name of an object.

   More than likely, the argument to `parseInt` will not be a literal, as in the previous example, but rather a string variable, as in this example:

```
String stringRepresentation = "5280";
int feetPerMile = Integer.parseInt(stringRepresentation);
```

As you will see in Segment 4.55, when you read data from the keyboard without the benefit of the class `Scanner`, you get a string as a result. If the string represents an integer, you use `parseInt` to extract the `int` value from the string.

4.45   You can create an object of the class `Integer` in one of three ways, as the following statements demonstrate:

```
Integer ten = new Integer(10);
Integer fiftyTwo = new Integer("52");
Integer eighty = 80;
```

In the first way, you supply an `int` value as a literal, a variable, or an expression. In the second way, you provide a string whose characters represent an integer value. The third way allows you to simply assign an `int` value without using the `new` operator. Recall that you could use an analogous shortcut to define a string.

4.46   Once you have defined `Integer` objects, you can compare them by using the methods `compareTo` and `equals`, much as you compare strings or the other objects we have discussed in this chapter.

   If you need the value of an `Integer` object as a primitive, you can use methods such as `intValue` or `doubleValue`. For example, if the variable `ten` is defined as in the previous segment, the expression

```
ten.intValue()
```

returns the `int` value 10, whereas

```
ten.doubleValue()
```

returns the `double` value 10.0. You also can simply assign the `Integer` object to an `int` variable, as in

```
int primitive10 = ten;
```

No type cast is necessary; however, using one is not an error.

4.47   **Autoboxing.** When performing arithmetic with `Integer` objects, you can use the same operators that you use to perform arithmetic with primitives. You also can intermix primitive integers with `Integer` objects. Thus, you can write statements such as those in Listing 4-3. Java converts between `int` and `Integer` as necessary. This process is called **autoboxing**.

Realize that the program in Listing 4-3 is just a demonstration of these concepts. In a real-world situation, using only primitive integers for this simple computation would certainly be adequate.

LISTING 4-3   A demonstration of arithmetic with `Integer` objects and primitive integers

```java
/** AgeDifference.java by F. M. Carrano
    Reads the ages of two people and displays the difference.
*/
import java.util.Scanner;
public class AgeDifference
{
    public static void main(String[] args)
    {
        Scanner keyboard = new Scanner(System.in);
        System.out.print("What is his age? ");
        int hisAge = keyboard.nextInt();

        System.out.print("What is her age? ");
        Integer herAge = keyboard.nextInt();

        Integer ageDifference = Math.abs(hisAge - herAge);
        System.out.println("He is " + hisAge + ", she is " + herAge +
                           ": a difference of " + ageDifference + ".");
    } // end main
} // end AutoBox
```

Sample Output

```
What is his age? 18
What is her age? 21
He is 18, she is 21: a difference of 3.
```

4.48   Figure 4-6 lists the other wrapper classes available in the Java Class Library. The classes that represent numeric values have methods analogous to those in the class `Integer`. The constants `MAX_VALUE` and `MIN_VALUE`, along with methods such as `parseInt`, are what you likely will use from these classes.

The class `Character` has some other useful methods that convert between uppercase and lowercase letters. You use the name of the class to invoke these methods. For example, if `ch` is a `char` variable, the expression

    Character.toUpperCase(ch)

returns the uppercase version of the letter in `ch`. If `ch` does not contain a letter, the expression returns `ch` unchanged. The method `toLowerCase` behaves in an analogous fashion.

`Character` also contains methods such as `isUpperCase`, `isLowerCase`, `isLetter`, and `isDigit` that test the nature of the character passed as an argument. For example, `isLetter(ch)` returns `true` if `ch` contains a letter.

FIGURE 4-6   Wrapper classes in the Java Class Library

Wrapper Class	Primitive Data Type
Boolean	boolean
Byte	byte
Character	char
Double	double
Float	float
Integer	int
Long	long
Short	short

Question 20 Suppose that the user types an integer as input to the following statement:

```
String input = keyboard.next();
```

What statement will extract the int value from the string input?

Question 21 The wrapper class Double is analogous to the class Integer. It has comparable methods and constants.

   a.   Define a Double object whose value is 12.8.
   b.   Display the largest possible double value.

The Class Random

4.49   Applications such as games, lotteries, and simulations depend upon numbers that are chosen at random. Since computers are programmed, we cannot expect them to produce truly random numbers. Instead we can create a sequence of numbers that does not repeat itself for a very long time. The numbers within any portion of this long sequence will appear to be random. Such numbers are called **pseudorandom numbers**, but we simply will call them random numbers.

   To begin a sequence of random numbers, you take some number—called the **seed**—from which you create the first random number. The seed could be the time of day or a number that the user provides, for example. If today you use a **random number generator** with a given seed to produce a sequence of *n* random numbers and tomorrow you use the same generator with the same seed to produce another sequence of *n* random numbers, the two sequences will be identical.

4.50   The package java.util within the Java Class Library contains the class Random that you can use to produce random numbers. An object of this class is a random number generator. You create such an object by writing a statement like

```
Random generator = new Random();
```

The seed of this random number generator is the time of day at which the statement executes, given in milliseconds.

Once you have created the generator object, you can use it any number of times to produce as many random numbers as you want. You can get random integers or random real numbers, as follows:

- `generator.nextInt()` returns a random integer of type `int`
- `generator.nextInt(n)` returns a random integer of type `int` that is greater than or equal to zero and less than n for a positive integer n
- `generator.nextDouble()` returns a random integer of type `double` that is greater than or equal to zero and less than 1

Note that the expression `Math.random()`, which we mentioned in the previous chapter, is equivalent to `generator.nextDouble()`. The first time `Math.random()` executes, a random number generator is created for you, and it is then used whenever you call `random`.

4.51   Listing 4-4 contains a program that demonstrates random numbers.

LISTING 4-4   Ways to generate random numbers

```java
/** RandomDemo.java by F. M. Carrano
    Demonstrates various ways to generate random numbers.
*/
import java.util.Random;

public class RandomDemo
{
    public static void main(String[] args)
    {
        Random generator = new Random();

        System.out.println("Two random integers:");
        int randomOne = generator.nextInt();
        int randomTwo = generator.nextInt();
        System.out.println(randomOne + "\n" + randomTwo + "\n");

        System.out.println("Two random integers that range from 0 to 6:");
        randomOne = generator.nextInt(7);
        randomTwo = generator.nextInt(7);
        System.out.println(randomOne + "\n" + randomTwo + "\n");

        System.out.println("Two random integers that range from 1 to 7:");
        randomOne = generator.nextInt(7) + 1;
        randomTwo = generator.nextInt(7) + 1;
        System.out.println(randomOne + "\n" + randomTwo + "\n");

        System.out.println("Three random real numbers that range " +
                           "from 0 to 0.999999999999999:");
        double realOne = generator.nextDouble();
        double realTwo = generator.nextDouble();
        double realThree = Math.random();
```

```
                System.out.println(realOne + "\n" + realTwo + "\n" +
                                   realThree + "\n");

                System.out.println("Two random real numbers that range " +
                                   "from 0 to 9.999999999999999:");
                realOne = 10 * generator.nextDouble();
                realTwo = 10 * generator.nextDouble();
                System.out.println(realOne + "\n" + realTwo + "\n");
        } // end main
} // end RandomDemo
```

Sample Output

```
    Two random integers:
    -818811660
    326079784

    Two random integers that range from 0 to 6:
    4
    5

    Two random integers that range from 1 to 7:
    6
    3

    Three random real numbers that range from 0 to 0.9999999999999999:
    0.7646410531137952
    0.4896647454209514
    0.8283467894955164

    Two random real numbers that range from 0 to 9.999999999999999:
    7.98994917249062
    2.938984865614466
```

Question 22 Suppose that m and n are two integers such that $m < n$. What expression will generate a random integer that ranges from m to n?

The Class **DecimalFormat**

Up to now, you have had little control over the **format** of output from println statements. For example, when you display a real value, the number of places shown after the decimal point is left to the system to choose. Sometimes that is good enough, but other times you always want a certain number of digits to appear. We'll look at a class in the Java Class Library that can help you produce the output that you desire.

4.52   The class DecimalFormat, in the package java.text of the Java Class Library, allows you to create a pattern that describes the desired format of a real number or an integer. The pattern is a string that you pass to the class's constructor as its argument. It is composed of the following characters:

- 0 represents a digit; leading and trailing zeros appear in the output.
- # represents a digit, but leading and trailing zeros do not appear in the output.
- % at the beginning or end of the pattern multiplies the value of the entire number by 100 and displays it as a percentage.

- • $ at the beginning of the pattern displays as a dollar sign.
- • - displays as a minus sign.
- • . displays as a decimal point.

After you create an object of type `DecimalFormat`, you use the object when invoking the method `format`, passing it the value that you want to format. The result is a string suitable as the argument to `println`.

4.53 **Example**. If `value` is a `double` variable whose value is 0.1, the statements

```
DecimalFormat formatter = new DecimalFormat("0.000");
System.out.println(formatter.format(value));
```

display

```
0.100
```

If you change the pattern to `"0.###"`, the output from these statements is

```
0.1
```

If you use the pattern `"0.0%"`, the output is

```
10.0%
```

Finally, if you use the pattern `"$0.00"`, the output is

```
$0.10
```

4.54 Figure 4-7 gives some examples of the output that results for various values and patterns.

 FIGURE 4-7   Examples of patterns used with the class `DecimalFormat`

Pattern	Value	Output
0.00	0.1	0.10
0.00	12.10	12.10
0.00	22	22.00
0.##	0.1	0.1
0.##	12.10	12.1
0.##	22	22
0.##	0.159	0.16
#.00	0.1	.10
#.00	12.10	12.10

Pattern	Value	Output
00.##	5.1	05.1
0.0%	0.16	16.0%
0.0%	0.165	16.5%
#.#%	0.16	16%
#.#%	0.165	16.5%
$0.00	20.16	$20.16
$0.00	20.5	$20.50

 Question 23 What `import` statement would you write for a program that uses the class `DecimalFormat`?

Question 24 What is displayed by the following statements?

```
DecimalFormat formatter = new DecimalFormat("#.00%");
System.out.println(formatter.format(0.15));
System.out.println(formatter.format(9.106));
System.out.println(formatter.format(30.007));
```

■ The Class **JOptionPane**

So far, we have written console applications that used the class Scanner to read input and the class System.out to display textual output. Instead, we can create a simple graphical user interface (GUI) using the class JOptionPane, which is in the package Swing. With this GUI, the communication between the user and the program uses strings and dialog boxes. A **dialog box** is a small window that either provides information for the user or requests input.

Using a Dialog Box to Read or Write a String

4.55   **Reading a string.** A simple way to read a string that the user types at the keyboard is to use a dialog box. This window contains a prompt, some space in which to type the input data, and a button to signal the end of the input.

To create a dialog box for input, you call the method showInputDialog of the class JOptionPane. You pass the method a string that serves as a prompt for the user, and the method returns the string that the user types. For example, if you wanted the user's name as a string, you could write the following statement:

```
String userName =
        JOptionPane.showInputDialog("Please type your name.");
```

The method showInputDialog displays a dialog box that is titled "Input" and contains both the message that was passed to it and a place for the user to type input data, as Figure 4-8 shows. The user then types input data at the position of the cursor and clicks the OK button. At that point, the dialog box disappears and the string that the user typed is returned and assigned to the variable userName.

FIGURE 4-8   An input dialog box

4.56   Suppose that you wanted to read an integer instead of a string. Although the user input is always read as a string, you can extract any numeric data by using a method from an appropriate wrapper class. Earlier in this chapter, Segment 4.44 showed how to extract an integer from a string. We will use that technique here.

For example, to read the user's age, you could write

```
String input = JOptionPane.showInputDialog("Please type your age.");
```

The user would see a dialog box similar to the one in Figure 4-8, but with a different prompt. After the user types his or her age as an integer and clicks OK, the data is read as a string and assigned to the variable input. If the user typed 21, for instance, input would contain the string "21". We now need to convert the string representation of 21 to an integer of type int. The following statement performs this task for us:

```
int age = Integer.parseInt(input);
```

To read a real number, such as the radius of a circle, you could write the following statements:

```
String input = JOptionPane.showInputDialog("Enter the circle's radius.");
double radius = Double.parseDouble(input);
```

4.57   **Displaying a string.** You also can use a dialog box to display a string. Instead of writing a statement like

```
System.out.println("I am " + myAge + " years old.");
```

to display the value of the integer variable myAge, you can write

```
JOptionPane.showMessageDialog(null, "I am " + myAge + " years old.");
```

The method showMessageDialog displays a dialog box that is titled "Message" and contains the string that was passed to it as an argument, as Figure 4-9 shows. Although myAge is not a string, its value is converted to a string, since it is joined to a string by the + operator, just as it would be when used with the method System.out.println.

FIGURE 4-9   An output dialog box

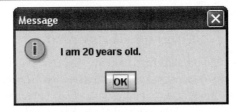

The first argument for this method specifies the window in which the dialog box will be displayed. By writing null for this argument, we indicate a default window. Notice that the method showInputDialog has one argument and assumes a default window.

4.58   **Ending execution.** When using a dialog box in your program, execution will continue even after the last statement in the main method has executed. The reason for this has to do with threads, which we introduced in the previous debugging interlude. Recall that a thread is a single sequential flow of logic within a program. A program can have several threads that can execute simultaneously. The thread that controls the input operation associated with a dialog box does not terminate unless you execute the statement

```
System.exit(0);
```

The zero is a code that indicates normal termination.

4.59   **A sample program.** Listing 4-5 shows a complete program that computes the area of a circle. Notice the import statement for the class JOptionPane, which is in the package javax.swing. You will learn more about the classes in this package in the next chapter.

LISTING 4-5   Using dialog boxes

```java
/** CircleArea.java by F. M. Carrano
    Demonstrates the use of an input dialog box in computing
    the area of a circle.
*/
import javax.swing.JOptionPane;
import java.text.DecimalFormat;

public class CircleArea
{
   public static void main(String[] args)
   {
      String input = JOptionPane.showInputDialog("Enter the circle's " +
                                                 "radius.");
      double radius = Double.parseDouble(input);
      double area = Math.PI * Math.pow(radius, 2);
      JOptionPane.showMessageDialog(null, "A circle whose radius is " +
                            radius + " has an area of " +
                            new DecimalFormat("0.##").format(area));

      System.exit(0);
   } // end main
} // end CircleArea
```

Sample Output

Input

? Enter the circle's radius.

2.8

OK   Cancel

Message

ⓘ A circle whose radius is 2.8 has an area of 24.63

OK

---

videonote
A problem
solved

Note: Using a dialog box for input or output is relatively easy. When used sparingly, dialog boxes provide a reasonable user interface. However, a barrage of dialog boxes can be annoying for a user. Other ways exist to create a graphical user interface.

CHAPTER SUMMARY

- The Java Class Library, which contains a collection of standard classes that you can use in your programs, is organized into packages of classes.

- You use the operator `new` to create a new object of a class type.

- A variable of a primitive data type contains the actual value of the data it represents. A variable of a class type contains a reference to the object that it represents.

- Characters within strings are represented by Unicode values.

- Certain escape characters are written as two characters. For example, the new-line character is \n.

- Methods within the class `String` enable you to manipulate strings. For example, you can join two strings end to end, get the length of a string, get the character at a certain position, locate a substring, and compare strings.

- You can use the class `Scanner` to extract tokens from a string that is either defined in your program or read as data. By default, white space separates the tokens, but you can define other characters as delimiters.

- An object of the class `Date` represents the time that it was created. You can compare two such objects and decide which one represents the earlier time.

- The class `BigDecimal` provides accurate decimal arithmetic with arbitrarily large numbers.

- A wrapper class such as `Integer` represents primitive data as an object. `Integer` contains the method `parseInt` that converts a string containing an integer to an `int`. It also defines constants that represent the minimum and maximum values of an `int` value.

- The class `Random` enables you to generate random numbers.

- The class `DecimalFormat` enables you to format the output of a real number or an integer according to a pattern that you create.

- You can use a dialog box to read a string from the user. If the string represents numeric data, you can convert it to an appropriate primitive type by using a method, such as `parseInt` or `parseDouble`, from a wrapper class. You also can use a dialog box to display a string.

- When using a dialog box in a program, you must use the method `System.exit` to terminate execution.

EXERCISES

1. What does it mean to instantiate an object?

2. What is a reference variable? How does it relate to an alias?

3. Display the following tabbed heading by using one `println` statement.
   ```
   Name     Address    City    State    Zip
   ```

4. In the expression `one.concat(two)`, what object is the receiving object?

5. What do the following statements display?

   ```
   String data = "54 Long Street";
   Scanner scan = new Scanner(data);
   System.out.println(scan.next());
   ```

6. What is the difference in meaning between the following two statements?

```
import java.util.Date;
import java.util.*;
```

7. Write statements that

   a. Define a `Date` object.
   b. Define a string that contains only the date portion of the `Date` object. For example, if the `String` representation of the `Date` object is `"Wed Jul 30 16:19:38 EDT 2010"`, define the string `"Jul 30, 2010"`.
   c. Define a string that contains only the time portion of the `Date` object.

8. When constructing a `BigDecimal` object, why is it desirable to pass the constructor a string that represents the numeric value?

9. By consulting the online documentation of the Java Class Library for the class `BigDecimal`, answer the following questions:

   a. What constructor would you use to construct a `BigDecimal` object from a string that is rounded toward positive infinity?
   b. What method would you use to convert a `BigDecimal` object to a floating-point value?
   c. What method would you use to move the decimal point of a `BigDecimal` object two places to the left?

10. Why is the method `equals` provided for the wrapper classes in the Java Class Library?

11. Complete the following table of maximum and minimum values for the wrapper classes:

Wrapper Class	MAX_VALUE	MIN_VALUE
Byte	$2^7 - 1$	-2^7
Character		
Double		
Float		
Integer		
Long		
Short		

12. After consulting the online documentation for the class `JOptionPane` in the Java Class Library, describe the differences among the methods `showConfirmDialog`, `showInputDialog`, and `showMessageDialog`.

13. Given a `Random` object called rand, what does the call `rand.nextDouble()` return?

14. What do the following statements display?

```
System.out.println(Integer.parseInt("17"));
System.out.println(Integer.parseInt("17", 10));
System.out.println(Integer.parseInt("17", 16));
```

15. Why must numeric input read from an input dialog box be parsed?

16. The program in Listing 4-1 uses the method `nextLine` to read the first and last names of a person. Revise the program using the method `next` instead of `nextLine` to read the first and last names into separate variables. Your revised program should produce the same output as the original program in Listing 4-1.

17. Many programs convert the information provided by the user to a consistent format. For example, we could require all data that is read to be converted to uppercase. Create a Java program that reads, converts to uppercase, and displays a person's name and full address.

18. Write a program that displays a tree, such as the following one, using text characters:

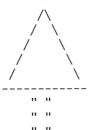

Remember to use escape sequences to display the characters \ and the ".

19. Write a Java program using the methods of the class JOptionPane to read a string containing an e-mail address. The string must begin as "My e-mail address is " and be followed by an e-mail address. Extract the e-mail address from the string using methods of the class Scanner, and display it using the methods of the class JOptionPane. Demonstrate that only bob@bob.com is extracted from the string "My e-mail address is bob@bob.com".

20. Write a program that generates and displays five random numbers within the range 0.0 to 1.0. Allow the user to provide the seed. Display the random numbers with four digits after the decimal point.

PROJECTS

1. Write a program that displays a random integer that lies within the range of two given integers. Include the given integers as possible values for the random integer. Ask the user to give the smaller of the two integers first. Use JOptionPane for all input and output.

2. Write a program that asks the user for two BigDecimal values and then displays the results when the given values are used with the BigDecimal methods add, subtract, multiply, divide, toString, equals, and compareTo. For example, your program's output might appear as follows:

```
This program displays the result of calls to various BigDecimal methods.

Enter your first BigDecimal number: 3.0
Enter your second BigDecimal number: 5.0

3 + 5 = 8
3 - 5 = -2
3 * 5 = 15
3 / 5 = 0.6
3.toString() is 3
5.toString() is 5
3.equals(5) is false
3.compareTo(5) is -1
```

3. A language game is an alteration of spoken words to make them incomprehensible to an untrained ear. Pig Latin is an example of such a game played on the English language. The first letter of a given word is moved to the end of the word and then followed by "ay." If the first letter is originally a capital letter, it is replaced by its lowercase. For example, Smart becomes martsay, and Java becomes avajay. Write a program that converts any given English word to Pig Latin.

4. Write a program that computes and displays the volume of ice cream that an ice cream cone can hold. Assume that the cone is entirely full of ice cream and has no scoops of ice cream on top. Ask the user for the height of the cone and the radius of its top. Use JOptionPane for all input and output. Format your decimal results to have two decimal places without leading and trailing zeros. The volume of a cone of height h and radius r is $\pi\, r^2\, h\, /\, 3$.

5. Augment the previous project by allowing optional scoops of ice cream on top of the cone in addition to all the ice cream in the cone itself. Assume that each scoop is perfectly spherical. The volume of a sphere of radius r is $4\pi r^3 / 3$.

6. Write a Java program that encodes a string supplied by the user. Replace all letters *a* with *@*, all letters *e* with *#*, all letters *i* with *!*, all letters *o* with *&*, and all letters *u* with *%*. Demonstrate that the string "It is a beautiful day in the neighborhood." is encoded as "!t !s @ b#@%t!f%l d@y !n th# n#!ghb&rh&&d."

ANSWERS TO SELF-TEST QUESTIONS

1.
```
String first = new String("Joe");
String last = "Java";
```

2.
```
System.out.println("During the first telephone call, " +
                   "Alexander Graham Bell said\n" +
                   "\"Watson, come here!\"");
```

3.
```
fullName = first + " " + last;
```

4.
```
nameLength = fullName.length();
```

5.
```
fullName = first.concat(" ")
fullName = fullName.concat(last);
```

6. If `fullName` contains "Joe Java", for example, `fullName.toLowerCase()` returns the string "joe java".

7. The string referenced by `line` is unchanged and contains "   Along came a spider,   ".

8. The string referenced by `trimmedLine` is unchanged.

9.
```
String myName = "Jill Java";
char firstInitial = myName.charAt(0);
char lastInitial = myName.charAt(5);
```

10. A single comma is displayed.

11. The first occurrence of the substring "a" is at index 7, so the expression has a value of 7. Remember that "a" is different from "A".

12.
```
spaceIndex = phrase.indexOf(" ");
```

13.
```
int spaceIndex = phrase.indexOf(" ");
String first = phrase.substring(0, spaceIndex);
String second = phrase.substring(spaceIndex + 1);
```

14. **a.** False.
    b. A negative integer.

15. In Listing 4-1, replace the statements between the first `print` statement and the assignment to `nameLength` with the following statements:
```
String firstName = keyboard.next();
firstName = firstName.trim();
String lastName = keyboard.next();
lastName = lastName.trim();
```

16.
```
Scanner keyboard = new Scanner(System.in);
keyboard.useDelimiter("/");
System.out.println(keyboard.next());
System.out.println(keyboard.next());
```

17. Its memory is recycled during garbage collection.

18.
```java
import java.util.Date;
public class Q18
{
    public static void main(String[] args)
    {
        Date dateAndTime1 = new Date();
        Date dateAndTime2 = new Date();
        System.out.println("First date and time is " +
                        dateAndTime1);
        System.out.println("Second date and time is " +
                        dateAndTime2);
        Date dateAndTime3 = new Date();
        System.out.println("Third date and time is " +
                        dateAndTime3);
        System.out.println("   " +
                dateAndTime2.before(dateAndTime3)); // true
        System.out.println("   " +
                dateAndTime2.after(dateAndTime3));   // false
        System.out.println("   " +
                dateAndTime2.compareTo(dateAndTime3)); // < 0
        System.out.println("   " +
                dateAndTime2.equals(dateAndTime3));   // false
        System.out.println("   " +
                dateAndTime2.equals(dateAndTime1));   // true
    } // end main
} // end Q18
```

19.
```java
BigDecimal base1 = new BigDecimal("5.4");
BigDecimal base2 = new BigDecimal("10.2");
Scanner keyboard = new Scanner(System.in);
System.out.print("Enter the height of the trapezoid: ");
BigDecimal height = keyboard.nextBigDecimal();
BigDecimal area = base1.add(base2);
area = area.multiply(height);
area = area.divide(new BigDecimal(2));
```

20.
```java
int value = Integer.parseInt(input);
```

21. **a.** Any one of the following statements will define the object:
```java
Double doubleObject = 12.8;
Double doubleObject = new Double(12.8);
Double doubleObject = new Double("12.8");
```

b. `System.out.println(Double.MAX_VALUE);`

22. `generator.nextInt(n - m + 1) + m`

23. `import java.text.DecimalFormat;`

24.
```
15.00%
910.60%
3000.70%
```

Chapter 5

Basic Graphics

Contents

Prerequisites

Objectives

After studying this chapter, you should be able to

• Write an application program that creates a window in which you can display graphics
• Display lines, rectangles, ovals, arcs, and strings in a window
• Use color in your graphic displays
• Use the method setFont to change the font that the Graphics method drawString uses to display text

U p to now, the programs in this book have been applications that display text as their output. We now will produce output that is graphical instead of textual. The tools we need are all contained in the standard Java Class Library. Thus, this chapter, like the previous one, continues to give examples of standard classes, their methods, and objects of those classes. With an increased understanding of these concepts, you will be ready to define your own classes in the next chapter.

As we progress through this book, we will use graphics from time to time to reinforce previous concepts in a visual and, hopefully, interesting way.

■ Creating a Window

videonote
Basic
graphical concepts

5.1   In computing, a **window** is any rectangular area that is a part of a user interface. A user can interact with a window by either providing data to a program or viewing textual or graphical output from a program. A **primary window** is an application's main window in which a user interacts with the application. Applications can have several primary windows, and a primary window can have several **secondary windows**, such as a dialog box.

A **frame** is an object that represents a primary window. Figure 5-1 shows an empty frame like the one we soon will create and display. A frame has a border—called the **title bar**—at its top that can contain a title and typically has buttons, such as a close button. The title bar is included in the overall size of the frame, and so reduces the area in which you can draw.

FIGURE 5-1   An empty frame

5.2   To create a frame, we construct an object of the standard class `JFrame`, which is in the package Swing. For example, the following statement creates a `JFrame` object and names it `aWindow`:

```
JFrame aWindow = new JFrame();
```

In other words, the statement instantiates a new object of the class `JFrame` by implicitly invoking `JFrame`'s constructor. At this point, the frame is empty and invisible; it has a blank title, and its height and width are each zero. We will use methods in the class `JFrame` to change these characteristics. Such methods are analogous to methods in the class `String`, which the previous chapter describes, in that you use an object like `aWindow` to invoke them, and you pass arguments to some of them.

The dimensions of a frame are given in terms of **pixels**, which are points of light that are evenly spaced in a rectangular grid within the frame. The statement

```
aWindow.setSize(300, 200); // width, height in pixels
```

gives our frame `aWindow` a width of 300 pixels and a height of 200 pixels. Remember that the actual area in which you can draw has smaller dimensions because of the title bar.

Clicking on the rightmost button in the title bar shown in Figure 5-1 closes the frame. However, your program will continue to run, even though you cannot see the frame. If you want the close button to end the execution of your program *and* close the frame, you must include the following statement:

```
aWindow.setDefaultCloseOperation(JFrame.EXIT_ON_CLOSE);
```

The `JFrame` method `setDefaultCloseOperation` specifies what action occurs when the user closes the frame. The constant `EXIT_ON_CLOSE`, which also is defined in the class `JFrame`, indicates that the application should exit. Three other actions can be specified by using other constants; however, we will not explore those possibilities.

As an option, we can place a title in the frame's title bar by calling JFrame's method setTitle. For example, to set the title shown in Figure 5-1, we would write

```
aWindow.setTitle("My Empty Window");
```

Finally, we need to make the frame visible by calling another method in JFrame, as follows:

```
aWindow.setVisible(true);
```

Incidentally, changing true to false hides the frame.

5.3   Listing 5-1 summarizes the steps we have just taken, within the context of a simple program, to create and display the empty frame shown in Figure 5-1.

LISTING 5-1   Creating and displaying an empty frame

```java
import javax.swing.JFrame;
public class EmptyWindow
{
    public static void main(String[] args)
    {
        JFrame aWindow = new JFrame();          // new empty invisible frame
        aWindow.setSize(300, 200);              // width and height in pixels
        aWindow.setDefaultCloseOperation(JFrame.EXIT_ON_CLOSE);
        aWindow.setTitle("My Empty Window"); // optional title
        aWindow.setVisible(true);               // make window visible
    } // end main
} // end EmptyWindow
```

Getting Ready to Draw

5.4   Unfortunately, we cannot draw directly on a frame. That is, we cannot draw on a JFrame object. A frame is really a kind of object known as a **container**. As its name implies, a container contains other objects. Thus, we must create a different object on which we can draw, and then add that object to our frame. One such object is called a **panel** and is an instance of the class JPanel, which is another standard class in the Swing package. You can think of a panel as the canvas on which we will draw and paint.

If we were to create a panel by writing, for example,

```
JPanel drawing = new JPanel();
```

it would be blank. We need to modify JPanel so that it displays our desired drawing. To do that, we need to define a new class. You will learn much more about writing your own classes in the next chapter, but we don't need all those details right now.

Question 1 Consider the Java statement that creates a panel in the previous segment.

    a. What is the data type of the variable drawing?
    b. What does drawing reference?
    c. What process creates an object of JPanel?
    d. During the process of creating an object of JPanel, what special method of JPanel is invoked?

5.5   Our new class—let's name it `DrawingPanel`—will have the following form:

```
public class DrawingPanel extends JPanel
{
   public void paintComponent(Graphics pen)
   {
      < Statements that draw go here. >
   } // end paintComponent
} // end DrawingPanel
```

The method `paintComponent` is responsible for painting the panel's background and any other drawings that you want to display. The statements within this method will call other methods defined in the standard class `Graphics`, which is included in the Java Class Library. The class `Graphics` is a part of the Abstract Window Toolkit (AWT) and provides basic support for graphics.

A Sample Drawing Panel

5.6   Listing 5-2 contains a complete definition of our new class, `DrawingPanel`. We are using two classes from the Java Class Library, `JPanel` and `Graphics`. We know that `JPanel` is in the Swing package and `Graphics` is in the package AWT. The `import` statements indicate these facts by using the actual package names, `javax.swing` and `java.awt`, respectively.

`DrawingPanel` builds upon, or **extends**, the class `JPanel`. This feature of Java is known as **inheritance**, whereby one class inherits the attributes and capabilities of another class. Later chapters in this book discuss inheritance in detail. In the meantime, we will use inheritance intuitively as we explore aspects of Java's graphics features.

LISTING 5-2   A panel that contains drawings of some basic shapes

```
import java.awt.Graphics;
import javax.swing.JPanel;

/** DrawingPanel.java by F. M. Carrano
    Demonstrates a panel containing some of the shapes we can draw.
*/
public class DrawingPanel extends JPanel
{
   public void paintComponent(Graphics pen)
   {
      // draw outlines of four shapes
      pen.drawRect(50,  50, 20, 20);        // square
      pen.drawRect(100, 50, 40, 20);        // rectangle
      pen.drawOval(200, 50, 20, 20);        // circle
      pen.drawOval(250, 50, 40, 20);        // oval

      // draw text
      pen.drawString("Square",    50,  90);
      pen.drawString("Rectangle", 100, 90);
      pen.drawString("Circle",    200, 90);
      pen.drawString("Oval",      250, 90);
```

```
      // paint areas of four shapes
      pen.fillRect(50,   100, 20, 20);           // square
      pen.fillRect(100, 100, 40, 20);            // rectangle
      pen.fillOval(200, 100, 20, 20);            // circle
      pen.fillOval(250, 100, 40, 20);            // oval

      // draw a line
      pen.drawLine(50, 150, 300, 150);           // line

      // draw an arc; paint the area of an arc
      pen.drawArc(50,   150, 250, 100, 0, 180); // arc
      pen.fillArc(100, 175, 200, 75,   90, 45); // arc
   } // end paintComponent
} // end DrawingPanel
```

Displaying a Panel

5.7   We now create a frame, as we did in Listing 5-1, and add an instance of our class DrawingPanel so that we can see the results of our drawing. Listing 5-3 contains a Java program that accomplishes these steps. We simply added the following two statements to those in Listing 5-1:

```
DrawingPanel panel = new DrawingPanel();
aWindow.add(panel);
```

The first of these statements creates an instance of our class DrawingPanel and names it panel. We then use the method add from the class JFrame to add the panel to the frame aWindow.

LISTING 5-3   A program that creates and displays a frame containing an
                   instance of DrawingPanel (Listing 5-2)

```
import javax.swing.JFrame;

/** DrawingSamples.java by F. M. Carrano
    Displays in a frame a panel demonstrating some of the shapes
    we can draw.
*/
public class DrawingSamples
{
   public static void main(String[] args)
   {
      JFrame aWindow = new JFrame();
      aWindow.setSize(350, 300); // width x height
      aWindow.setDefaultCloseOperation(JFrame.EXIT_ON_CLOSE);
      aWindow.setTitle("Samples of shapes we can draw");

      DrawingPanel panel = new DrawingPanel();
      aWindow.add(panel);
```

```
        aWindow.setVisible(true);
    } // end main
} // end DrawingSamples
```

Output

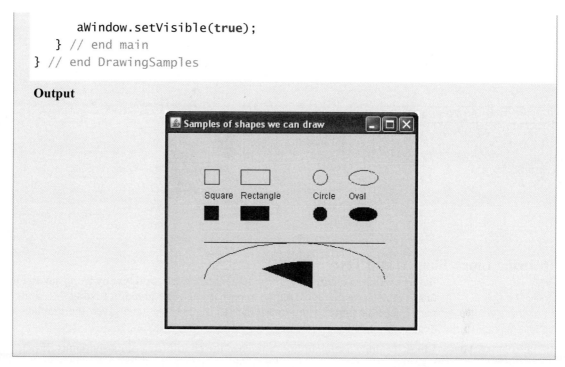

5.8   You can see the results of the calls to the Graphics methods. We'll explain these methods in the next section; for now, you should notice that we did not invoke the method paintComponent, which contains all the calls to the Graphics methods. What is going on?

The method paintComponent is invoked by the system automatically. How did the system know the name of the method paintComponent? The Java designers chose this name. The Java system contains a call to paintComponent, and we simply supplied its definition. If we had omitted a definition or given the method another name, our program would not work correctly. We did make one simplification in this definition, but we'll take care of that later. For now, don't worry about it!

Let's now turn to the details of the Graphics methods that we used to draw and fill the shapes.

■ The Class **Graphics**

An object of the class Graphics is called the **graphics context**, because it represents such attributes as the color of the drawing, the font of any text that is drawn, and so on. The Java runtime environment creates such an object and passes it to the method paintComponent when the system calls this method. Thus, within paintComponent you can use the methods of the Graphics object to display various shapes. Before we examine these methods, we need to consider the coordinate system that a typical graphics program uses.

The Coordinate System

5.9   You can display graphics within a panel or other **component** that is rectangular. The origin of the coordinate system is at the upper left corner of the component. The x-axis extends to the right from the origin along the top of the component. The y-axis extends downward from the origin along the left edge of the component. Each point then has an x- and a y-coordinate. As you move to the right, the x-coordinate increases, and as you move down, the y-coordinate increases. Figure 5-2 shows the axes, the origin (0, 0), and the point at the coordinates (5, 3). Coordinates are always given as a pair of integers, with the x-coordinate listed first, and represent a number of pixels. Thus, the point at (5, 3) is five pixels to the right of and three pixels below the origin.

FIGURE 5-2   The axes and some points in the coordinate system used for graphics

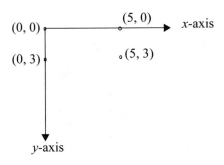

Drawing Lines, Shapes, and Text

In this section, we will draw lines, rectangles, ovals, and text by using several methods in the class Graphics. These methods, which appear in the code given in Listing 5-2, draw by using an imaginary **graphics pen**. To remind ourselves of this, we have given the graphics context, which is a Graphics object, the name pen.

5.10   **Lines.** To draw a straight line, you need the coordinates of its endpoints. If (x1, y1) and (x2, y2) are these coordinates, and pen is the graphics context, the following statement draws the desired line:

```
pen.drawLine(x1, y1, x2, y2);
```

The line is drawn in the current pen color, which by default is black. We will change this color later in the chapter.

5.11   **Rectangles and squares.** To draw a rectangle, you specify the coordinates of its upper left corner followed by its dimensions. The rectangle's width is given before its height. These dimensions are integers. So to draw a rectangle whose upper left corner is at the point (x, y) and whose dimensions are width and height, you write the following statement:

```
pen.drawRect(x, y, width, height);
```

The left and right edges of the rectangle have x-coordinates of x and x + width, respectively. Each of these edges involves height + 1 pixels. The top and bottom edges have y-coordinates of y and y + height, respectively, and involve width + 1 pixels each. Figure 5-3 is an expanded view of the pixels that are on the edges of a rectangle whose width is 5 and height is 4. Note the coordinates of the rectangle's corners.

To draw a square, you use drawRect with the width equal to the height.

FIGURE 5-3   The pixels on the edges of a rectangle whose width is 5 and
                  height is 4, as drawn by drawRect

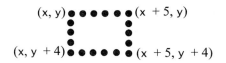

5.12 **Ovals and circles.** To draw an oval, you describe an imaginary rectangle that encloses the oval as tightly as possible, as shown in Figure 5-4. You provide to the method `drawOval`, the coordinates of the rectangle's upper left corner, and also its dimensions. Thus, the statement

```
pen.drawOval(x, y, width, height);
```

draws an oval that just fits within the imaginary rectangle whose upper left corner has the coordinates (x, y) and whose dimensions are `width` and `height`.

To draw a circle, you call `drawOval` and give it the circle's diameter as both width and height.

FIGURE 5-4   The imaginary rectangle enclosing an oval that is drawn

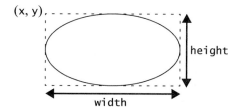

Question 2 Given the `Graphics` object `pen`, what Java statement will draw a square whose sides are 50 pixels each and whose upper left corner has the coordinates (100, 75)?

Question 3 What Java statement will draw a circle within the square you drew in the previous question? The edge of the circle should touch each side of the square.

Question 4 What Java statement will draw a circle whose radius is 50 pixels and whose center has the coordinates (75, 200)?

5.13 **Arcs.** An arc is a portion of an oval. You first specify the oval, as described in the previous segment. You then specify where the arc begins and its extent. Both of these specifications are given as angles in degrees. A horizontal line drawn from the center of the oval to the right edge of the oval is at zero degrees, as shown in Figure 5-5. Angles that are measured in a counterclockwise direction from this line have positive values, while angles measured in a clockwise direction have negative values. Note that the line at –45 degrees extends from the center of the oval through the lower right corner of the bounding rectangle.

Figure 5-5 shows an arc that begins at 40 degrees and extends for 50 degrees beyond its starting angle. To draw such an arc, you write

```
pen.drawArc(x, y, width, height, startAngle, extentAngle)
```

where the first four parameters describe the oval and the last two provide the arc's start angle and the angle of its extent. For example, the following statement draws the arc in Figure 5-5:

```
pen.drawArc(50, 200, 100, 75, 40, 50)
```

FIGURE 5-5   An arc as a piece of an oval, with its start and extent angles

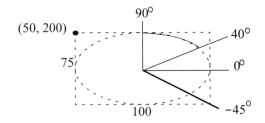

 Question 5 The arc in Figure 5-5 can be drawn by using either a negative starting angle or a negative extent angle. Give an example of a call to drawArc that uses one such angle.

5.14   **Strings.** You can display a string as printed text within the drawing area by using the method drawString. You provide the coordinates of the point at which you want the text to start. For example, the statement

```
pen.drawString("Java is great", 10, 20);
```

writes Java is great in a default font with the base of the first letter at the **base point** (10, 20). The rest of the string extends to the right of this point along a horizontal imaginary **baseline** whose *y*-coordinate is 20. Letters such as *g* will descend below this line, as Figure 5-6 illustrates.

FIGURE 5-6   Displayed text begins at a base point and extends along an
               imaginary baseline

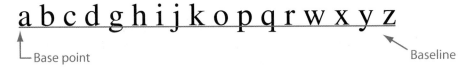

Painting Shapes

Previously, we saw the results of using the graphics pen to draw the outlines of rectangles and ovals. Here we will paint, or **fill**, rectangular and oval areas using the pen's current color. As before, the default color is black. We'll change this color in the next section.

5.15   **Rectangles and squares.** To fill a rectangular area, you specify its position and dimensions, much as you do for the method drawRect. That is, you specify the coordinates of a rectangle's upper left corner, its width, and its height. However, these dimensions have a slightly different meaning than they do for drawRect. For example, the statement

```
pen.fillRect(x, y, width, height);
```

fills a rectangular area whose upper left corner is at the point (x, y) and whose dimensions are width pixels by height pixels. The left and right edges of the rectangle have *x*-coordinates of x and x + width - 1. The top and bottom edges have *y*-coordinates of y and y + height - 1. Figure 5-7 shows an expanded view of the pixels that are in a rectangular area whose width is 5 and height is 4. Note the coordinates of the area's corners. Compare this figure with Figure 5-3.

To paint a square, you use fillRect with the width equal to the height.

FIGURE 5-7   The pixels in a rectangular area whose width is 5 and height is 4, as painted by fillRect

---

$$(x, y) \bullet \bullet \bullet \bullet \bullet (x + 4, y)$$
$$(x, y + 3) \bullet \bullet \bullet \bullet \bullet (x + 4, y + 3)$$

Note: The rectangular area that the statement

```
pen.fillRect(x, y, width, height);
```

fills does not include the bottom and right edges of the rectangle that is drawn by

```
pen.drawRect(x, y, width, height);
```

5.16   **Ovals and circles.** To fill an oval area, you describe an imaginary rectangular area that tightly encloses the oval. You provide the coordinates of the rectangle's upper left corner and its dimensions to the method fillOval. Thus, the statement

```
pen.fillOval(x, y, width, height);
```

fills an oval area within the rectangular area whose upper left corner is at the point (x, y) and whose dimensions are width and height.

To fill a circle, you call fillOval with the width the same as the height.

5.17   **Arcs.** As you learned in Segment 5.13, an arc is a portion of an oval that is bound by two lines originating at the oval's center, as shown previously in Figure 5-5. The area enclosed by these lines and the arc is filled by the method fillArc, as Figure 5-8 illustrates. The arguments are the same as those for the method drawArc.

FIGURE 5-8   A filled arc

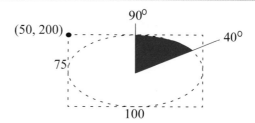

A Problem Solved: Displaying a Temperature

Write a program that draws a thermometer, such as the one shown in Figure 5-9, displaying a given temperature in both analog and digital form. The thermometer will register any temperature in the range 0 to 120 degrees Fahrenheit. Imagine that the temperature eventually will be read from a real thermometer. For now let's use a random number to simulate this data.

FIGURE 5-9   A thermometer

5.18   **Discussion.** For this discussion, "thermometer" will mean the entire picture shown in Figure 5-9, and "temperature column" will mean the thin vertical rectangle that indicates the temperature, including both the colored portion and the empty portion.

One key to a successful graphical design is to define named constants that describe the proposed drawing. Although this drawing is simple, beginning with a sketch that shows the meaning of these constants is a great help. Figure 5-10 shows such a sketch of a thermometer within a frame.

FIGURE 5-10   A schematic of our thermometer within a frame

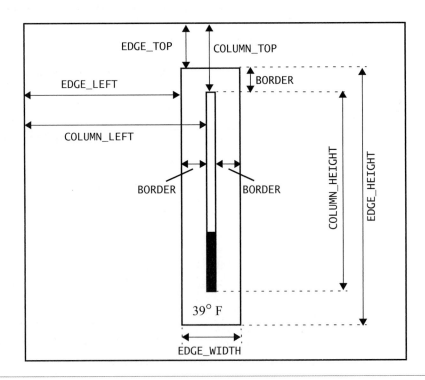

5.19   Now we can write some Java statements to define the named constants shown in the figure. We begin by positioning the upper left corner of the outer boundary, or edge, of the thermometer:

```java
final int EDGE_LEFT = 175;
final int EDGE_TOP  = 30;
```

To position the temperature column relative to the position of the entire thermometer, we first give a value to BORDER and then use it to define COLUMN_LEFT and COLUMN_TOP:

```java
final int BORDER = 20;       // distance between top/side edges and
                             // temperature column

final int COLUMN_LEFT = EDGE_LEFT + BORDER;
final int COLUMN_TOP  = EDGE_TOP  + BORDER;
```

As much as possible, the definition of a constant should show any dependence on other constants. For example, you can see that the temperature column is indented from the edges of the thermometer. More importantly, if you change the value of the border, for example, the value of the column coordinates—COLUMN_LEFT and COLUMN_TOP—will be computed for you. Such would not be the case if you gave these coordinates explicit values of 195 and 50, respectively.

Programming Tip
Many graphics programmers think in terms of left and top coordinates instead of *x*- and *y*-coordinates. Thinking this way is convenient for this problem.

5.20   Next, we give values to the dimensions of the temperature column and use them to compute the size of the thermometer:

```java
final int COLUMN_HEIGHT= 150;
final int COLUMN_WIDTH = 5;

final int EDGE_WIDTH = COLUMN_WIDTH + 2 * BORDER;
final int EDGE_HEIGHT = COLUMN_HEIGHT + (int)(2.5 * BORDER);
```

The value of EDGE_HEIGHT provides more room below the temperature column than above it to better accommodate the digital temperature reading.

5.21   **The solution.** The panel class containing the method paintComponent that solves this problem appears in Listing 5-4. The constants MIN_TEMPERATURE and MAX_TEMPERATURE specify the range of possible temperatures. Notice how we generate a random integer that lies within this range. Recall that Question 22 in Chapter 4 asked you to complete a similar task.

To get the height of the fluid in the temperature column—fluidHeight—we first compute the difference between the maximum and minimum temperatures and cast the result to double. Next, we form the ratio of the temperature and this difference. The earlier type cast avoids an integer division and its inherent truncation. We then multiply this ratio by the height of the temperature column to get the height of the filled rectangle that we will paint.

To display the temperature digitally, we have changed the font from its default setting. We discuss this aspect in the next section.

LISTING 5-4   A panel that draws a thermometer

```java
import java.awt.Font;
import java.awt.Graphics;
import javax.swing.JPanel;
import java.util.Random;
```

```java
/** ThermometerPanel.java by F. M. Carrano
    Represents a panel displaying a thermometer
    for a random temperature given in degrees Fahrenheit.
*/
public class ThermometerPanel extends JPanel
{
    public void paintComponent(Graphics pen)
    {
        final int BORDER = 20;      // distance between top/side edges and
                                    // temperature column
        final int EDGE_LEFT = 175;
        final int EDGE_TOP = 30;

        // temperature column geometry:
        final int COLUMN_LEFT = EDGE_LEFT + BORDER;
        final int COLUMN_TOP = EDGE_TOP + BORDER;
        final int COLUMN_HEIGHT= 150;
        final int COLUMN_WIDTH = 5;

        // thermometer dimensions
        final int EDGE_WIDTH = COLUMN_WIDTH + 2 * BORDER;
        final int EDGE_HEIGHT = COLUMN_HEIGHT + (int)(2.5 * BORDER);

        // key temperatures:
        final int MAX_TEMPERATURE = 120;
        final int MIN_TEMPERATURE = 0;

        // get temperature
        Random randomInteger = new Random();
        int temperature = randomInteger.nextInt(MAX_TEMPERATURE -
                          MIN_TEMPERATURE + 1) + MIN_TEMPERATURE;

        // paint fluid in temperature column
        double range = (double)(MAX_TEMPERATURE - MIN_TEMPERATURE);
        int fluidHeight = (int)(COLUMN_HEIGHT * temperature / range);
        int fluidTop = COLUMN_TOP + COLUMN_HEIGHT - fluidHeight;
        pen.fillRect(COLUMN_LEFT, fluidTop, COLUMN_WIDTH, fluidHeight);

        // draw edge of temperature column and the frame around it
        pen.drawRect(COLUMN_LEFT, COLUMN_TOP, COLUMN_WIDTH, COLUMN_HEIGHT);
        pen.drawRect(EDGE_LEFT, EDGE_TOP, EDGE_WIDTH, EDGE_HEIGHT);

        // show digital temperature
        int xLabel = COLUMN_LEFT - 2 * BORDER / 3;
        int yLabel = COLUMN_TOP + COLUMN_HEIGHT + BORDER;
        pen.setFont(new Font("Monospaced", Font.BOLD, 10));
        pen.drawString(temperature + "° F", xLabel, yLabel);
```

```
        } // end paintComponent
} // end ThermometerPanel
```

Programming Tip

Rather than passing an expression such as COLUMN_TOP + COLUMN_HEIGHT - fluidHeight to a method as an argument, assign it to a variable that can then become the argument. For example, the following statements appear in Listing 5-4:

```
int fluidTop = COLUMN_TOP + COLUMN_HEIGHT - fluidHeight;
pen.fillRect(COLUMN_LEFT, fluidTop, COLUMN_WIDTH, fluidHeight);
```

In this way, you document the meaning of the expression and make the call to the method easier to read and understand.

Question 6 In the statement that defines the constant EDGE_HEIGHT in Listing 5-4, why is the type cast necessary?

Question 7 In the statement that defines the variable range in Listing 5-4, what would happen if you omitted the type cast?

Question 8 In the statement that defines fluidHeight in Listing 5-4, why must the data type of range be double?

Question 9 In the statement that defines fluidHeight in Listing 5-4, why is the cast to int necessary? What would happen if you omitted it?

Question 10 In the statement that defines fluidHeight in Listing 5-4, what is the order of the operations in the expression COLUMN_HEIGHT * temperature / range?

5.22   The program in Listing 5-5 displays the thermometer by creating a frame and adding an instance of ThermometerPanel to this frame. The steps are much like those in the DrawingSamples program shown in Listing 5-3.

LISTING 5-5   A program that displays the thermometer panel defined in Listing 5-4

```java
import javax.swing.JFrame;

/** DisplayThermometer.java by F. M. Carrano
    Creates a frame that contains a thermometer panel.
*/
public class DisplayThermometer
{
    public static void main(String[] args)
    {
        final int WIDTH = 395;
        final int HEIGHT = 300;
        JFrame aWindow = new JFrame();
```

```
        aWindow.setSize(WIDTH, HEIGHT);
        aWindow.setDefaultCloseOperation(JFrame.EXIT_ON_CLOSE);
        aWindow.setTitle("Thermometer");

        ThermometerPanel panel = new ThermometerPanel();
        aWindow.add(panel);

        aWindow.setVisible(true);
    } // end main
} // end DisplayThermometer
```

Sample Output

Note: The dimensions of the frame

In Listing 5-5, we defined two named constants to specify the dimensions of the frame that will contain the thermometer panel. How did we arrive at the values for these constants? The sketch in Figure 5-10 shows the distance between the left edge of the frame and the left edge of the thermometer as the constant EDGE_LEFT. To center the thermometer between the left and right edges of the frame, we need the right edge of the frame to be EDGE_LEFT pixels from the right edge of the thermometer. The frame then should have a width of 2 * EDGE_LEFT + EDGE_WIDTH pixels. Since the values of EDGE_LEFT and EDGE_WIDTH are known only within the class ThermometerPanel, ideally the program DisplayThermometer in Listing 5-5 should be able to ask ThermometerPanel for its required frame width. You will learn how to do this in the next chapter. Meanwhile, we simply did the arithmetic and defined the constant WIDTH in DisplayThermometer. Similarly, we can find the frame height necessary to center the thermometer vertically. This computation is more involved, since the height of a frame includes the height of the title bar, which is platform dependent. However, the frame can give us the title-bar height after it is created. For now, we estimated the height of the title bar as 40 pixels when we defined the value of HEIGHT within DisplayThermometer.

Programming Tip

Changing the size of a frame by dragging its lower right corner has the effect of calling the method paintComponent again. As a result, the frame's content is redrawn. When paintComponent uses random numbers to affect the graphics, resizing a frame generates new random numbers. This action can help you debug your program.

Question 11 What Java expression, given in terms of constants defined by `ThermometerPanel`, will compute the height of the frame in which the thermometer will be centered vertically? Assume that the title bar is 40 pixels high.

The Class Font

videonote
Java classes for
graphical output

5.23   The class `Graphics` has a method `setFont` that sets the font for text that appears in a drawing, using the method `drawString`. You pass to `setFont` an object of the class `Font` that represents the desired font. This class is in the package `java.awt`.

To create a `Font` object, you write a statement such as

```
Font aFont = new Font(name, style, size);
```

where

- *name* is a string that gives the name of the font
- *style* is one of the integer constants `Font.BOLD`, `Font.PLAIN`, or `Font.ITALIC` that indicates the style of the font
- *size* is an integer, such as 10 or 12, that gives the point size of the font; the larger the point size, the larger the displayed characters

5.24   The name of the font that you choose can be either a physical name or a logical name. A **physical name** is the name of an actual font, such as Helvetica, Palatino, Times, Geneva, or Lucida. Using a physical font guarantees the appearance of your output, as long as the computer in question has that font available. A **logical name** is the name of one of five font families: Serif, SansSerif, Monospaced, Dialog, and DialogInput. Each family is associated with a physical font installed on the computer running your application. With a logical name, you do not have absolute control over the appearance of your output, but you know that your program will work. Figure 5-11 shows the names of some physical and logical fonts, written in the fonts that they represent.

Earlier in Listing 5-4, we chose a **monospaced font**, which means that every character has the same width, when we wrote the temperature digitally. Thus, the statement

```
pen.setFont(new Font("Monospaced", Font.BOLD, 10));
```

sets the font to a monospaced, bold, 10-point font. All subsequent calls to `drawString` will use this font until you make another call to `setFont`.

FIGURE 5-11   The Java names of some fonts and font families, written in 12-point type in the fonts they represent

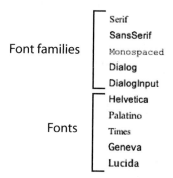

Font families
- Serif
- SansSerif
- Monospaced
- Dialog
- DialogInput

Fonts
- Helvetica
- Palatino
- Times
- Geneva
- Lucida

Question 12 What statements within a method `paintComponent` will display the word "Java" in an italic 12-point Palatino font at the point (x, y)?

■ The Class Color

5.25   You can create any color by mixing quantities of the three primary colors: red, green, and blue. In a programming language such as Java, the amount of each primary color is given by an integer between 0 and 255. The three integers that represent any given color make up the color's **RGB value**. For example, red is represented by the integers 255, 0, 0, and pink is represented by the integers 255, 200, 0.

Java's class Color defines several constants that represent some standard colors. For example, the constant Color.RED represents the color red. Such constants are actually instances of the class Color. Figure 5-12 lists these available constants and their RGB values.

You can define your own colors by using Color's constructor. You give the constructor three arguments representing the red, green, and blue portions of the color that you wish to define. For example, the statement

```
Color myRed = new Color(200, 0, 25);
```

creates a shade of red.

FIGURE 5-12   Predefined color constants within the class Color

Color	Java Constant	RGB Value
black	Color.BLACK	0, 0, 0
blue	Color.BLUE	0, 0, 255
cyan	Color.CYAN	0, 255, 255
dark gray	Color.DARK_GRAY	64, 64, 64
gray	Color.GRAY	128, 128, 128
green	Color.GREEN	0, 255, 0
light gray	Color.LIGHT_GRAY	192, 192, 192
magenta	Color.MAGENTA	255, 0, 255
orange	Color.ORANGE	255, 200, 0
pink	Color.PINK	255, 175, 175
red	Color.RED	255, 0, 0
white	Color.WHITE	255, 255, 255
yellow	Color.YELLOW	255, 255, 0

Programming Tip

The class Color is in the same package as the class Graphics, namely java.awt. Be sure to import the class before you use it.

5.26   Drawing or painting on a component involves both a background color and a foreground color. The **background color** is the color of the drawing surface, while the **foreground color** is the color of the "ink" in the pen. Both of these colors are set by default if you do not set them. For example, a standard background color is white and a standard foreground color is black. Thus, our previous drawings have been black on a white background.

You can set the foreground color—and hence the color of the pen—by invoking the Graphics method setColor. For example, to draw in blue within the graphics context pen, you would execute the statement

```
pen.setColor(Color.BLUE);
```

All subsequent drawing and painting operations will use a blue pen until you invoke setColor again.

> **Note:** The default pen color is black. To change this color, use the method setColor.

You can either use the default background color of a frame or specify a different color by calling the method setBackground. For example, the statement

```
aWindow.setBackground(Color.YELLOW)
```

sets the background color of the frame aWindow to yellow.

5.27   **Example.** Imagine a rectangle having a black edge and blue interior. How would you create such a figure? One way is to draw a black rectangle and fill its inside with blue. We could use the following statements to draw the black rectangle:

```
pen.setColor(Color.BLACK);
pen.drawRect(150, 50, 25, 15);
```

The interior area has its upper left corner at the point (151, 51). The right edge of the black rectangle has an *x*-coordinate of 175. By subtracting 151 from 175, we get 24 as the width of the interior area. The bottom edge of the black rectangle has a *y*-coordinate of 65. By subtracting 51 from 65, we get 14 as the height of the interior area. Thus, the following statements fill the interior of the black rectangle with blue:

```
pen.setColor(Color.BLUE);
pen.fillRect(151, 51, 24, 14);
```

5.28   There is an easier way to give a black rectangle a blue interior, however. Paint a blue rectangular area and then draw a black rectangle using the same arguments, as follows:

```
pen.setColor(Color.BLUE);
pen.fillRect(150, 50, 25, 15);
pen.setColor(Color.BLACK);
pen.drawRect(150, 50, 25, 15);
```

After the blue area is painted, its top and left edges are changed from blue to black by the call to drawRect. The bottom and right edges of the black rectangle are drawn adjacent to the blue area.

> **Note:** Drawing one color on top of another does not mix the colors, as would happen if you used actual paint. For example, drawing with a blue pen on a yellow area does not produce a green line, but rather a blue line. When the color of a pixel is changed by a Graphics method, its prior color is irrelevant.

5.29 Listing 5-6 contains a panel that demonstrates two ways to display a black rectangle with a blue interior, as described in the previous two segments. Listing 5-7 shows the program that displays the panel. Note the call to setBackground.

LISTING 5-6   A panel demonstrating the use of color

```
import java.awt.Color;
import java.awt.Graphics;
import javax.swing.JPanel;

/** BoxPanel.java by F. M. Carrano
    Two ways to color the inside of a rectangle.
*/
public class BoxPanel extends JPanel
{
   public void paintComponent(Graphics pen)
   {
      // display a solid blue rectangle with black edges
      pen.setColor(Color.BLACK);
      pen.drawRect(150, 50, 25, 15);
      pen.setColor(Color.BLUE);
      pen.fillRect(151, 51, 24, 14);

      // display an identical rectangle to the right of the previous one
      pen.setColor(Color.BLUE);
      pen.fillRect(200, 50, 25, 15);
      pen.setColor(Color.BLACK);
      pen.drawRect(200, 50, 25, 15);
   } // end paintComponent
} // end BoxPanel
```

LISTING 5-7   A program that displays the panel defined in Listing 5-6

```
import java.awt.Color;
import javax.swing.JFrame;

/** DisplayBoxes.java by F. M. Carrano
    Displays two identical rectangles that were formed in different ways.
*/
public class DisplayBoxes
{
   public static void main(String[] args)
   {
      JFrame aWindow = new JFrame();
      aWindow.setBackground(Color.LIGHT_GRAY);
```

```
        aWindow.setSize(370, 150);
        aWindow.setDefaultCloseOperation(JFrame.EXIT_ON_CLOSE);
        aWindow.setTitle("Two ways to color the inside of a rectangle");

        BoxPanel panel = new BoxPanel();
        aWindow.add(panel);

        aWindow.setVisible(true);
    } // end main
} // end DisplayBoxes
```

Output

Question 13 Imagine that you have called setBackground to set the background color to yellow and called setForeground to set the foreground color to blue. What color are your drawings?

Question 14 What Java statements will draw a black circle whose radius is 50 pixels, whose center has the coordinates (75, 200), and whose interior is painted blue?

A Problem Solved: The Happy Face

Write a Java program that displays a happy face like the one in Figure 5-13.

FIGURE 5-13   A happy face

5.30 **Discussion.** The specification of our problem is rather loose, so we have some flexibility in designing the face. Here are some of the decisions we must make:

- The shape, size, and color of the face
- The shape, size, color, and position of the eyes
- The shape, size, color, and position of the mouth
- The position of the face within the panel

5.31 The design steps for this application's graphical output are somewhat more involved than those for the thermometer. However, our approaches to both problems are similar. As we did for the previous example, we will define named constants that describe the face and its parts. When possible, these definitions should explicitly involve previously defined constants. For a circular face, for example, we can define constants for the coordinates of the circle's center as well as its radius and diameter. The following constants describe a face that will be centered in an area that is 300 pixels wide by 200 pixels high:

```
final int FACE_CENTER_X = 150;
final int FACE_CENTER_Y = 100;
final int FACE_RADIUS = 75;
final int FACE_DIAMETER = 2 * FACE_RADIUS;
```

We can clearly see that the diameter of the face is two times its radius, and if we change the value of the radius, the value of the diameter will be computed for us.

5.32 You might not think of the next constants until you begin to write the statements that actually paint the face—and that would be fine—but we will mention them now anyway. You know that to draw or paint a circle, you must provide the coordinates of the upper left corner of a square that encloses the circle. The *x*-coordinate of this corner is actually the distance between the left edge of the panel and the left side of the circle. Similarly, the *y*-coordinate of the corner is the distance between the top edge of the panel and the top of the circle. Thus, we define the following constants:

```
final int FACE_LEFT = FACE_CENTER_X - FACE_RADIUS;
final int FACE_TOP  = FACE_CENTER_Y - FACE_RADIUS;
```

We can now paint the face, as follows:

```
pen.fillOval(FACE_LEFT, FACE_TOP, FACE_DIAMETER, FACE_DIAMETER);
```

Notice that the constants FACE_LEFT and FACE_TOP depend upon other constants that were defined previously. Thus, if you change either the location or the radius of the circle, these constants will change automatically.

5.33 Now consider the mouth. We plan to form the mouth by painting a black oval area and then erasing part of it by painting another oval area in the face's color. Figure 5-14 shows the mouth and the constants we will need to paint it. Here are the definitions of these constants:

```
final int MOUTH_WIDTH = (int)(0.4 * FACE_DIAMETER);
final int MOUTH_HEIGHT = MOUTH_WIDTH / 4;

final int MOUTH_LEFT = FACE_CENTER_X - MOUTH_WIDTH / 2;
final int MOUTH_TOP = FACE_CENTER_Y + 2 * MOUTH_HEIGHT;
final int MOUTH_RIGHT = MOUTH_LEFT + MOUTH_WIDTH - 1;
```

The definitions of MOUTH_WIDTH and MOUTH_HEIGHT are somewhat arbitrary and reflect our judgment of reasonable proportions for the mouth based upon the size of the face. If you do not like the results for particular values of these two constants, you can change them without changing anything else. However, the width of the mouth should depend upon the size of the face. That way you could change the diameter of the face without changing the definition of the mouth's width.

FIGURE 5-14   The positions of the mouth and eyes of the happy face

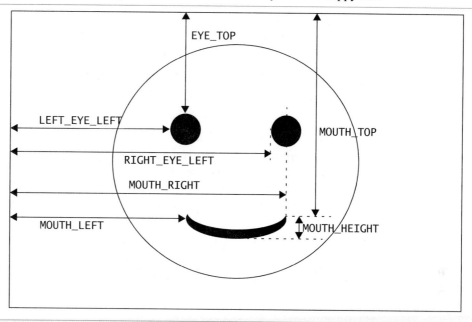

5.34   We now make the radius of each eye depend upon the radius of the face. We place their top edges with respect to the center of the face, the radius of the face, and the height of the mouth. And we align their centers with the corners of the mouth. Thus, we have the following definitions:

```
final int EYE_RADIUS = (int)(0.15 * FACE_RADIUS);
final int EYE_DIAMETER = 2 * EYE_RADIUS;

// distance from top of eyes to face center (used to define EYE_TOP)
final int EYES_FROM_CENTER = (FACE_RADIUS - 2 * MOUTH_HEIGHT) / 3;

// coordinates of eyes (centered over edges of mouth):
final int EYE_TOP = FACE_CENTER_Y - EYES_FROM_CENTER;
final int LEFT_EYE_LEFT = MOUTH_LEFT - EYE_RADIUS;
final int RIGHT_EYE_LEFT = MOUTH_RIGHT - EYE_RADIUS;
```

The coordinates for the eyes are illustrated in Figure 5-14.

5.35   **The solution.** Listing 5-8 shows the code for the panel that will display the happy face when it is added to a frame. Most of our effort went into defining the constants that describe the face. These constants document the relationship among the various components and enable you to easily change the position or size of the face.

LISTING 5-8   The happy-face panel

```
/** HappyFacePanel.java by F. M. Carrano
    Displays a happy face.
*/
import java.awt.Color;
import java.awt.Graphics;
import javax.swing.JPanel;
```

```java
public class HappyFacePanel extends JPanel
{
    public void paintComponent(Graphics pen)
    {
        final Color FACE_COLOR = Color.ORANGE;
        final Color EYE_COLOR = Color.BLACK;
        final Color MOUTH_COLOR = Color.BLACK;

        final int FACE_CENTER_X = 150;
        final int FACE_CENTER_Y = 100;
        final int FACE_RADIUS = 75;
        final int FACE_DIAMETER = 2 * FACE_RADIUS;
        final int FACE_LEFT = FACE_CENTER_X - FACE_RADIUS;
        final int FACE_TOP = FACE_CENTER_Y - FACE_RADIUS;

        final int MOUTH_WIDTH = (int)(0.4 * FACE_DIAMETER);
        final int MOUTH_HEIGHT = MOUTH_WIDTH / 4;
        final int MOUTH_LEFT = FACE_CENTER_X - MOUTH_WIDTH / 2;
        final int MOUTH_TOP = FACE_CENTER_Y + 2 * MOUTH_HEIGHT;
        final int MOUTH_RIGHT = MOUTH_LEFT + MOUTH_WIDTH - 1;

        final int EYE_RADIUS = (int)(0.15 * FACE_RADIUS);
        final int EYE_DIAMETER = 2 * EYE_RADIUS;

        // distance from top of eyes to face center
        // (used only to define EYE_TOP)
        final int EYES_FROM_CENTER = (FACE_RADIUS - 2 * MOUTH_HEIGHT) / 3;

        // coordinates of eyes (centered over edges of mouth):
        final int EYE_TOP = FACE_CENTER_Y - EYES_FROM_CENTER;
        final int LEFT_EYE_LEFT = MOUTH_LEFT - EYE_RADIUS;
        final int RIGHT_EYE_LEFT = MOUTH_RIGHT - EYE_RADIUS;

        // paint face
        pen.setColor(FACE_COLOR);
        pen.fillOval(FACE_LEFT, FACE_TOP, FACE_DIAMETER, FACE_DIAMETER);

        // paint eyes
        pen.setColor(EYE_COLOR);
        pen.fillOval(LEFT_EYE_LEFT, EYE_TOP, EYE_DIAMETER, EYE_DIAMETER);
        pen.fillOval(RIGHT_EYE_LEFT, EYE_TOP, EYE_DIAMETER, EYE_DIAMETER);

        // paint mouth: fill oval
        pen.setColor(MOUTH_COLOR);
        int ovalTop = MOUTH_TOP - MOUTH_HEIGHT;
        pen.fillOval(MOUTH_LEFT, ovalTop, MOUTH_WIDTH, 2 * MOUTH_HEIGHT);
        // then erase top of oval by painting it in face color
        pen.setColor(FACE_COLOR);
```

```
            pen.fillOval(MOUTH_LEFT, ovalTop, MOUTH_WIDTH, MOUTH_HEIGHT);
    } // end paintComponent
} // end HappyFacePanel
```

Design Decision: Frame size versus drawing size

For the happy-face problem, we based the size of the face on the frame dimensions. Earlier, we determined the frame dimensions from the size of the thermometer. One approach might be more suitable than the other for a particular situation. When the frame size is set first, it is necessary to adjust the size of the drawing to fit the frame. We call this adjusting process **scaling**. The interrelationship among the various constants defined in HappyFacePanel would facilitate scaling. Keep the possibility of scaling in mind as you design your drawings.

videonote
A problem
solved

SELF-TEST

Question 15 Write a program that displays the happy-face panel defined in Listing 5-8.

CHAPTER SUMMARY

- You can create a frame in which you display graphics by using methods in the class Graphics. You invoke these methods within a panel's method paintComponent.

- Graphical output is composed of points of light called pixels.

- You position drawings within a frame according to a coordinate system whose origin is at the upper left corner of the frame. The x-coordinate increases as you move to the right. The y-coordinate increases as you move down.

- The method drawLine draws a line between two points, given their coordinates.

- The method drawRect draws a rectangle, given both the coordinates of its upper left corner and its dimensions. You use this method to draw a square as well.

- The method drawOval draws an oval within an imaginary rectangle. You give the method the coordinates of this rectangle's upper left corner and its dimensions. You also use this method to draw a circle.

- The method drawArc draws an arc that is a portion of an oval. You pass to the method the position and dimensions of the rectangle that defines the oval, along with two angles that specify which portion of the oval is drawn.

- The method drawString displays text beginning at a given point.

- The method fillRect fills, or paints, the interior of a rectangle. Its arguments are the same as those of drawRect.

- The method fillOval fills the interior of an oval. Its arguments are the same as those of drawOval.

- The method fillArc fills the area bounded by the arc and the two lines that begin at the ends of the arc and end at the center of the oval that contains the arc.

- The class Font enables you to represent a font as an object. By passing such an object to the Graphics method setFont, you can set the font that the method drawString uses to display text. The classes Font and Graphics are in the same package, java.awt.

- The class Color contains constants that represent several standard colors, such as Color.BLUE.

- The class Graphics contains the method setColor that sets the color of the pen.
- A frame has the method setBackground that sets the color of the drawing surface.
- Defining named constants facilitates the creation of a drawing.

EXERCISES

1. Write statements to create and display a new frame that is 400 pixels by 600 pixels. Set the frame title to " First Frame."

2. Compare and contrast an object of JFrame and an object of JPanel.

3. Explain why an explicit call to paintComponent is not required when using a panel.

4. What is the default pen color used by the drawing methods of the Graphics class?

5. Write Java statements to draw an oval whose height is larger than its width.

6. Using the Graphics context pen, write Java statements to display the phrase " When pigs fly" beginning at point (x, y) in an 18-point sans serif font.

7. Write a Java statement to change the drawing color to blue.

8. What is the meaning of the arguments in the following Java statement?

```
Color customColor = new Color(200, 0, 25);
```

9. What is the difference between a background color and a foreground color?

10. Consult the documentation for the class Graphics in the Java Class Library.

    a. What method would you use to draw an outlined round-cornered rectangle using the graphics context's current color?
    b. What method would you use to reset the origin of the graphics context to a given point in the current coordinate system?

11. Consult the documentation for the class Font in the Java Class Library.

    a. What method would you use to test whether a string can be displayed in a particular font?
    b. What method would you use to see whether two Font objects are equivalent?

12. Consult the documentation for the class Graphics in the Java Class Library. What method would you use to draw a raised, filled three-dimensional rectangle? Using the Graphics object pen, write statements to draw a raised, filled three-dimensional rectangle at the point (10, 10). The rectangle should have a width of 200 pixels and a height of 300 pixels.

13. In Listing 5-4, could you replace the statement

```
final int EDGE_HEIGHT = COLUMN_HEIGHT + (int)(2.5 * BORDER);
```
with
```
final int EDGE_HEIGHT = (int)(COLUMN_HEIGHT + 2.5 * BORDER);
```
Explain.

14. Write a Java program to display your name on a panel within a frame.

15. Write a Java program to display your name within an ellipse on a panel.

16. Write a Java program using a combination of the shapes in the `Graphics` class to display a house like the following one:

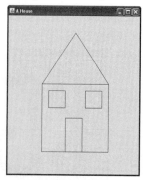

17. Write a Java program that draws a digital clock like the following one:

Use two random numbers for the values of the hours and minutes.

18. Write a Java program that reads each component of an RGB color value and displays a `JFrame` object in that color.

PROJECTS

1. Define a panel that includes the method `paintComponent` to draw the following diagram:

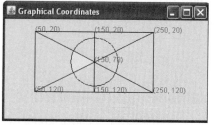

The rectangle is 200 pixels wide and 100 pixels high. The circle is centered within the rectangle and has a radius of 40 pixels. Display the coordinates in red. Fill the arc with yellow. Create a frame in which to display the diagram.

2. Design and write a program to draw a colorful face that is winking, similar to the following one:

3. Design and write a program to draw a picture of a snowman.

4. Design and write a program to draw a graphic of your first and last initials in block letters that overlap a circle. Use various colors. For example, Karen Gardner's initials appear as follows:

5. Design and write a program that graphically displays a three-dimensional rectangular prism, or box, of some sort. For example, you could draw an iPod, a cell phone, a gift box, a deck of cards, a calculator, a TV remote, and so on. Include color and details to demonstrate your knowledge of the topics discussed in this chapter.

ANSWERS TO SELF-TEST QUESTIONS

1. **a.** JPanel
   b. An object of JPanel
   c. Instantiation
   d. A constructor

2. `pen.drawRect(100, 75, 50, 50);`

3. `pen.drawOval(100, 75, 50, 50);`

4. `pen.drawOval(25, 150, 100, 100);`

5. `g.drawArc(50, 200, 100, 75, -320, 50); // same arc`
   or
   `g.drawArc(50, 200, 100, 75, 90, -50); // same arc`

6. Since the literal 2.5 is real, the result of the multiplication is real. Without casting this product to `int`, the sum would be real and could not be assigned to the `int` constant EDGE_HEIGHT.

7. Nothing. The integer difference would be cast to `double` implicitly. As Chapter 3 noted, this implicit cast is called coercion.

8. To avoid an integer division. If `range` were `int`, the result of the division would be zero.

9. The cast converts the `double` result to an `int` so that it can be stored in the `int` variable `fluidHeight`. Without it, a syntax error would occur.

10. Since the multiplication and division operators have the same precedence, they are performed from left to right in their order of appearance. The multiplication occurs before the division.

11. `EDGE_HEIGHT + 2 * EDGE_TOP + 40`

12. `pen.setFont(new Font("Palatino", Font.ITALIC, 12));`
    `pen.drawString("Java", x, y);`

13. Blue on a yellow background. The colors do not mix to form green.

14.
```
pen.setColor(Color.BLUE);
pen.fillOval(25, 150, 100, 100);
pen.setColor(Color.BLACK);
pen.drawOval(25, 150, 100, 100);
```

15.
```
/** DisplayHappyFace.java by F. M. Carrano
    Displays a happy face.
*/
import javax.swing.JFrame;
public class DisplayHappyFace
{
   public static void main(String[] args)
   {
      JFrame aWindow = new JFrame();
      aWindow.setSize(300, 240); // add 40 pixels to height to
                                 // accommodate title bar
      aWindow.setDefaultCloseOperation(JFrame.EXIT_ON_CLOSE);
      aWindow.setTitle("Happy Face");
      HappyFacePanel panel = new HappyFacePanel();
      aWindow.add(panel);
      aWindow.setVisible(true);
   } // end main
} // end DisplayHappyFace
```

Class Definitions: The Fundamentals

Contents

Prerequisites

Objectives

After studying this chapter, you should be able to

• Use and implement constructors
• Define data fields
• Describe the use of the access modifiers public and private
• Distinguish between formal parameters and arguments
• Write a method definition
• Describe the use of accessor methods and mutator methods, and write their definitions
• Call a method, given its header
• Describe the effect of a given call to a method
• Write a class definition

Chapter 4 discussed objects that belong to particular standard classes such as `String` and `BigDecimal`. We said that the data type of such objects is the name of their class. The objects have both data and behaviors that their class describes. The behaviors are the result of executing the methods defined by the class.

In this chapter, we will show you how to write your own classes and methods. By creating a class, you are in essence creating a new data type.

■ A Class Definition

A class is like a plan for building cars, as Figure 6-1 illustrates. Many cars can be built from the description given in one plan. The plan specifies that a car should have four wheels, among other things, but the actual wheels belong to the cars, not the plan.

FIGURE 6-1   A plan for building cars and the results of following it

Similarly, a class is a plan for creating certain objects. It describes the objects' data and behaviors. That is, a class contains declarations for the data associated with its objects, and definitions of methods that implement their behaviors.

We begin by considering a simple class called `Greeter`. First, we will imagine that someone has already written this class for us, and we will learn how to use it. Then we will actually define the class in Java.

Using the Class Greeter

6.1   Each object of the class Greeter contains a greeting that it can display. For example, Listing 6-1 contains a program that defines three different Greeter objects. Each object's greeting is established at the time that the object is created, that is, when the operator new executes. For example, when we define the object standardWelcomer, the expression

```
new Greeter()
```

creates a Greeter object, allocates space for a greeting, and assigns it a default value, such as "Hello, world!"

LISTING 6-1   A class that uses the class Greeter

```java
/** GreeterDemo by F. M. Carrano
    Demonstrates the class Greeter.
*/
public class GreeterDemo
{
    public static void main(String args[])
    {
        Greeter standardWelcomer = new Greeter();
        Greeter townCrier = new Greeter("It's 12 o'clock; all is well!");
        Greeter courtClerk = new Greeter("Order in the Court!");

        standardWelcomer.greet();
        townCrier.greet();
        courtClerk.greet();
    } // end main
} // end GreeterDemo
```

Output

```
Hello, world!
It's 12 o'clock; all is well!
Order in the Court!
```

6.2   As Chapter 4 pointed out, new is a Java operator that creates an object. The first time it is used in Listing 6-1, the new operator has one operand, the expression Greeter(). This expression represents a call to a special method, known as a constructor, which occurs during the object-creation process. A constructor initializes the newly created object. Constructors have the same name as the class. This particular constructor accepts no arguments, so you write nothing between the parentheses. Such a constructor is called a **default constructor**.

When we define the object townCrier, we involve another constructor. Note that a class can have several different constructors. This constructor has an argument that represents the object's greeting as a string. So townCrier's greeting is "It's 12 o'clock; all is well!"

When each of these objects receives an invocation for the method greet, its own greeting is displayed, as you can see from the output given in Listing 6-1. Although each object has the same method greet, a different string—the greeting associated with the object—is displayed each time.

> **Note:** The program component that uses a class is the **client** of the class. The **user** is the person using the program.

Beginning the Class Definition

videonote
Class definitions

6.3   The definition of the class Greeter has the following form:

```
public class Greeter
{
    . . .
} // end Greeter
```

The **access modifier** public indicates the class's availability. All clients may use this class. Next is the reserved word class and the name of the class. This initial portion of the definition is the **class header**. After the header, braces delineate the class's definition.

A class designer must decide what data, if any, will be represented by objects of the class. For example, each Greeter object has a string associated with it that is its greeting. Thus, in the class definition, we declare a string for this purpose. The class now appears as follows:

```
public class Greeter ◄─────────────── Header
{
    private String greeting;
    . . .
} // end Greeter
```

The variable greeting is a **data field**, or **field**, of the class. Its data type here is String. The access modifier private indicates that greeting is available by name within this class definition but nowhere else. Outside of this class, greeting is not defined. Although the class declares the field greeting, memory space is not allocated for it yet. Space for the greeting is allocated for any particular Greeter object when the object is created.

After the declaration of any fields are the definitions of the constructors and methods of the class. We discuss such definitions next, beginning with constructors. By the way, the fields and methods of a class are called the class's **members**.

> **Note: The name of a file containing a class definition**
> You store each public class in its own file that is named after the name of the class. For example, the class Greeter should be in the file Greeter.java. A file can contain several classes, as long as only one is public.

Defining Constructors

6.4   **The default constructor.** The definition of any constructor begins with the access modifier public, the name of the class—which is the name of the constructor—and a pair of parentheses. Nothing appears between these parentheses for a default constructor. For example, the definition of the default constructor for the class Greeter is

```
/** Creates a default Greeter object. */
public Greeter() ◄─────────────── Header
{
    greeting = "Hello, world!";
} // end default constructor
```

Looking back to Segment 6.1, we see that the statement

```
Greeter standardWelcomer = new Greeter();
```

creates a `Greeter` object and invokes the default constructor. Memory space is allocated for the new object, including space for a string called `greeting`. This memory allocation happens without any effort on our part. Thus, the new object has its own data field, or **instance variable**, `greeting`, that is a string, as shown in Figure 6-2. The declaration of `greeting` within the class is just that, a declaration. It indicates that a `Greeter` object will have a `String` variable called `greeting`. The process of creating the new object—instantiation—allocates memory for `greeting` and assigns it a value, using the default constructor that we just wrote.

FIGURE 6-2   The data field `greeting`: (a) declared within a class; (b) allocated within an object of the class

Sometimes, a default constructor has no statements in its body. In that case, the object is created, but any instance variables have default initializations. For example, instance variables that have primitive numeric types are initialized to zero. Instance variables of a class type are initialized to `null`, which is a predefined constant in Java. A variable that contains `null` does not reference any object.

> **Note:** An object, or instance, of a class has its own data fields that are declared within the class. The variables that represent the fields within an object are called instance variables because they belong to an instance of a class.

videonote
Defining
constructors

6.5   **Other constructors.** Any constructor other than the default constructor has a **parameter list** between the parentheses in its header. Such constructors—sometimes described as **parameterized constructors**—initialize data fields to values given when the constructors are invoked.

The parameter list of a constructor or any other method declares the **formal parameters**, or simply **parameters**, of the method. Each formal parameter corresponds to an argument when the method is invoked. The parameters, therefore, specify values or objects that are inputs to the method. You name formal parameters in the same way that you name variables. In fact, parameters within the body of a method behave as variables. You declare a formal parameter by writing the parameter's data type followed by its name. If you have more than one formal parameter, you separate their declarations using commas.

The following constructor creates a `Greeter` object, allocates space for the data field `greeting`, and initializes `greeting` to the string that the formal parameter `newGreeting` represents:

```
/** Creates a greeter object from the string newGreeting. */
public Greeter(String newGreeting)
{
   greeting = newGreeting;
} // end constructor
```

So when you write

```
Greeter joe = new Greeter("Hi");
```

in a method main, for example, the argument "Hi" corresponds to the formal parameter newGreeting. Thus, newGreeting represents "Hi" within the body of the constructor, and so "Hi" is assigned to the data field greeting.

Question 1 After a client assigns joe a new Greeter object, as we just did in the previous segment, will the following statement change the object's greeting? Explain your answer.

```
joe.greeting = "Hello";
```

Note: Constructors
A constructor is a special method within a class that creates an instance, or object, of the class, allocates memory for its data fields, and initializes them to particular values. A constructor is invoked when you use the new operator.

Typically, constructors should explicitly initialize the class's data fields instead of relying on default initializations. A class can have more than one constructor, with each one having a different list of parameters. A constructor without parameters is known as the default constructor.

Syntax: Constructors
Constructor definitions have the following general form:

access-modifier   class-name(*optional-parameter-list*)
{
    statement(s)
}

Note: Access modifiers
The words public and private are examples of access modifiers that indicate where a class, constructor, method, or data field can be used. Any class can use something that is public, regardless of where that item is defined. A private class, constructor, method, or data field can be used only by the class that defines it. A private data field, for example, is available by name only within the definitions of its class's constructors and methods. We will discuss private methods in Chapter 8 and private classes (in the form of inner classes, which are often private) in Chapter 17.

Defining Other Methods

6.6   You define a method that is not a constructor in much the same way that you define a constructor. Like constructors, methods have headers, but their syntax is slightly different, as you will see.

Note: Parameters and arguments
The declaration of a formal parameter occurs in the header of a method or constructor. When you write the call to a method or constructor, you pass to the method or constructor an argument for each of its formal parameters. We will consistently make this distinction between formal parameters and arguments, although we will sometimes say "parameter" instead of "formal parameter." Realize, however, that some people use the terms "parameter" and "argument" interchangeably.

6.7   **The method greet.** The public methods of a class define the behaviors that objects of the class have. Our class Greeter has the method greet, which displays an object's greeting. The definition of this method within the class appears as follows:

```
/** Displays the greeting. */
public void greet()  ◄──────────────── Header
{
    System.out.println(greeting);
} // end greet
```

The method displays the string that the data field greeting represents. Recall that data fields are available by name throughout the definition of the class. Thus, any method definition within the class can use greeting by name. Also remember that each object of the class Greeter has its own instance variable greeting, so this method displays the object's own greeting.

A method, such as greet, that performs an action but does not return a value as a result is known as a **void method**. This particular method has no formal parameters, although void methods can certainly have them.

6.8   Listing 6-2 contains the definition of the class Greeter as we have defined it so far. The data field greeting is private, as is typically the case for the data fields of a class. As a result, other classes cannot access or change the value of greeting directly by using the variable greeting. Although we can look at a Greeter object's greeting by calling the method greet to display it, as Figure 6-3 illustrates, we have no way to **get**—that is, to retrieve or access—the greeting as a string. Further-more, objects of the class Greeter, as it is given in Listing 6-2, cannot be changed. Recall from Segment 4.29 that such objects are said to be immutable.

LISTING 6-2   The class Greeter so far

```
/** Greeter.java by F. M. Carrano
    A class that represents a greeting.

    Data: A string

    Behaviors:
      Construct a new greeting
      Display the greeting
*/
public class Greeter
    private String greeting;

    /** Creates a default Greeter object. */
    public Greeter()
    {
        greeting = "Hello, world!";
    } // end default constructor

    /** Creates a Greeter object from the string newGreeting. */
    public Greeter(String newGreeting)
    {
        greeting = newGreeting;
    } // end constructor
```

```
/** Displays the greeting. */
public void greet()
{
    System.out.println(greeting);
} // end greet
} // end Greeter
```

Question 2 Imagine that you have created a new Greeter object by writing

```
Greeter sue = new Greeter("Good morning.");
```

and that later you write

```
sue = new Greeter("Good night.");
```

a. At the end of the previous segment, we said that Greeter objects are immutable. How is this fact consistent with the change in the value of sue?

b. What happens to the object whose greeting is "Good morning"?

FIGURE 6-3   A Greeter object jim hides its greeting, but displays it via its method greet

jim

jim.greet();

Hi!

6.9   **Accessor methods.** Often a class has methods that get the value of certain data fields. For example, we could add a method to Greeter that returns the value of the data field greeting. This method is called an **accessor method**, or a **get method**, or a **getter**. By convention, the names of such methods begin with "get."

A method that returns a value is called a **valued method**. It returns a value by executing a **return statement** of the form

```
return expression;
```

A valued method is like a mathematical function, since it returns a single value.

Thus, we can add the following accessor method to Greeter:

```
/** Returns the greeting as a string. */
public String getGreeting()
{
    return greeting;
} // end getGreeting
```

The data type String in the method's header is the method's **return type**. As a valued method, getGreeting must execute a return statement as its last action. The method returns the value of the expression in the return statement. The data type of this value must match the return type in the method's header. The method getGreeting returns a value of type String.

When an expression such as

```
courtClerk.getGreeting()
```

invokes the method from within a method `main`, for example, the string in `courtClerk`'s instance variable `greeting` is returned. We could assign the string to another variable or display it in a statement such as

```
System.out.println(courtClerk.getGreeting());
```

Programming Tip

Usually, a valued method should have only one `return` statement, and it should occur last in the body of the method.

Syntax: Methods

Methods other than constructors have the following general form:

access-modifier use-modifier return-type method-name(parameter-list)
{
    body
}

The access modifier is usually present, but later, when we talk about packages, you will see that sometimes you omit it. The **use modifier** is optional and often is omitted. You will learn about it later in this book. The return type is either the data type of the value returned by the method or `void`, which indicates that no value is returned. A method can return a value by executing a `return` statement of the form

```
return expression;
```

Methods that return a value are called valued methods. Methods that perform an action but do not return a value are called void methods.

Finally, not all methods have a parameter list.

Programming Tip

Do not write a data type before any argument that you pass to a method in its invocation. Although a formal parameter in the header of a method's definition is preceded by its data type, when you invoke the method, the arguments corresponding to the parameters are not accompanied by explicit data types.

Programming Tip

Do not write a return type, not even `void`, when you define a constructor. Doing so results in a syntax error in any statement that uses the constructor to create a new object. This error can confuse you, since the definition of the erroneous constructor will compile. However, it will appear to be an ordinary method, which is why the compiler will not let you use it as a constructor.

Programming Tip

Usually, your void methods should not contain a `return` statement. A void method can contain a `return` statement without a value, however. Such a statement causes the method to return to the point from which it was called.

videonote
Defining methods

6.10 **Mutator methods.** As we said in Segment 6.8, `Greeter` objects are immutable. Another class cannot modify the greeting associated with any existing `Greeter` object. If we want to modify the private data associated with an object, its class must define one or more methods for this purpose. A **mutator method**, or a **set method**, or a **setter**, is a method that changes the value of a data field. By convention, a method whose name begins with "set" is a set method.

For example, we could add the following set method to the class `Greeter`:

```
/** Sets the greeting to the string newGreeting. */
public void setGreeting(String newGreeting)
{
    greeting = newGreeting;
} //end setGreeting
```

This method is void, as it does not return a value. It has a formal parameter `newGreeting` that corresponds to an argument in the call to the method. For example, suppose that we add the following statement to the method `main` shown in Segment 6.1:

```
courtClerk.setGreeting("Here comes the judge.");
```

The formal parameter `newGreeting` represents the string `"Here comes the judge."` within the body of the method. This string is then assigned to `courtClerk`'s data field `greeting`.

Programming Tip: Data fields should be private

Within a class definition, you should make each data field private by beginning its declaration with the access modifier `private`. The client then cannot use the name of a data field to access or modify it. If needed, provide a set method for the client to use to change the value of a data field. The advantage of this approach is that the set method can check the value given to it by the client to ensure that the value assigned to a data field is valid. If the data field were public, a client could use the field's name to assign an illegal value to the field. A private data field does pose a slight disadvantage to the programmer, as the client must use a get method to access the field's value. However, within any of the class's method definitions, you can use the name of the data field in any way you wish. In particular, you can directly change the value of the data field.

Note: Naming methods

You name a method much as you name a variable. The name should begin with a lowercase letter. Since methods perform actions, we use a verb or action phrase to name them. For example, `greet` and `getGreeting` both describe the action of and name two `Greeter` methods.

Not all mutator methods have names beginning with "set." However, names that do begin with "set" should name mutator methods by convention.

Note: Objects having mutator methods are **mutable**. In other words, you can modify the private data associated with a mutable object.

Question 3 Suppose that we add a data field `name` to the class `Greeter` that names the greeter. The field is a string.

    a. What is the declaration within the class for this new data field?
    b. What change would you make to the default constructor?
    c. If we decide to add set and get methods for the new field, what are their definitions?

6.11   **The object this.** The method `setGreeting` contains the statement

```
greeting = newGreeting;
```

where `greeting` is a data field and `newGreeting` is a formal parameter of the method. Each object of the class contains an instance variable `greeting`. When you call `setGreeting` for a particular object, the object's `greeting` is involved. Within the body of a method, Java identifies the receiving object as `this`. In fact, you could write the previous statement as

```
this.greeting = newGreeting;
```

Programmers use `this` either for clarity or when they want to give the formal parameter the same name as the data field. For example, you could name `setGreeting`'s parameter `greeting` instead of `newGreeting` and write

```
this.greeting = greeting;
```

within its body. Although Java programmers tend to write statements such as the previous one within mutator methods, we will use `this` sparingly.

Note: Naming a method's formal parameters associated with data fields

The constructor of the class `Greeter` in Listing 6-2 and its method `setGreeting` given in Segment 6.10 set the class's data field `greeting` to a given value. In both cases we have used a parameter whose name differs from that of the data field. We could have given the parameter the same name as its corresponding data field `greeting`. Some programmers always use this style and think of it as a convention. In such cases, they must use the `this` object with the data fields. Other programmers distinguish between data fields and parameters by giving them different names. In those cases, the use of `this` is optional.

Local Variables

6.12   Let's consider our original version of the class `Greeter`, as shown in Listing 6-2. The class defines two constructors and the method `greet`. Suppose we want to define an additional method, `changeGreeting`, that changes the greeting to a string passed to it as an argument. In addition, let's make the method return the original greeting that it replaces. Thus, we could write the method's header as follows:

```
/** Changes the greeting to the string newGreeting
    and returns the old greeting. */
public String changeGreeting(String newGreeting)
```

To use this method, we might write

```
Greeter joe = new Greeter();
joe.greet();
String joeSaid = joe.changeGreeting("Have a good day.");
System.out.print("Joe said " + joeSaid + " but now says ");
joe.greet();
```

The output from these statements is

```
Hello, world!
Joe said Hello, world! but now says Have a good day.
```

6.13   Now let's think about the definition of `changeGreeting`. Changing the greeting is easy, as the following assignment statement within the method's body will suffice:

```
greeting = newGreeting;
```

But how will we return the original greeting? The previous statement destroys the reference to it. We need to save this reference in another variable before changing the value of the field `greeting`. Thus, we could write the following statements in the body of `changeGreeting`'s definition:

```
String oldGreeting = greeting; // retain original greeting
greeting = newGreeting;        // change greeting
```

All we need to do now is to return `oldGreeting`. Thus, the definition of the method `changeGreeting` is

```
/** Changes the greeting to the string newGreeting
    and returns the old greeting. */
public String changeGreeting(String newGreeting)
{
    String oldGreeting = greeting; // retain original greeting
    greeting = newGreeting;        // change greeting

    return oldGreeting;
} // end changeGreeting
```

The variable `oldGreeting`, which is declared within the body of the method `changeGreeting`, is said to be **local** to the body of the method. Thus, `oldGreeting` is available only within the body of `changeGreeting`. If `oldGreeting` appears outside of this method's definition but within the class `Greeter`, it is a different variable.

Note: Local variables
A **local variable** is a variable declared within the body of a method's definition. Its value is available only within the body of the method; it is unavailable elsewhere. Thus, a local variable within a method can have the same name as a local variable within another method. Such variables are different.

A method's formal parameters behave like local variables. Thus, if two methods each use the same name for a parameter, the parameters are different.

Question 4 If the class `Greeter` defines the method `changeGreeting` as given in the previous segment, what is displayed by the following statements?

```
Greeter joe = new Greeter();
System.out.print("Joe said " + joe.changeGreeting("Have a good day.")
                 + " but now says ");
joe.greet();
```

◼ Creating a New Class

We now will examine the steps you should take to invent an entirely new class. Imagine that your current programming project involves the names of people. You could represent the names as strings, but you would prefer that they were objects of a data type specifically designed for names. You decide to create your own data type. You do this by writing a class definition.

The Design

6.14   In designing a class, you need to take the following steps:

1. Name the class.
2. Choose and name the data fields, indicating their data types.
3. Describe the behaviors associated with objects of the class.
4. Name the methods that will implement these behaviors.
5. Specify the methods by writing a header and descriptive comments for each one.
6. Write statements that use the methods and could appear in a client.
7. Revise the method specifications, if necessary.

You would implement the class—by declaring the data fields and completing the body of each method—only after you are satisfied with the class design.

6.15 Let's call the class Name. For simplicity, we assume that a person's name consists only of a first name and a last name. These two components make up the data associated with a Name object. We can call them first and last, respectively, and note that each is a string.

Here are some basic behaviors that our objects can have:

- Set the first name to a given string.
- Set the last name to a given string.
- Set the first name and last name to given strings.
- Get, or retrieve, the first name as a string.
- Get the last name as a string.
- Get the first and last names as one string.

To make our example a bit more interesting, we add the following behavior:

- Give this object's last name to a given Name object.

6.16 Having described the class's behaviors, we name the methods and their parameters. We also choose the data types of the parameters and the values that the methods return. We can express the results of steps 4 and 5 by writing headers and descriptive comments for the methods in the context of a class definition, as Listing 6-3 shows. We have included a pair of braces for each one and have labeled each closing brace.

Notice in Listing 6-3 that a constructor and the method setName each have two formal parameters. A formal parameter is always preceded by its data type in the method's header. A comma separates each type-parameter pair. When you invoke these methods, you provide them with two arguments separated by a comma. You do not write the data types of these arguments, however.

LISTING 6-3   The partially completed class Name

```
/** The class Name, by F. M. Carrano.
    Represents a name that contains a first name and a last name.

    Data: the first and last names as strings

    Behaviors:
      Construct an empty name
      Construct a name given its first and last names
      Set the first name of an existing name
      Set the last name of an existing name
      Set the first and last names of an existing name
      Get the first name
      Get the last name
      Get the entire name
      Give the last name to another Name object
*/
public class Name
{
    private String first; // first name
    private String last;  // last name
```

```java
/** Creates a default name whose first and last names are empty. */
public Name()
{
} // end default constructor

/** Creates a name whose first and last names are the strings
    firstName and lastName, respectively. */
public Name(String firstName, String lastName)
{
} // end constructor

/** Sets the first name to the string firstName. */
public void setFirst(String firstName)
{
} // end setFirst

/** Sets the last name to the string lastName. */
public void setLast(String lastName)
{
} // end setLast

/** Sets the first and last names to the strings
    firstName and lastName, respectively. */
public void setName(String firstName, String lastName)
{
} // end setName

/** Returns the first name as a string. */
public String getFirst()
{
} // end getFirst

/** Returns the last name as a string. */
public String getLast()
{
} // end getLast

/** Returns the entire name as a string. */
public String getName()
{
} // end getName

/** Returns the entire name as a string. */
public String toString()
{
} // end toString

/** Gives the last name to otherName. */
public void giveLastNameTo(Name otherName)
```

```
      {
      } // end giveLastNameTo
} // end Name
```

6.17   As soon as we are satisfied with our work so far, we need only to fill in the body for each method. But before we do that, we should consider step 6 of our design process, as given in Segment 6.14. By writing statements that use the class, we test our understanding of the methods' specifications and our satisfaction with them. If necessary, we revise the specifications. If we are careful when we write these test statements, we can use them later to test the class after we finish its implementation. For example, the statements in Listing 6-4 invoke all of the methods in the class.

LISTING 6-4   Java statements that use the class Name

```java
Name joyce = new Name();
joyce.setName("Joyce", "Jones");

System.out.println("Joyce Jones' first name is " + joyce.getFirst());
System.out.println("Joyce Jones' complete name is " +
                    joyce.getFirst() + " " + joyce.getLast());
System.out.println("Joyce Jones' complete name is " +
                    joyce.getName());
System.out.println("Joyce Jones' complete name is " +
                    joyce.toString());
System.out.println("Joyce Jones' complete name is " + joyce);

joyce.setFirst("Joy");
joyce.setLast("Smith");
System.out.println("After changing Joyce Jones to Joy Smith, " +
                    "we have " + joyce);
Name derek = new Name("Derek", "Dodd");
System.out.println("Derek Dodd's complete name is " + derek);
derek.giveLastNameTo(joyce);
System.out.println("After giving Derek Dodd's last name to Joy Smith," +
                    "\nwe have " + joyce + " and " + derek);
```

6.18   **The method toString.** Notice the method toString in Listing 6-3. This method returns a string that contains the first and last names of a Name object. You can use this method to display the name that the object joyce represents by writing

```java
System.out.println(joyce.toString());
```

One significant aspect of this method is that Java invokes it automatically when you write a statement such as

```java
System.out.println(joyce);
```

For this reason, it is a good idea to write a method toString in all of your classes. The method should return a string that represents the data associated with a particular object.

If you do not define a method `toString`, Java will provide its own version of the method, with a return value that likely will have little meaning to you.

Notice that `toString` has the same purpose as the method `getName`. A class designer might specify more than one method to perform the same task for the convenience of the programmer who uses the class.

Programming Tip: Define a method `toString`

All classes include a method `toString`, whether you define one explicitly or not. Writing your own `toString` method for each class is a good idea in general, because the version that Java supplies will be of little use to you.

Note: For an object `myObject`, the following statements have the same effect:

```
System.out.println(myObject);
System.out.println(myObject.toString());
```

Note: The headers of the public methods of a class make up the class's **interface**.

Question 5 If you write

```
Greeter joe = new Greeter("Hello");
```

does the following statement display "Hello"? Why or why not?
```
System.out.println(joe);
```

Question 6 Create a `Name` object that represents your name. Then use this object to

- Display your name.
- Display your last name, a comma, a space, and your first name.
- Give your last name to another `Name` object in two different ways.

Question 7 Design a method `takeLastNameFrom` for the class `Name` that takes the last name of another `Name` object and assigns it to the receiving object. Write a comment that describes the method and a header for the method. Also, write statements that show how the method is used. Do not write the method's body.

The Implementation

6.19   We finally complete the implementation of the class, as Listing 6-5 shows. The default constructor sets the data fields to empty strings. If we did not initialize them, Java would set them each to `null`.

Notice that the method `setName` calls the methods `setFirst` and `setLast`. A method can invoke other methods in its class. We write

```
setFirst(firstName);
```

for example, in `setName`'s body without a receiving object. The object that receives the call to `setName` also receives the call to `setFirst`. You could write this statement as

```
this.setFirst(firstName);
```

if you prefer, but that is not necessary. Similarly, the method `toString` invokes the method `getName`.

Programming Tip

When feasible, call already defined methods from within the definition of another method in the same class. Doing so avoids repetition of code and simplifies both debugging and maintenance of the class.

6.20   The method `giveLastNameTo` must set its parameter's last name to the receiving object's last name. The statement

```
otherName.setLast(last);
```

does just that. Since `otherName` represents a `Name` object, you can use it to invoke the method `setLast`. However, you instead could write

```
otherName.last = last;
```

to accomplish the same task. Although the expression `otherName.last` would be illegal outside of the class `Name` because `last` is private, it is legal within the class and in particular within the definition of the method `giveLastNameTo`.

LISTING 6-5   An implementation of the class Name

```java
/** Name.java by F. M. Carrano.
    A class of names, each containing a first name and a last name.
*/
public class Name
{
   private String first; // first name
   private String last;  // last name

   /** Creates a default name whose first and last names are empty. */
   public Name()
   {
      first = ""; // empty string
      last  = "";
   } // end default constructor

   /** Creates a name whose first and last names are the strings
       firstName and lastName, respectively. */
   public Name(String firstName, String lastName)
   {
      first = firstName;
      last  = lastName;
   } // end constructor

   /** Sets the first name to the string firstName. */
   public void setFirst(String firstName)
   {
```

```
      first = firstName;
   } // end setFirst

   /** Sets the last name to the string lastName. */
   public void setLast(String lastName)
   {
      last = lastName;
   } // end setLast

   /** Sets the first and last names to the strings
       firstName and lastName, respectively. */
   public void setName(String firstName, String lastName)
   {
      setFirst(firstName);
      setLast(lastName);
   } // end setName

   /** Returns the first name as a string. */
   public String getFirst()
   {
      return first;
   } // end getFirst

   /** Returns the last name as a string. */
   public String getLast()
   {
      return last;
   } // end getLast

   /** Returns the entire name as a string. */
   public String getName()
   {
      return first + " " + last;
   } // end getName

   /** Returns the entire name as a string. */
   public String toString()
   {
      return getName();
   } // end toString

   /** Gives the last name to otherName. */
   public void giveLastNameTo(Name otherName)
   {
      otherName.setLast(last);
   } // end giveLastNameTo
} // end Name
```

Question 8 If you add the method `toString` to the class `Greeter` that appears in Listing 6-2, what is its definition?

Question 9 Implement the method `takeLastNameFrom` that Question 7 describes.

Note: Omitting Constructors

If you do not define a constructor in your class, Java will provide a default constructor, that is, a constructor that has no parameters. However, if every constructor that you define has parameters, Java will not define a default constructor for you. As a consequence, invoking a constructor without arguments will be illegal. For example, if we omit the default constructor from the previous definition of the class `Name`, one constructor would remain. Since Java will not provide another, we could not write the following statement in a program that uses the class:

```
Name someOne = new Name();
```

Programming Tip: Provide initial values for a class's data fields

Although Java initializes a class's data fields to default values, you should provide your own initial values when defining constructors. This can be especially important for data fields of a class type. In such cases, Java assigns `null` as a default value. If a method used such a field as a receiving object, an error would occur because of the `null` value. The next debugging interlude will show an example of this sort of mistake.

Programming Tip

If a class has two methods that perform the same task, you should ask yourself if you really need both methods. If you decide that you do, one method should call the other. Doing so helps to avoid errors both now and after any future changes to the code. For example, the class `Name` in Listing 6-5 has two methods, `getName` and `toString`, that return the same string. Rather than giving the same body to each of the methods, we make `toString` call `getName`.

Passing Arguments

6.21 When a formal parameter has a primitive type such as `int`, it is initialized to the value of the corresponding argument in the call to the method. This argument can be a literal constant—such as 51—or it can be a variable or any expression. This way of passing an argument to a method is known as a **call by value**. A method cannot change the value of an argument that has a primitive data type. Such an argument serves as an input value only.

Note: The arguments in a call to a method must match the formal parameters of the method's definition with respect to number, order, and data type. A match of data type need not be exact when the types are primitive, as Java allows certain implicit type casts, or coercions. An argument with a data type in the following list will match a formal parameter whose data type is either the same or appears to the right in this list:

```
byte → short → int → long → float → double
```

This list is the same as the one you saw in Segment 3.11 when we discussed assignments.

When a formal parameter has a class type, the corresponding argument in the method invocation must be an object of that class type. The formal parameter is initialized to the memory address of that object. The formal parameter, then, is just another name for the object. As a result, the method can change the data in the object, if the class has mutator methods. The method, however, cannot replace an object that is an argument with another object.

6.22   **Example.** For example, if you adopt a child, you might give that child your last name. If you use the previous class `Name` to represent names, you can use the method `giveLastNameTo` to make this change of name. Notice that the formal parameter of this method has the data type `Name`.

Now if Jamie Jones adopts Sam Smith, the following statements would change Sam's last name to Jones:

```
public static void main(String[] args)
{
    Name jamie = new Name("Jamie", "Jones");
    Name sam = new Name("Sam", "Smith");
    jamie.giveLastNameTo(sam);
    . . .
} // end main
```

Figure 6-4 shows the argument `sam` and the parameter `otherName` as the method `giveLastNameTo` executes.

FIGURE 6-4   The method `giveLastNameTo` modifies the object passed to it as an argument

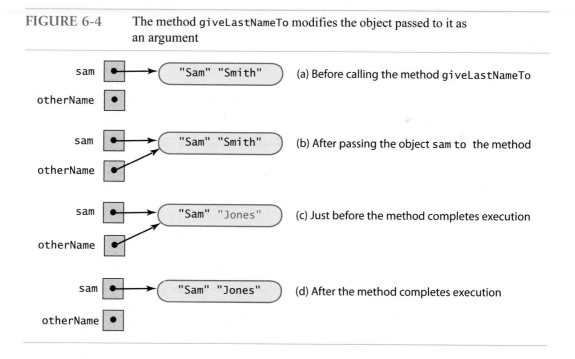

6.23   What happens if you change the method definition so that it allocates a new name, as follows?

```
public void giveLastNameTo2(Name otherName)
{
    otherName = new Name(otherName.getFirst(), last);
} // end giveLastNameTo2
```

With this change, the invoking statement

```
jamie.giveLastNameTo2(sam);
```

has no effect on `sam`, as Figure 6-5 illustrates. The parameter `otherName` behaves like a local variable, so its value is not available outside of the method definition. After the method ends its execution, the new `Name` object assigned to `otherName` is recycled.

Question 10 Consider a method definition that begins with the statement

```
public void process(int number, Name aName)
```

If `jamie` is defined as in Segment 6.22, and you invoke this method using the statement

```
someObject.process(5, jamie);
```

a. Can the method `process` change the data fields associated with `jamie`?
b. Can the method `process` assign a new object to `jamie`?

FIGURE 6-5   A method cannot replace an object passed to it as an argument

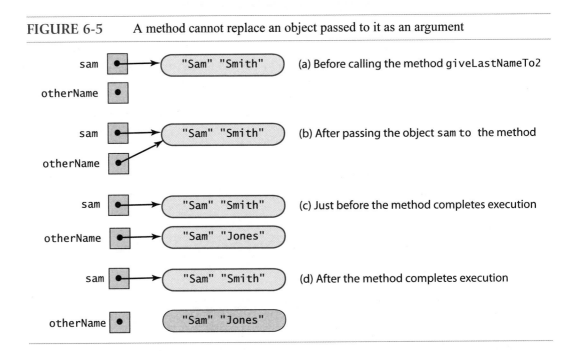

A Problem Solved: Comparing Classes of Squares

> As an exercise, imagine that you are asked to design and implement a class of square objects. Each object should be able to initialize the length of its side, change this length, and report its area.

6.24   **A brief design.** A square has four sides of equal length, and its area is the product of two of these lengths. Constructors can take care of any initialization, so we need only methods such as these:

- `setSide`—Sets or changes the length of the square's side to a given value
- `getSide`—Returns the length of the square's side
- `getArea`—Returns the area of the square

6.25   **Using the class.** Before we define the class, let's write some code that will use it. If we name the class Square, we might write the following statements:

```
Square box = new Square();
box.setSide(3.5);
System.out.println("A square whose side is " + box.getSide() +
                   " has an area of " + box.getArea());
```

The output from these statements would be

```
A square whose side is 3.5 has an area of 12.25
```

6.26   **An implementation.** The definition of this class is not difficult to write; you assume that everyone will write the same code. After a short time, two of your friends are asked to show and explain their implementations to the rest of the group. Joey's code appears in Listing 6-6. We'll get to Zoe's version later.

LISTING 6-6   A class of squares—first version

```java
/** Square.java by Joey
    A class of squares.
*/
public class Square
{
   private double side;

   public Square()
   {
      side = 1.0;
   } // end default constructor

   public Square(double initialSide)
   {
      side = initialSide;
   } // end constructor

   public void setSide(double newSide)
   {
      side = newSide;
   } // end setSide

   public double getSide()
   {
      return side;
   } // end getSide

   public double getArea()
   {
      return side * side;
   } // end getArea
} // end Square
```

Joey's code is straightforward. The class Square has one data field, side. A default constructor sets side to 1, an arbitrary but reasonable default value. A second constructor, as well as the set method setSide, sets side to a value given by the client. Finally, the method getArea computes and returns the area of the square.

Using the code that we wrote in Segment 6.25, Joey demonstrates that his implementation of Square works correctly.

Question 11 What would be the result of the code shown in Segment 6.25 if we changed the value of the square's side in the second statement from 3.5 to –3.5?

Question 12 Square's second constructor could call the method setSide instead of assigning a value to side directly. What would be the definition of this constructor in this case?

Question 13 Does the solution to the previous question offer a potential advantage over the original constructor?

Question 14 The method getArea could call the method getSide instead of using side directly. What would be the definition of getArea in this case?

6.27   **Another implementation.** Now let's consider Zoe's implementation of the class, as shown in Listing 6-7; it is fundamentally different from Joey's version in Listing 6-6. We have named it Square2 to differentiate the two versions.

In addition to the data field side, Zoe has defined a field area to hold the square's area. The value of this second field is set in each of the constructors as well as in the method setSide. That is, any time a square's side is set, its area is computed. The method getArea simply reports the value in the data field area instead of computing the area itself. These aspects are the significant differences between Joey's class Square and Zoe's class Square2.

LISTING 6-7   A class of squares—second version

```
/** Square2.java by Zoe
    A class of squares.
*/
public class Square2
{
    private double side;
    private double area;

    public Square2()
    {
        side = 1.0;
        area = 1.0;
    } // end default constructor

    public Square2(double initialSide)
    {
        side = initialSide;
        area = initialSide * initialSide;
    } // end constructor
```

```
   public void setSide(double newSide)
   {
      side = newSide;
      area = side * side;
   } // end setSide

   public double getSide()
   {
      return side;
   } // end getSide

   public double getArea()
   {
      return area;
   } // end getArea
} // end Square2
```

6.28   **Comparing implementations.** Although `Square` and `Square2` have different definitions, you can use them in the same way. That is, Zoe can use the same statements shown in Segment 6.25 to demonstrate `Square2` that Joey used for `Square`, with one minor change: Zoe simply changes each occurrence of `Square` to `Square2`.

Note that `Square` and `Square2` have the same interface. That is, their public methods have the same headers, are used in the same ways, and give the same results. These two classes illustrate the important point stated in the following Note.

Note: Two classes can differ in their implementations yet still provide the same behaviors. That is, *what* they do is the same, but *how* they go about it differs.

Is one class definition better than the other? The answer depends on our intended use of the class. Let's make some observations about these two classes:

- `Square` computes a square's area only when you call `getArea`, but it does so each time you call `getArea`. So if you call `getArea` frequently, the area would be computed over and over with the same result.
- In contrast, `Square2` always computes the area, but `getArea` simply reports the area without recomputing it. Even if you call `getArea` many times, the area is computed only once. But if you do not call `getArea` at all, the area is computed anyway.
- `Square2` uses more memory, because it has an additional data field.

Thus, if you needed to save memory, you would use `Square`; if you needed to save computer time, and you called `getArea` frequently, you would use `Square2`. Granted, the differences between these two classes in terms of their use of memory and computer time are small and likely insignificant. However, our discussion here should give you some insight into why the nature of an implementation is important and why a programmer might choose one over another.

Note: A class's implementation can affect the amount of memory and computer time it needs during execution.

6.29   **Why should data fields be private?** When you asked "Why?" as a child, didn't you hate the answer "Because I said so!"? Beginning Java programmers sometimes have the same reaction when told to make a class's data fields private. We gave you one reason for this rule in the programming tip right after Segment 6.10: Forcing a client to use a class method to give a value to a data field allows the class to enforce restrictions on the possible values.

Using the class `Square2`, we can show you another reason. Imagine that the data field `side` of `Square2` is public instead of private. Suppose we write the following code:

```java
Square2 squareTile = new Square2(4.0);
double edge = squareTile.getSide();
System.out.println("A " + edge + " by " + edge +
                   " tile has an area of " + squareTile.getArea());
squareTile.side = 3.0; // legal only if side is public
edge = squareTile.getSide();
System.out.println("A " + edge + " by " + edge +
                   " tile has an area of " + squareTile.getArea());
```

Because `side` is public, we can access it directly by name outside of the class and, in fact, change its value, as we have done in this example. The result of executing these statements is the output

```
A 4.0 by 4.0 tile has an area of 16.0
A 3.0 by 3.0 tile has an area of 16.0
```

Although we changed the value of `side` to a legal value, the value of `area` did not change. However, had we changed the value of `side` to 3.0 by writing `squareTile.setSide(3.0)`, the value of `area` would quickly have been changed to 9.0 by `setSide`. By making `side` private, we have restricted the ways in which a client can change its value, thus ensuring that any change to `side` also changes the value of `area`.

 Note: Because public data fields can be the source of data corruption in a class, data fields should be private.

6.30   **Yet another implementation.** Before you conclude that `Square` and `Square2` are the only possible implementations of a class of squares, let's look at `Square3` in Listing 6-8. This class has only one data field, `area`, to hold the square's area. The value of this field is set in each of the constructors as well as in the method `setSide`. That is, any time a square's side is set, its area is computed. The method `getArea` simply reports the value in the data field `area` instead of computing the area itself. However, the method `getSide` must compute the length of the side from the square's area.

LISTING 6-8   A class of squares—third version

```java
/** Square3.java
    A class of squares.
*/
public class Square3
{
    private double area;

    public Square3()
    {
```

```
      area = 1.0;
   } // end default constructor

   public Square3(double initialSide)
   {
      area = initialSide * initialSide;
   } // end constructor

   public void setSide(double newSide)
   {
      area = newSide * newSide;
   } // end setSide

   public double getSide()
   {
      return Math.sqrt(area);
   } // end getSide

   public double getArea()
   {
      return area;
   } // end getArea
} // end Square3
```

videonote
A problem
solved

Question 15 Can you use the statements shown in Segment 6.25, with each occurrence of Square changed to `Square3`, to demonstrate `Square3`?

Question 16 How do the behaviors of `Square3`'s methods `getSide` and `getArea` compare to those methods in `Square` and `Square2`?

CHAPTER SUMMARY

- A class is a plan for creating objects. It contains declarations for the data fields associated with its objects and definitions of methods that implement the objects' behaviors.

- The words `public` and `private` are examples of access modifiers that indicate where a class, method, or data field can be used. Any class can use something that is public. A private class, method, or data field can be used only by the class that defines it.

- When creating a class, you should specify its methods and write statements that use them. Only after you are satisfied with your design should you implement the methods.

- You should make each data field in a class private by beginning its declaration with the access modifier `private`. Doing so forces a client to use methods to assign values to these fields. In this way, an object's data is less likely to become corrupt.

- The first line of the definition of a class, constructor, or method is its header.

- When formal parameters occur in a method's header, each one appears with its data type. When you invoke a method, you pass it an argument that corresponds to each formal parameter. The same comments apply to constructors.

- A method that performs an action but does not compute a value as a result is known as a void method.

- A method that returns a value is known as a valued method. It returns a value by executing a `return` statement.

- An accessor method, or a get method, or a getter, is a method that returns the value of a data field. By convention, the names of such methods begin with "get."

- A mutator method, or a set method, or a setter, is a method that changes the value of a data field. By convention, methods whose names begin with "set" should be mutator methods.

- A method of class C can have a parameter of type C. Within the method's implementation, you can access the data fields of the argument that corresponds to this parameter by name.

- When a formal parameter has a primitive type, such as `int`, it is initialized to the value of the corresponding argument in the call to the method. This way of passing an argument to a method is known as a call by value. A method cannot change the value of an argument that has a primitive data type.

- When a formal parameter has a class type, the corresponding argument in the method invocation must be an object of that class type. The formal parameter is initialized to the memory address of that object. The method cannot replace an object that is an argument with another object. However, the method can change the state of such an object if the object is mutable.

- A constructor is a special method within a class that creates an instance, or object, of the class. The operator new uses a constructor to create a new object of the class.

- A class can have more than one constructor, with each one differing in its list of parameters. A constructor without parameters is known as the default constructor.

- If you do not define any constructor in your class, Java will provide a default constructor, that is, a constructor that has no parameters. However, if every constructor that you define has parameters, Java will not define a default constructor for you, so your class will have no default constructor.

- A local variable is a variable declared within the body of a method's definition. Its value is available only within the body of the method.

- The method `toString` returns a string that represents an object's data. If you fail to define a method `toString`, Java will provide its own version. However, Java's version of `toString` returns a string that likely will have no meaning to you.

- Within a method definition, you can write `this` to represent the method's receiving object.

EXERCISES

1. Describe the relationship between an object and its defining class.
2. In what way does the definition of a constructor differ from that of a method?
3. What are the naming conventions for accessor methods and mutator methods?
4. What is the purpose of the default constructor?
5. What is the purpose of a parameterized constructor?
6. What is the return type of a constructor?

7. What is the purpose of the access modifiers `public` and `private`?

8. Write Java statements to define a default constructor for a class named `Clock`. This class contains three integer and private data fields: `hour`, `minute`, and `second`.

9. Write a Java statement to create a new object named `wallClock` using the default constructor of the class `Clock`, as described in the previous exercise.

10. Write Java statements to define a parameterized constructor for the class `Clock`, as described in Exercise 8.

11. Write a Java statement to create a new object named `wallClock` using the parameterized constructor of the class `Clock`, as described in the previous exercise. Set the hour to 12, the minute to 15, and the second to 39.

12. Define a method for the class `Clock`, as described in Exercise 8, that displays the current time. Name your method `toString`.

13. Create accessor methods for the data fields defined in the class `Clock`. Refer back to Exercise 8 for a description of these fields.

14. Create mutator methods for the data fields defined in the class `Clock`. Refer back to Exercise 8 for a description of these fields.

15. When a data field is declared using the access modifier `private`, how does a client access the value of the data field? How does a client change the value of the data field?

16. Why are objects of the class `String` described as immutable?

17. What is the difference between a local variable and a data field?

18. Why should you define a method `toString` in the classes you create?

19. If you define a parameterized constructor for a class, must you define a default constructor? Explain.

20. Explain the difference between a void method and a valued method.

21. Describe the string that the method `toString` returns for each of the following classes in the Java Class Library:
    `java.math.BigDecimal`, `java.util.Date`, `java.lang.Integer`, `java.util.Random`, `java.awt.Rectangle`.
    (You pass a rectangle's width and height to the constructor of `Rectangle`.)

22. Implement a class `Car`, each of whose objects has a certain amount of gas in the gas tank, uses a specific amount of fuel per mile, and has a gas tank with a certain capacity.
    Provide a constructor that specifies the miles per gallon for the car. Define a method named `drive` that allows the car to be driven a certain distance and decrements the fuel supply appropriately. Also define a method named `refuel` that adds fuel to an existing `Car` object. Be sure to define appropriate accessor and mutator methods for the class.
    Test your class using a program that instantiates two different cars, one with a fuel efficiency of 32 miles per gallon and a 12-gallon tank, and one with a fuel efficiency of 21 miles per gallon and a 22-gallon tank. Each car is driven 121 miles with 10 gallons of fuel. Compute the amount of fuel remaining in each car.

23. Implement a class `Circle` whose constructor has a parameter to represent a circle's radius. Define the methods `getRadius`, `getArea`, `getCircumference`, and `toString`. The latter method should return a string containing the area and circumference of the circle.
    Test your class using a driver that creates two different circles and calls each method of each circle.

24. Implement a class `Counter` whose objects count things. An object of this class records a count as a nonnegative integer. Include methods to set the counter to 0, to increase the counter by 1, and to decrease the counter by 1. Define accessor and mutator methods as appropriate, as well as a `toString` method that displays the count as a string.
    Test your class using a driver that creates a counter and calls each of its methods.

25. Implement a class `Cylinder` whose constructor has a parameter to represent the radius of a cylinder's base and another parameter to represent a cylinder's height. Define the methods `getRadius`, `getAreaOfBase`, `getCircumference`, `getHeight`, `getVolume`, `getSurfaceArea`, and `toString`. Do not use the class `Circle` that Exercise 23 describes.

    Test your class using a driver that creates two different cylinders and calls each method of each cylinder.

26. Repeat the previous exercise, but this time use the class `Circle`, as described in Exercise 23, in `Cylinder`'s definition.

PROJECTS

1. Many games are played with dice, known as a die in the singular. A die is a six-sided cube whose sides are labeled with one to six dots. The side that faces up indicates the die's face value. Define a class `Die` that represents one *n*-sided die. The default value for *n* is 6. You should be able to roll the die and discover the value of its upper face. Thus, give the class the method `roll`, which returns a random integer ranging from 1 to *n*, and the method `getFaceValue`, which returns the current face value of the die. Note that a call to `roll` will return the same value as a subsequent call to `getFaceValue`. Demonstrate your class by creating several `Die` objects and rolling them.

    Often, games depend on the roll of two dice. Using your class `Die`, create a class `TwoDice`. An object of `TwoDice` represents two six-sided dice that are rolled together. Include at least the following methods: `rollDice`, `getFaceValueDieOne`, `getFaceValueDieTwo`, `isMatchingPair`, `isSnakeEyes`, `toString`, and `getValueOfDice`, which returns the sum of the two upper faces. Demonstrate your class by creating a `TwoDice` object and rolling it several times.

2. Design and implement a class `Frog`. Each `Frog` object has a name and keeps track of the number of times it leaps. Define two constructors, set and get methods for each data field, and the method `toString`. Also, define a method `jump` that simply increments the number of times the frog has jumped by 1. Demonstrate your class by creating three `Frog` objects. The output from this demonstration might appear as follows:

    ```
    Kermit has leapt 5 times.
    Kermit has leapt 8 times.
    Legs has leapt 0 times.
    Frogger has leapt 3 times.
    ```

3. Design and implement the class `CupDispenser`. Each `CupDispenser` object has a location and keeps track of the number of cups it currently contains. Define two constructors, set and get methods for each data field, and the method `toString`. Also, define a method `getOneCup` that simply decrements the number of cups in the dispenser by 1. Demonstrate your class by creating several `CupDispenser` objects. *Bonus*: Define the method `takeCupsFrom` that removes all the cups from its argument, a `CupDispenser` object, and adds them to its receiving object. For example, if `cd1` contains 10 cups, and `cd2` contains 20 cups, after the call `cd1.takeCupsFrom(cd2)`, `cd1` will contain 30 cups and `cd2` will be empty.

4. Design and implement the class `GeometricSequence` that represents the geometric sequence

    $$a, a \times r, a \times r^2, a \times r^3, a \times r^4, a \times r^5, ...$$

    The class should have the following private data fields:

    - The first term, *a*, in the sequence
    - The ratio *r* between successive terms in the sequence
    - The value of the current term in the sequence
    - The value of the exponent for the current term in the sequence

    Include a reasonable constructor, an accessor method for each data field, and a method `toString`. In addition, provide a mutator method for each of the following tasks:

    - Replace the current term in the sequence with the next term
    - Reset the current term in the sequence to the initial term in the sequence

    Write a program that tests your class definition.

5. A polygon is a closed figure with three or more sides. A regular polygon has sides that are all equal. Imagine that you have a circle of radius *r*, and you draw a regular polygon within the circle so that the polygon's corners just touch the circumference of the circle. For example, you might draw

If the polygon has *n* sides, you can use the following expression to compute the sum of its sides—that is, its perimeter:

$$n \times r \times \sqrt{2 \times (1 - \cos(360/n))}$$

Because the angle, 360 / *n*, in the previous expression is given in degrees, and the method `Math.cos` requires radians, you must convert from degrees to radians by using the formula

radians = degrees x π / 180

Design and implement a class of regular polygons. An object of this class should be able to report its number of sides and its perimeter. Demonstrate your class by writing a suitable program.

ANSWERS TO SELF-TEST QUESTIONS

1. No. The assignment is illegal, because `greeting` is private.

2. **a.** The value of `sue` is a reference to an object. Although `sue` references one object now and then a different object later, the objects themselves do not change.
   b. It is recycled during garbage collection.

3. **a.** `private String name;`
   b. Give name an initial value by adding an assignment such as

   ```
   name = "Default greeting";
   ```

   c.
   ```
   public void setName(String newName)
   {
      name = newName;
   } //end setName

   public String getName()
   {
      return name;
   } //end getName
   ```

4. `Joe said Hello, world! but now says Have a good day.`

5. No; `Greeter` does not define its own `toString` method.

6. ```
   Name me = new Name("Frank", "Carrano");
   System.out.println(me); // or System.out.println(me.toString());
   System.out.println(me.getLast() + ", " + me.getFirst());
   Name duke = new Name("Duke", "Java");
   me.giveLastNameTo(duke); // or duke.setLast(me.getLast());
   ```
   ```

7.
```
/** Changes the last name of this object to other's last name.*/
public void takeLastNameFrom(Name other)

// Use:
Name minnie = new Name("Minnie", "Mouse");
Name bugs = new Name("Bugs", "Bunny");
minnie.takeLastNameFrom(bugs); // minnie is now Minnie Bunny
```

8.
```
/** Returns the greeting as a string. */
public String toString()
{
    return greeting;
} // end toString
```

9.
```
/** Changes the last name of this object to other's last name.*/
public void takeLastNameFrom(Name other)
{
    last = other.last; // or last = other.getLast();
} // end takeLastNameFrom
```

10. **a.** Yes.
      b. No.

11. The output would be

> A square whose side is -3.5 has an area of 12.25

Clearly, a square cannot have a side whose length is negative. The next chapter will give you some tools to prevent a negative side within the class Square.

12.
```
public Square(double initialSide)
{
    setSide(initialSide);
} // end constructor
```

13. Yes. Suppose we defined setSide to ensure legal values for the side of a square, as described in the answer to Question 11. By calling setSide, the constructor will get the same protection without having to repeat the same code.

14.
```
public double getArea()
{
    double temp = getSide();
    return temp * temp;
} // end getArea
```

You could also write

```
public double getArea()
{
    return getSide() * getSide();
} // end getArea
```

but then getSide is called twice. In general, calling a method more than once to obtain the same result takes more time than calling it once and saving its result.

15. Yes. Square, Square2, and Square3 have the same interface.

16. Unlike both Square and Square2, Square3 computes a square's side each time you call getSide. Like Square2, Square3 always computes the area, but does so once; getArea simply reports the area without recomputing it. Even if you call getArea many times, the area is computed only once. If you do not call getArea at all, the area is computed anyway. On the other hand, Square computes the area each time getArea is called.

Debugging Interlude

2

Common Mistakes When Working with Classes

Contents

Prerequisites

We have just explored the basics of creating and using your own classes, as well as using classes written by someone else. These are major components of object-oriented programming. Before we introduce additional Java features, let's take a short break to continue our exploration of debugging. In this interlude, we will consider some common mistakes that you are apt to make while using or defining classes.

■ Working with Classes

Whether you are writing your own class or using one from the Java Class Library, mistakes can happen. Here are some of them.

A Silent Computational Error

D2.1

Imagine that your grandmother has asked you to help her make some candles. She has collected some cardboard mailing tubes to serve as molds. How much wax will she need? To find out, we can compute the volume of each cylindrical tube.

We begin by writing some pseudocode to describe what we need to do. It consists of three straightforward steps:

Prompt for and read the cylinder's height and radius.
Compute the volume.
Display the height, radius, and volume.

Since cylinders are the focus of this problem, let's define a class `Cylinder` to represent the various cylindrical mailing tubes.

A cylinder has a radius and a height, so these components can be the data fields of our class. In addition to creating a constructor, we can define accessor methods for the radius and height, as well as one for the volume. We need the formula for the volume of a cylinder. That volume is simply the area of the cylinder's circular cross-section multiplied by the cylinder's height. We know how to compute the area of a circle, since we did so in Chapter 4 (Segment 4.59, Listing 4-5). Thus, we have the following formula for the volume of a cylinder:

$$V_c = h \times \pi \times r^2$$

Listing D2-1 contains the definition of our class `Cylinder`.

LISTING D2-1   The class `Cylinder`, containing an error in its logic

```java
/** Cylinder.java by F. M. Carrano
    Represents cylinders, given their heights and radii.
*/
public class Cylinder
{
   private double radius;
   private double height;

   public Cylinder(double givenRadius, double givenHeight)
   {
      radius = givenRadius;
      height = givenHeight;
   } // end constructor

   public double getVolume()
   {
      return height * Math.PI * Math.pow(2.0, radius); // SILENT ERROR
   } // end getVolume

   public double getRadius()
   {
      return radius;
   } // end getRadius

   public double getHeight()
   {
      return height;
   } // end getHeight
} // end Cylinder
```

D2.2 Listing D2-2 contains a Java program to compute the volume of one cylinder by using our class `Cylinder`. It follows the logic of our earlier, brief algorithm.

LISTING D2-2   A test of the class `Cylinder`

```java
/** CylinderVolume.java by F. M. Carrano
    Computes the volume of a cylinder, given its height and radius.
*/
import java.text.DecimalFormat;
import java.util.Scanner;
public class CylinderVolume
{
    public static void main(String[] args)
    {
        Scanner keyboard = new Scanner(System.in);
        System.out.print("Enter the cylinder's radius " +
                         "and height in inches: ");
        double radius = keyboard.nextDouble();
        double height = keyboard.nextDouble();
        Cylinder aCylinder = new Cylinder(radius, height);
        double volume = aCylinder.getVolume();
        System.out.println("A cylinder whose radius is " +
                           aCylinder.getRadius() +
                           " and height is " + aCylinder.getHeight() +
                           "\nhas a volume of " +
                           new DecimalFormat("0.##").format(volume));
    } // end main
} // end CylinderVolume
```

Sample Output

```
Enter the cylinder's radius and height in inches: 2.8 6
A cylinder whose radius is 2.8 and height is 6.0
has a volume of 131.28
```

D2.3 Not only has our program compiled correctly, but also it ran and gave us results! However, if you use this program to compute the volumes of the remaining candle forms and then rush off to grandma's house with the indicated amount of wax, you both are likely to face disappointment. The computation performed by the program in Listing D2-2 is incorrect.

As reasonable as 131.28 might seem as a result, one computation does not test a program sufficiently. We should have started with a simple case whose answer is obvious. For example, a cylinder whose radius and height are each 1 would have a volume of π, or approximately 3.14. If we were to run our program again using these dimensions, we would get the following output:

```
Enter the cylinder's radius and height in inches: 1 1
A cylinder whose radius is 1.0 and height is 1.0
has a volume of 6.28
```

Clearly, we have a problem. Moreover, if you were to use a calculator to compute the volume using our original test data—a radius of 2.8 and height of 6—you would get approximately 147.7 instead of our program's value of 131.28.

What is wrong with the program in Listing D2-2?

D2.4   You might see the mistake right away, or you might scream in frustration. Silent errors need to be dealt with methodically. What could have gone wrong?

- The radius and height might be read incorrectly. You should always echo the input data. We did this, however, and the values are displayed correctly.
- The data types might be incorrect. The data type of each of the variables `radius`, `height`, and `volume` is `double`. This is correct.
- The `println` statement in the program uses `DecimalFormat` to format the output. Although clear output is desirable, trying to produce fancy output in the early drafts of a program is not a good idea. In this case, it would be better simply to display the value of `volume`. After your program works, you can go back and refine the appearance of the output. If we were to simplify the output here, however, we still would get a value like the one shown in Listing D2-2.

We have not found the problem.

Actually, the error is not in the program shown in Listing D2-2, but in the class `Cylinder`. Let's check the data types. Each of the fields `radius` and `height` is `double`, and the same is true of the constant `Math.Pi`. The method `Math.pow` needs two `double` arguments, which it has, and it returns a `double` value.

D2.5   It's time to trace the computation. We already know that the values of `height` and `radius` are correct in Listing D2-2, since we obtained and displayed them by using the method `getRadius` and `getHeight`. Let's display `Math.Pi` and `Math.pow(2.0, radius)`.

Suppose that we comment out the `return` statement in the method `getVolume` in Listing D2-1, and effectively replace it by inserting the following statements:

```
double pi = Math.PI;
double radiusSquared = Math.pow(2.0, radius);
double volume = height * pi * radiusSquared;
System.out.println(radius + " " + height);
System.out.println(pi + " " + radiusSquared + " " + volume);
return volume;
```

Now when we run the program in Listing D2-2 and enter 1 for both the radius and the height, the results are

```
1.0 1.0
3.141592653589793 2.0 6.283185307179586
A cylinder whose radius is 1.0 and height is 1.0
has a volume of 6.28
```

The value of `radiusSquared` is 2.0, but since `radius` is 1, its square should be 1.

Let's try another run of the program with different data:

```
3.0 6.0
3.141592653589793 8.0 150.79644737231007
A cylinder whose radius is 3.0 and height is 6.0
has a volume of 150.8
```

Since the radius is 3, its square should be 9, but we get 8.0. Do you see that we are computing 2^{radius} instead of the square of `radius`? Checking the documentation for `Math.pow` verifies that we have interchanged the arguments. That is, we should have written `Math.pow(radius, 2.0)` instead of Math.pow(2.0, radius). Since both arguments of pow have the same data type, our mistake did not alert the compiler. After we make this correction in Listing D2-1, the program will produce correct results.

Programming Tip: **Before using a standard method, check its documentation**

Mistakes, such as interchanging arguments or using incorrect data types, are easy to make. Check the documentation for methods in the Java Class Library on Sun's website. The compiler might catch some of these mistakes, but there is no guarantee that it will do so.

Programming Tip: **Use simple output until your computations are correct**

Designing correctly formatted output should be one of your last steps when writing a program. Worrying about the format of your output too soon likely will get in the way of writing and debugging a program that produces correct results. However, adding brief labels to the initial output will simplify your task. Notice how confusing the output in Segment D2.5 can be.

Undefined Variables of a Class Type

D2.6 Let's create two Square objects using the class Square given in Listing 6-6 of Chapter 6. The following program attempts this task but includes a common mistake that anyone might make. We have numbered the lines to clarify the error messages.

```
1 public class TwoSquares
2 {
3     public static void main(String[] args)
4     {
5         Square smallSquare, bigSquare;
6         smallSquare.setSide(1);
7         bigSquare.setSide(100);
8
9         System.out.println("Small square: side = " +
10                            smallSquare.getSide() + ", " +
11                       "area = " + smallSquare.getArea());
12        System.out.println("Big square: side = " +
13                            bigSquare.getSide() + ", " +
14                       "area = " + bigSquare.getArea());
15    } // end main
16 } // end TwoSquares
```

Error Messages

```
TwoSquares.java:6: variable smallSquare might not have been initialized
        smallSquare.setSide(1);
        ^

TwoSquares.java:7: variable bigSquare might not have been initialized
        bigSquare.setSide(100);
        ^

2 errors
```

This programmer has declared a variable of a class type—Square—and tried to initialize the object's data. What is the problem here? The statement

```
Square smallSquare;
```

declares smallSquare to be a variable of type Square but does not create an object of the class Square. So in the statement

```
smallSquare.setSide(1);
```

smallSquare does not reference an object. The compiler detects that we have not initialized this variable and complains. Although the error message is not definitive, this program would crash if executed.

To correct the problem, we need to add the following statements after the declaration of smallSquare and bigSquare in line 5:

```
smallSquare = new Square();
bigSquare = new Square();
```

Programming Tip: Remember to create objects

At some point after you declare a variable of a class type, you must use the operator new in conjunction with the class's constructor to create the object. Do this before using the variable in an invocation of a method of the class.

Constructors

D2.7

Missing default constructor. Recall from the previous chapter that Java defines a default constructor for a class only if you do not define any constructors. Once again, let's use the class Square, as given in Listing 6-6 of Chapter 6, but this time we will omit the definition of the default constructor. Since the resulting class—let's name it Square4—will still have a constructor defined, the compiler will not supply a definition of a default constructor. An attempt to invoke a default constructor would result in an error message from the compiler, as the following example demonstrates:

```
1  public class Square4Demo
2  {
3     public static void main(String[] args)
4     {
5        Square4 mySquare = new Square4();
6        mySquare.setSide(5.5);
7        . . .
```

Error Message

```
Square4Demo.java:5: cannot find symbol
symbol  : constructor Square4()
location: class Square4
        Square4 mySquare = new Square4();
                           ^
```

```
1 error
```

D2.8

Using a compiler-generated constructor. Now let's use the class Name in Listing 6-5 of the previous chapter, but without any constructor definitions. We name the revised class Name2. Since the class has no constructor definitions, the compiler will supply a default constructor. This constructor will create objects whose instance variables, first and last, are each initialized to null.

Suppose we use Name2 in a program that begins as follows:

```
1  public class Name2Demo
2  {
3     public static void main(String[] args)
```

```
 4     {
 5         Name2 myName = new Name2();
 6         String firstName = myName.getFirst();
 7         System.out.println("My first name is " + firstName);
 8         int length = firstName.length();
 9         System.out.println("My first name contains " + length +
10                            " characters.");
11         . . .
```

Executing these statements gives these results:

```
My first name is null
Exception in thread "main" java.lang.NullPointerException
        at Name2Demo.main(Nam2Demo.java:8)
```

The `println` statement at line 7 displays the value of `firstName`, which is `null`. In line 8, that `null` value is used in an attempt to invoke the `String` method `length`. That attempt results in an exception named `NullPointerException`. Even though `firstName` names a `String` object, the variable's current value is `null`. Thus, an invocation of the method `length` is not possible. The resulting error terminates execution of the program. The first programming tip at the end of Segment 6.20 in the previous chapter mentions this kind of error without naming the exception.

Note: **A compiler-generated constructor initializes data fields to default values**

A compiler-generated default constructor uses default values, such as zero or `null`, to initialize the data. These values are not always desirable. Such a constructor has the same effect as a programmer-defined default constructor that has an empty body. For example, if we were to add the following constructor definition to `Name2`, it would have the same effect as the compiler-generated default constructor:

```
public Name2()
{
} // end default constructor
```

Programming Tip: **Define a default constructor for most, but not all, classes**

By defining a default constructor, you can initialize an object's data to values that are more suitable than the compiler's default values. Doing so is especially important for data fields of a class type, as the previous and next segments show. But as the next note implies, not all classes should have a default constructor.

Note: **Set methods and default constructors**

If you rely on a compiler-generated default constructor, you should define set methods for the class so a client can provide acceptable values for the class's data. However, if you do not want set methods for your class, any default constructor must initialize the data fields to useful values. Otherwise, the default constructor will be useless; you should omit it and instead define a constructor that has parameters.

D2.9 Suppose we run the program given in the previous example, but replace the class `Name2` with the original class `Name` from Chapter 6. We would get the following output:

```
My first name is
My first name contains 0 characters.
```

No error this time!

While Name2 does not contain any constructor definitions, Name does. Its default constructor looks like this:

```java
public Name()
{
    first = ""; // empty string
    last = "";
} // end default constructor
```

This constructor initializes first and last to the empty string, whereas Name2's default constructor—which is compiler generated—initializes these variables to null. This latter value is the source of the error discussed in the previous example. Here, however, the expression firstName.getFirst() returns an empty string, which is assigned to the variable firstName. This empty string has a method length that returns 0 when it is invoked using the expression firstName.length().

 Note: An empty string is an object; null is not.

Omitting the Method toString

D2.10 We have previously mentioned the importance of a class having its own version of the method toString. Let's see what happens when you do not define toString. For example, let's remove the definition of the method toString from the class Name in Listing 6-5 of the previous chapter and call the revised class Name3. What happens if the following statements are in our program?

```java
Name3 joyce = new Name3("Joyce", "Jones");
System.out.println("Joyce's name is " + joyce);
```

We do not get an error. In fact, the println statement displays

```
Joyce's name is Name3@19821f
```

When an object's name—joyce, in this case—appears within a println statement and is not a part of a method invocation, the object's toString method is invoked. We mentioned this fact in the previous chapter, but we didn't define toString for Name3!

The method toString is special in that every class has one, even if you do not define it explicitly. However, this supplied method returns a string containing the class's name, the character '@', and a **hexadecimal** (base 16) number related to the receiving object—joyce in this example. This result is likely of little use. For this reason, we suggested in the previous chapter that each class generally should contain its own definition of toString.

■ A Problem Solved: Extracting Strings

> Read a person's name as a string, compute its length, and identify the first and last names and the person's initials. If the name is typed on one line, insist that only one space occur between the two names.

We already solved this problem in Chapter 4, but this time we'll make some mistakes and see how to find them. Although the improved solution that answered Question 15 in Chapter 4 would avoid some of the errors in this example, you might make the same errors while processing other strings or, as you will see in Chapter 18, arrays.

D2.11   **First-try solution.** Our first attempt at a solution appears in Listing D2-3. Although the program compiles, its execution results in an error message. An exception—`StringIndexOutOfBoundsException`—occurs because the value 1 is passed to the `String` method `charAt` in line 23 of the program. We have circled these key pieces of information in the program's output. As we study the code, we realize that the programmer mistakenly thinks that the characters in a string begin at index 1. Actually, the first character in a string is at index 0.

LISTING D2-3   A demonstration of `String` methods

```java
1  import java.util.Scanner;
2  public class StringDebug1
3  {
4     public static void main(String[] args)
5     {
6        Scanner keyboard = new Scanner(System.in);
7        System.out.print("Please type your first name, a space, and " +
8                         "your last name:");
9        String name = keyboard.nextLine();
10
11       // get indices:
12       int spaceIndex = name.indexOf(" "); // space between names
13       int firstNameStart = 1;
14       int firstNameEnd = spaceIndex - 1;
15       int lastNameStart = spaceIndex + 1;
16       int lastNameEnd = firstNameStart + name.length() - 1;
17
18       String firstName = name.substring(firstNameStart,
19                                         firstNameEnd);
20       String lastName  = name.substring(lastNameStart, lastNameEnd);
21       int nameLength = firstName.length() + lastName.length();
22
23       char firstInitial = firstName.charAt(1);
24       char lastInitial  = lastName.charAt(1);
25       String initials = firstInitial + ". " + lastInitial + ".";
26
27       System.out.println("Hi, " + name + ".\nYour name contains " +
28                          nameLength + " characters.");
29       System.out.println("Your first name is " + firstName + ".");
30       System.out.println("Your last name is " + lastName + ".");
31       System.out.println("Your initials are " + initials);
32    } // end main
33 } // end StringDebug1
```

Sample Output

```
Please type your first name, a space, and your last name:Joe Java
Exception in thread "main"
java.lang.StringIndexOutOfBoundsException: String index out of range: ①
        at java.lang.String.charAt(Unknown Source)
        at StringDebug1.main(StringDebug1.java:㉓)
```

D2.12 **Take two!** We need to change the arguments to the method charAt in lines 23 and 24 of Listing D2-3 from 1 to 0. Although we likely will be tempted to run the program again, first we really should see whether we made this same mistake elsewhere. In fact, the statement in line 13 assigns 1 instead of 0 to firstNameStart. So let's make the following three changes to the program:

```
13          int firstNameStart = 0;
            . . .
23          char firstInitial = firstName.charAt(0);
24          char lastInitial  = lastName.charAt(0);
```

When we run the corrected program, we get the following output:

```
Please type your first name, a space, and your last name: Joe Java
Hi, Joe Java.
Your name contains 5 characters.
Your first name is Jo.
Your last name is Jav.
Your initials are J. J.
```

This time, the program does not crash, but the first and last names are incorrect. Something might be wrong with the indices we passed to the method substring.

Wishing we had done this earlier, we add the following debugging statements to the program at line 22 of Listing D2-3:

```
System.out.println("DEBUG: first name: " + firstName + " indices " +
                      firstNameStart + " to " + firstNameEnd);
System.out.println("DEBUG: last name: " + lastName + " indices " +
                      lastNameStart + " to " + lastNameEnd);
```

Now the output is

```
Please type your first name, a space, and your last name: Joe Java
DEBUG: first name: Jo indices 0 to 2
DEBUG: last name: Jav indices 4 to 7
Hi, Joe Java.
Your name contains 5 characters.
Your first name is Jo.
Your last name is Jav.
Your initials are J. J.
```

D2.13 Given the values of the indices we just displayed, the invocations to substring are effectively name.substring(0, 2) and name.substring(4, 7). If we quickly sketch the string "Joe Java", we can number the characters and check the values of these indices. Our drawing in Figure D2-1 shows that the first name does indeed range from index 0 to index 2, and the indices for the last name range from 4 to 7. Everything appears to be correct—everything, that is, except for the results!

FIGURE D2-1 Indices 0 through 7 for the string "Joe Java"

J	o	e		J	a	v	a

Indices ➞ 0   1   2   3   4   5   6   7

D2.14   It is time to check our understanding of the method substring. Sun's online documentation[1] lists this method as follows:

```
String substring(int beginIndex, int endIndex)
Returns a new string that is a substring of this string.
```

The program's two invocations of this method use similar notation, and so they appear to be correct:

- name.substring(firstNameStart, firstNameEnd)
- name.substring(lastNameStart, lastNameEnd)

D2.15   **Take three!** We need to examine the detailed description of the method substring by clicking its name in the online documentation. That description includes the following:

> Returns a new string that is a substring of this string. The substring begins at the specified beginIndex and extends to the character at index endIndex - 1.

In other words, the second argument endindex passed to substring must be 1 larger than the last index of the desired string.

Thus, the correct calls to substring in Listing D2-3 are

- name.substring(firstNameStart, firstNameEnd + 1)
- name.substring(lastNameStart, lastNameEnd + 1)

D2.16   The program now gives us correct answers initially. After commenting out the debugging statements, we should try several different input strings. For example, here are the results of two runs of the program:

First run:

```
Please type your first name, a space, and your last name: Joe Java
Hi, Joe Java.
Your name contains 7 characters.
Your first name is Joe.
Your last name is Java.
Your initials are J. J.
```

Second run:

```
Please type your first name, a space, and your last name:      Jen Sun
Exception in thread "main" java.lang.StringIndexOutOfBoundsException:
String index out of range: 0
        at java.lang.String.charAt(Unknown Source)
        at StringDebug1.main(StringDebug1.java:28)
```

Notice that the input data for the second run has extra blanks at its beginning. Once again, the error occurs during the call to charAt. But the offending argument has a value of 0, which seems valid. We should have left those debugging statements in the program! Fortunately, we didn't delete them, just commented them out.

---

1. java.sun.com/javase/6/docs/api/

D2.17 After we've reinstated them, the debugging statements display the following output for the data entered in the second run:

```
DEBUG: first name:  indices 0 to -1
DEBUG: last name:   Jen Sun indices 1 to 9
```

For the first name, `firstNameStart` is 0 and `firstNameEnd` is -1. Thus, the call to `substring` that extracts the first name must be `name.substring(0, 0)`. This call is legal and results in the empty string, which the previous debugging results confirm. Notice that `lastName` encompasses the entire name, Jen Sun, including some leading blanks.

By examining the program, we are reminded of the importance of the space occurring between the first and last names. Its index is found by the statement

```
int spaceIndex = name.indexOf(" ");
```

However, since the string `name` contains leading blanks, `spaceIndex` is 0. This value corrupts our subsequent calculations.

The solution is to trim any leading—or trailing—blanks from the input data by adding the statement

```
name = name.trim();
```

right after the value of `name` is read.

D2.18 **A correct solution.** The corrected program appears in Listing D2-4. It, as well as the intermediate versions that we have discussed in this example, are included in the source code that is available for this book. Compare this program with the version given in Listing 4-1 of Chapter 4.

LISTING D2-4 A correct version of the program in Listing D2-3

```java
import java.util.Scanner;
public class StringDebug
{
    public static void main(String[] args)
    {
        Scanner keyboard = new Scanner(System.in);
        System.out.print("Please type your first name, a space, and " +
                         "your last name: ")
        String name = keyboard.nextLine();
        name = name.trim();

        // get indices:
        int spaceIndex = name.indexOf(" "); // space between names
        int firstNameStart = 0;
        int firstNameEnd = spaceIndex - 1;
        int lastNameStart = spaceIndex + 1;
        int lastNameEnd = firstNameStart + name.length() - 1;

        String firstName = name.substring(firstNameStart,
                                          firstNameEnd + 1);
        String lastName  = name.substring(lastNameStart, lastNameEnd + 1);
        int nameLength = firstName.length() + lastName.length();
/*
```

```
System.out.println("DEBUG: first name: " + firstName + " indices " +
                    firstNameStart + " to " + firstNameEnd);
System.out.println("DEBUG: last name: " + lastName + " indices " +
                    lastNameStart + " to " + lastNameEnd);
*/
      char firstInitial = firstName.charAt(0);
      char lastInitial  = lastName.charAt(0);
      String initials = firstInitial + ". " + lastInitial + ".";

      System.out.println("Hi, " + name + ".\nYour name contains " +
                          nameLength + " characters.");
      System.out.println("Your first name is " + firstName + ".");
      System.out.println("Your last name is " + lastName + ".");
      System.out.println("Your initials are " + initials);
   } // end main
} // end StringDebug
```

D2.19   **What did we learn?** Let's review some of the lessons illustrated in the previous example. The importance of testing a program with more than one set of data should be apparent. Future sections of this book will focus more on this step of program development.

videonote
Common errors

You saw in Segments D2.16 and D2.17 that leading blanks in the input data can cause problems for programs that work otherwise. To avoid these problems, you could just tell the user to avoid leading and trailing blanks, but a programmer should consider the convenience of the user by making a program deal with such situations. You might also simply assume that users would not use leading or trailing blanks, but that would be a poor assumption! As much as possible, a program should be able to cope with unexpected data without crashing. Such a program is said to be **robust**. A programmer who anticipates unusual situations and handles them in a suitable manner is said to be exercising **defensive programming**.

You also saw the importance of careful documentation. When naming methods, parameters, variables, and other components, use terms that are clear. Segment D2.14 showed how a programmer can misinterpret the meaning of substring's parameter endIndex to mean the index of the last character in a desired substring. Only after reading the details of the method's documentation, as pointed out in Segment D2.15, will one realize the meaning of this parameter.

Programming Tip: Debugging hints

- Choose your terminology carefully. You will help both yourself as a programmer and others who use your programs by choosing meaningful identifiers and writing clear comments and other documentation.
- Read the details in the documentation. When reading someone else's documentation, do not make rash assumptions based only on the identifiers used. Look for explanations of those terms.
- Perform some initial computations by hand. You should have some test data whose results you know. You also should be able to recognize unreasonable results.

- Test your code often and extensively. Isolate and test small pieces of code or individual methods.
- Poorly written code often is difficult, if not impossible, to debug. Don't be afraid to start over. Your initial attempts will give you insight into a better solution.
- Reduce the number of Java statements used, if doing so does not obscure your algorithm. The number of mistakes made by a typical programmer multiplies as the length of a program grows.

EXERCISE

1. Using the program given in Listing D2-2, test and debug the following version of the class Cylinder, which is included with the source code available for this book:

```java
public class Cylinder
{
    private double radius;
    private double height;
    private double volume;

    public Cylinder(double givenRadius, double givenHeight)
    {
        double radius = givenRadius;
        double height = givenHeight;
        double volume = height * Math.PI * Math.pow(radius, 2.0);
    } // end constructor

    public double getVolume()
    {
        return volume;
    } // end getVolume

    public double getRadius()
    {
        return radius;
    } // end getRadius

    public double getHeight()
    {
        return height;
    } // end getHeight
} // end Cylinder
```

Chapter

7

Decisions

Contents

Prerequisites

Objectives

After studying this chapter, you should be able to

- Write boolean expressions
- Use `if-else` statements to alter a program's flow of control
- Compare two primitive values of the same type
- Compare two objects
- Use assertions and `assert` statements in a program

If it isn't one thing, it's another. Making decisions is something we all do. And it is a task that Java programs can do. This chapter will show you the basics of how to write Java statements that can choose between two courses of action. Chapter 10 will complete this discussion by considering choices among several actions.

Flow of Control

7.1 The first Java statement that executes in an application program is the first one in the method `main`. Subsequent statements execute sequentially unless a statement alters this order. The order in which statements in a Java program execute is called the **flow of control**. If a statement contains a call to another method, control is given to that method, as shown in Figure 7-1. Eventually that method returns control to the method that called it. Execution ends when and if the closing brace in `main` is reached.[1]

In all of the examples you have seen so far, the statements in a program execute in the same order each time the program is run. You can alter this order during the execution of the program, however, by using one of several kinds of **decision statements**. The **if statement** and the **if-else statement** offer two courses of action according to the value of a certain kind of expression. Although we distinguish between these two statements here, they generally are both called `if` statements. Chapter 10 will show you how to choose among more than two possible actions.

FIGURE 7-1   Invoking a method

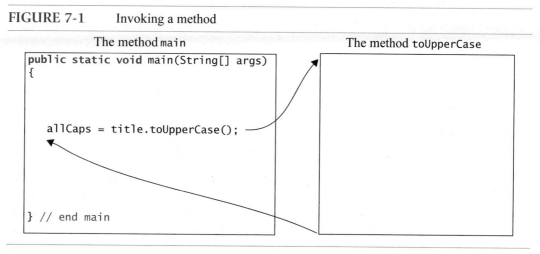

The `if` Statement

7.2 Your program can alter its flow of control according to a condition that you specify. If the condition is true, one or more specified statements will execute before program execution continues. The statement that makes this decision is called the `if` statement. It has the following form:

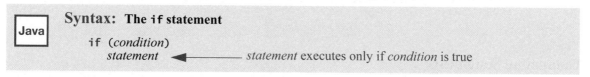

Syntax: The `if` statement

```
if (condition)
    statement  ◄──────── statement executes only if condition is true
```

---

1. Other ways of ending program execution are also possible.

If the condition is true, the statement that follows executes. If the condition is false, the statement that follows does not execute. In both cases, the flow of control continues sequentially. Figure 7-2 illustrates this logic.

Our first examples involve comparing primitives.

FIGURE 7-2   The logic of an `if` statement

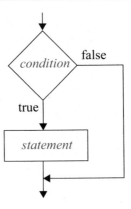

7.3   **Example.** Suppose that you have two `int` variables, `side1` and `side2`. The following `if` statement compares the contents of the two variables:

```
if (side1 < side2)
    System.out.println(side1 + " is smaller than " + side2);
System.out.println("Continuing computation."); // always executes
```

If the value of `side1` is less than the value of `side2`, the first `println` statement executes. Otherwise, this statement is skipped. In both cases, the second `println` statement executes.

The condition `side1 < side2` is an example of a **boolean expression**. The value of such an expression is either true or false. By convention, the statement that is executed if the boolean expression is true is indented. We will consider boolean expressions in detail shortly.

> **! Programming Tip**
> Indenting specific Java statements improves the readability of a program but does not affect the program's logic.

Compound Statements

You can execute more than one Java statement when a certain condition is true by placing those statements within braces after `if` (*condition*). The braces and the statements they enclose are a single construct called a **compound statement**. A compound statement can appear anywhere in a Java program that a single statement can appear.

7.4   **Example.** Imagine that your program asks its user whether he or she needs directions. You could read a one-character response—Y for yes, N for no—and use an if statement to decide what was read as follows:

```
Scanner keyboard = new Scanner(System.in);
System.out.println("Do you need help? (Answer Y or N)");
String response = keyboard.nextLine();
if (response.charAt(0) == 'Y')
{
    System.out.println("To evaluate launch conditions,");
    System.out.println("respond as prompted.");
    System.out.println("For technical support, call 888-555-5555.");
} // end if
```

If the user types Y in response to the question, all the statements within the compound statement execute. Notice that we do not indent the braces—they align with the if—but we do indent each statement within the braces.

In more complex situations, your program could contain a sequence of several closing braces, as you will see. Labeling each one with a comment helps to identify its matching open brace while you are writing the program.

Note that you use the **equality operator** == to test whether two primitives—characters in this example—have equal values.

Programming Tip: **Testing two primitive values for equality**

To test whether two primitives have equal values, use the equality operator ==. Do not use the assignment operator =. Doing so is a common mistake and leads to a syntax error that might be hard to understand at first.

Programming Tip: **Writing compound statements**

When writing a compound statement, type a pair of braces—each on its own line and aligned—label the closing brace, and then type the statements that are to appear between the braces. By using this technique, you are less likely to forget to write a closing brace. Typical IDEs, however, will prompt you to match braces.

Programming Tip: **Writing braces**

Always writing a pair of braces within an if statement, even when the braces enclose a single statement, is a style that many programmers use. The braces clarify the logic and are in place should you decide to replace a single statement with several. If you cannot remember whether to use braces, or you forget to add them where necessary, always use them. The examples in this book often will omit unnecessary braces to save space.

SELF-TEST

Question 1   In the previous example, why did we read the character as a string?

Question 2   In the previous example, a user's response of y instead of Y will be interpreted as "no" instead of "yes." How can you modify the code to ensure that the lowercase letter y is interpreted correctly?

Question 3   In the previous example, what happens if the user's response is Yes or No?

Question 4   Given a char variable ch, write statements that use a method in the class Character to decide whether ch contains an uppercase letter.

Basic Comparisons

Our previous examples compared two primitive values. In this section, we elaborate on how to compare two primitives that have the same type, and then discuss how to compare two objects.

Comparing Primitives

7.5 When comparing primitives, as in the previous examples, you use operators such as == or <. These operators are examples of **relational operators**. Figure 7-3 lists these operators and their meanings. Notice the two-character operators <= and >=. These exist because characters such as ≤ and ≥ are not on standard keyboards.

FIGURE 7-3   Relational operators that compare primitive values

Math Notation	Name	Java Operator	Java Examples
≥	Greater than or equal to	>=	points >= 60
≤	Less than or equal to	<=	expenses <= income
>	Greater than	>	expenses > income
<	Less than	<	pressure < max
=	Equal to	==	balance == 0 answer == 'y'
≠	Not equal to	!=	income != tax answer != 'y'

Question 5 Imagine that your job is to sell tickets in a movie theater. As you sell each ticket, a Java program counts how many you have sold so that you do not exceed the capacity of the theater. The program contains the integer constant THEATER_SIZE and the integer variable ticketCounter. The variable is initially 0 and is incremented by 1 for each ticket sold. Write statements that compare the values of ticketCounter and THEATER_SIZE and display a message when the theater's capacity has been reached or exceeded.

Question 6 At your summer job, you earn d dollars per hour. If you work h hours this week, your base pay will be $d \times h$ dollars. However, if you work more than 35 hours, you will earn an extra $d / 2$ dollars for each hour over 35. Write Java statements to compute your base pay and then adjust it if you work overtime.

Comparing Objects

Chapter 4 showed that all objects whose type is String, Date, or BigDecimal have the methods equals and compareTo. You use these methods, not the operators listed in Figure 7-3, to compare two objects of the same data type.

7.6   **Example.** Your program can respond to words that the user types at the keyboard as input. Suppose that you ask whether the user needs directions for using your program. Instead of requiring a one-letter response, as we did in Segment 7.4, you can ask for a response of Yes or No. You read the response as a string and use the method equals to compare the response with an expected one. Using a method such as toLowerCase before the comparison allows the user some typing flexibility.

```
final String YES = "yes";
System.out.println("Do you need help? (Answer Yes or No)");
String response = keyboard.nextLine();
response = response.toLowerCase();

if (response.equals(YES))
{
   System.out.println("To evaluate launch conditions,");
   System.out.println("respond as prompted.");
   System.out.println("For technical support, call 888-555-5555.");
} // end if
```

Question 7 In the previous example, instead of changing the user's response to lowercase, you can use the String method equalsIgnoreCase. How would you change the previous code to use this approach?

7.7   **Example.** What would happen if you wrote

```
if (response == YES)
```

in the previous example instead of

```
if (response.equals(YES))
```

You would not get a syntax error, but you also would not get the results you want.

   You learned in Segment 4.6 of Chapter 4 that a variable of a class type contains a reference to the object it represents. It does not contain the object itself. When comparing two variables of the same class type, the operator == compares the references, not the objects. In our example here, the operator == compares the reference in the variable response to the reference in the named constant YES. They are different because we have two different String objects, as Figure 7-4 illustrates. Even if both strings have the same value, namely "yes", the == comparison is false. The method equals, however, compares the values of the two strings and finds them equal.

FIGURE 7-4   Distinct references to strings whose values are the same

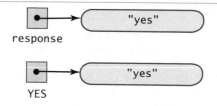

Programming Tip

To compare two characters, you use a relational operator such as <. But to compare two strings, you use one of the methosds equals, equalsIgnoreCase, or compareTo. Do not use the operators == and !=, as they will compare the addresses of the strings, not their values. Note that it is illegal to use the operators <, <=, >, and >= with references, and so it is also illegal to use them with strings. Using one of the relational operators when comparing objects is a common error.

7.8 **Example.** Consider the statements

```
String greeting = "Hi";
String salutation = "Hi";
```

Following their execution, the variables greeting and salutation each reference the literal "Hi". Even though "Hi" appears in two different assignment statements, the compiler creates only one String object, as Figure 7-5 illustrates. Both variables reference this string. Thus, the expression

```
greeting == salutation
```

is true, because both greeting and salutation contain the same reference. Moreover, the expression

```
greeting.equals(salutation)
```

is true because the value of the String object is compared with itself.

FIGURE 7-5   Two variables that reference the same string

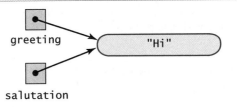

 Note: All classes have a method equals that decides whether two objects are equal. Only certain classes have a method compareTo. You'll learn more about these methods later in this book.

 Question 8 Assume that the object person has a method getFirstName. The expression person.getFirstName() returns the person's first name as a string.

   a.   What statements will display a greeting if the person's first name is Joe?
   b.   What statements will display a message if the person's first name contains more than five characters?

Question 9 If str is a String variable that references a one-character string, write statements that will display a message if the character is an uppercase letter.

Question 10 Suppose that balance is an instance of the class BigDecimal that represents the balance in your checking account. Write statements that display an error message if the balance is negative.

■ A Problem Solved: Day of the Week

7.9 Segment 3.16 presented a pseudocode solution to the problem of finding the day of the week on which a given date falls. At the time, we had not discussed the if statement. Now that we have done so, we can write a complete Java program to solve this problem. Listing 7-1 shows the program and some sample output. Notice that the program reports the day of the week as an integer 1 through 7, although the algorithm produces an integer 0 through 6. In a later chapter, we will transform this integer into a string that is the actual name of the day.

LISTING 7-1   Finding the day of the week for a given date

```java
/** DayOfWeek.java by F. M. Carrano

    Finds the day of week on which a given date falls.

    Input:   the month (1 - 12)
             the day (1 - 31)
             the 4-digit year
    Output: the date and an integer from 1 to 7 that indicates the
            day of the week (1 is Sunday, 2 is Monday, and so on)
*/
import java.util.Scanner;
public class DayOfWeek
{
   public static void main(String[] args)
   {
      Scanner keyboard = new Scanner(System.in);
      System.out.println("This program reports the day of the week " +
                         "for a given date.\n");

      System.out.println("Type the month, day, and year as " +
                         "integers separated by spaces: ");
      int month = keyboard.nextInt();
      int day   = keyboard.nextInt();
      int year  = keyboard.nextInt();

      // Adjust month and year so that January and February
      // are months 13 and 14 of the previous year
      int zellerMonth = month;
      int zellerYear = year;
      if (month < 3)
      {
         zellerMonth = month + 12;
         zellerYear = year - 1;
      } // end if
      // zellerMonth and zellerYear are ready for the computation;
      // month and year contain original values for output

      // Zeller's Congruence
      int computation = day + (26 * (zellerMonth + 1)) / 10 +
                        zellerYear + zellerYear / 4 +
                        6 * (zellerYear / 100) + zellerYear / 400;
      int dayOfWeek = computation % 7; // 0 - 6 for Saturday - Friday
      if (dayOfWeek == 0)
         dayOfWeek = 7;                         // adjust Saturday
```

```
            System.out.println();
            System.out.println(month + "/" + day + "/" + year + " is day " +
                              dayOfWeek + " of the week.");
    } // end main
} // end DayfWeek
```

Sample Output

```
This program reports the day of the week for a given date.

Type the month, day, and year as integers separated by spaces:
12 31 2010

12/31/2010 is day 6 of the week.
```

■ The `if-else` Statement

7.10   So far, we have used the `if` statement to do something if a certain condition is true, but not do it if the condition is false. Frequently, however, you want to do one thing if a certain condition is true and another thing if it is not, as Figure 7-6 illustrates. In these situations, an `if` statement can have an **else clause** that indicates what to do when the condition is false. This kind of `if` statement is sometimes called an `if-else` statement. It has the following form:

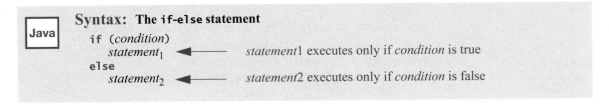

Syntax: **The `if-else` statement**
```
if (condition)
    statement₁          ←——— statement1 executes only if condition is true
else
    statement₂          ←——— statement2 executes only if condition is false
```

FIGURE 7-6   The logic of an `if-else` statement

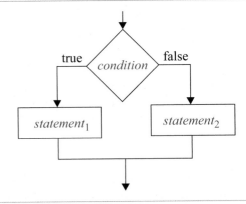

7.11   **Example.** A portion of a bank's program that maintains your checking account could use `BigDecimal` objects to represent monetary values, as you saw in Chapter 4. Suppose that `balance` and `checkAmount` are variables whose type is `BigDecimal`. Assume that they have been initialized to appropriate values.

The following statements process the check. Recall that the method compareTo returns an integer that is either negative, zero, or positive, depending on the results of the comparison.

```
if (checkAmount.compareTo(balance) <= 0)
    balance = balance.subtract(checkAmount);
else
    System.out.println("Insufficient funds to process check.");

System.out.println("Balance is $" + balance);
```

If the amount of the check does not exceed the account's current balance, it is deducted from the balance. Otherwise, a message is displayed. Regardless of the outcome of the comparison, the current balance is displayed.

What if we used int values instead of BigDecimal objects for monetary values? That is, suppose that the data type of the variables balance and checkAmount is int. Instead of the previous statements, you would write:

```
// same computation but with int variables
if (checkAmount <= balance)
    balance = balance - checkAmount;
else
    System.out.println("Insufficient funds to process check.");

System.out.println("Balance is $" + balance);
```

Here you compare the int values by using the operator <= instead of the method compareTo. Additionally, you use the operator - to perform the subtraction instead of the method subtract.

Programming Tip

Due to the way Java represents real numbers—that is, those numbers whose data type is either double or float—you should not expect two real values to be equal, even if they should be theoretically. When testing two real values for equality, allow for a small difference between them.

For example, if x and y are two double variables, you can treat them as equal if the difference between them is small. More precisely, x and y are approximately equal in value if the expression Math.abs(x - y) < SMALL_NUMBER is true. The value that you choose for the constant SMALL_NUMBER depends on the magnitude of x and y. It can be larger when x and y are large numbers and smaller when they are small.

To avoid having to look at the relationship among x, y, and SMALL_NUMBER for each computation, you can replace x - y with (x - y) / y in the previous boolean expression. Thus, if Math.abs((x - y) / y) < SMALL_NUMBER is true, you can take x and y as being almost equal. A value of 0.000005 for SMALL_NUMBER could be a reasonable choice. A course or book about numerical computation will explore this issue further.

Question 11 Each of the variables wordOne and wordTwo, whose data type is String, represents a word composed entirely of lowercase letters. Write statements that display these two words in alphabetical order.

Question 12 Given the variables wordOne and wordTwo, as described in the previous question, write statements that display one message if the two words have the same value, but another message if their values are different.

7.12 **Example.** Let's again consider the `if-else` statement shown in the previous example:

```java
if (checkAmount.compareTo(balance) <= 0)
    balance = balance.subtract(checkAmount);
else
    System.out.println("Insufficient funds to process check.");
```

Now consider this revision of the code:

```java
if (checkAmount.compareTo(balance) <= 0)
    balance = balance.subtract(checkAmount);
if (checkAmount.compareTo(balance) > 0)
    System.out.println("Insufficient funds to process check.");
```

Both the original code and the revision produce the same results. However, the revision is a poor design.

videonote
if and if-else
statments

Although situations arise in which successive `if` statements are warranted, this task is not one of them. The `if-else` statement makes one comparison and then executes one statement according to the result of that comparison. If something is true, one thing happens; otherwise something else happens. With successive `if` statements, two comparisons are made. Although these comparisons should negate each other, they will do so only if you, the programmer, have not made a mistake in writing the boolean expressions. Moreover, in this example, the method `compareTo` is called twice, increasing the time it takes to reach the same conclusion as the `if-else` statement.

Note: The selection operator

The **selection operator** `?:` provides the same logic as an `if-else` statement, and programmers sometimes use it because of its briefer syntax. This operator takes three operands, and is the only Java operator to do so. For this reason, it is also called the **ternary operator**.

The operator's first operand, written before the question mark, is a boolean expression whose value is tested. The next two operands precede and follow the colon. If the boolean expression is true, the result of the operation is the value of the second operand; otherwise the result is the value of the third operand. For example, the value of the expression

```java
(x >= 0) ? x : -x
```

is the absolute value of x. By assigning this value to a variable, we get the statement

```java
int y = (x >= 0) ? x : -x;
```

which has the same effect as the following `if-else` statement:

```java
if (x >= 0)
    y = x;
else
    y = -x;
```

Use the selection operator only if it clarifies the logic of your code. Usually, an `if-else` statement is easier to understand.

More Boolean Expressions in Comparisons

videonote
Booleans and
comparisons

As we mentioned earlier, an expression such as

```java
age >= 20
```

that we use as the condition within an `if` statement is called a boolean expression. These simple expressions use the relational operators given in Figure 7-3 to compare two operands—variables, constants, or other expressions—that have primitive data types. Each expression has a value of true or false. You can combine such expressions into more complex boolean expressions by using the **logical operators &&**, **||**, and **!**. These operators are named **and**, **or**, and **not**, respectively, and behave as follows:

> **Note: The logical operators &&, ||, and !**
> - *boolean-expression₁* **&&** *boolean-expression₂* is true if both boolean expressions are true; otherwise it is false. This operator is known as the "and" operator.
> - *boolean-expression₁* **||** *boolean-expression₂* is true if either or both boolean expressions are true; otherwise it is false. This operator is known as the " or" operator.
> - **!***boolean-expression* is true if *boolean-expression* is false; otherwise it is false. This operator is known as the "not" operator.

7.13   **The operator &&.** The statement

```
if ( (age >= 20) && (age < 30) )
    System.out.println("Your age is in the range 20 - 29.");
else
    System.out.println("Your age is outside the range 20 - 29.");
```

tests whether the value of age is within the range 20 to 29 and prints a message indicating the result. When two boolean expressions are joined by the "and" operator, &&, the result is true if both of the expressions are true. So if both age >= 20 and age < 30 are true, the expression

```
(age >= 20) && (age < 30)
```

is true. Note that the parentheses are optional, but they help make the expression easier to read.

7.14   Figure 7-7 shows the results of the operator && in four possible situations. In Java, if the result of an expression of the form *x* && *y* can be decided by looking only at the value of *x*, the expression *y* will not be evaluated. Is this ever possible? Yes. In the fourth example in Figure 7-7, 6 < 3 is false. The entire expression must therefore be false, regardless of the value of the second expression. Thus, the second expression is never evaluated. This phenomenon—called **short-circuit evaluation**—will become important later in your studies, and we will remind you of it then.

FIGURE 7-7   The operator &&

Operation	Result	Example
true && true	true	(6 > 3) && (4 == 4)
false && false	false	(6 < 3) && (4 < 4)
true && false	false	(6 > 3) && (4 < 4)
false && true	false	(6 < 3) && (4 == 4)

Programming Tip

When testing to determine whether a value lies within a certain range, you write two expressions joined with the operator &&. Each of these expressions compares the value with an endpoint of the range. For example, to see whether the value of age is between 20 and 29, you could write either (20 <= age) && (age < 30) or the equivalent expression (age >= 20) && (age < 30). Note that the variable age is written twice in either case. You could not write the expressions 20 <= age < 30 or age >= 20 && < 30, as they are syntactically incorrect.

Question 13 Several boolean expressions are equivalent to (20 <= age) && (age < 30). What are they?

7.15 **The operator ||.** The following if statement also indicates whether the value of age is within the range 20 to 29:

```
if ( (age < 20) || (age >= 30) )
    System.out.println("Your age is outside the range 20 - 29." );
else
    System.out.println("Your age is in the range 20 - 29." );
```

When two boolean expressions are joined by the "or" operator, ||, the result is true if one or both of the expressions is true. For example, if age is 19, age < 20 is true but age >= 30 is false. Together,

```
(age < 20) || (age >= 30)
```

is true.

To test whether age is within a certain range by using the operator ||, we use a boolean expression that is true if age is outside of the range. Earlier, in Segment 7.13, we used the operator && and a boolean expression that is true if age is within this range. The two approaches are equivalent, but to make them work, the clauses that follow if and those that follow else are reversed in the two examples.

7.16 Figure 7-8 shows the results of the operator || in four possible situations. In the third example, the value of the entire expression is known by looking only at the value of the first expression, 6 > 3. It is true, so the entire expression is true regardless of the value of the second expression. The second expression is not evaluated. Again, this is called short-circuit evaluation.

FIGURE 7-8 The operator ||

Operation	Result	Example
true || true	true	(6 > 3) || (4 == 4)
false || false	false	(6 < 3) || (4 < 4)
true || false	true	(6 > 3) || (4 < 4)
false || true	true	(6 < 3) || (4 == 4)

7.17 **The operator !.** The "not" operator, !, is a unary operator, taking only one operand. When it is applied to an expression that is true, the result is false and, conversely, when it is applied to an expression that is false, the result is true. For example, you can compare two strings and react if they are not equal by writing

```
if (!wordOne.equals(wordTwo))
    System.out.println("The strings are not equal." );
```

Although this is a fine example of using the ! operator, negating complex boolean expressions can lead to confusing logic and should be avoided if possible.

Programming Tip
To make your program easier to read, consider alternatives to !, if possible.

Note: **The order of operations in a boolean expression**
Operations in a boolean expression are performed in the following order:

1. Operations within parentheses
2. The unary operators +, -, and !
3. The operators *, /, and %
4. The binary operators + and -
5. The operators <, <=, >, and >=
6. The operators == and !=
7. The operator &&
8. The operator ||

Just as you saw in Chapter 3, operators at the same level in this list have the same precedence and are performed from left to right within the expression.

 Note: A boolean expression can contain boolean variables, that is, variables whose data type is boolean. In addition, the value of a boolean expression can be assigned to a boolean variable.

 Note: A **truth table** shows the value of a given boolean expression for all possible values of the variables that make up the expression. For example, a truth table for the operator && tabulates the value of the expression for every possible combination of operand values. Such a table could appear as follows:

x	y	x && y
true	true	true
true	false	false
false	true	false
false	false	false

 Question 14 Evaluate the following boolean expressions and indicate their values (true or false). Assume that the integer variables x, y, and z contain 2, 4, and 6, respectively.
    a. (x == y) || (y != z)
    b. (x == 2) && (z > 6) && (y <= 4)
    c. ((x < 1) || (y >= 4)) && (z <= 6)

Question 15 If ch is a char variable, write an if-else statement that tests whether ch contains an uppercase letter. Display one of two appropriate messages indicating the result. Do not use the class Character.

Question 16 Given the three sides of a triangle as double variables, write statements that test whether

    a. At least two sides are equal.
    b. All sides are equal.
    c. No sides are equal

A Problem Solved: Leap Years

> Is this year a leap year? Will the year 3000 be a leap year? Let's write a program to find out.

7.18   **The solution.** The overall logic of the program is not complicated, as you can see from the following pseudocode:

> *Describe the program's purpose*
> *Ask the user to type a year*
> *Read the year*
> *Test whether the year is a leap year*
> *Display the results*

Let's tackle the hardest part—testing whether a year is a leap year.
A year is a leap year if it is

- Divisible by 4 but not divisible by 100, or
- Divisible by 400

For example, the years 2000 and 2008 were leap years, but 2099 and 3000 will not be.
We need to translate the criteria for a leap year into Java. If year is an int variable containing the year, we can list each of the necessary tests in English and write its Java equivalent next to each one, as follows:

- Divisible by 4   `year % 4 == 0`

- Not divisible by 100   `year % 100 != 0`

- Divisible by 400   `year % 400 == 0`

For the year to be divisible by 4, the remainder after dividing the year by 4 must be 0. This will be the case if the expression year % 4 is 0, that is, if the expression year % 4 == 0 is true. Similarly, a year is not divisible by 100 if the remainder after dividing the year by 100 is not 0. In that case, the expression year % 100 != 0 is true. Both of these criteria must be true simultaneously to satisfy the requirement "Divisible by 4 but not divisible by 100." That is, year is a leap year if the expression

```
(year % 4 == 0) && (year % 100 != 0)
```

is true. If this expression is false, the year can still be a leap year if it is divisible by 400—that is, if year % 400 == 0 is true. By combining these observations, we determine that year is a leap year if the expression

```
( (year % 4 == 0) && (year % 100 != 0) ) || (year % 400 == 0)
```

is true. You can see this expression used in our leap-year program in Listing 7-2.

LISTING 7-2   Testing for a leap year

```
/** LeapYear.java by F. M. Carrano
    Tests whether a given year is a leap year.

    A year is a leap year if it is

      a) Divisible by 4 but not divisible by 100, or
      b) Divisible by 400
```

```
        Input: The 4-digit year
        Output: The year and a message about whether it is a leap year.
*/
import java.util.Scanner;
public class LeapYear
{
    public static void main(String[] args)
    {
        Scanner keyboard = new Scanner(System.in);
        System.out.println("This program tests whether a given year" +
                           " is a leap year.");
        System.out.print("Type the year: ");
        int year = keyboard.nextInt();
        if ( ((year % 4 == 0) && (year % 100 != 0)) || (year % 400 == 0) )
            System.out.println(year + " is a leap year.");
        else
            System.out.println(year + " is not a leap year.");
    } // end main
} // end LeapYear
```

Sample Output 1

```
This program tests whether a given year is a leap year.
Type the year: 2012
2012 is a leap year.
```

Sample Output 2

```
This program tests whether a given year is a leap year.
Type the year: 3000
3000 is not a leap year.
```

■ Assertions

7.19   An **assertion** is a statement of truth about some aspect of your program's logic. You can think of it as a boolean expression that is true, or that at least should be true, at a certain point. If an assertion is false, something is wrong with your program. You can state assertions as comments within your code. For example, if at some point in a method's definition you know that the variable sum should be positive, you could write the following comment:

```
// Assertion: sum > 0
```

Such comments point out aspects of the logic that might not be clear. Additionally, they provide places for you to check the accuracy of your code during debugging.

Java enables you to do more than simply write a comment to make an assertion. You can use an assert statement, such as

```
assert sum > 0;
```

to enforce the assertion. If the boolean expression that follows the reserved word assert is true, the statement does nothing. If it is false, an **assertion error** occurs and program execution terminates.

7.20   You can clarify the error message that Java provides by adding a second expression to the `assert` statement. The second expression must represent a value, since its representation as a string is displayed within the error message. For example, the statement

```
assert sum > 0 : sum;
```

adds the value of `sum` to the error message when `sum` is less than or equal to zero.

Programming Tip

Provide a second expression in an `assert` statement only when the expression's value will help you see why the assertion failed. The error message produced by an `assert` statement is meant for you, the programmer, not the user of your program.

Programming Tip

When the boolean expression in an `assert` statement involves several variables, the second expression should contain their values. For example, to confirm that the value of `sum` exceeds a certain minimum, you could write the following `assert` statement:

```
assert sum > min : "sum is " + sum + ", min is " + min;
```

7.21   By default, Java ignores `assert` statements at execution time, so you must give a command to enable them. If you are using the Java Development Kit (JDK)[2] from Sun Microsystems, the command

```
java -enableassertions³ MyProgram
```

executes the compiled program `MyProgram` with `assert` statements enabled. The next time you run the program, the assertions will be ignored, unless you once again use the previous command to enable them. Thus, you can leave the `assert` statements in place after you have finished debugging your program, without wasting execution time.

Note: Assertions within a program identify aspects of your logic that must be true. In Java, you use an `assert` statement to make an assertion.

Syntax: **The `assert` statement**

```
assert boolean-expression : valued-expression;
```

If *boolean-expression* is false, an assertion error occurs. The error message contains the value of the optional second expression. Note that *valued-expression* can be a call to a valued method but not a void method.

Programming Tip

Using the `assert` statement is a simple but effective way to find errors in your program's logic. After serving this purpose, assertions that are left in your program document the program's logic for those who want to revise or expand its capability. Remember that Java ignores `assert` statements unless you indicate otherwise when you run the program.

Programming Tip

An `assert` statement is not a substitute for an `if` statement. You should use `assert` statements as a programming aid, not as part of a program's logic.

---

2. If you are using an IDE, consult its documentation to learn how to enable assertions.
3. You can abbreviate `-enableassertions` as `-ea`.

Question 17 What assertion about z is true after the following statements execute? Write your assertion both as a comment and as an `assert` statement. Assume that x, y, and z are integer variables.

```
int z = x;
if (x < y)
    z = y;
assert
```

videonote
A problem
solved

Question 18 What `assert` statement can you add to the program in Listing 7-1 to verify that the value of the variable dayOfWeek is within the correct range?

CHAPTER SUMMARY

- A program's flow of control is the order in which its statements execute.

- An `if` statement tests a boolean expression and takes a course of action according to whether the expression is true or false.

- A statement within an `if` statement executes if a boolean expression is true. An optional `else` clause contains a statement that executes when the expression is false. Each of these statements can be compound, that is, a group of statements enclosed in braces.

- You use one of the operators ==, !=, <, <=, >, or >= to compare two primitive values. You use the method `equals` to test whether two objects have the same value. Certain objects also have the method `compareTo` that you can use to compare two objects.

- The "and" operator && returns true only when both of its operands are true. The "or" operator || returns true when one or both of its operands are true. The "not" operator ! changes the value of the boolean expression to which it applies from true to false or false to true.

- An assertion is a statement of truth about some aspect of your program's logic. In Java, you can add an assertion to your program by writing an `assert` statement.

EXERCISES

1. Write Java statements that assign the larger of two given integers to the variable `larger`.

2. Write Java statements that assign the smaller of two given integers to the variable `smaller`.

3. Write Java statements that compare two given integers and assign one of the following values to the variable `result`:
   - 0 if the integers are equal
   - –1 if the first integer is less than the second
   - 1 if the first integer is greater than the second

4. What test data should you use to test your answer to the previous exercise?

5. Distinguish between the comparison of primitives and the comparison of objects.

6. Distinguish between the `if` statement and the `if-else` statement, and give an example of each.

7. Given a person's age in the integer variable age, write Java statements to test whether a person is younger than 21 years of age. If so, display "Minor"; otherwise display "Of age."

8. An employee whose pay rate is given in the double variable payRate is evaluated on an integer scale from 1 to 100, and this evaluation is stored in the int variable evaluation. Write Java statements to increase the employee's pay rate by 3 percent if the evaluation is greater than 90; otherwise increase the pay rate by 1 percent.

9. Evaluate each of the following expressions, where x, y, and z contain 1, 3, and 5, respectively:

   a. (x == y) || (y > z)
   b. (z == 5) && (x > 0) || (y <= 3)
   c. ((x < 1) || (y >= 2)) && (z <= 6)

10. Complete the following truth table:

x	y	z	(x && y) || !z	!(x && (y || !z))
True	True	True	True	False
True	True	False		
True	False	True		
True	False	False		
False	True	True		
False	True	False		
False	False	True		
False	False	False		

11. Replace the following if-else statement with an equivalent assignment statement:

```
boolean result;
if (count % 10 == 0)
   result = true;
else
   result = false;
```

12. Is the following code a correct way to test whether the integer in the variable count is within the range 1 through 12? Give a reason for your answer.

```
if (count > 0) && (count < 13)
   System.out.println("The count is within range.");
else
   System.out.println("The count is out of range.");
```

13. Consider a class Clock whose data fields hour and minute are integers that store the current hour and minute, respectively. For each of the following situations, write an assert statement that could appear within the class definition to verify the described requirement.

   a. The value of hour neither exceeds 12 nor is less than 1.
   b. The value of minute neither exceeds 60 nor is less than 1.

14. Repeat the previous exercise, but write one assert statement to verify both requirements.

15. Repeat the previous exercise, but include an error message that displays the current values of hour and minute if either one is out of range.

16. Since Java can ignore assert statements, why should you use them?

17. While writing a program to track an inventory of soda, you design a class named SodaMachine. Among the class's methods are fill, which adds a given number of cans to the machine, and dispense, which subtracts a given number of cans from the machine. Implement the class SodaMachine. Then write a test program that informs the user when a soda machine's inventory drops below ten cans.

18. Write a Java program that reads the names of two of the user's friends and then displays them in alphabetical order.

19. Write a Java program that asks the user to guess a randomly generated integer between 1 and 1000. Display a message to indicate whether the user's guess is correct, higher than the random number, or lower than the random number.

20. Complete the methods getSmaller, getLarger, and getOrderedPair in the following class of pairs of integers:

```java
/** Represents pairs of integers. */
public class Pair
{
    private int one;
    private int two;

    public Pair(int oneNumber, int anotherNumber)
    {
        one = oneNumber;
        two = anotherNumber;
    } // end constructor

    /** Returns the smaller integer in this pair. */
    public int getSmaller()
    {
        . . .
    } // end getSmaller

    /** Returns the larger integer in this pair. */
    public int getLarger()
    {
        . . .
    } // end getLarger

    /** Returns a new pair whose integers are the same as in
        this pair, but whose first integer is the smaller one. */
    public Pair getOrderedPair()
    {
        . . .
    } // end getOrderedPair

    public String toString()
    {
        return one + ", " + two;
    } // end toString
} // end Pair
```

PROJECTS

1. The seasons in the Northern Hemisphere typically occur during the following date ranges:
   - Winter: December 22 to March 19
   - Spring: March 20 to June 20
   - Summer: June 21 to September 20
   - Autumn: September 21 to December 21

   Write a program that asks the user for the month and day as integers and then displays the season for that date. Sample output follows:

   ```
   This program reports the season for a given day and month.
   Type the month and day as integers separated by spaces: 7 22
   Month 7, Day 22 is in the summer.
   ```

2. Define a class `Triple` that is analogous to the class `Pair` described in Exercise 20. Objects of `Triple` contain three integers. Include in your definition the methods `getSmallest`, `getMiddle`, `getLargest`, and `getOrderedTriple`. Thoroughly test your new class by writing an appropriate client.

3. Define a class `Luggage` that represents pieces of luggage. Each `Luggage` object should have a length, width, and height—measured in inches—and a weight in pounds. These objects should be immutable. Using your new class, write a program that processes an airline passenger who has two pieces of luggage. Up-and-Away Airlines allows each passenger a total luggage weight of at most 50 pounds without an additional charge. Moreover, each piece of luggage must satisfy a size requirement; that is, the sum of its length, width, and height must be less than or equal to 62 inches. Oversized luggage is assessed a charge of $5 per piece. Overweight luggage is assessed a charge of $2 per pound over the 50-pound maximum.

   Your program should ask the user for the size and weight of each piece of luggage, indicate whether an additional charge is required and, if so, the amount of the charge. For example, the output of the program might appear as follows:

   ```
   Type the length, width, and height, in inches and separated by
   spaces, of the first piece of luggage: 36.5 24 9.5
   Type its weight in pounds: 48.5
   The dimensions 36.5 x 24.0 x 9.5 total 70.0 inches. This piece
   is oversized and incurs a $5 charge.

   Type the length, width, and height, in inches and separated by
   spaces, of the second piece of luggage: 24.5 8 6.5
   Type its weight in pounds: 37.25
   The dimensions 24.5 x 8.0 x 6.5 total 39.0 inches. This piece
   is acceptable. The total weight of the two pieces is 85.75
   pounds, which is 35.75 pounds over the limit. The charge at
   $2 per pound is $71.50

   Total luggage charge is $76.50.
   ```

4. Define a class that represents a coin. The coin has two sides, heads and tails. Only one side of the coin is up, or visible, at any time. A program that uses your class should be able to specify which side is up, detect which side is up, turn the coin over—that is, if it is heads, make it tails and vice versa—and toss the coin so that its visible face is a random event.

   After you design and implement the class, write a `main` method that demonstrates all the methods in the class.

5. Using two dice, we can play a simple game having the following rules:
   - The game has two players.
   - After deciding who throws the dice first, the players each roll both dice.
   - The player rolling the highest total face value of the dice wins; if the two totals are equal, it is a draw.
   - Two exceptional cases are possible:
     - A pair of ones (snake eyes) loses, unless both players roll snake eyes, in which case the game is a draw.
     - A matching pair (doubles) wins, unless both players roll doubles, in which case the highest score wins.

   Define the classes `Die` and `TwoDice`, as described in Project 1 of Chapter 6. Then define a class `DiceGame` that uses an instance of `TwoDice` to play the dice game just described. One player should be the user of the program; the other player should be the computer. Include at least the following methods in `DiceGame`: `giveDirections`, `play`, and `reportWinner`.

   Write a program that contains a `main` method to control the game. It should create an instance of `DiceGame`, interact with the user to decide which player rolls first, and invoke methods of `DiceGame` as necessary.

ANSWERS TO SELF-TEST QUESTIONS

1. `Scanner` has no method that returns a value of type `char`.

2. Add the statement
   ```
   response = response.toUpperCase();
   ```
   after `response` is read but before the `if` statement.

3. The result is the same as if the input had been Y or N.

4.
```java
if (Character.isUpperCase(ch))
    System.out.println("ch contains an uppercase letter.");
```

5.
```java
if (ticketCounter >= THEATER_SIZE)
    System.out.println("The theater is full!");
```

6.
```java
double pay = dollars * hours;
if (hours > 35)
    pay = pay + 0.5 * dollars * (hours - 35);
```

7. Omit the statement before the if statement, and in the if statement, change equals to equalsIgnoreCase.

8.
   a.
```java
String firstName = person.getFirstName();
if (firstName.equals("Joe"))
    System.out.println("Hi, Joe!");
```

or

```java
if (person.getFirstName().equals("Joe"))
    System.out.println("Hi, Joe!");
```

   b.
```java
String firstName = person.getFirstName();
if (firstName.length() > 5)
    System.out.println("Your name has more than five characters.");
```

9.
```java
char ch = str.charAt(0);
if (Character.isUpperCase(ch))
    System.out.println("str contains an uppercase letter.");
```

or

```java
if (str.compareTo("A") >= 0)
{
    if (str.compareTo("Z") <= 0)
        System.out.println("str contains an uppercase letter.");
} // end if
```

You might not think of the second solution. We will talk more about this construct in Chapter 10.

10.
```java
BigDecimal bigZero = new BigDecimal("0.0");
if (balance.compareTo(bigZero) < 0)
    System.out.println("Your account is overdrawn!");
```

11.
```java
if (wordOne.compareTo(wordTwo) <= 0)
    System.out.println(wordOne + " " + wordTwo);
else
    System.out.println(wordTwo + " " + wordOne);
```

12.
```java
if (wordOne.equals(wordTwo))
    System.out.println("The words are equal.");
else
    System.out.println("The words are not equal.");
```

13.
```java
(age >= 20) && (age < 30)
(age >= 20) && (30 > age)
(20 <= age) && (30 > age)
(age < 30) && (age >= 20)
(30 > age) && (age >= 20)
(30 > age) && (20 <= age)
```

14.
   a. True
   b. False
   c. True

15.
```java
if ((ch >= 'A') && (ch <= 'Z')
    System.out.println("Uppercase letter");
else
    System.out.println("Not an uppercase letter");
```

Compare this answer to the one given for Question 4.

16.
```java
a. if ((side1 == side2) || (side1 == side3) || (side2 == side3))
       System.out.println("At least two sides are equal");
b. if ((side1 == side2) && (side1 == side3))
       System.out.println("All sides are equal");
c. if ((side1 != side2) && (side1 != side3) && (side2 != side3))
       System.out.println("No sides are equal");
```

17.
```java
assert (z >= x) && (z >= y);
// Assertion: z is the larger of x and y
```

18.
```java
assert (dayOfWeek >= 0) && (dayOfWeek <= 6);
```

Chapter

8

Class Definitions: More Details

Contents

Prerequisites

Objectives

After studying this chapter, you should be able to
- Define boolean-valued methods within a class definition
- Define and use private methods within a class definition
- Use data fields that are final or both static and final when appropriate
- Define and use enumerations
- Write constructors that invoke another constructor within the same class

Chapter 6 began our discussion of class definitions. This chapter continues that introduction by first considering two categories of methods: boolean and private. Boolean-valued methods are simply methods that return a value of either true or false. A class has such methods so that a client can test for certain conditions. A private method is one that another method definition invokes as a "helping method." That is, the private method does a portion of the task of the public method. Private methods cannot be invoked by the client of the class. They are a part of the class's implementation, and so are hidden from public view.

This chapter also introduces enumerations. An enumeration defines a data type that represents a collection of known, discrete values, such as a limited set of numbers or letters. You can define an enumeration instead of defining a group of named constants. Java will then ensure that a variable of this new data type does not have a value outside of the enumeration. Finally, we look at how one constructor can call another.

Boolean-Valued Methods

Chapter 4 introduced the method `equals`, which compares two objects and returns either true or false according to the result of the comparison. In particular, Segment 4.21 described this method for the class `String`. Further, Segment 7.6 of Chapter 7 gave an example of using an `if` statement to react to the result of `String`'s equals method. Classes often include methods like `equals` that return a `boolean` value.

8.1 **Example: Using a class of dates.** Imagine a class that represents a date consisting of a month, day, and year, where each of these three components is an integer. The class has simple accessor methods, the methods `setDate` and `toString`, and the method `isLeapYear`, which tests whether a particular date occurs within a leap year. Recall that in Segment 7.18 of Chapter 7 we wrote a `main` method that determines whether a given year is a leap year. We will use the logic of that method in the definition of the method `isLeapYear`, as you will see.

Let's name the class `CalendarDate` to distinguish it from Java's class `Date` that we introduced in Chapter 4. The `LeapYearDemo` program in Listing 8-1 demonstrates the use of this class.

**LISTING 8-1   A demonstration of the method `isLeapYear` in the class
`CalendarDate`**

```
/** LeapYearDemo.java by F. M. Carrano
    Demonstrates the method isLeapYear in the class CalendarDate.
*/
import java.util.Scanner;
public class LeapYearDemo
{
   public static void main(String[] args)
   {
      Scanner keyboard = new Scanner(System.in);
      System.out.println("This program tests whether a given date " +
                         "occurs in a leap year.\n");
      System.out.println("Type the month, day, and year as " +
                         "integers separated by spaces: ");
      int month = keyboard.nextInt();
```

```
        int day = keyboard.nextInt();
        int year = keyboard.nextInt();

        CalendarDate theDate = new CalendarDate(month, day, year);
        System.out.print("You entered the date " + theDate + "; ");

        if (theDate.isLeapYear())
            System.out.println(theDate.getYear() + " is a leap year. ");
        else
            System.out.println(theDate.getYear() + " is not a leap year. ");
    } // end main
} // end LeapYear
```

Sample Output

```
This program tests whether a given date occurs in a leap year.

Type the month, day, and year as integers separated by spaces:
10 31 2010
The date is 10/31/2010; 2010 is not a leap year.
```

Notice that we can use the method isLeapYear much as we use the String method equals. In fact, both methods return a boolean value. Thus, the if statement that begins as

```
if (theDate.isLeapYear())
```

tests whether isLeapYear returns true or false. The longer statement

```
if (theDate.isLeapYear() == true)
```

is also correct, but programmers typically favor the first version.

8.2 **The class CalendarDate.** Listing 8-2 contains the class CalendarDate. Three data fields represent the date, which is set initially by the class's constructor. The remaining methods—an assortment of accessor methods and the methods setDate, toString, and isLeapYear—are as we described in the previous segment.

LISTING 8-2 The class CalendarDate

```
/** CalendarDate.java by F. M. Carrano
    Represents a date; defines a boolean-valued method.
*/
public class CalendarDate
{
    private int month;
    private int day;
    private int year;

    /** Constructs an object for the date newMonth/newDay/newYear. */
    public CalendarDate(int newMonth, int newDay, int newYear)
    {
```

```java
      month = newMonth;
      day = newDay;
      year = newYear;
   } // end constructor

   /** Sets the date to monthNumber/dayNumber/yearNumber. */
   public void setDate(int monthNumber, int dayNumber, int yearNumber)
   {
      month = monthNumber;
      day = dayNumber;
      year = yearNumber;
   } // end setDate
```

< *The* int-*valued accessor methods* getYear, getMonth, *and* getDay *are here.* >

```java
   /** Returns the date as a string in the numeric form month/day/year.
   */
   public String toString()
   {
      return month + "/" + day + "/" + year;
   } // end toString

   /** Returns true if the year is a leap year; otherwise, returns false.
   */
   public boolean isLeapYear()
   {
      // A year is a leap year if it is
      // a) Divisible by 4 but not divisible by 100, or
      // b) Divisible by 400
      boolean result;

      if (((year % 4 == 0) && (year % 100 != 0)) || (year % 400 == 0))
         result = true;
      else
         result = false;

      return result;
   } // end isLeapYear
} // end CalendarDate
```

8.3   **The method isLeapYear.** Let's focus for now on the method isLeapYear. Segment 7.18 of Chapter 7 described how to test for a leap year, and that test is the basis for the logic of this method. Notice how we declare a variable, result, to have the same data type as the method's return type—boolean—and then assign a value to result according to the logic of an if statement. In this way, the method needs only one return statement, which simply returns the value of result.

Although the definition of this method is fine, let's look at two variations. One strategy is to guess at the right answer—after all, it is only one of two choices—and then check to see whether our guess was correct. The body of the method would then appear as follows:

```
boolean result = false;
if ( ((year % 4 == 0) && (year % 100 != 0)) || (year % 400 == 0) )
   result = true;
return result;
```

As you can see, we can omit the `else` clause: If the boolean expression is false, execution continues with the `return` statement. In this case, `result` has the correct value—its original value, false.

In a second variation of the method definition, we can omit the variable `result` and the entire `if` statement. Instead, the body of the method could consist of the following one statement:

```
return ((year % 4 == 0) && (year % 100 != 0)) || (year % 400 == 0);
```

The expression in this `return` statement is the same one that appears in the previous `if` statement. If the expression is true, the `return` statement returns true; if the expression is false, the statement returns false.

Programming Tip: Naming boolean-valued methods
Programmers typically begin the name of a boolean-valued method with a word such as "is" or "has." When a method named in this way is called within an `if` statement, reading the statement suggests its meaning. For example, consider the following code that appears in Listing 8-1:

```
if (theDate.isLeapYear())
   System.out.println(theDate.getYear() + " is a leap year. ");
```

The `if` clause reads as "if theDate is a leap year." Following this naming convention can help you avoid confusion and logical errors.

Note: Using meaningful names for variables, methods, and classes contributes to programs that are **self-documenting**. Such code is easy to read and understand without much need for external documentation or lengthy comments.

Question 1 Specify a method `isWeekend` for the class `CalendarDate` that returns true if a date occurs on a Saturday or Sunday. What comments and header would you write for this method?

Question 2 If `getDayOfWeek` is another method defined in the class `CalendarDate`, what is the definition of the method `isWeekend`, described in the previous question? Assume that `getDayOfWeek` returns an integer from 1 to 7 to indicate Sunday through Saturday.

Private Methods

You saw previously in Segment 6.19 of Chapter 6 that one method can call another. The invoked method can belong to a different class or to the same class as the method that calls it. For example, in Listing 6-5, the method `setName` invokes `setFirst` and `setLast`. In this case, all three methods belong to the same class. The invoked methods are also public.

Sometimes the methods that a method calls are not suitable for use by the client of the class. Such methods usually perform only a part of a computation and are called by a method to help it complete its task. We make these methods private instead of public.

8.4 Consider the class `CalendarDate`, which appears in Listing 8-2. Both the constructor and the method `setDate` initialize the data fields `month`, `day`, and `year`. To eliminate this duplicated effort, we could replace the constructor's three assignment statements with a call to `setDate` as follows:

```
// A possible but undesirable definition of the constructor.
public CalendarDate(int newMonth, int newDay, int newYear)
{
    setDate(newMonth, newDay, newYear);
} // end constructor
```

More about methods

However, in Chapter 27, when we discuss inheritance, we will caution you about calling a public method from within a constructor and show you how to safely do so. Alternatively, we can give the constructor the desired behavior without calling a public method by defining a private method to initialize the data fields, as follows:

```
// Sets the date to monthNumber/dayNumber/yearNumber.
private void setFields(int monthNumber, int dayNumber,
                       int yearNumber)
{
    month = monthNumber;
    day = dayNumber;
    year = yearNumber;
} // end setFields
```

The constructor can then invoke this private method. To avoid duplication of code, we can revise `setDate` so that it also calls the private method:

```
public CalendarDate(int newMonth, int newDay, int newYear)
{
    setFields(newMonth, newDay, newYear);
} // end constructor

public void setDate(int monthNumber, int dayNumber, int yearNumber)
{
    setFields(monthNumber, dayNumber, yearNumber);
} // end setDate
```

With these changes, any method within the class `CalendarDate` can invoke the private method `setFields`, but no client of the class can.

 Note: Private methods of a class, like private data fields, are unavailable by name to a client of the class.

Checking the Validity of Data Fields

8.5 Let's remind ourselves of the reason for declaring a class's data fields as private. Basically, private fields protect an object's integrity. As we mentioned in the programming tip at the end of Segment 6.10 of Chapter 6, if a data field were public, a client could use its name to assign it an illegal value, avoiding a call to a set method. But regardless of whether a field is public or private, unless a class's constructors and set methods check the values of their arguments, they cannot ensure that the values assigned to the data fields are valid. For example, if `myCalendar` is an instance of `CalendarDate`, the statement

```
myCalendar.setDate(-2, -3, -4);
```

is legal but creates an invalid date.

With our suggested revision of CalendarDate, the private method setFields can check the validity of its arguments. In this way, both the constructor and the method setDate get this protection, as they both call setFields. Let's list the checks that setFields must make of the values of its arguments monthNumber, dayNumber, and yearNumber:

- monthNumber's value must be between 1 and 12, inclusive.
- dayNumber's value must be between 1 and 31, inclusive.
- yearNumber's value must be at least 1582, since that is the year that leap years were added to our present-day calendar.

8.6   If we add the named constant MIN_YEAR to the class CalendarDate, as follows:

```
private final int MIN_YEAR = 1582;
```

we can define the private method setFields as follows:

```
// Sets the date to monthNumber/dayNumber/yearNumber.
private void setFields(int monthNumber, int dayNumber,
                       int yearNumber)
{
   if ( (monthNumber >= 1) && (monthNumber <= 12) &&
        (dayNumber >= 1) && (dayNumber <= 31) &&
        (yearNumber >= MIN_YEAR) )
   {
      month = monthNumber;
      day = dayNumber;
      year = yearNumber;
   }
   else
   {
      System.out.println(monthNumber + "/" + dayNumber + "/" +
                         yearNumber + " is an illegal date.");
      System.exit(0);
   } // end if
} // end setFields
```

The class CalendarDate2 contains these revisions and is available in the online source code for this book.

Question 3 The method setFields, as given in the previous segment, ensures that the values for the month and year are valid, but its check of the day is not careful enough. For example, not all months have 31 days. Describe the checks that setFields should make.

Programming Tip
A method should be private if a client should never be able to call it. Such a method generally performs an implementation detail that should be hidden from the client.

Programming Tip
You should divide a large task into several smaller subtasks. The method that implements the large task can then call several private methods that each implement one smaller task.

Note: Constructors, like any other method, can invoke private methods.

Final Fields and Static Final Fields

8.7   As you learned in Chapter 6, ordinarily, the objects of a class have their own copies of the class's data fields. We call these variables instance variables. When objects of a class have an instance variable whose value is constant, those values might vary from object to object. For example, each object of a class Student could be given a fixed student number when it is created. The data field in Student could be declared as

```
private final int STUDENT_NUMBER;
```

The class's constructors, but no other methods, could assign a value to Student_Number. That is, the constructor could be defined as

```
public Student(int idNumber)
{
    STUDENT_NUMBER = idNumber;
} // end constructor
```

but the following set method would be illegal:

```
public void setStudentNumber(int idNumber)
{
    STUDENT_NUMBER = idNumber; // Syntax error!
} // end setStudentNumber
```

Figure 8-1 illustrates the two Student objects created by the following statements:

```
Student joe = new Student(1234);
Student emily = new Student(5678);
```

FIGURE 8-1   Two Student objects, each having an instance variable declared as final

---

Class definition	**Instances (objects) of the class**

```
public class Student
{
    private final int STUDENT_NUMBER;

    . . .

} // end Student
```

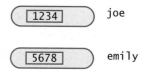

Each object of the class Student has its own copy of the final field STUDENT_NUMBER

 Programming Tip

You should declare a data field as final if its value will be initialized once when an object is constructed and will not change after that time. Doing so allows the compiler to check that no other code changes the field's value. Moreover, a final declaration clarifies your design to other programmers who read your class.

8.8 Now consider the class `CalendarDate2` as described in Segment 8.6. It defines the following named constant, combining its declaration and assignment of a value:

```
private final int MIN_YEAR = 1582;
```

Every object of `CalendarDate2` will have its own copy of the constant `MIN_YEAR`. We know, however, that all these constants have the same value. Thus, we are duplicating this constant unnecessarily. When the objects of a class, such as `CalendarDate2`, need access to the same constant, the objects could share one copy of the constant instead of each having its own copy. To create only one copy of `MIN_YEAR` that all objects of the class `CalendarDate2` can share, you declare `MIN_YEAR` as a **static field**, or **static variable**, or **class variable**. You declare a static field by adding the reserved word `static` to its declaration, as in

```
private static final int MIN_YEAR = 1582;
```

Figure 8-2 illustrates two `CalendarDate2` objects that share this static constant.

FIGURE 8-2   The static field `MIN_YEAR` shared by two objects of `CalendarDate2`

Class definition   **Instances (objects) of the class**

```
public class CalendarDate2
{
    public static final int MIN_YEAR = 1582;
    private int month;
    private int day;
    private int year;
    . . .

} // end CalendarDate2
```

Objects of the class `CalendarDate2` all reference the same static field but have their own copy of `month`, `day`, and `year`

! **Programming Tip**
Declare a data field as static if all objects of the class can share one copy of it.

8.9 Imagine a class of circles that declares a data field to represent a circle's radius, as follows:

```
public class Circle
{
    private double radius;
    . . .
```

Each object of this class has its own copy of `radius`.

Now suppose that we define a constant `PI` within the class to represent π, as follows:

```
private final double PI = 3.14159;
```

Each `Circle` object has its own copy of `PI`, but the objects could share one copy instead. Thus, we can declare `PI` as follows:

```
private static final double PI = 3.14159;
```

8.10   Since `PI` is a useful constant and cannot change, we can declare it as public so other classes can access it. The `final` modifier assures us that no one can alter `PI`'s value. Thus, imagine that the class `Circle` begins as follows:

```
public class Circle
{
    public static final double PI = 3.14159;
    private double radius;
    . . .
```

Within the class `Circle`, we know that we can write `PI` whenever we want the value of π. But what if we need π within another class? In that case, we write `Circle.PI` so that the compiler knows to look for `PI` within the class `Circle`. Recall from Chapter 3 that we can write `Math.PI` when we need the value of π. In fact, the class `Math` defines `PI` as a static named constant, much as we have just done for `Circle`. Because `Math` is a standard class in the Java Class Library, you should use `Math.PI` instead of defining your own constant for π.

Chapter 15 will discuss the modifier `static` further by presenting static variables and static methods.

Question 4   What happens if you do not declare a constant data field as static?

Note: A data field declared as final has a constant value that cannot change. A data field declared as static belongs to the class, not its individual objects. All of the objects of a class share the class's static fields. Some fields are static, some are final, some are both static and final, and some are neither static nor final.

Programming Tip
If a named constant is the same for all objects of a class, declare it as static and final. Since their values cannot change, you can safely give clients access to such constants by declaring them as public. Place them near the beginning of a class and outside of any method definitions. That way, the named constants are handy in case you need to modify them. You might, for example, want to change the number of digits you provide for a constant.

Note: Naming convention for data fields that are both static and final
As Segment 2.21 of Chapter 2 stated, the convention for naming constants is to capitalize all of the letters in the name. Until now, we declared named constants as final. Now that you know about the modifier `static`, we need to clarify the naming convention. A data field that is both static and final should have all letters in its name capitalized. Data fields or ordinary variables that are not static should not follow this convention, even if they are declared as final. All of the named constants in earlier chapters could and should be both static and final.

Programming Tip
Use `Math.PI` whenever you need the value of π. Do not define your own version.

■ Enumerations

8.11 Some computations can involve a variable whose value can be one of a seemingly endless array of possibilities. In other cases, a variable's value can have only certain values. For example, a boolean variable must be true or false. To represent a letter grade A, B, C, D, or F, we could use a char variable—grade, for example—but restrict its value to only those five letters. In reality, however, grade could contain any character, not just the letters A, B, C, D, and F. To prevent this, instead of declaring grade as a char, we can declare it as an **enumerated data type**, or **enumeration**. An enumeration itemizes the values that a variable can have.

For example, the following statement defines LetterGrade as an enumeration:

```
public enum LetterGrade {A, B, C, D, F}
```

LetterGrade behaves as a class type, so we can declare grade to have this type as follows:

```
LetterGrade grade;
```

The items listed between the braces in the definition of LetterGrade are the objects that grade can reference. For example, you can write

```
grade = LetterGrade.A;
```

to assign A to grade. You qualify each of these enumerated objects with the name of the enumeration, just as you qualify the named constant PI with the name of its class Math. Assigning an object other than A, B, C, D, or F to grade will cause a syntax error. Since these objects behave as constants, you name them as you would a constant by using uppercase letters and the rules for identifiers.

8.12 When the compiler encounters an enumeration, it creates a class that has several methods. Among them is toString, which displays the name of its receiving object. Thus, if you write

```
System.out.println(LetterGrade.A);
```

for example, toString is called implicitly and the letter A is displayed.

You also can compare enumerated objects by using the methods equals and compareTo. The order that compareTo uses is the order in which the objects appear in the definition of the enumeration. For example, if grade is an instance of LetterGrade,

```
grade.compareTo(LetterGrade.C)
```

tests whether grade is before, after, or equal to LetterGrade.C.

8.13 The position in which an object appears within its enumeration is called its **ordinal value**. These values begin at zero. Thus, in LetterGrade, the ordinal values of A and F are 0 and 4, respectively. You can use the method ordinal to access these values. For example, if

```
LetterGrade yourGrade = LetterGrade.A;
```

the expression

```
yourGrade.ordinal()
```

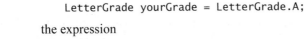
videonote
Constants and
enumerations

returns 0. Additionally, the expression

```
LetterGrade.B.ordinal()
```

returns 1.

8.14 The method valueOf takes a string and returns a matching object in a given enumeration. For example, the expression

```
LetterGrade.valueOf("A")
```

returns LetterGrade.A. The string passed to valueOf must match the name of the constant exactly.

Syntax: Enumerations

access-modifier **enum** *name* { *field*$_1$, *field*$_2$, . . . }

An enumeration is a class. Its fields are objects that resemble named constants.

Note: A public enumeration should be written in its own file, just as you would do with any other public class. A private enumeration is defined within another class but is always outside of method definitions. A private enumeration is available only within the class that contains it.

Programming Tip

Define and use an enumeration when you know all the possible values of a variable.

The next example uses some of the features that we have mentioned here. Chapter 15 will explore the capabilities of enumerations further.

A Problem Solved: Representing Coins

> Imagine that we need to represent coins in various programs. A coin has two sides, heads and tails. Additionally, a coin has a monetary value and shows the year in which it was minted. Let's decide that these characteristics are sufficient for our purposes and create a class of coins.

8.15 **Designing a class.** We'll name the class `Coin` and give it three data fields, as follows:

- `sideUp`—a designation for heads or tails
- `value`—a representation of the coin's value
- `year`—a positive integer denoting the year the coin was minted

Let's also give the class the following methods:

- Accessor methods that return the coin's visible side—heads or tails—its value in cents, and its mint year
- Boolean-valued methods that test whether the coin's visible side is heads or tails
- A method that simulates a coin toss by assigning a designation for heads or tails to `sideUp` at random
- The method `toString`

After naming these methods and refining their specifications, we can write the following comments and method headers:

```
/** Returns the string "HEADS" if the coin is
    heads side up; otherwise, returns "TAILS". */
public String getSideUp()

/** Returns the value of the coin in cents. */
public int getValue()

/** Returns the coin's mint year as an integer. */
public int getYear()

/** Returns true if the coin is heads side up. */
public boolean isHeads()
```

```
/** Returns true if the coin is tails side up. */
public boolean isTails()

/** Tosses the coin (sets sideUp randomly to one of two values). */
public void toss()

/** Returns the coin as a string in the form coin-name/year/side-up. */
public String toString()
```

Notice that we have not specified any set methods. Thus, once a `Coin` object is created, its value and mint date cannot be altered, just like a real coin. The method `getSideUp` could have returned the value of the third field `sideUp`, but instead we chose to have it return a string. We did this so that the data type we eventually choose for `sideUp` will not be a part of the method's specification and, in fact, will be hidden from the client.

A Simpler Problem: A Class of Valueless Coins

8.16   Instead of defining the entire class `Coin` according to the specifications we just listed, let's begin with a simpler version of the class. That is, let's omit the coin's value and mint year for now, along with their accessor methods `getValue` and `getYear`. Objects of this class, which we will call `Coin1`, would be suitable for a simple guessing game involving a coin toss. The program in Listing 8-3 uses the methods of the class `Coin1` in such a game. It creates a `Coin1` object, tosses the coin, asks the user to guess the outcome, and reports the results. The repetitive output is a result of demonstrating the methods `toString` and `getSideUp`, both of which return a string indicating the coin's visible side. Although we need not create a class of coins to write a coin-toss game, we are defining `Coin1` as a first step toward the more involved class `Coin`.

LISTING 8-3   Using the class `Coin1` for a guessing game

```
/** CoinToss.java by F. M. Carrano
    Using the class Coin1 in a guessing game.
*/
import java.util.Scanner;
public class CoinToss
{
    public static void main(String[] args)
    {
        System.out.println("Guess the result of a coin toss.");
        Scanner keyboard = new Scanner(System.in);

        // Define and toss a coin:
        Coin1 aCoin = new Coin1();
        System.out.println("Here's the coin: " + aCoin);
        System.out.println("Right now the coin is " +
                            aCoin.getSideUp() + " side up.");
        System.out.println("Here's the toss.");

        aCoin.toss(); // toss the coin

        // Get results
        String visibleSide = aCoin.getSideUp();
```

```
                visibleSide = visibleSide.toUpperCase();

                // Get user guess
                System.out.print("Call it: heads or tails? ");
                String userGuess = keyboard.nextLine();
                userGuess = userGuess.toUpperCase();

                // Show results
                System.out.print("\nThe tossed coin is ");
                if (aCoin.isHeads())
                    System.out.println("heads.");
                else
                    System.out.println("tails.");

                System.out.print("Your guess of " + userGuess + " is ");
                if (userGuess.equals(visibleSide))
                    System.out.println("correct!");
                else
                    System.out.println("wrong!");
        } // end main
} // end CoinToss
```

Sample Output 1

```
    Guess the result of a coin toss.
    Here's the coin: The coin is TAILS side up.
    Right now the coin is TAILS side up.
    Here's the toss.
    Call it: heads or tails? tails

    The tossed coin is tails.
    Your guess of TAILS is correct!
```

Sample Output 2

```
    Guess the result of a coin toss.
    Here's the coin: The coin is HEADS side up.
    Right now the coin is HEADS side up.
    Here's the toss.
    Call it: heads or tails? heads

    The tossed coin is tails.
    Your guess of HEADS is wrong!
```

8.17   **The class definition.** The data type of the field sideUp could be int, with values such as 0 and 1, or char, with values like 'H' and 'T'. But since we know that sideUp can have only two values, we can restrict its values by defining an enumeration as

```
private enum CoinSide {HEADS, TAILS}
```

Remember, we cannot place an enumeration within a method definition. The data type of the field sideUp, then, will be CoinSide. Note that as an alternative, we could define the enumeration as public and store it in its own file, CoinSide.java.

Listing 8-4 contains an implementation of the class `Coin1` using the same method headers given in Segment 8.15, but omitting `getValue` and `getYear`. Let's examine some of the details. The default constructor creates a heads-side-up coin by setting the field `sideUp` to `CoinSide.HEADS`. Notice that writing only `HEADS` here would not be correct.

The method `getSideUp` returns the string `sideUp.toString()`, indicating which side is facing up. Because of the way we defined the enumeration `CoinSide`, this string will contain all uppercase letters and be either `"HEADS"` or `"TAILS"`. If case is important to you, you can either use `String` methods to transform the string or change the definition of `getSideUp` to test the value of the field `sideUp` and return the desired string.

The method `isHeads` returns the value of the boolean expression `sideUp == CoinSide.HEADS`. Although we could have used an `if` statement here, doing so is unnecessary since such a statement would have tested this expression. The method `isTails` has a similar implementation. If you prefer, you can omit `isTails`, as a coin must be tails side up if `isHeads` returns false.

The most interesting method definition in this class is the one for the method `toss`. Since we want a coin toss to appear to have a random outcome, we must generate some sort of random number. The method `random` in the standard class `Math` will serve our purpose. Recall from Figure 3-1 in Chapter 3 that the invocation `Math.random()` returns a random number that is not negative but is less than 1.0. The method `toss` considers a random number less than 0.5 to indicate heads and larger numbers to mean tails.

Although defining the method `toString` for this class is important, its implementation is not particularly interesting—or difficult. The method can return the value of either the field `sideUp` or the method `getSideUp`, embedded into whatever string you feel is appropriate.

LISTING 8-4   The class `coin1`

```
/** Coin1.java by F. M. Carrano
    Represents a coin.
*/
public class Coin1
{
    private enum CoinSide {HEADS, TAILS}
    private CoinSide sideUp;

    /** Constructs an object for the coin.
        The new coin is heads side up. */
    public Coin1()
    {
        sideUp = CoinSide.HEADS;
    } // end constructor

    /** Returns "HEADS" if the coin is heads side up;
        otherwise, returns "TAILS". */
    public String getSideUp()
    {
        return sideUp.toString();
    } // end getSideUp

    /** Returns true if the coin is heads side up. */
```

```java
    public boolean isHeads()
    {
        return sideUp == CoinSide.HEADS;
    } // end isHeads

    /** Returns true if the coin is tails side up. */
    public boolean isTails()
    {
        return sideUp == CoinSide.TAILS;
    } // end isTails

    /** Tosses the coin by setting sideUp to either
        HEADS or TAILS randomly. */
    public void toss()
    {
        if (Math.random() < 0.5)
            sideUp = CoinSide.HEADS;
        else
            sideUp = CoinSide.TAILS;
    } // end toss

    /** Returns the coin as a string that includes its side up. */
    public String toString()
    {
        return "The coin is " + sideUp + " side up.";
//      return "The coin is " + getSideUp() + " side up."; // Alternate
    } // end toString
} // end Coin1
```

Question 5 Revise the definition of getSideUp to use an if statement and return either "Heads" or "Tails".

Question 6 Is the following definition of the method toss correct?

```java
public void toss()
{
    if (Math.random() < 0.5)
        sideUp = CoinSide.HEADS;
    else if (Math.random() >= 0.5)
        sideUp = CoinSide.TAILS;
} // end toss
```

Question 7 If a method within the definition of the class Coin1 contained an if statement that began as

```java
if (sideUp = CoinSide.HEADS)
```

it would generate the syntax error

```
incompatible types
found    : Coin.CoinSide
required: boolean
```

How would you correct the statement?

Question 8 Add the method `turnOver` to the class `Coin`. This method should turn a coin over from heads to tails or tails to heads.

Question 9 Suppose we defined the default constructor as follows:

```
public Coin1()
{
} // end default constructor
```

    a.   What value is assigned to the data field `sideUp` by this constructor?
    b.   What, if any, problem might this default constructor cause?

Question 10 Define a second constructor for the class `Coin1` that initializes `sideUp` according to the value of a string passed to it as an argument.

Enhancing the Class Definition

8.18   Now that we have defined the simpler class `Coin1`, we can enhance it to get the class `Coin`. Earlier, we made the design decision to have `Coin1`'s default constructor create a heads-up coin. Now let's change the constructor so that new coins will be either heads or tails at random. To do that, we could have the constructor call the public method `toss`, but as we noted earlier in Segment 8.4, calling a public method from within a constructor should be avoided for now. We can, however, define a private method `getToss` that does the same thing as `toss` and call it from both the constructor and `toss`, as follows:

```
public Coin(. . .)
{
   sideUp = getToss();
   . . .
} // end constructor

public void toss()
{
   sideUp = getToss();
} // end toss

// Returns a random value of either HEADS or TAILS.
private CoinSide getToss()
{
   CoinSide result;
   if (Math.random() < 0.5)
      result = CoinSide.HEADS;
   else
      result = CoinSide.TAILS;
   return result;
} // end getToss
```

8.19   **The data fields value and year.** Our original design calls for two more data fields to represent the coin's value and its mint year. We now want to add these fields to our enhanced class `Coin`. While the data type of `year` can be `int`, we should give some thought to the data type of `value`.

Design Decision: What should be the data type of `value`?
The coins in the United States are the penny, nickel, dime, quarter, fifty-cent piece, and dollar. Their respective values in cents are 1, 5, 10, 25, 50, and 100. Although the obvious conclusion may be that the data type of `value` should be `int`, let's not rush our decision. We need to coordinate the

data type of `value` with the data type of the argument a client passes to our class's constructor for initializing `value`, as well as the return type of the method `getValue`.

The number of coins in any currency is small, and these coins have distinct values. The U.S. currency has six coins, but an `int` variable can take on many more than six values! Suppose that we instead define an enumeration, such as the following one:

```
enum CoinName {PENNY, NICKEL, DIME, QUARTER, FIFTY_CENT, DOLLAR}
```

Should `CoinName` be the data type of `value`, the data type of the argument passed to the constructor, or the data type of both `value` and the argument? Let's consider the implications of each of these possibilities:

- If `CoinName` is the data type of `value`, and `int` is the data type of the constructor's argument, the constructor—in addition to having either a precondition or a validity check—must convert the integer argument to the appropriate enumerator for assignment to `value`. And since the method `getValue` will return an integer, it would have to convert the `CoinName` object referenced by `value` to an integer. Moreover, `getValue` would need to make this conversion every time it was called. Although we could change the specification of this method's return value from `int` to `CoinName`, by having `getValue` return an integer, we allow the client to readily perform arithmetic with the values of a number of coins.
- If `CoinName` is the data type of both `value` and the constructor's argument, the constructor could simply assign the value of its argument to `value`. But then `getValue` would have the same problem as in the previous possibility.
- If `int` is the data type of both `value` and the constructor's argument, once again the constructor could assign the value of its argument to `value`, but the client would be able to provide an illegal value. To protect against such an error,
  - The client could adhere to a precondition that required the coin value to be 1, 5, 10, 25, 50, or 100.
  - Without having a precondition, the constructor could check the validity of the value passed to it.
  - The constructor could make this check and have a precondition.
- If `int` is the data type of `value`, and `CoinName` is the data type of the constructor's argument, the constructor must convert the argument to the appropriate integer for assignment to `value`. However, once this conversion is done, `getValue` can simply return `value` as often as it is called.

Based on this discussion, we will make the following design decisions:

- The easiest and fastest way for `getValue` to return an integer value is for `value` to be declared as an `int`.
- Requiring the client to pass an object of `CoinName` to our class's constructor is an easy way to prevent the client from making a mistake.
- `CoinName` must be public to allow the client to use it.

8.20   Listing 8-5 shows the completed class. We have retained `CoinSide` as a private enumeration and assumed `CoinName` as a public one. The additional fields, `value` and `year`, are both integers, as we just discussed.

The revised constructor accepts as arguments a `CoinName` object and an integer mint year. The `if` statements that assign an integer to `value` based on the name of the desired coin do not provide the best logic for this task. When creating a nickel, for example, `name` is compared to several `CoinName` objects, even after 5 is assigned to `value`. Chapter 10 will give us the tools to improve this logic.

LISTING 8-5   The class Coin

```java
/** Coin.java by F. M. Carrano
    Represents a coin.
*/
public class Coin
{
   private enum CoinSide {HEADS, TAILS}
   private int value; // in cents
   private int year;   // mint year
   private CoinSide sideUp;

   /** Constructs an object for the coin having a given
       name and mint year. The visible side of the new
       coin is set at random. */
   public Coin(CoinName name, int mintYear)
   {
      if (name == CoinName.PENNY)
         value = 1;
      if (name == CoinName.NICKEL)
         value = 5;
      if (name == CoinName.DIME)
         value = 10;
      if (name == CoinName.QUARTER)
         value = 25;
      if (name == CoinName.FIFTY_CENT)
         value = 50;
      if (name == CoinName.DOLLAR)
         value = 100;

      year = mintYear;
      sideUp = getToss();
   } // end constructor

   /** Returns the value of the coin in cents. */
   public int getValue()
   {
      return value;
   } // end getValue

   /** Returns the coin's mint year as an integer. */
   public int getYear()
   {
      return year;
   } // end getYear
```

```
< The methods getSideUp, isHeads, and isTails are the same as in Listing 8-4. >

/** Tosses the coin; sideUp will be either HEADS or TAILS randomly.
*/
public void toss()
{
   sideUp = getToss();
} // end toss

/** Returns the coin as a string in the form value/year/side-up. */
public String toString()
{
   return value + "/" + year + "/" + sideUp;
} // end toString

// Returns a random value of either HEADS or TAILS.
private CoinSide getToss()
{
   CoinSide result = CoinSide.TAILS;
   if (Math.random() < 0.5)
      result = CoinSide.HEADS;

   return result;
} // end getToss
} // end Coin
```

8.21   Listing 8-6 contains a demonstration of the class Coin.

LISTING 8-6   A demonstration of the class Coin

```
/** CoinDemo.java by F. M. Carrano
    Demonstrates the class Coin.
*/
import java.util.Scanner;
public class CoinDemo
{
   public static void main(String[] args)
   {
      Scanner keyboard = new Scanner(System.in);

      Coin penny   = new Coin(CoinName.PENNY, 2008);
      Coin nickel  = new Coin(CoinName.NICKEL, 2000);
      Coin dime    = new Coin(CoinName.DIME, 1998);
      Coin quarter = new Coin(CoinName.QUARTER, 2010);
```

```
        System.out.println("Here are four coins:");
        System.out.println(penny +    ". It is " + penny.getSideUp() +
                            " side up.");
        System.out.println(nickel +   ". It is " + nickel.getSideUp() +
                            " side up.");
        System.out.println(dime +     ". It is " + dime.getSideUp() +
                            " side up.");
        System.out.println(quarter + ". It is " + quarter.getSideUp() +
                            " side up.");

        penny.toss();
        nickel.toss();
        dime.toss();
        quarter.toss();
        System.out.println("After tossing each of these coins, they are");

        System.out.println(penny.getSideUp()    + ", " +
                            nickel.getSideUp()    + ", " +
                            dime.getSideUp()      + ", " +
                            quarter.getSideUp());

        int totalValue = penny.getValue() + nickel.getValue() +
                            dime.getValue() + quarter.getValue();
        System.out.println("The four coins have a total value of " +
                            totalValue + " cents.");
    } // end main
} // end CoinDemo
```

Output

```
Here are four coins:
1/2008/HEADS. It is HEADS side up.
5/2000/TAILS. It is TAILS side up.
10/1998/TAILS. It is TAILS side up.
25/2010/TAILS. It is TAILS side up.
After tossing each of these coins, they are
TAILS, TAILS, HEADS, TAILS
The four coins have a total value of 41 cents.
```

Question 11 Define a method getCoinName for the class Coin whose return type is CoinName. What other changes, if any, must you make to the class Coin to support this new method?

Calling a Constructor from a Constructor

8.22 As you know, a class can define several constructors. Such constructors have different parameters but perform similar initializations of the class's data fields. For example, recall the beginning of the class Name, as given in Listing 6-5 of Chapter 6:

```java
public class Name
{
    private String first; // first name
    private String last;  // last name

    public Name()
    {
        first = ""; // empty string
        last  = "";
    } // end default constructor

    public Name(String firstName, String lastName)
    {
        first = firstName;
        last  = lastName;
    } // end constructor
    . . .
```

Although these two constructors perform simple and brief initializations, the actions are in fact repetitive. When several constructors or methods perform the same task, debugging or modifying the code becomes more difficult.

8.23 We have two ways to avoid this duplication of effort, one familiar and one new. We can define a private method to perform the task and have each constructor call this method. The following code is an example of this approach:

```java
public Name()
{
    initialize("", "");
} // end default constructor

public Name(String firstName, String lastName)
{
    initialize(firstName, lastName);
} // end constructor

private void initialize(String firstName, String lastName)
{
    first = firstName;
    last  = lastName;
} // end initialize
```

With this technique, correcting or modifying the initialization step can be done in one place instead of several places.

8.24 A second way to avoid duplicate code is to have one constructor actually invoke another. You cannot use the name of the constructor to call it from within another constructor. Instead, you use the reserved word this as the constructor's name. For example, we can write the two constructors for the class Name, as follows:

```java
public Name()
{
    this("", "");
} // end default constructor
```

```
public Name(String firstName, String lastName)
{
    first = firstName;
    last  = lastName;
} // end constructor
```

The default constructor invokes the second constructor, passing it two empty strings to use in the initialization of the data fields `first` and `last`. You write this call just as if you were calling any method, but you use `this` as the method's name.

Note: The constructor of a class can explicitly invoke another constructor in the same class by using the reserved word `this` as if it were a method name. This action can occur only within a constructor and must always be its first action.

We first encountered `this` in Segment 6.11 of Chapter 6 as the way Java identifies the receiving object within the body of a method. We now have seen another meaning for this reserved word.

Programming Tip

Rather than performing similar actions, multiple constructors in the same class should invoke either a common private method or another constructor.

Question 12 Write a default constructor for the class `Coin`, as given in Listing 8-5, to create a penny minted in 2010. This constructor should invoke the existing constructor by using the reserved word `this`.

videonote
A problem
solved

SELF-TEST

CHAPTER SUMMARY

- A boolean-valued method returns either true or false. By defining such methods within a class, you provide a way for a client to test certain conditions relevant to the class.

- A carefully chosen name for a boolean-valued method will help you to avoid logical errors. Typically, such method names begin with "is" or "has."

- A private method generally performs an implementation detail that should be hidden from the client. A private method can be called only from within its own class.

- You should divide a large task into several smaller subtasks. The public method that implements the large task can then call several private methods, each of which implements one smaller task.

- Declare a data field as final if its value will be initialized once when an object is constructed and will not change after that time.

- Declare a data field as static if all objects of the class can share one copy of it.

- An enumerated data type, or enumeration, lists the values that a variable can have. Define and use an enumeration when you know and can list the possible values for a variable before execution time.

- An enumeration is actually a class, and so it provides a new data type. It has the methods `compareTo`, `equals`, `ordinal`, `toString`, and `valueOf`.

- A public enumeration should be defined within its own file, just like any other public class. Such an enumeration is available for use within any other class.

- A private enumeration is defined within a class outside of all method definitions. Such an enumeration is available for use only within the class containing it.

- The constructor of a class can explicitly invoke another constructor in the same class by using the reserved word `this` as if it were a method name. This action can occur only within a constructor and must always be its first action.

EXERCISES

1. When should methods of a class use the access modifier `private`?

2. The class `CupDispenser` has a private data field, `numberOfCups`, which tracks the number of cups currently in the dispenser. Define the method `isEmpty` for this class. The method should return true if a `CupDispenser` object contains no cups, or false otherwise.

3. A *complex number* has a real part and an imaginary part and is represented as

   real-part + *imaginary-part* x *i*, where *i* is $\sqrt{-1}$.

   If the class `Complex`, which represents complex numbers, has two `double` data fields—`real` and `imaginary`—define the boolean-valued method `isZero` that detects whether the two fields of a `Complex` object are both zero.

4. The class `CalendarDate` appears in Listing 8-2. Define a method for this class that tests whether two `CalendarDate` objects are equal. Name the method `equals`, make its return type `boolean`, and invoke it by using an expression such as `obj1.equals(obj2)`.

5. Write Java statements to create two `CalendarDate` objects and compare them for equality by using the method `equals` described in the previous exercise. Display an appropriate message.

6. By consulting Sun's online documentation for the Java Class Library, state the names of two static fields of the class `System`.

7. Declare a static constant to represent a sales tax rate of 9.25 percent.

8. When would you declare a class's data field to be final?

9. Consider a class `Test` that begins as follows:

   ```
   public class Test
   {
      public static final int w = 1;
      public static int x = 2;
      private final int y = 3;
      private int z = 4;
      . . .
   ```

   a. Which of w, x, y, and z—if any—can have their values changed by a constructor of `Test`? Why?
   b. Which of w, x, y, and z—if any—can have their values changed by a client of `Test`? Why?

10. Define an enumeration that defines the days of the week.

    a. Write a Java statement to access Wednesday from the enumeration.
    b. What is the ordinal value of Wednesday?
    c. What Java expression would give you the ordinal value of Wednesday?

11. Given the enumeration LetterGrade, as defined in Segment 8.11, what is the output of the following statements?

```
LetterGrade jacksGrade = LetterGrade.A;
LetterGrade jillsGrade = LetterGrade.B;
LetterGrade johnsGrade = LetterGrade.C;
LetterGrade fredsGrade = LetterGrade.B;
LetterGrade charliesGrade = jillsGrade;

System.out.println(jacksGrade);
System.out.println(jillsGrade.toString());
System.out.println(johnsGrade.ordinal());
System.out.println(jillsGrade == fredsGrade);
System.out.println(jillsGrade == charliesGrade);
System.out.println(jillsGrade.equals(fredsGrade));
System.out.println(jillsGrade.equals(charliesGrade));
```

12. Consider a class called Person that has two data fields, one for the person's name and one for the person's age. Write two constructors for this class. The implementation of one constructor should invoke the other.

13. Consider a class named Fan to represent a fan. The class contains

- Three constants named, SLOW, MEDIUM, and FAST with values 1, 2, and 3, respectively, to denote the fan speed.
- An integer data field named speed that specifies the speed of the fan; the default value is SLOW.
- A boolean data field named isOn that specifies whether the fan is on; the default value is false.
- A real data field named radius that specifies the radius of the fan in inches; the default value is 5.
- A string data field named color that specifies the color of the fan; the default value is gray.
- A default constructor that creates a default fan.
- A method named toString that returns a string description for the fan as follows. If the fan is on, the string contains "On" as well as the fan speed, color, and radius. If the fan is off, the string contains "Off" as well as the fan color and radius.

Define the beginning of this class, including the data fields, a default constructor, and the method toString.

14. Repeat the previous exercise, but replace the three named constants with an enumeration named SpeedChoice. Also change the data type of the field speed from int to SpeedChoice.

PROJECTS

1. Complete the definition of the class Fan described in Exercise 13. Include accessor and mutator methods for all four data fields. Demonstrate your class by creating two Fan objects. The first of these fans should have a radius of 10, be yellow, and be on at maximum speed. The second fan should have a radius of 5, be gray, and be turned off. Display the fans by invoking their toString methods.

2. Repeat the previous project, but use the description of the class Fan in Exercise 14.

3. Design and implement a class `Triangle` that represents triangles. A constructor should accept the lengths of a triangle's three sides as integers and verify that they are valid by testing whether the sum of the lengths of any two sides exceeds the length of the third side. The class should define three boolean-valued methods `isRight`, `isIsosceles`, and `isEquilateral` that test whether a triangle is, respectively, a right, isosceles, or equilateral triangle. Demonstrate your class by writing an appropriate client.

4. As Exercise 3 described, a complex number has a real part and an imaginary part and is represented as

$$real\text{-}part + imaginary\text{-}part \times i, \text{ where } i \text{ is } \sqrt{-1}.$$

When writing a complex number, however, you omit the multiplication operator. For example, $2.5 + 6.2i$ is a complex number.

To add two complex numbers, you add the two real parts together and separately add the two complex parts together. The two sums make up the real and imaginary parts of the result of the addition. Likewise, to subtract two complex numbers, you subtract one real part from the other and separately subtract one complex part from the other. The two differences make up the real and imaginary parts of the result of the subtraction.

Design and implement a class `Complex` that represents complex numbers. In addition to defining at least two constructors, define the following methods:

- `Complex add(Complex number)`—Returns the sum of the receiving object and `number` without changing either of the operands
- `Complex subtract(Complex number)`—Returns the difference obtained by subtracting `number` from the receiving object without changing either of the operands
- `boolean equals(Complex number)`—Returns either true or false according to whether the receiving object and `number` are equal
- `String toString()`—Returns a string that represents the receiving object

5. Define two enumerations for a standard deck of playing cards, one to represent the four suits—spades, clubs, diamonds, and hearts—and another to represent the values of the cards—ace, two, three, ... , jack, queen, king.

Next, design and implement a class `Card` using your enumerations. The constructor should create an object with a randomly selected suit and value. Using `Card`, implement a guessing game, similar to `CoinToss` in Listing 8-3, that picks a card, asks the user to guess the outcome, and reports the results.

6. Design and implement a class `LinearMeasure` that represents a linear measurement in either yards, feet, inches, meters, centimeters, or millimeters. Use an enumeration to represent these units of measure.

Define a constructor that has two parameters. One parameter represents the value of the measurement, and the other is a string that names the unit of measure. The case of the letters in this string should be irrelevant.

Define methods that convert any measurement to any given unit. Each of these conversions should be performed by two methods: One should change the measure and units of the receiving object and return a reference to it; the other should not change the receiving object but simply return the value of the new measure as a real number. For example, statements such as

```
LinearMeasure length = new LinearMeasure(8.5, "yards");
System.out.println(length + " is " + length.inMeters() + " meters.");
System.out.println(length + ".");
System.out.println(length + " is " + length.toMeters() + ".");
System.out.println(length + ".");
```

should produce the following output:

```
8.5 yards is 7.7724 meters.
8.5 yards.
8.5 yards is 7.7724 meters.
7.7724 meters.
```

Demonstrate your class by writing an appropriate client.

ANSWERS TO SELF-TEST QUESTIONS

1.
```
/** Returns true if the date occurs on a Saturday or Sunday. */
public boolean isWeekend()
```

2.
```
public boolean isWeekend()
{
   result = false;
   int day = getDayOfWeek();
   if ( (day == 1) || (day == 7) )
      result = true;
   return result;
} // end isWeekend
```

3. For a date to be valid,
   1. yearNumber must be greater than or equal to MIN_YEAR.
   2. If monthNumber is 9, 4, 6, or 11, then
      (dayNumber >= 1) && (dayNumber <= 30) must be true.
   3. If monthNumber is 1, 3, 5, 7, 8, 10, or 12, then
      (dayNumber >= 1) && (dayNumber <= 31) must be true.
   4. If monthNumber is 2 and isLeapYear(yearNumber) is true, then
      (dayNumber >= 1) && (dayNumber <= 29) must be true.
   5. If monthNumber is 2 and isLeapYear(yearNumber) is false, then
      (dayNumber >= 1) && (dayNumber <= 28) must be true.

4. Each object of the class has its own copy of the constant.

5.
```
public String getSideUp()
{
   String result = "";
   if (sideUp == CoinSide.HEADS)
      result = "Heads";
   else
      result = "Tails";
   return result;
} // end getSideUp
```

or

```
public String getSideUp()
{
   String result = "Tails";
   if (sideUp == CoinSide.HEADS)
      result = "Heads";
   return result;
} // end getSideUp
```

6. If `Math.random()` in the `if` clause returns a number less than 0.5, the method will execute correctly. However, if that is not the case, the `else if` clause calls `random` again. If that results in another random number less than 0.5, `sideUp` will not have a new value.

7. `=` should be `==`.

8.
```
/** Turns the coin over. */
public void turnOver()
{
    if (sideUp == CoinSide.HEADS)
        sideUp = CoinSide.TAILS;
    else
        sideUp = CoinSide.HEADS;
} // end turnOver
```

9. **a.** `sideUp` is `null`.
   b. If the other methods of the class are the same as in Listing 8-4 for the class `Coin1`, the expression `sideUp.toString()` in the method `getSideUp` would cause a `NullPointerException`.

10.
```
/** Constructs an object for the coin having a given side up. */
public Coin1(String headsOrTails)
{
    if (headsOrTails.equalsIgnoreCase("heads"))
        sideUp = CoinSide.HEADS;
    else
        sideUp = CoinSide.TAILS;
} // end constructor
```

11.
```
public CoinName getCoinName()
{
    return myName;
} // end getCoinName
```

Add a data field to `Coin` declared as

```
private CoinName myName;
```

Add the following statement to the constructor:

```
myName = name;
```

12.
```
public Coin()
{
    this(CoinName.PENNY, 2010);
} // end default constructor
```

Chapter

9

Classes of Graphical Objects

Contents

Prerequisites

Objectives

After studying this chapter, you should be able to
• Write a class that represents a group of graphical objects
• Write an application that uses such a class

So far, we have drawn pictures based upon a series of named constants that we defined. Each picture had a fixed position and size. Altering a picture required changes to the constants within our code.

We now will create a class of objects that can be drawn. For example, we will begin with the happy face of Chapter 5 and define a class of happy-face objects. We also will create a class of thermometers and write an application to display one. This application will read a temperature from its user by means of a dialog box, which we introduced in Chapter 4.

A Problem Solved: The Happy Face Reprised

> In Chapter 5, we wrote a program to display a happy face. Here we will develop two versions of a class to represent happy faces. Our first version uses much of the code in Listing 5-8. Although everything that we will do in the first version is perfectly legal, see if you can suggest improvements.

The Class HappyFace: First Version

9.1 Listing 9-1 shows our first attempt at a class that represents a happy face. If you compare it to HappyFacePanel in Listing 5-8, you will see that we have taken the named constants and made them private fields of our class. Since the client of our new class will not be able to specify the characteristics of the face, we have made these constants static.

The statements in Listing 5-8 that paint the face are now in a method paintFace of our new class. Because this method requires a Graphics object to be able to draw, we give it one as a parameter. Ultimately, the system will provide this object, which the client of our class can pass to paintFace as an argument. Since our class uses the classes Graphics and Color, we must import them.

LISTING 9-1   A first attempt at a class of happy faces

```java
/** HappyFace1.java by F. M. Carrano
    Represents a happy face - FIRST ATTEMPT.
*/
import java.awt.Color;
import java.awt.Graphics;
public class HappyFace1
{
   private static final Color FACE_COLOR = Color.ORANGE;
   private static final Color EYE_COLOR = Color.BLACK;
   private static final Color MOUTH_COLOR = Color.BLACK;

   private static final int FACE_CENTER_X = 150;
   private static final int FACE_CENTER_Y = 100;
   private static final int FACE_RADIUS = 75;
   private static final int FACE_DIAMETER = 2 * FACE_RADIUS;

   private static final int FACE_LEFT = FACE_CENTER_X - FACE_RADIUS;
   private static final int FACE_TOP = FACE_CENTER_Y - FACE_RADIUS;

   private static final int MOUTH_WIDTH = (int)(0.4 * FACE_DIAMETER);
   private static final int MOUTH_HEIGHT = MOUTH_WIDTH / 4;

   private static final int MOUTH_LEFT = FACE_CENTER_X - MOUTH_WIDTH / 2;
   private static final int MOUTH_TOP = FACE_CENTER_Y + 2 * MOUTH_HEIGHT;
   private static final int MOUTH_RIGHT = MOUTH_LEFT + MOUTH_WIDTH - 1;

   private static final int EYE_RADIUS = (int)(0.15 * FACE_RADIUS);
   private static final int EYE_DIAMETER = 2 * EYE_RADIUS;
```

```
        // distance from top of eyes to face center
        // (used only to define EYE_TOP)
    private static final int EYES_FROM_CENTER =
                             (FACE_RADIUS - 2 * MOUTH_HEIGHT) / 3;

    // coordinates of eyes (centered over edges of mouth):
    private static final int EYE_TOP = FACE_CENTER_Y - EYES_FROM_CENTER;
    private static final int LEFT_EYE_LEFT = MOUTH_LEFT - EYE_RADIUS;
    private static final int RIGHT_EYE_LEFT = MOUTH_RIGHT - EYE_RADIUS;

    /** Displays the face. */
    public void paintFace(Graphics pen)
    {
        // paint face
        pen.setColor(FACE_COLOR);
        pen.fillOval(FACE_LEFT, FACE_TOP, FACE_DIAMETER, FACE_DIAMETER);

        // paint eyes
        pen.setColor(EYE_COLOR);
        pen.fillOval(LEFT_EYE_LEFT, EYE_TOP, EYE_DIAMETER, EYE_DIAMETER);
        pen.fillOval(RIGHT_EYE_LEFT, EYE_TOP, EYE_DIAMETER, EYE_DIAMETER);

        // paint mouth: fill oval, then erase top of oval by painting it
        // in face color
        pen.setColor(MOUTH_COLOR);
        int ovalTop = MOUTH_TOP - MOUTH_HEIGHT;
        pen.fillOval(MOUTH_LEFT, ovalTop, MOUTH_WIDTH, 2 * MOUTH_HEIGHT);

        pen.setColor(FACE_COLOR);
        pen.fillOval(MOUTH_LEFT, ovalTop, MOUTH_WIDTH, MOUTH_HEIGHT);
    } // end paintFace
} // end HappyFace1
```

9.2   As we did in Chapter 5, we now create a panel for the happy face. This panel has some similarities to the panel shown in Listing 5-8, but since most of the code is now in the class HappyFace, our panel is much simpler, as Listing 9-2 shows.

LISTING 9-2   The definition of a panel that contains a happy face

```
/** HappyFacePanel1.java by F. M. Carrano
    Displays a happy face.
*/
import java.awt.Color;
import java.awt.Graphics;
import javax.swing.JPanel;

public class HappyFacePanel1 extends JPanel
{
    private HappyFace1 face;
```

```
   /** Creates a HappyFace object. */
   public void HappyFacePanel1()
   {
      face = new HappyFace1();
   } // end default constructor

   /** Displays the face. */
   public void paintComponent(Graphics pen)
   {
      face.paintFace(pen);
   } // end paintComponent
} // end HappyFacePanel1
```

9.3   Listing 9-3 contains an application program that uses HappyFacePanel1 to display a happy face. Recall that Question 15 of Chapter 5 asked you to write such a program. The program shown in Listing 9-3 is like the one we gave as the answer to that question.

LISTING 9-3   An application that displays a happy face

```
/** DisplayHappyFace.java
    Displays a happy face.
*/
import javax.swing.JFrame;

public class DisplayHappyFace
{
   public static void main(String[] args)
   {
      JFrame aWindow = new JFrame();
      aWindow.setSize(300, 240); // add 40 pixels to height to
                                 // accommodate title bar
      aWindow.setDefaultCloseOperation(JFrame.EXIT_ON_CLOSE);
      aWindow.setTitle("Happy Face");

      HappyFacePanel1 panel = new HappyFacePanel1();
      aWindow.add(panel);

      aWindow.setVisible(true);
   } // end main
} // end DisplayHappyFace
```

Output

Question 1 What is wrong with HappyFace as a class?

The Class HappyFace: Improved Version

9.4   Hopefully, you have thought about the previous question and arrived at a reason why we should revise the class HappyFace. The class certainly works as is. It enables you to create a happy face and display it. But you can create only the happy face that we designed. It has a fixed location, a fixed size, and a fixed color. Although you could create several HappyFace objects, they would all display exactly the same picture in the same position.

The problem is that our class is too specific; it represents one happy face. Instead, it should be a blueprint for an entire group of happy faces: big, small, red, blue, here, or there. Why should you provide more than one option? Because in the real world, specifications will evolve, and programs will end up needing to do more than you first thought. By building in some flexibility, you can keep your classes and use them in the solutions to future problems.

Programming Tip

A good class is general and usually does more than what is absolutely necessary for the problem at hand. Novice programmers tend to take a more narrow approach, designing classes that describe one object to solve a very specific problem.

Note: Code reuse

Using previously written and tested software in current programming projects is known as **code reuse**. This technique enables programmers to save time by not re-creating what has already been done. The Java Class Library is an example of code available for reuse.

9.5   **The data fields.** Now that you have seen what not to do, let's write a class of happy faces that is more general. As class designers, we decide which aspects of the faces will be determined by the client and which, if any, we will set. Suppose that we decide to let the client specify a face's location, size, and color. In addition, once the client chooses these characteristics for a particular face, they will remain constant. We will control the face's general appearance, including its shape, eyes, and mouth.

The class in Listing 9-4 has private data fields x, y, radius, and color that represent a face's location, size, and color. These aspects are no longer represented by static constants, as they were in our first draft, HappyFace1. However, since the client cannot change the values of these fields once they are selected, the fields can be final. That is, the fields are constants, but each object will have its own constants with their own values. The constants will no longer be shared by all faces.

But what about the other constants in HappyFace1? As you can see from Listing 9-1, some constants depend on the size of the face, and some depend on each other. They can no longer be static fields to be shared by all, but they can be final. The only static constants we will retain specify the color of the eyes and mouth.

9.6   **The methods.** The computations indicated in the definitions of the constants in Listing 9-1 are now performed by a constructor of our new class. For example, the data field faceDiameter must be set to twice the value of faceRadius.

If we were to write only one constructor, its body would contain a sequence of assignment statements that set the data fields to their correct values based upon the face's radius. The radius would be one of several parameters for the constructor. If we also wanted a default constructor, it would need to make a similar set of assignments. Duplicating this effort would be both tedious and error prone. Instead, to ensure that both constructors assign the correct values to the data fields, we can have the default constructor call the parameterized constructor by using `this`, as described in the previous chapter. Using this approach allows us to make changes in the computations within only one constructor instead of two. Note that our default constructor creates the same face that the class in Listing 9-1 creates. The method `paintFace` is like the one in Listing 9-1, but it uses our data fields instead of static constants.

Note: Data fields declared as final can be initialized only within a constructor. If a constructor calls a private method to initialize such fields, syntax errors will occur.

Programming Tip

When a class defines several constructors, to avoid duplicate effort, reduce error, and simplify the maintenance of the class, the constructors should not contain similar statements. Two general approaches are possible:

- Place the statements that detail the initializations to be performed into one constructor. The other constructors should call that constructor by using the reserved word `this`, as described in Chapter 8.
- Define a private method that makes the initializations and let all the constructors call it. Note that this second approach is not possible for any fields declared as final.

LISTING 9-4   An improved version of a class of happy faces

```java
/** HappyFace.java by F. M. Carrano
    Represents a happy face.
*/
import java.awt.Color;
import java.awt.Graphics;
public class HappyFace
{
    private final int x, y; // coordinates of center of face
    private final int faceRadius;
    private final Color faceColor;

    private final int faceDiameter, faceLeft, faceTop;
    private final int mouthWidth, mouthHeight, mouthLeft, mouthTop;
    private final int eyeDiameter, eyeTop, leftEyeLeft, rightEyeLeft;

    private static final Color EYE_COLOR = Color.BLACK;
    private static final Color MOUTH_COLOR = Color.BLACK;

    /** Creates a default face. */
    public HappyFace()
    {
        this(200, 100, 75, Color.ORANGE);
    } // end default constructor
```

```java
/** Creates a face centered at a given point with a given radius and
    color. */
public HappyFace(int centerX, int centerY, int radius, Color color)
{
    faceColor = color;
    x = centerX;
    y = centerY;
    faceRadius = radius;
    faceDiameter = 2 * faceRadius;

    faceLeft = x - faceRadius;
    faceTop = y - faceRadius;

    mouthWidth = (int)(0.4 * faceDiameter);
    mouthHeight = mouthWidth / 4;

    mouthLeft = x - mouthWidth / 2;
    mouthTop = y + 2 * mouthHeight;
    int mouthRight = mouthLeft + mouthWidth - 1;

    int eyeRadius = (int)(0.15 * faceRadius);
    eyeDiameter = 2 * eyeRadius;

    // coordinates of eyes:
    eyeTop = y - (faceRadius - 2 * mouthHeight) / 3;
    leftEyeLeft = mouthLeft - eyeRadius;
    rightEyeLeft = mouthRight - eyeRadius;
} // end constructor

/** Displays the face. */
public void paintFace(Graphics pen)
{
    // paint face
    pen.setColor(faceColor);
    pen.fillOval(faceLeft, faceTop, faceDiameter, faceDiameter);

    // paint eyes
    pen.setColor(EYE_COLOR);
    pen.fillOval(leftEyeLeft, eyeTop, eyeDiameter, eyeDiameter);
    pen.fillOval(rightEyeLeft, eyeTop, eyeDiameter, eyeDiameter);

    // paint mouth: fill oval, then erase top of oval by painting it
    // in face color
    pen.setColor(MOUTH_COLOR);
    int ovalTop = mouthTop - mouthHeight;
    pen.fillOval(mouthLeft, ovalTop, mouthWidth, 2 * mouthHeight);

    pen.setColor(faceColor);
```

```
        pen.fillOval(mouthLeft, ovalTop, mouthWidth, mouthHeight);
   } // end paintFace
} // end HappyFace
```

Question 2 What changes would you make to the class `HappyFace` to add a method `setFace` that changes the location, size, and color of an existing `HappyFace` object?

9.7   **The panel.** We could use the same panel and application that appear in Listings 9-2 and 9-3 if we replace `HappyFace1` with `HappyFace`. However, we instead will create a new panel that displays two happy faces, to show you how to indicate the dimensions of the panel and window in a better way. Up to now, we indicated the size of the window. As you will see, stipulating the size of the panel is more convenient and often necessary.

Since we can now specify the position and size of the happy face, we want to define those characteristics within the panel. To do so, we begin with the size of the panel. The panel definition in Listing 9-5 defines `PANEL_WIDTH` and `PANEL_HEIGHT` as private named constants. We use them in the definitions of other constants that position and size two `HappyFace` objects.

The default constructor and `paintComponent` method are analogous to the ones shown earlier in Listing 9-2, but our new constructor takes the additional step of setting the panel's dimensions by calling the method `setPreferredSize`. Java can override your request, which explains the method's name: The method sets the size you prefer, which is not always the size you get. The argument to this method is an object of a standard class `Dimension`, which is in the AWT. `Dimension` provides a way to group the panel's width and height. For example, we could write

```
Dimension size = new Dimension(PANEL_WIDTH, PANEL_HEIGHT);
setPreferredSize(size);
```

However, we usually combine these statements into one, as follows:

```
setPreferredSize(new Dimension(PANEL_WIDTH, PANEL_HEIGHT));
```

videonote
Generalizing class
definitions

LISTING 9-5   The definition of a panel that contains two happy faces

```
/** HappyFacePanel.java by F. M. Carrano
    Displays two happy faces.
*/
import java.awt.Color;
import java.awt.Dimension;
import java.awt.Graphics;
import javax.swing.JPanel;

public class HappyFacePanel extends JPanel
{
   private HappyFace bigFace, smallFace;

   private static final int PANEL_WIDTH = 300;
   private static final int PANEL_HEIGHT = 325;
   private static final int BIG_FACE_X = PANEL_WIDTH / 2;
   private static final int BIG_FACE_Y = PANEL_HEIGHT / 2;
```

```java
   private static final int BIG_FACE_RADIUS = PANEL_WIDTH / 4;
   private static final Color BIG_FACE_COLOR = Color.ORANGE;

   private static final int SMALL_FACE_X = BIG_FACE_X -
                                       3 * BIG_FACE_RADIUS / 4;
   private static final int SMALL_FACE_Y = BIG_FACE_Y - BIG_FACE_RADIUS;
   private static final int SMALL_FACE_RADIUS = 2 * BIG_FACE_RADIUS / 3;
   private static final Color SMALL_FACE_COLOR = Color.BLUE;

   /** Creates two HappyFace objects. */
   public HappyFacePanel()
   {
      bigFace = new HappyFace(BIG_FACE_X, BIG_FACE_Y,
                             BIG_FACE_RADIUS, BIG_FACE_COLOR);
      smallFace = new HappyFace(SMALL_FACE_X, SMALL_FACE_Y,
                               SMALL_FACE_RADIUS, SMALL_FACE_COLOR);
      setPreferredSize(new Dimension(PANEL_WIDTH, PANEL_HEIGHT));
   } // end default constructor

   /** Displays the two faces. */
   public void paintComponent(Graphics pen)
   {
      bigFace.paintFace(pen);
      smallFace.paintFace(pen);
   } // end paintComponent
} // end HappyFacePanel
```

Note: The size of a component
The size of a graphical component depends not only on its content, but also on its **look and feel**, that is, aspects such as the shape, font, color, **layout**—or arrangement—of various parts, and any dynamic elements such as buttons and menus. Since the look and feel are platform dependent, Java might ignore the preferred size the programmer has provided for a component.

Note: The class Dimension
The class Dimension enables you to create an object that represents the width and height of a component. The class is a part of the Abstract Window Toolkit and is in the package java.awt. The JPanel method setPreferredSize sets a panel's dimensions and takes a Dimension object as its argument.

9.8   **The application.** Listing 9-6 contains the application program that creates our panel and a window in which to display it. If you compare this program with the one shown in Listing 9-3, you will see that we have omitted a call to the method setSize. Instead, we have invoked the method pack after adding the panel to the window. This JFrame method sets the size of the window to accommodate its contents.

LISTING 9-6   An application that displays the panel defined in Listing 9-5

```
/** DisplayHappyFaces.java by F. M. Carrano
    Displays two happy faces.
*/
import javax.swing.JFrame;

public class DisplayHappyFaces
{
   public static void main(String[] args)
   {
      JFrame aWindow = new JFrame();
      aWindow.setDefaultCloseOperation(JFrame.EXIT_ON_CLOSE);
      aWindow.setTitle("Happy Faces");

      HappyFacePanel panel = new HappyFacePanel();
      aWindow.add(panel);
      aWindow.pack();
      aWindow.setVisible(true);
   } // end main
} // end DisplayHappyFaces
```

Output

 Note: Setting the size of panels and windows
Instead of setting the size of a window, use the method `setPreferredSize` to set the size of each panel or component that you plan to display in the window. After adding these components to the window, call the method `pack` to make the window large enough for its contents.

 Note: Changing the location or size of panels and windows
Both `JFrame` and `JPanel` have the methods `setLocation` and `setBounds`. The method `setLocation` changes the location of a panel or window by changing the coordinates of its upper left corner to those passed to the method as its arguments. Similarly, `setBounds` changes both the location and dimensions of a window or panel to the coordinates and dimensions passed to it as arguments. For details about these methods, consult the online documentation for the class `Component`—the class ultimately extended by `JFrame` and `JPanel`—in the Java Class Library.

■ A Problem Solved: The Thermometer Reprised

We consider again the problem posed in "A Problem Solved: Displaying a Temperature" in Chapter 5. We want to display a thermometer that shows a given temperature. In Chapter 5, the temperature we displayed was randomly generated. Here, we will ask the user for a temperature by using a dialog box, as introduced in Chapter 4. We will define a class of thermometers and write a program to display an instance of this class.

The Class `Thermometer`

9.9   **Data fields.** The code given in Listing 5-4 of Chapter 5 defines several constants that are used in drawing the thermometer. If you examine them, you will see that the location of the thermometer is given by the constants `EDGE_LEFT` and `EDGE_TOP`. These constants represent the coordinates of the upper left corner of the thermometer's frame. We would like for our class of thermometers to let its client specify where the thermometer is drawn, so multiple thermometers can appear in the same window. Thus, the coordinates of the thermometer should be data fields of our class whose values the client can provide.

If you look at Listing 5-4 further, you will see that the coordinates of the temperature column—`COLUMN_LEFT` and `COLUMN_TOP`—depend on the coordinates of the thermometer itself. Since the latter coordinates are no longer constants for all thermometers, the coordinates of the temperature column cannot be static named constants. For simplicity, we will retain the remaining constants in Listing 5-4 and make them static named constants in our new class. Because most of these constants involve the implementation of the class, we make them private. However, a client might need the dimensions of the thermometer. We could define accessor methods for the width and height, but since they are shared by all thermometers, we choose to make the width and height public instead. Note that we have named these constants `WIDTH` and `HEIGHT`, instead of `EDGE_WIDTH` and `EDGE_HEIGHT` as we did in Listing 5-4.

Listing 9-7 contains the class `Thermometer`. Note the `import` statements for the classes `Color`, `Font`, and `Graphics` that we need to draw the thermometer. Also note the data fields `temperature`, `left`, `top`, `columnLeft`, and `columnTop`. The values of the first three fields are set by the client and affect the values of the last two fields. Except for `temperature`, the values of these fields remain fixed for a particular thermometer, so we declare them as final. The remaining data fields are static constants and have the same values as they did in Listing 5-4.

9.10   **The methods.** We have provided two constructors. The default constructor positions the thermometer at the coordinates (0, 0) and sets the temperature to zero degrees. The second constructor enables the client to specify these values. When the constructors set the data fields `left`, `top`, and `temperature`, they must also initialize `columnLeft` and `columnTop`. Rather than writing five assignment statements in both constructors, we have written them in one constructor, which the other calls.

LISTING 9-7   The class `Thermometer`

```
/** Thermometer.java by F. M. Carrano
    Represents a Fahrenheit thermometer that can display temperatures
    between 0 and 120 degrees. Temperatures below 32 degrees appear
    in blue; other temperatures are red.
*/
import java.awt.Color;
import java.awt.Font;
import java.awt.Graphics;
```

```java
public class Thermometer
{
    private int temperature;
    private final int left, top; // coordinates of upper left corner
                                 //    of thermometer
    private final int columnLeft,// coordinates of upper left corner
                      columnTop; //    of temperature column

    private static final int BORDER = 20; // distance between thermometer
                                          //    edges & temperature column

    // temperature column dimensions:
    private static final int COLUMN_HEIGHT= 150;
    private static final int COLUMN_WIDTH = 5;

    // thermometer dimensions:
    public static final int WIDTH = COLUMN_WIDTH + 2 * BORDER;
    public static final int HEIGHT = COLUMN_HEIGHT + (int)(2.5 * BORDER);

    // key temperatures:
    private static final int MAX_TEMPERATURE = 120;
    private static final int MIN_TEMPERATURE = 0;
    private static final int FREEZING_TEMPERATURE = 32; // of water

    /** Creates a default thermometer at the point (0, 0)
        set to zero degrees. */
    public Thermometer()
    {
        this(0, 0, 0);
    } // end default constructor

    /** Creates a thermometer at the point (xFrame, yFrame)
        set to the temperature initialTemperature;
        initialTemperature must not be less than
        MIN_TEMPERATURE nor more than MAX_TEMPERATURE */
    public Thermometer(int xFrame, int yFrame, int initialTemperature)
    {
        left = xFrame;
        top = yFrame;
        columnLeft = left + BORDER;
        columnTop = top + BORDER;
        temperature = initialTemperature;
    } // end constructor

    /** Sets the temperature to newTemperature. */
    public void setTemperature(int newTemperature)
    {
```

```java
      temperature = newTemperature;
} // end setTemperature

/** Returns the temperature. */
public int getTemperature()
{
   return temperature;
} // end getTemperature

/** Draws the thermometer. */
public void draw(Graphics pen)
{
   paintFluid(pen);
   drawEdges(pen);
   drawDigitalTemperature(pen);
} // end draw

// Sets the color of fluid in the temperature column:
// temperatures below freezing are blue; others are red.
private void setTemperatureColor(Graphics pen)
{
   if (temperature <= FREEZING_TEMPERATURE)
      pen.setColor(Color.BLUE);
   else
      pen.setColor(Color.RED);
} // end setTemperatureColor

// Paints the fluid in the temperature column.
private void paintFluid(Graphics pen)
{
   setTemperatureColor(pen);
   int fluidHeight = (int)(COLUMN_HEIGHT * (double)temperature /
                       (MAX_TEMPERATURE - MIN_TEMPERATURE));
   int fluidTop = columnTop + COLUMN_HEIGHT - fluidHeight;
   pen.fillRect(columnLeft, fluidTop, COLUMN_WIDTH, fluidHeight);
} // end paintFluid

// Draws the edges of the temperature column and the frame around it.
private void drawEdges(Graphics pen)
{
   pen.setColor(Color.BLACK);
   pen.drawRect(columnLeft, columnTop, COLUMN_WIDTH, COLUMN_HEIGHT);
   pen.drawRect(left, top, WIDTH, HEIGHT);
} // end drawEdges

// Draws the digital temperature.
private void drawDigitalTemperature(Graphics pen)
```

```
   {
      pen.setColor(Color.BLACK);
      int xLabel = columnLeft - 2 * BORDER / 3;
      int yLabel = columnTop + COLUMN_HEIGHT + BORDER;
      pen.setFont(new Font("Monospaced", Font.BOLD, 10));
      pen.drawString(temperature + "° F", xLabel, yLabel);
   } // end drawDigitalTemperature
} // end Thermometer
```

We have defined set and get methods for the temperature. These allow a client to change the temperature or to ask a thermometer for its temperature reading. The method draw draws the thermometer, given a Graphics object ultimately provided by the system. We have made one enhancement to the thermometer drawn in Listing 5-4. Whenever a temperature is above 32 degrees, it is shown in red; otherwise it appears in blue. A private method sets the color for us. We have also divided the statements in Listing 5-4 that draw the thermometer among three private methods. The method draw simply calls these private methods.

Question 3 Why is it possible to declare the data fields left, top, columnLeft, and columnTop in the class Thermometer as final?

Question 4 Instead of initializing the data fields in one constructor that the other constructor calls, could you define a private method to perform the initialization and call it from each of the constructors? Explain.

Note: Managing color
Drawing in Java is like drawing with one pen. You know that you can set the color of the pen by calling the Graphics method setColor. To draw in more than one color, you might need to change the pen's color several times, as we did in the class Thermometer in Listing 9-7. In such cases, it is easy to lose track of the pen's current color. Here are two possible ways to avoid problems:

- Each method that draws must set the pen's color before drawing. This is the technique we used in the class Thermometer. In this way, a method makes no assumption about the pen's prior color, but sets and manages the color itself. This approach to color management is appropriate when the logic involved is not complex, as is the case for Thermometer.
- Each method that draws must restore the pen's color to the value it had when the method was called. This approach is desirable when a method draws in one color and calls other methods in the same class to draw in different colors. The effect is like giving each method its own pen to manage. For example, if method *A* draws using a blue pen, calls method *B* to draw with a red pen, and then draws again when *B* is finished, *A* can assume that its pen will still be blue. The next note shows how a method can draw in one color without changing the pen color used by its client.

> **Note:** The method `getColor`
> In addition to the method `setColor`, the class `Graphics` defines the method `getColor` to return a `Color` object representing the current pen color. A method can call `getColor` to save the pen's color before changing it. Later, it can restore the pen to its original color. For example, the method could contain statements such as the following:
>
> ```
> Color originalColor = pen.getColor();
> pen.setColor(newColor);
> . . .
> pen.setColor(originalColor);
> ```

Displaying the Thermometer

9.11   **The panel.** As in our earlier example, we create a panel in which to display an instance of the class `Thermometer`. The panel in Listing 9-8 has a constructor that sets the size of the panel by invoking `JPanel`'s method `setPreferredSize` and then creates a `Thermometer` object set to the temperature passed to the constructor as an argument. To center the thermometer within the panel, notice how we use both the dimensions of the panel—which are local to the class—and the dimensions of the thermometer—which are public named constants within the class `Thermometer`.

The method `paintComponent` draws the thermometer by invoking the `Thermometer` method `draw`. We pass to `draw` the graphics context pen, which the system passed to `paintComponent`. Note that we declare the `Thermometer` object `myThermometer` as a private and final data field of the panel class, since it is used by both the constructor and `paintComponent` and it does not change.

LISTING 9-8   The definition of `ThermometerPanel`

```java
/** ThermometerPanel.java by F. M. Carrano
    Displays a thermometer.
*/
import java.awt.Dimension;
import java.awt.Graphics;
import javax.swing.JPanel;

public class ThermometerPanel extends JPanel
{
    private static final int PANEL_WIDTH = 400;
    private static final int PANEL_HEIGHT = Thermometer.HEIGHT + 50;

    private final Thermometer myThermometer;

    /** Creates a panel showing a thermometer set at a given
        temperature. */
    public ThermometerPanel(int temperature)
    {
        setPreferredSize(new Dimension(PANEL_WIDTH, PANEL_HEIGHT));

        // position thermometer within panel
        int thermometerX = PANEL_WIDTH / 2 - Thermometer.WIDTH / 2;
```

```
        int thermometerY = (PANEL_HEIGHT - Thermometer.HEIGHT) / 2;

        // create thermometer and set temperature
        myThermometer = new Thermometer(thermometerX, thermometerY,
                                        temperature);
    } // end default constructor

    /** Displays the thermometer */
    public void paintComponent(Graphics pen)
    {
        myThermometer.draw(pen);
    } // end paintComponent
} // end ThermometerPanel
```

9.12   **The application.** A program that creates a window in which to display our panel is shown in Listing 9-9. In addition to the steps taken by the happy-face program given in Listing 9-6, we read a temperature from the user and set the thermometer to this temperature before displaying the panel.

LISTING 9-9   An application that displays the panel defined in Listing 9-8

```
/** DisplayThermometer.java by F. M. Carrano
    Displays a thermometer.
*/
import javax.swing.JFrame;
import javax.swing.JOptionPane;

public class DisplayThermometer
{
    public static void main(String[] args)
    {
        JFrame aWindow = new JFrame();
        aWindow.setDefaultCloseOperation(JFrame.EXIT_ON_CLOSE);
        aWindow.setTitle("The Current Temperature");

        // get temperature from user
        String inputValue = JOptionPane.showInputDialog(
                                    "Please enter the temperature.");
        int temperature = Integer.parseInt(inputValue);

        // create a thermometer set at the given temperature
        ThermometerPanel panel = new ThermometerPanel(temperature);

        aWindow.add(panel);
        aWindow.pack();
        aWindow.setVisible(true);
    } // end main
} // end DisplayThermometer
```

Sample Output

SELF-TEST

Question 5 The class `Thermometer`, as given in Listing 9-7, contains an error. If a client sets a thermometer's temperature, displays it, sets the thermometer to another temperature, and displays it, the two drawings will overlap. For example, setting the initial temperature to 82 degrees and then changing it to 32 degrees results in a temperature column that is partially blue and partially red. Describe why this error occurs and what you can do to correct it.

Question 6 A client of the class `Thermometer` might find it useful to know the dimensions of the thermometer. One way to let a client access these dimensions is to make the constants `WIDTH` and `HEIGHT` public, as we described in Segment 9.9. What is another way, assuming that `WIDTH` and `HEIGHT` are private?

Question 7 What changes are necessary to the class `Thermometer` to enable a client to specify the dimensions of the temperature column?

Displaying Two Thermometers

9.13

videonote
Several objects
of a class

Suppose we want to display today's expected high and low temperatures in two separate thermometers, labeled and in one window. We already have the class `Thermometer`. We can create two `Thermometer` objects and display each one in its own panel. Since we want to display both thermometers in one window, we will add the two panels to a third panel before adding this third panel to the window. In effect, we create **subpanels** for the thermometers.

For labels, we can use the Swing class `JLabel`. Its constructor takes a `String` argument that forms the label. `JLabel` objects are components that we can add to a panel. Later, we will explore how to position, or lay out, components within other components, but for now, we will use default layouts.

> **Note:** The Swing class `JLabel`
> A `JLabel` object is a component that can display text and/or an image. You can add such components to a panel to label other objects displayed in the panel.

9.14

The subpanels. We want to create two panels, each containing a thermometer, that eventually will be subpanels of a larger panel. The class `ThermometerPanel` in Listing 9-8, with slight changes, will work for us. These changes are highlighted in Listing 9-10.

LISTING 9-10   The definition of `ThermometerPanel`

```
/** ThermometerSubpanel.java by F. M. Carrano
    Displays a thermometer that shows a particular temperature.
```

```java
*/
import java.awt.Dimension;
import java.awt.Graphics;
import javax.swing.JLabel;
import javax.swing.JPanel;

public class ThermometerSubpanel extends JPanel
{
    private static final int PANEL_WIDTH = 200;
    private static final int PANEL_HEIGHT = Thermometer.HEIGHT + 50;

    private final Thermometer myThermometer;

    /** Creates a panel showing a thermometer set at a given temperature
        and having a given label. */
    public ThermometerSubpanel(int temperature, String label)
    {
        setPreferredSize(new Dimension(PANEL_WIDTH, PANEL_HEIGHT));

        // position thermometer within panel
        int thermometerX = PANEL_WIDTH / 2 - Thermometer.WIDTH / 2;
        int thermometerY = (PANEL_HEIGHT - Thermometer.HEIGHT) / 2;

        // create thermometer and set temperature
        myThermometer = new Thermometer(thermometerX, thermometerY,
                                        temperature);

        // label thermometer
        JLabel thermometerLabel = new JLabel(label.toUpperCase());
        add(thermometerLabel);

    } // end default constructor

    /** Displays the thermometer */
    public void paintComponent(Graphics pen)
    {
        myThermometer.draw(pen);
    } // end paintComponent
} // end ThermometerSubpanel
```

We added an import statement for JLabel, changed the name of the class to distinguish it from the class in Listing 9-8, and added to the constructor a parameter that is used when creating an instance of JLabel. The constructor adds this label to the panel.

9.15 **The application.** Listing 9-11 provides a program that creates a window in which to display the two thermometers. We create two instances of ThermometerSubpanel and add them to an instance of JPanel. We then add the JPanel panel to the window.

LISTING 9-11   An application that displays two instances of the panel defined
                in Listing 9-10

```java
/** DisplayHighLowTemperatures.java by F. M. Carrano
    Displays two thermometers that show today's high
    and low temperatures as entered by the user.
*/
import javax.swing.JFrame;
import javax.swing.JOptionPane;
import javax.swing.JPanel;

public class DisplayHighLowTemperatures
{
   public static void main(String[] args)
   {
      JFrame aWindow = new JFrame();
      aWindow.setDefaultCloseOperation(JFrame.EXIT_ON_CLOSE);
      aWindow.setTitle("Today's High and Low Temperatures");

      // get high and low temperatures from the user
      String inputValue = JOptionPane.showInputDialog("Please enter " +
                                          "today's high temperature:");
      int highTemp = Integer.parseInt(inputValue);
      inputValue = JOptionPane.showInputDialog("Please enter " +
                                          "today's low temperature:");
      int lowTemp = Integer.parseInt(inputValue);

      ThermometerSubpanel panelHigh = new ThermometerSubpanel(highTemp,
                                                              "high");

      ThermometerSubpanel panelLow  = new ThermometerSubpanel(lowTemp,
                                                              "low");

      JPanel panel = new JPanel();

      panel.add(panelHigh);
      panel.add(panelLow);

      aWindow.add(panel);
      aWindow.pack();
      aWindow.setVisible(true);
   } // end main
} // end DisplayHighLowTemperatures
```

Sample Output

  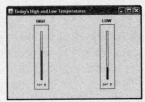

videonote
A problem
solved

CHAPTER SUMMARY

- When designing a class that can produce graphical output, think generally. Do not define a class that restricts itself to one particular drawing. Let the client specify aspects of the drawing, such as position, size, or color, as appropriate. Remember that a class describes a group of similar objects, not just one specific object.

- To avoid duplicate code, use private methods that several other methods can call.

- A panel can create a graphical object within its constructor and display it within the method paintComponent.

- A panel can use a dialog box to read a value from the user.

- Set the preferred size of a panel instead of setting the size of the window that will contain the panel.

- The Graphics method getColor returns a Color object representing the present pen color.

- You can add subpanels to the panel that you add to a window.

- Instances of the Swing class JLabel are components that can be added to a panel as labels.

EXERCISES

1. Why should the classes you design be as general as possible?

2. Consult the documentation for the class Dimension in the Java Class Library.

    a. What constructor would you use to create a new Dimension object from an existing Dimension object?
    b. What method would you use to retrieve the height of an existing Dimension object?
    c. What method would you use to change the width and height of an existing Dimension object?

3. Consult the documentation for the class JFrame in the Java Class Library.

    a. From which class does JFrame inherit the method pack?
    b. What four constants can you pass to the method setDefaultCloseOperation?

4. Write statements that will draw three squares side by side. First, draw the leftmost square using the current pen color. Next, draw the middle square in blue. Finally, draw the rightmost square using the same color as the leftmost square.

5. Imagine a cylinder of a given radius and height. Now imagine a class of cylinders that defines two private data fields, radius and height, whose data type is int. Define two constructors for this class, including a default constructor that creates a cylinder whose radius and height are each 20. Assume that the class has mutator methods, so that its data fields are not final. Thus, define a private method that each constructor can call.

6. Repeat the previous exercise, but do not define a private method. Instead, let the default constructor call the second constructor.

7. Consider the class of cylinders described in Exercise 5. Define the method draw within this class to draw the outline of a cylinder. For example, here are the outlines of two cylinders:

8. What changes to the class Thermometer, as given in Listing 9-7, will correct the error discussed in Self-Test Question 5?

9. Consult the documentation for the class FontMetrics in the Java Class Library. How do you find the

    a. Standard leading, or interline spacing, of the font?
    b. Descent of the font?
    c. Ascent of the font?
    d. Height of the font

10. Consider a class `MessagePanel` that extends `JPanel` and has a string named `message` as a data field. Using the class `FontMetrics` mentioned in the previous exercise, define the method `paintComponent` to display `message` centered within the panel.

11. The following code displays a digital clock within a panel:

```java
public class ClockPanel extends JPanel
{
    public void paintComponent(Graphics g)
    {
        final int hoursInDay = 12;
        final int minutesInHour = 60;
        // Draw the enclosing rectangle
        g.drawRect(20, 20, 345, 140);
        // Get random hour and minute
        Random generator = new Random();
        int hour = generator.nextInt(hoursInDay + 1);
        int minute = generator.nextInt(minutesInHour + 1);
        // Display the time
        g.setFont(new Font("Monospaced", Font.BOLD, 50));
        g.drawString(hour + ":" + minute, 150, 100);
    } // end paintComponent
} // end ClockPanel
```

Divide this code into two general classes, `DigitalClock` and `DigitalClockPanel`. The class `DigitalClock` defines data fields to represent the time, the position of the clock, and the color of the font to draw the time. The class should have only a default constructor that sets the clock's

- Time to the current time
- Position to the coordinates (20, 20)
- Width and height to 345 and 140, respectively
- Font color to blue

The class `DigitalClockPanel` should contain all the necessary methods to create an instance of `DigitalClock` and paint it on the panel. Provide a test driver that creates one instance of `DigitalClockPanel` centered within a frame.

12. Add three constructors to the class `DigitalClock` created in the previous exercise. Give them the following capabilities:

- Set the hour, minute, and second fields to given values
- Set the color field in addition to the previous fields to given values
- Set the dimensions of the digital clock in addition to the previous fields to given values

Create a test driver that allows the user to create either a default instance of a digital clock or an instance in which the user sets all of the fields of the digital clock.

13. Define a class `AnalogClock` to display an analog clock on a panel as shown next. Use the class `DigitalClock` developed in Exercise 11 to keep track of the time. To draw an analog clock, you can use a circle for the face and three lines for the hour, minute, and second hands. Each hand extends from the center of the clock to a point determined by the following formulas:

$$x_{end} = x_{center} + length_{hand} \times sin\ \Theta$$
$$y_{end} = y_{center} - length_{hand} \times cos\ \Theta$$

Since there are 60 seconds in one minute, the angle Θ for the second hand is

$$seconds \times (2\pi\ /\ 60)$$

and the angle Θ of the minute hand is

$$(minutes + seconds\ /\ 60) \times (2\pi\ /\ 60)$$

Because the clock face is divided into 12 hours, the angle for the hour hand is

$$(hours + minutes / 60 + seconds / 60^2) \times (2\pi / 12)$$

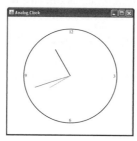

PROJECTS

1. Define a class Box to represent rectangles and squares. Four data fields should represent the coordinates of a box's upper left corner and the box's dimensions. Give the class two constructors, including a default constructor. In addition to appropriate accessor and mutator methods, give the class methods that return a box's area and perimeter, as well as one that draws the box. The method toString should return the values of a box's instance variables as a string.

2. Repeat Project 1 of Chapter 5, but represent the graphical coordinates as a class separate from the panel that displays it. The position and dimensions of the rectangle should be data fields of the class. The circle's diameter should be 80 percent of the rectangle's height.

3. Repeat Project 2 of Chapter 5, but represent the winking face as a class separate from the panel that displays it. Enable the client to choose which eye winks.

4. Repeat Project 3 of Chapter 5, but represent the snowman as a class separate from the panel that displays it.

5. Create a class Alphabet that displays capital letters in block form. Use your new class to draw your first and last initials in block letters that overlap a circle, as shown in Project 4 of Chapter 5. Complete Alphabet for at least five letters. Decide whether you will have 26 separate methods to draw the letters or one method that accepts a letter as an argument.

ANSWERS TO SELF-TEST QUESTIONS

1. The class HappyFace represents one face with fixed characteristics.

2. In addition to defining the method setFace, whose body would contain statements like those in the parameterized constructor, we would remove final from the declarations of the fields x, y, faceRadius, faceColor, faceDiameter, faceLeft, faceTop, mouthWidth, mouthHeight, mouthLeft, mouthTop, eyeDiameter, eyeTop, leftEyeLeft, and rightEyeLeft.

3. The class defines no public method to change the location of a Thermometer object, so the fields left, top, columnLeft, and columnTop can—and should be—declared as final.

4. No. Since the fields left, top, columnLeft, and columnTop are final, initializing them in a private method would cause syntax errors. Only a constructor can change the value of a final field.

5. The private method `paintFluid`, which the method `draw` invokes, draws over any existing drawing. So if `paintFluid` paints a red column representing 82 degrees and later paints a shorter blue column representing 32 degrees, a portion of the red column still remains. However, if the first temperature was 32, and the second temperature was 82, the longer red column for 82 would replace the blue column, obscuring the error. Notice that the digital version of the second temperature is written on top of that for the first temperature, which is still an error. To correct the errors, `draw` needs to first erase at least the temperature column and the digital temperature before drawing the current versions.

6. Add the methods `getWidth` and `getHeight` to return the values of `WIDTH` and `HEIGHT`, respectively. Note that the client cannot change these values.

7. Change `COLUMN_HEIGHT`, `COLUMN_WIDTH`, `WIDTH`, and `HEIGHT` to variables instead of constants and add set methods.

Chapter

10

Multiway Decisions

Contents

Prerequisites

Objectives

After studying this chapter, you should be able to
• Write nested if statements
• Use multiway if statements to cause one of several possible actions
• Use a switch statement to cause one of several possible actions

Imagine that you are an intern with a local health club. New members can stop at a kiosk and interact with a program that you are to write. The program will give some advice about appropriate facilities according to the person's age. Before the end of this chapter, you will be able to write this program.

Chapter 7 introduced the basic if statement, with and without an else clause. This statement enables our programs to choose between two options. Many times, however, we are faced with more than two choices, just as we will be when writing the program for the health club. This chapter discusses how to deal with these situations by nesting several if statements or by using a new statement, the **switch statement**. A switch statement chooses from among several possible actions according to the value of an expression whose data type is either int, char, or enumerated.

■ Nested **if** Statements

10.1   Chapter 7 gave the syntax of an **if** statement as follows:

```
if (condition)
    statement₁
else
    statement₂
```

Both *statement₁* and *statement₂* represent other Java statements, including **if** statements and compound statements. Recall that a compound statement consists of one or more Java statements enclosed in a pair of braces. The statements within these braces can also be other **if** statements.

When an **if** statement occurs within another **if** statement, we say that they are **nested**. Any of these statements can have an **else** clause.

10.2   **Example.** Suppose that you have two objects that represent two people. Each object has the method getAge that returns the age of a person as an integer. You wonder which person is older. The following statements will tell you:

```
if (person1.getAge() > person2.getAge())
   System.out.println("The first person is older.");
else
{
   if (person1.getAge() < person2.getAge())
      System.out.println("The second person is older.");
   else
      System.out.println("The two people are the same age.");
} // end if
```

Here the first **else** clause contains an entire **if-else** statement.

Observe that for any pair of ages, we have three possible outcomes: Either the first person is older, the second person is older, or they are the same age. Only one of these three cases is possible for two particular people. That is, the three cases are **mutually exclusive**.

Notice that the second **if-else** statement is a single statement, so the braces in this example are optional but desirable. Imagine, however, that we omit the braces to get

```
if (person1.getAge() > person2.getAge())
   System.out.println("The first person is older.");
else
   if (person1.getAge() < person2.getAge())
      System.out.println("The second person is older.");
   else
      System.out.println("The two people are the same age.");
```

Now let's write the second **if** on the same line as the first **else** and revise the indentation, as follows:

```
if (person1.getAge() > person2.getAge())
   System.out.println("The first person is older.");
else if (person1.getAge() < person2.getAge())
   System.out.println("The second person is older.");
else
   System.out.println("The two people are the same age.");
```

This form of the statement has exactly the same meaning as the first form, but it is easier for us to read and to understand. We will call it a **multiway if statement**. Although we have three possibilities here, any number is feasible.

Java

Syntax: The multiway `if` statement

```
if (condition₁)
    statement₁
else if (condition₂)
    statement₂
. . .
else if (conditionₙ)
    statementₙ
else
    statement_default
```

The logic of this statement is illustrated in Figure 10-1.

FIGURE 10-1   The logic of a multiway `if` statement

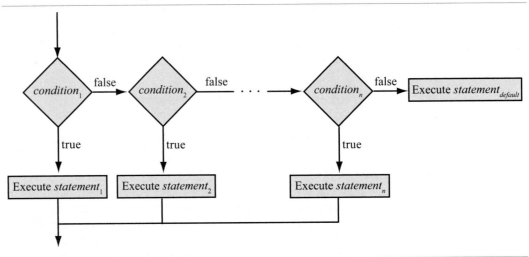

!

Programming Tip

Often, a multiway `if` statement should end with an `else` clause instead of an `else if`. Although not absolutely required or desired in every situation, an `else` clause accounts for all other conditions that earlier conditions do not specify.

10.3

Example. Suppose that age is an `int` variable that contains your age. The following `if-else` statement decides whether you are younger than 20, in your 20s, or older than 29:

```java
if (age >= 20)
{
    if (age < 30)
        System.out.println("You are in your 20s.");
    else
        System.out.println("You are older than 29.");
}
else
    System.out.println("You are younger than 20.");
```

The **if** clause contains an **if-else** statement, which is one Java statement. Thus, you can omit the braces, but they are desirable here to improve readability.

10.4   **Example.** Suppose that you did not care to indicate whether the age is over 29 in the previous example. You can omit the first **else** clause to get the following:

```java
if (age >= 20)
{
    if (age < 30)
        System.out.println("You are in your 20s.");
}
else
    System.out.println("You are younger than 20.");
```

This is fine, but what if you now omit the braces?

```java
// THIS LOGIC IS WRONG
if (age >= 20)
    if (age < 30)
        System.out.println("You are in your 20s.");
    else
        System.out.println("You are younger than 20.");
```

The **else** clause does not belong to the first **if**, despite what the indentation seems to indicate. An **else** clause corresponds to the nearest previous unmatched **if**. Thus, the meaning of the above statements is really

```java
// THIS LOGIC IS WRONG
if (age >= 20)
{
    if (age < 30)
        System.out.println("You are in your 20s.");
    else
        System.out.println("You are younger than 20.");
} // end if
```

If age is 35, for example, the resulting message is You are younger than 20, which is clearly incorrect.

Note: In the absence of braces, an **else** clause is paired with the preceding unmatched **if**.

The following advice from Chapter 7 is worth repeating here.

Programming Tip

Some programmers always use compound statements within other statements such as **if-else**, even when the compound statement contains only one other statement between braces. Doing so makes it easier to add another statement to the compound statement, but more importantly, it avoids the error that would occur if you forgot to add the braces. However, you need to know how an **if-else** statement behaves when some or all braces are omitted, since you likely will encounter such statements in working with code written by other programmers.

Question 1 What does the incorrect if statement in the previous example display when age is

a. 18.
b. 21.
c. 30.

Question 2 Write a multiway if statement that tests the value of the integer variable temperature. If temperature is less than or equal to 32, display the message FREEZING! If temperature is greater than or equal to 212, display BOILING! Otherwise, display NORMAL.

10.5

Example. Let's consider part of a program that assigns a letter grade—A through F—to an integer exam score ranging from 0 to 100. Grades are assigned as follows:

90 to 100	A
80 to 89	B
70 to 79	C
60 to 69	D
Below 60	F

We offer five different solutions to this problem. All are correct, but not all are good, as you will see. The first solution clearly indicates the range of scores for each letter grade.

```
// Solution 1 - Clear, efficient logic
if ((score >= 90) && (score <= 100))
   grade = 'A';
else if ((score >= 80) && (score <= 89))
   grade = 'B';
else if ((score >= 70) && (score <= 79))
   grade = 'C';
else if ((score >= 60) && (score <= 69))
   grade = 'D';
else
   grade = 'F';
```

The second solution is similar to the first one but omits the test of the higher limit in each range.

```
// Solution 2 - Faster execution than Solution 1,
//              but logic might not be as clear
if (score >= 90)
   grade = 'A';
else if (score >= 80)
   grade = 'B';
else if (score >= 70)
   grade = 'C';
else if (score >= 60)
   grade = 'D';
else
   grade = 'F';
```

For example, if a score is not 90 or higher, it must be 89 or lower. Thus, the first `else if` clause need not compare `score` with 89. Since this solution has less to do, it executes faster than the first solution. However, its logic might not be as clear to the reader.

Our third solution is much like the first one, but without any occurrences of `else`. Although its logic is correct, all of the `if` statements execute for any score. In contrast, each of the previous two solutions completes its execution as soon as it assigns a value to `grade`, ignoring the rest of the `if` statement.

```
// Solution 3 - Slower execution than Solution 1
if ((score >= 90) && (score <= 100))
   grade = 'A';
if ((score >= 80) && (score <= 89))
   grade = 'B';
if ((score >= 70) && (score <= 79))
   grade = 'C';
if ((score >= 60) && (score <= 69))
   grade = 'D';
if (score < 60)
   grade = 'F';
```

In the next solution, notice the two consecutive `if` clauses. Using the boolean operator `&&` instead is a clearer solution, as you can see in the first and third solutions. This solution is also like the third solution in that it has no `else` clauses. Exercise 6 at the end of this chapter pursues this solution further.

```
// Solution 4 - Logically like Solution 3, but awkward
if (score >= 90)
   if (score <= 100)
      grade = 'A';
if (score >= 80)
   if (score <= 89)
      grade = 'B';
if (score >= 70)
   if (score <= 79)
      grade = 'C';
if (score >= 60)
   if (score <= 69)
      grade = 'D';
if (score < 60)
   grade = 'F';
```

Complex decisions

The last solution is correct but has logic that is not immediately clear.

```
// Solution 5 - Logic is unclear
if (score < 90)
   if (score < 80)
      if (score < 70)
         if (score < 60)
            grade = 'F';
         else
            grade = 'D';
      else
         grade = 'C';
   else
      grade = 'B';
else
   grade = 'A';
```

Note: When writing a multiway `if` statement, clarity of logic should be your foremost concern. The `if`, `else if`, `else` form exhibited by solutions 1 and 2 usually provides the clearest logic. Although consecutive `if` statements are reasonable when cases are not mutually exclusive, you should see whether an `else` clause is possible. Since the cases in solution 3 are mutually exclusive, you should avoid the consecutive `if` statements in favor of solution 1 or solution 2. Consecutive `if` clauses (as shown in solution 4) and deeply nested `if` statements (as exhibited by solution 5) seldom provide clear logic.

Question 3 Each of the five solutions in the previous example assumes that the exam score is between 0 and 100. Suppose that the instructor gives bonus points, and one student gets a score of 101. What letter grade, if any, is assigned to this student by each solution?

Question 4 The program in Segment 7.9 of Chapter 7 displays an integer from 1 to 7 to indicate the day of the week for a given date. What statements will display the name of the day instead of an integer?

Question 5 Given the three sides of a triangle as the `int` variables `side1`, `side2`, and `side3`, write statements that decide whether all sides are equal, two sides are equal, or no sides are equal.

Question 6 Are the following statements a correct solution to Question 5? Explain your answer.

```
if ((side1 != side2) && (side1 != side3) && (side2 != side3))
   System.out.println("No sides are equal");
else if ((side1 != side2) || (side1 != side3))
   System.out.println("Two sides are equal");
else
   System.out.println("All sides are equal");
```

Question 7 Suppose that the `double` variable `area` contains the area of a circle. Write statements that display the following:

- `No circle` if area ≤ 0
- `Small circle` if $0 <$ area < 20
- `Moderate circle` if $50 \leq$ area < 50
- `Large circle` if area $>= 50$

Question 8 Listing 8-2 in Chapter 8 contains the class `CalendarDate`, which defines the method `isLeapYear`. If `theDate` is an instance of `CalendarDate`, what statements will test `theDate` and display a message indicating whether the date occurs within a leap year and, if it does, whether it occurs before, on, or after February 29?

A Problem Solved: Health Club Welcome

> At the beginning of this chapter, we suggested a program that you could write for a health club that asks for a person's age and gives some simple advice about available facilities that are age appropriate. To complete this program, we need to know the health club's policies and what it offers its members. A conversation with the club's fitness director provides us with the following information: Children under 10 should be directed to the children's center for either day care or organized and supervised activities. Older children under 13 can use the swimming pool and soccer fields. Teenagers under 17 are welcome to use the entire complex but should be cautioned about overtraining. People who are 17 to 49 years of age can use the entire complex. They should get a specific note about the swimming pool and the basketball league. Finally, those members who are 50 and older must have consulted a doctor before beginning an exercise program. The club has a physician on staff for this purpose.

10.6   The program in Listing 10-1 is a possible solution to this problem. We use a multiway `if` statement that ends with an `else` clause. This clause handles the unlikely event that the user has entered a negative or zero age. Notice the last `else if` clause for those in the oldest age group. It contains another `if` statement within a compound statement to deal with the physician consultation for this group.

LISTING 10-1   The health club program

```java
/** HealthClubWelcome.java by F. M. Carrano
    Provides the new members of a health club with
    age-appropriate advice about available facilities.

    Input:  name and age of the person
    Output: an appropriate message for these age groups:
            under 10
            10 - 13
            14 - 16
            17 - 49
            50 and over
*/
import java.util.Scanner;
public class HealthClubWelcome
{
    public static void main(String[] args)
    {
        Scanner keyboard = new Scanner(System.in);
        System.out.println("Welcome to the JavaJava Fitness Center!\n");
        System.out.print("What is your first name? ");
        String name = keyboard.nextLine();
        System.out.print("Welcome, " + name + ". What is your age? ");
        int age = keyboard.nextInt();
        keyboard.nextLine(); // get ready for next read by advancing
                             // beyond end of line

        System.out.println();
```

```
    if ((age > 0) && (age < 10))
       System.out.println("The Children's Center is available.");
    else if ((age >= 10) && (age < 13))
       System.out.println("The swimming pool and soccer fields " +
                            "are available.");
    else if ((age >= 13) && (age <= 16))
       System.out.println("The entire complex is available " +
                            "but do not overtrain.");
    else if ((age >= 17) && (age <= 49))
       System.out.println("The entire complex is available.\nNote " +
                    "the schedules for the pool and basketball leagues.");
    else if (age >= 50)
    {
       System.out.println("Anyone can begin an exercise program " +
                            "with the approval of a doctor. ");
       System.out.print("Have you consulted your doctor? ");
       String response = keyboard.nextLine();

       if (response.equalsIgnoreCase("yes"))
          System.out.println("The entire complex is available.");
       else
          System.out.println("The staff physician is available for " +
                            "consultation.");

    }
    else
       System.out.println("Input error: age is zero or negative.");
  } // end main
} // end HealthClubWelcome
```

Sample Output 1

```
Welcome to the JavaJava Fitness Center!

What is your first name? Chris
Welcome, Chris. What is your age? 18

The entire complex is available.
Note the schedules for the pool and basketball leagues.
```

Sample Output 2

```
Welcome to the JavaJava Fitness Center!

What is your first name? Mary
Welcome, Mary. What is your age? 57

Anyone can begin an exercise program with the approval of a doctor.
Have you consulted your doctor? no
The staff physician is available for consultation.
```

Question 9 What ages would you use to test the health club program?

The **switch** Statement

10.7　When a decision has several possible outcomes and is based on an expression's value whose data type is either int, char, or an enumeration, you can use a switch statement. For example, in Listing 7-1 of Chapter 7, the int variable dayOfWeek has a value that ranges from 1 to 7 to indicate one of the days Sunday through Saturday. The following switch statement assigns the day of the week as a string to the variable result:

```java
String result = null;
switch (dayOfWeek)
{
   case 1:
      result = "Sunday";
      break;
   case 2:
      result = "Monday";
      break;
   case 3:
      result = "Tuesday";
      break;
   case 4:
      result = "Wednesday";
      break;
   case 5:
      result = "Thursday";
      break;
   case 6:
      result = "Friday";
      break;
   case 7:
      result = "Saturday";
      break;
   default:
      assert false : "Error in dayOfWeek: " + dayOfWeek;
      break;
} // end switch
```

In this example, dayOfWeek is the expression that is tested. You must be able to list the values of the expression to be able to use a switch statement. Such is the situation here, since dayOfWeek has one of the values 1 through 7. Each value of the tested expression corresponds to a case within the switch statement. When the value of the expression matches the value in a case—called the **case label**—all statements after the case label execute until either a break statement or the end of the switch is encountered. So if dayOfWeek is 5, for example, result is assigned the string "Thursday" and execution continues with the statement after the switch's closing brace.

If the value of the expression does not match any of the case labels, either the statements after the keyword default execute or, if default is omitted, the switch ends normally. For example, if dayOfWeek is –2, the default case executes. Since dayOfWeek is computed by our earlier code, its value would be out of range only if that code was incorrect. Thus, as a debugging aid, we have written an `assert` statement as the default case that always produces an error message, assuming assertions are enabled.

Question 10 The code in Listing 7-1 of Chapter 7 first assigns a value that ranges from 0 to 6 to the `int` variable `dayOfWeek` to indicate one of the days Saturday through Friday. A subsequent `if` statement changes `dayOfWeek` to 7 if it had been 0. If we omit this `if` statement, what changes would you make to the `switch` statement given in the previous segment?

10.8 More than one value of the tested expression can result in the same action, but you must be able to list these values. For example, suppose that you want to know the number of days in a given month. You remember the following verse:

> *30 days hath September*
> *April, June, and November.*
> *All the rest have 31,*
> *Except February, which has 28 we find,*
> *Unless it's leap year, when it has 29.*

Suppose that the `int` variable `month` is an integer from 1 to 12, and the boolean variable `isLeapYear` is true if the year is a leap year. The following `switch` statement assigns the correct number of days to the variable `daysInMonth`:

```
switch (month)
{
    case 9: case 4: case 6: case 11: // Sept, Apr, June, Nov
        daysInMonth = 30;
        break;
    case 2:                          // Feb
        if (isLeapYear)
            daysInMonth = 29;
        else
            daysInMonth = 28;
        break;
    default:                         // All other months
        daysInMonth = 31;
        break;
} // end switch
```

To successfully use the default case for the months having 31 days, we must be assured that the variable `month` does not contain an illegal value.

Question 11 What multiway `if` statement is equivalent to the previous `switch` statement?

Question 12 The previous `switch` statement assumes that `month` is an integer from 1 to 12. If we did not verify this assumption prior to executing the `switch` statement, illegal values of `month` would assign 31 to `daysInMonth`. How can you modify the statement so illegal values of `month` will assign zero to `daysInMonth`?

Question 13 If, prior to executing the previous `switch` statement, we verified that `month` is an integer from 1 to 12, what `assert` statement could you add after that test and before the `switch` statement?

Note: The expression in a switch statement

- Cannot be boolean. For example, you cannot replace the if statement within the switch statement of the previous example with another switch statement, even though nested switch statements are possible in general.
- Cannot be a string.[1] For example, you could not use strings instead of integers in the previous example to designate the months.

Note: Writing a break statement at the end of a default case is a good programing practice, even though doing so is not absolutely required. That way, if you later decide to change the default case to an ordinary case that requires a break statement, one will be written already.

Syntax: **The switch statement**

```
switch (expression)        expression's type must be an integer type, char, or an enumeration
{
    case case-label:       case-label must be a constant whose type matches expression's
        statement(s);
        break;             break is optional; without it, execution continues to the next case

        . . .              Several cases are possible

    default:               default is optional; without it, a mismatch ends the switch
        statement(s);
        break;
} // end switch
```

Note that no statements can appear before the first case within a switch statement. The statements following case or default need not be—and usually are not—enclosed in braces.

10.9   **switch with char values.** The action of a switch statement can be based upon a character. For example, if the char variable grade contains a letter grade, the following switch statement assigns the correct number of quality points to the double variable qualityPoints:

```
double qualityPoints;
switch (grade)
{
    case 'A':
        qualityPoints = 4.0;
        break;
    case 'B':
        qualityPoints = 3.0;
        break;
    case 'C':
        qualityPoints = 2.0;
        break;
    case 'D':
        qualityPoints = 1.0;
        break;
```

---

1. This restriction is likely to be removed in a subsequent version of Java.

```
      case 'F':
         qualityPoints = 0.0;
         break;
      default:
         System.out.println("grade has an illegal value: " + grade);
         System.exit(0);
   } // end switch
```

Question 14 How would you revise the previous `switch` statement to accommodate letter grades given in lowercase?

Question 15 In the previous `switch` statement, would it be reasonable to replace the statements in the default case with one `assert` statement? Explain.

Question 16 If you could assume that grade's value was only `'A'`, `'B'`, `'C'`, `'D'`, or `'F'` prior to execution of the previous `switch` statement, would it be reasonable to replace the statements in the default case with the following assert statement? Explain.

```
assert false : "grade has an illegal value: " + grade;
```

10.10 **Omitting break in a switch.** Although break statements are typically used within a `switch` statement, the break itself is not a part of `switch`'s syntax. For example, you could use the following `switch` statement to compute the quality points for a given grade, instead of the one given in the previous segment:

```
double qualityPoints = 0.0;
switch (grade)
{
   case 'A':
      qualityPoints = qualityPoints + 1.0;
   case 'B':
      qualityPoints = qualityPoints + 1.0;
   case 'C':
      qualityPoints = qualityPoints + 1.0;
   case 'D':
      qualityPoints = qualityPoints + 1.0;
   case 'F':
      break; // needed to prevent sequencing to default
   default:
      System.out.println("grade has an illegal value: " + grade);
      System.exit(0);
} // end switch
```

When you omit a break statement, execution continues on to the statements in the next case. Thus, by the time the `switch` ends, `qualityPoints` will have the correct value. For example, if grade's value is `'C'`, case `'C'` executes, followed by case `'D'` and case `'F'`. These cases add 1 to `qualityPoints` twice, to get the correct value of 2, before break ends the `switch` statement. Since we have a default case, the break statement following case `'F'` prevents the default case from executing.

Occasionally, such a `switch` statement will be useful. This one, however, takes longer to execute and is less clear than the one given in the previous segment.

10.11 **switch with enumerated types.** In the previous example, the char variable grade could contain any character, not just the letters A, B, C, D, or F. Instead of declaring grade as a char, we can declare it as an enumerated data type and still use it within the switch statement. For example, we can define an enumeration to represent the letter grades A through F, as follows:

```
private enum LetterGrade {A, B, C, D, F}
```

Then, if we define grade as a variable of type LetterGrade and assign it a value, we could revise the switch statement that we wrote in Segment 10.9 as follows:

```
switch (grade)
{
   case A:
      qualityPoints = 4.0;
      break;
   case B:
      qualityPoints = 3.0;
      break;
   case C:
      qualityPoints = 2.0;
      break;
   case D:
      qualityPoints = 1.0;
      break;
   case F:
      qualityPoints = 0.0;
      break;
   default:
      assert false : "Illegal value for grade; should not occur";
      break;
} // end switch
```

videonote
Decisions with
distinct cases

Although this switch statement looks like the one in Segment 10.9, be sure to notice the lack of single quotation marks here in the case labels. These labels belong to an enumeration; they are not char values. Since the data type of the expression in the switch statement is an enumeration, the case labels are assumed to belong to that enumeration without qualification. Additionally, we know that grade cannot have other values, and so a default case is unnecessary. However, we have included one and have used an assertion during debugging. If you choose to omit the default case, you must initialize qualityPoints to a value before the switch statement executes, to avoid a syntax error. Without this initialization, the compiler will think it possible for qualityPoints to remain uninitialized after the switch statement.

 Question 17 By redefining the enumeration LetterGrade, you can assign the correct value to qualityPoints without using a switch statement or an if statement. How is this possible?

 Programming Tip
You always can use an if statement instead of a switch statement to make a decision. You must use an if statement when the decision is based upon a range of values or a comparison of objects, since a switch statement is not possible in those situations. However, when a decision is based upon discrete integer or char values that you can itemize, a switch statement is possible and can be clearer than an if statement, especially when there are more than two such values. The following note summarizes when you must use an if statement and when a switch statement is possible.

Note: Choosing between an `if` statement and a `switch` statement

You must use an `if` statement when a decision is based upon the following:	You can use a `switch` statement when a decision is based upon the following:
A range of values	An enumeration
A comparison of objects	Discrete integer or `char` values that can be itemized

■ A Problem Solved: Where To?

In this problem, we want to ask the user for a direction of travel—north, south, east, or west—and provide an appropriate comment.

10.12   We can read the user's response as a string, but we cannot use it as the expression in a `switch` statement. However, a `switch` statement will provide a clearer solution than an `if` statement. To solve our dilemma, we begin by defining an enumeration for the four main compass points:

```
private enum Compass {NORTH, SOUTH, EAST, WEST}
```

Since we can use the constants defined in this enumeration in a `switch` statement, we need a way to convert the user's response from a string to one of these constants. To do so, we can use the enumeration's method `valueOf`.

The program in Listing 10-2 reads the user's response as a string `direction` and converts it to uppercase by using the `String` method `toUpperCase`. An `if` statement then checks that the string matches the name of one of the enumerated constants. If it does, the expression

```
Compass.valueOf(direction)
```

returns the constant that matches the string. Once we have the appropriate constant in the enumeration `Compass`, we use it in a `switch` statement to perform the desired action. Here we simply display a suitable message.

LISTING 10-2   Using an enumerated data type with a `switch` statement

```java
/** WhereTo.java by F. M. Carrano
    Provides an encouraging message to a traveler
    going north, south east, or west.
*/
import java.util.Scanner;
public class WhereTo
{
    private enum Compass {NORTH, SOUTH, EAST, WEST}

    public static void main(String[] args)
    {
        Scanner keyboard = new Scanner(System.in);

        System.out.println("In which direction will you travel?");
```

```
                String direction = keyboard.next();
                direction = direction.toUpperCase();

                if (direction.equals("NORTH") || direction.equals("SOUTH") ||
                   direction.equals("EAST")  || direction.equals("WEST"))
                {
                   Compass way = Compass.valueOf(direction);
                   switch (way)
                   {
                      case NORTH:
                         System.out.println("North to Alaska!");
                         break;
                      case SOUTH:
                         System.out.println("Off to the sunny south!");
                         break;
                      case EAST:
                         System.out.println("Explore the fashionable east side!");
                         break;
                      case WEST:
                         System.out.println("Find adventure in the west!");
                         break;
                   } // end switch
                }
                else
                   System.out.println("Error in input.");
         } // end main
   } // end WhereTo
```

Sample Output

```
   In which direction will you travel?
   south
   Off to the sunny south!
```

■ A Problem Solved: Representing a Temperature

> Temperatures can be represented in degrees Fahrenheit, degrees Celsius, or in kelvins. You can think of a kelvin as one "degree" on the Kelvin scale; it just isn't called a degree. Scientists use the letters F, C, and K to represent the scale of a given temperature. For example, water freezes at 32 degrees Fahrenheit—that is, 32°F—0 degrees Celsius (0°C), and 273.15 kelvins (273.15 K).
>
> Write a class Temperature that represents temperatures. An object in this class should be able to convert from one scale to another and must keep track of its present scale.

10.13   A Temperature object has a temperature value and a scale as its data, and it could have the following behaviors:

- Returns its temperature value and scale as a string
- Converts its temperature to degrees Fahrenheit

- Converts its temperature to degrees Celsius
- Converts its temperature to kelvins

We should think some more about these behaviors. Do we want a `Temperature` object to change its scale and, therefore, its value, or do we want the object to remain unchanged but return an equivalent temperature in another scale? Rather than deciding this question, we will include both kinds of behavior. Thus, our list of behaviors becomes the following:

- Returns the temperature value and scale as a string
- Returns the temperature in degrees Fahrenheit
- Converts the temperature to degrees Fahrenheit
- Returns the temperature in degrees Celsius
- Converts the temperature to degrees Celsius
- Returns the temperature in kelvins
- Converts the temperature to kelvins

10.14   After naming and specifying methods to perform these behaviors, we have the following method headers:

- `public String toString()`
- `public Temperature toFahrenheit()`
- `public void convertToFahrenheit()`
- `public Temperature toCelsius()`
- `public void convertToCelsius()`
- `public Temperature toKelvin()`
- `public void convertToKelvin()`

Using these methods, we can write the program in Listing 10-3 to demonstrate the class `Temperature`. The class's constructor takes as arguments the temperature and a one-letter code that indicates the scale. We can use an enumeration for the scale, so assume that we have defined one called `Scale` whose constants are `F`, `C`, and `K`. We'll consider its definition momentarily.

In this example, we create an object that represents the freezing point of water on the Fahrenheit scale. We then display the temperature in degrees Fahrenheit, degrees Celsius, and kelvins. Finally, we convert the temperature to each of these scales and display the results. Notice that the expression `freezing.toCelsius()`, for example, returns the temperature in degrees Celsius but does not change the value or the scale of the object `freezing`. However, the statement

```
freezing.convertToCelsius();
```

changes the value and scale of `freezing`, as you can see after `freezing` is displayed. Recall that the `println` statements implicitly invoke the method `toString`, which implements the first behavior in the previous list.

LISTING 10-3   A demonstration of the class `Temperature`

```
/** TemperatureTest.java by F. M. Carrano
    Demonstrates the class Temperature.
*/
public class TemperatureTest
{
    public static void main(String args[])
    {
```

```
            Temperature freezing = new Temperature(32, Scale.F);
            System.out.println("Original temperature in Fahrenheit: " +
                            freezing);
            System.out.println("Temperature in Celsius: " +
                            freezing.toCelsius());
            System.out.println("Temperature in Kelvin: " +
                            freezing.toKelvin());

            System.out.println("\nTemperature in Fahrenheit: " + freezing);
            freezing.convertToCelsius();
            System.out.println("Temperature in Celsius: " + freezing);
            freezing.convertToKelvin();
            System.out.println("Temperature in Kelvin: " + freezing);
        } // end main
    } // end TemperatureTest
```

Output

```
    Original temperature in Fahrenheit: 32.00 degrees F
    Temperature in Celsius: 0.00 degrees C
    Temperature in Kelvin: 273.15 K

    Temperature in Fahrenheit: 32.00 degrees F
    Temperature in Celsius: 0.00 degrees C
    Temperature in Kelvin: 273.15 K
```

10.15   **The enumeration.** As we mentioned, we want to use an enumeration to represent the scale of the temperature. You can see from Listing 10-3 that the client of the class Temperature uses this enumeration. However, we also want Temperature itself to use it. If you define an enumeration within a class, it is private and can be used only within that class. Here we want the client and Temperature to use an enumeration. We mentioned in Chapter 8 that an enumeration is actually a class, so we can make an enumeration public and define it within its own file, just as we do with other classes that we write. So in the file Scale.java, we write the following definition:

```
    public enum Scale {F, C, K}
```

10.16   **Temperature's data fields.** A Temperature object must record the value and scale of the temperature that it represents. Thus, the class Temperature can define the following data fields:

```
    private double value;
    private Scale  scale;
```

The constructor will give these fields values according to the arguments it receives when it is invoked.

10.17   **The conversion methods.** Each one of the conversion methods must convert the temperature from its present scale to the desired scale. For example, the method convertToFahrenheit must be able to convert from either Celsius or Kelvin to Fahrenheit. The method should also recognize that a temperature in Fahrenheit needs no modification. Thus, the pseudocode for convertToFahrenheit could appear as follows:

```
if (the scale is C for Celsius)
    Convert the temperature from Celsius to Fahrenheit
else if (the scale is K for Kelvin)
    Convert the temperature from Kelvin to Fahrenheit
else
    Do nothing; the scale is already Fahrenheit
```

The other conversion methods have a similar logic.

These methods require that we be able to convert a temperature from

- Celsius to Fahrenheit
- Kelvin to Fahrenheit
- Fahrenheit to Celsius
- Kelvin to Celsius
- Fahrenheit to Kelvin
- Celsius to Kelvin

We will implement these conversions as the following private methods:

```
private void convertCelsiusToFahrenheit()
private void convertKelvinToFahrenheit()
private void convertFahrenheitToCelsius()
private void convertKelvinToCelsius()
private void convertFahrenheitToKelvin()
private void convertCelsiusToKelvin()
```

As you will see, this approach simplifies our logic, making it less likely that we will make an error.

10.18 **Using the private methods.** Let's implement the methods convertToFahrenheit and toFahrenheit so we can see how these private methods will be used. Even though the pseudocode we wrote in the previous segment for convertToFahrenheit uses if-else logic, we will use a switch statement in our implementation. Thus, the method convertToFahrenheit appears as follows:

```
public void convertToFahrenheit()
{
    switch (scale)
    {
        case C:
            convertCelsiusToFahrenheit();
            break;
        case K:
            convertKelvinToFahrenheit();
            break;
        default:
            assert scale.equals(Scale.F);
            break;
    } // end switch
} // end convertToFahrenheit
```

Each private method that convertToFahrenheit calls will change the values of the data fields value and scale appropriately. Thus, the Temperature object that invokes convertToFahrenheit will have its scale changed to Fahrenheit.

Notice the assert statement in the default case. It uses the method equals to compare enumerated constants, since they are objects. Also, we must write Scale.F instead of F here. However, the case labels can be unqualified constants, since the expression in the switch statement has the enumerated type Scale.

10.19 The method `toFahrenheit` does not change the value of its object's data fields. Instead, it returns a new `Temperature` object whose value is in degrees Fahrenheit. To do this, the method first uses the constructor to create a new object and gives its data fields the same values as those in the method's receiving object. The method then uses the method `convertToFahrenheit` to convert the scale of the new object before returning it to the client. Thus, `toFahrenheit` appears as follows:

```
public Temperature toFahrenheit()
{
    Temperature result = new Temperature(value, scale);
    result.convertToFahrenheit();

    return result;
} // end toFahrenheit
```

The other public conversion methods have similar implementations.

10.20 **Temperature conversions.** We now consider how to convert a temperature from one scale to another so that we can implement the private methods. On the Fahrenheit scale, the temperature difference between the freezing and boiling points of water is divided into 180 degrees. On the Celsius scale, this temperature difference is divided into 100 degrees. The ratio of 180 to 100 is 9 to 5. Since water freezes at 32°F, or 0°C, conversions between these two scales can be performed as follows:

- To convert a temperature from Celsius to Fahrenheit, multiply the Celsius temperature by 9 / 5 and add 32. That is, $f = (9 \times c / 5) + 32$.
- To convert a temperature from Fahrenheit to Celsius, subtract 32 from the Fahrenheit temperature and multiply the result by 5 / 9. That is, $c = (f - 32) \times 5 / 9$.

One unit on the Kelvin scale—that is, one kelvin—is the same size as one unit, or degree, on the Celsius scale. Absolute zero is 0 K, or –273.15°C. Thus, we have the following facts:

- To convert a temperature from Kelvin to Celsius, subtract 273.15. That is, $c = k - 273.15$.
- To convert a temperature from Celsius to Kelvin, add 273.15. That is, $k = c + 273.15$.

Conversions between Fahrenheit temperatures and Kelvin temperatures use the Celsius scale as an intermediary. Thus,

- To convert a temperature from Fahrenheit to Kelvin, first convert it to Celsius and then convert the result to Kelvin.
- To convert a temperature from Kelvin to Fahrenheit, first convert it to Celsius and then convert the result to Fahrenheit.

Note: **Conversions among temperature scales**

Conversion	Formula
Celsius to Fahrenheit	$f = (9 \times c / 5) + 32$
Fahrenheit to Celsius	$c = (f - 32) \times 5 / 9$
Kelvin to Celsius	$c = k - 273.15$
Celsius to Kelvin	$k = c + 273.15$
Fahrenheit to Kelvin	Convert Fahrenheit to Celsius, and then Celsius to Kelvin.
Kelvin to Fahrenheit	Convert Kelvin to Celsius, and then Celsius to Fahrenheit.

10.21 **The private methods.** Let's implement the private methods that convert a temperature to Fahrenhheit. These are the two methods that we used in the implementation of convertToFahrenheit.

The following method converts the temperature from Celsius to Fahrenheit:

```
private void convertCelsiusToFahrenheit()
{
   assert scale.equals(Scale.C) : "Unexpected scale: not Celsius";
   value = 9.0 * value / 5.0 + 32.0;
   scale = Scale.F;
} // end convertCelsiusToFahrenheit
```

This method assumes that the original temperature is in degrees Celsius. Since we, as class implementers, are the only ones who can use this method, we can assure that this condition is met. You can see that this is the case in the implementation of convertToFahrenheit in Segment 10.18.

To convert a temperature from Kelvin to Fahrenheit, we first convert it to Celsius and then to Fahrenheit. The following method performs this task, assuming that the current temperature is in kelvins:

```
private void convertKelvinToFahrenheit()
{
   assert scale.equals(Scale.K) : "Unexpected scale: not Kelvin";
   convertKelvinToCelsius();
   convertCelsiusToFahrenheit();
} // end convertKelvinToFahrenheit
```

No algebra is necessary to accomplish this task, so we are less likely to make a mistake. Additionally, our logic will be evident to other programmers who read our code.

10.22 Listing 10-4 contains the definition of the class Temperature. The remaining conversion methods are analogous to those we have examined already.

Notice that the method toString uses the class DecimalFormat to provide two decimal places for the value of the temperature. We discussed this class in Chapter 4 when we formatted the output produced by println statements.

LISTING 10-4 The class Temperature

```
/** Temperature.java by F. M. Carrano
    Represents a temperature in either Fahrenheit, Celsius, or Kelvin.
*/
import java.text.DecimalFormat;
public class Temperature
{
   private double value;
   private Scale  scale;
```

```java
/** Constructs a Temperature object, given a temperature
    and a scale of F (Fahrenheit), C (Celsius), or K (Kelvin). */
public Temperature(double initialTemperature, Scale initialScale)
{
   value = initialTemperature;
   scale = initialScale;
} // end constructor

/** Returns a string that contains the temperature and scale. */
public String toString()
{
   DecimalFormat formatter = new DecimalFormat("0.00");
   String result = formatter.format(value);
   switch (scale)
   {
      case F:
      case C:
         result = result + " degrees " + scale;
         break;
      case K:
         result = result + " " + scale;
         break;
   } // end switch
   return result;
} // end toString

/** Returns an equivalent temperature in Fahrenheit. */
public Temperature toFahrenheit()
{
   Temperature result = new Temperature(value, scale);
   result.convertToFahrenheit();
   return result;
} // end toFahrenheit

/** Converts the temperature to Fahrenheit. */
public void convertToFahrenheit()
{
   switch (scale)
   {
```

```java
         case C:
            convertCelsiusToFahrenheit();
            break;
         case K:
            convertKelvinToFahrenheit();
            break;
         default:
            assert scale.equals(Scale.F);
            break;
      } // end switch
} // end convertToFahrenheit

/** Returns an equivalent temperature in Celsius. */
public Temperature toCelsius()
{
   Temperature result = new Temperature(value, scale);
   result.convertToCelsius();

   return result;
} // end toCelsius

/** Converts the temperature to Celsius. */
public void convertToCelsius()
{
   switch (scale)
   {
      case F:
         convertFahrenheitToCelsius();
         break;
      case K:
         convertKelvinToCelsius();
         break;
      default:
         assert scale.equals(Scale.C);
         break;
   } // end switch
} // end convertToCelsius

/** Returns an equivalent temperature in Kelvin. */
public Temperature toKelvin()
{
   Temperature result = new Temperature(value, scale);
   result.convertToKelvin();
```

```java
         return result;
      } // end toKelvin

      /** Converts the temperature to Kelvin. */
      public void convertToKelvin()
      {
         switch (scale)
         {
            case F:
               convertFahrenheitToKelvin();
               break;
            case C:
               convertCelsiusToKelvin();
               break;
            default:
               assert scale.equals(Scale.K);
               break;
         } // end switch
      } // end convertToKelvin
// -------------------------------------------------
// Private methods
// -------------------------------------------------

// Convert the temperature to Fahrenheit:

      private void convertCelsiusToFahrenheit()
      {
         assert scale.equals(Scale.C) : "Unexpected scale: not Celsius";
         value = 9.0 * value / 5.0 + 32.0;
         scale = Scale.F;
      } // end convertCelsiusToFahrenheit

      private void convertKelvinToFahrenheit()
      {
         assert scale.equals(Scale.K) : "Unexpected scale: not Kelvin";
         convertKelvinToCelsius();
         convertCelsiusToFahrenheit();
      } // end convertKelvinToFahrenheit
// -------------------------------------------------
```

```
// Convert the temperature to Celsius:

   private void convertFahrenheitToCelsius()
   {
      assert scale.equals(Scale.F) : "Unexpected scale: not Fahrenheit";
      value = 5.0 * (value - 32.0) / 9.0;
      scale = Scale.C;
   } // end convertFahrenheitToCelsius

   private void convertKelvinToCelsius()
   {
      assert scale.equals(Scale.K) : "Unexpected scale: not Kelvin";

      value = value - 273.15;
      scale = Scale.C;
   } // end convertKelvinToCelsius

// -----------------------------------------------

// Convert the temperature to Kelvin:

   private void convertFahrenheitToKelvin()
   {
      assert scale.equals(Scale.F) : "Unexpected scale: not Fahrenheit";
      convertFahrenheitToCelsius();
      convertCelsiusToKelvin();
   } // end convertFahrenheitToKelvin

   private void convertCelsiusToKelvin()
   {
      assert scale.equals(Scale.C) : "Unexpected scale: not Celsius";
      value = value + 273.15;
      scale = Scale.K;
   } // end convertCelsiusToKelvin
} // end Temperature
```

videonote
A problem
solved

Question 18 Describe the behavior of each of the following methods, if added to the class Temperature:

   a. raise(n) and lower(n)
   b. setValue(n)
   c. changeScale(s)
   d. setTemperature(n, s)

Question 19 Describe the implementation of the method changeScale(s) that changes the scale of the current temperature to s.

CHAPTER SUMMARY

- An if statement can contain other if statements. Together, such if statements are said to be nested.

- When an else clause contains an if statement, it often is clearer to write the clause as an else if clause. Such a construct is a multiway if statement that provides several mutually exclusive choices.

- In the absence of braces, an else clause is paired with the preceding unmatched if.

- A switch statement provides multiple courses of action according to the value of an expression whose data type is int, char, or enumerated.

EXERCISES

1. Consider the following if statement:

```
if (x > 2)
{
   if (y > 2)
   {
      z = x + y;
      System.out.println("z is " + z);
   }
}
else
   System.out.println("x is " + x);
```

What is displayed if the values of x and y are, respectively,

   a. 3 and 2.
   b. 2 and 2.
   c. 3 and 4.

2. Write a multiway if statement to decide the percentage increase of an employee's salary based on the following merit rating scale:

Rating	% Increase
95 and above	5.0
80 to 94	2.5
Below 80	1.25

3. Write some code that displays a question whose answer is yes or no. Read the answer as a string. If the answer is yes, do something. If the answer is no, do something else. If the answer is neither of these choices, display an error message. If the response is longer than three characters, display Your response is too long.

4. Write a multiway `if` statement to decide how intense an earthquake was based on the following scale:

Richter Scale	Intensity
Less than 2.0	Micro
2.0 to 3.9	Minor
4.0 to 4.9	Light
5.0 to 5.9	Moderate
6.0 to 6.9	Strong
7.0 to 7.9	Major
8.0 to 9.9	Great
10.0 and above	Epic

5. A hexadecimal numeral uses the digits 0 through 9 and the letters *A* through *F* to denote its value. The letters *A* through *F* represent the decimal values 10 through 15. Assuming that `hexDigit` is a `char` variable that contains either a character 0 through 9 or a letter *A* through *F*, write Java statements to assign the character's decimal equivalent to the integer variable `decValue`.

6. Solution 4 to the grading problem shown in Segment 10.5 has no `else` clauses. Replace the third, fifth, seventh, and ninth occurrences of `if` with `else if`. If you now have a correct solution, describe why it is correct. If it is not correct, describe what you need to do to correct it.

7. Here is another solution to the grading problem given in Segment 10.5:

```
// Solution 6
if (score <= 100)
    if (score >= 90)
        grade = 'A';
    else if (score <= 89)
        if (score >= 80)
            grade = 'B';
        else if (score <= 79)
            if (score >= 70)
                grade = 'C';
            else if (score <= 69)
                if (score >= 60)
                    grade = 'D';
                else
                    grade = 'F';
```

Which comparisons, if any, can you omit because they are true in the logic at the point at which they occur?

8. Consider the following `if` statement that classifies people according to their age. The programmer who wrote this code was careless when indenting. The syntax, however, is correct. Assume that `age` is an `int` variable containing a positive value.

```
if (age < 12)
    System.out.println("You belong to Group 1");
else if (age > 12)
if (age <= 19)
    System.out.println("You belong to Group 2");
else if ( (age > 20) && (age < 55) )
    System.out.println("You belong to Group 3");
else
    System.out.println("You belong to Group 4");
else
    System.out.println("You belong to Group 5");
```

   a. How old are the people in Group 1?
   b. How old are the people in Group 2?
   c. How old are the people in Group 3?

d. How old are the people in Group 4?

e. How old are the people in Group 5?

f. Does the previous code account for all ages?

9. Suppose that the `int` variable `hour` contains the hour of the day in 24-hour notation. That is, it contains an integer that ranges from 0 to 23, where 0 is midnight. Write an `if` statement that displays a message for a café indicating the current meal offered. Use the following schedule:

   Breakfast is served from 6 a.m. to 10 a.m.
   Lunch is served from 11 a.m. to 2 p.m.
   Dinner is served from 5 p.m. to 8 p.m.
   The café is closed at all other times.

   a. What valid data types can be used with a `switch` statement?

   b. In a `switch` statement, is it a syntax error if the keyword `break` is not used after processing a case?

   c. Is it possible to use a `switch` statement to solve the earthquake problem given in Exercise 4? Why or why not

10. Rewrite the following multiway `if` statement as a `switch` statement:

```
if (a == 1)
    sum = sum + 2.5;
else if (a == 2)
    sum = sum + 5.0;
else if (a == 3)
    sum = sum + 7.5;
else if (a == 4)
    sum = sum + 10.0;
```

11. What value is assigned to `discount` by the following code?

```
double discount;
char   code = 'B';
switch (code)
{
   case 'A':
      discount = 0.0;
   case 'B':
      discount = 0.1;
   case 'C':
      discount = 0.2;
   default:
      discount = 0.3;
} // end switch
```

12. What value is assigned to `discount` by the following code?

```
double discount;
char   code = 'X';
switch (code)
{
   case 'A':
      discount = 0.0;
      break;
   case 'B':
      discount = 0.1;
      break;
   case 'C':
      discount = 0.2;
      break;
   default:
      discount = 0.3;
      break;
} // end switch
```

13. The answer to Self-Test Question 4 in this chapter uses a multiway if statement. Rewrite this if statement as a switch statement.

14. Revise the class Temperature, as given in Listing 10-4, by replacing the methods toFahrenheit, toCelsius, and toKelvin with one method, to, that accepts a scale as an argument. Similarly, replace the methods convertToFahrenheit, convertToCelsius, and convertToKelvin with one method, convertTo, that accepts a scale as an argument.

15. Write some Java statements that display an int value using a combination of numbers and the words "thousand," "million," and "billion." For example, display the number 2,147,483,647 as 2 billion 147 million 483 thousand 647.

16. Write a Java program that displays Do you want to continue? and then reads a user's response. If the response is either Y, Yes, OK, Sure, or Why not, display OK. If the response is either N or No, display Terminating. For any other input, display Invalid input. The case of the user's input should not matter.

17. Consider the classes Die and TwoDice, as described in Project 1 of Chapter 6, and assume that they are defined. Suppose a class DiceGame uses an instance of TwoDice to play the following dice game: You roll two dice and check the sum of the values shown on their upper faces. If the sum is

   • 7 or 11, you win.
   • 2, 3, or 12, you lose.
   • Any other value—4, 5, 6, 8, 9, or 10—you retain this value while another player rolls the dice.

   Write a method rollTwoDice for DiceGame. This method should roll two dice and return 0 for a losing roll, 1 for a winning roll, and the value rolled for any other outcome.

18. Add private methods that return the name of the day and the name of the month as strings to the class CalendarDate in Listing 8-2 of Chapter 8. Using these private methods, define the public method getDate that returns the date as a string such as

   Friday, December 31, 2010

19. Though ancient, roman numerals are still used to express a year on cornerstones, in movie credits, and on diplomas. Write a Java program that reads a four-digit year and displays its equivalent in roman numerals.

PROJECTS

1. Write a Java program that plays the game rock-paper-scissors. The program should randomly choose rock, paper, or scissors. The user should enter a choice, and the program should announce who has won. Recall that scissors cut paper, paper covers a rock, and a rock can smash scissors.

2. Write a Java program that asks for a user's tax filing status as a string, and gross annual income as an integer. Display the user's tax rate according to the following table:

Tax Rate	Gross Income			
	Single	Married (Filing Jointly)	Married (Filing Separately)	Head of Household
10%	0 to 8,350	0 to 16,700	0 to 8,350	0 to 11,950
15%	8,351 to 33,950	16,701 to 67,900	8,351 to 33,950	11,951 to 45,500
25%	33,951 to 82,250	67,901 to 137,050	33,951 to 68,525	45,501 to 117,450
28%	82,251 to 171,550	137,051 to 208,850	68,526 to 104,425	117,451 to 190,200
33%	171,551 to 372,950	208,851 to 372,950	104,426 to 186,475	190,201 to 372,950
35%	372,95 and over	372,951 and over	186,476 and over	372,951 and over

3. Consider a sequence of three integers, which we will call a "triple." Design and define a class of triples called Triple that has one parameterized constructor and the following methods:
   - getSmallest returns the smallest integer in a triple.
   - getLargest returns the largest integer in a triple.
   - getMiddle returns the integer in a triple that lies between the largest and smallest integers in the triple.
   - getOrderedTriple returns a new triple whose integers are the same as in this triple but are ordered from smallest to largest.
   - toString returns a string containing the integers in a triple in their given order.

   For example, if (5, 7, 2) is a triple, getMiddle returns 5, getOrderedTriple returns the triple (2, 5, 7), and toString returns a string such as "(5, 7, 2)".

4. To conserve water, Las Vegas assigns each of its households to a group and allows each group's members to water their yards only on certain days. There are six possible groups, A through E, and the watering schedule is shown in the following chart:

Group	Winter (Nov. to Feb.)	Spring/Fall (Mar., Apr., Sept., Oct.)	Summer (May to Aug.)
A	Monday	Monday, Wednesday, Friday	Any day
B	Tuesday	Tuesday, Thursday, Saturday	Any day
C	Wednesday	Monday, Wednesday, Friday	Any day
D	Thursday	Tuesday, Thursday, Saturday	Any day
E	Friday	Monday, Wednesday, Friday	Any day
F	Saturday	Tuesday, Thursday, Saturday	Any day

   Design and implement a class that uses one or more switch statements and one or more enumerations to determine whether the residents in a given watering group may water their yards today.

5. A weigh station is a checkpoint along a highway to inspect vehicular weights. This inspection is necessary to prevent heavy vehicles from damaging roads and bridges. Weigh stations measure each vehicle's gross weight and the weight on each axle using a set of in-ground truck scales. The Federal Bridge Gross Weight Formula of the U.S. Department of Transportation (DOT) is used to determine the appropriate maximum gross weight allowable for a commercial motor vehicle, based on axle spacing. This formula is

$$ w = 500 \times \left[\frac{L \times n}{n - 1} + 12 \times n + 36 \right] $$

where
   - w is the maximum weight in pounds that can be carried on a group of two or more axles to the nearest 500 pounds
   - L is the distance in feet between the outer axles of any two or more consecutive axles
   - n is number of axles considered

The truck in the following diagram is within the allowable gross weight

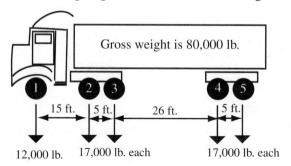

Experience has shown that the weights on axles 1 through 3, 1 through 5, and 2 through 5 are critical and are the ones that must be checked. If these weights, when considered with the distances between axles 1 and 3, 1 and 5, and 2 and 5, are within the limits imposed by the DOT formula, the truck will pass inspection.

Design and implement a class Truck that has as data fields the essential characteristics needed for the DOT formula. Also, design and implement a class WeighStation that has a method to determine whether a given Truck object is in compliance with or exceeds the allowable weight.

Finally, write a program that allows a user to enter the gross weight of a truck, the weight on each axle, and the distance between the various combinations of its five axles. Using the classes Truck and WeighStation, your program should display a message indicating whether the weight of the truck is within or exceeds the maximum allowable weight as determined by the DOT formula.

ANSWERS TO SELF-TEST QUESTIONS

1.   **a.** Nothing.
      b. You are in your 20s.
      c. You are younger than 20.

2.
```
if (temperature <= 32)
    System.out.println("FREEZING!");
else if (temperature >= 212)
    System.out.println("BOILING!");
else
    System.out.println("NORMAL");
```

3.   Solution 1: F
      Solution 2: A
      Solution 3: No grade is assigned
      Solution 4: No grade is assigned
      Solution 5: A

4.
```
if (dayOfWeek == 1)
    System.out.println("Sunday");
else if (dayOfWeek == 2)
    System.out.println("Monday");
else if (dayOfWeek == 3)
    System.out.println("Tuesday");
else if (dayOfWeek == 4)
    System.out.println("Wednesday");
else if (dayOfWeek == 5)
    System.out.println("Thursday");
else if (dayOfWeek == 6)
    System.out.println("Friday");
else if (dayOfWeek == 7)
    System.out.println("Saturday");
else
    System.out.println("Error");
```

5.
```
if ((side1 == side2) && (side1 == side3))
    System.out.println("All sides are equal");
else if ((side1 == side2) || (side1 == side3) || (side2 == side3))
    System.out.println("Two sides are equal");
else
    System.out.println("No sides are equal");
```

6.   Yes, but the use of the operator != makes this solution harder to understand than the solution we give for Question 5. Code based on confusing logic is more likely to contain errors.

7.
```java
if (area <= 0)
   System.out.println("No circle");
else if (area < 20)
   System.out.println("Small circle");
else if (area < 50)
   System.out.println("Moderate circle");
else
   System.out.println("Large circle");
// Note that the operator && is not necessary here
```

8.
```java
if (theDate.isLeapYear())
{
   if ( (theDate.getMonth() == 1) ||
       ((theDate.getMonth() == 2) && (theDate.getDay() <= 28)) )
   {
      System.out.print(theDate.getYear() + " is a leap year, but ");
      System.out.println(theDate + " occurs before February 29.");
   }
   else if (theDate.getMonth() > 2)
   {
      System.out.print(theDate.getYear() + " is a leap year, but ");
      System.out.println(theDate + " occurs after February 29.");
   }
   else
      System.out.println(theDate + " is February 29; it's leap year!!");
}
else
   System.out.println(theDate + " does not occur in a leap year.");
```

9. We need to ensure that the program correctly responds to any input data. Testing with the endpoints of each age range is especially important, as is trying illegal data. Thus, include at least the following ages in your test data: 1, 9, 10, 13, 14, 16, 17, 49, 50, 51, 0, -1.

10. Change case 7 for Saturday to case 0.

11.
```java
if ((month == 9) || (month == 4) || (month == 6) || (month == 11))
   daysInMonth = 30;
else if (month == 2)
{
   if (isLeapYear)
      daysInMonth = 29;
   else
      daysInMonth = 28;
}
else
   daysInMonth = 31;
```

12. Add cases to the switch statement and revise the default case as follows:
```java
switch (month)
{
   case 1: case 3: case 5: case 7: case 8: case 10: case 12:
                              // Jan, Mar, May, Jul, Aug, Oct, Dec
      daysInMonth = 31;
      break;
   case 4: case 6: case 9: case 11: // Apr, June, Sept, Nov
      daysInMonth = 30;
      break;
   case 2:                          // Feb
      if (isLeapYear)
         daysInMonth = 29;
      else
```

```
            daysInMonth = 28;
            break;
        default:
            System.out.println("Error in month: " + month);
            break;
    } // end switch
```

13.   `assert (month > 0) && (month <= 12);`

14. Revise the body of the `switch` statement, as follows:

```
case 'A':
case 'a':
    qualityPoints = 4.0;
    break;
case 'B':
case 'b':
    qualityPoints = 3.0;
    break;
    . . .
```

15. No. Since we do not know whether `grade` has a legal value, the `switch` statement must watch for illegal values. Assertions are used for debugging, not communicating with a user, since they can be disabled at execution time.

16. Yes. In this situation, we are really checking that our code satisfies a precondition of the `switch` statement. If it does not, we need to correct our code, not notify the user. An assertion is appropriate for alerting us to a problem.

17. By reversing the order of the enumerated values, the ordinal values will match the quality points for each grade. Thus, we can write

```
private enum LetterGrade {F, D, C, B, A}
    . . .
qualityPoints = grade.ordinal();
```

18.   **a.** Raises (lowers) the temperature by n units without changing the current scale.
   b. Sets the temperature to n units without changing the current scale.
   c. Changes the scale of the current temperature to the given scale s and converts the current value of the temperature to the new scale.
   d. Sets the value and scale of the temperature to the given values.

19. Use a `switch` statement on s. The cases invoke the public methods `convertToFahrenheit`, `convertToCelsius`, and `convertToKelvin`.

Chapter

11

Decisions and Object Interactions When Drawing

Contents

Prerequisites

Objectives

After studying this chapter, you should be able to
- Write Java code that displays simple graphics involving choices
- Write either an `if` statement or a `switch` statement that affects the characteristics of a graphical drawing
- Design and implement a group of classes whose objects interact

Although this chapter provides more examples of the `if` and `switch` statements, it more importantly develops several classes whose instances interact with one another. These examples are in the context of an application that produces graphical output. The solutions to our first three problems mainly demonstrate multiway `if` statements and `switch` statements within the context of graphics. Our last problem, however, uses five supporting classes in its solution, in addition to the classes that define a panel and a frame. The objects of several of these supporting classes must interact to solve the problem at hand. Finally, the examples in this chapter provide further illustration of the modifier `final`, either alone or in conjunction with `static`.

◼ A Problem Solved: The Thermometer Yet Again

Revise the class Thermometer, as given in Listing 9-7 of Chapter 9, so that the temperature column appears in color according to the following temperature ranges, which are given in degrees Fahrenheit:

°F	Less than 32	32 to 64	65 to 79	Higher than 80
Color	Blue	Cyan	Green	Red

For example, a thermometer that registers 30 degrees Fahrenheit should have a blue temperature column and should appear as shown in Figure 11-1.

FIGURE 11-1   A thermometer with a reading of 30 degrees Fahrenheit

11.1   **The solution.** To solve this new problem, we make some simple revisions to the class given in Listing 9-7. First, we add the following named constants:

```
private static final int COMFORTABLE_TEMPERATURE = 65;
private static final int HOT_TEMPERATURE = 80;
```

Then we replace Thermometer's private method setTemperatureColor, as shown in Listing 9-7, with the version given in Listing 11-1. This revision uses a multiway if statement to set the desired pen color according to the current temperature.

LISTING 11-1   The revised method setTemperatureColor

```
// Sets the color of fluid in the temperature column:
//   cold temperatures are blue; cool temperatures are cyan;
//   comfortable temperatures are green; hot temperatures are red.
private void setTemperatureColor(Graphics pen)
{
   if (temperature < FREEZING_TEMPERATURE)
      pen.setColor(Color.BLUE);
   else if (temperature < COMFORTABLE_TEMPERATURE)
      pen.setColor(Color.CYAN);
   else if (temperature < HOT_TEMPERATURE)
      pen.setColor(Color.GREEN);
   else
      pen.setColor(Color.RED);
} // end setTemperatureColor
```

Question 1 Is it possible to write a `switch` statement that is equivalent to the multiway `if` statement that appears in Listing 11-1? Explain.

■ A Problem Solved: Displaying a Random Color

> Paint a square in one of five colors chosen at random. Later, in Chapter 14, we will use such squares in a two-dimensional pattern to create a square quilt of colors.

11.2   **A class of squares.** We begin by defining a class of squares. Although we could give a "square" object typical attributes of size, position, and color, we choose to define only its size. The position and color will then be given as arguments to a method that displays the square. Listing 11-2 contains our definition of the class `Square`.

LISTING 11-2   A class of squares

```java
/** Square.java by F. M. Carrano
    A class of squares, each having its own size.
    A Square object can be painted at any location in any color.
*/
import java.awt.Color;
import java.awt.Graphics;

public class Square
{
    private final int side;

    public Square(int squareSide)
    {
        side = squareSide;
    } // end constructor

    /** Displays the square at a given position and in a given color.
        (xCorner, yCorner) are the coordinates of its upper left corner.*/
    public void display(int xCorner, int yCorner,
                        Color squareColor, Graphics pen)
    {
        pen.setColor(squareColor);
        pen.fillRect(xCorner, yCorner, side, side);
    } // end display
} // end Square
```

11.3   **The panel.** Next we need a panel to contain the displayed square. We must choose the size of the panel, as well as the size, location, and possible colors of the square. Suppose we decide to display the square in the center of a square panel. Listing 11-3 shows the definition of our panel. The constructor sets the panel size and creates a `Square` object of a constant size. In painting the square, the method `paintComponent` generates a random integer between 0 and 4 and uses it in a switch statement to choose the square's color from among five choices. Finally, from the coordinates of the panel's center, we compute the coordinates of the square's upper left corner before painting it.

LISTING 11-3   A panel that displays a square in its center in a randomly chosen color

```java
/** RandomColorPanel.java by F. M. Carrano
    Paints a square in one of five colors chosen at random.
*/
import java.awt.Color;
import java.awt.Dimension;
import java.awt.Graphics;
import javax.swing.JPanel;
import java.util.Random;

public class RandomColorPanel extends JPanel
{
   private static final int PANEL_SIDE = 300; // square panel

   private static final int X_CENTER = PANEL_SIDE / 2;
   private static final int Y_CENTER = X_CENTER;

   private static final int SQUARE_SIDE = 20;

   private static final int NUMBER_OF_COLORS = 5;
   private static final Color FIRST_COLOR = Color.RED;
   private static final Color SECOND_COLOR = Color.BLUE;
   private static final Color THIRD_COLOR = Color.GREEN;
   private static final Color FOURTH_COLOR = Color.CYAN;
   private static final Color FIFTH_COLOR = Color.ORANGE;
   private static final Color DEFAULT_COLOR = Color.BLACK;

   private final Square aSquare; // one square per panel

   // one random generator for all panels
   private static final Random generator = new Random();

   public RandomColorPanel()
   {
      setPreferredSize(new Dimension(PANEL_SIDE, PANEL_SIDE));
      aSquare = new Square(SQUARE_SIDE);
   } // end default constructor

   /** Displays a square in one of five colors chosen at random. */
   public void paintComponent(Graphics pen)
   {
      int colorChoice = generator.nextInt(NUMBER_OF_COLORS);
      Color squareColor;
```

```
          switch (colorChoice)
          {
            case 0:
               squareColor = FIRST_COLOR;
               break;
            case 1:
               squareColor = SECOND_COLOR;
               break;
            case 2:
               squareColor = THIRD_COLOR;
               break;
            case 3:
               squareColor = FOURTH_COLOR;
               break;
            case 4:
               squareColor = FIFTH_COLOR;
               break;
            default:
               squareColor = DEFAULT_COLOR;
               break;
         } // end switch

         int halfSide = SQUARE_SIDE / 2;
         int xCorner = X_CENTER - halfSide;
         int yCorner = Y_CENTER - halfSide;
         aSquare.display(xCorner, yCorner, squareColor, pen);
      } // end paintComponent
} // end RandomColorPanel
```

11.4   **The driver.** Listing 11-4 contains a program that displays our panel and shows a sample result. The program is much like others we have written before.

LISTING 11-4   A program that displays the panel defined in Listing 11-3

```
/** DisplayRandomColor.java by F. M. Carrano
    Displays a square in one of five colors chosen at random.
*/
import javax.swing.JFrame;

public class DisplayRandomColor
{
   public static void main(String[] args)
   {
      JFrame window = new JFrame();
      window.setDefaultCloseOperation(JFrame.EXIT_ON_CLOSE);
```

```
        window.setTitle("A Random Color");

        RandomColorPanel panel = new RandomColorPanel();
        window.add(panel);
        window.pack();
        window.setVisible(true);
    } // end main
} // end DisplayRandomColor
```

Sample Output

Question 2 What if statement is equivalent to the switch statement in Listing 11-3?

A Problem Solved: Displaying a Row of Dots

> Paint a circular disk, or dot, a random number of times in a row. The random number should be chosen from the integers 1 through 5. Varying the output will be our challenge.

11.5   **A class of dots.** Our class of dots is quite similar to the class of squares we wrote in Segment 11.2. Like a Square object, a Dot object "knows" only its size. Its position and color are given by the client as arguments to the method that displays the dot. Listing 11-5 gives the definition of the class Dot.

LISTING 11-5   A class of dots

```
/** Dot.java by F. M. Carrano
    A class of dots, each having its own diameter.
    A Dot object can be displayed at any location in any color.
*/
import java.awt.Color;
import java.awt.Graphics;

public class Dot
{
    private final int diameter;

    public Dot(int dotDiameter)
    {
```

```
          diameter = dotDiameter;
      } // end constructor

      /** Displays the dot at a given position and in a given color. */
      public void display(int xCenter, int yCenter,
                          Color dotColor, Graphics pen)
      {
         pen.setColor(dotColor);
         int radius = diameter / 2;
         pen.fillOval(xCenter - radius, yCenter - radius,
                      diameter, diameter);
      } // end display
} // end Dot
```

11.6   **The panel.** Listing 11-6 contains a panel that solves this problem by using an unusual switch state-ment, one that has no break statements. Typically, each case within a switch statement ends with a break statement. If you omit the break, execution continues with the statements in the next case. That behavior is exactly what we want here.

   We have written five calls to Dot's display method, one for each possible time we paint the dot. To paint a dot five times, for example, we enter the body of the switch statement at case 5. After painting the dot, we sequence into case 4 and paint it another time, and so on until we have painted it five times. To paint a dot only three times, we would enter the body of the switch state-ment at case 3 and sequence into case 2 and case 1.

LISTING 11-6   A panel that displays a row of dots

```
/** RowOfDotsPanel.java by F. M. Carrano
    Displays a dot 1, 2, 3, 4, or 5 times--at random--in a row.
*/
import java.awt.Color;
import java.awt.Dimension;
import java.awt.Graphics;
import javax.swing.JPanel;
import java.util.Random;

public class RowOfDotsPanel extends JPanel
{
   private static final int WIDTH = 350;
   private static final int HEIGHT = 200;

   // dot characteristics
   private static final Color COLOR = Color.BLUE;
   private static final int DIAMETER = 10;
   private static final int X_CENTER = 50;
   private static final int Y_CENTER = HEIGHT / 2;
   private static final int GAP = 3 * DIAMETER; // between dot edges
   private static final int MAX_NUMBER_OF_TIMES = 5; // must be <= 5
```

```java
private final Dot aDot;            // one Dot object per panel
private final int numberOfTimes;   // number of times to display a dot

// one random generator for all panels
private static final Random generator = new Random();

public RowOfDotsPanel()
{
   setPreferredSize(new Dimension(WIDTH, HEIGHT));
   aDot = new Dot(DIAMETER);
   numberOfTimes = generator.nextInt(MAX_NUMBER_OF_TIMES) + 1;
} // end default constructor

public void paintComponent(Graphics pen)
{
   switch (numberOfTimes)
   {
      case 5:
         aDot.display(X_CENTER + 4 * GAP, Y_CENTER, COLOR, pen);
      case 4:
         aDot.display(X_CENTER + 3 * GAP, Y_CENTER, COLOR, pen);
      case 3:
         aDot.display(X_CENTER + 2 * GAP, Y_CENTER, COLOR, pen);
      case 2:
         aDot.display(X_CENTER + GAP, Y_CENTER, COLOR, pen);
      case 1:
         aDot.display(X_CENTER, Y_CENTER, COLOR, pen);
   } // end switch
} // end paintComponent
} // end RowOfDotsPanel
```

Question 3 Is it possible to write an `if` statement that is equivalent to the `switch` statement that appears in Listing 11-6? Explain.

Question 4 Add a method to the class `Dot` that compares two `Dot` objects and returns

- 0 if the objects have the same diameter
- 1 if the receiving object has a larger diameter than the argument's diameter
- –1 if the receiving object has a smaller diameter than the argument's diameter

Give the method the following header:

```java
public int compareTo(Dot other)
```

11.7   **Repeating a task.** Although this is an interesting example of a `switch` statement, creating the cases needed to display a dot more than five times would soon become tedious. We will explore a much better way to repeat a task any given number of times in Chapter 12. To this end, we want to show you another `switch` statement that behaves like the one in Listing 11-6:

```java
int xCenter = X_CENTER;
switch (numberOfTimes)
```

```
   {
      case 5:
         aDot.display(xCenter, Y_CENTER, COLOR, pen);
         xCenter = xCenter + GAP;
      case 4:
         aDot.display(xCenter, Y_CENTER, COLOR, pen);
         xCenter = xCenter + GAP;
      case 3:
         aDot.display(xCenter, Y_CENTER, COLOR, pen);
         xCenter = xCenter + GAP;
      case 2:
         aDot.display(xCenter, Y_CENTER, COLOR, pen);
         xCenter = xCenter + GAP;
      case 1:
         aDot.display(xCenter, Y_CENTER, COLOR, pen);
   } // end switch
```

videonote

Simple decisions
when drawing

Here the statements in the first four cases are the same. The cumulative effect of adding GAP to xCenter changes the *x*-coordinate appropriately, as you should verify. In effect, we are repeating two statements a number of times with different results. This observation is key to our study of repetition in the next chapter.

11.8 **The driver.** Finally, we write a program that creates an instance of the panel class given in Listing 11-6. It is like other drivers you have seen in this chapter and is provided in Listing 11-7.

LISTING 11-7 A program that displays the panel defined in Listing 11-6

```java
/** DisplayRowOfDots.java by F. M. Carrano
    Displays a dot a random number of times in a row.
*/
import javax.swing.JFrame;

public class DisplayRowOfDots
{
   public static void main(String[] args)
   {
      JFrame window = new JFrame();
      window.setDefaultCloseOperation(JFrame.EXIT_ON_CLOSE);
      window.setTitle("A Random Number of Dots in a Row");

      RowOfDotsPanel panel = new RowOfDotsPanel();
      window.add(panel);
      window.pack();
      window.setVisible(true);
   } // end main
} // end DisplayRowOfDots
```

Sample Output

A Problem Solved: Where Is the Random Point?

> Imagine a randomly positioned point within the bounds of a given drawing area. If we know the coordinates of the point, we can see whether it lies to the left of, to the right of, or on a given vertical line. Likewise, we could learn where the point is relative to either a horizontal line, two perpendicular lines, or a square. Write a program that makes such determinations and illustrates the results graphically.

The Supporting Classes

11.9 We could dive right into a solution to this problem by defining a panel and using our knowledge of the class Graphics to create the drawings. We should resist the urge to do so, however, and first consider the various pieces of the problem. Let's list them:

- A point whose position is random
- A vertical line
- A horizontal line
- A pair of perpendicular lines
- A square
- A panel in which to display the previous items in this list
- A program to create the panel

videonote
Where is the
random point?

Points, lines, and squares certainly could be objects in our solution, so we should seriously think about writing a class for each of the items in the previous list. In fact, that is exactly what we will do.

11.10 **A class of random points.** We begin by considering the data associated with each point. Clearly, a point has x- and y-coordinates that specify its location. While we would like to position points randomly, we do not want them to be outside our drawing area. Thus, we need to provide limits—a smallest value and a largest value—for the coordinates of these points. These values, along with the point's coordinates, will be data fields in our class. In addition, we need an instance of the standard class Random to generate random numbers. Finally, we will define the diameter of each point—as a constant—for display purposes. To summarize, our class has the following data fields:

- The coordinates xCoord and yCoord
- The limits xMin, xMax, yMin, and yMax for the coordinates
- An instance generator of the class Random
- A constant for the diameter of a displayed point

You can see each of these items defined in the class RandomPoint in Listing 11-8.
    The following methods should be sufficient:

- A constructor that defines the limits on the coordinates of a point, a random-number generator, and a new point having random coordinates within the newly defined bounds
- A method changeLocation that assigns new random values to a point's coordinates
- Accessor methods getX and getY that return a point's coordinates
- A method display to draw the point as a small disk centered at the point

As you can see from Listing 11-8, these methods have simple definitions. However, generating the random values deserves some comment.

LISTING 11-8   The class RandomPoint

```java
import java.awt.Color;
import java.awt.Graphics;
import java.util.Random;

/** A class of points positioned randomly within given bounds.
*/
public class RandomPoint
{
   private int xCoord, yCoord;    // coordinates of point

   private final int xMin, xMax; // smallest and largest values for x-
   private final int yMin, yMax; //    and y-coordinates
   private static final int POINT_DIAMETER = 8;

   // one random generator for all panels
   private static final Random generator = new Random();

   /** Creates a point whose coordinates are random values
       that lie within given limits. */
   public RandomPoint(int minimumX, int maximumX,
                      int minimumY, int maximumY)
   {
      xMin = minimumX;
      xMax = maximumX;
      yMin = minimumY;
      yMax = maximumY;
      setRandomCoordinates();
   } // end constructor

   /** Changes the coordinates of this point to random values. */
   public void changeLocation()
   {
      setRandomCoordinates();
   } // end changeLocation

   /** Returns this point's x-coordinate. */
   public int getX()
   {
      return xCoord;
   } // end getX

   /** Returns this point's y-coordinate. */
   public int getY()
   {
      return yCoord;
   } // end getY
```

```
/** Displays this point as a small disk in a given color.
    The point is the center of this disk. */
public void display(Color penColor, Graphics pen)
{
   pen.setColor(penColor);
   int radius = POINT_DIAMETER / 2;
   pen.fillOval(xCoord - radius, yCoord - radius,
                POINT_DIAMETER, POINT_DIAMETER);
} // end display

// Changes the coordinates of this point to random values
// that lie within the given limits.
private void setRandomCoordinates()
{
   xCoord = generator.nextInt(xMax - xMin + 1) + xMin;
   yCoord = generator.nextInt(yMax - yMin + 1) + yMin;
} // end setRandomCoordinates
} // end RandomPoint
```

11.11   **The private method setRandomCoordinates.** Since both the constructor and the method changeLocation must generate random coordinates, we have them call the private method setRandomCoordinates. Notice that we create one random-number generator when we assign a new instance of Random to the data field generator. This field is both final and static. Thus, all RandomPoint objects will share this one random-number generator, that is, this one Random object. Even so, the RandomPoint objects will be able to generate their own random numbers by using the method setRandomCoordinates. This method uses generator to assign new values to xCoord and yCoord. Let's look at the details of this private method.

We know from Chapter 4 that generator.nextInt(n) returns a random integer of type int that is positive and less than n for a positive integer n. Thus, we can state the following facts:

- generator.nextInt(n) ranges from 0 to $n - 1$
- generator.nextInt(n + 1) ranges from 0 to n
- generator.nextInt(n - m + 1) ranges from 0 to $n - m$ for $0 \leq m \leq n$
- generator.nextInt(n - m + 1) + m ranges from m to n for $0 \leq m \leq n$

This last fact is the one we need for setRandomCoordinates. Its body is just

```
xCoord = generator.nextInt(xMax - xMin + 1) + xMin;
yCoord = generator.nextInt(yMax - yMin + 1) + yMin;
```

Later, when we study inheritance, an exercise will consider an improvement to the definition of RandomPoint.

11.12   **A class of vertical lines.** A line segment is completely determined by its two endpoints. To draw a line segment, we need the coordinates of these two points. If the line[1] is vertical, however, and if

---

1.   While a line has an infinite length, a line segment does not. Since we can draw only line segments, when we talk about lines, we actually mean line segments.

we know the length of the line and the coordinates of the uppermost endpoint, we can figure out the coordinates of the second endpoint, as Figure 11-2 illustrates.

FIGURE 11-2   A vertical line

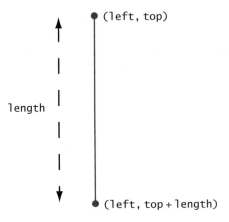

Let's create a class `VerticalLine` of vertical lines and note its data fields:

- The coordinates of the two endpoints

We can give the class the following methods:

- A constructor whose parameters are the coordinates of the line's uppermost endpoint and the line's length.
- Three accessor methods, `getUpperX`, `getUpperY`, and `getLength`.
- A method to draw the line in a given color.
- Three boolean-valued methods—`isPointLeft`, `isPointRight`, and `isPointOn`—that see whether a given point is positioned to the left of, to the right of, or on this line, respectively. Let's decide that these methods will behave as if the line segments were actually lines, that is, as if they had infinite lengths. For example, if a point lies on the imaginary extension of the line segment beyond its endpoints, `isPointOn` would return true.

Listing 11-9 gives a definition of the class `VerticalLine`. The constructor and accessor methods are straightforward. Note that a `VerticalLine` object is immutable—the class has no mutator methods—so we declare the data fields to be final. Each of the three boolean-valued methods is passed an instance of `RandomPoint`, and each uses an `if` statement to compare the *x*-coordinates of the point and the line.

LISTING 11-9   The class `VerticalLine`

```java
import java.awt.Color;
import java.awt.Graphics;

/** A class of vertical lines. Each line is specified by the
    coordinates of its uppermost endpoint and its length.
*/
public class VerticalLine
```

```java
{
    private final int left, top, bottom; // coordinates of endpoints

    /** Creates a vertical line, given its length and the
        coordinates of its uppermost endpoint. */
    public VerticalLine(int xCoord, int yCoord, int lineLength)
    {
        left = xCoord;
        top = yCoord;
        bottom = top + lineLength;
    } // end constructor

    /** Returns the x-coordinate of the line's uppermost endpoint. */
    public int getUpperX()
    {
        return left;
    } // end getUpperX

    /** Returns the y-coordinate of the line's uppermost endpoint. */
    public int getUpperY()
    {
        return top;
    } // end getUpperY

    /** Returns the line's length. */
    public int getLength()
    {
        return bottom - top;
    } // end getLength

    /** Returns true if a given point is to the
        left of this line; otherwise, returns false. */
    public boolean isPointLeft(RandomPoint aPoint)
    {
        boolean result = false;
        int xPoint = aPoint.getX();

        if (xPoint < left)
            result = true;

        return result;
    } // end isPointLeft

    /** Returns true if a given point is to the
        right of this line; otherwise, returns false. */
    public boolean isPointRight(RandomPoint aPoint)
    {
        boolean result = false;
        int xPoint = aPoint.getX();
```

```
      if (xPoint > left)
         result = true;

      return result;
   } // end isPointRight

   /** Returns true if a given point is on this line;
       otherwise, returns false. */
   public boolean isPointOn(RandomPoint aPoint)
   {
      boolean result = false;
      int xPoint = aPoint.getX();
      int yPoint = aPoint.getY();

      if ( (xPoint == left) && (yPoint >= top) && (yPoint <= bottom) )
         result = true;

      return result;
   } // end isPointOn

   /** Displays this line in a given color. */
   public void display(Color lineColor, Graphics pen)
   {
      pen.setColor(lineColor);
      pen.drawLine(left, top, left, bottom);
   } // end display
} // end VerticalLine
```

Design Decision: **What characteristics of a vertical line segment should we use to specify it?**

We know that a line segment is completely described by its two endpoints. When the line is vertical or horizontal, however, its length and one endpoint would also describe it. In defining the class VerticalLine, we decided that its client could provide a line's length and uppermost endpoint more conveniently than its two endpoints, but that the class would use only the line's endpoints as its data fields. As you can see, the methods in VerticalLine use both endpoints of a line in their definitions more often than they use the line's length. In fact, only the method getLength needs the length, and we chose to have this method compute the length from the endpoints. Although we could have included the line's length as an additional data field, doing so would describe the line in two ways. Since that approach would require us to ensure that these multiple descriptions are not contradictory, it generally is not a design that we would choose, especially if the class defines mutator methods. VerticalLine, however, does not define such methods. Thus, the decision to add the line length as a data field depends on how often you think getLength will be invoked.

Question 5 If you wanted to add a second constructor to the class `VerticalLine` that enabled its client to specify a vertical line by its two endpoints instead of its length and one endpoint, which of the following signatures would you choose? Why?

```
public VerticalLine(int topX, int topY, int bottomX, int bottomY)
```

or

```
public VerticalLine(int xCoord, int topY, int bottomY)
```

11.13 **A class of horizontal lines.** The class `HorizontalLine` is analogous to the previous class `VerticalLine`. If we know the length of the horizontal line and the coordinates of the leftmost endpoint, we can figure out the coordinates of the second endpoint, as Figure 11-3 illustrates. The class has the following data:

- The coordinates of the two endpoints

and the following methods:

- A constructor whose parameters are the coordinates of the line's leftmost endpoint and the line's length
- Three accessor methods, `getLeftX`, `getLeftY`, and `getLength`
- A method to draw the line in a given color
- Three boolean-valued methods—`isPointAbove`, `isPointBelow`, and `isPointOn`—that see whether a given point is positioned above, below, or on this line, respectively. Like the analogous methods in `VerticalLine`, these methods behave as if the line segments had infinite lengths.

Although we will use this class in the discussion that follows, we leave the details of its implementation to you as an exercise.

FIGURE 11-3 A horizontal line

(left, top) ●────────────────────● (left + length, top)

⟵ — — — — ⟶

length

11.14 **A class of perpendicular lines.** Let's consider only those pairs of perpendicular lines formed by a horizontal line and a vertical line that have equal lengths and intersect at their midpoints. Each such pair could be the axes in a typical *x-y* coordinate system. More importantly to us, the lines create four quadrants labeled 1, 2, 3, and 4, as shown in Figure 11-4.

This class, which we will name `FourQuadrants`, has an instance of each of the classes `HorizontalLine` and `VerticalLine` as its data fields. Let's name these objects `xAxis` and `yAxis`, respectively. Given the coordinates of the leftmost endpoint of the horizontal line—that is, the *x*-axis—and the length of the axes, the constructor creates the objects `xAxis` and `yAxis` such that they intersect at their midpoints. In addition to this constructor and a method to display the axes, our new class needs only one other method, `getQuadrant`, which returns as an integer the quadrant containing a given point.

FIGURE 11-4   The four quadrants formed by intersecting perpendicular lines

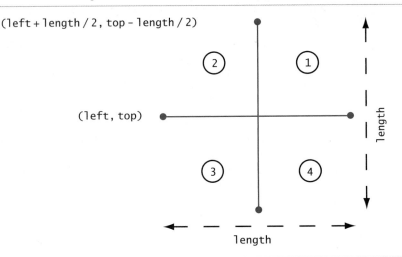

11.15   Let's consider the implementation of the method getQuadrant. Its argument will be an instance aPoint of RandomPoint. To see whether this point is in the first quadrant, for example, we would ask whether it is both above the *x*-axis and to the right of the *y*-axis. This determination is possible because of the functionality we built into the classes VerticalLine and HorizontalLine. That is, aPoint lies within the first quadrant if the boolean expression

        xAxis.isPointAbove(aPoint) && yAxis.isPointRight(aPoint)

is true. Similarly, the point aPoint is in the second quadrant if it is both above the *x*-axis and to the left of the *y*-axis, that is, if the boolean expression

        xAxis.isPointAbove(aPoint) && yAxis.isPointLeft(aPoint)

is true. Note that these determinations assume that the axes are infinitely long.

A multiway if statement involving these boolean expressions forms the heart of the definition of getQuadrant. Listing 11-10 contains the complete definition of the class FourQuadrants. The private method called by the method display to label the quadrants is tedious but not complex.

LISTING 11-10   The class FourQuadrants

```java
import java.awt.Color;
import java.awt.Graphics;

/** A class of objects, each of which represents four quadrants
    delineated by a pair of perpendicular lines. Each pair consists of a
    horizontal line (the x-axis) and a vertical line (the y-axis) having
    equal lengths and intersecting at their midpoints. The pair is
    specified by the coordinates of the leftmost endpoint of its x-axis
    and the length of the lines.
*/
public class FourQuadrants
{
```

```java
private final HorizontalLine xAxis;
private final VerticalLine   yAxis;

/** Creates four quadrants specified by the coordinates of the left
    endpoint of the x-axis and the length of the axes. */
public FourQuadrants(int xAxisLeft, int xAxisTop, int axisLength)
{
   xAxis = new HorizontalLine(xAxisLeft, xAxisTop, axisLength);
   int halfLength = axisLength / 2;
   int yAxisLeft = xAxisLeft + halfLength;
   int yAxisTop = xAxisTop - halfLength;
   yAxis = new VerticalLine(yAxisLeft, yAxisTop, axisLength);
} // end constructor

/** Returns the number of the quadrant that contains a given point. */
public int getQuadrant(RandomPoint aPoint)
{
   int result;

   if (xAxis.isPointAbove(aPoint) && yAxis.isPointRight(aPoint))
         result = 1; // first quadrant: above x-axis, right of y-axis
   else if (xAxis.isPointAbove(aPoint) && yAxis.isPointLeft(aPoint))
      result = 2; // second quadrant: above x-axis, left of y-axis
   else if (xAxis.isPointBelow(aPoint) && yAxis.isPointLeft(aPoint))
      result = 3; // third quadrant: below x-axis, left of y-axis
   else if (xAxis.isPointBelow(aPoint) && yAxis.isPointRight(aPoint))
      result = 4; // fourth quadrant: below x-axis, right of y-axis
   else
      result = 0; // on one of the axes

   return result;
} // end getQuadrant

/** Displays the two axes in a given color. */
public void display(Color axisColor, Graphics pen)
{
   xAxis.display(axisColor, pen);
   yAxis.display(axisColor, pen);
   labelQuadrants(pen); // label quadrants 1, 2, 3, 4
} // end display

// Labels four quadrants as 1, 2, 3, and 4.
private void labelQuadrants(Graphics pen)
{
   int axislength = xAxis.getLength();
   int indent = 2 * axislength / 5;
```

```
        int xAxisLeft = xAxis.getLeftX();
        int xAxisRight = xAxisLeft + axislength;

        int yAxisTop = yAxis.getUpperY();
        int yAxisBottom = yAxisTop + axislength;

        int x1 = xAxisRight - indent;
        int y1 = yAxisTop + indent;

        int x2 = xAxisLeft + indent;
        int y2 = y1;

        int x3 = x2;
        int y3 = yAxisBottom - indent;

        int x4 = xAxisRight - indent;
        int y4 = y3;

        pen.drawString("1", x1, y1);
        pen.drawString("2", x2, y2);
        pen.drawString("3", x3, y3);
        pen.drawString("4", x4, y4);
    } // end labelQuadrants
} // end FourQuadrants
```

Question 6 What boolean expression must be true for aPoint to be in the third quadrant?

Question 7 What boolean expression must be true for aPoint to be in the fourth quadrant?

Programming Tip: Design classes that provide sufficient functionality

Thinking about how you will use a class is critical to its design. As we have mentioned before, you should write some client code for your proposed class after you specify its public methods, but well before you begin their implementations. In this example, we are creating a group of classes to solve the problem at hand. You have just seen how the definition of the class FourQuadrants depends on the methods of the classes HorizontalLine and VericalLine. Had we not defined methods such as isPointAbove, the definition of FourQuadrants would be more difficult to write.

11.16   **A class of square boxes.** Our final supporting class describes squares that can be displayed and can tell us whether they contain a given point. We specify a square by providing the length of a side and the coordinates of its upper left corner, as Figure 11-5 shows. These values alone make up the data fields for the class. They are also the values used by the Graphics method drawRect. Calling drawRect within a display method that draws a square is sufficient for this problem. We need not form a square by using instances of our previous classes of horizontal and vertical lines.

FIGURE 11-5   A square

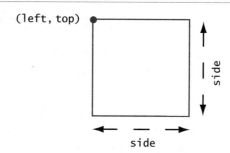

The most interesting part of our class, which appears in Listing 11-11, is the method isInside. However, we leave its definition for you as an exercise in Question 8. (If you get stuck, you can look at our answer at the end of this chapter.) To see whether a given point is inside a square, you can find the point's coordinates and compare them to the coordinates of the square's corners. Once we have the definition of isInside, the method isOutside is easy to write. If the expression !isInside(aPoint) is true, then isInside(aPoint) must be false, and we can conclude that aPoint must be outside of the square. While this might seem like cheating, defining isOutside in this way is the fastest and surest way to write a correct version of this method.

LISTING 11-11   The class SquareBox

```java
import java.awt.Color;
import java.awt.Graphics;

/** A class of squares that can detect whether they
    contain a given point. */
public class SquareBox
{
   private final int left, top; // coordinates of upper left corner
   private final int side;

   /** Creates a square at a given position and dimension. */
   public SquareBox(int xCoord, int yCoord, int sideLength)
   {
      left = xCoord;
      top = yCoord;
      side = sideLength;
   } // end constructor

   /** Returns true if a given point is either on or inside the
       boundaries of this box; otherwise, returns false. */
   public boolean isInside(RandomPoint aPoint)
   {
      < The implementation is left for you as an exercise. See Question 8. >
   } // end isInside
```

```
/** Returns true if a given point is outside the boundaries
    of this box; otherwise, returns false. */
public boolean isOutside(RandomPoint aPoint)
{
    return !isInside(aPoint);
} // end isOutside

/** Displays this box in a given color. */
public void display(Color boxColor, Graphics pen)
{
    pen.setColor(boxColor);
    pen.drawRect(left, top, side, side);
} // end display
} // end SquareBox
```

Question 8 What is the implementation of the method isInside for the class SquareBox?

The Panel

11.17 We need only the specifications for the previous classes to be able to define the panel for our solution. We do not need implementations of those classes until, of course, we are testing the panel. Thus, even though you might not have completed the implementations of HorizontalLine and SquareBox, we can use their methods in the definition of our panel.

Let's sketch our desired graphical output. We want to draw a vertical line and a randomly placed point. The program then should test where the point is relative to the line and report its findings within a dialog box. To avoid any ambiguity about this test, we set the line's length to the height of the panel. In this way, a point cannot be directly above or directly below an endpoint. The initial output might look something like the sketch shown in Figure 11-6.

FIGURE 11-6   A sketch of the proposed vertical-line output and the resulting dialog box

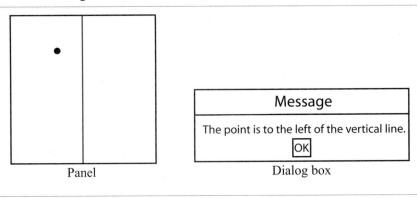

When the user clicks the OK button in the dialog box, the drawing should be replaced by a horizontal line and another randomly placed point. Another dialog box should appear that reports the location of the point relative to the new line. A similar sequence of events should take place to test the location of a random point relative to two perpendicular lines and then to a square box. After the user sees the results of the square and closes the dialog box, an all-done message should appear to indicate the end of the program.

11.18   **Initial pseudocode.** Let's write some pseudocode for our class, which we will name `WherePanel`. We can begin with the following outline:

```
public class WherePanel extends JPanel
{
    < Data fields. . . >

    public WherePanel()
    {
        Set panel size
        Initialize lines, shapes, and the point needed for drawings
    }

    public void paintComponent(Graphics pen)
    {
        Draw as needed
    }

    < Other methods . . . >
}
```

Even though we have written little detail, we are reminded of some key facts:

- Our panel must extend `JPanel`.
- We need data fields.
- A constructor will initialize the data fields and set the panel size. A default constructor will be sufficient.
- We must define the method `paintComponent`. It is the only method that can directly invoke methods in the class `Graphics`. Moreover, we do not—and cannot—invoke `paintComponent`; the system does that.

This last point is the challenge of this problem, since we have five cases—or scenes—to display in succession: the vertical line, the horizontal line, the perpendicular lines, the square, and the all-done message.

11.19   **Refined pseudocode for `paintComponent`.** Let's fill in some details for our pseudocode, beginning with the method `paintComponent`. Somehow, we need to control its behavior so that our scenes are displayed separately and in order. We do not want the scenes displayed all at once or successively on top of one another.

Our solution is to write a `switch` statement within `paintComponent` that has fives cases, one for each of our scenes. An integer data field, `scene`, can take on one of the values 1 through 5 and be used in the `switch` statement to choose the desired case, as the following pseudocode indicates:

```
/** Performs the drawing, under control of another method (action). */
public void paintComponent(Graphics pen)
{
    Clear drawing
    switch (scene)
    {
```

```
            case 1: Display the vertical line and the point
                break;
            case 2: Display the horizontal line and the point
                break;
            case 3: Display the perpendicular lines and the point
                break;
            case 4: Display the square box and the point
                break;
            case 5: Display "All done! Please click the window's close box."
                break;
            default: Display "Unexpected case in method paintComponent."
                break;
        } // end switch
    } // end paintComponent
```

Notice that the first action taken by paintComponent is to erase the drawing area. The switch statement then displays the appropriate figure according to the value of scene. But what sets this value?

11.20   **Pseudocode to set the scene.** One of our data fields will be scene, which we can define as follows:

```
    private int scene; // controls the progress of the drawing
```

We might initialize scene within the constructor, but we must do more. We need to change the value of scene in an appropriate and timely manner. Thus, we need another method that controls the action of our program. We can name such a method action and write the following pseudo-code for it:

```
    /** Controls the order of drawings and tests. */
    public void action()
    {
        scene = 1;
        Display vertical line and point
        Perform test and report results

        scene = 2;
        Display horizontal line and point
        Perform test and report results
        scene = 3;

        Display perpendicular lines and point
        Perform test and report results
        scene = 4;

        Display square box and point
        Perform test and report results
        scene = 5;

        Display exit message
    } // end action
```

After this method sets the value of scene, it somehow must execute the switch statement in paintComponent. We cannot call paintComponent directly, but we can ask the system to call it. We do that by invoking the method repaint. This method is defined in a class within the AWT on which JPanel is ultimately based. Since our panel class is based on JPanel—because we wrote extends JPanel—we can call repaint. Thus, we implement each pseudocode statement, such as

Display vertical line and point

within action by writing the Java statement

repaint();

11.21 **Data fields.** Before we can complete the definition of the method action, we should think more about what data fields we need in addition to scene. We will need the preferred dimensions of the panel, as well as objects to represent the various lines and figures within our drawings. We can express these requirements by writing the following pseudocode:

Constants giving the dimensions of the panel
Instances of VerticalLine, HorizontalLine, FourQuadrants, SquareBox, *and* RandomPoint
private int scene; // controls the progress of the drawing

We finally have used all the classes we defined earlier!

11.22 **Private methods.** We can now turn our attention back to the method action. The pseudocode for this method contains the statement

Perform test and report results

four times. Although it may seem as though action does the same thing at each of four places, the tests to be performed depend entirely on which line or figure we have drawn—that is, on which scene is executing.

We will write four methods, one for each scene, to perform the tests and display the results, and we will make each of these methods private, since they are an implementation detail. In fact, action will be the only method to invoke them. It is these methods that will use the decision statements if-else and switch. Since their logic is relatively straightforward, we will not write pseudocode for them. However, we at least will name them—verticalLineTest, horizontalLineTest, quadrantTest, and boxTest—so we can finish the definition of action.

11.23 **The completed panel.** Listing 11-12 contains the definition of our panel class. Look at the data fields, the methods action and paintComponent, and then the private methods that support action. Note that action is public, as the driver for the panel must be able to invoke it. You can leave examining the constructor until last.

LISTING 11-12   The class WherePanel

```
import java.awt.Color;
import java.awt.Dimension;
import java.awt.Graphics;
import javax.swing.JOptionPane;
import javax.swing.JPanel;

/** This class describes a square panel and controls the occurrence of
    various drawings and tests. A vertical line and a randomly positioned
    point will appear within the bounds of the panel. A dialog box will
    then state whether the point is to the left of, to the right of, or
```

```
         on the line. Similar events will occur in turn for a horizontal
      line, two perpendicular lines, and a square.
*/
public class WherePanel extends JPanel
{
   private static final int DRAWING_SIDE = 300;

   // minimum distance between random points and edges of drawing window
   private static final int BORDER = 50;

   private VerticalLine   vertical;
   private HorizontalLine horizontal;
   private FourQuadrants  quads;
   private SquareBox      box;
   private RandomPoint    aPoint;

   private int scene; // controls the progress of the drawing

   /** Creates a panel for the drawing area and initializes the
       planned drawings and associated components. */
   public WherePanel()
   {
      setPreferredSize(new Dimension(DRAWING_SIDE, DRAWING_SIDE));

      // A vertical line that bisects the drawing area:

      // coordinates
      int verticalLineX = DRAWING_SIDE / 2;
      int verticalLineTopEndY = 0;
      int verticalLineBottomEndY = DRAWING_SIDE;

      int lineLength = verticalLineBottomEndY - verticalLineTopEndY;
      vertical = new VerticalLine(verticalLineX, verticalLineTopEndY,
                                  lineLength);

      // A horizontal line that bisects the drawing area:

      // coordinates
      int horizontalLineY = verticalLineTopEndY + lineLength / 2;
      int horizontalLineLeftEndX = verticalLineX - lineLength / 2;
      int horizontalLineRightEndX = horizontalLineLeftEndX + lineLength;

      horizontal = new HorizontalLine(horizontalLineLeftEndX,
                                      horizontalLineY, lineLength);

      // Two perpendicular lines centered in the drawing area:
      quads = new FourQuadrants(horizontalLineLeftEndX, horizontalLineY,
                                lineLength);

      // A square box in the drawing area:
```

```java
      // coordinates
      int boxX = DRAWING_SIDE / 2;
      int boxY = DRAWING_SIDE / 3;
      int boxSide = DRAWING_SIDE / 4;

      box = new SquareBox(boxX, boxY, boxSide);

      // The coordinates of all random points are >= BORDER and
      // <= DRAWING_SIDE - BORDER.
      int maxValue = DRAWING_SIDE - 2 * BORDER;
      aPoint = new RandomPoint(BORDER, maxValue, BORDER, maxValue);
   } // end default constructor

   /** Controls the order of drawings and tests. */
   public void action()
   {
      scene = 1;
      repaint(); // draw vertical line
      verticalLineTest();

      scene = 2;
      repaint(); // draw horizontal line
      horizontalLineTest();

      scene = 3;
      repaint(); // draw perpendicular lines
      quadrantTest();

      scene = 4;
      repaint(); // draw square box
      boxTest();

      scene = 5; // exit message
      repaint();
   } // end action

   /** Performs the drawing, under control of the previous action method.
   */
   public void paintComponent(Graphics pen)
   {
      clearDrawing(pen);
      switch (scene)
      {
         case 1:
            vertical.display(Color.BLUE, pen);
            aPoint.display(Color.BLACK, pen);
            break;
         case 2:
            horizontal.display(Color.BLUE, pen);
```

```
                    aPoint.display(Color.BLACK, pen);
                    break;
                case 3:
                    quads.display(Color.BLUE, pen);
                    aPoint.display(Color.BLACK, pen);
                    break;
                case 4:
                    box.display(Color.BLUE, pen);
                    aPoint.display(Color.BLACK, pen);
                    break;
                case 5:
                    pen.setColor(Color.BLUE);
                    pen.drawString("All done! Please click the window's close " +
                                   "box.", 10, DRAWING_SIDE / 2);
                    break;
                default:
                    pen.setColor(Color.RED);
                    pen.drawString("Unexpected case in method paintComponent.",
                                   5, 5);
                    break;
        } // end switch
    } // end paintComponent

// Private methods:

    // Gets a random point and finds where it is relative to a
    // vertical line.
    private void verticalLineTest()
    {
        aPoint.changeLocation();
        String message;
        if (vertical.isPointLeft(aPoint))
            message = "The point is to the left of the vertical line.";
        else if (vertical.isPointRight(aPoint))
            message = "The point is to the right of the vertical line.";
        else
            message = "The point is on the vertical line.";

        showMessage(message);
    } // end verticalLineTest

    // Gets a random point and finds where it is relative to a
    // horizontal line.
    private void horizontalLineTest()
    {
        aPoint.changeLocation();
```

```
      String message;

      if (horizontal.isPointAbove(aPoint))
         message = "The point is above the horizontal line.";
      else if (horizontal.isPointBelow(aPoint))
         message = "The point is below the horizontal line.";
      else
         message = "The point is on the horizontal line.";

      showMessage(message);
   } // end horizontalLineTest

   // Gets a random point and finds which quadrant contains it.
   private void quadrantTest()
   {
      aPoint.changeLocation();
      int quadrant = quads.getQuadrant(aPoint);
      String message;

      switch (quadrant)
      {
         case 0:
            message = "The point is on the boundary of the quadrants.";
            break;
         case 1:
            message = "The point is in the first quadrant.";
            break;
         case 2:
            message = "The point is in the second quadrant.";
            break;
         case 3:
            message = "The point is in the third quadrant.";
            break;
         case 4:
            message = "The point is in the fourth quadrant.";
            break;
         default:
            message = "Unexpected case in method quadrantTest.";
            break;
      } // end switch

      showMessage(message);
   } // end quadrantTest

   // Gets a random point and finds whether it is inside or outside
   // of a square.
   private void boxTest()
```

```
   {
      aPoint.changeLocation();
      String message;

      if (box.isInside(aPoint))
         message = "The point is in the box.";
      else
         message = "The point is not in the box.";

      showMessage(message);
   } // end boxTest

   // Displays a dialog box containing a given message.
   private void showMessage(String message)
   {
      JOptionPane.showMessageDialog(null, message);
   } // end showMessage

   // Erases the drawing area by painting it in white.
   private void clearDrawing(Graphics pen)
   {
      pen.setColor(Color.WHITE);
      pen.fillRect(0, 0, DRAWING_SIDE, DRAWING_SIDE);
   } // end clearDrawing
} // end WherePanel
```

Note: The method repaint

Calling repaint() without arguments, as we have done here, causes the entire drawing to be rendered again. This occurs even if you have changed only a small part of the drawing. Although doing so is acceptable for our simple drawings, rendering more complex drawings repeatedly and in their entirety, when only a part of them is altered, wastes time. For those situations, repaint can take arguments that describe the portion of the drawing that is to be replaced. We will not consider this version of the method.

11.24 **The driver.** The driver for WherePanel is like our earlier drivers and appears in Listing 11-13, along with its output.

LISTING 11-13 A program that displays the panel defined in Listing 11-12

```
import javax.swing.JFrame;

/** Creates the frame and panel for graphic examples of decisions. */
public class WhereDriver
{
   public static void main(String[] args)
   {
```

```
        JFrame window = new JFrame();
        window.setDefaultCloseOperation(JFrame.EXIT_ON_CLOSE);
        window.setTitle("Examples of Decisions");

        WherePanel panel = new WherePanel();
        window.add(panel);
        window.pack();
        window.setVisible(true);
        panel.action();
    } // end main
} // end WhereDriver
```

Sample Output

CHAPTER SUMMARY

- You can use either an `if` statement or a `switch` statement to set the color of the pen. If the decision is based upon a range of values, use an `if` statement. If it is based upon discrete values, use a `switch` statement.

- You can use a `switch` statement to perform a variable number of tasks by omitting the `break` statements. If these tasks are all the same, however, a better way is possible, as you will see in Chapter 12.

- A call to the method `repaint` is a request for the system to call `paintComponent` again. Without arguments, `repaint` causes an entire panel to be drawn again. It is possible to specify that `repaint` draw only a portion of a panel to save time.

- The solution to a problem can involve objects of one or more classes. The last example in this chapter provides an example of such a situation.

EXERCISES

1. After replacing the `switch` statement in Listing 11-6 with the one given in Segment 11.7, what is the value of `xCenter` when the `switch` finishes execution and `numberOfTimes` is

    a. 5
    b. 2

2. Consider the class `RandomPoint`, as given in Listing 11-8. Define each of the following methods for this class:

    a. `toString`
    b. `equals`

3. Define the class `HorizontalLine`, as described in Segment 11.13.

4. Suppose that `lineA` and `lineB` are two instances of the class `VerticalLine`, which appears in Listing 11-9 of this chapter, and `aPoint` is an instance of the class `RandomPoint`, which appears in Listing 11-8. Write some code that decides whether `aPoint` lies between—but not on—the two vertical lines.

5. Define the method `getPoint` for the class `RandomPoint`, as given in Listing 11-8. This method should return a new `Point` object that represents the coordinates of the random point.

6. Consider a class named `Circle` that is analogous to the class `SquareBox`, as given in Listing 11-11. A `Circle` object can signal whether a given point lies within or outside of its boundary. Write definitions for the methods `isInside` and `isOutside`.

7. Define a class named `LineSegment` that represents line segments whose endpoints lie within a given square region. A `LineSegment` object should be able to report its endpoints as `Point` objects and draw itself. Define three parameterized constructors, each of which is given the length of the side of the bounding square region as a parameter, as follows:

    - Two additional parameters specify the line's endpoints as `Point` objects.
    - One additional parameter specifies one endpoint of the line as a `Point` object; the second endpoint is generated at random.
    - Both endpoints are generated at random as `Point` objects.

8. Define a class named `RandomRightTriangle` that represents right triangles whose sides lie entirely within a given square region. A `RandomRightTriangle` object should be able to report its vertices as `Point` objects and draw itself. Use the class `LineSegment`, as described in the previous exercise, to represent the triangle's sides. *Hint*: Define the hypotenuse of the triangle as a `LineSegment` object whose endpoints are chosen randomly. These endpoints are two vertices of the triangle. Let the third vertex be the vertex of the right angle, as you can determine its coordinates from the coordinates of the other two vertices.

9. The classes VerticalLine and HorizontalLine each have methods that involve the class RandomPoint. When defining such methods, what does the programmer need to know about RandomPoint, and what about RandomPoint can the programmer ignore?

10. Imagine that you've been asked to revise the class FourQuadrants, given in Listing 11-10. Instead of the data fields xAxis and yAxis, the revised class has four Point objects as its fields. These points are the endpoints of the axes and are named xAxis1, xAxis2, yAxis1, and yAxis2. Define the method getQuadrant for this definition of FourQuadrants.

PROJECTS

1. Write a graphical application that asks the user for a given emotion and displays a heart in an appropriate color. Use the following emotions and colors: anger/black, fear/orange, joy/yellow, love/red, sadness/blue, surprise/green. Display an unidentified emotion in gray. For example, your output might appear as follows:

2. Write a graphical application that displays a row of between one and five quarter moons. Choose both the number of moons and their color randomly. For example, your output might appear as follows:

3. Write a graphical application that has the following characteristics:
   - Its panel is 350 pixels wide by 200 pixels high.
   - It draws a horizontal line through the panel's center point.
   - It randomly paints either a circle or a square at a random location.
   - The color of the circle or square depends on its location relative to the horizontal line, as follows: It is blue if its center is above the line, green if its center is below the line, and red if its center is on the line.

   Generate two random integers that are the *x*- and *y*-coordinates of the center of the circle or square. Be sure that these coordinates lie within the window. Then generate another random integer. If it is even, paint a circle; otherwise paint a square. Let the diameter of the circle or the length of the side of the square be 20 pixels.

4. Write a graphical application that illustrates a randomly positioned point and a circle. Report within a dialog box whether the point lies within the circle. Use the class RandomPoint, as well as other classes that you define and that are analogous to the classes SquareBox, WherePanel, and WhereDriver, as given in this chapter.

5. Write a graphical application that draws a traffic light, such as the following:

The traffic light contains a red light, a yellow light, and a green light. Only one of them is lit at a time. Adhere to the following requirements:

- Define a class Light to represent the individual lights within the traffic light. A light needs to know and be able to report its position, size, color, and whether it is on. A method should draw a light as a solid painted circle if it is on or as an outline of a circle if it is off.
- Define a class TrafficLight to represent traffic lights. Each traffic light must contain three Light objects that have the same diameter. A traffic light needs to know and be able to report its position and size. A method should draw a traffic light by using methods from the class Light. Another method should report which light is on, and yet another should change which light is on. Typically, a traffic light changes from red to green, green to yellow, and yellow to red. So if you tell a traffic light to change colors, it will change to green if it was red, change to yellow if it was green, and change to red if it was yellow.

The program that demonstrates your traffic light should enable the user to change the light. Have the program issue at least three prompts to do so.

ANSWERS TO SELF-TEST QUESTIONS

1. Yes, but it would not be practical to do so. You would need to list each possible temperature between 0 and 120 as a separate case.

2.
```java
if (colorChoice == 0)
    pen.setColor(FIRST_COLOR);
else if (colorChoice == 1)
    pen.setColor(SECOND_COLOR);
else if (colorChoice == 2)
    pen.setColor(THIRD_COLOR);
else if (colorChoice == 3)
    pen.setColor(FOURTH_COLOR);
else if (colorChoice == 4)
    pen.setColor(FIFTH_COLOR);
else
    pen.setColor(DEFAULT_COLOR);
```

3. Yes, but it would not be practical to do so. You would need to write five calls to display when numberOfTimes was 5, four calls to display when numberOfTimes was 4, and so on.

4.
```java
public int compareTo(Dot other)
{
    int result;
    if (diameter < other.diameter)
        result = -1;
    else if (diameter > other.diameter)
        result = 1;
    else
        result = 0;

    return result;
} // end compareTo
```

5. The first choice allows a client to define a line that is not vertical, unless the constructor checks the coordinates to prevent that. The second choice avoids this possibility without requiring additional logic within the constructor. Thus, the constructor would begin as follows:
```java
/** Creates a vertical line at a given position.
    @param xCoord  the x-coordinate of the line's endpoints
    @param topY  the y-coordinate of the line's upper endpoint
    @param bottomY  the y-coordinate of the line's lower endpoint */
public VerticalLine(int xCoord, int topY, int bottomY)
```

6. To be in the third quadrant, a point must be below the *x*-axis and to the left of the *y*-axis. Thus, the following boolean expression must be true:

```
xAxis.isPointBelow(aPoint) && yAxis.isPointLeft(aPoint)
```

7. To be in the fourth quadrant, a point must be below the *x*-axis and to the right of the *y*-axis. Thus, the following boolean expression must be true:

```
xAxis.isPointBelow(aPoint) && yAxis.isPointRight(aPoint)
```

8.
```java
/** Returns true if a given point is either on or inside the
    boundaries of this box; otherwise, returns false. */
public boolean isInside(RandomPoint aPoint)
{
    boolean result = false;
    int xPoint = aPoint.getX();
    int yPoint = aPoint.getY();

    int right  = left + side;
    int bottom = top + side;

    if ( (xPoint >= left) && (xPoint <= right) &&
         (yPoint >= top)  && (yPoint <= bottom) )
        result = true;

    return result;
} // end isInside
```

Debugging Interlude

3

Introduction to Testing

Contents

Prerequisites

Let's pause once again to think about debugging. The best debugging strategy is to not make any mistakes! Although we cannot expect anyone to write flawless Java code, we can adopt programming techniques that help us avoid errors. We will continue to suggest such techniques, even while we explore ways to find our own mistakes in logic. Here we will focus on finding mistakes associated with decision statements.

Finding mistakes in logic is accomplished during **software testing**. In the process, we see whether our program meets its design requirements and behaves as needed and desired. During our discussion in this interlude, we will begin to explore this area of software development.

■ Avoiding Mistakes

D3.1

Modularity. When solving problems in previous chapters, we have written pseudocode to describe the steps in our solution. Each step often can be described by a sequence of even smaller steps, and these steps eventually will correspond to pieces, or **modules**, of our Java program. A module might be a class or, more likely, a method.

Avoiding mistakes

You have seen that the definition of a method can consist of calls to several private methods. For example, the class `Thermometer` in Listing 9-7 of Chapter 9 has a public method `draw` that calls three private methods. Its definition follows:

```
/** Draws the thermometer. */
public void draw(Graphics pen)
{
    paintFluid(pen);
    drawEdges(pen);
    drawDigitalTemperature(pen);
} // end draw
```

The intent of these steps is clear, and the definitions of the three private methods are each short, as you can see by examining Listing 9-7.

D3.2

Revising a module. The first example in Chapter 11 revised the class `Thermometer` to display the temperature in one of four colors instead of only two. Since the method `draw` called the private method `paintFluid`—which called a private method, `setTemperatureColor`, to set the color—we needed only to revise that latter method instead of revising `draw` or `paintFluid`.

In Chapter 9, the method `setTemperatureColor` is defined as follows:

```
// Sets the color of fluid in the temperature column:
// cold temperatures are blue, others are red.
private void setTemperatureColor(Graphics pen)
{
    if (temperature <= FREEZING_TEMPERATURE)
        pen.setColor(Color.BLUE);
    else
        pen.setColor(Color.RED);
} // end setTemperatureColor
```

In Chapter 11, we changed the method's `if` statement to a multiway `if` statement, after defining two more named constants:

```
// Sets the color of fluid in the temperature column:
// cold temperatures are blue; cool temperatures are cyan;
// comfortable temperatures are green; hot temperatures are red.
private void setTemperatureColor(Graphics pen)
{
    if (temperature < FREEZING_TEMPERATURE)
        pen.setColor(Color.BLUE);
    else if (temperature < COMFORTABLE_TEMPERATURE)
        pen.setColor(Color.CYAN);
    else if (temperature < HOT_TEMPERATURE)
        pen.setColor(Color.GREEN);
    else
        pen.setColor(Color.RED);
} // end setTemperatureColor
```

! **Programming Tip**

To reduce the chance of mistakes while writing or revising Java code, define methods that have a clear and focused purpose. If the logic is complex, divide it into portions that private methods can implement. A public method then can call these private methods. The resulting modularity, not only helps you avoid mistakes, but also helps you find any mistakes that you do make.

Programming Tip

Another way to avoid mistakes is to clearly document any conditions that must be met before a particular method is called. By doing so, you can more easily ensure that other methods satisfy these conditions before invoking the private methods. As you will learn in Chapter 15, the conditions that a client must meet before calling a method are called preconditions.

■ Displaying a Calendar

D3.3   Imagine a Java program that displays a complete calendar for any given year. In Chapter 7, you saw how to find the day of the week for any given date and how to detect when a year is a leap year. In Chapter 10, you learned how to use a switch statement to get the number of days in a given month. Using these basic ideas, we could begin the definition of a class of calendars.

The class shown in Listing D3-1 is still in development. The plan is to focus on computing the number of days in a month by writing and testing the private method getDaysInMonth. The class has temporary implementations, or **stubs**, for other methods in the class. Let's look at what we have.

One data field, year, and a constructor that initializes it, begin the class. The method display, which should display a complete calendar, produces only basic output. It can have a less tedious definition after we study the repetition statements in the next chapter. This method calls the private method displayMonth, which is a stub that in turn calls the private method getDaysInMonth. The latter method is the one we want to develop. Since getDaysInMonth calls the private method isLeapYear, writing a stub for isLeapYear would normally make sense. However, we wrote this method in Segment 8.3 of Chapter 8.

The class ends with a short main method that tests the class for two different years, one of which is a leap year.

LISTING D3-1   A draft of a class of calendars

```java
/** CalendarDebug3.java by F. M. Carrano
    A class to display a calendar for a given year.
*/
public class CalendarDebug3
{
    private final int year;

    public CalendarDebug3(int theYear)
    {
        year = theYear;
    } // end constructor

    /** Displays the 12 months in a year. */
    public void display()
    {
        System.out.println("For the year " + year + ", ");
        displayMonth(1);
        displayMonth(2);
        displayMonth(3);
        displayMonth(4);
        displayMonth(5);
```

```java
        displayMonth(6);
        displayMonth(7);
        displayMonth(8);
        displayMonth(9);
        displayMonth(10);
        displayMonth(11);
        displayMonth(12);
        System.out.println();
    } // end display

    // Displays the calendar for a given month.
    private void displayMonth(int month) // STUB
    {
        int numberOfDays = getDaysInMonth(month);
        System.out.println("    Month " + month + " has " +
                            numberOfDays + " days.");
    } // end displayMonth

    // Returns the number of days in a given month for a
    // specific year.
    private int getDaysInMonth(int month)
    {
        int daysInMonth;
        switch (month)
        {
            // Sept., Apr., June, Nov.
            case 9: case 4: case 6: case 11:
                daysInMonth = 30;
                break;
            // Feb.
            case 2:
                if (isLeapYear())
                    daysInMonth = 29;
                else
                    daysInMonth = 28;
            // all other months
            default:
                daysInMonth = 31;
        } // end switch

        return daysInMonth;
    } // end getDaysInMonth

    // Returns true if the year is a leap year;
    // otherwise, returns false.
    private boolean isLeapYear()
    {
        // A year is a leap year if it is
```

```
//    a) Divisible by 4 but not divisible by 100, or
//    b) Divisible by 400.
   return ((year % 4 == 0) && (year % 100 != 0)) ||
          (year % 400 == 0);
} // end isLeapYear
```

< *Other methods are here.* >

```
/** Tests this class. */
public static void main(String args[])
{
   CalendarDebug3 leapYear = new CalendarDebug3(2000);
   leapYear.display();
   System.out.println();
   CalendarDebug3 oddYear = new CalendarDebug3(2011);
   oddYear.display();
} // end main
} // end CalendarDebug3
```

Output

```
For the year 2000,
     Month 1 has 31 days.
     Month 2 has 31 days.
     Month 3 has 31 days.
     Month 4 has 30 days.
     Month 5 has 31 days.
     Month 6 has 30 days.
     Month 7 has 31 days.
     Month 8 has 31 days.
     Month 9 has 30 days.
     Month 10 has 31 days.
     Month 11 has 30 days.
     Month 12 has 31 days.

For the year 2021,
     Month 1 has 31 days.
     Month 2 has 31 days.
     Month 3 has 31 days.
     Month 4 has 30 days.
     Month 5 has 31 days.
     Month 6 has 30 days.
     Month 7 has 31 days.
     Month 8 has 31 days.
     Month 9 has 30 days.
     Month 10 has 31 days.
     Month 11 has 30 days.
     Month 12 has 31 days.
```

D3.4   The output shown in Listing D3-1 is correct, except for month 2. February does not have 31 days, even in a leap year. In fact, since 2000 was a leap year and 2021 is not, it seems that leap years do not affect our results.

You might immediately suspect that the method isLeapYear is incorrect. However, we wrote and tested that method in Chapter 8, so we can eliminate it as a suspect. Notice the advantage of having done this testing.

Programming Tip

Before writing a method that calls other methods, be sure that the other methods produce correct results. You can do this either by writing stubs for these auxiliary methods or by testing them separately in their own programs.

Even if isLeapYear is incorrect, it is called only within the second case of getDaysInMonth's switch statement. That case contains the following if statement:

```
if (isLeapYear())
    daysInMonth = 29;
else
    daysInMonth = 28;
```

Thus, we expect daysInMonth to contain either 28 or 29 at this point. Our expectation could be expressed as an assertion, and we could place the following assert statement immediately after the previous if-else statement:

```
assert (daysInMonth == 28) || (daysInMonth == 29): daysInMonth;
```

Recall two facts about assert from Segments 7.19 through 7.21 of Chapter 7:

- For assert to be effective, you must enable assertions when you run the program.
- If the boolean expression in the assert statement is false, the value of the expression after the colon is displayed in the resulting error message.

D3.5   We could simply run the program again, or we could focus only on February. Let's choose the latter approach by commenting out the calls to displayMonth in the method display except for the call displayMonth(2). After execution with assertions enabled, we would get the following output:

```
For the year 2000,
    Month 2 has 31 days.

For the year 2021,
    Month 2 has 31 days.
```

The output is still incorrect. However, since we did not receive an assertion error, we learned that daysInMonth contains either 28 or 29 at the point that the assert statement executes, as it should. How, then, did it become 31? Was case 2 and its assert statement skipped when getDaysInMonth(2) executed?

D3.6   One way to trace the execution of the switch statement in the method getDaysInMonth is to add some println statements that simply report their position. Rather than adding these statements directly to the method, however, a better way is to add to our class a private method that makes the same report when it is called from key places within the code. The effect of this trace can be controlled according to the value of the following named constant DEBUG:

```
private static final boolean DEBUG = true;
```

We place this constant near the beginning of the class, just before its first data field.

The additional private method could be defined as follows:

```
private void reportPosition(String method, String position)
{
    if (DEBUG)
        System.out.println("In method " + method + " at " +
                            position);
} // end reportPosition
```

If DEBUG is true, the method reports the position of its invocation. Otherwise, nothing happens.

Suppose we call reportPosition within the switch statement of getDaysInMonth, as follows:

```
switch (month)
{
    // Sept., Apr., June, Nov.
    case 9: case 4: case 6: case 11:
        reportPosition("getDaysInMonth", "cases 9, 4, 6, 11");
        daysInMonth = 30;
        break;
    // Feb.
    case 2:
        reportPosition("getDaysInMonth", "case 2");
        if (isLeapYear())
            daysInMonth = 29;
        else
            daysInMonth = 28;
        assert (daysInMonth == 28) || (daysInMonth == 29):
                                      daysInMonth;
    // all other months
    default:
        reportPosition("getDaysInMonth", "default case");
        daysInMonth = 31;
} // end switch
reportPosition("getDaysInMonth", "after switch");
```

Testing the class with assertions enabled results in the following output:

```
For the year 2000,
In method getDaysInMonth at case 2
In method getDaysInMonth at default case
In method getDaysInMonth at after switch
    Month 2 has 31 days.

For the year 2021,
In method getDaysInMonth at case 2
In method getDaysInMonth at default case
In method getDaysInMonth at after switch
    Month 2 has 31 days.
```

Since we are dealing with February, we enter the second case for both years. And since no assertion error occurs, daysInMonth must have a correct value of either 28 or 29 at the end of case 2. But then the default case executes. Our code indicates that the default case assigns 31 to daysInMonth, and that is the value we see in the previous output.

The switch statement, instead of ending after it assigns 28 or 29 to daysInMonth, sequences into its default case, which changes daysInMonth to 31. We are missing a break statement at the end of case 2. To correct this problem, we will add one after that case's assert statement.

Note: Execution of the last case in a switch statement will sequence into the default case, if any, if a break statement is not encountered.

Programming Tip: Retain the statements added for debugging

While you are developing the rest of this class, you should leave the calls to reportPosition in place. However, if you do not want tracing to occur, you can change the value of DEBUG to false. Later, when the class is completely written and tested, you could comment out these calls, along with the calls to any other debugging methods.

A Problem Solved: The Café Sign

> The cafés in a certain franchise all operate on the same meal schedule but have their own names. We have been employed to write the software for an electronic sign that displays the name of the café, an indication of whether it is open or closed, and the current meal served, if any. The meal schedule is as follows:
>
> | | |
> |---|---|
> | 6 a.m. to 10 a.m. | Breakfast |
> | 11 a.m. to 2 p.m. | Lunch |
> | 5 p.m. to 8 p.m. | Dinner |
> | Any other time | Closed |

D3.7 **Discussion.** We must be able to access the current time so that we can create a suitable message for the sign. Recall that Chapter 4 introduced the standard class `Date`, which is in the package `java.util`. If the statement

```
Date dateAndTimeNow = new Date();
```

executes, the expression `dateAndTimeNow.toString()` will return a string such as

```
"Wed Jul 30 16:19:38 EDT 2010"
```

During talks with the franchise owner, we have designed the sign's message. When Café Java is open for lunch, for example, its sign will display the following message:

> Café Java
>
> OPEN
>
> Serving Lunch
>
> Wed Jul 30 11:45

The last line gives the current date and time. A few hours later, when the café is closed, the sign will read the following:

> Café Java
>
> CLOSED
>
> See you at 5 p.m.
>
> Wed Jul 30 15:00

Notice that `Date` uses a 24-hour notation for the time of day. For now, we will use the same notation for the last line of our sign. To simplify our first solution even further, we can omit the third line, indicating the time that the café will reopen, from the message when the café is closed.

D3.8 **A trial program.** Temporarily ignoring certain requirements in a problem statement by omitting features from our initial solutions is a wise plan. Writing one or more short programs to try out our ideas is another good strategy. So before we tackle our simplified problem statement, let's write some code that gets the time of day and identifies the meal, if any, being served at that time. If you did Exercise 9 in Chapter 10, you've already given some thought to this identification task.

Here are some steps we must take:

Get a Date *object*
Extract the hour from the Date *object*
if (*it is breakfast time*)
   return "Breakfast"
else if (*it is lunchtime*)
   return "Lunch"
else if (*it is dinnertime*)
   return "Dinner"
else
   return "Closed"

Listing D3-2 translates this pseudocode into the public method getMealServed and the private method getHour.

LISTING D3-2   Trying our initial idea

```java
import java.util.Date;
public class CafeSign
{
   /** Returns the name of the meal currently being served or
       the word "Closed". */
   public String getMealServed()
   {
      String meal;
      Date now = new Date();
      int hour = getHour(now);

      if ((hour >= 6) && (hour <= 10))
         meal = "Breakfast";
      else if ((hour >= 11) && (hour <= 14))
         meal = "Lunch";
      else if ((hour >= 17) && (hour <= 20))
         meal = "Dinner";
      else
         meal = "Closed";

      return meal;
   } // end getMealServed

   private int getHour(Date now)
   {
      String nowString = now.toString();
      // nowString is "dow mon dd hh:mm:ss zzz yyyy"
System.out.println(nowString); // DEBUG

      String hourString = nowString.substring(11, 13);
      // hourString is "00" to "23"
System.out.println(hourString); // DEBUG
```

```
        int hour = Integer.parseInt(hourString); // 0 - 23

        return hour;
    } // end getHour

    /** Test program. */
    public static void main(String[] args)
    {
        CafeSign myCafe = new CafeSign();
        System.out.println(myCafe.getMealServed());
    } // end main
} // end CafeSign
```

Sample Output

```
Wed Jun 18 08:15:40 GMT-05:00 2010
08
Breakfast
```

D3.9   **Testing a time-dependent program.** Our trial program seems to work fine. It correctly displays the current the hour of the day and the meal being served. But shouldn't we test it some more? Hopefully, you think we should. We need to test the program with times both within and outside of the intervals that designate the three meals. We also should choose times at the endpoints of these intervals.

Usually, running a program with various test data is not a big deal. However, this program gets the actual time of day as its data. We could run it at various times of the day, but there is a faster way. We will begin by writing our own version of Date, as shown in Listing D3-3. Its constructor has one parameter, an integer that indicates to Date's toString method which date and time to return. The class does not have any other methods.

LISTING D3-3   A version of the class Date used to debug the class
                 CafeSign

```
/** A local version of Date used for debugging. */
public class Date
{
    private int which;

    public Date(int whichOne)
    {
        which = whichOne;
    } // end constructor

    public String toString()
    {
        String result = "";

        switch (which)
        {
```

```
        case 1:
            result = "Fri Oct 10 05:59:00 EDT 2010";
            break;
        case 2:
            result = "Fri Oct 10 06:00:00 EDT 2010";
            break;
        case 3:
            result = "Fri Oct 10 06:03:00 EDT 2010";
            break;

        < And so on, for a selection of times . . . >

    } // end switch

    return result;
} // end toString
} // end Date
```

While we are using our version of Date during testing, we add slashes to the statement

```
import java.util.Date;
```

to disable it. Of course, it is not a good practice to write a class with the same name as a class in the Java Class Library. However, our class Date is not intended to exist beyond our testing period.

D3.10   Next, we add the following method to the class CafeSign:

```
public String getMealServedTest(int whichOne)
{
    String meal;
    Date now = new Date(whichOne);
    int hour = getHour(now);

    if ((hour >= 6) && (hour <= 10))
        meal = "Breakfast";
    else if ((hour >= 11) && (hour <= 14))
        meal = "Lunch";
    else if ((hour >= 17) && (hour <= 20))
        meal = "Dinner";
    else
        meal = "Closed";

    return meal;
} // end getMealServedTest
```

This method is just like getMealServed, with three differences:

- It has a different name.
- It has a parameter whichOne.
- It passes whichOne to Date's constructor as an argument.

D3.11   Finally, we replace the main method used to test the class with the following one:

```
public static void main(String[] args)
{
    CafeSign myCafe = new CafeSign();
    System.out.println(myCafe.getMealServedTest(1) + "\n");
    System.out.println(myCafe.getMealServedTest(2) + "\n");
```

> *< And so on, for each of the times given in our class* Date.
> *The next chapter will introduce an easier way to handle this repetition. >*

```
} // end main
```

When we execute this code, the output will be as follows:

```
Fri Oct 10 05:59:00 EDT 2010";
05
Closed
Fri Oct 10 06:00:00 EDT 2010";
06
Breakfast
Fri Oct 10 06:03:00 EDT 2010";
06
Breakfast
Fri Oct 10 09:59:00 EDT 2010";
09
Breakfast
Fri Oct 10 10:00:00 EDT 2010";
10
Breakfast
Fri Oct 10 10:15:00 EDT 2010";
10
Breakfast
```

< And so on . . . >

D3.12 As you can see, we have a problem. At 10:15, the café is closed, but our message indicates that it is still serving breakfast. The rest of the output would show similar problems for times between 2 p.m. and 3 p.m., and between 8 p.m. and 6 a.m. Do you see what is wrong with our code?

The problem is that the method `getMealServed` does not look at the minutes portion of the time. Rather than adding code to correct the error, we will simply replace the three occurrences of `<=` in the method's multiway `if` statement with `<`. Thus, the statement becomes

```
if ((hour >= 6) && (hour < 10))
   meal = "Breakfast";
else if ((hour >= 11) && (hour < 14))
   meal = "Lunch";
else if ((hour >= 17) && (hour < 20))
   meal = "Dinner";
else
   meal = "Closed";
```

This change closes the café at 10 a.m., 2 p.m., and 8 p.m., rather than waiting one minute longer. This outcome is a reasonable interpretation of time periods that end at those times.

 Note: The method `getMealServedTest` duplicates much of the body of `getMealServed`. Having duplicate code in a class invites mistakes, due to the need to maintain it. For example, when we correct the mistake in `getMealServedTest` by changing the occurrences of `<=` to `<`, we need to make the same changes in `getMealServed`. It would be easy to forget to do so. We can remove the potential for this oversight by replacing the repeated code in both methods with a call to a new private method. Question 1 asks you to write such a method.

 Question 1 Write a private method that both `getMealServed` and `getMealServedTest` can call to avoid repeating the multiway `if` statement in both public methods.

Programming Tip: Sufficient testing of a program is essential

When a program checks the range of its input data, testing should include values within, outside of, and at the endpoints of each range. For programs that use real-time data, initial testing should use simulated but realistic data.

Note: Testing

Testing is performed at several levels. The previous testing of the class `CafeSign` is an example of **unit testing**, whereby you test small portions, or units, of code in isolation. Typically, a unit is a class, but to test a class, you must define and test each of its methods one at a time. Writing stubs makes this process easier. Including a main method that tests the class is a way to both test the class and indicate to other programmers the unit tests that you have performed.

When writing a software component that requires several classes, you first test each class individually. You then perform **integration tests** to test the classes' interaction with each other. Ultimately, you will perform **system tests**, during which the entire software system is tested.

Testing is also organized into several phases. The testing that we as programmers perform is an **alpha test**. During a **beta test**, software is given to people outside of the programmer's organization. Sometimes the general public is invited to participate in the beta phase.

Comparing Two Solutions

This final section is not about debugging, but instead returns to our opening theme of avoiding mistakes. We will continue to look at the café sign problem.

D3.13   **One solution.** Our first solution uses the previous ideas to refine the class `CafeSign` given in Listing D3-2. We add the name of the café to the class as a private data field, and define a constructor to initialize it. The class will have only one other public method, `getMessage`, which returns the sign's contents as a string. It calls several private methods, one of which is the method `getMealServedMessage`. This method has logic much like that of `getMealServed` in our early version of the class. Other private methods include `getHour`—which is based on our first version of `getHour` but has a different parameter—and `getDateAndTime`.

Imagine that we temporarily omit the opening time from the message "See you at . . . " in the sign's third line, as we suggested in Segment D3.7. Since we plan to add this information to the message as soon as we get the rest of the class written and tested, we will have the method `getMealServedMessage` call another private method `getNextMealTime`, which we stub. We should be able to get this much of the class written rather quickly, in light of our previous testing. Listing D3-4 gives the class so far.

LISTING D3-4   The class `CafeSign` with a stub for the method
`getNextMealTime`

```
/** CafeSign.java by F. M. Carrano
    Represents signs for a cafe.
*/
import java.util.Date;
public class CafeSign
{
    private final String name;
```

```java
public CafeSign(String cafeName)
{
   name = cafeName;
} // end constructor

/** Returns the message on the sign as a string. */
public String getMessage()
{
   Date now = new Date();
   String nowString = now.toString();
   // nowString has the form "dow mon dd hh:mm:ss zzz yyyy"
   String dateAndTime = getDateAndTime(nowString);
   String mealServedMessage = getMealServedMessage(nowString);

   return name + "\n" + mealServedMessage + "\n" + dateAndTime;
} // end getMessage

// Returns the date and time as the string "dow mon dd hh:mm".
private String getDateAndTime(String dateAndTime)
{
   // dateAndTime is "dow mon dd hh:mm:ss zzz yyyy"

   dateAndTime = dateAndTime.substring(0, 16);
   // dateAndTime is "dow mon dd hh:mm"

   return dateAndTime;
} // end getDateAndTime

// Returns a string indicating whether the cafe is open and,
// if it is, the name of the meal currently being served. */
private String getMealServedMessage(String dateAndTime)
{
   String message;
   int hour = getHour(dateAndTime);

   if ((hour >= 6) && (hour < 10))
      message = "OPEN\nServing Breakfast";
   else if ((hour >= 11) && (hour < 14))
      message = "OPEN\nServing Lunch";
   else if ((hour >= 17) && (hour < 20))
      message = "OPEN\nServing Dinner";
   else
      message = "CLOSED\nSee you at " + getNextMealTime(hour);

   return message;
} // end getMealServedMessage

// STUB
// Returns the next opening time, given the current hour.
```

```java
   private String getNextMealTime(int hour)
   {
      return "00 a.m.";
   } // end getNextMealTime

   // Returns the hour of the day as an integer.
   private int getHour(String dateAndTime)
   {
      String hourString = dateAndTime.substring(11, 13);
      int hour = Integer.parseInt(hourString);

      return hour;
   } // end getHour

   public static void main(String[] args)
   {
      CafeSign myCafe = new CafeSign("Cafe Java");
      System.out.println(myCafe.getMessage());
   } // end main
} // end CafeSign
```

D3.14   All we have left to do is define the method getNextMealTime. While not exceptionally difficult to write, the method requires some careful thought to avoid making a mistake. Here is our definition:

```java
private String getNextMealTime(int hour)
{
   String nextMealTime = "";

   if ((hour < 6) || (hour >= 20))
      nextMealTime = "6 a.m.";
   else if (hour == 10)
      nextMealTime = "11 a.m.";
   else if ((hour >= 14) && (hour < 17))
      nextMealTime = "5 p.m.";
   else
      nextMealTime = "ERROR";

   return nextMealTime;
} // end getNextMealTime
```

D3.15   **Another solution.** After designing and implementing a class, you should freely critique your own work. Both of the methods getNextMealTime and getMealServedMessage compare the current hour to the café's meal schedule. Why not combine these methods into one? If we order the various time segments and indicate the status of the café during those times, we are less likely to make a mistake.

So suppose that in addition to the data field name, we add the following definitions to our class:

```java
enum Status {BREAKFAST, AFTER_BREAKFAST, LUNCH, AFTER_LUNCH,
             DINNER, AFTER_DINNER}
private Status cafeStatus;
```

We then can define a private method, setStatus, that sets the field cafeStatus to one of the enumeration's values according to the time of day, using the following multiway if statement:

```java
if ((hour >= 6) && (hour < 10))
   cafeStatus = Status.BREAKFAST;
```

```
        else if (hour == 10)
            cafeStatus = Status.AFTER_BREAKFAST;
        else if ((hour >= 11) && (hour < 14))
            cafeStatus = Status.LUNCH;
        else if ((hour >= 14) && (hour < 17))
            cafeStatus = Status.AFTER_LUNCH;
        else if ((hour >= 17) && (hour < 20))
            cafeStatus = Status.DINNER;
        else
            cafeStatus = Status.AFTER_DINNER;
```

Subsequently, the method getMealServedMessage can examine the cafeStatus field in a switch statement to create the appropriate message, as follows:

```
switch (cafeStatus)
{
    case BREAKFAST:
        message = "OPEN\nServing Breakfast";
        break;
    case AFTER_BREAKFAST:
        message = "CLOSED\nSee you at 11 a.m.";
        break;
    . . .

    case AFTER_DINNER:
        message = "CLOSED\nSee you at 6 a.m.";
        break;
    default:
        message = "ERROR";
        break;
} // end switch
```

Since this code is easier to follow than our first solution, it should be easier to avoid mistakes.

> **!** **Programming Tip: Your initial class design might not be best**
>
> Novice programmers are generally content if their class implementation works. However, you should assess your design and seek better ways to implement a class. "Better" might mean easier, clearer, or faster to execute. A correctly working class with a complex implementation can help you see ways to improve it. Do not be afraid to start over using a different approach, as we did in the previous example.

ANSWER TO SELF-TEST QUESTION

```
1.    private String getMealName(Date now)
      {
          String meal;
          int hour = getHour(now);
          if ((hour >= 6) && (hour < 10))
              meal = "Breakfast";
          else if ((hour >= 11) && (hour < 14))
              meal = "Lunch";
          else if ((hour >= 17) && (hour < 20))
              meal = "Dinner";
          else
              meal = "Closed";
          return meal;
      } // end getMealName

      public String getMealServedTest(int whichOne)
```

```
    {
        Date now = new Date(whichOne);
        return getMealName(now);
    } // end getMealServedTest

    /*
    public String getMealServed()
    {
        Date now = new Date();
        return getMealName(now);
    } // end getMealServed
    */
```

Chapter

12

Repetition

Contents

Prerequisites

Chapter 7 Decisions

Objectives

After studying this chapter, you should be able to
• Design a loop for a specific situation requiring repetition
• Use a while statement to implement a given loop design
• Identify logical errors in a given while loop
• Control a while loop by using a boolean variable
• Write nested while loops

The console applications you have seen so far read some data from a user, perform one or more computations, and display some results. To repeat the process for another set of data, you need to run the program again. Or do you? Java has the ability to repeat a group of statements. You can repeat them verbatim or with different values or data. You can repeat them a given number of times or until a certain condition is met. Perhaps the condition is the answer to a yes-or-no question asked of the user. The statements that provide for this repetition, like the decision statements discussed in previous chapters, allow deviation from the normal sequential execution of code.

You can use one of three different statements to control the repetition of a group of statements. The controlling statement and the repeated group of statements together are called a **loop**. This chapter will look at one way to control a loop, and the next chapter will consider two others. A completely different approach to repetition is called **recursion**, which you will see in Chapter 24.

The Logic of a Loop

videonote
Repetition

12.1   The ability to repeat tasks rapidly is one of the keys to the power of computing. Whenever you are searching the web, playing video games, or using a bank ATM, you are experiencing the effects of this repetition. In Java, you can repeat a group of statements by using a controlling statement in a process known as **iteration**.

We can discuss the logic of a loop without knowing the syntax of the Java statements that control it. Typically, we consider four steps when we think of a loop, as Figure 12-1 illustrates. The first step involves getting ready to repeat a group of statements. You might initialize a counter or a condition that affects the number of times the statements will repeat, or iterate. You might also initialize certain parts of a computation that will be repeated during the loop. This initialization step is performed once.

Another step asks whether the iteration should continue by testing a given condition. The iteration continues as long as the condition is true. Often this step is second, right after the initialization step. However, the next chapter will show you a situation in which the test is the last of the four steps.

FIGURE 12-1   The steps of a typical loop

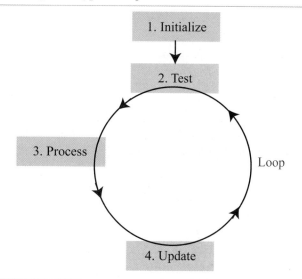

A third step—the process step—executes the statements that are to be repeated. These statements include the fourth step, which updates the condition that is tested in the second step. The fourth step often, but not always, is last. As Figure 12-1 shows, steps 2, 3, and 4 are repeated until the loop's execution ends.

The while Statement

12.2 The **while statement** controls the execution of a **while loop**, which is much like the loop pictured in Figure 12-2. It has the following form:

> **Syntax: The while statement**
>
> ```
> while (condition)
>     statement
> ```

Here, *condition* is a boolean expression like those you encountered in Chapter 7. It is the condition that is tested to see whether to continue the iteration. As long as *condition* is true, *statement* executes, as Figure 12-2 illustrates. *Statement* is called the **body** of the loop. *Statement* can be—and usually is—a compound statement. It includes both the process step and the update step shown in Figure 12-1. The initialization step—if one is needed—is performed separately before the while statement.

Our first examples are simple so that you can focus on how the loops are controlled.

FIGURE 12-2   The logic of a while statement

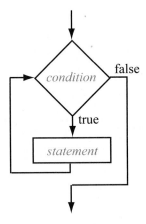

12.3 **Example: Counting.** The following loop displays the integers 1, 2, 3, and so on up to and including the given positive integer in the variable number.

```
// Purpose: Writes the integers 1, 2, ..., number
//          in ascending order, one per line.
// Given:   number is an integer > 0.
int counter = 1;                      Initialize
while (counter <= number)             Test
{
    System.out.println(counter);      Process
    counter = counter + 1;            Update
} // end while
```

The variable counter is initialized to 1 and then is compared with number. If counter is less than or equal to number, counter is displayed on its own line and incremented by 1. After this increase in value, counter is again compared with number. As soon as counter exceeds number, the loop ends and any statement after the closing brace executes.

Let's trace the execution of these statements when the value of number is 2:

counter is 1
1 <= 2 is true
Write 1
Add 1 to counter, so it becomes 2
2 <= 2 is true
Write 2
Add 1 to counter, so it becomes 3
3 <= 2 is false
Loop ends

Since this particular loop is controlled by a counter—that is, a variable that counts—it is called a **counted loop**.

 Note: The boolean expression in a while statement is evaluated, and if it is true, the body of the loop executes. If it is false, the statement after the body of the loop executes. If the boolean expression in a while statement is false initially, the body of the loop does not execute at all.

 Question 1 Revise the loop in the previous segment so that counter begins at 0.

12.4 **Example: Counting backward.** Sometimes it is desirable or necessary for a counted loop to count backward. If the variable number contains a positive integer n, the following loop displays the integers n, $n - 1$, $n - 2$, and so on down to 1.

```
// Purpose: Writes the integers number, number - 1, ..., 1 in
//          descending order, one per line.
// Given:   number is an integer > 0.
int counter = number;
while (counter >= 1)
{
   System.out.println(counter);
   counter = counter - 1;
} // end while
```

The variable counter will be zero when this loop ends.

The previous loop leaves the value of number unchanged. If you do not need its original value when the loop ends, you can write the loop as follows without the variable counter:

```
while (number >= 1)
{
   System.out.println(number);
   number = number - 1;
} // end while
```

The variable number will be zero when this loop ends.

12.5 **The operators ++ and --.** Adding 1 to a variable or subtracting 1 from a variable is common in a counted loop. Java has the operators ++ and -- for this purpose. The statement

```
counter++;
```

is equivalent to

```
counter = counter + 1;
```

and

```
counter--;
```

is equivalent to

```
counter = counter - 1;
```

You can use these operators in other contexts, not just in loops, as you will see in later chapters.

> **Programming Tip**
> The expression counter++ is equivalent to an assignment that changes the value of counter. It does not have the same meaning as the expression counter + 1. Analogously, counter-- does not mean counter - 1.

12.6 **Example: Exponentiation.** To compute r^i for a real number r and an integer i, you can use either the method pow in the class Math or repeated multiplication. For a specific exponent like 3, you could write r * r * r. But if the exponent is a variable whose value you do not know, you need to write a loop such as the following one:

```
// Purpose: Raises a real number to an integer power.
// Given:   base is the real number, exponent is the power,
//          exponent >= 0.
double product = 1;
while (exponent > 0)
{
   product = base * product;
   exponent--;
} // end while
// product is the result; exponent is zero
```

 Question 2 In the previous example, what happens if exponent is zero initially?

Question 3 In the previous example, the value of exponent is destroyed: It is zero after the loop ends. Revise the loop so that the value of exponent is not changed.

Question 4 Write a while loop that computes the sum $1 + 2 + ... + n$ for a positive integer n that is in the variable number. Then write a different while loop to compute the same thing.

12.7 **Example: A counted loop to add numbers that are read.** Suppose that you wanted to compute the average of a group of numbers that a user enters at the keyboard. You first would have to compute their sum. The logic of a loop to perform this first task might appear as follows:

```
sum = 0
while (there are more numbers to read)
{
   number = next number read from the keyboard
   sum = sum + number
}
```

How do we know how many numbers to read? The simplest way for the programmer to get the answer to this question is to ask the user, so that is what we will do here. A counter then controls the loop. The following code implements this idea:

```java
// Purpose: Computes the sum of numbers read from the user.
double number;
double sum = 0; // sum of the numbers read
int counter = 1;

System.out.print("How many numbers will you enter? ");
int howMany = keyboard.nextInt();

while (counter <= howMany)
{
   System.out.print("Please enter the next number: ");
   number = keyboard.nextDouble();

   sum = sum + number;
   counter++;
} // end while
```

At this point, sum contains the sum of the numbers read. You then can go on to compute the average by dividing sum by howMany.

Asking the user to tell you how many numbers you should read results in a straightforward loop. But does the user know this value? What if the user tells you to read 20 numbers but has 21? The next example gives another solution to this problem. It makes the user's life easier, but not yours!

12.8 **Example: A sentinel-controlled loop to add numbers that are read.** A solution to the difficulty just mentioned is to have the user signal you after he or she types the last number. The user could type another number whose value is known to you or is outside of the range of the other numbers typed. Such a number is called a **sentinel**, since it marks the end of the actual data entered into the program. A sentinel value restricts the user's data, so this approach can have its own disadvantage. But if, say, the user's data is always positive, you could have zero or a negative value serve as a sentinel without any disadvantage to the user.

The following loop computes the sum of the positive numbers read from the user. Since they are positive, we watch for a value that is not positive and use it as a signal to exit the loop. The variable number contains the value read, so it appears in the boolean expression in the while statement. Here are the initial steps that we will take to solve this problem:

```
sum = 0                                          // Initialize
number = the next number that the user types     // Initialize
number > 0 is true                               // Test
sum = sum + number                               // Process
number = the next number that the user types     // Update
number > 0 is true                               // Test
sum = sum + number                               // Process
. . . And so on
```

Where is the loop? The two statements after the step that tests the expression number > 0 form the body of the loop. The statements before the test are the initialization step. Thus, we have the following loop in Java:

```java
// Computes the sum of positive numbers read from the user.
// Given: Numbers to be added must be positive.
//        A nonpositive number will signal the end of the data.
double sum = 0;
```

```
System.out.print("Type the next positive number or 0 to end: ");
double number = keyboard.nextDouble();
while (number > 0)
{
    sum = sum + number;
    System.out.print("Type the next positive number or 0 to end: ");
    number = keyboard.nextDouble();
} // end while
```

At this point, sum contains the sum of the positive numbers that were read. To compute the average, you need a count of the numbers that you added. You would need to modify the previous code slightly to get this value. We leave this change to you as an exercise.

Question 5 What changes are necessary in the previous example to count the numbers that are added to sum?

Question 6 If you do not read a value into number before the while statement, you could try to assign it an arbitrary positive value. Would you be able to revise the loop in this way? Explain.

12.9   **Example.** Imagine that you have a program that accepts a Java reserved word as input and displays a description of its meaning. Suppose that the author of this program has created the class JavaWords to represent the reserved words and their descriptions. The method getMeaning in this class accepts a word as its argument and returns its meaning as a string. The following loop, which uses the string "QUIT" as a sentinel, could appear in the program:

```
JavaWords table = new JavaWords();
System.out.print("Enter a word or QUIT to exit: ");
String word = keyboard.next();
while (!word.equalsIgnoreCase("QUIT"))
{
    System.out.println(table.getMeaning(word));
    System.out.print("Enter a word or QUIT to exit: ");
    word = keyboard.next();
} // end while
```

A Problem Solved: A Guessing Game

> Vanessa used to play a guessing game with her grandfather. He would think of an integer from 1 to 100, and she would try to guess it. He would tell her whether her guess was correct, too high, or too low. She would continue guessing in this way until she guessed correctly. Write a Java program that plays this game, taking the role of Vanessa's grandfather.

12.10   **A pseudocode solution.** The logic of the guessing game can be described by the following pseudocode:

```
myInteger = a random integer in the range 1 to 100
guess = player's initial guess
while (guess is incorrect)
{
    Tell player whether guess is too high or too low
    guess = player's next guess
}
Tell player that the last guess was correct
```

12.11   **The program.** Listing 12-1 contains both the Java program that implements the previous pseudo-code and a sample of its output.

LISTING 12-1   The guessing game

```java
/** GuessingGame.java by F. M. Carrano
    A simple game in which the user guesses at an integer
    between 1 and 100 that was chosen randomly.
*/
import java.util.Random;
import java.util.Scanner;

public class GuessingGame
{
    public static void main(String[] args)
    {
        final int LIMIT = 100;
        Random generator = new Random();
        int myInteger = generator.nextInt(LIMIT) + 1; // 1 to LIMIT

        Scanner keyboard = new Scanner(System.in);
        System.out.println("I've picked an integer from 1 to " + LIMIT +
                           ".");
        System.out.print("Try to guess it: ");
        int guess = keyboard.nextInt();

        while (guess != myInteger)
        {
            if (guess < myInteger)
                System.out.print(guess + " is too low. ");
            else
                System.out.print(guess + " is too high. ");

            System.out.print("Try again: ");
            guess = keyboard.nextInt();
        } // end while

        System.out.println(guess + " is correct!");
    } // end main
} // end GuessingGame
```

Sample Output

```
I've picked an integer from 1 to 100.
Try to guess it: 50
50 is too high. Try again: 25
25 is too low. Try again: 37
37 is too low. Try again: 43
43 is too high. Try again: 40
40 is correct!
```

12.12 **A strategy for guessing.** As a player who runs the previous program, you might need as many as 100 guesses at the chosen random integer. Or you could be lucky and guess it correctly the first time. Although guessing randomly is a valid strategy, the output in Listing 12-1 shows a strategy that requires no more than seven guesses. Your first guess should be midway between 1 and 100. That guess, 50, was too high, so the correct answer must lie in the range from 1 to 49. Your next guess should be in the middle of this range. Thus, we guess 25 and find that it is too low. Now we know that the correct answer lies in the range from 26 to 49. After each guess, the range of possible choices is halved, as follows:

Range	Next Guess
1..100	50; too high
1..49	25; too low
26..49	37; too low
38..49	43; too high
38..42	40; correct

If lower is the lower end of a range of numbers and upper is the upper end, the midpoint occurs at (lower + upper) / 2. An integer division here will cause a truncation, which is fine. We then can describe our guessing strategy as follows:

```
lower = 1                     // the lower end of the range of possible numbers
upper = 100                   // the upper end of the range of possible numbers
guess = (lower + upper) / 2   // midway between lower and upper
while (guess is incorrect)
{
    if (guess is too low)
        lower = guess + 1
    else // guess is too high
        upper = guess - 1
    guess = (lower + upper) / 2
}
```

Later in this book, Chapter 23 will use a halving technique to quickly search a collection of items for a particular value.

Errors in Loops

videonote
Loop details
and errors

The typical errors that one makes when writing a loop affect the number of times that it iterates. Often a loop will cycle one too many times or one too few times. We call such errors **off-by-one errors**. Another common mistake causes a loop that never ends, that is, an **infinite loop**. We consider these two kinds of errors next.

Off-by-One Errors

12.13 A common mistake in loop design involves an incorrect condition that is tested. Maybe the condition uses a "less than" comparison when "less than or equals" is needed. Such mistakes cause the loop to cycle an incorrect number of times. Often this number is off by one.

For example, the loop in Segment 12.3 counted from 1 to n, where n is in the variable number:

```
int counter = 1;
while (counter <= number)
{
    System.out.println(counter);
    counter = counter + 1;
} // end while
```

If the `while` statement uses `<` instead of `<=`, the loop will count from 1 to $n - 1$. Thus, the loop cycles one too few times. Tracing the loop for a small value of `number` while you are designing the loop, as we did in Segment 12.3, will help you to avoid this error.

12.14   The steps of a loop that initialize, test, and update are interrelated. The values that you use in the initialize step affect both the condition that is tested and the location of the update step. Suppose that we begin `counter` at 0 in the previous example. If that is the only change we make, the loop will display the integers 0 through n. As a result, the loop will cycle one too many times. If we change the condition in the `while` statement to `counter < number`, the loop will display the integers 0 through $n - 1$. Although the loop will now cycle the correct number of times, we will not get the desired results. To correct the loop, we need to execute the update step before we display `counter`. Thus, we would have

```
int counter = 0;
while (counter < number)
{
    counter = counter + 1;
    System.out.println(counter);
} // end while
```

As you can see, and as you might expect, you can write a loop in more than one way to get the same result.

Infinite Loops

12.15   Errors in the condition that is tested can lead to a loop that never ends. Such a loop is said to be infinite. Intervention by the user, such as pressing Control-C, is needed to terminate execution of the program. For example, the code

```
int number = 6;
int counter = 1;
while (counter != number)
{
    System.out.println(counter);
    counter = counter + 2;
} // end while
```

displays odd integers beginning with 1. Since `counter` is always odd and `number` is even in this case, the condition `counter != number` is always true. Thus, the loop never ends. Notice that the loop would end if `number` contained a positive odd integer.

Question 7 What does the previous loop display when `number` contains 5?

Question 8 What revisions are necessary to correct the previous loop so that it displays the odd integers from 1 to n, where n is less than or equal to `number`?

Programming Tip: Stopping an infinite loop

When you see output flying by your eyes, or if your program seems to stall, you likely have an infinite loop in your program. You should learn how to terminate an infinite loop using your particular programming environment. The cause of an infinite loop is not always obvious. Debugging Interlude 4 will provide some advice for this situation.

12.16   **Equality or inequality of real numbers.** Using the operators `==` or `!=` in the condition of a loop often is not a good idea. Such is the case particularly when comparing real values. For example, suppose that you want to tabulate the values of cosine for angles between 0 and 1 at increments of 0.1. Although the following appears to be correct, in reality it is an infinite loop:

```
double angle = 0;
```

```
while (angle != 1.1)
{
    System.out.println(angle + " " + Math.cos(angle));
    angle = angle + 0.1;
} // end while
```

The value of `angle` never is 1.1 exactly. Recall that real values are not always represented exactly in binary. The slight error in the representation of 0.1 is compounded each time you add 0.1 to `angle`.

Replacing `!=` with `<` does not quite work either. Although the loop ends this time, the last computed value of the cosine is for the angle 1.09999. We actually wanted the loop to stop after computing the cosine of 1. You could use a counted loop instead, or you could iterate while the absolute difference between `angle` and 1.1 is greater than a small number such as 0.00005. A similar example of iteration with real numbers occurs in the problem solved at the end of this chapter.

12.17 **Missing or incorrect update step.** Forgetting the update step is another common mistake that can lead to an infinite loop. For example,

```
int counter = 1;
while (counter <= number)
{
    System.out.println(counter);
} // end while
```

displays 1 over and over for any positive value of `number`.

An incorrect update step can also cause an infinite loop. For example,

```
int counter = 1;
while (counter <= number)
{
    System.out.println(counter);
    counter = counter - 1;
} // end while
```

displays 1, 0, -1, -2, and so on.

12.18 **An extra semicolon.** Suppose that you accidentally place a semicolon at the end of the line that begins with `while`. The previous loop would look like this:

```
int counter = 1;
while (counter <= number); // incorrect semicolon
{
    System.out.println(counter);
    counter = counter - 1;
} // end while
```

The semicolon is not a syntax error; it represents an empty body for the `while` statement. The intended body in this example is a compound statement—it begins and ends with a brace—that will execute only once, if and when the `while` statement completes it execution. However, since the statement

```
while (counter <= number);
```

has an empty body, the value of the boolean expression never changes—and since the value of `counter <= number` is true, this loop is infinite. The compound statement is not a part of the loop, and it never executes.

Programming Tip

Do not write a semicolon after `while` (*condition*), as it can cause an infinite loop. Such a semicolon is not a syntax error, however, so you will not receive an error message from the compiler.

Boolean Variables in Loops

12.19 A boolean variable has a value that is either true or false. You can use such a variable to control a loop. Let's change the condition that controls the loop shown in Segment 12.8 to use a boolean variable, rather than a comparison of number to 0. Recall that this loop sums the positive numbers entered by a user. The logic of the original loop is as follows:

```
sum = 0
while (we are not done)
{
    number = the next number that the user types
    if (number > 0)
        sum = sum + number
    else
        We are done
}
```

In our revision, the user will still type a nonpositive number to indicate the end, but we will set a boolean variable to true to indicate when to end the loop. Suppose that we name the boolean variable done and initialize it to false. Then the while statement can be

```
while (!done)
```

which we read as "while not done." Since !done is true, the loop will execute until done becomes true. If we compare number with zero in an if statement, we can set done to true when number is less than or equal to zero.

The Java solution to this problem appears as follows:

```
double sum = 0;
boolean done = false;

while (!done)
{
    System.out.print("Type the next positive number or 0 to end: ");
    double number = keyboard.nextDouble();
    if (number > 0)
        sum = sum + number;
    else
        done = true;
} // end while
```

12.20   **Example.** Let's look at another example of using a boolean variable in a loop. In Listing 4-1 of Chapter 4, we located a person's first and last names within a string. We used the String method indexOf to locate the position of the blank that separates the first name from the last name. Suppose that we did not have that method available.

For simplicity, let's assume that the variable name represents a string that contains a first name, a blank, and a last name, without any leading or trailing blanks. We can use the method charAt to examine each character in the string until we find the blank that separates the two names. The following logic will solve our problem:

```
index = 0
while (the blank is not found and index < length of string)
{
    if (the character at index is a blank)
        We are done; exit the loop
    else
        index = index + 1
}
```

We can let the boolean variable found indicate whether we have found the blank character within the string. The following Java code implements the previous logic:

```java
int index = 0;
boolean found = false;
int stringLength = name.length();
while (!found && (index < stringLength))
{
    if (name.charAt(index) == ' ')
        found = true;
    else
        index++;
} // end while
```

When the loop ends, index indicates the position of the blank character within the string.

In this example, we assumed that the string name contains a blank character. Suppose, however, that we cannot make that assumption. If the string does not contain a blank, the loop will end, because index will equal stringLength. However, the variable found will be false. We can use an if statement after the loop to test found and discover whether we encountered a blank:

```java
if (found)
    System.out.println("A blank occurs at index " + index);
else
    System.out.println("No blanks are in the string.");
```

12.21   The problem described in the previous segment can also be solved without using a boolean variable. Suppose that we had described the solution as follows:

```
index = 0
while (index < length of string and the character at index is not a blank)
    index = index + 1
```

When this loop ends, either we will have found a blank at index or index will equal the length of the string.

We can translate this logic into Java as follows:

```java
int index = 0;
int stringLength = name.length();
while ((index < stringLength) && (name.charAt(index) != ' '))
    index++;
```

When the loop ends, we test the value of index to see whether we found a blank character. If index is less than stringLength, a blank was encountered.

Let's examine the boolean expression within the while statement. When the first part of the expression—index < stringLength—is true, the value of index is less than the length of the string. Therefore, it is safe to invoke name.charAt(index). But if the expression index < stringLength is false, invoking name.charAt(index) will cause an error because the value of index exceeds the last valid index associated with the string name. Fortunately, the second operand of the && operator will not execute when its first operand is false, due to short-circuit evaluation. Segment 7.14 of Chapter 7 introduced this notion. Note that it is important for the expression index < stringLength to be the first operand of &&. That is, we want to be sure that index is valid before using it in charAt.

▓ Nested Loops

12.22   Imagine that you want to display a square pattern of stars (asterisks), such as

```
* * * *
* * * *
* * * *
* * * *
```

where the number of rows and the number of stars per row are the same. This number is essentially the length of the side of the square. However, you do not know this length in advance. If you ask the user for this value—call it *n*—you need a loop to display *n* stars in one row. You need either *n* such loops—impossible since the value of *n* can change—or you need to execute one loop *n* times. That is, your loop needs to be within the body of another loop. Such loops are called **nested loops**.

The following logic is a first attempt at solving our problem:

```
while (another row must be displayed)
{
    while (another star must be displayed in this row)
        Display a star
    Go to a new line
}
```

The **inner loop** displays all the stars that are in one row. It executes once for each row. That is, each time the **outer loop** cycles, the inner loop executes completely, displaying *n* stars. The last step in the outer loop then begins a new line.

12.23   After asking the user for *n*, the length of the side of the square, we can control each of the loops by counting. Thus, we can refine the previous logic as follows:

```
sideLength = value entered by user
rowCount = 1
while (rowCount <= sideLength)
{
    starCount = 1
    while (starCount <= sideLength)
    {
        Display a star
        Add 1 to starCount
    }
    Go to a new line
    Add 1 to rowCount
}
```

The outer loop cycles sideLength times, since rowCount counts from 1 to sideLength. For each of those cycles, the inner loop cycles sideLength times, since starCount counts from 1 to sideLength. Thus, the inner loop displays sideLength stars in a row for each cycle of the outer loop, producing sideLength rows of sideLength stars.

Listing 12-2 shows a Java program that implements this logic.

LISTING 12-2   Displaying a square pattern of asterisks

```java
/** SquareOfStars.java by F. M. Carrano
    Displays a square pattern of asterisks (stars).
    Input: the number of stars per row.
*/
import java.util.Scanner;

public class SquareOfStars
{
    public static void main(String[] args)
    {
```

```
Scanner keyboard = new Scanner(System.in);
System.out.print("What is the length of the square's side? ");
int sideLength = keyboard.nextInt();

int rowCounter = 1;
while (rowCounter <= sideLength)
{
    int starCounter = 1;
    while (starCounter <= sideLength)
    {
        System.out.print("* ");
        starCounter++;
    } // end while

    System.out.println();
    rowCounter++;
} // end while
} // end main
} // end SquareOfStars
```

Sample Output

```
What is the length of the square's side? 3
* * *
* * *
* * *
```

Question 9 Modify the program in Listing 12-2 to draw stars in a pattern, such as

```
*
* *
* * *
* * * *
```

The Scope of a Variable

12.24   When you declare a variable, the portion of the program in which you can use that variable is called its **scope**. This portion extends from the declaration itself to the closing brace that encloses the declaration. That is, the closing brace ends the compound statement or method that contains the variable's declaration.

For example, Figure 12-3 contains the main method that appeared in Listing 12-2. The scope of starCount begins at its declaration and extends to the end of the outer while loop. Thus, starCount is available for use anywhere within this portion of the program. It would be undefined after the closing brace of the outer while loop, for example. Both rowCount and sideLength have a scope that begins at their respective declaration and extends to the end of the main method.

FIGURE 12-3   The scope of variables

```
public static void main(String[] args)
{
    Scanner keyboard = new Scanner(System.in);
    System.out.print("What is the length of the square's side? ");
    int sideLength = keyboard.nextInt();        Scope of sideLength

    int rowCount = 1;                           Scope of rowCount
    while (rowCount <= sideLength)
    {
        int starCount = 1;                      Scope of starCount
        while (starCount <= sideLength)
        {
            System.out.print("* ");
            starCount++;
        } // end while
        System.out.println();

        rowCount++;
    } // end while

} // end main
```

Notice how indentation helps the reader to identify a variable's scope. For this reason, a mistake in or disregard for indentation can confuse anyone who reads your program—including you.

Question 10 The following questions are about the `main` method that appears in Figure 12-3.

    a. Is it legal to display `sideLength` after the outer `while` loop?
    b. Is it legal to display `rowCount` within the inner `while` loop?
    c. Is it legal to display `starCount` after the outer `while` loop?

▰ A Problem Solved: The Root of an Equation

> As a certain particle travels, its velocity in meters per second is given as a function of the time t in seconds by the following formula:
>
> $$v_t = 4 \times e^{-t}$$
>
> At what time will the particle be traveling at 2 meters per second? That is, for what value of t is v_t equal to 2?

12.25   **Discussion.** We are asked to find a value of t such that $4 \times e^{-t} = 2$. An equivalent question asks for the value of t for which $4 \times e^{-t} - 2$ is zero. This value of t is said to be the *root* of the equation

$$4 \times e^{-t} - 2 = 0$$

The *Newton-Raphson method* is a repetitive technique to find the root of an equation. This method begins with a guess t_0 at the root and computes another, hopefully better, approximation of the root, t_1. For this particular equation, the method defines t_1 by the following formula:[1]

$$t_1 = 1 + t_0 - e^{t_0}/2$$

---

1. The details of how we arrived at this formula appear at the end of this section.

You then take the value of t_1 as a new guess t_0 and compute a new t_1. If all goes well, you generate a **sequence** of numbers that get closer and closer to the desired result. If that happens, the approximations themselves will get closer to each other. Thus, you stop computing when two successive estimates, t_0 and t_1, are almost the same. That is, you take t_1 as the result when

$$\left| t_1 - t_0 \right| \le \left| t_1 \right| \times \varepsilon$$

where the vertical bars indicate the absolute value, or magnitude, and ε is a small positive number. The smaller ε is, the closer together t_0 and t_1 must be to satisfy the inequality.

12.26   **The basic code.** Here are Java statements that compute the Newton-Raphson sequence for our given equation:

```java
final double EPSILON = 0.5e-5;
System.out.print("Please enter a guess at the root: ");
double newValue = keyboard.nextDouble();

double oldValue = 0;
while (Math.abs(newValue - oldValue) > EPSILON * Math.abs(newValue))
{
    oldValue = newValue;
    newValue = 1 + oldValue - Math.exp(oldValue)/2.0;
    System.out.println(newValue);
} // end while
```

With an initial guess of 1, the computed sequence is

```
0.6408590857704772
0.6918036762349127
0.6931462784620457
0.6931471805595384
```

You can take the last approximation as the root, although the digits beyond the first five are probably not significant. You can increase the precision of the final approximation by making EPSILON smaller.

12.27   **Preventing an infinite loop.** The Newton-Raphson method does not always work: The previous loop could be infinite. To guard against an infinite loop, you should limit the number of cycles by counting them and comparing the counter to some upper limit. If we make this change, the previous code would look like this:

```java
final double EPSILON = 0.5e-5;
final double LOOP_LIMIT = 25;

System.out.print("Please enter a guess at the root: ");
double newValue = keyboard.nextDouble();

int counter = 0;
double oldValue = 0;
while ((counter < LOOP_LIMIT) &&
       (Math.abs(newValue - oldValue) > EPSILON * Math.abs(newValue)))
{
    oldValue = newValue;
    newValue = 1 + oldValue - Math.exp(oldValue) / 2.0;
    counter++;
} // end while

if (counter < LOOP_LIMIT)
    System.out.println("The root is " + newValue);
else
    System.out.println("The method failed to find the root.");
```

12.28   The method `main` in Listing 12-3 now embeds this code within another loop that enables the user to try several guesses at the root.

LISTING 12-3   Finding the root of $4 \times e^{-t} - 2 = 0$

```java
/** RootOfEquation.java by F. M. Carrano
    Finds the root of the equation 4 * exp(-t) - 2 = 0,
    given an initial guess.
*/
import java.util.Scanner;
public class RootOfEquation
{
   public static void main(String[] args)
   {
      final double EPSILON = 0.5e-5;
      final double LOOP_LIMIT = 25;
      Scanner keyboard = new Scanner(System.in);

      char response = 'y';
      while (response == 'y' || response == 'Y')
      {
         System.out.print("Please enter a guess at the root: ");
         double newValue = keyboard.nextDouble();

         int counter = 0;
         double oldValue = 0;
         while ((counter < LOOP_LIMIT) &&
            (Math.abs(newValue - oldValue) > EPSILON * Math.abs(newValue)))
         {
            oldValue = newValue;
            newValue = 1 + oldValue - Math.exp(oldValue) / 2.0;
            counter++;
         } // end while

         if (counter < LOOP_LIMIT)
            System.out.println("The root is " + newValue);
         else
            System.out.println("The method failed to find the root.");

         System.out.print("\nTry again? (y or n): ");
         String input = keyboard.next();
         response = input.charAt(0);
      } // end while

      System.out.println("Done.");
   } // end main
} // end RootOfEquation
```

Sample Output

```
Please enter a guess at the root: 1
The root is 0.6931471805595384

Try again? (y or n): y
Please enter a guess at the root: 6
The method failed to find the root.

Try again? (y or n): n
Done.
```

Note: Recall that the floating-point representation of real numbers is seldom exact. For example, we can write the number 0.1 exactly in decimal, but in binary this value requires an infinite number of bits. On the other hand, certain values can be represented exactly in binary but not in decimal.

As you saw in Segment 12.16, when comparing two real numbers in Java, you should not expect that one number will be exactly equal to another, even if they theoretically should be. Although we do not expect two consecutive approximations of a root, as produced by the Newton-Raphson method, to be equal, they should be almost equal when the method is successful. That is, the magnitude of the difference $t_1 - t_0$ will be small. Just how small depends on the magnitude of the root. For example, if the root and, therefore, t_0 and t_1 are near 1,000,000, the magnitude of $t_1 - t_0$ will be larger than if the root were near 0.0007. To compensate for the magnitude of the root, we use $|t_1 - t_0| \leq |t_1| \times \varepsilon$ instead of $|t_1 - t_0|$ to terminate the loop.

12.29 **Alternate code.** When a lengthy boolean expression controls a loop, as is the case for the inner loop in Listing 12-3, you might prefer to let a boolean variable represent some or all of the expression. For example, the expression

```
Math.abs(newValue - oldValue) > EPSILON * Math.abs(newValue)
```

in the inner loop's while statement is rather long. Since the loop continues if this expression is true, we could replace the expression with the boolean variable stillLooking. Thus, we can revise the loop as follows. The differences between the previous loop and this one are highlighted.

```
int counter = 0;
boolean stillLooking = true;
while ((counter < LOOP_LIMIT) && stillLooking)
{
    double oldValue = newValue;
    newValue = 1 + oldValue - Math.exp(oldValue) / 2.0;
    if (Math.abs(newValue - oldValue) > EPSILON * Math.abs(newValue))
        counter++;
    else
        stillLooking = false;
} // end while

if (stillLooking)
    System.out.println("The method failed to find the root.");
else
    System.out.println("The root is " + newValue);
```

The `while` loop is still controlled by two conditions, even though the details of the second condition are contained within the loop's body instead of at the outset. If you find this technique easier to write and to understand, by all means use it. But resist the temptation to use a `break` statement to end a loop's execution. This should be done rarely, if ever.

Question 11 Does the previous code work correctly if we replace the `if` statement within the `while` loop with the following statements? Why?

```
stillLooking = Math.abs(newValue - oldValue) > EPSILON * Math.abs(newValue);
counter++;
```

Question 12 Another alternative to the lengthy boolean expression within the `while` loop is to define a private method that returns its value. You then replace the boolean expression in the `while` loop with a call to the private method. Define such a private method and revise the `while` loop accordingly.

Aside: The Formula for the Newton-Raphson Method

The Newton-Raphson method finds the root of an equation $f(t) = 0$. Beginning with a guess t_0 of the root, you compute a better approximation of the root, t_1, by using the following formula:

$$t_1 = t_0 - f(t_0) / f'(t_0)$$

For our problem,

$$f(t) = 4 \times e^{-t} - 2$$

so the derivative is

$$f'(t) = -4 \times e^{-t}$$

After some algebra, we get

$$t_1 = 1 + t_0 - e^{t_0}/2$$

which is the formula we used in Segment 12.25.

video*note*
A problem
solved

CHAPTER SUMMARY

- A loop typically involves four steps: initialization, testing, processing, and updating.

- A `while` statement tests its condition before executing the statements in its body. Thus, the body of the loop might not execute at all.

- The operator `++` can be used to add 1 to a variable. Similarly, the operator `--` can be used to subtract 1 from a variable.

- When read, a sentinel value signals the end of a data set.

- A common error in writing a loop causes the loop to cycle one too many or one too few times.

- Another common error in writing a loop causes the loop to cycle endlessly.

- You can use a boolean variable in the condition of a `while` statement to indicate when the repetition should end.

- When one loop is nested inside of another, the inner loop executes completely during each cycle of the outer loop.

EXERCISES

1. What are the four steps of a typical loop? Which steps are repeated?

2. Identify the four steps of the following `while` loop:

   ```
   int sum = 0;
   int count = 0;
   while (count < 10)
   {
       sum = sum + count;
       count = count + 1;
   }
   ```

3. What is the value of `sum` after the loop in the previous exercise completes its execution?

4. Revise the loop in Exercise 2 so that `count` decrements yet `sum` has the same value at the end of the loop as it does in the original loop.

5. Using the operators `++` and `--`, write statements equivalent to the following statements:

   ```
   sum = sum + 1;
   sum = sum - 1;
   ```

6. Two terms used to describe loop mistakes are "off by one" and "infinite loop." Explain the meaning of these terms and write loops that demonstrate each mistake.

7. What is the scope of a variable?

8. What is a sentinel value, and when should one be used?

9. Using the `String` method `charAt`, write a loop that computes the number of words in the sentence given as the string `sentence`.

10. Write a loop that repeatedly asks for user input until a negative number is entered. Display each value entered and a farewell message when the loop ends.

11. What does the following loop display?

    ```
    int n = 10;
    while (n > 0)
    {
        System.out.println(n);
        n = n - 3;
    }
    ```

12. What effect, if any, would replacing `>` with `<` in the loop given in the previous exercise have?

13. The *factorial* of a positive integer n is the product $1 \times 2 \times \ldots \times n$. It is denoted as $n!$. $0!$ is defined to be 1. Write a `while` loop that computes the factorial of the integer in the variable `number`. Then write a different `while` loop to compute the same thing.

14. Revise the class `SquareOfStars` in Listing 12-2 to use only one `while` loop. An `if` statement within the loop should output a new line when appropriate.

15. A *palindrome* is a word that is spelled the same both forward and backward. For example, the words "racecar" and "radar" are palindromes. Define a class of words that has a constructor and the boolean-valued method `isPalindrome`. Also write a driver to test your class.

16. Write a program that plays a guessing game with its user. The program chooses one of five colors at random and allows the player three turns to guess the color. Display messages to the player as appropriate. Define the class `ColorChooser` that has a constructor and a method `getRandomColor`. This method returns one of five colors at random as a string. This color is the one the user must guess. Define another class that plays the game.

17. Write a program that displays the first five multiples of the integer entered by the user. For example, the first five multiples of 3 are 3, 6, 9, 12, and 15.

18. Repeat the previous exercise, but instead of five multiples, let the user indicate the number of multiples.

19. Write a loop that displays the multiplication table for a given integer n. For example, the multiplication table for 5 is

×	1	2	3	4	5
1	1	2	3	4	5
2	2	4	6	8	10
3	3	6	9	12	15
4	4	8	12	16	20
5	5	10	15	20	25

20. Write a program that asks the user to enter an integer from 1 to 100 and then "guesses" at that integer by generating random integers until one matches the user's integer. Display both the guesses and the number of guesses the program takes to get the correct value.

21. A *square number*, or sometimes a *perfect square*, is an integer that can be written as the square of an integer. For example 16 is a square number, since it is the square of 4, that is, 4^2, or 4 x 4. Write a program that tests whether any positive integer entered by the user is a square number.

22. A *prime number* is an integer that is divisible only by 1 and itself. For example, 5 is a prime number, since 1 and 5 are the only divisors that result in a remainder of 0. Write a program that displays all the prime numbers from 2 to a given integer n.

PROJECTS

1. A *unique square* is a square number (see Exercise 21) that equals the sum of the consecutive integers from 1 to n. For example, 36 is a unique square, since it is equal to both 6 x 6 and the sum $1 + 2 + 3 + 4 + 5 + 6 + 7 + 8$. Define a class of integers that has the methods `isSquare` and `isUniqueSquare`. Use that class in a program that displays the first m unique square numbers for a positive integer m, as entered by the user.

2. Define a class of pyramids that use asterisks to display themselves. The height of a pyramid is given by the number of rows of asterisks in its display. For example, a pyramid having three rows would appear as follows:

```
  *
 ***
*****
```

3. Craps is a game played with two dice. Each die has six faces numbered 1 through 6. You roll the dice and sum the numbers on the two upper faces of the dice. The first roll of the dice in a craps round is called the "come out roll." In this variation of the game, if the come out roll is 2, 3, or 12—called craps—you lose. If the roll is 7 or 11—called natural—you win. If the roll is another value—that is, 4, 5, 6, 8, 9, or 10—that sum becomes the point. You continue to roll the dice until either a 7 is rolled (in which case you lose) or the same point value is rolled (in which case you win) or this was your fourth roll (the original roll and up to three more rolls). In the latter case, you pass the dice to the next player.

Write a program that plays two-player craps, where the program is one player and the user is the other. Continue play until one player either wins or loses.

4. In the poison apple game, the computer offers 15 apples to two players. The last apple is a poisonous apple and should be avoided. The players take turns removing one, two, or three apples. The player that is left having to select the last apple—the poisonous one—loses. Implement this game. Using either `Scanner` or `JOptionPane`, the program should ask for the names of the two players and, at each turn, the number of apples to be removed. Ensure that all user input is legal. Display the remaining apples after each turn, using either text characters or graphics. Determine when the game is over and announce the winner.

    For example, part of the output might appear as follows:

    ```
    Here are 15 apples:
     /  /  /  /  /  /  /  /  /  /  /  /  /  /  /
    () () () () () () () () () () () () () () ()
    Karen, choose 1, 2, or 3 of the 15 apples: 3
    We have 12 apples left:
     /  /  /  /  /  /  /  /  /  /  /  /
    () () () () () () () () () () () ()
    Dan, choose 1, 2, or 3 of the 12 apples: 1
    ```

5. The bisection method is another way to find a real root of an equation $f(x) = 0$. We begin by finding two values, a and b, such that $f(a)$ and $f(b)$ have opposite signs; that is $f(a) f(b) < 0$. In this case, a real root r will occur between a and b. If we arbitrarily let a be less than b, we have $a < r < b$. That is, the root r is in the interval (a, b). Here is an illustration of these points on the graph of $f(x)$:

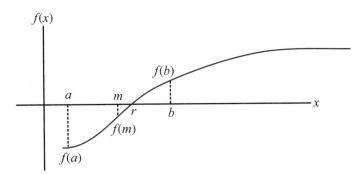

An approximation to the root r is the point m, midway between a and b. Thus,

$m = (a + b) / 2$

If $f(a) \times f(m) < 0$, the new smaller interval containing the root is (a, m). That is, we replace b with m. If $f(b) \times f(m) < 0$, the new interval containing r is (m, b). That is, we replace a with m. In case $f(m)$ is 0, m is the root. A more likely occurrence is that the interval (a, b) becomes small enough for us to conclude that either a, b, or the interval's midpoint is a reasonable approximation to the root.

In practice, two issues must be considered. Because both $f(a)$ and $f(b)$ are approaching zero, their product can be too small to represent in floating-point notation. To avoid an error, you should test the signs of $f(a)$ and $f(b)$ separately instead of testing the sign of their product. Second, because a and b are real numbers, not integers, the computation of their midpoint $(a + b) / 2$ can lead to an error. Instead use the algebraically equivalent expression $a + (b - a) / 2$.

Define a class that implements the bisection method to find the root of the equation given in Segment 12.25. Use a private method to evaluate $f(x)$.

Answers to Self-Test Questions

1.
```
int counter = 0;          Revised
while (counter < number)  Revised
{
    System.out.println(counter);
    counter = counter + 1;
} // end while
```

2. product is assigned 1 and the loop ends as soon as exponent is compared with 0.

3.
```
double product = 1;
int counter = exponent;
while (counter > 0)
{
    product = base * product;
    counter--;
} // end while
```

4.
```
int sum = 0;
int counter = 1;
while (counter <= number)
{
    sum = sum + counter;
    counter++;
} // end while
int sum = 0;
int counter = number;
while (counter > 0)
{
    sum = sum + counter;
    counter--;
} // end while
```

5.
```
double sum = 0;
int count = 0;
System.out.print("Type the next positive number or 0 to end: ");
double number = keyboard.nextDouble();
while (number > 0)
{
    sum = sum + number;
    count++;
    System.out.print("Type the next positive number or 0 to end: ");
    number = keyboard.nextDouble();
} // end while
// count is the number of positive numbers read
```

6. Not exactly. The loop requires the initial value to be added to sum, so it must be zero, not an arbitrary positive value. Thus, if number's initial value is zero, the sentinel could be -1 or any negative number.
```
double sum = 0;
double number = 0;
while (number >= 0)
{
    sum = sum + number;
    System.out.print("Type the next positive number or -1 to end: ");
    number = keyboard.nextDouble();
} // end while
```

7. 1
    3

8. Change != to <=.

9.
```java
import java.util.Scanner;
public class Question9
{
    public static void main(String[] args)
    {
        Scanner keyboard = new Scanner(System.in);
        System.out.print("How many stars in the triangle's base? ");
        int baseLength = keyboard.nextInt();
        int rowCounter = 1;
        int starsInRow = 1;
        while (rowCounter <= baseLength)
        {
            int starCounter = 1;
            while (starCounter <= starsInRow)
            {
                System.out.print("* ");
                starCounter++;
            } // end while
            System.out.println();
            rowCounter++;
            starsInRow++;
        } // end while
    } // end main
} // end Question9
```

10. **a.** Yes. **b.** Yes. **c.** No.

11. Yes, the loop still works correctly. The original code either increments counter or sets stillLooking to false. If stillLooking is false, the loop ends. If stillLooking is true, the loop only ends when counter becomes too large. In the proposed code, the same conditions exist. Although counter is always incremented, when stillLooking is false, the loop ends regardless of counter's value.

12.
```java
private static boolean stillLooking()
{
    return Math.abs(newValue - oldValue) > EPSILON * Math.abs(newValue)
} // end stillLooking
 . . .
while ((counter < LOOP_LIMIT) && stillLooking())
{
    double oldValue = newValue;
    newValue = 1 + oldValue - Math.exp(oldValue) / 2.0;
    counter++;
} // end while
```

Chapter

13

Repetition Continued

Contents

Prerequisites

Objectives

After studying this chapter, you should be able to
- Write a for loop or a do loop for a specific situation
- Transform a for loop into a while loop
- Identify logical errors in a given for loop or do loop
- Write nested for loops or do loops

The while statement that we introduced in Chapter 12 controls the repetition of any group of Java statements. Although you do not need any other way to control a loop, Java provides two other statements for this purpose. When a loop is controlled by counting, the for statement provides a convenient alternative to the while statement. And if you know that the body of a loop will execute at least once, you can use a do statement instead of a while statement. This chapter discusses both of these alternative loop-control statements.

■ The **for** Statement

13.1   When Chapter 12 introduced the notion of a loop, it presented four steps that usually occur during its execution: initialize, test, process, and update. These steps appear in a typical `while` loop as follows:

```
Initialize
while (condition) // Test
{
  Process
  Update
}
```

Any initialization precedes the `while` statement, and the process and update steps form the loop's body. The boolean expression *condition* appears in the `while` statement and is tested before the body executes.

In a **for statement**, or **for loop**, the process step forms the body, and the remaining steps are included explicitly right after the reserved word `for`. This statement has the following form:

Syntax: The for statement

```
for (initialize; condition; update)
    statement
```

Here, *initialize* is either a statement—commonly an assignment—or a comma-separated list of statements. This step occurs once, before any other aspect of the loop executes. *Condition* is a boolean expression—like the ones in a `while` statement—that is tested next. If the expression is true, the statement that forms the body of the loop executes. This statement, of course, can be a compound statement. After the body executes, the update step executes. *Update* has the same form as *initialize*. It specifies one or more statements that change the values of one or more variables in the boolean expression *condition* and possibly those in the body of the loop. Figure 13-1 illustrates the logic of a `for` statement.

> ♪ **Note:** A `for` loop has exactly the same logic as a `while` loop.

13.2   **Example.** Segment 12.3 of Chapter 12 showed a `while` loop that counted up from 1 to a given positive integer. We will now write that loop as a `for` loop instead of a `while` loop.

```
// Purpose: Writes the integers 1, 2, ..., number
//          in ascending order, one per line.
// Given:   number is an integer > 0.
int counter;
for (counter = 1; counter <= number; counter++)
   System.out.println(counter);
```

The trace of the logic given in Segment 12.3 applies to this loop as well.

Since we have declared `counter` before the `for` statement, it is available for use anywhere within the loop, as well as after the loop. You could also declare `counter` within the `for` statement, as follows:

```
for (int counter = 1; counter <= number; counter++)
   System.out.println(counter);
```

In this case, counter has meaning within the loop but not after the loop.

FIGURE 13-1   The logic of a for statement

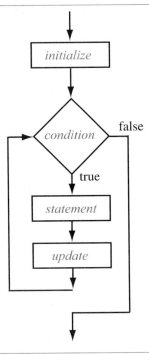

Programming Tip

Although you can always use a while loop instead of a for loop, you typically use a for statement for counted loops.

Question 1 Write a for statement that displays integers in descending order from number to 1.

13.3   **Example.** Exercise 13 of the previous chapter defined the factorial of a positive integer *n* as the product 1 x 2 x ... x *n*, and the factorial of 0 as 1. The notation *n*! denotes the factorial of *n*. That exercise asked you to write a while loop to compute it. Here we will write a for loop that makes the same computation.

The following statements compute the factorial of the integer in the variable number and place the result in the variable factorial:

```
// Purpose: Computes the factorial of an integer.
// Given:   number is an integer >= 0.
int factorial = 1;
for (int integer = 2; integer <= number; integer++)
   factorial = integer * factorial;
// factorial is the result
```

The variable factorial is declared before the for statement so that it will be available both within and after the loop. The variable integer is the loop counter, and since we do not need its value after the loop ends, we can declare it within the for statement. Notice that integer begins at 2. This approach avoids multiplying 1 by 1 for values of number greater than or equal to 2. For example, if number contains 3, the loop computes the product 3 x (2 x 1). If integer were to begin at 1 instead of 2, the loop would compute 3 x (2 x (1 x 1)). We get an added benefit when number is 0 or 1. In those cases, the expression integer <= number is false, so no multiplication takes place at all. The result in factorial is its initial value of 1, which is the correct answer.

Note: Since the boolean expression in a for statement is tested immediately after any initialization occurs, it is possible that the body of the loop will not execute at all.

13.4 **Example.** To show you various aspects of the for statement, we will revise the previous computation of the factorial in several ways. First, we could write the previous loop as follows:

```
int factorial, integer;
for (factorial = 1, integer = 2; integer <= number; integer++)
    factorial = integer * factorial;
// factorial is the result
```

Here the initialization step consists of two assignments that are separated by a comma.

Since both factorial and integer are int variables, we could declare them within the for statement as follows:

```
for (int factorial = 1, integer = 2; integer <= number; integer++)
    factorial = integer * factorial;
// factorial is unavailable here
```

Note that the data type int applies to both variables, but it is not repeated. However, the scope of these variables is the loop itself. Thus, factorial—and hence the result—is not available after the loop.

13.5 The following loop counts backward from number down to 2:

```
// Purpose: Computes the factorial of an integer.
// Given:   number is an integer >= 0.
int factorial = 1;
for (int integer = number; integer >= 2; integer--)
    factorial = integer * factorial;
// factorial is the result
```

If number is less than 2, no multiplication takes place and the result is 1.

The previous loop retains the original value of number, but if you do not need it, you can use number as the loop counter. Since we are assuming that number already has a value, we can write the following loop:

```
// Given: number is an integer >= 0.
int factorial = 1;
for (; number >= 2; number--)
    factorial = number * factorial;
// factorial is the result
```

We have omitted the initialization portion of the for statement, but have retained the semicolon.

Note: You can omit either the initialization or the update step or both in a for statement, but you must retain the two semicolons. Although you legally can omit the condition, doing so is not recommended.

Question 2 The following revision of the previous for loop is legal. What logical problem does it cause?

```
for (int factorial = 1; number >= 2; number--)
    factorial = number * factorial;
```

13.6   **Example.** Segment 12.7 in Chapter 12 used a while loop to compute the sum of numbers that a user enters at the keyboard so we could compute their average. Here we use a for loop to accomplish the same task. Note that the for statement, like the while statement, can have a compound statement for its body.

```
// Purpose: Computes the sum of numbers read from the user.
// Given:   howMany is the number of numbers to be read.
double sum = 0; // sum of the numbers read
for (int counter = 1; counter <= howMany; counter++)
{
    System.out.println("Please enter the next number: ");
    double number = keyboard.nextDouble();
    sum = sum + number;
} // end for
```

At this point, sum contains the sum of the numbers read. The average of these numbers is the quotient of sum and howMany.

If you wanted to initialize sum within the for statement, you would have to declare its data type and counter's data type before the for statement, because the two types are different. So you could begin the previous loop as follows:

```
double sum;       // sum of the numbers read
int    counter; // loop counter
for (sum = 0, counter = 1; counter <= howMany; counter++)
```

> **Note:** When you declare two or more variables within a for statement, the variables must have the same data type. If they do not, and you want to initialize them within the for statement, declare them before the for statement.

13.7   **Example: Nested loops.** The program in Listing 12-2 in the previous chapter uses nested while loops to display a square pattern of asterisks, such as

```
* * *
* * *
* * *
```

Here we use nested for loops to accomplish the same task:

```
System.out.print("What is the length of the square's side? ");
int sideLength = keyboard.nextInt();
for (int rowCount = 1; rowCount <= sideLength; rowCount++)
{
    for (int starCount = 1; starCount <= sideLength; starCount++)
        System.out.print("* ");
    System.out.println();
} // end for
```

The first (outer) for statement considers each row. For each row, an inner for statement displays the stars in that row. When the inner loop ends, a println advances to the next line of output, and rowCount in the outer loop is incremented.

13.8 **Examples: Loop control using characters or real values.** The variable that controls a counted loop need not have an integer data type. The following loop uses a char variable to display the letters in the alphabet:

```
System.out.println("The letters of the alphabet are\n");
for (char letter = 'a'; letter <= 'z'; letter++)
    System.out.print(letter + " ");
System.out.println();
```

Since letters are represented by consecutive integers in the Unicode system, the expression letter++ advances the variable letter to the next letter.

The following loop uses real values in its loop control:

```
System.out.println("The numbers 1 to 5 at steps of 0.25 are\n");
for (double real = 1; real <= 5.0; real = real + 0.25)
    System.out.print(real + " ");
System.out.println();
```

Although possible, using real numbers to control a loop is risky, since not all real numbers can be represented exactly. The previous loop causes no problem, because 0.25 has an exact representation in binary. Thus, the loop ends after displaying 5.0, as you would expect. However, if we changed the step to 0.2 instead of 0.25, the loop would end after displaying 4.800000000000002 and would thus cycle one time fewer than expected.

 Question 3 Write a for statement that displays every other uppercase letter in the alphabet.

13.9 **Example: An erroneous semicolon.** Suppose that you accidentally write a semicolon at the end of the line that begins with for. For example, the following loop is supposed to display the integers from 1 to 5 on separate lines:

```
int counter;
for (counter = 1; counter <= 5; counter++); // wrong semicolon
    System.out.println(counter);
```

Instead it displays 6. Because of the semicolon, the for statement has an empty body. The println statement displays the current value of counter, which is 6 after the loop finishes.

If you declared counter within the for statement, as in

```
for (int counter = 1; counter <= 5; counter++); // wrong semicolon
    System.out.println(counter); // syntax error: counter is undefined
```

The for statement

you would get a syntax error, because counter is undefined after the for loop.

It is possible for a correct for loop to have an empty body. If you decide to write such a loop, ending the for statement with a semicolon can cause confusion for those who read your program. A pair of braces to indicate an empty body can be a better alternative. In both cases, adding comments is helpful.

Using an Enumeration with a for Statement

13.10 The for statement has another form when you want to repeat statements for each object in an enumeration. For example, if you define

```
enum Suit {CLUBS, DIAMONDS, HEARTS, SPADES}
```

the for loop

```
for (Suit s : Suit.values())
    System.out.println(s);
```

displays

> CLUBS
> DIAMONDS
> HEARTS
> SPADES

You declare a variable to the left of a colon in the `for` statement. To the right of the colon, you represent the values that the variable will have. For the enumeration `Suit`, the expression `Suit.values()` represents the four possible values `CLUBS`, `DIAMONDS`, `HEARTS`, and `SPADES`.

This kind of loop—called a **for-each loop**—can be used with other collections of data, as you will see later in this book.

The do Statement

13.11   You have seen that the logic of a `for` loop is identical to the logic of a `while` loop. Both loops can end immediately after the first test of a given boolean expression without executing the body of the loop. This behavior is desirable for most loops, so these two statements are the ones that you usually will use for your loops.

Occasionally, however, you will know in advance that the body of a loop must execute at least once. Although you could choose either a `while` statement or a `for` statement to implement such a loop, you could also use the **do statement.** The do statement executes its body, which includes the update step, before evaluating a boolean expression to decide whether to continue the iteration.

The do statement has the following form:

Java

Syntax: The do statement

```
do
    statement
while (condition);   ◄────── The semicolon is required
```

Typically, *statement* is a compound statement. Note the semicolon at the end of the do statement.

---

videonote
The do statement

After executing the statement(s) in the body of a do statement, the boolean expression *condition* is evaluated. If it is true, the body of the loop executes again. Otherwise, the loop ends. Figure 13-2 illustrates this logic.

FIGURE 13-2   The logic of a do statement

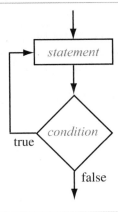

13.12   **Example.** Once more, we solve our simple problem of displaying the integers from 1 to a given

positive integer. Segments 12.3 and 13.2 used a `while` statement and a `for` statement, respectively, in their solutions to this problem. Here we use a do statement so that you can compare the three solutions:

```
// Purpose: Writes integers 1, 2, ..., number
//          in ascending order, one per line.
// Given:   number is an integer > 0.
int counter = 1;
do
{
   System.out.println(counter);
   counter++;
} while (counter <= number);
```

The do statement is more like a `while` statement than a `for` statement. Any initialization occurs before the statement itself. The body most often is a compound statement that contains the processing and update steps of the loop. It is not until the body executes completely that the boolean expression is evaluated. In this example, `counter` is displayed, incremented, and finally compared to `number` to see whether the loop should continue or end. Whether the `while` portion appears on the same line with the closing brace or on the next line is a matter of personal style. In either case, it must end with a semicolon.

For this example, the do statement offers no advantage over the `while` and `for` statements. Since this loop is counted, we would favor a `for` statement over the other choices.

13.13   **Example.** Segment 12.9 in Chapter 12 asked you to imagine a program that reads a Java reserved

word as input and displays a description of its meaning and use. Using a class `JavaWords` and its method `getMeaning`, we wrote a `while` loop that could appear in that program. That loop, however, did not check whether the user's input was a legal Java reserved word.

In this example, we insist that the user type a valid reserved word by using another method, `isValid`, of the class `JavaWords` and a do statement:

```
JavaWords table = new JavaWords();
String word;
do
{
   System.out.print("Enter a Java reserved word: ");
   word = keyboard.next();
} while (!table.isValid(word));
System.out.println(table.getMeaning(word));
```

If the input string does not match a word in `table`, the loop continues and prompts the user again to enter a reserved word. When the loop ends, the method `getMeaning` returns the description of the given word. Exercise 15 at the end of this chapter asks you to repeat this process for another reserved word, as was done in Segment 12.9.

Question 4 What `while` loop is equivalent to the previous do loop?

Question 5 Consider the do loop in Segment 13.13 and the `while` loop that answers the previous question. Which of these loops allows you to more easily notify the user when the input is an illegal word?

Question 6 Suppose that a program reads an integer and requires it to be nonzero. Write a do loop that continues to read integers until the value entered is not zero.

Question 7 Repeat the previous question, but use a while loop instead.

Question 8 Write a do loop that counts from 1 to 100, displaying ten integers per line. *Hint*: Every tenth integer is divisible by 10.

CHAPTER SUMMARY

- In a for loop, the process step forms the body. The initialization, test, and update steps are included explicitly right after the reserved word for.

- A for loop has exactly the same logic as a while loop. You typically use a for statement for counted loops.

- A for statement tests its condition immediately after any initialization occurs. Thus, the body of the loop might not execute at all.

- You can omit either the initialization or the update step or both in a for statement, but you must retain the two semicolons.

- When you declare two or more variables within a for statement, the variables must have the same data type. If they do not, declare them before the for statement.

- The do statement executes its body, which includes the update step, before evaluating a boolean expression to decide whether to continue the iteration.

- You must write a semicolon at the end of a do statement.

- Use a do statement when you know that the body of the loop will execute at least once.

EXERCISES

1. When should you use a for statement instead of a while statement? When should you use a while statement instead of a for statement?

2. What is the difference between a do statement and a while statement?

3. In the following code, label the four steps of a typical loop:

```
int count = 0;
for (int tracker = 0; tracker < 10; tracker++)
    count++;
```

4. Given a positive integer *n* in the variable number, write a for statement that computes the sum of the consecutive integers $1 + 2 + \ldots + n$.

5. Write a for statement that computes the sum of the first ten even integers. Perform the same computation using a while statement.

6. Write a for statement that raises a real number to an integer power. Perform the same computation using a while statement.

7. Given a positive integer *n* in the variable number, write a for statement that computes the sum of *n* real numbers entered by the user. Perform the same computation using a while statement.

8. Repeat Exercises 4 through 7, but write a do statement instead.

9. What is the scope of the variable counter in Segment 13.6?

10. Write a for-each statement to display each color in the following enumeration as a string on a separate line:

```
enum BasicColor {RED, BLUE, GREEN}
```

11. What output is displayed by the following code?

```
for (double sample = 2; sample > 0; sample = sample - 0.5)
    System.out.println(sample + " ");
```

12. What output is displayed by the following code?

```
int n = 1024;
int mark = 0;
for (int counter = 1; counter < n; counter = 2 * counter)
    mark++;
System.out.println(n + " " + mark);
```

13. Replace the following for statement with an equivalent while statement.

```
for (int timer = 10; timer > 0; timer = timer - 2)
    System.out.println("Hello " + timer);
```

14. Will the following loop end when the user enters either N or n as input? Explain.

```
Scanner keyboard = new Scanner(System.in);
char response;
do
{
    System.out.println("Processing ...\n");

    . . .

    System.out.print("Again? (Y or N): ");
    response = keyboard.next();
} while ((response != 'N') || (response != 'n'));
```

15. Embed the do loop given in Segment 13.13 into the while loop given in Segment 12.9 of Chapter 12 so that a user can enter as many words as desired. A sentinel value ends this process. If a word is a Java reserved word, its meaning is displayed. If it is illegal, it is ignored and another word is requested from the user.

16. The *Fibonacci sequence* is defined as follows:

F_0 and F_1 are 0 and 1, respectively.
$F_i = F_{i-1} + F_{i-2}$, when $i > 1$.

Write a Java program that uses a for statement to display the terms in the Fibonacci sequence from F_0 to F_n for a given nonnegative integer n provided by the user. What is the largest value of n for which your code computes F_n? What happens when n exceeds this largest value, and why does it happen?

17. Write a Java program that reads several real numbers entered by the user, computes their average, and finds the largest and smallest values among them. Display these values, along with the numbers that were read. Use a do statement.

18. Repeat the guessing game described in Exercise 20 of the previous chapter, but use a do statement instead of a while statement.

19. A *divisor*, or *factor*, of an integer n is an integer that divides n evenly without a remainder. A *proper divisor* of n is a divisor of n that is not equal to n. For example, the proper divisors of 8 are 1, 2, and 4. Two integers are said to be *amicable* if each is the sum of the proper divisors of the other. For example, 220 and 284 are amicable. The proper divisors of 220 are 1, 2, 4, 5, 10, 11, 20, 22, 44, 55, and 110. The sum of these divisors is 284. Further, the proper divisors of 284 are 1, 2, 4, 71, and 142, and the sum of these divisors is 220.

Write a Java program that finds the first five pairs of amicable integers.

20. One way to compute the square root of a real number x is to use the *Babylonian algorithm*. You begin by guessing that the square root of x is x / 2. The steps of this algorithm are as follows:

```
guess = x / 2
previousGuess = 0
Repeat until guess is within 1% of previousGuess
{
    r = x / guess
    previousGuess = guess
    guess = (guess + r) / 2
}
```

Write a program that reads a number and computes its square root by using the Babylonian algorithm. Display your results to two decimal places. You should get an accurate answer even for large numbers.

PROJECTS

1. Design, implement, and demonstrate a class of multiplication tables. An example of a multiplication table is given in Exercise 19 of the previous chapter.

2. Design, implement, and demonstrate a class of diamonds that display themselves as text using a character provided by the client. For example, a diamond of height 6 constructed from asterisks will display as follows:

```
   *
  ***
 *****
 *****
  ***
   *
```

Besides specifying a character, the client of your class also will specify one of three possible heights for each diamond—6, 12, or 22 characters—by providing one of the strings "short", "average", or "tall".

3. Project 3 in the previous chapter describes the dice game of craps. In this variation, one player continues to roll until he or she either wins or loses. The four-roll limit does not apply. Write a program that simulates a one-player game that ends in a win or loss. Without user intervention, simulate 10,000 games by this one player. After the last game is played, display the number of wins, the number of losses, and the probability of winning (the number of wins divided by 10,000).

4. In the Race to 100 game, a board has 100 consecutive squares. Beginning at the first square, two players alternate rolling two dice and advancing forward the number of spaces shown on the dice. The first player to reach the 100th square wins the game. A player who rolls a 7 must move backward either seven spaces or to the first square. A player who rolls a 2 or a 12 loses a turn. If a player lands on the other player's square, the other player must go back to the first square.

Design, implement, and demonstrate the classes needed to play this game. Display the board configuration after each move. You can write this game for either two human players or one human versus the program. Moreover, you could provide a choice of these two options.

ANSWERS TO SELF-TEST QUESTIONS

1.
```
for (int counter = number; counter >= 1; counter--)
    System.out.println(counter);
```

2. The result in `factorial` is not available after the loop.

3.
```java
for (char letter = 'A'; letter <= 'Z'; letter = letter + 2)
    System.out.print(letter + " ");
System.out.println();
```

4.
```java
JavaWords table = new JavaWords();
System.out.print("Enter a Java reserved word: ");
String word = keyboard.next();
while (!table.isValid(word))
{
    System.out.print("Enter a Java reserved word: ");
    word = keyboard.next();
} // end while
System.out.println(table.getMeaning(word));
```

5. The while loop cycles only for illegal words, so you can add a println statement to the beginning of its body to tell the user that the preceding input is illegal. The do loop would require an if statement after word is read to check its validity. This logic is awkward, as the same test is made in the while portion of the do loop.

6.
```java
int number;
do
{
    System.out.print("Enter a non-zero integer: ");
    number = keyboard.nextInt();
} while (number == 0);
```

7.
```java
System.out.print("Enter a non-zero integer: ");
int number = keyboard.nextInt();
while (number == 0)
{
    System.out.print("Enter a non-zero integer: ");
    number = keyboard.nextInt();
} // end while
```

8.
```java
int nextInteger = 1;
do
{
    System.out.print(nextInteger + " ");
    if ( (nextInteger % 10) == 0)
        System.out.println();
    nextInteger++;
} while (nextInteger <= 100);
```

Chapter

14

Repetition When Drawing

Contents

Prerequisites

Objectives

After studying this chapter, you should be able to
• Write an application that displays a simple drawing that involves repetition
• Write a loop that affects the characteristics of a graphical drawing

We will now use the statements introduced in the previous two chapters to produce graphical output. With the added ability of repetition, our graphics can be more complex, as the examples in this chapter will show.

A Problem Solved: Displaying a Row of Dots (Reprise)

> Paint a circular disk, or dot, a random number of times in a row. The random number should be chosen from the integers 1 through 5.

You saw a solution to this problem in Listing 11-6 of Chapter 11. That solution used a switch statement without break statements. Now that you know how to use the while statement, we can write a much better solution to this problem. As you will see, changing the maximum number of dots will be simple and will not add statements to the solution. Such would not be the case for the solution in Listing 11-6.

14.1   **The solution.** We begin with the class Dot, which we defined in Listing 11-5 of Chapter 11. Recall that a Dot object has a given diameter and the method display. This method enables us to display a dot at any given position in a given color.

The panel in Listing 11-6 uses a switch statement to paint dots repeatedly in a row from right to left. Here we use the same panel but replace the switch statement with a while statement. It paints a dot and then changes the *x*-coordinate of the dot's center in preparation for the next iteration. The effect is to paint the dot repeatedly, moving from left to right. To control the iteration, our while statement counts down from a random integer, numberOfTimes, to 1. Recall that numberOfTimes is a data field that the constructor initializes. In Listing 11-6, we declared numberOfTimes as final, since after its initialization by the constructor, its value does not change. Here, however, our loop control does change the value of this variable, so it cannot be final. Listing 14-1 shows the revised method paintComponent for the class RowOfDotsPanel. The driver and output for this panel are the same as shown in Listing 11-7.

LISTING 14-1   Using a loop to paint a row of dots

```
< The import statements for the class RowOfDotsPanel are the same as shown in Listing 11-6. >
. . .
public class RowOfDotsPanel extends JPanel
{
    private int numberOfTimes; // not final

    < Other data fields and the constructor for this class are the same as shown in Listing 11-6. >
    . . .

    public void paintComponent(Graphics pen)
    {
        int xCenter = X_CENTER;
        while (numberOfTimes > 0)
        {
            aDot.display(xCenter, Y_CENTER, COLOR, pen);
            xCenter = xCenter + GAP;
            numberOfTimes--;
        } // end while
    } // end paintComponent
} // end RowOfDotsPanel
```

Question 1 What changes would you make to the loop in Listing 14-1 so that it counts up instead of down?

Question 2 Since the loop in Listing 14-1 iterates a random number of times, how can you test it to be sure that it works correctly?

Question 3 What changes would you make to the loop in Listing 14-1 so that it paints the dot repeatedly from right to left without changing the result?

Question 4 What changes would you make to the loop in Listing 14-1 so that it uses xCenter instead of numberOfTimes to control the number of iterations?

Question 5 What changes would you make to the loop in Listing 14-1 so that it uses a for statement instead of a while statement?

■ A Problem Solved: The Quahog Shell

> A quahog (qwoh' hog) is a hard-shell clam found on the Atlantic coast of North America. The drawing in Figure 14-1a resembles this creature. We will define a class that displays this drawing.

FIGURE 14-1   (a) A drawing of a quahog shell; (b) the shell with lines added indicating the base and center of the ovals

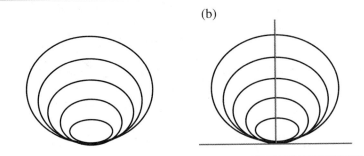

(a)   (b)

14.2   **The class Quahog.** Our class of quahogs will have only a constructor and a method display, as Listing 14-2 shows. The constructor sets the height of the quahog. Notice how the constructor ensures that this height is at least 40 pixels.

The drawing of a quahog consists of several ovals whose bottom edges meet at the same point. This point is on the horizontal line that just touches the base of each oval, as Figure 14-1b shows. From this point, we have drawn a vertical line that is perpendicular to the horizontal line. The center of each oval lies on this vertical line. Thus, the *x*-coordinates of the centers are equal, while the *y*-coordinates increase as the ovals become smaller. As you move from the outermost oval to the innermost one, the height and width of each oval decreases.

The method display begins by drawing the largest oval. It continues to draw smaller ovals until the height of the last oval drawn reaches a certain minimum value. Notice the variable height in the while statement that controls the repetition. The value of height decreases at each iteration until it reaches SMALLEST_OVAL. So here we are concerned with the height of the largest and smallest ovals and not with the number of ovals drawn. The computations used to decrease the size of the ovals are somewhat arbitrary but were chosen to yield a reasonable drawing.

The panel and driver needed to complete our program are similar to those we have written in the past.

LISTING 14-2   The class Quahog

```java
/** Quahog.java by F. M. Carrano
    Represents a quahog shell.
 */
import java.awt.Graphics;
public class Quahog
{
   private int height;
   private static final int OVAL_GAP = 20;
   private static final int SMALLEST_OVAL = 20;
   private static final int SHORTEST_QUAHOG = 2 * SMALLEST_OVAL;

   public Quahog(int quahogHeight)
   {
      height = Math.max(quahogHeight, SHORTEST_QUAHOG);
   } // end constructor

   public void display(int xCenter, int yCenter, Graphics pen)
   {
      while (height >= SMALLEST_OVAL)
      {
         int width = height + OVAL_GAP;
         int left = xCenter - width / 2;
         int top = yCenter - height / 2;
         pen.drawOval(left, top, width, height);
         yCenter = yCenter + OVAL_GAP / 2;
         height = height - OVAL_GAP;
      } // end while
   } // end display
} // end Quahog
```

Question 6 Will the method `display` always draw at least one oval? Why or why not?

Question 7 Is it possible to replace the `while` loop in `display` with a do loop? If so, write the loop. If not, explain why.

Question 8 Is it possible to replace the `while` loop in `display` with a for loop? If so, write the loop. If not, explain why.

■ A Problem Solved: Circles and Squares

> Randomly paint either a circle or a square in random positions and in random colors. Continue painting until the random point at which you would paint either a circle or a square has equal *x*- and *y*-coordinates. The diameter of the circles should equal the side of the squares. Figure 14-2 provides an example of the desired output from the program.

FIGURE 14-2   Sample output from the proposed program to paint circles and
squares

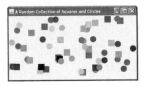

14.3   **A solution.** Let's make use of the class `Square`, as given in Listing 11-2, and the class `Dot`, as given
in Listing 11-5. The panel in Listing 14-3 has an instance of each of these classes as two of its data
fields. We use the `display` methods of these two objects to paint either the dot or the square in a
given color and position. The object, its color, and its position are chosen according to random
numbers that we will generate. This process, as well as the creation of the drawing, will be done
within the panel's `paintComponent` method.

LISTING 14-3   Painting circles and squares in random positions

```java
/** CirclesAndSquares.java by F. M. Carrano
    Paints a circle and a square in random colors and positions until
    one is encountered whose center has equal x- and y-coordinates.
*/
import java.awt.Color;
import java.awt.Dimension;
import java.awt.Graphics;
import javax.swing.JPanel;
import java.util.Random;

public class CirclesAndSquaresPanel extends JPanel
{
   private final Dot     aDot;
   private final Square aSquare;

   private static final Random randomInteger = new Random();

   private static final int PANEL_WIDTH = 400;
   private static final int PANEL_HEIGHT = 200;

   private static final int SIZE = 20; // circle diameter or square side
   private static final int HALF_SIZE = SIZE / 2;

   // minimum and maximum coordinates of center of circle or square
   private static final int X_MIN = HALF_SIZE;
   private static final int Y_MIN = HALF_SIZE;
   private static final int X_MAX = PANEL_WIDTH - HALF_SIZE;
   private static final int Y_MAX = PANEL_HEIGHT - HALF_SIZE;

   public CirclesAndSquaresPanel()
```

```
      {
         setPreferredSize(new Dimension(PANEL_WIDTH, PANEL_HEIGHT));
         aDot = new Dot(SIZE);
         aSquare = new Square(SIZE);
      } // end default constructor

      /** Displays the pattern of circles and squares. */
      public void paintComponent(Graphics pen)
      {
         // get coordinates of center of circle or square
         int xCenter = randomInteger.nextInt(X_MAX - X_MIN) + X_MIN;
         int yCenter = randomInteger.nextInt(Y_MAX - Y_MIN) + Y_MIN;
         while (xCenter != yCenter)
         {
            // RGB components of color
            int red   = randomInteger.nextInt(256);
            int green = randomInteger.nextInt(256);
            int blue  = randomInteger.nextInt(256);

            Color randomColor = new Color(red, green, blue);

            // paint the circle or square at a random position
            int whichOne = randomInteger.nextInt() % 2;
            if (whichOne == 0)
               aDot.display(xCenter, yCenter, randomColor, pen);
            else
            {
               int xCorner = xCenter - HALF_SIZE;
               int yCorner = yCenter - HALF_SIZE;
               aSquare.display(xCorner, yCorner, randomColor, pen);
            } // end if

            xCenter = randomInteger.nextInt(X_MAX - X_MIN) + X_MIN;
            yCenter = randomInteger.nextInt(Y_MAX - Y_MIN) + Y_MIN;
         } // end while
      } // end paintComponent
   } // end CirclesAndSquaresPanel
```

14.4   We begin by generating random x- and y-coordinates that will be the location of the next shape. Let's decide that the positions of the circle and square are defined by the coordinates of their centers. To paint these shapes completely within the drawing window, we set minimum and maximum values—x_{min}, y_{min}, x_{max}, and y_{max}—for their coordinates. These values depend on the size of the drawing window and the size of the circle or square, as Figure 14-3 shows. Note that s, w, and h in the figure correspond to the constants SIZE, PANEL_WIDTH, and PANEL_HEIGHT, respectively, in Listing 14-3.

FIGURE 14-3   The bounds on the coordinates for the centers of the circles and
                   squares

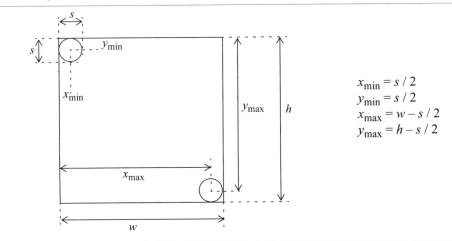

$$x_{\min} = s / 2$$
$$y_{\min} = s / 2$$
$$x_{\max} = w - s / 2$$
$$y_{\max} = h - s / 2$$

14.5   Using the class Random and its method nextInt, we can generate a random integer r_n such that

$$0 \le r_n < n$$

But what is n? Since the random x-coordinate must lie between $x_{\min}$ and $x_{\max}$, we can add $x_{\min}$ to the previous inequality to get

$$x_{\min} \le r_n + x_{\min} < n + x_{\min}$$

By naming this upper bound $x_{\max}$, we have

$$n + x_{\min} = x_{\max}$$

or

$$n = x_{\max} - x_{\min}$$

If the Java constants X_MIN and X_MAX represent $x_{\min}$ and $x_{\max}$, respectively, the expression randomInteger.nextInt(X_MAX - X_MIN) will give us r_n. Adding X_MIN to r_n gives us a random x-coordinate, as follows:

```
int xCenter = randomInteger.nextInt(X_MAX - X_MIN) + X_MIN;
```

Similarly, we can write

```
int yCenter = randomInteger.nextInt(Y_MAX - Y_MIN) + Y_MIN;
```

to get a random y-coordinate. Notice that the random coordinates are generated both prior to the while statement in Listing 14-3 and at the end of its body.

14.6   We also need to choose a color at random. Rather than choosing from among several predefined colors, such as Color.RED, we generate three random integers between 0 and 255 to represent the red, green, and blue components of a Color object. The class Color has several constructors, among which is the following one:

>
> **Note: A constructor in the class** `Color`
>
>   `public Color(int red, int blue, int green)`
>
> This constructor creates an object to represent a color having the specified red, blue, and green components. Each component must be between 0 and 255.

videonote
Repeatedly drawing
a shape

We use this constructor and the random integers to create a `Color` object. We then use this object to set the color of the pen before painting.

        Finally, to decide whether to paint a circle or a square, we generate a random integer. If it is even, we paint a circle; otherwise we paint a square.

▇ A Problem Solved: The Quilt

> Nancy wants to design a quilt composed of squares whose colors are chosen at random. The quilt will contain ten rows of ten squares each. Let's help her by writing a class `Quilt` of quilts. Figure 14-4 illustrates what a `display` method for a `Quilt` object might draw.

FIGURE 14-4   Sample output from a `Quilt` object's `display` method

14.7   **The class of quilts.** Once again, we can use the class `Square` given in Listing 11-2. An object of `Square` can be a data field of our new class `Quilt`, as Listing 14-4 shows. This `Square` object has a method `display` that paints the square in a given color and at a given position. By invoking this method from `Quilt`'s `display` method and within two nested `for` loops, we can paint the quilt. The inner loop will paint the squares in a row. The outer loop will cause the inner loop to execute completely for each of the required rows.

        Each of the `for` loops is a counted loop. The outer loop uses the variable `row` to count from 1 to `squaresPerSide`. The inner loop uses the variable `column` to count from 1 to `squaresPerSide`. Although this logic helps ensure that we will paint the correct number of squares, we must be sure to paint them in the correct locations. Thus, we need variables, `x` and `y`, to record the coordinates of each square. Changing the values of these variables is our challenge here.

        If the upper left corner of the quilt has the coordinates (`xCorner`, `yCorner`), we initialize `y` to `yCorner` before the outer loop. Thus, `y` is the *y*-coordinate of all of the squares in the first row. The body of the outer loop begins by initializing `x` to `xCorner`. Now `x` is the *x*-coordinate of the first square in the first row. Using `x`, the inner loop displays a row of squares. This inner loop begins by calling a private method `getRandomColor` to choose the color. We are now ready to paint a square by calling its `display` method. The inner loop ends by adding `squareSide` to `x` to get the *x*-coordinate of the next square. The inner `for` statement then increments its counter `column`. When the inner loop completes its execution, the outer loop adds `squareSide` to `y` to get the *y*-coordinate of the next row of squares and then increments its counter `row`.

The private method getRandomColor uses a switch statement to choose a color at random, as we did in Listing 11-3 of Chapter 11. That panel class paints a square in one of five colors chosen at random. By defining this private method, we were able to concentrate on the logic of the nested loops within the method display without the distraction of a lengthy switch statement. We could have defined and used this method in Listing 11-3, and simply reused it here. Note that we have carefully documented the method's requirements in case we want to use it elsewhere.

LISTING 14-4   The class Quilt

```java
/** Quilt.java by F. M. Carrano
    A square quilt composed of smaller squares,
    each painted in one of five colors chosen at random.
*/
import java.awt.Graphics;
import java.awt.Color;
import java.util.Random;

public class Quilt
{
    private final Square aSquare;
    private final int squaresPerSide;

    private static final int    NUMBER_OF_COLORS = 5;
    private static final Color FIRST_COLOR    = Color.RED;
    private static final Color SECOND_COLOR   = Color.BLUE;
    private static final Color THIRD_COLOR    = Color.GREEN;
    private static final Color FOURTH_COLOR   = Color.CYAN;
    private static final Color FIFTH_COLOR    = Color.ORANGE;
    private static final Color DEFAULT_COLOR = Color.BLACK;

    private static final Random generator = new Random();

    /** Constructs a square quilt having a given number of
        squares per side. Component squares are equal in size
        and have a given dimension. */
    public Quilt(int numberSquaresPerSide, int squareSide)
    {
        squaresPerSide = numberSquaresPerSide;
        aSquare = new Square(squareSide);
    } // end constructor

    /** Displays a quilt at a given position, where (xCorner, yCorner)
        are the coordinates of its upper left corner. */
    public void display(int xCorner, int yCorner, Graphics pen)
    {
        int y = yCorner;
        int squareSide = aSquare.getSide();
        for (int row = 1; row <= squaresPerSide; row++)
```

```
      {
         int x = xCorner;
         for (int column = 1; column <= squaresPerSide; column++)
         {
            Color squareColor = getRandomColor();
            aSquare.display(x, y, squareColor, pen);
            x = x + squareSide;
         } // end for

         y = y + squareSide;
      } // end for
   } // end display

   // Returns one of five colors at random.
   // Requirements: generator is an instance of Random;
   // NUMBER_OF_COLORS is a named integer constant;
   // FIRST_COLOR, SECOND_COLOR, THIRD_COLOR, FOURTH_COLOR,
   // FIFTH_COLOR, and DEFAULT_COLOR are named Color constants.
   private Color getRandomColor()
   {
      Color squareColor;
      int colorChoice = generator.nextInt(NUMBER_OF_COLORS);
      switch (colorChoice)
      {
         case 0:
            squareColor = FIRST_COLOR;
            break;
         case 1:
            squareColor = SECOND_COLOR;
            break;
         case 2:
            squareColor = THIRD_COLOR;
            break;
         case 3:
            squareColor = FOURTH_COLOR;
            break;
         case 4:
            squareColor = FIFTH_COLOR;
            break;
         default:
            squareColor = DEFAULT_COLOR;
            break;
      } // end switch

      return squareColor;
```

```
      } // end getRandomColor
} // end Quilt
```

The panel that creates and displays a Quilt object is straightforward, as is the driver for the panel. Both are left as exercises.

Question 9 How would you revise the loops in Listing 14-4 to use while statements instead of for statements?

Question 10 Define a class QuiltPanel that creates and displays a Quilt object.

Question 11 Define a driver for the panel you defined in the previous question.

14.8   **Alternate loop control.** Although the counted loops in Quilt's display method (Listing 14-4) ensure that we paint the correct number of squares, we could control the loops by comparing the coordinates of each square with appropriate limits. Such limits could be the *x*-coordinate of the quilt's right edge and the *y*-coordinate of its bottom edge. Thus, we could define the following variables:

```
int quiltSide = squaresPerSide * squareSide;
int xRight   = xCorner + quiltSide;
int yBottom = yCorner + quiltSide;
```

Varying repetition

The outer loop could use a while statement to compare the *y*-coordinate with yBottom, and the inner loop could use a while statement to compare the *x*-coordinate with xRight. The loops would then appear as follows:

```
int y = yCorner;
while (y < yBottom)
{
   int x = xCorner;
   while (x < xRight)
   {
      Color squareColor = getRandomColor();
      aSquare.display(x, y, squareColor, pen);
      x = x + squareSide;
   } // end while

   y = y + squareSide;
} // end while
```

This approach can be more difficult than using the counted loops shown in Listing 14-4, as computing the correct limits for the *x*- and *y*-coordinates can be elusive.

■ A Problem Solved: A Random Walk

Imagine that you are standing at the center of a square playing field. You may take a step in a direction that is perpendicular to any side. Suppose that you repeatedly take such steps in random directions. What path will you take before you reach one of the sides? Figure 14-5 shows one such path, assuming that your steps all have the same length. Notice that you might retrace or cross your path on your journey. Write a program that displays such paths. You will find that they can be quite complex.

FIGURE 14-5 A path from the center of a square to one of its sides, one step at a time

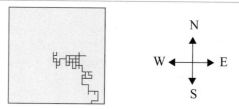

14.9 **The walker.** We begin by writing a class to represent a walker. With the square aligned to the points on a compass, the legal moves will be toward the north, south, east, and west. In Figure 14-5, north will be toward the top of the square, and east will be toward the right side.

This class must know the position and size of the square and be able to generate random numbers. A method `walk` will trace the path taken by a walker. Since the walker will always take at least one step to move from the center of the square to one of its sides, a loop within `walk` that controls the steps must execute at least once. Therefore, we can use a do statement to control it.

The class in Listing 14-5 begins with constants that define the square's location and size. We also define constants that represent four compass points and the step size. We will use these constants in a `switch` statement within the loop.

Since we know the coordinates of the square's upper left corner, we know the location of its top and left edges. We also will need the location of the square's bottom and right edges to know when the path has reached an edge. Thus, we define the variables `squareRight` and `squareBottom`. Next we compute the coordinates of the center of the square so that we can begin the path.

Each cycle of the loop within the method `walk` takes a step in a direction indicated by a random integer between 0 and 3. We draw a line segment to extend the path and adjust the coordinates of our current position accordingly. Then, if we have reached one of the square's sides, we exit the loop.

LISTING 14-5 The class `RandomWalker`

```java
/** RandomWalker.java by F. M. Carrano
    Draws the path of a random walker who starts at the center
    of a square and stops at the square's perimeter.
*/
import java.awt.Graphics;
import java.util.Random;

public class RandomWalker
{
   private final int left; // position of square's left edge
   private final int top;  // position of square's top edge
   private final int side; // length of square's side
   private final int step; // size of walker's step

   private static final Random generator = new Random();

   private static final int NORTH = 0, SOUTH = 1, EAST = 2, WEST = 3;
```

```java
public RandomWalker(int squareLeft, int squareTop, int squareSide,
                    int stepSize)
{
   left = squareLeft;
   top = squareTop;
   side = squareSide;
   step = stepSize;
} // end constructor

public void walk(Graphics pen)
{
   pen.drawRect(left, top, side, side); // draw square

   // describe rest of square
   int right = left + side;
   int bottom = top + side;
   int halfSide = side / 2;
   int xCenter = left + halfSide;
   int yCenter = top + halfSide;

   // current and next positions of walker
   int xCurrent = xCenter;
   int yCurrent = yCenter;
   int xNext, yNext;

   // take a walk
   do
   {
      int direction = generator.nextInt(4); // 0 - 3
      switch (direction)
      {
         case NORTH:
            xNext = xCurrent;
            yNext = yCurrent - step;
            break;
         case SOUTH:
            xNext = xCurrent;
            yNext = yCurrent + step;
            break;
         case EAST:
            xNext = xCurrent + step;
            yNext = yCurrent;
            break;
         case WEST:
            xNext = xCurrent - step;
            yNext = yCurrent;
```

```
                        break;
                    default:
                        xNext = 0;
                        yNext = 0;
                        break;
                } // end switch

                pen.drawLine(xCurrent, yCurrent, xNext, yNext);
                xCurrent = xNext;
                yCurrent = yNext;
            } while ((xCurrent > left) && (xCurrent < right) &&
                     (yCurrent > top) && (yCurrent < bottom));
        } // end walk
} // end RandomWalker
```

As usual, we need a panel and driver to create and display an instance of RandomWalker. We leave these for you as exercises.

videonote
A problem
solved

Question 12 How would you modify the class RandomWalker in Listing 14-5 so that the first step in the path is shown in green and the last step is shown in red?

Question 13 Define a class WalkPanel that creates and displays a RandomWalker object.

Question 14 Define a driver for the panel you defined in the previous question.

CHAPTER SUMMARY

- You can use a loop to draw or paint repeated shapes that can change in size, color, and position.

- If you know the number of times that you want to repeat a drawing, you can write a counted loop. You could use a while statement for this purpose, but usually you will want to use a for statement instead, as you learned in the previous chapter.

- You also can control a loop by using either the coordinates of a shape or the shape's size.

- If you always will draw a shape before deciding whether to repeat the drawing, you can use a do statement.

EXERCISES

1. Define a class QuahogPanel that creates a panel displaying two Quahog objects in different positions. Define a driver DisplayQuahog that creates a frame and adds a QuahogPanel object to it.

2. Add a constructor to QuahogPanel that sets its data fields to the two Quahog objects passed to it as arguments. Revise the class DisplayQuahog to demonstrate this new constructor.

3. Revise the class Quahog to give the drawing a client-specified color. Add a constructor to the class that has parameters for the color and height of the shell. The original constructor should set the shell color to black.

4. After revising the class Quahog as the previous exercise describes, what changes, if any, would you need to make to the method display to ensure that any change it makes to the pen's color is temporary? That is, after display completes execution, the pen's color should be the same as it was before display was called. You might need to consult the documentation for the class Graphics.

5. Consult the documentation for the class Color. What alternative is there for creating a custom color, other than the one presented in this chapter?

6. The method display in Listing 14-4 uses nested for statements. Could you replace the inner for statement with a do statement? If so, what change would you make to the code? If not, why not? Should you replace the inner for statement with a do statement?

7. Listing 14-5 contains a do statement. If all of the following relationships are true, how many times would the do statement repeat its body?
   - xCurrent < left
   - xCurrent > right
   - yCurrent < top
   - yCurrent > bottom

8. Using a for statement and the Graphics method drawRect, draw a pile of squares similar to the following one:

   The largest square at the bottom of the pile has a side equal to the value of the named constant BASE_SIDE. Each of the other squares has a side that is one-half the length of the side of the square below it. The pile contains a total of NUMBER_OF_SQUARES squares, where NUMBER_OF_SQUARES is a named constant.

9. Repeat the previous exercise, but with the following changes: Use a do statement instead of a for statement. Control the loop by checking the size of the square instead of the number of squares. That is, the length of the side of the smallest square at the top of the pile should not be less than the value of the named constant SMALLEST_SIDE.

10. Using a for statement and the Graphics method fillOval, draw a target such as the following one:

   The outermost disk has a diameter equal to the value of the named constant TARGET_SIZE. Each of the other disks has a diameter that is three-fourths the diameter of the next largest disk. The target contains a total of NUMBER_OF_DISKS disks, where NUMBER_OF_DISKS is a named constant.

11. Repeat the previous exercise, but with the following changes: Use a while statement instead of a for statement. Control the loop by checking the size of the disks instead of the number of disks. That is, the diameter of the smallest disk should not be less than the value of the named constant SMALLEST_DIAMETER.

12. Write a program that draws a conical shape such as the following one:

Beginning with a small circle, you draw more circles that increase in diameter and have centers whose *x*-coordinates increase and *y*-coordinates do not change.

13. Design a class that represents chessboards. Each chessboard is characterized by the coordinates of its upper left corner and its size. Each is eight squares wide by eight squares high. The square in the upper left corner of the board is red. Other squares alternate in color between red and black. Give the class a method display that paints a chessboard.

PROJECTS

1. The following optical illusion consists of parallel lines that do not seem to be parallel:

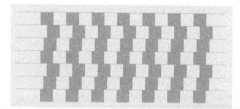

Using the class Square in Listing 11-2 of Chapter 11 and nested loops, produce the drawing in either a given or a random color. *Hints:* The length of each horizontal line must be at least the number of squares times twice the width of a square. The lines are separated by the height of a square. In the first row, draw seven squares separated by the width of a square. Position the first square in this row in any way you see fit. Draw each subsequent row in the same manner as the row before it, but move the first square either to the left or to the right of the first square in the previous row by a distance that is shorter than the side of a square.

2. Create a class Apple that displays a red apple with a black stem and a green leaf. Its method display should draw the apple at a given position. Using this class, implement the poison-apple game, as described in Project 4 of Chapter 12.

3. Implement the Race to 100 game, as described in Project 4 of Chapter 13. Illustrate the game board, updating it after each move. Define a class to represent the game board, giving it appropriate methods both to position the game pieces on the board and to display the board. During play, the board might look like this:

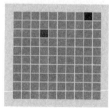

4. Write an application that draws a graph of the sine of *x* as *x* ranges from 0 to 2π radians. Plot 100 points at equally spaced values of *x*. Connect the points with straight lines.

You need to differentiate between the real value of *x* at which you evaluate the sine function and the *x*-coordinate that you will use for the plot. Remember that we really have two coordinate systems. One system has its origin at the intersection of the *x*- and *y*-axes that you will draw, while the other is the graphical system with its origin at the upper left corner of the window. To distinguish between the two systems, we will call the coordinates in the graphical system "left" and "top" instead of *x* and *y*.

For example, you would evaluate the sine of x at intervals of $(x_{max} - x_{min})$ / n, where n is the number of points. But if n is 100 and the x-axis is 100 pixels long, for instance, the distance between adjacent left coordinates is 1 pixel. Similarly, you need to scale the y values to fit the y axis by computing

yAxisLength x y / $(y_{max} - y_{min})$

and truncating the result to an integer. You subtract the result from the top coordinate of the x-axis to get the top coordinate of the point to be plotted.

ANSWERS TO SELF-TEST QUESTIONS

1.
```
int xCenter = X_CENTER;
int counter = 0;
while (counter < numberOfTimes)
{
    aDot.display(xCenter, Y_CENTER, COLOR, pen);
    xCenter = xCenter + GAP;
    counter++;
} // end while
```
Note that numberOfTimes can be final.

2. Set numberOfTimes to fixed values, such as 1, 3, and 5.

3.
```
int xCenter = X_CENTER + (numberOfTimes - 1) * GAP;
int counter = 0;
while (numberOfTimes > 0)
{
    aDot.display(xCenter, Y_CENTER, COLOR, pen);
    xCenter = xCenter - GAP;
    numberOfTimes--;
} // end while
```

4.
```
int xCenterMax = X_CENTER + numberOfTimes * GAP;
int xCenter = X_CENTER;
while (xCenter < xCenterMax)
{
    aDot.display(xCenter, Y_CENTER, COLOR, pen);
    xCenter = xCenter + GAP;
} // end while
```

5.
```
int xCenter = X_CENTER;
for (int counter = 1; counter <= numberOfTimes; counter++)
{
    aDot.display(xCenter, Y_CENTER, COLOR, pen);
    xCenter = xCenter + GAP;
} // end for
```

or

```
int xCenter = X_CENTER;
for (; numberOfTimes > 0; numberOfTimes--)
{
    aDot.display(xCenter, Y_CENTER, COLOR, pen);
    xCenter = xCenter + GAP;
} // end for
```

6. Yes. The constructor ensures that the value of height is at least SHORTEST_QUAHOG, which is larger than SMALLEST_OVAL. Thus, the while loop in display will cycle at least twice.

7.
```
do
{
   int width = height + OVAL_GAP;
   int left = xCenter - width / 2;
   int top = yCenter - height / 2;
   pen.drawOval(left, top, width, height);
   yCenter = yCenter + OVAL_GAP / 2;
   height = height - OVAL_GAP;
} while (height > SMALLEST_OVAL);
```

8.
```
for (; height > SMALLEST_OVAL; height = height - OVAL_GAP)
{
   int width = height + OVAL_GAP;
   int left = xCenter - width / 2;
   int top = yCenter - height / 2;
   pen.drawOval(left, top, width, height);
   yCenter = yCenter + OVAL_GAP / 2;
} // end for
```

9.
```
int row = 1;
while (row <= squaresPerSide)
{
   int x = xCorner;
   int column = 1;
   while (column <= squaresPerSide)
   {
      Color squareColor = getRandomColor();
      aSquare.display(x, y, squareColor, pen);
      x = x + squareSide;
      column++;
   } // end while
   y = y + squareSide;
   row++;
} // end while
```

10.
```
/** QuiltPanel.java by F. M. Carrano
    Paints a square quilt whose individual squares are each in
    one of five colors chosen at random.
*/
import java.awt.Color;
import java.awt.Dimension;
import java.awt.Graphics;
import javax.swing.JPanel;

public class QuiltPanel extends JPanel
{
   private final Quilt aQuilt;

   private static final int PANEL_SIDE = 250; // square panel

   // center of panel
   private static final int X_CENTER = PANEL_SIDE / 2;
   private static final int Y_CENTER = X_CENTER;

   // characteristics of quilt
   private static final int SQUARE_SIDE = 20;
   private static final int SQUARES_PER_SIDE = 10; // dimension of quilt

   // upper left corner of quilt
   private static final int X_CORNER = X_CENTER -
                              SQUARES_PER_SIDE * SQUARE_SIDE / 2;
   private static final int Y_CORNER = X_CORNER;
```

```
        public QuiltPanel()
        {
            setPreferredSize(new Dimension(PANEL_SIDE, PANEL_SIDE));
            aQuilt = new Quilt(SQUARES_PER_SIDE, SQUARE_SIDE);
        } // end default constructor

        /** Displays a quilt. */
        public void paintComponent(Graphics pen)
        {
            aQuilt.display(X_CORNER, Y_CORNER, pen);
        } // end paintComponent
    } // end QuiltPanel
```

11.
```
    /** DisplayQuilt.java by F. M. Carrano
        Displays a square quilt whose individual squares are
        each in one of five colors chosen at random.
    */
    import javax.swing.JFrame;
    public class DisplayQuilt
    {
        public static void main(String[] args)
        {
            JFrame window = new JFrame();
            window.setDefaultCloseOperation(JFrame.EXIT_ON_CLOSE);
            window.setTitle("A Colorful Quilt");
            QuiltPanel panel = new QuiltPanel();
            window.add(panel);
            window.pack();
            window.setVisible(true);
        } // end main
    } // end DisplayQuilt
```

12. Make the following changes to the method walk:

- Add the following statements before the do statement:

```
    int xPrev, yPrev;
    boolean firstStep = true;
```

- After the switch statement, replace

```
    pen.drawLine(xCurrent, yCurrent, xNext, yNext);
```

    with

```
    if (firstStep)
    {
        pen.setColor(Color.GREEN);
        pen.drawLine(xCurrent, yCurrent, xNext, yNext);
        firstStep = false;
        pen.setColor(Color.BLACK);
    }
    else
        pen.drawLine(xCurrent, yCurrent, xNext, yNext);

    xPrev = xCurrent;
    yPrev = yCurrent;
```

- After the do statement, add

```
    // draw last step again, but in red
    pen.setColor(Color.RED);
    pen.drawLine(xPrev, yPrev, xCurrent, yCurrent);
```

13.

```
/** WalkPanel.java by F. M. Carrano
    Draws the random path taken by a walker within a square area.
*/
import java.awt.Dimension;
import java.awt.Graphics;
import javax.swing.JPanel;

public class WalkPanel extends JPanel
{
    private final RandomWalker walker;

    private static final int PANEL_SIDE = 250; // square panel

    // center of panel
    private static final int X_CENTER = PANEL_SIDE / 2;
    private static final int Y_CENTER = X_CENTER;

    // characteristics of square area centered in panel window
    private static final int SQUARE_SIDE = 150;
    private static final int SQUARE_LEFT = X_CENTER - SQUARE_SIDE / 2;
    private static final int SQUARE_TOP  = Y_CENTER - SQUARE_SIDE / 2;
    private static final int STEP = 5;

    public WalkPanel()
    {
        setPreferredSize(new Dimension(PANEL_SIDE, PANEL_SIDE));
        walker = new RandomWalker(SQUARE_LEFT, SQUARE_TOP, SQUARE_SIDE,
                                  STEP);
    } // end default constructor

    /** Displays the walker's path. */
    public void paintComponent(Graphics pen)
    {
        walker.walk(pen);
    } // end paintComponent
} // end WalkPanel
```

14.

```
/** DisplayWalk.java by F. M. Carrano
    Displays a square and the random path taken by a walker.
*/
import javax.swing.JFrame;

public class DisplayWalk
{
    public static void main(String[] args)
    {
        JFrame window = new JFrame();
        window.setDefaultCloseOperation(JFrame.EXIT_ON_CLOSE);
        window.setTitle("A Random Walk");

        WalkPanel panel = new WalkPanel();
        window.add(panel);
        window.pack();
        window.setVisible(true);
    } // end main
} // end DisplayWalk
```

Debugging Interlude

4

Debugging Loops

Contents

Prerequisites

After introducing the while statement, Chapter 12 noted some typical errors programmers might make when coding a repetitive process. Loops that cycle one too few times, one too many times, or forever are common problems that we should try to avoid. These kinds of mistakes are not peculiar to the while statement; they can be made just as easily when writing for statements and do statements. Although our goal is to avoid mistakes, how do we find those that we do make?

■ Testing

D4.1

Before we can correct an error in logic, we must recognize that an error has occurred. To do so, we need to test the program. Thus, testing and debugging are interrelated activities. Ideally, a test should try all possible paths through a program's logic. When those paths depend on some sort of input data, designing the test data set is the immediate task.

Testing should proceed using the following:

- Typical data
- Extreme but acceptable data
- Unacceptable or incorrect data

We want our programs to behave well under all of these conditions. That is, a program should not crash or end in an infinite loop. A well-behaved program is robust.

D4.2

Example. Let's consider a simple example. Imagine that a class you intend to write needs a method to accept two integers, *m* and *n*, as arguments and return either

$$m^2 + (m + 1)^2 + ... + n^2, \text{ if } 0 < m \leq n$$

or

0 for other values of *m* and *n*

For example, if *m* is 3 and *n* is 5, our method should return $3^2 + 4^2 + 5^2$—that is, 9 + 16 + 25, or 50. If either *m* or *n*, or both, is less than or equal to zero, or if *m* is larger than *n*, the method should return zero. Mathematically speaking, we have a *function* that our method will evaluate. We can denote the value of this function as $f(m, n)$.

D4.3   Listing D4-1 contains a simple class that implements the previous function as the method sumSqs. To test this method, we call it with various values of *m* and *n*, as shown in Figure D4-1. In addition to displaying these values, we display each computed function value, as well as the expected value given in the figure. Including the expected value in the output makes it convenient and easy to check the results of your code. Output that is labeled and clear is just as important for you during debugging as it is to the eventual user of your programs.

FIGURE D4-1 Sample test data

m	*n*	*f(m, n)*	Comment
3	5	50	Typical values such that $0 < m \leq n$
1	5	55	*m* is positive and as close to zero as possible; $0 < m \leq n$
5	5	25	$0 < m = n$
5	2	0	$m > n$
–2	–5	0	$m > n$; both *m* and *n* are negative
–5	–2	0	*m* and *n* are negative
–2	5	0	*m* is negative
2	–5	0	*n* is negative
0	5	0	*m* is zero
5	0	0	*n* is zero
0	0	0	*m* and *n* are each zero

LISTING D4-1

```java
/** Debug4a.java by F. M. Carrano
    A class to test a method.
*/
public class Debug4a
{
   /** Returns the sum of the squares of the consecutive integers
       from m to n, if m > 0 and m <= n; otherwise, returns 0. */
   public int sumSqs(int m, int n)
   {
      int sum = 0;
      while ((m > 0) && (m <= n))
      {
         sum = sum + m * m;
         m++;
      } // end while

      return sum;
   } // end sumSqs

   public static void main(String[] args)
   {
      Debug4a tester = new Debug4a();
      System.out.println("sumSqs(3,5) = " + tester.sumSqs(3, 5) +
                         "; should be 50"); // 0 < 3 <= 5
                                            // 9 + 16 + 25
      System.out.println("sumSqs(1,5) = " + tester.sumSqs(1, 5) +
                         "; should be 55"); // 0 < 1 <= 5
                                            // 1 + 4 + 9 + 16 + 25
      System.out.println("sumSqs(5,5) = " + tester.sumSqs(5, 5) +
                         "; should be 25"); // 0 < 5 <= 5
                                            // 5 * 5
      System.out.println();
      System.out.println("sumSqs(5, 2) = " + tester.sumSqs(5, 2) +
                         "; should be 0."); // 5 > 2

      System.out.println("sumSqs(-2,-5) = " + tester.sumSqs(-2,-5)
                         + "; should be 0."); // -2&-5 < 0,-2 > -5
      System.out.println("sumSqs(-5,-2) = " + tester.sumSqs(-5,-2)
                         + "; should be 0."); // -5 < 0, -2 < 0
      System.out.println("sumSqs(-2,5) = " + tester.sumSqs(-2,5) +
                         "; should be 0.");   // -2 < 0
      System.out.println("sumSqs(2,-5) = " + tester.sumSqs(2,-5) +
                         "; should be 0.");   // -5 < 0
```

```
            System.out.println();
            System.out.println("sumSqs(0,5) = " + tester.sumSqs(0, 5) +
                               "; should be 0."); // 1st argument is 0
            System.out.println("sumSqs(5,0) = " + tester.sumSqs(5, 0) +
                               "; should be 0."); // 2nd argument is 0
            System.out.println("sumSqs(0,0) = " + tester.sumSqs(0, 0) +
                               "; should be 0."); // both arguments 0
    } // end main
} // end Debug4a
```

Output

```
    sumSqs(3,5) = 50; should be 50.
    sumSqs(1,5) = 55; should be 55.
    sumSqs(5,5) = 25; should be 25.

    sumSqs(5,2) = 0; should be 0.
    sumSqs(-2,-5) = 0; should be 0.
    sumSqs(-5,-2) = 0; should be 0.
    sumSqs(-2,5) = 0; should be 0.
    sumSqs(2,-5) = 0; should be 0.

    sumSqs(0,5) = 0; should be 0.
    sumSqs(5,0) = 0; should be 0.
    sumSqs(0,0) = 0; should be 0.
```

 Note: Exhaustive testing is impractical
Testing a program with every possible piece of data as input is seldom feasible. The data you use for testing should imply that the program will run correctly for other untested data. For example, testing the previous program when *m* is –2 and *n* is 5 almost certainly will have the same outcome as when *m* is –3 and *n* is 6. Of course, we might overlook possible input that would cause an error. This lapse is one reason that large software applications are not error free when they are released to users.

■ Debugging Loops

D4.4   The method in Listing D4-1 correctly implements our desired function, as you can see from the given output. But what if it hadn't? When debugging a method, we should examine the values of key variables at both the beginning and the end of the method. We can check the initial values of any input arguments and also check the computed results just before the method ends. Sometimes, knowing only that the method was called will be sufficient.

When debugging a loop, we examine key variables, including those used to control the loop, at the following places:

videonote
Debugging loops

- Before the loop begins
- At the beginning of the loop's body
- At the end of the loop's body
- After the loop ends

Listing D4-2 shows the method `sumSqs` from Listing D4-1 with additional statements that report the status of its computation at these four points, as well as at the beginning and end of the method. For now, we continue to use `println` statements for this purpose, but as you will see later, other techniques are available.

LISTING D4-2   Debugging statements in a method and loop

```java
public int sumSqs(int m, int n)
{
    System.out.println("\nEntering sumSqs with m = " + m +
                        " and n = " + n);
    int sum = 0;
    if (m > 0)
    {
        System.out.println("Before loop: m = " + m + ", n = " +
                            n + ", sum = " + sum);
        while (m <= n)
        {
            System.out.println("At top of loop body: m = " + m +
                                ", n = " + n + ", sum = " + sum);
            sum = sum + m * m;
            m++;
            System.out.println("At end of loop body: m = " + m +
                                ", n = " + n + ", sum = " + sum);
        } // end while
        System.out.println("After loop: m = " + m + ", n = " +
                            n + ", sum = " + sum);
    } // end if
    System.out.println("About to return " + sum +
                        " from sumSqs; m = " + m + ", n = " + n);
    return sum;
} // end sumSqs
```

D4.5   Let's examine some output from the method in Listing D4-2, using a selection of data from Figure D4-1. The call `sumSqs(3, 5)` would produce the following output:

```
Entering sumSqs with m = 3 and n = 5
Before loop: m = 3, n = 5, sum = 0
At top of loop body: m = 3, n = 5, sum = 0
At end of loop body: m = 4, n = 5, sum = 9
At top of loop body: m = 4, n = 5, sum = 9
At end of loop body: m = 5, n = 5, sum = 25
At top of loop body: m = 5, n = 5, sum = 25
At end of loop body: m = 6, n = 5, sum = 50
After loop: m = 6, n = 5, sum = 50
About to return 50 from sumSqs; m = 6, n = 5
```

From this output, we can see that the method was entered and the arguments were passed correctly. Also, the loop cycles three times before ending with the correct value. Had we made a mistake in logic, this output should help us to see it.

If m is positive and larger than n, the `while` loop will exit immediately, as the following call to `sumSqs(5, 2)` indicates the following:

```
Entering sumSqs with m = 5 and n = 2
Before loop: m = 5, n = 2, sum = 0
After loop: m = 5, n = 2, sum = 0
About to return 0 from sumSqs; m = 5, n = 2
```

Since m is positive, the `while` statement begins execution, but since m is larger than n, the loop exits without executing its body even once. Similar results will happen for calls such as `sumSqs(5, 0)` and `sumSqs(2, -5)`.

If m is not positive, the `if` statement will skip the loop entirely. For example, the call `sumSqs(0, 5)` produces the following output:

```
Entering sumSqs with m = 0 and n = 5
About to return 0 from sumSqs; m = 0, n = 5
```

Note: Tracing a program's logic

The previous examples show how we can trace the logic of our code. Not only have we verified the values of key variables, but we have been able to see when a method or loop begins and ends its execution. Moreover, we can tell whether a method or loop actually executes. Using `println` statements to trace a program is a useful technique, especially when the program is short. Other tools are available, however, that can be more convenient.

D4.6 **More testing.** Let's test our method with data that causes the loop to iterate many times. For example, suppose *m* is 2 and *n* is 2^{16}. For our first attempt, and to avoid lots of output, we will omit the debugging statements from the method, so that it appears as in Listing D4-1. The call to the method can be

```
tester.sumSqs(2, (int)Math.pow(2, 16))
```

We use the standard method `Math.pow` to compute 2^{16}. The arguments and return value for this method are `double`. Although we have passed the `int` arguments 2 and 16 to the method, Java will implicitly cast them to `double`. Such is not the case for pow's return value, however. Since it is `double`, and `sumSqs` expects `int` arguments, we must explicitly cast `Math.pow(2, 16)` to `int`.

The value returned by `sumSqs` is -715816961. Since a sum of squares cannot be negative, something is wrong. Let's insert the debugging statements shown in Listing D4-2. As soon as we run the program, we see output streaming by. After all, the loop iterates more than 65,000 times! If we had not already run the program without the debugging statements, we likely would assume that we had an infinite loop. Whether we terminate the program or let it continue to a normal conclusion, the output will show that m increases by 1 at each cycle of the loop. This is normal. But you will also see that sum increases, becomes negative, becomes positive again, decreases, and so on.

The last term added to our sum should be $(2^{16})^2$, or 2^{32}. The problem occurs because the largest `int` value is $2^{31} - 1$, as mentioned in Segment 4.43 of Chapter 4. Exceeding the maximum value supported by the architecture of a computer is called **overflow**. That is what has happened here.

D4.7 Although we cannot prevent overflow, we can avoid it by limiting the value of n. If necessary, we can increase this limit by changing the data type of the computation from `int` to `long`, as we have done in the following version of sumSqs:

```java
public long sumSqs(int m, int n)
{
    long sum = 0;
    if (m > 0)
    {
        while (m <= n)
```

```
         {
             long longM = (long)m;
             sum = sum + longM * longM;
             m++;
         } // end while
     } // end if

     return sum;
 } // end sumSqs
```

While the data type of the parameters m and n can remain as int, the type of the method's return value and the local variable sum is long. Note that we must cast m to long before squaring its value.

D4.8   **Taming lengthy debugging output.** As Segment D4.6 noted, debugging statements can produce many lines of output. Instead of displaying output each time the loop iterates, we can choose to do so less often. For example, we can revise the loop in Listing D4-1 by inserting a counter and an if statement, as follows:

```
int loopCounter = 0;
while (m <= n)
{
    sum = sum + m * m;
    m++;

    loopCounter++;
    if (loopCounter % 1000 == 0)
        System.out.println("At end of loop body: m = " + m +
                           ", n = " + n + ", sum = " + sum);
} // end while
```

The if statement displays output once in 1000 cycles of the loop. Using this restricted information, we often can learn enough about the behavior of a loop to correct it.

An Example

D4.9   **Background remarks.** If you answered Exercise 14 in Chapter 13 correctly, you would realize that a boolean expression such as

```
(response != 'N') || (response != 'n')
```

in which response is a variable whose type is char, is always true. Clearly, if response does not contain 'N', the expression response != 'N' is true, so the entire expression is true. If response does contain 'N', then response != 'n' must be true, which makes the entire expression true.

As you can see, the loop shown in Exercise 14 of Chapter 13 is infinite. One way to correct the loop is to change the operator || in the previous boolean expression to &&. That is, we can change the expression to

```
(response != 'N') && (response != 'n')
```

Now the loop cycles as long as response does not contain either 'N' or 'n'. A less error-prone way to write this loop is to avoid thinking negatively! As written, the loop cycles as long as response does *not* contain the particular values 'N' or 'n'. Why not cycle as long as response does contain other particular values, namely 'Y' or 'y'? That is, a loop of the form

```
do
{
    . . .

} while ((response == 'Y') || (response == 'y'));
```

is not only correct, but also easier to understand. Thus, you are more likely to avoid a logical error.

D4.10 Chapter 4 explored how to use the class `Scanner` to locate words within a string by searching for the delimiters that separate the words. Imagine that Joe was asked to write the code that implements the search used by `Scanner`. Listing D4-3 contains Joe's initial attempt to identify words separated by either a comma or a slash. The boolean expression in the `while` statement at line 21 of `WordFinder` is like the one in the previous segment. Notice that Joe correctly uses the operator `&&` instead of `||`. He wants the `while` loop to cycle while the next character is not a slash and not a comma, that is, while the next character is not a delimiter. The method `getNextChar` retrieves the next character from the string. When a delimiter is found, the `while` loop ends. The delimiter's index is recorded and used to copy the word preceding the delimiter in the string.

LISTING D4-3   The class `WordFinder`

```java
1 /** WordFinder.java by Joe
2     A class to locate words separated by either
3     a comma or a slash within a string.
4 */
5 public class WordFinder
6 {
7     private String aString;
8     private int index;
9
10    public WordFinder(String input)
11    {
12       aString = input;
13       index = -1;
14    } // end constructor
15
16    /** Returns the next word to appear in a string. */
17    public String getNextWord()
18    {
19       int before = index;
20
21       while ((getNextChar() != '/') && (getNextChar() != ','))
22       {
23       } // end while
24
25       int after = index; // index of separator / or ,
26       String word = aString.substring(before + 1, after);
27
28       return word;
29    } // end getNextWord
30
31    // Returns the next character in the string.
32    private char getNextChar()
33    {
34       index++;
```

```
35            return aString.charAt(index);
36     } // end nextChar
37 } // end WordFinder
```

D4.11 The output from the driver in Listing D4-4 shows that WordFinder does not work correctly. For the input string,

> ant,buffalo,cat/dog,eagle

the first word, ant, and the second word, buffalo, are found. They both are delimited by commas in the input string. The next recognized "word" is cat/dog, which again is followed by a comma in the input string. The slash has not been treated as a delimiter.

LISTING D4-4   The class WordFinderDemo

```
1 import java.util.Scanner;
2
3 /** WordFinderDemo.java by Joe
4     A class to demonstrate the class WordFinder.
5 */
6 public class WordFinderDemo
7 {
8     /** A simple test driver. */
9     public static void main(String[] args)
10    {
11       Scanner keyboard = new Scanner(System.in);
12       System.out.println("At the prompt, enter words " +
13                          "delimited by commas and/or slashes.");
14       System.out.println("Enter QUIT to exit.");
15       boolean proceed = true;
16       do
17       {
18          System.out.print("\nEnter delimited words or QUIT: ");
19          String aString = keyboard.nextLine();
20          if (aString.equalsIgnoreCase("QUIT"))
21             proceed = false;
22          else
23          {
24             System.out.println("Processing the string \"" +
25                                aString + "\"");
26             WordFinder finder = new WordFinder(aString);
27             String word1 = finder.getNextWord();
28             System.out.println(word1);
29             String word2 = finder.getNextWord();
30             System.out.println(word2);
```

```
31                     String word3 = finder.getNextWord();
32                     System.out.println(word3);
33               } // end if
34          } while (proceed);
35          System.out.println("All done!");
36     } // end main
37 } // end WordFinderDemo
```

Sample Output

```
At the prompt, enter words delimited by commas and/or slashes.
Enter QUIT to exit.

Enter delimited words or QUIT: ant,buffalo,cat/dog,eagle
Processing the string "ant,buffalo,cat/dog,eagle"
ant
buffalo
cat/dog

Enter delimited words or QUIT: QUIT
All done!
```

D4.12   Let's try some other strings. Since cat/dog causes a problem, let's place it at the beginning of the string. We'll follow it with a comma, as we know that worked last time. What would happen if the words were longer and delimited by slashes? Let's find out.

Using the input

```
cat/dog,clam/goat/
```

the program's output is

```
cat/dog
clam
goat
```

The first slash is ignored, but the subsequent ones are recognized.

Suppose the input ended with a comma instead of a slash? With the input

```
cat/dog,clam/goat,
```

the program's output is

```
cat/dog
clam
Exception in thread "main"
java.lang.StringIndexOutOfBoundsException: String index out of
range: 18
    at java.lang.String.charAt(String.java:686)
    at WordFinder.getNextChar(WordFinder.java:37)
    at WordFinder.getNextWord(WordFinder.java:21)
    at WordFinderDemo.main(WordFinderDemo.java:31)
```

D4.13   We need to do some tracing. Let's add some print statements to the loop in WordFinder, as follows:

```
    int before = index;
System.out.println("Before loop: index is " + index);       // DEBUG
    while ((getNextChar() != '/') && (getNextChar() != ','))
    {
```

```
System.out.println("In loop:    index is " + index);    // DEBUG
    } // end while
System.out.println("After loop:  index is " + index);    // DEBUG
    int after = index; // index of separator / or ,
```

Since cat/dog,clam/goat/ did not cause an exception, we will use it as input to the program. We get the following output:

```
Processing the string "cat/dog,clam/goat/"
Before loop: index is -1
In loop       index is 1
In loop:      index is 3
In loop:      index is 5
After loop:   index is 7
cat/dog
Before loop: index is 7
In loop:      index is 9
In loop:      index is 11
After loop:   index is 12
clam
Before loop: index is 12
In loop:      index is 14
In loop:      index is 16
After loop:   index is 17
goat
```

D4.14 Figure D4-2 illustrates the input string we just processed. The code correctly detects the comma at index 7, as well as the slashes at indices 12 and 17. Notice, however, that index increases by 2 during each cycle of the loop. As a result of the first call to getNextWord, happenstance causes the loop to bypass the first slash but exit at the comma. For each of the second and third calls to getNextWord, the loop exits at the slash.

FIGURE D4-2 The string "cat/dog,clam/goat/"

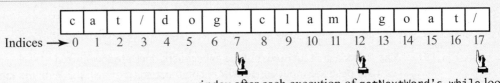

index after each execution of getNextWord's while loop

D4.15 Before the loop, index is –1. Only the method getNextChar increments index. Let's look more closely at what happens as the loop

```
while ((getNextChar() != '/') && (getNextChar() != ','))
{
} // end while
```

executes:

1. When the while statement begins, getNextChar is called; index is now 0.
2. Since the character at index 0 is not a slash, getNextChar is called; index is now 1.
3. Since the character at index 1 is not a comma, the empty body executes: That is, the loop cycles.
4. getNextChar is called, increasing index to 2.
5. The character at index 2 is not a slash; getNextChar is called again; index is now 3.
6. The character at index 3 is not a comma—it's a slash, but we aren't checking for that—so the empty body executes.

7. `getNextChar` is called, increasing `index` to 4.

8. The character at index 4 is not a slash; `getNextChar` is called again; `index` is now 5.

9. The character at index 5 is not a comma, so the empty body executes.

10. `getNextChar` is called, increasing `index` to 6.

11. The character at index 6 is not a slash; `getNextChar` is called again; `index` is now 7.

12. The character at index 7 *is* a comma! The loop falls through and the string `"cat/dog"` is returned.

D4.16   What did we learn? When the boolean expression used to control a loop contains a call to a method, that method should not be called again within the same expression. The correct way to write this loop is as follows:

```
char nextCharacter = getNextChar();
while ((nextCharacter != '/') && (nextCharacter != ','))
{
    nextCharacter = getNextChar();
} // end while
```

We also learned that tracing can be tedious! The debugging tools mentioned in the next section can help.

Programming Tip

Do not call the same method more than once within a boolean expression used to control a loop. The same advice applies to boolean expressions within `if` statements.

■ Overview of Debugging Tools

D4.17   In our previous examples, we needed to examine the intermediate results of Java statements at specific places within a program and at certain points in time. By doing so, we would likely uncover the source of a mistake in the program's logic. Up to now, we have exhibited these results simply by inserting `println` statements in our code. Although this technique uses a familiar statement, we ultimately are left with a program containing extraneous statements. If we remove these statements, we might find later that we need to insert them again to find more bugs. Embedding such `println`s within an `if` statement that tests the value of a boolean constant `DEBUG`, as Debugging Interlude 3 suggested, is one way to retain debugging statements but ignore them after debugging is finished. However, any time you change the value of `DEBUG`, you must compile the program again.

Although inserting `println` statements at key points in a program is useful, particularly for short programs, and should remain among your strategies for debugging, Java provides some standard classes that offer the debugging benefits of `println` statements without the downside mentioned previously. The statements that you use instead of `println` statements can be left in place after your program runs successfully. One simple method call indicates whether the debugging statements will be ignored. This alternate technique, called **logging**, will be described in Debugging Interlude 5.

D4.18   Typical integrated development environments, or IDEs, also provide powerful debugging tools. Although the details of how to access these tools varies from one IDE to another, they all share some basic features. For example, you can stop a program's execution and examine the values of key variables by setting a **breakpoint** at various places within the program. When program execution reaches a breakpoint, it stops until you indicate that it should resume. During the pause, you can look at, or **watch**, the values of certain variables to see whether the computation is progressing normally. To do so, just set a watch for each variable of interest before you run the program. Debugging Interlude 5 will trace a program's execution using this technique.

In addition to using breakpoints and watches, you can **single-step** through all or part of a program. That is, you can execute one statement at a time, examining the results along the way. If a method is called, you can either **step into** the method to trace its statements or **step over** the method to skip those details but continue with the method's result. You also can let a program run normally—and quickly—until it reaches a breakpoint, single-step through a portion that needs close examination, and finally resume normal execution.

Debugging Interlude 5 will provide an example of using an IDE to find the mistake in a program's logic.

The Command-Line Tool `jdb` (Optional)

D4.19   Java comes with a command-line tool, `jdb`, that has the same debugging features as those just described in general for IDEs. Finding the logical error in a program is much easier when you use an IDE's graphical debugging tools instead of the `jdb`. However, you might want to try Java's command-line tool to debug your code.

If you decide to use `jdb`, you first must tell the compiler to generate debugging information for `jdb`. You do this by providing the `-g` option for the `javac` command, as follows:

```
javac -g class_name.java
```

Then, instead of using the command `java` to run the program, you use `jdb`. For example, to compile and debug the program `MyProgram`, you would use the following sequence of commands:

```
javac -g MyProgram.java
jdb MyProgram
```

The response will be

```
Initializing jdb ...
>
```

At this prompt, you can enter various commands to the debugger.

D4.20   For example, to set a breakpoint in `MyProgram` at line 15, you would type the command

```
stop at MyProgram:15
```

The system response is

```
Deferring breakpoint MyProgram:15.
It will be set after the class is loaded.
>
```

After setting as many breakpoints as you like, you begin program execution by giving the command

```
run
```

When the breakpoint is reached, you will receive a message and the statement at line 15 will be displayed. This statement will execute next when you use the command

```
step
```

Each time you type this command, the statement at the current line executes and the debugger advances to the next line.

You can look at the current value of any variable by using the `print` command. For example, to see the current value of `index`, you would type

```
print index
```

You can continue single-stepping or you can resume execution until the next breakpoint by using the command

```
cont
```

To remove a breakpoint, you use the `clear` command. For example, to clear the breakpoint we set previously, you would use the command

```
clear MyProgram:15
```

After setting a breakpoint and beginning execution, you can trace when methods are entered and exited by giving the command

```
trace methods
```

Now each time you give the command `cont`, execution continues and then stops either at the beginning of a method or at its end. Tracing methods in this manner is just like setting breakpoints at the beginning and end of each method.

While in the debugger, you can get a list of available commands by typing

```
help
```

Finally, to end a debugging session, you use the command

```
exit
```

Note: Many more commands than the ones we have introduced here are available to you when you use the debugger `jdb`. To see a list of these commands, you can type the command `jdb` and then the command `help`, as follows:

```
jdb
Initializing jdb ...
> help
```

Similar debugging actions are available in a typical IDE, although the particulars of how to take those actions differ. If you are using an IDE, you should learn its debugging tools, as they will be more convenient to use than `jdb`. The approach to using these tools, however, is the same regardless of the form the tools take.

Designing Classes

Contents

Prerequisites

Objectives

After studying this chapter, you should be able to

- Use simple design tools to design a class before implementing it
- Describe the concepts of abstraction and encapsulation

- Write comments to specify a method, including a precondition and postcondition
- Develop a class that has an object as a data field
- Define and use static data fields
- Define and use static methods
- Use an enumeration's existing methods
- Define additional methods for an enumeration

When Chapter 6 showed how to define a class, it introduced the idea of designing the class before implementing it. This chapter expands on those design basics and presents some tools that class designers use in their work. We begin at an elementary level with some techniques for identifying the classes necessary for a particular solution and some notation for specifying a class during its design. As we do so, we will emphasize the importance of specifying methods before implementing them and of expressing these specifications as comments in your program. We will use these new tools when we develop a class to represent people. In doing so, we will consider using an existing class—written by either you or someone else—in the development of the new class. In particular, we will use the class Name from Chapter 6 when we design and implement a class of people objects.

We also will work with overloaded methods. These are methods in a class that have the same name. We will further explore the modifier static, which can affect a class's data fields and methods, and expand our knowledge of enumerations.

The next chapter will augment this introduction to class design.

■ Design Tools

We have designed classes in previous chapters, particularly in Chapters 6 and 8. Segment 6.14 of Chapter 6 listed some steps to take when designing a class. Let's recall those steps here:

1. Name the class.
2. Choose and name the data fields, indicating their data types.
3. Describe the behaviors associated with objects of the class.
4. Name the methods that will implement these behaviors.
5. Specify the methods by writing a header and descriptive comments for each one.
6. Write statements that use the methods and could appear in a client.
7. Revise the method specifications, if necessary.

This section will add to this design process by introducing some tools that professional class designers use in their work.

Choosing Classes

We have talked about specifying classes and implementing classes, but up to now, we have chosen the class that you are to specify or implement. If you must design an application from scratch, how will you determine the classes you need? You first need a clear description of the problem. Working from that description, you try to identify the classes you need in order to implement a solution. Some classes might already exist, such as those in the Java Class Library, while others need to be written. In this section, we introduce you to some techniques that software designers use when choosing and designing classes. Our intent is simply to expose you to these ideas. Future courses will develop ways to select and design classes.

15.1 Imagine that you are designing a registration system for your school. Where should you begin? A useful way to start would be to look at the system from a functional point of view, as follows:

- **Who or what will use the system?** A human user or a software component that interacts with the system is called an **actor**. So a first step is to list the possible actors. For a registration system, two of the actors could be a student and the registrar.
- **What can each actor do with the system?** A **scenario** is a description of the interaction between an actor and the system. Our second step, therefore, is to identify scenarios. One way to do this is to complete the question that begins "What happens when . . ." For example, what happens when a student adds a course? The basic scenario of adding a course successfully has variations that give rise to other scenarios. For instance, what happens when the student attempts to add a course that is closed?
- **Which scenarios involve common goals?** For example, the two scenarios we just described are related to the common goal of adding a course. A collection of such related scenarios is called a **use case**. Our third step, then, is to identify the use cases.

You can get an overall picture of the use cases involved in a system you are designing by drawing a **use case diagram**. Figure 15-1 shows a use case diagram for our simple registration system. Each actor—the student and the registrar—appears as a stick figure. The box represents the registration system, and the ovals within the box are the use cases. A line joins an actor and a use case if an interaction exists between the two.

Some use cases in this example involve one actor, and some involve both. For example, only the student applies for admission, and only the registrar enrolls a student. However, both the student and the registrar can add a course to a student's schedule.

Note: Use cases depict a system from the actors' points of view. They do not necessarily suggest classes within the system.

15.2 **Identifying classes.** Although drawing a use case diagram is a step in the right direction, it does not identify the classes that are needed for your system. Several techniques are possible, and you will probably need to use more than one.

One simple technique is to describe the system and then identify the nouns and verbs in the description. The nouns can suggest classes, and the verbs can suggest appropriate methods within the classes. Given the imprecision of natural language, this technique is not foolproof, but it can be useful.

For example, we could write a sequence of steps to describe each use case shown in Figure 15-1. Figure 15-2 gives such a description of the use case for adding a course from the point of view of a student. Notice the alternative actions taken in steps 2a and 4a when the system does not recognize the student or when a requested course is closed.

FIGURE 15-1   A use case diagram for a registration system

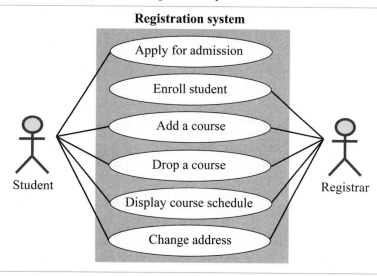

Registration system

- Apply for admission
- Enroll student
- Add a course
- Drop a course
- Display course schedule
- Change address

Student   Registrar

What classes does this description suggest? Looking at the nouns, we could decide to have classes to represent a student, a course, a list of all courses offered, and a student's schedule of courses. The verbs suggest actions that include deciding whether a student is eligible to register, seeing whether a course is closed, and adding a course to a student's schedule. One way to organize these actions with appropriate classes is to use CRC cards, which we describe next.

FIGURE 15-2   A description of a use case for adding a course

```
System:    Registration
Use case:  Add a course
Actor:     Student
Steps:
        1. Student enters identifying data.
        2. System confirms eligibility to register.
           a. If ineligible to register, ask student to enter identification data again.
        3. Student chooses a particular section of a course from a list of course offerings.
        4. System confirms availability of the course.
           a. If course is closed, allow student to return to step 3 or quit.
        5. System adds course to student's schedule.
        6. System displays student's revised schedule of courses.
```

CRC Cards

15.3   When thinking about a new class and its purpose, you should decide some of the details mentioned in the first few steps in the list given in Segment 6.14 of Chapter 6 and repeated at the beginning of this section. As you make your choices, you should write them down. A simple technique to represent a class at this early stage of the design involves using an index card. You write the class's name at the top of the card. You then list the behaviors, or **responsibilities**, of the class. Finally, you write the names of any other classes that have some sort of interaction with your new class. These interactions are called **collaborations**. Because of their content, these index cards are called **class-responsibility-collaboration**, or **CRC**, **cards**.

For example, consider the class Name that we wrote in Chapter 6. When designing this class, we listed its behaviors as follows:

- Construct an empty name
- Construct a name given the first and last names
- Set the first name of an existing name
- Set the last name of an existing name
- Set the first and last names of an existing name
- Get the first name
- Get the last name
- Get the entire name
- Give the last name to another Name object

After making this list, we could have written the CRC card shown in Figure 15-3. It gives the class's name, the behaviors in the previous list, and the class String as a collaboration, since a name is composed of strings.

FIGURE 15-3   A CRC card for the class Name

Name
Responsibilities
Construct an empty name
Construct a name given the first and last names
Set the first name
Set the last name
Set the first and last names
Get the first name
Get the last name
Get the entire name
Give the last name to another Name object
Collaborations
String

15.4   Notice that the small size of an index card forces you to write brief notes. The number of responsibilities must be small, which suggests that you think at a high level and consider small classes. For this reason, designers usually do not list constructors, set methods, and get methods on a CRC card, even though we did so in this example. Such methods are deemed common enough not to warrant being mentioned. For now, you should feel free to list them, if you find it helpful. You can use something other than index cards, if you like. The important point is to write about your new class.

    If you are designing a software system that requires more than one class, you will have a CRC card for each new class. As you think of these classes, write the name of each one on a new card. The size of the cards lets you arrange them on a table and move them around easily while you search for collaborations. When you see a collaboration, note it on the appropriate cards.

Note: **Class-responsibility-collaboration (CRC) cards**
CRC cards provide a way to organize your thoughts about the classes you need to create a particular application program. Their informal nature facilitates the revisions that are likely to occur at this early stage of the design process. Even so, capturing your ideas in writing not only records them but also helps to clarify your design.

Question 1 What should appear on a CRC card for the class `Greeter`, as given in Listing 6-2 of Chapter 6?

The Unified Modeling Language

15.5   To get a better picture of the relationships among the classes needed for a particular application, designers use a notation called the **Unified Modeling Language**, or **UML**. In fact, the use case diagram mentioned earlier in this chapter is a part of the UML, but CRC cards are not. A detailed description of the UML is beyond the scope of this book, but you should be aware of some basic elements of this notation. We plan to introduce you to the UML in small steps.

A **class diagram** in the UML contains a three-part box for each class. The first part of each box contains a class's name, the second part contains the data fields (called **attributes** in the UML), and the last part contains its methods (**operations**). For now, our diagrams will indicate only the names of the classes. Figure 15-4 contains a class diagram for the class `Name`, as given in Listing 6-5 of Chapter 6. This diagram shows the relationships, or **associations**, among `Name`, its client `DemoName`, and `String`. The arrows indicate these associations: `DemoName` can reference `Name` objects, and `Name` can reference `String` objects.

FIGURE 15-4   A class diagram showing the associations among the classes
Name, DemoName, and String

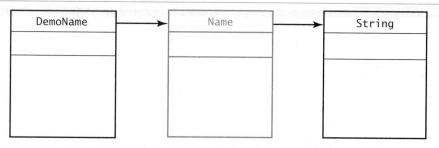

 Note: **Associations**
An association is a relationship between two objects of different classes. You indicate an association in a class diagram by drawing a line between the two boxes that represent the classes. The line can have an arrowhead at either or both of its ends. An arrow from class A pointing to class B indicates that an object of A references, and therefore depends on, an object of B.

The UML gives people an overall view of a complex system more effectively than either a natural language or a programming language can. English, for example, can be ambiguous, and Java code provides too much detail. Providing a clear picture of the interactions among classes is one of the strengths of the UML.

Specifying Methods

Once you have completed a CRC card for a class, you should specify what its methods do in more detail than the behaviors you described on the card. As you write these specifications, you should not think about any method's implementation. That is, you should not worry about *how* a method will accomplish its goals. Instead, you are seeking to identify what data and behaviors are important and specifying them without regard for how they will be defined in Java. This separation of specification from implementation allows you to concentrate on fewer details, thereby making your task easier and less error prone.

Abstraction and Encapsulation

15.6   The process that asks you to focus on *what* instead of *how* is called **abstraction**. When you abstract something, you identify its central ideas. For example, an abstract of a book is a brief description of the book, as opposed to the entire book. Separating the purpose of a class and its methods from their implementations is vital to a successful software project. Moreover, detailed, well-planned specifications facilitate an implementation that is more likely to be successful.

   Encapsulation is one of the design principles of object-oriented programming. To encapsulate means to enclose within a capsule or other container. When you practice encapsulation in Java, you enclose data and methods within a class. The class's implementation is, therefore, hidden from the client. A programmer needs to know only what each method does and how to call it. Thus, the programmer can use the class's methods without knowing—or worrying about—the details of their implementations. The resulting client code is then independent of the class's implementation.

   Is it hard for a programmer to use a class without knowing its implementation? You should know the answer to this question, because you have done this already! Chapter 4 showed you how to use several classes whose implementations you do not know that are in the Java Class Library. By using encapsulated software, you can write additional software more quickly, with less effort, and with fewer errors.

Note: **Encapsulation**
Encapsulation is a design principle of object-oriented programming that encloses data and methods within a class, thereby hiding the details of a class's implementation. A programmer should be able to use a class as though the body of every method was hidden from view. Thus, when you write a class, you should describe how to use it independently of any description of its implementation.

Note: **Information hiding**
When you separate the purpose of a class and its methods from their implementations, the goal is to avoid the need to change the class's clients if its implementation changes. As mentioned, you are hiding the implementation from the client. This process is called **information hiding**. Many people view information hiding and encapsulation as the same principle. Some, however, think of information hiding as the principle and encapsulation as the technique that achieves the principle.

Comments

15.7   Writing descriptions of the pieces of a program enables you to capture your ideas initially and to develop them so that they are clear enough to implement. Your written descriptions should be detailed enough to be useful as comments in your program. Taking this approach will help you go beyond the view that comments are something you add to satisfy an instructor or boss after you've written the program.

Although organizations tend to have their own style for comments, the developers of Java have specified a commenting style that you should follow. If you include comments in your program written in this style, you can run a utility program called javadoc to produce documents that describe your classes. This documentation tells people what they need to know to use your class, but omits all the implementation details, including the bodies of all method definitions.

The program javadoc extracts the header for your class, the headers for all public methods, and comments that are written in a certain form. Each such comment must appear immediately before either a public class definition or the header of a public method, and must begin with /** and end with */. We mentioned these comments briefly in Chapter 2 and have used them throughout the programs we have written so far. Certain **tags** are also used in javadoc. These begin with the symbol @ and appear within the comments to identify various aspects of the method. For example, you use @param to identify a description of a method's parameter, @return to identify the method's return value, and @throws to indicate an exception that the method throws. You will see some examples of these tags within the comments in this chapter. Appendix D provides the details for writing comments that are acceptable to javadoc and includes an example of the documentation that javadoc produces.

15.8   Whether or not you use javadoc to write comments, you should know what to write when you specify a method. The first step is to state the method's purpose or task concisely. Beginning this statement with a verb will help you to avoid many extra words that you really do not need.

In thinking about a method's purpose, you need to consider its input parameters, if any, and describe them. You also need to describe the method's results. Does it return a value, does it cause some action, or does it affect the state of an argument? When writing such descriptions, you should keep in mind the ideas in the following sections.

Preconditions and Postconditions

15.9   A **precondition** states the requirements necessary for executing a method. If a method's precondition is not met, you cannot expect the method to behave correctly. A precondition can be related to the description of a method's parameters. For example, a method that computes the square root of x can have $x \geq 0$ as a precondition.

videonote
Designing classes
formally

A **postcondition** is a statement of a method's effect after completing its execution. For a valued method, the postcondition describes the value returned by the method. For a void method, the postcondition describes the actions taken and any changes to the state of any object that either received the method invocation or is passed to the method. Thinking in terms of a postcondition can help you to clarify a method's purpose.

Writing a precondition and a postcondition for a method is a part of its design. The precondition states what a client must do for the method and what the method can assume is true before it executes. The postcondition states what a method does and what the client can assume is true after the method executes. Notice that going from precondition to postcondition leaves out the *how*— that is, we separate the method's specification from its implementation.

15.10   If the client is responsible for ensuring that certain conditions are met before calling the method, the method need not check these conditions. On the other hand, if the method is responsible for enforcing the conditions, the client does not check them. A clear statement of who must check a given set of conditions increases the probability that someone will do so and avoids duplication of effort.

For example, you could specify a method that computes a square root by writing the following comments before its header:

```
/** Computes the square root of a number.
    @param x   a real number >= 0
    @return the square root of x
*/
```

In this case, the method—by its precondition—assumes that the client will provide a nonnegative number as an argument.

On the other hand, the method could assume responsibility for checking the argument. In that case, its comments might read as follows:

```
/** Computes the square root of a number.
    @param x   a real number
    @return the square root of x if x >= 0
    @throws ArithmeticException if x < 0
*/
```

This method accepts any real number and either returns its square root, if that is possible, or throws an exception if not.

 Question 2 What precondition and postcondition can you write for the method `Math.cos(x)`?

 Programming Tip

Specify each public method fully in comments placed before the method's header. Be clear as to whether a method or its client is responsible for ensuring that the necessary conditions are met. In this way, checking is done but not duplicated. During debugging, however, a method should always check that its precondition has been met.

 Note: The steps in designing classes to solve a given problem

This chapter began with our seven-step list for class design. In light of the tools introduced here, we integrate those earlier steps into a new five-step list:

1. Study and understand the problem.
2. Propose classes, their responsibilities, and their collaborations. Record these ideas on CRC cards: Name the class. Choose and name the data fields, indicating their data types. Describe the behaviors associated with objects of the class. Name the methods that will implement these behaviors.
3. Draw a UML class diagram to formalize the relationships among the classes.
4. Write descriptive comments to document each class. Specify the methods by writing a header and comments for each one.
5. Write statements that use the methods and could appear in a client. Revise the method specifications, if necessary.

You now will be ready to implement the classes.

■ A Problem Solved: Creating a Class to Represent People

Design and implement a class of objects that can represent the customers of a bank or the students at a university.

A Class Design

15.11   We are creating a single class to represent people. For simplicity, assume that each one of these "person" objects has a name and a city of residence. Since we already have written the class Name in Chapter 6, let's use it to represent a person's name. Our new class—we'll call it Person—then can have two objects as data fields, an instance of the class Name and an instance of the class String, as follows:

```
private Name    myName;
private String myCity;
```

Figure 15-5 illustrates an object of type Person. It contains a Name object and a String object, and the Name object contains two String objects.

FIGURE 15-5   A Person object is made up of other objects

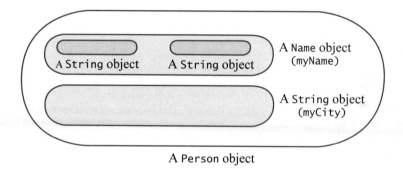

A Person object

We give the class Person constructors, as well as accessor and mutator methods and the method toString. Recall that the method toString is invoked when you use System.out.println to display an object, so it is a handy method to include in your class definitions. Suppose that we also want a method to decide whether two people live in the same city. Let's list these behaviors, as we did for the class Name in Segment 15.3, on the CRC card shown in Figure 15-6.

FIGURE 15-6   A CRC card for the class Person

Person
Responsibilities
Set person's name and city
Get person's name
Get person's city
Get person's name and city (toString)
Decide whether two people live in the same city
Collaborations
Name
String
DemoPerson (client of Person)

15.12   We continue the design of the class Person by writing a header and descriptive comments for each method. In doing so, we've refined the simple description of the task of each method, as listed on the CRC card, to include preconditions and postconditions. We've also added javadoc tags. Listing 15-1 shows the results of this task.

LISTING 15-1   An outline of the class `Person`

```java
/** Person.java by F. M. Carrano.
    Represents a person's name and place of residence.
*/
public class Person
{
   private Name    myName;
   private String myCity;

   /** Constructs a default Person object that has an empty name and
       city. */
   public Person()
   {
   } // end default constructor

   /** Constructs a Person object that has a given name and city.
       @param fullName   a Name object
       @param city       a string that names the person's city */
   public Person(Name fullName, String city)
   {
   } // end constructor

   /** Sets a person's name and city.
       @param fullName   a Name object
       @param city       a string that names the person's city */
   public void setPerson(Name fullName, String city)
   {
   } // end setPerson

   /** Sets a person's name and city.
       @param firstName   the person's first name as a string
       @param lastName    the person's last name as a string
       @param city        a string that names the person's city */
   public void setPerson(String firstName, String lastName, String city)
   {
   } // end setPerson

   /** Gets a person's name.
       @return the person's name */
   public Name getName()
   {
   } // end getName

   /** Gets a person's city of residence.
       @return the person's city */
   public String getCity()
   {
```

```
    } // end getCity

    /** Gets a person's name and city as a string.
        @return the person's full name and place of residence */
    public String toString()
    {
    } // end toString

    /** Tests whether a person lives in the same city as another person.
        @return true if the two people live in the same city, or
                false otherwise */
    public boolean isNeighbor(Person otherPerson
    {
    } // end isNeighbor
} // end Person
```

Question 3 Write a class diagram that shows the associations among the classes DemoPerson, Person, Name, and String.

A Client for Person

15.13   To clarify our specifications of the class Person and our understanding of them, we write a program that demonstrates Person before we actually implement it. In fact, a clear separation between these steps is not always present, as they often are performed in conjunction with each other. Writing a client for our proposed class can help us to decide what capabilities Person objects should have. Such client code can greatly influence our decisions about the design of this class. It also will help us write the headers for the methods.

Notice that we did not mention constructors on the CRC card in Figure 15-6. In writing the client DemoPerson, let's assume that Person will have a default constructor. We use this constructor to create our first Person object, joe, as follows:

```
Person joe = new Person();
```

If we do not want joe to be a generic person, we can use the method setPerson to set joe's name and city. We could decide to pass three String arguments—joe's first name, last name, and city—to setPerson, as follows:

```
joe.setPerson("Joe", "Java", "Kingston");
```

Thus, the header of setPerson would be

```
public void setPerson(String firstName, String lastName, String city)
```

If we had not already chosen this header for setPerson, we could do so now.

15.14   Let's use the default constructor again to create a second instance of Person, but this time we also create a Name object and pass it to setPerson. Thus, we might have

```
Person jill = new Person();
Name jillsName = new Name("Jill", "Jones");
jill.setPerson(jillsName, "Kingston");
```

This time `setPerson` receives two arguments, assuming that its header is

```java
public void setPerson(Name fullName, String city)
```

Notice that we have two separate versions of `setPerson`, each of which has different parameters. We'll discuss this aspect of Java in Segment 15.19.

A third instance of `Person` could use a second constructor, if we choose to define one, whose arguments are a `Name` object and a string:

```java
Name chrisName = new Name("Chris", "Robin");
Person chris = new Person(chrisName, "Providence");
```

Establishing the ways in which `Person` objects will be created and initialized, and writing other Java statements that use these objects, can help us to decide what capabilities `Person` objects should have. Such client code can greatly influence our decisions about the design of this class.

15.15   The program in Listing 15-2 begins by creating the `Person` objects given previously. The rest of the program invokes the methods of `Person`. Examine those calls and the output we expect after defining `Person`.

LISTING 15-2   A client for the proposed class `Person`

```java
/** DemoPerson.java by F. M. Carrano
    Demonstrates the class Person.
*/
public class DemoPerson
{
    public static void main(String args[])
    {
// 3 ways to create a Person object:
        Person joe = new Person();
        joe.setPerson("Joe", "Java", "Kingston");

        Person jill = new Person();
        Name jillsName = new Name("Jill", "Jones");
        jill.setPerson(jillsName, "Kingston");

        Name chrisName = new Name("Chris", "Robin");
        Person chris = new Person(chrisName, "Providence");

    // test other methods:
        System.out.println("Test toString(): ");
        System.out.println(joe + "\n");

        System.out.println("Test getName() and getCity(): ");
        System.out.println("My name is " + joe.getName() +
                            "; I live in " + joe.getCity() + ".\n");

        // do joe and jill live in the same city?
        System.out.println("Test isNeighbor(): ");
        if (joe.isNeighbor(jill))
            System.out.println(joe + " and " + jill +
                                " live in the same city.");
```

```
        else
            System.out.println(joe + " and " + jill +
                                " live in different cities.");

        // do joe and chris live in the same city?
        if (joe.isNeighbor(chris))
            System.out.println(joe + " and " + chris +
                                " live in the same city.");
        else
            System.out.println(joe + " and " + chris +
                                " live in different cities.");
    } // end main
} // end DemoPerson
```

Output

```
    Test toString():
    Joe Java (Kingston)

    Test getName() and getCity():
    My name is Joe Java; I live in Kingston.

    Test isNeighbor():
    Joe Java (Kingston) and Jill Jones (Kingston) live in the same city.
    Joe Java (Kingston) and Chris Robin (Providence) live in different cities.
```

Programming Tip

A program's output should be clear to its user, even when that user is you. When you define a new class, you undoubtedly will write additional code to test the class. Take some time to make the output from this code easy to understand.

Implementation of the Class Person

15.16   Listing 15-3 shows an implementation of the class Person. Let's examine some interesting aspects of this implementation. Notice that the default constructor initializes myName and myCity to specific values. If this constructor instead had an empty body, the data fields myName and myCity would be initialized by default to null, since they are objects. As long as myName remained null, it could not be used in calls to the methods of Name. Let's see how that might cause a problem.

After we create a default Person object within a client, how do we set its name and city? You saw in Listing 15-2 that we call the method setPerson. The first version of setPerson in Listing 15-3 causes no problem, as it assigns objects to the fields myName and myCity, as follows:

```
    myName = fullName;
    myCity = city;
```

But the second version of setPerson uses myName to invoke Name's method setName:

```
    myName.setName(firstName, lastName);
```

If myName is null, an error will occur.

15.17   To avoid this problem, we need to initialize myName to a Name object. Doing this only once per Person object is sufficient. So instead of assigning a new Name object to myName in setPerson, we make this assignment in the default constructor of Person. Thus, Person's default constructor executes

```
myName = new Name();
```

allowing setPerson to legally invoke

```
myName.setName(firstName, lastName);
```

Notice that you can access the name that myName represents only by calling Name's methods, not by using Name's data fields first and last.

The field myCity is assigned a string by both versions of setPerson, so its previous value is unimportant. It could be null or a value such as the empty string. We chose the latter value for Person's default constructor.

15.18   Within Person's method toString, we invoke Name's toString method to retrieve the person's name. Although the two methods have the same name, no problem results, as they belong to different objects of different classes.

The method isNeighbor has a parameter of type Person. This method causes one Person object to interact with another Person object to decide whether they have the same city. The expression joe.isNeighbor(jill) in Listing 15-2 is an example of how this method is used to compare the city fields of joe and jill. Within the body of the method, myCity is joe's city, while otherPerson.myCity is jill's. You can write otherPerson.myCity because it is within the definition of the class Person. You could also write otherPerson.getCity(). A similar situation is discussed in Segment 6.20 of Chapter 6 with respect to Name's method giveLastNameTo.

LISTING 15-3   The class Person

```
/** Person.java by F. M. Carrano
    Represents a person's name and city of residence.
*/
public class Person
{
   private Name myName;
   private String myCity;

   /** Constructs a default Person object that has an empty name and
       city. */
   public Person()
   {
      myName = new Name();
      myCity = "";
   } // end default constructor

   /** Constructs a Person object that has a given name and city.
       @param fullName  a Name object
       @param city      a string that names the person's city */
   public Person(Name fullName, String city)
   {
```

```
      myName = fullName;
      myCity = city;
   } // end constructor

   /** Sets a person's name and city.
      @param fullName   a Name object
      @param city       a string that names the person's city */
   public void setPerson(Name fullName, String city)
   {
      myName = fullName;
      myCity = city;
   } // end setPerson

   /** Sets a person's name and city.
      @param firstName   the person's first name as a string
      @param lastName    the person's last name as a string
      @param city        a string that names the person's city */
   public void setPerson(String firstName, String lastName, String city)
   {
      myName.setName(firstName, lastName);
      myCity = city;
   } // end setPerson

   /** Gets a person's name.
      @return the person's name */
   public Name getName()
   {
      return myName;
   } // end getName

   /** Gets a person's city of residence.
      @return the person's city */
   public String getCity()
   {
      return myCity;
   } // end getCity

   /** Gets a person's name and city as a string.
      @return the person's full name and city of residence */
   public String toString()
   {
      return myName.toString() + " (" + myCity + ")";
   } // end toString

   /** Tests whether a person lives in the same city as another person.
      @return true if the two people live in the same city, or
              false otherwise */
```

```
    public boolean isNeighbor(Person otherPerson)
    {
        return myCity.equals(otherPerson.myCity);
    } // end isNeighbor
} // end Person
```

Question 4 In the second version of the method `setPerson` given in Listing 15-3, what is another way to set the person's name? Do not create a new `Name` object.

Question 5 Assume that the default constructor of `Person` has an empty body. How can you revise the second version of the method `setPerson` so that it creates a new `Name` object for `myName`?

Question 6 Why is the implementation suggested by the previous question not as good as the one given in Listing 15-3?

Question 7 Recall that Segment 8.24 in Chapter 8 described how a constructor can call another constructor by using the reserved word `this`. Revise the definitions of `Person`'s constructors, as given in Listing 15-3, so that one calls the other.

Overloaded Methods

15.19   Notice the first responsibility on the CRC card in Figure 15-6 for our class `Person`:

Set person's name and city

In the design of this class, we named the method for this behavior `setPerson`. Given a `Name` object for the person's name and a string to represent the city, we wrote the following comment and header for this method:

```
/** Sets a person's name and city. */
public void setPerson(Name fullName, String city)
```

We also decided to provide the client some flexibility and convenience by designing another version of this method:

```
/** Sets a person's name and city. */
public void setPerson(String firstName, String lastName, String city)
```

videonote
Overloading

We certainly can have two different methods that initialize an instance of `Person` using different arguments, but can these methods have the same name? The answer is yes. Such methods are said to be **overloaded**. The rules for defining overloaded methods are summarized in the following note:

> **Note: Overloaded methods**
> A method in a class overloads one or more methods in the same[1] class when they have the same name but different parameter lists. That is, either one method must have a different number of parameters than the other method or the *n*th parameter in one method must have a different data type than the *n*th parameter in the other method. Since a method's **signature** is its name and the number, types, and order of its parameters, overloaded methods are those having the same name but different signatures.
>
> A class cannot have more than one method with the same signature, even if such methods have different return types, as the compiler cannot distinguish among them.

---

1. As you will see in the next chapter, one class can overload a method in another class, if the classes are related by inheritance.

15.20   Our previous classes have often contained more than one constructor, and so does the class Person. Having more than one constructor is not new to you. Recall that the note about constructors at the end of Segment 6.5 in Chapter 6 states, "A class can have more than one constructor, with each one differing in its list of parameters." We now can refine that statement to say that when a class has multiple constructors, they are overloaded. Thus, the constructors must differ in the number or types of their parameters.

Question 8 Is it possible to overload the method getCity in the class Person with a method that has the following header? Explain.

```
/** Gets a code for the person's city of residence.
    @return the zip code of the city's main post office */
public int getCity()
```

Class Relationships

The Java Class Library contains many classes for our use when we write our own classes. Moreover, we can use our own classes within other classes that we write. For example, our class Name uses the class String from the Java Class Library, and our class Person uses both Name and String. This section begins to investigate some of the details involved in using an already written class.

Clearly, when one class uses another, it is dependent on that other class. The degree of this dependence is also discussed in this section.

Reusing Classes

15.21   Object-oriented programming enables us to use existing classes in the definition of a new class. That is, you use classes that you or someone else has written to create new classes, rather than reinventing everything yourself. One way to do this is to declare an instance of an existing class as a data field of your new class. In fact, we have done this already when we defined classes that have a string as a data field. The class Name in Chapter 6 is such a class. Its fields are instances of the class String, as you can see by looking at Listing 6-5. Figure 15-7 illustrates this relationship between a Name object and its two String members. Since Name has an instance of String as a data field, the relationship between Name and String is called a ***has-a*** relationship.

FIGURE 15-7   A Name object contains String objects

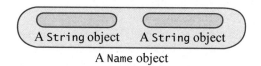

A Name object

Note: *Has-a* relationships

When class A "has a," or contains, an instance (object) of class B as one of its data fields, classes A and B are said to have a *has-a* relationship. This relationship is usually called **aggregation**. A variation of this relationship is called **composition**. These two concepts are similar but not the same, and their difference is subtle. For our current purposes, identifying a *has-a* relationship is more important than distinguishing between aggregation and composition. However, you should learn the differences between these concepts in your future studies, as they can have a significant impact on the design, implementation, and behavior of software.

Note: A class having an object as a data field has no special access to the object's private fields and private methods. Rather, the class must behave as a client would. That is, the class must use the object's public methods to manipulate the object's data.

 Note: Inheritance
Another way to reuse an existing class is through inheritance. A new class can inherit properties and behaviors from an existing class, augmenting or modifying them as desired. Although we have used inheritance in the graphics chapters, we will discuss it in detail in Chapters 16 and 27. As you will see, inheritance forms an *is-a* relationship between classes.

Note: Distinguishing between *is-a* relationships and *has-a* relationships is quite important. You need to know when to use aggregation and when to use inheritance. As important as inheritance is, aggregation is usually the more appropriate choice.

Coupling and Cohesion

videonote
Design guidelines
and concepts

15.22 **Coupling.** Two classes could be totally independent of each other, or one class could depend greatly on the other. The degree to which the classes in an application depend on one another is called **coupling**. Some coupling is necessary. After all, objects must collaborate to accomplish anything, and collaboration implies object dependency. For example, if an object of one class requires an object of another class to perform a task, coupling occurs between the two classes.

Such is the case for the classes Person and Name. If you look at the implementation of Person given in Listing 15-3, you will see that the method setPerson calls Name's method setName. Thus, a Person object uses the abilities of a Name object to carry out its tasks. If the definition of Name changes, the class Person might not work anymore. On the other hand, the Name object used by a Person object is oblivious to this relationship, because Name objects have no dependence on Person objects.

An application whose classes have minimal dependency is said to be loosely coupled. You should strive to reduce coupling in your designs, as loosely coupled designs have several benefits. For example, a loosely coupled application is

- Easier to understand. When a class depends on several other classes, understanding its implementation requires an understanding of all those other classes.
- Easier to maintain, enhance, or otherwise modify. If class A depends on class B, changing class B can adversely affect class A.
- Easier to reuse. The class Name, for instance, depends only on the class String, which is a part of the Java Class Library. String is not a class whose specifications might change tomorrow in a way that will damage Name. On the other hand, to use the class Person in an application, you must also have the class Name. In addition, you must know that the specifications of Name have not changed since you wrote Person.

15.23 When you draw a class diagram, you can and should show the dependency among classes. As mentioned in Segment 15.5 and illustrated in Figure 15-4, an arrow from class A to class B indicates a dependency of class A on class B. The class diagrams for two solutions to a given problem would show different dependencies among the classes, as Figure 15-8 illustrates. The design having the fewest dependencies has the lowest coupling. Such a design is not always the best, however, as sometimes other considerations take precedence.

FIGURE 15-8   Two class diagrams as examples of loosely coupled and highly coupled solutions

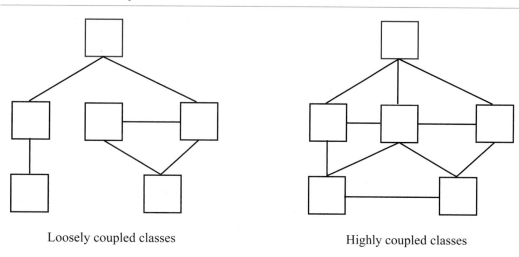

Loosely coupled classes   Highly coupled classes

15.24   **Cohesion.** Every method should perform one well-defined task, and each class should have a single well-defined responsibility. Such methods and classes are said to be highly **cohesive**. The methods of a class should be highly cohesive and should directly contribute to the class's responsibility. The class `Person` and its methods are highly cohesive.

A method should not have a secondary action, particularly if the action is subtle or undocumented. Such secondary actions are called **side effects**. For example, a method that returns a value should not also change the state of one of its arguments.

Using highly cohesive classes in an application promotes loose coupling. As the cohesion associated with a class decreases, that class does more unrelated work. The class is then more likely to become coupled with other classes in the program.

A highly cohesive class is easier to use in several distinct programs than one that is not cohesive. It is also easier to maintain, as it will have simpler logic. If you begin to design a class that has more than one responsibility, revise your design to use several classes, each with a single responsibility taken from your original design.

■ The Modifier `static`

As we mentioned in Segment 6.4 of Chapter 6, the objects of a class typically have their own copies of the class's data fields. Likewise, the objects have behaviors that are defined by the class's methods. Sometimes, you want the fields and behaviors to belong to the class instead of to the individual objects. In those cases, you use the modifier `static`.

Static Fields

15.25   We formally encountered the `static` modifier in Segment 8.8 of Chapter 8, when we talked about static fields. To review, if a class defines the named constant

```
private final int INCHES_PER_FOOT = 12;
```

every object of that class will have a copy of INCHES_PER_FOOT. But if we add the modifier static to the definition, as follows:

```java
private static final int INCHES_PER_FOOT = 12;
```

all objects of the class will share one copy of INCHES_PER_FOOT. This version of the constant is known as a static field.

Static fields can change in value if you omit the modifier final. Imagine that you want to count the number of Circle objects that a client creates. One variable within the class Circle could maintain this count. You would not want each Circle object to have its own counter. Thus, you would define the counter to be a static field, as follows:

```java
private static int numberOfCircles = 0;
```

Note that this field is not final, so its value can change.

Since the client invokes a constructor to create a Circle object, each constructor could increment numberOfCircles. Because numberOfCircles is private, you must define a get method within Circle so that the client can access the current value of numberOfCircles. Listing 15-4 shows a simple version of Circle that defines such a method, getNumberOfCircles. The client then simply invokes this method, as shown in Listing 15-5, to get the number of Circle objects created. The method getNumberOfCircles is a static method, which we discuss in the next section. As you will see, you use the class's name when invoking a static method, just as you do when calling methods of the standard class Math.

 Note: We initialize the data field numberOfCircles when we declare it, even though it is not a constant. Although this is legal, we prefer to perform initialization within constructors when possible. This static field cannot be initialized within a constructor, however, since the constructors must increment its value. If we had not initialized numberOfCircles to zero, its default initialization would have been zero anyway, but performing your own initialization instead of relying on default values is clearer to those who read your programs.

LISTING 15-4   A class that demonstrates a static field and a static method to access it

```java
/** Circle.java by F. M. Carrano
    A class having static fields and a static method.
*/
public class Circle
{
   private double radius;
   private static final double PI = Math.PI;
   private static int numberOfCircles = 0;

   /** Creates a circle of radius 1. */
   public Circle()
   {
      radius = 1.0;
      numberOfCircles++;
   } // end default constructor
```

```java
/** Creates a circle of radius newRadius. */
public Circle(double newRadius)
{
    radius = newRadius;
    numberOfCircles++;
} // end constructor

/** Returns a circle's radius. */
public double getRadius()
{
    return radius;
} // end getRadius

/** Returns a string that indicates the circle's radius. */
public String toString()
{
    return "A circle whose radius is " + radius;
} // end toString

/** Returns the number of Circle objects created by one client. */
public static int getNumberOfCircles()
{
    return numberOfCircles;
} // end getNumberOfCircles
} // end Circle
```

LISTING 15-5 A program that uses **Circle**'s static method

```java
/** StaticDemo.java by F. M. Carrano
    Demonstrates the use of a static method.
*/
public class StaticDemo
{
    public static void main(String[] args)
    {
        Circle unitCircle = new Circle();
        Circle myCircle   = new Circle(2.5);
        Circle yourCircle = new Circle(74.6);

        System.out.println(unitCircle);
        System.out.println(myCircle);
        System.out.println(yourCircle);
        System.out.println(Circle.getNumberOfCircles() +
                            " circles are defined.");
    } // end main
} // end StaticDemo
```

Output

```
A circle whose radius is 1.0
A circle whose radius is 2.5
A circle whose radius is 74.6
3 circles are defined.
```

Programming Tip

Use caution when defining a data field as static. A data field that is static but should not be will be difficult to find.

Note: The objects listed in the definition of an enumeration are static fields.

Static Methods

15.26   Sometimes you will have a task that is not a behavior of any object. For example, think of all of the computations that you can perform by using the class Math. This class has methods such as cos to compute the cosine of an angle and log to get a logarithm. These computations do not describe the behaviors of a Math object. In fact, we do not create Math objects when we want to use the methods in Math. Rather, we call these methods by using the class's name instead of an object name. Thus, we write statements such as

```
double cosAngle = Math.cos(angle);
double logX = Math.log(xValue);
```

A method such as cos or log is called a **static method** or **class method**. You define such a method by adding static to its header. For example, the header of the method cos is

```
public static double cos(double angle)
```

Notice that each main method is also static.

15.27   The method getNumberOfCircles in Listing 15-4 is a static method. Since it returns a count of the Circle objects that a client creates, the method really is appropriate for the class as a whole rather than for an individual object. Thus, in Listing 15-5, we have used the class's name to invoke the method rather than using a Circle object, such as myCircle. Although the latter is possible, you typically would not do that.

Note: Static methods: Restrictions

Within its class, a static method can

- Reference static data fields, but not nonstatic fields
- Call only static methods

These restrictions also apply to main methods, since they are static.
The second restriction has a loophole, which we point out next.

15.28   **Loophole.** When one method calls another method in its class, it usually names the method without qualifying it, using the name of the class or an object of that class. In these cases, a static method can call only static methods, as the previous note states. But if a static method creates an object of its class, it can use that object to invoke any method in the class, regardless of whether it is static. You are not likely to encounter such a situation.

Note: Instance methods
A method that defines a behavior of an object is called an **instance method**. Such methods are not static. A method that is not static must be an instance method. It can invoke any other method within its class and can reference any data field within its class.

Programming Tip
Use the modifiers `static` and `final` when you define named constants. Use `static` when you define a `main` method. You will seldom use `static` elsewhere.

Question 9 If a client creates three `Circle` objects, and then uses the second of these objects to invoke `getNumberOfCircles`, what is returned?

Question 10 Assume that in the class `Circle`, `numberOfCircles` and `getNumberOfCircles` are not static. If a client creates three `Circle` objects and then uses the third one to invoke `getNumberOfCircles`, what is returned?

An Enumeration as a Class

15.29   As Segment 8.12 in Chapter 8 mentioned, the compiler creates a class when it encounters an enumeration. These classes have methods such as `toString`, `ordinal`, `valueOf`, `equals`, and `compareTo`. For example, consider the following enumeration for the suits of playing cards:

```
enum Suit {CLUBS, DIAMONDS, HEARTS, SPADES}
```

We can use these methods in the following ways:

- `Suit.CLUBS.toString()` returns the string `"CLUBS"`.
- `System.out.println(Suit.CLUBS)` calls `toString` implicitly, and so displays CLUBS.
- `Suit.HEARTS.ordinal()` returns 2, the ordinal position of HEARTS in the enumeration.
- `Suit.valueOf("HEARTS")` returns `Suit.HEARTS`.
- `s.equals(Suit.DIAMONDS)` tests whether s, an instance of `Suit`, equals DIAMONDS.
- `s.compareTo(Suit.DIAMONDS)` compares s, an instance of `Suit`, to DIAMONDS, using their ordinal values to establish their sequence.

Note: An enumeration's method `valueOf` is static. Thus, you use the name of the enumeration when invoking this method, instead of using an instance of the enumerated type.

15.30   You can define data fields, constructors, and additional methods for an enumeration. If you define a private data field, you can assign it values for each of the objects in the enumeration. If you also add a get method, a client will be able to access these values. Listing 15-6 shows how these ideas are realized in a new definition for the enumeration `Suit`.

We have chosen strings as the values for the enumerated objects. Notation such as HEARTS("red") within the enumeration's definition invokes the constructor that we have provided and sets the value of HEARTS's private data field color. Note that the client cannot use the constructor, because it is private. Since color is final, its value cannot be changed by any other method. However, the method getColor provides public access to color's value.

Listing 15-7 demonstrates this enumeration.

LISTING 15-6   An enumeration that has a data field, constructor, and get method

```java
/** Suit.java by F. M. Carrano
    An enumeration of card suits.
*/
public enum Suit
{
    CLUBS("black"), DIAMONDS("red"), HEARTS("red"), SPADES("black");

    private final String color;

    private Suit(String suitColor)
    {
        color = suitColor;
    } // end constructor

    public String getColor()
    {
        return color;
    } // end getColor
} // end Suit
```

LISTING 15-7   A demonstration of the public enumeration Suit

```java
/** SuitDemo.java by F. M. Carrano
    A demonstration of the enumeration Suit.
*/
public class SuitDemo
{
    public static void main(String[] args)
    {
        for (Suit s : Suit.values())
            System.out.println(s + " are " + s.getColor());
    } // end main
} // end SuitDemo
```

Output

```
CLUBS are black
DIAMONDS are red
HEARTS are red
SPADES are black
```

videonote
A problem
solved

CHAPTER SUMMARY

- Use cases depict a system from the point of view of one or more actors. Use cases do not necessarily suggest classes within the system.

- A class-responsibility-collaboration, or CRC, card is a design tool that is simply an index card. It lists a class's name, proposed behaviors, and the names of other classes with which it has a relationship.

- The Unified Modeling Language, or UML, is a notation that class designers use to describe the relationships among classes.

- In software design, abstraction is a process that asks you to focus on *what* instead of *how*. You should identify what data and behaviors are important, and specify them without regard for how they will be defined in Java.

- Encapsulation is a design principle of object-oriented programming that encloses data and methods into a class, thereby hiding the details of a class's implementation. The programmer should be able to use a well-designed class as if the body of every method were hidden from view.

- Comments that precede a class or a method, and are written in a certain way, can be processed by a utility program called javadoc. The results are documents that describe the class and its methods.

- A method's precondition states the requirements necessary for executing the method. A client must satisfy the precondition before calling the method. A method's postcondition states the method's effect after completing its execution. A client can assume the truth of a postcondition after the method executes.

- A method in a class overloads one or more methods in the same class when they have the same name but differ in the number or types of parameters.

- You can use objects of one or more existing classes as the data fields of a new class. A relationship—called *has-a*—exists between the new class and each of the existing classes. The new class behaves as a client of the existing classes when it uses their data fields and methods. That is, the new class uses an object's methods to manipulate the object's data.

- A *has-a* relationship between two classes is usually called aggregation. Composition is a variation of aggregation that we will not consider in this book.

- Coupling is the degree to which the classes in an application depend on one another. Although some coupling is necessary to achieve collaboration among objects, loose coupling is desirable.

- A highly cohesive class has a single, well-defined responsibility. A highly cohesive method performs one well-defined task. High cohesion of classes and methods is desirable. Using highly cohesive classes in an application promotes loose coupling.

- A static field or static method is associated with the class and not the individual objects of the class.

- You should declare as static and final any data fields that are public constants.

- Since an enumeration is really a class, you can add data fields, a constructor, and methods to its definition.

EXERCISES

1. What is written on a CRC card?

2. List the behaviors of the class VerticalLine, as given in Listing 11-9 of Chapter 11, that would appear on a CRC card for that class.

3. Why do designers use index cards for CRC cards?

4. Why do designers separate the software's specification from its implementation?

5. What is abstraction, and how do software designers use it?

6. What is the purpose of the `javadoc` utility program?

7. Write comments in `javadoc` format for the following methods:

   - `isPointOn` of the class `VerticalLine`, as given in Listing 11-9 of Chapter 11
   - `display` of the class `SquareBox`, as given in Listing 11-11 of Chapter 11

8. What are preconditions and postconditions?

9. Why is cohesion important?

10. What data fields would you use in the definition of a class `Address` to represent a person's address? What new or existing classes are involved?

11. Add a data field to the class `Person` to represent a person's address. What new methods should you define for `Person`? What existing methods, if any, need to be changed in the class `Person` as a result of the additional field?

12.   a. When should a data field be static?
       b. When should a method be static?
       c. What is the difference between a static method and one that is not static?

13. Why are all the methods of the class `Math` static?

14. Draw a class diagram for the class `Quilt`, as given in Listing 14-4 of Chapter 14.

15. What is the UML notation for each of the following classes that appear in Chapter 11?

    - `RandomPoint` in Listing 11-8
    - `FourQuadrants` in Listing 11-10
    - `WherePanel` in Listing 11-12

16. Suppose you want to design software for a restaurant.

       a. Give use cases for placing an order and settling the bill.
       b. Identify a list of possible classes. Pick two of these classes, and write CRC cards for them.

17. When a customer of the Java International Bank opens a new savings account, the bank's software creates an instance of class named `BankAccount`. The initial balance for each new savings account must be greater than zero. When the customer makes deposits to or withdrawals from an account, appropriate methods of `BankAccount` are called.

       a. Write a CRC card for the class `BankAccount`.
       b. Write headers for each constructor and method in `BankAccount`. Include comments in `javadoc` format.
       c. What are the preconditions and postconditions for each constructor and method in `BankAccount`?

PROJECTS

1. Imagine that you want to keep track of your pet fish. Each fish is a certain kind and has a two-part name. For example, your clownfish is named Nemo Finding. You want to see whether any two given fish are the same kind. You also want to know how many fish you have. Design, implement, and demonstrate a class `Fish` that meets the previous requirements. Include a CRC card and a UML diagram that gives only the class names and the associations between them. Document each method with comments in `javadoc` format. Use the class `Name` from Chapter 6 to represent a fish's pet name.

2. Design a solution to either Project 2 or Project 3 of the previous chapter. Include a CRC card and a UML diagram that gives only the class names and the associations between them. Document each method with comments in javadoc format.

3. Listing 8-5 in Chapter 8 contains a definition for a class Coin. Using this class, or one like it, design, implement, and demonstrate a class of money jars. Each jar should be empty initially and should be able to accept any number of Coin objects representing quarters, dimes, nickels, and/or pennies. The jar should identify the value of each coin and be able to provide the total monetary value of its current contents. Include a CRC card in your design.

ANSWERS TO SELF-TEST QUESTIONS

1. Class name: Greeter
   Responsibility: greet
   Collaboration: String

2. Precondition: x is an angle in radians. Postcondition: The cosine of x is returned.

3.

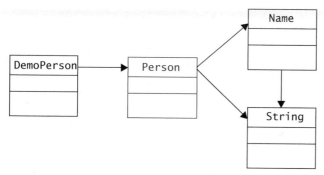

4. ```
   setFirst(firstName);
   setLast(lastName);
   ```

5. ```
   public void setPerson(String firstName, String lastName, String city)
   {
       myName = new Name(firstName, lastName);
       myCity = city;
   } // end setPerson
   ```

6. Suppose you were to set the name and city of an existing Person object more than once by invoking the version of setPerson suggested in Question 5. A new Name object would be created and soon deleted each time setPerson is called. This action would waste execution time.

7. ```
   public Person()
   {
       this(new Name(), "");
   } // end default constructor

   public Person(Name fullName, String city)
   {
       myName = fullName;
       myCity = city;
   } // end constructor
   ```
   ```

8. No. Although the two methods `getCity` have different return types, they have the same signatures. The compiler cannot distinguish between them.

9. 3

10. 1

Chapter 16

Object-Oriented Concepts

Contents

Prerequisites

Objectives

After studying this chapter, you should be able to
- Write a Java interface
- Represent interfaces and classes using UML notation
- Implement an existing Java interface
- Use a Java interface as a data type
- Describe the concept of polymorphism
- Describe the concept of inheritance
- Describe the class Object
- Describe overriding a method definition
- Override Object's method equals within a class
- Implement the Comparable interface

Object-oriented programming embodies three design concepts: encapsulation, polymorphism, and inheritance. The previous chapter introduced encapsulation as a technique that hides the details of a class's implementation from a client. Encapsulation relates directly to the importance of specifying methods before implementing them, which the previous chapter discussed. This chapter builds on that earlier presentation.

We use Java interfaces to indicate that a class must implement certain methods. Although our discussion of interfaces dominates this chapter, we go on to introduce inheritance as a way to create a new class that extends the behaviors of an existing class. Polymorphism is presented first in the context of interfaces and then again with inheritance. We include a discussion of the class Object as the ancestor of all classes and show you how to give your classes the methods equals and compareTo.

Java Interfaces

16.1   A class definition really has two parts, the **client interface** and the **implementation**. The client interface consists of the headers for the public methods of the class, the comments that tell a programmer how to use these public methods, and any publicly defined constants of the class. The implementation consists of the private data fields and the definitions of all methods, including those that are public and private. You should not need anything more than the client interface to be able to use a class in your program. Figure 16-1 illustrates an encapsulated implementation of a class and the client interface. Although the implementation is hidden from the client, the interface is visible and provides the client well-regulated communication with the implementation.

FIGURE 16-1   A client communicates with a class's hidden implementation through an interface

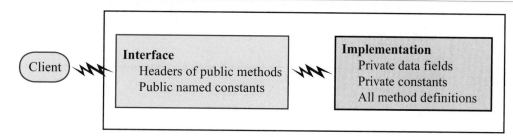

Question 1 Think of an everyday example that illustrates encapsulation. What part of your example corresponds to a client interface and what part to an implementation?

16.2   In the definition of a Java class, the client interface and implementation are not separated. They are mixed together. You can, however, create a separate **Java interface** that contains some or all of the headers for a class's public methods. You also can define public named constants within a Java interface. When you write an interface, you place it in its own file. In addition to writing your own interfaces, you can use those in the Java Class Library.

videonote
Java interfaces

Some interfaces describe all the public methods in a class, while others specify only certain public methods. If the interface includes comments to specify its methods, it will provide a programmer with the information necessary to implement those methods. One or more classes can be written to conform to an interface—that is, to **implement** the interface. Such a class must define a body for every method that the interface specifies. Notice that the method headers will appear in both the interface and the class.

Writing an Interface

16.3   A Java interface begins like a class definition, except that you use the word `interface` instead of `class`. That is, an interface begins with the statement

    public interface *interface-name*

rather than

    public class *class-name*

The interface can contain any number of headers for public methods, each followed by a semicolon. An interface does not declare the constructors for a class. Also note that methods within an interface are public by default, so you typically omit the modifier `public` from their headers. However, you can include the modifier if you prefer.

16.4   **Example.** Imagine such objects as circles, squares, or plots of land that have a perimeter and an area. Suppose that we want the classes of these objects to have get methods to access these quantities. If various programmers implemented these classes, they likely would not name or specify these get methods in the same way. To ensure that these classes provide our methods in a uniform way, we write an interface, such as the one in Listing 16-1. This interface provides a programmer with a handy summary of the methods' specifications. The programmer should be able to use these methods without looking at the class that implements them.

LISTING 16-1   The interface `Measurable`

```java
/** An interface for methods that return
    the perimeter and area of an object.
    @author F. M. Carrano1
*/
public interface Measurable
{
   /** Gets the perimeter.
       @return the perimeter */
   double getPerimeter();

   /** Gets the area.
       @return the area */
   double getArea();
} // end Measurable
```

You store an interface definition in a file whose name is the name of the interface followed by `.java`. For example, the interface in Listing 16-1 is in the file `Measurable.java`.

---

1. Note the `javadoc` tag `@author`.

Note: A Java interface is a good place to provide comments that specify each method's purpose, parameters, precondition, and postcondition. In this way, you can specify some or all of a class's methods in one file and implement them in another.

Note: An interface can declare data fields, but they must be public. By convention, a class's data fields are private, so any data fields in an interface should represent named constants. Thus, they should also be final and static.

Note: A Java interface does not specify constructors. Note that you never use the operator new with the name of an interface, as you would with the name of a class.

16.5 **Example.** Recall the class Name that we presented in Listing 6-5 of Chapter 6. Imagine that before we wrote the class, we had the interface shown in Listing 16-2. To save space, we have included comments for only the first two methods. This interface provides specifications of the desired methods for an entire class. You could use it when implementing a class such as Name. Additionally, you should be able to write a client for the class just by looking at the interface.

```
LISTING 16-2    The interface NameInterface

/** An interface for a class of names.
    @author F. M. Carrano
*/
public interface NameInterface
{
   /** Sets the first and last names.
       @param firstName  a string that is the desired first name
       @param lastName    a string that is the desired last name */
   void setName(String firstName, String lastName);

   /** Gets the full name.
       @return a string containing the first and last names */
   String getName();

   void setFirst(String firstName);
   void setLast(String lastName);

   String getFirst();
   String getLast();

   String toString();

   void giveLastNameTo(NameInterface otherName);
} // end NameInterface
```

Notice that the parameter of the method giveLastNameTo has NameInterface as its data type instead of Name, as it did in Chapter 6. You should write an interface independently of any class that will implement it. We will talk about interfaces as data types in Segment 16.10.

Programming Tip: **Naming an interface**

Interface names, particularly those that are standard in Java, often end in "-able," such as `Measurable`. That ending does not always provide a good name, so endings such as "-er" or "Interface" are also used.

Question 2 Imagine objects that have a string as a name. Write a Java interface, `Nameable`, that various classes of these objects could implement to provide an accessor and mutator for the name.

Question 3 Write a Java interface, `Circular`, that various classes could implement to provide an accessor and mutator for a real-valued radius.

Some UML Details

16.6 You represent an interface in UML in much the same way that you represent a class, but you precede its name with <<interface>>, as shown in Figure 16-2. As we mentioned in Segment 15.5 of the previous chapter, the middle portion of the notation is for a class's data fields and the last part is for its methods. The same is true for interfaces. To represent a method in the UML for either a class or an interface, you write its name and parameters, if any, as shown in the figure. The plus sign indicates that a method is public, while private methods are preceded by a minus sign. The colon and data type denote the type of a method's return value.

FIGURE 16-2 UML notation for the interface `Measurable`

```
              <<interface>>
               Measurable


          +getPerimeter(): double
          +getArea(): double
```

When a method has parameters, you use the same notation for their data types as you do for the method's return type. For example, Figure 16-3 shows the notation for the interface `NameInterface`, as given in Listing 16-2. We have shortened the parameter names to save space.

FIGURE 16-3 UML notation for the interface `NameInterface`

```
                 <<interface>>
                 NameInterface


    +setName(first: String, last: String): void
    +getName(): String
    +setFirst(first: String): void
    +setLast(last: String): void
    +getFirst(): String
    +getLast(): String
    +toString(): String
    +giveLastNameTo(other: NameInterface): void
```

Note: UML notation for interfaces and classes

Each interface and class is represented in UML by a three-part box. One part contains the component's name, a second contains its data fields, and the third contains its methods. You write the data type of any parameter or data field after a colon that follows the item's name. Similar notation is used for a method's return type. Private data fields and methods are preceded by a minus sign, while public members are preceded by a plus sign.

The only difference between the notations for an interface and a class is the appearance of <<interface>> before an interface's name.

Question 4 What UML notation represents the interface that you wrote in Question 2?

Question 5 What UML notation represents the class Name, as given in Listing 6-5 of Chapter 6?

Implementing an Interface

16.7   Any class that implements an interface must state so at the beginning of its definition by using an **implements clause**. For example, if a class C implements the Measurable interface given in Listing 16-1, it would begin as follows:

```
public class C implements Measurable
```

The class then must provide a definition for each method declared in the interface. In this example, the class C must implement the methods getPerimeter and getArea. Soon we will examine some classes that implement this interface.

If we wrote a class Name that implemented NameInterface, the class would begin as follows:

```
public class Name implements NameInterface
```

The rest of the class could look just like the one in Listing 6-5 of Chapter 6, except that the method giveLastNameTo would have a parameter whose data type is NameInterface instead of Name to match its declaration in the interface.

Note: Writing an interface is a way for a class designer to specify methods for another programmer. Implementing an interface is a way to guarantee that a class defines certain methods.

Note: A class can implement more than one interface. To do so, you list all the interface names, separated by commas, after the reserved word implements.

Note: Because all methods and fields declared in an interface must be public, you can omit their access modifiers. However, when a class implements an interface, you must write the access modifier public for each method in the interface. Although a method without an access modifier in an interface is assumed to be public, a method without an access modifier in a class is assumed to be private.

Question 6 Define two classes, Disk and Cylinder, that implement the interface Circular that Question 3 describes.

16.8 **Example: Measurable objects.** Imagine that we are writing components for a program to help architects. Each program component represents a part of a house. Thus, we might create classes such as Wall, Floor, Roof, Window, and Door. Each of the represented house parts has a perimeter and an area. In recognition of this fact, and to give some uniformity to our classes, we make each class implement the interface Measurable that appears in Listing 16-1.

Each of the classes Wall, Floor, and so on will implement the interface Measurable in its own way, and each can define additional methods. If other common behaviors are found during the design of these classes, you could form one or more additional interfaces that the classes could implement. For example, each of the building components mentioned has an associated cost. Methods relevant to their cost could make up an interface.

Instead of actually implementing these classes, we will experiment with simpler classes to further our understanding of interfaces.

16.9 Let's define two classes, Square and Circle, that implement the interface Measurable. We'll also write a demonstration program, ShapesDemo. Figure 16-4 shows a UML diagram that illustrates the relationships among our classes. Notice that an arrow having a dotted shaft and hollow head is drawn from a class to the interface that it implements.

The class Square in Listing 16-3 and the class Circle in Listing 16-4 each implement the interface Measurable in its own way. These two classes also implement methods that are not specified in the interface. The program ShapesDemo in Listing 16-5 creates an object of each class. We then use these objects in calls to the methods getPerimeter and getArea.

LISTING 16-3   A class of squares that implements the interface Measurable

```java
/** A class of squares.
    @author F. M. Carrano
*/
public class Square implements Measurable
{
    private double side;

    public Square(double newSide)
    {
        side = newSide;
    } // end constructor

    public double getSide()
    {
        return side;
    } // end getSide

    public String toString()
    {
        return "A square whose side is " + side;
    } // end toString

    public double getPerimeter()
    {
```

```
      return 4 * side;
   } // end getPerimeter

   public double getArea()
   {
      return side * side;
   } // end getArea
} // end Square
```

FIGURE 16-4   A UML class diagram for the ShapesDemo program

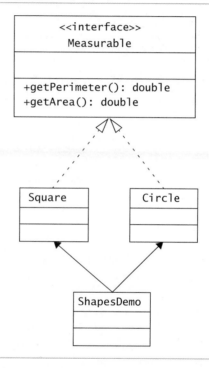

LISTING 16-4   A class of circles that implements the interface Measurable

```
/** A class of circles.
    @author F. M. Carrano
*/
public class Circle implements Measurable
{
   private double radius;

   public Circle(double newRadius)
   {
      radius = newRadius;
   } // end constructor
```

```java
   public double getRadius()
      return radius;
   } // end getRadius

   public String toString()
   {
      return "A circle whose radius is " + radius;
   } // end toString

   public double getPerimeter()
   {
      return 2 * Math.PI * radius;
   } // end getPerimeter

   public double getArea()
   {
      return Math.PI * radius * radius;
   } // end getArea
} // end Circle
```

LISTING 16-5   A program that demonstrates the classes `Square` and `Circle`

```java
/** Demonstrates the classes Square and Circle.
    @author F. M. Carrano
*/
import java.text.DecimalFormat;
public class ShapesDemo
{
   public static void main(String[] args)
   {
      Square mySquare = new Square(2.5);
      double mySquarePerimeter = mySquare.getPerimeter();
      double mySquareArea = mySquare.getArea();

      Circle myCircle = new Circle(2.5);
      double myCirclePerimeter = myCircle.getPerimeter();
      double myCircleArea = myCircle.getArea();

      DecimalFormat formatter = new DecimalFormat("0.00");
      System.out.println(mySquare + " inches");
      System.out.println("has a perimeter of " +
                         formatter.format(mySquarePerimeter) +
                         " inches and an area of " +
                         formatter.format(mySquareArea) +
                         " square inches.");
```

```
            System.out.println();

            System.out.println(myCircle + " feet");
            System.out.println("has a perimeter of " +
                        formatter.format(myCirclePerimeter) +
                        " feet and an area of " +
                        formatter.format(myCircleArea) +
                        " square feet.");
    } // end main
} // end ShapesDemo
```

Output

```
A square whose side is 2.5 inches
has a perimeter of 10.00 inches and an area of 6.25 square inches.

A circle whose radius is 2.5 feet
has a perimeter of 15.71 feet and an area of 19.63 square feet.
```

Question 7 How would you change the definition of the class `Circle`, as given in Listing 16-4, so that it implements the interface `Circular` described in Question 3?

An Interface as a Data Type

16.10   You can use a Java interface as you would a data type when you declare a variable, a data field, or a method's parameter or return type. For example, the method `giveLastNameTo` in `NameInterface`, as shown in Listing 16-2, has a parameter whose type is `NameInterface`:

```
public void giveLastNameTo(NameInterface otherName);
```

Any argument that you pass to this method must be an object of a class that implements `NameInterface`. Note that such a class must be defined with the clause `implements NameInterface`. Simply defining all the methods in the interface is insufficient.

Why didn't we declare `otherName`'s type to be `Name`, as we did in Listing 6-5 of Chapter 6? We want the interface to be independent of any class that implements it, since more than one class can implement an interface. By using `NameInterface` as the parameter's type, you ensure that the method's argument will be able to receive calls to all of the methods declared in `NameInterface`. In general, a method can be sure that an object passed to it as an argument is able to receive calls to methods declared in an interface if the data type of the argument's corresponding parameter is the interface.

Note: By using an interface as a variable's type, you indicate that the object referenced by the variable can receive calls to a certain set of methods, and only those methods.

16.11   **Implementation issues.** Since within `NameInterface` the data type of `giveLastNameTo`'s parameter is `NameInterface`, the definition of the method within any class that implements the interface must use the same method header as the one that appears in the interface. It must also add the modifier `public`, if it is not already present in the interface. For example, a correct definition of this method is

```
/** Gives the last name to otherName. */
public void giveLastNameTo(NameInterface otherName)
{
   otherName.setLast(last);
} // end giveLastNameTo
```

The body of the method is the same as in Listing 6-5 of Chapter 6.

Could the body be

```
otherName.last = last;
```

instead of

```
otherName.setLast(last);
```

If the data type of otherName is Name, as it is in Chapter 6, you can write otherName.last instead of invoking setLast. But here, since otherName's data type is NameInterface, otherName.last will cause a syntax error. After all, NameInterface does not—and cannot—declare a private data field such as last. The interface, however, does declare the method setLast.

16.12 In the ShapesDemo program of Listing 16-5, the statements that display the output for a square are like those for the circle. Let's create a new class that has a method to display the output for either of these objects. Listing 16-6 contains such a class, called ShapeWriter. Its method display has a parameter shape whose data type is Measurable. Thus, we can pass an object of any class that implements the interface Measurable to the method display. You also pass the units of measurement associated with the object shape to display. Listing 16-7 contains a new program, ShapesDemo2, that makes use of ShapeWriter's display method. Its output is the same as shown in Listing 16-5.

LISTING 16-6   The class ShapeWriter

```
/** A class to display a Measurable object.
    @author F. M. Carrano
*/
import java.text.DecimalFormat;
public class ShapeWriter
{
   /** Displays the perimeter and area of a Measurable object. */
   public void display(Measurable shape, String units)
   {
      double perimeter = shape.getPerimeter();
      double area = shape.getArea();

      DecimalFormat formatter = new DecimalFormat("0.00");
      System.out.println(shape + " " + units);
      System.out.println("has a perimeter of " +
                      formatter.format(perimeter) + " " + units +
                      " and an area of " +
                      formatter.format(area) +
                      " square " + units + ".");
   } // end display
} // end ShapeWriter
```

LISTING 16-7 A program that demonstrates the class ShapeWriter

```java
/** Demonstrates the classes ShapeWriter, Square, and Circle.
   @author F. M. Carrano
*/
public class ShapesDemo2
{
   public static void main(String[] args)
   {
      ShapeWriter writer = new ShapeWriter();

      Square mySquare = new Square(2.5);
      writer.display(mySquare, "inches");
      System.out.println();

      Circle myCircle = new Circle(2.5);
      writer.display(myCircle, "feet");
   } // end main
} // end ShapesDemo2
```

Output

```
A square whose side is 2.5 inches
has a perimeter of 10.00 inches and an area of 6.25 square inches.

A circle whose radius is 2.5 feet
has a perimeter of 15.71 feet and an area of 19.63 square feet.
```

Casting and Interfaces

16.13   Although using an interface as the data type of a variable is often a good idea, you must ensure compatible data types when passing arguments to methods or assigning values to variables. For example, within ShapeWriter, the data type of display's parameter shape is Measurable. You can pass the method a variable whose data type is either Measurable or a class, such as Square, that implements Measurable. However, if the data type of shape were Square, you could not pass the method a variable whose data type is Measurable. Nor could you assign a variable of type Measurable to one of type Square. A cast to Square would be required in both cases.

For instance, because Square implements Measurable, we can assign a Square object to a variable of type Measurable without a cast, as follows:

```java
Measurable box = new Square(2.5);
```

However, to subsequently assign box to a variable of type Square requires a cast:

```java
Square boxAlias = (Square)box;
```

Note: **Conversions between class types and interface types**

- Conversion from a class type to an interface type is implicit and legal.
- Conversion from an interface type to a class type requires a cast.

16.14 Again, consider the statement

```
Measurable box = new Square(2.5);
```

Since the interface `Measurable` declares the method `getArea` and the class `Square` implements `getArea`, we can invoke this method in a statement such as

```
double boxArea = box.getArea(); // Legal
```

However, `Square` defines the method `getSide`, which `Measurable` does not declare. Thus, the following statement is illegal and would cause a syntax error:

```
double side = box.getSide(); // ILLEGAL: getSide is not in Measurable
```

Because compilation occurs before execution, the compiler does not know that box will reference a Square object when this statement executes. But you do!

You can tell the compiler to assume that box will reference a Square object by casting box to Square. For example, you could write

```
Square mySquare = (Square)box;
double squareSide = mySquare.getSide(); // Legal
```

The compiler will accept your word. If, however, box does not reference a Square object when `getSide` is invoked, an exception will occur. For example, if box actually references a Circle object instead of a Square object, you cannot cast it to Square.

Question 8 In the `ShapesDemo` program given in Listing 16-5, what happens if you change the data types of `mySquare` and `myCircle` to `Measurable`?

Polymorphism and Interfaces

16.15 A variable declaration such as

```
Measurable shape;
```

where `Measurable` is an interface, makes shape a reference variable. Recall from Chapter 4 that a reference variable is used to reference an object. In particular, shape can reference any object of any class that implements `Measurable`. So if you have

```
shape = new Circle(3.1);
```

then `shape.getArea()`, for example, invokes the method `getArea` that the class `Circle` defines. If later you write

```
shape = new Square(3.1);
```

then `shape.getArea()` calls the method `getArea` defined in the class Square.

The version of `getArea` called is not determined by the data type of the variable shape, but rather by the data type of the object that shape references. This determination is made during program execution and is called **dynamic binding**. The variable shape is said to be **polymorphic**, since it can reference objects of different types. **Polymorphism**, which literally means "the ability to take many forms," is one of the features of object-oriented programming. We will give another example of this concept later in this chapter.

Note: Polymorphism is a feature of object-oriented programming whereby the correct version of a method is determined during program execution instead of during compilation. One method name in an instruction can cause different actions according to the kinds of objects that receive the call to the method. Through a mechanism called dynamic binding, the method invoked belongs to the receiving object. The class type of the variable that references the object does not affect the choice of method. Thus, different objects use different method actions for the same method name.

■ Inheritance Basics

If you want to define a new class, and an existing class does some of what you want your new class to do, you can use the existing class in the definition of the new class. In this way, you can avoid repeating what has been done already and concentrate on the new aspects of your class. The previous chapter introduced aggregation as a way to use an existing class in the definition of a new class. **Inheritance** provides another way to reuse an existing class by enabling you to take a general class and define more-specialized classes from it. Although we have mentioned inheritance and actually used it in the graphics chapters, we have not really discussed it. In this section, we begin our explanation of this important concept, and we will develop the details in Chapter 27.

16.16   A new class can **inherit** the properties and behaviors of an existing class and add to or revise its data fields and methods. For example, you might define a general class for vehicles and then define more specific classes for vehicles that travel on the land or sea, or in the air. The class of land vehicles would include the classes of automobiles and wagons. Figure 16-5 illustrates this hierarchy of classes. The Vehicle class is the **superclass** for the other **subclasses**. The LandVehicle class is the superclass for the subclasses Automobile and Wagon. Another term for superclass is **base class**, and another term for subclass is **derived class**. In the UML, a subclass points to its superclass with an arrow that has a hollow head.

A common way to describe subclasses is in terms of family relationships. For example, the class of vehicles is said to be an **ancestor** of the class of sailboats. Conversely, the class of sailboats is a **descendant** of the class of vehicles.

As you move up in the hierarchy in Figure 16-5, the classes become more general. A wagon is a land vehicle and therefore is also a vehicle. However, a vehicle is not necessarily a wagon. A sailboat is a sea vehicle and is also a vehicle, but a vehicle is not necessarily a sailboat.

FIGURE 16-5   A hierarchy of classes

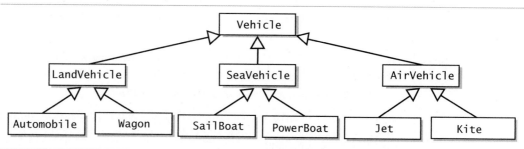

16.17   Java and other programming languages use inheritance to organize classes in this hierarchical way. A programmer then can use an existing class to write a new one that has more features but does not repeat existing code. For example, the class of vehicles has certain properties—such as miles traveled—that its data fields record. The class also has certain behaviors—such as going forward—that its methods define. The classes LandVehicle, AirVehicle, and SeaVehicle also have these properties and behaviors, since they are based on Vehicle. These derived classes can add to, revise, or hide the properties and behaviors that they inherit.

Note: Inheritance
Inheritance groups classes that have properties and behaviors in common. The common properties and behaviors are defined only once for all the classes. Thus, you can define a general class—the superclass, or base class—and later define a more specialized class—the subclass or derived class—simply by adding to or revising the details of the older, more general class definition.

Note: A class can have only one superclass. For the classes in Figure 16-5, for example, the class SailBoat has SeaVehicle as its superclass. Vehicle is simply an ancestor of SailBoat. Although SeaVehicle is also an ancestor of SailBoat, it specifically is SailBoat's superclass. A class can have many subclasses. For example Vehicle has three subclasses—LandVehicle, AirVehicle, and SeaVehicle. The subclasses of these three classes are descendants of Vehicle.

16.18   Since the Automobile class is derived from the LandVehicle class, it inherits all of LandVehicle's public data fields and public methods—except constructors. The Automobile class then defines additional fields for components such as its engine, and it also defines additional methods. Such fields and methods are not in the LandVehicle class, because they do not apply to all vehicles. For example, wagons have no engine.

Inheritance gives an object of a subclass all the behaviors of the superclass. For example, an automobile will be able to do everything that a land vehicle can do; after all, an automobile *is a* land vehicle. In fact, inheritance is known as an ***is-a*** relationship between classes. Since the subclass and the superclass share properties, you should use inheritance only when it makes sense to think of an object of the subclass as also being an object of the superclass. Otherwise, consider a *has-a* relationship, that is, use aggregation.

Note: Inheritance defines an *is-a* relationship
Inheritance makes an object of a subclass behave like an object of its superclass. Thus, you should use inheritance only when this *is-a* relationship between classes is meaningful.

Note: The definition of a subclass uses the Java reserved word extends to indicate its superclass. Thus, the definition of the class LandVehicle mentioned in Figure 16-5 begins as follows:

```
public class LandVehicle extends Vehicle
```

Again, a class can have only one superclass. In contrast, a class can implement several interfaces. When Chapter 27 discusses inheritance in detail, it will show you how to implement an interface when using inheritance.

Programming Tip
Although inheritance is a well-established term and concept in object-oriented programming, in Java it does not exactly match the everyday intuitive notion of inheritance. Rather, a subclass *extends* a superclass by adding data fields and methods. It may help you to understand how inheritance in Java works by thinking in this way.

Note: When we talk about inheritance, we will say either that a new class N extends an existing class E or that a new class N is derived from an existing class E.

Question 9 Revise the hierarchy in Figure 16-5 to categorize vehicles according to whether they have wheels.

The Class Object

16.19   Imagine that you define a class C, but you do not derive it from any other class. Java will behave as if you did derive C from the class Object. Object—which is in the Java Class Library—is the ancestor class of all other classes, as Figure 16-6 depicts.

Note: Every class is a descendant of the class Object, but Object has no ancestor.

FIGURE 16-6   Object is an ancestor class of all other classes

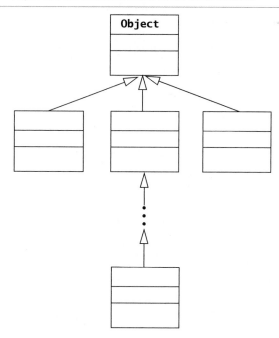

The class Object defines methods, such as toString and equals, that every class inherits. Thus, every object in a Java program has these methods. Unfortunately, the methods toString and equals, as defined in Object, likely will not behave reasonably for the classes you write. Object's toString, for example, returns a string that is not based on the values of the object's data. This string will probably have little meaning to you. You should write your own version of toString, as Segment 6.18 in Chapter 6 has already suggested.

Similarly, you should write your own version of the method equals, if you want your class to have this behavior. Several of the classes that Chapter 4 discussed—including String—have their own versions of equals.

What if a class does not define its own version of equals? Consider the class Name that we defined in Chapter 6. Since we did not define a method equals for this class, Name objects will use the version inherited from Object. Let's see what happens.

16.20 **Example: Object's method equals.** Consider the following objects of the class Name, which appears in Listing 6-5 of Chapter 6:

```
Name joyce1 = new Name("Joyce", "Jones");
Name joyce2 = new Name("Joyce", "Jones");
Name derek = new Name("Derek", "Dodd");
```

As defined here, joyce1 and joyce2 are two distinct objects that contain the same name. Typically, we would consider these objects to be equal, but in fact joyce1.equals(joyce2) is false. Object's equals method, which Name inherits, compares the addresses of the objects joyce1 and joyce2. These addresses are not equal, since they are two distinct objects. However, the expression joyce1.equals(joyce1) is true because we are comparing an object with itself.

> **Note:** Object's method equals reports whether two objects are identical—that is, have the same **identity**, or location in memory.

16.21 Realize that an object's identity might not be obvious. If we write

```
Name joyce3 = joyce1;
```

the expression joyce1.equals(joyce3) is true, because joyce1 and joyce3 are aliases. Therefore, these variables reference the same object. Figure 16-7 illustrates joyce1, its alias joyce3, and the distinct but equal object joyce2.

FIGURE 16-7   joyce1 is identical to its alias joyce3, but joyce1 equals joyce2

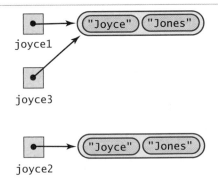

Finally, joyce1.equals(derek) is false because joyce1 and derek reference distinct objects, not because their names differ. Remember that this method equals belongs to the class Object.

Overriding the Method equals

16.22 **Name's method equals: First try.** To have equals behave correctly for Name objects, we must define our own version of the method in the class Name. The method should compare the names that the two objects represent. The following is our first attempt at an equals method for Name:

```
public boolean equals(Name other)
{
    return first.equals(other.first) && last.equals(other.last);
} // equals
```

With this method, if joyce1 and joyce2 are objects of the class Name, as defined in Segment 16.20, joyce1.equals(joyce2) is true.

Although it is perfectly fine to retain this version of the equals method, it does not completely prevent Object's equals from taking over occasionally. Object's equals has the following header:

```
public boolean equals(Object other)
```

Since Name inherits this method, Name effectively has two methods whose names are the same but whose parameters have different types. That is, we have overloaded the method equals.

Given these method definitions, if we write the following statements

```
Name joyce1 = new Name("Joyce", "Jones");
Object joyce2 = new Name("Joyce", "Jones");
```

the expression joyce1.equals(joyce2) will be false because Object's version of equals will be called. This occurs because the parameter of Object's equals method has the same data type as joyce2.

Note: A subclass can define a method that overloads a method inherited from the superclass.

16.23 **Name's method equals: Second try.** We need to effectively replace, or **override**, the equals method of Object by defining a method that has exactly the same header. Here is a method for the class Name that overrides the equals method in Object:

```
public boolean equals(Object other)
{
    Name otherName = (Name)other;
    return first.equals(otherName.first) &&
            last.equals(otherName.last);
} // equals
```

The parameter other has the type Object, so it does not have the data fields first and last. Thus, an expression such as other.first is illegal. Consequently, we cast other to the Name object, otherName. We then can write otherName.first and otherName.last within the method.

Now if we write

```
Name joyce1 = new Name("Joyce", "Jones");
Object joyce2 = new Name("Joyce", "Jones");
```

the expression joyce1.equals(joyce2) will invoke Name's method equals. Thus, the expression will be true, as it should be.

The previous definition of `equals` is not foolproof. You could pass an object of any class to the method, since the type of its parameter is `Object`. Someone could try to compare a `Name` object with an object of another, unrelated class. However, the cast within the method would not work, and you would get an error called `ClassCastException`. The optional Segment 16.24 tells you how to avoid the error and return false instead.

Note: Overriding a method definition

When a subclass defines a nonstatic method with the same header—that is, the same name, the same return type, and the same number and types of parameters—as a method in the superclass, the method definition in the subclass is said to override the definition in the superclass. Objects of the subclass that receive a call to the method will use the definition in the subclass instead of the one in the superclass.

Since a method's signature is its name and the number, types, and order of its parameters, overridden methods are those having the same signature and return type.

Note: Overriding versus overloading

- Overridden methods have the same signature and return type.
- Overloaded methods have different signatures but the same name.

- Overridden methods must be in different classes that are related by inheritance.
- Overloaded methods are in either the same class or different classes related by inheritance.

Note: Hiding a method definition

When a subclass defines a static method with the same header as a static method in the superclass, the method definition in the subclass is said to **hide** the definition in the superclass. The distinction between overriding and hiding is subtle and will be discussed in Chapter 27.

16.24   **Making `equals` foolproof (optional).** To ensure that the argument passed to the method `equals` is an object of the same class as the object that invokes the method, you use the Java operator `instanceof`. For example, the expression

        other instanceof Name

is true if `other` references an object of either the class `Name` or a class derived from `Name`. If `other` references an object of any other class, or if `other` is `null`, the expression will be false. Thus, our revised `equals` method appears as follows:

```
public boolean equals(Object other)
{
    boolean result = false;
    if (other instanceof Name)
    {
        Name otherName = (Name)other;
        result = first.equals(otherName.first) &&
                    last.equals(otherName.last);
    } // end if

    return result;
} // equals
```

Syntax: The operator `instanceof`

The Java operator `instanceof` has two operands, as follows:

object_name `instanceof` *class_name*

The first operand is a reference variable, and the second is a class name. The operator returns true if *object_name* references an object of either the class *class_name* or a class derived from *class_name*. If *object_name* references some other class or is `null`, `instanceof` returns false.

For example, if we have

```
String var1 = "Java";
Object var2 = "Java";
String var3 = null;
Name var4 = new Name("Gerry", "Java");
```

then

- `var1 instanceof String` is true.
- `var2 instanceof String` is true.
- `var3 instanceof String` is false.
- `var4 instanceof String` is false.

Notice that the expression `var2 instanceof String` is true even though var2's data type is not `String`. That is, `instanceof` examines the object referenced by a variable, not the variable's data type.

Programming Tip

The operator `instanceof` is written as one word entirely in lowercase

Question 10 Write an `equals` method for the class `Circle`, as given in Listing 16-4.

Question 11 Write an `equals` method for the class `Person`, as given in Listing 15-3 of Chapter 15, that decides whether two `Person` objects have the same name and city. Assume that the class `Name` has an `equals` method as described in the previous segments.

Question 12 Imagine two methods having the same name.

    a. Describe the methods if they are overloaded.
    b. Describe the methods if one overrides the other.

Note: The class `Enum`

When the Java compiler encounters an enumeration, it creates a class derived from the class `Enum`, which is in the package `java.lang` of the Java Class Library. `Enum` has the methods that we have used in conjunction with an enumeration, namely, `compareTo`, `equals`, `ordinal`, `toString`, and `valueOf`. Like all other classes, `Enum` is derived from `Object`. However, unlike most other classes, its constructor is not public. Thus, you cannot create objects of `Enum`. Only the Java compiler can do so.

Polymorphism and Inheritance

16.25   When a class inherits a method defined in an ancestor class, and also defines its own version of that method, the new version overrides the inherited method. We know that the signature and return type of the new method must exactly match those of the inherited method. Since every class inherits the method `toString` from the class `Object`, when you write your own version of `toString`, you are overriding the inherited one.

Now suppose that you write the following statements:

```
Object anObject = new Circle(3.5);
System.out.println(anObject.toString());
anObject = new Name("Joe", "Java");
System.out.println(anObject.toString());
```

where `Circle` is as given in Listing 16-4 and `Name` is as given in Listing 6-5 of Chapter 6. The output from these statements is

```
A circle whose radius is 3.5
Joe Java
```

videonote
Inheritance and
polymorphism

When anObject references a `Circle` object, `Circle`'s version of `toString` is called instead of `Object`'s version. When anObject references a `Name` object, `Name`'s version of `toString` is called. Just as you saw in Segment 16.15, the version of a method is determined by the data type of the object that a variable references, not by the data type of the variable. That is, polymorphism is at work here.

Note that we invoked `toString` explicitly for emphasis, but we could simply have written

```
System.out.println(anObject);
```

and invoked it implicitly with the same results.

When we look at the details of inheritance in Chapter 27, we will talk more about polymorphism.

Question 13 Consider the class `Name`, as given in Listing 6-5 of Chapter 6. Suppose that you add to this class the method `equals`, as it appears in Segment 16.23. Now imagine a client of `Name` that contains the following statements:

```
Name joyce1 = new Name("Joyce", "Jones");
Object joyce2 = new Name("Joyce", "Jones");
```

a. Does the expression joyce1.equals(joyce2) invoke a method from `Object` or from `Name`?
b. What is the result of the previous call to `equals`?
c. Repeat Parts a and b, but instead consider the expression joyce2.equals(joyce1).

Extending an Interface

16.26   Once you have an interface, you can define another interface to extend the original one by using inheritance. In fact, an interface can extend several interfaces, even though a class cannot extend several classes.

When an interface extends another interface, it has all the methods of the inherited interface. Thus, you can create an interface that consists of the methods in an existing interface plus some new methods. For example, consider the following interface, which Question 2 asked you to write:

```
public interface Nameable
{
    void setName(String name);
    String getName();
} // end Nameable
```

Imagine a plan to define a class of pets that implements this interface. We likely would decide to include other methods. We can extend `Nameable` to create the interface `Callable`:

```
public interface Callable extends Nameable
{
   public void come(String petName);
} // end Callable
```

A class that implements `Callable` must implement the methods `come`, `setName`, and `getName`.

16.27   You also can combine several interfaces into a new interface and add even more methods if you like. For example, suppose that in addition to the previous two interfaces, we define the following interfaces:

```
public interface Capable
{
   public void hear();
   public void respond();
} // end Capable

public interface Trainable extends Callable, Capable
{
   public void sit();
   public void speak();
   public void lieDown();
} // end Trainable
```

A class that implements `Trainable` must implement the methods `setName`, `getName`, `come`, `hear`, and `respond`, as well as the methods `sit`, `speak`, and `lieDown`.

 Note: A Java interface can extend several interfaces, even though a class cannot extend several classes.

 Question 14 Imagine a class `Pet` that contains the method `setName` yet does not implement the interface `Nameable` of Segment 16.26. Could you pass an instance of `Pet` as the argument of a method with the following header?

```
public void enterShow(Nameable petName)
```

■ The **Comparable** Interface

16.28   Earlier, in Segment 4.23 of Chapter 4, we described the method `compareTo` for the class `String`. This method returns an integer that indicates the result of a comparison, as follows. If `s` and `t` are strings, `s.compareTo(t)` is

- Negative if `s` comes before `t`
- Zero if `s` and `t` are equal
- Positive if `s` comes after `t`

videonote
Comparing objects

Many other classes have their own `compareTo` methods that behave in an analogous way. All such classes implement the following interface `Comparable`, which is in the Java Class Library:

```
public interface Comparable<T>
{
   int compareTo(T other);
} // end Comparable
```

The T in this interface designates a **generic type**. That is, T represents a class that implements this interface. The parameter of the method compareTo has T instead of Object as its data type. Using a generic type avoids the cast that is necessary when implementing a method such as equals, as given in Segment 16.23. Note that Chapter 32 will discuss generic types further.

16.29   **Implementing Comparable.** You add the method compareTo to a class definition by implementing the interface Comparable. For example, let's add compareTo to the class Circle that appears in Listing 16-4. Circle already implements the interface Measurable, so now it must implement two interfaces. Thus, we write

```
public class Circle implements Measurable, Comparable<Circle>
```

as shown in Listing 16-8. The name of the class appears in brackets after the interface name Comparable. That is, Circle corresponds to T in the interface and is then the data type of compareTo's parameter.

Our version of compareTo assumes that Circle has its own equals method, which Question 10 asked you to implement. Although compareTo need not invoke equals, it is usually a good idea for these two methods to at least return consistent results. That is, if object1.equals(object2) is true, object1.compareTo(object2) should return zero. The class BigDecimal, which you saw in Chapter 4, does not follow this suggestion, however. (See Exercise 12.)

LISTING 16-8   The method compareTo in the class Circle

```
/** A class of Comparable circles.
    @author F. M. Carrano
*/
public class Circle implements Measurable, Comparable<Circle>
{
    private double radius;

    < Definitions of the methods given in Listing 16-4 and
        the method equals described in Question 10 are here >

    public int compareTo(Circle other)
    {
        int result;
        if (this.equals(other))
            result = 0;
        else if (radius < other.radius)
            result = -1;
        else
            result = 1;

        return result;
    } // compareTo
} // end Circle
```

16.30   **The return value of compareTo.** Although we have returned either –1 or +1 for unequal objects, the specification of compareTo does not insist on these values. Only the sign of the result must be correct. Thus, when the comparison involves integers, a simple subtraction often produces a suitable return value. For example, if the data field `radius` in the class `Circle` were an integer instead of a real value, `compareTo` could have had the following simple definition:

```
// assumes radius is an integer
public int compareTo(Circle other)
{
   return radius - other.radius;
} // compareTo
```

16.31   You might wonder why `compareTo` does not belong to the class `Object`. It is omitted because not all classes should have a `compareTo` method. Classes of objects without a natural ordering are possible and not at all unusual. For example, consider a class of addresses. Deciding whether two addresses are equal is straightforward, but judging that one address is less than another is not.

Note: Not all classes should implement the interface `Comparable`. Those that do must define the method `compareTo`.

Programming Tip
Classes that implement the `Comparable` interface and, therefore, define a `compareTo` method should also define an `equals` method that overrides the `equals` method inherited from `Object`. Typically, both `compareTo` and `equals` should use the same test for equality.

16.32   As Segment 16.10 indicated, an interface name such as `Comparable` can serve as the data type in the declaration of a variable or parameter. A method whose header is

```
public void aMethod(Comparable item)
```

can invoke `item`'s `compareTo` method but none of its other methods. Thus, you can pass to `aMethod` an object of any class that implements the interface `Comparable`. What if a class `C` does not begin with the phrase `implements Comparable` yet still defines the method `compareTo`? You cannot pass an instance of `C` to `aMethod`.

Question 15   Revise the class `Name` given in Listing 6-5 of Chapter 6 so that it implements the interface `Comparable`.

Question 16   Repeat the previous question, but also implement `NameInterface`, as given in Listing 16-2.

Programming Tip: Subclasses that implement an interface
When a class implements an interface and is derived from another class, you write the name of the superclass before the name of the interface in the class header. For example, if the class `Jet` in Figure 16-5 implements the `Comparable` interface, you would begin its definition as follows:

```
public class Jet extends AirVehicle implements Comparable<Jet>
```

To remember this order, note that the reserved words `extends` and `implements` appear alphabetically in the definition of the class.

videonote
A problem solved

CHAPTER SUMMARY

- An interface contains the headers of the public methods that a class must implement. An interface also can define public named constants.

- The notation for an interface in the Unified Modeling Language, or UML, is the same as for a class, but you precede the interface's name with <<interface>>.

- A class that implements an interface has an `implements` clause in its header. The class must implement all the methods declared in the interface.

- You can use an interface name as a data type when you declare variables and parameters.

- Polymorphism is a feature of object-oriented programming whereby the correct version of a method is determined during program execution instead of during compilation. Through a mechanism called dynamic binding, the object that a variable references receives a call to a method defined in the class that is the object's data type, not the variable's type.

- Inheritance groups classes that have properties and behaviors in common. The common properties and behaviors are defined only once for all the classes. Thus, you can define a general class—the superclass, or base class—and later define more-specialized classes—the subclasses, or derived classes—simply by adding to or revising the details of the older, more general class definition.

- Use inheritance when you have an *is-a* relationship between two classes.

- A method in a subclass overrides a method in the superclass when both methods have the same name, the same return type, and the same number and types of parameters. That is, overridden methods have the same signature and return type.

- Every class is a descendant of the class `Object`. A typical class should override `Object`'s methods `toString` and `equals`.

- A subclass can define a method that overloads a method inherited from the superclass.

- The `Comparable` interface declares the method `compareTo`. A class that defines `compareTo` should implement `Comparable`.

- The definition of the `Comparable` interface uses the notation `Comparable<T>` to indicate a generic data type T. When a class implements the interface, it replaces T with its name.

EXERCISES

1. Name and describe the three principles of object-oriented programming.

2. What is the difference between a class's implementation and client interface?

3. What is the difference between a class and an interface?

4. What advantages does a Java interface offer a programmer?

5. All Java classes automatically extend what class in the Java Class Library?

6. What is the difference between overloading a method and overriding a method?

7. Consider the class `RandomPoint`, as given in Listing 11-8 of Chapter 11. If you had written a Java interface for this class before you defined it, what would it be? How would you change the class so that it implements your interface?

8. What is the UML notation for the interface you defined in the previous question?

9.   **a.** Define a class `Triangle` that implements the interface `Measurable`, as given in Listing 16-1.
   b. What statements could you add to the program in Listing 16-5 to demonstrate the class `Triangle`?

10. Consider the class `Triangle` described in Exercise 9. Would it be legal to pass a `Triangle` object to the method `display`, as defined in Listing 16-6, as an argument corresponding to the parameter `shape`?

11.   **a.** Choose and describe reasonable criteria for comparing two triangles.
   b. Revise the class `Triangle`, as described in Exercise 9, so that it also implements the interface `Comparable`.
   c. What statements could you add to the program in Listing 16-5 to demonstrate whether one `Triangle` object is equal to, greater than, or less than another `Triangle` object?

12. Show that the methods `compareTo` and `equals` are inconsistent for the class `BigDecimal`. That is, find two instances, `b1` and `b2`, of `BigDecimal` such that `b1.compareTo(b2)` is zero but `b1.equals(b2)` is false. *Hint*: Consider numbers with equal values but different precisions.

13. Define a Java interface called `Growable` to provide certain behaviors for various plant objects. Growable plants can be watered and fed. Define a class called `Rose` that implements the `Growable` interface. Create a client to demonstrate the use of your class.

14. Define a Java interface called `Priority` that declares three methods, `setPriority`, `getPriority`, and `comparePriorityTo`. This interface provides a way to establish numeric priority among a set of objects. The method `comparePriorityTo` is analogous to `compareTo`, but compares priorities.
   Define a class called `Email` that implements `Priority` and represents email messages. Create a client to demonstrate priorities among email messages.

15. Define an interface `Measureable3D` that extends the interface `Measurable`, as given in Listing 16-1. The new interface should declare the method `getVolume`.

16. Consider a class `C` that overrides the method `toString` of the class `Object`.

   a. What does this mean for `C`?
   b. If an object of `C` receives a call to `toString`, which version of the method is called, the one in `Object` or the one in `C`?
   c. Is the version of `toString` chosen by the compiler or at execution time?

17. Consider a class that provides a method to read integers one at a time from the keyboard. The class tracks the smallest, largest, and average of the integers it has read so far.

   a. Write an interface for the class. Include comments suitable for `javadoc` that specify the methods of the class.
   b. Implement and demonstrate the class.

PROJECTS

1. Define a Java class `LinearMeasure` that represents linear measurements in either yards, feet, inches, meters, centimeters, or millimeters. The class should implement the interface `Comparable` and override the method `toString`.
   Use an enumeration to represent these units of measure. Note that a measurement is given and represented in only one of these units. For example, 8.5 yards is *not* represented as 8 yards, 1 foot, and 6 inches.
   Define a constructor that has two parameters, one that represents the value of the measurement and another that names the unit of measure as a string. The case of the letters in this string should be irrelevant.

Define methods that convert any measurement to any given unit. These methods should not change the receiving object, but rather should return a new `LinearMeasure` object. For example, the statements

```
LinearMeasure length = new LinearMeasure(8.5, "yards");
System.out.println(length + " = " + length.toMeters());
```

should produce the following output:

```
8.5 yards = 7.7724 METERS
```

Write a client that fully demonstrates your class.

2. A pet has a breed, a name, and a sound. Write the UML notation for the interface `PetInterface` describing the behaviors all pets should have. Define the interface in Java as well as three classes that implement the interface. Finally, write a program that demonstrates the three classes.

3. Consider a class `Fraction` of fractions. Each fraction is signed and has a numerator and a denominator that are integers. Your class should be able to add, subtract, multiply, and divide two fractions. These methods should have a fraction as a parameter and should return the result of the operation as a fraction.

   The class should also be able to find the reciprocal of a fraction, compare two fractions, decide whether two fractions are equal, and convert a fraction to a string. Your class should handle denominators that are zero.

   Fractions should always occur in lowest terms, and the class should be responsible for this requirement. For example, if the user tries to create a fraction such as 4/8, the class should set the fraction to 1/2. Likewise, the results of all arithmetic operations should be in lowest terms. Note that a fraction can be improper—that is, its numerator can be larger than its denominator. Such a fraction, however, should be expressed in lowest terms.

   Design, but do not implement, the class `Fraction`. Begin by writing a CRC card for this class. Then write a Java interface that declares each public method. Include `javadoc`-style comments to specify each method.

4. Write a Java class `Fraction` that implements both the interface you designed in the previous project and the interface `Comparable`. Begin with reasonable constructors. Design and implement useful private methods, and include comments that specify them.

   To reduce a fraction such as 4/8 to its lowest terms, you need to divide both the numerator and the denominator by their greatest common denominator. The greatest common denominator of 4 and 8 is 4, so when you divide the numerator and denominator of 4/8 by 4, you get the fraction 1/2. The following algorithm finds the greatest common denominator of two positive integers:

   ```
   Algorithm gcd(integerOne, integerTwo)
   while (integerTwo != 0)
   {
       temp = integerOne % integerTwo
       integerOne = integerTwo
       integerTwo = temp
   }
   return integerOne
   ```

   It will be easier to determine the correct sign of a fraction if you force the fraction's denominator to be positive. However, your implementation must handle negative denominators that the client might provide.

   Write a program that adequately demonstrates your class.

5. An odometer records a car's mileage. It contains a number of counters that increment as the car travels. Each counter shows a digit from 0 to 9. The rightmost counter increments the fastest, increasing by 1 for every mile traveled. Once a counter reaches 9, it changes to 0 on the next mile and increases by 1 the value on the counter to its left.

You can generalize the behavior of such digit counters by giving them symbols other than the digits from 0 to 9. Examples of such digit counters include the following:

- A binary odometer whose counters each show either 0 or 1
- A desktop date display with three counters, one each for the year, month, and day
- A dice roll display whose counters each show the spots for a single die

Write a Java interface for any class that represents a digit counter. Also, write a Java interface for a general counter that has up to four digit counters. Include comments in `javadoc` style.

ANSWERS TO SELF-TEST QUESTIONS

1. One example is an iPod: The visible portion on the front of an iPod is its interface. Everything inside is its implementation. Other examples include a television, a cell phone, and an automobile.

2.
```java
public interface Nameable
{
    void setName(String name);
    String getName();
} // end Nameable
```

3.
```java
public interface Circular
{
    void setRadius(double newRadius);
    double getRadius();
} // end Circular
```

4.

```
┌─────────────────────────────────────┐
│          <<interface>>               │
│            Nameable                  │
├─────────────────────────────────────┤
│                                      │
├─────────────────────────────────────┤
│  +setName(name: String): void        │
│  +getName(): String                  │
└─────────────────────────────────────┘
```

5. The UML notation for the class `Name` is just like the UML notation given for `NameInterface`, but it omits `<<interface>>`.

6.
```java
public class Disk implements Circular
{
    double radius;

    void setRadius(double newRadius)
    {
        radius = newRadius;
    } // end setRadius

    double getRadius()
    {
        return radius;
    } // end getRadius

    < Various other method definitions are here. >
} // end Disk
```

The definition of the class `Cylinder` is analogous to the definition of `Disk`. The implementations for `setRadius` and `getRadius` happen to be the same as for `Disk`. The other methods of both classes need not be the same.

7. Change the class header to

```
public class Circle implements Measurable, Circular
```

and add a definition of the method setRadius:

```
public void setRadius(double newRadius)
{
    radius = newRadius;
} // end setRadius
```

8. It works, since getSide in Square and getRadius in Circle are not called. Note that toString also works correctly.

9.

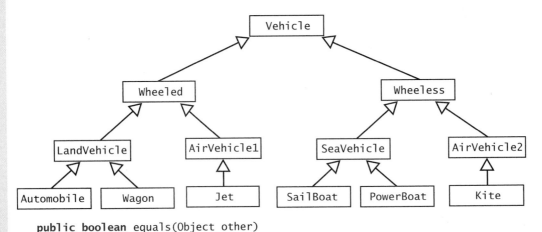

10.
```
public boolean equals(Object other)
{
    boolean result = false;
    if (other instanceof Circle)
    {
        Circle otherCircle = (Circle)other;
        result = (Math.abs(radius - otherCircle.radius) < 0.5E-5);
    } // end if
    return result;
} // end equals
```

11.
```
public boolean equals(Object other)
{
    boolean result = false;
    if (other instanceof Person)
    {
        Person otherPerson = (Person)other;
        result = myName.equals(other.myName) && myCity.equals(other.myCity);
    } // end if
    return result;
} // end equals
```

12. **a.** Overloaded methods are in either the same class or different classes that are related by inheritance. They have the same name but different signatures; that is, they have parameters that differ either in number or in data type.

   b. Overridden methods are in different classes that are related by inheritance. The methods have identical signatures and return types and are not static.

13. **a.** Name
   b. True
   c. The answers are the same.

14. No. Since Pet does not implement the interface Nameable, Pet objects are not of the data type Nameable.

15.
```java
public class Name implements Comparable<Name>
{
    . . .
    public int compareTo(Name other)
    {
        int result = last.compareTo(other.last);

        // if last names are equal, check first names
        if (result == 0)
            result = first.compareTo(other.first);

        return result;
    } // compareTo
} // end Name
```

16. Add NameInterface to the implements clause of Name's header, so that it appears as follows:
```java
public class Name implements Comparable<Name>, NameInterface
```
The rest of the class is like the one given in the previous answer.

Chapter

17

Inheritance and Interfaces in Swing and the AWT

Contents

Prerequisites

Objectives

After studying this chapter, you should be able to
- Describe the organization of the major classes and interfaces within Swing and the AWT
- Describe, define, and use action listeners and mouse listeners within a program
- Define and use buttons to provide input to a program
- Define and use an inner class
- Write programs that respond to mouse clicks
- Define and use text fields to provide input to a program

The previous chapter showed you how to write and use Java interfaces and also introduced inheritance. Although we still have not explored inheritance fully, we will begin to use it within chapters, such as this one, that discuss aspects of the Abstract Window Toolkit and Swing. Using the material covered in the previous chapter, this chapter will show the relationships among some of the classes in both Swing and the AWT. For the most part, however, this chapter will focus on implementing some of the interfaces in the AWT to enable our programs to respond to the click of a mouse.

■ The Organization of Major Classes Within the AWT and Swing

17.1   As we mentioned in Chapter 1, Swing builds on the classes within the AWT rather than replacing them. In fact, the developers of Java used inheritance to derive the classes in Swing from classes in the AWT. Figure 17-1 shows the hierarchy of the classes relevant to our discussion. As the previous chapter describes, a hollow-tipped arrow points to a class's superclass. Although both the AWT and Swing are available to us, we use Swing when possible, as it provides more powerful classes and enables us to do more.

FIGURE 17-1   The hierarchy of some classes in the AWT and Swing

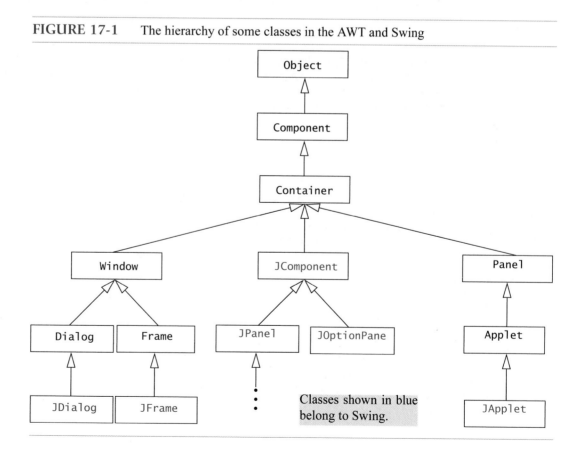

Three kinds of containers—frames, dialogs, and applets—are used for graphical user interfaces, and thus are called **top-level containers**, even though they appear at the bottom of Figure 17-1. You have seen how to write an application program that first creates a window, or frame, in which to display graphics. We use the Swing class JFrame to accomplish this. Another kind of container is the **dialog**, and one example is the dialog box that we created in Listing 4-5 of Chapter 4 by using the class JOptionPane. You also can use the class JDialog to create a custom dialog. The third kind of container is the applet. As we mentioned in Chapter 1, an applet is a Java program that runs within another program, such as an Internet browser. An applet can be run at a distant location and its graphical output viewed within a browser.

17.2 Every graphical user interface begins with a top-level container. Each top-level container has one **content pane**, which contains the graphical components to be displayed. A component such as a panel can be this content pane, thereby providing all of the drawing surface. Such a panel must be opaque. An **opaque panel** paints its entire area to hide anything that might have been drawn previously. Thus, you cannot see any components that are beneath an opaque panel. On the other hand, a **transparent panel** does not paint a background, so you can see some underlying components.

By default, the instances of a class derived from the Swing class JPanel usually are opaque panels. Whether a panel is opaque or transparent by default depends on your operating system. To ensure an opaque panel, you call setOpaque(true); on the other hand, setOpaque(false) makes a panel transparent.

By the way, when we discuss graphics, a **component**—or more precisely, a **graphical component**—is an object of a class that ultimately is based on the standard class JComponent. This distinction is especially important in this chapter when we talk about user interaction with components such as buttons.

17.3 In previous chapters, when we wanted graphical output we wrote application programs instead of applets, and we will continue to do so for the rest of this book. Figure 17-2 contains class diagrams for the classes we use when writing application programs that produce graphical output, and includes a selection of their methods. The figure also indicates the packages to which the relevant classes belong.

■ Using Button Input

Our next application program will use buttons to affect the appearance of its graphical output. A **button** is an object of the Swing class JButton. It is a component that a user can click with the mouse to indicate a choice, thus providing input to a program. As you've probably guessed, a button click is simply a mouse click on a button. Our classes will use inheritance, and one of them will implement the AWT interface ActionListener and deal with the button clicks. Let's examine the details of using buttons in a program.

The Class JButton

17.4 **Constructors.** A Swing button appears as a rectangular graphic that optionally contains text and/or a small picture called an **icon**. For example, the statement

```
JButton labeledButton = new JButton("Click Here");
```

creates the button shown in Figure 17-3a, while the statement

```
JButton plainButton = new JButton();
```

creates the empty button illustrated in Figure 17-3b.

FIGURE 17-2   Classes and methods in the Java Class Library used for graphics in an application program

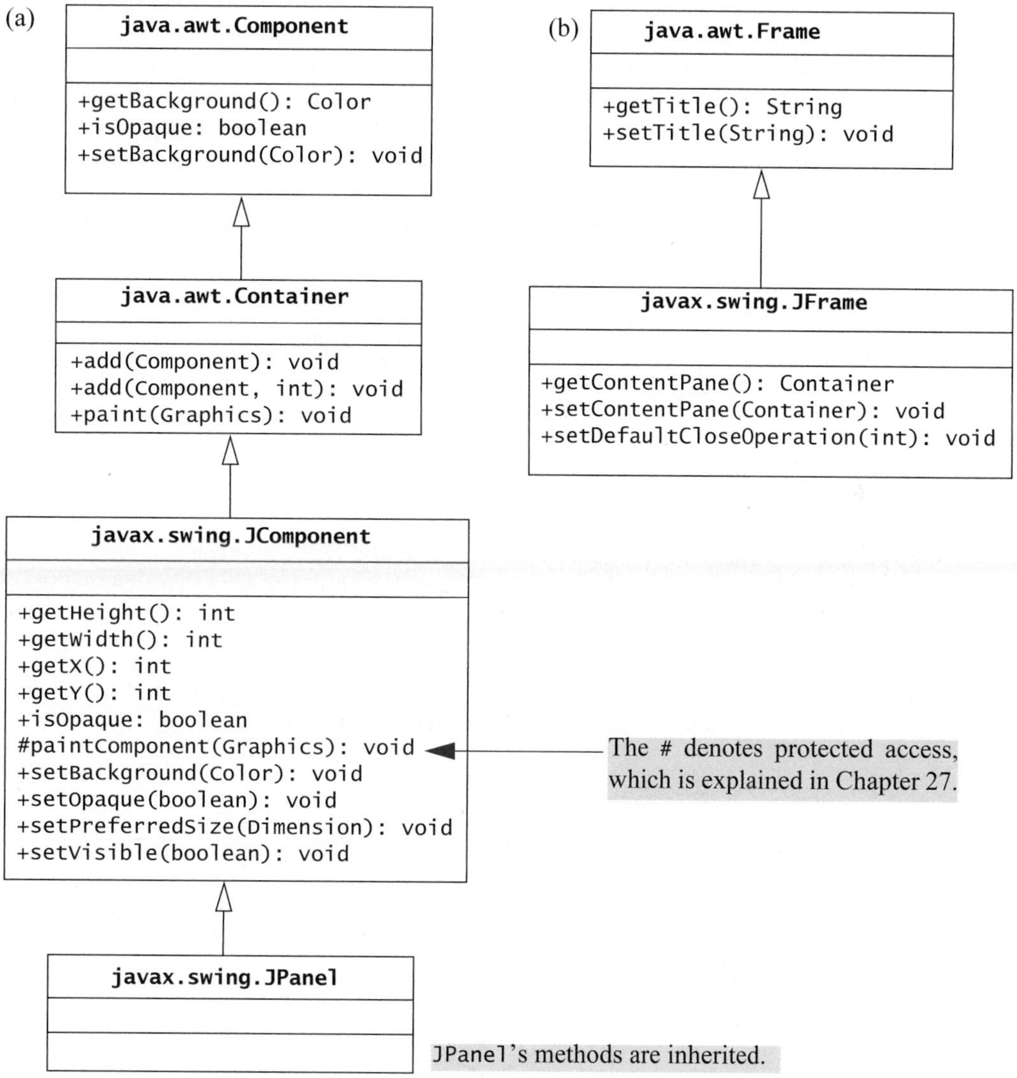

(a)

```
java.awt.Component
```
```
+getBackground(): Color
+isOpaque: boolean
+setBackground(Color): void
```

(b)

```
java.awt.Frame
```
```
+getTitle(): String
+setTitle(String): void
```

```
java.awt.Container
```
```
+add(Component): void
+add(Component, int): void
+paint(Graphics): void
```

```
javax.swing.JFrame
```
```
+getContentPane(): Container
+setContentPane(Container): void
+setDefaultCloseOperation(int): void
```

```
javax.swing.JComponent
```
```
+getHeight(): int
+getWidth(): int
+getX(): int
+getY(): int
+isOpaque: boolean
#paintComponent(Graphics): void
+setBackground(Color): void
+setOpaque(boolean): void
+setPreferredSize(Dimension): void
+setVisible(boolean): void
```

The # denotes protected access, which is explained in Chapter 27.

```
javax.swing.JPanel
```

JPanel's methods are inherited.

FIGURE 17-3   Examples of buttons that contain (a) text; (b) nothing

(a)

Click Here

(b)

You can retrieve or change a button's text by calling the button's methods `getText` and `setText`. Buttons also can display an icon in addition to or instead of text, but we will let you explore this feature as an exercise.

17.5   Action commands. Clicking a button is an **action**. An action generates an **event**, which is an object of the class `ActionEvent`. A button event contains the button's **action command**, which is a string that identifies the button causing the event. By invoking an accessor method of the event, we can retrieve the action command and thereby identify which button was clicked. We then can react appropriately.

By default, a button's action command is the same as its text. You can set a different action command by calling the button's method `setActionCommand`. For instance, we could set `labeledButton`'s action command to the string `"start"` by writing

```
labeledButton.setActionCommand("start");
```

When a button is displayed, its text is visible but its action command is not.

Note: A selection of methods in the class `JButton`
The class `JButton` is in the package `javax.swing` of the Java Class Library.

```
/** Creates a button without a label. */
public JButton()

/** Creates a button whose text is the given string. */
public JButton(String buttonText)

/** Sets or changes a button's text to the given string. */
public void setText(String buttonText)

/** Returns a button's text. */
public void getText()

/** Sets a button's action command to the given string. */
public void setActionCommand(String command)

/** Returns a button's action command. */
public String getActionCommand()

/** Adds an action listener to a button (see next section). */
public void addActionListener(ActionListener listener)
```

Question 1 What Java statements create a button called `myButton` whose displayed text is "My Button" and whose action command is "Button One" ?

Question 2 Once a button is created, can you change its text? If so, change `myButton`'s text; if not, explain why not.

The Interface `ActionListener`

17.6 **Action listeners.** An **action listener** is an object that reacts to certain events, such as the click of a button. By using an action listener for a button, for example, you can indicate the action associated with a particular button.

The class that defines an action listener must implement the AWT interface `ActionListener`, as you will see. This interface declares only one method:

```
public void actionPerformed(ActionEvent event)
```

When a button click occurs, the system calls this method and passes it an event as an argument. The method then can determine the course of action by calling the event's method `getActionCommand`, which returns the button's action command. Thus, the method `actionPerformed` defines what you want to do when a button is clicked.

To make all of this interaction work, the button needs to know about the action listener. That is, we must **register** the action listener with the button by calling the button's method `addActionListener`. But first we need to write the class of action listeners.

Note: **The interface `ActionListener`**
The interface `ActionListener` is in the package `java.awt.event` of the Java Class Library. This interface declares one method, which defines the action that occurs when a certain event, such as a button click, takes place:

```
/** Defines the action to occur when an event
    such as a button click occurs. */
public void actionPerformed(ActionEvent event)
```

Note that the class `ActionEvent` is also in the package `java.awt.event`.

Note: **The class `ActionEvent`**
Objects of the class `ActionEvent`, which is in the package `java.awt.event`, are created for us, so we need not worry about the class's constructors. When certain events—such as a button click—occur, the system invokes the method `actionPerformed` and passes it an `ActionEvent` object as an argument.

Only one method of this class is important to us right now, since it returns the action command associated with the clicked button or other event that has occurred:

```
/** Returns the action command associated with the event. */
public String getActionCommand()
```

17.7 **The relevant classes and methods.** Figure 17-4 contains class diagrams for the classes relevant to using a button, and includes a selection of their methods. Italics and the tag `{abstract}` in the figure indicate an **abstract class**. Such a class is used only as the superclass for other classes. You cannot create objects of an abstract class. These classes will be covered later in Chapter 27.

FIGURE 17-4   Classes and methods in the Java Class Library relevant to buttons

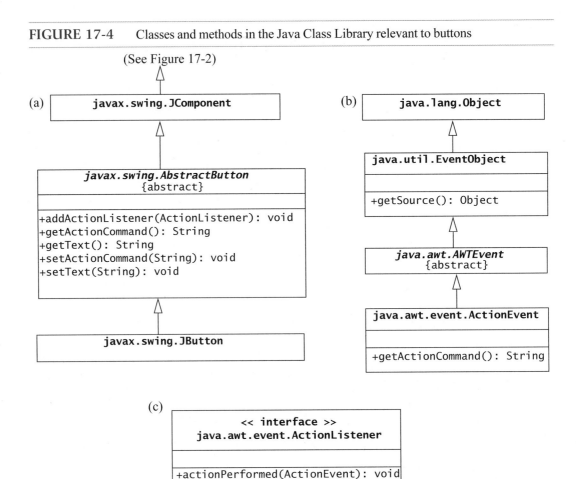

(c)

| << interface >> java.awt.event.ActionListener |

17.8   **Implementing the interface `ActionListener`.** The class that implements the interface `ActionListener` describes a listener for an action occurring on a certain component. Usually, this class is considered an implementation detail and is not used anywhere outside of the relevant panel or frame. You can define such a class as a private **inner class** within the class representing a panel or frame.

Note: Inner classes

An inner class is a class defined within another class, the **outer class**. An inner class can have its own data fields, constructors, and other methods. Methods of an inner class can access by name the data fields and methods of the outer class. If an inner class is a detail of the outer class's implementation, it should be private, because such details should be hidden from the client.

For example, consider a panel that contains two buttons, one of which has the action command "Add". The following class—arbitrarily called `ButtonListener`—could be an inner class of the panel class:

```java
private class ButtonListener implements ActionListener
{
   public void actionPerformed(ActionEvent event)
   {
      String command = event.getActionCommand();
      if (command.equals("Add"))
      {
         < Statements that define the action to occur when the "Add" button is clicked. >
      }
      else
      {
         < Statements that define the action to occur when a different button is clicked. >
      }
   } // end actionPerformed
} // end ButtonListener
```

Since the interface `ActionListener` declares only one method, we have only one method definition to write within the inner class. The parameter `event` represents the action event that the system generates when the user clicks a button, and the expression `event.getActionCommand()` is that button's action command.

Question 3 Assume that we have registered an action listener with both the button `myButton` that you created in Question 1 and a second button. Define the action listener's method `actionPerformed` so that the method `myButtonAction` is called when `myButton` is clicked, but nothing happens when the second button is clicked.

Registering an Action Listener

17.9   Suppose that the outer class for `ButtonListener` is a panel that contains the buttons as well as any other graphics associated with the application. The constructor for this outer class contains statements like those in Segments 17.4 and 17.5 to define `labeledButton` and `plainButton` and set `labeledButton`'s action command. To register a listener for `labeledButton`, we first create an instance of the inner class `ButtonListener` by writing either

```java
ButtonListener listener = new ButtonListener();
```

or

```java
ActionListener listener = new ButtonListener();
```

videonote
Input using buttons

Recall from the previous chapter that we can use an interface name as a data type.
We then register this listener with `labeledButton` by writing

```java
labeledButton.addActionListener(listener);
```

We can register the same listener with our second button, `plainButton`, by writing

```java
plainButton.addActionListener(listener);
```

Although we could have separate listeners for these two buttons, one is sufficient, since the action command will tell us which button was clicked.

Question 4 If myButtonListener is an action listener for the button myButton, how do you register the listener with the button?

Question 5 Can one action listener be used for more than one button?

Question 6 Can several buttons each have their own action listener?

Question 7 If each button has its own action listener, must the method actionPerformed call the method getActionCommand?

Responding to a Button Click

17.10   **Example.** The class in Listing 17-1 describes a panel containing two buttons and a label. Recall our use of the Swing class JLabel in Segment 9.14 of Chapter 9 to create a label. We will use such a label to report which of the two buttons has been clicked. You should recognize the statements in Listing 17-1 that create and process the buttons, as they are like the ones presented earlier in this chapter. Listing 17-2 contains a driver for this class, along with the results of clicking the buttons.

LISTING 17-1   The class ButtonDemoPanel

```java
/** ButtonDemoPanel.java by F. M. Carrano
    A simple demonstration of two buttons.
*/
import javax.swing.JButton;
import javax.swing.JLabel;
import javax.swing.JPanel;

import java.awt.Color;
import java.awt.Dimension;
import java.awt.Graphics;

import java.awt.event.ActionEvent;
import java.awt.event.ActionListener;

public class ButtonDemoPanel extends JPanel
{
   private final JButton redButton, greenButton;
   private final JLabel messageOut;
   private static final String redMessage = "Red button clicked.";
   private static final String greenMessage = "Green button clicked.";
   private static final int PANEL_WIDTH = 250, PANEL_HEIGHT = 100;

   public ButtonDemoPanel()
   {
      ButtonListener listener = new ButtonListener();
//    ActionListener listener = new ButtonListener(); // Alternate
      redButton = new JButton("Red");
      redButton.setActionCommand("Button One");
```

```java
        redButton.addActionListener(listener);
        add(redButton);

        greenButton = new JButton("Green");
// Alternate statements instead of the previous one:
//      greenButton = new JButton();
//      greenButton.setText("Green");

        greenButton.setActionCommand("Button Two");
        greenButton.addActionListener(listener);
        add(greenButton);

        messageOut = new JLabel();
        add(messageOut);

        setPreferredSize(new Dimension(PANEL_WIDTH, PANEL_HEIGHT));
    } // end default constructor

    private class ButtonListener implements ActionListener
    {
        public void actionPerformed(ActionEvent buttonClick)
        {
            String command = buttonClick.getActionCommand();
            if (command.equals("Button One"))
                messageOut.setText(redMessage);
            else // assume second button clicked
                messageOut.setText(greenMessage);
        } // end actionPerformed
    } // end ButtonListener
} // end ButtonDemoPanel
```

LISTING 17-2   The class ButtonDriver

```java
/** ButtonDemoDriver.java by F. M. Carrano
    A driver for the class ButtonDemoPanel.
*/
import javax.swing.JFrame;

public class ButtonDemoDriver
{
    public static void main(String[] args)
    {
        JFrame window = new JFrame();
        window.setDefaultCloseOperation(JFrame.EXIT_ON_CLOSE);
        window.setTitle("Button Demo");

        ButtonDemoPanel panel = new ButtonDemoPanel();
```

```
        window.add(panel);
        window.pack();
        window.setVisible(true);
    } // end main
} // end ButtonDemoDriver
```

Sample Output (Before and After a Button Click)

Note: A user can "click" a button by pressing a key on the keyboard instead of by using the mouse. For example, you likely have pressed the Enter key when logging onto a website, instead of using a mouse to click a button. Although we will not discuss how to enable this feature, a class such as JButton responds to a key press by using a listener for a key event in much the same way that it responds to a mouse event. Later in this chapter, you will learn how to respond to mouse events.

Question 8 What relationship, if any, exists between a button's action command and its text?

Question 9 What happens when a button is clicked that makes it possible for us to learn which button it is?

Programming Tip

Since a button's default action command is its text, you might wonder why you should bother to use a distinct action command. Doing so separates what the user sees—that is, the button's text—from the logic of reacting to a button click. This separation is useful, however, if your application is used internationally. For example, if the buttons' text is in English, you can simply change the text to another language without altering the statements that process the action commands.

A Problem Solved: Smile or Frown

In Chapter 9, we wrote a class of happy faces. Let's create a similar face, but one that smiles or frowns according to which button the user clicks.

17.11   **The face.** We begin with a class of faces. This class is quite similar to the class HappyFace that you saw in Listing 9-4 of Chapter 9. As you can see in Listing 17-3, the class Face has a boolean data field that controls whether the face smiles or frowns. The methods smile and frown set this field, and the method paintFace paints the face's mouth according to the field's value. We have highlighted the differences between this class and HappyFace.

LISTING 17-3   The class Face

```
/** Face.java by F. M. Carrano
    Represents a face that can smile or frown.
*/
```

```java
import java.awt.Color;
import java.awt.Graphics;

public class Face
{
   private boolean smile; // true for smile, false for frown
   private final int x, y; // coordinates of center of face
   private final int faceRadius;
   private final Color faceColor;
   private final int faceDiameter, faceLeft, faceTop;
   private final int mouthWidth, mouthHeight, mouthLeft, mouthTop;
   private final int eyeDiameter, eyeTop, leftEyeLeft, rightEyeLeft;

   private static final Color EYE_COLOR = Color.BLACK;
   private static final Color MOUTH_COLOR = Color.BLACK;

   /** Creates a default face. */
   public Face()
   {
      this(200, 100, 75, Color.ORANGE);
   } // end default constructor

   /** Creates a face centered at a given point with a given radius
       and color. */
   public Face(int centerX, int centerY, int radius, Color color)
   {
      smile = true;
      faceColor = color;
      x = centerX;
      y = centerY;
      faceRadius = radius;
      faceDiameter = 2 * faceRadius;

      faceLeft = x - faceRadius;
      faceTop  = y - faceRadius;

      mouthWidth = (int)(0.4 * faceDiameter);
      mouthHeight = mouthWidth / 4;
      mouthLeft = x - mouthWidth / 2;
      mouthTop = y + 2 * mouthHeight;
      int mouthRight = mouthLeft + mouthWidth - 1;

      int eyeRadius = (int)(0.15 * faceRadius);
      eyeDiameter = 2 * eyeRadius;
      // coordinates of eyes:
      eyeTop = y - (faceRadius - 2 * mouthHeight) / 3;
      leftEyeLeft = mouthLeft - eyeRadius;
      rightEyeLeft = mouthRight - eyeRadius;
   } // end constructor
```

```
/** Makes the face smile. */
public void smile()
{
    smile = true;
} // end smile

/** Makes the face frown. */
public void frown()
{
    smile = false;
} // end frown

/** Displays the face. */
public void paintFace(Graphics pen)
{
    // paint face
    pen.setColor(faceColor);
    pen.fillOval(faceLeft, faceTop, faceDiameter, faceDiameter);

    // paint eyes
    pen.setColor(EYE_COLOR);
    pen.fillOval(leftEyeLeft, eyeTop, eyeDiameter, eyeDiameter);
    pen.fillOval(rightEyeLeft, eyeTop, eyeDiameter, eyeDiameter);

    // paint mouth: first fill oval,
    pen.setColor(MOUTH_COLOR);
    int ovalTop = mouthTop - mouthHeight;
    pen.fillOval(mouthLeft, ovalTop, mouthWidth, 2 * mouthHeight);

    // then erase top or bottom of oval by painting it in face color
    pen.setColor(faceColor);
    if (smile)
        pen.fillOval(mouthLeft, ovalTop, mouthWidth, mouthHeight);
    else
        pen.fillOval(mouthLeft, ovalTop + mouthHeight, mouthWidth,
                     mouthHeight);

} // end paintFace
} // end Face
```

17.12   **A panel for the face.** Let's paint the face in its own panel. The class `FacePanel`, shown in Listing 17-4, is a subclass of `JPanel`. The constructor creates a `Face` object and sets the panel's size. The method `paintComponent`, which overrides the corresponding method in `JPanel`, paints the face. One additional method, `setMouth`, sets the shape of the mouth so the panel can react to the user's button clicks. Another panel that contains the buttons will invoke this method.

LISTING 17-4   The panel that contains the face

```
/** FacePanel.java by F. M. Carrano
    A panel containing a face that can smile or frown.
```

```
*/
import javax.swing.JPanel;
import java.awt.Color;
import java.awt.Dimension;
import java.awt.Graphics;

public class FacePanel extends JPanel
{
   private static final int PANEL_WIDTH = 300;
   private static final int PANEL_HEIGHT = 350;
   private static final int FACE_X = PANEL_WIDTH / 2;
   private static final int FACE_Y = PANEL_HEIGHT / 2;
   private static final int FACE_RADIUS = PANEL_WIDTH / 4;
   private static final Color FACE_COLOR = Color.ORANGE;

   private final Face aFace;

   /** Constructs a panel containing a face. */
   public FacePanel()
   {
      aFace = new Face(FACE_X, FACE_Y, FACE_RADIUS, FACE_COLOR);
      setPreferredSize(new Dimension(PANEL_WIDTH, PANEL_HEIGHT));
   } // end FacePanel

   /** Paints the panel. */
   public void paintComponent(Graphics pen)
   {
      aFace.paintFace(pen);
   } // end paintComponent

   /** Sets the shape of the mouth according to the
       value of the parameter smile. */
   public void setMouth(boolean smile)
   {
      if (smile)
         aFace.smile();
      else
         aFace.frown();

      repaint();
   } // end setMouth
} // end FacePanel
```

17.13   **The buttons.** The application at hand has two buttons, one to make the face smile and one to make it frown. We can create the two buttons and place them into a panel. That panel and an instance of FacePanel are subpanels of a larger panel. The class FaceAndButtonPanel, given in Listing 17-5, describes one way to create this larger panel. The two subpanels, one for the face and one for the buttons, are data fields that the constructor creates using statements like the ones you have seen already. The rest of the class is the definition of the inner class ButtonListener. Within this inner class, the method actionPerformed calls FacePanel's method setMouth, passing it an argument according to the value of the action command. Notice that these arguments are named constants for either true or false to make the code easier to read. Remember that the face panel defines the method paintComponent, so no painting is done explicitly within the class FaceAndButtonPanel.

LISTING 17-5   The class FaceAndButtonPanel

```
/** FaceAndButtonPanel.java by F. M. Carrano
    A panel containing a face and two buttons to control it.
*/
import javax.swing.JButton;
import javax.swing.JPanel;
import java.awt.Dimension;

import java.awt.event.ActionListener;
import java.awt.event.ActionEvent;

public class FaceAndButtonPanel extends JPanel
{
    private final FacePanel facePanel;
    private final JPanel    buttonPanel;
    private static final boolean SMILE = true, FROWN = false;

    public FaceAndButtonPanel()
    {
        facePanel = new FacePanel();
        add(facePanel);

        buttonPanel = new JPanel();
        ButtonListener listener = new ButtonListener();
   //   ActionListener listener = new ButtonListener(); // Alternate

        JButton smileButton = new JButton("Smile");
        smileButton.setActionCommand("smile-button");
        smileButton.addActionListener(listener);
        buttonPanel.add(smileButton);

        JButton frownButton = new JButton("Frown");
        frownButton.setActionCommand("frown-button");
        frownButton.addActionListener(listener);
        buttonPanel.add(frownButton);

        add(buttonPanel);
    } // end constructor

    private class ButtonListener implements ActionListener
    {
        public void actionPerformed(ActionEvent event)
        {
```

```
            if ("smile-button".equals(event.getActionCommand()))
                facePanel.setMouth(SMILE);
            else
                facePanel.setMouth(FROWN);
        } // end actionPerformed
    } // end ButtonListener
} // end FaceAndButtonPanel
```

17.14   **Displaying the final results.** Finally, we instantiate `FaceButtonPanel` within the class `FaceDriver`. Listing 17-6 shows this class and two views of the output from the program.

LISTING 17-6   The frame containing `FaceAndButtonPanel`

```java
/** FaceDriver.java by F. M. Carrano
    Displays a face that smiles or frowns according to the
    click of one of two buttons.
*/
import javax.swing.JFrame;
public class FaceDriver
{
    public static void main(String[] args)
    {
        JFrame window = new JFrame();
        window.setDefaultCloseOperation(JFrame.EXIT_ON_CLOSE);
        window.setTitle("Happy or Sad Face");

        FaceAndButtonPanel panel = new FaceAndButtonPanel();

        window.add(panel);
        window.pack();
        window.setVisible(true);
    } // end main
} // end FaceDriver
```

Output (Initially and After Clicking the "Smile" Button)

Output (After Clicking the "Frown" Button)

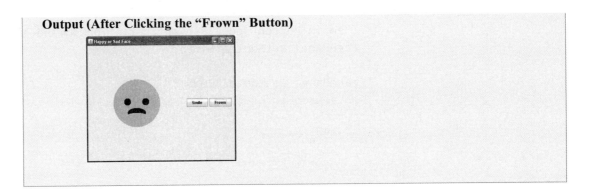

Question 10 What changes can you make to the class `FaceAndButtonPanel` in Listing 17-5 so that each of the two buttons has its own action listener?

▪ Using Mouse Input

Have we not already responded to mouse clicks in our treatment of buttons? You might think so, but button events are different from mouse events in Java. A button event occurs in response to a mouse click on a button. The class `JButton` hides the mouse click from us and creates a button event. Your class, however, can respond to a mouse event directly when you deal with components other than buttons. Let's see how this is done.

The Interface `MouseListener`

17.15   A **mouse event** is generated when any of the following **mouse actions** occurs on a component that implements the interface `MouseListener`:

- The mouse is on a component and the mouse is clicked—that is, pressed and released.
- The mouse is on a component and the mouse is pressed.
- The mouse is on a component and the mouse is released.
- The mouse enters a component.
- The mouse leaves a component.

Although we speak of the position of the mouse, we mean the position of its cursor on the screen.
When any mouse event occurs, the system calls one of the following methods, depending on the cause of the event:

- `mouseClicked`
- `mousePressed`
- `mouseReleased`
- `mouseEntered`
- `mouseExited`

Each of these methods is passed the mouse event as its argument. A mouse event actually is an object of the standard class `MouseEvent`.

17.16   By defining the previous five methods, we can respond to certain mouse actions. These methods are declared in the standard interface `MouseListener`.

Note: The interface `MouseListener`

The interface `MouseListener` is in the package `java.awt.event` of the Java Class Library. Each method in this interface defines the response to a certain mouse action:

```java
/** Defines the response to a click of a mouse button. */
public void mouseClicked(MouseEvent event)

/** Defines the response to a press of a mouse button. */
public void mousePressed(MouseEvent event)

/** Defines the response to a release of a mouse button. */
public void mouseReleased(MouseEvent event)

/** Defines the response when the mouse enters a component. */
public void mouseEntered(MouseEvent event)

/** Defines the response when the mouse exits a component. */
public void mouseExited(MouseEvent event)
```

Note that the class `MouseEvent` is also in the package `java.awt.event`.

17.17   A **mouse listener** is an object of a class that implements the interface `MouseListener`. Typically, this class is a private inner class of a component class, such as a derived class of `JPanel`. You register a mouse listener by passing it to the method `addMouseListener`—which `JPanel` inherits from the class `Component`—much as you register an action listener for a button.

Although the code necessary to deal with a mouse event is similar to the code we wrote for button events, a mouse does not have an action command. Instead, the `MouseEvent` object that is generated and passed to one of the methods declared in `MouseListener` can report the position of the mouse cursor at the time of the event. You can obtain and react to this position when you define the `MouseListener` methods.

Note: The class `MouseEvent`

The class `MouseEvent` is in the package `java.awt.event`. Like action events, objects of this class are created for us, so we need not worry about `MouseEvent`'s constructors. When a mouse action occurs, the system calls the appropriate method declared in the interface `MouseListener` and passes it a `MouseEvent` object as the argument.

The following methods of `MouseEvent` report the position of the mouse cursor at the time of the mouse action:

```java
/** Returns the x-coordinate of the mouse cursor
    associated with the mouse event. */
public int getX()

/** Returns the y-coordinate of the mouse cursor
    associated with the mouse event. */
public int getY()

/** Returns the position of the mouse cursor
    associated with the mouse event. */
public Point getPoint()
```

Responding to a Mouse Click

17.18   **Example.** Let's look at a simple example that summarizes what we must do to respond to a mouse click. The class in Listing 17-7 describes a panel that marks and reports the location of any mouse click within its boundaries. An inner class implements the interface `MouseListener` and captures the location of the mouse click within the method `mouseClicked`. Once again, we use a `JLabel` object for our message, and we set the message within the method `mouseClicked`. Since we want to mark the location of the mouse click, we also must define the method `paintComponent`. Notice the call to `repaint` as the last action of the mouse listener's method `mouseClicked`.

LISTING 17-7   The class `MouseDemoPanel`

```
/** MouseDemoPanel.java by F. M. Carrano
    Marks and reports the location of mouse clicks.
*/
import javax.swing.JLabel;
import javax.swing.JPanel;

import java.awt.Color;
import java.awt.Dimension;
import java.awt.Graphics;

import java.awt.event.MouseEvent;
import java.awt.event.MouseListener;

public class MouseDemoPanel extends JPanel
{
    private int mouseX, mouseY;
    private final JLabel messageOut;

    private static final int PANEL_WIDTH = 300;
    private static final int PANEL_HEIGHT = 200;

    // size and color of dot to mark mouse location
    private static final int RADIUS = 2;
    private static final int DIAMETER = 2 * RADIUS;
    private static final Color DOT_COLOR = Color.BLUE;

    public MouseDemoPanel()
    {
        mouseX = 0;
        mouseY = 0;
        messageOut = new JLabel();
        add(messageOut);
        addMouseListener(new ClickListener()); // listen for mouse clicks
        setPreferredSize(new Dimension(PANEL_WIDTH, PANEL_HEIGHT));
    } // end default constructor
```

```java
    public void paintComponent(Graphics pen)
    {
        // clear previous marks by painting background
        pen.setColor(getBackground());
        pen.fillRect(0, 0, getWidth(), getHeight());

        // paint dot centered at mouse click
        pen.setColor(DOT_COLOR);
        pen.fillOval(mouseX - RADIUS, mouseY - RADIUS, DIAMETER, DIAMETER);
    } // end paintComponent

    // Listens for mouse clicks
    private class ClickListener implements MouseListener
    {
        public void mouseClicked(MouseEvent click)
        {
            // the mouse button has been clicked on this panel;
            // get coordinates of mouse click
            mouseX = click.getX();
            mouseY = click.getY();

            messageOut.setText("Mouse click at (" + mouseX + ", " +
                                    mouseY + ").");
            repaint();
        } // end mouseClicked

        // Ignore these actions on this panel:
        public void mousePressed(MouseEvent e) {}
        public void mouseReleased(MouseEvent e){}
        public void mouseEntered(MouseEvent e) {}
        public void mouseExited(MouseEvent e)  {}
    } // end ClickListener
} // end MouseDemoPanel
```

The interface
MouseListener

We are interested only in mouse clicks in this example, so we want to ignore other mouse actions. However, since the interface MouseListener declares five methods, and the inner class ClickListener implements MouseListener, ClickListener must define all five methods. To satisfy this requirement, the definitions of the methods associated with the ignored mouse actions have empty bodies, as shown in the highlighted area of the listing.

Note: The class MouseAdapter
The class MouseAdapter is a class that implements the methods in the interface MouseListener. These method definitions have empty bodies. Thus, this class provides a convenient way to create a listener class for mouse events.

For example, instead of implementing MouseListener, the inner class ClickListener in Listing 17-7 could extend the class MouseAdapter as follows:

```
private class ClickListener extends MouseAdapter
{
    public void mouseClicked(MouseEvent click)
    {
        < The body of this method, as given in Listing 17-7, is here. >
    } // end mouseClicked
} // end ClickListener
```

In this way, ClickListener would define only the method mouseClicked and omit the method definitions in Listing 17-7 that have empty bodies.

MouseAdapter is in the same package as MouseListener, namely java.awt.event.

17.19 The driver in Listing 17-8 creates a window for our panel and gives a sample of its output. Initially, a dot appears at the point (0, 0), but no message is displayed. A message is displayed as soon as the user clicks the mouse somewhere on the panel.

LISTING 17-8   A driver for MouseDemoPanel

```
/** MouseDemoDriver.java by F. M. Carrano
    A driver for the class MouseDemoPanel.
*/
import javax.swing.JFrame;

public class MouseDemoDriver
{
    public static void main(String[] args)
    {
        JFrame window = new JFrame();
        window.setDefaultCloseOperation(JFrame.EXIT_ON_CLOSE);
        window.setTitle("Mouse Demo");

        MouseDemoPanel panel = new MouseDemoPanel();
        window.add(panel);
        window.pack();
        window.setVisible(true);
    } // end main
} // end MouseDemoDriver
```

Sample Output (Before and After a Mouse Click)

17.20 **The relevant classes and methods.** Figure 17-5 shows the elements of the Java Class Library that are relevant to using the mouse. The problem in the next section uses some of these elements in its solution.

FIGURE 17-5   Mouse methods in the Java Class Library

Question 11 When you run the program given in Listing 17-8, a dot appears at the point (0, 0), but no message is displayed. A message will be displayed as soon as the user clicks the mouse somewhere on the panel. How will the program behave if, in `MouseDemoPanel`, you move the statement

```
messageOut.setText("Mouse click at (" + mouseX + ", " +
                   mouseY + ").");
```

from the method `mouseClicked` to the method `paintComponent`, placing it right after the call to `fillRect`?

Question 12 Since we have no use for the methods `mousePressed`, `mouseReleased`, `mouseEntered`, and `mouseExited` that appear in Listing 17-7, may we simply omit their definitions completely? Why or why not?

Design Decision: Choosing the data type of the mouse-click location

The method mouseClicked given in Listing 17-7 uses the methods getX and getY of the class MouseEvent to retrieve the location of the mouse when it is clicked by the user. Notice that these integer values are saved in the data fields mouseX and mouseY. In turn, these data fields are accessed by the method paintComponent when it draws the dot to mark the mouse location.

An alternate way to record the location of the mouse click uses one data field, mouseLocation, whose data type is Point. The method mouseClicked then would use MouseEvent's method getPoint instead of the methods getX and getY to retrieve this location. This decision forces paintComponent to get the *x*- and *y*-coordinates of the mouse click by using Point's methods getX and getY. For example, paintComponent could contain the following statements:

```
int dotCornerX = (int)mouseLocation.getX() - RADIUS;
int dotCornerY = (int)mouseLocation.getY() - RADIUS;
pen.setColor(DOT_COLOR);
pen.fillOval(dotCornerX, dotCornerY, DIAMETER, DIAMETER);
```

Note that mouseClicked must call the same getX and getY, since in this example we want to display the coordinates of the mouse click.

Although using the class Point can be a convenient way to record the location of a mouse event, doing so in the previous example is awkward. However, the problem solved in the next section does use Point in this way, as Listing 17-10 will show.

Note: Be aware of a method's return type

The classes MouseEvent and Point each define methods named getX and getY. These methods return the coordinates of a point. However, while the MouseEvent versions return int values, Point's methods return double values. Notice that we had to cast these double values to int in the statements given in the previous Design Decision. Forgetting to do so is easy, particularly when working with both of these classes in the same program.

A Problem Solved: Changing Color at the Click of a Mouse

Imagine a disk represented by a circular area painted in a given color other than gray. If you position the mouse cursor within the disk and click the mouse button, the disk will become gray. Another click will return the disk to its original color, and so on.

17.21 **Designing a solution.** What classes should we define? Let's begin with a class of disks. These disks must be more sophisticated than the simple squares we created in Chapter 6. Each disk must be able to display itself, change color, and tell us whether a given point is within its boundary. These behaviors require that a disk know its color, position, and size. Figure 17-6 summarizes our decisions about this class on a CRC card.

FIGURE 17-6   A CRC card for a class of graphical disks

```
                         ClickDisk
  Responsibilities
    Display
    Change color
    Is this point inside?


  Collaborations
    Color
    Graphics
    Point
```

17.22   Note that our disks do not interact directly with the mouse. Instead, a panel, which is a graphical component, will handle the mouse events and give the mouse's position to a disk. The panel class should create a disk, define the method paintComponent to paint the disk, and define an inner class that implements the interface MouseListener. Finally, a driver will create a window containing an instance of the panel class. Figure 17-7 contains a UML diagram for our proposed solution to this problem. To indicate an inner class, the arrow indicating the association has a crossed circle on the end near the outer class.

We can enhance the UML diagram in Figure 17-7 by adding the specifications for the class of disks, as shown in Figure 17-8. We named the class, its methods, and the methods' parameters. We also chose relevant data types where appropriate.

FIGURE 17-7   A UML diagram of a proposed solution

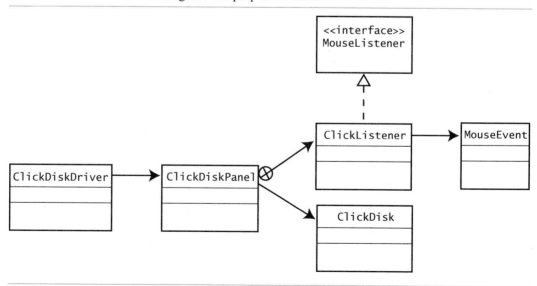

FIGURE 17-8   UML details for the class `ClickDisk`

ClickDisk
-center: Point
-radius: int
-currentColor: Color
-isGray: boolean
+getCenter(): Point
+getRadius(): int
+getColor(): Color
+changeColor(): void
+inDisk(aPoint: Point): boolean
+display(pen: Graphics): void

17.23   **The class `ClickDisk`.** After writing comments and a header for each method, we complete the class definition given in Listing 17-9. The client can choose the size and location of the disk, as well as a color other than gray. These three values are stored in data fields. We also retain the disk's current color in another data field. To facilitate a color change, we have a boolean field `isGray` to indicate whether the disk's color is gray. The method `changeColor` changes both the disk's current color and the value of `isGray` according to the present value of `isGray`.

The method `inDisk` tests whether a given point is within the circular disk. What may seem like a challenging task is actually quite simple. The class `Point` has a method `distance`, which returns the distance between the receiving point and another point that is passed as an argument to the method. For example, if `myPoint` and `yourPoint` are `Point` objects, `myPoint.distance(yourPoint)` returns the distance between the two points as a `double` value. To implement `inDisk`, we need only to see whether the distance between the given point and the disk's center is less than or equal to the radius of the disk. The method's definition is then

```
public boolean inDisk(Point mouseLocation)
{
    return (int)mouseLocation.distance(center) <= radius;
} // end inDisk
```

LISTING 17-9   The class `ClickDisk`

```
/** ClickDisk.java by F. M. Carrano
    A class of disks that can be displayed, change color, and
    recognize when a given point lies within its boundaries.
*/
import java.awt.Color;
import java.awt.Graphics;
import java.awt.Point;

public class ClickDisk
{
    private final Point center;
    private final int radius;
    private final Color aColor; // a color other than gray
```

```java
   private Color currentColor; // disk's color at the moment
   private boolean isGray;      // true if currentColor is gray

   /** Creates a disk having a given center, radius, and color. */
   public ClickDisk(Point diskCenter, int diskRadius, Color diskColor)
   {
      center = diskCenter;
      radius = diskRadius;
      aColor = diskColor;
      currentColor = aColor;
      isGray = false;
   } // end constructor
```

< The accessor methods getCenter, getRadius, *and* getColor *are here. >*

```java
   /** Changes the disk's color either from or to gray. */
   public void changeColor()
   {
      if (isGray)
      {
         currentColor = aColor;
         isGray = false;
      }
      else
      {
         currentColor = Color.GRAY;
         isGray = true;
      } // end if
   } // end changeColor

   /** Returns true if the given point is within the disk.
       Otherwise, returns false. */
   public boolean inDisk(Point aPoint)
   {
      return (int)aPoint.distance(center) <= radius;
   } // end inDisk

   /** Displays a disk in its current color. */
   public void display(Graphics pen)
   {
      int xCorner = (int)center.getX() - radius;
      int yCorner = (int)center.getY() - radius;
      int diameter = 2 * radius;
      pen.setColor(currentColor);
      pen.fillOval(xCorner, yCorner, diameter, diameter);
   } // end display
} // end ClickDisk
```

17.24 **The class `ClickDiskPanel`.** The class `ClickDiskPanel`, shown in Listing 17-10, describes the panel that displays a `ClickDisk` object and is analogous to the class `FaceAndButtonPanel` in Listing 17-5. Its constructor creates both the `ClickDisk` object and a mouse listener, and registers the latter as a listener for mouse clicks on this panel. The method `paintComponent` simply invokes the `display` method of the `ClickDisk` object.

The significant part to notice is the private inner class `ClickListener`, which is highlighted in the listing. An object of this class is the mouse listener that the constructor creates and registers. `ClickListener` contains the statements that process and react to a mouse click. The method `mouseClicked` gets the location of the mouse click and, if this location is within the bounds of the disk, changes the disk's color. If `disk` is the name of the `ClickDisk` object, the method's definition is

```
public void mouseClicked(MouseEvent mouseClick)
{
   Point mouseLocation = mouseClick.getPoint();
   if (disk.inDisk(mouseLocation))
   {
      disk.changeColor();
      repaint();
   } // end if
} // end mouseClicked
```

Recall that this method is called automatically by the system as a result of a mouse click on the panel.

As before, the other four methods declared in the interface `MouseListener` must be defined with the inner class, but we give them empty bodies, since we do not want to respond to the mouse actions they represent.

LISTING 17-10 The class `ClickDiskPanel`

```
/** ClickDiskPanel.java by F. M. Carrano
    A panel for ClickDisk that processes mouse clicks.
*/
import javax.swing.JPanel;

import java.awt.Color;
import java.awt.Dimension;
import java.awt.Graphics;
import java.awt.Point;

import java.awt.event.MouseEvent;
import java.awt.event.MouseListener;

public class ClickDiskPanel extends JPanel
{
   private static final int PANEL_SIDE = 200; // square panel
   private static final int MID = PANEL_SIDE / 2;
   private static final Point DISK_CENTER = new Point(MID, MID);
   private static final int DISK_RADIUS = 40;
   private static final Color DISK_COLOR = Color.CYAN;
   private final ClickDisk disk;
```

```
    public ClickDiskPanel()
    {
        disk = new ClickDisk(DISK_CENTER, DISK_RADIUS, DISK_COLOR);

        ClickListener listener = new ClickListener();
        addMouseListener(listener); // sees clicks on this panel

        setPreferredSize(new Dimension(PANEL_SIDE, PANEL_SIDE));
    } // end default constructor

    public void paintComponent(Graphics pen)
    {
        disk.display(pen);
    } // end paintComponent


    private class ClickListener implements MouseListener
    {
        public void mouseClicked(MouseEvent mouseClick)
        {
            Point mouseLocation = mouseClick.getPoint();
            if (disk.inDisk(mouseLocation))
            {
                disk.changeColor();
                repaint();
            } // end if
        } // end mouseClicked

        // Ignore these actions on this panel:
        public void mousePressed(MouseEvent e) {}
        public void mouseReleased(MouseEvent e){}
        public void mouseEntered(MouseEvent e) {}
        public void mouseExited(MouseEvent e)   {}
    } // end ClickListener
} // end ClickDiskPanel
```

17.25   **The driver.** Finally, the program in Listing 17-11 creates the frame for the panel whose class is
ClickDiskPanel.

LISTING 17-11   An application whose frame contains an instance of
ClickDiskPanel

```
/** ClickDiskDriver.java by F. M. Carrano
    A driver that demonstrates ClickDisk within ClickDiskPanel.
*/
import javax.swing.JFrame;

public class ClickDiskDriver
{
```

```
    public static void main(String[] args)
    {
        JFrame window = new JFrame();
        window.setDefaultCloseOperation(JFrame.EXIT_ON_CLOSE);
        window.setTitle("Click Disk");

        ClickDiskPanel panel = new ClickDiskPanel();
        window.add(panel);
        window.pack();
        window.setVisible(true);
    } // end main
} // end ClickDiskDriver
```

Sample Output

Question 13 Run the program given in Listing 17-11. What happens when you press, move, and then release the mouse button?

Question 14 Repeat Question 13, but first replace the method mouseClicked with mouse-Pressed.

Question 15 Repeat Question 13, but first replace the method mouseClicked with mouse-Released.

The Interface MouseMotionListener

17.26   When a user either moves or drags the mouse, a **mouse motion event** occurs, and a MouseEvent object is generated. Two methods, which are declared in the interface MouseMotionListener, enable you to react to such an event.

> **Note:** The interface MouseMotionListener
> The interface MouseMotionListener is in the package java.awt.event of the Java Class Library. Each method in this interface defines the action that occurs when a certain mouse motion event takes place:
> ```
> /** Defines the response when a mouse moves onto a component
>     but is not pressed. */
> public void mouseMoved(MouseEvent event)
>
> /** Defines the response when a mouse is pressed, held, and moved
>     while on a component. */
> public void mouseDragged(MouseEvent event)
> ```

You use this interface and implement its methods in much the same way that you use the interface MouseListener. By implementing the method mouseMoved, you could, for example, paint a dot that follows the cursor as it moves.

Using Text Fields

We end this chapter by showing you how to read data from the user in a new way by using an instance of the Swing class JTextField.

The Class JTextField

17.27   A **text field** is an instance of the Swing class JTextField. To create one, we invoke the constructor of JTextField, giving it the number of columns of input data it should be able to contain. For example, we could write

        JTextField textInput = new JTextField(9);

to define a text field accommodating a nine-character input value. We then can add textInput to a panel, just as we added buttons or labels to a panel.

Although the panel displays the text field for us, we will not know when the user has entered data into it unless we activate an action listener. For example, we can detect when the user has clicked a button or pressed the Enter key after typing a line of input. Either action causes the system to generate an event and call the method actionPerformed. As you saw earlier in this chapter, this method is declared in the interface ActionListener, and so the action listener is an instance of a class that implements this interface. Additionally, after creating the action listener, we need to register it with the text field by writing a statement of the form

        textInput.addActionListener(*the_action_listener*);

17.28   The method actionPerformed can get the input data entered into the text field by calling JTextField's method getText. For example, the statement

        String inputString = textInput.getText();

retrieves the input data as a string. If the data is meant to have a type other than String, we must convert it in much the same way that we did in Chapter 4 when obtaining input by using JOptionPane.

Figure 17-9 shows a class diagram for the classes JTextField and JLabel.

Note: When an application uses several text fields for its input, you typically should provide a button for the user to click after completing all the text fields. In such cases, your text fields would not respond to the Enter key.

Question 16 Assume that textInput is the text field created in Segment 17.27, and that we have written an action listener for the text field and registered it. What statement(s) should be in the definition of the method actionPerformed to retrieve the single integer entered into the text field by the user? Assign this integer to the int variable result.

FIGURE 17-9   The classes `JTextField` and `JLabel` within the Java Class
Library

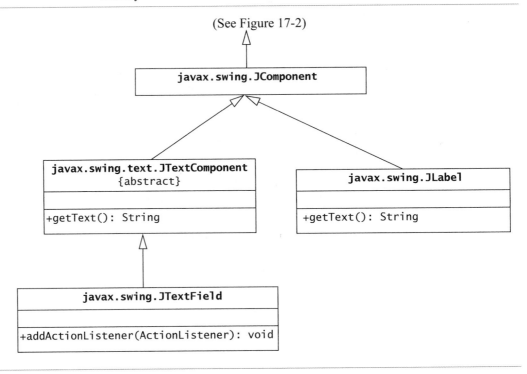

A Problem Solved: Displaying RGB Colors

Segment 5.25 in Chapter 5 explains how differing amounts of the three primary colors—red, green, and blue—represented by integers between 0 and 255 are used by computer applications to create any given color. These integers are the color's RGB value.

Write an application that displays the color represented by any given RGB value.

17.29   **The general approach to a solution.** We can implement our application as two classes, one for a panel and one for a frame. The panel will contain two subpanels. One subpanel can handle the input and will contain a prompt to the user within a `JLabel` object. The second subpanel will display the output, which is simply the RGB value in the form of another `JLabel` object displayed over the background color it represents.

Let's ask the user to enter a color's red, green, and blue components as integers in the range 0 to 255. In particular, suppose we ask the user to enter each component as a three-digit integer, one after the other, in one text field. Thus, the user actually types a nine-digit integer, which the text field returns as a string.

Once we have the input data as a string, we use the method `parseInt` of the class `Integer` to convert the data to a nine-digit integer. After breaking this integer into its three component parts, we create a `Color` object and use it to set the background color of a panel. A call to `repaint` forces the panel to paint its background, thus displaying the color specified by the user.

17.30 **The data fields and constructor.** Listing 17-12 shows the definition of the panel class. A text field, two subpanels, and a label for the output are data fields, which the constructor creates. The constructor then adds both the prompt, as a locally defined label, and the text field to the input panel. The order in which we add these components to the panel dictates the order in which they appear when displayed. Finally, the constructor adds an empty label to the output panel and then adds both subpanels to the larger panel represented by this class.

   Notice two details handled by the constructor: First, it sets the preferred sizes of the panel and its two subpanels. More significantly, it creates and registers an action listener for the text field. This listener is an object of the inner class that we describe next.

17.31 **The inner class.** While the constructor sets up the panel and prepares for the user's input, the method `actionPerformed` within the inner class processes the input and produces the output. After converting the input string to an integer, we use integer division and the remainder operator to break the nine-digit input into three integers representing the red, green, and blue components of the desired color. A `Color` object having these components represents the background color for the output panel. The output label is set to show the numeric RGB value, and the text in the text field is cleared in anticipation of subsequent input. A final call to `repaint` displays the results.

LISTING 17-12   The class `ColorPanel`: Using a text field for input

```java
/** ColorPanel.java by F. M. Carrano
    Displays the color represented by given RGB values.
*/
import javax.swing.JLabel;
import javax.swing.JPanel;
import javax.swing.JTextField;
import javax.swing.SwingConstants;

import java.awt.Color;
import java.awt.Dimension;
import java.awt.Graphics;

import java.awt.event.ActionEvent;
import java.awt.event.ActionListener;

public class ColorPanel extends JPanel
{
    private final JTextField textInput; // input field for color numbers
    private final JPanel inputPanel;
    private final JPanel outputPanel;
    private final JLabel outputLabel;

    private static final int PANEL_WIDTH = 500;
    private static final int SUBPANEL_HEIGHT = 50;

    public ColorPanel()
    {
        // create the input panel for the prompt and text field
        inputPanel = new JPanel();
```

```
        Dimension subpanelDimension = new Dimension(PANEL_WIDTH,
                                                    SUBPANEL_HEIGHT)
        inputPanel.setPreferredSize(subpanelDimension);

        // create the text field and a listener for it
        textInput = new JTextField(9); // three 3-digit numbers
        textInput.addActionListener(new InputListener());

        // add a prompt and the text field to the input panel
        inputPanel.add(new JLabel("Enter Red-Green-Blue components " +
                                  "as rrrgggbbb, then press Enter:"));
        inputPanel.add(textInput);

        // create the label and panel for output
        outputLabel = new JLabel();
        outputPanel = new JPanel();
        outputPanel.setPreferredSize(subpanelDimension));
        outputPanel.add(outputLabel);

        // add subpanels to this panel
        add(inputPanel);
        add(outputPanel);

        setPreferredSize(new Dimension(PANEL_WIDTH, 2 * SUBPANEL_HEIGHT));
    } // end default constructor

    private class InputListener implements ActionListener
    {
        public void actionPerformed(ActionEvent event)
        {
            String inputString = textInput.getText();

            int red   = Integer.parseInt(inputString.substring(0, 3));
            int green = Integer.parseInt(inputString.substring(3, 6));
            int blue  = Integer.parseInt(inputString.substring(6));
/*
            // alternate code using integer division and remainders:
            int integerInput = Integer.parseInt(inputString);
            int blue = integerInput % 1000;     // get last 3 digits

            integerInput = integerInput / 1000; // discard last 3 digits
            int green = integerInput % 1000;

            integerInput = integerInput / 1000;
            int red = integerInput % 1000;
*/
            Color theColor = new Color(red, green, blue);
            outputPanel.setBackground(theColor);

            textInput.setText(""); // clear input
            outputLabel.setText("RGB = " + red + " " + green + " " + blue);
```

```
            repaint();
        } // end actionPerformed
    } // end InputListener
} // end ColorPanel
```

17.32   Listing 17-13 shows the driver for our panel and some sample output.

LISTING 17-13   A driver for the class `ColorPanel`

```
/** ColorDriver.java by F. M. Carrano
    A driver for the class ColorPanel.
*/
import javax.swing.JFrame;
public class ColorDriver
{
    public static void main(String[] args)
    {
        JFrame window = new JFrame();
        window.setDefaultCloseOperation(JFrame.EXIT_ON_CLOSE);
        window.setTitle("RGB Color Display");

        ColorPanel panel = new ColorPanel();
        window.add(panel);
        window.pack();
        window.setVisible(true);
    } // end main
} // end ColorDriver
```

Sample Output (Before and After Entering Data, but Before Pressing Enter)

Sample Output (After Pressing Enter)

videonote
A problem
solved

CHAPTER SUMMARY

- The Java Class Library provides three kinds of top-level containers: frames, dialogs, and applets.

- Frames, dialogs, and applets each have a content pane. You add components such as panels, buttons, text fields, and labels to the content pane.

- A button is an object of the Swing class `JButton` that can be clicked by the user to provide input to a program.

- A button can display text and have an action command.

- Clicking a button is an action that generates an event. The event contains data that indicates which button was clicked.

- An action listener responds to and processes certain events, such as a button click or the press of the Enter key after a line of input is typed into a text field.

- An action listener is an object of a class that implements the AWT interface ActionListener. The class typically is an inner class. The interface declares one method, actionPerformed. This method defines the response to the action that occurred.

- You register an action listener with the object that will cause the relevant event. For example, you can register an action listener with a button or a text field.

- Clicking, pressing, releasing, or moving the mouse are actions that generate a mouse event. The event generates an object of the class MouseEvent. This object contains data that indicates the location of the mouse when the action occurred. When a mouse event occurs, the appropriate method in either of the interfaces MouseListener or MouseMotionListener is called and receives a MouseEvent object as its argument. This object can be asked for the position of the mouse at the time of the event.

- You can define an inner class within another class, which becomes the outer class. Methods of an inner class have the same access to data fields and methods as the outer class. Generally, you make a class an inner class because it is a detail of the implementation of the outer class, and such details should be hidden from the client.

- A mouse listener is an object of a class that implements the AWT interface MouseListener. Likewise, a mouse motion listener is an object of a class that implements the AWT interface MouseMotionListener. Either class typically is an inner class. The interface MouseListener declares the methods mouseClicked, mousePressed, mouseReleased, mouseEntered, and mouseExited. The interface MouseMotionListener declares the methods mouseDragged and mouseMoved.

- You register either a mouse listener or a mouse motion listener with the component that will interact with the mouse.

- A text field is an object of the Swing class JTextField that enables a user to provide a string as input to a program. An action listener responds to the press of the Enter key by the user who has typed data into the text field. You create an action listener for a text field in much the same way that you create one for a button.That is, you implement the interface ActionListener and pass an instance of the implementing class to JTextField's method addActionListener. You then add the text field to a panel or a content pane. You use JTextField's method getText to get the input data as a string.

EXERCISES

1. Write a Java statement to create a button containing the text "Cancel."

2. After consulting the documentation for the class JButton, write a Java statement to create a button containing the icon in the file cncl.ico.

3. Suppose you create three buttons in a panel. The text in those buttons consists of the strings "Button 1", "Button 2", and "Button 3". Define a private inner class for the panel that determines which of the three buttons has been clicked.

4. Within the panel described in the previous question, create a button listener and register it with each of the three buttons. Assume that the variables oneButton, twoButton, and threeButton reference the buttons. Then add the buttons to the panel.

5. What useful information can you obtain from a MouseEvent object?

6. Revise the class ClickDiskPanel, shown in Listing 17-10, so that the disk turns gray when the mouse button is pressed but returns to blue when the mouse button is released.

7. If you omit the phrase `implements ActionListener` from the inner class `InputListener` in Listing 17-12, will the class compile? If it compiles, will it run with no error messages? Explain your answer.

8. Revise the inner class `ClickListener` of the class `MouseDemoPanel` given in Listing 17-7 to extend `MouseAdapter` instead of implementing the interface `MouseListener`.

9. Revise the class `ColorPanel`, as given in Listing 17-12, so that it uses three text fields instead of one. Provide a separate text field for each color component, and label the three fields "Red," "Green," and "Blue." Also, provide one button for the user to click after completing the input in all the text fields. The user should not press the Enter key for each text field.

10. Create a Java application for a one-player guessing game. The program chooses an integer at random, and the player enters each guess within a text field. Tell the player whether the guess is higher or lower than the secret number. Allow the player to continue until he or she guesses the number.

11. Create a simple one-player dice game using two dice. The player enters a bet in a text field and then clicks a button to enter the bet and roll the dice. If the roll is 7 or 11, the player wins three times the bet. Otherwise, the player loses the bet.

12. Create a Java application that paints a square. The user specifies the position and size of the square by positioning and clicking the mouse twice, once for the upper left corner of the square and once for the lower right corner.

13. Create a Java application that draws a triangle. The user specifies the position and size of the triangle by positioning and clicking the mouse three times, once for each vertex of the triangle.

14. Using the interface `MouseMotionListener`, write an application in which a red dot follows the cursor as the mouse moves. You will need the method `addMouseMotionListener`.

PROJECTS

1. Combine Exercises 12 and 13 to produce an application that allows a user to paint squares in one half of a drawing area and to draw triangles in the other half.

2. Consider the class `RandomColorPanel`, as given in Listing 11-3 of Chapter 11. Add an inner class to `RandomColorPanel` that implements the interface `MouseListener`. Each time a user clicks the mouse on an object of `RandomColorPanel`, a square whose upper left corner is at the mouse click should appear in a random color.

3. Implement a two-player tic-tac-toe game. Use nine buttons arranged in a three-by-three grid to form the game board. Initially, all button text should be blank, as shown here:

When a player clicks on an empty button, an appropriate "X" or "O" should appear on the button. Use `JOptionPane` to display the outcome of each game. *Notes*: The dimensions of the panel will affect the buttons' arrangement. (Try a width of 125 and a height of 165.) For an extra challenge, use the class `java.awt.GridLayout` to arrange the buttons.

4. Design a class that displays a login screen for a website. Provide space for the user name and password. Also provide two buttons labeled "Enter" and "Cancel." For now, do not check the validity of the name and password, but instead simply display a welcome message that includes the user name.

5. Experiment with the methods in the interfaces `MouseListener` and `MouseMotionListener`. Design a program that allows the user to drag shapes from one place to another. For example, create a face and let the user choose eyes, ears, nose, and mouth and drag them to appropriate places on the face.

ANSWERS TO SELF-TEST QUESTIONS

1.
```java
JButton myButton = new JButton("My Button");
myButton.setActionCommand("Button One");
```

or

```java
JButton myButton = new JButton();
myButton.setText("My Button");
myButton.setActionCommand("Button One");
```

2. Yes; `myButton.setText("New Label");`

3.
```java
public void actionPerformed(ActionEvent event)
{
    String command = event.getActionCommand();
    if (command.equals("Button One"))
        myButtonAction();
} // end actionPerformed
```

4. `myButton.addActionListener(myButtonListener);`

5. Yes.

6. Yes.

7. No. Each listener reacts to only one button, so its version of `actionPerformed` simply reacts to that button click. The method has no need to ask which button was clicked.

8. By default, the action command is the same as the text. However, you can set the action command to be a string that is distinct from the button's text. Although a button's text is visible, its action command is not. A program uses the action command to identify the button that was clicked.

9. An event is generated and passed to the method `actionPerformed` as it is called. This method can ask the event for the button's action command and thereby decide which button was clicked.

10. Remove the statement that defines `listener`. Replace the statements

    `smileButton.addActionListener(listener);`

and

    `frownButton.addActionListener(listener);`

with

    `smileButton.addActionListener(new SmileButtonListener());`

and

    `frownButton.addActionListener(new FrownButtonListener());`

respectively. Also replace the inner class `ButtonListener` with the following two inner classes:

```java
private class SmileButtonListener implements ActionListener
{
    public void actionPerformed(ActionEvent event)
    {
        facePanel.setMouth(SMILE);
    } // end actionPerformed
} // end ButtonListener
```

```
    private class FrownButtonListener implements ActionListener
    {
      public void actionPerformed(ActionEvent event)
      {
        facePanel.setMouth(FROWN);
      } // end actionPerformed
    } // end ButtonListener
```

11. Before you click the mouse, a dot appears at the point (0, 0) and the message `Mouse click at (0, 0).` is displayed.

12. No. The interface `MouseListener` declares all of these methods and, since the inner class `ClickListener` implements `MouseListener`, the class must provide a definition for each method, even if these definitions have empty bodies.

13. The action has no effect. If you move the mouse before releasing it, the event is not treated as a mouse click.

14. As soon as the mouse is pressed while the mouse is within the disk, the disk changes color.

15. As soon as the button is released while the mouse is within the disk, the disk changes color.

16.   `int result = Integer.parseInt(textInput.getText());`

Debugging Interlude 5

Debugging Tools

Contents

Prerequisites

In Debugging Interlude 4, we talked about tracing the execution of a program using `println` statements. We also mentioned that there are other tools to use than `println` statements. This debugging interlude elaborates on those other ways to trace the logic of a program.

Using Breakpoints and Watches in an IDE

At the end of Debugging Interlude 4, we mentioned the use of breakpoints and watches within an integrated development environment (IDE) to find logical errors in a program. These tools essentially have the same purpose from one IDE to another, even though each IDE has its own way to initiate them. Recall that we set a breakpoint in our code as a place for program execution to pause while we examine, or watch, the contents of the variables for which we have defined.

D5.1 For example, let's consider the method sumSqs, given in Listing D4-1 of Debugging Interlude 4, and give the class a new name. Listing D5-1 shows this class. We'll trace this program.

LISTING D5-1   A sample program to demonstrate breakpoints and watches

```java
/** IDE_Tracing.java by F. M. Carrano
    A program to demonstrate tracing using an IDE.
*/
public class IDE_Tracing
{
   public int sumSqs(int m, int n)
   {
      int sum = 0;
      if (m > 0)
      {
         while (m <= n)
         {
            sum = sum + m * m;
            m++;
         } // end while
      } // end if

      return sum;
   } // end sumSqs

   public static void main(String[] args)
   {
      IDE_Tracing tester = new IDE_Tracing();
      int result = tester.sumSqs(3, 5);
      System.out.println("sumSqs(3, 5) = " + result);
   } // end main
} // end IDE_Tracing
```

D5.2   Suppose that we compile and run the program given in Listing D5-1 within an IDE such as NetBeans or BlueJ. Let's set four breakpoints, as indicated in Figure D5-1, and watch the variables m, n, sum, and result. The numbering of the breakpoints in the figure serves only to identify them and does not indicate the order in which they are reached during execution. Now, if we run the program in the IDE's debugging mode, execution will pause at the first breakpoint within the main method—labeled "Breakpoint 3" in the figure. Before a value is assigned to the variable result, it is not initialized, and neither are the other three variables under watch. Figure D5-2a shows their status at this point. When we continue execution, another pause will occur at the while statement in the method sumSqs. This point is labeled "Breakpoint 1" in Figure D5-1. Before this statement executes for the first time, the parameters m and n, as well as the local variable sum, have values, as Figure D5-2b illustrates. By continuing execution after each pause at a breakpoint, we can observe the values of our watched variables as they change, as shown in the rest of Figure D5-2. Since the logic of this program is correct, these values are as expected. On the other hand, if we had made an error in logic, these values should help us to locate our mistake.

FIGURE D5-1 The program shown in Listing D5-1 after four breakpoints are set

```
/** IDE_Tracing.java by F. M. Carrano
    A demonstration of tracing a program using an IDE.
*/
public class IDE_Tracing
{
    public int sumSqs(int m, int n)
    {
        int sum = 0;
        if (m > 0)
        {
            while (m <= n)          ← Breakpoint 1
            {
                sum = sum + m * m;
                m++;
            } // end while
        } // end if

        return sum;                 ← Breakpoint 2
    } // end sumSqs

    public static void main(String[] args)
    {
        IDE_Tracing tester = new IDE_Tracing();
        int result = tester.sumSqs(3, 5);              ← Breakpoint 3
        System.out.println("sumSqs(3,5) = " + result); ← Breakpoint 4
    } // end main
} // end IDE_Tracing
```

FIGURE D5-2 The values of the four watched variables as the program shown in Figure D5-1 pauses at each breakpoint

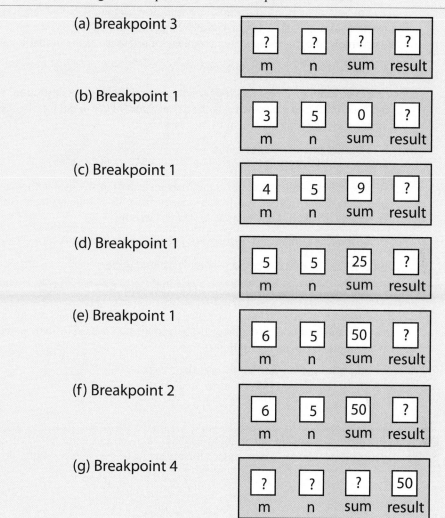

(a) Breakpoint 3

?	?	?	?
m	n	sum	result

(b) Breakpoint 1

3	5	0	?
m	n	sum	result

(c) Breakpoint 1

4	5	9	?
m	n	sum	result

(d) Breakpoint 1

5	5	25	?
m	n	sum	result

(e) Breakpoint 1

6	5	50	?
m	n	sum	result

(f) Breakpoint 2

6	5	50	?
m	n	sum	result

(g) Breakpoint 4

?	?	?	50
m	n	sum	result

Logging

A program can generate and report, or **log**, messages about occurrences during its execution. For a correctly running program in production, these messages might simply report the program's progress as it completes the steps in a particular process. For a program still in development, such messages can help us to debug its logic. This technique, called **logging**, can replace the use of println statements in debugging.

The Class Logger

D5.3   To log a message, we create a **logger**, that is, an object of the class Logger, which is in the package java.util.logging of the Java Class Library. The class Logger is unusual in that it does not have a public constructor. Rather, we create a logger by calling Logger's static method getLogger. The method takes a string as its argument and returns a reference to a Logger object. The string identifies the logger. If a logger has a given identification and already exists, getLogger returns it. Otherwise, the method creates and returns a new logger.

For our debugging purposes, we will use Logger's global logger, identified by the static String constant GLOBAL_LOGGER_NAME. To get the global logger, we pass this string to getLogger. For example, the following statement places a reference to the global logger in the variable log:

```
Logger log = Logger.getLogger(Logger.GLOBAL_LOGGER_NAME);
```

If you want to access this logger within a particular class definition, you can define it as a private data field. And since we really need only one logger to debug, we can make it static. Thus, we can add the following statement to the class:

```
private static Logger log =
        Logger.getLogger(Logger.GLOBAL_LOGGER_NAME);
```

D5.4 We now will use calls to Logger's methods instead of println statements to trace the logic of some code. One simple method for this purpose is info. Its string argument is the message logged when the method is called. For example, instead of writing

```
System.out.println("Entering isEven with argument n = " + n);
```

at the beginning of the method isEven, we could write

```
log.info("Entering isEven with argument n = " + n);
```

The message logged includes the date, the time, and the names of the class and the method, followed on the next line by the label INFO: and the text passed to info as its argument. For the previous example, the message might be

```
Jan 15, 2010 1:48:34 PM MyClass isEven
INFO: Entering isEven with argument n = 12
```

Question 1 Consider the method sumSqs, as given in Listing D4-2 of Debugging Interlude 4. What calls to log.info can replace the six println statements used to debug this method?

An Example

D5.5 Listing D5-2 shows a sample class that contains the method sumSqs, as given previously in Listing D5-1. We have added some calls to log.info, but—to save space—not as many as in the answer to Question 1. Notice the output from the program. The highlighted lines are the strings that we defined in the calls to info and println. The remaining portion of the output is generated by the method info.

The first statement in the main method tells the logger to report all messages. After we have corrected the bugs in the program, we can change the identifier ALL in this statement to OFF. When we do so, the logger will not report any messages. The only output from this program will be the one line written by println. Although we will have left all of the logging statements in the program, they will be ignored. If ever we need them again, we can simply change OFF to ALL. This ability makes logging more convenient than using println statements when tracing a program's logic.

The identifiers ALL and OFF name public static constants in the class Level, which is in the same package as the class Logger. Note that we import both classes and use notation such as Level.ALL to reference the constants. The next section will expand on the use of Level.

LISTING D5-2 A simple example of using a logger to trace a program's logic

```java
import java.util.logging.Level;
import java.util.logging.Logger;

/** SimpleLoggerDemo.java by F. M. Carrano
    A simple demonstration of logging.
*/
public class SimpleLoggerDemo
{
   private static Logger log =
           Logger.getLogger(Logger.GLOBAL_LOGGER_NAME);

   public int sumSqs(int m, int n)
   {
      log.info("Entering sumSqs with m = " + m + " and n = " + n);

      int sum = 0;
      if (m > 0)
      {
         while (m <= n)
         {
            sum = sum + m * m;
            m++;
         } // end while
      } // end if

      log.info("Exiting sumSqs and returning " + sum);

      return sum;
   } // end sumSqs

   public static void main(String[] args)
   {
      log.setLevel(Level.ALL);
      log.info("Entering SimpleLoggerDemo main");

      SimpleLoggerDemo tester = new SimpleLoggerDemo();
      int result = tester.sumSqs(3, 5);
      System.out.println("sumSqs(3, 5) = " + result);

      log.info("Exiting SimpleLoggerDemo main");
   } // end main
} // end SimpleLoggerDemo
```

Output

```
Jan 15, 2010 1:48:34 PM SimpleLoggerDemo main
INFO: Entering SimpleLoggerDemo main
Jan 15, 2010 1:48:34 PM SimpleLoggerDemo sumSqs
INFO: Entering sumSqs with m = 3 and n = 5
Jan 15, 2010 1:48:34 PM SimpleLoggerDemo sumSqs
INFO: Exiting sumSqs and returning 50
sumSqs(3, 5) = 50         ◄──────── Written by the one println
Jan 15, 2010 1:48:34 PM SimpleLoggerDemo main       statement in main
INFO: Exiting SimpleLoggerDemo main
```

Programming Tip

The method and class names that the method `info` gives after the date and time are not always accurate. Repeating these names in the messages you give to `info` for it to place in the output will help you avoid confusion, should `info` make a mistake in its own determination. Segment D5.8 describes an alternative method to `info` that always provides accurate names for the class and method containing its invocation.

Note: At this stage of your Java education, the elements of logging demonstrated in Listing D5-2 are all you really need to know when using this technique for debugging your own programs. You should be aware, however, that professional programmers use features of logging not shown in our simple example. The next section, which is optional, provides some more insight into logging. The complete details are beyond our present scope.

■ More Logging (Optional)

Message Levels

D5.6   The class `Level`, which we mentioned and used in the previous section, defines named, static constants that indicate the **level** of importance of a message. In descending order of importance, these constants are as follows:

```
SEVERE   ◄─── Highest level
WARNING
INFO
CONFIG
FINE
FINER
FINEST   ◄─── Lowest level
```

`Logger` has methods to specify the level of a message. For example, when we call the method `info` to log a message, we implicitly ask it to log the message at level `INFO`. Other methods in `Logger` request logging at other levels. The names of these methods are like their corresponding levels. For example, the method `warning` asks to log a `WARNING`-level message.

D5.7   The logger itself is given a level—by its method `setLevel`—that it uses to screen messages. Any request to log a message at a level lower than the logger's currently set level is ignored. Requests at or above the logger's level are logged. In our example, each call to `Logger.info` attempts to log an

INFO-level message. Since the logger's level is set to ALL, messages at all levels are logged. If, instead of ALL, the logger's level was WARNING, for example, all requests by the method info would be ignored because INFO is at a lower level than WARNING.

In addition to controlling the level at which we log a message, we can specify which of these messages should become part of a program's output. After a message is logged, it has to pass the scrutiny of another object called a **handler**. The handler decides whether and how to output, or **publish**, the message. The handler also has a level, and it publishes all messages logged at or above its level. Figure D5-3 illustrates the fate of three messages at various levels.

The handler used in our previous example in Listing D5-2 is a **default handler**, so the code contains no evidence of it. The level of the default handler is INFO. Thus, messages logged at or above the INFO level are published and appear in the program's output. If we had called the Logger method fine, for instance, the message would be logged at level FINE, since the logger's level is ALL. However, the message would not be published, since the handler's level is INFO, and FINE is a lower level.

FIGURE D5-3 Screening messages according to their levels by both a logger and a handler: A message (a) blocked by the logger; (b) logged by the logger but blocked by the handler; (c) logged by the logger and published by the handler

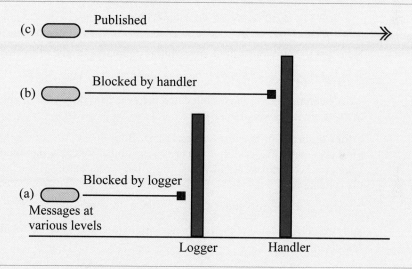

Other Logger Methods

As we mentioned, Logger has the methods severe, warning, info, config, fine, finer, and finest that ask to log a message at the level implied by their names—that is, SEVERE, WARNING, and so on. Each message has the form shown earlier in the output for Listing D5-2, where INFO is replaced by the appropriate level. These Logger methods are called **convenience methods**, as they are easier to use but less precise than the next method we will describe.

D5.8 **The method logp.** The method logp behaves like the previous convenience methods but requires a level, class name, method name, and message as its arguments. For example, the statement

```
log.logp(Level.FINE, "LoggerDemo", "sumSqs" "Entering loop");
```

is equivalent to

```
log.fine("Entering loop");
```

if fine can deduce correctly the names of the class and method from which it is called. Recall that a convenience method has only a string as its argument, so the method must infer these names. Even though logp is more cumbersome to use than the convenience methods, the names of the class and method that appear in a logged message are of your choosing, and so they should be correct. The identifier logp suggests *log precisely*.

D5.9 **Other forms of logp.** We can pass an object as a fifth argument to logp. This object can be either a parameter of the method to be traced or an array of several parameters. In this way, the value(s) of the parameter(s) will appear in the logged message. (You will learn about arrays in the next chapter.) Instead of using an array, you could call the method several times, once for each parameter that you want to see.

D5.10 **The methods entering and exiting.** Logger also defines two methods—entering and exiting—that you can use to signal the beginning and end of a method's execution. Each method takes the names of the invoking class and method as arguments. For example, we could begin the body of the method sumSqs in Listing D5-2 with the statement

```
log.entering("LoggerDemo", "sumSqs");
```

By default, the log request will be at the level FINER. If the handler publishes messages at this level, the output will be

```
Jan 15, 2010 1:48:34 PM LoggerDemo sumSqs
FINER: ENTRY
```

Note that the previous call to entering is equivalent to the following call to logp:

```
log.logp(Level.FINER, "LoggerDemo", "sumSqs" "ENTRY");
```

The method exiting is called and behaves just like entering but uses the word RETURN instead of ENTRY in its message.

D5.11 **Other forms of entering and exiting.** Both of the methods entering and exiting can have a third argument. We can pass entering an object that is a parameter of the method to be traced. Likewise, we can pass exiting an object that is the return value of the traced method. For example, the statement

```
log.entering("LoggerDemo", "sumSqs", new Integer(m));
```

adds the current value of the parameter m right after the word ENTRY in the logged message. Similarly, the statement

```
log.exiting("LoggerDemo", "sumSqs", sum);
```

adds the current value of the return value sum right after the word RETURN in the logged message. Because the data type of sum is int, Java implicitly converts sum to an Integer object.

Instead of passing only one parameter of the traced method to entering, we can pass it several parameters in an array, just as we can for the method logp.

Logging Messages at Levels Lower Than INFO

D5.12 As stated in Segment D5.7, only messages at or above the level INFO are published by default. Thus, the program in Listing D5-2 uses the method info to log messages at the INFO level, and it does not call the methods entering and exiting, as the level of their requests—FINER—is below INFO. To publish messages logged at levels below INFO, we must disable the default handler and create another one. To disable the default publication of messages for the logger log, we write

```
log.setUseParentHandlers(false);
```

To create a new handler, we use the class ConsoleHandler from the Java Class Library. The next segment describes this class.

D5.13   **The class `ConsoleHandler`.** To create a handler as a substitute for the default handler, we simply invoke the constructor for the class `ConsoleHandler` and set the desired level of the resulting object. For example, we could add a data field to our class by writing

```
private static ConsoleHandler myHandler = new ConsoleHandler();
```

and then later set the new handler's level as follows:

```
myHandler.setLevel(Level.ALL);
```

This handler will publish all messages, but we could have it ignore some messages by setting its level accordingly.

Finally, we must add the handler to our logger by writing

```
log.addHandler(myHandler);
```

where `log` is the logger.

Listing D5-3 contains a revision of the program in Listing D5-2 that uses `ConsoleHandler`. Note that `ConsoleHandler` is in the package `java.util.logging`. Just prior to the loop, we log a message at the `FINE` level rather than at the `INFO` level, as was done in Listing D5-2. This is a convention that developers follow. As you can see from the program's output, the methods `entering` and `exiting` log their messages at the level `FINER`.

LISTING D5-3   Creating and using a handler when tracing a program's logic

```java
import java.util.logging.ConsoleHandler;
import java.util.logging.Level;
import java.util.logging.Logger;

/** LoggerDemo.java by F. M. Carrano
    A demonstration of a custom handler.
*/
public class LoggerDemo
{
    private static Logger log =
            Logger.getLogger(Logger.GLOBAL_LOGGER_NAME);

    private static ConsoleHandler myHandler = new ConsoleHandler();

    public int sumSqs(int m, int n)
    {
        log.entering("LoggerDemo", "sumSqs", m);
        log.entering("LoggerDemo", "sumSqs", n);

        int sum = 0;
        if (m > 0)
        {
            log.fine("Before loop: m = " + m + ", n = " +
                    n + ", sum = " + sum);
            while (m <= n)
            {
```

```
            sum = sum + m * m;
            m++;
        } // end while
    } // end if

    log.exiting("LoggerDemo", "sumSqs", sum);

    return sum;
} // end sumSqs


public static void main(String[] args)
{
    log.setLevel(Level.ALL);
    log.entering("LoggerDemo", "main");

    myHandler.setLevel(Level.ALL);
    log.addHandler(myHandler);

    LoggerDemo tester = new LoggerDemo();
    int result = tester.sumSqs(3, 5);
    System.out.println("sumSqs(3, 5) = " + result);

    log.exiting("LoggerDemo", "main");
} // end main
} // end LoggerDemo
```

Output

```
Jan 15, 2010 1:48:34 PM LoggerDemo sumSqs
FINER: ENTRY 3
Jan 15, 2010 1:48:34 PM LoggerDemo sumSqs
FINER: ENTRY 5
Jan 15, 2010 1:48:34 PM LoggerDemo sumSqs
FINE: Before loop: m = 3, n = 5, sum = 0
Jan 15, 2010 1:48:34 PM LoggerDemo sumSqs
FINER: RETURN 50
sumSqs(3, 5) = 50    ◀──────────────    Written by the one println
Jan 15, 2010 1:48:34 PM LoggerDemo main               statement in main
FINER: RETURN
```

Note: When logging messages to debug a program, if you plan to leave the logging statements in your final code, follow the convention of professional programmers by logging your messages at the FINE level. In this way, you can prevent the appearance of any debugging output when users run the final version of your program. To do so, you must use your own handler, as Listing D5-3 demonstrates. For your own purposes, however, you can log messages at and above the INFO level by using the default handler, as shown in Listing D5-2.

Question 2 What output does the following program produce?

```java
public class Question2
{
    private static Logger log =
            Logger.getLogger(Logger.GLOBAL_LOGGER_NAME);

    public static void main(String[] args)
    {
        log.setUseParentHandlers(false);
        log.setLevel(Level.ALL);
        log.entering("Question2", "main");
        log.info("informative message");
        log.severe("severe message");
        log.warning("warning message");
        log.fine("fine message");
        log.finer("finer message");
        log.finest("finest message");
        log.exiting("Question2", "main");
    } // end main
} // end Question2
```

Question 3 Repeat Question 2 after removing the call to setUseParentHandlers.

■ A Problem Debugged: The Click Disk

> Chapter 17 developed the class ClickDisk. An object of this class is displayed as a circular disk. If we click on such a disk using the mouse, the disk's color changes to gray. A second click restores it to its original color. Listing 17-11 in Chapter 17 contains an example of this output.
>
> Imagine that during development, the class appears as shown in Listing D5-4. Testing the class using one disk, as we demonstrated in Chapter 17, results in expected behaviors. It would be a mistake, however, to conclude that our class is correct. Let's see what happens when we create more than one disk.

D5.14   The mistake in our solution is subtle, even though it might become obvious to you due to our presentation. In practice, you would be faced with the complete listings of not only the class ClickDisk, but also the classes ClickDiskPanel and ClickDiskDriver. The latter classes are given in Listings 17-10 and 17-11, respectively, of Chapter 17. Since ClickDiskPanel defines only one disk, we must revise it for our additional testing. ClickDiskDriver can remain as it appears in Chapter 17.

LISTING D5-4   A possible draft of the class ClickDisk during its development

```java
< Appropriate comments and import statements are here. >

public class ClickDisk
{
    private final Point center;
    private final int radius;
    private final Color aColor;       // a color other than gray

    private Color currentColor;       // disk's color at the moment
    private static boolean isGray;    // true if currentColor is gray
```

```
/** Creates a disk having a given center, radius, and color. */
public ClickDisk(Point diskCenter, int diskRadius, Color diskColor)
{
    center = diskCenter;
    radius = diskRadius;
    aColor = diskColor;
    currentColor = aColor;
    isGray = false;
} // end constructor

/** Changes the disk's color from or to gray. */
public void changeColor()
{
    if (isGray)
    {
        currentColor = aColor;
        isGray = false;
    }
    else
    {
        currentColor = Color.GRAY;
        isGray = true;
    } // end if
} // end changeColor
```

< *The accessor methods* getCenter, getRadius, *and* getColor *are here.* >

< *The methods* inDisk *and* display, *as given in Listing 17-9 of Chapter 17, are here.* >

```
} // end ClickDisk
```

D5.15 **Revisions of the class ClickDiskPanel.** The revisions to the panel to add a second disk are not complicated. We change the named constants to position two disks rather than one. Likewise, we declare two disks as data fields, create them in the constructor, and display them in the method paintComponent. Finally, we need to revise the method mouseClicked in the private inner class ClickListener, as follows:

```
public void mouseClicked(MouseEvent click)
{
    Point mouseLocation = click.getPoint();
    if (disk1.inDisk(mouseLocation))
        disk1.changeColor();
    else if (disk2.inDisk(mouseLocation))
        disk2.changeColor();
    repaint();
} // end mouseClicked
```

D5.16 **The results.** Figure D5-4 illustrates the results of running the program ClickDiskDriver after our revisions to ClickDiskPanel. Part a of the figure shows the initial configuration of the two disks. Each additional part shows the effect after a mouse click on a disk. Note that each check mark indicates a click on the disk to its left, resulting in the disk to its right. For example, Parts a and b show that a click on the top disk changes its color to gray. Clicking that disk once more returns it to its original color, as Part c shows.

All proceeds as it should until we click the bottom disk in Part f. Its color should change to gray, but it does not, as Part g indicates. A second click to the bottom disk does change its color to gray (Part h), and a third click changes it back to its original color (Part i). A click on the top disk, which is gray, leaves it unchanged (Part j) until another click changes its color (Part k).

FIGURE D5-4   Two ClickDisk objects as they are clicked

(a)   (b)   (c)   (d)   (e)   (f)   (g)   (h)   (i)   (j)   (k)

D5.17   **Where's the error?** Two mouse clicks, indicated by the blue check marks in Figure D5-4, are ignored. That is, clicking the bottom disk in Part f and clicking the top disk in Part i do not change the disk's color. We might not notice that sometimes a second click is needed to make a disk react, but if we do, we might ignore the problem. After all, the program works correctly for one disk. Do we have a sticky mouse? (Our program must be correct!) Have we encountered a mysterious timing problem? (Maybe no one will notice.) Have we actually uncovered a mistake in the operating system? (We are heroes!) Excuses like these are far-fetched and counterproductive. As soon as we feel that the mistake is not our own, the prospect of finding it diminishes.

Let's try to isolate the error. Because the disks are displayed, the main method in the driver is likely correct. The same is true of the panel's constants, constructor, and method paintComponent. What aspects of the program affect the disk's color? We revised the method mouseClicked in the panel's inner class. It seems correct, and its behavior depends on two methods in ClickDisk: inDisk and changeColor. So we turn our attention to ClickDisk. However, if we don't find the mistake soon, we should trace mouseClicked's behavior.

D5.18   **Looking closer at ClickDisk.** The previous discussion suggests that we examine ClickDisk's methods inDisk and changeColor. Since our earlier test of a panel that defined only one disk was successful, the method inDisk is probably correct. One might question whether a click on a disk's edge is in the disk, but if we were careful to position the cursor well within the disk before clicking the mouse button, inDisk is probably not the problem.

Let's trace the execution of changeColor and observe the values of the two fields that affect a disk's color: currentColor and isGray. For a first try, we can look at the values of these two fields as soon as the method changeColor is entered and again right before it returns. Notice that changeColor is called from within ClickDiskPanel each time the mouse is clicked. Either logging or an IDE's debugging features will provide the evidence we seek. Figure D5-5 gives these results, both textually and pictorially, for the sequence of mouse clicks illustrated in Figure D5-4.

When we clicked on the bottom disk shown in Figure D5-4f, it did not change color. When changeColor is entered, isGray is true and currentColor is cyan, as you can see in the highlighted portion of Figure D5-5f. The disk is cyan, so isGray must be incorrect. That explains why the disk's color did not change: Since isGray is true, changeColor sets currentColor to cyan and isGray to false. Our trace agrees with those values when changeColor exits. An analogous explanation applies to the ignored click in Figure D5-4i.

FIGURE D5-5   The results of tracing the method changeColor

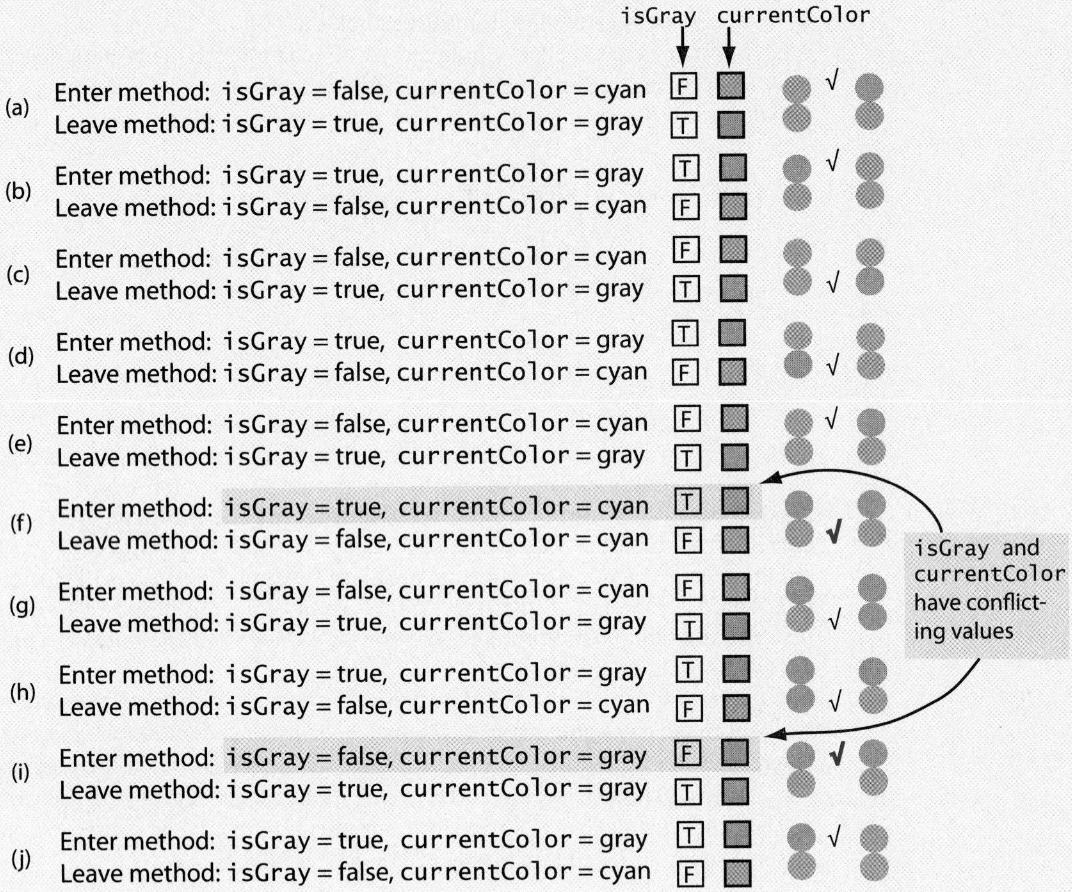

D5.19   **Further analysis.** We now have found incorrect values and explained why those values cause the behavior we observed. In fact, no mouse click is ignored; currentColor is set each time, even though its value sometimes does not change. But why are the values incorrect?

Let's look at Part e of Figure D5-5. Both disks are cyan. A click on the top disk causes a call to changeColor. When the method is entered, the values of currentColor and isGray are correct, since

isGray is false, and currentColor is cyan

according to our traced values. When the method exits,

isGray is true, and currentColor is gray

These values also are correct, since the clicked disk changes to gray.

Next, a click on the bottom disk in Part f causes another call to changeColor. When the method is entered,

isGray is true, and currentColor is cyan

according to our trace. Notice that the value of currentColor has changed from gray to cyan; after all, the disk is cyan when changeColor is entered. However, isGray is still true—it should be false. Although currentColor always reflects the color of the disk we click, as it should, the value of isGray does not. It still has the value set by the previous call to changeColor. Why is this?

D5.20   The explanation. The class ClickDisk contains a mistake in the declaration of isGray. This field should not be static. Because it is, it belongs to the class and is shared by all objects of the class. Thus, each object of ClickDisk does not have its own copy of isGray. The one copy of isGray that exists cannot record the status of more than one ClickDisk object. Our modified program[1] worked fine when we had one disk but failed with two disks.

An error like this one is hard to detect. The best strategy is to avoid making this mistake. Data fields that describe an object are seldom static unless they are constant, that is, final.

Note: Although Figure D5-5 lists the colors as cyan and gray, the actual program output will involve values like the following ones:

- java.awt.Color[r=0, g=255, b=255] for cyan
- java.awt.Color[r=128, g=128, b=128] for gray

The integers are the red, green, and blue components of the color. The exact integer values are not important; we simply need to distinguish the two colors.

videonote
Debugging
tools

ANSWERS TO SELF-TEST QUESTIONS

```
1.    public int sumSqs(int m, int n)
      {
          log.info("Entering sumSqs with m = " + m + " and n = " + n);
          int sum = 0;
          if (m > 0)
          {
              log.info("Before loop: m = " + m + ", n = " + n +
                      ", sum = " + sum);

              while (m <= n)
              {
                  log.info("At top of loop body: m = " + m + ", n = " +
                          n + ", sum = " + sum);
                  sum = sum + m * m;
                  m++;
                  log.info("At end of loop body: m = " + m + ", n = " +
                          n + ", sum = " + sum);
              } // end while
```

---

1. The class ClickDisk, as given in Listing 17-9 of Chapter 17, is correct as is. We added the modifier static to isGray for our demonstration here.

```
        log.info("After loop: m = " + m + ", n = " + n + ",
                sum = " + sum);
    } // end if

    log.info("About to return " + sum + " from sumSqs; m = " +
            m + ", n = " + n);

    return sum;
} // end sumSqs
```

2. No output is produced because no handler is available to publish messages.

3.
```
Jan 15, 2010 1:48:34 PM Question2 main
INFO: informative message
Jan 15, 2010 1:48:34 PM Question2 main
SEVERE: severe message
Jan 15, 2010 1:48:34 PM Question2 main
WARNING: warning message
```

Chapter

18

Arrays

Contents

Objectives

After studying this chapter, you should be able to
• Declare and allocate a one-dimensional array
• Initialize the elements in an array
• Write a loop that searches an array for a given value, the smallest value, or the largest value
• Define methods that accept an entire array as an argument
• Define methods that return an array
• Copy the entries from one array to another
• Test whether two arrays are equal

Programmers often must keep track of a group of items. These items might be as simple as primitive values or as complex as large objects. In most programming languages, the underlying construct that allows us to gather such items together is called an **array**, and Java is no exception. This chapter will introduce this language feature and show you how to use it to perform various tasks. As you will see, arrays enable us to manipulate large groups of data concisely.

■ Motivation

18.1   Imagine a class in grade school during an arithmetic lesson. The teacher has planned an exercise in using a calculator. She will announce ten numbers, and each student is to find the numbers' sum. After that, she has some other calculations planned.

   The twins, Vandee and Vander—Dee and Der to their friends—are anxious to show off their skills. As the teacher announces each of the ten numbers, the students key each one into their calculators. Dee likes to keep track of everything, so she carefully writes the number in her notebook before keying it into her calculator. Der, on the other hand, immediately enters it into his calculator without writing it down.

   Both Dee and Der get the right answer. The teacher now asks them to divide their sum by 10 to get the average of the numbers she has given them. Again, Dee and Der calculate this value correctly. The teacher discusses the concept of average, using familiar examples, such as the average height of all the students in the room. "Are you taller or shorter than average?" she asks. "If you subtract the average height from your height, the difference will be positive, zero, or negative. This result indicates, respectively, whether you are taller than average, average, or shorter than average."

   She now gives them another challenge. "Suppose that the ten numbers I just gave you are the heights of ten students. You just computed their average. How does the height of each student compare with the average?"

   Der panics. He doesn't remember the ten numbers. Dee, however, has them all recorded in her notebook. She quickly performs ten subtractions on her calculator and notes the results.

18.2   Dee could have used a Java array to record the ten numbers instead of a page in her notebook. With an array, not only could she compute the sum and average of these numbers, but she could also later compute the differences between the numbers and their average. By the way, these differences are called *deviations*.

   Der, meanwhile, does not need an array to compute the sum and subsequently the average of the ten numbers. But his approach does not allow him to find the deviation of each student's height from the average height. Let's look at the code in Listing 18-1 to see why.

LISTING 18-1   Some Java code to compute the sum and then the average of
                given numbers

```java
// computes the average of numbers read - no array needed

// find out how many numbers will be read
Scanner keyboard = new Scanner(System.in);
System.out.print("How many numbers do you plan to type? ");
int numberCount = keyboard.nextInt();

// read the numbers and compute their sum
double sum = 0;
for (int counter = 1; counter <= numberCount; counter++)
{
    System.out.print("Please enter next number: ");
    double numberRead = keyboard.nextDouble();

    sum = sum + numberRead;
} // end for

// compute the average
double average = sum / numberCount;
System.out.println("The average of the " + numberCount +
                   " numbers is " + average);

// we cannot compute deviations here, since we no longer have
// the original numbers
```

Sample Output

```
How many numbers do you plan to type? 5
Please enter next number: 2.1
Please enter next number: 3.2
Please enter next number: 4.3
Please enter next number: 5.4
Please enter next number: 6.5
The average of the 5 numbers is 4.3
```

As you can see, this code contains nothing new. You can read a given quantity of numbers, compute their sum, and then compute their average using your current knowledge of Java. But computing the deviations of these numbers from the average is impossible here, since we've saved only the most recently read number.

You could, of course, ask the user to enter the numbers again. Not only would that approach be tiresome for the user, but it also would be susceptible to mistakes in typing. You could store each number into its own variable, but you would need to know how many numbers would be entered before you wrote the code. For example, if you planned to use five numbers, you could declare five variables. However, 1000 numbers would require 1000 variables, clearly a tedious, impractical approach.

▪ Array Basics

18.3   Although creating many distinctly named variables is not a reasonable way to represent a group of data, an array enables us to conveniently group numerous items together and yet have the ability to reference any individual item in the group.

  We can picture an array much as we pictured the string in Figure 4-4 of Chapter 4. Just as we do for the characters of the string, we number the items in an array with consecutive integers beginning with zero, and we call each of these integers an index. Figure 18-1 illustrates an array of characters. Although this depiction of an array is identical to our depiction of a string in Figure 4-4, strings and arrays are different things in Java.

FIGURE 18-1   An array of 20 characters

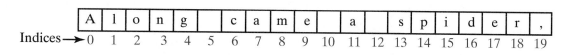

Declaring and Creating an Array

18.4   You use a variable to name and represent an array. The data type of an **array variable** is written as any data type followed by a pair of square brackets. For example, if primes is the name of the array of prime integers pictured in Figure 18-2, we would declare it as follows:

```
int[] primes;
```

Although this declaration does not reserve memory for the array, it does create the variable primes, which is the gray box in the figure. To allocate ten memory locations for the array primes, we would write

```
primes = new int[10];
```

Often, we will combine this allocation with the array's declaration, as in the following assignment statement:

```
int[] primes = new int[10];
```

Notice that you create an array using the new operator, much as you create an object of a class. Java treats arrays as special kinds of objects, as you will see in Segment 18.9. The array variable primes contains a reference to the array object.

FIGURE 18-2   An array of prime integers

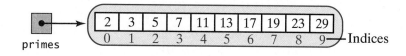

18.5   The number of memory locations, or **elements**, in an array is called its **length** or sometimes its **capacity**. You use an integer value—given as either a literal, a named constant, a variable, or an expression—to specify its length when you create the array. Once it is created, you can reference the array's length by writing its name, a dot, and the word "length." For example, primes.length is the notation for the length of the array primes we created in the previous example. The value of primes.length is 10.

The values in the array are called **entries**. For example, the entries in the array `primes` are the prime integers 2, 3, 5, and so on.

Syntax: Declaring and creating an array

entry-type`[]` *array-name* `= new` *entry-type*`[`*length*`];`

where *entry-type* is any primitive type or class type, and *length* is an integer value. The portion on the left side of the assignment operator is the array declaration; the portion on the right side creates the array.

Examples:

```
int[] ages = new int[100];       // ages.length is 100
String[] notes = new String[50]; // notes.length is 50
```

Referencing Array Elements

18.6   An array does not have an explicit method, such as `String`'s `charAt`, to access its individual elements. Instead, Java uses a square-bracket notation to reference its elements. For example, if `phrase` is the array pictured in Figure 18-1, we reference the element at index 4 by writing `phrase[4]`. In this example, the entry in `phrase[4]` is the character `'g'`. The statement

```
System.out.println(phrase[4]);
```

displays the letter *g*, while the assignment statement

```
phrase[4] = 'G';
```

changes the character in the fifth element of `phrase` to the capital letter *G*.

This notation can provide us with much more power if we use a variable or expression as the index instead of a literal. For example, the following loop displays the characters in the array `phrase`:

```
// display the characters in the array phrase
for (int index = 0; index < phrase.length; index++)
    System.out.print(phrase[index]);
System.out.println();
```

The expression `phrase[index]` takes on the values of `phrase[0]` through `phrase[19]` as index ranges in value from 0 to 19.

Note that terms such as `phrase[19]` and `phrase[index]` are sometimes called **indexed variables**.

Declaring and Initializing an Array

18.7   Although the elements of an array are initially given default entries when the array is created, you can initialize the elements explicitly when you declare the array. To do so, you write the data type of its elements, a pair of square brackets, the assignment operator, and a list of values separated by commas and enclosed in curly brackets. For example, to define an array of three integers, you write

```
int[] data = {10, 20, 30};
```

Now `data[0]` is 10, `data[1]` is 20, and `data[2]` is 30. Also note that `data.length` is 3. That is, the length of the array is the minimum number of elements required for the values listed between the curly brackets. In other words, the previous Java statement is equivalent to the following sequence of statements:

```
int[] data = new int[3];
data[0] = 10;
data[1] = 20;
data[2] = 30;
```

Syntax: **Initializing an array when it is declared**

> *entry-type*[] *array-name* = {v_1, v_2, ..., v_n};

where *entry-type* is any primitive type or class type, and the entries v_i are values of type *entry-type*.

Example:

```
String[] notes = {"do", "re", "mi", "fa", "so", "la", "ti", "do"};
```

Here, notes.length is 8.

Array Index Out of Bounds

18.8   When programming with arrays, making a mistake with an index is easy. This is especially true if that index is an expression. If the array temperature has seven elements, but an index is some integer other than 0 through 6, the index is said to be **out of bounds**. An out-of-bounds index expression will compile without any error message, but will cause an error when you run your program. In particular, you will get an exception that belongs to the class IndexOutOfBoundsException, which is in the Java Class Library. As we mentioned in Segment 4.16 of Chapter 4, a similar situation can occur when you work with strings. Chapter 28 will discuss exceptions further.

Note: **Arrays**

An array is an ordered group of values that have either the same or compatible data types. The values can be either primitive values or references to objects. An identifier names the group. You use this name and a bracketed index to reference the individual elements in the group.

Examples:

```
int[] ages = new int[100];
```
- ages[0] is the first integer in the array ages.
- ages[9] is the tenth integer in the array ages.

```
String[] notes = new String[50];
```
- notes[49] is the last string in the array notes.
- notes[index] is the third string in the array notes if the value of index is 2.
- notes[2 * index + 1] is the sixth string in the array notes if the value of index is 2.

Note: **Terminology**

When speaking of an array, we will use the term "element" to mean a location in an array, such as phrase[4], that holds a value. Some people use "element" to mean the value, while others use the term to mean both things. That is, some do not make a clear distinction between a location in an array and the value contained therein. This book, however, will refer to a value within an array as an entry and the location containing the value as an element.

Question 1 Write some Java code that declares and creates an array of five integers. Then write a loop that sets each entry in this array to 3.

Question 2 Write one Java statement that declares and creates an array of five integers, each of which has a value of 3.

Question 3 Write some Java code that reads a positive integer *n* from the user and then declares and allocates an array of *n* strings.

Question 4 What, if anything, is wrong with the following piece of Java code?

```
String[] names;
names[0] = "Josh";
names[1] = "Isabella";
names[2] = "Dan";

for (int index = 0; index < names.length; index++)
    System.out.println(names[index]);
```

Question 5 What, if anything, is wrong with the following piece of Java code?

```
String[] names = {"Josh", "Isabella", "Dan");
for (int index = 0; index <= names.length; index++)
    System.out.println(names[index]);
```

18.9 **Arrays as objects.** Java arrays are objects—strange objects. An array does not belong to any class in the Java Class Library,[1] but its class is created for you. The name of this class is the data type of the array. For example, an array of strings belongs to the class `String[]`, and an array of integers belongs to the class `int[]`. These arrays extend the class `Object`, which Chapter 16 introduced as a class in the Java Class Library. Thus, an array can be assigned to a variable of type `Object`.

An array has one instance variable, `length`, and it is public and final. Because it is public, we can reference the length of the array `myArray` as `myArray.length`, as we mentioned earlier in Segment 18.5. Because `length` is final, moreover, you cannot change its value. For example, you cannot write

```
myArray.length = 100; // Illegal!
```

videonote
Array basics

An array has methods, such as `toString` and `equals`, that are defined in the class `Object` and which every class inherits. However, these methods are not suitable for any specific array, and so they are not used. An array does have one public method, `clone`, that creates a duplicate of it. We will defer discussing this method until Appendix E.

In Segment 2.11, we called the data type of an object a class type. We also called it a reference type. Even though an array technically belongs to a class, we will call its data type an **array type**, rather than a class type. Both class types and array types are reference types.

Note: Reference types
By a reference type, we mean either a class type or an array type. Primitive types are not reference types.

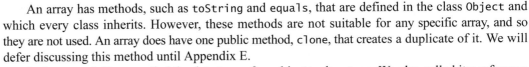

Note: Be careful when speaking about an array and its reference variable. For example, consider the variable `myArray` that references an array. An assignment of an entry to an element such as `myArray[index]` changes the contents of the array that `myArray` references. An assignment to `myArray` itself—for example, `myArray = null`—changes the value of this reference variable; in fact, the array is lost unless an alias to it exists.

---

1. The Java Class Library contains two classes, `Array` and `Arrays`, that provide static methods for creating and working with arrays. Java arrays do not belong to either class.

Examples of Processing an Array

Let's look at some examples that demonstrate the basics of working with an array.

Computing Deviations

18.10 We can now modify the code given in Listing 18-1 so that it also computes the deviation of each number from the average of all the numbers read. As you can see in Listing 18-2, we create an array `numbers` that is just large enough to accommodate the numbers we plan to read as data. As we read those numbers, we save them in the array as well as accumulate their sum. After we read all of the input data and compute their average, a second loop computes and displays the deviation of each number from the average. Note the loss of precision in the results due to the way a computer represents real numbers.

LISTING 18-2   Java code to compute the sum of given numbers, their average, and the deviation of each number from this average

```java
// find out how many numbers will be read
Scanner keyboard = new Scanner(System.in);
System.out.print("How many numbers do you plan to type? ");
int numberCount = keyboard.nextInt();

// create an array for the numbers
double[] numbers = new double[numberCount];

// read, save, and sum the numbers
double sum = 0;
for (int index = 0; index < numberCount; index++)
{
   System.out.print("Please enter next number: ");
   double numberRead = keyboard.nextDouble();
   numbers[index] = numberRead;
   sum = sum + numberRead;
} // end for

// compute the average
double average = sum / numberCount;
System.out.println("The average of the " + numberCount +
                   " numbers is " + average);

// compute and display the deviations
System.out.println("Number\tDeviation from Average");
System.out.println("------\t---------------------");
for (int index = 0; index < numberCount; index++)
{
   double deviation = numbers[index] - average;
   System.out.println(numbers[index] + "\t" + deviation);
} // end for
```

Sample Output

```
How many numbers do you plan to type? 5
Please enter next number: 2.1
Please enter next number: 3.2
Please enter next number: 4.3
Please enter next number: 5.4
Please enter next number: 6.5
The average of the 5 numbers is 4.3

Number  Deviation from Average
------  ----------------------
2.1     -2.1999999999999997
3.2     -1.0999999999999996
4.3     0.0
5.4     1.1000000000000005
6.5     2.2
```

Instead of reading the numbers into an ordinary variable numberRead, we could read them directly into the array. That is, the loop could be written as

```
for (int index = 0; index < numberCount; index++)
{
    System.out.print("Please enter next number: ");
    numbers[index] = keyboard.nextDouble();
    sum = sum + numbers[index];
} // end for
```

Reading values directly into an array is fine in this example, but it is not always a good idea. Segment 18.12 shows an example in which you should read data into an ordinary variable before storing it in an array.

Question 6 Suppose that you want to retain all of the deviations after you compute them. What changes would you make to the code given in Listing 18-2 to accomplish this?

Partially Filled Arrays

18.11   In our previous examples shown in Listings 18-1 and 18-2, we asked the user for the size of the input data set and then created an array of that size. Suppose that our program, not the user, counts the items in the data set. For example, let's read up to 50 positive integers, counting them and saving them in an array. As soon as we read an integer that is not positive, we will stop. Recall that the signal to stop—in this case, a zero or negative number—is called a sentinel.

Although we do not know exactly how many integers we will read, we have decided that we will allow the user to enter up to 50 numbers. Thus, we can create an array of 50 locations to accommodate the largest possible data set as follows:

```
public static final int CAPACITY = 50;
int[] data = new int[CAPACITY];
```

Although this array has 50 locations, we might not use all of them. That is, this array might be **partially filled**. If we read ten integers into the array, elements data[0] through data[9] will contain those integers, but the remaining 40 elements will be unused. In contrast, the array in Listing 18-2 is created after we know how many numbers we will store in it. If that number is ten, we create an array of ten elements and place ten numbers into the array. It will have no unused elements.

Note: **Array capacity versus array contents**
When an array is created, a fixed number of locations are reserved for its elements. This number is the array's capacity. That is, the array has room for a certain number of entries. The number of entries that an algorithm actually stores in the array often is less than the array's capacity. In such cases, we say that the array is partially filled. In other words, an array is partially filled if you do not use all of its elements.

The entries that an algorithm stores in an array are the array's **contents**. If myArray is a partially filled array, myArray.length is its capacity, but it is not the number of entries it contains. A partially filled array actually has entries in the unused elements, but we ignore them. Those entries could be default values or values left from a prior computation.

18.12 Imagine a group of no more than 50 people. Let's place the age of each person into an array of integers. Listing 18-3 contains some code that reads and counts these ages, which are positive integers, as given by the user. This data is stored into the array ageList. In the sample output, we have entered five positive integers followed by a sentinel value of zero. After this code executes, the variable ageCount contains 5. Note that ageList.length, which is the length of the array ageList, is 50. That is, the capacity of this array is 50, but we have placed only 5 entries into it. The remaining entries are not meaningful to us.

LISTING 18-3   Reading, counting, and saving integers using an array

```java
// Counts and saves the ages of up to 50 people
// until a negative number or zero is read.
public static final int CAPACITY = 50;
Scanner keyboard = new Scanner(System.in);

int[] ageList = new int[CAPACITY];
int ageCount = 0;

System.out.print("Please enter the next age or 0 to end: ");
int age = keyboard.nextInt();

while ( (age > 0) && (ageCount < CAPACITY) )
{
   ageList[ageCount] = age;
   ageCount++;

   System.out.print("Please enter next age or 0 to end: ");
   age = keyboard.nextInt();
} // end while

System.out.println(ageCount + " ages have been read.");

// ageList.length equals CAPACITY, not how many numbers were read
```

Sample Output

```
Please enter the next age or 0 to end: 55
Please enter the next age or 0 to end: 44
Please enter the next age or 0 to end: 33
Please enter the next age or 0 to end: 22
Please enter the next age or 0 to end: 11
Please enter the next age or 0 to end: 0
5 ages have been read.
```

Take special notice of the logic in this code segment, which we can describe with the following pseudocode:

Read an integer
while (*the integer is positive and we have room to store it*)
{
    Save the integer in the array and count it
    Read another integer
}

By reading the data into an ordinary variable instead of directly into the array, we can examine the data before saving it in the array. In this way we ensure that the array will contain only positive integers.

Question 7 What are the purposes of ageCount and CAPACITY in Listing 18-3?

Question 8 In the while statement of Listing 18-3, why is the comparison of ageCount with CAPACITY strictly "less than" instead of "less than or equal to"?

Question 9 When the code in Listing 18-3 executes, what happens if the first integer entered by the user is zero?

Question 10 When the code in Listing 18-3 executes, what happens if the user enters 50 positive integers followed by a zero?

Question 11 Repeat the previous question for a user who enters 51 positive integers.

Question 12 After the code in Listing 18-3 executes, will the array ageList ever contain the sentinel value?

Question 13 When the code in Listing 18-3 executes, what happens if the user enters -1 instead of 0 as the sentinel value?

Counting Occurrences in an Array

18.13 The code shown in Listing 18-3 in the previous segment results in an array, ageList, of positive integers. The variable ageCount contains the number of ages in the array, and we know that ageCount does not exceed 50, the array's capacity. Suppose that we now want to know how many people in our group are 18 years old.

To count the number of times a given value occurs in an array, we compare it to every entry in the array. Here we compare the age, 18, to every age in ageList. We use a loop to cycle through the array's indices from 0 to ageCount – 1. If index represents these index values, we must compare 18 with each value in ageList[index]. Each time we find a match, we increment a counter. When the loop ends, the value of the counter is the desired result.

Here is a for loop that performs this task:

```
// count the number of times the value 18 occurs in the array ageList
int count18 = 0;

for (int index = 0; index < ageCount; index++)
{
   if (ageList[index] == 18)
   {
      count18++;
   } // end if
} // end for

// count18 is the number of 18-year-olds in the array ageList
```

Question 14 How would you modify the previous loop to count the number of people who are 18 or older?

Question 15 Given an array, nameList, of strings, write some Java code to count the number of times that the string "Brady" appears in the array. Assume that the variable nameCount contains the number of strings in the array, and that the number is both positive and does not exceed nameList.length.

Finding the Smallest Entry in an Array

18.14 When the entries in an array can be compared with each other, we can find the smallest (or largest) among them. For example, let's assume that we have an array data of numberCount positive integers. We know that numberCount does not exceed data.length, the capacity of the array. Let's make the additional assumption that numberCount is greater than zero; that is, we'll assume that the array contains at least one integer.

Our strategy is to examine each integer in the array and to ask "Is this the smallest value we have seen so far?" The first integer in the array is the smallest so far. If the second integer is larger, we go on to examine the third one. But if the second integer is smaller, it becomes the smallest we have seen so far. We would then compare it with the third integer, and so on. Figure 18-3 illustrates this strategy. An arrow marks the next integer in the array to be considered, while blue shading highlights the smallest integer so far.

FIGURE 18-3 Finding the smallest entry in an array

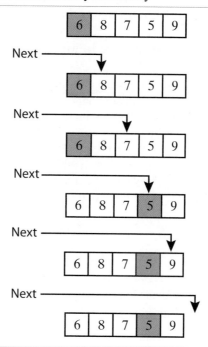

18.15 The implementation of this strategy is straightforward, as you can see by looking at the code in Listing 18-4. The variable smallestValue contains the highlighted integer in Figure 18-3. The loop variable index is like the "Next" arrow in the figure. Its value begins at 1, which is the index of the array's second element. At each iteration of the loop, we ask whether the entry in the current element, data[index], is smaller than the smallest value we have seen so far. If it is, the current entry becomes the smallest we have seen so far. When index exceeds numberCount − 1, which is the index of the last element in the array, the loop ends, and smallestValue contains the smallest entry in the array.

LISTING 18-4   Code to find the smallest integer in an array

```
// find the smallest integer in the array data;
// assume numberCount > 0 and numberCount <= data.length
int smallestInteger = data[0];
for (int index = 1; index < numberCount; index++)
{
   if (data[index] < smallestValue)
      smallestInteger = data[index];
} // end for

System.out.println("The smallest integer is " + smallestInteger + ".");
```

Question 16 If the array elements data[0] and data[1] are equal in value, which one of them is assigned to smallestInteger after the first cycle of the loop in Listing 18-4?

Question 17 What changes would you make to the code in Listing 18-4 so that it finds the largest integer in the array data?

Question 18 What changes would you make to the code in Listing 18-4 so that it finds the alphabetically earliest name in the array of strings nameList?

Finding the Index of the Smallest Entry in an Array

18.16   Although the code in Listing 18-4 finds the smallest entry in an array, we do not know where in the array this entry is. We know only its value. Sometimes that is enough, but other times knowing the index of the smallest entry is important. We can find this index by making some small changes to the code in Listing 18-4.

   We can track this index using a variable indexOfSmallestInteger. Although we could add this variable to Listing 18-4 in addition to the variable smallestInteger, we really do not need smallestInteger anymore. After all, the smallest entry so far is in data[indexOfSmallestInteger]. Listing 18-5 shows the result of these changes.

LISTING 18-5   Code to find the index of the smallest integer in an array

```
// find the index of the smallest integer in the array data;
// assume numberCount > 0 and numberCount <= data.length
int indexOfSmallestInteger = 0;
for (int index = 1; index < numberCount; index++)
{
   if (data[index] < data[indexOfSmallestInteger])
      indexOfSmallestInteger = index;
} // end for
```

```
System.out.println("The smallest integer is " +
                    data[indexOfSmallestInteger] + " at index " +
                    indexOfSmallestInteger + ".");
```

Question 19 What changes would you make to the code in Listing 18-5 so that it finds the index of the largest integer in the array data?

Searching an Array for a Given Entry

18.17   To see whether an array contains a particular entry, we use a loop much like the ones we used in the previous segments. Although those loops cycle through all of the array, the loop we need here should stop as soon as the first occurrence of the desired entry is found in the array. We do not care whether the entry occurs more than once.

The following pseudocode describes the basic logic of the loop:

> **while** (givenEntry *is not found and we have more array elements to check*)
> {
>   **if** (givenEntry *equals the next array entry*)
>   givenEntry *is found in the array*
> }

This loop terminates under one of two conditions: Either givenEntry has been found in the array or the entire array has been searched without success.

18.18   We can refine the previous pseudocode as follows:

> index = 0
> **while** (givenEntry *is not found and* index < numberOfEntries)
> {
>   **if** (givenEntry *equals* myArray[index])
>   givenEntry *is found in the array*
>   **else**
>   index++
> }

Segment 12.20 of Chapter 12 described how we can use a boolean variable in such a loop. Let's use the boolean variable found to indicate whether we have found givenEntry in the array. Initially, found will be false. If and when we find givenEntry in the array, we will change the value of found to true, and the loop will then terminate. Our pseudocode now looks like this:

> index = 0
> found = **false**
> **while** (!found && index < numberOfEntries)
> {
>   **if** (givenEntry *equals* myArray[index])
>   found = **true**
>   **else**
>   index++
> }

18.19   This pseudocode is almost Java code at this point. To implement the "equals" comparison, we need to know whether the array's entries are primitive values or objects. Lets assume that the entries, as well as givenEntry, are strings. Thus, we must use the String method equals instead of the operator == to make the comparisons. Although we could use a while loop, we have chosen to use a for loop, as follows:

videonote
Array processing

```
// test whether an array contains a given entry
boolean found = false;

for (int index = 0; !found && (index < numberOfEntries); index++)
{
    if (givenEntry.equals(myArray[index]))
    {
        found = true;
    } // end if
} // end for

if (found)
    System.out.println(givenEntry + " occurs in the array.");
else
    System.out.println(givenEntry + " does not occur in the array.");
```

More Fundamentals

This section furthers our investigation into the nature of arrays and how to use them in Java.

Arrays of Objects

18.20   While the entries in an array of primitive values are actually those values, the entries in an array of objects are only references to the objects, not the objects themselves. So even though our discussions and figures often will save space by depicting arrays as if they actually contained objects, they do not. Figure 18-4 shows two different illustrations of an array of String objects. The first drawing is how we usually will show an array of strings, while the second one illustrates that the array actually contains references to the strings.

FIGURE 18-4   Two illustrations of an array of String objects: (a) as if the strings were in the array; (b) the actual situation—the array contains references to the strings

(a)

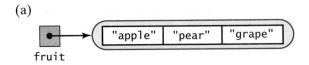

(b)

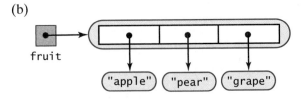

18.21   **Creating an array of objects.** Let's recall the class `Name` that appears in Listing 6-5 of Chapter 6. To create an array of our friends' names, we begin by declaring and naming the array:

```
Name[] friends;
```

This step allocates memory for the array variable `friends`, which will reference the array. Next, we create the array, making room for at most 20 friends:

```
friends = new Name[20];
```

We still have not created any `Name` objects. This statement simply reserves memory for the array. To create the `Name` objects, we can write a loop, such as

```
for (int index = 0; index < 20; index++)
    friends[index] = new Name();
```

Figure 18-5 illustrates the effect of these three steps.

 Note: The syntax for allocating an array of objects and for creating one of those objects is similar and can be confusing:
- `new Name[20]` allocates an array of 20 elements, each of which can reference a `Name` object. This expression does not create any `Name` objects.
- `new Name()` creates one `Name` object using `Name`'s default constructor.

FIGURE 18-5   Three steps in creating an array of `Name` objects

```
// Declare a reference variable
Name[] friends;
```
friends

```
// Allocate 20 array elements
friends = new Name[20];
```
friends

```
// Create 20 Name objects
for (int index = 0; index < 20; index++)
    friends[index] = new Name();
```
friends

Name objects

 Question 20   Since we invoked `Name`'s default constructor when creating the objects for the array `friends`, what statement would call `Name`'s method `setName` to set our first friend's name to Jesse Java?

Passing an Array to a Method

18.22 An entire array can be an argument to a method. To write a parameter for an array in the header of the method's definition, you follow the same rules as for any other parameter. It consists of the data type of the array followed by its name. Since an array's data type is the type of its entries followed by a pair of square brackets, an array parameter has the following form:

> *entry-type*[]   *array-name*

For example, suppose that a driver program uses an array of numbers to test a particular class. At some point in the program, we might need to set these numbers to zero. The driver could define the following static method to accomplish this step:

```java
/** Sets all values in an array to zero. */
public static void clearArray(double[] anArray)
{
   for (int index = 0; index < anArray.length; index++)
      anArray[index] = 0.0;
} // end clearArray
```

Notice that you pass to the method a reference to an entire array. You give no indication of the array's length in the parameter list.

Syntax: Array parameters

Within a method's header, a parameter can represent an entire array by having the form

> *entry-type*[]   *array-name*

where *entry-type* is the data type of the entries in the array and *array-name* is the array's name. The array's length is not written explicitly.

Example:

```java
public int countWords(String[] paragraph)
```

18.23 **Array arguments.** When we call the previous method `clearArray`, we pass it a reference to an array of `double` values, as in this example:

```java
double[] testData = {1.1, 2.2, 3.3, 4.4, 5.5};
. . .
clearArray(testData);
// Assertion: testData contains zeros
. . .
double[] moreData = new double[100];
for (int index = 0; index < moreData.length; index++)
   moreData[index] = index;
. . .
clearArray(moreData);
// Assertion: moreData contains zeros
```

Arguments, such as `testData` and `moreData`, are array names without brackets, but more importantly, they are references to actual arrays. For example, when `testData` is passed to `clearArray`, the reference in `testData` is copied to `clearArray`'s parameter `anArray`, as Figure 18-6 illustrates. Recall from Segment 6.21 of Chapter 6 that Java passes arguments by value. Although `clearArray` cannot alter the reference in `testData`, it can alter the contents of the array that `testData`—and hence `anArray`—references. In fact, following a call to `clearArray`, all entries in the array argument have been set to zero.

FIGURE 18-6   Passing an array reference to a method

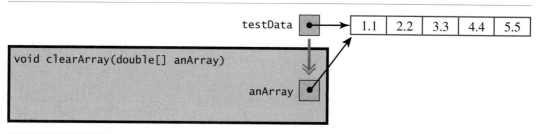

Notice that we can pass an array of any size to the method. The length of the array argument `testData` is 5, while the length of `moreData` is 100. Within the method's definition, `anArray.length` is the length of the particular array argument.

Note: Array arguments
When you call a method that has an entire array as a parameter, you give only a reference to the array as the corresponding argument. Note that an array argument

- Has no index
- Can be of any length
- Can have its values changed by the method

Example:

```
clearArray(myArray);
```

Note: An array element as an argument
An element of an array—that is, an indexed variable—has a value just like any other variable. Thus, if you pass it as an argument to a method, its data type must match that of the corresponding parameter in the method's header. For example, if a method's parameter is an integer whose declaration in the method's header is

```
int anInteger
```

and `myArray` is an array of `int` values, you could pass an argument corresponding to `anInteger`, such as `myArray[2]` or `myArray[index]`.

Question 21 Write a static method that is given an array of integers as its argument and returns the index of the smallest value in the array.

Question 22 What changes would you make to the answer to the previous question when the array argument is only partially filled?

18.24 **An array of objects as a parameter.** Recall the class Coin, as given in Listing 8-5 of Chapter 8. A Coin object has both a name, which is an instance of the enumeration CoinName, and a value in cents. The following static method accepts both an array of Coin objects and the name of a particular coin and returns the total value of all coins in the array having the given name:

```
/** Computes the total value of all coins having a given name in a
    given array.
    @param coins           an array of Coin objects
    @param numberOfCoins   the number of coins in the array
    @param coinToCount     the name of the kind of coin to consider
    @return the total value in cents of all coins in the given
            array that have the name coinToCount */
public static int getValueOfCoins(Coin[] coins, int numberOfCoins,
                                  CoinName coinToCount)
{
   int totalValue = 0;
   for (int counter = 0; counter < numberOfCoins; counter++)
   {
      CoinName name = coins[counter].getCoinName();
      if (coinToCount.equals(name))
         totalValue = totalValue + coins[counter].getValue();
   } // end for

   return totalValue;
} // end getValueOfCoins
```

In the body of the for statement, notice that coins[counter] is a Coin object whose name is coins[counter].getCoinName() and whose value is coins[counter].getValue(). Recall that Question 11 in Chapter 8 asked you to define a method getCoinName for the class Coin.

If the method getValueOfCoins belongs to the class CoinCounter, the following statement invokes the method to compute the value of all nickels in the array coinArray:

```
int value = CoinCounter.getValueOfCoins(coinArray, coinArray.length,
                                        CoinName.NICKEL);
```

Array Assignments

18.25 You know that when you assign a variable of a primitive type to another variable of the same type, the value in one variable replaces the value in the other. For example, Figure 4-1 in Chapter 4 illustrated the effect of the following statements:

```
int size = 12;
int newSize = 30;
size = newSize;
```

Both size and newSize contain 30 after these statements execute. Thus, you can use assignment to copy primitive values.

On the other hand, you cannot use assignment to make a copy of an object. If we execute

```
String greeting = "Hello";
String salutation = "Hi";
greeting = salutation;
```

for example, both greeting and salutation will reference the same string, "Hi", as Figure 4-2 in Chapter 4 showed. Rather than making a copy of "Hi", we have copied a reference to it.

18.26 Since arrays are objects, you cannot copy an array by assigning one array variable to another. For example, the statements

```
String[] fruit = {"apple", "pear", "grape"};
String[] citrusFruit = {"orange", "lemon", "lime"};
```

create the arrays shown in Figure 18-7a. The assignment statement

```
fruit = citrusFruit;
```

creates an alias for the array {"orange", "lemon", "lime"}. That is, we will have two variables that name the same array, as Figure 18-7b illustrates. Regardless of whether the array contains objects, as in this example, or primitive values, assignment of one array to another produces aliases, not duplicate arrays. So how can we make a duplicate copy of an array?

FIGURE 18-7 Two array variables that reference (a) two distinct arrays; (b) the same array

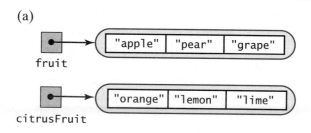

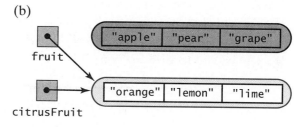

Copying an Array

Sometimes you must make a distinct copy of an array. Perhaps you want to modify the contents of an array but retain the original data. By first copying the array, you can make your changes to the copy and still have the original version. At other times, an algorithm might require you to copy all or part of an array to another array. You can perform such tasks in one of several ways. Our first examples will create duplicate arrays of integers, as pictured in Figure 18-8.

FIGURE 18-8 Duplicate arrays of integers

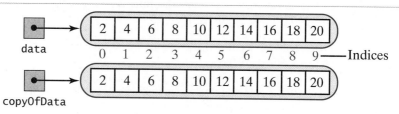

18.27 **Using a loop.** Given an existing array that already contains values, you can create a second array of the same length and data type as the existing array. You then can copy each value in the first array to a corresponding element in the new array, as in the following example:

```
int[] data = {2, 4, 6, 8, 10, 12, 14, 18, 20};
int[] copyOfData = new int[data.length];
for (int index = 0; index < data.length; index++)
    copyOfData[index] = data[index];
```

Although this code is not difficult to write, faster and easier ways to copy an array are possible, as you will now see.

18.28 **System.arraycopy.** You have used the class System from the Java Class Library when you performed input and output, likely without thinking much about it. This class defines several static methods, among which is arraycopy. We can use this method instead of the loop that we wrote in the previous segment to copy values from one array to another, as follows:

```
int[] data = {2, 4, 6, 8, 10, 12, 14, 18, 20};
int[] copyOfData = new int[data.length];
System.arraycopy(data, 0, copyOfData, 0, data.length);
```

Notice that the array copyOfData must be declared and allocated before arraycopy is called, but it need not contain specific values. The second argument—0—in the call to arraycopy is the index of the first element in data to be copied. The fourth argument—0—is the index of the first element in copyOfData to be given a value. The last argument is the number of values to be copied.

You can use arraycopy to copy only some of the values in an array to either all or a portion of another array. You also can move a portion of an array to another part of the same array. The following note indicates how:

Note: The method System.arraycopy
The standard class System in the Java Class Library defines the static method arraycopy, which copies all or a part of a given array to a specified destination array. Its header is

```
public static void arraycopy(Object sourceArray, int sourceIndex,
                             Object destinationArray, int destIndex,
                             int count)
```

The method copies count consecutive values from the array sourceArray, beginning at sourceIndex, to consecutive elements in the array destinationArray, beginning at destIndex. If sourceArray and destinationArray reference the same array, the result is the same as if values from sourceArray were first copied to a temporary array and then copied from the temporary array into destinationArray.

Since the class System is in the package java.lang and is included automatically in every Java program, no import statement is needed when you use System.arraycopy. Note that the method's name is entirely lowercase.

Question 23 Given the arrays data and copyOfData, as defined in Segment 18.28, what call to arraycopy will copy the integers 6, 8, 10, 12, and 14 from data to the portion of copyOfData that begins at index 0?

Question 24 Repeat the previous question, but place the integers such that 14 is in the last element of copyOfData.

Question 25 Consider the header for arraycopy as given in the previous note. What are the indices of the elements in sourceArray that arraycopy copies to destinationArray? Express your answer in terms of sourceIndex and count.

Question 26 Consider the header for `arraycopy` as given in the previous note. What are the indices of the elements in `destinationArray` that are affected by `arraycopy`? Express your answer in terms of `destIndex` and `count`.

18.29 **Arrays.copyOf.** The class `Arrays` in the package `java.util` of the Java Class Library defines several static methods that manipulate arrays. In particular, the method `copyOf` returns a copy of a given array. For example, the following statements define an array `data` and then make a duplicate copy of it:

```
int[] data = {2, 4, 6, 8, 10, 12, 14, 18, 20};
int[] copyOfData = Arrays.copyOf(data, data.length);
```

These two arrays have the same length and contents.

If we replace the second argument in the previous example with a value that is less than `data`'s length, fewer values are copied from `data`, and the size of the returned array is reduced accordingly. For example,

```
int[] copyOfData = Arrays.copyOf(data, 3);
```

copies 2, 4, and 6 into `copyOfData` so that `copyOfData.length` is 3.

On the other hand, if the second argument given to `copyOf` is larger than `data.length`, the size of the returned array will be larger than the size of the given array. Elements after the one containing the last value copied from the given array will contain either zero, false, or `null`, according to the data type of the array's entries.

Note: **The method `Arrays.copyOf`**
The standard class `Arrays` in the package `java.util` of the Java Class Library defines several static methods, each named `copyOf`. Each of these methods returns a new array of a given length containing values copied from a given array, as the following specifications indicate. Note that *entry-type* is any data type:

`public static` *entry-type*`[] copyOf(`*entry-type*`[] sourceArray, int newLength)`

The method returns a new array of length `newLength` containing values copied from consecutive values in the array `sourceArray`. If `newLength` is greater than the length of `sourceArray`, the additional elements in the returned array are given values of zero, false, or `null`, as appropriate for the data type of the array. If `newLength` is less than the length of `sourceArray`, the additional values in `sourceArray` are ignored.

An `import` statement is necessary when you use `Arrays.copyOf` in a program.

Note: **`Arrays.copyOf` versus `System.arraycopy`**
The method `copyOf` was added to the class `Arrays` with the introduction of Java 6. `System.arraycopy`, on the other hand, was a part of the original version of Java. Both methods copy an array faster than you could using code you have written. The newer method `copyOf` allows you to copy an array using less code, and so it is preferable to `arraycopy`. For example, as Segments 18.28 and 18.29 have shown, you can copy the array `data` by using either of the following statements:

```
int[] copyOfData = new int[data.length];
System.arraycopy(data, 0, copyOfData, 0, data.length);
```

or

```
int[] copyOfData = Arrays.copyOf(data, data.length);
```

Before calling `System.arraycopy`, you must create an array. The newer method `Arrays.copyOf` does this step for you.

18.30 **Copying arrays of objects.** An array of primitive values actually contains those values. When we copy primitive values from one variable or array to another, duplicate values are created. Such is the case when we duplicate an array of integers, as Figure 18-8 shows. However, an array of objects contains only references to the objects, not the objects themselves. Thus, copying such an array copies the references.

If you were to duplicate an array of strings, for example, using any of the techniques we have just introduced, you would get two distinct arrays. The references, but not the strings, would be copied from one array to the other. Thus, each array would contain its own references, but there would be only one set of strings, as Figure 18-9 shows. The copy of the array is called a **shallow copy**.

If we were to create duplicates of both the strings and the array, we would have a **deep copy**. The original array and the duplicate array would each reference their own set of strings, as Figure 18-10 illustrates.

Since any string, once created, cannot be altered, sharing it causes no problems. Thus, a shallow copy of an array of strings is perfectly acceptable. But when the objects in an array can be modified—perhaps by a set method—you should create a deep copy.

FIGURE 18-9   A shallow copy of an array of strings

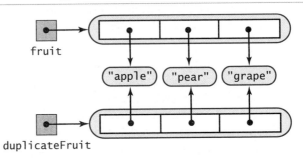

FIGURE 18-10   A deep copy of an array of strings

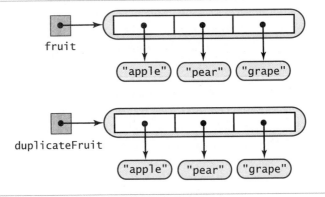

Methods that Return an Array

18.31 As you know, the header of a method that returns a value contains the data type of the value. Chapter 6 gave the form of such headers as

access-modifier   use-modifier   return-type   method-name(parameter-list)

When the method returns an array, *return-type* is the data type of the array. That is, *return-type* has the form *entry-type*[], where *entry-type* is the data type of the entries in the array. Thus, the header of a method that returns an array has the following form:

access-modifier   use-modifier   entry-type[]   *method-name*(*parameter-list*)

For example, the method `Arrays.copyOf`—described in Segment 18.29—returns an array. Its header has the form

```
public static type[] copyOf(type[] sourceArray, int newLength)
```

where *type* is any data type.

Syntax: Methods that return an array

The return type of a method that returns an array is the data type of the array. In other words, the return type is *entry-type*[], where *entry-type* is the data type of the array's entries.

Programming Tip

When a method returns an array that you want to assign to an array variable, you should declare the variable but not allocate memory for an array. For example, to invoke the method `Arrays.copyOf`, as described in Segment 18.29, you do not write

```
double[] copyOfArray = new double[10]; // WRONG!
copyOfArray = Arrays.copyOf(originalArray, 10);
```

The first statement allocates ten locations for a new array, but these locations are discarded when the second statement executes.

Instead, you just declare an array variable and assign to it the array returned by the method, as follows:

```
double[] copyOfArray;
copyOfArray = Arrays.copyOf(originalArray, 10);
```

Of course, you can combine the previous statements into one as follows:

```
double[] copyOfArray = Arrays.copyOf(originalArray, 10);
```

Array Equality

18.32   If you have two distinct arrays, what does it mean to say that the arrays are equal? Arrays are equal if their corresponding entries are equal. For example, the following two arrays are equal:

```
String[] names = {"alpha", "beta", "gamma", "delta"};
String[] tags  = {"alpha", "beta", "gamma", "delta"};
```

The arrays have the same length, and the strings in corresponding elements are equal in value. That is, `names[index]` equals `tags[index]` as `index` ranges in value from 0 to 3. Since the arrays contain strings, we could test the equality of these entries by evaluating the boolean expression `names[index].equals(tags[index])` for all values of `index`.

18.33   **Comparing entries.** The following static method is an example of how you can test whether two arrays are equal:

```
/** Tests whether two arrays of strings are equal.
    @return true if the arrays have equal lengths and contain
    equal strings in the same order */
public static boolean areEqual(String[] arrayOne, String[] arrayTwo)
{
    boolean arraysAreEqual = true; // for now
    if (arrayOne.length == arrayTwo.length)
    {
        int index = 0;
        while (arraysAreEqual && (index < arrayOne.length))
        {
            if (arrayOne[index].equals(arrayTwo[index]))
                index++;
            else
                arraysAreEqual = false;
        } // end while
    }
    else
        arraysAreEqual = false;

    return arraysAreEqual;
} // end areEqual
```

If this method belongs to the class ArrayTasks, for example, the expression

```
ArrayTasks.areEqual(names, tags)
```

returns true, given the arrays names and tags as defined in Segment 18.32.

18.34   **Arrays.equals.** The class Arrays, which we introduced in Segment 18.29, defines a method equals that has the same effect as the method we defined in the previous segment. Thus, given the arrays names and tags as defined in Segment 18.32, the expression

```
Arrays.equals(names, tags)
```

returns true.

 Note: Testing arrays for equality

To be equal, two arrays must contain the same entries in the same order. That is, they must have the same number of entries, and the entries in one array must be equal to the corresponding entries in the other array. To see whether two arrays are equal, you can write your own method, as we did in Segment 18.33, or use the method Arrays.equals.

18.35   **Incorrect tests for equality.** Let's again consider the arrays names and tags, as defined earlier in Segment 18.32. To see whether the arrays are equal, you might be tempted to write an if statement that begins as

```
if (names == tags)
```

However, the expression names == tags is false, even though the arrays are, in fact, equal. The expression actually tests whether the two variables contain the same references. Since the two arrays are distinct, they are in different portions of memory. Thus, the references to the two arrays are not the same.

When used with objects—and arrays are objects—the operator == tests for identity, not equality. Recall from Segment 16.20 in Chapter 16 that two objects have the same identity if they have

videonote
Using an array

the same location in memory. Although the arrays names and tags are equal, they are not identical. An alias for names, however, would be identical to names. That is, given the following assignment

```
String[] namesAlias = names;
```

the expression names == namesAlias would be true. Figure 18-11 illustrates the difference between equality and identity.

Arrays do have an inherited equals method, as Segment 18.9 mentioned, but it does not behave like either our method areEqual or the method Arrays.equals. Rather, it tests for identity instead of equality. Thus, the expression names.equals(tags) is false.

Question 27 If one and two are two arrays having the same type, the expression one == two is almost always false. Under what circumstance(s) would the expression be true?

FIGURE 18-11   (a) Equal arrays; (b) identical arrays

(a)

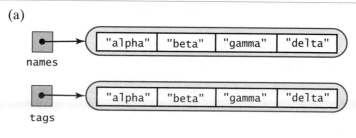

(b)

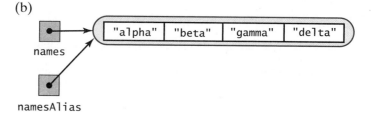

Time Out

videonote
A problem
solved

18.36   Although we have more to say about arrays, we have covered the most important points. The next chapter will use what we have covered here by developing a class that uses an array in its implementation. Although the chapter will not introduce anything new about arrays, it will reinforce what you have learned so far. It also will talk more about class design and development. The new class is relevant to the study of data structures, which is an important topic in computer science that you undoubtedly will encounter before long. In fact, Chapter 32 will introduce it. So take some time to digest the material in this chapter and then go on to the next one to see how it is used. After that, Chapter 20 will present additional array concepts.

CHAPTER SUMMARY

- An array is a construct in a programming language that enables you to group items having the same or related data types.

- Declaring an array defines a variable and gives the data type of the array's entries.

- Creating an array allocates memory for a fixed number of entries.

- The number of elements allocated for an array is called the array's length. The length of the array a is written in Java as a.length, and its value cannot be changed.

- An array contains at most one value, or entry, per element. Thus, the length of an array is also its capacity. If you place fewer entries into an array than its capacity, the array is said to be partially full.

- To reference an array element, you write the array's name followed by an integer expression enclosed in square brackets. The expression is known as an index.

- Loops are used frequently to process the entries in an array.

- Assigning one array variable to another does not copy the array. Rather, it results in two names for the same array.

- To copy an array, you can call one of the methods System.arraycopy or Arrays.copyOf. Alternatively, you can write a loop that copies each entry in one array to another array.

- Two arrays are equal if they contain the same entries in the same order. You cannot use the operator == to test whether two arrays are equal.

- To see whether two arrays are equal, you can either call the method Arrays.equals or write your own code that compares the entries in the arrays.

- You can pass an entire array as an argument to a method. The parameter for such a method has the form *data_type*[] *array-name*. The corresponding argument is simply the array name.

- A method can return an entire array. The method's return type is given in its header as *data_type*[].

EXERCISES

1. Write Java statements to declare and allocate an array capable of containing 20 integers.

2. Write Java statements to fill the array you created in the previous exercise with the first 20 odd integers.

3. Write Java statements to declare and initialize an array of seven strings to the days of the week.

4. Write Java statements to display the contents of the array you created in the previous exercise.

5. What is the result of executing the following code?

```java
char[] letter = {'a', 'b', 'c', 'd', 'e', 'f'};
for (int index = 1; index < letter.length; index++)
   System.out.print(letter[index] + ", ");
```

6. What is the result of executing the following code?

```java
int[] sampleArray = new int[10];
for (int index = 1; index <= sampleArray.length; index++)
{
   sampleArray[index] = 3 * index;
   System.out.print(sampleArray[index] + ", ");
} // end for
```

7. What is the result of executing the following code?

```java
int[] sampleArray;
sampleArray[0] = 21;
sampleArray[1] = 22;
sampleArray[2] = 23;
for (int index = 0; index < sampleArray.length; index++)
   System.out.print(sampleArray[index] + ", ");
```

8. Write a Java statement to declare an array of 25 BankAccount objects.

9. Define a static method to return the average of the floating-point numbers in a given array.

10. Using the method System.arraycopy, copy an array of integers, numbers, to a new array named numbersCopy.

11. Repeat the previous exercise, but instead use the method Arrays.copyOf.

12. Consider a class Person that has two data fields: a string for a name and an integer for an age. Assume that the class has typical set and get methods for these fields and whatever constructors you deem reasonable.

    a. Write Java statements that declare an array group that can hold up to 50 Person objects and allocate memory for it.
    b. Write Java statements that set the first element of this array to a Person object representing Jill, who is 21 years old.

13. Define a static void method, reverseArray, that reverses the order of the integers in an array given as the method's argument. *Hint*: Swap pairs of integers, beginning at the ends of the array and working toward the center. If the array contains an odd number of integers, the middle integer does not move.

14. Define a static valued method, getReversedArray, that returns an array whose entries are in the reverse order of the entries in the array given as the method's argument. The method should not alter its argument. Consider the hint given in the previous exercise.

15. Consider a class CardGame. Write descriptive comments and the header for a void method, shuffleDeck, of this class that accepts an array of Card objects and shuffles them.

16. Repeat the previous exercise, but this time specify a valued method getShuffledDeck that returns a shuffled array of cards without altering the array given to it as an argument.

17. Suppose that you define an array of names by writing

    ```
    String[] names = {"Joe", "Maria", "Chad", "Kim"};
    ```

    Is the following statement legal? Explain your answer.

    ```
    names[4] = "Jodi";
    ```

18. Suppose that you want to read an integer size, define an array names that has size locations, and read up to size names into the array. Imagine that the user types one name per line and types ## instead of a name as a signal to the program to stop reading names.

    After reading the names, the program should display a message that indicates why it stopped reading: Either it read ## or it read size names and could read no more.

    Complete the following Java statements to accomplish these tasks:

    ```
    int size = keyboard.nextInt();
    // define an array called names that can hold exactly size strings

    // read the strings
    int index =
    boolean done =
    while (                              )
    {
        String input = keyboard.next();
        if (                        )

        else

    } // end while
    ```

```
      // display a message
      if (                              )
         System.out.println("Sentinel read.");
      else
         System.out.println(size + " names read.");
```

19. Imagine that you have an array, words, of one-word strings, some of which might be duplicates. Write a static method that accepts the array as an argument and counts the number of times each word occurs in the array. The method should return an array, counts, of these counts such that words[i] occurs counts[i] times.

20. Consider a class that has an array, myStrings, of strings as a data field and the following accessor method:

```
      public String[] getStrings()
      {
         return myStrings;
      } // end getStrings
```

Explain why and how you would improve this definition.

PROJECTS

1. Write a program to allow passengers to reserve seats in a small seven-row airplane, whose seats are numbered as follows:

```
1   A B   C D
2   A B   C D
3   A B   C D
4   A B   C D
5   A B   C D
6   A B   C D
7   A B   C D
```

The program should display this seat pattern each time a passenger wants to choose a seat. An "X" should mark seats already reserved. For example, after seats 1A, 2B, and 4C are reserved, the display should look like this:

```
1   X B   C D
2   A X   C D
3   A B   C D
4   A B   X D
5   A B   C D
6   A B   C D
7   A B   C D
```

After the passenger chooses a seat, the seat pattern should be updated and displayed. If the passenger chooses an already occupied seat, display an error message.

The program should continue until either all seats are assigned or a signal is entered to end execution.

2. The function

$$a_0 + a_1 \times x + a_2 \times x^2 + a_3 \times x^3 + \ldots + a_n \times x^n$$

is a polynomial in x whose coefficients are the real numbers $a_0, a_1, \ldots, a_n$, where a_n is not zero. The number n is called the polynomial's degree. You can evaluate a polynomial at a given real value of x—call it x_0—by computing the following sequence of numbers:

$$b_n = a_n$$
$$b_{n-1} = a_{n-1} + b_n \times x_0$$
$$b_{n-2} = a_{n-2} + b_{n-1} \times x_0$$
$$\ldots$$
$$b_0 = a_0 + b_1 \times x_0$$

The value of the polynomial is then b_0. This way of evaluating a polynomial is called Horner's method and requires n additions and n multiplications. Any other way of evaluating a polynomial will require at least this many additions and multiplications.

Write a program that reads a polynomial's coefficients into an array and then evaluates it for various values of x, as entered by the user.

3. Given the class Coin, as shown in Listing 8-5 of Chapter 8, design, implement, and demonstrate a class CoinJar. An object of CoinJar should be able to accept and contain Coin objects. It should also be able to report various statistics about its Coin contents, including the number of a particular coin, the number of all of its coins, and their total value.

4. Design and implement a class Quiz that administers a short-answer quiz of up to 25 questions. Provide a method that adds a question and its answer to a quiz. The user should be able to enter a desired number of questions and answers. Provide another method to present each question in turn to the user, accept an answer for each one, and keep track of the results. Create a client that populates a quiz, presents it, and then displays the final results.

Clearly, running one program to both create and administer a quiz is not practical. However, after you learn about text files in Chapter 29, you will be able to write one client that uses the class Quiz to create the quiz and another client to administer the quiz.

5. A cryptoquote is an encoded quotation obtained by substituting one letter for another. For example, the phrase "To be or not to be" could be encoded as "AB CD BE FBA AB CD," by making the following substitutions: *A* for *t*, *B* for *o*, *C* for *b*, *D* for *e*, *E* for *r*, and *F* for *n*. Note that letters need not be substituted in alphabetical order, as we have done here.

Write a program that presents a cryptoquote and enables the user to replace letters to solve the puzzle. Along with the cryptoquote, the program should indicate the frequency with which each letter occurs in the cryptoquote. For example, using the previous cryptoquote, the program's output might begin as follows:

```
AB CD BE FBA AB CD
A B C D E F G H I J K L M N O P Q R S T U V W X Y Z
3 4 2 2 1 1                              <--Frequency
Solve the puzzle!
Replace: C b
AB bD BE FBA AB bD
Replace: A n
nB bD BE FBn nB bD
Replace: n t
tB bD BE FBt tB bD
```

Use an array of characters instead of a string to represent the cryptoquote. Notice that the user can change a replacement, as shown with n in the last two lines of the example.

ANSWERS TO SELF-TEST QUESTIONS

1.
```
int[] myArray = new int[5];
for (int index = 0; index < myArray.length; index++)
   myArray[index] = 3;
```

2.
```
int[] myArray = {3, 3, 3, 3, 3};
```

3.
```
Scanner keyboard = new Scanner(System.in);
System.out.print("How many numbers do you plan to type? ");
int n = keyboard.nextInt();
String[] strings = new String[n];
```

4. The first statement declares the array names, but does not allocate memory for it. The first statement should be something like

```
String[] names = new String[3];
```

5. The comparison in the for statement should be < instead of <=.

6. Create an array of deviations and change the loop as follows:

```
double[] deviations = new double[numberCount];
for (int index = 0; index < numberCount; index++)
{
    deviations[index] = number[index] - average;
    System.out.println(number[index] + "\t" + deviations[index]);
} // end for
```

7. The constant CAPACITY indicates the number of elements created for the array ageList. The array can contain that number of ages. However, ageCount counts the number of ages read and prevents the code from storing more than CAPACITY ages in the array.

8. Since ageCount is used as an array index, it must be strictly less than CAPACITY. The index of the last element in the array is 49, not 50.

9. The output is

```
Please enter next positive integer or 0 to end: 0
0 numbers have been read.
```

10. 50 integers are placed into the array. The program reports that 50 integers have been read.

11. 50 integers are placed into the array. The loop ends, the program reports that 50 integers have been read, and the 51st integer remains in age.

12. No.

13. –1 will have the same effect on the program as 0. Any integer that is less than or equal to zero will act as a sentinel value for this code.

14. Change the comparison operator in the if statement from == to >=.

15.
```
// count the number of times the string "Brady" occurs in the
// array nameList
String givenName = "Brady";
int counter = 0;
for (int index = 0; index < nameCount; index++)
{
    if (nameList[index].equals(givenName))
    {
        counter++;
    } // end if
} // end for
// counter is the number of times givenName occurs in the array nameList
```

16. data[0] remains in smallestInteger, because data[1] is not smaller than smallestInteger.

17. You must change the comparison operator from < to >. Although you should also change the comments and the name of the variable smallestInteger, these changes do not affect the logic.

```
// find the largest integer in the array data;
// assume numberCount > 0 and numberCount <= data.length
int largestInteger = data[0];
for (int index = 1; index < numberCount; index++)
{
   if (data[index] > largestInteger)
      largestInteger = data[index];
} // end for
System.out.println("The largest integer is " + largestInteger + ".");
```

18. The most significant change is to use the String method compareTo instead of the comparison operator <.

```
// find the alphabetically earliest name in the array nameList;
// assume nameCount > 0 and nameCount <= nameList.length
int earliestName = nameList[0];
for (int index = 1; index < nameCount; index++)
{
   if (nameList[index].compareTo(earliestName) < 0)
      earliestName = nameList[index];
} // end for
System.out.println("The earliest name is " + earliestName + ".");
```

19. You must change the comparison operator from < to >. Although you should also change the comments and the name of the variable indexOfSmallestInteger, these changes do not affect the logic.

```
// find the index of the largest integer in the array data;
// assume numberCount > 0 and numberCount <= data.length
int indexOfLargestInteger = data[0];
for (int index = 1; index < numberCount; index++)
{
   if (data[index] > data[indexOfLargestInteger])
      indexOfLargestInteger = index;
} // end for
System.out.println("The largest integer is " + data[indexOfLargestInteger]
                   + " at index " + indexOfLargestInteger + ".");
```

20. friends[0].setName("Jesse", "Java");

21.
```
/** Returns the index of the smallest integer in the
    entire array anArray. */
public static int getIndexOfSmallest(int[] anArray)
{
   int indexOfSmallestInteger = 0;
   for (int index = 1; index < anArray.length; index++)
   {
      if (data[index] < data[indexOfSmallestInteger])
         indexOfSmallestInteger = index;
   } // end for

   return indexOfSmallestInteger;
} // end getIndexOfSmallest
```

22. Add a parameter to specify the number of entries in the array. That is, begin the method as follows:

    ```
    /** Returns the index of the smallest integer in the
        first count integers in the array anArray. */
    public static int getIndexOfSmallest(int[] anArray, int count)
    ```

    Then, in the for statement, replace anArray.length with count.

23. `System.arraycopy(data, 2, copyOfData, 0, 5);`

24. `System.arraycopy(data, 2, copyOfData, 4, 5);`

25. sourceIndex through sourceIndex + count – 1

26. destIndex through destIndex + count – 1

27. The expression one == two is true only if one and two are aliases for the same array.

Chapter 19

An Array-Based Data Structure

Contents

Prerequisites

Objectives

After studying this chapter, you should be able to

• Describe the data organization known as a bag
• Use an array to implement a bag
• Identify a proposed class's core methods
• Write a partial implementation of a class that includes definitions of its core methods
• Complete the definition of a class by using a strategy that tests each method as it is defined

The previous chapter introduced you to arrays, which are Java constructs for grouping either primitive values or objects of the same type. You saw how to declare an array; allocate memory for it; and initialize, set, or change its contents. The chapter provided several examples of ways to manipulate the contents of an array. Along the way, you saw how to pass an entire array to a method and to return an array from a method.

This chapter will begin to generalize the idea of grouping objects. In Java, a **collection** is an object that groups other objects and provides various services to its client. In particular, a typical collection enables a client to add, remove, retrieve, and query the objects it represents. Typically, the objects contained in a collection are related by their data type.

Various collections exist for different purposes. Their behaviors are specified abstractly and can differ in purpose according to the collection. Likewise, a specific collection can have several implementations as classes. Some implementations use arrays to hold the objects in the collection. This chapter will use much of the material in the previous chapter to define a nontrivial class that implements a particular collection. It will also give you some practical advice about developing the definition of a class.

■ The Bag

19.1   Imagine a paper bag, a reusable cloth bag, or even a plastic bag. People use bags when they shop, pack a lunch, or eat potato chips. Bags contain things. In everyday language, a bag is a kind of container. In Java, however, a container is an object whose class extends the standard class `Container`. Such containers are used in graphics programs, as you saw in Chapter 5. Rather than being considered a container, a **bag** in Java is a kind of collection.

videonote
Designing a data
structure

What distinguishes a bag from other collections? A bag doesn't do much more than contain its items. It doesn't order them in a particular way, nor does it prevent duplicate items. Most of its behaviors could be performed by other kinds of collections. While describing the behaviors that we want for the collection we'll design in this chapter, let's keep in mind that we are specifying a programming abstraction inspired by an actual physical bag. For example, a paper bag holds things of various dimensions and shapes. So just as the capacity of a physical bag is limited by its size and shape, the capacity of an abstract bag is limited by the amount of memory assigned to its implementation. Since our abstract bag will hold objects of the same type, this limit is conveniently expressed as a maximum number of objects. Unless clearly stated otherwise, from now on when we refer to a bag we will mean a Java object representing an abstract bag.

 Note: Java collections conform to the specifications given in the interface `Collection`, which is a part of the package `java.util` in the Java Class Library. While this interface will influence our design of a bag in this chapter, we will not conform to all of its requirements right now. Chapter 32 will expand upon this introduction to collections in Java.

A Bag's Behaviors

19.2   Since a bag has an upper limit on the number of objects it can contain, we'll specify this capacity when we create the bag. Reporting this capacity could be one of a bag's behaviors:

Get the bag's capacity

Likewise, we should be able to see how many objects are in a bag:

Get the number of items currently in the bag

Two related behaviors detect whether a bag is full or empty:

See whether the bag is full
See whether the bag is empty

19.3   We should be able to add and remove objects:

Add a given object to the bag
Remove an unspecified object from the bag
Remove an occurrence of a particular object from the bag, if possible
Remove all objects from the bag

While you hope that the bagger at the grocery store does not toss six cans of soup into a bag on top of your bread and eggs, our add operation does not indicate where in the bag an object should go. Remember, that a bag does not order its contents. Likewise, the first remove operation just removes any object it can. This operation is like reaching into a grab bag and pulling something out. On the other hand, the second remove operation looks for a particular item in the bag. If you find it, you take it out. If the bag contains several equal objects that satisfy your search, you remove any one of them. If you can't find the object in the bag, you can't remove it, and you just say so. Finally, the last remove operation simply empties the bag of all objects.

19.4   How many cans of dog food did you buy? Did you remember to get anchovy paste? Just what is in that bag? The answers to these questions can be answered by the following operations:

Count the number of times an object occurs in the bag
Test whether the bag contains a particular object
Look at all objects in the bag

We have enough behaviors for now. At this point, we would have written all 11 behaviors on a piece of paper or, as Chapter 15 suggested, on a CRC card.

FIGURE 19-1   A CRC card for a class `BagOfStrings`

BagOfStrings
Responsibilities
Get the bag's capacity
Get the number of strings currently in the bag
See whether the bag is full
See whether the bag is empty
Add a given string to the bag
Remove an unspecified string from the bag
Remove an occurrence of a particular string from the bag, if possible
Remove all strings from the bag
Count the number of times a given string occurs in the bag
Test whether the bag contains a particular string
Retrieve all strings that are in the bag
Collaborations
String

19.5 What type of objects will our bag contain? Although we might be tempted to accept all types of objects by using Object[1] as the data type, we mentioned earlier that all objects in a bag should have the same data type. Let's use String as this type and define a bag of strings. Later, Chapter 32 will show us how to define a bag or other collection that accepts objects whose type is chosen by the client of the class. We have begun a design for a class we'll name BagOfStrings. Figure 19-1 illustrates a CRC card for this class.

Specifying a Bag

Before we implement the class BagOfStrings, we need to specify in detail the methods that correspond to the bag's behaviors. We'll name the methods, choose their parameters, decide their return types, and write comments to fully describe their behaviors. Our goal, of course, is to write a Java header and comments for each method, but first we will express the methods in pseudocode and then in UML notation.

19.6 The first two behaviors on our CRC card give rise to two methods that return either the bag's capacity or a count of its current contents. Each of these methods has no parameters and returns an integer. In pseudocode, we have the following specifications:

```
// Returns the capacity of this bag.
getCapacity()

// Returns the current number of strings in this bag.
getCurrentSize()
```

We can express these methods using UML as

```
+getCapacity(): integer
+getCurrentSize(): integer
```

and add these two lines to a class diagram. Finally, the Java headers for these methods are

```
/** Gets the capacity of this bag.
    @return the integer number of strings that this bag can hold */
public int getCapacity()

/** Gets the current number of strings in this bag.
    @return the integer number of strings currently in this bag */
public int getCurrentSize()
```

19.7 Testing whether the bag is full or empty can be performed by two boolean-valued methods, again without parameters. Their specifications in pseudocode and UML are

```
// Returns true if this bag is full.
isFull()

// Returns true if this bag is empty.
isEmpty()
```

and

```
+isFull(): boolean
+isEmpty(): boolean
```

We add these two lines to our class diagram.

---

1. The class Object is introduced in Chapter 16. If you have not read this chapter, just know that all classes are based on Object and, therefore, all references to objects can be assigned to variables whose data type is Object.

The Java headers for these two methods are

```
/** Sees whether this bag is full.
    @return true if this bag is full, or false if not */
public boolean isFull()

/** Sees whether this bag is empty.
    @return true if this bag is empty, or false if not */
public boolean isEmpty()
```

19.8 We now want to add a given string to the bag. We can name the method add and give it a parameter to represent the given string. We might write the following pseudocode:

```
// Adds a new string to this bag.
add(newString)
```

Clearly, the data type of `newString` is `String`. We might be tempted to make `add` a void method, but remember that a bag has a finite capacity. If the bag is full, we cannot add a new string to it. What should we do in this case? Here are two options when dealing with a full bag:

- Do nothing. We cannot add another item, so we ignore it and leave the bag unchanged.
- Leave the bag unchanged, but signal the client that the addition is impossible.

The first option is easy, but it leaves the client wondering what happened. Of course, we could state as a precondition of add that the bag must not already be full. Then the client has the responsibility to avoid adding a new string to a full bag.

The second option is the better one, and it is not too hard to specify or implement. How can we indicate to the client whether the addition was successful? The interface `Collection` specifies that an exception should occur if the addition is not successful. You will see how to work with exceptions in Chapter 28, but for now we will use another approach. Displaying an error message is not a good choice, as you should leave all written output up to the client. Since the addition is either successful or not, we can simply have the method add return a boolean value. Thus, we can specify the method in UML as

```
+add(newString: String): boolean
```

and in Java as

```
/** Adds a new string to this bag.
    @param newString  the string to be added
    @return true if the addition is successful, or false if not */
public boolean add(String newString)
```

19.9 Three behaviors involve removing strings from a bag: remove all strings, remove any one string, and remove a particular string. Suppose we name the methods and any parameters and specify them in pseudocode as follows:

```
// Removes all strings from this bag.
clear()

// Removes one unspecified string from this bag.
remove()

// Removes one occurrence of a particular string from this bag, if possible.
remove(aString)
```

What return types are these methods?

19.10 The method `clear` can be a void method: We just want to empty the bag, not retrieve any of its contents. Thus, we write

```
+clear(): void
```

in UML and the following header in Java:

```
/** Removes all strings from this bag. */
public void clear()
```

If the first `remove` method removes a string from the bag, the method can easily return the string it has removed. Its return type is then `String`. In UML, we have

```
+remove(): String
```

and in Java

```
/** Removes one unspecified string from this bag.
    @return either the removed string, if the removal
            was successful, or null */
public String remove()
```

Notice that we respond to an attempt to remove a string from an empty bag by returning `null`.

The second `remove` method won't be able to remove a particular string from the bag if the bag does not contain the string. We could have the method return a boolean value, much as add does, so it can indicate success or not. Or the method could return either the removed string or `null` if it can't remove the string. Here are the specifications for these two possible versions of the method, first in UML and then in Java—we must choose one:

```
+remove(aString: String): boolean
```

```
/** Removes one occurrence of a given string from
    this bag, if possible.
    @param aString  the string to be removed
    @return true if the removal was successful, or false if not */
public boolean remove(String aString)
```

or

```
+remove(aString: String): String
```

```
/** Removes one occurrence of a given string from
    this bag, if possible.
    @param aString  the string to be removed
    @return either the removed string, if the removal was successful,
            or null */
public String remove(String aString)
```

Even though the first version of this method does not return the removed string, the client does have the string it passed to `remove` as its argument. This argument string is equal to a successfully removed string. We will choose this first version, to be consistent with the interface `Collection`.

Question 1 Is it legal to have both versions of `remove(aString)`, which were just described, in one class? Explain.

Question 2 Is it legal to have two versions of `remove`, one that has no parameter and one that has a string as a parameter, in the same class? Explain.

19.11 The remaining behaviors do not change the contents of the bag. One of these behaviors counts the number of times a given string occurs within the bag. We specify it first in pseudocode, then in UML, and finally in Java, as follows:

```
// Counts the number of times a given string appears in this bag
getFrequencyOf(aString)
```

```
+getFrequencyOf(aString): integer
```

```
/** Counts the number of times a given string appears in this bag.
    @param aString  the string to be counted
    @return the number of times aString appears in this bag */
public int getFrequencyOf(String aString)
```

Another method tests whether the bag contains a given string. Its specifications in pseudocode, UML, and Java are

```
// Tests whether this bag contains a given string.
contains(aString)
```

```
+contains(aString: String): boolean
```

```
/** Tests whether this bag contains a given string.
    @param aString  the string to locate
    @return true if this bag contains aString, or false otherwise */
public boolean contains(String aString)
```

19.12   Finally, we want to look at the contents of the bag. Rather than providing a method that displays the strings in the bag, we will define one that returns an array of these strings. The client is then free to display any or all of them in any way desired. Here are the specifications for our last method:

```
// Look at all objects in this bag.
toArray()
```

```
+toArray(): String[]
```

```
/** Retrieves all strings that are in this bag.
    @return a newly allocated array of all the strings in this bag */
public String[] toArray()
```

Recall that the data type of an array of strings is String[]. When a method returns an array, it usually should define a new one to return, as we have done here.

19.13   As we developed the previous specifications for the bag's methods, we represented them using UML notation. Figure 19-2 shows the result of doing so.

At this point, we should write some statements that test the proposed class. Although we cannot execute these statements yet—after all, we have not implemented the class BagOfStrings yet —we can use them to confirm or revise both our decisions about the design of the methods and the accompanying documentation. We will skip the details of this step, but you will see sample programs that test the class later in this chapter.

FIGURE 19-2   UML notation for the class BagOfStrings

```
+---------------------------------------------+
|              BagOfStrings                   |
+---------------------------------------------+
|                                             |
+---------------------------------------------+
| +getCapacity(): integer                     |
| +getCurrentSize(): integer                  |
| +isFull(): boolean                          |
| +isEmpty(): boolean                         |
| +add(newString: String): boolean            |
| +clear(): void                              |
| +remove(): String                           |
| +remove(aString: String): boolean           |
| +getFrequencyOf(aString: String): integer   |
| +contains(aString: String): boolean         |
| +toArray(): String[]                        |
+---------------------------------------------+
```

An Interface

19.14   If you read about interfaces in Chapter 16, now would be the time to organize the Java headers that we have just written into an interface. Listing 19-1 contains such an interface. Although writing an interface before implementing a class is certainly not required, doing so is a way to document your specifications in a concise way. You then can use the code in the interface as an outline for the actual class. Having an interface also provides a data type for a bag that is independent of a particular class definition. We plan to use an array in the implementation here, but later in Chapter 32 you will see that we can use a structure other than an array. Code written with respect to an interface allows us to more easily replace one implementation of a bag with another.

LISTING 19-1   A Java interface for a bag of strings

```java
/**
    An interface that describes the operations of a bag of strings.
    @author Frank M. Carrano
*/
public interface BagOfStringsInterface
{
   /** Gets the capacity of this bag.
       @return the integer number of strings that this bag can hold */
   public int getCapacity();

   /** Gets the current number of strings in this bag.
       @return the integer number of strings currently in this bag */
   public int getCurrentSize();

   /** Sees whether this bag is full.
       @return true if this bag is full, or false if not */
   public boolean isFull();

   /** Sees whether this bag is empty.
       @return true if this bag is empty, or false if not */
   public boolean isEmpty();

   /** Adds a new string to this bag.
       @param newString  the string to be added
       @return true if the addition is successful, or false if not */
   public boolean add(String newString);

   /** Removes all strings from this bag. */
   public void clear();

   /** Removes one unspecified string from this bag.
       @return either the removed string, if the removal
               was successful, or null */
   public String remove();

   /** Removes one occurrence of a given string from this bag,
       if possible.
```

```
            @param aString   the string to be removed
            @return true if the removal was successful, or false if not */
    public boolean remove(String aString);

    /** Counts the number of times a given string appears in this bag.
        @param aString   the string to be counted
        @return the number of times aString appears in this bag */
    public int getFrequencyOf(String aString);

    /** Tests whether this bag contains a given string.
        @param aString   the string to locate
        @return true if this bag contains aString, or false otherwise */
    public boolean contains(String aString);

    /** Retrieves all strings that are in this bag.
        @return a newly allocated array of all the strings in this bag */
    public String[] toArray();
} // end BagOfStringsInterface
```

Implementing and Testing a Bag

The definition for the class Bag could be fairly involved. The class certainly has quite a few methods. For such classes, you should not define the entire class and then attempt to test it. Instead, you should identify a group of **core methods** to both implement and test before continuing with the rest of the class definition. By leaving the definitions of the other methods for later, you can focus your attention and simplify your task. But what methods should be part of this group? In general, such methods should be central to the purpose of the class and allow reasonable testing. We sometimes will call a group of core methods a **core group**.

A Group of Core Methods

19.15   When dealing with a collection such as a bag, you cannot test most methods until you have created the collection. Thus, adding objects to the collection is a fundamental operation. If the method add does not work correctly, testing other methods such as remove would be pointless. Thus, the bag's add method is part of the group of core methods that we implement first.

videonote

Implementing and testing

To test whether add works correctly, we need a method that allows us to see the bag's contents. The method toArray serves this purpose, and so it is a core method. The constructors are also fundamental and are in the core group. Similarly, any methods that a core method might call are part of the core group as well. For example, since we cannot add a string to a full bag, the method add will need to call isFull.

 Note: Methods such as add and remove that can alter the underlying structure of a collection are likely to have the most involved implementations. In general, you should define such methods before the others in the class. But since we can't test remove before add is correct, we will delay implementing it until after add is completed and thoroughly tested.

 Programming Tip
When defining a class, implement and test a group of core methods. Begin with methods that add to a collection of objects and/or have involved implementations.

19.16   We have identified the following core methods to be a part of the first draft of the class `BagOfStrings`:

- Constructors
- `public boolean add(String newString)`
- `public boolean isFull()`
- `public String[] toArray()`

With this core, we will be able to construct a bag, add strings to it, and look at the result. When these methods work correctly, we can begin to implement the remaining methods.

Before we define any of the core methods, we need to consider the class's data fields. Since the bag will hold a group of strings, one field can be an array of these strings. The length of the array defines the bag's capacity. We can let the client specify this capacity, as well as provide a default capacity that the client can use instead. We also will want to track the current number of strings in a bag. Thus, we can define the following data fields for our class,

```
private final String[] bag;
private static final int DEFAULT_CAPACITY = 25;
private int numberOfStrings;
```

and add them to our earlier UML representation of the class in Figure 19-2. The augmented notation appears in Figure 19-3.

FIGURE 19-3   UML notation for the class `BagOfStrings`, updated to include the class's data fields

```
┌─────────────────────────────────────────────┐
│                BagOfStrings                   │
├─────────────────────────────────────────────┤
│ -bag: String[]                                │
│ -DEFAULT_CAPACITY: integer                    │
│ -numberOfStrings: integer                     │
├─────────────────────────────────────────────┤
│ +getCapacity(): integer                       │
│ +getCurrentSize(): integer                    │
│ +isFull(): boolean                            │
│ +isEmpty(): boolean                           │
│ +add(newString: String): boolean              │
│ +clear(): void                                │
│ +remove(): String                             │
│ +remove(aString: String): boolean             │
│ +getFrequencyOf(aString: String): integer     │
│ +contains(aString: String): boolean           │
│ +toArray(): String[]                          │
└─────────────────────────────────────────────┘
```

Design Decision: When the array bag is partially full, which array elements should contain the bag's entries?

In the previous chapter, the first entry in an array is always in the first element of the array, that is, the element whose index is 0. Although this characteristic is typical of many arrays, it is not a requirement, especially for arrays that implement collections. For example, some collection implementations can benefit by ignoring the array element whose index is 0 and using the elements that begin at index 1. Sometimes you might want to use the elements at the end of the array before the ones at its beginning. For the bag, we have no reason to be atypical, and so the objects in our bag will begin at index 0 of the array.

Another consideration is whether the bag's objects should occupy consecutive elements of the array. Requiring the add method to place objects into the array bag consecutively is certainly reasonable, but why should we care, and is this really a concern? We need to establish certain truths, or assertions, about our planned implementation so that the action of each method is not detrimental to other methods. For example, the method toArray must "know" where add has placed the bag's entries. Our decision now also will affect what must happen later when we remove an entry from the bag. Will the method remove ensure that the array entries remain in consecutive elements? It must, because for now at least, we will insist that bag entries occupy consecutive array elements.

19.17   **The constructors.** A constructor for this class must create the array bag. Notice that the declaration of the data field bag in the previous segment does not create an array. Forgetting to create an array in a constructor is a common mistake. To create the array, the constructor must specify the array's length, which is the bag's capacity. And since we are creating an empty bag, the constructor should also initialize the field numberOfStrings to zero.

The following constructor performs these steps, using a capacity given as an argument:

```
/** Creates an empty bag having a given capacity.
    @param capacity  the integer capacity desired */
public BagOfStrings(int capacity)
{
   bag = new String[capacity];
   numberOfStrings = 0;
} // end constructor
```

The default constructor can invoke the previous one, passing it the default capacity as an argument, as follows:

```
/** Creates an empty bag whose capacity is 25. */
public BagOfStrings()
{
   this(DEFAULT_CAPACITY);
} // end default constructor
```

Recall from Chapter 8 that a constructor can invoke another constructor in the same class by using the keyword this as a method name.

19.18   **The method add.** If the bag is full, we cannot add anything to it. In that case, the method add should return false. Otherwise, we simply add newString immediately after the last entry in the array bag by writing the following statement:

```
bag[numberOfStrings] = newString;
```

If we are adding to an empty bag, numberOfStrings would be zero, and the assignment would be to bag[0]. If the bag contained one string, an additional string would be assigned to bag[1], and so on. After each addition to the bag, we increase the counter numberOfStrings. These steps are illustrated in Figure 19-4 and accomplished by the following definition of the method add:

```
/** Adds a new string to this bag.
    @param newString  the string to be added
    @return true if the addition is successful, or false if not */
public boolean add(String newString)
{
   boolean result = true;
   if (isFull())
   {
      result = false;
   }
   else
   {  // assertion: result is true here
```

```
        bag[numberOfStrings] = newString;
        numberOfStrings++;
    } // end if

    return result;
} // end add
```

Notice that we call isFull as if it has been defined already. Had we not considered isFull as a core method earlier, its use now would indicate to us that it should be in the core group.

 Note: The entries in a bag have no particular order. Thus, the method add can place a new entry into a convenient element of the array bag. In the previous definition of add, that element is the one immediately after the last element used.

FIGURE 19-4   Adding entries to an array that represents a bag until it becomes full

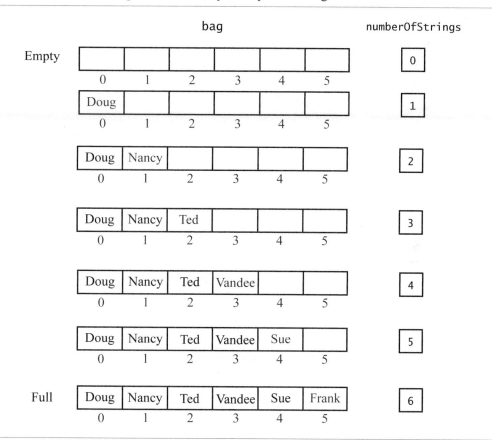

19.19   **The method isFull.** A bag is full when it contains as many strings as the array bag can accommodate. That situation occurs when numberOfStrings is equal to the capacity of the array. Thus, isFull has the following straightforward definition:

```
/** Sees whether this bag is full.
    @return true if this bag is full, or false if not */
public boolean isFull()
{
    return numberOfStrings == bag.length;
} // end isFull
```

19.20 **The method `toArray`.** The last method, `toArray`, in our initial core group retrieves the strings that are in a bag and returns them to the client within an array. We have already indicated the header for this method in Segment 19.12. The method will create and return a new array that contains the strings in the bag. The length of this new array can equal the number of strings in the bag—that is, `numberOfStrings`—rather than the length of the array bag.

After `toArray` creates the new array, a simple loop can copy the references in the array bag to this new array before returning it. Thus, the definition of `toArray` can appear as follows:

```java
/** Retrieves all strings that are in this bag.
    @return a newly allocated array of all the strings in this bag */
public String[] toArray()
{
    String[] result = new String[numberOfStrings];
    for (int index = 0; index < numberOfStrings; index++)
    {
        result[index] = bag[index];
    } // end for

    return result;
} // end toArray
```

Recall from Segment 18.30 in the previous chapter that `toArray` returns a shallow copy of the array bag, since it does not duplicate the strings in the bag. Segment 18.30 also said, however, that a shallow copy of an array of strings is perfectly acceptable because strings cannot be altered.

Design Decision: **Should the method `toArray` return the array bag instead of a copy?**

Suppose that we define `toArray` as follows:

```java
public String[] toArray()
{
    return bag;
} // end toArray
```

This simple definition would certainly return an array of the bag's contents to a client. For example, the statement

```java
String[] bagArray = myBag.toArray();
```

provides a reference to an array of the strings in `myBag`. A client could use the variable `bagArray` to display the contents of `myBag`.

The reference `bagArray`, however, is to the array bag itself. That is, `bagArray` is an alias for the private instance variable bag within the object `myBag`, and therefore gives the client direct access to this private data. Thus, a client could change the contents of the bag without calling the class's public methods. For instance, if `myBag` is the full bag pictured in Figure 19-4, the statement

```java
bagArray[2] = null;
```

would change the entry Ted to `null`. Although this approach might sound good to you if the intent is to remove Ted from the bag, doing so could destroy the integrity of the bag. For example, the entries in the array bag would no longer be consecutive, and the count of the number of entries in the bag would be incorrect.

Programming Tip
A class should not return a reference to an array that is a private data field.

Question 3 In the previous method `toArray`, does the value of `numberOfStrings` equal `bag.length` in general?

Question 4 Suppose that the previous method `toArray` gave the new array `result` the same length as the array `bag`. How would a client get the number of strings in the returned array?

Question 5 Suppose that the previous method `toArray` returned the array `bag` instead of returning a new array such as `result`. If `myBag` is a bag of five strings, what effect would the following statements have on the array `bag` and the field `numberOfStrings`?

```
String[] bagArray = myBag.toArray();
bagArray[0] = null;
```

19.21   **The class so far.** Listing 19-2 shows the definition of the class `BagOfStrings` at this point in its development.[2] It contains only the core methods we have identified. We will test these methods in the next segment before we continue the implementation of the class.

LISTING 19-2   A partial definition of the class `BagOfStrings`

```java
/**
   A class that implements a bag of strings by using an array.
   @author Frank M. Carrano
*/
public class BagOfStrings
{
   private final String[] bag;
   private static final int DEFAULT_CAPACITY = 25;
   private int numberOfStrings;

   /** Creates an empty bag whose capacity is 25. */
   public BagOfStrings()
   {
      this(DEFAULT_CAPACITY);
   } // end default constructor

   /** Creates an empty bag having a given capacity.
       @param capacity  the integer capacity desired */
   public BagOfStrings(int capacity)
   {
      bag = new String[capacity];
      numberOfStrings = 0;
   } // end constructor

   /** Adds a new string to this bag.
       @param newString  the string to be added
       @return true if the addition is successful, or false if not */
```

---

2.   The source code available on the book's website identifies this version of the class as `BagOfStrings1`.

```java
public boolean add(String newString)
{
   boolean result = true;
   if (isFull())
   {
      result = false;
   }
   else
   {  // assertion: result is true here
      bag[numberOfStrings] = newString;
      numberOfStrings++;
   } // end if

   return result;
} // end add

/** Retrieves all strings that are in this bag.
    @return a newly allocated array of all the strings in this bag */
public String[] toArray()
{
   String[] result = new String[numberOfStrings];
   for (int index = 0; index < numberOfStrings; index++)
   {
      result[index] = bag[index];
   } // end for

   return result;
} // end toArray

/** Sees whether this bag is full.
    @return true if this bag is full, or false if not */
public boolean isFull()
{
   return numberOfStrings == bag.length;
} // end isFull
} // end BagOfStrings
```

19.22 **Testing the class.** Listing 19-3 shows a program to test the core methods defined in Listing 19-2. Let's discuss the tests performed, as well as the program's structure and use of arrays.

Initially, the main method creates an empty bag by using the default constructor. Since we wrote the class BagOfStrings, we know that the capacity of this bag is 25. If you add fewer than 25 strings to the bag, it should not be full. Thus, isFull should return false after these additions. The program's output, in fact, indicates that both this bag's contents and isFull are correct.

Next in the main method, we consider a full bag by creating a bag whose capacity is seven and then adding seven strings to it. This time, isFull should return true. Again, the program's output shows that our methods are correct.

LISTING 19-3   A test program for the version of the class BagOfStrings given
                in Listing 19-2

```java
/** A demonstration of the first draft of the class BagOfStrings
    @author Frank M. Carrano
*/
public class BagDemo1
{
   public static void main(String[] args)
   {
      // a bag that is not full
      BagOfStrings aBag = new BagOfStrings();
      String[] contentsOfBag1 = {"A", "A", "B", "A", "C", "A"};

      System.out.println("Adding to an empty bag: A, A, B, A, C, A");
      addToBag(aBag, contentsOfBag1);
      displayBag(aBag);

      if (aBag.isFull())
         System.out.println("This bag is full but should not be.");
      else
         System.out.println("This bag is not full.");
      System.out.println();

      // a full bag
      aBag = new BagOfStrings(7);
      String[] contentsOfBag2 = {"A", "B", "A", "C", "B", "C", "D"};

      System.out.println("Adding to an empty bag: A, B, A, C, B, C, D");
      addToBag(aBag, contentsOfBag2);
      displayBag(aBag);

      if (aBag.isFull())
         System.out.println("This bag is full.");
      else
         System.out.println("This bag is not full but should be.");
   } // end main

   public static void addToBag(BagOfStrings aBag, String[] content)
   {
      for (int index = 0; index < content.length; index++)
      {
         aBag.add(content[index]);
      } // end for
   } // end addToBag

   public static void displayBag(BagOfStrings aBag)
   {
```

```
            System.out.print("The bag contains ");
            String[] bagArray = aBag.toArray();
            for (int index = 0; index < bagArray.length; index++)
            {
                System.out.print(bagArray[index] + " ");
            } // end for

            System.out.println();
    } // end displayBag
} // end BagDemo1
```

Output

```
Adding to an empty bag: A, A, B, A, C, A
The bag contains A A B A C A
This bag is not full.

Adding to an empty bag: A, B, A, C, B, C, D
The bag contains A B A C B C D
This bag is full.
```

19.23   **Programming details of BagDemo1.** Notice that, in addition to the main method, BagDemo1 has two other methods. Since main is static and calls these other methods, they must be static as well. (If you need to review static methods, see Chapter 15.)

The method displayBag takes a bag as its argument and uses the bag's method toArray to access its contents. Once we have an array of the bag's strings, a simple loop can display them. The method addToBag accepts as its arguments a bag and an array of strings. The method uses a loop similar to the one in displayBag to add each string in the array to the bag.

Notice how an array is written as a parameter in the heading of addToBag. You write the array's data type, which in this case is String[], followed by the name of the array. An argument corresponding to this parameter and passed to the method will be a reference to an entire array.

Note: A method can change the state of an object passed to it as an argument
You pass two arguments to the method addToBag: a bag and an array of strings. Both of these arguments are references to objects that exist in the main method. The method addToBag stores copies of these references in its parameters, which, as you should recall, behave as local variables. Although addToBag cannot change the references as they exist in the main method, it can alter the referenced objects. In particular, it changes the bag—that is, the BagOfStrings object —by adding strings to it. That bag, remember, is local to main and is outside of addToBag. Although addToBag does not change the entries in its array argument, it could.

Question 6 What is the result of executing the following statements within the main method of BagDemo1?

```
BagOfStrings aBag = new BagOfStrings();
displayBag(aBag);
```

Implementing More Methods

Now that we can add strings to a bag, we can implement the remaining methods, beginning with the easiest ones. We will postpone the definitions of remove momentarily until we see how to search a bag.

19.24 The methods isEmpty, getCapacity, and getCurrentSize have straightforward definitions, as you can see:

```
/** Sees whether this bag is empty.
    @return true if this bag is empty, or false if not */
public boolean isEmpty()
{
   return numberOfStrings == 0;
} // end isEmpty

/** Gets the capacity of this bag.
    @return the integer number of strings that this bag can hold */
public int getCapacity()
{
   return bag.length;
} // end getCapacity

/** Gets the number of strings currently in this bag.
    @return the integer number of strings currently in this bag */
public int getCurrentSize()
{
   return numberOfStrings;
} // end getCurrentSize
```

19.25 **The method getFrequencyOf.** To count the number of times a given string occurs in a bag, we count the number of times the string occurs in the array bag. This situation is similar to the one described in Segment 18.13 and Question 15 of Chapter 18. Using a for loop to cycle through the array's indices from 0 to numberOfStrings – 1, we compare the given string to every string in the array. Each time we find a match, we increment a counter. When the loop ends, we simply return the value of the counter. Note that we must use the method equals to compare strings. That is, we must write

```
aString.equals(bag[index])
```

and not

```
aString == bag[index] // WRONG!
```

The method definition follows:

```
/** Counts the number of times a given string appears in this bag.
    @param aString   the string to be counted
    @return the number of times aString appears in this bag */
public int getFrequencyOf(String aString)
{
   int counter = 0;

   for (int index = 0; index < numberOfStrings; index++)
   {
      if (aString.equals(bag[index]))
      {
         counter++;
      } // end if
   } // end for

   return counter;
} // end getFrequencyOf
```

19.26   **The method contains.** To see whether a bag contains a given string, we once again search the array bag. We developed a loop for this task in Segments 18.17 through 18.19 of the previous chapter. To adapt that loop for use in the method contains, we simply change variable names, and instead of testing the value of found after the loop ends, we return its value. Here, then, is our definition of the method contains:

```java
/** Tests whether this bag contains a given string.
    @param aString  the string to locate
    @return true if this bag contains aString, or false otherwise */
public boolean contains(String aString)
{
   boolean found = false;

   for (int index = 0; !found && (index < numberOfStrings); index++)
   {
      if (aString.equals(bag[index]))
      {
         found = true;
      } // end if
   } // end for

   return found;
} // end contains
```

Note: Two kinds of loops

To count how many times a string occurs in an array, the method getFrequencyOf uses a loop that cycles through all of the array's strings. In fact, the body of the loop executes numberOfStrings times. In contrast, to indicate whether a given string occurs in an array, the loop in the method contains ends if, and as soon as, the desired string is discovered. The body of this loop executes between one and numberOfStrings times. You should be comfortable writing loops that execute either a definitive or a variable number of times.

19.27   **Testing the additional methods.** As you define additional methods for the class BagOfStrings, you should test them by adding statements to BagDemo1. Although the program in Listing 19-4, BagDemo2, tests all the methods we have defined so far, the program should be formed and tested incrementally. The tests shown in BagDemo2 are performed on a bag that is not full. As we did in BagDemo1, you should run similar tests on a full bag. The version of BagDemo2 that is available on the book's website includes such tests and identifies this version of the class BagOfStrings as BagOfStrings2.

LISTING 19-4   A test program for the methods isEmpty, getCapacity, getCurrentSize, getFrequencyOf, and contains

```java
/** A demonstration of the second draft of the class BagOfStrings
    @author Frank M. Carrano
*/
public class BagDemo2
{
   public static void main(String[] args)
   {
      // a bag that is not full
      BagOfStrings aBag = new BagOfStrings();
```

```java
if (aBag.isEmpty())
   System.out.println("The first bag is empty.");
else
   System.out.println("The first bag is not empty but should be.");

System.out.println("The capacity of the bag is " +
                   aBag.getCapacity() + ".");

String[] contentsOfBag1 = {"A", "A", "B", "A", "C", "A"};
System.out.println("\nAdding to the bag: A, A, B, A, C, A");
addToBag(aBag, contentsOfBag1);
displayBag(aBag);

System.out.println("This bag contains " + aBag.getCurrentSize() +
                   " strings.");

if (aBag.isEmpty())
   System.out.println("This bag is empty but should not be.");
else
   System.out.println("This bag is not empty.");

if (aBag.isFull())
   System.out.println("This bag is full but should not be.");
else
   System.out.println("This bag is not full.");
System.out.println();

System.out.println();
System.out.println("In this bag, the count of A is " +
                   aBag.getFrequencyOf("A"));
System.out.println("In this bag, the count of B is " +
                   aBag.getFrequencyOf("B"));
System.out.println("In this bag, the count of C is " +
                   aBag.getFrequencyOf("C"));
System.out.println("In this bag, the count of D is " +
                   aBag.getFrequencyOf("D"));

System.out.println();
System.out.println("Does this bag contain A? " +
                   aBag.contains("A"));
System.out.println("Does this bag contain B? " +
                   aBag.contains("B"));
System.out.println("Does this bag contain C? " +
                   aBag.contains("C"));
System.out.println("Does this bag contain D? " +
                   aBag.contains("D"));
System.out.println();
```

< Similar code for a full bag should be here. >
```
   } // end main
```

< The static methods `addToBag` *and* `displayBag` *from Listing 19-3 appear here. >*
```
} // end BagDemo2
```

Output
```
   The first bag is empty.
   The capacity of the bag is 25.

   Adding to the bag: A, A, B, A, C, A
   The bag contains A A B A C A
   This bag contains 6 strings.
   This bag is not empty.
   This bag is not full.

   In this bag, the count of A is 4
   In this bag, the count of B is 1
   In this bag, the count of C is 1
   In this bag, the count of D is 0

   Does this bag contain A? true
   Does this bag contain B? true
   Does this bag contain C? true
   Does this bag contain D? false

   . . .
```

Methods That Remove Strings

We have postponed the methods to remove strings from a bag until now because defining a method to remove a specific string is somewhat more difficult and involves a search much like the one we performed in the method `contains`. We begin, however, with two related methods that are not as difficult to define.

19.28   **The method `clear`.** The method `clear` removes the strings from a bag, one at a time. The following definition of `clear` calls the method `remove` until the bag is empty:

```java
/** Removes all strings from this bag. */
public void clear()
{
   while (!isEmpty())
      remove();
} // end clear
```

Exactly which string is removed by each cycle of the loop is unimportant. Thus, we call the `remove` method that removes an unspecified string. Moreover, we do not save the string that the method returns.

Question 7 Revise the definition of the method `clear` so that it does not call `isEmpty`, and so the `while` statement has an empty body.

19.29   **Removing an unspecified string.** The method `remove` that has no parameter removes any string from a bag, as long as the bag is not empty. Recall from the specification in Segment 19.10 that the method returns the string it removes. If the bag is empty before the method executes, `null` is returned.

Removing a string from a bag involves removing it from an array. While we can access any string in the array bag, the last one is easy to remove. To do so, we

- Access the string so it can be returned
- Set the string's array element to `null`
- Decrement `numberOfStrings`

Decrementing `numberOfStrings` causes the last entry to be ignored, meaning that it is effectively removed, even if we did not set its location in the array to `null`.

A literal translation of the previous steps into Java leads to the following definition of the method:

```java
public String remove()
{
   String result = null;
   if (numberOfStrings > 0)
   {
      result = bag[numberOfStrings - 1];
      bag[numberOfStrings - 1] = null;
      numberOfStrings--;
   } // end if

   return result;
} // end remove
```

Note that this method computes `numberOfStrings - 1` three times. The following refinement avoids this repetition:

```java
/** Removes an unspecified string from this bag.
    @return either the removed string, if the removal
            was successful, or null otherwise */
public String remove()
{
   String result = null;
   if (numberOfStrings > 0)
   {
      numberOfStrings--;
      result = bag[numberOfStrings];
      bag[numberOfStrings] = null;
   } // end if

   return result;
} // end remove
```

Question 8 Why does the method `remove` set `bag[numberOfStrings]` to `null`?

Question 9 The previous `remove` method removes the last string in the array bag. Why might removing a different string be more difficult to accomplish?

19.30   **Removing a given string: the hard way.** Given a string—call it `aString`—we will remove it from the bag. If the string occurs more than once in the bag, we will remove only one occurrence. Exactly which occurrence is removed is unspecified. We will simply remove the first occurrence of `aString` that we encounter while searching for it. As we discussed in Segment 19.10, we will return either true or false, according to whether we find the string in the bag.

Assuming that the bag is not empty, we search the array bag much as the method `contains` did in Segment 19.26. If `aString` equals `bag[index]`, we note the value of `index`. Figure 19-5 illustrates the array after a successful search.

FIGURE 19-5   The array bag after a successful search for the string "Alice"

bag[index]

Doug	Alice	Nancy	Ted	Vandee	Sue	

Indices → 0   1   2   3   4   5   6

We now need to remove the string in bag[index]. If we simply write

bag[index] = null;

the reference in bag[index] to the string will be removed, but we will have a gap in the array. That is, the contents of the bag will no longer be in consecutive array locations, as Figure 19-6a illustrates. We could get rid of that gap by shifting the subsequent strings, as shown in Figure 19-6b. This time-consuming approach is not necessary, however, as we discuss next.

FIGURE 19-6   (a) A gap in the array bag after clearing the entry in bag[index];
(b) the array after shifting subsequent entries to avoid a gap

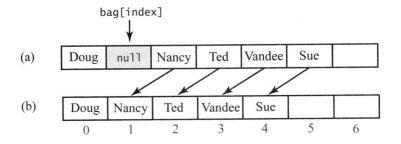

19.31   **Removing a given string: an easier way.** Remember that we are not required to maintain any particular order for a bag's entries. So instead of shifting array entries after removing an entry, we can replace the entry being removed with the last entry in the array, as follows. After locating aString in bag[index], as Figure 19-7a indicates, we copy the entry in bag[numberOfStrings - 1] to bag[index] (Figure 19-7b). We then replace the entry in bag[numberOfStrings - 1] with null, as Figure 19-7c illustrates, and finally decrement numberOfStrings.

FIGURE 19-7   Avoiding a gap in the array while removing an entry

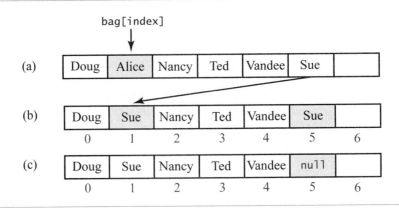

19.32 **Pseudocode for removing a string.** Let's organize our discussion by writing some pseudocode to remove the given string aString from a bag that contains it:

> *Locate* aString *in the array* bag; *assume it occurs at* bag[index]
> bag[index] = bag[numberOfStrings - 1]
> bag[numberOfStrings - 1] = null
> *Decrement the counter* numberOfStrings
> **return true**

This pseudocode assumes that the bag contains aString.

After adding some details to the pseudocode to accommodate the situation in which aString is not in the bag, and to avoid computing numberOfStrings - 1 more than once, as we did in Segment 19.29, the pseudocode appears as follows:

> *Search the array* bag *for* aString
> **if** (aString *is in the bag at* bag[index])
> {
>   *Decrement the counter* numberOfStrings
>   bag[index] = bag[numberOfStrings]
>   bag[numberOfStrings] = **null**
>   **return true**
> }
> **else**
>   **return false**

19.33 **Avoiding duplicate effort.** We can easily translate this pseudocode into the Java method remove. However, if we were to do so—and you might want to—we would see much similarity between our new method and the remove method we wrote earlier in Segment 19.29. In fact, if aString occurs in bag[numberOfStrings - 1], both remove methods will have exactly the same effect. To avoid this duplicate effort, both remove methods can call a private method that performs the removal. We can specify such a method as follows:

```
// Removes and returns the array entry at a given index.
// If no such entry exists, returns null.
private String removeEntry(int giveIndex)
```

Before we implement this private method, let's see if we can use it by revising the remove method in Segment 19.29. Since that method removes and returns the last entry in the array bag, that is, bag[numberOfStrings - 1], its definition can make the call removeEntry(numberOfStrings - 1). Proceeding as if removeEntry were defined and tested, we can define remove as follows:

```
/** Removes one unspecified string from this bag.
    @return either the removed string, if the removal was successful,
    or null otherwise */
public String remove()
{
    String result = removeEntry(numberOfStrings - 1);
    return result;
} // end remove
```

This definition looks good; let's implement the second remove method.

19.34 **The second remove method.** The first remove method does not search for the entry to remove, as it removes the last entry in the array. The second remove method, however, does need to perform a search. Rather than thinking about the details of locating a string in an array right now, let's delegate that task to another private method, which we specify as follows:

```
// Locates a given string within the array bag.
// Returns the index of the string, if located, or -1 otherwise.
private int getIndexOf(String aString)
```

Assuming that this method is defined and tested, we can define our public method as follows:

```java
/** Removes one occurrence of a given string from this bag.
    @param aString  the string to be removed
    @return true if the removal was successful, or false if not */
public boolean remove(String aString)
{
    int index = getIndexOf(aString);
    String result = removeEntry(index);
    return aString.equals(result);
} // end remove
```

Notice that removeEntry returns either the string it removes or null. That is exactly what the first remove method needs, but the second remove method has to return a boolean value. Thus, we need to compare the string we want to remove with the one removeEntry returns to get the desired boolean value.

Question 10 Can the return statement in the previous definition of remove be written as follows?

```java
return result.equals(aString);
```

19.35   **The definition of the private method removeEntry.** Let's look back at the pseudocode we wrote in Segment 19.32 for removing a particular string from the bag. The private method removeEntry assumes that the search for the string is done already, but the basic logic of removing the string is the same as that pseudocode describes. We can revise the pseudocode as follows:

```
// Removes and returns the array entry at a given index.
// If no such entry exists, returns null.
if (the bag is not empty and the given index is not negative)
{
    result = bag[givenIndex]
    Decrement the counter numberOfStrings
    bag[givenIndex] = bag[numberOfStrings]
    bag[numberOfStrings] = null
    return result
}
else
    return null
```

The definition of the method remove given in the previous segment passes the integer returned by getIndexOf to removeEntry. Since getIndexOf can return −1, removeEntry must watch for such an argument. Thus, if the bag is not empty—that is, if numberOfStrings is greater than zero —and givenIndex is greater than or equal to zero, removeEntry removes and returns the array entry at givenIndex by replacing it with the last entry and decrementing the bag's size. Otherwise, the method returns null.

The code for the method is

```java
// Removes and returns the array entry at a given index.
// If no such entry exists, returns null.
private String removeEntry(int givenIndex)
{
    String result = null;
    if (!isEmpty() && (givenIndex >= 0))
    {
        result = bag[givenIndex];                 // entry to remove
        numberOfStrings--;
        bag[givenIndex] = bag[numberOfStrings];   // replace entry with
                                                  // last entry
        bag[numberOfStrings] = null;              // remove last entry
    } // end if
```

```
   return result;
} // end removeEntry
```

19.36   **Locating the string to remove.** We now need to think about locating the string to remove from the bag so we can pass its index to `removeEntry`.

> **Note:** The method `contains` performs the same search that we will use to locate `aString` within the definition of `remove`. Unfortunately, `contains` returns true or false; it does not return the index of the string it locates in the array. Thus, we cannot simply call that method within our method definition.

Design Decision: Should the method `contains` return the index of a located entry?

Should we change the definition of `contains` so that it returns an index instead of a boolean value? No. As a public method, `contains` should not provide a client with such implementation details. Recall our discussion of information hiding and encapsulation in Segment 15.6 of Chapter 15. The client should have no expectation that a bag's entries are in an array, since they are in no particular order. Instead of changing the specifications for `contains`, we will follow our original plan to define a private method to search for a string and return its index.

The definition of `getIndexOf` will be like the definition of `contains`, which we recall here:

```
public boolean contains(String aString)
{
   boolean found = false;

   for (int index = 0; !found && (index < numberOfStrings); index++)
   {
      if (aString.equals(bag[index]))
      {
         found = true;
      } // end if
   } // end for

   return found;
} // end contains
```

The structure of the loop is suitable for the method `getIndexOf`, but we must save the value of `index` when the string is found. The method will return this index instead of a boolean value.

19.37   **The definition of `getIndexOf`.** To revise the loop in `contains` for use in `getIndexOf`, we define an integer variable `where` to record the value of `index` when `aString` equals `bag[index]`. Thus, the loop looks like this:

```
int where = -1;
boolean found = false;

for (int index = 0; !found && (index < numberOfStrings); index++)
{
   if (aString.equals(bag[index]))
   {
      found = true;
      where = index;
   } // end if
} // end for

// Assertion: If where > -1, aString is in the array bag, and it
// equals bag[where]; otherwise, aString is not in the array
```

With this loop as its body, the method getIndexOf returns the value of where. Notice that we initialize where to –1, which is the value to return if aString is not found.

Question 11 What assert statement can you add to the definition of the method getIndexOf just before the return statement to indicate the possible values that the method can return?

Question 12 Revise the definition of the method getIndexOf so that it does not use a boolean variable.

Aside: Thinking positively

Within the method contains, the variable found provides the correct boolean value for the method to return. However, the method getIndexOf returns the value of where instead of the value of found. Since found is used only to control the loop and not as a return value, we can modify the logic somewhat to avoid the use of the not operator !.

Let's use a variable stillLooking instead of found and initialize it to true. Then we can replace the boolean expression !found with stillLooking, as you can see in the following definition of the method getIndexOf:

```java
// Locates a given string within the array bag.
// Returns the index of the string, if located, or -1 otherwise.
private int getIndexOf(String aString)
{
    int where = -1;
    boolean stillLooking = true;

    for (int index = 0; stillLooking && (index < numberOfStrings); index++)
    {
        if (aString.equals(bag[index]))
        {
            stillLooking = false;
            where = index;
        } // end if
    } // end for

    return where;
} // end getIndexOf
```

If aString is found within the array, stillLooking is set to false to end the loop. Some programmers prefer to think positively, as in this revision, while others find !found to be perfectly clear.

19.38   **A revised definition for the method contains.** Having completed the definitions of remove and the private methods they call, we realize that the method contains can call the private method getIndexOf, resulting in a simpler definition than the one given in Segment 19.26. Recall that the expression getIndexOf(aString) returns an integer between 0 and numberOfStrings – 1 if aString is in the bag, or –1 otherwise. That is, getIndexOf(aString) is greater than –1 if aString is in the bag. Thus, we can define contains as follows:

```java
/** Tests whether this bag contains a given string.
    @param aString  the string to locate
    @return true if this bag contains aString, or false otherwise */
public boolean contains(String aString)
{
    return getIndexOf(aString) > -1;
} // end contains
```

We should repeat the tests of `contains` that we made in Listing 19-4. By testing this version of `contains`, we are also testing the private method `getIndexOf`.

Note: Both the method `contains` and the second `remove` method must perform similar searches for a string. By isolating the search in a private method that both `contains` and `remove` can call, we make our code easier to debug and to maintain. This strategy is the same one we used when we moved the removal operation to the private method `removeEntry` that both `remove` methods call.

Programming Tip

Even though you might have written a correct definition of a method, do not hesitate to revise it if you think of a better implementation.

19.39 **Testing `remove` and `clear`.** Our class `BagOfStrings` is essentially complete. Since we have tested all methods except `remove` and `clear`, we assume that they are correct, and we can use them in the tests for `remove` and `clear`. The program `BagDemo3` in Listing 19-5 removes strings from a bag that is not full. As we did earlier in this chapter, you should run similar tests on a full bag. The source code available on the book's website includes such tests in `BagDemo3` and identifies the complete version of the class as `BagOfStrings`.

LISTING 19-5   A program that tests the method `clear` and both `remove` methods

```
/** A demonstration of the methods remove and clear
    in the class BagOfStrings
    @author Frank M. Carrano
*/
public class BagDemo3
{
    public static void main(String[] args)
    {
        // a bag that will not be full

        BagOfStrings aBag = new BagOfStrings();
        System.out.println("A new empty bag:");

        // Removing a string from an empty bag:
        removeFromBag(aBag, null);
        removeFromBag(aBag, "B");

        System.out.println("\nAdding to the bag: A, A, B, A, C, A");
        String[] contentsOfBag1 = {"A", "A", "B", "A", "C", "A"};
        addToBag(aBag, contentsOfBag1);
        displayBag(aBag);
```

```java
      if (aBag.isFull())
         System.out.println("This bag is full but should not be.");
      else
         System.out.println("This bag is not full.");

      removeFromBag(aBag, null);
      displayBag(aBag);
      removeFromBag(aBag, "B");
      displayBag(aBag);

      removeFromBag(aBag, "A");
      displayBag(aBag);

      removeFromBag(aBag, "C");
      displayBag(aBag);

      removeFromBag(aBag, "Z");
      displayBag(aBag);

      System.out.println("\nClearing the bag:");
      aBag.clear();

      if (aBag.isEmpty())
         System.out.println("The bag is empty.");
      else
         System.out.println("The bag is not empty but should be.");

      < Similar code for a full bag should be here. >
   } // end main

   public static void removeFromBag(BagOfStrings bag, String aString)
   {
      if (aString == null)
      {
         System.out.println("\nRemoving a string from the bag:");
         String removedString = bag.remove();
         System.out.println("remove() returns " + removedString);
      }
      else
      {
         System.out.println("\nRemoving \"" + aString +
                            "\" from the bag:");
         boolean result = bag.remove(aString);
         System.out.println("remove(\"" + aString + "\") returns " +
                            result);
      } // end if
   } // end removeFromBag

   < The static methods addToBag and displayBag from Listing 19-3 appear here. >
} // end BagDemo3
```

Output

```
A new empty bag:

Removing a string from the bag:
remove() returns null

Removing "B" from the bag:
remove("B") returns false

Adding to the bag: A, A, B, A, C, A
The bag contains A A B A C A
This bag is not full.

Removing a string from the bag:
remove() returns A
The bag contains A A B A C

Removing "B" from the bag:
remove("B") returns true
The bag contains A A C A

Removing "A" from the bag:
remove("A") returns true
The bag contains A A C

Removing "C" from the bag:
remove("C") returns true
The bag contains A A

Removing "Z" from the bag:
remove("Z") returns false
The bag contains A A

Clearing the bag:
The bag is empty.
. . .
```

Question 13 The output from the program in Listing 19-5 indicates the results of two calls to `remove("B")`. Prior to the second of these calls, the contents of the bag are displayed as A A B A C. Explain why removing "B" from this bag results in the output A A C A.

The Class Definition

19.40   Listing 19-6 gathers the previous method definitions into our final implementation of the class `BagOfStrings`. Notice that the class implements `BagOfStringsInterface`, as given in Listing 19-1. If you haven't learned about interfaces, you can omit the clause `implements BagOfStringsInterface`, which is highlighted in the listing.

LISTING 19-6   The class `BagOfStrings`

```java
/**
   A class that implements a bag of strings by using an array.
   @author Frank M. Carrano
*/
public class BagOfStrings implements BagOfStringsInterface
```

```
{
   private final String[] bag;
   private static final int DEFAULT_CAPACITY = 25;
   private int numberOfStrings;

   /** Creates an empty bag whose capacity is 25. */
   public BagOfStrings()
   {
      this(DEFAULT_CAPACITY);
   } // end default constructor

   /** Creates an empty bag having a given capacity.
       @param capacity  the integer capacity desired */
   public BagOfStrings(int capacity)
   {
      bag = new String[capacity];
      numberOfStrings = 0;
   } // end constructor

   /** Adds a new string to this bag.
       @param newString  the string to be added
       @return true if the addition is successful, or false if not */
   public boolean add(String newString)
   {
      boolean result = true;
      if (isFull())
      {
         result = false;
      }
      else
      {  // assertion: result is true here
         bag[numberOfStrings] = newString;
         numberOfStrings++;
      } // end if

      return result;
   } // end add

   /** Retrieves all strings that are in this bag.
       @return a newly allocated array of all the strings in this bag */
   public String[] toArray()
   {
      String[] result = new String[numberOfStrings];
      for (int index = 0; index < numberOfStrings; index++)
      {
         result[index] = bag[index];
      } // end for

      return result;
```

```java
   } // end toArray

   /** Sees whether this bag is full.
       @return true if this bag is full, or false if not */
   public boolean isFull()
   {
      return numberOfStrings == bag.length;
   } // end isFull

   /** Sees whether this bag is empty.
       @return true if this bag is empty, or false if not */
   public boolean isEmpty()
   {
      return numberOfStrings == 0;
   } // end isEmpty

   /** Gets the capacity of this bag.
       @return the integer number of strings that this bag can hold */
   public int getCapacity()
   {
      return bag.length;
   } // end getCapacity

   /** Gets the number of strings currently in this bag.
       @return the integer number of strings currently in this bag */
   public int getCurrentSize()
   {
      return numberOfStrings;
   } // end getCurrentSize

   /** Counts the number of times a given string appears in this bag.
       @param aString  the string to be counted
       @return the number of times aString appears in this bag */
   public int getFrequencyOf(String aString)
   {
      int counter = 0;
      for (int index = 0; index < numberOfStrings; index++)
      {
         if (aString.equals(bag[index]))
         {
            counter++;
         } // end if
      } // end for

      return counter;
   } // end getFrequencyOf

   /** Tests whether this bag contains a given string.
       @param aString  the string to locate
```

```
       @return true if this bag contains aString, or false otherwise */
public boolean contains(String aString)
{
   return getIndexOf(aString) > -1;
} // end contains

/** Removes all strings from this bag. */
public void clear()
{
   while (!isEmpty())
      remove();
} // end clear

/** Removes one unspecified string from this bag.
    @return either the removed string, if the removal
            was successful, or null otherwise */
public String remove()
{
   String result = removeEntry(numberOfStrings - 1);
   return result;
} // end remove

/** Removes one occurrence of a given string from this bag.
    @param aString  the string to be removed
    @return true if the removal was successful,
            or false if not */
public boolean remove(String aString)
{
   int index = getIndexOf(aString);
   String result = removeEntry(index);

   return aString.equals(result);
} // end remove

// Locates a given string within the array bag.
// Returns the index of the string, if located, or -1 otherwise.
private int getIndexOf(String aString)
{
   int where = -1;
   boolean found = false;
   for (int index = 0; !found && (index < numberOfStrings); index++)
   {
      if (aString.equals(bag[index]))
      {
         found = true;
         where = index;
      } // end if
   } // end for
```

```
        return where;
    } // end getIndexOf

    // Removes and returns the entry at a given index within the array.
    // If no such entry exists, returns null.
    private String removeEntry(int givenIndex)
    {
        String result = null;

        if (!isEmpty() && (givenIndex >= 0))
        {
            result = bag[givenIndex];                    // entry to remove
            numberOfStrings--;
            bag[givenIndex] = bag[numberOfStrings];      // replace entry to
                                                         // remove with last entry

            bag[numberOfStrings] = null;                 // remove last entry
        } // end if

        return result;
    } // end removeEntry
} // end BagOfStrings
```

19.41   **Final tests.** We should consolidate our tests and run them again. This time, we will make use of BagOfStringsInterface, as you can see in the outline of the test program in Listing 19-7. If you have not studied interfaces, simply substitute BagOfStrings for BagOfStringsInterface, shown highlighted in the listing. Note that the complete program is in the source code available on the book's website.

LISTING 19-7   An outline of the class BagDemo

```
/** A demonstration of the class BagOfStrings
    @author Frank M. Carrano
*/
public class BagDemo
{
    public static void main(String[] args)
    {
        BagOfStringsInterface bag = new BagOfStrings();
        . . .
    } // end main

    public static void addToBag(BagOfStringsInterface aBag,
                                String[] content)
    {
        < The body of addToBag is the same as in Listing 19-3. >
    } // end addToBag

    public static void removeFromBag(BagOfStringsInterface aBag,
                                     String aString)
```

videonote
A problem
solved

```
    {
        < The body of removeFromBag is the same as in Listing 19-5. >
    } // end removeFromBag

    public static void displayBag(BagOfStringsInterface aBag)
    {
        < The body of displayBag is the same as in Listing 19-3. >
    } // end displayBag
```

CHAPTER SUMMARY

- A collection is an object that holds a group of other objects.

- A bag is a collection whose entries are in no particular order. When you add an object to a bag, you cannot indicate where in the bag it will be placed.

- You can remove from a bag an object having either a given value or one that is unspecified.

- Carefully specify the methods for a proposed class before you begin to implement them, using tools such as CRC cards and UML notation.

- Identifying and implementing a class's central, or core, methods before any others is a good strategy to use when you expect the class to be lengthy or complex. Use stubs for the remaining methods.

- Test a class at each stage of its development, particularly after adding a significant method.

- You can use a Java array to implement a bag, but other implementations are possible.

- Adding an entry right after the last entry in an array does not disturb the position of existing entries. Likewise, deleting the last entry from an array does not disturb the position of existing entries.

- Because a bag does not maintain its entries in a specific order, deleting an entry does not require you to move subsequent array entries to the next lower position. Instead, you can replace the entry that you want to delete with the last entry in the array and replace the last entry with null.

EXERCISES

1. In the class BagOfStrings, what is the difference between the methods getCapacity and getNumberOfStrings?

2. Why are the methods getIndexOf and removeEntry in the class BagOfStrings private instead of public?

3. To define a new class BagOfCoins to represent a bag of Coin objects, where the class Coin is as defined in Chapter 8, what changes would you need to make to the class BagOfStrings?

4. Suppose that groceryBag is a bag filled to its capacity with ten strings that name various groceries. Write Java statements that remove and count all occurrences of "soup" in groceryBag. Do not remove any other strings from the bag. Report the number of times that "soup" occurred in the bag. Accommodate the possibility that groceryBag does not contain any occurrence of "soup".

5. The *union* of two collections consists of their contents combined into a new collection. Define a method `union` for the class `BagOfStrings` that returns as a new bag the union of the bag receiving the call to the method and the bag that is the method's one argument. Note that the union of two bags might contain duplicate items. For example, if object *x* occurs five times in one bag and twice in another, the union of these bags contains *x* seven times. Specifically, suppose that `bag1` and `bag2` are `BagOfStrings` objects; `bag1` contains the `String` objects a, b, and c; and `bag2` contains the `String` objects b, b, d, and e. After the statement

       BagOfStrings everything = bag1.union(bag2);

   executes, the bag `everything` contains the strings a, b, b, b, c, d, and e. Note that `union` does not affect the contents of `bag1` and `bag2`.

6. The *intersection* of two collections is a new collection of the entries that occur in both collections. That is, it contains the overlapping entries. Define a method `intersection` for the class `BagOfStrings` that returns as a new bag the intersection of the bag receiving the call to the method and the bag that is the method's one argument. Note that the intersection of two bags might contain duplicate items. For example, if object *x* occurs five times in one bag and twice in another, the intersection of these bags contains *x* twice. Specifically, suppose that `bag1` and `bag2` are `BagOfStrings` objects; `bag1` contains the `String` objects a, b, and c; and `bag2` contains the `String` objects b, b, d, and e. After the statement

       BagOfStrings commonItems = bag1.intersection(bag2);

   executes, the bag `commonItems` contains only the string b. If b had occurred in `bag1` twice, `commonItems` would have contained two occurrences of b, since `bag2` also contains two occurrences of b. Note that `intersection` does not affect the contents of `bag1` and `bag2`.

7. The *difference* of two collections is a new collection of the entries that would be left in one collection after removing those that also occur in the second. Define a method `difference` for the class `BagOfStrings` that returns as a new bag the difference of the bag receiving the call to the method and the bag that is the method's one argument. Note that the difference of two bags might contain duplicate items. For example, if object *x* occurs five times in one bag and twice in another, the difference of these bags contains *x* three times. Specifically, suppose that `bag1` and `bag2` are `BagOfStrings` objects; `bag1` contains the `String` objects a, b, and c; and `bag2` contains the `String` objects b, b, d, and e. After the statement

       BagOfStrings leftOver1 = bag1.difference(bag2);

   executes, the bag `leftOver1` contains the strings a and c. After the statement

       BagOfStrings leftOver2 = bag2.difference(bag1);

   executes, the bag `leftOver2` contains the strings b, d, and e. Note that `difference` does not affect the contents of `bag1` and `bag2`.

8. Define a method `equals` for the class `BagOfStrings` that tests whether two bags have exactly the same contents.

9. A *set* is a special bag that does not allow duplicates. Specify each operation for a set of strings by stating its purpose; by describing its parameters; and by writing preconditions, postconditions, and a pseudocode version of its header. Then write a Java interface for the set that includes `javadoc`-style comments.

10. Suppose the class `SetOfStrings` defines the set you specified in Exercise 9. Consider an object of `SetOfStrings` representing an empty set and an object of the class `BagOfStrings` that contains several strings. Write statements at the client level that create a set from the given bag.

11. Write code that accomplishes the following tasks: Consider two bags that can hold strings. One bag is named `letters` and contains several one-letter strings. The other bag is empty and is named `vowels`. One at a time, remove a string from `letters`. If the string contains a vowel, place it into the bag `vowels`; otherwise, return the string to the bag `letters`. After you have checked all of the strings in `letters`, report the number of vowels in the bag `vowels` and the number of times each vowel appears in the bag.

12. A *ring* is a collection of items that has a reference to a current item. An operation—let's call it advance—moves the reference to the next item in the collection. When the reference reaches the last item, the next advance operation will move the reference back to the first item. A ring also has operations to get the current item, add an item, and remove an item. The details of where an item is added and which one is removed are up to you.

Design a class to represent a ring of strings. Specify each operation by stating its purpose, by describing its parameters, and by writing a pseudocode version of its header. Then write a Java interface for the ring that includes javadoc-style comments.

PROJECTS

1. You might have a piggy bank or some other receptacle to hold your spare coins. The piggy bank holds the coins but gives them no other organization. And certainly the bank can contain duplicate coins. A piggy bank is like a bag, but it is simpler, as it has only three operations: You can add a coin to the bank, remove one (you shake the bank, so you have no control over what coin falls out), or see whether the bank is empty.

Design a class PiggyBank, assuming that you have the class Coin from Chapter 8. Specify each method of PiggyBank by stating the method's purpose; by describing its parameters; and by writing preconditions, postconditions, and a pseudocode version of its header. Then write a Java interface for these methods that includes javadoc-style comments.

2. Implement the class PiggyBank, as described in the previous project. Use a bag to hold the Coin objects. This bag belongs to the class BagOfCoins, which is like BagOfStrings but uses Coin instead of String as the data type of the objects it contains.

3. Repeat the previous project, but use an array instead of a bag to hold the Coin objects.

4. Define a class SetOfStrings that represents a set and implements the interface described in Exercise 9. Use the class BagOfStrings in your implementation.

5. Repeat the previous project, but use an array instead of the class BagOfStrings.

6. Imagine a pile of books on your desk. Each book is so large and heavy that you can remove only the top one from the pile. You cannot remove a book from under another one. Likewise, you can add another book to the pile only by placing it on the top of the pile. You cannot add a book beneath another one.

If you represent books by their titles alone, design and implement a class PileOfBooks that you can use to track the books in the pile on your desk.

7. Define a class RingOfStrings that represents a ring and implements the interface described in Exercise 12.

ANSWERS TO SELF-TEST QUESTIONS

1. No. The two methods have identical signatures. Recall that a method's return type is not a part of its signature. These methods have the same name and parameter list.

2. Yes. The two methods have different signatures. They are overloaded methods.

3. No. The two values are equal only when a bag is full.

4. The client would have to call the method getCurrentSize to learn how many strings were in the array that was returned. With the present design, if the client contained a statement such as

```
String[] bagContents = myBag.toArray();
```

bagContents.length would be the number of strings in the bag.

5. The statements set the first element of bag to null. The value of numberOfStrings does not change, so it is 5.

6. The bag aBag is empty. When displayBag is called, the statement

```
String[] bagArray = aBag.toArray();
```

executes. When toArray is called, the statement

```
String[] result = new String[numberOfStrings];
```

executes. Since aBag is empty, numberOfStrings is zero. Thus, the array result is empty. The loop in toArray is skipped and the empty array is returned and assigned to bagArray. Since bagArray.length is zero, the loop in displayBag is skipped. The result of the call displayBag(aBag) is simply the line

The bag contains

7.
```
public void clear()
{
   while (remove() != null)
   {
   } // end while
} // end clear
```

8. Since numberOfStrings is decremented, the string in bag[numberOfStrings] will be ignored by all methods. If this element contains the only reference to the string, the string will continue to exist, thereby wasting memory. Setting bag[numberOfStrings] to null causes the memory assigned to the string to be recycled.

9. A string in the array bag, other than the last one, would be set to null. The remaining strings would no longer be in consecutive elements of the array. We could either rearrange the strings to get rid of the null entry or modify other methods to skip any null entry.

10. No. If result were null—and that is quite possible—a NullPointerException would occur.

11.
```
assert ((where >= 0) && (where < numberOfStrings)) || (where == -1);
```

12.
```
private int getIndexOf(String aString)
{
   int where = -1;
   for (int index = 0; (where == -1) && (index < numberOfStrings);
        index++)
   {
      if (aString.equals(bag[index]))
         where = index;
   } // end for

   return where;
} // end getIndexOf
```

or

```
private int getIndexOf(String aString)
{
   int where = numberOfStrings - 1;
   while ((where > -1) && !aString.equals(bag[index]))
      where--;

   return where;
} // end getIndexOf
```

13. After locating "B" in the bag, the remove method replaces it with the last entry in the array bag, which is "C". The method also decreases the current number of strings in the bag so that only the relevant array entries are displayed.

Chapter

20

Arrays Continued

Contents

Prerequisites

Objectives

After studying this chapter, you should be able to
- Write a for-each loop to cycle through all entries in an array
- Resize an array
- Define a method whose invocation can contain an arbitrary number of arguments
- Make use of the parameter in the method `main`
- Create and use an array having more than one dimension
- Describe and use a ragged array.
- Use parallel arrays but know how to avoid them

Chapter 18 described the essentials of defining and using an array, while Chapter 19 used those fundamentals in developing a class. This chapter introduces more array features, some more important than others.

The ordinary one-index arrays that we have used up until now are known as one-dimensional arrays. We make this distinction now because this chapter will introduce you to arrays that use more than one index. Such arrays are said to be multidimensional. But before we examine them, we will talk more about one-dimensional arrays.

More About One-Dimensional Arrays

Among our topics in this section are using a for-each loop with arrays, resizing a full array, and writing a method that has a variable number of parameters.

The For-Each Loop Applied to Arrays

20.1 Segment 13.10 in Chapter 13 introduced the for-each loop, which is a variant of the `for` loop used with collections of data. In that segment, we used a for-each loop to iterate through all the objects in an enumeration. We can use a similar for-each loop to process all the values in an array.

For example, the following statements compute the sum of the integers in an array:

```java
int[] anArray = {1, 2, 3, 4, 5};
int sum = 0;
for (int element : anArray)
   sum = sum + element;
System.out.println(sum);
```

Similarly, the following statements display all the strings in an array:

```java
String[] friends = {"Gavin", "Gail", "Jared", "Jessie"};
for (String name : friends)
   System.out.println(name);
```

Syntax: The for-each statement with arrays

You can use a variant of the `for` statement, called the for-each statement, to cycle through every entry in a group of values. When that group is an array, the for-each statement has the following form:

> **for** (*entry-type variable* : *array-name*)
>   *body*

The body of the loop executes once for each entry in the array and has a reference to each entry in *variable*. The data type of the entries in the array is *entry-type*. Note that you should not use for-each loops with partially filled arrays.

Question 1 What for-each loop could you use to process the entire array, `text`, of strings instead of the following loop?

```java
int index = 0;
while (index < text.length)
{
   System.out.println(text[index]);
   index++;
} // end while
```

Question 2 What for loop could replace the for-each loop given in the previous segment to compute the sum of the integers in the array `anArray`?

Resizing an Array

20.2   An array has a fixed size, which is chosen by either the programmer or the client before the array is created. A fixed-size array is like a classroom. If the room contains 40 desks but only 30 students, we waste 10 desks. If 40 students are taking the course, the room is full and cannot accommodate anyone else. Likewise, if we do not use all of the locations in an array, we waste memory. If we need more, we are out of luck.

Some applications can use an array that has a limited length. For instance, the number of passengers on a given aircraft or the number of ticket holders to a movie must not exceed a known maximum. For other applications, however, the size of a collection can grow without bound. For example, the previous chapter uses a fixed-size array to represent the entries in a bag. When the array, and hence the bag, becomes full, subsequent requests to add an entry to it are denied. That is, calls to the add method return false.

We will now show you how a group of items can be as large as you want—within the limits of your computer's memory—but still use an array to represent it.

20.3   **The strategy.** When a classroom is full, one way to accommodate additional students is to move to a larger room. In a similar manner, when an array becomes full, you can move its contents to a larger array. This process is called **resizing** an array. Figure 20-1 shows two arrays: an original array of five consecutive memory locations and another array—twice the size of the original array—that is in another part of the computer's memory. If you copy the data from the original smaller array to the beginning of the new larger array, the result will be like expanding the original array. The only glitch in this scheme is the name of the new array: You want it to be the same as the name of the old array. You will see how to accomplish this momentarily.

FIGURE 20-1   Resizing an array copies its contents to a larger second array

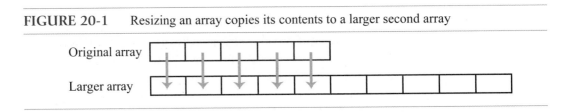

Suppose we have an array that myArray references, as Figure 20-2a illustrates. We first define an alias oldArray that also references the array, as Figure 20-2b shows. The next step is to create a new array that is larger than the original array and let myArray reference this new array. As pictured in Figure 20-2c, the new array typically doubles the size of the original array. The final step copies the contents of the original array to the new array (Figure 20-2d) and then discards the original array. The following pseudocode summarizes these steps:

```
oldArray = myArray
myArray = a new array whose length is 2 * oldArray.length
Copy entries from the original array—oldArray—to the new array—myArray
oldArray = null // discard old array
```

FIGURE 20-2 (a) An array; (b) two references to the same array; (c) the original array variable now references a new, larger array; (d) the entries in the original array are copied to the new array

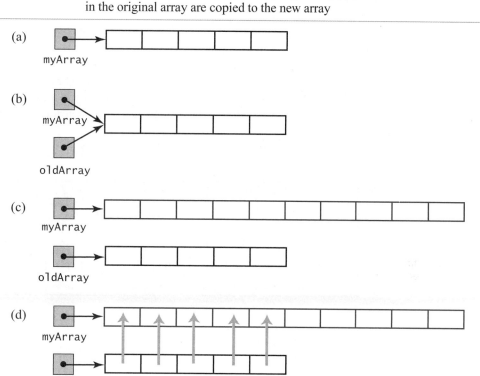

(a) myArray

(b) myArray
oldArray

(c) myArray
oldArray

(d) myArray
oldArray

 Note: To say that we "resize" an array is really a misnomer, since an array's length cannot be changed. The process of resizing an array creates a completely new array that contains the entries of the original array. The new array is given the name of the original array—in other words, a reference to the new array is assigned to the variable that had referenced the original array. The original array is then discarded.

 Note: When an array is no longer referenced, its memory is recycled during garbage collection, just as occurs with any other object.

20.4 **The code.** While we could simply translate the previous pseudocode into Java, much of the work can be done by using the method `Arrays.copyOf`, which Segment 18.29 of Chapter 18 introduced. For example, let's work with a simple array of integers:

```
int[] myArray = {10, 20, 30, 40, 50};
```

At this point, `myArray` references the array, as Figure 20-3a shows. Next, we'll call `Arrays.copyOf`. The method's first parameter, `sourceArray`, is assigned the reference in the variable `myArray`, as Figure 20-3b implies. Next the method creates a new, larger array and copies the entries in the argument array to it (Figure 20-3c). Finally, the method returns a reference to the new array (Figure 20-3d), and we assign this reference to myArray as follows:

```
myArray = Arrays.copyOf(myArray, 2 * myArray.length);
```

FIGURE 20-3   The effect of the statement
myArray = Arrays.copyOf(myArray, 2 * myArray.length);
(a) The argument array; (b) the parameter that references the argument array; (c) a new, larger array that gets the contents of the argument array; (d) the return value that references the new array

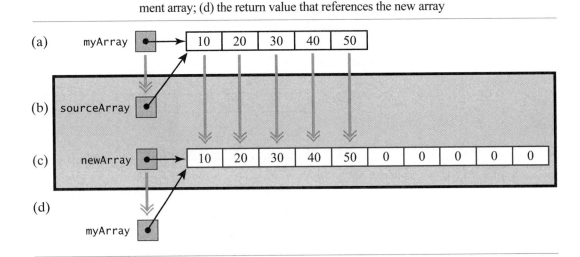

20.5   Resizing an array is not as attractive as it might first seem. Each time you expand the size of an array, you must copy its contents. If you were to expand an array by one element each time you needed additional space in the array, the process would be expensive in terms of computing time. For example, if a 50-element array is full, accommodating another entry would require you to copy the array to a 51-element array. Adding yet another entry would require that you copy the 51-element array to a 52-element array, and so on. Each addition would cause the array to be copied. If you added 100 entries to the original 50-entry array, you would copy the array 100 times.

However, expanding the array by *m* elements spreads the copying cost over *m* additions instead of just one. Doubling the size of an array each time it becomes full is a typical approach. For example, when you add an entry to a full array of 50 entries, you copy the 50-element array to a 100-element array before completing the addition. The next 49 additions then can be made quickly without copying the array. Thus, you will have added 50 entries to the original list but will have copied the array only once.

 Note: When increasing the size of an array, its entries are copied to a larger array. You should expand the array sufficiently to reduce the impact of the cost of copying. A common practice is to double the size of the array.

Question 3 Consider the array of strings that the following statement defines:

```
String[] text = {"cat", "dog", "bird", "snake"};
```

What Java statements will increase the capacity of the array text by five elements without altering its current contents?

Question 4 Consider an array, text, of strings. If the number of strings placed into this array is less than its length (capacity), how could you decrease the array's length without altering its current contents? Assume that the number of strings is in the variable size.

A Problem Solved: An Expandable Bag

> The previous chapter developed a class to represent a data organization known as a bag. That implementation uses a fixed-size array to hold the data, and so the bag could become full. We want to revise the class so that a bag can hold as many entries as we desire. Thus, if the array gets full, we will create a larger array—using what we just learned—the next time a client requests another addition.

20.6   **The approach.** By examining Listing 19-6 in Segment 19.40 of the previous chapter, we can see what we need to revise. Let's itemize these tasks:

- Change the name of the class to ExpandableBagOfStrings so we can distinguish between our two implementations.
- Remove the modifier final from the declaration of the array bag to enable its resizing.
- Change the name of the constant DEFAULT_CAPACITY to DEFAULT_INITIAL_CAPACITY. Although unnecessary, this change simply clarifies the new purpose of the constant, since the bag's capacity will increase as necessary. Make the same change in the default constructor, which uses the constant.
- Change the names of the constructors to match the new class name.
- Revise the definition of the method add to always accommodate a new entry. The method will never return false.
- Revise the definition of the method isFull to always return false. A bag will never become full.

The rest of the class will remain unchanged.

20.7   **The method add.** Revising the method add is the only substantial task in this list, so let's focus on it. Here is its original definition as it appears in Listing 19-6:

```java
/** Adds a new string to the bag.
    @param newString  the string to be added
    @return true if the addition is successful, or false if not */
public boolean add(String newString)
{
   boolean result = true;
   if (isFull())
   {
      result = false;
   }
   else
   {  // assertion: result is true here
      bag[numberOfStrings] = newString;
      numberOfStrings++;
   } // end if
```

```
      return result;
   } // end add
```

Since the bag will never be full, the method isFull will always return false. Thus, we can no longer call isFull to see whether the array bag is full. We instead can define a private method to both make this check and resize the array bag, if necessary. Let's name the method ensureCapacity. Assuming that we have this private method, we can revise the method add as follows:

```
/** Adds a new string to the bag.
    @param newString  the string to be added
    @return true */
public boolean add(String newString)
{
   ensureCapacity();
   bag[numberOfStrings] = newString;
   numberOfStrings++;

   return true;
} // end add
```

20.8   **The private method ensureCapacity.** The array bag is full when numberOfStrings equals bag.length. When that is the case, we will resize bag using the technique described earlier in Segment 20.4. Thus, the definition of ensureCapacity is straightforward:

```
private void ensureCapacity()
{
   if (numberOfStrings == bag.length)
      bag = Arrays.copyOf(bag, 2 * bag.length);
} // end ensureCapacity
```

20.9   **The class ExpandableBagOfStrings.** Listing 20-1 contains our revised class.

LISTING 20-1   The class ExpandableBagOfStrings

```
import java.util.Arrays;
/**
   A class that implements a bag of strings by using an array.
   The bag is never full.
   @author Frank M. Carrano
*/
public class ExpandableBagOfStrings implements BagOfStringsInterface
{
   private String[] bag; // cannot be final due to doubling
   private static final int DEFAULT_INITIAL_CAPACITY = 25;
   private int numberOfStrings;

   /** Creates an empty bag whose initial capacity is 25. */
   public ExpandableBagOfStrings()
   {
      this(DEFAULT_INITIAL_CAPACITY);
   } // end default constructor

   /** Creates an empty bag having a given initial capacity.
       @param capacity  the integer capacity desired */
```

```java
public ExpandableBagOfStrings(int capacity)
{
    bag = new String[capacity];
    numberOfStrings = 0;
} // end constructor

/** Adds a new string to the bag.
    @param newString  the string to be added
    @return true */
public boolean add(String newString)
{
    ensureCapacity();
    bag[numberOfStrings] = newString;
    numberOfStrings++;

    return true;
} // end add

/** Sees whether this bag is full.
    @return true if this bag is full, or false if not */
public boolean isFull()
{
    return false;
} // end isFull
```

< *All of the remaining methods that appear in Listing 19-6 are here.* >

```java
private void ensureCapacity()
{
    if (numberOfStrings == bag.length)
        bag = Arrays.copyOf(bag, 2 * bag.length);
} // end ensureCapacity
} // end ExpandableBagOfStrings
```

Note: **Inheritance**

Instead of the definition of ExpandableBagOfStrings just given, we could have used inheritance to extend the class BagOfStrings. Such an approach would eliminate the redundancy in the definitions of these two classes and explicitly show their relationship. After you study Chapter 27, you will be able to use inheritance to define ExpandableBagOfStrings.

Design Decision: You might wonder about some of the decisions we made while defining the class ExpandableBagOfStrings in Listing 20-1, such as the following:

- Why is the method add a boolean method and not a void method? It always returns true!
- Why did we bother to define isFull? The bag is never full!
- Why did we define the private method ensureCapacity? Only one method, add, calls it!

The answers to the first two questions are the same: We implemented BagOfStringsInterface, so we followed its specifications. As a result, we have two different implementations, each of which can be used by the same client. Our answer to the third question reflects our approach to problem solving. To implement add, we needed to answer two questions: When is an array full, and how do we expand a full array? Rather than risking the distraction of answering these questions while we were defining the method add, we chose to specify a private method to provide those answers. Admittedly, the definition of this private method turned out to be short. We could now integrate the body of the private method into that of add, but we have no pressing reason to do so.

Question 5 What is the definition of a constructor that you could add to the class ExpandableBagOfStrings to initialize the bag to the contents of a given array?

Question 6 In the definition of the constructor described in the previous question, is it necessary to copy the entries from the argument array to the array bag, or would a simple assignment (bag = contents) be sufficient?

20.10   **Testing the class.** The program in Listing 20-2 demonstrates the class ExpandableBagOfStrings. Notice that we create a bag whose initial capacity is only 3. This allows us to easily test the bag's ability to increase its capacity. For example, when the fourth item is added, the bag's capacity is doubled to 6. At the seventh addition, the capacity is doubled again, this time to 12.

LISTING 20-2   A program that demonstrates the class ExpandableBagOfStrings

```
/** A demonstration of the class ExpandableBagOfStrings
    @author Frank M. Carrano
*/
public class ExpandableBagDemo
{
   public static void main(String[] args)
   {
      // a bag whose initial capacity is small
      BagOfStringsInterface aBag = createEmptyBag(3);

      System.out.println("\nAdding to the bag more strings than" +
                   "\nits initial capacity: A, D, B, A, C, A, D");
      String[] contentsOfBag = {"A", "D", "B", "A", "C", "A", "D"};
      addToBag(aBag, contentsOfBag);

      displayBag(aBag);
      testIsEmpty(aBag, false);
      testIsFull(aBag, false);

      System.out.println("\nRemoving B from the bag: " +
                   "remove(\"B\") returns " + aBag.remove("B"));
      removeFromBag(aBag, 5);
```

```java
      displayBag(aBag);
      testIsEmpty(aBag, false);
      testIsFull(aBag, false);
   } // end main

   private static BagOfStringsInterface
              createEmptyBag(int initialCapacity)
   {
      BagOfStringsInterface bag = new ExpandableBagOfStrings(3);
      testIsEmpty(bag, true);
      System.out.println("The initial capacity of the bag is " +
                      bag.getCapacity());

      return bag;
   } // end createEmptyBag

   // Precondition: If bag is empty, empty should be true, else false.
   private static void testIsEmpty(BagOfStringsInterface bag,
                                   boolean empty)
   {
      System.out.print("\nTesting isEmpty with ");
      if (empty)
         System.out.println("an empty bag:");
      else
         System.out.println("a bag that is not empty:");

      System.out.print("isEmpty finds the bag ");
      if (empty && bag.isEmpty())
         System.out.println("empty: OK.");
      else if (empty)
         System.out.println("not empty, but it is: ERROR.");
      else if (!empty && bag.isEmpty())
         System.out.println("empty, but it is not empty: ERROR.");
      else
         System.out.println("not empty: OK.");
   } // end testIsEmpty

   // Precondition: If bag is full, full should be true, else false.
   private static void testIsFull(BagOfStringsInterface bag,
                                  boolean full)
   {
      < The body of this method is analogous to the body of testIsEmpty. >
   } // end testIsFull

   < The static methods addToBag and displayBag from Listing 19-3 and removeFromBag from
     Listing 19-5 of Chapter 19 appear here. >
} // end ExpandableBagDemo
```

Output

```
The bag is empty.
The initial capacity of the bag is 3

Adding to the bag more strings than
its initial capacity: A, D, B, A, C, A, D
The bag contains A D B A C A D
The capacity of the bag is 12
The bag contains 7 strings.
The bag is not empty.
The bag is not full.

Removing B from the bag:
Removing 5 more strings from the bag: D A C A D
The bag contains A
The capacity of the bag is 12
The bag contains 1 strings.
The bag is not empty.
The bag is not full.
```

An Arbitrary Number of Arguments

20.11   You can write one parameter in a method's header to correspond to any number of arguments—including none—in the call to the method. This feature is called **varargs**, and the parameter sometimes is called a **varargs parameter**. For example, let's write a method that returns the largest integer among any number of integers given to it as arguments. The class MyMath in Listing 20-3 defines such a method, maximum, which we can invoke as follows:

```
int large1 = MyMath.maximum(2, 4, 6, 0, 1, 3); // 6
int large2 = MyMath.maximum(-1);                // -1
int large3 = MyMath.maximum(99, 4, -55, 0, 1);  // 99
```

The variable large1 is assigned the value 6, large2 is −1, and large3 is 99.

The definition of the method maximum has one parameter in its header to represent the arguments in each of its invocations. As you might have guessed, the parameter is actually a reference to an array—in this case, an array of integers. You do not use array notation, however, when you write the method's header. Instead, three dots and a space immediately follow the data type of the arguments. For example, the header of the method maximum is

```
public static int maximum(int... integers)
```

As you can see in the method's definition given in Listing 20-3, you treat the parameter integers as you would any other array parameter.

Since maximum initializes the variable result to integers[0], this particular method must be given at least one argument.

LISTING 20-3   A class defining a method that accepts any positive number
                of arguments

```
/** A class that defines a method having a varargs parameter.
    @author Frank M. Carrano
*/
```

```
public class MyMath
{
   /** Finds the largest of any positive number of integers.
       @return the largest of the given integers */
   public static int maximum(int... integers)
   {
      int result = integers[0];
      for (int number : integers)
         result = Math.max(result, number);

      return result;
   } // end maximum
} // end MyMath
```

Note: You can call a method having a varargs parameter by passing it either a list of values separated by commas, as in the previous examples, or an array of values, as in the following example:

```
int largestInArray = MyMath.maximum(intArray);
```

Here, `intArray` is an array of integers; the method `maximum` returns the largest integer in `intArray`.

The converse is not true, however. For example, if a method has the header

```
public static int minimum(int[] integers)
```

you could not call it by using a statement such as this one:

```
int smallestInArray = MyMath.minimum(99, 4, -55, 0, 1); // ILLEGAL!
```

Note: **The parameter for an arbitrary number of arguments**
A method header can declare a parameter that will correspond to any number of arguments, separated by commas, in the call to the method. Such a parameter has the following form:

argument-type... parameter-name

The three dots indicate that the method's body will treat *parameter-name* as a one-dimensional array of the corresponding arguments. The data type of these arguments—that is, the entries in the implicit array—is *argument-type*.

The following rules apply:

- A method can have only one varargs parameter
- If a method declares several parameters, any varargs parameter must appear last in the header

Note that a client could pass an array of values to a varargs parameter instead of writing a comma-separated sequence of arguments.

20.12 **Constructors.** Since a constructor can declare parameters, it can have a varargs parameter. For example, we could add the following constructor to the class ExpandableBagOfStrings, as given in Listing 20-1:

```
/** Creates a bag containing the given strings. */
public ExpandableBagOfStrings(String... contents)
{
    bag = Arrays.copyOf(contents, contents.length);
    numberOfStrings = contents.length;
} // end default constructor
```

If aBag is an object of ExpandableBagOfStrings, the statement

```
aBag = new ExpandableBagOfStrings("alpha", "beta", "gamma");
```

creates a bag containing the three given strings. The bag's initial capacity is 3.

Why did we make a copy of contents before assigning it to bag? As the previous segment noted, you can pass a reference to an array as the argument corresponding to a varargs parameter. For example, suppose we define the following array of strings:

```
String[] stringData = {"alpha", "beta", "gamma");
```

The statement

```
aBag = new ExpandableBagOfStrings(stringData);
```

passes stringData to the previous constructor and creates a bag containing the three strings in the array. Assigning a copy of the argument array to the array bag is necessary, because otherwise the client could use the reference that it has to the argument array—stringData in this example—to corrupt the bag's data after the bag has been created.

Note: **Caution!**
When a class defines a default constructor—remember that it has no parameters—you cannot invoke another constructor having one varargs parameter, and no others, without passing it arguments. For example, the class ExpandableBagOfStrings has a default constructor. If it also has the constructor defined in this segment, a statement such as

```
aBag = new ExpandableBagOfStrings();
```

would call the default constructor. This is good.

If, however, ExpandableBagOfStrings did not define a default constructor, but did define the previous constructor having a varargs parameter, the previous statement would invoke this constructor and create an empty bag. This might seem fine at first, but it really is not! Not only is the bag empty, but also its capacity is zero. That is, both numberOfStrings and bag.length are zero. What happens when you try to add an entry to this bag? The method add calls ensureCapacity, which tries to double the length of the array. Two times zero is still zero! A bag with a capacity of zero is useless.

Programming Tip
Use varargs parameters with caution, and avoid using one with a constructor when it is the only parameter. Using a parameter that has an explicit array type will avoid the problems highlighted in the previous note.

Question 7 If you were to add a constructor like the one just given in Segment 20.12 to the class BagOfStrings, given in Listing 19-6 of the previous chapter, what special considerations, if any, would be necessary?

Question 8 What is the effect of calling the method maximum, as given in Listing 20-3, without any arguments?

Question 9 What method definition could you add to the class MyMath, as given in Listing 20-3, to compute the smallest value among any number of double values given to it as arguments?

The Parameter in the Method main

20.13   We have written many main methods. Each begins as

```
public static void main(String[] args)
```

and up to now, you likely have written this line without giving it much thought. But having learned about arrays, you should now recognize that the parameter args represents an array of strings. Although most main methods ignore this parameter, you can make use of it.

videonote
Advanced array
manipulation

When you execute a Java program, you can provide strings, called **command-line arguments**, to the method main. The Java runtime environment (JRE) places these strings into an array, which it passes to main as it calls the method. Within main, you can access these strings by referencing the elements in the array args, just as you do for any other array.

For example, if you use the command

```
java MyProgram Hello out there!
```

to execute the program MyProgram, three strings—"Hello", "out", and "there!"—are placed into an array and passed to MyProgram's main method. If args is main's parameter, you can reference these strings as args[0], args[1], and args[2], respectively. You can use command-line arguments, in conjunction with decision statements within the main method, to affect the method's logic. Even if you use an IDE instead of the command line to run your programs, you will be able to pass command-line arguments to the JRE. The IDE's documentation should tell you how to do this.

■ Multidimensional Arrays

20.14   Until now, the data that we have organized into an array has been like the items on a grocery list. The entries appear one after the other. But other everyday data organizations are two-dimensional. Some examples are a spreadsheet, a chessboard, a tic-tac-toe game, or a Sudoku puzzle, as Figure 20-4 illustrates. You can store the data from any one of these organizations in an array having two indices.

FIGURE 20-4   Everyday data organizations that are two-dimensional

  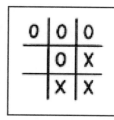 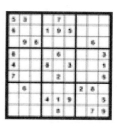

For example, suppose we wanted to store the 60 dollar amounts shown in Figure 20-5, ignoring the bold items, which are just labeling. If we use an array with one index, the array will have a length of 60, and keeping track of which entry goes with which index would be difficult and confusing. On the other hand, if we allow ourselves two indices, we can use one index for the row and one index for the column. This arrangement is illustrated in Figure 20-6. As was true for the simple arrays you have already seen, you begin numbering indices with 0 rather than 1. If the array is named `table`, and it has two indices, the Java notation `table[3][2]` specifies the entry in the fourth row and third column. By convention, we think of the first index as denoting the row and the second as denoting the column.

Arrays that have exactly two indices can be displayed on paper as a two-dimensional table and are called **two-dimensional arrays**. Arrays, however, can have several indices. A **multidimensional array** simply has more than one index. An *n*-dimensional array has *n* indices. The ordinary one-index arrays that we have used up to now are **one-dimensional arrays**.

FIGURE 20-5   A table of dollar amounts

The effect of various interest rates on $1000 when compounded annually (rounded to whole dollars)						
Year	**5.00%**	**5.50%**	**6.00%**	**6.50%**	**7.00%**	**7.50%**
1	$1050	$1055	$1060	$1065	$1070	$1075
2	$1103	$1113	$1124	$1134	$1145	$1156
3	$1158	$1174	$1191	$1208	$1225	$1242
4	$1216	$1239	$1262	$1286	$1311	$1335
5	$1276	$1307	$1338	$1370	$1403	$1436
6	$1340	$1379	$1419	$1459	$1501	$1543
7	$1407	$1455	$1504	$1554	$1606	$1659
8	$1477	$1535	$1594	$1655	$1718	$1783
9	$1551	$1619	$1689	$1763	$1838	$1917
10	$1629	$1708	$1791	$1877	$1967	$2061

FIGURE 20-6   Row and column indices for an array named `table`; `table[3][2]` is the element in the fourth row and third column

Row index 3		table[3][2]		Column index 2		
Indices	0	1	2	3	4	5
0	1050	1055	1060	1065	1070	1075
1	1103	1113	1124	1134	1145	1156
2	1158	1174	1191	1208	1225	1242
3	1216	1239	1262	1286	1311	1335
4	1276	1307	1338	1370	1403	1436
5	1340	1379	1419	1459	1501	1543
6	1407	1455	1504	1554	1606	1659
7	1477	1535	1594	1655	1718	1783
8	1551	1619	1689	1763	1838	1917
9	1629	1708	1791	1877	1967	2061

The Basics

20.15 Arrays having multiple indices are handled in much the same way as arrays having only one index. To declare and create the array `keyData` of integers that has 4 rows and 6 columns, we write

```java
int[][] keyData = new int[4][6];
```

You can have arrays with any number of indices. To get more indices, you just use more square brackets in the declaration.

Indexed variables for multidimensional arrays are just like indexed variables for arrays of one dimension, except that they have multiple indices. Each index is enclosed in a pair of square brackets. For example, the following statements set all the elements in `keyData` to zero:

```java
for (int row = 0; row < 4; row++)
    for (int column = 0; column < 6; column++)
        keyData[row][column] = 0;
```

Note that we used two `for` loops, one nested within the other. This is a common way of stepping through the indexed variables in a two-dimensional array. If we had three indices, we would use three nested loops, and so on for higher numbers of indices.

As was true of the indexed variables for a one-dimensional array, indexed variables for a multidimensional array all have the same data type and can be used anywhere that a variable of that type is allowed. For example, for the two-dimensional array `keyData`, an indexed variable such as `keyData[3][5]` is a variable of type `int` and can be used anyplace that an ordinary `int` variable can be used.

Programming Tip

When writing an indexed variable for a multidimensional array, enclose each index in square brackets. For example, `keyData[3][5]` is the element in the fourth row and sixth column of the array `keyData`. Some programming languages use the notation `keyData[3, 5]` for this element, but Java does not. This notation will cause a syntax error.

20.16 **Method parameters and return values.** A multidimensional array can be a parameter of a method. For example, the following method header has a two-dimensional array as a parameter:

```java
public static void clearArray(double[][] array)
```

The array's data type is `double[][]`, so it has two indices, and each entry is a `double` value.

Likewise, a method can return a multidimensional array. A method that returns a two-dimensional array of strings could have a header such as the following one:

```java
public String[][] getTable()
```

Note: Array parameters and return types do not indicate the size of the array.

Java's Representation

20.17 Java implements a multidimensional array as a one-dimensional array of other array objects. For example, consider the array

```java
int[][] keyData = new int[4][6];
```

The array `keyData` is in fact a one-dimensional array of length 4, and the data type of its elements is `int[]`. Thus, each entry in the array `keyData` is a reference to a one-dimensional array of length 6, as Figure 20-7 illustrates. The previous Java statement actually declares and creates `keyData` as follows:

1. It allocates the variable `keyData` (the gray box in the figure) and declares that it will reference a two-dimensional array:

    ```
    int[][] keyData;
    ```

2. It allocates a one-dimensional array whose elements will reference one-dimensional arrays:

    ```
    keyData = new int[4][];
    ```

3. It allocates four one-dimensional arrays that can hold up to six integers each and assigns them to the elements of the array created in step 2:

    ```
    for (int index = 0; index < keyData.length; index++)
        keyData[index] = new int[6];
    ```

Thus, a two-dimensional array is a one-dimensional array of one-dimensional arrays. A three-dimensional array is a one-dimensional array of two-dimensional arrays, and so on.

FIGURE 20-7   A two-dimensional array is really a one-dimensional array of one-dimensional arrays

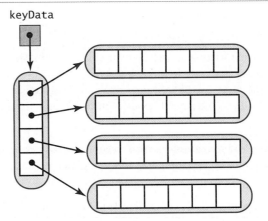

Normally, you can ignore how Java represents a multidimensional array, since this detail is handled automatically by the compiler. However, sometimes you can profit from this knowledge. For example, consider the nested `for` loops in Segment 20.15 that filled the two-dimensional array `keyData` with zeros. We used the constants 4 and 6 to control the `for` loops, but it would be better style to use the data field `length` instead. To do so, we need to think in terms of an array of arrays. In this example, `keyData.length` is the number of rows in `keyData`, and `keyData[row].length` is the number of columns in the row whose index is `row`. Using these observations, we can revise the nested loops as follows:

```
for (int row = 0; row < keyData.length; row++)
    for (int column = 0; column < keyData[row].length; column++)
        keyData[row][column] = 0;
```

20.18 **Declaring and initializing a two-dimensional array.** Segment 18.6 in Chapter 18 showed you how to declare and initialize a one-dimensional array. We can use a similar notation for a two-dimensional array, now that we know how Java represents it.

```
String[][] greek = { {"alpha", "beta", "gamma", "delta"},
                     {"Alpha", "Beta", "Gamma", "Delta"},
                     {"ALPHA", "BETA", "GAMMA", "DELTA"} };
```

The array greek has three rows and four columns. The first row contains lowercase strings, each string in the second row begins with a capital letter, and the last row contains strings in uppercase.

Note: Avoiding zero as an array index
Although you need to get used to using 0 as an array index, some applications involve integer numbering schemes that begin at 1 instead of 0. For example, anything to do with a calendar involves 1 through 31 for the dates in a month. Typically, a programmer would adjust a date by subtracting 1 before using it as an index to an array. Another approach is to reserve extra memory for the array and then ignore the elements having 0 as an index.

For example, if you want to represent your schedule for a month, you might create a one-dimensional array of Schedule objects as follows:

```
public static final int DAYS_PER_MONTH = 31;
Schedule[] month = new Schedule[DAYS_PER_MONTH + 1];
```

Since we plan to use the indices 1 through 31, we create one extra element for the array month. To prevent us from using month[0] accidentally, we should not change its default initial value of null—although setting it to null yourself is a good idea.

To record our schedule for a year, we could use a two-dimensional array such as the following:

```
public static final int DAYS_PER_MONTH = 31;
public static final int MONTHS_PER_YEAR = 12;
Schedule[][] year =
            new Schedule[DAYS_PER_MONTH + 1][MONTHS_PER_YEAR + 1];
```

By creating one extra row and one extra column, we can use 1 through 31 as row indices and 1 through 12 as column indices, thereby avoiding 0 as an index. We are wasting one row of 13 elements and one column of 32 elements. We can return the extra row to the system and prevent its use by writing

```
year[0] = null;
```

This is possible because year is an array of rows. We cannot, however, deallocate the extra column.

Programming Tip
Consider the space you would waste before deciding to avoid using 0 as an index.

Question 10 The following specifications are for a method that doubles the integer values given to it in a two-dimensional array. What is the method's definition?

```
/** Returns a two-dimensional array whose values are twice those
    in the given two-dimensional array. The argument is unchanged. */
public static int[][] doubleArray(int[][] anArray)
```

Question 11 What will the following statements display?

```java
int[][] x = new int[5][3];
for (int r = 0; r < 5; r++)
   for (int c = 0; c < 3; c++)
      x[r][c] = r + c;

for (int[] row : x)
{
   for (int v : row)
      System.out.print(v + " ");
   System.out.println();
} // end for
System.out.println();
```

A Problem Solved: Processing a Digital Image

> Imagine that we need to locate the brightest features of a given digital picture. When the numeric value of a pixel is above a certain threshold value, we should assume that it is bright enough to retain. We will ignore any pixels that do not exceed this threshold. The threshold value is the product of a given factor and the average of all the pixel values in the array.

20.19   **Discussion.** When Chapter 5 introduced graphical drawing in Java, it defined a pixel as a point of light. Any digital image typically is formed as a rectangular arrangement of evenly spaced pixels. This arrangement can be represented in Java as a two-dimensional array of real numbers. Each number describes the color and intensity of its corresponding pixel. Various programs can adjust these values and thereby manipulate the picture they represent. The computations necessary for manipulating a digital image can become involved. The solution to the problem at hand, however, is not complicated, and so the mathematics should not distract us from learning about two-dimensional arrays.

Let's assume that our picture is represented by a two-dimensional array, pixels, that is nRows by nCols. The following pseudocode computes the average of the pixel values and then multiplies that average by the given factor to obtain the threshold value:

```
sum = 0
for (row = 0; row < nRows; row++)
   for (col = 0; col < nCols; col++)
      sum = sum + pixels[row][col]

average = sum / (nRows * nCols)
threshold = factor * average
```

Now we can compare each pixel value, pixels[row][col], to the value of threshold, as the problem statement describes. We can record whether or not a pixel value exceeds the threshold as a boolean value in another array, result, having the same dimensions as the array pixels. If pixels[row][col] exceeds threshold, we will set result[row][col] to true. Otherwise, this entry will be false.

20.20   **The class Picture.** Let's define a class Picture to represent a digital image and perform the computation we just described. We can specify the following method to create and return the desired boolean array:

```java
/** Locates the brightest features in the picture.
    @param factor  a real value used to identify the features
    @return a 2-D array of boolean values that indicate where
            the brightest features are in the picture */
public boolean[][] getFeatures(double factor)
```

The client will supply the factor that will be multiplied by the average pixel value to arrive at the threshold used to select the brightest features in the picture. While getFeatures could compute this average pixel value, we decided to define another method and make it publicly available. Its specification is

```
/** Computes the average of all pixel values in the picture.
    @return the real average of all pixel values */
public double getPixelAverage()
```

Listing 20-4 shows the definition of our class. Let's examine its details.

LISTING 20-4   The class Picture

```java
/** A representation of a digital picture.
    @author Frank M. Carrano
*/
public class Picture
{
   private double[][] pixels; // declare array
   private int nRows, nCols;

   /** Creates a Picture object.
       @param content  a 2-D array of real pixel values */
   public Picture(double[][] content)
   {
      nRows = content.length;
      nCols = content[0].length;
      pixels = new double[nRows][nCols]; // allocate array

      // fill array
      for (int row = 0; row < nRows; row++)
         for (int col = 0; col < nCols; col++)
            pixels[row][col] = content[row][col];
   } // end constructor

   /** Locates the brightest features in the picture.
       @param factor  a real value used to identify the features
       @return a 2-D array of boolean values that indicate where
               the brightest features are in the picture */
   public boolean[][] getFeatures(double factor)
   {
      boolean[][] result = new boolean[nRows][nCols];
      double threshold = factor * getPixelAverage();

      for (int row = 0; row < nRows; row++)
      {
         for (int col = 0; col < nCols; col++)
         {
            result[row][col] = (pixels[row][col] > threshold)
         } // end for
      } // end
```

```
            return result;
        } // end getFeatures

        /** Computes the average of all pixel values in the picture.
            @return the real average of all pixel values */
        public double getPixelAverage()
        {
            double sum = 0;
            for (int row = 0; row < nRows; row++)
                for (int col = 0; col < nCols; col++)
                    sum = sum + pixels[row][col];

            return sum / (nRows * nCols);
        } // end getPixelAverage
    } // end Picture
```

20.21   **The data fields.** The major data field in Picture is a two-dimensional array that represents the pixels in the digital image. Its declaration is

```
private double[][] pixels; // declare array
```

The constructor will allocate memory for the array and initialize its contents, as you will soon see. Even though any method in this class could obtain this array's dimensions directly from the array, we will have the constructor set two more fields, nRows and nCols, to these dimensions. In this way, the dimensions are defined once and the result is shared by the rest of the class. The declaration of these fields is simply

```
private int nRows, nCols;
```

20.22   **The constructor.** The constructor accepts a two-dimensional array of pixel values from the client as a representation of a picture. The constructor's header is

```
public Picture(double[][] content)
```

Its definition begins by assigning values to nRows and nCols and then allocating the array pixels:

```
nRows = content.length;
nCols = content[0].length;
pixels = new double[nRows][nCols]; // allocate array
```

The constructor then copies entries from the given array content to the data field pixels:

```
for (int row = 0; row < nRows; row++)
    for (int col = 0; col < nCols; col++)
        pixels[row][col] = content[row][col];
```

Since these arrays contain primitive values, the values are actually copied, and we get two distinct arrays that contain the same values. As Segment 20.12 noted, when a constructor initializes a data field that is an array with an array passed to it as an argument, it should make a copy of the argument array to prevent the possible corruption of the class's data by the client.

20.23   **The method getFeatures.** The definition of getFeatures begins by allocating a two-dimensional boolean array that it will initialize and return to the client:

```
boolean[][] result = new boolean[nRows][nCols];
```

The array is the same size as the array passed to the constructor by the client.

Next, the method calculates the threshold value to be used in identifying the picture's brightest features by multiplying the given factor by the average pixel value that the method getPixelAverage returns:

```
double threshold = factor * getPixelAverage();
```

To compare each pixel value with threshold, we assign the boolean result of the comparison to an array element within two nested for statements that will cycle through the entire two-dimensional array, as follows:

```
for (int row = 0; row < nRows; row++)
{
   for (int col = 0; col < nCols; col++)
   {
      result[row][col] = (pixels[row][col] > threshold);
   } // end for
} // end for
```

The method then returns the array result.

Question 12 What if statement is equivalent to the assignment statement within the previous nested for statements?

Question 13 Could we use one for-each statement instead of the two nested for statements given in the previous segment to assign values to the array result? Why or why not?

20.24 **The method getPixelAverage.** As you can see in Listing 20-4, the definition of the method getPixelAverage closely follows the pseudocode given in Segment 20.19. Although that pseudocode includes the computation of the threshold, this method returns only the pixel average. The threshold is computed in getFeatures.

Question 14 How would you write the body for the method whose header follows, as a member of the class Picture?

```
/** Gets the picture's pixels.
    @return a 2-D array of real pixel values */
public double[][] getPixels()
```

Note: Protect private arrays from damage
Did you get the correct answer to Question 14? If you haven't tried to define the method getPixels, take a moment to at least think about a solution.

What would happen if you defined this method as follows?

```
public double[][] getPixels()
{
   return pixels;
} // end getPixels
```

At first glance, this definition might seem to be a reasonable accessor method for the private array pixels. After all, the body of an accessor method for the integer field nRows, for example, would be

```
return nRows;
```

Although a client of such an accessor method would be able to get the value of nRows, it could not change it. Such is not the case for the previous definition of getPixels.

Imagine a Picture object—call it aPicture—and the invocation

```
double[][] myPixels = aPicture.getPixels();
```

The client's variable myPixels is now an alias for the private field pixels. So any change apparently made to the array referenced by myPixels is actually made to the array referenced by pixels. That is, a statement such as

```
myPixels[2][3] = 0;
```

changes aPicture's private data. This discussion is like the one in the previous chapter for the class BagOfStrings.

Note that the solution to Question 14 makes a copy of the array referenced by pixels that getPixels returns to the client. In this way, any changes the client might make are to the copy, not to the private data in the array referenced by pixels.

20.25 **Demonstrating the class Picture.** Listing 20-5 contains a program to demonstrate the results of using the class Picture. A more useful program would read the picture's data from a file using techniques that Chapters 29 and 30 will cover.

LISTING 20-5 The class PictureDemo

```java
/** A demonstration of the class Picture.
    @author Frank M. Carrano
*/
public class PictureDemo
{
   private static double[][] pictureContent =
                             { {0.1, 3.2, 4.3, 5.4, 6.5, 7.6},
                               {8.2, 7.3, 6.4, 5.5, 4.6, 3.7},
                               {6.0, 5.2, 3.4, 1.6, 0.8, 0.2},
                               {0.0, 2.1, 1.4, 6.9, 1.1, 0.0} };
   public static void main(String[] args)
   {
      Picture aPicture = new Picture(pictureContent);
      boolean[][] features = aPicture.getFeatures(1.2);
      double average = aPicture.getPixelAverage();
      System.out.println("The average of all pixels is " + average);
      System.out.println("The threshold is 1.2 times this average, or " +
                        1.2 * average);
      display(features);
      System.out.println();
   } // end main

   /** Displays a 2-D array of boolean values,
       using a dot for false and X for true. */
```

```java
    public static void display(boolean[][] array)
    {
        int nRows = array.length;
        int nCols = array[0].length;
        for (int row = 0; row < nRows; row++)
        {
            for (int col = 0; col < nCols; col++)
            {
                if (array[row][col])
                    System.out.print("X");
                else
                    System.out.print(".");
            } // end for
            System.out.println();
        } // end for
    } // end display
} // end PictureDemo
```

Output

```
The average of all pixels is 3.8125
The threshold is 1.2 times this average, or 4.575
...XXX
XXXXX.
XX....
...X..
```

Question 15 Can you replace the nested for statements in the method display, as shown in Listing 20-5, with nested for-each statements? If so, revise the method; if not, explain why not.

Arrays of Three or More Dimensions

Typically, when a programmer uses an array, the array is one-dimensional. A two-dimensional array likely is appropriate when the problem naturally involves tables or charts of data associated with scientific, statistical, or mathematical problems. A three-dimensional array could represent image data or certain measurements taken at various places within a cubic space of a given width, depth, and height. One might even have a fourth dimension by considering the time the measurements were taken. Rarely will a programmer use an array having more than four dimensions, unless the problem at hand involves data that can be represented naturally in multiple dimensions.

20.26 **Example.** Imagine a refrigerator manufacturer that wants to test how well its new appliance holds cold temperatures during a power outage. Suppose that one can measure the temperature within the refrigerator at 1-inch intervals each hour for ten hours. If the interior dimensions of the refrigerator are 30 inches wide, 50 inches high, and 20 inches deep, we could record the temperature measurements over the course of ten hours in the following four-dimensional array:

```java
double[][][][] temperatures = new double[30][50][20][10];
```

This statement reserves 30 x 50 x 20 x 10, or 300,000, elements for the array and one reference—temperatures—to the array. We can view this array in any of the following ways:

- `temperatures[width]` is a 50 x 20 x 10 three-dimensional array. Since `width` can range from 0 to 29, we have 30 such arrays.
- `temperatures[width][height]` is a 20 x 10 two-dimensional array. Since `width` can range from 0 to 29, and `height` can range from 0 to 49, we have 1500 such arrays.
- `temperatures[width][height][depth]` is a one-dimensional array of 10 elements. Since `width` can range from 0 to 29, `height` can range from 0 to 49, and `depth` can range from 0 to 19, we have 30,000 such arrays.

20.27   **Allocating multidimensional arrays.** You need not allocate a multidimensional array all at once, even though that is what we did in the previous example when we allocated the array `temperatures`. Instead, you can allocate each dimension separately, beginning with the dimension associated with the first pair of square brackets. Thus, we could allocate the array `temperatures` as follows:

```java
double[][][][] temperatures = new double[30][][][];
for (int i = 0; i < temperatures.length; i++)
{
    temperatures[i] = new double[50][][];
    for (int j = 0; j < temperatures[i].length; j++)
    {
        temperatures[i][j] = new double[20][];
        for (int k = 0; k < temperatures[i][j].length; k++)
        {
            temperatures[i][j][k] = new double[10];
        } // end for k
    } // end for j
} // end for i
```

videonote
Multidimensional
arrays

Clearly, this is a harder way to allocate an array when you know its dimensions in advance. This example shows, however, that you can allocate each dimension without knowing the subsequent dimensions.

Ragged Arrays

20.28   Since Java stores a multidimensional array as an array of arrays, you might wonder whether the arrays that are elements of another array must all be the same size. In fact, they do not. For example, each row of a two-dimensional array can have a different length. Such mutidimensional arrays are said to be **ragged**.

Mileage charts show the distances between two cities. Typically, such charts are two-dimensional, in which the cities label the rows and columns of the chart. Figure 20-8a shows an example of such a chart for some U.S. cities. Since the distance from Boston to San Francisco is the same as the distance from San Francisco to Boston, for example, this chart includes that value twice. That is, the value in row *i* and column *j* is the same as the value in row *j* and column *i* for all values of *i* and *j*. We can represent this chart as a two-dimensional array that is **symmetrical**. If we omit the duplicate mileages, the chart will appear as in Figure 20-8b. It can be represented by a **triangular**—and ragged—two-dimensional array.

20.29   **Initializing a ragged array.** We can create a ragged two-dimensional array in Java that represents the mileages shown in Figure 20-8b as follows:

```java
int[][] mileageChart =
        { {1110},
          {710, 1000},
          {1430, 2000, 1020}

          < and so on . . . >

          {2480, 3130, 2170, 1260, 2290, 2930, 2900, 640}
          {2630, 3020, 2050, 1340, 2250, 2840, 2820, 170, 810} };
```

FIGURE 20-8   Mileage between cities given as a two-dimensional table that is (a) symmetrical; (b) triangular and ragged

(a)

	Atlanta	Boston	Chicago	Denver	Indianapolis	New York City	Philadelphia	Portland, OR	San Francisco	Seattle
Atlanta	—	1110	710	1430	530	850	750	2660	2480	2630
Boston	1110	—	1000	2000	930	210	320	3140	3130	3020
Chicago	710	1000	—	1020	190	810	790	2120	2170	2050
Denver	1430	2000	1020	—	1060	1790	1740	1260	1260	1340
Indianapolis	530	930	190	1060	—	730	660	2240	2290	2250
New York City	850	210	810	1790	730	—	110	2910	2930	2840
Philadelphia	750	320	790	1740	660	110	—	2860	2900	2820
Portland, OR	2660	3140	2120	1260	2240	2910	2860	—	640	170
San Francisco	2480	3130	2170	1260	2290	2930	2900	640	—	810
Seattle	2630	3020	2050	1340	2250	2840	2820	170	810	—

(b)

	Atlanta	Boston	Chicago	Denver	Indianapolis	New York City	Philadelphia	Portland, OR	San Francisco
Boston	1110								
Chicago	710	1000							
Denver	1430	2000	1020						
Indianapolis	530	930	190	1060					
New York City	850	210	810	1790	730				
Philadelphia	750	320	790	1740	660	110			
Portland, OR	2660	3140	2120	1260	2240	2910	2860		
San Francisco	2480	3130	2170	1260	2290	2930	2900	640	
Seattle	2630	3020	2050	1340	2250	2840	2820	170	810

Question 16 Assuming the definition of mileageChart just given, what Java expression represents the number of cities?

20.30   **Allocating a ragged array.** Instead of creating and initializing a ragged array for our mileage chart, as in the previous segment, we could declare and allocate the array and later read values into it. After declaring it, we would allocate references for all the rows. Then, in a loop, we would allocate memory for the elements in each row. For example, we could declare and allocate a mileage chart as follows, where CITY_COUNT is an integer constant equal to the number of cities:

```
int[][] myMileageChart;
myMileageChart = new int[CITY_COUNT][]; // allocate array of rows
// allocate each row
for (int row = 0; row < CITY_COUNT; row++)
    myMileageChart[row] = new int[row + 1];
```

Although myMileageChart has a fixed number of rows, we allocate each row so that it has one more element than the preceding row.

When creating the two-dimensional array myMileageChart, we provided a specific value for the first dimension but then allocated the rest of the array in a separate step. When creating any multidimensional array, you must specify the first dimension at the very least. For example, our initial allocation of a four-dimensional array could be

```
double[][][][] myArray = new double[10][][][];
```

We now must allocate each dimension for the rest of the array.

Question 17 In the for statement given in the previous segment, what expression involving myMileageChart can replace CITY_COUNT?

Question 18 What is the capacity of the array `myMileageChart` created by the code given in the previous segment?

Question 19 If `triArray` is a triangular array of integers, such as the one pictured in Figure 20-8b and created in Segment 20.29, what Java statements will display it?

Parallel Arrays

20.31 Imagine a party planner who needs to maintain a list of the guests at a particular event. We offer to write a Java program to take over this task. How can we represent this list? One way is to use a one-dimensional array of strings, such as the one pictured in Figure 20-9a. However, this approach does not separate a guest's first name and last name. It might be better to use a two-dimensional array of strings in which one column is the first name and another column is the last name. Figure 20-9b shows an example of such an array.

FIGURE 20-9 (a) A one-dimensional array of names; (b) a two-dimensional array of names

(a)

0	"Kathy Kruller"
1	"Pita Chip"
2	"Vanilla Wafer"
3	"Chrissy Crisp"
4	"Graham Kracker"
5	"Coco Puff"

(b)

	0	1
0	"Kathy"	"Kruller"
1	"Pita"	"Chip"
2	"Vanilla"	"Wafer"
3	"Chrissy"	"Crisp"
4	"Graham"	"Kracker"
5	"Coco"	"Puff"

20.32 Our party planner likely must retain other information about the guests, such as the tables at which they will be seated and, if this is a fundraiser, how much each contributes. You might think that we could simply add more columns to the array in Figure 20-9b to accommodate the additional data, but all elements in an array must have the same data type. We could represent table numbers and dollar amounts as strings in these additional columns, but doing so would be inconvenient, especially if we want to get a tally of the contributions or perform other arithmetic computations.

Since we cannot have a two-dimensional array whose columns contain values of different data types, we could use several one-dimensional arrays. For example, of the four arrays in Figure 20-10, two contain strings, and two contain integers. For a given index `i`, the entries `first[i]`, `last[i]`, `table[i]`, and `gift[i]` describe one guest. Arrays that have this correspondence are called **parallel arrays**. Note that parallel arrays have the same length.

The following Java statements create the parallel arrays illustrated in Figure 20-10:

```
String[] first = {"Thornton", "Perry", "Mary", "Venus"};
String[] last =  {"Rose", "Winkle", "Gold", "Flytrap"};
int[] table =    {2, 1, 3, 2};
int[] gift =     {50, 75, 35, 20};
```

The following statements provide an example of how you could display the contents of these parallel arrays:

```
for (int index = 0; index < first.length; index++)
{
   System.out.println(first[index] + " " + last[index] +
                     " at table " + table[index]);
   System.out.println("contributed $" + gift[index] + ".");
} // end for
```

FIGURE 20-10   Parallel arrays representing a guest list

	first	last		
0	"Thorton"	"Rose"	2	50	0
1	"Perry"	"Winkle"	1	75	1
2	"Mary"	"Gold"	3	35	2
3	"Venus"	"Flytrap"	2	20	3

first   last   table   gift

20.33   Sometimes parallel arrays are useful, but usually they are thought of as an old technique used when programming languages were not object oriented. Instead of using parallel arrays, we can encapsulate associated data into an object and create a one-dimensional array of these objects. Objects that represent the data shown in Figure 20-10 can be described by the class Guest, which is outlined in Listing 20-6. Figure 20-11 illustrates an array—named guestList—of Guest objects that we can use instead of parallel arrays.

LISTING 20-6   An outline of the class Guest, using two strings to represent a guest's name

```
/** A class that represents a guest at a fund raiser.
    @author Frank M. Carrano
*/
public class Guest
{
   private String firstName;
   private String lastName;
   private int tableNumber;
   private int gift;

   public Guest(String firstName, String lastName,
                int tableNumber, int gift)
   {
      this.firstName = firstName;
      this.lastName = lastName;
      this.tableNumber = tableNumber;
      this.gift = gift;
   } // end constructor
```

> *< Accessor methods* `getFirstName`, `getLastName`, `getTableNumber`, *and* `getGift`
> *are defined here. >*
> `} // end Guest`

FIGURE 20-11   An array of `Guest` objects, where `Guest` is as outlined in
Listing 20-6

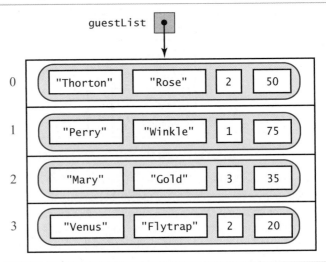

20.34   Another way to define the class `Guest` is to use the class `Name`, as defined in Listing 6-5 of Chapter 6, to represent a guest's name. This version of `Guest` is outlined in Listing 20-7, and an array of its objects is illustrated in Figure 20-12.

LISTING 20-7   Another version of the class `Guest`, using a `Name` object to represent a guest's name

```
/** A class that represents a guest at a fund raiser.
    @author Frank M. Carrano
*/
public class Guest
{
   private Name guestName;
   private int tableNumber;
   private int gift;

   public Guest(Name guestName, int tableNumber, int gift)
   {
      this.guestName = guestName;
      this.tableNumber = tableNumber;
      this.gift = gift;
   } // end constructor
```

```
    < Accessor methods getName, getTableNumber, and getGift are defined here. >
} // end Guest
```

FIGURE 20-12   An array of Guest objects, where Guest is as outlined in
               Listing 20-7

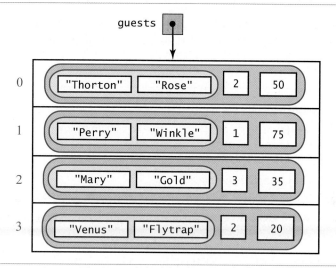

Programming Tip

Use an array of objects instead of parallel arrays when possible. Parallel arrays were useful when programming languages were not object oriented, but Java programmers tend not to use them today. The standard class Graphics, however, does use parallel arrays when drawing polygons, as you will see in Chapter 22. This fact is the main reason we introduce parallel arrays here. Note that Segments 18.20 and 18.21 of Chapter 18 introduced arrays of objects.

videonote
A problem
solved

Question 20 Assuming the version of Guest given in Listing 20-7, what Java statements will create the array illustrated in Figure 20-12?

Question 21 Given the array that you defined in the previous question, what Java statements will have the same effect as the for loop given in Segment 20.32?

CHAPTER SUMMARY

- You can use a for-each loop to process all the values in an array.

- Although every array has a fixed size, you can make it appear to change size by allocating a new array, copying the entries from the original array to the new array, and using the original variable to reference the new array.

- By increasing an array's capacity, you can implement collections whose contents are limited in number only by the size of the computer's memory.

- Any method can declare one parameter that represents an arbitrary number of arguments passed to it by a client.

- The parameter in a method `main` represents an array of any command-line arguments given when a program begins execution.

- An array can have any number of dimensions. Most arrays are either one- or two-dimensional.

- A multidimensional array in Java is actually a one-dimensional array of other arrays.

- A multidimensional array can be ragged. That is, the arrays that are entries of another array need not have the same size. For example, a two-dimensional array can have rows of unequal lengths.

- Arrays are said to be parallel when the entry at a given index in one array corresponds to the entries in other arrays at the same index. Typically, you should avoid parallel arrays and use an array of objects instead.

EXERCISES

1. Consider the following code segment:

   ```
   double[] tenths = {.1, .2, .3, .4, .5, .6, .7, .8, .9};
   for (double item : tenths)
       System.out.println(item);
   ```

   a. What, if any, output is produced?
   b. Revise the loop so that only the first five entries in the array are displayed.

2. What steps are taken by the method `copyOf` as a result of the following invocation?

   ```
   Arrays.copyOf(myArray, 2 * myArray.length)
   ```

3. If you know that you will have 1000 entries to add to a one-dimensional array, and you know how to resize an array, what length should the array have when it is first allocated? Explain your answer.

4. Define a static method `doubleArray` that accepts a one-dimensional array of strings as an argument and returns a one-dimensional array of the same strings, but with a length that is twice the length of the argument array.

5. Define a static method `doubleSquareArray` that accepts a square two-dimensional array of integers as an argument and returns a square two-dimensional array that has twice the number of rows and columns as the argument array and contains the same integers.

6. Given a two-dimensional array of strings, define a static method that returns the number of times a given string appears in the array.

7. The class `ThreeD` has a three-dimensional array of strings as one of its data fields. Define a method for the class that searches this array for the string passed to it as an argument. If the given string exists in the array, the method should return an array containing the three indices of the array element that contains the string. If the given string is not found in the array, the method should return `null`.

8. A *magic square* is a square two-dimensional array of positive integers such that the sum of each row, column, and diagonal is the same constant. For example, the following is a magic square:

18	99	86	61
66	81	98	19
91	16	69	88
89	68	11	96

because the sum of the integers in each row is 264, the sum of the integers in each column is 264, and the sum of the integers in each of the two diagonals (18 + 81 + 69 + 96 and 61 + 98 + 16 + 89) is 264. The size of the square array shown above is 4 because it has four rows and four columns.

The following Java class represents a square array of integers, but its method implementations are missing:

```
public class Square
{
    private int     mySize;
    private int[][] array;

    public Square(int initialSize) {}
    public void set(int[][] values) {}
    public boolean isMagicSquare() {}

    < Other methods are defined here. >
    . . .
} // end Square
```

   a. Complete the definition of the constructor.
   b. Complete the definition of the method `set` to copy integers from the given array to the data field `array`.
   c. Complete the definition of the method `isMagicSquare` so that it returns true if `array` contains a magic square, or false if it does not.

9. Consider a two-dimensional array of strings. The array has NUM_ROWS rows and NUM_COLS columns, where NUM_ROWS and NUM_COLS are named constants whose values are positive integers. Write one loop that displays all of the strings in the array, one per line. Do the strings in your output appear in row-wise or column-wise order?

10. Consider the two-dimensional array of strings described in the previous exercise. Write two nested loops to copy the array into a one-dimensional array of strings whose length is NUM_ROWS * NUM_COLS.

11. Repeat the previous exercise, but use only one loop.

12. Consider a one-dimensional array of strings. The length of the array is N * M, where N and M are named constants whose values are positive integers. Write two nested loops that display all of the strings in the array, one per line.

13. If `myArray` is a two-dimensional *n*-by-*m* array, the *transpose* of `myArray` is the *m*-by-*n* array `transpose`, such that `transpose[i][j]` is equal to `myArray[j][i]`. Define a static method that accepts a two-dimensional array as an argument and returns its transpose as a new array.

14. Define a static method that accepts a two-dimensional *n*-by-*n* array as an argument and transforms it into its transpose (see the previous exercise), using the least amount of additional storage possible.

PROJECTS

1. Tic-tac-toe is a game for two players that is played on a three-by-three arrangement of squares that we will call the game board. Players alternately claim a square by marking it in a distinctive way, traditionally with Xs and Os. The first player to claim three squares that are adjacent either horizontally, vertically, or diagonally wins. Tie games, which have no winner, are possible.

Define a Java class that represents the game board of tic-tac-toe. This class is responsible for displaying the board, reporting its status, and marking the squares with Xs and Os, all under control of its client.

Number the squares on the board as follows:

```
1  2  3
4  5  6
7  8  9
```

The players use these numbers to indicate their moves.

Write a program that uses your class to play tic-tac-toe. Display the empty board with its squares numbered, as just shown. Alternate turns between player X and player O, marking each move on the board. For example, if player X makes the first move by choosing square 5, if the move is legal, display the board as

```
1  2  3
4  X  6
7  8  9
```

and tell player O to make the next move. When the game ends, announce the outcome.

You can allow either two human players or one player who plays against your program. In the latter case, you must develop a strategy for choosing squares. This strategy can be as simple or complex as you choose. You can use a strategy that never loses or one that chooses squares randomly.

2. A *histogram* is a bar chart that represents the frequency distribution of a set of data. The length of each bar is proportional to the frequency of occurrence of certain data values. For example, the following histogram shows the distribution of given integers, whose values are between 1 and 50, inclusive, within the ranges 1 to 10, 11 to 20, and so on:

```
 1 - 10 # # #
11 - 20 # # # #
21 - 30 # # # # #
31 - 40 # # # #
41 - 50 # #
```

Each pound sign (#) represents one integer in the range, so in our example, three integers are in the range 1 to 10, and so on. Define and demonstrate a Java class that creates a histogram like the one just shown.

3. Define two Java classes, Classroom1 and Classroom2, that represent the students in a classroom. Classroom1 should provide as data fields four parallel arrays to contain the following student information: first name (String), last name (String), age (int), and grade point average, or GPA (double). Define a method getClassList that returns as a string a list of students in a particular object of this class. Classroom2 should provide, as one data field, an array of type Student, where the class Student contains the same information for a student as described for the previous parallel arrays. Classroom2 should also define a method getClassList. Each class should be able to resize the classroom if necessary.

Demonstrate each class. Compare the implementations of Classroom1 and Classroom2, and discuss their pros and cons.

4. A *Latin square* is an *n*-by-*n* two-dimensional array of positive integers such that each row and each column contains the integers 1, 2, ..., *n*. For example, the following is a three-by-three Latin square:

2	3	1
3	1	2
1	2	3

Latin squares for a given value of *n* are not unique. Define a class of Latin squares whose constructor has a parameter to represent *n*. Include a method to return a valid *n*-by-*n* Latin square.

5. Design and implement a class ToDoList. An object of this class—let's call it a to-do list—is a collection of strings that describe tasks a user wants to accomplish. Strings on this list appear in order, one after the other, just as they would had you written a list of tasks on paper. In other words, each string has a position on the list beginning with 1, as in the following example:

> 1. Read Chapter 20
> 2. Begin Project 3
> 3. Order pizza

The list should be as long as the user desires.
Give the to-do list the following behaviors:

- add—Add a new task to the end of the list
- remove—Remove and return the first task from the list
- replace—Replace and return a particular task, designated by its number, with a new task
- getCurrentSize—Return the current number of tasks on the list
- isEmpty—Return true if the list is empty or false if it is not
- clear—Erase all tasks from the list

Demonstrate your class ToDoList.

ANSWERS TO SELF-TEST QUESTIONS

1.
```
for (String line : text)
   System.out.println(line);
```

2.
```
int sum = 0;
for (int index = 0; index < anArray.length; index++)
   sum = sum + anArray[index];
```

3.
```
text = Arrays.copyOf(text, text.length + 5);
```
or
```
String[] origText = text;            // save reference to array
text = new String[text.length + 5]; // increase length of array
System.arraycopy(origText, 0, text, 0, origText.length);
```

4.
```
text = Arrays.copyOf(text, size);
```
or
```
String[] origText = text; // save reference to array
text = new String[size];   // decrease length of array
System.arraycopy(origText, 0, text, 0, size);
```

5.
```
/** Creates a bag containing the given array of strings. */
public ExpandableBagOfStrings(String[] contents)
{
   bag = Arrays.copyOf(contents, contents.length);
   numberOfStrings = contents.length;
} // end constructor
```

6. A simple assignment statement would be a poor choice, since then the client could use the reference to the array that it passes to the constructor as an argument to corrupt the bag's data. Copying the argument array to the array bag is necessary to protect the integrity of the bag's data.

7. Except for its name, BagOfString's constructor would be the same as the one given for ExpandableBagOfStrings in Segment 20.12. The only consideration would be for the client to know when the capacity of the bag is the same as its size, that is, when the bag is full.

8. An ArrayIndexOutOfBoundsException occurs when an attempt is made to reference integers[0].

9.
```
/** Finds the smallest of any number of real numbers.
    @return the smallest of the given numbers */
public static double minimum(double... numbers)
{
    int result = numbers[0]; // or Double.MAX_VALUE
    for (int value : numbers)
        result = Math.min(value, number);
    return result;
} // end minimum
```

10.
```
public static int[][] doubleArray(int[][] anArray)
{
    int numberOfRows = anArray.length;
    int numberOfCols = anArray[0].length;
    int[][] result = new int[numberOfRows][numberOfCols];
    for (int row = 0; row < numberOfRows; row++)
        for (int col = 0; col < numberOfCols; col++)
            result[row][col] = 2 * anArray[row][col];

    return result;
} // end doubleArray
```

11.
```
0 1 2
1 2 3
2 3 4
3 4 5
4 5 6
```

12.
```
if (pixels[row][col] > threshold)
    result[row][col] = true;
else
    result[row][col] = false;
```

13. No. If we were to write

```
for (double[] row : pixels)
```

we would need another loop to process row. If we were to write

```
for (double value : pixels)
    if (value > threshold)
```

we would get a syntax error. Moreover, we wouldn't have indices for the element in result that needed to be assigned a value.

14.
```
/** Task: Gets the picture's pixels.
    @return a 2-D array of real pixel values */
public double[][] getPixels()
{
    double[][] copy = new double[nRows][nCols];
    for (int row = 0; row < nRows; row++)
        for (int col = 0; col < nCols; col++)
            copy[row][col] = pixels[row][col];
```

```
        return copy;
    } // end getPixels
```

15. Yes, you can do so as follows:

```
    for (boolean[] row : array)
    {
        for (boolean bValue : row)
        {
            if (bValue)
                System.out.print("X");
            else
                System.out.print(".");
        } // end for
        System.out.println();
    } // end for
    System.out.println();
```

16. `mileageChart.length`

17. `myMileageChart.length`

18. The first row has one element, the second row has two elements, and so on until we get to the last row, which has CITY_COUNT elements. In all, the array contains $1 + 2 + 3 + ... +$ CITY_COUNT elements, which is CITY_COUNT x (CITY_COUNT + 1) / 2 elements.

19.
```
    for (int row = 0; row < triArray.length; row++)
    {
        for (int col = 0; col <= row; col++) // or col < triArray[row].length
            System.out.print(triArray[row][col] + " ");
        System.out.println();
    } // end for
```

20.
```
    Guest[] guests = new Guest[4];
    guests[0] = new Guest(new Name("Thornton", "Rose"), 2, 50);
    guests[1] = new Guest(new Name("Perry", "Winkle"), 1, 75);
    guests[2] = new Guest(new Name("Mary", "Gold"), 3, 35);
    guests[3] = new Guest(new Name("Venus", "Flytrap"), 2, 20);
```

or

```
    Guest[] guests = {new Guest(new Name("Thornton", "Rose"), 2, 50),
                      new Guest(new Name("Perry", "Winkle"), 1, 75),
                      new Guest(new Name("Mary", "Gold"), 3, 35),
                      new Guest(new Name("Venus", "Flytrap"), 2, 20)};
```

21.
```
    for (int index = 0; index < guests.length; index++)
    {
        Name guestName = guests[index].getName();
        int tableNumber = guests[index].getTableNumber();
        int gift = guests[index].getGift();
        System.out.println(guestName + " at table " + tableNumber +
                           " contributed $" + gift + ".");
    } // end for
```

Debugging Interlude

6

Debugging Arrays

Contents

Prerequisites

This debugging interlude talks about typical execution-time errors that programmers make while using arrays in Java programs.

An Unallocated Array

D6.1   Chapter 19 used an array of strings in the definition of the class `BagOfStrings`. You learned to focus on a core group of methods when beginning the definition of a new class, instead of tackling the entire class at once. Even so, our development of this core group likely would progress in smaller steps than Chapter 19 describes.

For example, Listing D6-1 shows an early draft of this class. Imagine that we have begun in a simple manner by defining only two data fields—bag and `numberOfStrings`—a default constructor, a simplified method add, and a stub for `toArray`. Our goal is to get something to work and then refine the definitions to their final form. Thus, the method add does not check for a full bag; it just assigns the new string to bag[numberOfStrings] before incrementing `numberOfStrings`. The method `toArray` merely returns the array bag. Although this action is sufficient for testing the class, as you saw in Chapter 19, we ultimately need to return a copy of bag, not bag itself. Hence, we tag both methods as stubs.

LISTING D6-1   An early version of the class `BagOfStrings`

```
1  /** A class that implements a bag of strings by using an array.
2      @author Frank M. Carrano
3  */
4  public class BagOfStrings
5  {
6     private final String[] bag;
7     private int numberOfStrings;
8
9     /** Creates an empty bag. */
10    public BagOfStrings()
11    {
12       numberOfStrings = 0;
13    } // end default constructor
14
15    /** Adds a new string to this bag.
16        @param newString  the string to be added
17        @return true if the addition is successful,
18               or false if not */
19    public boolean add(String newString)
20    {
21       bag[numberOfStrings] = newString;
22       numberOfStrings++;
23
24       return true; // STUB
25    } // end add
26
27    /** Retrieves all strings that are in this bag. */
28    public String[] toArray()
29    {
30       return bag; // STUB
31    } // end toArray
32  } // end BagOfStrings
```

D6.2   Listing D6-2 contains a driver for `BagOfStrings`. It creates an instance of the class and adds three strings to the bag. After one line of expected output, an exception occurs at line 21 of `BagOfStrings` due to an invocation of the method add at line 10 of the driver. A `NullPointerException` indicates a null value in a variable used in line 21. At that point, `numberOfStrings` is zero and `newString` is "A". If we were to look at the value of the variable bag by using one of the techniques described in the previous debugging interlude, it would be `null`. This value causes the `NullPointerException` when we try to reference bag[0].

The variable bag is `null` because the constructor did not allocate the array. It should contain a statement such as

```
bag = new String[CAPACITY];
```

where CAPACITY is an integer constant that specifies the size of the array. Figure D6-1 illustrates the array prior to and after its allocation. This figure is similar to Figure 18-5 in Chapter 18.

LISTING D6-2   An initial test of the class BagOfStrings

```
1 /** A test of the class BagOfStrings
2     @author Frank M. Carrano
3 */
4 public class BagDemo
5 {
6    public static void main(String[] args)
7    {
8       BagOfStrings aBag = new BagOfStrings();
9       System.out.println("Adding to the bag: A, B, C");
10      aBag.add("A");
11      aBag.add("B");
12      aBag.add("C");
13      displayBag(aBag);
14   } // end main

       < The definition of the method displayBag, as given in Listing 19-3 of Chapter 19,
         is here. >
27 } // end BagDemo
```

Output

```
Adding to the bag: A, B, C
Exception in thread "main" java.lang.NullPointerException
      at BagOfStrings.add(BagOfStrings.java:21)
      at BagDemo.main(BagDemo.java:10)
```

Programming Tip

Declaring an array but failing to allocate it is an easy-to-make mistake. Allocate an array soon after writing its declaration. You're more likely to forget the allocation if you get distracted by other programming details. Moreover, from a stylistic point of view, the declaration and allocation of an array should be close to each other. A reader of your code should not have to look far to discover the length of an array.

Note: If the array bag is allocated and index is a nonnegative integer that is less than the number of array elements, bag[index] contains null prior to having a value assigned to it.

FIGURE D6-1   The array, bag, of strings after (a) its declaration; (b) its allocation; (c) strings are assigned to its first two elements

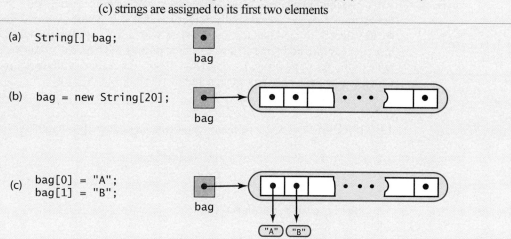

(a)   `String[] bag;`

(b)   `bag = new String[20];`

(c)   `bag[0] = "A";`
      `bag[1] = "B";`

■ A Silent Error

D6.3   Suppose we further develop the class `BagOfStrings` by detecting when the bag is full. Thus, we give the bag a default capacity, complete two constructors as well as the methods `add` and `isFull`—as given in Listing 19-2 of Chapter 19—and define the methods `isEmpty`, `getCapacity`, and `getCurrentSize`, as shown in Segment 19.24 of Chapter 19. Listing D6-3 shows the class at this stage.

LISTING D6-3   The class `BagOfStrings` after further development

```
1  /** A class that implements a bag of strings by using an array.
2      @author Frank M. Carrano
3  */
4  public class BagOfStrings
5  {
6     private final String[] bag;
7     private static final int DEFAULT_CAPACITY = 3;
8     private int numberOfStrings;
9

      < Two constructors and the method add are here. >

43    /** Retrieves all strings that are in this bag. */
44    public String[] toArray() // STUB
45    {
46       return bag;
47    } // end toArray
48

      < The methods isFull, isEmpty, getCapacity, and getCurrentSize are here. >
76 } // end BagOfStrings
```

The Method toArray as a Stub

D6.4 After making the changes to BagOfStrings, as shown in Listing D6-3, suppose we decide to test the method toArray, accidentally forgetting that it is a stub. We had given DEFAULT_CAPACITY a small value, 3, to facilitate testing the class with a full bag. We can leave that value as is while we test toArray. We add three strings to a bag, display the bag, call toArray, and then display the contents of the resulting array. Listing D6-4 shows the results of these actions. As you would expect, the output contains the same strings in both the bag and the array.

LISTING D6-4 A test of the method toArray in the class BagOfStrings

```
1  /** A test of the class BagOfStrings
2      @author Frank M. Carrano
3  */
4  public class BagDemo
5  {
6     public static void main(String[] args)
7     {
8        BagOfStrings aBag = new BagOfStrings();
9        System.out.println("Adding to the bag: A, B, C");
10       aBag.add("A");
11       aBag.add("B");
12       aBag.add("C");
13       displayBag(aBag);
14
15       String[] bagArray = aBag.toArray();
16       System.out.print("An array of the strings in the bag: ");
17       for (int index = 0; index < bagArray.length; index++)
18          System.out.print(bagArray[index] + " ");
19       System.out.println();
20
21       System.out.print("\nChange the contents of the array.");
22       for (int index = 0; index < bagArray.length; index++)
23          bagArray[index] = "Z");
24
25       displayBag(aBag);
26    } // end main
27
       < The definition of the method displayBag, as given in Listing 19-3 of Chapter 19,
         is here. >
39 } // end BagDemo
```

Output

```
Adding to the bag: A, B, C
The bag contains A B C
An array of the strings in the bag: A B C

Change the contents of the array.
The bag contains Z Z Z
```

D6.5 Since bagArray exists in the client, what happens if we alter its contents? The loop at lines 22 and 23 assigns the string "Z" to each element of the array. When we display the contents of the bag again, we find that they have changed, too. The method toArray in Listing D6-3 is a stub and simply returns bag. The client in Listing D6-4 assigns this return value to its local variable bagArray, which now becomes an alias for bag. Any change to bagArray[index] within the client is a change to bag[index] within the object aBag. This occurs despite the private declaration of the array bag within the class BagOfStrings.

While the "silent" error in this example becomes rather apparent when you examine the program's output, it is less likely to be this obvious in practice.

Highlighting our earlier caution again is worthwhile:

Programming Tip

Do not define a public method within a class that returns a reference to any data field that is an array or other object. Doing so enables a client to corrupt an object of the class, even if the data fields in the class are private.

Array Index Out of Bounds

Let's complete the definition of the method toArray so that it is no longer a stub.

Defining the Method toArray

D6.6 Instead of returning a reference to the array in BagOfStrings, toArray should return a reference to a copy of the array to ensure that the client cannot damage the bag's contents. Listing D6-5 shows this method definition within the class BagOfStrings. After creating a new array of strings to hold the current contents of the bag, we copy the references in the array bag to this new array and return the result to the client.

LISTING D6-5   The class BagOfStrings after defining toArray

```
1 /** A class that implements a bag of strings by using an array.
2     @author Frank M. Carrano
3 */
4 public class BagOfStrings
5 {
6    private final String[] bag;
7    private static final int DEFAULT_CAPACITY = 3;
8    private int numberOfStrings;
9
```

```
        < Two constructors and the method add are here. >
43      /** Retrieves all strings that are in this bag.
44          @return a newly allocated array of all the strings
45                  in this bag */
46      public String[] toArray()
47      {
48          String[] result = new String[numberOfStrings];
49          for (int index = 1; index <= numberOfStrings; index++)
50              result[index] = bag[index];
51
52          return result;
53      } // end toArray
54
        < The methods isFull, isEmpty, getCapacity, and getCurrentSize are here. >

82 } // end BagOfStrings
```

D6.7 Listing D6-6 shows our test driver. After adding four strings to a bag whose capacity is 3, we display the bag. Note that main now invokes both getCapacity and getCurrentSize, which it didn't do earlier. As you can see in the listing, an exception occurs.

LISTING D6-6 Another test of the class BagOfStrings

```
 1 /** A test of the class BagOfStrings
 2     @author Frank M. Carrano
 3 */
 4 public class BagDemo
 5 {
 6    public static void main(String[] args)
 7    {
 8       BagOfStrings aBag = new BagOfStrings();
 9       System.out.println("Adding to the bag: A, B, C, D");
10       aBag.add("A");
11       aBag.add("B");
12       aBag.add("C");
13       aBag.add("D");
14       int capacity = aBag.getCapacity();
15       int count = aBag.getCurrentSize();
16       System.out.println("The bag's capacity is " + capacity +
17                          " strings; it contains " + count +
18                          " strings:");
```

```
19        displayBag(aBag);
20    } // end main
21
22    public static void displayBag(BagOfStrings bag)
23    {
24        String[] bagArray = bag.toArray();
25        for (int index = 0; index < bagArray.length; index++)
26            System.out.print(bagArray[index] + " ");
27        System.out.println();
28    } // end displayBag
29 } // end BagDemo
```

Output

```
Adding to the bag: A, B, C, D
The bag's capacity is 3 strings; it contains 3 strings:
Exception in thread "main" java.lang.ArrayIndexOutOfBoundsException: 3
        at BagOfStrings.toArray(BagOfStrings.java:50)
        at BagDemo.displayBag(BagDemo.java:24)
        at BagDemo.main(BagDemo.java:19)
```

D6.8   In the output given in Listing D6-6, notice that the bag contains three strings, as it should, since the bag's capacity is 3. Our attempted addition of "D" to the full bag does not change the bag, as you can see by examining the definition of add given in Chapter 19. We simply ignore add's return value of false.

   The error message indicates an exception due to an index value of 3, which is too large for the array. The problem occurred at lines 19 and 24 of BagDemo. Line 19 is within the body of main at the call to displayBag, and line 24 is within the body of displayBag at the call to toArray. Additionally, execution was at line 50 of the class BagOfStrings within the method toArray when the exception occurred. (See Listing D6-5.)

D6.9   The exception, ArrayIndexOutOfBoundsException, occurs at line 50 because index is out of bounds. The error message gives its value as 3. Thus, index is too large for either or both of the arrays result and bag. Since the bag's default capacity is 3, the array bag has room for only three entries. The bag contained three strings when the exception occurred, as the program's output indicates. Thus, the method getCurrentSize must have returned 3, which implies that the value of the field numberOfStrings is also 3. We now know that the array result has three elements. That is, both arrays result and bag have the same size, 3.

In Listing D6-5, toArray's for loop is

```
49          for (int index = 1; index <= numberOfStrings; index++)
50              result[index] = bag[index];
```

The loop variable index ranges from 1 to 3. But indices for a three-element array should range from 0 to 2. The exception occurred when index became too large. The correct loop should be

```
49          for (int index = 0; index < numberOfStrings; index++)
50              result[index] = bag[index];
```

The variable index must start at 0 instead of 1, and the comparison must be strictly "less than" instead of "less than or equal to."

■ Another Silent Error

For this discussion, imagine that we are back in Chapter 19 at Segment 19.30 when we define a method to remove a particular string from a bag.

The Method remove

D6.10   The method remove calls the private methods getIndexOf and removeEntry. After we add these method definitions to the class in Listing D6-5, it might look like the one in Listing D6-7. Once again, we use a small default capacity for our initial tests, but since we plan to remove entries, it is slightly larger than in the previous examples.

LISTING D6-7   The class BagOfStrings after adding the method remove

```java
/** A class that implements a bag of strings by using an array.
    @author Frank M. Carrano
*/
public class BagOfStrings
{
    private final String[] bag;
    private static final int DEFAULT_CAPACITY = 4; // for testing
    private int numberOfStrings;

    < Two constructors and the method add are here. >

    /** Removes one occurrence of a given string from this bag.
        @param aString  the string to be removed
        @return true if the removal was successful,
                or false if not */
    public boolean remove(String aString)
    {
        int index = getIndexOf(aString);
        String result = removeEntry(index);
        return aString.equals(result);
    } // end remove

    // Removes and returns the array entry at a given index.
    // If no such entry exists, returns null.
```

```
private String removeEntry(int givenIndex)
{
   String result = null;
   if (!isEmpty() && (givenIndex >= 0))
   {
      result = bag[givenIndex]; // entry to remove
      bag[givenIndex] = null; // remove reference to last entry
      numberOfStrings--;
   } // end if

   return result;
} // end removeEntry

// Locates a given string within the array bag.
// Returns the index of the string, if located,
// or -1 otherwise.
private int getIndexOf(String aString)
{
   int where = -1;
   boolean stillLooking = true;

   for (int index = 0; stillLooking &&
                        (index < numberOfStrings); index++)
   {
      if (aString.equals(bag[index]))
      {
         stillLooking = false;
         where = index;
      } // end if
   } // end for

   return where;
} // end getIndexOf
```

< *The methods* toArray, isFull, isEmpty, getCapacity, *and* getCurrentSize
   are here. >

```
} // end BagOfStrings
```

D6.11 **Testing.** The test driver in Listing D6-8 is similar to the one in Listing D6-6 for our previous test.
After adding four entries to the bag, we remove the last one and see successful results. If we stop
our tests here, however, we will fail to detect a mistake in our logic.

LISTING D6-8   A test of the method remove

```
/** A test of the class BagOfStrings
    @author Frank M. Carrano
*/
```

```java
public class BagDemo
{
    public static void main(String[] args)
    {
        BagOfStrings aBag = new BagOfStrings();
        System.out.println("Adding to the bag: A, B, C, D");
        aBag.add("A");
        aBag.add("B");
        aBag.add("C");
        aBag.add("D");
        int capacity = aBag.getCapacity();
        int count = aBag.getCurrentSize();
        System.out.println("The bag's capacity is " + capacity +
                           " strings; " + "it contains " + count +
                           " strings:");
        displayBag(aBag);

        aBag.remove("D");
        count = aBag.getCurrentSize();
        System.out.println("\nAfter removing \"D\" from the bag, " +
                           "it contains " + count + " strings:");
        displayBag(aBag);
    } // end main

    < The method displayBag, as given in Listing D6-6, is here. >
} // end BagDemo
```

Output

```
Adding to the bag: A, B, C, D
The bag's capacity is 4 strings; it contains 4 strings:
A B C D

After removing "D" from the bag, it contains 3 strings:
A B C
```

Programming Tip: **Test extensively**
Insufficient testing can hide logical errors in a program that appears to execute correctly.

D6.12   **More tests.** At the end of the main method in Listing D6-8, the bag contains the three strings "A", "B", and "C". Let's add statements to main to remove "B" and display the bag again, as follows:

```java
aBag.remove("B");
count = aBag.getCurrentSize();
System.out.println("\nAfter removing \"B\" from the bag, " +
                   "it contains " + count + " strings:");
displayBag(aBag);
```

The output from these additional statements is

```
After removing "B" from the bag, it contains 2 strings:
A null
```

Although the bag contains two strings, as it should, its displayed contents are incorrect. Although "B" is no longer in the bag, we see null instead of C in the output.

What will happen if we now add two more strings to the bag? Let's see. The additional statements

```
aBag.add("E");
aBag.add("F");
count = aBag.getCurrentSize();
System.out.println("\nAfter adding E and F to the bag, " +
                   "it contains " + count + " strings:");
displayBag(aBag);
```

produce the following output:

```
A null E F
```

Since at this point the bag should contain the strings "A", "C", "E", and "F", it apparently treats the null as an entry and has lost the string "C".

D6.13   **What's wrong?** Figure D6-2 illustrates the effect of the previous additions and removals on the array bag that contains the strings in the bag aBag. You can deduce this information by examining the array bag within the class BagOfStrings, using a technique described in the previous debugging interlude.

FIGURE D6-2   The effect of the incorrect program in Listing D6-7 and D6-8 on the array bag

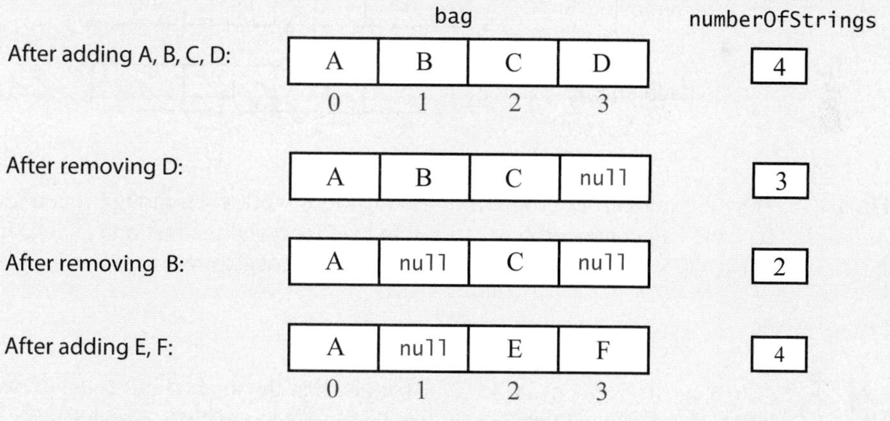

When we designed and implemented BagOfStrings in Chapter 19, we said we had to avoid the mistake we made here. Replacing an entry in an array with null leaves a gap that causes the problems we see in Figure D6-2. To correct the problem, we could shift array entries to remove the gap, as illustrated in Figure 19-6 in Chapter 19. However, since a bag does not order its entries, shifting is much more work than necessary. Instead of shifting, and instead of replacing the entry to remove with null, we replace it with the last entry in the array.

During a removal operation, the array bag is revised by the private method `removeEntry`. Thus, that method should be redefined as follows:

```
private String removeEntry(int givenIndex)
{
   String result = null;
   if (!isEmpty() && (givenIndex >= 0))
   {
      result = bag[givenIndex];              // entry to remove
      numberOfStrings--;
      bag[givenIndex] = bag[numberOfStrings];// replace entry
      bag[numberOfStrings] = null;           // remove reference
   } // end if

   return result;
} // end removeEntry
```

This definition is the same one that appears in Chapter 19 in Listing 19-6.

Figure D6-3 shows the effect of the corrected program on the same array.

FIGURE D6-3   The effect of the program on the array bag after `removeEntry` is corrected

bag   numberOfStrings

After adding A, B, C, D:

A	B	C	D
0	1	2	3

4

After removing D:

| A | B | C | null |

3

After removing B:

| A | C | null | null |

2

After adding E, F:

A	C	E	F
0	1	2	3

4

D6.14   Why did our earlier program in Listing D6-8 work even though it contained a mistake? In our first test, the bag contained four strings and we removed the last one. Replacing the last entry with `null` is exactly what needed to happen. However, doing so for other entries is wrong.

videonote
Debugging arrays

> **Note:** In Segment D6.13, we assumed that the method `getIndexOf` was correct. What if we could not find a mistake in our logic for `removeEntry`? We would have to check that `getIndexOf` was indeed correct by tracing its execution. Trying to debug a method that calls other methods that have not been debugged likely will waste your time. If we had written and debugged `getIndexOf`, then done the same with `removeEntry`, finding any error in `remove` would have been much easier.

Chapter

21

Array Lists

Contents

Prerequisites

Objectives

After studying this chapter, you should be able to

- Describe and use the standard interface List
- Create an object of the class ArrayList
- Distinguish between an array list's size and its capacity
- Use the methods of the standard class ArrayList to add, retrieve, search for, replace, or remove entries
- Distinguish between an array list and an array

You have seen how to keep a collection of objects or primitive values in a Java array. The array, however, is a rather basic construct. While the ability to use arrays is essential for any Java programmer, we have other ways to store objects of the same type. For example, Chapter 19 defined a collection as an object that groups other objects and provides various services to its client. In particular, Chapter 19 introduced the bag as one kind of collection. Different collections have different purposes and behaviors, which we specify abstractly. We can implement a specific collection as a class in several ways. Some implementations hold a collection's objects in an array, while others use different techniques.

This chapter is about another kind of collection, the **list**. While a bag does not organize its contents, the entries in a list have an order and, therefore, a position within the list, as Figure 21-1 illustrates. These entries then are referenced by their position. This chapter discusses a specification and one implementation of the list as they appear in the Java Class Library.

FIGURE 21-1 (a) A bag and (b) a list

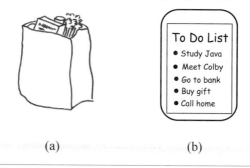

(a) (b)

The List

21.1 It's hard to imagine life without at least one list! We all make lists: to-do lists, gift lists, address lists, grocery lists, even lists of lists. These lists provide a useful way for us to organize our lives. In a program, a list provides a way to organize data. Each list has a first item, a last item, and usually items in between. That is, the items in a list have a position: first, second, and so on. An item's position might be important to you, or it might not. When adding an item to your list, you might always add it at the end, or you might insert it between two other items that are already in the list.

What can you do to an everyday list? Typically, you can

- Add a new entry at the end of the list, at its beginning, or between items
- Look at any entry
- Find out whether the list contains a particular entry
- Replace an entry
- Remove an entry
- Remove all entries
- Count the number of entries on the list
- See whether the list is empty

21.2 You might wonder about the difference between a list and a bag, which we introduced in Chapter 19. Although both the list and the bag are examples of collections, a list maintains the order of its entries, and a bag does not. Thus, the entries in a list have an order determined by the client, but the entries in a bag have no particular order. When you work with a list, you decide where an entry should be. Although you might not be conscious of the exact position of an entry on an everyday list, a program must be. A convenient way to identify a particular entry is by numbering the positions of the entries within the list. In Java, the position numbers, or indices, begin at zero, just as they do for an array. This convention allows us to describe, or specify, the operations on a list more precisely.

On the surface, a list is similar to an array: Both objects use indices to reference their entries. A list, however, is a more powerful object than an array. You work with a list by using its methods. Although an array inherits a few methods from Object, most are not useful. At this point, you should not worry about how to represent a list in your program or how to implement its operations. In fact, a list's implementation need not use an array.

The Behaviors of a List

21.3   **Example.** If you add three objects, a, b, and c, one at a time and in the order given, to the end of an initially empty list, the list will appear as

a
b
c

The object a is first, at index 0; b is at index 1; and c is last at index 2. To save space here, we will sometimes write a list's contents on one line. For example, we might write this list as

a b c

This list is not empty; it contains three entries, so its size is 3. Notice that adding entries to the end of a list does not change the positions of entries already in the list. Figure 21-2 illustrates these add operations as well as the operations that we describe next.

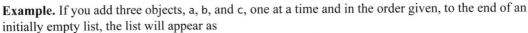
FIGURE 21-2   The effect of adding entries to an initially empty list

<table>
<tr><td>Add a</td><td>Add b</td><td>Add c</td></tr>
<tr><td>a</td><td>a
b</td><td>a
b
c</td></tr>
</table>

<table>
<tr><td>Add d at index 1</td><td>Add e at index 0</td><td>Remove entry at index 2</td></tr>
<tr><td>a
d
b
c</td><td>e
a
d
b
c</td><td>e
a
b
c</td></tr>
</table>

21.4   Now suppose that we add entries at various positions within the list. For example, adding d at index 1 places d second—that is, at index 1—within the list. Doing so, however, moves b to index 2 and c to index 3, so that the list now contains

a d b c

If we add e to the beginning of the list by adding it at index 0, the current entries in the list move to the next higher position. The list then contains

e a d b c

Look at Figure 21-2 again to see the effect of these operations.

21.5 What happens when we remove an entry? For example, if we remove the entry at index 2, we remove the third entry—d in the previous example—from the list. The list then contains

```
e a b c
```

Notice that entries after the one that was removed shift to the next lower position within the list. Figure 21-2 illustrates this change to the list.

We can replace the entry b of our list with f to get

```
e a f c
```

No other entries move or change.

 Note: The objects in a list have an order determined by the client of the list. To add, remove, or retrieve an entry, you must specify the entry's position, or index, within the list. The first entry in the list is at index 0.

 Question 1 Write pseudocode statements that add some objects to a list, as follows. First add c, then a, then b, and then d, such that the order of the objects in the list will be a, b, c, d. Your pseudocode should include an index for each addition to the list.

◼ The Interface **List**

21.6 The package `java.util` of the Java Class Library specifies the behaviors of a list by providing the standard interface `List`. Listing 21-1 contains a partial definition of `List` and includes the methods that are most important to us now. The methods appear alphabetically by name. You can see all of `List`'s methods by visiting Sun's website at http://java.sun.com/javase/6/docs/api/.

Segment 16.28 of Chapter 16 introduced the notion of a generic data type in discussing the interface `Comparable`. The interface `List` also specifies a generic type `T` instead of `Object` for the data type of its entries. Thus, the entries in a list are objects whose class types are either the same or related by inheritance. If we were to allow a list to contain objects of differing data types—that is, if we declared their data type to be `Object` rather than a generic type—we would need to determine the data type of any entry retrieved from a list and then perform a cast to that type.

LISTING 21-1 A partial definition of the interface `List`

```java
/** An interface that describes the operations of a list. */
public interface List<T>
{
   /** Adds a new entry to the end of this list.
       @param newEntry  the object to be added
       @return true */
   public boolean add(T newEntry);

   /** Adds a new entry to this list by inserting it at a given position.
       @param index  the desired index for the new entry
       @param newEntry  the object to be added */
   public void add(int index, T newEntry);
```

```java
/** Removes all entries from this list. */
public void clear();

/** Sees whether a given entry occurs in this list.
    @param anEntry  the entry to be located
    @return true if anEntry is in this list or false if not */
public boolean contains(Object anEntry);

/** Gets the entry at the given position within this list.
    @param index  the index of desired entry
    @return a reference to the desired entry */
public T get(int index);

/** Gets the index of the first occurrence of an entry in this list.
    @param anEntry  the entry to be located
    @return the index of the first occurrence of anEntry, or
            -1 if anEntry is not in this list */
public int indexOf(Object anEntry);

/** Sees whether this list is empty.
    @return true if the list is empty, or false if not */
public boolean isEmpty();

/** Gets the index of the last occurrence of an entry in this list.
    @param anEntry  the entry to be located
    @return the index of the last occurrence of anEntry, or
            -1 if anEntry is not in this list */
public int lastIndexOf(Object anEntry);

/** Removes the entry at the given position in this list.
    @param index  the index of the entry to be removed
    @return a reference to the removed entry */
public T remove(int index);

/** Removes the first occurrence of a given entry from the list,
    if possible.
    @param anEntry  the entry to be removed
    @return true if the removal was successful or false otherwise */
public boolean remove(Object anEntry);

/** Replaces the entry at the given position within this list.
    @param index  the index of the entry to be replaced
    @param newEntry  the replacement entry
    @return a reference to the entry originally at the given index */
public T set(int index, T newEntry);

/** Gets the size of this list.
    @return the number of entries in this list. */
public int size();
```

```
/** Retrieves all entries in this list.
    @param anArray  an array
    @return an array of all the entries in this list; if anArray is
            large enough to contain the entries, it will be returned;
            otherwise, a newly allocated array of the list's entries
            is returned; entries in the array are in the same order
            as in the list */
public <T> T[] toArray(T[] anArray);
```

< Other method declarations are here. >

```
} // end List
```

21.7 You could either define a class that implements the interface List or use one of several existing classes in the Java Class Library that implement List. In particular, the classes ArrayList and LinkedList, which are in the package java.util, each implement this interface. As you might suspect, the class ArrayList uses an array to contain the objects in a list. The class LinkedList, however, does not use an array. Chapter 32 will give you some insight into the way it organizes the objects in a list. You should be able to use these classes or define your own class, as appropriate, when you need a list. Since we have been thinking about arrays recently, this chapter will focus on the class ArrayList.

When we speak of a list, we are not concerned about its implementation. If a particular implementation is significant to a discussion, we will call an instance of ArrayList an **array list** and an instance of LinkedList a **linked list**.

Note: An ArrayList object is called an array list. Although it uses an array to hold its entries, you should not think of an array list as an array. Both an array list and an array are objects, but they are different kinds of objects. A list, be it an array list or a linked list, has many methods that manipulate its contents for you. You would need to program these operations for an array if you did not use a list.

Note: Chapter 19 created a bag of strings whose entries have String as their data type. We could have defined a class Bag, for example, that uses a generic data type instead of the specific data type String. We chose not to do so at that time, but you will learn how to write a class that uses generic data types in Chapter 32. Since the interface List included in the Java Class Library uses generic data types, we must use them in this chapter. Using an existing interface or class that involves generic data types, however, is easier than writing their definitions.

■ The Class **ArrayList**

We will use an object of the class ArrayList to demonstrate the behaviors of any list, as specified in the interface List. When appropriate, we will mention details particular to ArrayList's implementation of List.

An Array List's Size and Capacity

21.8 As Chapter 18 discussed, the length, or capacity, of an array is the number of elements allocated for its entries. The actual number of entries that are currently in an array often is smaller than the array's length and has no special name. For a list, however, the current number of entries is called its **size**. This number can grow without limit, other than the amount of memory available. Abstractly, a list does not have a definitive capacity, although a particular implementation might impose one. In particular, an object of ArrayList has a **capacity** that is the number of entries it can hold before it has to allocate more memory. That is, if the size of an array list reaches its capacity, a subsequent addition will cause it to increase its capacity. Figure 21-3 illustrates an array list whose size and capacity differ. Although you can ask an array list for its size, you cannot ask it for its current capacity. Also notice that the interface List does not specify a capacity for a list.

FIGURE 21-3   An array list of strings whose size is 5 and current capacity is 8

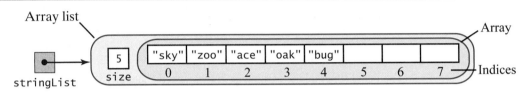

21.9   Two methods in the interface List involve a list's size; their headers are as follows:

```
/** Sees whether this list is empty.
    @return true if the list is empty, or false if not */
public boolean isEmpty()

/** Gets the size of this list.
    @return the number of entries in this list. */
public int size()
```

If nameList is an empty list, nameList.isEmpty() returns true and nameList.size() returns zero. However, if nameList is a list of five entries, nameList.isEmpty() returns false and nameList.size() returns 5.

Creating an Array List

21.10   **The constructors.** In Segment 16.29 of Chapter 16, we wrote Comparable<Circle> in the header of the class Circle that implements the interface Comparable. We use a similar notation when instantiating an object of ArrayList. For example, let's create an array list of Guest objects, where Guest is the class outlined in both Listing 20-6 and Listing 20-7 of the previous chapter, by using the default constructor of ArrayList:

```
ArrayList<Guest> guestList = new ArrayList<Guest>();
```

ArrayList<Guest> is the data type of guestList and the name of the constructor given to the new operator. In this example, the constructor involved is the default constructor; it creates an empty array list whose initial capacity—by default—is ten objects of type Guest.

A second constructor is similar to the default constructor in both its use and its effect, except that the client provides the initial capacity of the array list as an argument. For example, if we plan to add 25 Name objects to an array list, we could define it as follows:

```
ArrayList<Name> nameList = new ArrayList<Name>(25);
```

Question 2   What are two ways to create an array list that can hold ten strings?

21.11 **The method `ensureCapacity`.** You just saw that you can specify the initial capacity of an array list as an argument to ArrayList's constructor. After creating the list, you can increase its capacity by calling the method ensureCapacity. Its header is

```
/** Increases the capacity of this list, if necessary, to ensure
    that it is at least as large as the given minimum.
    @param minCapacity  the minimum capacity desired */
public void ensureCapacity(int minCapacity)
```

Since an array list can adjust its capacity without your intervention, you could simply ignore this detail. Thus, you could always use ArrayList's default constructor to create an array list and never think about its capacity. Completely ignoring the capacity, however, can waste computer time. Small but frequent increases in the capacity take more time than larger, infrequent increases. The same is true of resizing an array, as you saw in Segment 20.5 of the previous chapter. Thus, before adding a great number of objects to an array list, you should call the method ensureCapacity. For a modestly sized list, you can ignore its capacity and let the list resize itself as needed.

 Note: Abstractly, a list does not have a capacity. Its size is the current number of entries it contains, and this number can grow as necessary. Although the method ensureCapacity belongs to ArrayList, it is not a method that would belong to all implementations of a list, and so the interface List does not include it.

21.12 **Using `List` as a data type.** Segment 16.10 in Chapter 16 shows how to use an interface as a data type. Since the class ArrayList implements the interface List, you can assign an array list to a variable of type List. For example, you could write

```
List<String> myList = new ArrayList<String>();
```

The array list referenced by myList has all the methods declared in the interface List. Although ArrayList defines other methods that are not in List, they are not available to myList.

For example, consider ArrayList's method ensureCapacity. This method is not declared in the interface List, since it is not relevant to all lists. Thus, you could not write

```
myList.ensureCapacity(100); // ILLEGAL!
```

On the other hand, if your program uses only methods declared in List, you can easily change your mind about which implementation of a list you will use. For instance, you could change the previous assignment to myList to

```
List<String> myList = new LinkedList<String>();
```

without having to change anything else in the program.

 Question 3 Suppose that myList is the array list created in Question 2.

a. What does myList.isEmpty() return?

b. What does myList.size() return?

c. Would your answer to either of the previous parts of this question change if we first executed myList.ensureCapacity(25)?

Adding Entries to a List

The interface List provides two methods that add objects to a list. One method adds an entry to the end of a list, and the other adds an entry at a specified position within the list. Note that you can add duplicate entries to a list. For an ArrayList object, if the list has reached its capacity before an addition, the list will increase its capacity to accommodate a new entry without further action from you. The amount of this increase is unspecified.

21.13 **Adding to the end of an list.** Recall the header for the first add method:

```
/** Adds a new entry to the end of this list.
    @return true */
public boolean add(T newEntry)
```

Here, T represents the class type of the list's entries. The following statements provide an example of this method when used with an array list of strings; the comments show the contents of the list after each addition:

```
List<String> buddyList = new ArrayList<String>();
buddyList.add("Jake");  // Jake
buddyList.add("Emily"); // Jake, Emily
buddyList.add("Julie"); // Jake, Emily, Julie
buddyList.add("Dan");   // Jake, Emily, Julie, Dan
```

In these examples, we have ignored the boolean value that add returns, since it is always true.

Recall that the method add for the class BagOfStrings in Chapter 19 returns either true or false, according to whether the addition is successful. On the other hand, the method add for the class ExpandableBagOfStrings always returns true, just as ArrayList's method add does. In fact, ArrayList resizes its array in much the same way that ExpandableBagOfStrings does. Since an object of either of these classes can hold as many entries as the computer's memory permits, its add method can always return true.

Situations other than a lack of room in an array can prevent a successful addition to an array list, in which case an exception will occur.

21.14 **Adding within a list.** The header for the second add method is

```
/** Adds a new entry to this list by inserting it at
    a given position.
    @param index  the desired index for the new entry
    @param newEntry  the object to be added */
public void add(int index, T newEntry)
```

Let's use this method to add more entries to buddyList, as follows:

```
// Current buddyList:         Jake, Emily, Julie, Dan
buddyList.add(2, "Josh"); // Jake, Emily, Josh, Julie, Dan
buddyList.add(0, "Liz");  // Liz, Jake, Emily, Josh, Julie, Dan
buddyList.add(6, "Joe");  // Liz, Jake, Emily, Josh, Julie, Dan, Joe
```

Notice how current entries shift within the list to make room for an inserted entry. However, if the insertion occurs after all entries in the list, no shifting is necessary.

Figure 21-4a pictures the addition of Josh to the array list. Dan moves to its next higher position, then Julie moves to its next higher position, and finally Josh is inserted at the position formerly occupied by Julie. In Part b, Josh is added after the last entry currently in the list. No other entries must move.

videonote
The class ArrayList

FIGURE 21-4   Adding Josh to an array list (a) before an existing entry, Julie; (b) after all entries

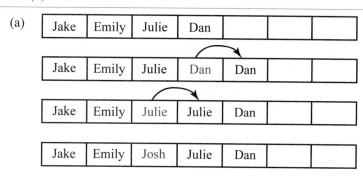

21.15   **IndexOutOfBoundsException.** When adding entries at specific positions within any list, the value of the index given to the method add must be within range. That is, it must be greater than or equal to zero and less than or equal to the number of entries currently in the list. Because of this requirement, each entry you add must be adjacent to an existing entry. Thus, an array list will have no gaps between entries.

   If the index given to add is out of range—that is, if the index is negative or exceeds the number of current entries—an IndexOutOfBoundsException occurs. Figure 21-5 shows where additions to an array list are legal.

FIGURE 21-5   Positions at which an entry can be added to a list

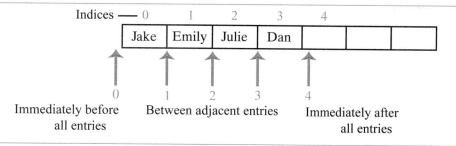

 Note: ArrayList objects cannot contain primitive values
Objects whose data type is List can contain objects only. If you want to work with a collection of primitive values, you can use either an array or an appropriate wrapper class with a list. For example, to create an array list of integers, you could use the class Integer when creating an object of ArrayList, as follows:

```
List<Integer> ages = new ArrayList<Integer>();
```

You then could either create and add `Integer` objects to this array list or rely on autoboxing, which Chapter 4 describes. Autoboxing will cause Java to convert your integers to `Integer` objects. Thus, you could write statements such as

```
ages.add(21);
```

instead of

```
ages.add(new Integer(21));
```

Note that the use of a primitive type for the element type of an `ArrayList` object will cause a syntax error:

```
ArrayList<int> ages = new ArrayList<int>(); // SYNTAX ERROR!
```

Question 4 What are the contents of `myList` after the following statements execute?

```
ArrayList<Integer> myList = new ArrayList<Integer>(3);
myList.add(5);
myList.add(10);
myList.add(2, 15);
myList.add(2, 20);
myList.add(1, 25);
```

Question 5 What is the effect of adding the following statement after the addition of 15 to `myList` in the previous question?

```
myList.ensureCapacity(75);
```

Question 6 What is the effect of each of the following calls to add on the list `yourList`? Assume that prior to each call, `yourList` is a list of the `Integer` objects represented by the following integers: 5, 10, 15, 20, 25.

   a. `yourList.add(6, 30)`
   b. `yourList.add(5, 35)`
   c. `yourList.add(0, 40)`
   d. `yourList.add(yourList.size(), 30)`

Retrieving Entries

21.16   **Retrieving one entry.** You can access any entry within a list by invoking the method get. Its header has the following form:

```
/** Gets the entry at the given position within this list.
    @param index  the index of desired entry
    @return a reference to the desired entry */
public T get(int index)
```

For example, if the list `buddyList` contains the strings `"Jake"`, `"Emily"`, `"Julie"`, and `"Dan"`, as shown in Figure 21-5, `buddyList.get(2)` returns the string `"Julie"`, because `"Julie"` is at index 2 within the list.

The value of `index` must be greater than or equal to zero and less than the current number of entries in the array list. If `index` is negative or is greater than or equal to the number of current entries, an `IndexOutOfBoundsException` occurs.

21.17 **Retrieving all entries.** The method `toArray` returns an array of all the entries in a list. Its header is

```
/** Retrieves all entries in this list.
    @param anArray  an array
    @return an array of all the entries in this list; if anArray is
            large enough to contain the entries, it will be returned;
            otherwise, a newly allocated array of the list's entries
            is returned; entries in the array are in the same order
            as in the list */
public <T>  T[] toArray(T[] anArray)
```

This header uses a strange notation to indicate that the method returns an array of type `T[]`.

Suppose `buddyList` is a list of strings, like the one that Segment 21.13 creates. To get all the strings in `buddyList`, for example, you could write

```
String[] anArray = new String[buddyList.size()];
String[] buddies = buddyList.toArray(anArray);
```

Note that the data type of both the argument `anArray` and the array `buddies` is `String[]`, since `buddyList` contains strings. Because the length of the array `anArray` is the same as the size of the list, `toArray` places the list's entries into `anArray` and returns a reference to it. By assigning the returned reference to `buddies`, we cause both `anArray` and `buddies` to reference the same array. That is, they are aliases.

You can invoke `toArray` in any of the following alternate ways:

- ```
  String[] buddies = new String[buddyList.size()];
  buddyList.toArray(buddies);
  ```
- ```
  String[] buddies = buddyList.toArray(new String[buddyList.size()]);
  ```
- ```
  String[] buddies = buddyList.toArray(new String[0]);
  ```

The first two ways simply avoid the alias `anArray`. In the last way, `anArray`'s argument cannot accommodate the list's entries, and so the method creates a new array containing the entries and returns a reference to it.

21.18 Another way to retrieve all the entries in an array list is to call the method `toString`. All classes inherit this method from `Object`, and so it is not declared in the interface `List`. `ArrayList`'s version of `toString` calls the `toString` method for each object in the array list and returns those strings, separated by commas and all enclosed in a pair of square brackets. For example, if `buddyList` contains `"Jake"`, `"Emily"`, and `"Josh"`, `buddyList.toString()` would return the string `"[Jake, Emily, Josh]"`. To get meaningful results, the objects in an array list must have their own version of `toString`, not the default version provided by the class `Object`.

Question 7 What is the result of executing the following statements?

```
ArrayList<Integer> integers = new ArrayList<Integer>();
for (int i = 1; i < 6; i++)
   integers.add(2 * i);
for (int index = 1; index < 6; index++)
   System.out.print(integers.get(index) + " ");
System.out.println();
```

Question 8 If `buddyList` contains `"Suzie"`, `"Joe"`, and `"Maria"`, what does the following statement display?

```
System.out.println(buddyList);
```

Question 9 If `buddyList` contains five strings, why is the call `buddyList.add(5, "Jim")` legal but `buddyList.get(5)` is not?
```

Searching for Entries

21.19   You can search an existing list to see whether it contains a given object. The method `contains` is passed an object as an argument and returns either true if the object occurs in the list or false otherwise. Its specification is

```
/** Sees whether a given entry occurs in this list.
    @param anEntry  the entry to be located
    @return true if anEntry is in this list or false if not */
public boolean contains(Object anEntry)
```

You also can get the index of any entry within an array list by calling either the method `indexOf` or the method `lastIndexOf`. The method `indexOf` locates the first occurrence of the entry, while `lastIndexOf` locates the entry's last occurrence. In case the entry is not in the list, each of these methods returns –1. Their specifications follow:

```
/** Gets the index of the first occurrence of an entry in this list.
    @param anEntry  the entry to be located
    @return the index of the first occurrence of anEntry, or
            -1 if anEntry is not in this list */
public int indexOf(Object anEntry)

/** Gets the index of the last occurrence of an entry in this list.
    @param anEntry  the entry to be located
    @return the index of the last occurrence of anEntry, or
            -1 if anEntry is not in this list */
public int lastIndexOf(Object anEntry)
```

Because each of the previous three methods searches a list for a particular object, the method `equals` is called. This `equals` method belongs to the class used to instantiate the objects in the list and must have a meaningful definition in order for `contains`, `indexOf`, and `lastIndexOf` to work correctly.

Question 10 If `buddyList` contains "Suzie", "Joe", "Maria", and "Joe", what is the value of each of the following expressions?

   a. `buddyList.contains("Joe");`
   b. `buddyList.indexOf("Joe");`
   c. `buddyList.lastIndexOf("Joe");`
   d. `buddyList.contains("Emma");`
   e. `buddyList.indexOf("Emma");`

Replacing Entries

21.20   `ArrayList` has the method `set`, which you can use to replace any existing entry in the list. You give the method the index of the entry to be replaced as well as its replacement. The method not only replaces the entry, but it also returns a reference to the entry originally at the specified position. The method's header follows:

```
/** Replaces the entry at the given position within this list.
    @param index  the index of the entry to be replaced
    @param newEntry  the replacement entry
    @return a reference to the entry originally at the given index */
public T set(int index, T newEntry)
```

If `buddyList` contains "Liz", "Jake", "Emily", and "Josh", the statement

```
String oldEntry = buddyList.set(1, "John")
```

changes the list so that it now contains "Liz", "John", "Emily", and "Josh". The statement also sets `oldEntry` to reference "Jake", which is the string originally at index 1 in the list.

Removing Entries

21.21   Three methods remove entries from an array list. The method `clear` removes all entries, leaving the list empty. The method `remove` has two forms: One removes the entry at a given position, and the other removes the first occurrence of a specific entry. Their specifications follow:

```
/** Removes all entries from this list. */
public void clear()

/** Removes the entry at the given position in this list.
    @param index  the index of the entry to be removed
    @return a reference to the removed entry */
public T remove(int index)

/** Removes the first occurrence of a given entry from the list,
    if possible.
    @param anEntry  the entry to be removed
    @return true if the removal was successful, or false otherwise */
public boolean remove(Object anEntry)
```

21.22   For example, if `buddyList` contains

        "Liz", "Jake", "Emily", and "Josh"

The statement

        String removedEntry = buddyList.remove(1)

removes "Jake" from the list and assigns the string to `removedEntry`. The list now contains

        "Liz", "Emily", and "Josh"

Notice how current entries are shifted within the list to avoid a gap at the position of the removed entry, as Figure 21-6a illustrates.

FIGURE 21-6   Removing an entry from an array list when the entry is (a) before an existing entry; (b) after all other entries

(a)

| Liz | Jake | Emily | Josh | | | |

| Liz | Emily | Emily | Josh | | | |

| Liz | Emily | Josh | Josh | | | |

| Liz | Emily | Josh | | | | |

(b)

| Liz | Jake | Emily | Josh | | | |

| Liz | Jake | Emily | | | | |

However, if the entry being removed is at the end of the list, no shifting is necessary. For example, the invocation

    buddyList.remove("Josh")

removes "Josh" from the list, as Figure 21-6b shows, and returns true. The invocation

    buddyList.remove("John")

leaves the list unchanged and returns false. Finally, the statement

    buddyList.clear()

leaves the list buddyList empty.

videonote
Arrays, array lists,
and interfaces

21.23   When removing an entry by its position, the index given to remove must be greater than or equal to zero and less than the current number of entries in the array list. If index is negative or is greater than or equal to the number of current entries, an IndexOutOfBoundsException occurs.

Question 11 What is the effect of each of the following calls to remove on the list buddyList, and what does the method return? Assume that prior to each call, the list buddyList contains "Liz", "Jake", "Josh", "Emily", and "Josh".

    a.   buddyList.remove("Josh")
    b.   buddyList.remove(1)
    c.   buddyList.remove("Derek")
    d.   buddyList.remove(5)

Question 12 Write pseudocode statements that exchange the third and seventh entries in a list of ten objects. Your pseudocode should include an index for each operation on the list.

Question 13 Why does removing an entry from an array list involve shifting array entries, but removing an entry from a bag does not?

> **Note:** **Avoiding an IndexOutOfBoundsException when working with a list**
>
> When retrieving, replacing, or removing an entry in a list, the index given to the method must be greater than or equal to zero and less than the current number of entries in the list. If index is negative or is greater than or equal to the number of current entries, an IndexOutOfBoundsException occurs. Figure 21-7 shows where in a list these operations are legal.

FIGURE 21-7   Positions at which an entry can be retrieved, replaced, or removed in a list

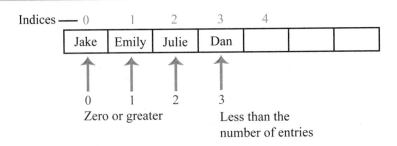

21.24 **Example.** A professor wants an alphabetical list of the names of the students who arrive for class today. As each student enters the room, the professor adds the student's name to a list. It is up to the professor to place each name into its correct position in the list so that the names will be in alphabetical order. The list does *not* choose the order of its entries.

The following Java statements place the names Amy, Ellen, Bob, Drew, Aaron, and Carol in an alphabetical list. The comment at the end of each statement shows the list after the statement executes.

```
// make an alphabetical list of names as students enter a room
List<String> alphaList = new ArrayList<String>();
alphaList.add("Amy");        // Amy
alphaList.add("Ellen");      // Amy Ellen
alphaList.add(1, "Bob");     // Amy Bob Ellen
alphaList.add(2, "Drew");    // Amy Bob Drew Ellen
alphaList.add(0, "Aaron");   // Aaron Amy Bob Drew Ellen
alphaList.add(3, "Carol");   // Aaron Amy Bob Carol Drew Ellen
```

After initially adding Amy to the empty list and Ellen to the end of the list (at index 1), the professor inserts

- Bob between Amy and Ellen at index 1
- Drew between Bob and Ellen at index 3
- Aaron before Amy at index 0
- Carol between Bob and Drew at index 3

This technique of inserting each name into a collection of alphabetized names is called an **insertion sort.** We will discuss this and other ways of ordering items in Chapter 23.

If we now remove the entry at index 3—Carol—by writing

```
alphaList.remove(3);
```

Drew and Ellen will then be at indices 3 and 4, respectively. Thus, `alphaList.get(3)` would return a reference to Drew.

Finally, suppose that we want to replace a name in this list. We cannot replace a name with just any name and expect that the list will remain in alphabetical order. Replacing Bob with Ben by writing

```
alphaList.set(2, "Ben");
```

would maintain alphabetical order, but replacing Bob with Nancy would not. The list's alphabetical order resulted from our original decisions about where to add names to the list. The order did not come about automatically as a result of list operations. That is, the client, not the list, maintained the order.

 Question 14 Suppose that `alphaList` contains a list of the four names Amy, Ellen, Bob, and Drew as strings. Write pseudocode statements that swap Ellen and Bob and that then swap Ellen and Drew so that the list will be in alphabetical order.

 Note: A list of objects having unrelated or unknown data types
Seldom will you want to store objects of unrelated or unknown classes in a list. If you do, however, use `Object` as the data type of the entries when you create the list. For example, you can use `ArrayList<Object>` as the list's data type.

Note: Using `ArrayList` instead of `ArrayList<T>`
If you write a statement such as

```
ArrayList myList = new ArrayList();
```

instead of

```
ArrayList<String> nameList = new ArrayList<String>();
```

for example, you will get an array list whose entries have the data type `Object`. Although you would be able to add an object of any class type to `myList`, you would have to cast it to the appropriate class type when retrieving it from the list. For instance, you can add a string to `myList` by writing a statement such as

```
myList.add("Josh");
```

However, if you invoke the method `get` to retrieve `"Josh"`, you must cast the resulting object to `String` before assigning it to a `String` variable. That is, you would write something like

```
String firstName = (String)myList.get(0);
```

On the other hand, if you add `"Josh"` to `nameList` by writing

```
nameList.add("Josh");
```

you can retrieve it without a cast, as follows:

```
String firstName = nameList.get(0);
```

Before generic data types were added to Java, you had no choice but to use `ArrayList` without the `<T>` notation, thus creating an array list of `Object` entries. Java still allows you to use `ArrayList` in this way, enabling older code, written before the language was enhanced, to execute. You should not write new code that omits the `<T>` notation, however. Instead, if you want a list of `Object` entries, you should follow the advice in the previous note.

■ Arrays Versus Array Lists

21.25   We conclude this chapter by comparing the syntax for an array of objects and an array list of the same objects. We will use objects of the class `Guest`, which was outlined in Listing 20-7 in the previous chapter. Let's begin by creating four `Guest` objects, as follows:

```
Guest guest1 = new Guest(new Name("Anna", "Baker"), 1, 75);
Guest guest2 = new Guest(new Name("Charlie", "Dodge"), 1, 100);
Guest guest3 = new Guest(new Name("Emma", "Frank"), 2, 25);
Guest guest4 = new Guest(new Name("Garth", "Henry"), 2, 50);
```

21.26   **Creating an array.** To create an array of 15 elements and add these `Guest` objects to it, we write the following statements:

```
Guest[] guests = new Guest[15];
guests[0] = guest1;
guests[1] = guest2;
guests[2] = guest3;
guests[3] = guest4;
```

Although the expression `guests.length` gives us the length—15—of the array, this array is partially filled, and so we must count the number of entries ourselves. We'll store this count in the integer variable `guestCount`:

```
int guestCount = 4;
```

21.27 **Creating an array list.** Now let's create an array list whose initial capacity is 15 and add the four Guest objects to it:

```
ArrayList<Guest> guests = new ArrayList<Guest>(15);
guests.add(guest1);
guests.add(guest2);
guests.add(guest3);
guests.add(guest4);
```

The array list—not the programmer—keeps track of how many entries we have added to it. We can ask it for this value as follows:

```
int guestCount = guests.size();
```

21.28 **Displaying the entries in an array.** For an appropriate value of index, guests[index] is a Guest object within the array. To display the entry's data, we use the accessor methods for the class Guest. Thus, we have the following:

- guests[index].getName() is the guest's name
- guests[index].getTableNumber() is the guest's table number
- guests[index].getGift() is the guest's contribution

By using these expressions in the following loop, we can display the guests' data:

```
for (int index = 0; index < guestCount; index++)
{
   Name guestName    = guests[index].getName();
   int tableNumber   = guests[index].getTableNumber();
   int gift          = guests[index].getGift();

   System.out.println(guestName + " at table #" + tableNumber +
                          " gave $" + gift + ".");
} // end for
```

This loop displays the following output:

```
Anna Baker at table #1 gave $75.
Charlie Dodge at table #1 gave $100.
Emma Frank at table #2 gave $25.
Garth Henry at table #2 gave $50.
```

Question 15 Is it possible to revise the previous loop using a for-each statement? If so, write the loop; if not, explain why not.

21.29 **Displaying the entries in an array list.** For an appropriate value of index, guests.get(index) is a Guest object within the array list. Using Guest's accessor methods once again, we have

- guests.get(index).getName() is the guest's name
- guests.get(index).getTableNumber() is the guest's table number
- guests.get(index).getGift() is the guest's contribution

By using these expressions in the following loop, we can display the guests' data:

```
for (int index = 0; index < guestCount; index++)
{
   Name guestName    = guests.get(index).getName();
   int tableNumber   = guests.get(index).getTableNumber();
   int gift          = guests.get(index).getGift();

   System.out.println(guestName + " at table #" + tableNumber +
                          " gave $" + gift + ".");
} // end for
```

As an alternative to this loop, we can use a for-each loop, as follows:

```
for (Guest aGuest : guests)
{
   Name guestName   = aGuest.getName();
   int tableNumber = aGuest.getTableNumber();
   int gift        = aGuest.getGift();

   System.out.println(guestName + " at table #" + tableNumber +
                         " gave $" + gift + ".");
} // end for
```

These loops each display the same output as the loop given in the previous segment.

21.30   **Using `toString` when displaying a collection.** A class's `toString` method is not always appropriate when you want to display an object's data in a particular format. In those cases, you would use the object's accessor methods, as we have shown in the previous two segments. However, if `toString` does provide appropriate output, the loops we have just written can be simplified greatly.

Let's suppose that the class `Guest` defines the following version of `toString`:

```
public String toString()
{
   return guestName + " at table #" + tableNumber +
                         " gave $" + gift + ".";
} // end toString
```

Notice that it returns the same string that is displayed by the code given in the previous two segments. Thus, the following loop displays the contents of the array `guests`:

```
for (int index = 0; index < guestCount; index++)
   System.out.println(guests[index]);
```

You can display the contents of the array list `guests` by using either of the following two loops:

```
for (int index = 0; index < guestCount; index++)
   System.out.println(guests.get(index));
```

or

```
for (Guest aGuest : guests)
   System.out.println(aGuest);
```

Each of these loops results in the same output shown in Segment 21.28.

Since `ArrayList` has its own `toString` method, you can use it instead of writing a loop to display the contents of an array list. However, the results may not be to your liking, as the following statement and output show:

```
System.out.println(guests); // uses ArrayList's toString method

// Output:
[Anna Baker at table #1 gave $75., Charlie Dodge at table #1 gave $100., Emma
Frank at table #2 gave $25., Garth Henry at table #2 gave $50.]
```

Syntax: The for-each statement with collections

Recall from Chapters 13 and 20 (Segments 13.10 and 20.1) that you can use a for-each statement to cycle through every entry in a group of values such as an enumeration or an array. When that group is a collection, the for-each statement has the following form:

```
for (entry-type   variable : collection-name)
    body
```

The body of the loop executes once for each entry in the collection and has a reference to each entry in *variable*. The data type of the entries in the collection is *entry-type*. In the case of a list, the loop cycles *collection-name*.size() times.

Question 16 If you have not kept track of the capacity of the array myArray, can you find out what it is? If so, how?

Question 17 If you have not kept track of the number of entries you placed into the array myArray, can you find that number from the array? If so, how?

Question 18 If you have not kept track of the capacity of the array list myList, can you find it? If so, how?

Question 19 If you have not kept track of how many entries are actually in the array list myList, can you find that number? If so, how?

Note: Arrays versus array lists

We began this chapter by citing some advantages of array lists over arrays. In general, an array list is easier to use than an array. However, an array list can consume more computer time than an array used for the same purpose. This increase in time is usually not a major concern.

Note: The size of arrays, strings, and array lists

Suppose myArray is an array, myString is a string, and myList is an array list. Then

- myArray.length is the number of elements reserved for the array. An array cannot tell you how many entries it actually contains. Note that length is a public data field.
- myString.length() is the number of characters in the string. Note that length is a public method in the class String.
- myList.size() is the current number of entries in the array list. The public method size belongs to the class ArrayList. No method is available to obtain a list's current capacity.

videonote
A problem
solved

CHAPTER SUMMARY

- A list is a collection that maintains a client-determined order for its entries. You reference these entries by their positions within the list. The positions, like array indices, begin at zero.

- The interface List declares the methods that a list should have. The classes ArrayList and LinkedList are two standard implementations of this interface. Each of these classes defines more methods than are declared in the interface List. The objects of ArrayList are called array lists; the objects of LinkedList are called linked lists.

- ArrayList is defined in terms of a generic data type. When you create an array list, you indicate the data type of its entries. This data type must be a class type.

- The capacity of an array list is the maximum number of entries it can hold before having to allocate more space.

- An array list has an initial capacity, which you can specify. If you omit an initial capacity, the default capacity is 10.

- The size of a list is the number of entries it currently contains.

- You can add entries at the beginning or the end of a list or at any position within the list.

- You can retrieve entries from a list either individually by position or all at once as an array.

- You can see whether a list contains a particular entry or get the index of its first or last occurrence in the list.

- You can replace the entry at a given position within a list.

- You can remove an entry from a list by specifying either its value or its position. You also can delete all the entries in a list.

- Arrays and array lists are two different kinds of objects. In general, array lists are easier to use.

EXERCISES

1. What are the advantages of using a list instead of an array to hold a group of objects?

2. Write a Java statement to create an array list, named studentList, that will contain Student objects. The initial capacity of the list should be

   a. 10
   b. 100

3. Explain why an addition to an array list might require significantly more execution time than the addition that precedes it.

4. If you know that you will have 1000 entries to add to an array list, what capacity should the array list have when it is first created? Explain your answer.

5. Imagine a main method that creates the array list studentList, as Exercise 2 describes. Assume that the class containing main also defines the static method getStudent, which interacts with the user and returns either a new Student object or null. Write statements for the main method that add each Student object returned by getStudent to studentList.

6. After you add several Student objects to the list studentList, as created in the previous exercise, what Java expression represents the number of entries in the list?

7. What Java statements will tell the user whether the Student object aStudent is in the list studentList?

8. What Java statements will replace an occurrence of the Student object aStudent in the list studentList with the Student object substitute? Accommodate the possibility that aStudent does not occur in the list.

9. Write Java statements to display a given array list of Student objects. Be sure to accommodate an empty array list.

10. Consider an array list of strings, some of which might be duplicates. Create another array list of all the strings in the first list, but without duplicates.

11. Suppose that the class ArrayList did not have the method set. Write Java statements at the client level that replace an object in the array list myList. The object's position in the list is givenPosition and the replacement object is newObject.

12. Suppose that the class ArrayList did not have the method contains. If myList is an array list of strings, write Java statements at the client level that see whether the string aString is in the list myList.

13. A *permutation* is one of several possible ways in which you can order or arrange a group of things. Write a program that displays a new random permutation of the integers 0 to 9 at the request of its user. For example, the program's output could be as follows:

```
2 8 0 1 9 3 5 4 6 7
Another permutation? yes
6 5 3 1 0 9 7 4 2 8
Another permutation? no
Bye!
```

Use a list to contain your permutation. Each time you generate a random integer between 0 and 9, check to see whether the integer is in the list. If it is, generate another random integer. If it is not, add it to the list. Continue this process until the list contains ten integers.

14. Repeat the previous exercise, but use the following approach. In addition to a list that will contain the permutation, create a second list that contains the integers 0 through 9. Remove an integer at random from the second list and add it to the end of the first list. Repeat this process until the second list is empty.

15. Think about how you would solve Exercises 13 and 14 using arrays instead of lists. Which approach is easier to code? Why?

16. Exercise 8 in the previous chapter defined a magic square as a square n-by-n array of positive integers such that the sum of each row, column, and diagonal is the same constant. A *normal magic square* is an n-by-n magic square composed of the integers 1, 2, ..., n^2. For example, the following magic square is a normal magic square composed of the integers 1 through 16, or 4^2:

16	3	2	13
5	10	11	8
9	6	7	12
4	15	14	1

The sum of each row, column, and diagonal is 34. Normal magic squares exist that are three by three or larger.

If you have an array list of n^2 objects of type Integer, where n is greater than 2, write code that tests whether a normal magic square can contain only the integers represented by the objects in the list.

17. Write code that accomplishes the following tasks: Consider two array lists that can hold objects of the class Coin, which appears in Listing 8-5 of Chapter 8. One list is named myList and contains several of these objects, while the other list is empty and is named yourList. One at a time, remove a coin from myList and toss it. If the result of the toss is heads, the coin is yours to keep: Place it into yourList. If the coin toss is tails, you must return the coin to myList in the same position from which you removed it. After all coins have been tossed once, compute the total value of the coins in each list.

18. Suppose that you have an array list that is created by the following statement:

```
List<Name> nameList = new ArrayList<Name>();
```

Imagine that someone has added to the list several instances of the class `Name` as defined in Listing 6-5 of Chapter 6.

   a. Write Java statements that display the last names of the people in the list in the same order in which they appear in the list. Do not alter the list.

   b. Write Java statements that interchange the two names that occur first and last in the list.

19. Suppose that you have a list that is created by the following statement:

```
List<Double> quizScores = new ArrayList<Double>();
```

Imagine that someone has added to this list the quiz scores received by a student throughout a course. The professor would like to know the average of these quiz scores, ignoring the lowest score.

   a. Write Java statements at the client level that will find and remove the lowest score in the list.

   b. Write Java statements at the client level that will compute the average of the scores remaining in the list.

PROJECTS

1. Define a class that implements the interface `BagOfStringsInterface`, as given in Listing 19-1 of Chapter 19. Use an array list to hold the strings in a bag.

2. Define a class `RingOfStrings` that represents a ring and implements the interface described in Exercise 12 of Chapter 19. Use an array list to hold the strings in a ring.

3. A recipe contains a title, a list of ingredients, and a list of directions. An entry in the list of ingredients contains an amount, a unit, and a description. For example, an object that represents 2 cups of flour could be an entry in this list. An entry in the list of directions is a string.

Design and implement a class of recipes. Create any other classes that you need, but use the class `ArrayList` for the two lists in a recipe.

4. Santa Claus allegedly keeps lists of those who are naughty and those who are nice. On the naughty list are the names of those who will get coal in their stockings. On the nice list are those who will receive gifts. Each object in this list contains a name (an instance of the class `Name` in Listing 6-5 of Chapter 6) and a list of that person's gifts (an instance of `ArrayList`). Design and implement a class of the objects on the nice list. Write a client that creates and demonstrates Santa's nice list.

5. Create a vocabulary drill for a foreign language. Begin by creating a class, `Vocabulary`, of word pairs. For each pair, one word or phrase is in the primary language—English, for example—and the other is in the language to be learned. Associated with each word is a count of the number of times the user of the drill has answered correctly.

Now create an array list of `Vocabulary` objects, each of which contains one pair of words. At random, select an object in this list, and randomly present one of the words in the object for the user to translate. Indicate whether the user's translation is correct. If it is, count it; if it is not, present another word at random. If the user is able to translate a particular word correctly a predetermined number of times, do not present that word again.

For example, a drill for an English-speaking user who is learning German might contain the following dialogue:

```
good
haben Incorrect! The correct response is "guten"
tag
day Correct!
```

6. Consider the following interface for a list of strings:

```java
public interface ListOfStringsInterface
{
    public boolean add(String newEntry);
    public void add(int index, String newEntry);
    public void clear();
    public boolean contains(String anEntry);
    public String get(int index);
    public int indexOf(String anEntry);
    public boolean isEmpty()
    public int lastIndexOf(String anEntry);
    public String remove(int index);
    public boolean remove(String anEntry);
    public String set(int index, String newEntry);
    public int size();
} // end ListOfStringsInterface
```

   a. Write comments in javadoc style to describe each method in this interface. Assume that the behavior of the methods is analogous to that specified in Listing 21-1.

   b. Define a class ListOfStrings that implements this interface. Begin by identifying and defining a group of core methods as described just prior to Segment 19.15 of Chapter 19. Write a program that demonstrates your new class.

ANSWERS TO SELF-TEST QUESTIONS

1. *Add* c *at index* 0 *(or Add* c *to the end of the list)*
   Add a *at index* 0
   Add b *at index* 1
   Add d *at index* 3

2. `ArrayList<String> integerList = new ArrayList<String>();`

   and

   `ArrayList<String> integerList = new ArrayList<String>(10);`

3. a. True
   b. 0
   c. No

4. myList contains the Integer objects represented by the following integers: 5, 25, 10, 20, 15.

5. The capacity of the list increases to 75, which is likely much larger than the list's original capacity if ensureCapacity had not been called. The contents of the list, however, are unaffected.

6. a. An IndexOutOfBoundsException occurs.
   b. 35 is added to the end of the list, so it contains 5, 10, 15, 20, 25, 35.
   c. 40 is added to the beginning of the list, so it contains 40, 5, 10, 15, 20, 25.
   d. 30 is added to the end of the list, so it contains 5, 10, 15, 20, 25, 30.

7. The call integers.get(5) causes an IndexOutOfBoundsException.

8. [Suzie, Joe, Maria]

9. To add an entry at a given index, the index must be greater than or equal to zero and less than or equal to the number of entries currently in the list. The list buddyList contains five strings, and its last string has an index of 4. Thus, adding "Jim" at index 5 is legal. On the other hand, since the index of the last string in buddyList is 4, buddyList.get(4) is legal, but buddyList.get(5) is not. The index given to the method get as an argument must be greater than or equal to zero and less than the current number of entries in the array list.

10.
   a. True
   b. 1
   c. 3
   d. False
   e. −1

11.
   a. The first occurrence of "Josh" is removed, so buddyList now contains "Liz", "Jake", "Emily", and "Josh". The method remove returns true.
   b. The entry at index 1, which is "Jake", is removed, so buddyList now contains "Liz", "Josh", "Emily", and "Josh". The method remove returns true.
   c. The method remove returns false, and the list is unchanged.
   d. An IndexOutOfBoundsException occurs.

12. The third and seventh entries in the list have indices of 2 and 6, respectively.

```
seven = myList.remove(6)
three = myList.remove(2)
myList.add(2, seven)
myList.add(6, three)
```

Another solution:

```
seven = myList.get(6)
three = myList.get(2)
myList.set(2, seven)
myList.set(6, three)
```

13. A list must maintain the order of its entries, so when any entry except the last one is removed from the array, the subsequent entries must be shifted. This approach ensures that the entries remain in adjacent array elements. A bag does not maintain any order for its entries. Even if you use an array to contain a bag's entries, you can remove an entry simply by replacing it with the last entry in the array. For both a list and a bag, you then decrease the count of entries.

14.
```
bob = alphaList.remove(2)
ellen = alphaList.remove(1)
alphaList.add(1, bob)
alphaList.add(2, ellen)
drew = alphaList.remove(3)
ellen = alphaList.remove(2)
alphaList.add(2, drew)
alphaList.add(3, ellen)
```

Another solution uses get and set, much as the second solution to Question 12 does.

15. A for-each loop cycles once for each element in an array. It is not appropriate if guestCount is less than guests.length. A for-each loop is appropriate for a full array, that is, if guestCount is equal to guests.length.

16. Yes; myArray.length is the capacity, or length, of the array.

17. In general, no. If you know something about the array's contents, you might be able to search for an element that does not contain a valid entry. For example, an array of strings likely has null in its unoccupied elements.

18. No

19. Yes; myList.size() returns the number of entries in the list.

Chapter

22

Arrays When Drawing

Contents

Prerequisites

Objectives

After studying this chapter, you should be able to

• Use the Graphics methods drawPolygon and fillPolygon to draw or paint a polygon
• Use the class Polygon to represent or manipulate a polygon
• Use the Graphics method drawPolyline to draw a polyline
• Use the class Point to represent or modify a point on a two-dimensional surface
• Define and use an array of buttons or other graphical objects

Arrays give us more programming power in general and allow us to create more-complex graphical applications. We'll begin this chapter by drawing a polygon—a closed figure having several sides—given the *x*- and *y*-coordinates of its vertices, which are stored in parallel arrays. Using the same arrays, we also can draw a polyline, which is like a polygon but without one of its sides. Unfortunately, some classes in the Abstract Window Toolkit (AWT) use parallel arrays—as you will see—even though we now discourage their use.

We will also investigate the classes Polygon and Point from the Java Class Library. Although we will use them to define a class of right triangles, you also can create more-complex shapes. Using four right-triangle objects, we will form a diamond shape and create a quilt using a two-dimensional array of squares that contain these diamonds.

The chapter ends by creating a keypad represented by an array of buttons, that is, JButton objects. A user can click buttons on the keypad to give a program integer input data.

■ Polygons

22.1   The quilt created in Chapter 14 uses simple squares of various colors. Let's try something more complicated. Suppose each square is black and contains a diamond shape whose vertices bisect the sides of the square, as Figure 22-1 illustrates. The diamond itself is divided into four triangular regions of different colors. These four triangles are actually right triangles whose right angles share a common vertex at the diamond's center.

FIGURE 22-1   A square containing a diamond design

Although we could draw the sides of a triangle without difficulty by using the method drawLine, we will treat the triangle as a polygon. A *polygon* is simply a closed two-dimensional figure composed of straight lines that do not cross. Triangles, rectangles, and octagons are examples of polygons. We think of these shapes as polygons because the Java Class Library provides classes and methods to represent and display them.

Polygon Methods in the Class Graphics

22.2   To describe a polygon, we need the coordinates of its vertices. Java expects these coordinates to be in two arrays that are parallel. One array contains the *x*-coordinates of the vertices, and the other contains their *y*-coordinates. For example, a five-sided polygon, commonly called a pentagon, could have vertices at the points (150, 200), (150, 150), (175, 125), (200, 150), and (200, 200). The following arrays represent these vertices:

```java
int[] xVertices = {150, 150, 175, 200, 200};
int[] yVertices = {200, 150, 125, 150, 200};
```

If pen is a Graphics object and vertexCount is the number of vertices, the statement

```java
pen.drawPolygon(xVertices, yVertices, vertexCount);
```

draws the outline of the pentagon shown in Figure 22-2a. To fill the interior of the pentagon, as shown in Figure 22-2b, we would write

```java
pen.fillPolygon(xVertices, yVertices, vertexCount);
```

If we do not draw one side of the polygon, we get an open figure called a *polyline*. The statement

```java
pen.drawPolyline(xVertices, yVertices, vertexCount);
```

draws the polyline shown in Figure 22-2c. Note that the first point (150, 200) and last point (200, 200) given by the arrays xVertices and yVertices are the two that are not connected by a line. If those two points happen to be the same, drawPolyline and drawPolygon would have the same effect: That is, the figure would be closed.

FIGURE 22-2　　(a) The outline of a polygon; (b) a filled polygon; (c) a polyline

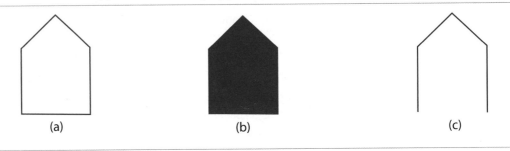

(a)   (b)   (c)

Note: Graphics methods for polygons and polylines

The methods drawPolygon, fillPolygon, and drawPolyline in the class Graphics take the same arguments, as follows:

- xCoords is an array of *x*-coordinates
- yCoords is an array of *y*-coordinates
- count is the number of points defined by the arrays of coordinates

The headers for these methods follow:

```java
/** Draws the outline of the polygon having the given vertices. */
public void drawPolygon(int[] xCoords, int[] yCoords, int count)

/** Fills the interior of the polygon having the given vertices. */
public void fillPolygon(int[] xCoords, int[] yCoords, int count)

/** Draws lines between the points (xCoords[i], yCoords[i]) and
    (xCoords[i + 1], yCoords[i + 1]) for i = 0, 1, ..., count - 2. */
public void drawPolyline(int[] xCoords, int[] yCoords, int count)
```

Each of the methods drawPolygon and fillPolygon has another form that accepts a Polygon object as its only argument. We will give an example of these methods in the next section, when we describe the standard class Polygon.

Note: Why do standard classes such as `Graphics` and `Polygon` use parallel arrays? The classes `Graphics` and `Polygon` have existed since the first version of Java. For whatever reasons, the designers of these classes chose to use parallel arrays. Since we now discourage the use of parallel arrays, why do these classes remain as is? The Java designers strive to accommodate code that other programmers have written already, even as Java and its library of classes evolve. Thus, these original classes continue to exist. We need to either work with what we have or design our own classes.

Question 1 Consider a triangle whose base and height are each 50 pixels. The vertex opposite the base is at the top edge of the drawing area, and the base's leftmost point is at the left edge of the drawing area. What are the coordinates of the triangle's vertices? What Java statements define parallel arrays that represent these coordinates?

Question 2 What Java statement draws the triangle described by your answer to the previous question? Assume that `pen` is a `Graphics` object.

Question 3 If the arrays that answer Question 1 are named `xVertices` and `yVertices`, what is the result of the following statement?

```
pen.drawPolyline(xVertices, yVertices, 3);
```

The Class Polygon

Instead of representing a polygon only by its vertices, we can create an object of the standard class `Polygon`, which is a part of the AWT, from the coordinates of the polygon's vertices. Using a `Polygon` object to represent a polygon gives us a more convenient way to work with the figure than if we used only arrays of vertex coordinates. `Polygon` defines methods that perform tasks on an existing polygon, such as testing whether a given point is within its boundary, adding a vertex, and changing the polygon's position. We will describe only the latter two methods here. But first we will look at the class's constructors. You can refer to the documentation for the Java Class Library on Sun's website to learn more about this class.

22.3 **The constructors.** One of `Polygon`'s constructors accepts the same arguments as the method `drawPolygon`. The specifications for this constructor follow:

```
/** Creates a polygon having the given vertices. */
public Polygon(int[] xCoords, int[] yCoords, int count)
```

For example, if `xVertices` and `yVertices` are the arrays of vertices given in Segment 22.2, and `vertexCount` is the number of vertices, the following statement creates a `Polygon` object:

```
Polygon myPentagon = new Polygon(xVertices, yVertices, vertexCount);
```

Sometimes creating arrays of coordinates just so you can invoke the previous constructor is inconvenient. In such cases, you can invoke `Polygon`'s default constructor to get an empty polygon and then add points to it. To add points to a polygon, you use the class's method `addPoint`, which we introduce next.

22.4 **The method addPoint.** You can add a vertex to any existing `Polygon` object by using the method `addPoint`, passing it the integer coordinates of the point as arguments. Its specification is

```
/** Adds a vertex, given its coordinates, to this polygon. */
public void addPoint(int xCoordinate, int yCoordinate)
```

For example, the following statements create a `Polygon` object that represents the triangle whose vertices are (0, 50), (25, 0), and (50, 50). This is the same triangle that you created earlier when answering Question 1.

```
Polygon triangle = new Polygon();
triangle.addPoint(0, 50);
triangle.addPoint(25, 0);
triangle.addPoint(50, 50);
```

22.5 **The method translate.** The method `translate` moves the position of a polygon by adjusting the values of the coordinates of its vertices. In effect, the method moves the polygon by a given amount along the *x*-axis and by another amount along the *y*-axis. Its specification appears as follows:

```
/** Changes the location of this polygon by adding the
    given amounts to the coordinates of its vertices. */
public void translate(int xIncrement, int yIncrement)
```

For example, consider the `Polygon` object `triangle` that we created in the previous segment. The following statements will move the triangle to the right by 75 pixels and down by 50 pixels, as Figure 22-3 shows:

```
triangle.translate(75, 50);
```

FIGURE 22-3   The effect of the method `translate` on a `Polygon` object: (a) before; (b) after

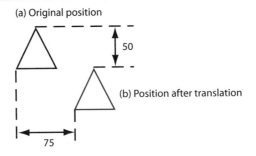

Question 4 If you did not have the class `Polygon`, what statements could you use to draw the two triangles pictured in Figure 22-3?

Note: Graphics methods for Polygon objects

As mentioned in an earlier note, each of the methods `drawPolygon` and `fillPolygon` has another form that takes a `Polygon` object as its only argument. Their specifications follow:

```
/** Draws the outline of a given polygon. */
public void drawPolygon(Polygon poly)

/** Fills the interior of a given polygon. */
public void fillPolygon(Polygon poly)
```

To draw the polygon shown previously in Figure 22-2a and created in Segment 22.3, we can write

```
pen.drawPolygon(myPentagon);
```

where pen is a `Graphics` object. Likewise, the statement

```
pen.fillPolygon(myPentagon);
```

displays the filled polygon in Figure 22-2b.

Note: Constructors and selected methods of the class Polygon

```
/** Creates an empty polygon. */
public Polygon()

/** Creates a polygon having the given vertices. */
public Polygon(int[] xCoords, int[] yCoords, int count)

/** Adds a vertex, given its coordinates, to this polygon. */
public void addPoint(int xCoordinate, int yCoordinate)

/** Changes the location of this polygon by adding the
    given amounts to the coordinates of its vertices. */
public void translate(int xIncrement, int yIncrement)
```

A Class of Right Triangles

Let's design and implement a class of right triangles. Restricting the triangles to those having right angles will make our task simpler yet still rich enough to investigate some design trade-offs. Moreover, we can use right triangles to create patterns like the one pictured in Figure 22-1. We begin by deciding what is needed to describe a triangle, and what we want objects of this class to do.

Data Fields and Methods

22.6   **Data fields.** The size of a right triangle is completely determined by the lengths of its base and height. The third side—its hypotenuse—is determined from these dimensions. We can position the triangle by placing its right angle, formed by the intersection of its base and height, at a certain point and indicating its orientation. Let's imagine that the vertex of the right angle is at the intersection of imaginary x- and y-axes and that the triangle's base and height lie on these axes. The axes form four quadrants, which by convention are numbered from 1 to 4 in counterclockwise fashion, starting with the upper-right quadrant. We then can use the coordinates of the right-angle vertex and the number of the quadrant containing the hypotenuse to describe the triangle's position and orientation, as Figure 22-4 illustrates. In fact, since we also have the lengths of the triangle's base and height, we have enough data to calculate the coordinates of the triangle's two other vertices. Furthermore, using these coordinates, we can form a polygon to represent the triangle.

We now can list the following data fields for the class:

- The triangle's base and height
- The quadrant containing the hypotenuse
- The coordinates of the triangle's three vertices

FIGURE 22-4   Right triangles in various quadrants

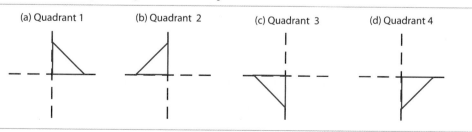

22.7   **Choosing methods.** A triangle should have basic accessor methods. Since the coordinates of a triangle's vertices completely describe its location, size, and orientation, one method should return them as an array. Although a client could calculate any characteristic of a triangle from its vertices, let's provide some convenience methods that report the base, height, quadrant, and location.

What about displaying the triangle? Should we specify a method to draw a triangle and another to paint its interior? Note that Polygon does not have such methods. In fact, we use methods in the class Graphics to display a Polygon object. However, our previous graphical objects had methods to display themselves, and so we also will include such methods for our triangles. Since we can represent a triangle as a Polygon object, let's specify a method in our class that returns such an object. This method will allow the client to display the triangle as desired.

The CRC card in Figure 22-5 summarizes our decisions so far. Notice that we really need to represent the vertices as objects if we plan to create methods that return a vertex or an array of vertices. The CRC card notes this requirement as a collaboration of our planned class RightTriangle. Without a class of vertices, we would need a pair of methods to return the coordinates of any particular point. Fortunately, we do not have to invent our own class Vertex, because the Java Class Library contains the class Point, which we can use instead. The next section introduces this class.

videonote
Arrays of shapes and coordinates

FIGURE 22-5   A CRC card for a class of right triangles

RightTriangle
Responsibilities
Construct a right triangle given its base, height, quadrant, and right-angle vertex
Get the base
Get the height
Get the quadrant
Get the right-angle vertex
Get an array of all vertices
Get the triangle as a Polygon object
Draw the triangle's outline in a given color
Paint the triangle's outline and interior in a given color
Collaborations
Polygon
A class to represent vertices

The Class Point

22.8   Like the classes Graphics and Polygon, the class Point is in the AWT. It represents points (x, y) in two-dimensional coordinate space. As such, it is well suited to represent a triangle's vertices. Since it is not a complex class, we will list a selection of its methods, along with their specifications. As usual, you can learn more about Point by referring to the documentation for the Java Class Library on Sun's website.

Note: **Constructors and selected methods of the class `Point`**

```
/** Creates a point whose coordinates are (0, 0). */
public Point()

/** Creates a point whose coordinates are (x, y). */
public Point(int x, int y)

/** Creates a new point whose coordinates are the same as
    those of a given Point object. */
public Point(Point aPoint)

/** Returns a duplicate of this point. */
public Point getLocation()

/** Returns the x-coordinate of this point. */
public double getX()

/** Returns the y-coordinate of this point. */
public double getY()

/** Sets the coordinates of this point to those of a
    given Point object. */
public void setLocation(Point aPoint)

/** Sets the coordinates of this point to (x, y). */
public void setLocation(int x, int y)

/** Changes the location of this point by adding the given
    amounts to the coordinates of its vertices. */
public void translate(int xIncrement, int yIncrement)
```

Question 5 Define one array of `Point` objects that represent the following three vertices of a triangle: (0, 50), (25, 0), (50, 50).

22.9   As we mentioned, we plan to use `Point` objects as the vertices of our right triangles. Before we do, note the following things about `Point`'s methods: The method `getLocation` returns a new point having the same coordinates as the point receiving the method's call. As you soon will see, this aspect of the method will enable a triangle to return copies of its vertices, thus protecting its actual vertices from being altered by a careless or devious client.

   The methods `getX` and `getY` each return their respective coordinate as a `double` value, even though the value is an integer. We must remember this fact when we invoke them. Lastly, the method `translate` is analogous to `Polygon`'s `translate` method. By the way, `Polygon` makes little use of `Point`. Although it has one method that sees whether a polygon contains a given `Point` object, `Polygon`'s constructors and other methods, such as `addPoint`, accept integer coordinates, not points, as arguments. You will see how this aspect of `Polygon` makes our implementation of `RightTriangle` less elegant.

Question 6 Basing your answer only on the methods specified for the class `Point` in the previous Note, is a definition for `Point`'s method `translate` possible? If so, write such a definition; if not, explain why not.

Question 7 Repeat the previous question for the method `getLocation` instead of `translate`.

Specifications for the Class `RightTriangle`

22.10 We now return our attention to the CRC card for our class of right triangles, as shown in Figure 22-5, and our discussions of the class's data fields and methods. As we name these aspects of the class, we can note refinements to its specification by using the UML. Figure 22-6 shows the result of this step. Remember that the vertices are `Point` objects.

FIGURE 22-6   UML notation for the class `RightTriangle`

```
                    RightTriangle
-base: int
-height : int
-quadrant: int
-vertices: Point[]

+getBase(): int
+getHeight(): int
+getQuadrant(): int
+getLocation(): Point
+getVertices(): Point[]
+getPolygon(): Polygon
+draw(triangleColor: Color,
        pen: Graphics): void
+fill(triangleColor: Color,
        pen: Graphics): void
```

22.11 Our final step in specifying the class `RightTriangle` is to write comments and headers for the constructors and methods, as follows:

```java
/** Creates a right triangle given its base, height, quadrant
    containing its hypotenuse, and vertex of its right angle. */
public RightTriangle(int triangleBase, int triangleHeight,
                     int hypotenusQuadrant, Point rightAngleVertex)

/** Returns the triangle's base. */
public int getBase()

/** Returns the triangle's height. */
public int getHeight()

/** Returns the quadrant number (1 - 4) containing the hypotenuse. */
public int getQuadrant()

/** Returns a copy of the triangle's right-angle vertex. */
public Point getLocation()

/** Returns an array of copies of the triangle's vertices. */
public Point[] getVertices()

/** Returns a polygon that represents the triangle. */
public Polygon getPolygon()

/** Displays the outline of this triangle in a given color. */
public void draw(Color triangleColor, Graphics pen)

/** Displays the interior of this triangle in a given color. */
public void fill(Color triangleColor, Graphics pen)
```

Question 8 Given an implementation of the class `RightTriangle` and the previous specification for its constructor, what statement(s) will create a right triangle whose base and height each equal 50 pixels and whose right-angle vertex is at the point (100, 150)? Orient the triangle like the one shown in Figure 22-4c.

Question 9 Given the `RightTriangle` object you created in the previous question and an implementation of the class `RightTriangle`, as previously specified, what statement will assign a `Polygon` object that represents the triangle to the variable `myPoly`?

Question 10 Under the same assumptions described in the previous question, what statement will define an array of `Point` objects representing the triangle's vertices?

Implementing `RightTriangle`

22.12   **Data fields.** We begin the implementation of the class `RightTriangle` by declaring its data fields. Since the class has no mutator methods, we can make the fields final as follows:

```
private final int base, height;
private final int quadrant;     // containing the hypotenuse
private final Point[] vertices; // vertices[0] = right-angle vertex
```

Using the numbering system shown earlier in Figure 22-4, quadrant is the quadrant containing the triangle's longest side—the hypotenuse. We arbitrarily chose `vertices[0]` to reference the triangle's right-angle vertex. These two decisions will affect the definition of the class's constructor. The values of `vertices[1]` and `vertices[2]` depend not only on `vertices[0]`, but also on the triangle's base, its height, and the quadrant containing the hypotenuse. Figure 22-7 illustrates these relationships, assuming a base of b pixels and a height of h pixels.

FIGURE 22-7   The vertices of a right triangle in various quadrants

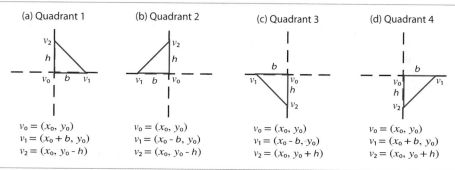

While these data fields are sufficient for now, thinking ahead to what the method definitions will require might revise our choices.

Design Decision: **Should the class `RightTriangle` have a `Polygon` object as a data field?**

- **Choice 1: A `Polygon` object as a data field instead of an array of vertices.**

    If we did not have an array of vertices as a data field, we would need such an array locally within the constructor so we could define the polygon. However, since a `Polygon` object cannot give us its vertices, we could not implement the method `getVertices` using this approach. The method `getPolygon` also presents a problem. Suppose `triangle` is the name of the data field that is the

Polygon object. If getPolygon simply returns triangle, the client could change or corrupt the object it references. This method really should return a copy of the Polygon object, triangle, but Polygon has no method to make a copy.

- **Choice 2: An array of vertices, but no Polygon object as a data field.**

  To display a triangle, the methods draw and fill can conveniently treat it as a polygon and call one of the Graphics methods drawPolygon or fillPolygon. These methods, however, require either a Polygon object as an argument or parallel arrays that give the coordinates of the triangle's vertices. To satisfy this requirement, each method could either invoke the method getPolygon or use a loop to extract the required coordinates from the array vertices of Point objects. For example, with the first alternative, the method draw would contain an invocation such as pen.drawPolygon(getPolygon()). Because there is no Polygon object as a data field, one would be created each time draw or fill was invoked.

- **Choice 3: A Polygon object and an array of vertices as two data fields.**

  With a Polygon object named triangle as a data field, the methods draw and fill can simply pass triangle to the appropriate Graphics method. To initialize triangle, the constructor can call the method getPolygon. If the client also invokes getPolygon, it will get a Polygon object that is separate from the one triangle references. As a result, the client cannot alter the right triangle. Note that no method should return the data field triangle to the client. We can declare RightTriangle's data fields as final to guard against such change.

Let's add a Polygon object as a data field, as just described in Choice 3. Thus, the data-field declarations are

```
private final int base, height;
private final int quadrant;      // containing the hypotenuse
private final Point[] vertices;  // vertices[0] = right-angle vertex
private final Polygon triangle;
```

At this point, we should update the UML representation of our class, as shown in Figure 22-6. Question 11 asks you to do this.

Question 11 How would you revise the UML representation of the class RightTriangle, as shown in Figure 22-6, to reflect the addition of the data field triangle?

22.13   **The logic of the constructor.** We now turn our attention to writing a constructor that defines and initializes the data fields. The calculation of the coordinates for the triangles' vertices, as pictured in Figure 22-7, can be simplified by using the method translate from the class Point. For example, Figure 22-7a indicates the relationship between v_0 and each of the vertices v_1 and v_2. Instead of incrementing coordinates, we can begin with a copy of v_0 and use translate to shift it by b pixels along the x-axis to get v_1. Similarly, beginning with another copy of v_0, we use translate to shift it by h pixels along the y-axis to get v_2. Thus, if vertices[0], vertices[1], and vertices[2] are v_0, v_1, and v_2, respectively, the following statements in pseudocode assign correct values to these three array elements:

vertices[0] = *a copy of the* Point *object for the right-angle vertex*
vertices[1] = *another copy of the* Point *object for the right-angle vertex*
vertices[2] = *another copy of the* Point *object for the right-angle vertex*

vertices[1].translate(*b*, 0)   // *Move to the right*
vertices[2].translate(0, *-h*) // *Move up*

Analogous uses of translate apply to triangles in the other quadrants.

22.14 **Some Java details.** The key parts of the constructor's definition are initializing the array `vertices` and choosing the appropriate arguments for the `translate` method. The latter should be evident given our previous discussion, but the array initialization contains a subtlety. If `rightAngleVertex` is the `Point` object representing the triangle's right-angle vertex, we first initialize each element in the array `vertices` to this point. You might be tempted to write the following loop, but it is incorrect:

```
for (int index = 0; index < 3; index++)
    vertices[index] = rightAngleVertex; // INCORRECT!
```

What's wrong with this loop? It assigns the same reference to each element of the array of vertices, as Figure 22-8 illustrates. Thus, each element references the same `Point` object. As a result, no matter which array element receives the call to `translate`, the same point is moved. The triangle has one vertex; it needs three!

FIGURE 22-8   Incorrect initialization of the array `vertices`

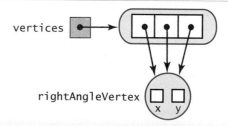

We can correct the previous loop by assigning copies of `rightAngleVertex` to the elements in `vertices` before using `translate` to adjust their positions. The `Point` method `getLocation` is ideal for this task, as it returns a copy of the point receiving its call. The correct loop, then, is

```
for (int index = 0; index < 3; index++)
    vertices[index] = rightAngleVertex.getLocation();
```

Figure 22-9 illustrates the effect of this loop.

FIGURE 22-9   The array `vertices` after its correct initialization

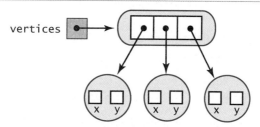

Three distinct copies of `rightAngleVertex`

22.15 **The constructor's definition.** The following definition of the constructor summarizes the discussion in the previous segments:

```
/** Creates a right triangle given its base, its height, the
    quadrant containing its hypotenuse, and the location of its
    right-angle vertex. */
public RightTriangle(int triangleBase, int triangleHeight,
                     int hypotenusQuadrant, Point rightAngleVertex)
```

```
{
    base = triangleBase;
    height = triangleHeight;
    quadrant = hypotenusQuadrant;
    vertices = new Point[3];

    for (int index = 0; index < 3; index++)
        vertices[index] = rightAngleVertex.getLocation(); // duplicates

    switch (quadrant)
    {
        case 1:
            vertices[1].translate(base, 0);
            vertices[2].translate(0, -height);
            break;
        case 2:
            vertices[1].translate(-base, 0);
            vertices[2].translate(0, -height);
            break;
        case 3:
            vertices[1].translate(-base, 0);
            vertices[2].translate(0, height);
            break;
        case 4:
            vertices[1].translate(base, 0);
            vertices[2].translate(0, height);
            break;
    } // end switch
    triangle = getPolygon();
} // end constructor
```

22.16   **The method getLocation.** Recall that we decided to store the right-angle vertex in `vertices[0]`. The method `getLocation` needs to return a copy of this point. An easy way to get a copy of `vertices[0]` is to invoke this point's own `getLocation` method, as you can see in the following definition of our triangle's version of `getLocation`:

```
/** Returns a copy of the triangle's right-angle vertex. */
public Point getLocation()
{
    return vertices[0].getLocation(); // calls Point's getLocation
} // end getLocation
```

Instead of the point `vertices[0].getLocation()`, we could have returned either of the following points:

- **new** Point(vertices[0]), or
- **new** Point((**int**)vertices[0].getX(), (**int**)vertices[0].getY())

In the latter expression, notice the necessary casts to `int` of the `double` values returned by `getX` and `getY`.

22.17   **The method getVertices.** This method is similar to the previous `getLocation` method, but it returns an array of points that are copies of the triangle's vertices. Like `getLocation`, `getVertices` calls Point's `getLocation`:

```
/** Returns an array of copies of the triangle's vertices. */
public Point[] getVertices()
{
    Point[] result = new Point[3];
    for (int index = 0; index < 3; index++)
        result[index] = vertices[index].getLocation();

    return result;
} // end getVertices
```

Question 12 What expressions could you use instead of `vertices[index].getLocation()` in the definition of the method `getVertices`?

22.18   **The method getPolygon.** To create a `Polygon` object that represents a right triangle, we use the same technique that we used in Segment 22.4. That is, we create an empty polygon by invoking `Polygon`'s default constructor and then use the method `addPoint` to add the triangles' vertices to the polygon. Doing so here is more convenient than creating parallel arrays of coordinates and invoking `Polygon`'s other constructor.

Unfortunately, as we noted earlier, `addPoint`'s arguments are the coordinates of the point instead of a `Point` object. To get the coordinates, we must call `Point`'s two methods `getX` and `getY`. Again, the `double` values these methods return must be cast to `int` before they are passed to `addPoint`. The method's definition, then, is as follows:

```
/** Returns a polygon that represents the triangle. */
public Polygon getPolygon()
{
    Polygon triPoly = new Polygon();

    // add vertices to the polygon
    for (int index = 0; index < 3; index++)
    {
        int xVertex = (int)vertices[index].getX();
        int yVertex = (int)vertices[index].getY();
        triPoly.addPoint(xVertex, yVertex);
    } // end for

    return triPoly;
} // end getPolygon
```

22.19   **The methods draw and fill.** The last two methods use the `Graphics` methods `getColor`, `setColor`, `drawPolygon`, and `fillPolygon` to achieve their effect. Their definitions follow:

```
/** Displays the outline of this triangle in a given color. */
public void draw(Color triangleColor, Graphics pen)
{
    Color saveColor = pen.getColor(); // get current pen color
    pen.setColor(triangleColor);      // set pen color
    pen.drawPolygon(triangle);        // draw triangle
    pen.setColor(saveColor);          // restore pen color
} // end draw

/** Displays the interior of this triangle in a given color. */
public void fill(Color triangleColor, Graphics pen)
{
    Color saveColor = pen.getColor(); // get current pen color
    pen.setColor(triangleColor);      // set pen color
    pen.fillPolygon(triangle);        // paint triangle
    pen.setColor(saveColor);          // restore pen color
} // end fill
```

After changing the pen's color, both methods restore it to its original value right after displaying the triangle.

22.20   **The complete definition.** Listing 22-1 contains the definition of `RightTriangle`, including the accessor methods `getBase`, `getHeight`, `getQuadrant`, and `getPolygon`.

LISTING 22-1   The class `RightTriangle`

```java
/** RightTriangle.java
    A class of right triangles, each having its own dimension and
    location.
    @author Frank M. Carrano
*/
import java.awt.Color;
import java.awt.Graphics;
import java.awt.Point;
import java.awt.Polygon;

public class RightTriangle
{
   private final int base, height;
   private final int quadrant; // assumes the right-angle vertex is at
                               // the origin of imaginary x- and y-axes
   private final Point[] vertices; // vertices[0] = right-angle vertex
   private final Polygon triangle;

   /** Creates a right triangle given its base, its height, the
       quadrant containing its hypotenuse, and the location of its
       right-angle vertex. */
   public RightTriangle(int triangleBase, int triangleHeight,
                        int hypotenusQuadrant, Point rightAngleVertex)
   {
      base = triangleBase;
      height = triangleHeight;
      quadrant = hypotenusQuadrant;
      vertices = new Point[3];

      for (int index = 0; index < 3; index++)
         vertices[index] = rightAngleVertex.getLocation();

      switch (quadrant)
      {
         case 1:
            vertices[1].translate(base, 0);
            vertices[2].translate(0, -height);
            break;
         case 2:
            vertices[1].translate(-base, 0);
            vertices[2].translate(0, -height);
            break;
```

```
            case 3:
                vertices[1].translate(-base, 0);
                vertices[2].translate(0, height);
                break;
            case 4:
                vertices[1].translate(base, 0);
                vertices[2].translate(0, height);
                break;
        } // end switch
        triangle = getPolygon();
    } // end constructor

    /** Returns the triangle's base. */
    public int getBase()
    {
        return base;
    } // end getBase

    /** Returns the triangle's height. */
    public int getHeight()
    {
        return height;
    } // end getHeight

    /** Returns the quadrant containing the triangle's hypotenuse. */
    public int getQuadrant()
    {
        return quadrant;
    } // end getQuadrant

    /** Returns a copy of the triangle's right-angle vertex. */
    public Point getLocation()
    {
        return vertices[0].getLocation(); // calls Point's getLocation
    } // end getLocation

    /** Returns an array of copies of the triangle's vertices. */
    public Point[] getVertices()
    {
        Point[] result = new Point[3];
        for (int index = 0; index < 3; index++)
            result[index] = vertices[index].getLocation();
        return result;
    } // end getVertices

    /** Returns a polygon that represents the triangle. */
    public Polygon getPolygon()
```

```
{
    Polygon triPoly = new Polygon();

    // add vertices to the polygon
    for (int index = 0; index < 3; index++)
    {
        int xVertex = (int)vertices[index].getX();
        int yVertex = (int)vertices[index].getY();
        triPoly.addPoint(xVertex, yVertex);
    } // end for
    return triPoly;
} // end getPolygon

/** Displays the outline of this triangle in a given color. */
public void draw(Color triangleColor, Graphics pen)
{
    Color saveColor = pen.getColor(); // get current pen color
    pen.setColor(triangleColor);       // set pen color
    pen.drawPolygon(triangle);         // draw triangle
    pen.setColor(saveColor);           // restore pen color
} // end draw

/** Displays the interior of this triangle in a given color. */
public void fill(Color triangleColor, Graphics pen)
{
    Color saveColor = pen.getColor(); // get current pen color
    pen.setColor(triangleColor);       // set pen color
    pen.fillPolygon(triangle);         // paint triangle
    pen.setColor(saveColor);           // restore pen color
} // end fill
} // end RightTriangle
```

 Note: Reflections on our design decisions
Although we chose the third design option for RightTriangle—using a Polygon object and an array of vertices as data fields—it can be dangerous to represent an object's data in two different ways. If a RightTriangle object had a method—translate, for example—that changed the triangle's position, we would need to update both the polygon representation and the triangle's vertices, assuming, of course, that we removed the modifier final from the declarations of the class's data fields. Since our version of RightTriangle defines no such methods, we are less likely to have a conflict between the various data representations.

One more concern: What if the client does not call either of the methods draw or fill? The constructor will have called getPolygon and assigned the result to triangle, even though that Polygon object will go unused. To avoid this possibility, the constructor could assign null to triangle. If either draw or fill found that triangle is null, the method would assign the value returned by getPolygon to triangle before using it in performing its task. The details of this change are considered in the following question.

Question 13 If `RightTriangle`'s constructor assigns `null` to the data field `triangle`, what revisions would you make to the definitions of the methods `draw` and `fill` so that `triangle` will reference the `Polygon` object used by these methods in displaying the triangle?

A Problem Solved: A New Quilt

> At the beginning of this chapter, we suggested a new pattern for the quilt created in Chapter 14. The new square, which is pictured in Figure 22-1, contains a diamond shape composed of four right triangles. Figure 22-10 shows a sample quilt made from such squares. Define a class of such quilts.

FIGURE 22-10   A sample quilt of diamonds

A Class of Squares

22.21   The previous sections of this chapter created the class `RightTriangle`. Our first task now is to build a class of the squares shown in Figure 22-1. The simple squares used in Chapter 14 did not have coordinates and could be drawn at any point. However, the squares here will have specific positions so that we can place the triangles correctly.

Listing 22-2 shows a class of such squares. The constructor creates each square, given its upper left corner and its dimension. An array of four `RightTriangle` objects form the diamond shape within a square. The right angles of these triangles share a single vertex, which is at the center of the square. Note how the constructor makes use of the `Point` methods `getLocation` and `translate` to find the center point and then forms the array of triangles.

LISTING 22-2   The class `DiamondSquare`

```
/** DiamondSquare.java
    A class of squares, each containing a diamond composed
    of four triangles in different colors.
    @author Frank M. Carrano
*/
import java.awt.Color;
import java.awt.Graphics;
import java.awt.Point;

public class DiamondSquare
{
   private final Point squareCorner;
   private final int side;
   private final RightTriangle[] sectors;
```

```java
/** Creates a square at a given position and of a given size. */
public DiamondSquare(Point upperLeftCorner, int squareSide)
{
    squareCorner = upperLeftCorner.getLocation();
    side = squareSide;

    int triangleBase = side / 2;
    int triangleHeight = triangleBase;

    // get center of square; triangles meet here
    Point squareCenter = upperLeftCorner.getLocation();
    squareCenter.translate(triangleBase, triangleBase);

    // define one triangle per quadrant
    sectors = new RightTriangle[4];
    for (int index = 0; index < 4; index++)
        sectors[index] = new RightTriangle(triangleBase, triangleHeight,
                                        index + 1, squareCenter);
} // end constructor

/** Returns the square's upper left vertex. */
public Point getUpperLeftCorner()
{
    return squareCorner.getLocation();
} // end getUpperLeftCorner

/** Returns the square's side. */
public int getSide()
{
    return side;
} // end getSide

/** Returns the side of the diamond within the square. */
public int getDiamondEdge()
{
    // diamond edge is hypotenuse of triangle
    int base = side / 2; // triangle base
    double edge = base / Math.round(Math.sin(Math.toRadians(45)));
    return (int)edge
} // end getDiamondEdge

/** Displays the square in given colors. */
public void display(Color backgroundColor, Color[] sectorColors,
                    int colorIndex, Graphics pen)
{
    int xCorner = (int)squareCorner.getX();
    int yCorner = (int)squareCorner.getY();
```

```
        pen.setColor(backgroundColor);
        pen.fillRect(xCorner, yCorner, side, side);
        for (int index = 0; index < sectorColors.length; index++)
        {
            sectors[index].fill(sectorColors[colorIndex], pen);
            colorIndex = (colorIndex + 1) % sectorColors.length;
        } // end for
    } // end display
} // end DiamondSquare
```

22.22   The display method first paints a square in a background color—black in our example—and then paints the four triangles over this background. Colors for the triangles are chosen from an array of colors given to the method by the client. The client also provides the index of the first color to be chosen. Subsequent colors are taken from consecutive array elements, assuming that the last element is followed by the first one. Note how the Java operator % is used in the following loop to make the indices behave in this manner:

```
for (int index = 0; index < sectorColors.length; index++)
{
    sectors[index].fill(sectorColors[colorIndex], pen);
    colorIndex = (colorIndex + 1) % sectorColors.length;
} // end for
```

The accessor methods getUpperLeftCorner, getSide, and getDiamondEdge are provided for completeness but are not used in this example.

A Class of Quilts

22.23   To form a quilt of DiamondSquare objects, we will use a two-dimensional array and define it as a data field of our new class. The array's declaration in the class is

```
private final DiamondSquare[][] quiltArray;
```

The class's constructor allocates the array, as follows:

```
quiltArray = new DiamondSquare[squaresPerSide][squaresPerSide];
```

where squaresPerSide is a data field initialized by the constructor using a value given to it by the client as an argument. The constructor then creates the squares and assigns them to elements in this array using the following nested loops:

```
Point rowCorner = quiltCorner.getLocation();      // copy point
Point squareCorner = rowCorner.getLocation();     // copy point
for (int row = 0; row < squaresPerSide; row++)
{
    for (int col = 0; col < squaresPerSide; col++)
    {
        quiltArray[row][col] = new DiamondSquare(squareCorner,
                                                 squareSide);

        squareCorner = squareCorner.getLocation(); // copy point
        squareCorner.translate(squareSide, 0);     // move point
    } // end for
```

```
            rowCorner.translate(0, squareSide);           // move point
            squareCorner = rowCorner.getLocation();        // copy point
        } // end for
```

Note how we compute the position of each small square, beginning with the `Point` object `quiltCorner`, which positions the entire quilt. The `Point` method `translate` moves the square's corner both to the right and down. Copying each point by calling the `Point` method `getLocation` is vital to the success of this loop.

Question 14 What happens if we do not call the method `getLocation` in the previous code for `DiamondQuilt`'s constructor? That is, what is the effect of the following code?

```
Point rowCorner = quiltCorner;
Point squareCorner = rowCorner;
for (int row = 0; row < squaresPerSide; row++)
{
    for (int col = 0; col < squaresPerSide; col++)
    {
        quiltArray[row][col] = new DiamondSquare(squareCorner,
                                                 squareSide);
        squareCorner.translate(squareSide, 0);   // move point
    } // end for

    rowCorner.translate(0, squareSide);          // move point
    squareCorner = rowCorner;
} // end for
```

22.24   Listing 22-3 contains the complete class of quilts. The method `display` depends on the `display` method defined in the class `DiamondSquare`, as you can see from the following statement:

```
quiltArray[row][column].display(BACKGROUND_COLOR, COLOR_CHOICES,
                                colorIndex, pen);
```

Note that the value of `colorIndex` is chosen at random but lies within the legal bounds of the array `COLOR_CHOICES`.

You should glance back at the class `Quilt` in Listing 14-4 of Chapter 14. That class used a `switch` statement to select a color at random. Notice how much easier it is to use an array of colors, as we have done here, instead of a `switch` statement.

The panel and driver for `DiamondQuilt` are like those given as answers to Questions 10 and 11 in Chapter 14, but with appropriate changes to the arguments passed to constructors and methods. The code for these two classes is included in the source code distributed with this book.

LISTING 22-3   The class `DiamondQuilt`

```
/** DiamondQuilt.java
    A square quilt composed of smaller squares,
    each containing a four-sector diamond.
    @author Frank. M Carrano
*/
import java.awt.Color;
import java.awt.Graphics;
import java.awt.Point;
import java.util.Random;
```

```java
public class DiamondQuilt
{
   private final Point quiltCorner;
   private final int squaresPerSide;
   private final DiamondSquare[][] quiltArray;
   private final Random generator;

   private static final Color BACKGROUND_COLOR = Color.BLACK;
   private static final Color[] COLOR_CHOICES =
                  {Color.RED, Color.BLUE, Color.GREEN, Color.ORANGE};
   private static final int NUMBER_OF_COLORS = COLOR_CHOICES.length;

   /** Constructs a square quilt having a given number of squares per
       side. Component squares are equal in size and have a given
       dimension. */
   public DiamondQuilt(Point upperLeftCorner, int numberSquaresPerSide,
                       int squareSide)
   {
      quiltCorner = upperLeftCorner;
      squaresPerSide = numberSquaresPerSide;
      quiltArray = new DiamondSquare[squaresPerSide][squaresPerSide];
      generator = new Random();

      Point rowCorner = quiltCorner.getLocation();    // copy point
      Point squareCorner = rowCorner.getLocation();   // copy point
      for (int row = 0; row < squaresPerSide; row++)
      {
         for (int col = 0; col < squaresPerSide; col++)
         {
            quiltArray[row][col] = new DiamondSquare(squareCorner,
                                                     squareSide);
            squareCorner = squareCorner.getLocation(); // copy point
            squareCorner.translate(squareSide, 0);    // move point
         } // end for

         rowCorner.translate(0, squareSide);           // move point
         squareCorner = rowCorner.getLocation();       // copy point
      } // end for
   } // end constructor

   /** Displays this quilt. */
   public void display(Graphics pen)
   {
      for (int row = 0; row < squaresPerSide; row++)
      {
         for (int column = 0; column < squaresPerSide; column++)
         {
```

```
                    int colorIndex = generator.nextInt(NUMBER_OF_COLORS);
                    quiltArray[row][column].display(BACKGROUND_COLOR,
                                                   COLOR_CHOICES, colorIndex, pen);
            } // end for
        } // end for
    } // end display
} // end DiamondQuilt
```

A Problem Solved: Connecting the Dots

> Segments 17.15 through 17.19 of Chapter 17 show how to use the interface MouseListener and the class MouseEvent to locate the positions of mouse clicks. Let's mark those positions with dots and connect them with line segments, as shown in Figure 22-11.

FIGURE 22-11   Line segments that connect the points of mouse clicks

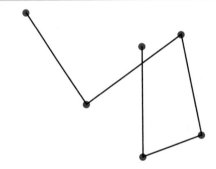

Using Parallel Arrays of Coordinates

22.25   Rather than using the Graphics method drawLine to draw the lines between the points, we can use the method drawPolyline. Doing so requires parallel arrays containing the coordinates of the points. Thus, let's define the following data fields in a class LinesPanel, which describes the panel we will display:

```
private final int[] xPoints;
private final int[] yPoints;
private int pointCount;
```

videonote
Parallel arrays

The constructor for LinesPanel should initialize pointCount and allocate the arrays xPoints and yPoints, as follows:

```
xPoints = new int[50];
yPoints = new int[50];
pointCount = 0;
```

This constructor must also register a listener for mouse clicks.

22.26   The listener's method `mouseClicked` will add the coordinates of new mouse clicks to the arrays `xPoints` and `yPoints` and then increment `pointCount`. The following statements perform these steps, given the point `mouseClick`:

```
xPoints[pointCount] = mouseClick.getX();
yPoints[pointCount] = mouseClick.getY();
pointCount++;
```

To draw the lines between the points, we can write the statement

```
pen.drawPolyline(xPoints, yPoints, pointCount);
```

within the panel's method `paintComponent`. If we also want to mark the points themselves, we can use the method `fillOval` within the following loop, where the named constants `RADIUS` and `DIAMETER` describe the size of the dot:

```
for (int index = 0; index < pointCount; index++)
   pen.fillOval(xPoints[index] - RADIUS, yPoints[index] - RADIUS,
                DIAMETER, DIAMETER);
```

22.27   The complete panel is described by the class `LinesPanel` in Listing 22-4. A driver and sample output are given in Listing 22-5.

LISTING 22-4   The class `LinesPanel`, using parallel arrays of coordinates

```java
/** LinesPanel.java
    A panel in which lines are drawn between dots whose positions
    are indicated by the user's mouse clicks.
    @author Frank M. Carrano
*/
import javax.swing.JPanel;

import java.awt.Color;
import java.awt.Dimension;
import java.awt.Graphics;

import java.awt.event.MouseEvent;
import java.awt.event.MouseListener;

public class LinesPanel extends JPanel
{
   private final int[] xPoints;
   private final int[] yPoints;
   private int pointCount;

   // size and color of dot to mark mouse location
   private static final int RADIUS = 2;
   private static final int DIAMETER = 2 * RADIUS;
   private static final Color DOT_COLOR = Color.BLUE;

   private static final Color LINE_COLOR = Color.BLACK;
   private static final int PANEL_SIDE = 300; // square panel

   public LinesPanel()
   {
```

```java
      xPoints = new int[50];
      yPoints = new int[50];
      pointCount = 0;

      addMouseListener(new MyListener());
      setPreferredSize(new Dimension(PANEL_SIDE, PANEL_SIDE));
   } // end default constructor

   public void paintComponent(Graphics pen)
   {
      // draw line segments
      pen.setColor(LINE_COLOR);
      pen.drawPolyline(xPoints, yPoints, pointCount);

      // paint dots centered at the points
      pen.setColor(DOT_COLOR);
      for (int index = 0; index < pointCount; index++)
         pen.fillOval(xPoints[index] - RADIUS, yPoints[index] - RADIUS,
                      DIAMETER, DIAMETER);
   } // end paintComponent

   private class PointListener implements MouseListener
   {
      public void mouseClicked(MouseEvent mouseClick)
      {
         // the mouse button has been pressed and released
         // (clicked) on this panel
         xPoints[pointCount] = mouseClick.getX();
         yPoints[pointCount] = mouseClick.getY();
         pointCount++;
         repaint();
      } // end mouseClicked

      // the following methods are not used in this panel:
      public void mouseEntered(MouseEvent e) {}
      public void mouseExited(MouseEvent e)  {}
      public void mousePressed(MouseEvent e) {}
      public void mouseReleased(MouseEvent e){}
   } // end PointListener
} // end LinesPanel
```

LISTING 22-5   The class `LinesDriver`

```java
/** LinesDriver.java
    A driver for LinesPanel.
    @author Frank M. Carrano
*/
import javax.swing.JFrame;
```

```
public class LinesDriver
{
    public static void main(String[] args)
    {
        JFrame window = new JFrame();
        window.setDefaultCloseOperation(JFrame.EXIT_ON_CLOSE);
        window.setTitle("Connect the Dots");

        LinesPanel panel = new LinesPanel();
        window.add(panel);
        window.pack();
        window.setVisible(true);
    } // end main
} // end LinesDriver
```

Sample Output

Question 15 The class LinesPanel in Listing 22-4 declares the data fields xPoints and yPoints. These fields are arrays that the constructor allocates, but the method mouseClicked within the inner class PointListener sets the entries in the arrays. Why then are these arrays declared as final?

Question 16 During the execution of LinesDriver, and before the user has clicked the mouse, a window appears and the method paintComponent is called. What, if anything, does the method draw? Why?

Using an Array of Points

22.28   We used parallel arrays of *x*- and *y*-coordinates in the definition of LinesPanel, as given in Listing 22-4 because we could pass them as arguments to the method drawPolyline. But Chapter 20 suggested that we use an array of objects instead of several parallel arrays of related values. As you saw in Chapter 17, a MouseEvent object can give us the location of a mouse click as a Point object instead of as integer *x*- and *y*-coordinates. We can save these objects in an array. Let's see how LinePanel would change if we replaced the parallel arrays of coordinates with an array of points. The revised class is shown in Listing 22-6.

22.29   **Easy changes.** After importing the class Point, we replace as data fields the parallel arrays xPoints and yPoints in Listing 22-4 with one array, points, of Point objects. The constructor allocates this array instead of the parallel arrays. In the method mouseClicked within the inner listener class PointListener, we replace the two assignment statements

```
xPoints[pointCount] = mouseClick.getX();
yPoints[pointCount] = mouseClick.getY();
```

with the following one:

```
points[pointCount] = mouseClick.getPoint();
```

The rest of the changes are more substantial, as you will see.

LISTING 22-6   A revised version of the class LinesPanel, using an array of points

```java
/** LinesPanel.java
    A panel in which lines are drawn between dots whose positions
    are indicated by the user's mouse clicks.
    @author Frank M. Carrano
*/
import javax.swing.JPanel;

import java.awt.Color;
import java.awt.Dimension;
import java.awt.Graphics;
import java.awt.Point;

import java.awt.event.MouseEvent;
import java.awt.event.MouseListener;

public class LinesPanel extends JPanel
{
    private final Point[] points;
    private int pointCount;

    // size and color of dot to mark mouse location
    private static final int RADIUS = 2;
    private static final int DIAMETER = 2 * RADIUS;
    private static final Color DOT_COLOR = Color.BLUE;

    private static final Color LINE_COLOR = Color.BLACK;
    private static final int PANEL_SIDE = 300; // square panel

    public LinesPanel()
    {
        points = new Point[50];
        pointCount = 0;

        addMouseListener(new PointListener());
        setPreferredSize(new Dimension(PANEL_SIDE, PANEL_SIDE));
    } // end default constructor

    public void paintComponent(Graphics pen)
    {
```

```
      if (pointCount == 1)
         paintDot(points[0], pen);
      else if (pointCount > 1)
      {
         for (int index = 0; index < pointCount - 1; index++)
            joinAndMarkPoints(points[index], points[index + 1], pen);
      }
      // else if pointCount == 0, do nothing before first mouse click
} // end paintComponent

// Draws a line segment between two given points and
// marks the points with dots.
private void joinAndMarkPoints(Point one, Point two, Graphics pen)
{
   joinPoints(one, two, pen);
   paintDot(one, pen);
   paintDot(two, pen);
} // end joinAndMarkPoints

// Draws a line segment between two given points.
private void joinPoints(Point one, Point two, Graphics pen)
{
   pen.setColor(LINE_COLOR);
   pen.drawLine((int)one.getX(), (int)one.getY(),
                (int)two.getX(), (int)two.getY());
} // end joinPoints

// Paints a dot at a given point.
private void paintDot(Point aPoint, Graphics pen)
{
   pen.setColor(DOT_COLOR);
   pen.fillOval((int)aPoint.getX() - RADIUS,
                (int)aPoint.getY() - RADIUS, DIAMETER, DIAMETER);
} // end paintDot

private class PointListener implements MouseListener
{
   public void mouseClicked(MouseEvent mouseClick)
   {
      // the mouse button has been pressed and released (clicked)
      // on this panel
      points[pointCount] = mouseClick.getPoint();
      pointCount++;
      repaint();
   } // end mouseClicked
```

```
        // the following methods are not used in this panel:
        public void mouseEntered(MouseEvent e) {}
        public void mouseExited(MouseEvent e)  {}
        public void mousePressed(MouseEvent e) {}
        public void mouseReleased(MouseEvent e){}
    } // end PointListener
} // end LinesPanel
```

22.30   **Working with points.** Although we must deal with coordinates at some level, avoiding parallel arrays in this class definition means that we cannot use `drawPolyline`. Instead, we write our own methods to draw lines between two given `Point` objects and mark the points with dots. After some thought, we can specify the following private methods to replace `drawPolyline`:

```
// Draws a line segment between two given points and
// marks the points with dots.
private void joinAndMarkPoints(Point one, Point two, Graphics pen)

// Draws a line segment between two given points.
private void joinPoints(Point one, Point two, Graphics pen)

// Paints a dot at a given point.
private void paintDot(Point aPoint, Graphics pen)
```

As Listing 22-6 shows, the definitions of these methods are not difficult. We do need to use `Point`'s accessor methods to get the coordinates of a point, and we need to remember to cast the returned `double` values to `int`.

22.31   **The method `paintComponent`.** We can use the previous private methods to entirely redefine the method `paintComponent`. The approach we used earlier in Listing 22-4 hid a concern that we should have considered: What happens if the system calls `paintComponent` before the user has clicked the mouse to indicate a point? After all, we cannot prevent the system from calling this method. In Listing 22-4, `paintComponent` calls `drawPolyline`. If `pointCount` is zero, `drawPolyline` simply does nothing. The same is true of the loop that marks the points with dots. Thus, calling `paintComponent` before we have points to work with causes no problem. We need to ensure the same behavior now. Thus, we write the following pseudocode for `paintComponent`:

```
if (pointCount == 1)
    Mark the point in pointCount[0]
else if (pointCount > 1)
    Join and mark the pointCount points in the array points
else
    Do nothing
```

The definition of `paintComponent` shown in Listing 22-6 is a straightforward translation of this pseudocode into Java, using the three private methods we specified in the previous segment.

Design Decision: **One array of points and parallel arrays of coordinates**

The definition of LinesPanel given earlier in Listing 22-4 uses parallel arrays of coordinates and calls drawPolyline. The revision of LinesPanel given in Listing 22-6 uses one array of Point objects but does not call drawPolyline. Could we have called drawPolyline in this revised class? Yes, but to do so, we would need parallel arrays of coordinates. Let's consider three ways we could have defined both an array of points and parallel arrays of the points' coordinates:

- **Choice 1: The class's data fields are points—the array of Point objects—and the integer pointCount.**

  In this scenario, the data fields, constructor, and inner listener class are the same as given in Listing 22-6. The rest of the class—that is, the method paintComponent and the private methods it calls—is replaced by the following definition of paintComponent:

  ```java
  public void paintComponent(Graphics pen)
  {
     int[] xPoints = new int[50];
     int[] yPoints = new int[50];

     for (int index = 0; index < pointCount; index++)
     {
        Point nextPoint = points[index];
        xPoints[index] = (int)nextPoint.getX();
        yPoints[index] = (int)nextPoint.getY();
     } // end for
  ```

  < Statements to draw line segments and paint dots, just as in Listing 22-6. >

  ```java
  } // end paintComponent
  ```

  The parallel arrays xPoints and yPoints are local to this method, since they aren't used anywhere else. Although this might seem like a reasonable solution, we need to consider that paintComponent could be called often. Each time it is called, it reallocates the two local arrays and assigns values to their elements. Most of these values are not changed, but they are reassigned anyway. These occurrences waste computer time and can delay the appearance of the drawing.

- **Choice 2: The class's data fields are points (the array of Point objects), the parallel arrays xPoints and yPoints, and the integer pointCount.**

  The arrays xPoints and yPoints are allocated in the constructor along with the array points. Thus, they are no longer allocated in paintComponent. The reassignment of values to the parallel arrays, however, is still done each time paintComponent is called, which wastes time.

- **Choice 3: The class's data fields are the same as in Choice 2—points, xPoints, yPoints, and pointCount—but the loop that assigns values to xPoints and yPoints is removed from paintComponent.**

  To remove the loop from paintComponent, we can revise the definition of the method mouseClicked as follows:

  ```java
  public void mouseClicked(MouseEvent mouseClick)
  {
     Point nextPoint = mouseClick.getPoint();
     xPoints[pointCount] = (int)nextPoint.getX();
     yPoints[pointCount] = (int)nextPoint.getY();
     points[pointCount] = nextPoint;
     pointCount++;
     repaint();
  } // end mouseClicked
  ```

You should see now that the array of Point objects is essentially useless. We can get the co-ordinates of a mouse click directly from the mouse event without first getting a Point object.

If we want to use the method drawPolyline, we should avoid an array of points and use only two parallel arrays of coordinates, as is done in Listing 22-4. If we want to work with Point objects, we should write our own method to join them with lines, since no Graphics method exists to do so. This is the approach we took in Listing 22-6. As was mentioned in the note at the end of Segment 22.20, representing an object's data in two different ways can cause logical errors if we forget to keep both representations up to date.

Using a List of Points

22.32   Instead of using arrays in Listings 22-4 and 22-6, we could use lists—that is, instances of the class ArrayList—which the previous chapter discussed. For example, in Listing 22-6 we could save the Point objects in a list instead of an array. Let's see how using such a list would change the definition of LinesPanel given in Listing 22-6.

After importing the class ArrayList from the Java Class Library, the next change is the declaration of the list as a data field. Thus, we replace the declaration of the array points in LinesPanel with

```
private final ArrayList<Point> points;
```

Since a list can report the number of items it currently holds, the data field pointCount is no longer needed.

The next changes are to the constructor. Instead of allocating the array points and initializing pointCount, which no longer exists, we create an instance of ArrayList as follows:

```
points = new ArrayList<Point>();
```

The rest of the constructor remains as it is in Listing 22-6.

22.33   The method paintComponent in Listing 22-6 has access to the data field pointCount. Since this field no longer exists, we make pointCount a local variable by beginning the body of the revised method with the statement

```
int pointCount = points.size();
```

Thus, we ask the array list for the number of points it contains.

The last change is to the method mouseClicked within the inner class that describes the mouse listener. This method must obtain the point at which the user clicks the mouse and store it in the list points. Thus, we replace the statements

```
points[pointCount] = mouseClick.getPoint();
pointCount++;
```

given in Listing 22-6 with

```
points.add(mouseClick.getPoint());
```

This definition is much simpler.

■ A Problem Solved: The Keypad

Often when a program requires numeric input, the user can simply type digits on a keypad. Some applications, however, simulate tangible things—such as a calculator or a telephone—by providing the user with a keypad that is drawn on the screen. The user then clicks the keys to enter a number. Create a program that draws such a keypad.

Establishing the Design

22.34   Before we can solve this problem, we must clarify exactly what to ask of a user. Someone has a decision to make.

Design Decision: **When has the user finished clicking keys?**

If the user clicks the keys 1, 2, and 3 to enter the integer 123, how will we know whether the user plans to click another key? When you use a telephone, you enter a number. Some phones require you to press a special key to initiate the call, while others detect when the expected number of digits has been entered.

Our keypad could have an "Enter" key that the user clicks after entering an entire number. Without such a key, we must "tell" the keypad the number of digits to expect. For example, we could pass that number as an argument to the constructor. Either approach is reasonable, but let's arbitrarily choose the first one.

Our keypad will have keys labeled 0 through 9, as well as a key to enter the input. Let's also add a key to clear the input. A sketch of the keypad's appearance is shown in Figure 22-12.

FIGURE 22-12   A sketch of a 12-key keypad

22.35   Rather than defining a class of keys, we can use `JButton` objects. Thus, our keypad can be represented as an array of buttons. This array can be one-dimensional, since the two-dimensional arrangement of the keys on the keypad is a cosmetic detail that need not be related to how the keys are stored in memory.

As Chapter 17 discussed, buttons require action listeners. Our keypad, then, can be a panel whose class has a private inner class of these listeners. Since we are dealing with buttons and panels, we do not have to worry about displaying them. That is, we will not write a `paintComponent` method. The keypad only needs to report the value that is entered via its keys. Let's display this value as a label in a separate panel.

What classes shall we define? So far, we want a class for a keypad panel and one for an output panel. The keypad panel will communicate with the output panel. These two panels could be subpanels of a third panel that the client could use. To simplify our example, however, we will have the output panel be a subpanel of the keypad panel. Figure 22-13 illustrates our design.

FIGURE 22-13   A class diagram showing the associations among the classes for
                   a proposed solution to the keypad problem

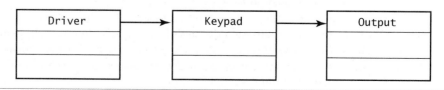

The Class OutputPanel

22.36 The panel on which the keypad will display the digits entered by a user is not complicated, so we will define its class. As you can see in Listing 22-7, the class's data field is a JLabel object. In addition to a default constructor, the class defines one method, which sets text on the label to a given string.

LISTING 22-7   The class OutputPanel

```java
/** OutputPanel.java
    A panel to display the values entered on a keypad.
    @author Frank M. Carrano
*/
import javax.swing.JLabel;
import javax.swing.JPanel;

import java.awt.Color;
import java.awt.Dimension;

public class OutputPanel extends JPanel
{
    private final JLabel display;

    private static final int PANEL_WIDTH = 150;
    private static final int PANEL_HEIGHT = 20;
    private static final Color OUTPUT_BACKGROUND = Color.CYAN;

    public OutputPanel()
    {
        display = new JLabel();
        add(display);
        setPreferredSize(new Dimension(PANEL_WIDTH, PANEL_HEIGHT));
        setBackground(OUTPUT_BACKGROUND);
    } // end default constructor

    public void setMessage(String theMessage)
    {
        display.setText(theMessage);
        repaint();
    } // end setMessage
} // end OutputPanel
```

The Class KeypadPanel

22.37 Let's make a list of things our keypad class needs:

- Data fields, including an array of buttons, a string to record the keys clicked, an object of OutputPanel, and some constants to name the keys and describe the panel.
- A default constructor.
- An inner class describing a listener for the buttons. It will implement the interface ActionListener, and so it will need a definition for the method actionPerformed.
- The standard classes JButton, JPanel, Color, Dimension, and ActionEvent, as well as the interface ActionListener. You might not think of all the necessary classes now, but that shouldn't stop you from trying.

We begin by declaring as a data field the array of buttons that will be the keys on the keypad. Once established, the reference to this array will not change, and so its declaration can be

```
private final JButton[] keys;
```

Because we plan to label the keys using digits and letters, we define the following array of strings as a data field:

```
private static final String[] KEY_NAMES = {"1","2","3","4","5","6",
                                           "7","8","9","C","0","E"};
```

The declarations for the object of OutputPanel and the string to record the keys clicked are

```
private final OutputPanel output;
private String keysClicked;
```

Once the object of OutputPanel is created, the reference to it will not change. Thus, its declaration can include the modifier final. The remaining data fields are named constants for the panel's dimensions and background color.

22.38 **The constructor.** To allocate memory for the array of buttons, we can write

```
keys = new JButton[KEY_NAMES.length];
```

The constructor now must create the individual buttons, label them, register them with the action listener—call it listener—that it also creates, and add each button to the panel. The following statements accomplish these tasks:

```
ButtonListener listener = new ButtonListener();

for (int index = 0; index < KEY_NAMES.length; index++)
{
    keys[index] = new JButton(KEY_NAMES[index]);
    keys[index].addActionListener(listener);
    add(keys[index]);
} // end for
```

In addition, the constructor initializes both keysClicked to the empty string and output to an instance of OutputPanel. It then adds output as a subpanel of this panel.

22.39 **The method actionPerformed.** When the user clicks a key—that is, a button—on the keypad, the method actionPerformed within the private inner listener class is called. This method must identify the key and act accordingly. Since we are using a button's text as its action command, we can identify the key by calling the method getActionCommand and assigning the text it returns to the local variable buttonLabel as follows:

```
String buttonLabel = buttonClick.getActionCommand();
```

Each numeric key causes its one-digit label to be concatenated to the end of the string keysClicked, as Figure 22-14 illustrates. To enter the value 987, for example, the user would click the keys "9," "8," and "7" in that order, forming the string "987". Each key causes the text in the OutputPanel object to be displayed again. The user then clicks the "E" key to process the string keysClicked. To simulate this processing, we will convert the string to an integer value and display it as Entered 987, for example. Finally, the "C" key sets keysClicked to the empty string.

The following if statement implements these steps and appears in the method actionPerformed:

```
if (buttonLabel.equals("C"))                    // "Clear" key
{
    keysClicked = "";
    output.setMessage("");                      // clear output
}
```

```
      else if (buttonLabel.equals("E"))          // "Enter" key
      {
         int result = Integer.parseInt(keysClicked);
         output.setMessage("Entered " + result);
      }
      else                                        // numeric keys
      {
         keysClicked = keysClicked + buttonLabel; // record key
         output.setMessage(keysClicked);          // update output
      } // end if
```

FIGURE 22-14 Recording the value entered on a keypad

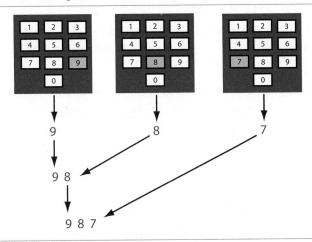

22.40 **The class KeypadPanel.** The complete class KeypadPanel is given in Listing 22-8.

LISTING 22-8

```
/** KeypadPanel.java
    A keypad, having the keys 0 through 9, that
    enables a user to enter integer values.
    @author Frank M. Carrano
*/
import javax.swing.JButton;
import javax.swing.JPanel;

import java.awt.Color;
import java.awt.Dimension;
import java.awt.event.ActionEvent;
import java.awt.event.ActionListener;

public class KeypadPanel extends JPanel
{
   private final JButton[] keys;
   private final OutputPanel output;
   private String keysClicked;
```

```java
   private static final String[] KEY_NAMES = {"1", "2", "3",
                                              "4", "5", "6",
                                              "7", "8", "9",
                                              "C", "0", "E"};
   private static final int PANEL_WIDTH = 150;
   private static final int PANEL_HEIGHT = 160;
   private static final Color BUTTON_BACKGROUND = Color.BLUE;

   public KeypadPanel()
   {
      keys = new JButton[KEY_NAMES.length];
      keysClicked = "";
      output = new OutputPanel();
      add(output);

      ButtonListener listener = new ButtonListener();
      for (int index = 0; index < KEY_NAMES.length; index++)
      {
         keys[index] = new JButton(KEY_NAMES[index]);
         keys[index].addActionListener(listener);
         add(keys[index]);
      } // end for

      setPreferredSize(new Dimension(PANEL_WIDTH, PANEL_HEIGHT));
      setBackground(BUTTON_BACKGROUND);
   } // end default constructor

   private class ButtonListener implements ActionListener
   {
      public void actionPerformed(ActionEvent buttonClick)
      {
         String buttonLabel = buttonClick.getActionCommand();
         if (buttonLabel.equals("C"))                   // "Clear" key
         {
            keysClicked = "";
            output.setMessage("");                      // clear output
         }
         else if (buttonLabel.equals("E"))              // "Enter" key
         {
            int result = Integer.parseInt(keysClicked);
            output.setMessage("Entered " + result);
         }
         else                                           // numeric keys
         {
            keysClicked = keysClicked + buttonLabel;    // record key
            output.setMessage(keysClicked);             // update output
```

```
            } // end if
        } // end actionPerformed
    } // end ButtonListener
} // end KeypadPanel
```

The Class KeypadDriver

22.41   Listing 22-9 defines a driver for the class KeypadPanel and shows some sample results.

LISTING 22-9   The class KeypadDriver

```java
/** KeypadDriver.java
    A driver for KeypadPanel.
    @author Frank M. Carrano
*/
import javax.swing.JFrame;

public class KeypadDriver
{
    public static void main(String[] args)
    {
        JFrame window = new JFrame();
        window.setDefaultCloseOperation(JFrame.EXIT_ON_CLOSE);
        window.setTitle("Keypad");

        KeypadPanel panel = new KeypadPanel();
        window.add(panel);
        window.pack();
        window.setVisible(true);
    } // end main
} // end KeypadDriver
```

Sample Output

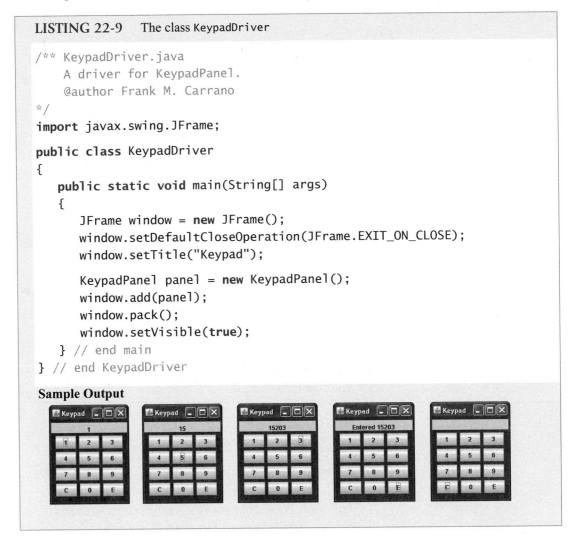

---

videonote
A problem
solved

Question 17 After the user of the program KeypadDriver, as given in Listing 22-9, clicks the "E" key, what happens if a numeric key is clicked next?

Question 18 Suppose an object of the class KeypadPanel does not have a "C" key to clear the previous input. How could you modify the class definition so that additional numeric input will be treated as a new entry instead of as digits being added to the previous entry?

CHAPTER SUMMARY

- A polygon is a closed two-dimensional figure composed of straight lines that do not cross.

- You can represent a polygon either by two parallel arrays containing the *x*- and *y*-coordinates of its vertices or by an object of the AWT class `Polygon`.

- The `Graphics` method `drawPolygon` draws a polygon given either parallel arrays of the *x*- and *y*-coordinates of its vertices or an object of the class `Polygon`.

- The `Graphics` method `fillPolygon` is analogous to `drawPolygon` but paints the interior of the figure.

- A polyline is an open two-dimensional figure composed of straight lines that do not cross. If you erase one side of a polygon, a polyline remains.

- The `Graphics` method `drawPolyline` draws a polyline given parallel arrays of the *x*- and *y*-coordinates of its vertices.

- The class `Point` in the AWT represents points in two-dimensional coordinate space.

- Representing an object's data in more than one way can cause logical errors, if the representations are not always equivalent.

EXERCISES

1. What is the difference between the two `Graphics` methods `drawPolygon` and `drawPolyline`?

2. Consider a square whose side has a length of 100 pixels.

   a. What are the coordinates of the square's vertices?
   b. What Java statements define parallel arrays that represent the vertices of this square?
   c. What Java statements define an array of `Point` objects that represents the vertices of this square?

3. If `pen` is a `Graphics` object, write one or more Java statements that draw the square represented by the arrays described in Question 2b.

4. Repeat the previous question, but instead use the arrays described in Question 2c.

5. Given the `Polygon` object created by the statement

   ```
   Polygon star = new Polygon();
   ```

   write statements to add the following points to `star`: (20, 50), (35, 70), and (50, 50).

6. Consider the polygon `star` you defined for the previous question.

   a. What statements test whether the `Point` object `aPoint` lies within the interior of `star`?
   b. What statements move `star` to the left 5 pixels and up 10 pixels?
   c. What statements remove all points from `star`, resulting in an empty polygon?

7. Write a program that draws a picture of a given one-dimensional array of integers. You can limit the size of the given array so that its illustration fits into the window that you create.

8. Repeat the previous exercise for a given two-dimensional array of integers.

9. Consider a number of same-sized squares arranged in an *n*-by-*n* grid, much like the squares on the board used for the games of checkers and chess. Place either a black or a white tile in each square. After arranging the tiles, you should be able to move the grid of tiles to another location without disturbing the pattern of tiles and without re-creating the tiles. Implement classes for the tiles and the grid.

PROJECTS

1. Imagine that you want to display the upper face of a die for a particular game. Suppose you define a class `Die` to represent a die face and use an array of seven `Dot` objects to represent the dots on the face. Each `Dot` object has a position, and they are arranged on a square as follows:

   Each `Dot` object also has a method to make it either visible or invisible. After generating a random integer between 1 and 6 to simulate the roll of the die, you would make the appropriate dot or dots visible, thereby displaying the die's upper face as one of the previous configurations.

   Since the `Dot` objects are in an array, you should arrange them so that visible dots are in adjacent elements of the array. Then you can use a loop (or loops) to display the dots on the die's face. To this end, number the positions of the dots on the die face from 0 to 6.

   Define the classes `Dot` and `Die`, as well as a driver that demonstrates the behavior of your classes.

2. Create a graphical version of a histogram, as described in Project 2 of Chapter 20.

3. Implement the following puzzle: Each square in a row of squares can be either blue or black. A square can change color only under certain conditions, as follows. The first square will change color anytime you click it. Each of the other squares will change color when you click it, but only if the preceding one is blue and all other squares before it are black.

   To begin the puzzle, the user chooses a number *n*, between 1 and 10, by clicking a button on a keypad. Given a row of *n* blue squares, the user's challenge is to make all of the squares black.

4. Create a graphical version of the game tic-tac-toe, as described in Project 1 of Chapter 20. Provide a three-by-three array of buttons for the players to use to indicate their choices.

5. Write a program that enables two people to play the game Concentration. In this game, 15 pairs of pictures are hidden behind a board of 30 numbered squares. The first player chooses two squares, revealing the figures behind them as each is chosen. If the figures match, they are removed from the board and the player gets a point and takes another turn. However, if the two figures do not match, they are hidden again and the second player takes a turn. The game ends when a player earns 8 points. Note that ties are impossible.

   Let the board contain six rows and five columns of squares. Players can choose squares by either clicking buttons or entering numbers in a dialog box. For the figures, you can use colors, letters, digits, or other characters, depending on the fonts available to you.

   Here are some tasks that your program must accomplish:

   - Draw the closed board.
   - Get 15 pairs of figures and shuffle them.
   - Hide the figures behind the board.
   - Keep track of the player's turns.
   - Identify chosen squares.
   - Open a square to reveal its figure.
   - Close a square to hide its figure and show its number again.
   - Identify when two chosen figures match.
   - Keep score.
   - Identify when the game ends and who the winner is.

ANSWERS TO SELF-TEST QUESTIONS

1. The vertices are (0, 50), (25, 0), and (50, 50). The following statements define parallel arrays that represent these coordinates:

```
int[] xVertices = {0, 25, 50};
int[] yVertices = {50, 0, 50};
```

2.
```
pen.drawPolygon(xVertices, yVertices, 3);
```

You could express the number of vertices as xVertices.length, yVertices.length, or some equivalent expression instead of as the literal 3.

3. The statement draws the following polyline:

4.
```
int[] xVertices = {0, 25, 50};
int[] yVertices = {50, 0, 50};
int vertexCount = xVertices.length;
pen.setColor(Color.BLACK);
pen.drawPolygon(xVertices, yVertices, vertexCount);
// adjust vertices to reposition triangle
for (int index = 0; index < vertexCount; index++)
{
   xVertices[index] = xVertices[index] + 75;
   yVertices[index] = yVertices[index] + 50;
} // end for
pen.setColor(Color.BLUE);
pen.drawPolygon(xVertices, yVertices, vertexCount);
```

5.
```
Point[] vertices = {new Point(0, 50), new Point(25, 0), new Point(50, 50)};
```

6.
```
public void translate(int xIncrement, int yIncrement)
{
   setLocation((int)getX() + xIncrement,
               (int)getY() + yIncrement);
} // end translate
```

7.
```
public Point getLocation()
{
   return new Point((int)getX(), (int)getY());
} // end getLocation
```

8.
```
Point vertex = new Point(100, 150);
RightTriangle myTriangle = new RightTriangle(50, 50, 3, vertex);
```

9.
```
Polygon myPoly = myTriangle.getPolygon();
```

10.
```
Point[] vertices = myTriangle.getVertices();
```

11. Add

```
-triangle: Polygon
```

after and in the same box as

```
-vertices: Point[]
```

12. Either

```
new Point(vertices[index])
```

or

```
new Point((int)vertices[index].getX(), (int)vertices[index].getY())
```

13. Add the following statements to the beginning of each method's body:

```
if (triangle == null)
    triangle = getPolygon();
```

14. The variables `rowCorner`, `squareCorner`, and `quiltCorner` reference the same `Point` object. The `translate` method moves the point by `squareSide` pixels to the right `squaresPerSide` times, down once, to the right `squaresPerSide` times, down once, and so on. Thus, each row of the quilt will not appear directly beneath the preceding row, but rather will be shifted to the right by the length of the row. If your window is large enough, the output will appear, as follows:

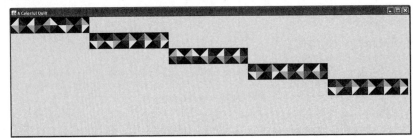

15. The reference variables `xPoints` and `yPoints` do not change in value—they continue to reference the same arrays —even though the entries in the array might change.

16. Since `pointCount` is zero, both `drawPolyline` and the `for` loop draw nothing

17. Suppose the user enters 123 and then clicks the "E" key. The displayed output is `Entered 123`. If "9" is clicked next, for example, the output becomes 1239.

18. Ignoring any changes necessary to remove the "C" key, the essential change is to set `keysClicked` to the empty string as the last action caused by the "E" key. Thus, the "E" key causes the following statements to execute:

```
int result = Integer.parseInt(keysClicked);
output.setMessage("Entered " + result)
keysClicked = "";
```

Chapter

23

Sorting and Searching

Contents

Prerequisites

Objectives

After studying this chapter, you should be able to

- Sort the entries in an array into ascending order by using a selection sort and an insertion sort
- Assess and compare the performances of these two sorting methods
- Search an array for a particular entry by using a linear search and a binary search
- Assess and compare the performance of these two searching methods

We are all familiar with arranging objects in order from smallest to largest or from largest to smallest. Not only do we order numbers this way, but we also can arrange people by height, age, or name; music by title, artist, or album; and so on. Arranging things into either ascending or descending order is called **sorting**. We can sort any collection of items that can be compared with one another. Likewise, in Java we can sort any primitive values or any objects that are Comparable—that is, objects of any class that implements the interface Comparable and, therefore, defines the method compareTo. Sorting is such an important task that many sorting algorithms exist. This chapter examines two basic algorithms for sorting data, to give you a feeling for the technique. These algorithms are not particularly fast, and better ones exist. In fact, we will present one such algorithm in Chapter 25 when we discuss recursive array processing.

As important as sorting is, searching is more common. Just think of how many times you search the World Wide Web. This chapter looks at two simple search strategies, the linear search and the binary search. A binary search is usually much faster than a linear search when the data is sorted. Realize, however, that Web searches utilize more sophisticated algorithms than the ones we will introduce here.

Sorting data usually takes much more time than searching it. The performance of an algorithm is a significant issue, particularly when large amounts of data are involved. We will look at the performance of the algorithms in this chapter and see how computer scientists talk about this aspect. Since people naturally want to improve the way they do things, it should not be a surprise that many algorithms exist for both sorting and searching.

■ Sorting

23.1 Suppose that you have a collection of items that need to be sorted in some way. For example, you might want to arrange an array of numbers from lowest to highest or from highest to lowest, or you might want to create a list of strings in alphabetical order. This chapter discusses and implements two simple algorithms that sort items into ascending order. Since typical sorting algorithms sort an array, our algorithms will rearrange the first *n* values in an array a so that

$$a[0] \leq a[1] \leq a[2] \leq \ldots \leq a[n - 1]$$

With only small changes to our algorithms, we will be able to sort entries into descending order.

Selection Sort

23.2 Imagine that you want to rearrange the books on your bookshelf by height, with the shortest book on the left. You might begin by tossing all of the books onto the floor. You then could return them to the shelf one by one, in their proper order. If you first return the shortest book to the shelf, and then the next shortest, and so on, you would perform a kind of **selection sort**. But using the floor—or another shelf—to store your books temporarily uses extra space needlessly.

videonote
Basic sorting

Instead, you could approach your intact bookshelf and *select* the shortest book. Since you want it to be first on the shelf, you remove the first book on the shelf and put the shortest book in its place. You still have a book in your hand, so you put it into the space formerly occupied by the shortest book. That is, the shortest book has traded places with the first book, as Figure 23-1 illustrates, and is now in its correct position. You now ignore the shortest book and repeat the process for the rest of the bookshelf.

FIGURE 23-1   Before and after exchanging the shortest book and the first book

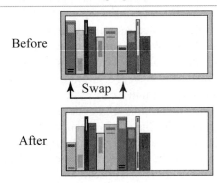

Before

Swap

After

23.3   In terms of an array a, the selection sort finds the smallest entry in the array and exchanges it with the entry in a[0]. Then, ignoring a[0], the sort finds the next smallest entry and swaps it with the one in a[1], and so on. Notice that we use only one array. We sort it by making entries trade places with other entries.

We could have copied the array into a second array and then moved the entries back to the original array in their proper order. But that would be like using the floor to store books temporarily. Fortunately, all of that extra space is unnecessary.

Figure 23-2 shows how a selection sort rearranges an array of integers by interchanging values. Beginning with the original array, the sort locates the smallest value in the array, that is, the 2 in a[3]. The value in a[3] is interchanged with the value in a[0]. After that interchange, the smallest value is in a[0] where it belongs.

The next smallest value is the 5 in a[4]. The sort then interchanges the value in a[4] with the value in a[1]. Now the values in a[0] and a[1] are the smallest in the array and are in their correct position within the final sorted array. The algorithm then interchanges the next smallest entry—the 8—with the value in a[2], and so on until the entire array is sorted.

23.4   **The algorithm.** The following pseudocode describes an algorithm for the selection sort:

Algorithm selectionSort(a)
// Sorts the array a into ascending order.

```
last = a.length - 1;
for (index = 0; index < last; index++)
{
    indexOfNextSmallest = the index of the smallest value among
                          a[index], a[index + 1], . . . , a[last]
    Interchange the values of a[index] and a[indexOfNextSmallest]
    // Assertion: a[0] <= a[1] <= . . . <= a[index], and these are the smallest
    // of the original array entries. The remaining array entries begin at a[index + 1].
}
```

During the last iteration of the for loop, notice the value of index. It is last - 1, even though the last array element is a[last]. Once the entries in a[0] through a[last - 1] are in their correct places, only the entry in a[last] remains to be positioned. But since the other entries are correctly positioned, it must already be in the correct place as well.

FIGURE 23-2   A selection sort of an array of integers into ascending order

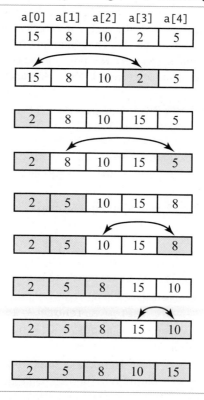

 Note: Notation

In mathematics, one-letter variable names are common. Recognizing this, and seeking to save some space, we use a and n within the text and pseudocode to represent, respectively, an array and its number of entries. Within Java code elsewhere, we have tried to avoid one-letter identifiers, using them only sparingly. However, the code that you will see in this chapter uses a and n to maintain consistency with the text.

23.5   **The Java definition.** One way to organize methods that sort an array is to create a class of static methods that perform the various sorts. For example, to sort integers, our class could begin as follows:

```
public class IntegerSorter
{
   public static void selectionSort(int[] a)
   {
      . . .
```

A client could include the statement

```
IntegerSorter.selectionSort(myArray);
```

to sort an array, myArray, of integers, for instance.

The class in Listing 23-1 contains the public method selectionSort and two private methods that assist in sorting. We can add other sorting methods as we develop them. It is easy to see that the definition of selectionSort is a direct translation of the previous pseudocode into Java code. The method getIndexOfSmallest searches the array elements a[first] through a[last] and returns the index of the element containing the smallest entry. The method uses two local variables, min and indexOfMin. At any point in the search, min references the smallest value found so far. That value occurs at a[indexOfMin]. At the end of the search, the method returns indexOfMin.

LISTING 23-1   A class containing a static method that performs a selection sort

```java
/** A class of static methods for sorting an array of integers
    from smallest to largest.
    @author Frank M. Carrano
*/
public class IntegerSorter
{
   /** Sorts the integers in an array into ascending order.
       @param a  an array of integers */
   public static void selectionSort(int[] a)
   {
      int last = a.length - 1;
      for (int index = 0; index < last; index++)
      {
         int indexNextSmallest = getIndexOfSmallest(a, index, last);
         swap(a, index, indexNextSmallest);
         // Assertion: a[0] <= a[1] <=...<= a[index] <= all other a[i]
      } // end for
   } // end selectionSort

   // Returns the index of the smallest value among the entries in
   // a[first], a[first + 1], . . . , a[last], where
   // 0 <= first <= last < a.length
   private static int getIndexOfSmallest(int[] a, int first, int last)
   {
      int indexOfMin = first;
      for (int index = first + 1; index <= last; index++)
      {
         if (a[index] < a[indexOfMin])
            indexOfMin = index;
         // Assertion: min is the smallest of a[first] through a[index]
      } // end for
      return indexOfMin;
   } // end getIndexOfSmallest

   // Swaps the values in the array elements a[i] and a[j], where
   // 0 <= i < = j < a.length
```

```
   private static void swap(int[] a, int i, int j)
   {
      int temp = a[i];
      a[i] = a[j];
      a[j] = temp;
   } // end swap
```

< Other sorting methods are here. >

```
} // end IntegerSorter
```

23.6 We gave getIndexOfSmallest a third parameter, last, even though selectionSort always passes it a.length – 1 as the corresponding argument, because sorting methods often have the same three parameters. Such methods enable us to sort a portion of an array as well as an entire array. For example, we could define selectionSort as follows:

```
/** Sorts a portion of an array of integers into ascending order.
    @param a      an array of integers
    @param first  an integer >= 0 that is the index of the first
                  array element to consider
    @param last   an integer >= first and < a.length that is the
                  index of the last array element to consider */
public static void selectionSort(int[] a, int first, int last)
{
   for (int index = first; index < last; index++)
   {
      int indexNextSmallest = getIndexOfSmallest(a, index, last);
      swap(a, index, indexNextSmallest);
      // Assertion: a[first] <= a[first + 1] <= . . . <= a[index] <=
      // all other a[i]
   } // end for
} // end selectionSort
```

For the convenience of the client, we can include both this version of the method and the one given in Listing 23-1. The bodies of the methods are quite similar; so to avoid the possible mistakes caused by duplication, we revise the one-parameter version so that it calls the three-parameter version, as follows:

```
public static void selectionSort(int[] a)
{
   selectionSort(a, 0, a.length - 1);
} // end selectionSort
```

Recall from Chapter 15 that since the two methods are in the same class and have the same name but different signatures, they are overloaded.

Question 1 What steps does a selection sort take when sorting the following array into ascending order? 9 6 2 4 8.

Question 2 In the previous question, how many comparisons between integers in the array did the selection sort make?

Question 3 To sort an entire array, myArray, of integers, we can call the method selectionSort in one of two ways. What are those two ways?

Question 4 Is it possible to add a method definition to the class given in Listing 23-1 so that we can sort the first ten integers in the array myArray by using the following invocation?

```
IntegerSorter.selectionSort(myArray, 10);
```

If so, define such a method; otherwise, explain why not.

Question 5 What change to the given algorithm for a selection sort will enable it to sort an array into descending order?

Question 6 What steps would a selection sort take when sorting the following array into descending order? 2 4 9 6 8

23.7 **A driver.** The program in Listing 23-2 demonstrates the class IntegerSorter, assuming that we have made the changes to it described in the previous segment.

LISTING 23-2   A driver for the class IntegerSorter

```java
/** A driver that demonstrates the class IntegerSorter.
    @author Frank M. Carrano
*/
public class SortDriver
{
   public static void main(String[] args)
   {
      int[] array = {40, 200, -55, 148, 0, 75, 21, 5, 150, 10, 3};
      System.out.println("Before sorting, the array contains:");
      display(array);
      IntegerSorter.selectionSort(array, 1, 6);
      System.out.println("\nAfter sorting a[1] through a[6], " +
                         "the array contains:");
      display(array);

      IntegerSorter.selectionSort(array);
      System.out.println("\nAfter sorting the entire array, " +
                         "it contains:");
      display(array);
   } // end main

   public static void display(int[] array)
   {
      for (int index = 0; index < array.length; index++)
         System.out.print(array[index] + " ");
      System.out.println();
```

```
        } // end display
} // end SortDriver
```

Output

```
    Before sorting, the array contains:
    40 200 -55 148 0 75 21 5 150 10 3

    After sorting a[1] through a[6], the array contains:
    40 -55 0 21 75 148 200 5 150 10 3

    After sorting the entire array, it contains:
    -55 0 3 5 10 21 40 75 148 150 200
```

Question 7 If an array of integers is sorted into ascending order, how does each entry—except for the last one—compare to the entry that follows it?

Question 8 Consider a method that you could add to the client of `IntegerSorter` that detects whether a given array is sorted. What is a definition of such a method if its header is

```
public static boolean isSorted(int[] array)
```

Detecting When an Array Is Sorted

23.8   The program shown in Listing 23-2 demonstrates a selection sort. Although we could use it to test the sorting methods more extensively, doing so would be tedious, since someone must read the output to verify its accuracy. If we were to use large arrays, a mistake in sorting could quite possibly be overlooked.

A better approach uses the two methods named `isSorted` in Listing 23-3. They address the task raised by Questions 7 and 8 by checking whether all or a portion of an array is sorted. Although the `main` method in this listing simply demonstrates the use of these methods, serious testing likely would omit much of the output shown here—but only after a sufficient test of the test program itself!

The method `main` defines the array `data`, whose entries will not change. They, of course, could be set in various other ways. We pass a copy of `data` to the sort method each time the method is called by using the method `Arrays.copyOf`, which Segment 18.29 of Chapter 18 introduced. In this way, we can begin each sort with the same data.

Note: Extensive Testing

A program that uses many and/or large data sets in its test of a method should indicate whether or not the outcome is correct. This information should be presented in a brief and easily understood fashion. We should not have to read through pages of output to see whether a method has executed correctly. If a method fails the test, however, the program should provide us with sufficient output to help us locate the source of the errors.

LISTING 23-3   A program that checks sorting results

```java
import java.util.Arrays; // for copyOf

/** A driver that tests the class IntegerSorter.
    @author Frank M. Carrano
*/
public class SortDriver
{
   public static void main(String[] args)
   {
      final int[] data = {40, 200, -55, 148, 0, 75, 21, 5, 150, 10, 3};
      int[] array = Arrays.copyOf(data, data.length);
      System.out.println("Before sorting, the array contains:");
      display(array);
      IntegerSorter.selectionSort(array, 1, 6);
      System.out.println("\nAfter sorting a[1] through a[6], " +
                         "the array contains:");
      display(array);
      check(array, 1, 6);

      array = Arrays.copyOf(data, data.length); // restore array
      IntegerSorter.selectionSort(array);
      System.out.println("\nAfter sorting the entire array, " +
                         "it contains:");
      display(array);
      check(array);
   } // end main

   public static boolean isSorted(int[] array, int first, int last)
   {
      boolean sorted = true;
      for (int index = first; sorted && (index < last); index++)
      {
         if (array[index] > array[index + 1])
            sorted = false;
      } // end for

      return sorted;
   } // end isSorted

   public static boolean isSorted(int[] array)
   {
      return isSorted(array, 0, array.length - 1);
   } // end isSorted

   public static void check(int[] array, int first, int last)
   {
      System.out.print("The sort is ");
```

```
            if (isSorted(array, first, last))
                System.out.println("correct.");
            else
                System.out.println("INCORRECT!");
        } // end check

        public static void check(int[] array)
        {
            check(array, 0, array.length - 1);
        } // end check

        public static void display(int[] array)
        {
            for (int index = 0; index < array.length; index++)
                System.out.print(array[index] + " ");
            System.out.println();
        } // end display
} // end SortDriver
```

Output

```
Before sorting, the array contains:
40 200 -55 148 0 75 21 5 150 10 3

After sorting a[1] through a[6], the array contains:
40 -55 0 21 75 148 200 5 150 10 3
The sort is correct.

After sorting the entire array, it contains:
-55 0 3 5 10 21 40 75 148 150 200
The sort is correct.
```

Insertion Sort

23.9   Another intuitive sorting algorithm is the **insertion sort**. Why would we want another sorting algorithm when we already have the selection sort? The insertion sort has an advantage over the selection sort, as you will see.

Suppose again that you want to rearrange the books on your bookshelf by height, with the shortest book on the left. If the leftmost book on the shelf was the only book, your shelf would be sorted. But you have many books to sort. Consider the second book. If it is taller than the first book, you now have two sorted books. If not, you remove the second book, slide the first book to the right, and *insert* the book you just removed into the first position on the shelf. The first two books are now sorted.

Now consider the third book. If it is taller than the second book, you now have three sorted books. If not, remove the third book and slide the second book to the right, as Parts a through c of Figure 23-3 illustrate. Now see whether the book in your hand is taller than the first book. If so, insert the book into the second position on the shelf, as shown in Part d of the figure. If not, slide the first book to the right, and insert the book in your hand into the first position on the shelf. If you repeat this process for each of the remaining books, the books on your bookshelf will be arranged by height.

FIGURE 23-3   The placement of the third book during an insertion sort

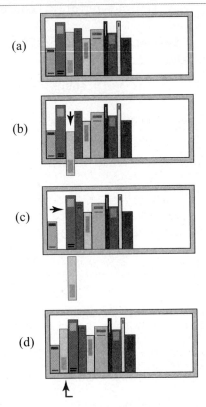

Figure 23-4 shows the bookshelf after several steps of the insertion sort. The books on the left side of the shelf are sorted. You remove the next unsorted book from the shelf and slide sorted books to the right, one at a time, until you find the right place for the book in your hand. You then insert this book into its new sorted location.

FIGURE 23-4   An insertion sort of books

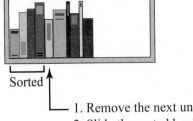

Sorted

1. Remove the next unsorted book.
2. Slide the sorted books to the right one by one until you find the right spot for the removed book.
3. Insert the book into its new position.

23.10   An insertion sort of an array **partitions**—that is, divides—the array into two parts. One part is sorted and initially contains just the first element in the array. The second part contains the remaining elements. The algorithm moves the first entry from the unsorted part and inserts it into its proper sorted position within the sorted part. Just as you did with the bookshelf, you choose the proper position by comparing the unsorted entry with the sorted entries, beginning at the end of the sorted part and continuing toward its beginning. As you compare, you shift array entries in the sorted part to make room for the insertion.

Figure 23-5 illustrates these steps for a sort that has already positioned the first three entries of the array. The 3 is the next entry that must be placed into its proper position within the sorted region. Since 3 is less than 8 and 5, but is greater than 2, the 8 and 5 are shifted to make room for the 3.

Figure 23-6 illustrates an entire insertion sort of an array of integers. At each pass of the algorithm, the sorted part expands by one element as the unsorted part shrinks by one element. Eventually, the unsorted part is empty and the array is sorted.

Note: Array partitioning by sorting algorithms

The insertion sort is not the only sorting algorithm that partitions an array. In fact, the selection sort also partitions the array into a sorted region and an unsorted region. Initially, the sorted region for a selection sort is empty. By exchanging array entries, the selection sort expands the sorted region while shrinking the unsorted region. You can see this effect in Figure 23-2 by thinking of the blue portion of the array as the sorted region.

23.11   **The algorithm.** The following iterative algorithm describes an insertion sort of the entries at indices `first` through `last` of the array a. The loop in the algorithm processes the unsorted part and invokes another method—`insertInOrder`—to perform the insertions. Since the sort begins with `a[first]` in the sorted portion of the array, the index `unsorted`, which accesses each of the other entries to be sorted, ranges from `first + 1` to `last`.

FIGURE 23-5   Inserting the next unsorted integer into its proper location within the sorted portion of an array during an insertion sort

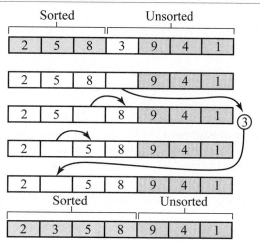

FIGURE 23-6   An insertion sort of an array of integers into ascending order

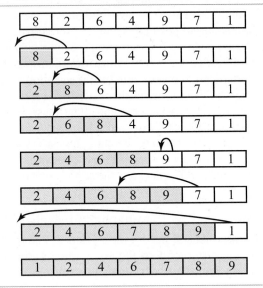

Algorithm insertionSort(a, first, last)
// *Sorts the entries in the array elements* a[first] *through* a[last].

```
for (unsorted = first + 1 through last)
{
   firstUnsorted = a[unsorted]
   insertInOrder(firstUnsorted, a, first, unsorted - 1)
}
```

Algorithm insertInOrder(entry, a, begin, end)
// *Inserts* entry *into the sorted array segment extending from* a[begin] *to* a[end].

```
index = end
while ( (index >= begin) and (entry < a[index]) )
{
   a[index + 1] = a[index] //  make room
   index--
}
//  Assertion: a[index + 1] is available
a[index + 1] = entry // insert

//  Assertion: a[begin] <= a[begin + 1] <= ... <= a[end + 1]
```

23.12   **The Java definition.** As Listing 23-4 shows, the Java code for an insertion sort closely follows the pseudocode given in the previous segment. We can add these methods to the class `IntegerSorter` shown in Listing 23-1.

LISTING 23-4   A Java implementation of an insertion sort of an array of integers

```java
public static void insertionSort(int[] a)
{
   insertionSort(a, 0, a.length - 1);
} // end insertionSort
```

```java
public static void insertionSort(int[] a, int first, int last)
{
    for (int unsorted = first + 1; unsorted <= last; unsorted++)
    {
        // Assertion: a[first] <= a[first + 1] <= ... <= a[unsorted - 1]
        int firstUnsorted = a[unsorted];
        insertInOrder(firstUnsorted, a, first, unsorted - 1);
    } // end for
} // end insertionSort

// Inserts a given entry into the sorted array segment
// extending from a[begin] to a[end].
private static void insertInOrder(int entryToInsert, int[] a,
                                  int begin, int end)
{
    int index = end;
    while ((index >= begin) && (entryToInsert < a[index]))
    {
        a[index + 1] = a[index];   // make room
        index--;
    } // end while

    // Assertion: a[index + 1] is available
    a[index + 1] = entryToInsert; // insert
    // Assertion: a[begin] <= a[begin + 1] <= ... <= a[end + 1]
} // end insertInOrder
```

Question 9 What steps does an insertion sort take when sorting the following array into ascending order? 9 6 2 4 8

Question 10 In the previous question, how many comparisons between integers in the array did the insertion sort make?

Sorting Objects

23.13   So far, we have sorted arrays of integers. How would we sort an array of objects? Sorting depends on our ability to compare items. We compare two integers—or two other primitive values—by using Java's comparison operators. Exactly how we compare two objects depends on the nature of the objects. For example, we can arrange a row of books on a bookshelf in several ways: by title, by author, by height, by color, and so on. The designer of a class of book objects would choose one of these ways and then define the method compareTo to implement that comparison. That is, we must use compareTo instead of the comparison operators when comparing objects. However, as Chapter 16 noted, not all classes define compareTo. Only classes that implement the interface Comparable—or extend a class that implements Comparable—have a compareTo method. Thus, not all objects can be sorted by using algorithms, such as the selection sort and insertion sort, that depend on compareTo.

23.14 **Sorting strings.** As an example of how we can sort objects, we will sort an array of strings. Recall that the class `String` defines the method `compareTo`. Listing 23-5 revises the insertion sort of integers shown in Listing 23-4 to work with strings, and places it within a class. Highlighting indicates where we changed the original code. In addition to changing the data type of the entries from `int` to `String`, we must use `String`'s `compareTo` method instead of the operator `<` to compare entries.

For now, we can use such customized methods for each class of objects to be sorted. After you learn more about generics in Chapter 32, you will be able to write methods that can sort an array of any class's objects, as long as the class implements the interface `Comparable`.

videonote
Sorting objects

LISTING 23-5 Insertion sort for an array of strings

```java
/** A class of static methods for sorting an array of strings
    into ascending order.
    @author Frank M. Carrano
*/
public class StringSorter
{
   public static void insertionSort(String[] a)
   {
      insertionSort(a, 0, a.length - 1);
   } // end insertionSort

   public static void insertionSort(String[] a, int first, int last)
   {
      for (int unsorted = first + 1; unsorted <= last; unsorted++)
      {
         // Assertion: a[first] <= a[first + 1] <=...<= a[unsorted - 1]
         String firstUnsorted = a[unsorted];
         insertInOrder(firstUnsorted, a, first, unsorted - 1);
      } // end for
   } // end insertionSort

   // Inserts a given entry into the sorted array
   // segment extending from a[begin] to a[end].
   private static void insertInOrder(String entryToInsert, String[] a,
                                     int begin, int end)
   {
      int index = end;
      while ((index >= begin) &&
             (entryToInsert.compareTo(a[index]) < 0))
      {
         a[index + 1] = a[index]; // make room
         index--;
      } // end while

      // Assertion: a[index + 1] is available
      a[index + 1] = entryToInsert;  // insert
      // Assertion: a[begin] <= a[begin + 1] <= ... <= a[end + 1]
   } // end insertInOrder
} // end StringSorter
```

23.15   The program in Listing 23-6 tests the methods shown in Listing 23-5. It is like the program given earlier in Listing 23-3, but has the changes described in the previous segment.

LISTING 23-6   A driver for StringSorter

```java
import java.util.Arrays; // for copyOf

/** A driver that tests the class StringSorter.
    @author Frank M. Carrano
*/
public class SortDriver
{
   public static void main(String[] args)
   {
      final String[] names = {"Jamie", "Colbie", "Andrew", "Corwin",
                              "Kyle", "Sasha", "Cooper", "Ali", "Nolan",
                              "Brady", "Blake", "Ethan"};

      String[] array = Arrays.copyOf(names, names.length);
      System.out.println("Before sorting, the array contains:");
      display(array);

      StringSorter.insertionSort(array, 1, 6);
      System.out.println("\nAfter sorting a[1] through a[6], " +
                         "the array contains:");
      display(array);
      check(array, 1, 6);

      array = Arrays.copyOf(names, names.length); // restore array
      StringSorter.insertionSort(array);
      System.out.println("\nAfter sorting the entire array, " +
                         "it contains:");
      display(array);
      check(array);
   } // end main

   public static boolean isSorted(String[] array, int first, int last)
   {
      boolean sorted = true;
      for (int index = first; sorted && (index < last); index++)
      {
         if (array[index].compareTo(array[index + 1]) > 0)
            sorted = false;
      } // end for

      return sorted;
   } // end isSorted
```

```
public static boolean isSorted(String[] array)
{
    return isSorted(array, 0, array.length - 1);
} // end isSorted

public static void check(String[] array, int first, int last)
{
    System.out.print("The sort is ");
    if (isSorted(array, first, last))
        System.out.println("correct.\n");
    else
        System.out.println("INCORRECT!\n");
} // end check

public static void check(String[] array)
{
    check(array, 0, array.length - 1);
} // end check

public static void display(Object[] array)
{
    for (int index = 0; index < array.length; index++)
        System.out.print(array[index] + " ");
    System.out.println();
} // end display
} // end SortDriver
```

Question 11 The method display in Listing 23-6 has a parameter whose data type is Object[]. Why can we pass an array of strings to this method when we call it?

Question 12 Why does the method isSorted in Listing 23-6 have a parameter whose data type is String[] instead of Object[]?

Sorting Methods in the Java Class Library

23.16   Both selection sort and insertion sort are examples of how we can sort an array. But neither method is especially fast. While they are certainly fast enough for small arrays—say those containing no more than 100 entries—they are too slow for large arrays.

The class Arrays in the package java.util of the Java Class Library defines several versions of a static method sort that arranges an array into ascending order. These methods are fast and can be used with any array of primitive values or Comparable objects. The methods occur in pairs, as follows:

```
public static void sort(type[] a)
```

sorts an entire array a, while the method

```
public static void sort(type[] a, int first, int after)
```

sorts the elements a[first] through a[after - 1]. Notice that after is 1 more than the index of the last entry in the array segment to be sorted, whereas our sorting methods used the index of the last entry. Also, *type* is either byte, char, double, float, int, long, short, or Object. The objects in an array of objects must belong to a class that implements the interface Comparable.

Searching

We are always looking for something. Like the people in Figure 23-7, you can search your desk for a pen, your closet for your favorite sweater, or a list of names to see whether you are on it. Searching for a particular item—sometimes called the **target**—among a collection of many items is a common task. As we mentioned at the start of this chapter, we will consider two simple search strategies, the linear search and the binary search.

FIGURE 23-7   Searching is an everyday occurrence

A Linear Search of an Unsorted Array

23.17   A **linear**, or **sequential**, **search** of an array compares the desired item—the target—with the first entry in the array, the second entry in the array, and so on until it either locates the desired entry or looks at all the entries without success. The code that Chapter 18 developed in Segments 18.17 through 18.19 actually uses a linear search to locate a given string within an array of strings. We can use those ideas to define a static method that searches an unsorted array of strings. The class in Listing 23-7 contains such a method, as well as one that searches a portion of an array. Providing two versions of a search method is analogous to our previous sorting methods.

videonote
Searching

If the loop in the method `linearSearch` locates an entry in the array that matches the desired string `target`, the current array index is recorded in `result`, and the boolean variable `searching` becomes false, causing the loop to exit. On the other hand, if the loop examines all the entries in the array without finding one that matches `target`, `searching` remains true as the loop ends. Figure 23-8 provides an example of these two outcomes. For simplicity, this figure—and, later, Figure 23-11—use integers.

LISTING 23-7   The class `StringSearcher`

```
/** A class whose static methods search an array of strings.
    @author Frank M. Carrano
*/
public class StringSearcher
{
   /** Performs a linear (sequential) search of a portion of an array.
       @param target   the string to find
       @param strings  an array of strings
```

```
                @param first    an integer >= 0 that is the index of the first
                                 array element to consider
                @param last     an integer >= first and < a.length that is the
                                 index of the last array element to consider */
            @return the index of an occurrence of target,
                     if it is in the array, or -1 if not. */
     public static int linearSearch(String target, String[] strings,
                                    int first, int last)
     {
        boolean searching = true;
        int result = -1;
        for (int index = first; searching && (index <= last); index++)
        {
           if (target.equals(strings[index]))
           {
              result = index;
              searching = false;
           } // end if
        } // end for

        return result;
     } // end linearSearch

     /** Performs a linear (sequential) search of an array.
         @param target   the string to find
         @param strings  an array of strings
         @return the index of an occurrence of target,
                 if it is in the array, or -1 if not. */
     public static int linearSearch(String target, String[] strings)
     {
        return linearSearch(target, strings, 0, strings.length - 1);
     } // end linearSearch
  } // end StringSearcher
```

FIGURE 23-8a   An iterative sequential search of an array that finds its target

A search for 8

Look at 9:

9	5	8	4	7

$8 \neq 9$, so continue searching.

Look at 5:

9	5	8	4	7

$8 \neq 5$, so continue searching.

Look at 8:

9	5	8	4	7

$8 = 8$, so the search has found 8.

FIGURE 23-8b   An iterative sequential search of an array that does not find its
target

A search for 6

Look at 9:

9	5	8	4	7

6 ≠ 9, so continue searching.

Look at 5:

9	5	8	4	7

6 ≠ 5, so continue searching.

Look at 8:

9	5	8	4	7

6 ≠ 8, so continue searching.

Look at 4:

9	5	8	4	7

6 ≠ 4, so continue searching.

Look at 7:

9	5	8	4	7

6 ≠ 7, so continue searching.

No entries are left to consider, so the search concludes that 6 is not in the array.

23.18   The program in Listing 23-8 demonstrates the linear search provided by the class StringSearcher. We define an array names of strings to search as well as a second array of target strings. The method linearSearch is invoked for each target string, and the results of each search are given. Notice that we report the position of a located string as an everyday value 1 through 12 instead of an array index. Also, our tests search for three strings in the array names—at its beginning, middle, and end—as well as one string not in the array. Incidentally, notice our use of a for-each loop to consider each string in the array targets.

Question 13 How many comparisons to strings in the array names, as defined in Listing 23-8, did linearSearch make while searching for "Matt"?

Question 14 What is the final value of the variable searching within the method linearSearch after the method completes its search for the string "Turtle"?

Question 15 If the array names contained only two strings, and both were occurrences of the string "Chris", which occurrence would linearSearch report when searching for "Chris"?

LISTING 23-8   A demonstration of a linear search

```
/** A driver that demonstrates the class StringSearcher.
    @author Frank M. Carrano
*/
public class SearchDriver
{
   private static String[] names =
```

```
                {"Chris", "Tyler", "Josh", "Kirk", "Luke", "Madison",
                 "Matt", "Ashley", "Derek", "Sam", "Taylor", "Melinda"};
    private static String[] targets =
                {"Chris", "Matt", "Melinda", "Turtle"};

    public static void main(String args[])
    {
        // display array of names
        System.out.println("Here are " + names.length + " names:");
        displayArray(names, names.length / 2);
        System.out.println();

        // search for names
        for (String target : targets)
        {
            System.out.print("Searching for " + target + ": ");
            int index = StringSearcher.linearSearch(target, names);
            if (index > -1)
                System.out.println("Found at position " + (index + 1) + ".");
            else
                System.out.println("Not found.");
        } // end for
    } // end main

    /** Displays an array of strings in rows of a specified
        number of strings. */
    public static void displayArray(String[] array, int stringsPerRow)
    {
        int rowStart = 0;
        int rowEnd = rowStart + stringsPerRow - 1;
        while (rowEnd < array.length)
        {
            for (int index = rowStart; index <= rowEnd; index++)
                System.out.print(array[index] + " ");
            System.out.println();
            rowStart = rowEnd + 1;
            rowEnd = rowStart + stringsPerRow - 1;
        } // end while
    } // end displayArray
} // end SearchDriver
```

Output

```
Here are 12 names:
Chris Tyler Josh Kirk Luke Madison
Matt Ashley Derek Sam Taylor Melinda

Searching for Chris: Found at position 1.
Searching for Matt: Found at position 7.
Searching for Melinda: Found at position 12.
Searching for Turtle: Not found.
```

Design Decision:

Although our method `linearSearch` in Listing 23-7 could have returned true or false—that is, the boolean value `searching`—to indicate the outcome of the search, we chose to return either –1 or the index of the array entry matching `target`. Because of this design decision, we could have omitted the boolean variable `searching` and used `result` to control the method's loop. However, we retained the boolean variable to make our logic clearer in this version of the code. Question 16 asks you to revise `linearSearch` by omitting the boolean variable.

Why did we choose to return –1 to indicate an unsuccessful search? Because it could not be an array index. The method returns an array index when the search is successful, and so we had to choose a value that could not be an index when the search is not successful. Any negative integer would suffice as a return value in this case.

Question 16 Revise the definition of the four-parameter version of the method `linearSearch`, as given in Listing 23-7, by omitting the boolean variable.

A Linear Search of a Sorted Array

23.19   Imagine that you are looking through a jar of coins for one minted during the year of your birth. A linear search of 10 coins is not a problem. With 1000 coins, however, the search might be lengthy. But suppose that, before you begin searching your coins, someone arranges them in sorted order by their dates. If you searched the sorted coins in Figure 23-9 sequentially for the date 1992, you would look at the coins dated 1988 and 1990 before arriving at 1992. If instead you looked for the date 1993, you would look at the first four coins without finding it. Should you keep looking? If the coins are sorted into ascending order and you have reached the one dated 1994, you know that you will not find 1993 beyond it. If the coins are not sorted, you have to examine all of them to see that 1993 is not present.

FIGURE 23-9   Coins sorted by their mint dates

23.20   If our array is sorted into ascending order, we can use the previous ideas to revise the linear search, as follows:

```java
public static int linearSearch(String target, String[] strings)
{
   int result = -1;
   // search the array until either the target is found or passed,
   // or the entire array is considered
   int index = 0;
   while ((index < strings.length) &&
          (target.compareTo(strings[index]) > 0))
      index++;

   // did we find the target?
   if ((index < strings.length) && target.equals(strings[index]))
      result = index; // target is found

   return result;
} // end linearSearch
```

The searching loop is somewhat different from the one we used previously when the array wasn't sorted. We search the array as long as index is legal and the target string is greater than the array entry at index. The loop ends when one of the following conditions occurs:

- target is found, that is, it equals the array entry at index.
- target is less than the array entry at index.
- The entire array has been searched without success.

The if statement after the loop detects which of these conditions is true. Observe that index is declared outside of the loop, making it available after the loop, as is required by this if statement. Also notice the absence of a boolean variable resembling searching in Listing 23-7.

23.21   **Refining the code.** If the target happens to be at the end of the array, the previous code compares target to strings[strings.length - 1] twice, once in the while statement and once in the if statement. We can avoid this duplicate operation by iterating one fewer time. With this change, index would never exceed the length of the array, and so we could remove the test of its value from the if statement. Listing 23-9 shows these changes in our final version of linearSearch.

LISTING 23-9   The class SortedStringSearcher

```java
/** A class whose static method searches a sorted array of strings.
    @author Frank M. Carrano
*/
public class SortedStringSearcher
{
   /** Performs a linear (sequential) search of an array
       sorted into ascending order.
       @param target   the item to find
       @param strings  an array of sorted strings
       @return the index of an occurrence of target
               if it is in the array, or -1 if not. */
   public static int linearSearch(String target, String[] strings)
   {
      int result = -1;
      // search the array until either the target is found or passed,
      // or all but the last entry in the array is considered
      int index = 0;
      while ((index < strings.length - 1) &&
             (target.compareTo(strings[index]) > 0))
         index++;

      // did we find the target?
      if (target.equals(strings[index]))
         result = index; // target is found

      return result;
   } // end linearSearch
} // end SortedStringSearcher
```

23.22 We can use the program shown in Listing 23-8 to test `SortedStringSearcher` by first replacing `StringSearcher` with `SortedStringSearcher` in the call to `linearSearch`. We also must search a sorted array instead of the unsorted one given in Listing 23-8. For example, suppose that we define the array `names` as follows:

```
private static String[] names =
        {"Ashley", "Chris", "Derek", "Josh", "Kirk", "Luke",
         "Madison", "Matt", "Melinda", "Sam", "Taylor", "Tyler"};
```

As before, we will search for those names in the array that occur first, last, and near the middle—in particular, Ashley, Tyler, and Madison. We also need to search for names that are not in the array, but this time we should choose ones according to when the search will stop. Thus, we will choose a name alphabetically before Ashley, one between existing names, and one after Tyler. Consequently, we can define the array `targets` as follows:

```
private static String[] targets =
        {"Ashley", "Tyler", "Madison", "Aaron", "Emma", "Zachary"};
```

With the changes just described, the program produces the following output:

```
Here are 12 names:
Ashley, Chris, Derek, Josh, Kirk, Luke,
Madison, Matt, Melinda, Sam, Taylor, Tyler

Searching for Ashley: Found at position 1.
Searching for Tyler: Found at position 12.
Searching for Madison: Found at position 7.
Searching for Aaron: Not found.
Searching for Emma: Not found.
Searching for Zachary: Not found.
```

23.23 The linear search of an unsorted array—given earlier in Listing 23-7—always examines the entire array before it can confirm the absence of an item. The modified linear search of a sorted array, however, often makes far fewer comparisons to reach the same conclusion. But after expending the effort to sort an array, we usually can search it even faster by using the technique that we discuss next.

Question 17 The method `linearSearch` given in Listing 23-9 can be revised to work for arrays that are sorted into descending order. How would you change the method?

A Binary Search of a Sorted Array

Think of a number between 1 and 1 million. When I guess at your number, tell me whether my guess is correct, too high, or too low. At most, how many attempts will I need before I guess correctly? You should be able to answer this question by the time you reach the end of this chapter!

23.24 If you had to find a new friend's telephone number in a printed directory, what would you do? You could open the book, glance at the entries, and quickly see whether you were on the correct page. If you were not, you would decide whether you had to look at earlier pages (those in the left portion of the book) or at later pages (those in the right portion). What aspect of a telephone directory enables you to make this decision? The alphabetical order of the names.

If you decided to look in the left portion, you could ignore the entire right portion. In fact, you could tear off the right portion and discard it, as Figure 23-10 illustrates. You have reduced the size of the search problem, as you have only part of the book left to search. By repeating this process, you eventually would either find the telephone number or discover that it is not there.

A **binary search** is like searching a telephone directory by opening it to a page near its middle. At each step of the search, you reduce the number of pages left to search by one-half.

23.25   Let's adapt these ideas to searching an array a of n integers that are sorted into ascending order. (Descending order would also work with a simple change in our algorithm.) We know that

a[0] ≤ a[1] ≤ a[2] ≤ . . . ≤ a[n - 1]

Because the array is sorted, we can rule out whole sections of the array that could not possibly contain the number we are looking for—just as you ruled out an entire half of the telephone directory.

For example, if we are looking for the number 7, and if we know that a[5] is equal to 9, then we know that 7 is less than a[5]. But we also know that 7 cannot appear after a[5] in the array, because the array is sorted. That is,

7 < a[5] ≤ a[6] ≤ . . . ≤ a[n - 1]

We know this without looking at the elements beyond a[5]. We therefore can ignore these elements, as well as a[5]. Similarly, if the sought-after number is greater than a[5]—for example, if we were looking for 10—we could ignore a[5] and all the elements before it.

23.26   Replacing the index 5 in the preceding example with whatever index—call it mid—is midway between 0 and n − 1 is a first step to drafting an algorithm for a binary search of an array. We need a way to consider half of the array and ignore the other half. If target does not equal the entry in a[mid], we search either the elements indexed by 0 through mid - 1 or the elements indexed by mid + 1 through n - 1.

We can search portions of the array by using the variables first and last, as we did for sorting, to indicate the first and last indices of the subrange of the array to be searched. That is, we search a[first] through a[last] for target. To find the approximate midpoint of this portion of the array, we could set mid to (first + last) / 2. Combining these ideas with a loop leads to the following draft of an algorithm:

Algorithm to search a[0] *through* a[n - 1] *for* target, *assuming* n >= 1

```
first = 0
last = n - 1
while (the search for target continues)
```

```
    {
        mid = (first + last) / 2
        if (target equals a[mid])
            result = mid
        else if (target < a[mid])
            last = mid - 1   // target is in first half
        else   // target > a[mid]
            first = mid + 1 // target is in second half
    }
    return result
```

To search the entire array, we initially set first to 0 and last to n - 1. Each repetition of the loop will then use some other values for first and last. For example, at the end of the first repetition, if the sought item is greater than a[mid], first would be set to mid + 1, and last would still be n - 1.

23.27   Figure 23-11 provides an example of a binary search. Note that Segment 12.12 of Chapter 12 described a strategy for a guessing game that is like a binary search.

FIGURE 23-11   A binary search of a sorted array that (a) finds its target; (b) does not find its target

(a) A search for 8

Look at the middle entry, 10:

2	4	5	7	8	**10**	12	15	18	21	24	26
0	1	2	3	4	5	6	7	8	9	10	11

8 < 10, so search the left half of the array.

Look at the middle entry, 5:

2	4	**5**	7	8
0	1	2	3	4

8 > 5, so search the right half of the array.

Look at the middle entry, 7:

7	8
3	4

8 > 7, so search the right half of the array.

Look at the middle entry, 8:

8
4

8 = 8, so the search has found 8.

(b) A search for 16

Look at the middle entry, 10:

2	4	5	7	8	**10**	12	15	18	21	24	26
0	1	2	3	4	5	6	7	8	9	10	11

16 > 10, so search the right half of the array.

Look at the middle entry, 18:

12	15	**18**	21	24	26
6	7	8	9	10	11

16 < 18, so search the left half of the array.

Look at the middle entry, 12:

12	15
6	7

16 > 12, so search the right half of the array.

Look at the middle entry, 15:

15
7

16 > 15, so search the right half of the array.
That is, set `first` to 8.

Since `last` is 7, `first` > `last`. No entries are left to consider,
so the search concludes that 16 is not in the array.

23.28   When will the loop end? If the sought-after item is in the array, the algorithm considers smaller and smaller portions of the array until it finds the item and ends the loop. But what if the item is not anywhere in the array? Will the loop end? Unfortunately not, but that is not hard to fix.

Note that either the value of `first` increases or the value of `last` decreases during each repetition of the loop. If the value of `first` actually becomes larger than the value of `last`, the algorithm will have no more array entries to check. In that case, `target` is not in the array. We need to add this test to our pseudocode and have the algorithm return –1 when the search is unsuccessful. Thus, we get the following more complete algorithm:

Algorithm to search a[0] *through* a[n - 1] *for target*

```
result = -1
first = 0
last = n - 1
while (result is -1 and first <= last)
{
    mid = (first + last) / 2
    if (target equals a[mid])
        result = mid
    else if (target < a[mid])
        last = mid - 1   // target is in first half
    else   // target > a[mid]
        first = mid + 1  // target is in second half
}
return result
```

23.29 Listing 23-10 contains the definition of the method `binarySearch` as a member of the class `SortedStringSearcher`, which appeared earlier in Listing 23-9. We call the method in the same way that we call the method `linearSearch`.

Notice that the Java computation of the midpoint `mid` is

```
int mid = first + (last - first) / 2;
```

instead of

```
int mid = (first + last) / 2;
```

as the pseudocode would suggest. If you were to search an array of at least 2^{30}, or about one billion, elements, the sum of `first` and `last` could exceed the largest possible `int` value of $2^{31} - 1$. Thus, the computation `first + last` would overflow to a negative integer and result in a negative value for `mid`. If this negative value of `mid` was used as an array index, an `ArrayIndexOutOfBoundsException` would occur. The computation `first + (last - first) / 2`, which is algebraically equivalent to `(first + last) / 2`, avoids this error. Note that we first encountered an overflow in Segment D4.6 of Debugging Interlude 4.

LISTING 23-10 The static method `binarySearch`

```java
/** A class of static methods for searching a sorted array of strings.
    @author Frank M. Carrano
*/
public class SortedStringSearcher
{
   /** Performs a binary search of an array sorted into ascending order.
       @param target   the item to find
       @param strings  an array of sorted strings
       @return the index of an occurrence of target,
               if it is in the array, or -1 if not. */
   public static int binarySearch(String target, String[] strings)
   {
      boolean searching = true;
      int result = -1;
      int first = 0;
      int last = strings.length - 1;
      while (searching && (first <= last))
      {
         int mid = first + (last - first) / 2;
         if (target.equals(strings[mid]))
         {
            result = mid;       // target found at a[mid]
            searching = false;
         }
         else if (target.compareTo(strings[mid]) < 0)
            last = mid - 1;   // target in first half
         else
            first = mid + 1;   // target in second half
      } // end while
```

```
        return result;
    } // end binarySearch
```

    < *The method* `linearSearch`, *as given in Listing 23-9, is here.* >

```
} // end SortedStringSearcher
```

Question 18 When a binary search searches the array in Figure 23-11 for 8 and for 16, how many comparisons to an array entry are necessary in each case?

Question 19 During a binary search, which entries in the array

    "C" "F" "J" "M" "T" "W"

are compared to the target when the target is **a.** "A"; **b.** "F"; **c.** "R".

Question 20 Define another version of the method `binarySearch` so that it has two more parameters, `first` and `last`, and searches the portion of the array `strings` ranging from `strings[first]` to `strings[last]`.

Question 21 If you were to add the method that you defined in the previous question to the class `SortedStringSearcher`, as defined in Listing 23-10, how would you avoid the duplication of code?

Question 22 What changes to the binary search algorithm are necessary when the array is sorted in descending order (from largest down to smallest) instead of ascending order, as we have assumed during our discussion?

Note: The previous method `binarySearch` calls both the method `equals` and the method `compareTo`. If the objects in the array did not have an appropriate `equals` method, `binarySearch` would not execute correctly. Note, however, that you could use `compareTo` instead of `equals` to test for equality.

Programming Tip

If a class `C` implements the interface `Comparable` and therefore defines a `compareTo` method, and if the class also overrides `Object`'s `equals` method—as it ought—both `compareTo` and `equals` should use the same test for equality. That is, for any two objects one and two of `C`, the expressions `one.equals(two)` and `one.compareTo(two) == 0` should have the same boolean value. Sun's documentation for the interface `Comparable` strongly recommends—but does not require—that this be so. In fact, almost all classes in the Java Class Library that implement `Comparable` follow this recommendation.

Question 23 What class in the Java Class Library does not adhere to the recommendation for the methods `compareTo` and `equals` that the previous programming tip describes? *Hint*: Consult the documentation for the interface `Comparable`.

Searching Methods in the Java Class Library

23.30   The class `Arrays` in the package `java.util` defines several versions of a static method `binarySearch` to perform a binary search of an array. These methods can search any array of primitive values or `Comparable` objects that are sorted into ascending order. The methods occur in pairs, as follows:

```
public static int binarySearch(type[] a, type target)
```

searches an entire array a, while the method

```
public static int binarySearch(type[] a, int first, int after, type target)
```

searches the elements a[first] through a[after - 1]. Notice that after is 1 more than the index of the last entry in the array segment to be searched, whereas our search methods used the index of the last entry. Here, *type* can be `Object` or any of the primitive types byte, char, double, float, int, long, or short, and both occurrences must be the same. The objects in an array of objects must belong to a class that implements the interface `Comparable`. Each method returns either the index of the array element that equals target or the value -belongsAt - 1, where belongsAt is the index of the array element that should contain target.

Programming Tip

When you define a method compareTo for the objects in an array that you pass to a method in any class—such as Arrays—in the Java Class Library, you must follow the specifications for compareTo as described in the interface Comparable. You might not like those specifications, but they are the ones that a method such as Arrays.binarySearch assumes.

Note: The indices that indicate a portion of an array

This chapter defines methods to sort or search a portion of an array a ranging from a[first] to a[last]. To call any of these methods, you provide the indices first and last as arguments. To call the standard methods Arrays.sort and Arrays.binarySearch, however, you would provide first and last + 1 as arguments.

We have defined our methods in a way that is easier for you to understand. The authors of the Java Class Library defined the methods Arrays.sort and Arrays.binarySearch in a way that is easier for programmers to use. For example, to sort the first howMany entries in the array a, the call to sort could be

```
Array.sort(a, 0, howMany);
```

whereas the call to our insertion sort would be

```
StringSorter.insertionSort(a, 0, howMany - 1);
```

As you can see, the methods in the standard class Arrays enable you to avoid subtracting 1.

Exercise 15 at the end of this chapter asks you to revise the methods defined in this chapter to use the same indices for parameters as are used by Arrays.sort and Arrays.binarySearch.

Programming Tip

In the interest of consistency and to avoid confusion, you should define your own methods to be consistent with other existing methods, such as those in the Java Class Library. Unfortunately, not all programmers follow this advice.

> **Aside: The hidden error in binary search**
>
> Until 2006, implementations of the binary search—including the method `Arrays.binarySearch`—used the expression `(first + last) / 2` to compute the midpoint `mid`. For decades, this computation caused no problem, as memory—and therefore arrays—was never large enough to cause an overflow. Eventually, a search of a large array caused an `ArrayIndexOutOfBoundsException`, as mentioned in Segment 23.29. According to Joshua Block, the author of `Arrays.binarySearch`, this error was corrected in 2006.[1]

The Performance of Algorithms

23.31 In this chapter, we have encountered two algorithms for sorting an array and two for searching it. Which method should we choose when sorting or searching an array? Usually the "best" solution to a problem balances various criteria such as execution time, memory space requirements, programming effort, generality, and so on. Computer scientists measure and often consider an algorithm's time and space requirements, called its **complexity**, as the main basis for choosing a solution. The process of measuring the complexity of algorithms is called the **analysis of algorithms**.

When we assess an algorithm's complexity, we are not measuring how involved or difficult it is—although that could be a secondary consideration after complexity. Instead, we are measuring the algorithm's **time complexity** (the time it takes to execute) or its **space complexity** (the amount of memory it needs to execute). Typically we analyze these requirements separately. So a "best" algorithm might be either the fastest one or the one that uses the least memory. An inverse relationship often exists between an algorithm's time complexity and its space complexity. If we revise an algorithm to save execution time, we usually will need more space. If we reduce an algorithm's space requirement, it likely will require more time to execute. Sometimes, however, we are able to save both time and space. We will concentrate on the time complexity of algorithms in this discussion.

23.32 The measure of an algorithm's complexity is expressed in terms of the size of the problem. For example, if we are searching a collection of data, the size of the problem is the number of items in the collection. Such a measure enables us to compare the relative cost of algorithms as a function of the size of the problem. Typically, we are interested in large problems; a small problem is likely to take little time, even if the algorithm is inefficient.

It is important to understand that we do not compute the actual time requirement of an algorithm. After all, we have not implemented the algorithm in Java and have not chosen the computer. Instead, we look for a function of the problem size that behaves like the algorithm's actual time requirement. That is, as the time requirement increases by some factor, the value of the function increases by the same factor, and vice versa. The value of the function is said to be *directly proportional* to the time requirement. Such a function is called a **growth-rate function** because it measures how an algorithm's time requirement grows as the problem size grows.

Because they measure time requirements, growth-rate functions have positive values. By comparing the growth-rate functions of two algorithms, we can see whether one algorithm is faster than the other for large-size problems.

---

1. "Extra, Extra—Read All About It: Nearly All Binary Searches and Mergesorts Are Broken," Joshua Block, Google Research Blog, June 2, 2006. www.googleresearch.blogspot.com/2006/06/extra-extra-read-all-about-it-nearly.html.

23.33   For any given problem of a fixed size, we can estimate the maximum time that an algorithm could take—that is, its **worst-case time**. If we can tolerate this worst-case time, our algorithm is acceptable. We also can estimate the minimum or **best-case time**. If the best-case time is still too slow, we need another algorithm. For many algorithms, the worst and best cases rarely occur. A more useful measure in practice is the **average-case time** requirement of an algorithm. This measure, however, is usually harder to determine than the best and worst cases.

   To find an algorithms's growth-rate functions in the worst, best, and average cases, we count or estimate the number of significant operations in a particular case as a function of the problem size n. With this function in hand, computer scientists use several notations to represent the algorithm's complexity. Instead of saying that an algorithm has a time requirement proportional to n, for example, we say that it is **O(n)**. We call this notation **Big Oh** since it uses the capital letter O. We read O(n) as either "Big Oh of n" or "order of n." Similarly, if an algorithm's time requirement is proportional to n^2, we say that it is O(n^2). If an algorithm has the same time requirement regardless of the problem size, the algorithm is O(1). Other notations, such as *Omega* and *Theta*, are used, but we will not cover them here.

23.34   **An example.** Imagine that you are at a wedding reception, seated at a table of n people. In preparation for the toast, the waiter pours champagne into each of n glasses. That task is O(n). Someone makes a toast. It is O(1), even if the toast seems to last forever, because it is independent of the number of guests. If you clink your glass with everyone at your table, one at a time, you perform an O(n) operation. If everyone at your table does likewise, a total of O(n^2) clinks take place. If only one clink occurs at a time, we have an O(n^2) operation.

The Performance of Sorting Methods

23.35   **Selection sort.** When the method `selectionSort` in Listing 23-1 sorts an array of n entries, its loop executes $n - 1$ times. Thus, the method invokes the methods `getIndexOfSmallest` and `swap` $n - 1$ times each. In the $n - 1$ calls to `getIndexOfSmallest`, `last` is $n - 1$ and `first` ranges from 0 to $n - 2$. Each time `getIndexOfSmallest` is invoked, its loop executes `last - first` times. Thus, this loop executes a total of

$$(n - 1) + (n - 2) + \ldots + 1$$

times. This sum is $n \times (n - 1) / 2$. Since the execution time of the individual operations in the loop is independent of the problem size—that is, they are each O(1)—the time complexity of the selection sort is directly proportional to n^2. Notice that our discussion does not depend on the arrangement of the data in the array. It could be wildly out of order, nearly sorted, or completely sorted; in any case, selection sort's time complexity is O(n^2). This measure, however, assumes that the comparison of two entries in the array is an O(1) operation.

 Note: **You can ignore all but the largest term in a growth-rate function**
You are not likely to notice the effect of an inefficient algorithm when the problem is small. Thus, an analysis of a solution's time requirement should focus on large problems. If we care only about large values of n when comparing the algorithms, we can consider only the dominant term in each growth-rate function.

   For example, $n \times (n - 1) / 2$ is $(n^2 - n) / 2$. This expression behaves like $n^2 - n$, which behaves like n^2 when n is large because n^2 is much larger than n in that case. In other words, the difference between the value of $(n^2 - n) / 2$ and that of n^2 is relatively small and can be ignored when n is large. So instead of using $n \times (n - 1) / 2$ as the growth-rate function for selection sort, we can use n^2—the term with the largest exponent—and say that selection sort requires time proportional to n^2.

Question 24 Show that $(n-1) + (n-2) + \ldots + 1$ is equal to $n \times (n-1) / 2$. *Hint*: Write $(n-1) + (n-2) + \ldots + 1$; beneath it write $1 + 2 + \ldots + (n-1)$. Add the corresponding terms in the two lines. The result is twice the sum you seek.

23.36   **Insertion sort.** When the insertion sort given in Listing 23-4 sorts an array of *n* entries, `first` is 0 and `last` is $n - 1$. Thus, the for loop executes $n - 1$ times, and so the method `insertInOrder` is invoked $n - 1$ times. Within `insertInOrder`, `begin` is 0 and `end` ranges from 0 to $n - 2$. The loop within `insertInOrder` makes at most end – begin + 1 cycles each time the method is invoked. Hence, this loop executes at most a total of

$$1 + 2 + \ldots + (n-1)$$

times. This sum is $n \times (n-1) / 2$.

    This analysis provides a worst-case scenario, and so in the worst case, the insertion sort is $O(n^2)$. In the best case, the loop in `insertInOrder` would exit immediately. Such is the case if the array is sorted already. In the best case, then, insertion sort is $O(n)$. In general, the more sorted an array is, the less work `insertInOrder` needs to do. This fact and its relatively simple implementation make the insertion sort popular for applications in which the array does not change much. For example, some customer databases add only a small percentage of new customers each day.

23.37   **Choosing between a selection sort and an insertion sort.** Figure 23-12 summarizes the performance of our two sorting methods. The selection sort is an $O(n^2)$ algorithm in the best, worst, and average cases. Regardless of the original order of an array's entries, a selection sort will do the same work to sort the array. For example, suppose that the entries in your array are totally mixed up, but my array is in perfect ascending order. The method `selectionSort` given in this chapter will take the same amount of time to sort each of our arrays!

FIGURE 23-12   Summary of sorting performance

	Best Case	Average Case	Worst Case
Selection sort	$O(n^2)$	$O(n^2)$	$O(n^2)$
Insertion sort	$O(n)$	$O(n^2)$	$O(n^2)$

    The insertion sort is $O(n^2)$ in both the average and worst cases. But in its best case, it is $O(n)$, and so is faster than the selection sort in this case. The best case for an insertion sort is when the array is already sorted. Even if that extreme case does not occur, the closer an array's entries are to being sorted, the less work an insertion sort does, meaning that the insertion sort will be faster than a selection sort.

    Typically, however, the average-case behavior applies, and in such situations both the selection sort and the insertion sort are $O(n^2)$. Although these methods are fine for small arrays, much faster sorting algorithms are available. Generally speaking, you should use one of the several overloaded `sort` methods in the class `java.util.Arrays`, which are described earlier in this chapter, instead of writing your own. These sorting methods offer $O(n \times \log n)$ performance and in general are much faster than either selection sort or insertion sort. Chapter 25 will examine the algorithm that `sort` uses to sort an array of objects.

The Performance of Searching Methods

23.38   **Linear search.** How quickly will the method `linearSearch` locate the item we seek? Counting the comparisons that occur when searching an array of *n* items will provide a measure of the algorithm's performance. In the best case, it will find the desired item at the very beginning of the array. It will make only one comparison. In the worst case, the method will search the entire array. Either it will find the desired item at the end of the array, or it will not find it at all. In either event, it will make *n* comparisons for an array of *n* entries. In general, we say that a linear search is an $O(n)$ algorithm.

A linear search of an unsorted array is rather easy to understand and implement. When the array contains relatively few entries, the search is fast enough to be practical. However, when the array contains many entries, a linear search can be time-consuming. Although the modified linear search of a sorted array is faster than an ordinary linear search when the target is not in the array, if your array is sorted, you should use a binary search.

23.39   **Binary search.** How quickly will the method `binarySearch` find the desired item in a sorted array? The algorithm eliminates about half of the array from consideration after examining only one entry. It then eliminates another quarter of the array, and then another eighth, and so on. Thus, most of the array is not searched at all, saving much time. Intuitively, the binary search algorithm is quite fast, much faster in general than a linear search.

But just how fast is it? Again, we can count comparisons. Comparisons are made each time the algorithm divides the array in half. In the best case, the binary search finds the desired item immediately, that is, at the array's midpoint. If it does, the method will make only one comparison. To see the algorithm's worst-case behavior, we can calculate the maximum number of comparisons that can occur during a search.

Suppose that n is a power of 2; that is, $n = 2^k$ for some positive value of k. After each division, about one-half of the items are left to search. In other words, beginning with n items, we would be left with either $n / 2$ or $n / 2 - 1$ items to search. In the worst case, we would have to search the $n / 2$ items. Halving those items would leave either $n / 4$ or $n / 4 - 1$ items to search, and so on. In the worst case, the search would continue until only one item was left. That is, $n / 2^k$ would equal 1. This value of k gives us the number of times the array is divided in half, or the number of array entries that are compared to the target. Since n equals 2^k, we have $k = \log_2 n$ by the definition of a logarithm.

If n is not a power of 2, we can find a positive integer k so that n lies between 2^{k-1} and 2^k. For example, if n is 14, $2^3 < 14 < 2^4$. Thus, we have for some $k \geq 1$,

$$2^{k-1} < n < 2^k$$
$$k - 1 < \log_2 n < k$$
$$k = 1 + \log_2 n \text{ rounded down}$$
$$= \log_2 n \text{ rounded up}$$

To summarize,

$k = \log_2 n$ when n is a power of 2
$k = \lceil \log_2 n \rceil$ when n is not a power of 2 (the brackets indicate rounding up)

In general, k—the number of array entries compared to the target—is $\lceil \log_2 n \rceil$.

Each repetition of the algorithm's loop, with the possible exception of the last one, makes two comparisons between the target and the middle entry in an array segment: One comparison tests for equality and one for "less than." Thus, the binary search performs at most $2 \times \lceil \log_2 n \rceil$ comparisons. We conclude that a binary search is O(log n) in the worst case. An O(log n) algorithm is considerably faster than an O(n) one. Note that it is customary to omit a multiplier of a term and the base of the logarithm when speaking of an algorithm's order, because they really do not matter. For example, since $2 \times \log_2 n$, $\log_2 n$, and $\log_{10} n$ increase at the same rate at which n increases, an O($2 \times \log_2 n$) algorithm is also an O($\log_2 n$) algorithm and an O($\log_{10} n$) algorithm, and so it is simply an O(log n) algorithm.

23.40   **Choosing between a linear search and a binary search.** When searching an array of objects, certain considerations are necessary before you choose a search method. You need to know which algorithms are applicable. To use a linear search, the objects must have a method `equals` that ascertains whether two distinct objects are equal in some sense. Since all objects inherit `equals` from the class `Object`, you must ensure that the objects' class has overridden `equals` with an appropriate version. If not, a method `compareTo` will suffice, but not all classes define this method. A binary search on an array of objects, on the other hand, requires that the objects have a `compareTo` method and that the array be sorted. If these conditions are not met, you must use a linear search.

If both search algorithms are applicable to your array—and they are for sorted arrays of primitive values—what search should you use? To search an array of 1000 entries, the binary search will compare the target to about 10 array entries in the worst case. In contrast, a simple linear search could compare the target to all 1000 array entries, and on average will compare it to about 500 array entries. For an array of one million entries, a binary search compares the target to at most 20 entries. So how many guesses at a number chosen between 1 and 1 million will you need? At most 20.

Figure 23-13 summarizes the performance of our three search methods. If the array is small, you can simply use a linear search. If the array is large and already sorted, a binary search is typically much faster than either a linear search or a modified linear search. But if the array is not sorted, should you sort it and then use a binary search? The answer depends on how often you plan to search the array. Sorting takes time, typically more time than a linear search would. If you will search an unsorted array only a few times, sorting the array so that you can use a binary search likely will not save you time; you should use a linear search instead.

FIGURE 23-13   Summary of searching performance

	Best Case	Average Case	Worst Case
Linear search (unsorted data)	O(1)	O(n)	O(n)
Linear search (sorted data)	O(1)	O(n)	O(n)
Binary search (sorted array)	O(1)	O(log n)	O(log n)

videonote
A problem
solved

CHAPTER SUMMARY

- A selection sort of an array selects the smallest entry and swaps it with the first one. Ignoring the new first entry, the sort then finds the smallest entry in the rest of the array and swaps it with the second entry, and so on.

- A selection sort is O(n^2) in all cases.

- An insertion sort divides an array into two portions, sorted and unsorted. Initially, the array's first entry is in the sorted portion. The sort takes the next unsorted entry and compares it with entries in the sorted portion. As the comparisons continue, each sorted entry is shifted by one position toward the end of the array until the unsorted entry's correct position is located. The sort then inserts the entry into its correct position, which has been vacated by the shifts.

- An insertion sort is O(n^2) in the worst case but is O(n) in the best case. The more sorted an array is, the less work an insertion sort does.

- A linear search of an array looks at the first entry, then the second entry, and so on until it either finds a particular entry or discovers that the item does not occur in the array.

- The average-case performance of a linear search is O(n).

- A linear search will search an array whose entries are in any order—that is, the entries are either unsorted or sorted—but will have no advantage if the array is sorted.

- The modified linear search of a sorted array generally takes less time to detect whether an item does not occur in an array than a linear search of an unsorted array.

- A binary search of an array requires that the array be sorted. It looks first to see whether the desired item is at the middle of the array. If it is not, the search decides in which half of the array the item can occur and repeats this strategy on only this half.

- A binary search is O(log n) in the worst case. Generally, it is much faster than a modified linear search.

EXERCISES

1. Consider the array of integers 10 3 7 1 5.

   a. Trace the steps of a selection sort as it sorts this array into ascending order. Write the array contents every time two integers are swapped.
   b. How many swaps and how many comparisons did the sort require?

2. Repeat the previous exercise, but instead use an insertion sort.

3. Repeat the previous two exercises for the array 80 90 70 85 60 40.

4. How would you change the selection sort algorithm to sort in descending order?

5. Consider the array of integers 50 20 60 80 40. Trace the steps of a selection sort as it sorts this array into descending order. Write the array contents every time two integers are swapped.

6. How would you change the insertion sort algorithm to sort in descending order?

7. Suppose a given algorithm requires a total of $n \times (n + 4) + 1$ major operations. What is the growth rate of the algorithm?

8. What steps does the linear search algorithm take in locating "car" in the following array of three-letter words? dog bat cat pot car dot big

9. What steps does the linear search take when locating a coin minted in 1992 among the coins shown in Figure 23-9?

10. Repeat the previous exercise, but instead use a binary search.

11. Consider the array of integers 20 30 40 50 60 70 80 90. List the integers that a search of this array examines, in the order that they are considered, when searching for 80 by using the following:

    a. Linear (sequential) search
    b. Binary search

12. How many comparisons does each of the following search algorithms make before discovering that 45 is not present in the array given in the previous exercise?

    a. Linear (sequential) search
    b. Binary search

13. Consider the array of integers 2 6 9 14 18 22 27 33 44 47 51 53. List the integers that a search of this array examines, in the order that they are considered, when searching for 10 by using the following:

    a. Linear (sequential) search
    b. Binary search

Stop the search as soon as you either find 10 or know that 10 is not in the array. Show how you arrived at your answer.

14. Consider a revised selection sort algorithm so that on each pass it finds both the largest and smallest values in the unsorted portion of the array. The sort then moves each of these values into its correct location by swapping them with other array entries.

    a. How many comparisons are necessary to sort n values?

    b. Is the answer to Part a greater than, less than, or equal to the number of comparisons required by the original version of selection sort?

15. Revise the methods defined in this chapter to use the same indices for parameters as are used by the methods `Arrays.sort` and `Arrays.binarySearch` in the Java Class Library.

16. A **bubble sort** can sort an array of n entries into ascending order by making $n - 1$ passes through the array. On each pass, it compares adjacent entries and swaps them if they are out of order. For example, on the first pass, it compares the first and second entries, then the second and third entries, and so on. At the end of the first pass, the largest entry is in its proper position at the end of the array. We say that it has bubbled to its correct spot. Each subsequent pass ignores the entries at the end of the array, since they are sorted and are larger than any of the remaining entries. Thus, each pass makes one fewer comparison than the previous pass. Implement the bubble sort.

    The following diagram gives an example of a bubble sort:

Original array

| 8 | 2 | 6 | 4 | 9 | 7 | 1 |

After pass 1   Sorted

| 2 | 6 | 4 | 8 | 7 | 1 | 9 |

After pass 2   Sorted

| 2 | 4 | 6 | 7 | 1 | 8 | 9 |

After pass 3   Sorted

| 2 | 4 | 6 | 1 | 7 | 8 | 9 |

After pass 4   Sorted

| 2 | 4 | 1 | 6 | 7 | 8 | 9 |

After pass 5   Sorted

| 2 | 1 | 4 | 6 | 7 | 8 | 9 |

After pass 6   Sorted

| 1 | 2 | 4 | 6 | 7 | 8 | 9 |

17. The bubble sort in the previous exercise always makes *n* passes. However, it is possible for the array to become sorted before all *n* passes are complete. For example, a bubble sort of the array

   9 2 1 6 4 7 8

is sorted after only two passes:

   2 1 6 4 7 8 9 (end of pass 1)

   1 2 4 6 7 8 9 (end of pass 2)

But since a swap occurred during the second pass, the sort needs to make one more pass to check that the array is in order. Additional passes, such as the ones that the algorithm in the previous exercise would make, are unnecessary.

   You can skip these unnecessary passes and even do less work by remembering where the last swap occurred. During the first pass, the last swap is of the 9 and the 8. The second pass checks up to the 8. But during the second pass, the last swap is of the 6 and the 4. You now know that 6, 7, 8, and 9 are sorted. The third pass needs only to check up to the 4, instead of to the 7 as an ordinary bubble sort would do. No swaps occur during the third pass, so the index of the last swap during this pass is taken as zero, indicating that no further passes are necessary. Implement this revised bubble sort.

PROJECTS

1. Define a class Student whose instances store the identification number, name, and grade point average for a student. This class should define the methods equals and compareTo, basing a comparison on identification numbers.

   Modify one sorting method and one searching method to process an array of Student objects. Create an array of Student objects having unique identification numbers.

   a. Sort the array according to identification numbers, using your selected algorithm, and display the results.
   b. Search either the original unsorted array or the sorted array for each student, given an identification number.
   c. Search for each student, given a name. You will need another search method that does not use Student's equals and compareTo methods.

2. Create an array of 50,000 random integers that are in the range from 1 to 10,000. Sort this array using selection sort and insertion sort. Time the execution of both of these sorting methods and determine which is more efficient. Write a summary of which algorithm you find to be more efficient and why.

   To time a section of Java code, you can use the class java.util.Date, which was described in Segment 4.30 of Chapter 4. A Date object contains the time at which it was constructed. Its method getTime returns the time as a long integer equal to the number of milliseconds that have passed since 00:00:00.000 GMT on January 1, 1970. By subtracting the starting time in milliseconds from the ending time in milliseconds, you get the run time—in milliseconds—of a section of code.

   For example, suppose that thisMethod is the name of a method you wish to time. The following statements will compute the number of milliseconds that thisMethod requires to execute:

```
Date current = new Date();              // get current time
long startTime = current.getTime();
thisMethod();                           // code to be timed
current = new Date();                   // get current time
long stopTime = current.getTime();
long elapsedTime = stopTime - startTime; // milliseconds
```

3. Create a sorted array as described in the previous project. Create another array of 1000 unsorted integers selected at random from the sorted array.

    a. Search the sorted array for each value in the unsorted array by using a linear search.

    b. Search the sorted array for each value of the unsorted array by using a binary search.

    c. Calculate the average execution time for each of the previous two searches and compare the efficiencies of the two algorithms.

ANSWERS TO SELF-TEST QUESTIONS

1.
```
9 6 2 4 8
2 6 9 4 8
2 4 9 6 8
2 4 6 9 8
2 4 6 8 9
```

2. Using the notation $x:y$ to indicate a comparison between x and y, the sort makes the following comparisons:

    9:6, 6:2, 2:4, 2:8; 6:9, 6:4, 4:8; 9:6, 6:8; 9:8

    Thus, it makes ten comparisons.

3.
```
IntegerSorter.selectionSort(a);
IntegerSorter.selectionSort(a, 0, a.length - 1);
```

4. Yes, we can overload `selectionSort` another time by adding the following method to the class in Listing 23-1:

```
public static void selectionSort(int[] a, int count)
{
    selectionSort(a, 0, count - 1);
} // end selectionSort
```

5. You can swap the smallest entry with the last entry in the array. Then, ignoring the last entry, you find the smallest one among the other entries and swap it with the next-to-last entry, and so on. Or you can find the largest entry in the array and swap it with the first one. Then, ignoring the first entry, you find the largest one among the other entries and swap it with the second entry, and so on.

6.

First way:	Second way:
2 4 9 6 8	2 4 9 6 8
8 4 9 6 2	9 4 2 6 8
8 6 9 4 2	9 8 2 6 4
8 9 6 4 2	9 8 6 2 4
9 8 6 4 2	9 8 6 4 2

7. Each entry before the last one in an array is less than or equal to the entry that follows it. That is, for each entry a[i] in the sorted array a of n items, a[i] $\leq$ a[i + 1] for i = 0, 1, . . . , $n-2$.

8.
```
public static boolean isSorted(int[] array)
{
    boolean sorted = true;
    int last = array.length - 1;
    for (int index = 0; sorted && (index < last); index++)
    {
        if (array[index] > array[index + 1]))
            sorted = false;
    } // end for

    return sorted;
} // end isSorted
```

9.
```
9 6 2 4 8
6 9 2 4 8
2 6 9 4 8
2 4 6 9 8
2 4 6 8 9
```

10. Using the notation $x{:}y$ to indicate a comparison between x and y, the sort makes the following comparisons:

    6:9; 2:9, 2:6; 4:9, 4:6, 4:2; 8:9, 8:6

    Thus, it makes eight comparisons.

11. `String`, like all classes, has `Object` as an ancestor. This fact makes such a call legal. The `print` method in the body of `display` invokes the method `toString`. Polymorphism, which Segment 16.25 in Chapter 16 describes, enables `print` to invoke `String`'s version of `toString` instead of `Object`'s version. And since `display` does not invoke `compareTo`, we can call `display` and pass it an array of objects of any type. As you saw in Listing 23-6, such is not the case for the other methods in `SortDriver`, since the objects to be sorted must have a `compareTo` method.

12. This method invokes `compareTo` for each object in the array passed to it as an argument. If such objects had the data type `Object`, they would not have a `compareTo` method. That is, `Object` does not implement the interface `Comparable`.

13. `"Matt"` is compared with `"Chris"`, `"Tyler"`, `"Josh"`, `"Kirk"`, `"Luke"`, `"Madison"`, and `"Matt"`. Thus, there are seven comparisons.

14. True. Because `"Turtle"` does not exist in the array, the method searches the entire array. Thus, `searching` retains its original value as the method returns its result.

15. The first one. That is, `linearSearch` would return 0, and the program given in Listing 23-8 would report the position as 1.

16.
```
public static int linearSearch(String target, String[] strings,
                               int first, int last)
{
    final int NOT_FOUND = -1;
    int result = -1;
    for (int index = first; (result == NOT_FOUND) && (index <= last); index++)
    {
        if (target.equals(strings[index]))
            result = index;
    } // end for

    return result;
} // end linearSearch
```

17. In the `while` statement, change the > operator in

    `target.compareTo(strings[index]) > 0`

    to <.

18. Searching for 8 requires seven comparisons, as follows:

8 == 10?
8 < 10?
8 == 5?
8 < 5?
8 == 7?
8 < 7?
8 == 8?

Searching for 16 requires eight comparisons, as follows:

16 == 10?
16 < 10?
16 == 18?
16 < 18?
16 == 12?
16 < 12?
16 == 15?
16 < 15?

19. **a.** "J" and "C"
b. "J", "C", and "F"
c. "J", "T", and "M"

20.
```
public static int binarySearch(String target, String[] strings,
                               int first, int last)
{
   boolean searching = true;
   int result = -1;
   while (searching && (first <= last))
   {
      < The body of this loop is the same as it is in Listing 23-10 >
   } // end while

   return result;
} // end binarySearch
```

21. Replace the definition of binarySearch shown in Listing 23-10 with the following one:

```
public static int binarySearch(String target, String[] strings)
{
   return binarySearch(target, strings, 0, strings.length - 1);
} // end binarySearch
```

22. In the else if, change < to >.

23. Math.BigDecimal

24.
$$(n - 1) + (n - 2) + \ldots + 1$$
$$1 \quad\quad + 2 \quad\quad + \ldots + (n - 1)$$

$$\overline{n \quad\quad + n \quad\quad + \ldots + n}$$

The sum contains $(n - 1)$ occurrences of n and so is equal to $n \times (n - 1)$. Since this result is two times the one we seek, divide by 2 to get $n \times (n - 1) / 2$.

Chapter

24

Recursion

Contents

Prerequisites

Objectives

After studying this chapter, you should be able to
- Write a recursive method
- Decide whether a given recursive method will end successfully in a finite amount of time
- Discuss in general terms the pros and cons of recursion and iteration
- Identify occurrences of tail recursion and mutual recursion

Repetition is a major feature of many algorithms. In fact, repeating actions rapidly is a key ability of computers. Two problem-solving processes, called iteration and recursion, involve repetition, and most programming languages provide two kinds of repetitive constructs, iterative and recursive.

You know about iteration because you know how to write a loop. Regardless of the loop construct you use—`while`, `for`, or `do`—the loop contains the statements that you want to repeat and a mechanism for controlling the number of repetitions. You might have a counted loop that counts repetitions as 1, 2, 3, 4, 5, or 5, 4, 3, 2, 1. Or the loop might execute repeatedly while a boolean variable or expression is true. Iteration often provides a straightforward and efficient way to implement a repetitive process.

At times, however, iterative solutions are elusive or hopelessly complex. For some problems, discovering or verifying such solutions is not a simple task. In these cases, recursion can provide an elegant alternative. Some recursive solutions can be the best choice, some provide insight for finding a better iterative solution, and some should not be used at all because they are grossly inefficient. Recursion, however, remains an important problem-solving strategy.

Learning recursion is important for another reason. Segments 15.6 through 15.10 of Chapter 15 talked about the importance of abstraction in software design, whereby you initially focus on what a method does instead of how it performs its task. This focus will help you understand recursion, and truly understanding recursion will help develop your ability to think abstractly. This chapter and the next one will teach you about recursion.

What Is Recursion?

24.1   We can build a house by hiring a contractor. The contractor in turn hires several subcontractors to complete portions of the house. Each subcontractor might hire other subcontractors to help. We use the same approach when we solve a problem by breaking it into smaller problems. In one special variation of this problem-solving process, the smaller problems are identical except for their size. This special process is called **recursion**.

Suppose that we can solve a problem by solving an identical but smaller problem. How will we solve the smaller problem? If we use recursion again, we will need to solve an even smaller problem that is just like the original problem in every other respect. How will replacing a problem with another one ever lead to a solution? One key to the success of recursion is that eventually we will reach a smaller problem, known as the **base case** or **stopping case**, whose solution we know because either it is obvious or it is given. The solution to this base case is probably not the solution to the original problem, but it can help us complete the solution to the previous larger problem. Continuing back in this manner, we solve larger and larger problems until we complete the solution to the original problem.

 Note: Recursion is a problem-solving process that breaks a problem into identical but smaller problems.

Example: The Countdown

24.2
It's New Year's Eve and the giant ball is falling in Times Square. The crowd counts down the last ten seconds: "10, 9, 8, . . ." Suppose that I ask you to count down to 1 beginning at some positive integer like 10. You could shout "10" and then ask a friend to count down from 9. Counting down from 9 is a problem that is exactly like counting down from 10, except that there is less to do. It is a smaller problem.

To count down from 9, your friend shouts "9" and asks a friend to count down from 8. This sequence of events continues until eventually someone's friend is asked to count down from 1. That friend simply shouts "1." No other friend is needed. Figure 24-1 illustrates these events.

FIGURE 24-1   Counting down from 10

videonote
What is recursion?

In this example, I've asked you to complete a task. We saw that you could contribute a part of the task and then ask a friend to do the rest. We know that your friend's task is just like the original task, but it is smaller. We also know that when your friend completes this smaller task, your job will be done. What is missing from the process just described is the signal that each friend gives to the previous person at the completion of his or her task.

To provide this signal, when you count down from 10, I need you to tell me when you are done. I don't care how—or who—does the job, as long as you tell me when it is done. I can take a nap until I hear from you. Likewise, when you ask a friend to count down from 9, you do not care how your friend finishes the job. You just want to know when it is done so you can tell me that you are done. You can take a nap while you are waiting.

24.3   Ultimately, we have a group of napping people waiting for someone to say "I'm done." The first person to make that claim is the person who shouts "1," as Figure 24-1 illustrates, since that person needs no help in counting down from 1. At this time in this particular example, the problem is solved, but I don't know that because I'm still asleep. The person who shouted "1" says "I'm done" to the person who shouted "2." The person who shouted "2" says "I'm done" to the person who shouted "3," and so on, until you say "I'm done" to me. The job is done; thanks for your help; I have no idea how you did it, and I don't need to know!

What does any of this have to do with Java? In the previous example, you play the role of a Java method. I, the client, have asked you, the recursive method, to count down from 10. When you ask a friend for help, you are invoking a method to count down from 9. But you do not invoke another method; you invoke yourself!

Note: A method that calls itself is a **recursive method**. The invocation is a **recursive call** or **recursive invocation**.

Implementation Details

24.4   The following Java method counts down from a given positive integer, displaying one integer per line.

```
/** Counts down from a given positive integer.
    @param integer  an integer > 0 */
public static void countDown(int integer)
{
    System.out.println(integer);
    if (integer > 1)
        countDown(integer - 1);
} // end countDown
```

Since the given integer is positive, the method can display it immediately. This step is analogous to you shouting "10" in the previous example. Next the method asks whether it is finished. If the given integer is 1, nothing is left to do. But if the given integer is larger than 1, we need to count down from integer – 1. We've already noted that this task is smaller but otherwise identical to the original problem. How do we solve this new problem? We invoke a method, but countDown is such a method. Thus, we write a call to countDown, the same method that we are defining. It does not matter that we have not finished writing it at this point!

24.5   Will the method countDown actually work? Shortly we will trace the execution of countDown, both to convince you that it works and to show you how it works. But traces of recursive methods are messy, and we usually do not have to trace them. If we follow certain guidelines when writing a recursive method, we can be assured that it will work.

In designing a recursive solution, we need to answer certain questions:

Note: Questions to answer when designing a recursive solution

- What part of the solution can you contribute directly?
- What smaller but identical problem has a solution that, when taken with your contribution, provides the solution to the original problem?
- When does the process end? That is, what smaller but identical problem has a known solution, and how will you know when you have reached this problem, the base case?

For the method `countDown`, we have the following answers to these questions:

- The method `countDown` displays the given integer as the part of the solution that it contributes directly. This happens to occur first here, but it need not always occur first.
- The smaller problem is counting down from `integer - 1`. The method solves the smaller problem when it calls itself recursively.
- The `if` statement asks if the process has reached the base case. Here the base case occurs when `integer` is 1. Because the method displays `integer` before checking it, nothing is left to do once the base case is identified.

Note: Design guidelines for successful recursion

To write a recursive method that behaves correctly, you generally should adhere to the following design guidelines:

- The method must be given an input value, usually as an argument, but sometimes as a value read from the user.
- The method definition must contain logic that involves this input value and leads to different cases. Typically, such logic includes an `if` statement or a `switch` statement.
- One or more of these cases must provide a solution that does not require recursion. These are the base cases. Yes, it is possible to have more than one base case.
- One or more cases must include a recursive invocation of the method. These recursive invocations should in some sense take a step toward a base case by using "smaller" arguments or solving "smaller" versions of the task performed by the method.

Programming Tip: Infinite recursion

A recursive method that does not check for a base case, or that misses the base case, will execute "forever." This situation is known as **infinite recursion**. Its apparent effect is like that of an infinite loop. As Chapter 12 warned, you should learn how to terminate a program using your particular programming environment. Finding the cause of infinite recursion can be a challenge, but Debugging Interlude 7 will assist you in this situation.

24.6 Before we trace the method `countDown`, we should note that we could have written it in other ways. For example, a first draft of this method might have looked like this:

```
public static void countDown(int integer)
{
    if (integer == 1)
```

```
            System.out.println(integer);
        else
        {
            System.out.println(integer);
            countDown(integer - 1);
        } // end if
    } // end countDown
```

Here the programmer considered the base case first. The solution is clear and perfectly acceptable, but we can avoid the redundant `println` statement that occurs in both cases.

24.7 Removing the redundancy just mentioned could result in either the version given earlier in Segment 24.4 or the following one:

```
public static void countDown(int integer)
{
    if (integer >= 1)
    {
        System.out.println(integer);
        countDown(integer - 1);
    } // end if
} // end countDown
```

When `integer` is 1, this method will display 1 and produce the recursive call `countDown(0)`. This call turns out to be the base case for this method, and nothing more is displayed.

For integer arguments greater than 1, all three versions of `countDown` produce correct results. There are probably other versions as well; choose the one that is clearest to you.

Programming Tip

Your first draft of a recursive method might not be elegant, but once its logic is correct, you can revise it. This advice is no different for recursion than for any other code that you write.

24.8 Let's compare the version of `countDown` just given in the previous segment with the following iterative version:

```
// Iterative version.
public static void countDown(int integer)
{
    while (integer >= 1)
    {
        System.out.println(integer);
        integer--;
    } // end while
} // end countDown
```

The two methods have a similar appearance. Both compare `integer` with 1, but the recursive version uses an `if` and the iterative version uses a `while`. Both methods display `integer`. Both compute `integer – 1`.

Programming Tip

An iterative method contains a loop. A recursive method calls itself. Although some recursive methods contain a loop *and* call themselves, if you have written a `while` statement within a recursive method, be sure that you did not mean to write an `if` statement.

Question 1 Write a recursive void method that displays *n* blank lines of output, where *n* is a positive integer, effectively skipping *n* lines. Use `System.out.println()` to display one blank line.

Question 2 Describe a recursive algorithm that draws a given number of concentric circles. The innermost circle should have a given diameter. The diameter of each of the other circles should be four-thirds the diameter of the circle just inside it.

Tracing a Recursive Method

24.9   Now let's trace the method `countDown` given in Segment 24.4:

```java
public static void countDown(int integer)
{
    System.out.println(integer);
    if (integer > 1)
        countDown(integer - 1);
} // end countDown
```

For simplicity, suppose that we invoke this method with the statement

```java
countDown(3);
```

from within a `main` method of the class that defines `countDown`. This call behaves like any other call to a nonrecursive method. The value of the argument 3 is copied into the parameter `integer` and the following statements are executed:

```java
System.out.println(3);
if (3 > 1)
    countDown(3 - 1); // first recursive call
```

The integer 3 is displayed, and the recursive call `countDown(2)` occurs, as Figure 24-2a shows.
    Execution of the method is then suspended until the results of `countDown(2)` are known. In this particular method definition, no statements appear after the recursive call. So although it appears that nothing will happen when execution resumes, it is here that the method will return to the client.

24.10   Continuing our trace, `countDown(2)` causes the following statements to execute:

```java
System.out.println(2);
if (2 > 1)
    countDown(2 - 1); // second recursive call
```

The integer 2 is displayed, and the recursive call `countDown(1)` occurs, as shown in Figure 24-2b. Execution of the method is then suspended until the results of `countDown(1)` are known.
    The call `countDown(1)` causes the following statements to execute:

```java
System.out.println(1);
if (1 > 1)
```

The integer 1 is displayed, as Figure 24-2c shows, and no other recursive call occurs.

FIGURE 24-2   The effect of the method call `countDown(3)`

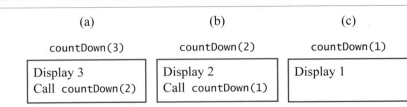

24.11   Figure 24-3 illustrates the sequence of events from the time that countDown is first called. The numbered arrows indicate the order of the recursive calls and the returns from the method. The first three arrows trace the steps that we just discussed. After 1 is displayed, the method completes execution and returns to the point (arrow 4) after the call countDown(2 - 1). Execution continues from there, and the method returns to the point (arrow 5) after the call countDown(3 - 1). Ultimately, a return to the point (arrow 6) after the initial method call in main occurs.

Although tracking these method returns seems like a formality that has gained us nothing, it is an important part of any trace because some recursive methods will do more than simply return to their calling method. We will encounter an example of such a method shortly.

FIGURE 24-3   Tracing the recursive call countDown(3)

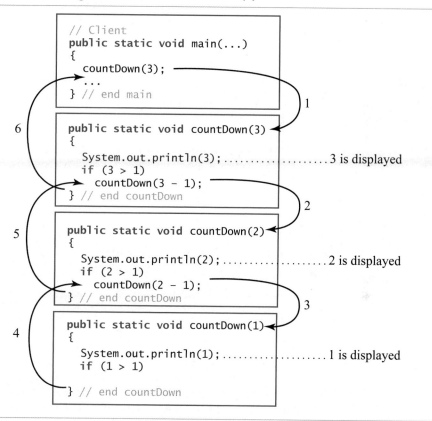

24.12   Figure 24-3 appears to show multiple copies of the method countDown. In reality, however, multiple copies do not exist. Instead, for each call to a method—be it recursive or not—Java records the current state of the method's execution, including the values of its parameters and local variables as well as the location of the current instruction. Each record, called an **activation record**, provides a snapshot of the method's state during its execution. The records are placed into a data structure called a **stack**, much as you would stack photos one on top of the other. The stack organizes the records chronologically, so that the record of the currently executing method is on top. In this way, Java can suspend the execution of a recursive method and invoke it again with new argument values. The boxes in Figure 24-3 correspond roughly to the activation records shown in Figure 24-4 that are added to the stack as a result of the call countDown(3) in the main method.

FIGURE 24-4 The stack of activation records during the execution of
countDown(3)

(a)

main(. . .):

(b)

main(. . .):

countDown(3):

integer: 3
Return to calling point
in main

(c)

main(. . .):

countDown(3):

countDown(2):

integer: 2
Return to calling point
in countDown

(d)

main(. . .):

countDown(3):

countDown(2):

countDown(1):

integer: 1
Return to calling point
in countDown

(e)

main(. . .):

countDown(3):

countDown(2):

integer: 2
Return to calling point
in countDown

(f)

main(. . .):

countDown(3):

integer: 3
Return to calling point
in main

(g)

main(. . .):

Note: The stack of activation records
Each call to a method generates an activation record that captures the state of the method's
execution and that is placed into a stack. In general, a recursive method uses more memory
than an iterative method, because each recursive call generates an activation record.

Programming Tip: Stack overflow
Too many recursive calls can cause the stack of activation records to become full, causing a
"stack overflow" error message. In essence, the method has used too much memory. Infinite
recursion or large-size problems are the likely causes of this error. Your operating system or
IDE will allow you to increase the size of the stack to accommodate lengthy recursions that
are not infinite.

Question 3 Write a recursive void method countUp(n) that counts up from 1 to *n*, where *n*
is a positive integer. *Hint:* A recursive call will occur before you display anything.

Question 4 Given your answer to the previous question, trace the call countUp(3) by listing the calls to countUp and println in the order in which they occur with their appropriate
arguments.

Recursive Methods That Return a Value

24.13 The recursive method `countDown` in the previous sections is a void method. Valued methods can also be recursive. The guidelines for successful recursion given in Segment 24.5 apply to valued methods as well, with an additional note. Recall that a recursive method must contain a statement such as an `if` that chooses among several cases. Some of these cases lead to a recursive call, but at least one case has no recursive call. For a valued method, each of these cases must provide a value for the method to return.

24.14 **Example: Compute the sum $1 + 2 + \ldots + n$ for any integer $n > 0$.** The given input value for this problem is the integer n. Beginning with this fact will help us to find the smaller problem because its input will also be a single integer. The sum always starts at 1, so that can be assumed.

Suppose that I have given you a positive integer n and asked you to compute the sum of the first n integers. You need to ask a friend to compute the sum of the first m integers for some positive integer m. What should m be? Well, if your friend computes the sum of the first $n - 1$ integers—that is, $1 + \ldots + (n - 1)$—you can simply add n to that sum to get your sum. Thus, if `sumOf(n)` is the method call that returns the sum of the first n integers, n is added to your friend's sum in the expression `sumOf(n - 1) + n`.

What small problem can be the base case? That is, what value of n results in a sum that you know immediately? One possible answer is 1. If n is 1, the desired sum is 1.

With these thoughts in mind, we can write the following method:

```java
/** Computes the sum of the first n positive integers.
    @param n   an integer > 0
    @return the sum 1 + 2 + ... + n */
public static int sumOf(int n)
{
   int sum;
   if (n == 1)
      sum = 1;                    // base case
   else
      sum = sumOf(n - 1) + n; // recursive call

   return sum;
} // end sumOf
```

 Question 5 Does the previous method `sumOf` satisfy the design guidelines for successful recursion given in Segment 24.5? Justify your answer.

24.15 The definition of the method `sumOf` satisfies the design guidelines for successful recursion. Therefore, we can be confident that the method will work correctly, and we don't need to trace its execution. However, a trace will be instructive here because it will not only show us how a valued recursive method works, but also demonstrate actions that occur after a recursive call is complete.

Suppose that we invoke this method with the statement

```java
System.out.println(sumOf(3));
```

The computation occurs as follows:

1. `sumOf(3)` is `sumOf(2) + 3`; `sumOf(3)` suspends execution, and `sumOf(2)` begins.
2. `sumOf(2)` is `sumOf(1) + 2`; `sumOf(2)` suspends execution, and `sumOf(1)` begins.
3. `sumOf(1)` returns 1; this is the base case.

Once the base case is reached, the suspended executions resume, beginning with the most recent one. Thus, sumOf(2) returns 1 + 2, or 3; then sumOf(3) returns 3 + 3, or 6. Figure 24-5 illustrates this computation.

FIGURE 24-5   Tracing the execution of sumOf(3)

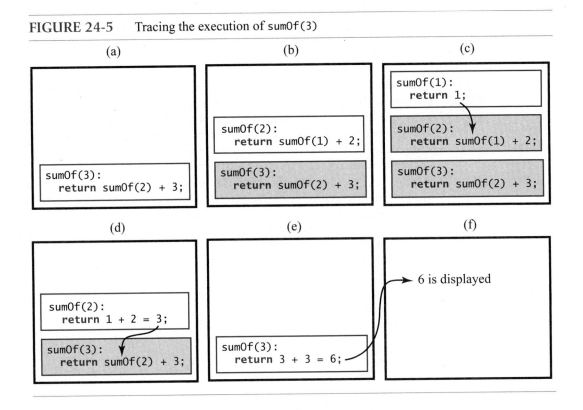

Question 6 Write a recursive valued method that computes the product of the integers from 1 to *n*, where *n* > 0.

Note: Should you trace a recursive method?

We have traced the execution of a recursive method primarily to illustrate how recursion works and to provide some insight into how a typical compiler implements recursion. Should you ever trace a recursive method? Possibly. You certainly should not trace a recursive method while you are writing it. If the method is incomplete, your trace will be, too, and you are likely to become confused. If a recursive method does not work, follow the suggestions given in the next programming tip. You should trace a recursive method only as a last resort.

Programming Tip: Debugging a recursive method

If a recursive method does not work, answer the following questions. Any "no" answers should guide you to the error.

- Does the method have at least one input value?
- Does the method contain a statement that tests an input value and leads to different cases?
- Did you consider all possible cases?
- Does at least one of these cases cause at least one recursive call?
- Do these recursive calls involve smaller arguments, smaller tasks, or tasks that get closer to the solution?
- If these recursive calls produce or return correct results, will the method produce or return a correct result?
- Is at least one of the cases a base case that has no recursive call?
- Are there enough base cases?
- Does each base case produce a result that is correct for that case?
- If the method returns a value, does each of the cases return a value?

Debugging Interlude 7 will provide some examples of debugging recursive methods.

24.16   Our previous examples were simple so that you could study the construction of recursive methods. Since you could have solved these problems iteratively with ease, should you actually use their recursive solutions? Nothing is inherently wrong with these recursive methods. However, given the way that typical present-day systems execute recursive methods, a stack overflow is likely for large values of n. Iterative solutions to these simple examples would not have this difficulty and are easy to write. You should realize, however, that future computing systems might be able to execute these recursive methods without difficulty.

The next two problems have recursive solutions that are easier to find than iterative versions.

Note: A key to writing successful recursion

When you read a recursive algorithm or method, you should be able to understand that it is a correct solution without tracing its recursive calls. You should have the same mind-set when you write a recursive method. Focus on the result of each method call without thinking about the calls it will make recursively. Remember, *what* instead of *how*.

■ A Problem Solved: Speaking the Digits in a Number[1]

Automated customer support systems that are available by telephone often ask you to enter a number, such as a telephone number, an account number, or a postal code. After you do so, the system typically repeats the number digit by digit, for your confirmation.

To simulate such a system, we will read a positive integer and display its digits as words.

1. Based on Reingold, Edward M. "Four Apt Elementary Examples of Recursion" in *Lecture Notes in Computer Science: Language, Culture, Computation: The Yaacov Choueka Jubilee Volume*, edited by N. Dershowitz and E. Nissan (Berlin: Springer-Verlag, 2009).

24.17   Given a positive integer, such as 1234, we need to isolate its digits, 1, 2, 3, and 4, in the order in which they occur. If the integer is less than 10, it consists of a single digit. After speaking the digit, we would be done, and so this is the base case. For multidigit integers, we must speak the digits in their order of occurrence, but isolating the rightmost digit is easier than finding the leftmost one. If someone would speak all the digits but the last one—this is the recursive step—we could speak the last one.

These ideas are expressed by the following pseudocode:

Algorithm speak(integer)

```
if (integer < 10)
    Speak the one-digit integer
else
{
    Speak all but the last digit of integer
    Speak the last digit of integer
}
```

24.18   So how do we isolate the last digit in an integer? Division by 10 leaves an integer's last digit as a remainder. That is, if integer is a positive integer, the expression integer % 10 is the last digit. Moreover, integer / 10 is the rest of the original integer. The recursive method speak, then, can have the following definition, which assumes a method, speakDigit, that speaks single digits:

```
private void speak(int integer)
{
    if (integer < 10)
        speakDigit(integer);
    else
    {
        speak(integer / 10);      // speak all digits but the last one
        speakDigit(integer % 10); // speak the last digit
    } // end if
} // end speak
```

24.19   Although the method speak could be public and static, as a private method it can belong to a class of spoken integers. Such a class is given in Listing 24-1. The public method speak calls the private method speak, passing it the data field anInteger. In this way, a client creates an object of the class and invokes the public speak without passing it an integer. The private method speakDigit simply displays the digit, thus simulating the actual method that would speak each digit. For the purpose of this example, we have chosen to display each digit as a word.

LISTING 24-1   A class of integers that can report their digits

```
/** A representation of integers that can report their digits.
    @author Frank M. Carrano
*/
public class SpokenInteger
{
    private int anInteger;

    /** Creates a spoken integer.
        @param integer  a positive integer */
```

```java
   public SpokenInteger(int integer)
   {
      anInteger = integer;
   } // end constructor

   /** Speaks the digits in this integer. */
   public void speak()
   {
      speak(anInteger);
   } // end speak

   // Recursively speaks the digits in a given positive integer.
   private void speak(int integer)
   {
      if (integer < 10)
         speakDigit(integer);
      else
      {
         speak(integer / 10);      // speak all digits but the last one
         speakDigit(integer % 10); // speak the last digit
      } // end if
   } // end speak

   // Speaks a given digit that is >= 0 and <= 9.
   private void speakDigit(int digit)
   {
      switch (digit)
      {
         case 0:
            System.out.print("zero"); break;
         case 1:
            System.out.print("one"); break;
         . . .

         case 9:
            System.out.print("nine"); break;
         default:
            System.out.println("error"); break;
      } // end switch
      System.out.print(" ");
   } // end speakDigit
} // end SpokenInteger
```

24.20 Listing 24-2 contains a simple driver for the class `SpokenInteger` and shows some sample output from the program. Note that any leading zeros in the input are ignored.

LISTING 24-2 A driver for the class `SpokenInteger` and sample output

```java
/** A driver that demonstrates the class SpokenInteger.
    @author Frank M. Carrano
*/
import java.util.Scanner;
public class Driver
{
    public static void main(String args[])
    {
        Scanner keyboard = new Scanner(System.in);
        System.out.print("Please enter your number: ");
        int integer = keyboard.nextInt();
        while (integer > 0)
        {
            SpokenInteger anInteger = new SpokenInteger(integer);
            System.out.print("You entered ");
            anInteger.speak();
            System.out.println();

            System.out.print("Please enter your number: ");
            integer = keyboard.nextInt();
        } // end while
        System.out.println("All done!");
    } // end main
} // end Driver
```

Sample Output
```
Please enter your number: 26
You entered two six
Please enter your number: 904670
You entered nine zero four six seven zero
Please enter your number: 09008  ◄──────── Leading zeros are ignored
You entered nine zero zero eight
Please enter your number: 0
All done!
```

Question 7 If you entered 123 in response to the prompt given by the program in Listing 24-2, what calls to the methods `speak` and `speakDigit` would occur? List these calls in the order they occur, giving their arguments as values instead of variables.

Question 8 Repeat the previous question, but instead assume that you've entered 090.

Question 9 In the previous question, why isn't the leading zero displayed?

A Problem Solved: Writing a Number in Words[2]

> When a bank or other business prints a check, the dollar amount shown on the check must appear in words as well as numerals. For example, the amount 4321 would be written as "four thousand three hundred twenty-one." What class could represent positive integers that would display themselves in this manner?

24.21 Let's begin our discussion by thinking about the words we use to name numbers. The numbers 1 through 19 each have their own unique name, that is, "one" through "nineteen." After 19, the numbers 20 through 99 have names that follow a pattern, such as twenty, twenty-one, twenty-two, and so on. Thus, we need the words "twenty," "thirty," and so on up to "ninety" to express this segment of numbers. For the numbers 100 through 999, we count in hundreds: five hundred eighty-two, for instance. Finally, after 999, we count in thousands, millions, billions, and so on. We'll refer to the latter terms as "powers of 1000."

Before we can consider a solution, we need to know how many names for the various powers of 1000 we will need. That is, we must know how large an integer can be. The largest value of type `int` has 10 digits and is approximately two billion. In contrast, the largest value of type `long` has 19 digits and is approximately nine quintillion. That should be large enough, so let's work with `long` integers.

24.22 Now that we know the data type of the integer, we can write a portion of a class of integers that can display themselves in words, as follows:

```java
public class VerbalInteger
{
   private long anInteger;

   /** Creates a verbal integer.
       @param integer  a nonnegative integer */
   public VerbalInteger(long integer)
   {
      anInteger = integer;
   } // end constructor

   /** Writes this integer in words. */
   public void write()
   {
      . . .
   } // end write

   < Several private methods are here. >
   . . .
} // end VerbalInteger
```

Although this class is similar to the one shown in Listing 24-1, it will have more private methods, as you will see.

2. *Ibid.*

24.23   Our previous discussion notes some special cases when naming the numbers 1 through 999. Suppose the method `writeUnderThousand` handles these integers that are less than 1000. The numbers after 999 have names involving the powers of 1000. Let's consider an integer such as 1,234,567. We know how to express 567 because we have—or soon will have—the method `writeUnderThousand`. If someone will write the words for the first portion of the number, we can express the rest. However, we cannot simply ask to have 1,234 expressed in words, since the response would begin as "one thousand" instead of "one million." Rather we should ask someone to write out the words for 1,234,000 before we write out 567.

Thus, when we ask to have part of a number expressed in words, we also must indicate which power of 1000 needs to be given. Let's do a little arithmetic to see what this exponent should be. If we have an integer i, we can write

$$i = i \times 1000^0$$

since the value of 1000^0 is 1. We now can divide and multiply by 1000 and still get i:

$$i = \frac{i}{1000} \times 1000^1$$

Each time we might repeat the division, we would add 1 to the exponent of 1000 to maintain the equality.

24.24   Although these operations do not affect the value of i mathematically, in Java the integer division `integer / 1000` truncates. But that is fine. In our earlier example, we needed someone to express 1,234,000. We see now that we can give this person both the value of `integer / 1000`—which is 1,234—and the exponent 1. This person could ask another for help, passing the result of another division by 1000 and the exponent 2, and so on.

The following pseudocode captures these ideas:

Algorithm write(integer, power)
// integer *is positive; initially,* power *is 0*

```
if (integer > 0)
{
    write(integer / 1000, power + 1) // write the first part of the integer
    Write integer % 1000, if it is not zero   // write the rest of the integer
}
```

The base case for this algorithm occurs when `integer` is divided by 1000 so often that nothing is left for our assistant to do. For example, beginning with 1,234,567, we first pass 1,234 and the exponent 1 to our helper. Next, we pass the 1 and an exponent 2. Finally, we are left with 0. It does not mean that the original number was 0, but rather that the recursive calls should end. Thus, the algorithm does nothing in this case, instead of displaying the word "zero."

24.25   We can add some detail to the previous pseudocode as follows:

Algorithm write(integer, power)
// integer *is positive; initially,* power *is 0*

```
if (integer > 0)
{
    write(integer / 1000, power + 1)  // write the first part of the integer
    if (integer % 1000 > 0)            //  if the rest of the integer is not 000
    {
        writeUnderThousand(integer % 1000) // write the 3-digit integer
```

Write the word for the value of 1000 *raised to* power
```
      }
   }
```

The implementation of this algorithm will result in a private method that the public method write, outlined in Segment 24.22, will call. Thus, the definition of the public method write is

```
public void write()
{
   write(anInteger, 0);
} // end write
```

The first argument passed to the private method is the data field anInteger; the second argument is zero, so that write's parameter power is zero initially.

24.26 We now must treat the special cases. The previous algorithm for write uses the method writeUnderThousand to handle integers less than 1000. However, that method must consider integers that it knows are less than 100 as well as those that it knows are less than 20 as special cases. Thus, let's assume that the methods writeUnderHundred and writeUnderTwenty will deal with these cases, and write pseudocode for the method writeUnderThousand:

Algorithm writeUnderThousand(integer)
// Precondition: 0 < integer < 1000

```
if (integer < 100)
   writeUnderHundred(integer)
else // integer >= 100, integer < 1000
{
   writeUnderTwenty(integer / 1000)  // write hundreds (first) digit
   Write the word "hundred"
   writeUnderHundred(integer % 1000) // write remaining 2-digit integer
}
```

Integers less than 100 are passed to the method writeUnderHundred. Other integers range from 100 to 999, so their first digits range from 1 to 9 but are certainly less than 20. The method writeUnderTwenty can deal with this first digit, which is computed as integer / 1000. Similarly, the remaining two digits in integer represent a value less than 100, and so are given to writeUnderHundred to process.

24.27 The method writeUnderHundred might encounter integers under 20 and need to call the method writeUnderTwenty. Its algorithm follows:

Algorithm writeUnderHundred(integer)
// Precondition: 0 < integer < 100

```
if (integer < 20)
   writeUnderTwenty(integer)
else // integer >= 20, integer < 100
{
   Write the word for the appropriate multiple of 10
   writeUnderTwenty(integer % 10)
}
```

The method writeUnderTwenty contains a simple switch statement with 20 cases. Other methods to produce the labels mentioned in the previous algorithms are similar to writeUnderTwenty.

24.28 Listing 24-3 shows the completed class `VerbalInteger`. Its method definitions closely follow the pseudocode we have developed. Note the casts from `long` to `int` in the `switch` statements of the methods `writeUnderTwenty` and `writeMultipleOfTen`.

LISTING 24-3 The class `VerbalInteger`

```java
/** A representation of an integer that can be written as words.
    @author Frank M. Carrano
*/
public class VerbalInteger
{
   private long anInteger;

   /** Creates a verbal integer.
       @param integer  a nonnegative integer */
   public VerbalInteger(long integer)
   {
      anInteger = integer;
   } // end constructor

   /** Writes this integer in words. */
   public void write()
   {
      write(anInteger, 0);
   } // end write

   // Recursively writes in words a given positive integer
   // whose form is integer * 1000^power, where integer > 0
   // and power >= 0.
   private void write(long integer, int power)
   {
      if (integer > 0)
      {
         write(integer / 1000, power + 1); // write all but last 3 digits
         if (integer % 1000 > 0) // if the last 3 digits are not 000
         {
            writeUnderThousand(integer % 1000); // write 3-digit integer
            writePowerOfThousand(power);         // label it
         } // end if
      } // end if
   } // end write

   // Writes the name of a value between 1 and 999; ignores 0.
   // Precondition: 0 < integer < 1000.
   private void writeUnderThousand(long integer)
   {
      if (integer < 100)
```

```
         writeUnderHundred(integer);
      else // integer >= 100 but < 100
      {
         writeUnderTwenty(integer / 100); // write hundreds (first) digit
         System.out.print("hundred ");     // label it
         writeUnderHundred(integer % 100);// write the 2-digit integer
      } // end if
} // end writeUnderThousand

// Writes the name of a value between 1 and 99; ignores 0.
// Precondition: 0 < integer < 100.
private void writeUnderHundred(long integer)
{
   if (integer < 20)
      writeUnderTwenty(integer);
   else // integer >= 20 but < 100
   {
      writeMultipleOfTen(integer / 10);
      writeUnderTwenty(integer % 10);
   } // end if
} // end writeUnderHundred

// Writes the name of a value between 1 and 19; ignores 0.
private void writeUnderTwenty(long integer)
{
   switch ((int)integer)
   {
      case 0: // ignore 0
         break;
      case 1:
         System.out.print("one "); break;
      case 2:
         System.out.print("two "); break;
      . . .

      case 19:
         System.out.print("nineteen "); break;
      default:
         System.out.print("error in writeUnderTwenty "); break;
   } // end switch
} // end writeUnderTwenty

// Writes a multiple of 10 as one word, where 1 <= multiple < = 9.
private void writeMultipleOfTen(long multiple)
{
   switch ((int)multiple)
```

```java
        {
           case 1:
              System.out.print("ten "); break;
           case 2:
              System.out.print("twenty "); break;
           . . .
           case 9:
              System.out.print("ninety "); break;
           default:
              System.out.print("error in writeMultipleOfTen "); break;
        } // end switch
     } // end writeMultipleOfTen

     // Writes a power of 1000 as one word, where 1 <= power <= 6;
     // ignores 0.
     private void writePowerOfThousand(int power)
     {
        switch (power)
        {
           case 0: // ignore 0
              break;
           case 1:
              System.out.print("thousand "); break;
           case 2:
              System.out.print("million "); break;
           . . .
           case 6:
              System.out.print("quintillion "); break;
           default:
              System.out.print("error in writePowerOfThousand "); break;
        } // end switch
     } // end writePowerOfThousand
} // end VerbalInteger
```

24.29 Listing 24-4 contains a driver for the class VerbalInteger and shows some sample output from the program.

LISTING 24-4 A driver for the class VerbalInteger and sample output

```java
/** A driver that demonstrates the class VerbalInteger.
    @author Frank M. Carrano
*/
```

```
import java.util.Scanner;
public class Driver
{
    public static void main(String args[])
    {
        Scanner keyboard = new Scanner(System.in);

        System.out.print("Please enter an integer: ");
        long integer = keyboard.nextLong();
        while (integer > 0)
        {
            VerbalInteger anInteger = new VerbalInteger(integer);
            System.out.print("You entered ");
            anInteger.write();
            System.out.println();

            System.out.print("Please enter an integer: ");
            integer = keyboard.nextLong();
        } // end while
        System.out.println("All done!");
    } // end main
} // end Driver
```

Sample Output

```
Please enter an integer: 904670
You entered nine hundred four thousand six hundred seventy
Please enter an integer: 12345678900
You entered twelve billion three hundred forty five million six
hundred seventy eight thousand nine hundred
Please enter an integer: 9223372036854775807
You entered nine quintillion two hundred twenty three quadrillion
three hundred seventy two trillion thirty six billion eight hundred
fifty four million seven hundred seventy five thousand eight hundred
seven
Please enter an integer: 0
All done!
```

Question 10 If you entered 12300 in response to the prompt given by the program in Listing 24-4, what method calls would occur? List these calls in the order they occur, giving their arguments as values instead of expressions.

Question 11 Suppose the private method write of the class VerbalInteger in Listing 24-3 displayed the word "zero" as its base case. What output would the program given in Listing 24-4 produce in response to the input 12300?

Question 12 You can replace the method writeUnderThousand in the class VerbalInteger, as given in Listing 24-3, with the following recursive version:

```
// Writes the name of a value between 1 and 999;
// ignores 0. Precondition: 0 < integer < 1000.
private void writeUnderThousand(long integer)
{
   if (integer < 20)
      writeUnderTwenty(integer);
   else if (integer < 100)
   {
      writeMultipleOfTen((int)integer / 10);
      writeUnderTwenty(integer % 10);
   }
   else // integer >= 100 but < 1000
   {
      writeUnderTwenty(integer / 100);
      System.out.print("hundred ");
      writeUnderThousand(integer % 100);
   } // end if
} // end writeUnderThousand
```

After this replacement, the method writeUnderHundred is unnecessary. Why is the logic of this recursive method writeUnderThousand the same as that of the original nonrecursive version given in Listing 24-3?

Recursion Versus Iteration

24.30 Do programmers actually use recursion, or is it simply a fun mental exercise? As strange and confusing as recursion might seem to you at first, it is an important problem-solving tool. And yes, programmers use it. In fact, the programmers of the Java Class Library used recursion—as you will see in the next chapter—when they defined the sort methods in the class Arrays. But should *we* use recursion? Should we forget about loops and never use iteration again?

videonote
More about recursion

Both recursion and iteration are important; professional programmers use both techniques, and so should we. Sometimes an iterative solution is easier to write, and sometimes a recursive one is. The previous two problems of converting integers to words have solutions that are easier to write using recursive methods than iterative ones. These methods have straightforward logic and behave acceptably. However, some recursive solutions are so inefficient that you should avoid them. The next solution is among those you should not use.

Fibonacci Numbers: A Poor Use of Recursion

The problem that we will look at now is simple, occurs frequently in mathematical computations, and has a recursive solution that is so natural that you likely will be tempted to use it. Don't!

24.31 Early in the 13th century, the mathematician Leonardo Fibonacci proposed a sequence of integers to model the number of descendants of a pair of rabbits. Later named the *Fibonacci sequence*, these numbers occur today in surprisingly many applications.

The first two terms in the Fibonacci sequence are 1 and 1. Each subsequent term is the sum of the preceding two terms. Thus, the sequence begins as 1, 1, 2, 3, 5, 8, 13, ... Typically, the sequence is defined by the equations

$$F_0 = 1$$
$$F_1 = 1$$
$$F_n = F_{n-1} + F_{n-2} \text{ when } n \geq 2$$

These equations naturally lead us to writing the following recursive algorithm:

Algorithm fibonacci(n)

```
if (n <= 1)
    return 1
else
    return fibonacci(n - 1) + fibonacci(n - 2)
```

24.32   This algorithm makes two recursive calls. That fact in itself is not the difficulty. The next chapter will show you perfectly good algorithms—displayArray in Segment 25.5 and mergeSort in Segment 25.18—that make two recursive calls. The trouble here is that the same recursive calls are made repeatedly. A call to fibonacci(n) invokes fibonacci(n - 1) and then fibonacci(n - 2). But the call to fibonacci(n - 1) has to compute fibonacci(n - 2), so the same Fibonacci number is computed twice.

Things get worse. The call to fibonacci(n - 1) calls fibonacci(n - 3) as well. The two previous calls to fibonacci(n - 2) each invoke fibonacci(n - 3), so fibonacci(n - 3) is computed three times. Figure 24-6a illustrates the dependency of F_6 on previous Fibonacci numbers and so indicates the number of times a particular number is computed by the method fibonacci. In contrast, an iterative computation of F_6 computes each prior term once, as Figure 24-6b shows. The recursive solution is clearly less efficient. In fact, the time required to compute F_n recursively increases exponentially as n increases. In other words, the time required is proportional to C^n for some constant C greater than 1.

FIGURE 24-6   The computation of the Fibonacci number F_6 using (a) recursion; (b) iteration

(a)

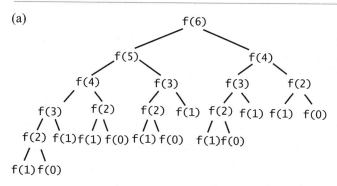

Each f(n) represents the call fibonacci(n) and returns the value F_n

f(0) is called 5 times, returning F_0
f(1) is called 8 times, returning F_1
f(2) is called 5 times, returning F_2
f(3) is called 3 times, returning F_3
f(4) is called 2 times, returning F_4
f(5) is called once, returning F_5
f(6) is called once, returning F_6

(b) $F_0 = 1$
      $F_1 = 1$
      $F_2 = F_1 + F_0 = 2$
      $F_3 = F_2 + F_1 = 3$
      $F_4 = F_3 + F_2 = 5$
      $F_5 = F_4 + F_3 = 8$
      $F_6 = F_5 + F_4 = 13$

Each F_n is a variable whose value is computed once

24.33 At the beginning of this section, we observed that each Fibonacci number is the sum of the preceding two Fibonacci numbers in the sequence. This observation should lead us to an iterative solution, which Question 13 will explore. An iterative computation of a Fibonacci number is O(n). That is, the time required to compute F_n iteratively increases linearly as n increases, instead of exponentially as occurs for the recursive computation. It turns out that we also can compute F_n directly, as follows:

$$F_n = (a^n - b^n) / \sqrt{5}$$

where $a = (1 + \sqrt{5}) / 2$ and $b = (1 - \sqrt{5}) / 2$. This direct approach is O(1); that is, the time to evaluate the expression for F_n is independent of n.

Although the clarity and simplicity of this recursive solution make it a tempting choice, it is much too inefficient to use. Exercise at the end of this chapter shows a recursive way to compute the Fibonacci numbers that is O(n). Even so, an iterative or direct solution is easier to write.

> **Programming Tip**
> Do not use a recursive solution that repeatedly solves the same problem in its recursive calls.

Question 13 Write two methods that each compute the Fibonacci sequence by using iteration instead of recursion. Given an integer $n > 1$, one method should return an array of the Fibonacci numbers F_0, F_1, . . ., F_n. The other method should use three variables to contain the current term in the sequence and the two terms before it. It should return only F_n.

Question 14 If you compute the Fibonacci number F_6 recursively, how many recursive calls are made and how many additions are performed?

Question 15 If you compute the Fibonacci number F_6 iteratively, how many additions are performed?

Kinds of Recursion

Some of the ways in which recursion can occur are given special names. We end this chapter by briefly discussing a few standard classifications.

Tail Recursion

24.34 **Tail recursion** occurs when the last action performed by a recursive method is a recursive call. For example, the following method countDown from Segment 24.7 is tail recursive:

```
public static void countDown(int integer)
{
   if (integer >= 1)
   {
      System.out.println(integer);
      countDown(integer - 1);
   } // end if
} // end countDown
```

A method that implements the algorithm fibonacci given in Segment 24.31 will not be tail recursive, even though a recursive call *appears* last in the method. A closer look reveals that the last *action* is an addition.

24.35   The tail recursion in a method simply repeats the method's logic with changes to parameters and variables. We can perform the same repetition by using iteration. Converting a tail-recursive method to an iterative one is usually a straightforward process. For example, let's see how to convert the recursive method countDown just given. First we replace the if statement with a while statement. Then, instead of the recursive call, we assign its argument integer - 1 to the method's formal parameter integer. Doing so gives us the following iterative version of the method:

```
public static void countDown(int integer)
{
  while (integer >= 1)
  {
    System.out.println(integer);
    integer = integer - 1;
  } // end while
} // end countDown
```

This method is essentially the same as the iterative method given in Segment 24.8.

Because converting tail recursion to iteration is often uncomplicated, some compilers convert tail-recursive methods to iterative methods to save the overhead involved with recursion. Most of this overhead involves memory, not time. If you need to save space, you should consider replacing tail recursion with iteration.

> **Note:** In a tail-recursive method, the last action is a recursive call. This call performs a repetition that can be done with iteration. Converting a tail-recursive method to an iterative one is usually a straightforward process.

Direct, Indirect, and Mutual Recursion

24.36   A method uses **direct recursion** if it contains an explicit call to itself. The method countDown shown in Segment 24.34 uses direct recursion, as do the other examples shown earlier in this chapter. Some recursive algorithms, however, make their recursive calls indirectly. For example, we might have the following chain of events: Method A calls method B, method B calls method C, and method C calls method A. Such recursion—called **indirect recursion**—is more difficult to understand and to trace, but it does arise naturally in certain applications.

For example, the following rules describe strings that are valid algebraic expressions:

- An *algebraic expression* is either a term or two terms separated by a + or – operator.
- A *term* is either a factor or two factors separated by a * or / operator.
- A *factor* is either a variable or an algebraic expression enclosed in parentheses.
- A *variable* is a single letter.

These rules are circular and lead to a natural solution to the problem of detecting valid algebraic expressions by using indirect recursion.

videonote
Kinds of recursion

For example, suppose that the methods isExpression, isTerm, isFactor, and isVariable detect whether a string is, respectively, an expression, a term, a factor, or a variable. The method isExpression calls isTerm, which in turn calls isFactor, which then calls isExpression and isVariable. Figure 24-7 illustrates these calls. Such a recursive solution to this problem is easier to write than an iterative one.

FIGURE 24-7 An example of indirect recursion

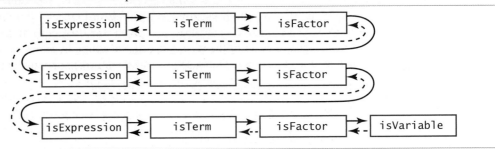

24.37 When two methods call each other, the indirect recursion is called **mutual recursion**. For example, the following two methods, which determine whether a given nonnegative integer is even or odd, are mutually recursive. Their logic is based on these observations about nonnegative integers:

- 0 is even.
- A nonzero integer n is even if $n - 1$ is odd.
- A nonzero integer n is odd if $n - 1$ is even.

```java
/** Tests whether a given integer is even.
    @param integer  a nonegative integer
    @return true if integer is even, otherwise returns false */
public static boolean isEven(int integer)
{
   boolean result;
   if (integer == 0)
      result = true;
   else
      result = isOdd(integer - 1);

   return result;
} // end isEven

/** Tests whether a given integer is odd.
    @param integer  a nonegative integer
    @return true if integer is odd, otherwise returns false */
public static boolean isOdd(int integer)
{
   boolean result;
   if (integer == 0)
      result = false;
   else
      result = isEven(integer - 1);

   return result;
} // end isOdd
```

videonote
A problem
solved

CHAPTER SUMMARY

- Recursion is a problem-solving process that breaks a problem into identical but smaller problems.

- The definition of a recursive method must contain logic that involves an input—often a parameter—to the method and leads to different cases. One or more of these cases are base cases, or stopping cases, because they provide a solution that does not require recursion. One or more cases include a recursive invocation of the method that takes a step toward a base case by solving a "smaller" version of the task performed by the method.

- For each call to a method, Java records the values of the method's parameters and local variables in an activation record. The records are placed into a stack that organizes them chronologically. The record most recently added to the stack is of the method that is currently executing. In this way, Java can suspend the execution of a recursive method and invoke it again with new argument values.

- Recursion can be used to solve problems whose iterative solution would be more complex or more difficult to discover.

- You should not use a recursive solution that repeatedly solves the same problem in its recursive calls. For example, the recursive computation of a Fibonacci number computes previous numbers several times each.

- Tail recursion occurs when the last action of a recursive method is a recursive call. This recursive call performs a repetitive process that can also be done by using iteration. Converting a tail-recursive method to an iterative one is usually a straightforward process.

- Direct recursion occurs when a method calls itself. A tail-recursive method exhibits direct recursion.

- Indirect recursion results when a method calls a method that calls another method, and so on until the first method is called again.

- Mutual recursion is a special case of indirect recursion whereby two methods call each other.

EXERCISES

1. What are three characteristics that every recursive method must have?

2. What is the base case in the method countdown, as given in Segment 24.6? What is the recursive call?

3. Why can a recursive method cause a stack overflow?

4. As a surprise for your young cousin's birthday, you have placed your small gift into a box, placed the box into a larger box, and continued placing smaller boxes into larger boxes until you ran out of boxes. Write a recursive algorithm that your cousin can follow to open your gift.

5. Write a recursive method to compute 2^n for a positive integer n.

6. Write a recursive method and an iterative method that each compute $n!$, the factorial of n. What happens when you execute these methods?

7. What is the output of the following program?

```java
public class Exercise7
{
    public static void main(String[] args)
    {
        System.out.println("Sum = " + guessOutput(4));
    } // end main

    public static int guessOutput(int n)
    {
        boolean result;
        if (n == 1)
            result = 1;
        else
            result = n + guessOutput(n - 1);
        return result;
    } // end guessOutput
} // end Exercise7
```

8. What is the output of the following program?

```java
public class Exercise8
{
   public static void main(String[] args)
   {
      guessOutput(7654321);
   } // end main

   public static void guessOutput(int n)
   {
      if (n > 0)
      {
         System.out.print(n % 10 + " ");
         guessOutput(n / 10);
      } // end if
   } // end guessOutput
} // end Exercise8
```

9. Identify and fix the errors in the following program:

```java
public class Exercise9
{
   public static void main(String[] args)
   {
      guessOutput(7654321);
   } // end main

   public static void guessOutput(int n)
   {
      if (n != 0)
      {
         System.out.println(n);
         guessOutput(n / 10);
      } // end if
   } // end guessOutput
} // end Exercise9
```

10. Identify and fix the errors in the following program:

```java
public class Exercise10
{
   public static void main(String[] args)
   {
      Exercise10 ex = new Exercise10();
      System.out.println(ex);
   } // end main

   public Exercise10()
   {
      Exercise10 ex = new Exercise10();
   } // end default constructor
} // end Exercise10
```

11. Consider the method displayRowOfCharacters that displays any given character the specified number of times on one line. For example, the call

```java
displayRowOfCharacters('*', 5);
```

produces the line

```
*****
```

Implement this method in Java by using recursion.

12. Write a recursive method that asks the user for integer input that is between 1 and 100, inclusive. If the input is out of range, the method should recursively ask the user to enter a new input value.

13. Write a recursive method that displays the entries in a given array in backward order. That is, display the last entry first and the first entry last. *Hint*: Consider the last entry of the array first.

14. Repeat Exercise 13, but have your solution instead consider the first entry of the array first.

15. Repeat Exercises 13 and 14, but write a string backward instead of an array.

16. Write a recursive method that displays a given message n times.

17. Write a recursive method that finds the number of occurrences of a specified letter in a given string.

18. Repeat Exercise 15 in Chapter 12, but use a recursive definition of the method isPalindrome.

19. Define a recursive method f that, given a nonnegative integer n, returns
    - n % 2 when n ranges from 0 to 9
    - f(n / 10) + (n % 10) % 2 when n is greater than or equal to 10

20. Jack and Jill take turns using a one-gallon pail to empty a tank of water. On his turn, Jack always removes one gallon of water. Jill, however, removes one or two gallons so that either an even number of gallons are left in the tank or the tank becomes empty. Using recursion, how many turns in total must Jack and Jill make to empty the tank, if it initially contains *n* gallons?

21. Trace the call f(16) to the following method by showing a stack of activation records:

```
public int f(int n)
{
  int result = 0;
  if (f <= 4)
    result = 1;
  else
    result = f(n / 2) + f(n / 4);

  return result;
} // end f
```

22. Trace the call fibonacci(6) to the following method:

```
/** Computes the (n + 1)-st Fibonacci number F(n).
    @param n   an integer >= 0.
    @return the Fibonacci number F(n) */
public static int fibonacci(int n)
{
  int result = 0;
  if (n <= 1)
    result = 1;
  else
    result = fibonacci(1, 1, n);
  return result;
} // end fibonacci

private static int fibonacci(int one, int two, int n)
{
  int result = 0;
  if (n == 1)
    result = one;
  else
    result = fibonacci(two, one + two, n - 1);
  return result;
} // end fibonacci
```

List any recursive calls in the order they occur, giving their arguments as values instead of variables. How does this method compare to an iterative Fibonacci method with respect to required execution time?

PROJECTS

1. The following algorithm finds the square root of a positive number:

    ```
    Algorithm squareRoot(number, lowGuess, highGuess, tolerance)
    newGuess = (lowGuess + highGuess) / 2
    if ((highGuess - newGuess) / newGuess < tolerance)
        return newGuess
    else if (newGuess * newGuess > number)
        return squareRoot(number, lowGuess, newGuess, tolerance)
    else if (newGuess * newGuess < number)
        return squareRoot(number, newGuess, highGuess, tolerance)
    else
        return newGuess
    ```

    To begin the computation, you need a value `lowGuess` that is less than the square root of the number and a value `highGuess` that is larger. You can use zero as `lowGuess` and the number itself as `highGuess`. The parameter `tolerance` controls the precision of the result independently of the magnitude of `number`. For example, computing the square root of 250 with `tolerance` equal to 0.00005 results in 15.81. This result has four digits of accuracy.

    Implement this algorithm.

2. Design and implement a class of vending machines. Each machine contains an assortment of products ranging in price from $0.01 to $1.00. The machine accepts only a one-dollar bill, but it returns change when necessary. Include a recursive method to compute the change using the fewest coins possible selected only from the following coins: quarter ($0.25), dime ($0.10), nickel ($0.05), and penny ($0.01).

3. Imagine a row of n lights that can be turned on or off only under certain conditions, as follows. The first light can be turned on or off anytime. Each of the other lights can be turned on or off only when the preceding light is on and all other lights before it are off. If all the lights are on initially, how can you turn them off? For three lights numbered 1 to 3, you can take the following steps, where 1 is a light that is on and 0 is a light that is off:

    1 1 1 All on initially

    0 1 1 Turn off light 1

    0 1 0 Turn off light 3

    1 1 0 Turn on light 1

    1 0 0 Turn off light 2

    0 0 0 Turn off light 1

    You can solve this problem in general by using both direct recursion and mutual recursion, as follows:

    ```
    Algorithm turnOff(n)
    // Turns off n lights that are initially on.

    if (n == 1)
        Turn off light 1
    else
    {
        if (n > 2)
            turnOff(n - 2)
        Turn off light n
        if (n > 2)
    ```

```
        turnOn(n - 2)
      turnOff(n - 1)

}
```

Algorithm `turnOn(n)`
// Turns on n *lights that are initially off.*

```
if (n == 1)
```
    Turn on light 1
```
else
{
    turnOn(n - 1)
    if (n > 2)
        turnOff(n - 2)
```
    Turn on light n
```
    if (n > 2)
        turnOn(n - 2)
}
```

Implement these algorithms in Java. Use the results in a program to produce a list of directions to turn off *n* lights that initially are on.

4. A *polygon* is a closed *n*-sided figure composed of *n* straight line segments, joined end to end. The point at which two sides join is called a *vertex*. For example, a triangle is a three-sided polygon, and a rectangle is a four-sided polygon. Using recursion, compute the area of a polygon. If you cut off a triangle, compute its area, and sum these areas as you repeat the process, you eventually will get the area of the polygon. Note that a triangle whose vertices are at the coordinates (x_1, y_1), (x_2, y_2), and (x_3, y_3) has an area equal to

$$(x_1 \times y_2 + x_2 \times y_3 + x_3 \times y_1 - x_1 \times y_3 - x_2 \times y_1 - x_3 \times y_2) / 2$$

5. The Towers of Hanoi is a classic puzzle in computer science whose solution is not obvious. Imagine three poles and a number of disks of varying diameters. Each disk has a hole in its center so that it can fit over each of the poles. Suppose that the disks have been placed on the first pole in order from largest to smallest, with the smallest disk on top. Here is the initial configuration for three disks:

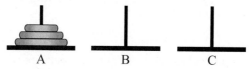

The goal is to move the entire stack of disks to either of the others so that they remain piled in their original order. You can move only one disk—the topmost one—at a time from one pole to another, and disks can only be stacked on top of larger disks. You can store disks on another pole temporarily, as long as you observe the previous restrictions.

If we label the poles A, B, and C and place *n* disks on pole A, a recursive algorithm will move the disks to pole C, as follows:

```
if (n == 1)
```
    Move the disk from pole A to pole C
```
else
{
```
    Move n - 1 *disks from pole A to pole B, leaving the largest disk alone on pole A*
    Move the disk from pole A to pole C
    Move n - 1 *disks from pole B to pole C*
```
}
```

Implement a recursive solution to the Towers of Hanoi puzzle. Your program should display a list of the moves necessary to solve the puzzle. For example, if three disks are on pole A, the following sequence of seven moves will move the disks to pole C, using pole B temporarily:

Move a disk from pole A to pole C
Move a disk from pole A to pole B
Move a disk from pole C to pole B
Move a disk from pole A to pole C
Move a disk from pole B to pole A
Move a disk from pole B to pole C
Move a disk from pole A to pole C

Use a value of 3 for *n* while you are developing your solution. Test your program with values of *n* up to 9.

6. Solve the previous Towers of Hanoi puzzle iteratively instead of recursively by using the following algorithm. Beginning with pole A and moving from pole to pole in the order pole A, pole C, pole B, pole A, and so on, make at most one move per pole according to the following rules:

- Move the topmost disk from a pole to the next possible pole in the specified order. Remember that you cannot place a disk on top of a smaller one.
- If the disk that you are about to move is the smallest of all the disks and you just moved it to the present pole, do not move it. Instead, consider the next pole.

This algorithm should make the same moves as the recursive algorithm given in the previous project. Take note of the differences in logic that arise from not using recursion.

ANSWERS TO SELF-TEST QUESTIONS

1.
```java
public static void skipLines(int givenNumber)
{
    if (givenNumber >= 1)
    {
        System.out.println();
        skipLines(givenNumber - 1);
    } // end if
} // end skipLines
```

2. *Algorithm* drawConcentricCircles(givenNumber, givenDiameter, givenPoint)

```
if (givenNumber >= 1)
{
    Draw a circle whose diameter is givenDiameter and
        whose center is at givenPoint
    givenDiameter = 4 * givenDiameter / 3
    drawConcentricCircles(givenNumber - 1, givenDiameter, givenPoint)
}
```

3.
```java
public static void countUp(int n)
{
    if (n >= 1)
    {
        countUp(n - 1);
        System.out.println(n);
    } // end if
} // end countUp
```

4. Given the answer to Question 3, the trace is

```
countUp(3);
countUp(2);
countUp(1);
countUp(0);
System.out.println(1);
System.out.println(2);
System.out.println(3);
```

5. Yes, for the following reasons:

   - The method has an input value, the parameter n.
   - The method's logic involves cases based on the value of n.
   - One case, when n is 1, requires no recursion.
   - Another case, when n is greater than 1, involves a recursive call.
   - The recursive call has an argument whose value, n - 1, is smaller than the original argument n.

6.
```
public static int productOf(int n)
{
    int result = 1;
    if (n > 1)
        result = n * productOf(n - 1);

    return result;
} // end productOf
```

7.
```
anInteger.speak();
speak(123);
speak(12);
speak(1);
speakDigit(1);
speakDigit(2);
speakDigit(3);
```

8.
```
anInteger.speak();
speak(090);
speak(9);
speakDigit(9);
speakDigit(0);
```

9. 090 / 10 is 9, which is the first digit displayed.

10.
```
anInteger.write();
write(12300, 0);
write(12, 1);
write(0, 2);
writeUnderThousand(12);
writeUnderHundred(12);
writeUnderTwenty(12);
writePowerOfThousand(1);
writeUnderThousand(300);
writeUnderTwenty(3);
writeUnderHundred(0);
writeUnderTwenty(0);
writePowerOfThousand(0);
```

11. You entered zero twelve thousand three hundred

12. The if and else if clauses of the revised method are exactly equivalent to the logic of the method writeUnderHundred given in Listing 24-3. The final else clause in the recursive version begins just like the nonrecursive version in Listing 24-3. At this point, we must write a number less than 100, that is, integer % 100. Although the next statement in the original version invokes writeUnderHundred, the recursive version calls itself. But again notice that the beginning of the recursive writeUnderThousand performs the same steps as writeUnderHundred. Thus, the logic of the two versions is equivalent.

13.
```
/** A class whose static methods compute the Fibonacci numbers.
    @author Frank M. Carrano
*/
public class Fibonacci
{
   /** Computes a portion of the Fibonacci sequence.
       @param n  an integer > 1
       @return an array of the first n + 1 Fibonacci numbers */
   public static int[] fibonacci1(int n)
   {
      int[] fib = new int[n + 1];
      fib[0] = 1;
      fib[1] = 1;
      for (int index = 2; index <= n; index++)
         fib[int] = fib[index - 1] + fib[index - 2];

      return fib;
   } // end fibonacci1

   /** Computes the (n + 1)-st Fibonacci number F(n).
       @param n  an integer > 1
       @return the Fibonacci number F(n) */
   public static int fibonacci2(int n)
   {
      int fib0 = 1;
      int fib1 = 1;
      int fib2 = 0; // the compiler wants fib2 initialized
      for (int index = 2; index <= n; index++)
      {
         fib2 = fib1 + fib0;
         fib0 = fib1;
         fib1 = fib2;
      } // end for

      return fib2;
   } // end fibonacci2
} // end Fibonacci
```

14. 24 recursive calls and 12 additions

15. 5 additions

Chapter

25

Recursive Array Processing

Contents

Prerequisites

Objectives

After studying this chapter, you should be able to
- Perform operations on an array's data by using recursion
- Search an array by using a recursive linear search and a recursive binary search
- Sort an array by using a recursive merge sort
- Decide between recursion and iteration when processing an array

Chapter 23 talked about sorting the entries in an array and searching an array for a particular item. The previous chapter introduced you to recursion as a way to perform a repetitive process. Recursion can be an especially powerful technique when processing a data structure such as an array. In fact, some of the best sorting and searching algorithms often are stated recursively. After examining some basic ways of working with an array recursively, we will present some recursive algorithms for sorting and searching the entries in an array.

■ Basic Techniques

In this section, we consider a simple task—displaying the integers in an array—so that we can focus on recursively processing an array without the distraction of the task. In fact, many recursive algorithms use one of the techniques you are about to see. Subsequent sections will use these techniques to search or sort an array recursively.

25.1 Suppose that we have an array of integers, and we want a method that displays it. So that we can display either all or part of the array, the method will display the array entries whose indices range from `first` to `last`. Thus, we can declare the method as follows:

```
/** Displays the integers in an array.
    @param array  an array of integers
    @param first  the index of the first integer displayed
    @param last   the index of the last integer displayed
    Precondition: 0 <= first <= last < array.length */
public static void displayArray(int[] array, int first, int last)
```

This task is simple and could readily be implemented using iteration. You might not imagine, however, that we could also implement it recursively in a variety of ways. But we can and will.

25.2 **Starting with `array[first]`.** An iterative solution would certainly start at the first element, `array[first]`, so it is natural to have our first recursive method begin there also. If I ask you to display the array, you could display `array[first]` and then ask a friend to display the rest of the array. Displaying the rest of the array is a smaller problem than displaying the entire array. You wouldn't have to ask a friend for help if you had to display only one value—that is, if `first` and `last` were equal. This is the base case. Thus, we could write the method `displayArray` as follows:

```
/** Precondition: 0 <= first <= last < array.length */
public static void displayArray(int array[], int first, int last)
{
    System.out.print(array[first] + " ");   // display first entry
    if (first < last)                        // more to display?
        displayArray(array, first + 1, last); // display rest of array
} // end displayArray
```

For simplicity, we assume that the integers will fit on one line. Notice that the client would follow a call to `displayArray` with `System.out.println()` to get to the next line.

25.3 **Not so fast!** If the base case is when `first` equals `last`, why didn't we test for that case? Although the previous method does not explicitly test the expression `first == last`, no recursive call occurs when `first` and `last` are equal. However, suppose that we began by asking about the base case explicitly and wrote the following pseudocode:

Algorithm displayArray(array, first, last)
if (*we have only one entry to display*)
    Display the entry
else if (*we have more than one entry to display*)
    {

Display the first entry
```
    displayArray(array, first + 1, last)
}
```

Translating this logic into Java results in the following method:

```
/** Precondition: 0 <= first <= last < array.length */
public static void displayArray(int array[], int first, int last)
{
    if (first == last)
        System.out.print(array[first] + " "); // display sole entry
    else if (first < last)
    {
        System.out.print(array[first] + " "); // display first entry
        displayArray(array, first + 1, last); // display rest of array
    } // end if
} // end displayArray
```

Notice, however, that both clauses of the if statement begin with the same print statement. Thus, we can move it before the if statement. Doing so leads us to the method given previously in Segment 25.2.

25.4 **Starting with array[last].** Strange as it might seem, we can begin with the last entry in the array and still display the array from its beginning. Rather than displaying the last entry right away, you would ask a friend to display the rest of the array. After the entries in array[first] through array[last - 1] had been displayed, you would display array[last]. The resulting output would be the same as for the previous versions of displayArray.

The method that implements this plan follows:

```
/** Precondition: 0 <= first <= last < array.length */
public static void displayArray(int array[], int first, int last)
{
    if (first <= last)
    {
        displayArray(array, first, last - 1);// display up to last entry
        System.out.print(array[last] + " "); // display last entry
    } // end if
} // end displayArray
```

25.5 **Dividing the array in half.** A common way to process an array recursively divides—or partitions, as we said in Chapter 23—the array into two pieces. You then process each of the pieces separately. Since each of these pieces is an array that is smaller than the original array, each defines the smaller problem necessary for recursion. Our first examples also divided the array into two pieces, but one of the pieces contained only one element. Here we divide the array into two approximately equal pieces. To divide the array, we find the element at or near the middle of the array. The index of this element is

```
    int mid = (first + last) / 2;
```

As Segment 23.29 of Chapter 23 noted, we should use the following statement instead to avoid a possible out-of-bounds index:

```
    int mid = first + (last - first) / 2;
```

Figure 25-1 shows two arrays and their middle elements. Suppose that we include array[mid] in the left "half" of the array, as the figure shows. In Part b, the two pieces of the array are equal in length; in Part a they are not. This slight difference in length doesn't matter.

FIGURE 25-1   Two arrays with their middle elements within their left halves

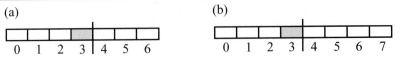

Once again, the base case is an array of one element, which we can display without help. But if the array contains more than one element, we divide it into halves. We then ask a friend to display one half and another friend to display the other half. These two friends, of course, represent the two recursive calls in the following method:

```
/** Precondition: 0 <= first <= last < array.length */
public static void displayArray(int array[], int first, int last)
{
   if (first == last)
      System.out.print(array[first] + " ");
   else
   {
      int mid = first + (last - first) / 2;
      displayArray(array, first, mid);     // display first half
      displayArray(array, mid + 1, last); // display second half
   } // end if
} // end displayArray
```

Question 1   In the previous segment, suppose that the array's middle element is treated separately, and is not in either "half" of the array. You then can recursively display the left half, display the middle entry, and recursively display the right half. What is the implementation of displayArray if you make these changes?

   Note: When you process an array recursively, you can partition it into two pieces. For example, the first or last element could be one piece, and the rest of the array could be another piece. Or you could divide the array into halves or in some other way. You could even divide it into more than two pieces. These strategies can apply to collections in general and to many other situations for which you seek a recursive solution.

■ Searching an Array Recursively

videonote
Searching recursively

Chapter 23 presented three algorithms for searching an array. Each was stated iteratively, but each also has a recursive solution. This section examines those recursive solutions using the ideas just given in the previous section.

A Recursive Linear Search

25.6   A linear search of an unsorted array compares the target with the array entries, one at a time, until it either finds a match or examines the entire array without success. Let's compare the target with the array's first entry. If they match, we are done. If the target and the first entry do not match, we will ask a friend to search the rest of the array. The friend's problem is a smaller occurrence of our original searching problem, so a recursive solution could be possible. We need a base case. If the array is empty, it cannot contain the target. That's our base case.

We can write some pseudocode to summarize these ideas. Our algorithm will return an integer— either an array index when the target is found or –1 if the search is unsuccessful:

Algorithm linearSearch(target, a, first, last)
// Searches a[first] *through* a[last] *for* target.

```
if (first > last)
   return -1
else if (target equals a[first])
```

```
         return first
     else
         return linearSearch(target, a, first + 1, last)
```

25.7   Listing 25-1 contains an implementation of this algorithm to search an array of strings. The recursive method searches the portion of the array beginning at `strings[first]` and continuing through `strings[last]`. A second public method having the same name searches an entire array, and so has only two parameters. This method simply calls the first method, passing it 0 and `string.length - 1` as the arguments corresponding to the parameters `first` and `last`. Since both static methods are useful to a client, they are both public.

LISTING 25-1   The class `StringSearcher`, whose methods search an unsorted array of strings using a recursive linear search

```java
/** A class whose static methods search an array of strings.
    @author Frank M. Carrano
*/
public class StringSearcher
{
   /** Performs a linear search of a portion of an array.
       @param target   the string to find
       @param strings  an array of strings
       @param first  the index of the first string in the array segment
       @param last   the index of the last string in the array segment
       @return the index of an occurrence of target,
               if it is in the array, or -1 if not. */
   public static int linearSearch(String target, String[] strings,
                                     int first, int last)

   {
      int result = -1;
      if (first > last)
         result = -1;
      else if (target.equals(strings[first]))
         result = first;
      else
         result = linearSearch(target, strings, first + 1, last);

      return result;
   } // end linearSearch

   /** Performs a linear search of an array.
       @param target   the string to find
       @param strings  an array of strings
       @return the index of an occurrence of target,
               if it is in the array, or -1 if not. */
   public static int linearSearch(String target, String[] strings)
   {
      return linearSearch(target, strings, 0, strings.length - 1);
   } // end linearSearch
} // end StringSearcher
```

SELF-TEST

Question 2 The algorithm `linearSearch`, as given in Segment 25.6, begins its search at the array's first entry. What pseudocode describes a recursive linear search that begins its search at the array's last entry?

Question 3 The algorithm `linearSearch`, as given in Segment 25.6, uses an empty array as its base case. What changes would you make to the algorithm so that the base case is an array consisting of one entry and a precondition is `first <= last`?

Question 4 Like a linear search of an unsorted array, the modified linear search of a sorted array, as described in Chapter 23, can be recursive. What pseudocode describes a modified linear search recursively?

Searching a Bag Recursively

25.8 As you will recall from Chapter 19, a bag is a collection whose entries are in no particular order. One of its methods, `contains`, returns either true or false according to whether its argument is equal to one of the items in the bag. That method, whose iterative definition is in Segment 19.26, is a member of the class `BagOfStrings`. From our study of searching an array in Chapter 23, we recognize the search algorithm used by `contains` as a linear search.

We just defined a recursive linear search of an unsorted array that returns an integer—either –1 for an unsuccessful search or an array index when the target is found. The `contains` method, however, simply returns true or false. While `contains` could call the method `linearSearch` given in Listing 25-1, we instead can revise its algorithm slightly as follows:

```
Algorithm linearSearch(target, a, first, last)

if (first > last)
    return false
else if (target equals a[first])
    return true
else
    return linearSearch(target, a, first + 1, last)
```

25.9 As you can see in Listing 25-2, the public method `contains` calls a private method that implements the previous algorithm. Since the array to be searched is a data field of the class, it need not be a parameter of the private method `linearSearch`, even though the algorithm just given indicates that it is.

LISTING 25-2   BagOfStrings's method `contains` and the recursive method it calls

```
/**
    A class that implements a bag of strings by using an array.
    @author Frank M. Carrano
*/
public class BagOfStrings
{
    private final String[] bag;
    private static final int DEFAULT_CAPACITY = 25;
    private int numberOfStrings;

    < Constructors and all methods given in Listing 19-6—except contains—appear here. >

    /** Tests whether the bag contains a given string.
        @param aString  the string to locate
```

```
        @return true if the bag contains aString, or false otherwise */
    public boolean contains(String aString)
    {
        return linearSearch(aString, 0, numberOfStrings - 1);
    } // end contains

    private boolean linearSearch(String target, int first, int last)
    {
        boolean result;
        if (first > last)
            result = false;
        else if (target.equals(bag[first]))
            result = true;
        else
            result = linearSearch(target, first + 1, last);

        return result;
    } // end linearSearch
} // end BagOfStrings
```

Note: A recursive method that requires its class's client to have knowledge of the class's private fields should be private. For example, a client of the class BagOfStrings, as given in Listing 25-2, would need to know how a bag's entries were stored to be able to call the method linearSearch. For that reason, linearSearch cannot be public.

A Recursive Binary Search

25.10   Chapter 23 introduced the binary search of a sorted array. A binary search sees whether the middle entry in an array is the desired target. If it is, the search is over, but otherwise the search can ignore about one-half of the array's entries as it continues looking for the target. This search can be described by the following recursive algorithm:

> *Algorithm to search* a[0] *through* a[n - 1] *for* target
>
> mid = *approximate midpoint between* 0 *and* n - 1
> **if** (target *equals* a[mid])
>   **return** mid
> **else if** (target < a[mid])
>   **return** *the result of searching* a[0] *through* a[mid - 1]
> **else** // target > a[mid]
>   **return** *the result of searching* a[mid + 1] *through* a[n - 1]

Notice that to

> *Search* a[0] *through* a[n - 1]

you start by looking for the target in a[mid]. If it is not there, you have to

> *Search* a[0] *through* a[mid - 1]

and, if necessary, you have to

> *Search* a[mid + 1] *through* a[n - 1]

These two searches of a portion of the array are smaller versions of the very task we are solving, and so can be accomplished by calling the algorithm itself recursively. Recall the examples of a binary search shown in Figure 23-11.

25.11   Just as for the iterative version of the binary search developed in Chapter 23, the recursive version must have two indices to delimit the portion of the array that still needs to be searched. But instead of declaring `first` and `last` as local variables, we make them parameters of a recursive method. So instead of the pseudocode given in the previous segment, we have the following version of the algorithm:

```
Algorithm binarySearch(target, a, first, last)

mid = first + (last - first) / 2
if (first > last)
   return -1
else if (target equals a[mid])
   return mid
else if (target < a[mid])
   return binarySearch(target, a, first, mid - 1)
else  // target > a[mid]
   return binarySearch(target, a, mid + 1, last)
```

25.12   Listing 25-3 contains the definition of the method `binarySearch` as a member of the class `SortedStringSearcher`. The public method searches an entire array by calling a recursive private method to perform a recursive binary search.

LISTING 25-3   A class containing the static method `binarySearch`

```java
/** A class containing a static method for recursively searching
    a sorted array of strings.
    @author Frank M. Carrano
*/
public class SortedStringSearcher
{
   /** Performs a binary search of an array of strings
       sorted into ascending order.
       @param target   the string to find
       @param strings  an array of sorted strings
       @return the index of an occurrence of target,
               if it is in the array, or -1 if not. */
   public static int binarySearch(String target, String[] strings)
   {
      return binarySearch(target, strings, 0, strings.length - 1);
   } // end binarySearch

   private static int binarySearch(String target, String[] strings,
                                   int first, int last)
   {
      int result;
      int mid = first + (last - first) / 2;
```

```
      if (first > last)
         result = -1; // target not in array
      else if (target.equals(strings[mid]))
         result = mid; // target found at a[mid]
      else if (target.compareTo(strings[mid]) < 0)
         result = binarySearch(target, strings, first, mid - 1);
      else
         result = binarySearch(target, strings, mid + 1, last);

      return result;
   } // end binarySearch
} // end SortedStringSearcher
```

Question 5 In Chapter 23, Question 18 asked you to count the number of comparisons between the target and an array entry made by the iterative binary search algorithm when it searches the array shown in Figure 23-11 for 8 and for 16. Perform the same counts for the recursive method just given in Listing 25-3. How do these new counts compare to the ones made earlier?

Question 6 Can you revise the public method `binarySearch` given in Listing 25-3 so that it returns true or false without revising the private method? If so, make this change; if not, explain why not.

Question 7 How can you revise both the public and private methods `binarySearch` given in Listing 25-3 so that each returns true or false?

Question 8 What changes to the binary search algorithm are necessary when the array is sorted in descending order (from largest down to smallest) instead of ascending order, as we have assumed during our discussion?

Question 9 Could you use a recursive binary search in a definition of a bag's method `contains`? If so, revise the method; if not, explain why not.

■ A Recursive Merge Sort

25.13   The sorting methods described in Chapter 23 often are sufficient when you want to sort small arrays. They even can be a reasonable choice when sorting a larger array once. However, if you need to sort very large arrays frequently, those methods take too much time. We now consider a sorting algorithm that is much faster in general and is best described recursively.

videonote
The merge sort

The **merge sort** divides an array into halves, sorts the two halves, and then merges them into one sorted array. To sort each half of the array, merge sort uses a merge sort. Thus, the algorithm for merge sort is usually stated recursively. As you soon will see, most of the work during the execution of a merge sort occurs during the merge step. Since this step also involves most of the programming effort, we will begin by describing how to merge two sorted arrays into one sorted array.

Note: Divide and conquer
A recursive algorithm expresses the solution to a problem in terms of a smaller version of the same problem. When we divide a problem into two or more smaller but *distinct* problems, solve *each* new problem, and then combine their solutions to solve the original problem, the strategy is said to be a **divide-and-conquer** algorithm. That is, we divide the problem into pieces and conquer each piece to reach a solution. Although divide-and-conquer algorithms often are expressed recursively, this is not a requirement.

A recursive divide-and-conquer algorithm makes two or more recursive calls. For example, the recursive method `displayArray` given earlier in Segment 25.5 uses the divide-and-conquer strategy when it displays one half of an array and then the other half. The binary search, however, is not a divide-and-conquer algorithm even though it has two recursive calls in its definition. Only one of these calls actually executes. And although the recursive linear search shown in the previous section considers smaller and smaller arrays, it does not divide the problem into two searching problems.

Merging Arrays

25.14   Imagine two distinct and sorted arrays. Merging them into one sorted array is not difficult, but it is somewhat tedious. Processing both arrays from beginning to end, we compare the first entry in one array with the first entry in the other array and copy the smaller of the two entries to a new third array, as Figure 25-2 shows. After reaching the end of one array, we simply copy the remaining entries from the other array to the new third array.

FIGURE 25-2   Merging two sorted arrays into one sorted array

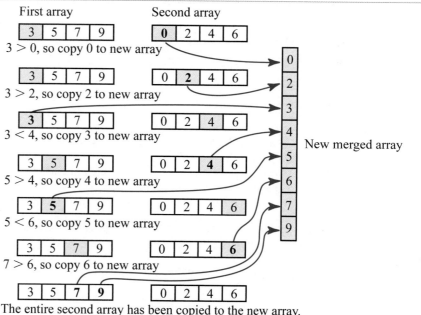

The Merge-Sort Algorithm

25.15 As we mentioned in Segment 25.13, a merge sort sorts and then merges two halves of an array. In doing so, it uses a temporary array for the merge step. It then copies the temporary array back to the original array, as Figure 25-3 shows.

FIGURE 25-3   The major steps in a merge sort

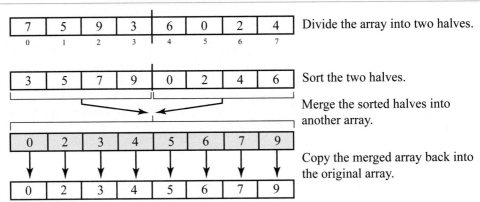

Divide the array into two halves.

Sort the two halves.

Merge the sorted halves into another array.

Copy the merged array back into the original array.

This sounds like a simple plan, but how do we sort the two halves of the array? By using a merge sort, of course! If mid is the index of the approximate midpoint of an array of n elements, we sort the entries indexed by 0 through mid and then the entries indexed by mid + 1 through n - 1. Since we perform these sorts by making recursive calls to the merge-sort algorithm, the algorithm needs two parameters—first and last—to specify the first and last indices of the subrange of the array to be sorted. We will use the notation a[first..last] to mean the array elements a[first], a[first + 1],...,a[last].

25.16 Merge sort has the following recursive formulation:

Algorithm mergeSort(a, tempArray, first, last)
// *Sorts the array entries in* a[first] *through* a[last] *recursively.*

if (first < last)
{
    mid = first + (last - first) / 2
    mergeSort(a, tempArray, first, mid)
    mergeSort(a, tempArray, mid + 1, last)
    Merge the sorted halves a[first..mid] *and* a[mid + 1..last] *using the*
       array tempArray
}

Notice that the algorithm ignores arrays of one or fewer elements.
The following pseudocode describes the merge step:

Algorithm merge(a, tempArray, first, mid, last)
// *Merges the adjacent subarrays* a[first..mid] *and* a[mid + 1..last].

beginHalf1 = first
endHalf1 = mid
beginHalf2 = mid + 1
endHalf2 = last

// *While both subarrays are not empty, compare the first entry in one subarray with*
// *the first entry in the other; then copy the smaller entry into the temporary array*

```
index = 0 // next available location in tempArray
while ( (beginHalf1 <= endHalf1) and (beginHalf2 <= endHalf2) )
{
   if (a[beginHalf1] < a[beginHalf2])
   {
      tempArray[index] = a[beginHalf1]
      beginHalf1++
   }
   else
   {
      tempArray[index] = a[beginHalf2]
      beginHalf2++
   }
   index++
}
// Assertion: One subarray has been completely copied to tempArray.
```

Copy remaining entries from other subarray to tempArray
Copy entries from tempArray *to array* a

Question 10 What entries are compared two at a time, and in which order, when the following two sorted arrays are merged into one sorted array?

0 2 4 8 9
1 5 7

25.17 **Tracing the steps in the algorithm.** Let's examine what happens when we invoke mergeSort on the array halves. Figure 25-4 shows that mergeSort divides an array into two halves and then recursively divides each of those halves into two halves until each half contains only one element. At this point in the algorithm, the merge steps begin. Pairs of one-element subarrays are merged to form two-element subarrays. Pairs of two-element subarrays are merged to form four-element subarrays, and so on. Remember that each merge step copies entries from one array to another and finally back again.

The numbers on the arrows in the figure indicate the order in which the recursive calls and the merges occur. Notice that the first merge occurs after four recursive calls to mergeSort and before

FIGURE 25-4   The effect of the recursive calls and the merges during a merge sort

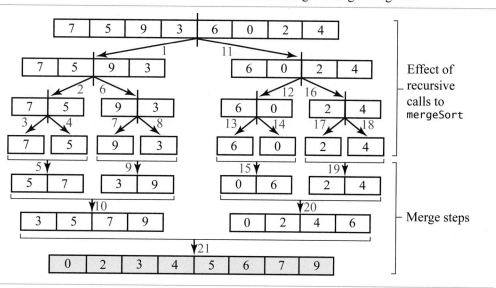

other recursive calls to mergeSort. Thus, the recursive calls to mergeSort are interwoven with calls to merge. The actual sorting takes place during the merge steps and not during the recursive calls.

Note: Merge sort rearranges the entries in an array during its merge steps.

Question 11 Trace the steps that a merge sort takes when sorting the following array into ascending order: 9 6 2 4 8 7 5 3.

A Merge-Sort Method

25.18   Although the implementation of the recursive mergesort is straightforward, a pitfall awaits us. Since a second but temporary array is an implementation detail in the merge step, we might be tempted to hide this array's allocation within the method merge. But doing so would allocate and initialize the temporary array many times, because merge is called each time mergesort is called recursively. To avoid this excessive execution time, we can allocate the temporary array in the following public version of mergesort and pass it to a private method, sort, that implements the pseudocode given previously:

```java
public static void mergeSort(String[] a, int first, int last)
{
   String[] tempArray = new String[a.length];
   sort(a, tempArray, first, last);
} // end mergeSort
```

Listing 25-4 shows the details of a Java implementation of a merge sort. You can test the method mergeSort by using a program analogous to the one given in Listing 23-3 of Chapter 23 for a selection sort of integers.

LISTING 25-4   A class containing the static method mergeSort

```java
/** A class of static methods for recursively sorting an array
    of strings into ascending order.
    @author Frank M. Carrano
*/
public class StringSorter
{
   /** Sorts an array into ascending order using a merge sort.
       @param a  an array of strings */
   public static void mergeSort(String[] a)
   {
      mergeSort(a, 0, a.length - 1);
   } // end mergeSort

   /** Sorts an array segment into ascending order using a merge sort.
       @param a  an array of strings
```

```
          @param first  the index of the first string in the segment
          @param last   the index of the last string in the segment */
public static void mergeSort(String[] a, int first, int last)
{
   String[] tempArray = new String[a.length];
   sort(a, tempArray, first, last);
} // end mergeSort

// Sorts the array segment a[first..last] using a temporary
// array tempArray.
private static void sort(String[] a, String[] tempArray,
                         int first, int last)
{
   if (first < last)
   {
      // sort each half
      int mid = first + (last - first) / 2;  // index of midpoint
      sort(a, tempArray, first, mid);        // sort left half
      sort(a, tempArray, mid + 1, last);     // sort right half

      merge(a, tempArray, first, mid, last); // merge the halves
   } // end if
} // end sort

// Merges the sorted subarrays a[first..mid] and a[mid + 1..last]
// into tempArray.
private static void merge(String[] a, String[] tempArray,
                          int first, int mid, int last)
{
   // partition the array into two pieces
   int beginHalf1 = first;
   int endHalf1 = mid;
   int beginHalf2 = mid + 1;
   int endHalf2 = last;

   // while both subarrays are not empty, copy the smaller of
   // the subarrays' first entries into the temporary array
   int index = beginHalf1; // next available location in tempArray
   while ((beginHalf1 <= endHalf1) && (beginHalf2 <= endHalf2))
   {
      // Assertion: tempArray[beginHalf1..index - 1] is in order
      if (a[beginHalf1].compareTo(a[beginHalf2]) < 0)
      {
         tempArray[index] = a[beginHalf1];
         beginHalf1++;
      }
```

```
      else
      {
          tempArray[index] = a[beginHalf2];
          beginHalf2++;
      } // end if

      index++;
   } // end while

   // copy rest of nonempty subarray to the temporary array
   if (beginHalf1 > endHalf1) // if first subarray is empty
      System.arraycopy(a, beginHalf2, tempArray, index,
                          endHalf2 - beginHalf2 + 1);
   else
      System.arraycopy(a, beginHalf1, tempArray, index,
                          endHalf1 - beginHalf1 + 1);

   // copy the result into the original array
   System.arraycopy(tempArray, first, a, first, last - first + 1);
   } // end merge
} // end StringSorter
```

Question 12 If you changed the two recursive calls to sort within the private sort in Listing 25-4 to

```
sort(a, tempArray, first, mid - 1); // sort left half
sort(a, tempArray, mid, last);      // sort right half
```

what else, if anything, would you need to change to correctly sort the array?

Question 13 Imagine replacing the private method sort in Listing 25-4 with the following version:

```
private static void sort(String[] a, String[] tempArray, int first, int last)
{
   if (first < last)
   {
      // sort each half
      int mid = first + (last - first) / 2   // index of midpoint
      megeSort(a, first, mid);               // sort left half
      megeSort(a, mid + 1, last);            // sort right half
      merge(a, tempArray, first, mid, last); // merge the halves
   } // end if
} // end mergeSort
```

Notice that this method calls the public mergeSort method. Will the method sort an array? Explain.

Merge Sort in the Java Class Library

25.19 As you learned in Segment 23.16 of Chapter 23, the class Arrays in the package java.util defines several versions of a static method sort to sort an array into ascending order. For an array of objects, sort uses a recursive merge sort. This version of merge sort, however, skips the merge step if none of the entries in the left half of the array are greater than the entries in the right half. Since both halves are sorted already, the merge step is unnecessary in this case.

Question 14 What change to the merge sort given in Listing 25-4 is necessary to skip any unnecessary merges, as just described?

Note: The time complexity of merge sort

Merge sort is $O(n \times \log n)$ in the worst, best, and average cases, regardless of the initial order of the array. Merge sort is much faster on average than either a selection sort or an insertion sort. A disadvantage of merge sort is the need for a temporary array during the merge step.

Note: Quick sort

Quick sort is another algorithm that sorts in $O(n \times \log n)$ time in the average case without a second array. In fact, the static method sort in the class Arrays of the Java Class Library uses a recursive quick sort when sorting arrays of primitive values. Theoretically, quick sort's worst-case behavior is $O(n^2)$ and occurs when the array is already sorted. Even a nearly sorted array causes problems for a quick sort. Fortunately, implementations of this sort take steps to avoid this degradation in performance. Although the details of a quick sort are beyond our present scope, you likely will study it in a future course.

The Performance of Merge Sort (Optional)

This section will show why merge sort is an $O(n \times \log n)$ algorithm.

25.20   Assume for now that n—the number of entries in the array—is a power of 2, so that we can divide n by 2 evenly. Such is the case for the array in Figure 25-4, which contains eight entries. The initial call to the private method sort makes two recursive calls to sort, dividing the array into two subarrays of $n / 2$, or 4, elements each. Each of the two recursive calls to sort makes two recursive calls to sort, dividing the two subarrays into four subarrays of $n / 2^2$, or 2, elements each. Finally, recursive calls to sort divide the four subarrays into eight subarrays of $n / 2^3$, or 1, element each. It takes three levels of recursive calls to obtain subarrays of one element each. Notice that the original array contained 2^3 entries. The exponent 3 is the number of levels of recursive calls. In general, if n is 2^k, k levels of recursive calls occur.

Now consider the merge steps, because that is where the real work occurs. The merge step makes at most $n - 1$ comparisons among the n entries in the two subarrays. Figure 25-5 provides an example of a merge that requires $n - 1$ comparisons, while earlier, Figure 25-2 gave an example in which fewer than $n - 1$ comparisons occur. Each merge also requires n moves to a temporary array and n moves back to the original array. In total, each merge requires at most $3n - 1$ operations.

FIGURE 25-5   A worst-case merge of two sorted arrays

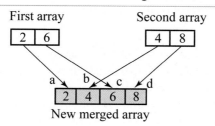

a. $2 < 4$, so copy 2 to new array

b. $6 > 4$, so copy 4 to new array

c. $6 < 8$, so copy 6 to new array

d. Copy 8 to new array

25.21   Each call to sort calls merge once. The merge operation associated with the first call to sort requires at most $3 \times n - 1$ operations. It is O(n). An example of this merge appears as step 21 in Figure 25-4. The two recursive calls to sort result in two more calls to merge. Each call merges $n / 2$ elements in at most $(3 \times n) / 2 - 1$ operations. The two merges together then require at most $3 \times n - 2$ operations. They are O(n). The next level of recursion involves 2^2 calls to sort, resulting in four calls to merge. Each call to merge merges $n / 2^2$ elements in at most $(3 \times n) / 2^2 - 1$ operations. Together these four merges use at most $3 \times n - 2^2$ operations, and so they are O(n).

If n is 2^k, the k levels of recursive calls to sort result in k levels of merges. The merges at each level are O(n). Since k is $\log_2 n$, sort is O($n \times \log n$). If n is not a power of 2, we can find an integer k so that $2^{k-1} < n < 2^k$. For example, when n is 15, k is 4. Thus,

$$k - 1 < \log_2 n < k$$

If we round $\log_2 n$ up, we will get k. Therefore, merge sort is O($n \times \log n$) in this case as well. Notice that the merge steps are O(n) regardless of the initial order of the array. Merge sort is then O($n \times \log n$) in the worst, best, and average cases.

▪ Recursion Versus Iteration

As we did in the previous chapter, let's compare recursion and iteration, but this time with respect to the binary search and the merge sort.

Binary Search

25.22   Chapter 23 introduced the binary search and defined the Java method binarySearch, which used a loop in its implementation. We learned that a binary search is faster in general than a linear search when the array is already sorted. Earlier in this chapter, however, we realized that this search algorithm has a recursive formulation, so we examined a recursive definition of the method binarySearch. Which version should we use?

Both versions of binarySearch make the same comparisons while searching for the target. In fact, each method is O($\log n$) in the average case. Thus, execution time should not be a major concern when choosing a version of a binary search. Let's consider the search's memory needs.

25.23   We know that a recursive method can use more memory than an iterative method, because each recursive call generates an activation record. A binary search makes a recursive call when it divides the array in half, which is when it compares the target to an array entry. As Segment 23.39 in Chapter 23 shows, the binary search compares the target to at most $\lceil \log_2 n \rceil$ array entries. Thus, a recursive binary search makes at most $\lceil \log_2 n \rceil$ recursive calls and generates at most $\lceil \log_2 n \rceil$ activation records.

For small arrays—when n is small—the number of activation records generated by a recursive binary search is insignificant. The same is true for an array of one million items, where at most 20 activation records would be generated. The memory requirements of a recursive binary search are a possible concern only for exceptionally large arrays.

Note: The algorithm for a binary search is naturally recursive. The recursive definition of binarySearch is shorter than its iterative counterpart, easier to understand, and easier to write correctly. However, the iterative version is not horrendous. If you have access to both versions, use whichever one you choose. If you were to write your own method, you likely would find the recursive approach easier.

Merge Sort

25.24   The algorithm for merge sort also is naturally recursive. Thus, implementing the recursive merge sort is easy once we have developed the details of merging two sorted arrays. Defining an iterative merge sort is not as simple.

Let's first make some observations about the recursive solution. The recursive calls simply divide the array into *n* one-element subarrays, as you saw in Figure 25-4. Although we do not need recursion to isolate the entries in an array, the recursion controls the merging process. To replace the recursion with iteration, we will need to control the merges. Such an algorithm will need less memory space and execution time than the recursive algorithm, since it will eliminate the recursive calls and, therefore, the stack of activation records. But an iterative merge sort will be trickier to code without error.

25.25   Basically, an iterative merge sort starts at the beginning of the array and merges pairs of individual elements to form two-element subarrays. Then it returns to the beginning of the array and merges pairs of the two-element subarrays to form four-element subarrays, and so on. After merging all pairs of subarrays of a particular length, if no entries are left over, the array is sorted and we are done. However, we might have elements left over. If so, they will have one of the following forms:

- One full subarray and a partial second subarray
- One full subarray only
- One partial subarray

For the first case, we use the method merge to merge the two subarrays into one sorted subarray, which we leave in place. The result is like the other two cases: The leftovers are in one sorted subarray. We therefore treat these three situations in the same way by merging the subarray with the rest of the sorted array. In doing so, you can avoid some of the copying between a temporary array and the original array, thereby saving execution time during the merges. The implementation of an iterative merge sort requires more effort and care than a recursive one.

Note: The merge-sort algorithm is naturally recursive. Coding a recursive implementation is straightforward, with the merge method requiring the most work. An iterative solution is much trickier to code, as it must control the merging of pairs of subarrays and still requires the same merge method as a recursive solution. A carefully coded iterative solution can save some execution time as well as memory that otherwise would be allocated to activation records. However, the recursive merge sort remains a fine choice.

videonote
A problem
solved

CHAPTER SUMMARY

- A recursive method that processes an array often divides the array into two or more portions. Recursive calls to the method work on each of these array portions. Sometimes a portion might contain only one entry.

- A recursive method whose parameters require a client to have knowledge of a class's private fields should be private. Such a method can be called by a public method that passes the appropriate arguments to the private method, thereby hiding them from the client.

- A linear search can be performed recursively, but such a search has no advantage over an iterative version.

- A binary search is naturally recursive, so its recursive definition is easier to understand, and easier to write correctly, than its iterative counterpart. Moreover, this recursive method is practical to use.

- Merge sort is another algorithm that is stated recursively. Its recursive definition is much easier to write than an iterative version and is useful in practice.

- Merge sort is O($n \times \log n$) in the worst, best, and average cases, regardless of the initial order of the array. It is generally much faster than either a selection sort or an insertion sort, but it does require a temporary array during the merge step.

- Merge sort is an example of a divide-and-conquer algorithm. Such an algorithm divides a problem into two or more smaller but distinct problems, solves each new problem, and then combines their solutions to solve the original problem.

EXERCISES

1. Revise the recursive linear search, as given in Listing 25-1, to search an array of integers.

2. Revise the recursive binary search, as given in Listing 25-3, to search an array of integers.

3. Revise the recursive merge sort, as given in Listing 25-4, to sort an array of integers.

4. Write a static recursive method to count the number of occurrences of a given string in a one-dimensional array of strings.

5. Repeat the previous exercise for a two-dimensional array. *Hint*: Consider calling the method you wrote for a one-dimensional array.

6. Write a static recursive method to count the number of uppercase letters in a given string.

7. Write a static recursive method to count the number of occurrences of a specified character in a given string.

8. Write four different recursive methods that each compute the sum of integers in an array of integers. Model your methods after the displayArray methods given in Segments 25.2, 25.4, and 25.5 and described in Question 1.

9. Trace the actions of the method displayArray, as given in Segment 25.5, for the array 10 20 30 40 50.

10. Trace the actions of the method binarySearch, as given in Listing 25-3, as it searches the array 20 30 40 50 60 70 80 90 for the following:

    a. 10
    b. 45
    c. 60

11. Write a recursive method that returns the smallest integer in an array of integers. If you divide the array into two pieces—halves, for example—and find the smallest integer in each of the two pieces, the smallest integer in the entire array will be the smaller of the these two integers. Since you will be searching a portion of the array—for example, the elements array[first] through array[last]—give your method three parameters: the array and the two indices first and last. *Hint*: Study the method displayArray given in Segment 25.5.

12. Write a program to demonstrate mergeSort in the class StringSorter, as given in Listing 25-4. Model your program after the one given in Listing 23-3 of Chapter 23 for a selection sort of integers.

13. If n is a positive integer in Java, n % b is the rightmost digit in the base b representation of n. Moreover, n / b is the value of the integer after dropping the rightmost digit of n. Write a recursive method that displays a positive integer in a given base between 2 and 10.

14. Spilling a dark liquid on a white tablecloth causes a stain. Let's divide the tablecloth into a rectangular arrangement of square *cells*, such as the following one:

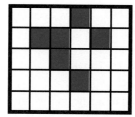

The blue cells represent the stain. We want to know the stain's size, that is, how many blue cells are connected to one another either on their edges or at their corners. For example, the stain shown here is of size 6.

Given the location of a cell in the stain, recursively determine the stain's size. Use a two-dimensional array to represent the cells. Each cell can be either blue or white and has either been counted or not.

15. After examining and rejecting the middle entry in an array, the binary search algorithm continues its search by dividing the array into two pieces and then ignoring one of the pieces. Create an analogous recursive search method that divides the array into three pieces after examining two entries and failing to locate the desired target.

PROJECTS

1. Create an unsorted array of 50,000 random integers that are in the range from 1 to 10,000. Sort this array using the method `Arrays.sort`. Create a second array of 1000 integers randomly selected from the sorted array. Search the sorted array for each integer in the second array, using an iterative linear search, a recursive linear search, an iterative binary search, and a recursive binary search. Using the technique described in Project 2 of Chapter 23, calculate the total execution time of the 1000 searches for each searching method. What, if anything, are you able to conclude?

2. Repeat Project 2 of Chapter 23, but include the recursive merge sort. Comment on the relative speeds of the three sorting algorithms.

3. Project 1 in Chapter 23 asked you to modify either selection sort or insertion sort to sort an array of Student objects according to the identification numbers of the students. Define another method that sorts the array of students using the recursive merge-sort algorithm. Then repeat the previous project, using Student objects instead of integers. Generate random identification numbers for the students.

4. Imagine an array of *n* items from which you can choose. You will place the items you choose into a backpack of size *k*. Each item has a size and a value. Of course, you cannot take more items than you have space for in the backpack. Your goal is to maximize the total value of the items you take.

   Design a recursive algorithm maxBackpack to solve this backpack problem. The parameters to the algorithm are the backpack, the array of items, and the position within the array of the next item to consider. The algorithm chooses the items for the backpack and returns a backpack containing the chosen items. *Hint*: If all items in the array have not been considered, retrieve the next item in the array. You can either ignore the item or, if it fits, put it in the backpack. To decide, make a recursive call for each of these two cases. Compare the backpacks returned by these calls to see which one has the most valuable contents. Then return that backpack.

   Design and implement the classes BackpackItem and Backpack. A backpack can report its size, its contents, the total value of its contents, and the overall size of its contents. Then write a program that defines the method maxBackpack. The program should read the size of the backpack and then the size, value, and name of each available item. After displaying the available items, call maxBackpack. Then display the chosen items, their individual values, and their total value.

Test your program with a backpack of size 10 and the following available items:

Size	Value	Name
1	7000	vintage subway token
2	50000	gold coin
4	10000	treasure map
4	11000	tapestry
5	12000	computer science textbook
10	60000	glass vase

Note: You can use array lists instead of arrays in this project.

5. Consider a maze made up of a rectangular array of squares, such as the following one:

```
X X X X X X X X X X X X
    X         X X X X   X
X X       X         X   X
X X   X X   X   X   X   X
X X     X       X       X
X X   X X X X
X X X X X X X X X X X X
```

The Xs represent a blocked square and form the walls of the maze. Let's consider mazes that have only one entrance and one exit on opposite sides of the maze, as in our example. Beginning at the entrance at the top left side of the maze, find a path to the exit at the bottom right side. You can move only up, down, left, or right.

Each square in the maze can be in one of four states: clear, blocked, path, or visited. Initially, each square is either clear or blocked. If a square lies on a successful path, mark it with a period. If you enter a square but it does not lead to a successful path, mark the square as visited.

Let a two-dimensional array represent the maze. Use a recursive algorithm to find a path through the maze. Some mazes might have more than one successful path, while others have no path.

ANSWERS TO SELF-TEST QUESTIONS

1.
```java
public static void displayArray(int[] array, int first, int last)
{
   if (first == last)
      System.out.print(array[first] + " ");
   else
   {
      int mid = first + (last - first) / 2;
      displayArray(array, first, mid - 1); // display first half
      System.out.print(array[mid] + " ");  // display middle entry
      displayArray(array, mid + 1, last);  // display second half
   } // end if
} // end displayArray
```

2. The following algorithm begins a search of an array at the array's last entry:

Algorithm linearSearch(target, a, first, last)

```
if (first > last)
   return -1
else if (target equals a[last])
   return last
else
   return linearSearch(target, a, first, last - 1)
```

3. A correct but awkward algorithm follows:

Algorithm linearSearch(target, a, first, last)

```
if (first == last)
   if (target equals a[first])
      return first
   else
      return -1
else if (target equals a[first])
   return first
else
   return linearSearch(target, a, first + 1, last)
```

This pseudocode can be simplified as follows:

Algorithm linearSearch(target, a, first, last)

```
if (target equals a[first])
   return first
else if (first == last)
   return -1
else
   return linearSearch(target, a, first + 1, last)
```

4. The following algorithm searches a sorted array:

Algorithm linearSearch(target, a, first, last)

```
if (first > last)
   return -1
else if (target equals a[first])
   return first
else if (target > a[first])
   return linearSearch(target, a, first + 1, last)
else
   return -1
```

5. They are the same. Searching for 8 requires seven comparisons; searching for 16 requires eight comparisons.

6. Yes. Revise the public method as follows:

```
public static boolean binarySearch(String target, String[] strings)
{
   return binarySearch(target, strings, 0, strings.length - 1) > -1;
} // end binarySearch
```

7. In the public method, change its return type from int to boolean. Revise the private method as follows: Change the return type of the method, as well as the type of the variable result, from int to boolean. In the first two assignments to result, change -1 to false and change mid to true.

8. In the second else if of the algorithm given in Segment 25.11, change < to >.

9. No. A binary search requires a sorted array. The array in our implementation of a bag is not sorted, since a bag does not order its entries.

10. 0:1, 2:1, 2:5, 4:5, 8:5, 8:7

11.

```
        9 6 2 4 8 7 5 3
     9 6 2 4          8 7 5 3
   9 6     2 4     8 7     5 3
  9   6   2   4   8   7   5   3
   6 9     2 4     7 8     3 5
     2 4 6 9          3 5 7 8
        2 3 4 5 6 7 8 9
```

12. Since you would be sorting each of the subarrays a[first..mid - 1] and a[mid..last], the method merge must merge the same subarrays. Currently, it merges the subarrays a[first..mid] and a[mid + 1..last]. To change merge, you would initialize endHalf1 to mid - 1 instead of mid, and initialize beginHalf2 to mid instead of mid + 1.

13. Yes. The recursion is now indirect. However, each time the public mergeSort executes, it allocates a new temporary array before invoking the private method sort. These extra steps waste time.

14. In the private method sort, the merge step is not necessary if the last entry in the first half of the array (that is, a[mid]) is less than or equal to a[mid + 1] (that is, the first entry in the second half of the array). We can test for this case by placing the call to merge in an if statement, as follows:

```
if (a[mid].compareTo(a[mid + 1]) > 0)
    merge(a, tempArray, first, mid, last); // merge the two halves
// else skip the merge step
```

Chapter

26

Recursive Drawings

Contents

Prerequisites

Objectives

After studying this chapter, you should be able to
• Write an application that uses recursion to display a drawing
• Identify when a problem has a natural recursive solution

Producing graphical output can be an enjoyable way to practice recursion. Certain drawings, such as those of fractals, allow us to visually appreciate the effect of recursion. It is in this spirit that we approach the problems set forth in this chapter. We hope they will inspire you to create your own recursive drawings or those suggested by the exercises and projects at the end of this chapter.

We begin with a simple drawing that is easily produced either iteratively or recursively. Both approaches are reasonable, and although most programmers would choose the iterative solution, the problem affords us a simple way to hone our skills in using recursion. The subsequent problems, which might seem impossible to solve using iterative techniques, have straighforward recursive solutions, as you will see.

A Problem Solved: The Target

> Create a class of bull's-eye targets. Each target should be composed of concentric circular bands of alternating colors.

26.1   Figure 26-1 shows an example of a target like the ones we want to create. Although the proposed class—let's call it `Target`—is not complex, we should begin by writing some notes about its characteristics. The CRC card given in Figure 26-2 shows the behaviors, or responsibilities, we assign to a target, along with the supporting classes we will need. But we also should think about the class's data fields. A target needs the coordinates of its center, a radius, the number of bands, and two colors. Since we do not plan any mutator methods for `Target`, we can declare these fields to be final. Thus, our class can have the following fields:

```
private final int xCenter;
private final int yCenter;
private final int radius;
private final int bandCount;
private final Color firstColor;
private final Color secondColor;
```

FIGURE 26-1   A bull's-eye target

FIGURE 26-2   A CRC card for the proposed class `Target`

Target
Responsibilities
Construct a specific target
Display the target
Get the target's center point
Get the target's radius
Collaborations
Graphics, Color, Point

26.2   Do we want the client to provide the number of bands, or should the constructor compute this number based on the target's radius? Arbitrarily, let's choose the latter approach. We can specify a fixed width for each band and use it along with the radius to calculate the number of bands. If we count the center bull's-eye as a band, having an even number of bands will guarantee that the outermost band and the center bull's-eye will have different colors. Thus, if we define BAND_WIDTH as a named constant, the constructor can contain the following computation:

```
bandCount = radius / BAND_WIDTH;
if (bandCount % 2 != 0) // ensure that bandCount is even
   bandCount++;
```

Of course, if bandCount is originally odd and we make it even, the bands will be thinner than BAND_WIDTH. Let's ignore that, since these decisions are hidden from and not made by the client.

Assuming the class's data fields, as given in the previous segment, the constructor can have the following definition:

```
/** Constructs a target with a given center and radius. */
public Target(Point center, int outerRadius, Color outerColor,
              Color bullseyeColor)
{
   xCenter = (int)center.getX();
   yCenter = (int)center.getY();
   radius = outerRadius;

   bandCount = radius / BAND_WIDTH;
   if (bandCount % 2 != 0) // ensure that bandCount is even
      bandCount++;

   firstColor = outerColor;
   secondColor = bullseyeColor;
} // end constructor
```

26.3   How shall we paint a target recursively? We could paint the innermost band and let the recursive call—our assistant—paint the rest of the target. That strategy would require that each band, like the one shown in Figure 26-3, be painted. This is more work for us than necessary.

FIGURE 26-3   One band of a bull's-eye target

Instead of painting bands, we will paint entire disks. For example, let's paint a disk the size of the target, as Figure 26-4 shows. Painting smaller and smaller disks in alternating colors on top of this one will give us the bands we want. This description sounds iterative, however, so let's try to think recursively: To paint a two-color target whose outer band is one color, we paint a disk in that color and then paint a smaller target that is centered within the disk and whose outer band is the other color. When do we stop? When we have painted the desired number of bands.

Realize that beginning with the smallest disk will not work. Imagine painting a blue disk as the target's bull's-eye and then painting a larger white disk on top of it. The blue disk would no longer be visible.

FIGURE 26-4   A disk the size of a target

 Note: To paint a target, we paint a disk the size of the entire target and then paint a smaller target centered at the center of the larger one. Thus, the solution to the target problem performs one part of the drawing and uses recursion to solve the rest.

26.4   As is often the case when using recursion, Target's public method display calls a private recursive method to perform the actual drawing. This private method, paintTarget, has the following definition:

```java
private void paintTarget(int outerRadius, int numberOfBands, Graphics pen)
{
   if (numberOfBands > 0)
   {
      paintDisk(outerRadius, nextColor(numberOfBands), pen);
      paintTarget(outerRadius - BAND_WIDTH, numberOfBands - 1, pen);
   } // end if
} // end paintTarget
```

The method paintDisk is another private method that paints a disk of a given radius and color. This disk serves as the target's outer band. To alternate colors, we call the private method nextColor. It simply returns one of two colors according to whether an integer is even or odd. The parameter numberOfBands serves as this integer.

The recursive call to paintTarget must both decrease the radius of the inner target to be painted and decrement the number of bands. Decreasing the radius by BAND_WIDTH at each recursive call will cause the bands to have the same thickness. But because we force the number of bands to be even, the center bull's-eye might be larger than we would like. The version of paintTarget shown in Listing 26-1 uses a radius of outerRadius − outerRadius / numberOfBands instead of outerRadius − BAND_WIDTH. This version results in a smaller bull's-eye at the risk of slightly unequal bands. The choice is a matter of preference and is not relevant to the recursion.

LISTING 26-1   The class Target

```java
/** Target.java by F. M. Carrano
    Represents a bull's-eye target of concentric
    circular bands of alternating colors.
*/
```

```java
import java.awt.Color;
import java.awt.Graphics;
import java.awt.Point;
public class Target
{
    private final int xCenter;
    private final int yCenter;
    private final int radius;
    private final int bandCount;
    private final Color firstColor;
    private final Color secondColor;
    private static final int BAND_WIDTH = 15;

    /** Constructs a target with a given center and radius. */
    public Target(Point center, int outerRadius, Color outerColor,
                  Color bullseyeColor)
    {
        xCenter = (int)center.getX();
        yCenter = (int)center.getY();
        radius = outerRadius;

        bandCount = radius / BAND_WIDTH;
        if (bandCount % 2 != 0) // ensure that bandCount is even
            bandCount++;

        firstColor = outerColor;
        secondColor = bullseyeColor;
    } // end constructor

    /** Displays the target. */
    public void display(Graphics pen)
    {
        paintTarget(radius, bandCount, pen);
    } // end display

    // Paints a target having a given outer radius and number of bands.
    private void paintTarget(int outerRadius, int numberOfBands,
                             Graphics pen)
    {
        if (numberOfBands > 0)
        {
            paintDisk(outerRadius, nextColor(numberOfBands), pen);
            paintTarget(outerRadius - outerRadius / numberOfBands,
                        numberOfBands - 1, pen);
        } // end if
    } // end paintTarget
```

```
// Paints a circular area having a given radius and color.
private void paintDisk(int radius, Color circleColor, Graphics pen)
{
   pen.setColor(circleColor);
   int diameter = 2 * radius;
   pen.fillOval(xCenter - radius, yCenter - radius, diameter,
                diameter);
} // end paintDisk

// Returns one of two colors according to a given positive integer.
private Color nextColor(int integer)
{
   Color result = secondColor; // assume integer is odd
   if (integer % 2 == 0)
      result = firstColor;      // integer is even

   return result;
} // end nextColor

/** Gets the target's center.
    @return a point whose coordinates equal those of the target's
            center */
public Point getCenter()
{
   return new Point(xCenter, yCenter);
} // end getCenter

/** Gets the target's radius.
    @return an integer equal to the target's radius */
public int getRadius()
{
   return radius;
} // end getRadius
} // end Target
```

26.5   The panel and driver for our class Target are uneventful but are given in Listings 26-2 and 26-3.

LISTING 26-2   The class TargetPanel

```
/** TargetPanel.java by F. M. Carrano
*/
import javax.swing.JPanel;
import java.awt.Color;
import java.awt.Dimension;
import java.awt.Graphics;
import java.awt.Point;
```

```java
public class TargetPanel extends JPanel
{
   private static final int PANEL_SIDE = 300;
   private final Target myTarget;

   public TargetPanel()
   {
      setPreferredSize(new Dimension(PANEL_SIDE, PANEL_SIDE));
      int center = PANEL_SIDE / 2;
      myTarget = new Target(new Point(center, center), 100,
                            Color.BLUE, Color.WHITE);
   } // end default constructor

   public void paintComponent(Graphics pen)
   {
      myTarget.display(pen);
   } // end paintComponent
} // end TargetPanel
```

LISTING 26-3   A driver for `TargetPanel`

```java
/** TargetDriver.java by F. M. Carrano
*/
import javax.swing.JFrame;

public class TargetDriver
{
   public static void main(String[] args)
   {
      JFrame window = new JFrame();
      window.setDefaultCloseOperation(JFrame.EXIT_ON_CLOSE);
      window.setTitle("Bull's-Eye Target");

      TargetPanel panel = new TargetPanel();
      window.add(panel);
      window.pack();
      window.setVisible(true);
   } // end main
} // end TargetDriver
```

videonote
Using recursion
when drawing

Output

Question 1 What base case does `paintTarget` use?

Question 2 Is it possible to change `paintTarget`'s base case to one band? If so, make the change. If not, explain why not.

Question 3 Is it possible to make `paintTarget` iterative instead of recursive? If so, make the change. If not, explain why not.

Question 4 How does a recursive `paintTarget` compare to an iterative version with respect to programming difficulty and efficiency of execution?

■ A Problem Solved: Painting Like Mondrian

> Piet Mondrian was a Dutch painter who was born in the Netherlands in 1872 and died in New York City in 1944. At one point in his career, his paintings were made up of rectangular areas of red, yellow, blue, or black, separated by thick black straight lines, all on a white field. In fact, paintings in this group usually have large areas of white. Create a class that represents drawings in the style of Mondrian.

26.6 Figure 26.7 shows a print of Mondrian's *Composition with Red Blue Yellow*. Mimicking his style can involve random selections of color and randomly placed black lines of random thicknesses. Of course, we must set some constraints to avoid a totally ugly painting! So let's plan our strategy.

FIGURE 26-5   *Composition with Red Blue Yellow* by Piet Mondrian

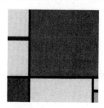

To "paint a Mondrian," we can fill the entire area with a random color selected from among red, blue, yellow, and white. We then divide the area into two pieces by drawing a randomly placed horizontal or vertical line. The next step is to recursively paint a Mondrian in each of these two pieces. If a piece is smaller than a certain size, we'll do nothing. That's the base case.

Describing our strategy in pseudocode gives us the following algorithm:

Algorithm `paintMondrian`(*a rectangular area*)

if (*the area exceeds a given minimum*)
{
    Choose a color at random from a selection of colors
    Paint the area in the chosen color
    At random, draw either a horizontal or vertical line at a random position across
       the entire area
    if (*a horizontal line was drawn*)
    {
        `paintMondrian`(*the upper portion of the area*)
        `paintMondrian`(*the lower portion of the area*)
    }
}

```
        else // a vertical line was drawn
        {
            paintMondrian(the left portion of the area)
            paintMondrian(the right portion of the area)
        }
    }
```

 Note: The solution to the Mondrian problem divides the painting into two pieces and uses recursion on each piece.

26.7   If we were to implement this algorithm in Java, the paintings would contain many lines and few white spaces. Mondrian's paintings were simpler and often had few areas of color. We can adjust the algorithm during its implementation to achieve more realistic results by biasing the color selection toward white and by randomly omitting some of the divisions and their associated lines. Listing 26-4 contains a class Mondrian whose definition makes these adjustments. Let's examine its details.

LISTING 26-4   The class Mondrian

```java
/** Mondrian.java by F. M. Carrano
    Represents a rectangular painting in the style of Mondrian.
*/
import java.awt.Color;
import java.awt.Graphics;
import java.awt.Point;
import java.util.Random;

public class Mondrian
{
    private final int xCorner;
    private final int yCorner;
    private final int width;
    private final int height;
    private final Random generator;
    private static final Color[] COLORS =
                            {Color.RED, Color.BLUE, Color.YELLOW};

    /** Constructs a painting having a given position and size.
    */
    public Mondrian(Point canvasCorner, int canvasWidth, int canvasHeight)
    {
        xCorner = (int)canvasCorner.getX();
        yCorner = (int)canvasCorner.getY();
        width = canvasWidth;
        height = canvasHeight;
        generator = new Random();
    } // end constructor
```

```java
/** Displays the painting. */
public void display(Graphics pen)
{
   paintMondrian(xCorner, yCorner, width, height, pen);
} // end display

private void paintMondrian(int left, int top, int width, int height,
                           Graphics pen)
{
   if ( (width > 25) && (height > 25) )
   {
      pen.setColor(getRandomColor());
      pen.fillRect(left, top, width, height);

      // at random, divide the canvas by either a horizontal line
      // or a vertical line, or do nothing; each line has a random
      // position and thickness
      switch (generator.nextInt(3))
      {
         case 0: // horizontal line
            int topHeight = generator.nextInt(height);
            paintMondrian(left, top, width, topHeight, pen); // above
            paintMondrian(left, top + topHeight,
                          width, height - topHeight, pen);   // below
            drawHorizontalLine(left, top + topHeight, width, pen);
            break;
         case 1: // vertical line
            int leftWidth = generator.nextInt(width);
            paintMondrian(left, top, leftWidth, height, pen); // left
            paintMondrian(left + leftWidth, top,
                          width - leftWidth, height, pen);     // right
            drawVerticalLine(left + leftWidth, top, height, pen);
            break;
         case 2: // do nothing
            break;
      } // end switch
   } // end if
   // else base case: canvas is too small to continue
} // end paintMondrian

// Returns either Color.WHITE or a color chosen at random from
// the array COLORS. WHITE is returned about 50% of the time.
private Color getRandomColor()
{
   Color randomColor;
   if (generator.nextInt(2) == 0)
```

```
        {
            int randomIndex = generator.nextInt(COLORS.length);
            // randomIndex >= 0 and < colors.length
            randomColor = COLORS[randomIndex];
        }
        else
            randomColor = Color.WHITE;

        return randomColor;
    } // end getRandomColor

    // Draws a horizontal black line at a given position with a given
    // length and random thickness.
    private void drawHorizontalLine(int left, int top, int length,
                                    Graphics pen)
    {
        int thickness = generator.nextInt(4) + 1; // 1, 2, 3, or 4 pixels
        pen.setColor(Color.BLACK);
        pen.fillRect(left, top, length, thickness);
    } // end drawHorizontalLine

    // Draws a vertical black line at a given position with a given
    // length and random thickness.
    private void drawVerticalLine(int left, int top, int length,
                                  Graphics pen)
    {
        int thickness = generator.nextInt(4) + 1; // 1, 2, 3, or 4 pixels
        pen.setColor(Color.BLACK);
        pen.fillRect(left, top, thickness, length);
    } // end drawVerticalLine
} // end Mondrian
```

26.8   Four data fields of the class Mondrian position the drawing and give its dimensions. Another field is an instance of the class Random for the random numbers we will need. The constructor gives values to these fields, which are declared as final. The only other public method is display, which calls the private, recursive method paintMondrian. This private method implements the algorithm given earlier in Segment 26.6, but with a few adjustments.

To decide whether to draw a horizontal line or a vertical one, we generate a random integer. To reduce the number of times the painting area is divided by a line, we introduce a third choice—do nothing. These three possibilities are the cases in a switch statement that examines the random integer.

If we were to draw a black line before the recursive calls to paintMondrian, we would need to be careful not to paint over the line. A simpler approach is to draw the line after the recursive calls, and that is what we have done here.

The method `paintMondrian` also calls the private method `getRandomColor`, which randomly chooses a color. However, we bias the color selection toward white. About one-half of the calls to `getRandomColor` result in white, while the other ones result in a color chosen at random from the array `COLORS`. The remaining private methods in the class draw the horizontal and vertical lines. To add black to the paintings, we draw lines of random thickness. To achieve these lines, we use the method `fillRect` instead of `drawLine`, passing it a random thickness of between one and four pixels.

Question 5 Is it possible to make `paintMondrian` iterative instead of recursive? Explain.

Question 6 What changes to `paintMondrian` would be necessary to draw the vertical or horizontal line before the two recursive calls instead of after?

26.9   As before, the panel and driver for the class `Mondrian` are like others we have written; they are given in Listings 26-5 and 26-6. A sample painting created by the class `Mondrian` is included in Listing 26-6.

LISTING 26-5   The class `MondrianPanel`

```java
/** MondrianPanel.java by F. M. Carrano
*/
import javax.swing.JPanel;
import java.awt.Dimension;
import java.awt.Graphics;
import java.awt.Point;

public class MondrianPanel extends JPanel
{
   private static final int PANEL_SIDE = 300;
   private final Mondrian painting;

   public MondrianPanel()
   {
      painting = new Mondrian(new Point(0, 0), 300, 300);
      setPreferredSize(new Dimension(PANEL_SIDE, PANEL_SIDE));
   } // end default constructor

   public void paintComponent(Graphics pen)
   {
      painting.display(pen);
   } // end paintComponent
} // end MondrianPanel
```

LISTING 26-6   A driver for `MondrianPanel`

```java
/** MondrianDriver.java by F. M. Carrano
*/
import javax.swing.JFrame;
```

```
public class MondrianDriver
{
    public static void main(String[] args)
    {
        JFrame window = new JFrame();
        window.setDefaultCloseOperation(JFrame.EXIT_ON_CLOSE);
        window.setTitle("In the style of Mondrian");

        MondrianPanel panel = new MondrianPanel();
        window.add(panel);
        window.pack();
        window.setVisible(true);
    } // end main
} // end MondrianDriver
```

Sample Output

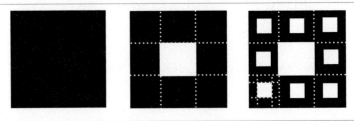

■ A Problem Solved: The Sierpinski Carpet

> Beginning with a square area, divide it into nine equal subsquares with two vertical lines and two horizontal lines, like those used for the game tic-tac-toe. Remove the center square. Repeat the process recursively on each of the remaining eight subsquares. Design a class that represents the result, which is known as a *Sierpinski carpet*.

26.10   The Sierpinski carpet is named after its inventor, Waclaw Sierpinski (1882–1969), a Polish mathematician who first described the configuration in 1916. It is a kind of *fractal*, which is a shape whose parts are smaller versions of the whole shape.

Figure 26-6 illustrates the first steps in the construction of a Sierpinski carpet. Rather than removing squares, we can paint square white areas. We begin with a square black area and then paint a smaller white square at the black square's center. The side of the white square is one-third the length of the black square's side. Imaginary extensions of the sides of the white square outline eight smaller black squares. We then repeat the entire process recursively on each of these black squares.

FIGURE 26-6   The initial steps in the construction of a Sierpinski carpet

> **Note:** Painting a Sierpinski carpet is similar to our solution to the Mondrian problem: We paint an area, divide it into smaller pieces, and recursively paint a Sierpinski carpet in each of these smaller pieces.

videonote
More about
recursive drawing

26.11   Listing 26-7 contains our class of Sierpinski carpets. Its data fields and constructor are straightforward. As in our earlier examples, a public method—display—invokes a private method to perform the recursion. The recursion continues until the side of the subsquares becomes too small to divide.

The steps taken by the recursive method are not complex. It paints a large black square and, at its center, a white square one-third the size of the black square. Eight recursive calls follow. The hardest part in writing these calls is providing the correct coordinates of the upper left corners of the smaller squares. Figure 26-7 shows these coordinates. Using extra local variables can help avoid some confusion. Note that since we are using integer arithmetic, the drawing is sensitive to the coordinates and dimensions of the carpet.

FIGURE 26-7   Key points for drawing a Sierpinski carpet and their coordinates

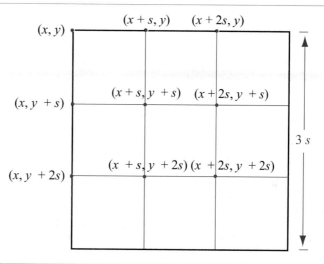

LISTING 26-7   A class of Sierpinski carpets

```java
/** Carpet.java by F. M. Carrano
    A class of Sierpinski carpets.
*/
import java.awt.Color;
import java.awt.Graphics;
import java.awt.Point;

public class Carpet
{
    private final int xCorner, yCorner; // upper left corner
    private final int carpetSide;

    public Carpet(Point corner, int side)
    {
```

```
            xCorner = (int)corner.getX();
            yCorner = (int)corner.getY();
            carpetSide = side;
        } // end constructor

        public void display(Graphics pen)
        {
            display(xCorner, yCorner, carpetSide, pen);
        } // end display

        private void display(int x, int y, int side, Graphics pen)
        {
            if (side > 3)
            {
                // paint large black square
                pen.setColor(Color.BLACK);
                pen.fillRect(x, y, side, side);

                // paint smaller white square at center
                side = side / 3;
                pen.setColor(Color.WHITE);
                pen.fillRect(x + side, y + side, side, side);

                // get key coordinates for black subsquares
                int xMiddle = x + side;
                int xRight = x + 2 * side;
                int yMiddle = y + side;
                int yBottom = y + 2 * side;

                // use recursion on each black subsquare
                display(x, y, side, pen);                 // top left
                display(xMiddle, y, side, pen);           // top middle
                display(xRight, y, side, pen);            // top right
                display(x, yMiddle, side, pen);           // middle left
                display(xRight, yMiddle, side, pen);      // middle right
                display(x, yBottom, side, pen);           // bottom left
                display(xMiddle, yBottom, side, pen);     // bottom middle
                display(xRight, yBottom, side, pen);      // bottom right
            } // end if
        } // end display
} // end Carpet
```

26.12   A panel and driver for the class Carpet are given in Listings 26-8 and 26-9, along with the driver's output.

LISTING 26-8   A panel for the class Carpet
```
/** CarpetPanel.java by F. M. Carrano
*/
import javax.swing.JPanel;
```

```java
import java.awt.Dimension;
import java.awt.Graphics;
import java.awt.Point;

public class CarpetPanel extends JPanel
{
   private static final int PANEL_SIDE = 300;
   private final Carpet aCarpet;

   public CarpetPanel()
   {
      setPreferredSize(new Dimension(PANEL_SIDE, PANEL_SIDE));
      aCarpet = new Carpet(new Point(0, 0), PANEL_SIDE);
   } // end default constructor

   public void paintComponent(Graphics pen)
   {
      aCarpet.display(pen);
   } // end paintComponent
} // end CarpetPanel
```

LISTING 26-9   A driver for `CarpetPanel` and its output

```java
/** CarpetDriver.java by F. M. Carrano
*/
import javax.swing.JFrame;
public class CarpetDriver
{
   public static void main(String[] args)
   {
      JFrame window = new JFrame();
      window.setDefaultCloseOperation(JFrame.EXIT_ON_CLOSE);
      window.setTitle("Sierpinski Carpet");

      CarpetPanel panel = new CarpetPanel();
      window.add(panel);
      window.pack();
      window.setVisible(true);
   } // end main
} // end CarpetDriver
```

Output

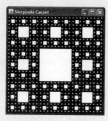

Question 7 Is it possible to make `Carpet`'s private method `display` iterative instead of recursive? Explain.

Question 8 If the first call to `Carpet`'s private method `display` is

```
display (x, y, 300, pen);
```

what are the first four recursive calls to the method?

Question 9 What recursive call occurs next?

Note: You have seen that you can draw involved patterns rather easily by using recursion. Our solutions, however, involve painting over already painted areas. While this technique makes our code easier to write, it requires more execution time. Since our drawings are small, any delay caused by an increase in execution time likely is not noticeable. However, this technique should be abandoned if the overpainting would cause a noticeable delay for the user. Our emphasis here is to look at techniques for recursion, not to find the most efficient approach. In practice, providing a user with rapidly drawn graphical output is an important consideration.

videonote
A problem
solved

CHAPTER SUMMARY

- A drawing of a bull's-eye target can be made recursively or iteratively with equal ease. The recursive solution paints a disk the size of the target and then paints a smaller target centered in this disk.

- The recursive solution to the target problem performs one part of the drawing and performs a recursive process on the rest. However, the drawing must proceed from the outermost band toward the center.

- Creating a painting in the style of the artist Mondrian can be accomplished recursively by dividing the canvas into two pieces and painting each piece in Mondrian's style.

- The Sierpinski carpet is an example of a fractal. Fractals are drawn most easily by using recursion.

- To draw a Sierpinski carpet recursively, you divide a black square into nine equal squares, paint the center square white, and draw Sierpinski carpets in each of the other eight squares.

EXERCISES

1. What base case is used by the private recursive method `paintMondrian` in Listing 26-4?

2. What base case is used by the private recursive method `display` in Listing 26-7 to draw a Sierpinski carpet?

3. The example at the beginning of Chapter 14 painted a circular disk, or dot, a random number of times in a row. Revise the solution given in that chapter to use recursion instead of iteration.

4. Repeat Exercise 8 in Chapter 14 to draw a pile of squares, but use recursion instead of iteration.

5. Repeat Exercise 12 in Chapter 14 to draw a conical shape, but use recursion instead of iteration.

6. Revise the class `Quahog`, as given in Listing 14-2 of Chapter 14, to use recursion instead of iteration when drawing the quahog shell.

7. Repeat Exercise 13 in Chapter 14 to draw a chessboard, but use recursion instead of iteration.

8. Write a program to draw the following recursive design:

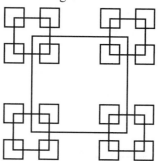

Begin with a square. Then draw a smaller square at and centered on each corner. Recursively repeat drawing smaller squares at the corners of squares until either a maximum number of recursive levels is reached or the squares become smaller than a predetermined size.

9. An *H tree* of order *n* is a recursive design based on the letter H. The following are H trees of orders 0, 1, and 2:

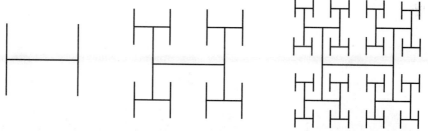

Each H is centered at a given point and consists of three line segments of equal length. Each H has a half-sized H centered on each of its four tips.
    Write a program to draw an H tree of order *n* using recursion.

10. Write a program to draw the following recursive design:

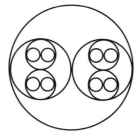

Beginning with a circle, you inscribe two circles whose diameters are one-half of the given circle's diameter and that are tangent to both the larger circle and to each other. An imaginary line joining the centers of the three circles is horizontal. You recursively repeat this process on each circle. At each successive level of the recursion, the imaginary line joining the inscribed circle centers alternates between horizontal and vertical.

11. A rectangle whose short side has length *s* is called a *golden rectangle* if the length of its long side is $s \times (1 + \sqrt{5}) / 2$. If you divide the rectangle into two pieces by drawing a line of length *s* to form an *s*-by-*s* square, the remaining piece will be a golden rectangle.

   Recursively subdivide a golden rectangle to form a design such as the following one:

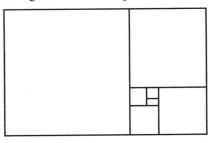

PROJECTS

1. A *Sierpinski triangle* is analogous to a Sierpinski carpet. To create one, you begin with an equilateral triangle. Connect the midpoints of the sides of the triangle to form four subtriangles, and remove the inner subtriangle. The result is a Level 1 Sierpinski triangle. Repeat the process on each of the remaining three subtriangles to get a Level 2 Sierpinski triangle, as follows:

Level 1   Level 2

   Theoretically, you could continue up to any level, but in practice you will reach a point where you will not be able to see additional triangles.

   Write a program that uses recursion to draw a level *n* Sierpinski triangle for any integer *n* between 1 and 7, inclusive, that the user specifies. The user must also provide the vertices and side length of the original outer triangle.

2. Repeat Project 1 in Chapter 14 to draw an optical illusion, but use recursion instead of iteration.

3. An *m-star* of order *n* consists of *m* line segments of equal lengths that begin at a common point, pass through the vertices of an *m*-sided regular polygon centered at the point, and end at the center of an *m*-star of order *n* − 1 whose line segments are shorter than those in the star of order *n*. An *m*-star of order 0 is empty. Note that *m* must be 3 or greater.

For example, a 5-star of order 3 appears as follows:

Write a recursive program that creates an m-star of order n. Continue the recursion until either a maximum number of recursive levels is reached or the line segments become too small. You can choose a fixed value of m, but for more of a challenge, let the user specify m.

4. One example of a fractal curve is the *Koch curve* introduced by the Swedish mathematician Helge von Koch in 1904. You can draw a Koch curve by beginning with a line segment and taking the following steps:

- Divide the line segment into three equal parts.
- Draw an equilateral triangle using the middle part as its base.
- Erase the middle part.

The result is

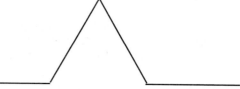

You then recursively apply the previous three steps to each of the four line segments. Koch curves display an intricate beauty as the number of recursive levels increases.

Write a recursive program that creates a Koch curve.

5. A figure even more remarkable than the Koch curve described in the previous project is the *Koch snowflake* or *Koch star*. You can create this snowflake by applying the three-step recursive process used to create a Koch curve to each side of an equilateral triangle rather than to only one line segment:

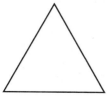  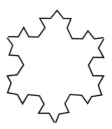

Write a recursive program that creates a Koch snowflake.

ANSWERS TO SELF-TEST QUESTIONS

1. When numberOfBands is zero, the method does nothing.

2. Yes.
```
    private void paintTarget(int outerRadius, int numberOfBands, Graphics pen)
    {
       paintDisk(outerRadius, nextColor(numberOfBands), pen);
       if (numberOfBands > 1)
          paintTarget(outerRadius - outerRadius / numberOfBands, numberOfBands - 1, pen);
    } // end paintTarget
```

3. Yes.
```
    private void paintTarget(int outerRadius, int numberOfBands, Graphics pen)
    {
       while (numberOfBands > 0)
       {
          paintDisk(outerRadius, nextColor(numberOfBands), pen);
          outerRadius = outerRadius - outerRadius / numberOfBands;
          numberOfBands--;
       } // end while
    } // end paintTarget
```

4. The programing effort for both the recursive and iterative versions of paintTarget is about the same. The choice in this regard is likely a matter of preference. Execution efficiency also is comparable. Additionally, since targets have relatively few bands, the number of recursive calls will be small and should not require much more memory than a loop.

5. Any recursive method can be converted to an iterative one, but doing so is not always easy. The algorithm used in paintMondrian is naturally recursive. A recursive definition of this method is easier to write and to understand than an iterative version would be. And as with paintTarget, the number of recursive calls to paintMondrian is small, making its overhead insignificant.

6. Besides the obvious need to move the calls to drawHorizontalLine and drawVerticalLine, the arguments to the recursive calls to paintMondrian would have to be adjusted to avoid painting over the lines. However, to do so, we would need to know the thickness of the lines. This value is random and is generated and hidden within the methods that draw the lines. Changing this aspect of the code would require that thickness be either a data field of the class or determined within paintMondrian and passed to the methods that draw the lines. Neither choice is attractive.

7. The answer to this question is like the answer to Question 5. Any recursive method can be converted to an iterative one, but doing so is not always easy. The algorithm used in creating a Sierpinski carpet is naturally recursive, so a recursive definition of the method is easier to write and to understand than an iterative version would be. As long as the number of recursive calls to display is small, its overhead will be small. However, painting a large carpet will increase the method's memory requirement, perhaps to the point of causing a stack overflow.

8.
```
    display(x, y, 100, pen); // top left
    display(x, y, 33, pen);  // top left
    display(x, y, 11, pen);  // top left
    display(x, y, 3, pen);   // top left
```

9.
```
    display(xMiddle, y, 3, pen); // top middle
```

Debugging Recursive Methods

Contents

Prerequisites

Finding errors in a program's logic is always challenging, but debugging a recursive method can be even more so. This interlude will give you some guidance in fixing recursion that has gone astray. The examples here include errors we made while writing the code for the previous chapters about recursion. Note, however, that the techniques we use here are applicable to debugging any method, including those that are not recursive.

■ Infinite Recursion

As Chapter 24 warned, infinite recursion occurs when a base case is either omitted or never reached. The apparent effect of infinite recursion in your program is like that of an infinite loop: The program will execute "forever." Once again, you must know how to terminate a program's execution. Usually, you will have time to react to an infinite loop, but infinite recursion can cause more grief. While a program caught in an infinite loop typically wastes only execution time, infinite recursion claims more and more memory at each recursive call.

Carpeting Trouble: Base-Case Omission

D7.1   Chapter 26 defined and pictured a Sierpinski carpet, a kind of fractal. Even if you have not read Chapter 26—or studied graphics—you can understand this example. The first recursive steps of displaying a Sierpinski carpet are illustrated in Figure 26-6, and the program's output appears in Listing 26-9. To paint a Sierpinski carpet, we begin with a large black square and, at its center, we paint a smaller white square. We then recursively paint eight smaller Sierpinski carpets around the white square, in effect dividing the large black square into nine subsquares of equal size.

To accomplish this, we defined the class Carpet, as Listing D7-1 shows. It contains a public method display, which calls a private recursive method display to perform the painting. This private method calls itself recursively eight times. Each call requires the coordinates of a subsquare as arguments. As you can imagine, passing the correct values to these recursive calls requires a good deal of concentration. Anyway, that's our excuse for the results you are about to see.

LISTING D7-1   A draft of the class Carpet, which is in need of debugging

```java
1  /** A class of Sierpinski carpets.
2      @author Frank M. Carrano
3  */
4  import java.awt.Color;
5  import java.awt.Graphics;
6  import java.awt.Point;
7
8  public class Carpet
9  {
10     private final int xCorner, yCorner;
11     private final int carpetSide;
12
13     public Carpet(Point corner, int side)
14     {
15        xCorner = (int)corner.getX();
16        yCorner = (int)corner.getY();
17        carpetSide = side;
18     } // end constructor
19
20     public void display(Graphics pen)
21     {
22        display(xCorner, yCorner, carpetSide, pen);
23     } // end display
24
25     private void display(int x, int y, int side, Graphics pen)
26     {
27        // paint large black square
28        pen.setColor(Color.BLACK);
29        pen.fillRect(x, y, side, side);
30
```

```
31          // paint smaller white square at center
32          side = side / 3;
33          pen.setColor(Color.WHITE);
34          pen.fillRect(x + side, y + side, side, side);
35
36          // get key coordinates for black subsquares
37          int xMiddle = x + side;
38          int xRight = x + 2 * side;
39          int yMiddle = y + side;
40          int yBottom = y + 2 * side;
41
42          // perform recursion on each black subsquare
43          display(x, y, side, pen);                    // top left
44          display(xMiddle, y, side, pen);              // top middle
45          display(xRight, y, side, pen);               // top right
46          display(x, yMiddle, side, pen);              // middle left
47          display(xRight, yMiddle, side, pen);         // middle right
48          display(x, yBottom, side, pen);              // bottom left
49          display(xMiddle, yBottom, side, pen);        // bottom middle
50          display(xRight, yBottom, side, pen);         // bottom right
51      } // end display
52 } // end Carpet
```

D7.2   Using the supporting classes `CarpetPanel` and `CarpetDriver`, which appear respectively in Listings 26-8 and 26-9 of Chapter 26, we get undesired results when the program executes. For example, the messages in NetBeans' output window begin as follows:

```
Exception in thread "AWT-EventQueue-0" java.lang.StackOverflowError
        at sun.java2d.loops.SurfaceType.pixelFor(SurfaceType.java:384)
        at sun.java2d.SurfaceData.pixelFor(SurfaceData.java:621)
        at sun.java2d.SunGraphics2D.setColor(SunGraphics2D.java:1747)
        at Carpet.display(Carpet.java:28)
        at Carpet.display(Carpet.java:43)
        at Carpet.display(Carpet.java:43)
        at Carpet.display(Carpet.java:43)
        . . .
```

As you can see, the message

```
    at Carpet.display(Carpet.java:43)
```

repeats over and over. This portion of the message could continue to appear until either we explicitly terminate execution or the IDE stops displaying it. Even so, we must act to stop execution.

The beginning of the message indicates a stack overflow error, about which Chapter 24 warned. A typical cause of a stack overflow is infinite recursion. The three lines in the message that begin with `at sun.java2d` indicate what part of the code was executing when the stack overflow occurred. In fact, each part of the message steps back in time, tracing the method calls that occurred. Thus, the overflow occurred when executing line 384 as a result of the call at line 621, which was reached due to the call at line 1747. These three locations are within the Java Class Library, so they really do not mean too much to us. However, our call from line 28 of our class `Carpet` is responsible for the jump to line 1747. Line 28 in Listing D7-1 is the invocation `pen.setColor(Color.BLACK)`. So far, this trace-back information is not too informative. However, the rest of the error message shows that the method `display` is invoked repeatedly at line 43 of the class `Carpet`. This is the first of the eight recursive calls in the method `display`. This call is responsible for drawing a smaller carpet in the upper left portion of a carpet. In fact, the drawing produced by the program, and given in Figure D7-1, shows the center squares for these smaller carpets.

FIGURE D7-1 The drawing produced by a call to `Carpet`'s method `display`

 Note: If you run this program from the command line instead of an IDE, the error message shown in Listing D7-1 will display so quickly that you likely will see only the latter lines involving the statement at line 43. Although the program will create a window, it probably will not contain the picture shown in Figure D7-1.

D7.3   Notice that the private method `display` shown in Listing D7-1 has no base case. This omission is the cause of the infinite recursion and stack overflow. We were distracted while coding `display` by the need to concentrate on the coordinates in the recursive calls. The best way to deal with this type of error is not to make it. Maybe, however, we were simply unsure of the base case. Thinking about the main computation could help us discover the base case, but thinking and coding are two different things. As you can see, jumping right into code invites mistakes that should be avoided.

So what should we have done, assuming that we were unsure of the details of a base case? We could begin with some pseudocode, as follows:

> *Algorithm* `SierpinskiCarpet(x, y, side)`
>
> **if** (*base case*)
>   *Do nothing*
> **else**
> { . . .
> }

By at least documenting that we need a base case, we are less likely to omit it.

In Segment 26.11 of Chapter 26, we stated "The recursion continues until the side of the sub-squares becomes too small to divide." We can now improve our pseudocode by first writing

> *Algorithm* `SierpinskiCarpet(x, y, side)`
>
> **if** (`side` *is too small*)
>   *Do nothing*
> **else**
> { . . .
> }

and then refining this version to

```
Algorithm SierpinskiCarpet(x, y, side)

if (side > some minimum size)
{ . . .
}
```

Note: A checklist for debugging a recursive method

Once again, the best way to debug a program is not to make mistakes. Facetious as this rule may be, since everyone makes mistakes, we can strive to avoid them. Taking extra care while writing recursive code is especially important. Segment 24.5 of Chapter 24 listed some design guidelines for writing a recursive method. We can revise these guidelines as questions to ask ourselves as we either check our work or look for errors in a recursive method:

- Does the method receive input from either a parameter or a value read?
- Does the method definition involve this input value in a way that leads to different cases?
- Does at least one of these cases provide a solution without recursion?
- Does at least one case make a recursive call to the method to perform a "smaller" version of the method's task?

■ Incorrect Results

Our next examples involve programs that execute normally but have incorrect logic. Although we would expect incorrect results from such programs, sometimes their results can be correct. Insufficient testing can lead us to believe that all is well.

Sorting and Merging, Merging and Sorting

D7.4   The merge sort of an array, which Chapter 25 introduced, is not particularly complicated, nor is it hard to code. But confusion certainly is possible. The algorithm for a merge sort is recursive: We divide the array into two parts, use a merge sort to sort each part, and then merge the two sorted pieces into one sorted array.

Recall the class StringSorter, given in Listing 25-4. The recursive merge-sort algorithm is implemented within a private method sort, which is called by a public method mergeSort. Imagine a programmer who confuses when to sort with when to merge and writes the following version of the private method sort:

```java
// Sorts the array segment a[first..last] using a
// temporary array tempArray.
private static void sort(String[] a, String[] tempArray,
                         int first, int last)
{
   if (first < last)
   {
      int mid = first + (last - first) / 2;
      merge(a, tempArray, first, mid, last);
      sort(a, tempArray, first, mid);
      sort(a, tempArray, mid + 1, last);
   } // end if
} // end sort
```

D7.5   Assuming that the rest of the class `StringSorter` is the same as shown in Listing 25-4, let's test it using the driver shown in Listing D7-2. This program is analogous to the one that appears in Listing 23-3 of Chapter 23 and is like the program that Exercise 12 of Chapter 25 asked you to write. Notice that the driver, in addition to displaying the array before and after the sort, checks and reports whether the array is, in fact, sorted. As Segment 23.8 of Chapter 23 mentioned, such checks are important, especially for large arrays, since a human check would be unreliable. Also notice that our test data is in an array, `names`, that we do not alter. We copy the strings from `names` into another array, which we then sort. In this way, we have the original unsorted array if we want to add another test to the driver. For example, we could sort a part of the array or use a different sorting method.

LISTING D7-2   A driver for the class `StringSorter`

```java
import java.util.Arrays; // for copyOf
/** A driver that tests the class StringSorter.
    @author Frank M. Carrano
*/
public class SortDriver
{
    public static void main(String[] args)
    {
        final String[] names = {"Jamie", "Colbie", "Andrew",
                                "Corwin", "Kyle", "Ali"};

        // initialize array
        String[] array = Arrays.copyOf(names, names.length);
        System.out.println("Before sorting, the array contains:");
        display(array);
        StringSorter.mergeSort(array);
        System.out.println("\nAfter sorting, the array contains:");
        display(array);
        check(array);
    } // end main

    public static boolean isSorted(String[] array, int first,
                                   int last)
    {
        boolean sorted = true;
        for (int index = first; sorted && (index < last); index++)
        {
            if (array[index].compareTo(array[index + 1]) > 0)
                sorted = false;
        } // end for

        return sorted;
    } // end isSorted
```

```java
   public static boolean isSorted(String[] array)
   {
      return isSorted(array, 0, array.length - 1);
   } // end isSorted

   public static void check(String[] array)
   {
      System.out.print("The array is ");
      reportResult(isSorted(array));
   } // end check

   public static void check(String[] array, int first, int last)
   {
      System.out.print("Entries at index " + first + " to " +
                         last + " are ");
      reportResult(isSorted(array, first, last));
   } // end check

   private static void reportResult(boolean inOrder)
   {
      if (inOrder)
         System.out.println("sorted.\n");
      else
         System.out.println("NOT sorted!\n");
   } // end reportResult

   public static void display(Object[] array)
   {
      for (int index = 0; index < array.length; index++)
         System.out.print(array[index] + " ");
      System.out.println();
   } // end display
} // end SortDriver
```

Output

```
Before sorting, the array contains:
Jamie Colbie Andrew Corwin Kyle Ali

After sorting, the array contains:
Colbie Corwin Jamie Ali Andrew Kyle
The array is NOT sorted!
```

D7.6 The output shown in Listing D7-2 indicates that mergeSort is in error. As we have mentioned, tracing the calls to a recursive method is usually difficult to do by hand. Using the tools described earlier in Debugging Interlude 5 will enable us to trace the logic accurately, but such a trace is not always helpful. Confusion is likely as we trace a recursion deeper and deeper.

More useful than tracing the recursive calls and their arguments in this example is seeing how the array changes during the sort. You can see these changes by using the breakpoints and watches provided by an IDE. Alternatively, and with minimal change to the class StringSorter, you can define a class of static methods to display the array. In this way, you can format the output to your liking. An example of such a class, ArrayDebugger, is shown in Listing D7-3.

LISTING D7-3   The class ArrayDebugger

```
** A class of static methods for displaying
   an array of strings.
   @author Frank M. Carrano
*/
public class ArrayDebugger
{
   /** Displays the two pieces of an array, a[first..mid] and
       a[mid + 1..last].
       @param debug   a boolean value to indicate whether to
                      display anything
       @param action  a string that precedes " the pieces:" in a
                      label for the output */
   public static void display(boolean debug, Object[] a,
                              int first, int mid, int last,
                              String action)
   {
      if (debug)
      {
         System.out.println(action + " the pieces:");
         display(a, first, mid);    // a[first..mid]
         System.out.print("| ");
         display(a, mid + 1, last); // a[mid + 1..last]
         System.out.println();
      } // end if
   } // end display

   /** Displays the array a[first..last].
       @param debug   a boolean value to indicate whether to
                      display anything */
   public static void display(boolean debug, Object[] a,
                              int first, int last)
   {
      if (debug)
      {
         display(a, first, last);
         System.out.println();
      } // end if
   } // end display
```

```
// Displays the subarray a[first..last].
private static void display(Object[] a, int first, int last)
{
    for (int index = first; index <= last; index++)
        System.out.print(a[index] + " ");
} // end display
} // end ArrayDebugger
```

D7.7 To use the class `ArrayDebugger`, we add the following statement to the private method `sort` immediately after the definition of the local variable `mid`:

```
ArrayDebugger.display(DEBUG, a, first, mid, last, "Sorting");
```

Next we add two statements to the method `merge` shown in Listing 25-4 of Chapter 25, as follows: We add

```
ArrayDebugger.display(DEBUG, a, first, mid, last, "Merging");
```

as the first statement in its body, and add

```
ArrayDebugger.display(DEBUG, a, first, last);
```

as its last statement. Finally, we add the following statement at the beginning of the class `StringSorter`:

```
public static final boolean DEBUG = true;
```

Simply by changing `DEBUG` to `false`, we can disable the debugging statements we just added.

D7.8 After making the previous changes to `StringSorter` and executing `SortDriver` again, we will get the following output:

```
Before sorting, the array contains:
Jamie Colbie Andrew Corwin Kyle Ali
Sorting the pieces:
Jamie Colbie Andrew | Corwin Kyle Ali  ◄——— Array is halved correctly
Merging the pieces:
Jamie Colbie Andrew | Corwin Kyle Ali  ◄——— Halves are not sorted, so
Corwin Jamie Colbie Andrew Kyle Ali              merge is incorrect
Sorting the pieces:
Corwin Jamie | Colbie
Merging the pieces:
Corwin Jamie | Colbie
Colbie Corwin Jamie
Sorting the pieces:
Colbie | Corwin
Merging the pieces:
Colbie | Corwin
Colbie Corwin
Sorting the pieces:
Andrew Kyle | Ali
Merging the pieces:
Andrew Kyle | Ali
Ali Andrew Kyle
Sorting the pieces:
Ali | Andrew
Merging the pieces:
Ali | Andrew
Ali Andrew
```

```
After sorting, the array contains:
Colbie Corwin Jamie Ali Andrew Kyle
The array is NOT sorted!
```

The sort seems to begin correctly. As it divides the array into two halves, however, the halves are merged immediately. Then the first half is divided into two pieces and these pieces are merged. Which method is at fault, sort or merge? Since we can test merge independently of sort—but not the other way around—doing so is essential. Knowing that merge is correct would allow us to focus on, and more confidently blame, sort.

In its introduction to the merge sort, Chapter 25 said that it divides the array into halves, sorts each half, merges the sorted halves into a second temporary array, and then copies the temporary array back to the original array. Whoever wrote the sort method given in Segment D7.4 did not adhere to this description. The call to merge should be after, not before, the two recursive calls to sort.

Question 1 Would the method sort, as given in Segment D7.4, ever produce a correctly sorted array? If so, give an example; if not, describe why.

Question 2 Using the code for the classes StringSorter, SortDriver, and ArrayDebugger, which is given on the book's website, replace the method sort in StringSorter with the following version:

```
private static void sort(String[] a, String[] tempArray,
                         int first, int last)
{
    if (first < last)
    {
        int mid = first + (last - first) / 2;
        sort(a, tempArray, first, mid - 1);
        sort(a, tempArray, mid + 1, last);
        merge(a, tempArray, first, mid, last);
    } // end if
} // end sort
```

Run SortDriver first with the array {"Colbie", "Andrew", "Corwin", "Kyle", "Sasha", "Cooper"} and then with {"Jamie", "Colbie", "Andrew", "Corwin", "Kyle", "Ali"}. What are the results? What, if anything, is wrong with the method sort?

Verbalizing Integers: Saying Too Much

The method sort given in Segment D7.4 produces incorrect results almost all of the time, while the version shown in Question 2 is right sometimes but more often is incorrect. In contrast, our next example gives correct results in many but not all instances. Extensive testing is needed to avoid accepting a defective method as correct.

D7.9   Recall the class VerbalInteger, which we developed in Chapter 24 and is given in Listing 24-3. This class represents an integer as an object whose write method displays the integer in words. Now imagine a class identical to the one shown in Listing 24-3 except for the private method write. In this new class, write has the following definition instead of the one given in Listing 24-3:

```
// Recursively writes in words a given positive integer
// whose form is integer * 1000^power, where integer > 0
// and power >= 0.
private void write(long integer, int power)
{
    if (integer < 1000)
        writeUnderThousand(integer);
```

```
      else
      {
         write(integer / 1000, power + 1);
         writeUnderThousand(integer % 1000);
      } // end if

      writePowerOfThousand(power);
   } // end write
```

D7.10 The method conforms to our earlier checklist. It has input parameters, a base case, and a recursive call involving the parameters. Moreover, the argument `integer / 1000` in the recursive call takes a step toward the base case.

Let's test the class. The driver given in Listing 24-4 of Chapter 24 requires user input. Using it to extensively test our class would be tedious, due to all the input that we must type. The driver given here in Listing D7-4 defines an array of integers and uses each one to test the method `write`. As the output indicates, each of these integers is expressed correctly in words.

Note: **Literals of type long**

The L at the end of some integers in the definition of the array `numbers` in the class `Tester` might be new to you. It tells the compiler that the integer should have the type `long`. We could have written an L after every integer, since this is an array of `long` integers. For most of the integers this isn't necessary, though, because the compiler converts them to `long`. However, an 11-digit integer, for example, is larger than the largest possible value for an `int`. Without an L suffix, the compiler would see an 11-digit integer as a syntax error.

LISTING D7-4 A driver for the class `VerbalInteger`

```java
/** A driver that tests the class VerbalInteger.
    @author Frank M. Carrano
*/
public class Tester
{
   private static long[] numbers = {1, 12, 19, 20, 25, 246, 999,
         9870, 1034, 12305, 123456, 1234567, 12345678, 123456789,
         1234567890, 12345678900L, 123456789000L, Long.MAX_VALUE};

   public static void main(String args[])
   {
      for (long integer : numbers)
      {
         System.out.print(integer + " is ");
         VerbalInteger anInteger = new VerbalInteger(integer);
         anInteger.write();
         System.out.println();
      } // end for
```

```
    } // end main
} // end Tester
```

Output

```
1 is one
12 is twelve
19 is nineteen
20 is twenty
25 is twenty five
246 is two hundred forty six
. . .
12345678 is twelve million three hundred forty five thousand six hundred
seventy eight
```
. . . *< and so on; all results are correct for the integers in the array* numbers *>*

D7.11 Although our revised method write behaves correctly for the integers shown in Listing D7-4, it contains an error. To see this, look what happens if we define the array numbers as follows:

```
private static long[] numbers = {123000000L, 100000000000L,
                                 100000000000000L};
```

The program Tester will produce the following output:

```
123000000 is one hundred twenty three million thousand
100000000000 is one hundred billion million thousand
100000000000000 is one hundred trillion billion million thousand
```

The highlighted words are extraneous and should not appear in the output.

D7.12 Suppose that we trace this program's execution for just one of these troublesome integers, one hundred billion (100000000000L), for example. As a result of the call anInteger.write() in the main method of the class Tester, the following calls to the VerbalInteger methods write, writeUnderThousand, and writePowerOfThousand occur:

```
write(100000000000L, 0);
write(100000000L, 1);
write(100000L, 2);
write(100L, 3);
writeUnderThousand(100L);
writePowerOfThousand(3);
writeUnderThousand(0);       // 100000L % 1000
writePowerOfThousand(2);
writeUnderThousand(0);       // 100000000L % 1000
writePowerOfThousand(1);
writeUnderThousand(0);       // 100000000000L % 1000
writePowerOfThousand(0);
```

Clearly, writePowerOfThousand is called too often, but we knew this already from the program's output. Unfortunately, this trace might prompt us to patch the code with if statements that try to prevent the extraneous output. In this example, the problem is more profound than a missing if statement. The recursion is amiss.

In fact, the base case is incorrect. Although the base case might appear to include all integers less than 1000, the if statement in the method write compares integer to 1000 and ignores the value of power. The correct base case, as was noted in Segment 24.24 of Chapter 24, occurs when integer is zero, in which case you do nothing. The best course of action here is to start over by describing an algorithm like the one given in Chapter 24.

We end this interlude with reminders of some points we mentioned earlier in this book.

Programming Tip: **Tracing the execution of a recursive method is usually not productive**

Although tracing the execution of methods that are not recursive is useful, such usually is not the case for recursive methods.

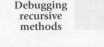

videonote
Debugging
recursive
methods

Programming Tip: **Sometimes the fastest way to debug a seriously incorrect program is to discard it and start over**

Although you may be reluctant to toss out your program and begin again, realize that all will not be lost if you do so. You will have gained some insight into the problem and can use it to design a better solution. Patching the logic of a program instead of truly understanding it can lead to unreliable and complex code.

ANSWERS TO SELF-TEST QUESTIONS

1. Yes. Any array that is already sorted will remain sorted after it is manipulated by this version of sort.

2. The first array is sorted correctly, even though sort is logically incorrect. However, the second array is not sorted by the method. In the first recursive call to sort, the argument mid - 1 should be mid.

Chapter

27

Inheritance Continued

Contents

Prerequisites

Objectives

After studying this chapter, you should be able to

- Know when to use inheritance and when to not use it
- Derive a class from another class by using inheritance
- Use super to invoke a superclass constructor or method from a subclass constructor or method
- Define and use protected methods
- Define and use packages
- Define and use abstract classes and methods
- Distinguish among overriding, hiding, and overloading methods
- Define and use final classes and methods

Inheritance is a major principle of object-oriented programming and a significant feature of Java. Chapter 16 introduced inheritance, even though we used it earlier to extend classes of the Java Class Library whenever we added graphics to a program. However, we have yet to use inheritance to extend any of our own classes. We shall do so now.

■ A Problem Solved: Designing a Hierarchy of Classes

> A typical member of an online community must choose and register a user name and a password. Such a registered user has full access to the group's features and files. In some cases, a user can be an unregistered guest who can participate only in minimal ways. And certain users either own the group or are responsible for its maintenance. Design several classes, related by inheritance, to represent these kinds of users.

27.1   The people who interact with an online community fall into one of the following categories:

- Registered user: A user who has a user name and a password and can participate fully in the group.
- Guest: A user who has not registered and has limited use of the available features and files.
- Administrator: A registered user who maintains the group, performing tasks such as approving memberships, organizing or deleting files, and so on. An administrator is a special registered user with more rights than a registered user.

Within the software that implements our online community, we can represent these three groups of users by the three classes `RegisteredUser`, `Guest`, and `Administrator`. Since objects of these classes represent users of various types, we expect their behaviors to be similar. A major distinction is the access that each has to the community's data. A simple way to make this distinction is to ask each object for a code that represents its rights. In particular, each object can have a method `getUseCode` that returns a code such as `LIMITED` for guests, `REGULAR` for registered users, and `ALL` for administrators. We can define these three codes in a public enumeration, for example:

```
public enum UseCode {LIMITED, REGULAR, ALL}
```

An `Administrator` object has the same attributes and behaviors as a registered user but also has the right to examine or change anything within the community. Thus, in addition to a use code, both an administrator and a registered user should have a name and password, each of which can be a string. Since a registered user typically completes a profile when registering with the community, another field can be an instance of a class `Profile` that we would define. The details of the user profile are not important to our discussion of inheritance, so we will not concern ourselves with the definition of the class `Profile`. Finally, let's require accessor methods to the data fields. If we were to think of our other three classes independently of one another, we might arrive at the designs illustrated in Figure 27-1.

FIGURE 27-1   Preliminary designs for the classes RegisteredUser, Guest,
and Administrator

RegisteredUser
-name: String -password: String -info: Profile -code: UseCode
+getName(): String +getPassword(): String +getProfile(): Profile +getUseCode(): UseCode

Administrator
-name: String -password: String -info: Profile -code: UseCode
+getName(): String +getPassword(): String +getProfile(): Profile +getUseCode(): UseCode

Guest
-code: UseCode
+getUseCode(): UseCode

27.2   The redundancy shown in Figure 27-1 for the classes RegisteredUser and Administrator is clear, but inheritance can help us to avoid the duplicate code that seems inevitable in this design. Since an object of any of these three classes represents a user, we can organize the classes as descendants of a general class, User, as Figure 27-2 shows. The relationships illustrated among the classes are just as we described earlier: A guest is a user, a registered user is a user, and an administrator is a registered user. These *is-a* relationships are realized using the inheritance hierarchy shown in the figure.

Although a guest has no name in our first design shown in Figure 27-1, a guest is a user and so has a name in our second design given in Figure 27-2. To accommodate this difference, the system can assign the string "Guest" to the data field name of any user who is a guest.

 Note: Why is Administrator a subclass of RegisteredUser, rather than vice versa?
As we just noted, an administrator is a registered user. A registered user, however, is not necessarily an administrator. In fact, few registered users are administrators. An administrator is a special registered user. Inheritance is appropriate when specialization is involved.

■ The Basic Rules of Inheritance

Chapter 16 gave a brief introduction to inheritance, enough to help you more fully understand the use of the Swing library when adding graphics to your programs. You need more details, however, and this section will begin to provide them as we implement the design shown in Figure 27-2.

What Is Inherited?

27.3   Let's think some more about the design shown in Figure 27-2 before we implement it. User is the superclass of RegisteredUser, so RegisteredUser inherits all public members of User; in this

FIGURE 27-2   A hierarchy of users of an online community

```
                            ┌─────────────────────────────┐
                            │            User             │
                            ├─────────────────────────────┤
                            │ -name: String               │
                            │ -code: AccessCode           │
                            ├─────────────────────────────┤
                            │ +getName(): String          │
                            │ +getUseCode(): UseCode      │
                            └─────────────────────────────┘
                                  △                  △
                       ┌──────────┘                  └──────────┐
          ┌─────────────────────────────┐      ┌─────────────────────────────┐
          │        RegisteredUser       │      │            Guest            │
          ├─────────────────────────────┤      ├─────────────────────────────┤
          │ -password: String           │      │                             │
          │ -info: Profile              │      ├─────────────────────────────┤
          ├─────────────────────────────┤      │                             │
          │ +getPassword(): String      │      └─────────────────────────────┘
          │ +getProfile(): Profile      │
          └─────────────────────────────┘
                         △
                         │
          ┌─────────────────────────────┐
          │        Administrator        │
          ├─────────────────────────────┤
          │                             │
          ├─────────────────────────────┤
          │                             │
          └─────────────────────────────┘
```

case, it inherits the methods getName and getUseCode. RegisteredUser does not inherit the private data fields of User, but since it has indirect access to them via getName and getUseCode, it does not define its own copies of User's fields. However, RegisteredUser does define the additional fields password and info, as well as the additional accessor methods getPassword and getProfile.

Note: Private data fields and private methods are not inherited

A subclass does not inherit the private data fields and private methods of its superclass. No other class can know about a class's private portions. Thus, a subclass cannot reference by name the private fields in its superclass and cannot invoke by name the private methods in its superclass. However, a subclass can invoke a public method in its superclass, and that public method can invoke a private method in the superclass as well as access or modify the value of the superclass's private data fields.

Note: Constructors are not inherited

A class C does not inherit the constructors of its superclass B. If it did, C would have a constructor named B, and that makes no sense. For example, if a class CollegeStudent is derived from the class Student, CollegeStudent cannot have a constructor named Student.

Question 1 Which class is the superclass of the class Guest?

Question 2 What data fields and methods, if any, does the class Guest inherit?

Question 3 Which classes are ancestors of the class Administrator?

Question 4 What data fields and methods, if any, does the class Administrator inherit?

Constructors of the Superclass and Subclass

27.4   No set methods appear in our design, and so the constructors will have to initialize the data fields of the particular objects they create. Specifically, User's constructor sets the values of its fields name and code. Likewise, RegisteredUser's constructor sets the values of its fields password and info. But a registered user needs a name and a use code, and only User's constructor can set them. Although a subclass does not inherit the constructors of its superclass, a subclass's constructor can invoke a constructor of its superclass, as you will see. Let's focus on these aspects.

The class User can have the following definition:

```java
public class User
{
    public enum UseCode {LIMITED, REGULAR, ALL}
    private final String name;
    private UseCode code;

    public User(String newName, UseCode newUseCode)
    {
        name = newName;
        code = newUseCode;
    } // end constructor

    < The accessor methods getName and getUseCode are defined here. >
} // end User
```

27.5   Now RegisteredUser can extend User, as follows:

```java
public class RegisteredUser extends User
{
    private String password;
    private Profile info;

    public RegisteredUser(String newName, Profile newProfile,
                          String newPassword)
    {
        super(newName, UseCode.REGULAR);
        password = newPassword;
        info = newProfile;
    } // end constructor

    < The accessor methods getPassword and getProfile are defined here. >
} // end RegisteredUser
```

RegisteredUser's constructor initializes its own fields—password and info—as any constructor would. However, it also must give the user a name and the use code REGULAR. Since RegisteredUser does not have direct access to User's data fields name and info, its constructor must call User's constructor. Within a subclass, super is the name of the superclass's constructor. We use super in the same way that we used this in Segment 8.24 of Chapter 8 to call a constructor from another constructor within the same class. Note that if we use super in this way, it must be first in the constructor's body.

Note: **Calling the constructor of the superclass**

Even though a subclass does not inherit the constructors of its superclass, its constructors always call the superclass's constructors. The constructor of a subclass can explicitly invoke the constructor of its superclass, or base class, by using the reserved word super. This action can occur only within another constructor and must always be its first action. You cannot use the name of the constructor instead of super. If you omit super, each constructor of a subclass implicitly calls the default constructor of the superclass. Sometimes this action is what you want, but sometimes it is not. The superclass might not define a default constructor—in which case, a syntax error occurs—or the default constructor might provide the wrong initialization for the situation.

Programming Tip

To avoid an error, either syntactical or logical, you should always use super within a subclass's constructors to explicitly invoke the appropriate constructor of the superclass.

27.6 The class Administrator is derived from RegisteredUser. Although Administrator does not define additional data fields and methods of its own, it does inherit the public methods of RegisteredUser. Moreover, since RegisteredUser inherits methods from User, Administrator also inherits them. Thus, an Administrator object has the methods getName, getUseCode, getPassword, and getProfile.

The definition of Administrator contains only a constructor, which invokes the constructor of its superclass RegisteredUser as follows:

```
public class Administrator extends RegisteredUser
{
   public Administrator(String newName, Profile newProfile,
                        String newPassword)
   {
      super(newName, newProfile, newPassword);
      < Set use code to UseCode.ALL. >
         . . .
   } // end constructor
} // end Administrator
```

Administrator's constructor calls RegisteredUser's constructor, which in turn calls User's constructor with UseCode.REGULAR as an argument. Thus, the use code of an Administrator object will be incorrect unless we change it to UseCode.ALL.

Design Decision: **Should RegisteredUser's constructor have a use code as a parameter?**

Notice that User's constructor has a use code as a parameter and uses it to initialize the data field code. Also notice that RegisteredUser's constructor invokes User's constructor and passes it UseCode.REGULAR to correctly set the use code. If RegisteredUser's constructor had a use code as a parameter, Administrator could simply pass it the correct use code.

videonote
Inheritance details

However, if that were the situation, a programmer could mistakenly give a RegisteredUser object an incorrect use code, that is, incorrect access rights. We do not want any user to have too much or too little access. But a programmer could create User objects having any use code. Why, then, is it all right for User's constructor to have a use code as a parameter, but not for RegisteredUser's constructor to have such a parameter?

When we designed the classes User, RegisteredUser, Administrator, and Guest, we had no intention of actually creating User objects. User helps us to organize our classes and to simplify their code. Later in this chapter, we will prevent clients from instantiating User by making it an abstract class. We can also, however, remove the use code as a parameter of User's constructor, as you will soon see.

Note: **Java does not allow multiple inheritance**

Some programming languages allow one class to have several different superclasses. That is, class C could extend both classes A and B. This feature, known as **multiple inheritance**, is not allowed in Java. In Java, a class can have only one superclass. Class B, however, can extend class A and then class C can extend class B, since this is not multiple inheritance. In fact, we did this when we derived RegisteredUser from User and then derived Administrator from RegisteredUser.

Recall that a class can implement any number of interfaces in addition to extending any one superclass. This capability gives Java an approximation to multiple inheritance without the complications that arise with multiple superclasses.

Protected Access

27.7   Because RegisteredUser's constructor does not have a use code as a parameter in the present design, the only way for Administrator to set the use code is for one of its ancestor classes to have a set method such as setUseCode. We intentionally omitted this set method because we did not want objects of RegisteredUser and Guest to be able to change their use code. Can we give User the method setUseCode so that descendant classes can invoke it but their clients cannot?

You know that you control access to a class's data fields and methods by using an access modifier such as public or private. Any client can invoke a class's public methods. No client or descendant class can invoke a class's private methods. We need an access modifier that falls between public and private whereby a descendant class can invoke an ancestor's method but a client cannot. That access is called **protected access**, and the access modifier that specifies it is protected. If a method of the class C is marked protected, you can invoke it from within any method definition within either C, a subclass of C, or a class within the same package as C. However, a protected method behaves as if it were private within classes that are not derived from C or that are not in the same package as C.

Note: **Protected access**
A method or data field within a class C and that is modified by protected can be accessed by name only within

- The class C
- Any subclass of C
- Any class within the same package as C

Thus, let's add the following set method to the definition of the class User:

```java
protected void setUseCode(UseCode newUseCode)
{
   code = newUseCode;
} // end setUseCode
```

Any descendant class of User can invoke setUseCode, so we can complete the definition of Administrator's constructor by inserting the statement

```java
setUseCode(UseCode.ALL);
```

after the call to super.

Programming Tip

When you design a class, consider the classes derived from it, either now or in the future. They might need access to your class's data fields. If your class does not have public accessor or mutator methods, you can provide protected versions of such methods. However, always make the data fields private. Although protected data fields are possible, private data fields having protected accessor or mutator methods are preferable.

The Implementation So Far

27.8   Giving User the protected method setUseCode means that User's constructor no longer needs the use code as a parameter. Instead, the constructor can leave Java's default value, null, in the data field code or assign it null explicitly. With those changes, RegisteredUser can invoke setUseCode, just as Administrator does, to set the use code. Listings 27-1 through 27-4 show the definitions of the classes User, RegisteredUser, Administrator, and Guest, with the revisions we have just described.

LISTING 27-1   The class User

```java
/** User.java by F. M. Carrano
    A superclass for users of an online community.
*/
public class User
{
   public enum UseCode {LIMITED, REGULAR, ALL}
   private final String name;
   private UseCode code;
```

```java
    /** Creates a User object having a given name. */
    public User(String newName)
    {
        name = newName;
        code = null;
    } // end constructor

    /** Retrieves the user's name as a string. */
    public String getName()
    {
        return name;
    } // end getName

    /** Retrieves the user's use code. */
    public UseCode getUseCode()
    {
        return code;
    } // end getUseCode

    // Sets the user's use code.
    protected void setUseCode(UseCode newUseCode)
    {
        code = newUseCode;
    } // end setUseCode
} // end User
```

LISTING 27-2   The class RegisteredUser

```java
/** RegisteredUser.java by F. M. Carrano
    A class of registered users in an online community.
*/
public class RegisteredUser extends User
{
    private String password;
    private Profile info;

    /** Creates a RegisteredUser object having a given name,
        password, and profile. */
    public RegisteredUser(String newName, String newPassword,
                          Profile newProfile)
    {
        super(newName);
        password = newPassword;
        info = newProfile;
        setUseCode(UseCode.REGULAR);
    } // end constructor
```

```
   /** Retrieves the user's password as a string. */
   public String getPassword()
   {
      return password;
   } // end getPassword

   /** Retrieves the user's profile as a Profile object. */
   public Profile getProfile()
   {
      return info;
   } // end getProfile
} // end RegisteredUser
```

LISTING 27-3   The class Administrator

```
/** Administrator.java by F. M. Carrano
    A class of administrators of an online community.
*/
public class Administrator extends RegisteredUser
{
   /** Creates an Administrator object having a given name,
       password, and profile. */
   public Administrator(String newName, String newPassword,
                        Profile newProfile)
   {
      super(newName, newPassword, newProfile);
      setUseCode(UseCode.ALL);
   } // end constructor
} // end Administrator
```

LISTING 27-4   The class Guest

```
/** Guest.java by F. M. Carrano
    A class of guests of an online community.
*/
public class Guest extends User
{
   /** Creates a Guest object. */
   public Guest()
   {
      super("Guest");
      setUseCode(UseCode.LIMITED);
   } // end constructor
} // end Guest
```

27.9   Listing 27-5 contains a demonstration driver for these classes. Its output is correct, but suppose we add the following statement immediately after the Guest object aGuest is created:

      aGuest.setUseCode(User.UseCode.ALL);

Can a Guest object call the protected method setUseCode? Although we want the answer to this question to be no, in fact the invocation aGuest.setUseCode() is perfectly legal unless we also place our classes into a package that does not contain the class Driver. Presently, aGuest can change its use code and become an administrator! We need to investigate packages.

LISTING 27-5   A driver for the classes RegisteredUser, Administrator, and Guest

```java
/** Driver.java by F. M. Carrano
    A demonstration of the classes RegisteredUser, Administrator,
    and Guest.
*/
public class Driver
{
    public static void main(String args[])
    {
        RegisteredUser joe = new RegisteredUser("Joe", "abcd",
                                            new Profile());
        System.out.println(joe.getName() +
                    " is a registered user whose use code is " +
                    joe.getUseCode());
        Administrator jill = new Administrator("Jill", "xyz",
                                            new Profile());
        System.out.println(jill.getName() +
                    " is an administrator whose use code is " +
                    jill.getUseCode());
        Guest aGuest = new Guest();
        System.out.println(aGuest.getName() +
                    " is a guest whose use code is " +
                    aGuest.getUseCode());

    } // end main
} // end Driver
```

Output

```
Joe is a registered user whose use code is REGULAR
Jill is an administrator whose use code is ALL
Guest is a guest whose use code is LIMITED
```

Question 5 Let's add a protected method setName to the class User. What is its definition?

Question 6 Assuming the method setName, as described in the previous question, let's replace the call super(newName) in RegisteredUser's constructor with setName(newName). What is the effect of this change?

27.10 **Reprise: Using this to invoke a constructor.** As you saw in Segment 8.24 of Chapter 8, we use the reserved word this much as we used super here to call a constructor from within another constructor. However, this calls a constructor of the same class instead of a constructor of the superclass, as super does. Any use of either this or super must be the first action in a constructor definition. Thus, a constructor definition cannot contain both a call using super and a call using this. But what if we want both kinds of call? In that case, we would use this to call a constructor that has super as its first action.

Packages and Package Access

27.11 You know that the Java Class Library is organized into units called packages. Using several related classes is more convenient if you group them together within a package. To identify a class as part of a particular package, you precede the class's definition with a statement like

```
package myStuff;
```

You then place the class's file and the files of the related classes—they begin with the same package statement—into one directory or folder and give it the same name as the package. As you know, to use a package in your program, you begin the program with an import statement.

 Note: A client of a class that is within the same package has access to the protected members of the class.

Although the classes User, RegisteredUser, Administrator, and Guest are not in a package, if they are in the same directory as the client Driver, the client can call the protected method setUseCode. This is the situation described in Segment 27.9.

27.12 **Correcting the problem.** We can create a package of the classes User, RegisteredUser, Administrator, Guest, and Profile by beginning each of their files with a package statement such as the following one:

```
package UserPackage;
```

We then place the files for the classes within a folder named UserPackage. To use this package, the client Driver—which is not in the folder UserPackage—imports each class that it needs from the package with the statements

```
import UserPackage.RegisteredUser;
import UserPackage.Administrator;
import UserPackage.Guest;
import UserPackage.Profile;
```

Now the client Driver cannot call any protected method within the package; in particular, it cannot call setUseCode. This restriction occurs even if Driver imports the class User.

27.13 **Package access.** A public class—whether it is within a package or not—is available to any other class. If you omit the class's access modifier entirely, the class is available only to other classes within the same package. This kind of class is said to have **package access**. If you omit public from the header of the class User, for example, the client Driver will be unable to import and use it. Similarly, if you omit the access modifier from the declaration of a data field or the header of a method, the field or method is available by name inside the definition of any class within the same package but not outside of the package.

Package access is more restricted than protected access and gives you more control when defining classes. You can use package access in situations where you have a package of cooperating classes that act as a single encapsulated unit. If you control the package directory, you control who is allowed to access the package.

Figure 27-3 illustrates the various kinds of access modifiers.

FIGURE 27-3   Public, private, protected, and package access of the data fields and methods of a class C

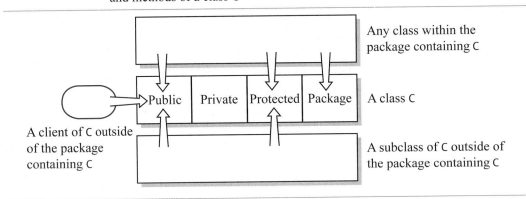

Type Compatibility

27.14   Consider the driver in Listing 27-5 for the classes RegisteredUser, Administrator, and Guest. Imagine a method in this driver that has a formal parameter of type User and begins as follows:

```
public void someMethod(User someone)
```

Within the body of someMethod, we can use the object someone to invoke public methods that are defined in the class User. For example, the definition of someMethod could contain the expression someone.getName(). That is, someone has User behaviors.

In Listing 27-2, you saw that the class RegisteredUser extends the class User. Consider an object joe of the class RegisteredUser. Since RegisteredUser inherits all the public methods of the class User, joe has those inherited methods. That is, joe can behave like an object of User. (It happens that joe can do more, since it is an object of RegisteredUser, but that is not relevant right now.) Therefore, joe can be the argument of someMethod. That is, the main method of the driver could contain the statement

```
someMethod(joe);
```

Thus, the argument in an invocation of someMethod can be an object of type RegisteredUser, even though someMethod's formal parameter is of type User. As an object of the class RegisteredUser, joe can behave as if it were of type User. Explicit type casting is unnecessary.

We can take this idea further. The class Administrator in Listing 27-3 extends the class RegisteredUser. Every object of the class Administrator can behave like an object of the class RegisteredUser and also like an object of the class User. If we have a method whose formal parameter is of type User, the argument in an invocation of this method can be an object of type Administrator. Thus, an object can take on several data types as a result of inheritance. Although an object belongs to only one class, a reference to that object can be assigned to variables of different but related data types.

 Note: The public behaviors of an object of an ancestor class are also behaviors of objects of any descendant class.

27.15 Because an object of a subclass also has the behaviors of all of its ancestor classes, we can assign a reference to an object of a class to a variable of any ancestor type, but not the other way around. For example, since the class `Administrator` is derived from the class `RegisteredUser`, which is derived from the class `User`, the following assignments are legal:

```
User user1 = new RegisteredUser( . . . );
User user2 = new Administrator( . . . );
RegisteredUser user3 = new Administrator( . . . )
```

A `RegisteredUser` object can perform `User` behaviors, and an `Administrator` object can perform both `User` behaviors and `RegisteredUser` behaviors. In other words, a registered user is a user, and an administrator is both a registered user and a user. As we mentioned in Chapter 16, some programmers find the phrase "is a" to be useful in deciding what assignments to variables are legal.

The following statements will be flagged by the compiler as illegal:

```
RegisteredUser user4 = new User( . . . );          // ILLEGAL
Administrator  user5 = new User( . . . );          // ILLEGAL
Administrator  user6 = new RegisteredUser( . . . ) // ILLEGAL
```

This is as it should be: A user is not necessarily a registered user, and a registered user is not necessarily an administrator. For example, `user4` might be expected to, but cannot, perform `RegisteredUser` behaviors: Its declared data type is `RegisteredUser`, but it is assigned a `User` object.

 Note: An object of a subclass has at least the same, and typically more, behaviors than those defined in its superclass.

 Question 7 `Guest` is a descendant class of `User`. Can you assign an object of `Guest` to a variable of type `User`? Why or why not?

Question 8 Can you assign an object of `User` to a variable of type `Guest`? Why or why not?

27.16 As we noted in the previous segment, assigning an object of the class `RegisteredUser` to a variable of type `User` is perfectly legal. For example, the following statements are legal:

```
RegisteredUser rob = new RegisteredUser( . . . );
User aUser = rob;
```

Here the variable `aUser` is just another name for the object that `rob` references, as Figure 27-4 illustrates. That is, `aUser` and `rob` are aliases. The object still "remembers" that it was created as a `RegisteredUser` object.

FIGURE 27-4   The variable `aUser` is another name for a `RegisteredUser` object

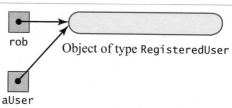

A variable's **static type** is the type that appears in its declaration. For example, the static type of the variable aUser is User. The static type is fixed and determined when the code is compiled. A variable's **dynamic type** can change as execution progresses, depending on the type of object that the variable references during execution. For example, when aUser is assigned an object of RegisteredUser, the dynamic type of aUser is RegisteredUser. Thus, if we assign an Administrator object to aUser, aUser's dynamic type changes to Administrator. Since the dynamic type of a variable of a reference type can differ from its static type and change during execution, it is called a **polymorphic variable**.

Although we can assign an object of type RegisteredUser to a variable aUser of type User, aUser cannot receive a call to a method defined in RegisteredUser but not in User. Figure 27-5 illustrates this situation. However, if a method in RegisteredUser overrides a method in User, aUser can receive a call to that method, and the version in RegisteredUser will be used.

 Note: For a method call v.aMethod(...), the static type of the variable v determines what method names are legal, but its dynamic type determines which definition of the method is used.

FIGURE 27-5 Legal and illegal calls

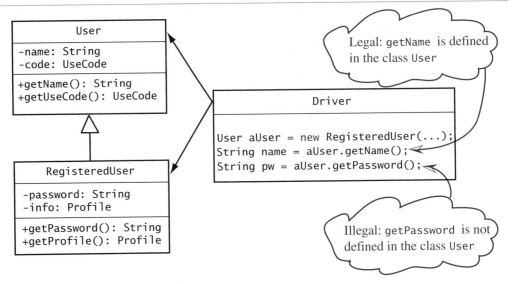

 Note: Objects "know" how they are supposed to act

When an object receives a call to either an overridden method or a method that calls an overridden method, the action of that method is the one defined in the class whose constructor created the object. The choice of action is not affected by the static type of the variable naming the object. A variable of any ancestor class can reference an object of a descendant class, but the object will always take the actions defined in the class used to create it, because Java uses dynamic binding.

Casting Object Types

27.17 In Segment 27.15, when we write

```
User user1 = new RegisteredUser( . . . );
```

user1's static type is User and its dynamic type is RegisteredUser. No explicit cast is needed here, although an implicit cast does occur. We also know that the assignment

```
RegisteredUser userOne = user1; // ILLEGAL
```

is illegal. The compiler does not know that user1 will reference a RegisteredUser object during execution. However, if we explicitly cast user1 to RegisteredUser, all will be fine:

```
RegisteredUser userOne = (RegisteredUser)user1; // OK
```

The cast tells the compiler that user1 will reference a RegisteredUser object by the time this statement executes. The cast is like making a promise to the compiler. The compiler's response is to place an execution-time check that user1 does indeed reference a RegisteredUser object. If you break your promise, and user1 does not reference a RegisteredUser object, an exception will occur.

 Note: When to use inheritance
Some programmers don't understand inheritance, so they either avoid it or use it inappropriately. Inheritance provides a powerful way to organize classes, eliminate redundant code, and reduce programming time, so you should know how and when to use it.

Before you decide to use inheritance in your code, however, you should consider your design carefully to ensure that inheritance is the right choice. Because an object of a subclass can behave as an object of the superclass, a subclass object must be able to replace a superclass object and behave in a manner consistent with the specifications of the superclass. Do not use inheritance if an *is-a* relationship does not exist between your proposed subclass and an existing superclass. Even if you want class C to have some of the methods of class B, if these classes do not have an *is-a* relationship, you should not use inheritance; consider using composition instead. A desire to disable some public methods or fields that would be inherited from a proposed superclass is another indication that you should avoid inheritance.

Abstract Classes and Methods

videonote
Abstract classes
and methods

27.18 The class User defined previously in Listing 27-1 is a superclass for other classes such as RegisteredUser. We really do not need or want to create objects of type User, although presently it is legal to do so. After all, every user is either a guest, a register user, or an administrator. A User object is none of these. To prevent a client from creating objects of a class like User, we can declare the class to be an **abstract class** by including the reserved word abstract in the header of the class definition, as follows:

```
public abstract class User
{
  . . .
```

In our case, we can make this change to User without affecting the rest of its definition or the definitions of its descendant classes.

 Note: An abstract class will be the superclass of another class. Thus, an abstract class is sometimes called an **abstract superclass**. An abstract class cannot be instantiated.

27.19   Often when programmers define an abstract class, they declare one or more methods that have no body. The intention in doing so is to require that every subclass implement such methods in an appropriate way for that class. For example, imagine classes for various geometric forms, such as circles, spheres, and cylinders, that have a radius. Let's define an abstract superclass that classes like Circle, Sphere, and Cylinder could extend. The class Round, shown in Listing 27-6, is such a superclass.

LISTING 27-6   The abstract class Round

```java
/** Round.java by F. M. Carrano
    An abstract superclass that describes geometric
    shapes having a radius.
*/
public abstract class Round
{
   private double radius;

   public void setRadius(double newRadius)
   {
      radius = newRadius;
   } // end setRadius

   public double getRadius()
   {
      return radius;
   } // end getRadius

   public abstract double getArea();
} // end Round
```

This class declares the private data field radius and defines set and get methods for it. The class also declares the method getArea. We might want every subclass of Round to implement a method getArea, each in its own way. We certainly cannot implement such a method that would be appropriate for a future class that is not yet defined. Any definition we might give getArea should be, but would not have to be, overridden by a subclass. Instead, we can require every subclass to write its own version of getArea without defining it ourselves by declaring it as an **abstract method**. Such a declaration includes the reserved word abstract in the method's header and ends in a semicolon; the method has no body.

If a class has at least one abstract method, Java requires that you declare the class itself as abstract. This makes sense, for otherwise you could create an object of an incomplete class. For example, a Round object would have a method getArea without an implementation. If you omitted the declaration of getArea from Round, you could still make Round abstract, but you would not need to.

 Note: An abstract method declaration within an abstract class consists of the method's header followed by a semicolon. The header must include the reserved word abstract. An abstract method cannot be private, static, or final.

Question 9 In `Round`, can we make the methods `setRadius` and `getRadius` abstract and omit their implementations? If so, revise the class accordingly; if not, explain why not.

27.20 The class `Circle`, as given in Listing 27-7, is derived from the superclass `Round`. `Circle` implements `Round`'s abstract method `getArea`. Since `Circle` cannot reference `Round`'s data field `radius` by name, `getArea` must invoke the inherited method `getRadius` to access `radius`'s value.

LISTING 27-7   A class `Circle`, which extends the abstract superclass `Round`

```
/** Circle.java by F. M. Carrano
    A class of circles, derived from the abstract superclass Round.
*/
public class Circle extends Round
{
   public double getArea()
   {
      double circleRadius = getRadius();
      return Math.PI * circleRadius * circleRadius;
   } // end getArea
} // end Circle
```

Question 10 In the method `getArea`, as given in Listing 27-7, would changing the identifier `circleRadius` to `radius` be legal? Why or why not?

27.21 What if the subclass of an abstract class does not implement all of the abstract methods? For example, what if the class `Circle` did not implement `getArea`? `Circle` would have to be abstract. If it was not, a syntax error would occur. Java expects the subclass of an abstract class to either implement all of the abstract methods or to be abstract itself.

 Note: A class with at least one abstract method must be declared as an abstract class. Thus, abstract methods can appear only within an abstract class.

 Programming Tip
You should implement a method in an abstract class when doing so makes sense. In this way, you include as much detail as possible in the abstract class, detail that need not be repeated in descendant classes. For example, not all methods of the abstract class `Round` are abstract. Some are full definitions that do not use the reserved word `abstract`.

 Note: Constructors cannot be abstract
Since a class cannot override a constructor in its superclass, constructors are never abstract. If a constructor were abstract, a subclass could not implement it.

Note: Abstract classes can have constructors
Even though you cannot create an object of an abstract class, you can define constructors in an abstract class. In fact, if you do not define any constructors, Java will provide a default constructor. After all, when an abstract class is extended and all of its methods are given a definition, the subclass's constructor will call the constructor in the abstract class.

Interfaces Versus Abstract Classes

27.22   The purpose of an interface, which Chapter 16 introduced, is similar to that of an abstract superclass. However, an interface is not a superclass. In fact, it is not a class of any kind. When should you use an interface and when should you use an abstract superclass? You should use an abstract superclass if you want to provide a method definition or declare a private data field that your classes will have in common. Otherwise, you should use an interface. Remember that a class can implement several interfaces but can extend only one class.

Instead of deriving the class `Circle` from the abstract superclass `Round`, we could define the following interface that `Circle` could implement:

```java
public interface Circular
{
   void setRadius(double newRadius);
   double getRadius();
   double getArea();
} // end Circular
```

This interface recognizes that a radius will exist, and so it declares both set and get methods for it. However, an interface cannot declare a private field for the radius. The class that implements the interface will do that.

A class `Circle` that implements this interface could appear as given in Listing 27-8. The class defines a private data field `radius` and implements the three methods declared in the interface `Circular`.

LISTING 27-8   An implementation of the interface `Circular`

```java
/** Circle.java by F. M. Carrano
    A class of circles that implements the interface Circular.
*/
public class Circle implements Circular
{
   private double radius;

   public void setRadius(double newRadius)
   {
      radius = newRadius;
   } // end setRadius

   public double getRadius()
   {
      return radius;
   } // end getRadius
```

```
    public double getArea()
    {
        return Math.PI * radius * radius;
    } // end getArea
} // end Circle
```

> **! Programming Tip**
>
> If you want to declare a private data field or provide an implementation of a public method that your classes will have in common, use an abstract superclass. Otherwise, use an interface.

▣ Overriding Methods, Hiding Methods

Chapter 16 introduced the concept of overriding a method definition and briefly mentioned hiding a method. This section develops those concepts in the context of the details we have seen so far in this chapter. We begin by reviewing what we've already covered about overriding methods and then give an example involving the abstract class Round.

Overriding Revisited

27.23   As you saw in Segment 16.23 of Chapter 16, when a subclass defines a nonstatic method having the same signature and return type as a method in the superclass, the method definition in the subclass overrides the definition in the superclass. Objects of the subclass that receive a call to the method will use the definition in the subclass instead of the one in the superclass.

Consider again the classes Round and Circle, as given in Listings 27-6 and 27-7. Let's add another method to the class Round, one that invokes the abstract method getArea. Before you point out that we're invoking a method that has no body, remember that Round is an abstract class. When we finally derive a class—such as Circle—from Round that is not abstract, getArea will be implemented.

The method we have in mind is toString, which we define as follows:

```
public String toString()
{
    return "radius of " + radius + " and an area of " + getArea();
} // end toString
```

This method overrides the method toString that Round inherits from the class Object. Recall that Object is the ultimate ancestor of all classes. Within our version of toString, the call to the abstract method getArea serves as a placeholder for a method that will be defined in a future subclass. Notice that toString is not abstract, even though it calls an abstract method.

27.24   The class Circle extends the class Round, and so it inherits the latter's method toString. Let's override this inherited method. Suppose we want Circle's toString to return the string "This circle has a " followed by the string returned by the inherited toString. Can we override a method and still call it? We can, as the following definition of Circle's toString demonstrates:

```
public String toString()
{
    return "This circle has a " + super.toString();
} // end toString
```

When a Circle object receives a call to toString, the previous method is invoked. It, in turn, invokes Round's toString using the expression super.toString().

Note: When a method in a subclass overrides a method in the superclass, an object of the subclass no longer has the behavior defined by the method in the superclass.

Note: Overriding applies only to instance methods in the superclass, that is, methods that are not static.

Note: The method paintComponent
The class JPanel in the Swing package of the Java Class Library defines the method paintComponent. When you define your own panel class, you extend JPanel and override paintComponent. The first statement of your definition should be a call to paintComponent in JPanel. For example, this statement could be

```
super.paintComponent(pen);
```

where pen is the parameter of type Graphics in your method.

For the graphics programs we have written in previous chapters, no harm was done by omitting this statement. However, to ensure that your graphics will appear correctly, you should always make this call.

Note: Although an instance method in a subclass can use super to invoke an overridden method defined in the superclass, the method cannot invoke an overridden method that is defined in the superclass's superclass. That is, the construct super.super is illegal. The use of super in a static method to invoke an overridden method is illegal.

Hiding Methods

27.25   As we mentioned in Chapter 16, when a static method in a subclass has the same signature and return type as a static method in the superclass, the method in the subclass hides the method in the superclass. The concepts of hiding and overriding are quite similar, but hiding involves static methods and overriding involves those that are not static, that is, instance methods. Additionally, with hiding, the compiler decides which static method to call, whereas the Java Virtual Machine (JVM) chooses between an overriding and overridden method during the execution of a program.

For example, consider the following two simple classes:

```java
public class BaseClass
{
    public void objectAction()
    {
        System.out.println("Object action in BaseClass.");
    } // end objectAction

    public static void classAction()
    {
        System.out.println("Class action in BaseClass.");
```

```
        } // end classAction
    } // end BaseClass

    public class DerivedClass extends BaseClass
    {
        public void objectAction()
        {
            System.out.println("Object action in DerivedClass.");
        } // end objectAction

        public static void classAction()
        {
            System.out.println("Class action in DerivedClass.");
        } // end classAction
    } // end DerivedClass
```

Given these classes, if derivedObject is an object of DerivedClass, the statement

    derivedObject.objectAction();

invokes the method objectAction in DerivedClass, and the statement

    DerivedClass.classAction();

invokes the method classAction in DerivedClass. Note that

    derivedObject.classAction();

also invokes the method classAction in DerivedClass. However, using the class name instead of an object to invoke a static method is the preferable style.

Note: **The access modifier for overridden or hidden methods in a subclass**
When a method in a subclass either overrides or hides a method in the superclass, its access modifier cannot restrict the access of the overridden or hidden method. It must provide either the same or more access, as the following table indicates:

Access of the Overridden or Hidden Method in the Superclass	Access of the Overriding or Hiding Method in the Subclass
Public	Public
Protected	Protected or public
Package	Package, protected, or public

Failure to adhere to these restrictions will result in a syntax error at compilation time.

Note: An instance method in a superclass can be overridden in a subclass only by another instance method. A static method in a superclass can be hidden in a subclass only by another static method. That is, when overriding or hiding methods, you cannot add or delete the modifier static in a method's heading.

Note: A subclass can overload a method it inherits from its superclass. The subclass method neither overrides nor hides the inherited method.

 Note: If a superclass defines a public or protected inner class, a subclass will inherit the inner class. (Inner classes were introduced in Segment 17.8 of Chapter 17.)

Final Classes and Methods

27.26   When we define a class, we can prevent another programmer from extending it by adding the `final` modifier to the class's header. A **final class** cannot be used as the superclass for any subclass. Java's `String` class is an example of a final class. Its definition begins as

```
public final class String
```

 Note: `String` cannot be the superclass for any other class because it is a final class.

For classes that are not final, we can prevent a subclass from overriding a method definition in the superclass by adding the `final` modifier to the method header. For example, we can write

```
public final void myMethod()
{
   . . .
}
```

A **final method** cannot be overridden by a new definition in a subclass of its class. Note that private methods are automatically final methods, since they cannot be overridden at all.

27.27   Suppose that a constructor calls a public method `m`. For simplicity, imagine that this method is in the same class `C` as the constructor, as follows:

```
public class C
{
   . . .
   public C()
   {
      m();
      . . .
   } // end default constructor
   public void m()
   {
      . . .
   } // end m
   . . .
} // end C
```

Now imagine that we define a new class by extending `C`, and we override the method `m`. If we invoke the constructor of our new class, it will call `C`'s constructor, which will call our overridden version of the method `m`. This method might use data fields that the constructor has not yet initialized, causing an error. Even if no error occurs, we will, in effect, have altered the behavior of the superclass's constructor. As a precaution, we should declare `m` as a final method by adding `final` to its header.

Programming Tip

If a constructor invokes a public or protected method in its class, declare that method to be final so that no subclass can override the method and hence change the behavior of the constructor.

Note: Constructors cannot be final. Since a subclass does not inherit, and therefore cannot override, a constructor in its superclass, final constructors are unnecessary.

Programming Tip

Most classes and methods should not be final. Those that are final cannot be extended or overridden, thus limiting your design choices. Always ask yourself whether making a class or method final is really necessary or desirable. On the other hand, you should also ask yourself why a data field is not final. Final data fields have several advantages, as Chapter 8 discussed. Many fields can be final without any disadvantage.

videonote
A problem
solved

CHAPTER SUMMARY

- A class can extend another class and inherit all of its public and protected members. The new class is a subclass; the older class is the superclass.

- A subclass can declare new data fields and define new methods.

- A subclass can invoke any public or protected methods defined in its superclass.

- A client of a subclass can invoke any public methods that are either defined in the subclass or inherited from the superclass.

- A subclass cannot invoke a private method of its superclass directly by name. However, an inherited public or protected method can invoke a private method defined within its class.

- A subclass cannot reference by name any private data field defined in its superclass.

- A subclass does not inherit the constructors of its superclass. However, a constructor of the subclass invokes a constructor of the superclass. By default, the invoked constructor of the superclass is its default constructor.

- You can use super within a subclass constructor to invoke a particular superclass constructor explicitly. This must be the first action within the constructor's body and replaces the implicit invocation of the superclass's default constructor.

- Although a subclass can reference by name any protected field declared in its superclass, a class's data fields should be private. Protected access to the fields can be achieved by providing protected methods.

- Java does not allow multiple inheritance. A subclass can have only one superclass. It can, however, implement several interfaces.

- A class, method, or data field has package access when its declaration has no access modifier.

- A class within a package has access to any class, method, or data field that is in the same package and is not private.

- A class outside of a package has access only to public members of classes within the package.

- A subclass outside of the package containing its superclass has access to public and protected members of the superclass.

- You can assign an object of a class to a variable whose type is any ancestor of the class. No cast is needed.

- You can assign a variable of a class type to a variable whose type is any descendant of the class, if you use a cast. The cast is an indication to the compiler that, at execution time, the assigned variable will reference an object of the type indicated by the cast.

- Use inheritance only when an *is-a* relationship exists between your proposed subclass and an existing superclass. Remember that an object of a subclass must also be an object of the superclass. That is, a subclass object must be able to replace a superclass object and behave in a manner consistent with the specifications of the superclass.

- An abstract class exists only as the superclass of another class. You cannot create objects of an abstract class. The header of an abstract class must include the reserved word abstract.

- An abstract method has no body. Its declaration consists of the method's header followed by a semicolon. The header must include the reserved word abstract. Abstract methods can exist only within an abstract class.

- An abstract method cannot be private, static, or final.

- A subclass of an abstract class must either implement all inherited abstract methods or be itself abstract.

- Constructors cannot be abstract.

- If you want to declare a private data field or provide an implementation of a public method that your classes will have in common, use an abstract base class. Otherwise, use an interface.

- Overriding applies only to instance methods in the superclass, that is, methods that are not static. When a method in a subclass overrides a method in the superclass, an object of the subclass no longer has the behavior defined by the method in the superclass.

- An instance method in a subclass can invoke an overridden method defined in the superclass by using the reserved word super. However, the method cannot invoke an overridden method that is defined in the superclass's superclass.

- Hiding is similar to overriding but applies to static methods instead of instance methods.

- An instance method in a superclass can be overridden in a subclass only by another instance method. A static method in a superclass can be hidden in a subclass only by another static method.

- A method in a subclass that overloads an inherited method neither overrides nor hides the inherited method.

- A final class cannot be used as the superclass for any subclass. A final method cannot be overridden by a new definition in a subclass.

- Constructors cannot be declared as final, since a subclass does not inherit them.

EXERCISES

1. What is the difference between a superclass and a subclass?

2. Since a subclass does not inherit the superclass's constructors and private data fields, how does the subclass's constructor initialize those data fields?

3. Must a constructor's definition in a subclass explicitly invoke a constructor in the superclass by using super? Explain.

4. Java does not support multiple inheritance. How can a Java class inherit behaviors from more than one class?

5. What is the difference between a static type and a dynamic type?

6. To guarantee that a class defines particular methods, you can use an interface or an abstract class.

   a. When can you use an interface instead of an abstract class?
   b. When must you use an abstract class instead of an interface?

7. What is the difference between overridden methods and hidden methods?

8. Can an abstract class ever implement an interface?

9. Consider the following outline of a class Student:

```java
public class Student
{
    private String name;
    private String ident;

    public Student() { ... }
    public Student(String studentName, String studentId) { ... }
    public void setStudent(String studentName, String studentId) { ... }
    public String getName() { ... }
    public String getId() { ... }
    public String toString() { ... }
} // end Student
```

Now consider the following outline of a class CollegeStudent:

```java
public class CollegeStudent extends Student
{
    private int year;
    private String degree;

    public CollegeStudent() { ... }
    public CollegeStudent(String studentName, String studentId,
                        int graduationYear, String degreeSought) { ... }
    public void setStudent(String studentName, String studentId,
                        int graduationYear, String degreeSought) { ... }
    public String getYear() { ... }
    public String getDegree() { ... }
    public String toString() { ... }
} // end CollegeStudent
```

   a. Does the method setStudent in CollegeStudent overload or override the method setStudent in the class Student? Explain.
   b. The class CollegeStudent does not define methods that get the student's name and identification number. Why?
   c. Define the constructors for CollegeStudent. Can you omit a call to super in the default constructor? Can you omit it in the second constructor? Give reasons for your answers.
   d. Define the method setStudent for CollegeStudent.

e. Can the method setStudent for CollegeStudent contain the following statement?

```
name = studentName;
```

Explain.

f. If joe is an object of the class CollegeStudent, write Java statements that display joe's name.

g. If the method toString in Student returns a string containing the student's name and identification number, and toString in CollegeStudent returns a string containing the student's name, identification number, year, and degree, can CollegeStudent's toString call Student's toString? If so, what statement will make this call? If not, why not?

10. Given the classes Student and CollegeStudent, as described in the previous exercise, which of the following statements are legal and which are not?

    a. Student bob = new Student();
    b. Student bob = new CollegeStudent();
    c. CollegeStudent bob = new Student();
    d. CollegeStudent bob = new CollegeStudent();

11. Given the classes Student and CollegeStudent, as described in Exercise 9, suppose that joe is an object of Student and jill is an object of CollegeStudent.

    a. Can joe be the argument of a method whose parameter's type is CollegeStudent? Why or why not?
    b. Can jill be the argument of a method whose parameter's type is Student? Why or why not?
    c. Is joe.getYear() legal? Why or why not?
    d. Is jill.getName() legal? Why or why not?

12. Consider the classes Student and CollegeStudent, as described in Exercise 9, and the following methods:

```
public static void main(String args[])
{
    Student s = new CollegeStudent(...);
    CollegeStudent cs = new CollegeStudent(...);
    process(s);
    process(cs);
} // end main

public static void process(Student aStudent)
{
    System.out.println(aStudent.getName());
    ...
} // end process
```

    a. What are the static and dynamic types of s, cs, and aStudent when the code is executed?
    b. If we change the data type of the parameter aStudent from Student to CollegeStudent, will the main method execute correctly? If so, explain why; if not, explain why not and correct the method.

13. Revise the definition of the class RandomPoint, as given in Listing 11-8 of Chapter 11, so that it extends the standard class java.awt.Point.

14. Define a class Triangle that extends the standard class java.awt.Polygon. Then define the class RightTriangle as an extension of Triangle.

15. Listing 20-1 in Chapter 20 gives a definition for the class ExpandableBagOfStrings. Revise this definition by extending the class BagOfStrings, as given in Listing 19-6 of Chapter 19.

PROJECTS

1. The class Name given in Listing 6-5 of Chapter 6 represents a person's first and last names. Derive the class ProperName from Name, adding data fields for a middle initial and a title such as Ms., Mrs., Mr., or Dr. Provide reasonable constructors and set and get methods for the new fields. Override the toString method so that it behaves correctly for the new class.

   Explain why inheritance is appropriate in the definition of ProperName but would not be a reasonable choice for the definition of the class NickName.

2. Define a class Time that represents the time of day in 24-hour notation. Give the class appropriate constructors, mutators, and accessors. Also define the methods toString and equals. Then extend Time to get the class ZonedTime. This new class represents the time of day in 24-hour notation for a given time zone. In addition to appropriate constructors, mutators, accessors, and the methods toString and equals, define methods to change from standard time to daylight saving time and conversely. Finally, write a client that demonstrates the two classes.

3. Define an abstract superclass named BankAccount that provides the basic behaviors for a bank's checking and savings accounts. All accounts have an account number and a current balance, and they all provide for deposits and withdrawals. Define the classes CheckingAccount and SavingsAccount, each of which extends BankAccount. Also define the class BonusSaverAccount, which extends SavingsAccount.

   Assume that checking accounts do not pay interest but do have overdraft protection. A savings account pays interest at a certain rate. A bonus savings account pays a bonus in addition to the interest a regular savings account pays, as long as the balance is higher than a certain given amount. This account also charges a fixed penalty for every withdrawal from the account.

   Write a client that demonstrates your classes.

4. Implement the classes Student and CollegeStudent—described in Exercise 9—as abstract classes. CollegeStudent should extend Student. Then define UndergradStudent and GradStudent by extending CollegeStudent. The classes UndergradStudent and GradStudent should each ensure that the degree field of CollegeStudent is set to a legal value. For example, you could restrict an undergraduate student to B.A. and B.S. degree programs and a graduate student to M.S. and Ph.D. programs. Consider using an enumeration for this aspect.

   Write a client that demonstrates your classes.

ANSWERS TO SELF-TEST QUESTIONS

1. The class User

2. The class Guest inherits the methods getName and getUseCode from the class User. It does not inherit any data fields, since they are private in User. Note that both Guest and RegisteredUser inherit the same members from User.

3. The classes RegisteredUser and User

4. The class Administrator inherits the methods getPassword and getProfile from the class RegisteredUser as well as the methods getName and getUseCode from the class User. It does not inherit any data fields, since they are private in both User and RegisteredUser.

5.
```
protected void setName(String newName)
{
   name = newName;
} // end setName
```

With this added method, the class's data field name cannot be final.

6. RegisteredUser's constructor no longer has an explicit call to User's constructor, so the compiler will generate a call to User's default constructor. But User has no default constructor, so a syntax error will result. You can either add a default constructor to User or revert to the original code for RegisteredUser's constructor.

7. Yes. You can assign an object of a class to a variable of any ancestor type. An object of type Guest can do anything that an object of type User can do.

8. No. The User object might not have all the behaviors of a Guest object. Even though the class Guest given in Listing 27-4 doesn't do more than a User object, the assignment is still illegal.

9. If Round simply declared setRadius and getRadius as abstract—omitting their implementations—a descendant class would be unable to implement them because it would be unable to access radius.

10. Yes. In the method getArea, circleRadius is a local variable. Naming it radius instead has no effect on the method and does not conflict with the data field radius in Round.

Chapter

28

Exceptions

Contents

Prerequisites

Objectives

After studying this chapter, you should be able to
- Distinguish between checked and unchecked exceptions and give examples of each
- Handle a checked exception by using try, catch, and finally blocks
- Use the throws clause in a method's heading to postpone the handling of an exception
- Use the throw statement to throw an exception
- Define your own class of exceptions
- Override a method that has a throws clause

Earlier in the book, in the first debugging interlude and again in Chapter 4, we described an exception as an unusual circumstance or event that interrupts the execution of a program. Since then, we have noted when certain exceptions will occur, and you likely have encountered them while developing your own programs. Those exceptions indicated mistakes in our code. By correcting those mistakes, we avoided the exceptions and no longer had to worry about them. In fact, our final code gave no indication that an exception could occur. Furthermore, if our code was entirely correct, an exception would not occur.

Dealing with exceptions involves more than learning how to debug a program. A programmer can intentionally cause an exception to occur under certain conditions. In fact, the programmers who wrote the code for the Java Class Library did so. If you peruse the documentation for this library, you will see lists of the exceptions that might occur during the execution of certain methods. We need to know about exceptions so we can use these methods. What should we do when such an exception occurs? Should we ever intentionally cause an exception in our own programs, and if so, how would we do so? These are some of the questions that this chapter will answer. This knowledge will be particularly important to us when we talk about file input and output in the next chapter.

■ The Basics

We begin by considering some terminology, looking at the various kinds of exceptions, and introducing errors (which look like exceptions, but technically are not).

Kinds of Exceptions

28.1   Despite our earlier description of an exception as an unusual event or circumstance, an **exception** is actually an object. This object is created when an unusual event or circumstance occurs during the execution of a method. When the method creates such an object, we say that the method **throws** the exception. An exception is a signal to the rest of the program that something unexpected has happened. Our code can react appropriately to the exception based on its class type and what the exception, as an object, can tell us via its methods. We **handle** the exception when we detect and react to it.

Exceptions belong to various classes, but all of these classes have the standard class Exception as an ancestor. Exception is in the Java Class Library and is available to us without an import statement. Exceptions are classified into two groups:

- Checked exceptions, which must be handled
- Unchecked, or runtime, exceptions, which need not be—and usually are not—handled

28.2   **Checked exceptions** are the result of a serious occurrence during program execution. For example, if a program is reading data from a disk—as the next chapter will describe—and the system cannot find the file that contains the data, a checked exception will occur. The name of the class to which this exception belongs is FileNotFoundException. This name, like the names of all exception classes in the Java Class Library, is meant to describe the cause of the exception. A common practice is to describe an exception by its class name. For example, we might say that a FileNotFoundException has occurred.

Note: **Checked exceptions in the Java Class Library**
The following classes in the Java Class Library represent some of the checked exceptions that you might encounter:

```
ClassNotFoundException
FileNotFoundException
IOException
NoSuchMethodException
WriteAbortedException
```

28.3 **Unchecked exceptions** often are called by their alternate name, **runtime exceptions**, so that is what we will call them. The cause of a runtime exception usually is a logical error in the program. For example, an out-of-bounds array index causes an exception of the class `ArrayIndexOutOfBounds`. A division by zero causes an `ArithmeticException`. Although we could add code that would handle a runtime exception, we usually just need to fix the mistakes in our program.

> **Note: Runtime (unchecked) exceptions in the Java Class Library**
> The following classes in the Java Class Library represent some of the runtime exceptions that you are likely to encounter:
>
> ```
> ArithmeticException
> ArrayIndexOutOfBoundsException
> ClassCastException
> IllegalArgumentException
> IllegalStateException
> IndexOutOfBoundsException
> NoSuchElementException
> NullPointerException
> StringIndexOutOfBoundsException
> UnsupportedOperationException
> ```

> **Note: All exception classes have the standard class `Exception` as an ancestor**
> The standard class `RuntimeException` extends `Exception`, and all classes for runtime exceptions either extend or are descended from `RuntimeException`. The classes of checked exceptions either extend or are descended from `Exception` but do not have `RuntimeException` as an ancestor.

> **Note:** Many exception classes are in the package `java.lang`, and so do not need to be imported. Some classes, however, are in another package, and these do need to be imported. For example, when we use the class `IOException` in a program, we will need the `import` statement
>
> ```
> import java.io.IOException;
> ```
>
> We will encounter this exception in the next chapter.

Question 1 Consult the documentation for the class `ArithmeticException` in the Java Class Library, and give an example of a Java statement that would cause an exception of this type.

Question 2 What happens to program execution when an `ArithmeticException` is thrown? Run a simple test program to see.

Question 3 Consult the documentation for the class `NullPointerException` in the Java Class Library, and give an example of Java statements that would cause an exception of this class.

Errors

28.4 An **error** is an object of either the standard class `Error` or one of its descendant classes. Since the class `Error` is not derived from the class `Exception`, an error is not an exception, even though errors appear to be similar to exceptions. In general, an error indicates the occurrence of an abnormal situation, such as running out of memory. If your program uses more memory than is available, you must either revise your program to make it more efficient in its use of memory, change a setting to let Java access more memory, or buy more memory for your computer. These situations are too serious for a typical program to handle. Hence, errors need not be handled, even though doing so is legal.

Figure 28-1 shows the hierarchy of some exception and error classes. Runtime exceptions, such as `ArithmeticException`, are descended from `RuntimeException`. Checked exceptions, such as `IOException`, are descended from `Exception` but not `RuntimeException`. An assertion error,

FIGURE 28-1   The hierarchy of some standard exception and error classes

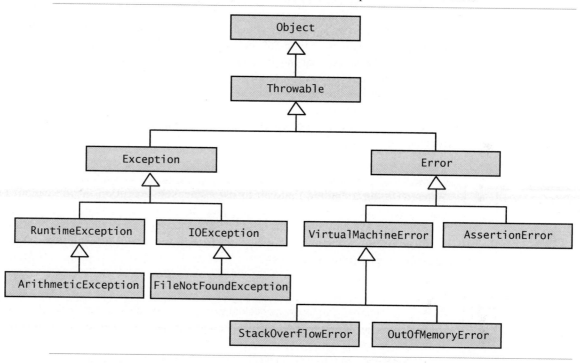

videonote
Exception basics

which Segment 7.19 of Chapter 7 defined, is an object of the class `AssertionError`, which has the class `Error` as its superclass. When we discussed recursion in Chapter 24, we mentioned a stack overflow error. This error belongs to the class `StackOverflowError`. Both `StackOverflowError` and `OutOfMemoryError` are derived from the abstract class `VirtualMachineError`, which has `Error` as its superclass. Knowing only that `StackOverflowError`, `OutOfMemoryError`, and `AssertionError` have `Error` as an ancestor class instead of `Exception` is what is important to us right now.

Handling an Exception

When a checked exception might occur, it must be handled somewhere. For a method that might cause a checked exception, you have two choices: Handle the exception within the method or tell the method's client to do so.

Postpone Handling: The `throws` Clause

28.5   Imagine a method that returns the string it reads from a disk. Since we will learn how to write such a method in the next chapter, let's not worry about how this method accomplishes its task. However, something might go wrong while reading from the disk. That something could generate an IOException. Since an IOException is a checked exception, it must be handled. We could handle the exception within the method's body. Sometimes, however, a programmer is not sure what action is best for a client when an exception occurs. Should execution end, or would another action make more sense? We can leave the handling of the exception to the method's client. As long as the exception is handled at some point, we need not handle it within the method itself.

A method that can cause but does not handle a checked exception must declare in its header that it might throw an exception. For example, if the method readString might throw an IOException but does not handle it, its header would look like this:

```
public String readString(. . .) throws IOException
```

The highlighted portion is a **throws clause**. It frees the method readString of the responsibility of handling any exceptions of type IOException that might occur during its execution. If, however, another method calls readString, it must deal with the exception. That invoking method can either handle the IOException itself or tell its client to handle the exception by including it in a throws clause in its header. Eventually, however, every thrown, checked exception should be handled somewhere in the program.

You can list more than one checked exception in a throws clause by separating the exceptions with commas.

Programming Tip

When defining a method that can throw a checked exception, if you cannot provide a reasonable reaction to the exception, pass it on to the method's client by writing a throws clause in the method's header. Avoid using Exception in a throws clause, as doing so provides the programmer with little if any useful information. Instead, use as specific an exception as you can.

Note: If a method can throw a checked exception, you must either declare the exception in the method's header by writing a throws clause or handle the exception within the method. Failure to do so will cause a syntax error.

If a method can throw an unchecked exception, you could declare it in a throws clause or handle it, but neither action is required.

Note: A method's execution ends if it throws but does not handle an exception

If a method throws an exception but does not handle it, the method's execution ends. For example, if the previous method readString throws an IOException, its execution ends immediately. Program execution continues, however, and the exception is passed to readString's client.

Syntax: The throws clause

access-modifier use-modifier return-type method-name (parameter-list) **throws** *exception-list*

A method's header can contain a throws clause that lists the possible exceptions the method can throw but will not handle. The exception names listed in *exception-list* are separated by commas. Their order here is unimportant.

Handle It Now: The try-catch Blocks

28.6 To handle an exception, we first must identify the Java statements that can cause it. We also must decide which exception to look for. A method's documentation and throws clause will tell us which checked exceptions might occur. It is those exceptions that we will handle.

The code to handle an exception consists of two pieces. The first piece, the **try block**, contains the statements that might throw an exception. The second piece consists of one or more catch blocks. Each **catch block** contains code to react to, or **catch**, a particular type of exception. Thus, the code to handle an IOException as a result of invoking the method readString would have the following form:

```
try
{
    < Possibly some code >
    object.readString(. . .); // might throw an IOException
    < Possibly some more code >
}
catch (IOException e)
{
    < Code to react to the exception, probably including the following: >
    System.out.println(e.getMessage());
}
```

28.7 The statements within the try block execute just as they would if the block was not there. If no exception occurs and the try block completes execution, execution continues with the statement after the catch block. However, if an IOException occurs within the try block, execution immediately transfers to the catch block. The exception now has been caught.

The syntax for a catch block resembles that of a method definition. The identifier e is called a **catch block parameter**; it represents the object of IOException that the catch block will handle. Although a catch block is not a method definition, throwing an exception within a try block is like calling a catch block, in that the parameter e represents an actual exception.

As an object, every exception has the accessor method getMessage, which returns a descriptive string created when the exception is thrown. By displaying this string, we provide the programmer with an indication of the nature of the exception.

28.8 After the catch block executes, the statements after it execute. But what if the problem is serious, and the best reaction to it is to terminate the program? The catch block can end the program by calling the exit method, introduced in Segment 4.58 of Chapter 4, as follows:

```
System.exit(0);
```

The number 0 given as the argument to System.exit indicates a normal termination of the program. Although we have encountered a serious problem, we intentionally terminate the program, which, in the view of the operating system, is normal.

Note: If you do not handle a checked exception or declare it in a throws clause, the compiler will complain. A method can handle some exceptions itself and can declare some in its throws clause. Generally, you do not handle or declare runtime (unchecked) exceptions, since they indicate a bug in your program. Such exceptions terminate program execution when they are thrown.

Note: A catch block whose parameter has the type C can catch exceptions of the class C and any of C's descendant classes.

Multiple catch Blocks

28.9 The statements within a single `try` block can throw any one of a number of different types of exceptions. For example, suppose that the code within the previous `try` block in Segment 28.6 could throw more than one type of checked exception. The `catch` block after this `try` block can catch exceptions of the class `IOException` and any class derived from `IOException`. To catch exceptions of other types, we can write more than one `catch` block after the `try` block. When an exception is thrown, execution continues with the first `catch` block—in order of appearance—whose parameter matches the exception in type. Thus, the order in which `catch` blocks appear is significant.

28.10 **A poor order for catch blocks.** For example, the following sequence of `catch` blocks is poor, because the `catch` block for `FileNotFoundException` never executes:

```
catch (IOException e)
{
   . . .
}
catch (FileNotFoundException e)
{
   . . .
}
```

With this ordering, any I/O exception will be caught by the first `catch` block. Because `FileNotFoundException` extends `IOException`, a `FileNotFoundException` is a kind of `IOException` and will match the parameter of the first `catch` block. Fortunately, this ordering likely will receive a warning from the compiler.

28.11 **A good order for catch blocks.** The correct ordering places the more specific exception before its ancestor class, as follows:

```
catch (FileNotFoundException e)
{
   . . .
}
catch (IOException e) // handle all other IOExceptions
{
   . . .
}
```

Programming Tip

Since all exception classes have `Exception` as an ancestor, avoid using `Exception` in a `catch` block. Instead, catch as specific an exception as you can, and catch the most specific one first.

Java

Syntax: try-catch blocks

```
try
{
   < Statements that can cause an exception >
}
catch (exceptionType e)
{
   < Code to react to the exception, probably including the following: >
   System.out.println(e.getMessage());
}
< Possibly other catch blocks >
```

Question 4 The static void method `anythingCanHappen` might throw an exception, but it does not handle any. The method has no parameters. What, if anything, is wrong with the following try-catch blocks?

```
try
{
    anythingCanHappen();
}
catch (Exception e)
{
    System.out.println("Exception in anythingCanHappen");
}
```

Question 5 If the static method `anythingCanHappen`, which the previous question describes, might throw only the checked exceptions `IOException` and `EOFException` but does not handle them, what is the method's header?

Question 6 Under the assumptions stated in the previous question, what `catch` blocks should a client have after the `try` block given in Question 4? Is the order of the `catch` blocks important in this case? Why? *Hint*: Consult the documentation for these two exceptions, which are in the Java Class Library.

Programming Tip: Avoid nested try-catch blocks, if possible

Although nesting `try-catch` blocks within either a `try` block or a `catch` block is legal, you should avoid doing so if possible. First see whether you can organize your logic differently to avoid the nesting. Failing that, move the inner blocks to a new method that you call within what was an outer block.

Note: Where to next?

At this point in our study of Java, handling an exception thrown by an invoked library method is our greatest concern. This ability will be essential to learning how to perform input and output with external files, as you will see in the next chapter. If you want, you can skip the rest of this chapter for now and read the next one.

Aside: Nested try-catch blocks

If you must nest `try-catch` blocks, the following guidelines apply. When a `catch` block appears within another `catch` block, they must use different identifiers for their parameters. If you plan to nest `try-catch` blocks within a `try` block, you could omit the inner `catch` blocks if the outer `catch` blocks deal with the relevant exceptions appropriately. In such a case, an exception thrown within an inner `try` block is caught in the outer `try` block.

Throwing an Exception

Although the ability to handle an exception is most useful, knowing how to throw an exception and how to define a class of exceptions is also important. This section looks at how exceptions are thrown. You should throw an exception within a method only in unusual or unexpected situations that you cannot address in a reasonable way.

28.12 **The `throw` statement.** A method intentionally throws an exception by executing a `throw` statement. Its general form is

> `throw` *exception_object*;

Rather than creating the exception object in a separate step, programmers usually create the object within the `throw` statement, as in the following example:

> `throw new IOException();`

This statement creates a new object of the class `IOException` and throws it. Just as we should catch as specific an exception as possible, the exceptions we throw should be as specific as possible.

Although we can invoke the default constructor of the exception class, as in the previous example, we also can provide the constructor with a string as an argument. The resulting object will contain that string in a data field, and both the object and this string will be available to the `catch` block that handles the exception. The `catch` block then can use the exception's method `getMessage` to retrieve the string, as you saw earlier. The default constructor provides a default value for such a string.

Syntax: The `throw` statement

> `throw` *exception_object*;

where *exception_object* is an instance of a class of exceptions, typically created by one of the following invocations of the class's constructor:

> `new` *class_name*()

or

> `new` *class_name*(*message*)

Either the string provided by the default constructor or the string *message* is available to the code that catches the exception, via the exception's method `getMessage`.

Programming Tip: If an unusual situation occurs, should I throw an exception?

- If you can resolve the unusual situation in a reasonable manner, you likely can use a decision statement instead of throwing an exception.
- If several resolutions to an abnormal occurrence are possible, and you want the client to choose one, you should throw a checked exception.
- If a programmer makes a coding mistake by using your method incorrectly, you can throw a runtime exception. However, you should not throw a runtime exception simply to enable a client to avoid handling it.
- You should throw only exceptions, never errors.

Programming Tip

If a method contains a `throw` statement to throw an exception, add a `throws` clause to its header rather than catching the exception within the method's body. In general, throwing an exception and catching one should occur in separate methods.

Question 7 What is the difference in purpose between the Java keywords `throw` and `throws`?

■ Programmer-Defined Exception Classes

You can define your own exception classes by extending existing exception classes. An existing superclass could be one in the Java Class Library or one of your own. The constructors in an exception subclass are the most important—and often the only—methods you need to define. Other methods are inherited from the superclass.

A Sample Definition

28.13 For example, consider the method sqrt provided by Java's class Math to compute the square root of a real number. Since sqrt returns a double value, it computes the square root of only nonnegative numbers. If we give the method a negative number, it returns the special value NaN, which stands for "not a number." If displayed, this value appears as NaN. If it is involved in arithmetic, the result is NaN.

Imagine, instead, a square root method that requires a nonnegative argument. Let's treat the passing of a negative number to the method as a programming mistake and throw a runtime exception. The method certainly could throw an instance of RuntimeException, but a more specific exception would be better. So let's define our own class, SquareRootException, as shown in Listing 28-1. Because we want a runtime exception, our class extends RuntimeException. Each of the two constructors for this class uses super to invoke RuntimeException's constructor, passing it a string as a message. The default constructor passes a default message, but the second constructor passes the message provided as its argument when it is called. Most programmer-defined exception classes are as straightforward as SquareRootException.

LISTING 28-1   The exception class SquareRootException

```java
/** SquareRootException.java by F. M. Carrano
    A class of runtime exceptions thrown when an attempt
    is made to find the square root of a negative number.
*/
public class SquareRootException extends RuntimeException
{
   public SquareRootException()
   {
      super("Attempted square root of a negative number.");
   } // end default constructor

   public SquareRootException(String message)
   {
      super(message);
   } // end constructor
} // end SquareRootException
```

28.14 Note that SquareRootException's default constructor could use this instead of super, as follows:

```java
public SquareRootException()
{
   this("Attempted square root of a negative number.");
} // end default constructor
```

By using this, the constructor calls the second constructor, which in turn calls RuntimeException's constructor. In contrast, the default constructor shown in Listing 28-1 uses super to call RuntimeException's constructor directly. Although the version in Listing 28-1 is more direct and might seem better, using this to link one constructor to another is usually preferable, as the technique tends to reduce mistakes.

Question 8 Suppose that you plan to throw a checked exception when a division by zero is about to occur. What is a definition of a class `DivisionByZeroException` that you could use in this situation?

Using Our Own Exception Class

28.15

videonote

Creating our own
exception classes

We have imagined a square root method that throws a runtime exception when given a negative number as its argument. Now that we have an appropriate class of exceptions, let's define this method within a class of static methods, as shown in Listing 28-2, that is much like the class `Math`. We have numbered the lines in this listing to make the output in the next listing easier for you to understand.

The header for the method `squareRoot` is similar to the header of `Math.sqrt` but also includes a `throws` clause to indicate that the method might throw a `SquareRootException`. Notice the new tag `@throws` in the javadoc comment preceding the header. It provides documentation of the exception that might occur. If the method could throw more than one exception, we would include a separate `@throws` tag for each one and list the exceptions alphabetically by name. Since `SquareRootException` is a runtime exception, listing it in a `throws` clause and documenting it in javadoc are optional.

Within the body of the method `squareRoot` is a `throw` statement. It throws a `SquareRootException` if the method's argument is negative. If the argument is not negative, the method simply returns the square root as computed by the method `Math.sqrt`.

LISTING 28-2   The class `OurMath` and its static method `squareRoot`

```
1 /** OurMath.java by F. M. Carrano
2     A class of static methods to perform various mathematical
3     computations, including the square root.
4 */
5 public class OurMath
6 {
7    /** Computes the square root of a nonnegative real number.
8        @param value  a real value whose square root is desired
9        @return the square root of the given value
10       @throws SquareRootException if value < 0 */
11   public static double squareRoot(double value)
12        throws SquareRootException
13   {
14      if (value < 0)
15         throw new SquareRootException();
16      else
17         return Math.sqrt(value);
18   } // end squareRoot

   < Other methods not relevant to this discussion are here. >

99 } // end OurMath
```

Programming Tip: Do not confuse the keywords throw and throws

You use the Java reserved word `throws` in a method's header to declare the exceptions that the method might throw. The reserved word `throw` is used within the body of a method to actually throw an exception.

Note: **The javadoc tag @throws**

A javadoc comment that precedes a method's header should contain a separate line for each exception the method might throw. Each of these lines begins with the tag @throws, and they should be ordered alphabetically by the names of the exceptions. All checked exceptions must be documented.

Documenting runtime exceptions is optional and is generally not done. However, a designer can document those runtime exceptions that a client might reasonably want to handle. In fact, you will encounter some documented runtime exceptions in the Java Class Library. Realize, however, that your use of a method might cause a runtime exception that is undocumented. If you decide to document runtime exceptions, they must not depend on how the method is defined. Thus, identifying the exceptions a method might throw should be done as part of its design and specification, and not its implementation.

28.16 A demonstration of the class `OurMath` is given in Listing 28-3. Note the message displayed as a result of the exception. Also note that execution stops when the exception occurs.

LISTING 28-3   A driver for the class `OurMath`

```
 1 /** OurMathDriver.java by F. M. Carrano
 2     A demonstration of a runtime exception using the class OurMath.
 3 */
 4 public class OurMathDriver
 5 {
 6    public static void main(String[] args)
 7    {
 8       System.out.print("The square root of 9 is ");
 9       System.out.println(OurMath.squareRoot(9.0));
10
11       System.out.print("The square root of -9 is ");
12       System.out.println(OurMath.squareRoot(-9.0));
13
14       System.out.print("The square root of 16 is ");
15       System.out.println(OurMath.squareRoot(16.0));
16    } // end main
17 } // end OurMathDriver
```

Output

```
The square root of 9 is 3.0
The square root of -9 is Exception in thread "main"
   SquareRootException: Attempted square root of a negative number.
at OurMath.squareRoot(OurMath.java:15)
at OurMathDriver.main(OurMathDriver.java:12)
```

Question 9 What change can you make to the class `OurMath`, as given in Listing 28-2, to replace the message

```
Attempted square root of a negative number
```

with

```
OurMath has thrown an exception
```

Question 10 What change can you make to the driver in Listing 28-3 to handle the exception and thereby report, but ignore, the attempted square root? The program should continue by computing the square root of 16.

28.17 Imagine that our class OurMath is widely available to other programmers. Joe wants to use our class to compute the square root, but he doesn't want to receive an error message when squareRoot encounters a negative argument. Instead, he wants the method to return a complex[1] number involving *i*, which is an abbreviation for the square root of –1. For example, the square root of –9 is 3*i*, because

$$\sqrt{-9} = \sqrt{9(-1)} = \sqrt{9}\sqrt{-1} = 3i$$

To accommodate results that involve *i* and those that do not, Joe has his method return a string. Thus, Joe envisions a method that would return the string "3i" as the square root of –9 and would return the string "3" as the square root of 9.

Joe's method will invoke OurMath.squareRoot. As this invocation must appear within a try block, Joe writes

```
String result = "";
try
{
    Double temp = OurMath.squareRoot(value);
    result = temp.toString();
}
```

All is fine, as long as value is not negative, but if it is negative, a SquareRootException is thrown. Instead of displaying an error message, as the driver in Listing 28-3 does, Joe wants his method to return the correct value for a negative argument. He writes the following pseudocode to get his ideas on paper:

```
// assume value is negative
catch (SquareRootException e)
{
    Double temp = the square root of -value
    result = temp.toString() followed by "i"
}
```

Joe then translates this pseudocode into the following catch block:

```
catch (SquareRootException e)
{ // Assertion: value is negative
    Double temp = OurMath.squareRoot(-value);
    result = temp.toString() + "i";
}
```

28.18 Listing 28-4 shows Joe's method squareRoot within his class JoeMath, and Listing 28-5 provides a demonstration of the class.

LISTING 28-4 The class JoeMath

```
/** JoeMath.java by Joe
    A class of static methods to perform various mathematical
```

---

1. Only a rudimentary knowledge of complex numbers is needed here. Complex numbers build on real numbers by adding an imaginary part involving *i*. Every complex number has the form $a + b\,i$, where *a* and *b* are real numbers. To represent a real number in this notation, you would have *b* be zero.

```
         computations, including the square root.
 */
public class JoeMath
{
   /** Computes the square root of a real number.
       @param value  a real value whose square root is desired
       @return a string containing the square root of the given value */
   public static String squareRoot(double value)
   {
      String result = "";
      try
      {
         Double temp = OurMath.squareRoot(value);
         result = temp.toString();
      }
      catch (SquareRootException e)
      {
         Double temp = OurMath.squareRoot(-value);
         result = temp.toString() + "i";
      }

      return result;
   } // end squareRoot
```

< Other methods not relevant to this discussion could be here. >

```
} // end JoeMath
```

LISTING 28-5   A driver for the class `JoeMath`

```
/** JoeMathDriver.java by F. M. Carrano
    A demonstration of a runtime exception using the class JoeMath.
 */
public class JoeMathDriver
{
   public static void main(String[] args)
   {
      System.out.print("The square root of 9 is ");
      System.out.println(JoeMath.squareRoot(9.0));

      System.out.print("The square root of -9 is ");
      System.out.println(JoeMath.squareRoot(-9.0));

      System.out.print("The square root of 16 is ");
      System.out.println(JoeMath.squareRoot(16.0));

      System.out.print("The square root of -16 is ");
      System.out.println(JoeMath.squareRoot(-16.0));
```

```
        } // end main
} // end JoeMathDriver
```

Output

```
    The square root of 9 is 3.0
    The square root of -9 is 3.0i
    The square root of 16 is 4.0
    The square root of -16 is 4.0i
```

Question 11 How can you revise the statements in the catch block shown in Listing 28-4 so that JoeMath.squareRoot calls itself instead of OurMath.squareRoot?

Question 12 Would the definition of JoeMathDriver, as given in Listing 28-5, have to be different if the class SquareRootException, as shown in Listing 28-1, extended Exception instead of RuntimeException? If so, explain why and how. If not, explain why not.

■ A Problem Solved: Groups of People

> Create a class Group to represent a group of people, in no particular order. Give the group the following methods: addPerson, removePerson, isEmpty, isFull, getSize, and toString. The method addPerson should throw a GroupException if a new person cannot be added to the group because it is full. Similarly, removePerson should throw a GroupException if the group is empty prior to an attempted deletion from the group. Assume that the classes Name and Person—as given, respectively, in Listing 6-5 of Chapter 6 and Listing 15-3 of Chapter 15—are available.

28.19   Because this is a chapter about exceptions, let's first define the class GroupException. As you can see from Listing 28-6, its definition is much like that for SquareRootException, as given in Listing 28-1. This time, however, we will use a checked exception, and so we derive GroupException from the standard class Exception. GroupException's default constructor invokes the class's second constructor, passing it a suitable string. This second constructor, in turn, calls a constructor of the superclass Exception.

LISTING 28-6   The class GroupException

```java
/** GroupException.java by Frank Carrano
    Represents a checked exception appropriate for a group of objects.
*/
public class GroupException extends Exception
{
    public GroupException()
    {
        this("Unspecified GroupException.");
    } // end default constructor
```

```
      public GroupException(String message)
      {
         super(message);
      } // end constructor
   } // end GroupException
```

28.20   The definition of the class Group is fairly straighforward and is given in Listing 28-7. We use an array to store the Person objects added to a group and an integer variable to track the group's size. Both of these items are data fields of the class and are declared as follows:

```
   private final Person[] personArray;
   private int        size;
```

Since the problem description allows the group to become full, we do not resize the array, as Chapter 20 described, when it is full. Therefore, the array needs a maximum size, which we provide in the constant data field MAX_SIZE.

The default constructor creates an empty group. In addition to setting the group's size to zero, the constructor allocates memory for the array personArray. Failing to perform this allocation is a common oversight among novice programmers.

LISTING 28-7   The class Group

```
/** Group.java by Frank Carrano
    Represents a group of Person objects.
*/
public class Group
{
   private final Person[] personArray;
   private int size;
   private static final int MAX_SIZE = 25;

   /** Creates an empty group. */
   public Group()
   {
      size = 0;
      personArray = new Person[MAX_SIZE];
   } // end default constructor

   /** Adds a new person to the group.
       @param newPerson  a Person object
       @throws GroupException if the group is full before the
               attempted addition */
   public void addPerson(Person newPerson) throws GroupException
   {
      if (isFull())
         throw new GroupException("Attempted addition to a full group.");
      else
      {
```

```java
            personArray[size] = newPerson; // add to end of array
            size++;
        } // end if
    } // end addPerson

    /** Removes and returns one person from the group.
        @return the Person object that is deleted from the group
        @throws GroupException if the group is empty before the
                deletion is attempted */
    public Person removePerson() throws GroupException
    {
        if (isEmpty())
            throw new GroupException(
                            "Attempted deletion from an empty group.");
        else
        {
            size--;
            Person removed = personArray[size];
            personArray[size] = null;
            return removed;
        } //end if
    } // end removePerson

    /** Tests whether the group is empty.
        @return true if the group is empty */
    public boolean isEmpty()
    {
        return size == 0;
    } // end isEmpty

    /** Tests whether the group is full.
        @return true if the group is full. */
    public boolean isFull()
    {
        return size == MAX_SIZE;
    } // end isFull

    /** Gets the size of the group.
        @return the number of objects in the group */
    public int getSize()
    {
        return size;
    } // end getSize

    /** Gets a listing of the people in the group.
        @return the contents of the group as one string. */
    public String toString()
```

```
    {
        String contents = "";
        for (int index = 0; index < size; index++)
            contents = contents + personArray[index] + "\n";
        return contents;
    } // end toString
} // end Group
```

28.21   **Adding an entry to the group.** The method `addPerson` adds a `Person` object to the group if the group is not full already. If the group is full, however, the method should throw an exception. Since `addPerson` does not specify where to add a new entry to the group, we can add it anywhere in the array. The easiest place to add an entry to an array is right after its last entry, as Figure 28-2 illustrates. Since `size` contains the number of current entries, the new entry should be placed in `personArray[size]`. Following the addition, we must increment `size` to reflect the increase in the group's size. We can summarize these actions by writing the following pseudocode:

> *Algorithm* `addPerson(newPerson)`
> *// Adds a* `Person` *object to the group.*
>
> **if** (*the group is full*)
>   **throw** GroupException
> **else**
> {
>   personArray[size] = newPerson
>   size++
> }

The Java code for `addPerson`, as given in Listing 28-7, closely follows this pseudocode. Note the `@throws` tag in the method's comment, the `throws` clause in the method's header, the call to `isFull` to test whether the group is full, and the `throw` statement that throws an exception. The latter statement invokes `GroupException`'s constructor, passing it a description of the problem.

FIGURE 28-2   The array element available for the next addition to the group

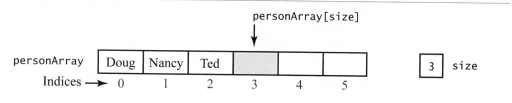

28.22   **Removing an entry from the group.** The method `removePerson` removes a `Person` object from the group, if possible. If the group is empty, the method throws an exception. The decisions we made about the definition of `addPerson` affect how we can define `removePerson`. By adding objects into consecutive array locations, we avoid intermingling the occupied locations and the unoccupied locations. That is, they form two distinct clusters, as Figure 28-3a shows. The occupied location having the largest index is `personArray[size - 1]`. In fact, this location contains the last entry added to the group. If we remove this last entry, return it, and decrement `size`, the array will still have two distinct clusters of occupied and unoccupied locations, as Figure 28-3b illustrates.

FIGURE 28-3 (a) Before and (b) after removing an entry from a nonempty group

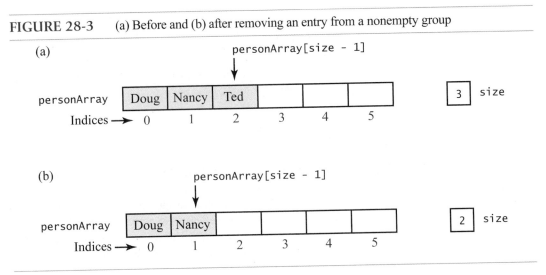

The following pseudocode reflects the steps we just described:

Algorithm removePerson()
// Removes and returns one Person *object from the group.*

```
if (the group is empty)
    throw GroupException
else
{
    size--
    removed = personArray[size]
    personArray[size] = null
    return removed
}
```

The Java code for removePerson, as given in Listing 28-7, closely follows this pseudocode. Once again, notice the @throws tag in the method's comment and the throws clause in the method's header. Also note the call to isEmpty to test whether the group is empty and the throw statement that throws an exception. The latter statement is similar to the analogous statement in the method addPerson; however, it passes a different message to GroupException's constructor.

The methods addPerson and removePerson act in conjunction with each other: The action of one maintains the validity of the other. While this consideration might not be evident to us when we specify these methods, it must be at the forefront when we define them in Java.

28.23 **Further discussion.** Our definition of the method removePerson sets the array's reference to the removed entry to null. In this way, only the client retains a reference to this object. By decrementing size, the method ensures that a subsequent call to either itself or addPerson by a client will behave correctly and ignore this null reference. If an addition occurs after a removal, a reference to the new entry will replace the null value. If no addition occurs after a removal, the null reference will remain in the array but will be ignored.

Notice how the method toString forms a string from each entry in the group using the expression

```
contents + personArray[index] + "\n"
```

because the data type of the variable contents is String, + is the concatenation operator, which interprets personArray[index] as if it were personArray[index].toString(). The array entries are Person objects, so Person's toString method is invoked. The string returned by the method is then followed by the new-line character. As a result, Group's toString returns one string, which, when displayed, lists the names and cities of each group member, one member per line.

28.24   The program in Listing 28-8 demonstrates some of Group's behaviors. In particular, an exception is thrown by the method removePerson when an attempt is made to remove a person from the group csc211 after all of its entries have been removed.

LISTING 28-8   A demonstration of an exception thrown by the class Group

```java
/** GroupDriver.java by F. M. Carrano
    A demonstration of the class Group.
*/
public class GroupDriver
{
   public static void main(String args[])
   {
      Group csc211 = new Group();
      try
      {
         csc211.addPerson(new Person(new Name("Aly", ""), "Atlanta"));
         csc211.addPerson(new Person(new Name("Brady", ""), "Boston"));
         csc211.addPerson(new Person(new Name("Colbie", ""), "Chicago"));
         csc211.addPerson(new Person(new Name("Decker", ""), "Denver"));

         System.out.println("The group contains the following people:");
         System.out.println(csc211);

         System.out.println("Removing the following people from " +
                            "the group:");
         while (csc211.getSize() > 0)
         {
            Person aPerson = csc211.removePerson();
            System.out.println(aPerson);
         } // end while

         Person anotherPerson = csc211.removePerson();
         System.out.println(anotherPerson);
      }
      catch (GroupException unusualEvent)
      {
         System.out.println(unusualEvent.getMessage());
         System.out.println("Execution cannot continue.");
      }
   } // end main
} // end GroupDriver
```

Output

```
The group contains the following people:
Aly  (Atlanta)
Brady  (Boston)
Colbie  (Chicago)
Decker  (Denver)
```

```
Removing the following people from the group:
Decker  (Denver)
Colbie  (Chicago)
Brady  (Boston)
Aly  (Atlanta)
Attempted deletion from an empty group.
Execution cannot continue.
```

Question 13 Imagine a revision to the program in Listing 28-8 that adds 26 Person objects to the group csc211 by calling the method csc211.addPerson 26 times. What output would the program produce?

Question 14 Imagine a class Group2 that is just like the class Group, as given in Listing 28-7, but with the following changes: The data type Person is replaced by String, and the names of the methods addPerson and removePerson are changed to add and remove, respectively. The resulting Group2 methods add and remove will have similarities to the methods add and remove of the class BagOfStrings, which is given in Listing 19-6 of Chapter 19. How are they different?

■ Inheritance and Exceptions

28.25   Imagine a class whose method someMethod has a throws clause in its header. Can we override someMethod in a subclass and list additional checked exceptions in its throws clause? No, Java will not let us; we will get a syntax error if we do.

For example, consider the following superclass and subclass:

```
public class BaseClass
{
    public void someMethod() throws Exception1
    { . . .
    } // end someMethod
} // end BaseClass

public class DerivedClass extends BaseClass
{
    public void someMethod() throws Exception1, Exception2 // ERROR!
    { . . .
    } // end someMethod
} // end DerivedClass
```

The throws clause in the overriding method will be flagged as syntactically incorrect. Let's think about why this is an error.

Suppose a program creates an instance of DerivedClass, assigns the object to a variable of BaseClass—let's call it baseObject—and places the call baseObject.someMethod() within a try block, as follows:

```
public class Driver
{
    public static void main(String[] args)
    {
        BaseClass baseObject = new DerivedClass();
        try
        {
            baseObject.someMethod();
        }
```

```
        catch (Exception1 e)
        {
            System.out.println(e.getMessage());
        }
    } // end main
} // end Driver
```

Since baseObject references an instance of DerivedClass, DerivedClass's version of someMethod is called. But since baseObject's static type is BaseClass, the compiler sees only BaseClass's definition for someMethod. Thus, it checks only that Exception1 is caught. If the throws clause in DerivedClass was legal, we could call DerivedClass's someMethod without catching Exception2.

28.26 The rule governing which exceptions can appear in a throws clause of an overriding method is relaxed somewhat if the exceptions are related by inheritance. For example, if Exception2 extends Exception1, the following is legal:

```
public class BaseClass
{
    public void someMethod() throws Exception1
    { . . .
    } // end someMethod
} // end BaseClass

public class DerivedClass extends BaseClass
{
    public void someMethod() throws Exception2 // OK, assuming
    // Exception2 extends Exception1
    { . . .
    } // end someMethod
} // end DerivedClass
```

 Note: An overriding method in a subclass cannot list exceptions in a throws clause that aren't listed in a throws clause of the overridden method in the superclass, unless they are derived from the exception classes listed in the overridden method. However, an overriding method can list fewer exceptions in its throws clause or none at all.

 Question 15 If the throws clause of someMethod in BaseClass, as given in the previous segment, lists only the class Exception, what throws clauses would be legal for someMethod in DerivedClass?

Question 16 Consider the class Group2, as Question 14 describes. Since the classes Group2 and BagOfStrings share similarities, could we derive Group2 from BagOfStrings? If so, should we? For simplicity, assume that BagOfStrings does not have an implements clause in its header.

Question 17 Under the assumptions of the previous question, could we derive BagOfStrings from Group2? If so, should we?

Question 18 Consider the previous question again. Looking only at the remove method that has no parameter, and assuming that we are deriving BagOfStrings from Group2, define remove in BagOfStrings.

■ The `finally` Block

28.27   If you have code that must execute regardless of whether an exception occurs, you could place it at the end of the `try` block and at the end of each `catch` block. An easier way to accomplish this, however, is to place one copy of the code in question within a `finally` block that follows the last `catch` block. Code within a `finally` block executes after either the `try` block or an executing `catch` block ends. Although optional, the `finally` block is a good way to provide clean-up services, such as closing a file or releasing system resources.

The following code shows the placement of the `finally` block:

```
try
{
    < Code that might throw an exception, either by executing a throw statement
      or by calling a method that throws an exception >
}
catch (AnException e)
{
    < Code that handles exceptions of type AnException or a subclass of anException >
}

< Possibly other catch blocks to handle other types of exceptions >

finally
{
    < Code that executes after either the try block or an executing catch block ends >
}
```

 Note: Statements within a `finally` block execute regardless of whether an exception occurs, but they do not execute if either the `try` block or a `catch` block calls `System.exit`. If no exception takes place, the `finally` block executes after its corresponding `try` block completes its execution. (If the `try` block contains a `return` statement, the `finally` block executes before the return.) However, if an exception occurs, and it is caught by one of the `catch` blocks, the `finally` block executes after that `catch` block executes.

28.28   **Example.** Imagine that you open the refrigerator door and reach for the milk. Whether you find milk or not, you should close the door. In the following code, the method `takeOutMilk` will throw an exception if no milk is found. Whether an exception occurs or not, `closeRefrigerator` is called within the `finally` block.

```
try
{
    openRefrigerator();
    takeOutMilk();
    pourMilk();
    putBackMilk();
}
catch (NoMilkException e)
{
    System.out.println(e.getMessage());
}
finally
{
    closeRefrigerator();
}
```

28.29   Let's explicitly demonstrate the behavior of a `finally` block by executing the code given in the previous example. The program in Listing 28-9 provides simple definitions for the methods called in this example. All but `takeOutMilk` simply display an appropriate message. The method `takeOutMilk`, however, displays a message some of the time at random but throws a NoMilkException the rest of the time. The definition of the class NoMilkException is analogous to the definition of the class GroupException shown earlier in Listing 28-6.

In the first sample output shown in Listing 28-9, no exception occurs. Each method within the try block executes in turn, as the output indicates. Lastly, the method closeRefrigerator within the finally block executes. In the second sample output, openRefrigerator executes normally, but then takeOutMilk throws an exception. After the exception is caught by the catch block, the finally block executes as expected.

LISTING 28-9   A demonstration of a finally block

```java
/** GetMilk.java by F. M. Carrano.
    Demonstrates the behavior of a finally block.
*/
public class GetMilk
{
   public static void main(String[] args)
   {
      try
      {
         openRefrigerator();
         takeOutMilk();
         pourMilk();
         putBackMilk();
      }
      catch (NoMilkException e)
      {
         System.out.println(e.getMessage());
      }
      finally
      {
         closeRefrigerator();
      }
   } // end main

   public static void openRefrigerator()
   {
      System.out.println("Open the refrigerator door.");
   } // end openRefrigerator

   public static void takeOutMilk() throws NoMilkException
   {
      if (Math.random() < 0.5)
         System.out.println("Take out the milk.");
      else
         throw new NoMilkException();
   } // end openRefrigerator
```

< *The methods* pourMilk, putBackMilk, *and* closeRefrigerator *are analogous to*

```
        openRefrigerator and are here. >
    . . .
} // end GetMilk
```

Sample Output 1 (no exception is thrown)

```
Open the refrigerator door.
Take out the milk.
Pour the milk.
Put the milk back.
Close the refrigerator door.
```

Sample Output 2 (exception is thrown)

```
Open the refrigerator door.
Out of milk!
Close the refrigerator door.
```

28.30   **Nested `try-finally` blocks.** Some programmers find the `try-catch-finally` sequence confusing and prefer to place the `finally` block after a `try` block instead of after a `catch` block. Doing so, however, requires the `try-finally` blocks to be nested within another `try` block. For example, the program in Listing 28-10 revises the `try-catch-finally` blocks shown in Segment 28.28.

If `takeOutMilk` throws an exception, the `finally` block executes and then the exception propagates to the outer `try` block and is caught by the `catch` block. The output shown in Listing 28-10 demonstrates this behavior. Thus, when an exception is thrown, the `finally` block executes before the exception is caught, whereas the reverse is true for the code shown in Listing 28-9.

LISTING 28-10   A demonstration of a nested `finally` block

```java
/** GetMilk2.java by F. M. Carrano.
    Demonstrates the behavior of a nested finally block.
*/
public class GetMilk2
{
   public static void main(String[] args)
   {
      try
      {
         try
         {
            openRefrigerator();
            takeOutMilk();
            pourMilk();
            putBackMilk();
         }
         finally
         {
            closeRefrigerator();
         }
      }
```

```
      catch (NoMilkException e)
      {
          System.out.println(e.getMessage());
      }
   } // end main
   < The remaining methods are identical to those given in Listing 28-9. >
   . . .
} // end GetMilk
```

Sample Output 1 (no exception is thrown) ◄— Same as the output shown in Listing 28-9

```
Open the refrigerator door.
Take out the milk.
Pour the milk.
Put the milk back.
Close the refrigerator door.
```

Sample Output 2 (exception is thrown) ◄— Different from the output shown in Listing 28-9

```
Open the refrigerator door.
Close the refrigerator door.
Out of milk!
```

videonote
A problem solved

Note: Despite our earlier advice about not nesting `try-catch` blocks, nesting `try-finally` blocks can be a reasonable choice. However, the unnested sequence of a `try` block followed by a `finally` block followed by one or more `catch` blocks is illegal.

CHAPTER SUMMARY

- An exception is an object that is created, or thrown, when an unusual event or circumstance occurs. A program can detect and react to, that is, handle, the exception.

- All classes of exceptions are descendants of the standard class `Exception`. All classes of runtime, or unchecked, exceptions are descendants of the standard class `RuntimeException`, which extends `Exception`. Exceptions that are not runtime exceptions are checked exceptions.

- Checked exceptions must be handled, but runtime exceptions need not be handled.

- A method handles an exception by using `try-catch` blocks that could involve a `finally` block. The `try` block detects when an exception is thrown, the `catch` blocks deal with it, and the optional `finally` block provides code that must execute regardless of whether an exception occurs.

- Although every exception class is a descendant of the class `Exception`, and you can use `Exception` in a `catch` block, catching more-specific exceptions is preferable, since doing so enables you to provide more accurate messages.

- Catch the most specific exception first.

- A method that can cause but does not handle a checked exception must declare the exception in a `throws` clause within its header. This approach is warranted when you cannot provide a reasonable reaction to the exception. The method's client must either handle the exception or declare it in a `throws` clause of its own. If the exception actually occurs, the method's execution ends but program execution continues.

- Avoid using `Exception` in a `throws` clause. Instead, use as specific an exception as you can.

- Statements within a `finally` block execute regardless of whether an exception occurs but do not execute if either the `try` block or a `catch` block calls `System.exit`. If no exception takes place, the `finally` block executes after its corresponding `try` block completes its execution. (If the `try` block contain a `return` statement, the return is deferred until the `finally` block executes.) However, if an exception occurs, and it is caught by one of the `catch` blocks, the `finally` block executes after that `catch` block.

- A method can throw an exception by executing a `throw` statement.

- You can define your own classes of exceptions by extending either `Exception` or `RuntimeException`. As a general rule, if you insert a `throw` statement in your code, it is probably best to define your own exception class.

- An error is an object of either the standard class `Error` or one of its descendant classes. Although similar to an exception, an error is not an exception. The occurrence of an error is too serious for a typical program to handle. Hence errors need not be caught or declared, even though doing so is legal.

- A `javadoc` comment that precedes a method's header should contain a separate line for each checked exception the method might throw. Each of these lines begins with the tag `@throws`, and they should be ordered alphabetically by the names of the exceptions. Documenting a runtime exception is at the discretion of the software designer. Any documented exception must be a part of a method's design and specification, and must not depend on how the method is defined.

- An overriding method in a subclass cannot list exceptions in a `throws` clause that aren't listed in a `throws` clause of the overridden method in the superclass, unless they are derived from the exceptions listed in the overridden method. However, an overriding method can list fewer exceptions in its `throws` clause or none at all.

- Although you can nest `try-catch` blocks within either a `try` block or a `catch` block, you should avoid doing so if possible. Nesting `try-finally` blocks within a `try` block, however, can be reasonable, but the unnested sequence of a `try` block followed by a `finally` block followed by one or more `catch` blocks is illegal.

EXERCISES

1. Consult the documentation for the class `IndexOutOfBoundsException` in the Java Class Library.
   a. What classes in the Java Class Library are subclasses of this class?
   b. What is the superclass of this class?
   c. Is an exception of this class checked or unchecked? Why?
   d. What happens to an executing program if this exception occurs?

2. Repeat Exercise 1 for the class `StringIndexOutOfBoundsException`.

3. Repeat Exercise 1 for the class `NoSuchFieldException`.

4. Consult the documentation for the class `ArrayList` in the Java Class Library. Which methods, if any, that `ArrayList` defines might throw an exception? Must any of these possible exceptions be handled? Why? Do not consider the methods defined in `ArrayList`'s ancestor classes.

5. Write a program that causes and recovers from a `StringIndexOutOfBoundsException`.

6. What is the header for a method named `exercise6` that returns an `int` value and has an array of integers as a parameter. Instead of handling a possible `IOException`, the method's author expects its client to do so.

7. Repeat the previous exercise, but this time assume that the method `exercise7` handles any checked exception.

8. Must you either handle an unchecked exception or declare it in a method's header?

9. In what order should you write multiple `catch` blocks after a single `try` block?

10. Define a class NeedlessOperationException of checked exceptions that are thrown to indicate an integer multiplication by 1.

11. Define a method that throws but does not handle a NeedlessOperationException, as described in Exercise 10.

12. Define a main method that calls the method you defined in the previous exercise and handles a possible NeedlessOperationException.

13. Define a method that might throw a NeedlessOperationException, as described in Exercise 10, and handles it.

14. Define a main method that calls the method you defined in the previous exercise.

15. Add a method to the class OurMath, as given in Listing 28-2, that performs integer division and throws a DivisionByZeroException, as described in Question 8 in Segment 28.14.

16. Add statements to the driver given in Listing 28-3 to test the method you defined for the previous exercise.

17. The class DooDad has a default constructor that might throw a DooDadConstructorException. The class FoeFum has a DooDad object as a data field. Write a default constructor for FoeFum that creates the class's data field. In the event a DooDadConstructorException is thrown, invoke DooDad's static method getDefaultDooDad and assign the returned DooDad object to FoeFum's data field.

18. Given the classes Name in Listing 6-5 of Chapter 6, Person in Listing 15-3 of Chapter 15, GroupException in Listing 28-6, and Group in Listing 28-7, write a program that creates a group of Person objects created from data entered by a user.

19. Write a program that demonstrates the behavior of try-catch-finally blocks when
    a. The try block causes an exception
    b. The catch block causes a runtime exception
    c. No exception occurs

20. If the try block of a try-catch-finally sequence contains a return statement, the finally block executes before the return. Write a program that demonstrates this behavior.

PROJECTS

1. Design and create a class UserData whose methods provide a client with valid integers and valid real numbers. Use Scanner to read input data from a user. Handle the possible exceptions to guarantee the validity of the data, have the user replace any invalid data, and finally return the validated data to the client.

2. Repeat Project 1 of Chapter 20 to play the game of tic-tac-toe. The class that represents the game board should assume that values that are input to its methods are legal. Its game-playing client should interact with the user and ensure that legal data is sent to the game board. To facilitate checking the validity of input data, handle the exceptions that Scanner methods such as nextInt might throw. Consult the documentation for the Java Class Library as needed.
   If a client were to pass invalid data to the game-board class, an exception—an ArrayIndexOutOfBoundsException, for example—likely would occur. Make the game-board class more robust by handling any possible runtime exception that might occur, thus avoiding a program crash during play.

ANSWERS TO SELF-TEST QUESTIONS

1. A division by zero will cause an ArithmeticException. For example, the statement
   ```
   int result = 5 / 0;
   ```
   will cause such an exception.

2. A message is displayed to indicate the exception, and then execution ends.

3.
```java
String myString = null;
System.out.println("My string has " + myString.length() +
                    "characters.");
```

4. The `try-catch` blocks are syntactically correct, but the `catch` block will catch any exception that is thrown. Although that might be what you want to do, you almost always should be more specific when catching exceptions.

5.
```java
public static void anythingCanHappen() throws IOException, EOFException
```

Note that the order of `IOException` and `EOFException` in the `throws` clause is irrelevant.

6.
```java
try
{
    anythingCanHappen();
}
catch (EOFException e)
{
    System.out.println("EOFException in anythingCanHappen");
}
catch (IOException e)
{
    System.out.println("IOException in anythingCanHappen");
}
```

The order of the `catch` blocks is important, since `EOFException` extends `IOException`. If you were to reverse the order of the `catch` blocks, an `EOFException` would be caught by the first `catch` block as an `IOException`.

7. The keyword `throw` is used to throw an exception, whereas the keyword `throws` begins a clause in a method's header that indicates to its client the exceptions that the method might throw.

8.
```java
public class DivisionByZeroException extends Exception
{
    public DivisionByZeroException()
    {
        this("Attempt to divide by zero."); // or replace 'this' with 'super'
    } // end default constructor

    public DivisionByZeroException(String message)
    {
        super(message);
    } // end constructor
} // end DivisionByZeroException
```

9. Change the statement
```java
throw new SquareRootException();
```
to
```java
throw new SquareRootException("OurMath has thrown an exception");
```

10. Replace statements 11 and 12 of the `main` method with the following statements:
```java
try
{
    System.out.print("The square root of -9 is ");
    System.out.println(OurMath.squareRoot(-9.0));
}
catch (SquareRootException e)
{
    System.out.println(e.getMessage());
}
```

The output is then

```
The square root of 9 is 3.0
The square root of -9 is Attempted square root of a negative number.
The square root of 16 is 4.0
```

11.
```
catch (SquareRootException e)
{
    String posResult = squareRoot(-value); // recursive call
    result = posResult + "i";
}
```

12. No. Although SquareRootException would be a checked exception, JoeMath.squareRoot already handles it. This method does not throw an exception, so JoeMathDriver has no exception to handle.

13.
```
Attempted addition to a full group.
Execution cannot continue.
```

14. The major difference between these Group2 methods and the BagOfStrings methods is how they signal to the client their inability to perform their task. The Group2 method add throws an exception if the group is full, whereas the BagOfStrings method add returns false if the bag is full. Similarly, the Group2 method remove throws an exception if the group is empty, but the BagOfStrings method remove returns null if the bag is empty.

15. The method someMethod in DerivedClass could omit a throws clause or list Exception and/or any exceptions derived from Exception.

16. No, Group2 cannot extend BagOfStrings. Let's consider the remove method. Its header in BagOfStrings is

```
public String remove(String aString)
```

Since this header has no throws clause, we cannot write remove's header in Group2 as

```
public String remove() throws GroupException
```

The same is true of the add method, but add poses yet another problem. In BagOfStrings, add returns a boolean value, while in Group2, it is a void method. An overriding method must have the same return type as the overridden method.

Even if we could derive Group2 from BagOfStrings, we should not. Group2 would inherit all methods of BagOfStrings, so it would have more methods than originally desired.

17. No, BagOfStrings cannot extend Group2. Group2 does not provide the methods necessary to implement the following methods in BagOfStrings: toArray, getCapacity, countOccurrences, contains, clear, the remove method that has a parameter, and the constructor that has a parameter. BagOfStrings could not override add in Group2 because the two methods have different return types. However, add's throws clause in Group2 would not be a problem. Note that BagOfStrings could override Group2's parameterless remove method.

18.
```
public String remove()
{
    String result = null;

    if (!isEmpty())
    {
        try
        {
            result = super.remove();
        }
        catch (GroupException e)
        {}
    } // end if

    return result;
} // end remove
```

Chapter 29

Text Files

Contents

Prerequisites

Objectives

After studying this chapter, you should be able to
- Describe the purpose of files
- Describe the kinds of files available in Java
- Create a text file
- Read a text file
- Append data to a text file
- Change existing data in a text file

Until now, input to a program has come from the keyboard or the mouse. Output has been displayed on a screen either textually or graphically. These forms of input and output occur in real time and are temporal. When the program ends, the input and output vanish.

You undoubtedly are aware of more persistent forms of data, such as your music, video, and photo collections. Each item in these collections is a **file**, which is simply data on a particular storage medium, such as a disk. Files are created by programs. For example, you can use a text editor to write your Java programs or a word processor to write an essay. Files also can be read by programs. This chapter will show why you might want to create and read files within a Java program and how to do so.

Preliminaries

We begin by looking at some generalities about files.

Why Files?

29.1   You own files such as Java programs, songs, photos, and so on. Each of these files was created by a program. You might have run the program yourself—such as when you used a text editor to write a Java program—or obtained the result of someone else's program in the form of a song or picture. In any event, you clearly do not want the output of the program to disappear when program execution stops. You want the data to last, to be persistent. By "persistent," we mean "to last beyond program execution." The contents of a file last until a program changes them or they become damaged. We want to use our files—that is, we want to run our programs, listen to our music, and watch our videos. The reason for creating files should be obvious.

Would you ever use a file as input to a program? You have done so if you ever have edited a photo or revised an essay you wrote yesterday. Java programs—like the ones we have written—can read data from an input file rather than the keyboard. Thus, files provide a convenient way to deal with large data sets.

Note: Reasons why a program creates a file

- A program creates and saves a file so it can be used over and over by other programs.
- A program creates a file for its own use as temporary storage for numerous intermediate results. The program writes data into the file and later reads the data, but does not save the file.

Streams

29.2   In Java, all input and output of data—including reading a file or writing a file—involves streams. A **stream** is an object that represents a flow of data. The data is a collection of eight-bit bytes representing numbers, characters, music, and so on. A stream either

- Sends data from your program to a destination, such as a file or the screen—in which case it is called an **output stream**—or
- Takes data from a source, such as a file or the keyboard, and delivers it to your program—in which case it is called an **input stream**

For example, the object `System.out` is an output stream that moves data from a program to a display. If an output stream is connected to a file, data will move from the program to the file. That is, the program will write the file. Likewise, `System.in` is an input stream that moves data from the keyboard to a program. If an input stream is connected to a file, the program will read data from the file.

> **Note:** Input and output are done from the perspective of the program. Thus, "input" means that data moves *into* your program from an input device such as a disk or keyboard. The word "output" means that data moves *out of* your program to an output device such as a disk or the screen.

> **Note:** Streams in Java are objects of certain classes in the Java Class Library. In particular, these classes are in the package `java.io`. Thus, to use these classes, you must import them from `java.io`.

29.3   Before you can read or write a file, you must connect the file to an appropriate stream and associate it with your Java program. You accomplish these steps, or **open** the file, when you create the stream by invoking the constructor of the stream's class. After you are finished with the file you must **close** it, or disconnect it from the stream, and hence from your program, by calling a particular stream method named `close`. We will examine the details of these steps shortly.

The Kinds of Files

29.4   All files are written as representations of ones and zeros, that is, binary digits, or bits. Java, however, treats files as either text files or binary files. A **text file** represents a collection of characters. The streams associated with text files provide methods that interpret the file's binary contents as characters. The files that contain your Java programs are most likely text files. A text editor can read a text file and make it appear to you as a sequence of characters. Any file other than a text file is called a **binary file**. For example, your song and picture files are binary files.

A Java program can create or read text files and binary files. The steps for processing—that is, writing or reading—a text file are analogous to those for a binary file. The kind of file determines which stream classes we use to perform the input or output. This chapter will focus on text files; we will discuss binary files in the next two chapters.

> **Programming Tip: Choosing the kind of file**
> Your Java program should use a text file if you will use a text editor to
>
> - Create files that the program will read
> - Read or edit files that the program will create
>
> If you will not use a text editor to create or read a file, consider using a binary file, as such files typically require less disk space than text files.

> **Note: The contents of a text file**
> A text file contains a sequence of characters in which each character is represented by the system's default encoding. As Chapter 4 noted, Java uses the Unicode character set, which includes many letters in natural languages that are quite different from English. The Unicode representation of each character requires two bytes. Many text editors, operating systems, and programming languages other than Java use the ASCII character set. The ASCII character set is a subset of the Unicode character set and contains the characters normally used for English and typical Java programs. The representation of each character in ASCII requires one byte.

A typical text file is organized as lines, each ending with a special end-of-line character. The lines in a text file are analogous to the lines you see when a program displays its output. In reality, however, the file is a sequence of data. For this reason, we say that a text file offers **sequential access** to its contents. That is, before you can read the nth line of the file, you start at the file's beginning and read through its first $n - 1$ lines.

File Names

29.5   Although Java does not specify the characters that can make up a file name, your operating system does. Typically, you use letters, digits, and a dot in the name of a data file, ending it with a suffix, such as .txt. This suffix is simply a convention, not a Java rule, although your operating system can give it meaning. This book uses the suffix .txt to indicate a text file.

Within a Java program, the name of a file is a string. Although our examples will use a String constant as a file name, our programs could have asked the user for the file's name and stored it in a String variable.

■ Creating a Text File

The standard class PrintWriter, which is in the package java.io of the Java Class Library, has the familiar methods print and println. As you will see, these methods behave like System.out.print and System.out.println. Thus, we will use this class to create an output stream for a text file.

Opening, Writing, and Closing a Text File

29.6   **Opening a text file for output.** Before you can write to a text file, you must open it by writing a statement like

```
PrintWriter toFile = new PrintWriter(fileName);
```

The call to PrintWriter's constructor creates an output stream and connects it to the file named by the String variable fileName. The **stream variable** toFile references this stream. Once the stream is created, your program always refers to the file by using the stream variable instead of its actual file name.

When you connect a file to an output stream in this way, your program always starts with an empty text file. If the file named by fileName did not exist before the constructor was called, a new, empty file is created and given that name. However, if the file named by fileName already exists, its old contents will be lost.

29.7   PrintWriter's constructor can throw a checked exception—FileNotFoundException—while attempting to open a file. For this reason, its invocation must appear within either a try block that is followed by an appropriate catch block or a method whose header lists this exception in a throws clause. For example, we could write the following statements to open a text file named data.txt for output:

```
String fileName = "data.txt";
PrintWriter toFile = null;
try
{
   toFile = new PrintWriter(fileName);
}
catch (FileNotFoundException e)
{
   System.out.println("PrintWriter error opening the file " +
                    fileName);
```

```
        System.out.println(e.getMessage());
        < Possibly other statements to deal with this exception. >
    }
```

Notice that we declared the variable `toFile` outside of the `try` block so that `toFile` is available outside of this block. Remember, anything declared in a block—even a `try` block—is local to the block. Declaring `toFile` in this way enables us to use it to write to the file, as you will see.

A `FileNotFoundException` does not necessarily mean that the file was not found. After all, if you are creating a new file, it doesn't already exist. In that case, an exception is thrown if the file could not be created because, for example, the file name is already used as a folder (directory) name.

Note: A `FileNotFoundException` will occur if a file cannot be opened for output, either because it does not exist and cannot be created or because it is inaccessible.

29.8 **Writing a text file.** The methods `println` and `print` of the class `PrintWriter` work the same for writing to a text file as the respective methods `System.out.println` and `System.out.print` work for writing to the screen. Thus, when a program writes a value to a text file, the number of characters written is the same as if it had written the value to the screen. For example, writing the `int` value 12345 to a text file places five characters in the file. In general, writing an integer of type `int` places between 1 and 11 characters in a text file.

The following statements write four lines to the text file we created in the previous segment:

```
for (int counter = 1; counter < 5; counter ++)
    toFile.println("Line " + counter);
```

Notice that we use the stream variable `toFile` when calling `println`, not the actual name of the file. Additionally, we did not place the call to `println` within a `try` block, as `println` does not throw any checked exceptions. The same is true of `print`.

Note: `System.out` is an object of the standard class `PrintStream`. Because both `PrintStream` and `PrintWriter` define the same `print` and `println` methods, objects of `PrintWriter` have the same `print` and `println` methods as `System.out`. However, `System.out` directs its output stream to a different destination than `PrintWriter` objects do.

29.9 **Buffering.** Instead of sending output to a file immediately, `PrintWriter` waits to send a larger packet of data. Thus, the output from `println`, for example, is not sent to the output file right away. Instead, it is saved and placed into a portion of memory called a **buffer**, along with the output from other invocations of `print` and `println`. When the buffer is too full to accept more output, its contents are written to the file. Thus, the output from several `print` and `println` statements is written at the same time, instead of each time one statement executes. This technique is called **buffering**, and it saves execution time.

29.10 **Closing a text file.** When we are finished using a file, we must disconnect it from the stream. Every stream class, including `PrintWriter`, has a method named `close` to accomplish this task. Thus, to close the file associated with the stream variable `toFile`, we write

```
    tofile.close();
```

When closing a file, the system writes any data still left in the buffer to the file and releases any resources it used to connect the stream to the file. Note that `close` will not throw an exception.

Programming Tip

If you do not close a file, Java will close it for you, but only if your program ends normally. To avoid any possible loss of data or damage to a file, you should close it as soon as possible after you are finished using it.

29.11 **Flushing an output file.** You can force any pending output that is currently in a buffer to be written to its destination file by calling PrintWriter's method flush, as follows:

```
toFile.flush();
```

The method close automatically calls the method flush, so for most simple applications, you do not need to call flush explicitly. However, if you continue to program, you will eventually encounter situations in which you will have to use flush.

Question 1 What Java statements will create a new text file that contains the English alphabet in uppercase, one letter per line? Name the file alpha.txt.

Question 2 What, if anything, is wrong with the following try block that opens a text file for output?

```
try
{
    PrintWriter toFile = new PrintWriter("myFile.txt");
}
```

Question 3 Must you place the call to the method close within a try block? Why or why not?

A Class for Creating Text Files

29.12 The class TextFileMaker given in Listing 29-1 encapsulates the details of opening, writing, and closing a text file. We will need the classes PrintWriter and FileNotFoundException from the Java Class Library. Our new class has three data fields: a stream variable toFile, the file's name as a string, and a boolean variable that signals whether the file is open. The constructor simply initializes these fields.

The public method openFile opens a text file by calling PrintWriter's constructor with the file's name as its argument. Notice how openFile handles the exception that PrintWriter's constructor might throw and sets the boolean data field open according to whether the file is opened. The method writeLine checks that the file is open and, if so, writes a given string as the next line in the file. To make our class simple, we did not overload writeLine to accommodate data of various data types. The client, therefore, must pass a string to writeLine. However, you certainly could overload writeLine—much as PrintWriter overloads both println and print—to give the client's programmer less to worry about. The method closeFile calls PrintWriter's close method and also sets the field open to false. Finally, the methods getName and isOpen are straightforward.

The next section will use this class to create a text file of strings.

videonote
Text files and streams

LISTING 29-1   The class TextFileMaker

```
import java.io.PrintWriter;
import java.io.FileNotFoundException;
/** TextFileMaker.java
    A class for creating text files.
```

```java
      @author Frank M. Carrano
*/
public class TextFileMaker
{
   private PrintWriter toFile;
   private final String name;
   private boolean open;

   public TextFileMaker(String fileName)
   {
      toFile = null;
      name = fileName;
      open = false;
   } // end constructor

   public void openFile()
   {
      try
      {
         toFile = new PrintWriter(name);
         open = true;
      }
      catch (FileNotFoundException e)
      {
         System.out.println("Cannot open the file " + name);
         System.out.println(e.getMessage());
         open = false;
      }
   } // end openFile

   public void writeLine(String line)
   {
      if (open)
         toFile.println(line);
   } // end writeLine

   public void closeFile()
   {
      toFile.close();
      open = false;
   } // end closeFile

   public String getName()
   {
      return name;
   } // end getName
```

```
    public boolean isOpen()
    {
       return open;
    } // end getName
} // end TextFileMaker
```

Question 4 Repeat Question 1, but this time use the class `TextFileMaker` as given in Listing 29-1.

A Problem Solved: Creating a Text File of Colleges and Universities

> The United States is home to many colleges and universities. To maintain a list of them, let's create a text file that contains the following data for each school: name, city, state, and current enrollment.

29.13   **Discussion.** Although the easiest way for a staff member to create this text file is to use a text editor, we will write a Java program that prompts its user for the necessary data and writes these facts to a new text file. Let's name the file `CollegeFile.txt`.

The design of this program requires no lengthy discussion, as it uses the class `TextFileMaker` in Listing 29-1. Most of the program's effort involves the interaction with the user. Let's note the major steps the program should take:

- Give directions to the user.
- Open the text file.
- Write data to the file as the user supplies it.
- Close the file.

We need the class `Scanner` to obtain the data entered by the user at the keyboard.

29.14   **The program.** Listing 29-2 contains a program to create the desired text file. The program is straightforward, but one detail concerning the interaction with the user requires some care. Let's see what we have.

After importing `Scanner` from the Java Class Library, we begin the class `CreateCollegeFile` by defining a string constant for the file's name. Within the `main` method, we call the method `giveDirections` simply to provide some directions to the user. After creating the object, `maker`, of the class `TextFileMaker`, we use its methods to open the text file, write user data to the file, and then close the file. The tasks of obtaining the data from the user and then writing it to the file are organized as the private method `writeFile`. Let's examine the details of this method.

29.15   **The method `writeFile`.** We use the class `Scanner` to read from the keyboard, as we have done many times before. A `while` loop controls the repeated requests for input and exits when the user types `DONE` at the prompt for a school name. Notice how the `String` method `equalsIgnoreCase` gives the user case flexibility when entering the sentinel value.

After the data is read for one university, it is written to the file by the statements

```
maker.writeLine(name);
maker.writeLine(city + ", " + state + " " + zip);
maker.writeLine("" + enrollment);
```

We've written this as three lines to facilitate reading the file later.

The `while` loop ends by reading another university name. Unless we are careful, the program will not behave as we hope. The last value read was the enrollment as an integer, and we are about to read a string. If the relevant statements were juxtaposed as

```
int enrollment = keyboard.nextInt();
name = keyboard.nextLine();
```

`nextLine` would stay on the same line and read whatever exists immediately after the enrollment data, rather than moving to the next line before beginning to read. You might not see anything there, but `nextLine` would see—and read—a character or two that marks the end of the line. The loop would then cycle to its beginning, leaving the user no opportunity to enter the name of the next university. To avoid this mistake, we call `nextLine` before trying to read the next university name. Thus, the loop ends with the statements

```
int enrollment = keyboard.nextInt();
keyboard.nextLine(); // flush end-of-line after last integer entered
```

< The statements that write to the file. >

```
System.out.print("\nSchool name: ");
name = keyboard.nextLine();
```

Had we read the enrollment as a string by using the method `nextLine` instead of reading it as an integer using `nextInt`, we would have had no problem: The end-of-line characters would have been handled correctly. Reading data of both numeric and `String` types requires care, however. Although we encountered this problem in an earlier chapter while reading from the keyboard, it can also occur when we read from a text file.

 Note: When you read a value at the end of a line using any `Scanner` method other than `nextLine`, the character or characters marking the end of the line remain as the next to be read. Only `nextLine` reads past these characters. So regardless of whether you read from the keyboard or from a text file using `Scanner`, you must read beyond these ending characters—by using `nextLine`—before trying to read the next string.

LISTING 29-2   A program that creates a text file of colleges and universities

```
import java.util.Scanner;
/** CreateCollegeFile.java
    Creates a text file of U. S. colleges and universities.
    @author Frank M. Carrano
*/
public class CreateCollegeFile
{
    private static final String FILE_NAME = "CollegeFile.txt";
    private static final String SENTINEL = "DONE";

    public static void main(String[] args)
    {
        giveDirections();
        TextFileMaker maker = new TextFileMaker(FILE_NAME);
```

```java
      maker.openFile();
      if (maker.isOpen())
      {
         writeFile(maker);
         maker.closeFile();
         System.out.println("All data entered; file is created.");
      }
      else
         System.out.println("TextFileMaker cannot create a file.");
   } // end main

   // Gives directions to the user.
   private static void giveDirections()
   {
      System.out.println("You are about to create a text file\n" +
                         "of U. S. colleges and universities.");
      System.out.println("At the prompts, enter\n" +
                         "  the school name;\n" +
                         "  its city, state, and zip code; and\n" +
                         "  its enrollment.\n");
      System.out.println("When finished, enter " + SENTINEL +
                         " instead of a school name.\n");
   } // end giveDirections

   // Writes into the text file the data supplied by a user at the
   // keyboard; maker is a TextFileMaker object that represents
   // a text file open for output
   private static void writeFile(TextFileMaker maker)
   {
      Scanner keyboard = new Scanner(System.in);

      System.out.print("School name: ");
      String name = keyboard.nextLine();
      while (!name.equalsIgnoreCase(SENTINEL))
      {
         System.out.print("City: ");
         String city = keyboard.nextLine();
         System.out.print("State: ");
         String state = keyboard.nextLine();
         System.out.print("Zip code: ");
         String zip = keyboard.nextLine();
         System.out.print("Current enrollment: ");
         int enrollment = keyboard.nextInt();
         keyboard.nextLine(); // flush end-of-line after
                              // last integer entered
```

```
            maker.writeLine(name);
            maker.writeLine(city + ", " + state + " " + zip);
            maker.writeLine("" + enrollment);

            System.out.print("\nSchool name: ");
            name = keyboard.nextLine();
      } // end while
   } // end writeFile
} // end CreateCollegeFile
```

Sample Output

```
You are about to create a text file
of U. S. colleges and universities.
At the prompts, enter
   the school name,
   its city, state, and zip code; and
   its enrollment.

When finished, enter DONE instead of a school name.

School name: University of Rhode Island
City: Kingston
State: RI
Zip code: 02881
Current enrollment: 15904


. . .


School name: San Francisco State University
City: San Francisco
State: CA
Zip code: 94132
Current enrollment: 30014


School name: done
All data entered; file is created.
```

Question 5 The argument in the call

```
maker.writeLine("" + enrollment);
```

concatenates the empty string to the value of enrollment. Is doing so necessary? In other words, could the argument simply be enrollment?

29.16   If we were to use a text editor to examine the text file created by the program in Listing 29-2, it would look like this:

```
University of Rhode Island
Kingston, RI 02881
15904

. . .
San Francisco State University
San Francisco, CA 94132
30014
```

Let's turn our attention to reading a text file like this one.

Reading a Text File

You know how to use the class Scanner to read data from the keyboard. We can use this same class to read data from a text file. Let's see how. Realize, however, that Scanner is not a stream class.

Opening, Reading, and Closing a Text File

29.17 **Opening a text file for input.** Previously, we invoked PrintWriter's constructor to open a text file for output. In an analogous way, we might invoke Scanner's constructor to open a text file for input. You might guess that we would accomplish this step by using a statement such as

```
Scanner fromFile = new Scanner(fileName);// does NOT open a text file
```

where fileName is a String variable representing the file's name. Unfortunately, this statement has nothing to do with any text file! Instead, the Scanner object fromFile extracts portions of the string fileName, as Chapter 4 describes, beginning with Segment 4.26.

Note: **A Scanner object is not a stream**
We will, in fact, use Scanner to get data from a text file, but Scanner is not a stream class. In fact, it belongs to the package java.util, not java.io. According to the constructor we use to create it, a Scanner object can process a string

- Entered at the keyboard or
- Read from a text file or
- Given to its constructor as an argument

The Scanner objects we will use to read a text file actually contain a stream object that reads the file. The Scanner methods then translate, or parse, the input string, convert the data to the desired data type, and pass it to our program.

videonote
Reading and writing
text files

Scanner has several constructors, one of which takes an instance of the standard class File. This latter class, which is in the package java.io, represents a file in a system-independent and abstract way. Moreover, one of File's constructors accepts a string that is the file's name as its argument. Thus, to access the file whose name is referenced by the String variable fileName, we would write

```
Scanner fileData = new Scanner(new File(fileName));
```

Although the Scanner object fileData is not a stream object, it creates an input stream, thus opening the file for input. We chose the name fileData as a reminder that it is not a stream variable.

Unlike the two previous constructors of Scanner, this new constructor can throw a FileNotFoundException. Thus, its invocation must appear within either a try block that is followed by an appropriate catch block or a method whose header lists this exception in a throws clause. For example, the following statements ultimately open the text file named data.txt for input:

```
String fileName = "data.txt";
Scanner fileData = null;
try
{
    fileData = new Scanner(new File(fileName)); // can throw FileNotFoundException
}
```

```
catch (FileNotFoundException e)
{
    System.out.println("Scanner error opening the file " + fileName);
    System.out.println(e.getMessage());
    < Possibly other statements that react to this exception. >
}
```

Note: The Scanner constructor, whose parameter is a File object, will throw a FileNot-FoundException if it cannot open a file for input, because the file either does not exist or is inaccessible.

Note: Input from a text file

Opening a text file for input enables you to read data from it sequentially, starting from the file's beginning. Note that other standard classes exist that let you open a text file directly, rather than indirectly by using Scanner. However, Scanner offers you a convenient way to read from a text file.

29.18 **Reading a text file.** All of Scanner's methods are available to you when reading a text file. If you do not know the format of the data in the file, you can use the Scanner method nextLine to read it line by line. For example, the following statements read and display the lines in the existing text file data.txt:

```
String fileName = "data.txt";
Scanner fileData = null;
System.out.println("The file " + fileName +
                    " contains the following lines:");
try
{
    fileData = new Scanner(new File(fileName));
}
catch (FileNotFoundException e)
{
    System.out.println("Error opening the file " + fileName);
    System.out.println(e.getMessage());
    System.exit(0);
}

while (fileData.hasNextLine())
{
    String line = fileData.nextLine();
    System.out.println(line);
} // end while

fileData.close();
```

If nextLine were to read beyond the end of a file, it would throw a runtime (unchecked) exception, NoSuchElementException. We use Scanner's method hasNextLine to prevent nextLine from reading beyond the end of the file. Thus, the while loop ends when the end of the file is reached. At that point we close the file. Notice that we use the Scanner method close to indirectly close the text file.

Note: The class `File`

Segment 29.17 introduced the standard class `File`, whose constructor accepts as its argument a string that is a file's name. Because `Scanner` has no constructor that accepts a file name as an argument, but `File` does, we can open a text file for input by using a statement such as

```
Scanner fileData = new Scanner(new File(fileName));
```

This `Scanner` constructor accepts a `File` object as its argument and instantiates an input stream connected to the file. Although this stream belongs to the `Scanner` object `fileData` and is hidden from us, we can use `fileData` to read from the file.

The class `File` is useful in other ways as well. For example, you can

- Test whether a file exists, using the method `exists`
- Test whether a file exists and can be read, using the method `canRead`
- Test whether a file exists and can be written, using the method `canWrite`
- Change the name of a file, using the method `renameTo`
- Delete a file, using the method `delete`

We will use some of these methods in the next program and later in this chapter. Meanwhile, you should consult the online documentation for this class in the Java Class Library.

Question 6 Suppose that a file named `data.txt` does not exist.

   a. What happens if you execute the statement

```
Scanner fileData = new Scanner(new File("data.txt"));
```

   b. What happens if you execute the statement

```
Scanner fileData = new Scanner("data.txt");
```

   c. What happens if you execute the statement

```
PrintWriter toFile = new PrintWriter("data.txt");
```

Question 7 Write some statements that test whether the file `data.txt` exists and can be read. If so, open it for input.

A Problem Solved: Displaying a List of Colleges and Universities

> The program in Listing 29-2 created a text file, named `CollegeFile.txt`, of colleges and universities. Write a program to read the file and produce a report that lists the school names, enrollments, and locations in three labeled columns.

29.19 **Discussion.** Although we could display the lines in the file using Java statements like the ones shown in Segment 29.18, the result might not be in a form we want. After all, the file contains three lines for each school, as Segment 29.16 shows. Moreover, the desired report lists the data in a different order than it appears in the file. That is, for each school, the file contains its name, location, and enrollment, but our report should list the name, enrollment, and location in three columns.

To do more than simply echo the contents of a text file line by line, we should know the format of the file. Fortunately, we do know this, since we wrote the program in Listing 29-2. Had we not created the file ourselves, we could either examine its contents by using a text editor or get a description of the file's contents from the person who did write the file. With this knowledge, we can draft the following pseudocode to describe what we need to do:

Open the file
while (*the file has an unread line*)
{
    name = *the string in the next line*
    location = *the string in the next line*
    enrollment = *the integer in the next line*

    Display name, enrollment, *and* location
}
Close the file

Since this text file contains a mixture of strings and integers, we will have the problem we described in Segment 29.15. Recall that if you read the last value on a line by using a Scanner method other than nextLine, you must call nextLine to skip over the character or characters that mark the end of the line before you read from the next line. This caution applies to reading from a text file as well as reading from the keyboard.

29.20 **The program.** The implementation of the previous pseudocode appears in the program given in Listing 29-3. Having a structure similar to that of the program that created the file, this program begins by calling the method getFileScanner to create a scanner that opens the text file for input. The method readAndDisplayFile implements the loop given in the previous pseudocode. Notice again the extra call to nextLine after the integer enrollment is read.

We have attempted to align the columnar data and its headings, but without knowledge of the maximum length of each item, we can only guess. Clearly, this first attempt is not successful.

LISTING 29-3 A program to display and format the data read from a text file

```java
import java.io.File;
import java.io.FileNotFoundException;
import java.util.Scanner;

/** ReadCollegeFile.java
    Reads a text file of U. S. colleges and universities
    and displays its contents.
    @author Frank M. Carrano
*/
public class ReadCollegeFile
{
   private static final String FILE_NAME = "CollegeFile";
   private static Scanner fileData;

   public static void main(String[] args)
   {
      fileData = getFileScanner(FILE_NAME);
```

```java
      readAndDisplayFile();
      fileData.close();
   } // end main

   // Returns a Scanner object ready to read from the named text file.
   private static Scanner getFileScanner(String fileName)
   {
      Scanner input = null;
      try
      {
         input = new Scanner(new File(fileName));
      }
      catch (FileNotFoundException e)
      {
         System.out.println("Cannot open the file " + fileName);
         System.out.println(e.getMessage());
         System.out.println("Program execution cannot continue.");
         System.exit(0);
      }

      return input;
   } // end getFileScanner

   // Reads and displays the contents of a text file
   private static void readAndDisplayFile()
   {
      displayHeading();

      while (fileData.hasNextLine())
      {
         String name = fileData.nextLine();
         String location = fileData.nextLine(); // city, state, and zip
         int enrollment = fileData.nextInt();
         fileData.nextLine(); // flush end-of-line

         System.out.println(name + "\t" + enrollment + "\t\t" +
                              location);
      } // end while
   } // end readAndDisplayFile

   // Displays the heading for the table of data
   private static void displayHeading()
   {
      System.out.println("A List of U. S. Colleges and Universities");
      System.out.println();
      System.out.println("School Name\t\t\tEnrollment\tLocation");
      System.out.println();
```

```
        } // end displayHeading
    } // end ReadCollegeFile
```

Sample Output

```
A List of U. S. Colleges and Universities

School Name                        Enrollment     Location

University of Rhode Island         15904          Kingston, RI 02881
Binghamton University    14435                    Vestal, NY 13902
    . . .
University of Iowa        30500                  Iowa City, IA 52242
San Francisco State University   30014           San Francisco, CA 94132
```

29.21 **Fixing the output cheaply.** Although aligning the data into columns has nothing to do with files, we take this brief diversion as a prelude to our next topic. An easy way to adjust our output is to assume that the school names are no longer than a certain value. For example, let's assume that all names have 30 or fewer characters and define the following named constant at the beginning of the class:

```
private static final int NAME_WIDTH = 30;
```

Now, after we read a school name, we will add a sufficient number of blank characters, if necessary, to make it have 30 characters. That is, we **pad** the name with blanks. We can define the following method to accomplish this task:

```
// Returns a string containing the given string followed by a
// sufficient number of blanks to give it the specified length.
private static String padString(String name, int newLength)
```

Assuming this method, which we leave for you to define, we make the following changes[1] to the program given in Listing 29-3:

- In displayHeading replace the statement

```
System.out.println("School Name\t\t\tEnrollment\tLocation");
```

with

```
System.out.println(padString("School Name", NAME_WIDTH) +
                        "\tEnrollment\tLocation");
```

- In readAndDisplayFile, replace the variable name in the statement

```
System.out.println(name + "\t" + enrollment + "\t\t" + location);
```

with padString(name, NAME_WIDTH) to get

```
System.out.println(padString(name, NAME_WIDTH) +
                        "\t" + enrollment + "\t\t" + location);
```

With these changes, the program's output will begin as follows:

```
A List of U. S. Colleges and Universities

School Name                        Enrollment     Location

University of Rhode Island         15904          Kingston, RI 02881
Binghamton University              14435          Vestal, NY 13902
    . . .
```

---

1. The modified program, ReadCollegeFile2, is included in the source code available on the book's website.

Question 8 Consider the following method to open a text file for output:

```
public static void openFile(String fileName, PrintWriter toFile)
                    throws FileNotFoundException
{
   toFile = new PrintWriter(fileName);
} // end openFile
```

Suppose that we invoke this method using statements such as the following within the main method of the program that contains openFile:

```
PrintWriter toFile = null;
try
{
   openFile("MyFile", toFile);
}
catch (FileNotFoundException e)
{
   System.out.println(e.getMessage());
   System.exit(0);
}
toFile.println("Here is the first line for MyFile");
```

Why do these statements throw an exception?

Reading a Text File More Than Once

29.22   Reading a file can be time consuming, particularly when it is quite large. Therefore, you should not read a file more than once, if at all possible. Some algorithms, however, do require you to process data more than once. Doing so is not a problem when the data is in memory, but accommodating the data from a large file in an array, for example, might be impossible. In those cases, you might want to read the file several times.

   In the previous example, we assumed a maximum length for the name of a school. While the output shown in the previous segment has neatly aligned columns, they might be spaced farther apart than necessary. Additionally, if the program encounters a name having more than 30 characters, it will shift the associated enrollment figure to the right beyond the beginning of the second column. We could modify the code to truncate the name to 30 characters, but that is not ideal. If your own name is lengthy, how do you feel when you see only part of your name on printed forms?

29.23   To solve our difficulty, we should replace our assumed name length of 30 with the actual length of the longest name in our data set. To compute that value, we must look at all of the names, which, of course, requires us to read the file. Since we need this value before we can display anything, we will have to either read the file a second time or store its data in an array. For really large files, the latter choice would be impossible.

   If we can define a method, getLengthOfLongestName, to compute the width to use for the name column, we can make the following changes to the revisions[2] we just made in Segment 29.21:

- Delete the definition of the named constant NAME_WIDTH.
- In readAndDisplayFile, replace the call to displayHeading with the statements

```
int nameWidth = getLengthOfLongestName() + 1;
displayHeading(nameWidth);
```

---

2. The modified program, ReadCollegeFile3, is included in the source code available on the book's website.

- In readAndDisplayFile, replace the one occurrence of NAME_WIDTH with nameWidth.
- In displayHeading, replace the one occurrence of NAME_WIDTH with nameWidth.

The definition of getLengthOfLongestName follows:

```java
private static int getLengthOfLongestName()
{
    int longestLength = 0;
    while (fileData.hasNextLine())
    {
        String name = fileData.nextLine();
        int nameLength = name.length();
        if (longestLength < nameLength)
            longestLength = nameLength;

        // read and ignore other data about this school
        String location = fileData.nextLine();
        String enrollment = fileData.nextLine();
    } // end while

    // reset to beginning of file
    fileData.close();
    fileData = getFileScanner(FILE_NAME);

    return longestLength;
} // end getLengthOfLongestName
```

Once the file is read completely, the method closes it by closing the scanner referenced by fileData, and opens it again so that readAndDisplayFile can complete its task.

After these changes, the program is able to align the columns in its output regardless of the length of the institution's name.

Note: Sorting the data in a file

Searching a data set for a particular entry is a common task. As Chapter 23 showed, searching sorted data can be faster than searching unsorted data. That chapter not only discussed searching, but also showed how to sort the data in an array. When your data is in a file, however, the data might not fit entirely into an array: The file is simply too large for the computer's memory to accommodate it.

The merge sort, which Chapter 25 presented, can be adapted to sort the data in a file. Although the details of this modification are beyond our scope, its basic idea is not hard to understand. The sort reads a portion of the file into an array, sorts the array, and writes the sorted data to another file. This process is repeated for successive portions of the original file until all data has been processed. In the next phase, pairs of sorted blocks of data are read from the new file and merged into a larger block, which is then written to the original file. This merging continues until the second file is processed and is then repeated on the original file, and so on until all the data has been sorted. Note that merging involves small portions of sorted data at a time, so that only a small amount of memory is needed to sort a large file.

■ Appending Data to an Existing Text File

Preparing a text file that includes every college and university in the United States would involve a good deal of data entry. Once completed, what happens if we must add another school? And how can we keep the enrollment data current? Suppose a school changes its name or no longer exists? Let's tackle the first question here and leave the others for later.

29.24 When you add a line to the end of an existing text file, you **append** it to the file. Since we actually will write a new line to the file, we want to use the class PrintWriter, as we did earlier in this chapter to create a text file. When we consult the documentation for PrintWriter, however, we find no constructor that will open an existing file and append data to it. As we mentioned before, when you open a file for output, you ordinarily lose any existing data.

Although PrintWriter does not have an appropriate constructor, it is still the class we want to use to write the file. What we need is another class to help us open the file in the way we want. Much as we use the class File in conjunction with Scanner to open a text file for input, we can use the class FileWriter, which is in the package java.io of the Java Class Library. The appropriate FileWriter constructor is declared as follows:

```
public FileWriter(String fileName, boolean append)
```

This constructor opens the text file named by the String variable fileName for output. If the argument append is true, any data written to the file will be appended to its end. Otherwise, if append is false, any existing data in the file is lost.

Conveniently, PrintWriter has a constructor that accepts a FileWriter object as its argument. Thus, we can use FileWriter to open the text file so that it will accept additional output, and then use PrintWriter to provide methods such as print and println to write the output. Note that FileWriter does not have such methods.

29.25 Most of FileWriter's constructors, including the one given in the previous segment, can throw an IOException if they cannot open the designated file. The reasons for such an occurrence are the same as we encountered before: Either no such file exists and one cannot be created; fileName names an existing text file, but it cannot be opened; or fileName is actually the name of a folder instead of a text file.

Since the constructors of both FileWriter and PrintWriter can throw an exception, we invoke them within a try block. For example, to append another line to the existing text file CollegeFile.txt, we could open it as follows:

```
try
{
    FileWriter fw = new FileWriter(fileName, true);// IOException?
    toFile = new PrintWriter(fw);                   // FileNotFoundException?
}
catch (FileNotFoundException e)
{
    System.out.println("PrintWriter error opening the file " +
                        fileName);
    System.out.println(e.getMessage());
    System.exit(0);
}
catch (IOException e)
{
    System.out.println("FileWriter error opening the file " +
                        fileName);
    System.out.println(e.getMessage());
    System.exit(0);
}
```

We now can add one or more lines of data to the end of the file by using statements of the form

```
toFile.println(. . .);
```

>
> **Note:** Why do we need `PrintWriter`? Isn't `FileWriter` enough?
> Although the class `FileWriter` has the constructor we need to append to a file, it provides only basic support for text files. The class `PrintWriter` lacks the necessary constructor, but it has useful methods such as `println`. Using both classes provides an appropriate constructor and convenient methods.

Question 9 If the `FileWriter` constructor throws an `IOException`, why will it not be caught by the first catch block?

Question 10 Why did we catch `FileNotFoundException` before `IOException`, even though `FileWriter`'s constructor is invoked before `PrintWriter`'s?

■ Changing Existing Data in a Text File

29.26 Once we have created a text file of colleges and universities, as we did earlier in this chapter, the enrollment data will change and must be updated at some point. Although we can add lines at the end of an existing text file, we cannot add them anywhere else. Moreover, we cannot delete lines, and in general, we cannot modify lines. However, as we read a text file, we can copy lines that require no changes to another text file, skip lines that we no longer want to keep in the file, and write additional or modified lines to the new file. Changing the data in a file, therefore, is like reading one file and writing another. Most of the logic in a program that makes the changes must decide where and what changes are needed.

When the new file is complete, we can delete the old file and—if we like—give the new file the name of the old file. Although we can use the operating system to rename or delete a file after the program has run, our Java program can perform these task for us by using the class `File`. For example, to change the name of the existing file `MyData.txt`, we could write statements such as

```java
File originalFile = new File("MyData.txt");
File newFile = new File("MyUpdatedData.txt");
originalFile.renameTo(newFile);
```

The `File` method `renameTo` changes the name of the file and returns a boolean value to indicate whether the change was successful. Although the previous example ignores this returned value, we could have written something like

```java
if (originalFile.renameTo(newFile))
    System.out.println("Name change successful.");
else
    System.out.println("Attempted name change unsuccessful.");
```

Note that rename has a `File` object as its argument instead of a string containing the new name.

The `File` method `delete` deletes an existing file and returns either true or false to indicate whether the operation was successful. For example, to delete the previous file, we could write

```java
originalFile.delete();
```

29.27   As an example of how to update a text file, the program in Listing 29-4 rounds each enrollment in the file `CollegeFile.txt`, which we created in Listing 29-2, to the nearest hundred. Our approach takes the following steps:

- Change the name of the file `CollegeFile.txt` to `OldCollegeFile.txt`.
- Create a new text file named `CollegeFile.txt`.
- Copy the contents of `OldCollegeFile.txt` to `CollegeFile.txt`, but round each enrollment before writing it.

We have chosen not to delete the original data, now in `OldCollegeFile.txt`, as a precaution. The user can choose to either retain the file or delete it by using a simple system-level action or command. If `OldCollegeFile.txt` is retained, however, the program cannot be run another time until this file is deleted.

LISTING 29-4   The program `UpdateCollegeFile`

```java
import java.io.File;
import java.io.FileNotFoundException;
import java.io.PrintWriter;
import java.util.Scanner;

/** UpdateCollegeFile.java
    Updates a text file of U. S. colleges and universities
    by rounding their enrollments to the nearest hundred.
    @author Frank M. Carrano
*/
public class UpdateCollegeFile
{
   private static final String FILE_NAME = "CollegeFile.txt";
   private static Scanner fileData = null;
   private static PrintWriter toFile = null;

   public static void main(String[] args)
   {
      openFiles(FILE_NAME);
      roundEnrollments();
      fileData.close();
      toFile.close();
      System.out.println("The file has been updated successfully.");
   } // end main

   // Opens the named input file and creates a new output file.
   private static void openFiles(String fileName)
   {
      File original = new File(fileName);
      File renamedSource = new File("Old" + fileName);
      original.renameTo(renamedSource); // change file name
```

```java
        try
        {
            fileData = new Scanner(renamedSource); // open input file
            toFile = new PrintWriter(fileName);    // create new output file
        }
        catch (FileNotFoundException e)
        {
            System.out.println(e.getMessage());
            System.exit(0);
        }
    } // end openFiles

    // Rounds all enrollments to the nearest hundred.
    private static void roundEnrollments()
    {
        while (fileData.hasNextLine())
        {
            String name = fileData.nextLine();
            toFile.println(name);
            String location = fileData.nextLine(); // city, state, and zip
            toFile.println(location);
            int enrollment = fileData.nextInt();
            fileData.nextLine(); // flush end-of-line after integer entered
            toFile.println(round(enrollment));
        } // end while
    } // end roundEnrollments

    // Rounds the given integer to the nearest hundred.
    private static int round(int integer)
    {
        int result = integer / 100 * 100; // round down
        if ((integer % 100) >= 50)
            result = result + 100;          // round up

        return result;
    } // end round
} // end UpdateCollegeFile
```

Programming Tip: Avoid a silent program

Without the `println` statement at the end of the method `main` in Listing 29-4, a successful execution of the program would produce no visible output to the user. All output would be written to a file. A program without visible output is called a **silent program**. Such a program can bewilder its user. Did the program actually do anything? Always provide at least one message to the user to indicate the program's status.

videonote
A problem
solved

CHAPTER SUMMARY

- A program can create and save a file to be used over and over by other programs.

- A program can create a file for its own use as temporary storage for intermediate results. In other words, the program writes data into the file and later reads the data, but does not save the file.

- A stream is an object that represents a flow of data. An output stream sends data from a program to a destination, such as a file or the screen. An input stream takes data from a source, such as a file or the keyboard, and delivers it to a program.

- When you open a file, you connect it to an appropriate stream, thereby associating it with your Java program. This step is accomplished by invoking the constructor of the stream's class.

- When a program no longer needs an open file, you must close, or disconnect, it from the stream and, hence, from your program by calling a particular stream method named `close`.

- A text file represents a collection of characters. The streams associated with text files provide methods that interpret the file's binary contents as characters. Files other than text files are called binary files.

- Use a text file if you want to use a text editor to create or read it.

- A text file provides sequential access to its contents. Before you can read a particular line of the file, you must read all lines before it.

- File names are represented as strings within a program.

- Once a file is open, you use a stream variable or a `Scanner` object to work with the file instead of the file's name.

- When you use the class `PrintWriter` to open a text file for output, either a new file is created or the data in an existing file is lost.

- `PrintWriter`'s constructor throws a `FileNotFoundException` if a file cannot be opened for output either because it does not exist and cannot be created or because it is inaccessible.

- You use `PrintWriter`'s methods `print` and `println` to write data to a text file.

- If you do not close a file, Java will close it for you, but only if your program ends normally. To avoid any possible loss of data or damage to a file, you should close it as soon as possible after you are finished using it.

- You can use the class `Scanner` to read a text file. Although a `Scanner` object is not an input stream, it can create one that is connected to a text file. `Scanner` has no constructor that accepts the name of a file, but the class `File` does. Thus, you use both classes to create a `Scanner` object that opens a text file for input.

- After creating a `Scanner` object to access a text file as input, you use `Scanner`'s methods, such as `nextLine`, to read the file.

- By using methods of the class `File`, you can test whether a file exists, change a file's name, or delete a file.

- After reading a file, you can return to its beginning again by first closing the file and then opening it again. The class `Scanner` can do this for you.

- You can append data to the end of a text file by using the class `FileWriter` in conjunction with the class `PrintWriter` when you open it for output.

- To change the data in an existing text file, you must create a new file.

EXERCISES

1. What is the difference between a text file and a binary file?

2. What is the meaning of sequential access?

3. What happens when you close a text file?

4. What happens when you flush a text file?

5. What is a buffer? What is its purpose?

6. Imagine a program that performs operations on a text file. The program does not ask for or get any input from its user. Suppose that the operations last ten minutes. Should the program communicate with the user? If so, how and why? If not, why not?

7. Write statements to create an output stream to a text file named customers.txt. Be sure to handle any checked exceptions that might occur.

8. Write statements that place two lines of text into the text file created in the previous exercise and then close the file.

9. Write statements to read and display the text file you created in Exercises 7 and 8.

10. Write statements to add two more lines of text to the end of the text file created in Exercises 7 and 8.

11. Write statements to remove the second line of text from the text file you updated in the previous exercise.

12. Write a program that reads and displays a text file that you create by using a text editor.

13. Define a static method that makes a copy of a text file. The method should accept as an argument the name of the original file. The name of the copy should be "copyOf" followed by the name of the original file. The client of your method should use the class File to ensure that the original file exists and can be read before calling the method.

14. Revise the private method round in Listing 29-4 so that it rounds to the nearest 10^n, where n is an additional parameter.

PROJECTS

1. Design and implement a class StudentDatabase that creates and maintains a text file of student data obtained from objects of the classes UndergradStudent and GradStudent, as described in Project 4 of Chapter 27. A driver should create objects of UndergradStudent and GradStudent and then interact with StudentDatabase to create the text file. Subsequently, the driver should ask StudentDatabase for the data from the text file and create appropriate objects of UndergradStudent and GradStudent.

2. Create a simple text editor that maintains its text in a text file. The user should be able to create a new document or retrieve an existing one by providing a specific name. If the document exists, display each of its lines with the appropriate line numbers. If the document does not exist, create a blank one. Enable the user to add, replace, or delete lines anywhere in the document by specifying a line number and desired text. Allow the user the option of ending the program with or without saving the document.

3. The class URL in the package java.net of the Java Class Library represents a Uniform Resource Locator (i.e., a web address). You can use this class to access and read the HTML that defines a particular web page. For example, the following statements read and display the first line of text on the home page for the University of Rhode Island:

```
URL urlAddress = new URL("http://uri.edu/index.html");
InputStream inStream = urlAddress.openStream();
Scanner webReader = new Scanner(inStream);
String line = webReader.nextLine();
System.out.println(line);
```

When you write statements such as these, you must handle the exceptions that might be thrown.

Write a program that searches the home page of your choice and displays any URLs that it finds that are enclosed in quotes. In other words, it should search for URLs of the form "http:// ...". Next, modify the program so that it searches for and lists the URLs found at the first URL found on a web page. Enhance your program as much as you can to search the web for given strings.

ANSWERS TO SELF-TEST QUESTIONS

1.
```
PrintWriter toFile = null;
try
{
    toFile = new PrintWriter("alpha.txt");
}
catch (FileNotFoundException e)
{
    System.out.println("PrintWriter error opening the file " + fileName);
    System.out.println(e.getMessage());
    System.exit(0);
}

for (char letter = 'A'; letter <= 'Z'; letter++)
    toFile.println(letter);

tofile.close();
```

2. The file variable toFile is declared within the try block, so it will be unavailable to the rest of the program. Thus, you will not be able to write to the file or close it.

3. No; close does not throw a checked exception.

4.
```
TextFileCreater creater = new TextFileCreater("alpha.txt");
creater.openFile();
for (char letter = 'A'; letter <= 'Z'; letter++)
    creater.writeLine(letter);

creater.closeFile();
```

5. Within the class TextFileCreater, the definition of the method writeLine declares the data type of its parameter as String. A corresponding argument of enrollment would cause a syntax error, because the argument's data type is int, not String. When we write the argument as "" + enrollment, Java sees a String argument, and so converts the numeric value of enrollment to a string. Concatenation with the empty string does not alter the resulting string.

6.   **a.** A `FileNotFoundException` occurs.

b. This statement has nothing to do with files. The `Scanner` object `fileData` is created and is able to process the string `"data.txt"`.

c. A new text file named `data.txt` is created.

7.

```
File aFile = new File("data.txt");
Scanner fileData = null;
try
{
    if (aFile.canRead())
        fileData = new Scanner(aFile);
    else
        throw new FileNotFoundException();
}
catch (FileNotFoundException e)
{
    System.out.println("Error opening the file " + fileName);
    System.out.println(e.getMessage());
    System.exit(0);
}
```

8. The local variable `toFile` within `main` is `null`. It is passed to `openFile` but is not modified by this method. Thus, the `println` statement in `main` causes a `NullPointerException`.

9. An `IOException` is not a descendant of `FileNotFoundException`, and so it is not caught by the first `catch` block.

10. Since `FileNotFoundException` is a descendant of `IOException`, if we reversed the order of the `catch` blocks, a `FileNotFoundException` would be caught by the block that catches an `IOException`.

Getting Java for Free

The following list provides an overview of, and links to, several Java compilers and integrated development environments (IDEs) that you can obtain and use without charge. Installation instructions for each of these resources are available at the given URLs.[1]

- **Java SE Development Kit (JDK)**
  The JDK for Linux, Solaris, and Windows is available from Sun Microsystems at

  java.sun.com/javase/downloads/

  It includes the Java Runtime Environment (JRE) and command-line tools that you can use to write applications and applets.

  All Linux, Solaris, and Windows users must install the JDK before using any of the IDEs that follow in this list. MacOS users will already have Java installed by default. Note that MacOS users can use the JDK command-line tools in Terminal.

- **NetBeans**
  NetBeans is an open-source IDE for Linux, MacOS, Solaris, and Windows that is available at either

  java.sun.com/javase/downloads/

  or

  www.netbeans.info/downloads/index.php

  NetBeans requires that Linux, Solaris, and Windows users download and install the appropriate JDK from Sun, as described previously. MacOS users will already have Java installed by default.

- **BlueJ**
  BlueJ is an IDE developed specifically for beginning Java students. It is available for Debian, MacOS, Windows, and other systems at

  www.bluej.org/download/download.html

  BlueJ requires that Debian and Windows users download and install the JDK from Sun, as described previously. MacOS users will already have Java installed by default.

- **Eclipse**
  Eclipse is an open-source IDE for Linux, MacOS, and Windows that is available at

  www.eclipse.org/downloads/

  Eclipse requires that Linux and Windows users download and install the appropriate JDK from Sun, as described previously. MacOS users will already have Java installed by default.

---

1. Oracle acquired Sun Microsystems on January 27, 2010. As this book went to press, there were no plans to change the URLs of the Java websites.

Reserved Words

The meanings of the following identifiers—called reserved words or keywords—are determined by the Java language. You may not redefine any of them. Therefore, you cannot use any of these reserved words for variable names, method names, or class names.

abstract	false	package	void
assert	final	private	volatile
boolean	finally	protected	while
break	float	public	
byte	for	return	
case	goto	short	
catch	if	static	
char	implements	strictfp	
class	import	super	
const	instanceof	switch	
continue	int	synchronized	
default	interface	this	
do	long	throw	
double	native	throws	
else	new	transient	
enum	null	true	
extends		try	

Appendix C

Unicode Characters

The printable characters in the Unicode character set make up the ASCII character set. The numbering is the same whether the characters are considered to be members of the Unicode character set or members of the ASCII character set. Note that the code for the blank character is 32.

32		56	8	80	P	104	h
33	!	57	9	81	Q	105	i
34	"	58	:	82	R	106	j
35	#	59	;	83	S	107	k
36	$	60	<	84	T	108	l
37	%	61	=	85	U	109	m
38	&	62	>	86	V	110	n
39	'	63	?	87	W	111	o
40	(	64	@	88	X	112	p
41	)	65	A	89	Y	113	q
42	*	66	B	90	Z	114	r
43	+	67	C	91	[	115	s
44	,	68	D	92	\	116	t
45	-	69	E	93	]	117	u
46	.	70	F	94	^	118	v
47	/	71	G	95	_	119	w
48	0	72	H	96	`	120	x
49	1	73	I	97	a	121	y
50	2	74	J	98	b	122	z
51	3	75	K	99	c	123	{
52	4	76	L	100	d	124		
53	5	77	M	101	e	125	}
54	6	78	N	102	f	126	~
55	7	79	O	103	g		

Documentation and Programming Style

Contents

Most programs are used many times and are changed either to fix bugs or to accommodate new demands by the user. If the program is not easy to read and to understand, it will not be easy to change. It might even be impossible to change without heroic efforts. Even if you use your program only once, you should pay some attention to its readability. After all, you will have to read the program to debug it.

In this appendix, we discuss three techniques that can help make your program more readable: meaningful names, indenting, and comments.

Naming Variables and Classes

D.1

Names without meaning are almost never good variable names. The name you give to a variable should suggest what the variable is used for. If the variable holds a count of something, you might name it `count`. If the variable holds a tax rate, you might name it `taxRate`.

In addition to choosing names that are meaningful and legal in Java, you should follow the normal practice of other programmers. That way it will be easier for them to read your code and to combine your code with their code, should you work on a project with more than one person. By convention, each variable name begins with a lowercase letter, and each class name begins with an uppercase letter. If the name consists of more than one word, use a capital letter at the beginning of each word, as in the variable `numberOfTries` and the class `StringBuffer`.

Use all uppercase letters for named constants to distinguish them from other variables. Use the underscore character to separate words, if necessary, as in `INCHES_PER_FOOT`.

■ Indenting

D.2 A program has a structure: Smaller parts are within larger parts. You use indentation to indicate this structure and thereby make your program easier to read. Although Java ignores any indentation you use, indenting consistently is essential to good programming style.

Each class begins at the left margin and uses braces to enclose its definition. For example, you might write

```
public class CircleCalculation
{
   . . .
} // end CircleCalculation
```

The data fields and methods appear indented within these braces, as illustrated in the following simple program:

```
public class CircleCalculation
{
   public static final double PI = Math.PI;

   public static void main(String[] args)
   {
      double radius; // in inches
      double area;   // in square inches
      . . .
   } // end main
} // end CircleCalculation
```

Within each method, you indent the statements that form the method's body. These statements in turn might contain compound statements that are indented further. Thus, the program has statements nested within statements.

Each level of nesting should be indented from the previous level to show the nesting more clearly. The outermost structure is not indented at all. The next level is indented. The structure nested within that is double indented, and so on. Typically, you should indent two or three spaces at each level of indentation. You want to see the indentation clearly, but you want to be able to use most of the line for the Java statement.

If a statement does not fit on one line, you can write it on two or more lines. However, when you write a single statement on more than one line, you should indent the successive lines more than the first line, as in the following example:

```
System.out.println("The volume of a sphere whose radius is " +
                    radius + " inches is " + volume +
                    " cubic inches.");
```

Ultimately, you need to follow the rules for indenting—and for programming style in general—given by your instructor or project manager. In any event, you should indent consistently within any one program.

■ Comments

D.3 The documentation for a program describes what the program does and how it does it. The best programs are **self-documenting**. That is, their clean style and well-chosen names make the program's purpose and logic clear to any programmer who reads the program. Although you should strive for such self-documenting programs, your programs will also need a bit of explanation to make them completely clear. This explanation can be given in the form of **comments**.

Comments are notations in your program that help a person understand the program, but that are ignored by the compiler. Many text editors automatically highlight comments in some way, such as showing them in color. In Java, there are several ways of forming comments.

Single-Line Comments

D.4   To write a comment on a single line, begin the comment with two slashes //. Everything after the slashes until the end of the line is treated as a comment and is ignored by the compiler. This form is handy for short comments, such as

```
String sentence; // Spanish version
```

If you want a comment of this kind to span several lines, each line must contain the symbols //.

Comment Blocks

D.5   Anything written between the matching pair of symbols /* and */ is a comment and is ignored by the compiler. This form is not typically used to document a program, however. Instead, it is handy during debugging to temporarily disable a group of Java statements. Java programmers do use the pair /** and */ to delimit comments written in a certain form, as you will see in Segment D.7.

When to Write Comments

D.6   It is difficult to explain just when you should write a comment. Too many comments can be as bad as too few. Too many comments can hide the really important ones. Too few comments can leave a reader baffled by things that were obvious to you. Just remember that you also will read your program. If you read it next week, will you remember what you did just now?

Every program file should begin with an explanatory comment. This comment should give all the important information about the file: what the program does, the name of the author, how to contact the author, the date that the file was last changed, and in a course, what the assignment is. Every method should begin with a comment that explains the method.

Within methods, you need comments to explain any nonobvious details. Notice the poor comments on the following declarations of the variables radius and area:

```
double radius; // the radius
double area;   // the area
```

Because we chose descriptive variable names, these comments are obvious. But rather than simply omitting these comments, can we write something that is not obvious? What units are used for the radius? Inches? Feet? Meters? Centimeters? We will add a comment that gives this information, as follows:

```
double radius; // in inches
double area;   // in square inches
```

Java Documentation Comments

D.7   The Java language comes with a utility program named **javadoc** that will generate HTML documents that describe your classes. These documents tell people who use your program or class how to use it, but omit all the implementation details.

The program javadoc extracts the header for your class, the headers for all public methods, and comments that are written in a certain form. No method bodies and no private items are extracted.

For `javadoc` to extract a comment, the comment must satisfy two conditions:

- The comment must occur immediately before a public class definition or the header of a public method.
- The comment must begin with `/**` and end with `*/`.

Segment D.12 contains an example of a comment in this style.

You can insert HTML commands in your comments so that you gain more control over `javadoc`, but that is not necessary and we have not done so in this book.

D.8   **Tags.** Comments written for `javadoc` usually contain special **tags** that identify such things as the programmer and a method's parameters and return value. Tags begin with the symbol @. We will describe only four tags in this appendix.

The tag `@author` identifies the programmer's name and is required of all classes and interfaces. The other tags of interest to us are used with methods. They must appear in the following order within a comment that precedes a method's header:

```
@param
@return
@throws
```

We will describe each of these tags next.

D.9   **The `@param` tag.** You must write a `@param` tag for every parameter in a method. You should list these tags in the order in which the parameters appear in the method's header. After the `@param` tag, you give the name and description of the parameter. Typically, you use a phrase instead of a sentence to describe the parameter, and you mention the parameter's data type first. Do not use punctuation between the parameter name and its description, as `javadoc` inserts one dash when creating its documentation.

For example, the comments

```
* @param code      the character code of the ticket category
* @param customer  the string that names the customer
```

will produce the following lines in the documentation:

```
code - the character code of the ticket category
customer - the string that names the customer
```

D.10   **The `@return` tag.** You must write a `@return` tag for every method that returns a value, even if you have already described the value in the method's description. Try to say something more specific about this value here. This tag must come after any `@param` tags in the comment. Do not use this tag for `void` methods and constructors.

D.11   **The `@throws` tag.** Next, if a method can throw a checked exception, you name it by using a `@throws` tag, even if the exception also appears in a `throws` clause in the method's header. You can list unchecked exceptions if a client might reasonably catch them. Include a `@throws` tag for each exception, and list them alphabetically by name.

D.12   **Example.** Here is a sample `javadoc` comment for a method. We usually begin such comments with a brief description of the method's purpose. This is our convention; `javadoc` has no tag for it.

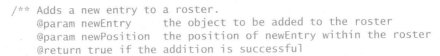

```
/** Adds a new entry to a roster.
    @param newEntry      the object to be added to the roster
    @param newPosition   the position of newEntry within the roster
    @return true if the addition is successful
```

```
@throws RosterException if newPosition < 1 or newPosition >
                    1 + the length of the roster */
```
public boolean add(Object newEntry, **int** newPosition) **throws** RosterException

The documentation that javadoc prepares from the previous comment appears as follows:

add

```
public boolean add(java.lang.Object newEntry,
                   int newPosition)
            throws RosterException
```

Adds a new entry to a roster.

> **Parameters:**
> newEntry - the object to be added to the roster
> newPosition - the position of newEntry within the roster
> **Returns:**
> true if the addition is successful
> **Throws:**
> RosterException - if newPosition < 1 or newPosition > 1 + the length of the roster

To save space in this book, we sometimes omit portions of a comment that we would include in our actual programs. For example, some methods might have only a description of their purpose, and some might have only a @return tag. Note that javadoc accepts these abbreviated comments.

Running javadoc

D.13   You run javadoc on an entire package. However, if you want to run it on a single class, you can make the class into a package simply by inserting the following at the start of the file for the class:

package *package_name*;

Remember that the package name should describe a relative path name for the directory or folder containing the files in the package.

To run javadoc, you must be in the folder that contains the package's folder, but not in the package folder itself. Then you execute the following command:

javadoc -d *document_folder   package_name*

Replace *document_folder* with the name of the folder in which you want javadoc to place the HTML documents it produces. The folder must already exist; javadoc will not create it for you.

For example, suppose you want to use javadoc to generate documentation for the class MyClass. Create a folder to hold a package; for instance, you might call the folder—and the package—MyStuff. Place the file MyClass.java in the folder MyStuff, and place the following at the start of the file MyClass.java:

package MyStuff;

The package MyStuff now contains the class MyClass.

Next, create a folder to receive the HTML documents. For example, you might call this folder MyDocs. Place MyDocs in the folder containing MyStuff. Do not place it within MyStuff.

Finally, use the command cd to change to the directory that contains both MyStuff and MyDocs, and give the following command:

javadoc -d MyDocs MyStuff

If you then look in the folder MyDocs, you will see a number of HTML documents whose names end in .html. You can view these files by using your browser. The HTML documents will describe the package MyStuff, including the class MyClass.

If you wish, you can use the folder MyStuff in place of MyDocs, so that both the source file MyClass.java and the HTML documents end up in the same folder.

Further details about javadoc are available at java.sun.com/j2se/javadoc/index.jsp.

Cloning

Contents

Prerequisites

■ Cloning an Object

E.1   In Java, a **clone** is a copy of an object. Typically, we clone only mutable objects. A mutable object is one that has public methods, such as set methods, that can change its state. Since sharing an immutable object is safe, cloning it is usually unnecessary.

The class Object contains a protected method clone that returns a copy of an object. The method has the following header:

```
protected Object clone() throws CloneNotSupportedException
```

Since clone is protected, and since Object is the ultimate ancestor of all other classes, the implementation of any method can contain the invocation

```
super.clone()
```

But clients of a class cannot invoke clone unless the class overrides it and declares it to be public. Making copies of objects can be expensive, so it might be something you do not want a class to do. By making clone a protected method, the designers of Java force you to think twice about cloning.

Programming Tip

Not all classes should have a public clone method. In fact, most classes, including read-only classes, do not have one.

E.2   If you want a class to contain a public method clone, the class must state this fact by implementing the Java interface Cloneable, which is in the package java.lang of the Java Class Library. Such a class would begin as follows:

```
public class MyClass implements Cloneable
{ . . .
```

The interface `Cloneable` is simply

```
public interface Cloneable
{
}
```

As you can see, the interface is empty. It declares no methods and serves only as a way for a class to indicate that it implements `clone`. If you forget to write `implements Cloneable` in your class definition, instances of your class that invoke `clone` will cause the exception `CloneNotSupportedException`. This result can be confusing at first, particularly if you did implement `clone`.

Programming Tip

If your program produces the exception `CloneNotSupportedException` even though you implemented a method `clone` in your class, you probably forgot to write `implements Cloneable` in your class definition.

Note: The `Cloneable` interface

The empty `Cloneable` interface is not a typical interface. A class implements it to indicate that it will provide a public `clone` method. Since the designers of Java wanted to provide a default implementation of the method `clone`, they included it in the class `Object` and not in the interface `Cloneable`. But because the designers did not want every class to automatically have a public `clone` method, they made `clone` a protected method.

Note: Cloning

Cloning is not an operation that every class should be able to do. If you want your class to have this ability, you must

- Declare that your class implements the `Cloneable` interface
- Override the protected method `clone` that your class inherits from the class `Object` with a public version

This second step assumes that your class either does not extend another class or extends a class that does not define a `clone` method. However, if your class's superclass defines its own public method `clone`, your class would override it with its own public version instead of overriding `Object`'s protected method.

E.3 **Example: Cloning a Name object.** Let's add a method `clone` to the class `Name` given in Listing 6-5 of Chapter 6. Before we begin, we should add `implements Cloneable` to the first line of the class definition, as follows:

```
public class Name implements Cloneable
```

The public method `clone` within `Name` must invoke the method `clone` of its superclass by executing `super.clone()`. Because `Name`'s superclass is `Object`, `super.clone()` invokes `Object`'s protected method `clone`. `Object`'s version of `clone` can throw an exception, so we must enclose each call to it in a `try` block and write a `catch` block to handle the exception. The method's final action should return the cloned object.

Thus, Name's method clone could appear as follows:

```
public Object clone()
{
   Name theCopy = null;

   try
   {
      theCopy = (Name)super.clone();
   }
   catch (CloneNotSupportedException e)
   {
      System.out.println("Name cannot clone: " + e.getMessage());
   }

   return theCopy;
} // end clone
```

Since super.clone() returns an instance of Object, we must cast this instance to Name. After all, we are creating a Name object as the clone. The return statement will implicitly cast theCopy to Object to match the method's return type.

The exception that Object's method clone can throw is CloneNotSupportedException. Since we are writing a clone method for our class Name, this exception will never occur. Even so, we still must use try and catch blocks when invoking Object's clone method. Instead of the println statement in the catch block, we could write the simpler statement

```
throw new Error(e.getMessage());
```

Programming Tip

Every public clone method must invoke the method clone of the base class by executing super.clone. Ultimately, Object's protected clone method will be invoked. That invocation must appear in a try block, even though a CloneNotSupportedException will never occur.

E.4   **Two ways to copy.** What does this method clone actually do? You want it to make copies of the data fields associated with the object receiving the method's invocation. As Segment 18.30 of Chapter 18 mentioned, you can make two kinds of copies of an object, a shallow copy and a deep copy. In particular, you can

- Copy the reference to the object and share the object with the clone, as illustrated in Figure E-1a. This copy is a shallow copy, and the clone is a **shallow clone**.
- Copy the object itself, as illustrated in Figure E-1b. This copy is a deep copy, and the clone is a **deep clone**.

Note: Object's clone method returns a shallow clone.

FIGURE E-1   (a) A shallow clone; (b) a deep clone

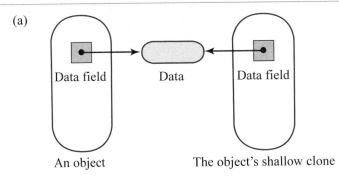

(a)

An object   The object's shallow clone

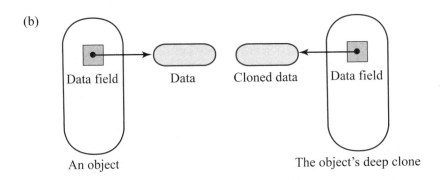

(b)

An object   The object's deep clone

E.5   **Name's clone is shallow.** The class Name has the data fields first and last, which are instances of String. Each field contains a reference to a string. It is these references that are copied when clone invokes super.clone(). For example, Figure E-2 illustrates the objects that the following statements create:

```
Name april = new Name("April", "Jones");
Name twin = (Name)april.clone();
```

The clone twin is a shallow clone because the strings that are the first and last names are not copied.

FIGURE E-2   An instance of Name and its shallow clone

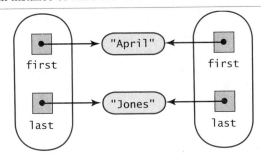

april, an instance of Name   april.clone(), the shallow clone

A shallow clone is good enough for the class Name. Recall that instances of String are immutable. It is not a problem for a Name object and its clone to share the same strings because no one can change the strings. This is good news since, like many classes that Java provides, String does not override clone. Thus, if we change the clone's last name by writing

```
twin.setLast("Smith");
```

twin's last name will be "Smith", but april's will still be "Jones", as Figure E-3 shows. That is, setLast changes twin's data field last so that it references another string "Smith". It does not change april's last, so it still references "Jones".

FIGURE E-3   The clone twin after the statement twin.setLast("Smith") changes one of its data fields

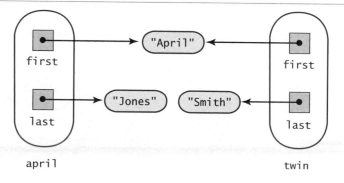

 Programming Tip

Shallow copies of data fields that reference immutable objects are typically sufficient for a clone. Sharing an immutable object is usually safe.

E.6 **Example: Creating a deep clone of a single field.** Sometimes a shallow clone is unsuitable. If a class has mutable objects as data fields, you must clone those objects and not simply copy their references. For example, let's add a method clone to the class Person that is given in Listing 15-3 of Chapter 15. Recall that the class has the following form:

```
public class Person
{
    private Name    myName;
    private String myCity;

    < Constructors and the methods setPerson, getName, getCity, toString, and
      isNeighbor >
      . . .
} // end Person
```

Since the class Name has set methods, the data field myName is a mutable object. Therefore, we should be sure to clone myName within the definition of Person's clone method. We can do that because we added a clone method to Name in Segment E.3. Since myCity is a String object, it is immutable, and so cloning it is unnecessary. Thus, we can define a clone method for the class Person as follows:

```
public Object clone()
{
    Person theCopy = null;

    try
    {
        theCopy = (Person)super.clone();
    }
```

```
    catch (CloneNotSupportedException e)
    {
        throw new Error(e.getMessage());
    }

    theCopy.myName = (Name)myName.clone();
    return theCopy;
} // end clone
```

After invoking super.clone(), we clone the mutable data field myName by calling Name's public clone method. This latter invocation need not be within a try block. Only Object's clone method contains a throws clause and must be called within a try block.

Figure E-4 illustrates an instance of Person and the clone that this method returns. As you can see, the Name object that represents the person's full name is copied, but the strings that represent the first and last names, as well as the city, are not.

FIGURE E-4   An instance of Person and its clone, including a deep copy
              of myName

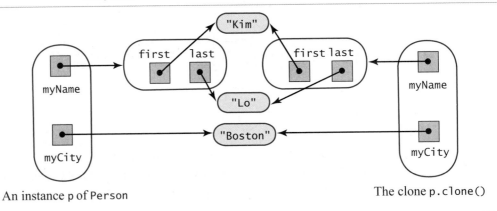

An instance p of Person   The clone p.clone()

Had we failed to clone the data field myName—that is, had we omitted the statement

    theCopy.myName = (Name)myName.clone();

the person's full name would be shared by the original instance and its clone. Figure E-5 illustrates this situation.

FIGURE E-5   An instance of Person and its clone, including a shallow copy
              of myName

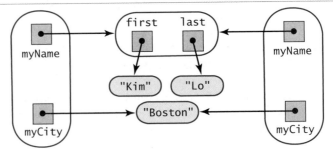

An instance of Person   The shallow clone

Question 1 Suppose that x is an instance of Person and y is its clone; that is,

```
Person y = (Person)x.clone();
```

a. If you change x's last name by executing

```
Name xName = x.getName();
xName.setLast("Smith");
```

does y's last name change? Explain.

b. If you fail to clone myName within Person's clone method, will changing x's last name change y's last name as well? Explain.

Note: Within each public clone method, you typically perform the following tasks:

- Invoke the clone method of the superclass by writing super.clone().
- Enclose this call to clone in a try block, and write a catch block to handle the possible exception CloneNotSupportedException. You can skip this step if super.clone() invokes a public clone method.
- Clone the mutable data fields of the object that super.clone() returned, when possible.
- Return the clone.

Cloning an Array

E.7 The class BagOfStrings that you saw in Listing 19-6 of Chapter 19 uses an array to implement a bag. Suppose that we want to add a clone method to this class. While making a copy of the bag, clone needs to copy the array and all the objects in it. Thus, the objects in the bag must have a clone method as well. Since these objects are strings, which are immutable, the method clone that String inherits from Object will suffice.

We can begin BagOfStrings as follows:

```
public class BagOfStrings implements BagOfStringsInterface, Cloneable
```

Note that BagOfStrings implements two interfaces, BagOfStringsInterface and Cloneable.

E.8 Now we can implement clone. We will invoke super.clone() within a try block but perform the rest of the tasks after the catch block. Thus, we have the following outline for BagOfStrings' method clone:

```
public Object clone()
{
   BagOfStrings theCopy = null;

   try
   {
      theCopy = (BagOfStrings)super.clone(); // not enough by itself
   }
   catch (CloneNotSupportedException e)
   {
      throw new Error(e.getMessage());
   }

   theCopy.bag = bag.clone();                // clone the array
   return theCopy;
} // end clone
```

The method first invokes `super.clone` and casts the returned object to `BagOfStrings`. To perform a deep copy, we need to clone the data fields that are or could be mutable objects. Thus, we need to clone the array bag. Arrays in Java have a public `clone` method; in other words, their class implements `Cloneable`. So we can add the following statement to the bag's `clone` method:

```
theCopy.bag = bag.clone();
```

No `try` and `catch` blocks are necessary here. An array's `clone` method creates a shallow copy of each object in the array, but since these objects are strings, shallow copies are sufficient.

E.9   **Cloning a bag of names.** Now imagine a class `BagOfNames` that represents bags of `Name` objects. You can create such a class by replacing most occurrences of `String` in `BagOfStrings` with `Name`. When we clone a bag of names, we not only must clone the array bag, but we also need to clone each `Name` object in the array. We have already defined a public `clone` method for `Name`, so we can write a loop whose body contains the following statement:

```
theCopy.bag[index] = bag[index].clone();
```

We can control the loop by using `BagOfNames`'s data field `numberOfNames`, which records the number of entries in the bag.

Thus, we have the following definition of `clone` for the class `BagOfNames`:

```
public Object clone()
{
    BagOfNames theCopy = null;

    try
    {
        theCopy = (BagOfNames)super.clone();
    }
    catch (CloneNotSupportedException e)
    {
        throw new Error(e.getMessage());
    }

    theCopy.bag = bag.clone();

    for (int index = 0; index < numberOfNames; index++)
        theCopy.bag[index] = bag[index].clone();

    return theCopy;
} // end clone
```

 Note: To make a deep clone of an array a of cloneable objects, you invoke `a.clone()` and then clone each object in the array. For example, if `myArray` is an array of `Thing` objects, and `Thing` implements `Cloneable`, you would write

```
Thing[] clonedArray = (Thing[])myArray.clone();

for (int index = 0; index < myArray.length; index++)
    clonedArray[index] = (Thing)myArray[index].clone();
```

ANSWER TO SELF-TEST QUESTION

1.   **a.** No. The clone y has a `Name` object that is distinct from x's `Name` object because a deep copy was made. (See Figure E-4.)
     b. Yes. Both objects share one `Name` object. (See Figure E-5.)

Index